# EXPLORE ECONOMICS ONLINE

Whether you need a little extra help understanding the material or want to practice for a test, we offer online options to help you when you need it.

Our free Book Companion Site (BCS) offers convenient, hands-on tools to make learning fun and easy.

**www.worthpublishers.com/ExplorationsinEconomics1e**

- Use the free graphic organizers and watch the animated graphs.
- Test yourself with the vocabulary flash cards.
- Take the online quizzes to see if you are ready for an exam.
- Click on the link to the St. Louis Federal Reserve's website and download the "Economics Lowdown Podcasts" and other helpful tutorials.

Sapling Learning's interactive study program helps you with economics homework when and where you need it.

**www.saplinglearning.com**

- Sapling's easy-to-use interface lets you focus on solving problems instead of struggling with the system.
- Sapling's practice problems range from easy to challenging to help you fully understand the content.
- Sapling gives you immediate feedback on every answer and guides you through areas where you need extra practice.
- The *Explorations in Economics* e-Book is included in Sapling so you can easily refer to the book and read it on a PC, Mac, iPad, or other device.

# Explorations in Economics

## Alan B. Krueger
Princeton University

## David A. Anderson
Centre College

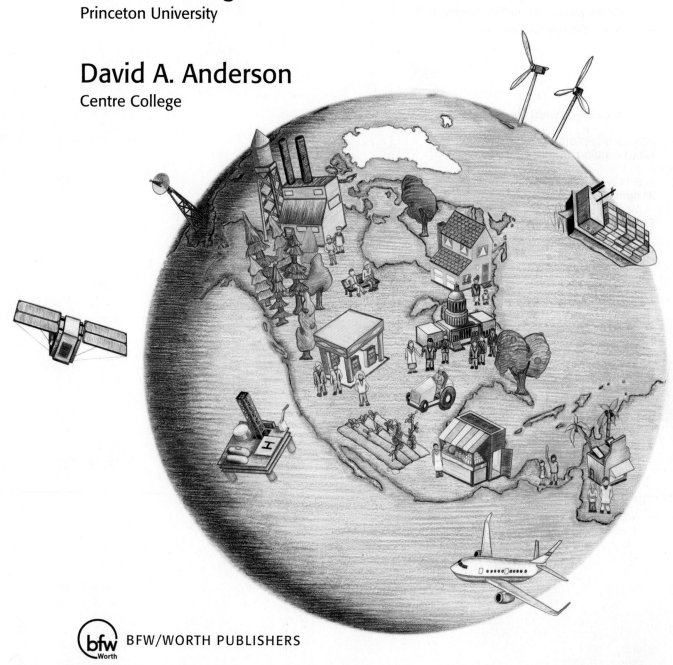

bfw
Worth

BFW/WORTH PUBLISHERS

*Publisher:* Ann Heath
*Assistant Editor:* Enrico Bruno
*Associate Editor:* Dora Figueiredo
*Development Editor:* Rebecca Kohn/Sharon Balbos
*Senior Marketing Manager:* Janie Pierce-Bratcher
*Marketing Assistant:* Rachel Sachs
*Project Editor:* Mark Parker Miller, Scribe Inc.
*Art Director:* Diana Blume
*Text Designer:* Tom Carling, Carling Design Inc.
*Photo Editor:* Cecilia Varas
*Photo Researcher:* Dena Digilio Betz
*Production Manager:* Sarah Segal
*Text and Cover Illustration:* Joe BelBruno
*Copy Editor:* Brittney Todd, Scribe Inc.
*Proofreader:* Daniel J. King, Scribe Inc.
*Composition:* Melissa Tarrao/Tim Durning, Scribe Inc.
*Printing and Binding:* RR Donnelley

Library of Congress Control Number: 2013930579

ISBN-10: 0-7167-0107-3
ISBN-13: 978-0-7167-0107-1

Printed in the United States of America

Fifth Printing

BFW/Worth Publishers
41 Madison Ave.
New York, NY  10010


highschool.bfwpub.com/economics

I dedicate this book to my parents, Rhoda and Norman Krueger,
a schoolteacher and a public accountant, who taught me the
value of education and public service.
*Alan B. Krueger*

To the students of today, whose economic literacy
will serve the well-being of society tomorrow.
*David A. Anderson*

# About the Authors

### ALAN B. KRUEGER

Alan B. Krueger is the Bendheim Professor of Economics and Public Affairs at Princeton University. He received a BS from Cornell University and an AM and PhD in economics from Harvard University. Krueger currently serves as chair of President Obama's Council of Economic Advisers and is a member of the president's cabinet. He previously served as assistant secretary for economic policy and chief economist of the U.S. Department of the Treasury (2009–2010) and chief economist of the U.S. Department of Labor (1994–1995). He has been a member of the Executive Committee of the American Economic Association (2005–2007) and was chief economist for the Council for Economic Education (CEE, 2003–2009). While at the CEE, Krueger helped draft the Voluntary National Content Standards in Economics and served as cochair of the committee. He was also a columnist for the *New York Times*. Among his many scholarly publications are *What Makes a Terrorist: Economics and the Roots of Terrorism* and *Education Matters: A Selection of Essays on Education*. When not in Washington, DC, Krueger lives in Princeton, New Jersey, with his wife, Lisa, a high school math teacher. They have two adult children.

### DAVID A. ANDERSON

David Anderson is the Paul G. Blazer Professor of Economics at Centre College. He received his BA in economics from the University of Michigan and his MA and PhD in economics from Duke University. Anderson is a leading authority on AP Economics and currently serves as chief reader for the AP Microeconomics exam. He has authored dozens of scholarly articles and many books, including *Krugman's Economics for AP*, *Cracking the AP Economics Exam*, *Economics by Example*, *Favorite Ways to Learn Economics*, *Environmental Economics and Natural Resource Management*, *Contemporary Economics for Managers*, and *Treading Lightly*. His research is primarily on economic education, environmental economics, law and economics, and labor economics. Anderson teaches courses in each of these fields and loves teaching introductory economics. He is an accomplished runner who is making great strides toward his goal of completing a marathon in every state in the union. He lives in Danville, Kentucky, with his wife and two children.

# KEY CONTRIBUTORS

### JAMES CHASEY
Homewood-Flossmoor High School
Homewood, IL (retired)
*Assessments and Test Bank*

James Chasey earned a BA from Purdue University and an MA from the University of Illinois. As the Christa McAuliffe Fellow for Illinois, he received advanced training at the University of Chicago Graduate School of Business. He has received the Freedoms Foundation Leavey Award, the Money Smart Award from the Federal Reserve Bank of Chicago, and the Purdue University Outstanding Education Alumni Award. He taught AP Economics and general economics at Homewood-Flossmoor High School and served as adjunct professor of economics at the College of DuPage and at Governors State University.

### PEGGY PRIDE
St. Louis University High School
St. Louis, MO (retired)
*Assessments and Teacher's Edition*

Peggy Pride earned a BA in history and economics and an MA in business education from Southern Illinois University–Edwardsville. She retired in 2008 after a 35-year teaching career at St. Louis University High School in St. Louis, Missouri, where she taught AP Economics. Pride served on the Test Development Committee for AP Economics from 1999 to 2004 and then as a table leader and micro question leader for 12 years. She was honored to receive the GATE Teacher of the Year Award in 2005. She was the primary author of the College Board publication *Advanced Placement Economics Teacher's Guide* and has written curriculum for the College Board and Junior Achievement.

### LAURA ADAMS
*Personal Finance Handbook*

Laura Adams is an award-winning personal finance author. She earned a BS from the University of the South and an MBA from the University of Florida. She received the Excellence in Financial Literacy Education (EIFLE) Award from the Institute for Financial Literacy for her book *Money Girl's Smart Moves to Grow Rich*. She is the author of several e-Books and audiobooks published by Macmillan, as well as hundreds of personal finance articles. Adams hosts the Money Girl podcast, a top-10 Internet show on iTunes that has been downloaded more than 45 million times. She is frequently quoted in the media and has been featured on national broadcast, radio, print, and online outlets.

### JOSEPH BELBRUNO
*Illustrator*

Joseph BelBruno is an artist living and working in Los Angeles, California. He graduated from the California College of the Arts in San Francisco in 2010 with a degree in painting and drawing. *Explorations in Economics* is the first textbook he has illustrated. In addition to this illustration work, BelBruno is an avid painter.

### ELIZABETH CURTIS
Dartmouth College
*Headline Economics*

# CONTENT ADVISORS AND SUPPLEMENT AUTHORS

## DAVID BREMER
**Las Lomas High School, Walnut Creek, CA**
*CEE and CA Standards Consultant*

David Bremer has taught general economics for 15 years and also currently teaches AP Macroeconomics and Specially Designed Academic Instruction in English (SDAIE) Economics for English language learners. He earned a BS in business administration from Cal Poly, San Luis Obispo, and an MA in political science from the University of California–Davis. Before becoming a teacher, Bremer worked in the business world for several years.

## DIANNA MILLER
**Florida Virtual School, FL**
*Teacher's Edition*

Dianna Miller earned a BA in social studies education and an MA in history from the University of North Florida and a specialist in education degree from the University of Florida. She currently teaches AP Economics for Florida Virtual School, an online public school in Florida. She has served as an AP Economics reader since 2005 and is currently a table leader for AP Macroeconomics. She is the 2011 Florida Council for the Social Studies Trimble Award winner and was a finalist for the National Online Teacher of the Year Award in 2010.

## JAMES MCCALIP
**Singley Academy, Irving, TX**
*TX Standards Consultant*

James McCalip has taught economics at Jack E. Singley Academy for 10 years. He serves as the adviser for the academy's National Honor Society. He received a BA in philosophy and religion from Dallas Baptist University and an MDiv from Southwestern Baptist Theological Seminary. He is currently enrolled in the MA program in Economic and Entrepreneurship Education at the University of Delaware.

## MIKE FULLINGTON
**Port Charlotte High School, Port Charlotte, FL**
*Teacher's Edition*

Mike Fullington earned his BS from Concordia University in Mequon, Wisconsin. He teaches AP Economics at Port Charlotte High School and is a reader for the AP Economics exam. He has been published in the Council for Economic Education's *Advanced Placement Economics: Teacher Resource Manual*. He was chosen as the 2011 Harvard Club Teacher of the Year and was a finalist for Teacher of the Year for Charlotte County, Florida.

## PAMELA M. SCHMITT
**U.S. Naval Academy, Annapolis, MD**
*Content Advisor*

Pamela M. Schmitt earned her PhD in economics from Indiana University in 2000. She is currently an associate professor of economics at the U.S. Naval Academy, where she has been the recipient of numerous teaching awards. She has worked as an AP Economics reader and table leader since 2001 and is currently serving as chair of the ETS Test Development Committee for the AP Microeconomics exam.

## DAVID MAYER
**Churchill High School, San Antonio, TX**
*Content Advisor and Teacher's Edition*

David Mayer received a BS in economics from Texas A&M University and an MA from the University of Texas at San Antonio. In addition to teaching the general economics course, he has taught the AP Economics course since 2004 and has worked as an AP Economics reader and then table leader since 2006. David is a College Board–endorsed consultant for economics and conducts several professional development workshops and institutes each year.

**DEE MECHAM**
The Bishop's School, La Jolla, CA
*Content Advisor*

Dee Mecham joined The Bishop's School in fall 2005 after 11 years in Hawai'i, where he taught at the Kamehameha Schools and the University of Hawai'i. He has been involved in AP Reading for many years and currently serves on the ETS Test Development Committee for the AP Microeconomics exam. This year, Mecham teaches tenth, eleventh, and twelfth graders in both general economics and AP Economics.

**WOODROW W. HUGHES JR.**
Converse College, Converse, GA
*Content Advisor*

Woodrow W. Hughes Jr. worked in the banking industry after graduating from Furman University with a BA in economics. He earned his PhD in economics from the University of South Carolina in 1989 and has been on the Converse College faculty since 1986. In 2006, he was awarded the Kathryne Amelia Brown teaching award. Hughes is also active in the AP Economics community, having served as a reader and coauthored a number of AP publications.

**LESLIE PAIGE WOLFSON**
The Pingry School, Martinsville, NJ
*Teacher's Edition*

Leslie Paige Wolfson holds an MA in economics and finance and is the author of *INSIGHTS: A New View of Economics and Nature*. She has been teaching AP Economics and Economic Principles and Issues for 18 years and coordinates her school's Financial Literacy program. She was awarded the Research Fellowship Award and the Woodruff J. English Faculty Award for New Jersey. She has been listed in *Who's Who in American Educators* and was voted an Outstanding Woman in Education.

## ACCURACY CHECKERS

**Andreas Bentz**, formerly Dartmouth College, NH

**Darcy Brodison**, Coronado High School, AZ

**Dixie Dalton**, Southside Virginia Community College, VA

**Joyce Jacobson**, Wesleyan College, CT

**Lisa Krueger**, Princeton High School, NJ

**John Shea**, University of Maryland, MD

**Amy Shrout**, Holy Cross College, IN

*Explorations in Economics* benefited from the input of hundreds of reviewers and focus group participants. A complete list may be found at the back of the book beginning on page R-1.

# Brief Contents

# Contents

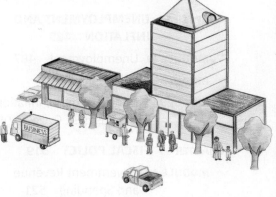

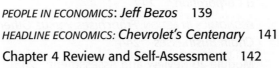

**PART 5  MACROECONOMICS**

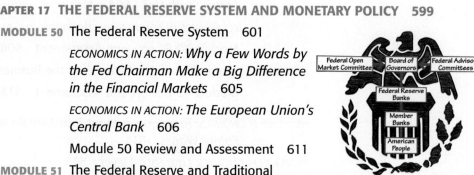

# Special Features

## ECONOMICS IN ACTION

**ECONOMICS IN ACTION**

### Opportunity Cost Doesn't Always Mean Dollars Paid Out

People often confuse the opportunity cost of a decision with the direct dollar cost of that decision. If you've ever missed a sports practice to take a make-up exam after school, you've experienced an opportunity cost that doesn't involve money at all. And even if you're not Ben Kaufman, the opportunity cost of attending college includes more than the cost of tuition. College students also give up the best alternative to attending college, which is typically going straight to work. Suppose you would earn $25,000 a year in the best available job right after high school. Then the opportunity cost of attending college would be the tuition cost plus the forgone income of $25,000 for each of four years, or $100,000. Although it isn't actually paid out, that money you would have earned is part of the cost, too.

The first step in making good decisions is to understand that the true cost of any decision is the opportunity cost, and not just the amount of money spent as a result of the decision. This applies to life's big decisions, such as whether to attend college, and to everyday decisions, such as whether to make up an exam.

*The opportunity cost of attending college is the tuition and the forgone income that you would have earned had you been working instead.*

# PEOPLE IN ECONOMICS

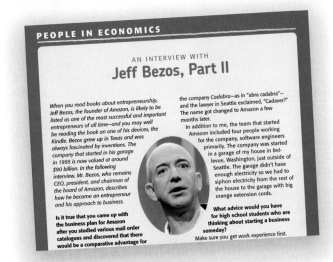

PEOPLE IN ECONOMICS

AN INTERVIEW WITH
Jeff Bezos, Part II

# HEADLINE ECONOMICS

HEADLINE ECONOMICS

USA TODAY

# Burger King Tries Home Delivery
BY BRUCE HOROVITZ, USA TODAY

102

# Figures and Tables

The graphs highlighted in blue are featured as interactive, animated graphs on the Book Companion Site.
**www.worthpublishers.com/ExplorationsinEconomics1e**

# How to Get the Most from This Program

Are you taking Economics because it was a required course or because you are interested in learning more about the economy? Either way, learning how to use the *Explorations in Economics* program effectively will help you achieve success in the class and in life.

**CHAPTER 1 & YOU** On a typical weekend afternoon you probably have some tough decisions to make: will you watch a movie, hang out with friends, study for a big test, or do some odd jobs for neighbors? And with the money in your pocket, will you buy a pizza, donate to charity, download an album, or save for the future? Other tough decisions must be made at the national level. For example, should new tax dollars go toward building better schools or strengthening our national defense? And should new workers produce donuts or dream homes? This chapter explains how the tools of economics apply to tough calls like these. Even if you never make decisions about donuts or national defense, what you learn will help you make better choices at school, at home, and with the money in your pocket on a weekend afternoon.

CHAPTER 1

# Exploring Economics

MODULE 1: **What Is Economics?**
MODULE 2: **Production Possibilities for a Nation**
MODULE 3: **The World of Economics**

## WHAT TO EXPECT FROM ECONOMICS

Now that you're studying economics, don't be surprised if people start asking you questions like "What's going to happen with the stock market?" If you don't know exactly what the stock market is, don't worry—you'll learn about it later in this book. But here's a secret: even if you memorized every bit of economic wisdom ever written, you still wouldn't be able to predict whether the stock ... you will learn in Chapter ... to the stock market. B... make sense of the daily ... money; and lead a happ...

How can economics ... understanding the worl... making tools for indivi... Economics can help you ... a successful business, a... as many have recently, ... on to their jobs and ho... weather, oil spills, and ... prepare for jolts to foo...

Your study of econo... advertisers, the media ... capture your hard-earn... the stock market is u...

> Each chapter in the book is divided into two to four short modules.
>
> REVIEW the MODULE OUTLINE and read the CHAPTER INTRODUCTION to get a feel for the ideas that will be introduced in the chapter.
>
> For example, Chapter 1 lets you know what to expect and why an understanding of economics is important.

**CHAPTER 1 & YOU** On a typical weekend afternoon you probably have some tough decisions to make: will you watch a movie, hang out with friends, study for a big test, or do some odd jobs for neighbors? And with the money in your pocket, will you buy a ... donate to charity, download an album, or save for the future? ... tough decisions must be made at the national level. For example, ... new tax dollars go toward building better schools or strengthening ... national defense? And should new workers produce donuts or ... homes? This chapter explains how the tools of economics ap... tough calls like these. Even if you never make decisions about d... or national defense, what you learn will help you make better choices at school, at home, and with the money in your pocket on a weekend afternoon.

> READ the CHAPTER & YOU paragraph to see how the economic ideas in the chapter relate to your life.

---

What Is Economics?    **3**

## MODULE 1

# What Is Economics?

**KEY IDEA:** Economics deals with the choices we make, individually and
as a society, under conditions of scarcity.

**OBJECTIVES**
- To explain what economics is and why it is important.
- To define opportunity costs.
- To differentiate between wants and needs.
- To name society's key economic resources.

*You can't always get what you want!*

### Economics Is about More Than Money

What you're doing right now—reading this book—is the result of an economic
decision. That might surprise you. When people think of *economics*, they
usually think about money, complicated graphs and charts, or factories
producing cars. Or they think about words like *prices*, *unemployment*, and
*stocks*. Economics is about all of these things, as you will see. But it is also
about you, right now, making the choice to sit down and read this book.
Because economics, at its core, is about choices: **economics** is the study
of choice under conditions of *scarcity*.

**Scarcity** exists if we desire more of something than we can have. For
example, individuals face a scarcity of time, businesses face a scarcity of the materials used to
make what they sell, governments face a scarcity of tax dollars, and countries face a scarcity
of energy sources. A good way to understand scarcity is to think about your own life.

### SCARCITY AND YOU

What is scarce for you? In other words,
what do you desire that you can't have?
If you would like a better cell phone, your
own car, more clothes, and more time
playing your favorite sport, these things
are scarce for you. Behind these examples are two more basic forms of scarcity.
One is the scarcity of money available for
you to spend—as you know, it doesn't
exactly grow on trees. The other is time.
Everything you do takes time
eating, doing chores, relaxing
ily or friends, going to concerts
ing events, reading, surfing the
and your favorite: studying ec
But there are only so many hou
day. You don't have as much tir
would like, so your time is scarc

Each of us must deal with the scarcity
of time and money. So when economists
study choices, they usually focus on how
people spend their time and money.

**Scarcity Implies Tradeoffs**
Whenever the scarcity of money
or time forces you to make a choice, you
face a *tradeoff*. You make a **tradeoff**
when you give up one thing to get something else. For example, suppose you
have $25 to spend. You've considered

**Economics** is the study of
choice under conditions of
scarcity.

**Scarcity** exists if we desire
more of something than we
can have.

You make a **tradeoff** when
you give up one thing to get
something else.

---

# Glossary/Glosario

This Glossary/Glosario includes all of the definitions
found in the margins of the text.

Cómo usar el glosario en español:
1. Busca el término en inglés que desees encontrar.
2. El término en español, junto con la definición,
   se encuentra en la columna de la derecha.

| English | Español |
|---|---|
| **A** | |
| **Absolute advantage**—the ability to produce more of a good than a trading partner using a given quantity of resources. | **Ventaja absoluta**—la capacidad de producir más de un bien que otra persona, usando una cantidad dada de recursos. |
| **ACH (automated clearing house) transfers**—transfers between payers' and payees' accounts carried out without the use of checks on a secure electronic s-transfer network | **Transferencias de caja de compensación**—transferencias entre las cuentas de quienes pagan y quienes reciben, efectuadas sin en un red segura para la |

---

**Each module presents a handful of concepts central to the study of economics.**

**PREVIEW those concepts by reading the KEY IDEA and OBJECTIVES at the beginning of each module.**

**STUDY the KEY TERMS as you read. Notice that the most important vocabulary words are printed in blue and defined in the margin.**

**These words are also defined in the English and Spanish Glossary/Glosario appendix at the end of the book.**

**PRACTICE your mastery of the language of economics with the ONLINE FLASHCARDS.**

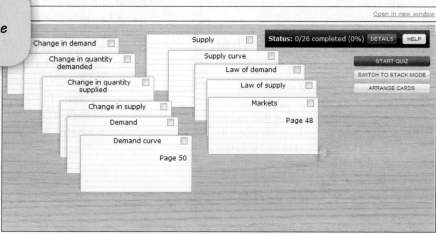

Open in new window

| Change in demand | Supply | Status: 0/26 completed (0%)  DETAILS  HELP |
| Change in quantity demanded | Supply curve | START QUIZ |
| Change in quantity supplied | Law of demand | SWITCH TO STACK MODE |
| Change in supply | Law of supply | ARRANGE CARDS |
| Demand | Markets | |
| Demand curve | Page 48 | |
| Page 50 | | |

the market price is lower than the equilibrium price, there is excess demand and the market price rises. In both cases, unless something like government price controls prevents the market price from fully adjusting, it will keep moving until it reaches the equilibrium price.

 **DID YOU GET IT?**
Why can we expect the price of a good to reach the equilibrium price?

*Even though no one really needs the latest electronic gadget, prices tend to be high when long lines of customers form for gadgets that are in short supply.*

demand relative to supply—is the key to price determination. When there is a lot of demand for something that is in short supply, like gold, Super Bowl tickets, a[nd] Picasso paintings, the relative scarc[ity] causes the good to be expensive ev[en] though no one really "needs" it to s[ur-] vive. The same idea explains why ma[ny] goods that are very important to u[s—] such as food and clothing—are availa[ble] at much lower prices. For these goo[ds,] prices are low because supply is high re[la-] tive to demand.

are high and others are low. The *relative scarcity* of a good—meaning the size of

**STOP and think about the DID YOU GET IT? questions, which are sprinkled throughout the text and figures. If you can answer each question correctly and defend your point of view, you are on your way to mastering the content!**

**Did you ever wonder why the latest Apple product is so expensive? LOOK at the PHOTOS and READ the CAPTIONS, which review and illustrate the explanations in the text. Sometimes pictures really are worth a thousand words!**

## ECONOMICS IN ACTION
## The Diamond-Water Paradox

**WATCH OUT for CAUTION BOXES, which identify common mistakes made by economics students, like this one on page 64.**

 **Markets Are More Than Supermarkets**

It's tempting to think of a market as a physical place, such as your local supermarket. But remember that *market* has a special meaning in economics; it refers to a group of buyers and sellers of a specific product or resource. The exchanges in a single market may take place in many different locations, including online.

## YOUR TURN

Think about your favorite food (pizza? chocolate?) and your least favorite food (sushi? liverwurst?). Is your favorite food sold in many restaurants or stores? Is your favorite food easier to find than your least favorite food? If so, resources are being allocated well to serve you and others like you and you can commend your country for its answer to the first key economic question.

**GET INVOLVED with the content. Spend time reflecting on YOUR TURN questions and activities, like this example from page 40. YOUR TURN questions help connect your personal experiences to the economics concept you just learned.**

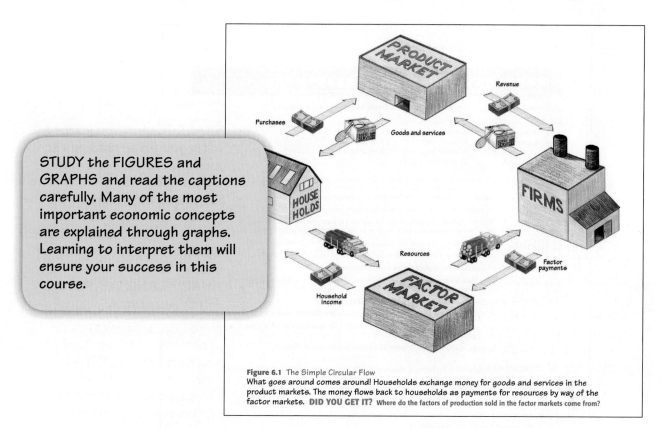

STUDY the FIGURES and GRAPHS and read the captions carefully. Many of the most important economic concepts are explained through graphs. Learning to interpret them will ensure your success in this course.

**Figure 6.1**  The Simple Circular Flow
What goes around comes around! Households exchange money for goods and services in the product markets. The money flows back to households as payments for resources by way of the factor markets.  **DID YOU GET IT?**  Where do the factors of production sold in the factor markets come from?

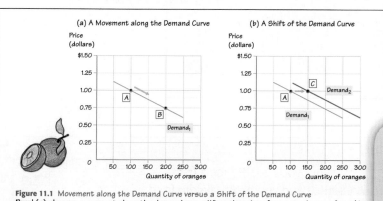

**Figure 11.1**  Movement along the Demand Curve versus a Shift of the Demand Curve
Panel (a) shows a movement along the demand curve. When the price of oranges changes from $1 to $0.75, consumers are willing to buy 100 more oranges. Panel (b) shows what happens if people want to purchase more oranges at every price; the entire demand curve shifts to the right.

VISIT the Book Companion Site to get help with graphing.

LEARN how to read and interpret graphs with with the interactive GraphExplore tool and PRACTICE drawing your own graphs.

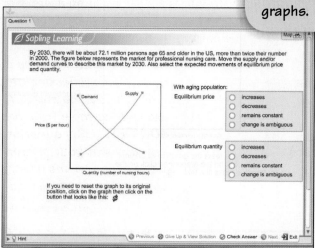

# MODULE 13 REVIEW AND ASSESSMENT

**Summing Up the Key Ideas:** Match the following terms to the correct definitions.

A. Profit
B. Quantity supplied
C. Unit-elastic supply
D. Elastic supply
E. Supply schedule
F. Supply curve
G. Market supply curve
H. Elasticity of supply
I. Law of supply
J. Inelastic supply
K. Perfect competition

_____ 1. A condition that exists when every unit of the good sold in the market is identical, the g
produced by many firms, new firms are free to enter the market, existing firms are free
market, and consumers are aware of the prices charged by the various firms.

_____ 2. The tendency for the price and quantity supplied to move in the same direction.

_____ 3. When the quantity supplied is moderately sensitive to price changes, such that the perc
change in the quantity supplied is the same as the percentage change in the price.

_____ 4. A graphical representation of the supply schedule, showing the quantity supplied at eac

_____ 5. The total revenue a firm receives from selling its product minus the total cost of produc

_____ 6. Measures how responsive firms are to price changes.

_____ 7. When the quantity supplied is so sensitive to price changes that it changes by a larger p
than the price.

_____ 8. A table that lists the quantity supplied at specified prices.

_____ 9. A graphical representation of the quantity supplied by all firms in the market at various

_____ 10. The quantity of a good or service that firms would be willing and able to sell at a particula
over a given period of time.

_____ 11. When the quantity supplied changes by a smaller percentage than the price.

**Analyze and Explain:** In the following situations, identify if the supply is **elastic** or **inelastic** and then
provide an explanation for your answer.

| | ELASTIC OR INELASTIC? | EXPLANATION |
|---|---|---|
| 1. the supply of houses | | |
| 2. the supply of a service such as car washing | | |
| 3. the supply of computers, which producers can supply more of by next year | | |
| 4. the supply of tickets for a professional tennis match | | |

PRACTICE what you learned after you finish reading each module. Each module ends with a short set of questions for you to quiz yourself. Do the matching exercises to make sure you know the KEY TERMS. Check your understanding of the key ideas by answering the ANALYZE AND EXPLAIN and APPLY questions.

VISIT the Book Companion Site or access our SAPLING LEARNING interactive study program for lots of extra help and opportunities to practice what you've learned.

WORK lots and lots of problems with guided feedback in Sapling Learning's interactive study program so you know you are ready to ace your teacher's tests.

Question 1

**Sapling Learning** Map

By 2030, there will be about 72.1 million persons age 65 and older in the US, more than twice their number
. The figure below represents the market for professional nursing care. Move the supply and/or
curves to describe this market by 2030. Also select the expected movements of equilibrium price
ntity.

Demand    Supply

per hour)

Quantity (number of nursing hours)

you need to reset the graph to its original
position, click on the graph then click on the
button that looks like this:

With aging population:
Equilibrium price
○ increases
○ decreases
○ remains constant
○ change is ambiguous

Equilibrium quantity
○ increases
○ decreases
○ remains constant
○ change is ambiguous

Hint    Previous   Give Up & View Solution   Check Answer   Next   Exit

# CHAPTER 5 REVIEW AND SELF-ASSESSMENT

## REVIEW

### Points to Remember

**MODULE 13: UNDERSTANDING SUPPLY**

1. **Profit** is the total revenue a firm receives from selling its product minus the total cost of producing it.

2. The **quantity supplied** is the amount of a good that firms are willing to supply at a particular price over a given period of time.

3. There is **perfect competition** in a market when there are many firms selling identical goods, firms are free to enter and exit the market, and consumers have full information about the price and availability of goods.

4. According to the **law of supply**, an increase in the price of a good leads to an increase in the quantity supplied.

5. The **supply schedule** for a good is a table l... quantity of t...

11. When there is a movement along the supply curve, this is called a **change in the quantity supplied**.

12. **Inventory** consists of goods that are held in temporary storage.

**MODULE 15: PRODUCTION, COST, AND THE PROFIT-MAXIMIZING OUTPUT LEVEL**

13. The **short run**... the quantity o...

14. The **long run**... quantities of ...

15. The **marginal**... by which tota... worker is hire...

> TEST YOURSELF after completing the modules in each chapter. REVIEW the POINTS TO REMEMBER for each module. This easy-to-follow outline will help fill in any gaps you may have in your notes.
>
> ANSWER the SELF-ASSESSMENT Multiple-Choice and Constructed Response questions to make sure you understand all the material and will do well on tests.

## SELF-ASSESSMENT

The following questions are the type your teacher might ask you on a quiz or a... improve your performance on class tests.

### Multiple-Choice Questions

| PRICE (DOLLARS) | QUANTITY SUPPLIED |
|---|---|
| $5.00 | 100 |
| 4.50 | 90 |
| 4.00 | 75 |
| 3.50 | 55 |
| 3.00 | 30 |
| 2.50 | 0 |

1. As the price falls from $4.50 to $4.00,

   a. the quantity supplied decreases from 90 to 75.

   b. the ... upplied increases from 75 to 90.

2. When a perfectly competitive firm shuts down in the short run, there is still the obligation to pay

   a. all the variable costs, but not the fixed cost.

   b. no costs at all.

   c. the variable costs.

   d. the fixed costs.

3. Which of the following correctly defines *profit*?

   a. marginal revenue minus marginal cost

   b. fixed cost minus variable cost

   c. marginal revenue minus marginal product

   d. total revenue minus total cost

### Constructed Response Question

1. Complete the blank spaces in this table of costs and revenue for a typical firm:

| NUMBER OF WORKERS | TOTAL PRODUCT | MARGINAL PRODUCT | FIXED COST (DOLLARS) | VARIABLE COST (DOLLARS) | TOTAL COST (DOLLARS) | MARGINAL COST (DOLLARS) | PRODUCT PRICE (DOLLARS) | TOTAL REVENUE (DOLLARS) | PROFIT (DOLLARS) |
|---|---|---|---|---|---|---|---|---|---|
| 0 | 0 | | | | $200 | | $10 | | |
| 1 | 20 | | | $60 | | | 10 | | |
| 2 | 50 | | | 120 | | | 10 | | |
| 3 | 70 | | | 180 | | | 10 | | |
| 4 | 80 | | | 240 | | | 10 | | |
| 5 | 85 | | | 300 | | | 10 | | |
| 6 | 88 | | | 360 | | | 10 | | |
| 7 | 90 | | | 420 | | | 10 | | |
| 8 | 91 | | | 480 | | | 10 | | |

2. Answer these questions using the data in the chart:

   a. How much are the fixed costs for this firm?

   b. In what type of market does this firm sell i... product? Exp...

   d. At what point (if any) do diminishing returns set in? Explain.

   e. What is the profit-maximizing ...tput level for this firm? Explain.

> **SEE HOW CONCEPTS APPLY**
> to the real world in the special boxed content that is sprinkled throughout the book

## ECONOMICS IN ACTION

# The Wages of Economics

Economists work in many places, including government agencies like the Central Intelligence Agency and the Bureau of Labor Statistics; consulting ...pany; and large ...d, and Bank of America. ...ics is also helpful for a ...ness. Because people ...ave skills that help them ...nd markets, they are ...d.

...ssociation of Colleges ...rveys new college ...each year, asking ...ng salaries. Different ...ajors earn different ...alaries. As the table ...conomics is among the ...aying specialties.

| COLLEGE MAJOR | STARTING SALARY (DOLLARS) |
|---|---|
| Engineering | $58,581 |
| Computer science | 56,383 |
| Economics | 54,800 |
| Business administration | 49,200 |
| Accounting | 47,800 |
| Math and sciences | 40,939 |
| Communications | 40,022 |
| Political science | 38,400 |
| Education | 37,423 |

**Median Starting Salary for Selected Majors, College Class of 2012**

SOURCE: National Association of Colleges and Employers, "Salary Survey: Starting Salaries for New College Graduates—April 2012 Executive Summary." Available online at www.naceweb.org/salary-survey-data/?referal=research&menuID=71&nodetype=4.

**DID YOU GET IT?**
Why are people with training in economics valued in the workplace?

(ISTOCKPHOTO/THINKSTOCK)

## ECONOMICS IN ACTION

# Lowering the Price of TV Downloads

In early 2010, Apple wanted to lower the price it charged on iTunes for downloading TV shows from $1.99 to $0.99 per episode. But Apple first needed permission from the TV networks that supplied the shows. Apple's managers believed that lowering the price would cause so many more people to download shows that total spending on the shows—and the total revenue of the TV networks—would rise. If they were right, the TV networks would come out ahead, and so would Apple, which kept a portion of the sales revenue for itself.

The managers at the TV networks weren't so sure. They agreed that lowering the price would increase the number of downloads, but each download would bring in less money than before. The TV executives worried that the rise in quantity demanded might not make up for the fall in price and that their total revenue would decrease.

Who was right, the managers at Apple or those at the TV networks? In making their case, the Apple managers were essentially arguing that the demand for downloaded TV shows was elastic. If that were true, then the rise in quantity demanded would more than make up for the lower price, causing an increase in total spending on downloads and the total revenue for the networks and for Apple.

The TV networks, by contrast, were concerned that the demand for downloaded TV shows might be inelastic. If they were right, then the quantity demanded would not rise by enough to make up for the price drop, and total revenue would fall.

In February 2010, the TV networks decided to dip their toes in the water. They gave Apple permission to charge $0.99 for certain shows only, on an experimental basis. Their goal was to determine if demand was elastic or inelastic. Based on the results, they would decide whether to allow Apple to lower the price of all TV shows. Because the networks didn't announce the revenue for specific shows, no one knows for sure how the experiment turned out. But we can make a good guess about the results, because six months after the experiment began, the networks were still charging the higher $1.99 price on almost all their shows. This suggests that the demand for TV downloads was inelastic and that the revenue from the experimental shows fell when the price fell.

*The demand for TV downloads is inelastic. That is, a price change leads to a relatively small change in the quantity of downloads demanded.*

> **ECONOMICS IN ACTION** are found in every module and show you how the economic concepts you're studying apply to the world around you.

## PEOPLE IN ECONOMICS

### AN INTERVIEW WITH **Jeff Fluhr of StubHub**

*Jeff Fluhr was a cofounder of StubHub, an Internet trading website for buying and selling tickets to sporting and entertainment events. He attended Morristown High School in Morristown, New Jersey. Although he didn't take an economics class in high school, economics has had a big impact on his life. In 2007, he sold StubHub to eBay for $310 million and looked for other ventures to start.*

**When did you think of the idea for StubHub?**
I was a first-year student getting my MBA in business school in 2000 when I started the company. Prior to this, I had the uncomfort... experience of buy... and selling ticket... ...king lots h...

people would prefer to pay a higher price rather than not go. And at higher prices, some people with tickets would prefer to sell them, because they have better things to do with the money. The higher price brings supply and demand back into balance. StubHub provides a market to create that balance.

**Can you give an example?**
For the Miley Cyrus concert tour that began in October 2007, tickets were first sold by Ticketmaster at $65—far below the equilibrium price. People were not permitted to buy more than four tickets each, but all the tickets sold out within minutes anyway. Many devoted fans— even if they were willing to p... ...uld ...en unable to go...

## HEADLINE ECONOMICS

### AP

# "Sneakerheads" Hype Shoes for Credit and Profit

CHICAGO—They are lined up in the freezing rain, waiting patiently, stubbornly. All night. All for a few pairs of shoes. Sean Rivera is among the 60 or so die-hards on this sidewalk along Chicago's Magnificent Mile shopping district. He looks a little crazy, smiling and squinting through fogged glasses.

It's all part of the life of "sneakerheads," people who spend hundreds, even thousands of dollars on shoes, many of which carry the name of professional basketball stars, past and present. Chicagoans proudly point out that it started here with Michael Jordan and his Nike Air Jordan brand.

Jesus Estrella, a blogger who has become a self-made sneaker guru on YouTube, filmed one recent melee outside a mall in Orlando, Florida. "This shoe game officially has gone bananas," Estrella, who is known as

"JStar" in the sneakerhead community, said as he watched police arrive and then begin sending people home.

You don't always know which shoe is going to be "the shoe" of the ones that are released, Estrella says. But often, the shoes that go the quickest are those that are "reissued"—new versions of old standards, including Air Jordans and the Nike "Mag" sneakers worn by the character Marty McFly in the movie "Back to the Future." Consignment shops and online auctions have seen some of those shoes resell for thousands of dollars, while others sit on shelves longer and sell for less. A pair of original Air Jordans in good condition—bought by the most serious collectors—can sell today for $4,000 to $5,000. "Back to the Future" Mags, originally released to raise money for the Michael J. Fox

Foundation and Parkinson's research, go for that much, or more.

Often, sneakerheads are young men in their teens, 20s and 30s, many of whom now use the Internet to show off their "kicks." And companies like Nike are using that instant, word-of-mouth communication to their benefit, marketing experts say.

Limiting the supply—a tactic sometimes called "artificial scarcity"— also fuels the demand in an age when young people are [...] products and looki[...] out. "It's harder a[...] yourself different [...] body has access to [...] Gary Rudman, pre[...] based GTR Consu[...] the habits of young[...]

For sneakerhe[...] showing off your [...] ibility with your p[...] an associate profes[...] Yale University, rel[...] as "social sign[...] yourself with a h[...] build status. So [...] turn, limiting acc[...] service to create [...] tion of coolness. [...] leagues have, for [...] Google and Spotif[...] service—both of w[...] made some service[...] sumers by invitation[...]

"It's a bit of a puzzle—why would the company early on try to slow down the adoption of their product?" she says. She found that the goal for Google, with Google+, or Spotify was to eventually draw in even more members who wanted what the initial members had. Michael Carberry, marketing professor at American University in Washington, says when you factor in what it costs to design and promote the limited edition shoes, Nike may not make as much money on them as it would if they were mass produced, but the publicity they generate is priceless. "The buzz is what works for them and it just enhances the aura of Nike," he says—and, in turn, generates more overall shoe sales to those

AP PHOTO/MARTHA IRVINE

**220**

> HEADLINE ECONOMICS boxes include articles featured in leading newspapers and economics magazines. These articles help link larger economic concepts to the world around you. Questions at the end of each article ask you to summarize and reflect on the article, like this one on page 220.

> PEOPLE IN ECONOMICS features introduce you to both influential economists, like Adam Smith, and new names in economics, like Jeff Fluhr and Alexa von Tobel. Some of the boxes feature extensive interviews while others offer a short biographical sketch.

## PEOPLE IN ECONOMICS

# Alexa von Tobel, LearnVest.com

When she graduated from Harvard College, Alexa von Tobel realized that although she was about to start a job on Wall Street, she did not feel comfortable managing her own money. In fact, she had never taken a personal finance class and wasn't sure how to deal with credit cards, insurance, and taxes. It occurred to her that many young women must be in a similar situation.

A few years later, in 2008, von Tobel took a leave of absence from Harvard Business School (to which she had since returned) to start LearnVest.com. Her goal was to explain personal finance in clear and understandable ways, and to provide tools that would help women manage their financial situation. LearnVest offers features for tracking expenditure and budgeting, as well as tutorials on saving money and reducing debt. Users can also pay to receive advice from financial experts and enroll in online finance courses. Alexa von Tobel believes that financial planning is something that everyone should be able to do and that taking control of your finances can help you achieve your dreams.

# Skills Handbook

SECTION 1: **Critical Thinking Skills**

SECTION 2: **Data Bank**

SECTION 3: **Atlas**

SECTION 4: **Reading Graphs and Other Visual Resources**

SECTION 5: **Test-Taking Skills**

> CHECK OUT the SKILLS HANDBOOK at the end of the book for study tips and information that will help you be successful in this and other courses.

> If you need a little extra help with reading articles or interpreting graphs, consult Sections 1 and 4.

**Practice Reading Primary and Secondary Sources**

## NEW YORK NEWS

*October 29, 1929*

### STOCK MARKET CRASHES

New York—A massive decline in stock mar prices took place yesterday on the New Yo Stock Exchange. More than 16 million sha changed hands as buyers rushed to sell stoc The Dow Jones Industrial Average lost 12 p cent to close at just 198, down from a high 381 in September.

Stock prices have been falling for wee General Electric closed the day at 210 a peaking at 396 on September 3. RCA hit earlier this year but bottomed out at 26 y terday. "I'm ruined," investor Andrew Adams told reporters on Wall Street. "I only hope the market recovers soon."

 **CHECK YOUR UNDERSTANDING**
Answer the following questions about the practice selection to check your understanding.

1. Is the text a primary or secondary source? How can you tell?
2. What is the main idea of this text?
3. Restate the events of the text using your own words.

> Review Section 5 as you prepare to take your first text.

## SECTION 4

# Reading Graphs and Other Visual Resources

### READING LINE GRAPHS

Line graphs are visual depictions of numerical values. The line on the graph shows the changing levels of a certain measurement or measurements. Usually, line graphs show change over time. More than one line may appear on a graph to allow the viewer to compare and contrast data.

### Prepare to Read Line Graphs

Learning how to find information on a line graph is important to reading it correctly.

**d the title.**
e tells t

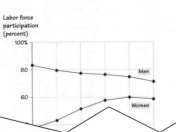

## SECTION 5

# Test-Taking Skills

### EFFECTIVELY ANSWERING A MULTIPLE-CHOICE QUESTION

Answering multiple-choice questions may seem challenging, but having a plan to address each question can make the test-taking process less intimidating.

### Parts of a Multiple-Choice Question

All multiple-choice questions are set up in a similar way. Study this question to know what to expect.

> The **question stem** asks the question you must answer.

Which statement best describes the circular flow of income?

Fou **oices** give just one best

- **Read each answer choice carefully.**
  Consider each answer choice one by one. Look for key words in the answer choices. Choices that include words such as *always* or *never* are often wrong.

- **Choose the best answer.**
  Determine which answer choice best fits the question. Make sure that the answer choice addresses the important terms and ideas you identified while reading the question.

### General Practices

Make sure that you mark your answer choice clearly and neatly. If you change an answer, be sure to completely erase your first choice. Use any time at the end of the test to double-check your earlier answers.

### EFFECTIVELY ANSWERING AN
**AY QUESTION**

# Personal Finance Handbook

FH

> PREPARE FOR THE FUTURE and learn how to manage your money by reading the PERSONAL FINANCE HANDBOOK.

> Lots of activities, tips, links to useful websites, and other valuable information will help you get on the road to financial independence.

## ACTIVITY

### Create a Resume

If you applied for a job today, what information could you list on your resume? Create a sa... using the template below:

YOUR NAME HERE
123 Any Street, City, State, Zip Code
Phone: (000) 000-0000 | Email: yourname@youremail.com

**PROFESSIONAL OBJECTIVE**

State the kind of work you want to do and why you are qua...

Example: To sell technology products and services for a gl... electronics and experience in customer service.

Write your objective here:

_____

**...RIENCE**

## CREATE A BUDGET

Take a look at Avery's financial situation and help him create a realistic spending plan that will lead to a better financial future.

### Current Situation

Avery is 24 years old and works in the mail room at a large company. His gross pay is $2,500 per month, which gives him $2,000 in net pay (after taxes and health insurance are taken out). He's been spending more than his take-home pay for a year and has accumulated over $8,000 in credit card debt. Avery can ...nancing a lifestyle that he can't afford. Additionally, ...tirement.

...thly Spending*

| AMOUNT (DOLLARS) |
| --- |
| $2,000 |
| $700 |

## ACTIVITY

### What Is a Job Application?

In addition to your resume, most potential employers require you to complete a job or employment application. The application can be customized by the employer, but it typically asks for personal information, references, and specifics about the job you're applying for. Submitting an impressive resume and application will make you stand out from other applicants.

Here's a tip to save time when you're applying for a job: Complete the sample application below and make a copy to bring with you to each job interview.

### Employment Application Information Sheet

**POSITION APPLYING FOR:**_____

First Name: _____ Middle Initial:_____ Last Name: _____

Current Address

Street and Apt #: _____ City _____ State:____ Zip Code: _____
Telephone:_____ E-mail:_____
Social Security #: _____ - ____ - _____ Driver's License #: _____ State: ____

I am an U.S. Citizen or otherwise authorized to work in the
United States on an authorized basis: _____Yes ____No

Have you ever been convicted of a felony? _____Yes ____No

**CHAPTER 1 & YOU** On a typical weekend afternoon you probably have some tough decisions to make: will you watch a movie, hang out with friends, study for a big test, or do some odd jobs for neighbors? And with the money in your pocket, will you buy a pizza, donate to charity, download an album, or save for the future? Other tough decisions must be made at the national level. For example, should new tax dollars go toward building better schools or strengthening our national defense? And should new workers produce donuts or dream homes? This chapter explains how the tools of economics apply to tough calls like these. Even if you never make decisions about donuts or national defense, what you learn will help you make better choices at school, at home, and with the money in your pocket on a weekend afternoon.

# Exploring Economics

MODULE 1:   **What Is Economics?**

MODULE 2:   **Production Possibilities for a Nation**

MODULE 3:   **The World of Economics**

## WHAT TO EXPECT FROM ECONOMICS

Now that you're studying economics, don't be surprised if people start asking you questions like "What's going to happen with the stock market?" If you don't know exactly what the stock market is, don't worry—you'll learn about it later in this book. But here's a secret: even if you memorized every bit of economic wisdom ever written, you still wouldn't be able to predict whether the stock market will rise or fall tomorrow. In fact, as you will learn in Chapter 12, not even the experts know what will happen to the stock market. But economics has a lot to offer. It can help you make sense of the daily news; make good decisions about your time and money; and lead a happier, more satisfying life.

How can economics do all that? Economics provides a framework for understanding the world around you. It offers a powerful set of decision-making tools for individuals, businesses, organizations, and governments. Economics can help you figure out what to do with your earnings, develop a successful business, and plan for the future. When businesses stumble, as many have recently, economics shapes policies to help workers hold on to their jobs and homes. Throughout the world, in the wake of severe weather, oil spills, and other disasters, economic forecasts help people prepare for jolts to food and energy prices.

Your study of economics will also help you evaluate messages from advertisers, the media, and the troubling number of tricksters out to capture your hard-earned money. For example, you've already read that the stock market is unpredictable, so you know to be wary of claims

*Economics connects the dots between natural disasters and high food prices.*

that a particular stock investment is a "sure thing." Economic education can also boost your earnings: people with training in economics often earn high salaries because they have acquired skills valued in fields such as business, finance, and government.

Beyond that, you can expect familiarity with economics to help you become a better citizen. Before long, as a voter, a member of a household, and a participant in the life of your community, you will have opportunities to make important decisions. Economic literacy will help you navigate the swirling debates over budgets, the environment, health care, and taxes. Your exposure to economics might even inspire you to seek public office or change the world in some other way! In fact, many former presidents, members of Congress, business executives, rock stars, and philanthropists were economics majors.

An introduction to economics will not give you all the answers, but it will teach you the right kinds of questions to ask and give you a logical way to approach decision making. Ultimately, the economic way of thinking will help you explore your possibilities for success and happiness. And that's why this book is titled *Explorations in Economics*! Let's get started . . .

## BOTTOM LINE
Economics provides a logical way for people to think about decisions at every level—personal, family, organizational, business, and governmental—and what these decisions mean for society.

# MODULE 1

# What Is Economics?

**KEY IDEA:** Economics deals with the choices we make, individually and as a society, under conditions of scarcity.

**OBJECTIVES**

- To explain what economics is and why it is important.
- To define opportunity costs.
- To differentiate between wants and needs.
- To name society's key economic resources.

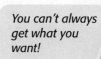

*You can't always get what you want!*

## Economics Is about More Than Money

What you're doing right now—reading this book—is the result of an economic decision. That might surprise you. When people think of *economics*, they usually think about money, complicated graphs and charts, or factories producing cars. Or they think about words like *prices*, *unemployment*, and *stocks*. Economics is about all of these things, as you will see. But it is also about you, right now, making the choice to sit down and read this book. Because economics, at its core, is about choices: **economics** is the study of choice under conditions of *scarcity*.

**Scarcity** exists if we desire more of something than we can have. For example, individuals face a scarcity of time, businesses face a scarcity of the materials used to make what they sell, governments face a scarcity of tax dollars, and countries face a scarcity of energy sources. A good way to understand scarcity is to think about your own life.

## SCARCITY AND YOU

What is scarce for you? In other words, what do you desire that you can't have? If you would like a better cell phone, your own car, more clothes, and more time playing your favorite sport, these things are scarce for you. Behind these examples are two more basic forms of scarcity. One is the scarcity of money available for you to spend—as you know, it doesn't exactly grow on trees. The other is time. Everything you do takes time—sleeping, eating, doing chores, relaxing with family or friends, going to concerts or sporting events, reading, surfing the Internet, and your favorite: studying economics. But there are only so many hours in the day. You don't have as much time as you would like, so your time is scarce.

Each of us must deal with the scarcity of time and money. So when economists study choices, they usually focus on how people spend their time and money.

###  Scarcity Implies Tradeoffs

Whenever the scarcity of money or time forces you to make a choice, you face a *tradeoff*. You make a **tradeoff** when you give up one thing to get something else. For example, suppose you have $25 to spend. You've considered buying a new cat, but you're fond of eating at the ice cream shop. If you spend your $25 on a pet, you can't also spend it on banana splits. With an unlimited amount of money, you would not face a tradeoff—you could have a personal zoo and still eat ice cream every day. But because money is scarce, the tradeoff is

**Economics** is the study of choice under conditions of scarcity.

**Scarcity** exists if we desire more of something than we can have.

You make a **tradeoff** when you give up one thing to get something else.

© VICTOR MARTELLO/ISTOCKPHOTO.COM

*Using your time to study today will have big payoffs in the future.*

The **opportunity cost** of a choice is the value of the next-best alternative given up when that choice is made.

*The movies or shooting hoops? What you give up is part of the opportunity cost of a choice.*

necessary: you can't have your cat and eat banana splits, too.

Choices involving time have tradeoffs, too. For example, right now, you've made a choice to read this book. Even if a teacher or parent told you to read it, you still chose to do it rather than face the consequences of disappointing them. But you could be using your time in many other ways instead, like watching television, talking to friends, or reading a different book. Are you still here? If so, your choice to keep reading means you cannot do those other activities, at least

for now. That's the tradeoff involved in choosing to read this chapter.

Economists are interested in how people like you respond to tradeoffs. If you're wise, you consider the consequences of choices that arrive far into the future. For example, your choice to read this chapter is part of a larger decision to become more educated. Your education, in turn, will help determine the types of jobs you can obtain, your lifestyle, and your understanding of the world around you.

Next we'll look at more aspects of tradeoffs that wise decision makers never neglect.

**DID YOU GET IT?**
Name a good that is scarce for you. What tradeoff must you make to get it?

## OPPORTUNITY COST

As you study economics, you'll learn valuable new ways to think about some familiar concepts. One of these concepts is *cost*. For example, if you go to a movie, what does it cost you? You might be tempted to say that the cost is what you pay for the ticket. If the price of the ticket is $10, that's the cost of going to the movie.

Economics uses a more complete way of thinking about cost, called *opportunity cost*. The **opportunity cost** of a choice is the value of the next-best alternative given up when that choice is made. The opportunity cost captures the full tradeoff involved in a choice.

What is the opportunity cost of seeing a movie? The $10 price of the ticket is part of the opportunity cost. If you pay for a movie ticket, you will have $10 less to spend on other things. In addition to scarce money, the movie uses up some of your scarce time. If you do not go to the movie, you can spend both your money and your time on something else. The activity that you would give up for the movie is part of its opportunity cost.

Let's be more specific. What would you do with that time if you did not see the movie? Would you go to the mall with friends? Practice basketball? Study? If you didn't see the movie, you would choose the best of these other options. Suppose the best alternative would be to practice basketball. Then to see the movie you must give up practicing basketball during that time. You don't actually give up a trip to the mall or study time, because you would not have chosen those activities anyway. The basketball practice you do give up is one part of the opportunity cost of the movie. The other part is the $10 you actually pay for the ticket.

Because opportunity cost is central to the economic way of thinking, you will see the concept in many chapters of this book. Always remember that the opportunity cost of a choice is whatever you must give up for the choice, not just the amount of money you spend. If a choice uses up time, the next-best alternative for using that time is part of the opportunity cost.

**DID YOU GET IT?**
What is your opportunity cost if you go to the movies tonight?

# SCARCITY AND SOCIETY

In addition to choices for individuals, economics deals with choices for *society*. By **society**, we mean any collection of people who share a common bond, such as those living in the same city or country. Tradeoffs for society arise from scarcity, just as they do for individuals. To understand what scarcity means to society, we must first consider our desires and how we attempt to satisfy them.

## Needs and Wants

Everyone in a society has **needs** that must be met for survival. These include food, water, and shelter. In addition, we have **wants**—things we desire that are not essential. A television is an example of a want. Your life might be less fun without a television, but you don't need it to survive. People often confuse needs and wants. Do you ever say that you "need" something—a haircut, a candy

bar, a new outfit—that you could live without? If so, an economist would say you really meant "want." You want a candy bar. You need enough food to stay alive.

It is vitally important to satisfy needs, but most of the tradeoffs in our society involve wants. That's because our needs are limited but our wants are unlimited. No matter how well we live, we can usually think of ways to live better. You can probably imagine having a more luxurious home, a snazzier bike, nicer clothes, and so on. *Economies* form as societies seek to satisfy their needs and wants. An **economy** is a system for coordinating the production and distribution of *goods* and *services*.

## Goods and Services

**Goods** are physical items produced in an economy. Jeans, tennis rackets, popcorn, cars, and even houses are goods. **Services** are activities produced in an economy. A doctor's exam, a teacher's lesson, and a beauty treatment are all services. Services are used up at the same time they are produced, leaving no physical object behind.

When a doctor checks your throat or listens to your heart, you are receiving medical services. True, the doctor uses some goods during the examination, such as a tongue depressor and a stethoscope, but the checkup itself is a service. You cannot put the checkup in a bag and carry it home.

You use many services every day—perhaps more than you think. The teacher in your economics course provides educational services. If you ride the bus to school, your driver provides transportation services. The janitor at your school provides cleaning services. Your phone and computer wouldn't be the same without phone and Internet service providers. And your favorite musicians provide entertainment services. You may also benefit from services provided by waiters, lifeguards, police officers, plumbers, government officials, and mechanics, among others. Most of the discussions of goods in this book apply

An **economy** is a system for coordinating the production and distribution of goods and services.

**Goods** are physical items produced in an economy, such as jeans, tennis rackets, popcorn, cars, and homes.

**Services** are activities produced in an economy, such as education, entertainment, and health care.

A **society** is a collection of people who share a common bond, such as those living in a city, a country, or even the entire world.

**Needs** are minimal requirements of things such as food, water, and shelter that are necessary for survival.

**Wants** are things that are desired but are not essential to life.

**Labor** is the time and effort people contribute to the production process.

**Capital** is anything long lasting that is created by humans for use in production.

**Physical capital** is any long-lasting good that is used to make other goods or services.

**Human capital** refers to the skills and knowledge of workers.

**Resources** are the basic elements from which all goods and services are produced.

**Entrepreneurship** is the willingness of people to organize, operate, and assume the risks involved with business ventures.

**Land** is anything drawn from nature for use in the production of goods or services.

equally to services, although sometimes the services category goes unmentioned for the sake of brevity.

 **DID YOU GET IT?**
What is the difference between a need and a want?

## SCARE RESOURCES

To create any good or service, we must tap into our limited supply of *resources*. In economics, the term *resources* has a very specific meaning: **resources** are the basic elements from which all goods and services are produced.

Economists classify resources into four types: *land, labor, capital,* and *entrepreneurship*. Let's take a closer look at each.

**1.    Land** describes anything drawn from nature for use in the production of goods or services. This includes the fields where strawberries are grown and the properties where Taco Bell restaurants are built. Land also includes the *natural resources* found on or under the ground, such as the forests used to make books, the water sprayed to irrigate cotton

fields, the oil refined to make gasoline, and the iron ore smelted to make steel.

**2.    Labor** is the time and effort people contribute to the production process. Labor is provided whenever a farmer plants strawberries, a cook makes a burrito, a lumberjack cuts down a tree, or an engineer designs an irrigation system.

**3.    Capital** is anything long lasting that is created by humans for use in the production of other things. There are two types of capital: **Physical capital** is any long-lasting *good* that is used to make other goods or services. Examples include tractors, pans, axes, irrigation systems, and oil refineries. Although oil itself is used to fuel everything from tractors to chain saws, it is not considered capital because it is used up in the production process. **Human capital** refers to the skills and knowledge of workers. If you've ever tried to drive a tractor, cook a fancy meal, or cut down a tree, you know these acts take more than time and effort. People with more skills and knowledge produce better results. If you have surgery, fly in an airplane, or eat out, the human capital of the people providing the service matters to you!

**4.    Entrepreneurship** is the willingness of people to organize, operate, and assume the risks involved with business ventures. Entrepreneurs bring together the land, labor, and capital to produce goods and services that satisfy our needs and wants. Although most towns have the land, labor, and capital required for a Taco Bell restaurant, they will have no restaurant unless there is an entrepreneur willing to make it happen. Entrepreneur

Glen Bell opened the first Taco Bell in Downey, California, in 1962. Among other examples of entrepreneurs, Oprah Winfrey started the giant media company Harpo (Oprah spelled backward), Larry Page and Sergey Brin founded Google, and Mark Zuckerberg created Facebook.

The term **inputs** is used to describe the four types of resources, along with anything made with these resources that is in turn used to make something else, such as cement, steel, lumber, and plastic. Because all inputs are either resources or made with resources, it is safe to say that resources are the building blocks of every good and service you consume.

## Society's Tradeoffs

We've seen that to address some of our needs and wants, we must use resources to produce goods and services. The more resources we have, the more goods and services we can produce. Unfortunately, we cannot wave Harry Potter's magic wand and make resources appear out of thin air. Instead, we are limited by the availability of resources. At any point in time, a country has a given number of people who can provide labor, a set amount of land, fixed amounts of physical and human capital, and only so many entrepreneurs. Countries, like people, face a scarcity of resources.

*Writer, producer, and TV personality Tyra Banks is president and chief creative officer of Bankable Enterprises. After Banks became a successful entrepreneur with her show* America's Next Top Model, *she enrolled in a program at Harvard Business School. It's never too late to develop your human capital further!*

Resource scarcity forces every society to make tradeoffs. If more resources are committed to the production of one good or service, fewer resources remain for making other things. To make more bicycles, the manufacturers would need more rubber for the wheels, metal for the frames, and space for the factories, and thus more land. They would also need more capital in the form of machinery to make bicycle frames and parts, labor for assembling and selling the bicycles, and entrepreneurs to organize the bicycle-making businesses. The resources used in the bicycle industry would be drawn away from the production of other things such as computers and cars. So the decision to have more bicycles means we must give up something else.

**Inputs** include the four types of resources— land, labor, capital, and entrepreneurship—along with anything made with these resources that is then used to make something else, such as cement, steel, lumber, and plastic.

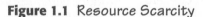

**Figure 1.1** *Resource Scarcity*
**With limited resources and unlimited wants, society is forced to make tradeoffs. DID YOU GET IT?** How does the scarcity of resources affect society's ability to satisfy its wants?

Resource scarcity

Limited ability to produce goods and services

Limited ability to satisfy unlimited wants

Even if a country buys goods from other countries, it still faces scarcity and tradeoffs. Imagine you buy a bicycle made in Canada. That bicycle was made using Canadian resources instead of U.S. resources. Did we escape a tradeoff by getting the bicycle in a different country? Not at all. Purchases across international borders go both ways! The U.S. dollars used to purchase Canadian goods are likely to return home as Canadians purchase U.S. goods. The result is really a trade: Canada provides bicycles to the United States in exchange for goods made in the United States using U.S. resources. So to obtain the bicycle from Canada, we end up using some of our own resources to make goods for Canadians—resources that could otherwise have been used to produce something else. In general, a country cannot escape the scarcity of resources and the tradeoffs it creates. The next module takes a closer look at these tradeoffs.

 **DID YOU GET IT?**
Name the four types of resources.

# MODULE 1 REVIEW AND ASSESSMENT

## Summing Up the Key Ideas: Match the following terms with the correct definition.

A. Economics
B. Scarcity
C. Tradeoff
D. Opportunity cost
E. Society
F. Needs
G. Wants
H. Economy
I. Goods
J. Services
K. Resources
L. Land
M. Labor
N. Capital
O. Physical capital
P. Human capital
Q. Entrepreneurship
R. Inputs

__B__ 1. Exists if we desire more of something than we have.

__I__ 2. Physical items produced in our economy.

__Q__ 3. The willingness of people to organize, operate, and assume the risks involved with business ventures.

__R__ 4. The four types of resources, along with anything created from these resources that is then used to make something else (e.g., cement, steel, lumber, and plastic).

__A__ 5. The study of choice under conditions of scarcity.

__C__ 6. The term for what happens when you give up something to get something else.

__D__ 7. The value of the next-best alternative.

__P__ 8. The skills and knowledge of workers.

__O__ 9. Anything long lasting that is created by humans for use in production.

__E__ 10. Any collection of people who share a common bond, such as those living in the same city or country.

__F__ 11. Minimal amounts of food, water, and shelter necessary for survival.

__J__ 12. Activities produced in an economy.

__G__ 13. Things we desire that are not essential.

__H__ 14. A system for coordinating the production and distribution of goods and services.

__m__ 15. The time and effort people contribute to the production process.

__L__ 16. Anything drawn from nature for use in the production of goods and services.

_____N_____ 17. Any long-lasting good that is used to make other goods or services.

_____K_____ 18. The basic elements from which all goods are produced.

**Analyze:** After you finish this chapter, you might want to take inventory of the scarce resources you own. Classify each of the following items as **land, labor, physical capital, human capital, entrepreneurship,** or **not counted as a scarce resource**.

| | CLASSIFICATION |
|---|---|
| 1. the tools you own | _physical capital_ |
| 2. the area in your yard where you plant vegetables | _land_ |
| 3. the lawn mower you purchased to cut the grass | _physical capital_ |
| 4. gasoline purchased to run the lawn mower | _not counted_ |
| 5. the workers hired to build the planting beds in the garden | _entrepreneurship, human capital_ |
| 6. the knowledge and skills acquired in your college degree program | _human capital_ |
| 7. the money in your pocket | _not accounted_ |
| 8. the water and fertilizer used in your garden | _physical capital_ |
| 9. the organizational skills you possess and use in the operation of your business to sell the vegetables you grow | _entrepreneurship_ |
| 10. the effort you exert in tending your garden | _physical capital_ |

**Apply:** List an opportunity cost for each of the following activities.

| | OPPORTUNITY COST |
|---|---|
| 1. completing this problem set | _time, energy_ |
| 2. watching television tonight | _time, energy_ |
| 3. going to bed early | _reading a book or watching T.V. missed opportunity_ |
| 4. playing a high school sport | _time, energy, homework time_ |
| 5. having an after-school job | _time, energy, HW time_ |
| 6. going to school after high school | _money, time_ |
| 7. going to work directly out of high school | _missed opportunities, further education_ |

## MODULE 2

# Production Possibilities for a Nation

**KEY IDEA:** **A production possibilities frontier illustrates the tradeoffs society makes in its use of scarce resources.**

### OBJECTIVES

- **To explain why economists use models.**
- **To present and interpret the production possibilities frontier model.**
- **To explain the law of increasing opportunity cost.**
- **To define the concepts of efficiency and growth.**

## Managing Complexity

The U.S. economy consists of millions of buyers and sellers of goods and services. Think about all the economic activity near where you live. Even in a small town there are dozens of businesses, hundreds of workers, and thousands of items that could be purchased on any given day. You could not possibly keep track of all the decisions that affect the economy of a small town.

Now imagine the number of decisions that affect the economy of an entire country. On eBay alone, more than $1,000 worth of products are traded every second! Even if computers could track everything that goes on in an economy, that information would not be enough to explain the underlying behavior. Data on production and sales could not explain why these activities take place or how they would change in response to new developments, such as an increase in the price of oil. To gain understanding we must boil the complexity of the economy down to a manageable level. Economists do that with *models*.

*eBay handles $1,000 worth of trades every second. Imagine the complexity of the economy as a whole! Economists use models to simplify their analyses.*

## ECONOMIC MODELS

> A **model** is a simplified representation of reality. Models help you focus on a few aspects of the real world by stripping away nonessential details.

A **model** is a simplified representation of reality. For example, a roadmap is a model because it leaves out details such as buildings, trees, and bumps in the road. It shows you the key streets and highways that will get you from where you are to where you want to be. The lack of details makes a roadmap less realistic but more useful. In economics, we use models to focus on a few aspects of the real world. In the same way, a good economic model leaves out many details of the real world but helps you focus on what is important and find your way in the world of economics.

Economic models are used to understand and predict economic activity. Just as one map helps you find your way around town and another helps you find your way around a new school, it takes different models to help you understand different principles of economics. You are about to learn the first of several models introduced in this book. The *production possibilities frontier model* will allow you to visualize and better understand the tradeoffs a country makes when using its scarce resources.

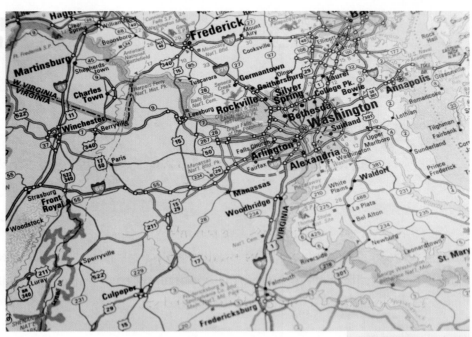

*By leaving out some details, maps and other models make it easier to find what you're looking for.*

# THE PRODUCTION POSSIBILITIES FRONTIER MODEL

Consider a basic choice every country faces: how to divide its scarce resources among different types of production. In a 1976 speech about military threats from the Soviet Union, British prime minister Margaret Thatcher stated, "The Soviets put guns over butter, but we put almost everything over guns." Like many countries, Britain was struggling with the division of resources between goods and services for general consumption, represented by *butter*, and goods and services for use by the military, represented by *guns*. We will continue with that symbolic use of guns and butter.

Imagine a country that produces only guns and butter. Of course, no country produces just two goods, but a realistic model with millions of goods and services would be hard to work with! The table in Figure 2.1 shows several quantities of butter that the country could choose to produce in a week. For each listed quantity of butter, the table also shows the largest quantity of guns that could be made with the resources not used to make butter. For example,

the row labeled *A* indicates that if the country makes no butter and uses all of its resources to make guns, it can produce 1,000 guns. Row *B* indicates that if the country makes 100 tons of butter, there will be enough resources left to make only 900 guns.

If you run your finger down the column for butter, you'll see that as you move from row to row, butter production increases. But producing more butter requires the country to pull resources out of gun production, so gun production falls. Finally, when you arrive at row *F*, the country uses all of its resources for butter and produces 500 tons. Because no resources are left for guns, no guns can be made.

The graph in Figure 2.1 shows the country's *production possibilities frontier*. The **production possibilities frontier**, or **PPF**, is a curve that shows the maximum quantity of one good that can be produced for each possible quantity of another good produced. The quantity of butter is measured on the horizontal axis and the quantity of guns is measured on the vertical axis. Each labeled point on the graph corresponds to a row of the table. For example, the point labeled *B* on the graph represents the information in the row labeled *B* in the table. At point *B*, the

A **production possibilities frontier**, or **PPF**, is a curve that shows the maximum quantity of one good that can be produced for each possible quantity of another good produced.

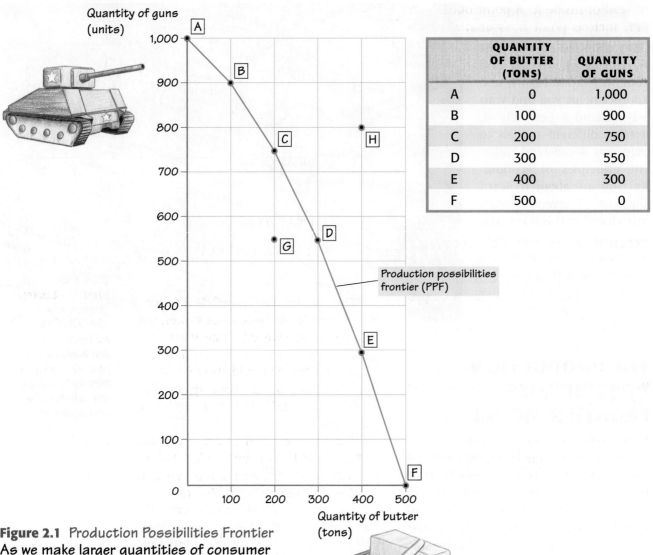

**Figure 2.1** *Production Possibilities Frontier*
*As we make larger quantities of consumer goods like butter, fewer resources are available to make military goods like guns.*
**DID YOU GET IT?** What is the largest quantity of guns that can be made if 400 tons of butter are made?

| | QUANTITY OF BUTTER (TONS) | QUANTITY OF GUNS |
|---|---|---|
| A | 0 | 1,000 |
| B | 100 | 900 |
| C | 200 | 750 |
| D | 300 | 550 |
| E | 400 | 300 |
| F | 500 | 0 |

graph shows that along with 100 tons of butter, at most 900 guns can be made.

The production possibilities frontier is the smooth curve connecting points *A* through *F*. Between the labeled points on the curve are many unlabeled points that also represent combinations of a quantity of butter and a quantity of guns that can be made using all available resources. The word *frontier* means "boundary" or "border," and the production possibilities frontier represents a border between what the country can produce and what it cannot produce using the available resources.

The country can choose the production levels represented by any point on the PPF. It can also choose any point inside the PPF. For example, point *G* represents a combination of 200 tons of butter and 550 guns. The country could produce at point *G* if it wanted to. But the PPF shows us that if 200 tons of butter are produced, the country has enough resources to produce 750 guns (point *C*). So the country would prefer to make better use of its resources and produce at point *C* rather than at point *G*. In general, a country is better off producing on the production possibilities frontier instead of inside it. A point outside the PPF, such as point *H*, is unattainable—there are not enough resources available to produce the combination of goods that point *H* represents.

**DID YOU GET IT?**
What does a production possibilities frontier represent?

# OPPORTUNITY COST FOR SOCIETY

"There is no such thing as a free lunch." Have you ever heard that saying? Economist Milton Friedman used it to refer to the practice at some schools of providing free lunches to students. Friedman pointed out that even if the lunch appears to be free to the students who eat it, it is not really free to society. Producing a meal requires resources. As you now know, those resources could have been used for something else. So to have more "free lunches," we must have less of some other goods or services. We cannot pretend that school lunches or other items are really free when society faces tradeoffs to provide them. Even goods that are "free" to individuals usually take time to produce and have an opportunity cost for society.

The production possibilities frontier allows us to visualize a country's opportunity cost when it produces more of one good. Continuing with our story of guns and butter, suppose the country starts at point *C* in Figure 2.2, producing 200 tons of butter and 750 guns. What is the opportunity cost of producing 100 more tons of butter? Producing more butter would require the country to move rightward and downward along the production possibilities frontier, in this case from point *C* to point *D*. At point *D*, the country produces 300 tons of butter, 100 more tons than at point *C*. It also produces 550 guns at point *D*, 200 fewer than at point *C*. So the opportunity cost of the additional 100 tons of butter is 200 guns. This is because to produce 100 more tons of butter, the country gives up 200 guns.

*BTW, economists aren't particularly good at using abbreviations when texting, but they like this one: TNSTAAFL. It means that, due to opportunity costs, "there's no such thing as a free lunch!"*

The production possibilities frontier shows that to have more butter, the country must give up some guns. The guns sacrificed are the opportunity cost of more butter. We could also reverse the example. Suppose the country, starting at point *C*, decides that it wants more guns instead of more butter. Then it will have to move leftward and upward along the PPF, to a point like *B*. Gun production will increase, but butter production will decrease. In this case, the country sacrifices 100 tons of butter for 150 more guns. The butter it gives up is the opportunity cost of the additional guns.

## The Law of Increasing Opportunity Cost

Maybe you've heard of Murphy's Law: if something can go wrong, it will. This type of law is not written by lawmakers or enforced by police; it is called a "law" simply because it is so commonly observed. Economists have laws like that, too.

Notice the shape of the production possibilities frontier in Figure 2.2. It is curved like the right half of a rainbow.

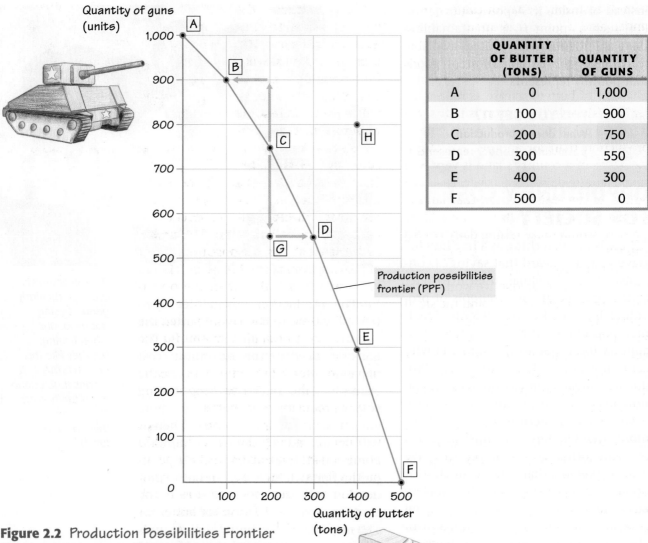

| | QUANTITY OF BUTTER (TONS) | QUANTITY OF GUNS |
|---|---|---|
| A | 0 | 1,000 |
| B | 100 | 900 |
| C | 200 | 750 |
| D | 300 | 550 |
| E | 400 | 300 |
| F | 500 | 0 |

**Figure 2.2** Production Possibilities Frontier
The production possibilities frontier illustrates opportunity costs: looking along the frontier, we see that as more of one good is made, the country must make less of another.

The **law of increasing opportunity cost** states that the opportunity cost of a good rises as more of the good is produced.

The numbers in the table determine this shape. As we go down the table, butter production increases by a constant 100 tons in each new row. But notice that gun production falls by larger and larger amounts each time butter production increases by 100 tons. For example, moving from row *A* to row *B* (or point *A* to point *B* along the PPF), butter production rises by 100 tons, and gun production falls by 100, from 1,000 to 900. So the opportunity cost of the first 100 tons of butter is 100 guns. What if we move from row *B* to row *C*? While butter production again rises by 100 tons, gun production falls by 150, from 900 to 750. So

the opportunity cost of the second 100 tons of butter is 150 guns. As you continue down the rows, the opportunity cost of an additional 100 tons of butter continually increases. The more butter we produce, the greater the opportunity cost of producing still more butter.

The tendency for the opportunity cost of a good to rise as more of the good is produced is called the **law of increasing opportunity cost**. This is the first of several economic "laws" you will learn in this book. Note that the conditions for economic laws are not always met and these laws do not hold 100 percent of the time. However, learning the laws of economic behavior can help you understand a great deal about how the economy works.

What is behind the law of increasing opportunity cost? Why does the opportunity cost of butter increase as more butter is produced? The reason is that some resources are better suited for one type of production than for another. For example, some of a country's land is very well suited to raise dairy cows needed to make butter. In the United States, that land is known as Wisconsin. Other land, such as a desert, would make raising dairy cows a struggle but is a fine place for a gun factory. Labor is also specialized. Some workers are happy and productive working on a dairy farm. Others can't stand the smell of manure but are high achievers in a factory setting. As for capital, those red barns and milking machines are less than ideal for making guns, and the metal stamping machines used to form guns aren't great for milking cows.

Let's apply these ideas to the guns and butter PPF by examining Figure 2.3. Suppose a country begins at point A, where it produces only guns but no butter. At point A, all of the country's resources are used to make guns. Even those resources that would be much more useful for making butter, such as farmers and their equipment, are employed in gun production. Now suppose the country decides to produce butter, too. To make its first 100 tons of butter, moving from A to B, the country will have to shift resources out of gun production and into butter production. To make as much as possible of both goods, it will shift those resources that are the most useful for making butter and the least useful for making guns—those farmers and barns and milking machines. Gun production will not fall much, because the resources taken away were not doing a lot of good in gun production anyway. So the opportunity cost of the first 100 tons of butter is only 100 guns.

Now suppose the country wants to produce *an additional* 100 tons of butter, moving from point B to point C. This time, the country will have to shift some resources that are better suited for making guns—and less suited for making butter—than the resources it shifted before. Shifting away these resources will cause gun production to fall by even more than before. This is why, as the figure shows, the opportunity cost of moving from point B to point C is 150 guns, which is higher than the opportunity cost of moving from point A to point B. Likewise, the law of increasing opportunity cost applies to any further increases in butter production as well: the more butter the country is already producing, the greater the opportunity cost of producing more butter.

An economy must choose where to operate among the many possible points on its current production possibilities frontier. That is, a country must decide how much food and how much other stuff to make. There are also decisions to be made between types of food, like pizza and tofu, and types of other stuff, like cars and education. How are these decisions made? That depends on how the economy is organized.

In the United States, the choices of individuals play an important role. If more people decide to purchase a college education than a car, more resources are devoted to education services than car manufacturing. Some of these decisions are also made by your elected government officials, who decide how much money is spent on bridges and roads and those guns we discussed for the military. In Chapter 6 you'll learn how increases in the demand for a good or service increase prices and signal producers to provide

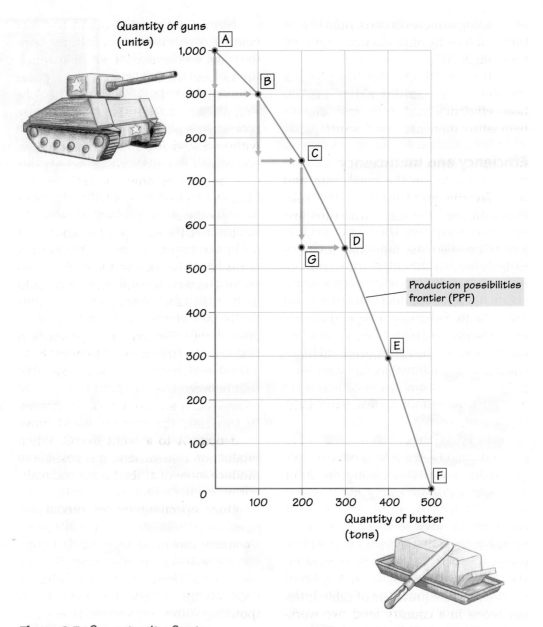

**Figure 2.3** *Opportunity Costs*
The first 100 tons of butter are made with resources specialized for making butter and of little use for making guns, so the opportunity cost is only 100 guns. As more and more butter is made, it must be made using resources better and better suited for making guns, so the opportunity cost rises.
**DID YOU GET IT?** What is the opportunity cost of producing 400 tons of butter rather than 300 tons?

more of it. Chapter 2 explains other systems countries use to divide their limited resources among education, cars, food, and all other stuff.

**DID YOU GET IT?**
Why does the opportunity cost generally increase as more of something is made?

# EFFICIENCY AND GROWTH

More than one billion people in the world today do not have enough health care, education, food, or housing to lead a healthy and happy life. Billions more would be happier if more goods and services were available to them. If you would enjoy going to more concerts, riding faster trains, or owning more electronic gadgets, for example, then you can count yourself in that group. This section uses the production possibilities frontier to explain how efficiency and economic growth help satisfy more needs and wants.

## Efficiency and Inefficiency

Suppose you're on the track team and your favorite event is the mile. Your friend on the track team, who runs just as fast as you in each event, has no preference between the mile and the 100-meter dash. It would be unfortunate if your coach signed you up to run the 100-meter dash and had your friend run the mile. By switching your events, you would be made better off and your friend would be no worse off. Efforts to achieve efficiency are about finding opportunities to make improvements such as this.

The economy of a country is **efficient** if the country takes every opportunity to make some people better off without making other people worse off. This means the country is getting the most out of its available resources. It would be inefficient to use more resources than necessary to produce a good. By eliminating such waste, more of at least one good could be made available to customers without making less of other goods.

Suppose the providers of cable Internet access in a country send two workers to connect each home with Internet service, even though one worker could do the job just as quickly. Production in this country would be inefficient. If the cable companies adopted the efficient method of sending one worker instead, fewer workers would be needed in the cable industry and the country could expand its production of other goods or services. You can see why in Figure 2.4. In this model, a country uses all of its resources to produce one of two things: Internet connections or T-shirts. Point A represents the combination of connections and T-shirts made when cable companies send two workers to connect each home: 500 homes are connected and 1,000 T-shirts are produced in a week.

Notice that point *A* lies in the area below the production possibilities frontier. This area represents points at which production is inefficient. At any point below the frontier, the country is not getting the most from its resources because more of at least one good could be made without sacrificing any of the other. By changing how resources are used—in this case, by sending only one cable worker to each home—the country could move to a point on its production possibilities frontier. For example, the labor freed up by sending only one worker to each home could be used in the cable industry to connect more homes. This could move the country from point *A* to point *D*. Or the extra labor could be used to make more T-shirts, and production would move from point *A* to point *B*. As a third option, the extra labor could be split between the two industries to make more T-shirts and connect more homes. In this case, the country would move from point *A* to a point like *C*. When production is inefficient, it is possible to produce more of at least one good without producing less of any other good.

Once operating on its production possibilities frontier, as we have seen, a country can make more of one good only by making less of another. Because movements along the frontier offer no opportunities for gains without corresponding losses, production is efficient at every point on the production possibilities frontier. Outside the frontier are points the country can only wish for. These points are out of reach because the country does not have enough resources to produce at those levels. Later in this module we'll consider ways to reach those points.

## Idle Resources

At times, a country's entire economy goes a bit haywire, and production falls in many industries at the same time. For example, from 2007 to 2009, production of many goods and services decreased in the United States, in Europe, and in many other countries. (You'll learn why this happened in Chapter 13.) With

An economy is **efficient** if there is no opportunity to make someone better off without making anyone else worse off.

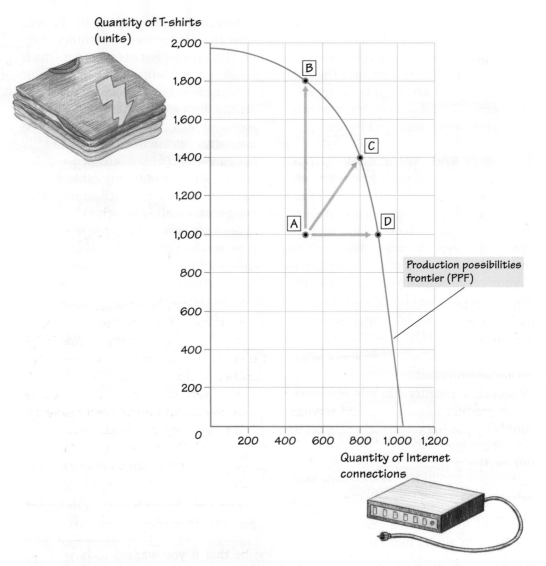

**Figure 2.4** Efficiency in Production
It would be inefficient for a country to produce at a point below the production possibilities frontier, as shown by point A. Among the better alternatives are points B, C, and D. At point B, more T-shirts could be made without giving up any Internet connections. At point D, more Internet connections could be provided without decreasing the quantity of T-shirts. And at point C, more T-shirts and more Internet connections could be produced.

fewer goods and services being produced, fewer workers were needed to produce them. Less capital was needed, so many factories shut down, assembly lines sat motionless, and computers were unplugged. At times like this, an economy has *idle resources*, which are resources that could be used to make some good or service but are not being used to produce anything.

Idle resources cause a country to operate below its production possibilities frontier. As with inefficient production, idle resources result in production at a point like *A* in Figure 2.4. However, the reasons for being inside the production possibilities frontier instead of on it are different. When production is inefficient, the country might be using all of its resources, yet it is not using them in the most productive way. This is true, for instance, when two cable installers are sent out to do the work of one. When resources are idle, the resources that are

*Idle workers prevent a country from reaching its production possibilities frontier.*

actually in use might be employed as productively as possible, but other resources are sitting on the sidelines—perhaps some factories are closed or some workers are unemployed.

When a country has idle resources, it can produce more goods and services simply by putting those idle resources to use. There is no need to shift resources out of the production of one good to make more of another. So as with inefficiency, the usual opportunity cost of production does not apply when there are idle resources.

## Economic Growth

Time cures all wounds, or so they say, but can it help with problems of resource scarcity? Yes! Most countries experience **economic growth**, which is an increase in the ability to produce goods and services over time. One source of economic growth is an increase in resources. For example, if a population grows over time, the labor supply generally increases as well. A country's physical capital can increase with investments in new factories, office buildings, machinery, and stores. Human capital rises with educational opportunities (thank you for reading this book in the service of your country). With more resources available, a country can produce more goods and services.

Consider the Internet connections discussed above. It's clear that more connections can be provided with more workers, more vans for the cable workers to drive, or more training that helps the workers complete a connection faster. Another source of economic growth is the discovery of new ways to produce goods and services using fewer resources. Wi-Fi technology that sends Internet signals through the air has allowed far more people to connect their computers to the Internet and reduced the need for workers, vans, and training classes. And think about the resource-saving changes in the way people buy and sell music. It used to be that if you wanted to buy music, you had to go to a store and buy a compact disc. Selling music required a lot of capital—thousands of stores around the country, delivery trucks, and cash registers. It also required a lot of labor, including store clerks, security guards, and truck drivers. Today, you can purchase and download your music over the Internet. This leaves more resources for the production of other things.

**Economic growth** is an increase in the ability to produce goods and services over time.

We can use the production possibilities frontier model to show the effects of economic growth. Start by looking at the left panel of Figure 2.5. The horizontal axis indicates the quantity of food produced in a country. The vertical axis indicates the quantity of "all other goods," meaning all goods and services other than food, produced in the country. These general categories of goods are useful when discussing aspects of the entire economy rather than the tradeoff between two specific goods. It is relatively hard to pin down what a unit of "food" or a unit of "all other goods" is, but think of these units as bundles of all types of food and all types of other goods and services.

Suppose the country initially chooses point *X*. Are the citizens content with what they have? No—wants are unlimited! They want more of everything from pizza and electric cars to health care and education. This motivates the development of resource-saving production methods and investment in new capital. Over time, this results in economic growth, which shifts the entire production possibilities frontier outward. The right panel of Figure 2.5 shows the original production possibilities frontier and the new one. Thanks to economic growth, the country can produce more food, more of all other goods, or more food *and* more of all other goods. The last option—more of both—is shown

by the movement from point *X* on the original production possibilities frontier to point *Y* on the new production possibilities frontier.

Economic growth is a common goal because it enables a country to produce more goods and services and do a better job satisfying the needs and wants of its citizens. When the economy grows, the country can produce more of everything. However, there are opportunity costs connected with economic growth. For a country to enjoy the benefits of economic growth in the future, it must make economic sacrifices in the present. It must take resources that could be used to make goods for consumption now and instead use them to make capital and develop improved production methods for the future. It's like when you forgo purchases of things you would enjoy now in order to save money for college and other ways to improve your life later on. You'll learn more about economic growth, and the types of sacrifices it requires, in Chapter 13.

**? DID YOU GET IT?**
**What is the difference between achieving efficiency and achieving economic growth?**

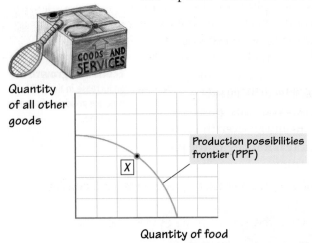

Quantity of all other goods

Production possibilities frontier (PPF)

*X*

Quantity of food

Quantity of all other goods

*Y*

Production possibilities frontier after economic growth

*X*

Quantity of food

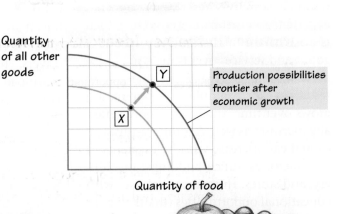

**Figure 2.5** Economic Growth and the PPF
Economic growth shifts the entire production possibilities frontier outward, allowing a country to produce more of any or all goods. **DID YOU GET IT?** What does it mean for a country if its production possibilities frontier shifts outward?

## PEOPLE IN ECONOMICS

# Adam Smith The Father of Economics

Although strands of economic ideas can be found throughout recorded history, the systematic study of economics began with the publication in 1776 of a remarkable book by Adam Smith, *An Inquiry into the Nature and Causes of the Wealth of Nations*, or *The Wealth of Nations* for short. Smith, a Scottish scholar who lived from 1723 to 1790, researched his book while working as a tutor for two high school–aged students on a tour of France. Smith saw economic behavior as guided mainly by the force of self-interest. He viewed the economy as a system in which regular patterns emerged from people buying and selling in markets. He stressed that people should be free to make decisions without meddling from the government or other outside forces. A major point in Smith's writing was that the market system—in which everyone makes decisions that are best for themselves individually—can create the best outcome for society as a whole. Even when people act from selfish motives, the market encourages them to make the kind of

selfish decisions that will benefit others. This effect has become known as the "invisible hand" of the market. We'll learn a lot more about the market economy in Chapter 2. *The Wealth of Nations* was published in the first year of the American Revolution. Founding Fathers such as Alexander Hamilton, James Madison, and Thomas Jefferson closely read and debated the claims in the book.

 **DID YOU GET IT?**
According to Adam Smith, what guides the behavior of buyers and sellers?

## MODULE 2 REVIEW AND ASSESSMENT

**Summing Up the Key Ideas:** Match the following terms with the correct definition.

A. Model
B. Production possibilities frontier
C. Law of increasing opportunity cost
D. Efficient
E. Economic growth
F. Economic model

_B_ 1. A curve that shows the maximum quantity of one good that can be produced for each possible quantity of another good produced.

_C_ 2. The tendency for the opportunity cost of a good to rise as more of the good is produced.

_F_ 3. Something used to understand and predict economic activity.

_E_ 4. An increase in the ability to produce goods and services over time.

_A_ 5. A simplified representation of reality.

_D_ 6. A condition that exists when a country takes every opportunity to make some people better off without making other people worse off.

## Analyze and Explain: Use Figure 2.1, shown here, to answer the following questions.

1. How many units of butter are produced at point *F*? _500_ How many guns are produced at point *F*? _0_

2. How many units of butter are produced at point *A*? _0_ How many guns are produced at point *A*? _1,000_

3. How many more guns are produced by switching from point F to point E? _300_

4. How much less butter is produced at point F than at point E? _0 or -100_

5. Why would production at point G be inefficient? _G is has an idle resource_

6. Why isn't production at point H currently a possibility? _the resources for butter are better suited somewhere else—law of increasing opportunity cost_

7. If the PPF were a straight, downward-sloping line, would the law of increasing opportunity cost still hold? _yes_ Explain your answer. _Still a positive slope more butter_

8. To be efficient, where is the optimum place to be on a graph like Figure 2.1? _D_

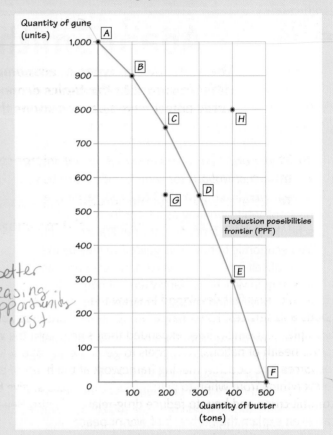

## Apply: The country of Whatselvania faces a **production possibilities frontier (PPF)** like the one in Figure 2.1, shown here. Indicate the effect (**shift of the frontier**, **movement along the frontier**, or **no change**) of each of the following events.

| OCCURENCE | EFFECT ON ECONOMIC GROWTH |
|---|---|
| 1. The number of farm and factory workers in the country increases. | _shift along the front_ |
| 2. The amount of butter that the citizens of Whatselvania want to consume increases. | _movement front_ |
| 3. Some farms and gun factories in Whatselvania close, and workers are now unemployed. | _shift_ |
| 4. New resources are discovered that permit more production of guns and butter. | _shift_ |
| 5. A new technology is developed that frees up existing resources that can be used for making guns or butter. | _shift ppf_ |
| 6. There is an increased need by the military for guns. | _movement_ |
| 7. Resources used to produce goods or services other than guns and butter have been depleted. | _no change_ |

# MODULE 3

# The World of Economics

**KEY IDEA:** There are several types of economics that differ in regard to the topics economists study and the types of questions they ask.

## OBJECTIVES

- To explain the difference between microeconomics and macroeconomics.
- To differentiate between positive and normative economics.
- To identify terms that have special meanings in economics.

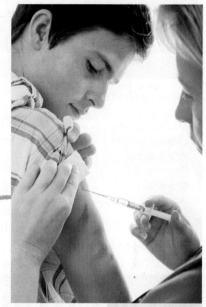

*Economics: it's not just about money and stores.*

## The Many Uses of Economic Tools

Economics was first developed to study the production and distribution of goods and services. The boundaries of the field are much broader now. For example, economists have expanded their sights from the wealth of nations to the health of nations, with goals to get more out of our limited health care resources. The decision-making framework at the heart of economics applies to everything from when to get married and where to give birth to whether to commit crime and how to reduce drug-related deaths. Believe it or not, the tools of economics can even explain the outbreak of war or peace.

Likewise, the tools of economics shed light on topics as surprising as cheating on standardized tests, participation in terrorism, bribery of public officials, and the popularity of reality television shows. There are more surprises to come. For now, be assured that the tools of economics apply to a pleasing assortment of questions. Our goal in writing this book is to provide you with those tools. In this module we will take a closer look at what economists study and give you a roadmap of what's ahead.

## MICROECONOMICS AND MACROECONOMICS

Economics is divided into two major areas: *microeconomics* and *macroeconomics*. **Microeconomics** is the study of how people make decisions and how those decisions affect others in the economy. Our discussion in Module 1 of the opportunity cost of a movie is an example of microeconomics, because it is about how you make decisions. The decisions people make when running a business are also examined in microeconomics. Examples of questions explored in the microeconomics sections of this book include the following:

- How many hours should you work for pay each week?

- Is a college education a good investment?

- How will faster Internet connections affect the film industry?

- How does a natural disaster like the Gulf oil spill in 2010 affect the price businesses charge for fish in the United States and the earnings of people who fish for a living?

**Macroeconomics** is the study of the economy as a whole. This includes the ups and downs of the economy and the interactions between its various

**Microeconomics** is the study of how people make decisions and how those decisions affect others in the economy.

**Macroeconomics** is the study of the economy as a whole.

*Microeconomics helps us understand the choices people make about how much time to spend on work and play.*

parts. Our earlier discussions of production possibilities and economic growth are examples of macroeconomics. The following questions are addressed in the macroeconomics sections of this book:

• Why do the prices of goods and services tend to rise over time?

• What effect does government borrowing have on the economy?

• Why are some nations poor and others rich?

• Why is an economy sometimes not able to provide jobs for everyone who wants to work?

The next chapter will discuss both microeconomic and macroeconomic perspectives on how economies work. In Chapters 3–12 we turn to detailed discussions of microeconomic topics. Chapters 13–17 cover macroeconomic topics. Finally, Chapters 18 and 19 combine microeconomics and macroeconomics to address critical questions about how countries develop and trade in the global economy.

 **DID YOU GET IT?**
**What is the difference between microeconomics and macroeconomics?**

# ECONOMICS IN ACTION

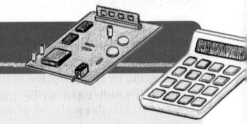

# The Wages of Economics

Economists work in many places, including government agencies like the Central Intelligence Agency and the Bureau of Labor Statistics; consulting firms like McKinsey and Company; and large corporations like Google, Ford, and Bank of America. An understanding of economics is also helpful for a career in law, politics, or business. Because people with training in economics have skills that help them solve problems and understand markets, they are very much in demand.

The National Association of Colleges and Employers surveys new college graduates each year, asking their starting salaries. Different college majors earn different starting salaries. As the table shows, economics is among the highest-paying specialties.

| Median Starting Salary for Selected Majors, College Class of 2012 | |
|---|---|
| **COLLEGE MAJOR** | **STARTING SALARY (DOLLARS)** |
| Engineering | $58,581 |
| Computer science | 56,383 |
| Economics | 54,800 |
| Business administration | 49,200 |
| Accounting | 47,800 |
| Math and sciences | 40,939 |
| Communications | 40,022 |
| Political science | 38,400 |
| Education | 37,423 |

SOURCE: National Association of Colleges and Employers, "Salary Survey: Starting Salaries for New College Graduates—April 2012 Executive Summary." Available online at www.naceweb.org/salary-survey-data/?referal=research&menuID=71&nodetype=4.

 **DID YOU GET IT?**
**Why are people with training in economics valued in the workplace?**

# POSITIVE AND NORMATIVE ECONOMICS

Beyond covering questions on everything from the macroeconomics of the world economy to the microeconomics of your Saturday afternoon, economics covers questions both on the way things are and about the way things should be. **Positive economics** is the study of what the world is like and why it works the way it does. It is about facts and cause-and-effect relationships. Positive questions include the following:

- How many teenagers live in poverty?

- Do people buy more or less Coke when their incomes increase?

- How do salary limits for professional soccer players affect team performance?

Economists seek answers to questions like these with scientific methods rather than relying on opinions about what is good or bad. Positive economics also allows predictions to be made. By studying how one thing, like the availability of jobs, affects another thing, like the amount of crime, we can make predictions such as this: a country that is losing jobs can expect more crime. The predictions are not always right, but they help individuals, businesses, and governments plan for the future.

**Normative economics** is the study of the way things should be rather than the way things are. Normative economics brings opinions and ideals into the process of answering questions. Normative questions include the following:

- Should our country do more to help the poor?

- Should Coke be sold in high school vending machines?

- Should college athletes be paid?

Different people have different opinions. Although there are no right or wrong answers, economics still helps us think about normative questions. For example, economics helps us study the efficiency of

*Should college athletes be paid? That's a normative question.*

**Positive economics** is the study of what the world is like and why it works the way it does.

plans to help the poor, so that any efforts that are made will serve as many people as possible. Consider the plan, adopted in several cities, to limit the amount of money owners can charge for apartments. Economists studied the situation and found that with these limits, fewer apartments were made available, housing shortages increased, and fewer people were served than under alternative programs.

**DID YOU GET IT?**
What is the difference between positive and normative economics?

# THE LANGUAGE OF ECONOMICS

It's been said that economists have their own language. There's some truth to that. Economists assign precise meanings to words and sometimes use them in special ways. You've already seen that in economics, *capital* is anything long lasting that is created by humans and used to produce goods and services. In ordinary language, people use *capital* to mean money. An entrepreneur might say, "I want to open up a restaurant, but first I need to raise enough capital to buy cooking equipment." To an economist, the cooking equipment itself is capital.

The word *market* is another with special meaning in economics. In standard

**Normative economics** is the study of the way things should be rather than the way things are.

English, a market is a place where you buy goods, such as a supermarket, a flea market, or a farmers' market. In economics, a **market** is not a place but a collection of buyers and sellers, wherever they may be. The market for cellular phone service in the United States, for example, includes everyone in the country who buys cellular phone service and every company that sells it. The market is made up of the buyers and sellers themselves rather than being a particular location where they happen to be when they buy or sell phone service. We'll discuss the idea of a market further when we discuss economic systems in the next chapter.

In economics, a **market** is not a place but a collection of buyers and sellers, wherever they may be.

In your economic explorations you will discover many more words with distinct meanings in this field. Chapter 16 explains that even the word *money* receives special treatment in economics. You'll also learn new words and phrases, like *opportunity cost*, that are used almost exclusively in economics. Understanding this language will help you grasp what you read and hear about the economy and share what you learn, clearly and precisely, with others.

To help you find and learn important terms, this book presents each key term in three different places. You will find definitions in the text, in the page margin, and in the glossary at the back of the book.

## PEOPLE IN ECONOMICS

# Milton Friedman

Milton Friedman (1912–2006), a Nobel Prize–winning economist, was a leading figure in the Chicago school of economics. He also served as an informal economic adviser to President Reagan. Friedman is considered one of the most influential economists of the twentieth century.

Friedman spent much of the 1950s and 1960s challenging the ideas that government spending (fiscal policy) was the most significant factor in combating an economic downturn and that the quantity of money available in the economy was of little importance. By contrast, Friedman theorized that money supply and prices are directly linked. He suggested that the Federal Reserve needed to regulate the money supply in order to prevent price inflation. This theory was not new, but it had fallen out of fashion in the first part of the twentieth century. In recent years, it has once again become more widely accepted.

Friedman was also a strong advocate for the free-market economy. His books *Capitalism and Freedom* and *Free to Choose* (coauthored with his wife, Rose Director Friedman), along with a PBS television series, explained his ideas about individual freedom to a general audience. In his books, he promoted policies such as a negative income tax, a school voucher program, and the elimination of the draft.

**DID YOU GET IT?**
What are some words that economists use in a different way than noneconomists?

**YOUR TURN**
Start good study habits early in your study of economics. Make flash cards for each of the bold key terms in this chapter. Write the term on one side of an index card and write the definition on the back. Quiz yourself, learn the terms, and impress your friends and family with your mastery of the language of economics.

# MODULE 3 REVIEW AND ASSESSMENT

**Summing Up the Key Ideas:** Match the following terms with the correct definition.

A. Microeconomics    C. Positive economics    E. Market
B. Macroeconomics    D. Normative economics   F. Capital

_F_ 1. Created by humans and used to produce goods and services.

_C_ 2. The study of what the world is like and why it works the way it does.

_A_ 3. The study of how people make decisions and how those decisions affect others in the economy.

_D_ 4. The study of the way things should be rather than the way things are.

_E_ 5. A collection of buyers and sellers, wherever they may be.

_B_ 6. The study of the economy as a whole.

**Analyze:** Identify each of the following as **normative** or **positive** statements.

NORMATIVE OR POSITIVE?

1. The United States should end poverty. — _normative_

2. Movie tickets cost $7.50 to see a first-run movie. — _positive_

3. Senior citizens should pay less to go to the movies. — _normative_

4. Markets are collections of buyers and sellers. — _positive_

5. Resources are scarce. — _positive_

6. The best way to address the lack of government funding is to raise taxes. — _positive_

7. Unemployment is a worse problem for society than inflation. — _positive_

8. Products that are harmful to consumers should be removed from the market by the government. — _normative_

9. Factories should be required to install clean air devices that protect the environment. — _normative_

**Apply:** Identify each of the following as questions that would be answered in the study of **microeconomics (micro)** or the study of **macroeconomics (macro)**.

MICRO OR MACRO?

1. How are the prices of textbooks determined?

   *micro*

2. What effect does government borrowing have on the economy?

   *macro*

3. What causes the relative price of the U.S. dollar and the Canadian dollar to change?

   *macro*

4. What is the value of goods and services produced in the U.S. economy last year?

   *macro*

5. How do rent control laws affect the availability of housing in New York City?

   *micro*

6. How does a farmer decide how many jalapeño peppers to produce?

   *micro*

## Bloomberg Businessweek®

# It's a Man vs. Machine Recovery

### Companies have been buying technology instead of hiring

BY DAVID J. LYNCH

The U.S. in 2011 produced almost one-quarter more goods and services than it did in 1999, while using almost precisely the same number of workers. It's as if $2.5 trillion worth of stuff—the equivalent of the entire U.S. economy circa 1958—materialized out of thin air.

Although businesses haven't added many people, they've certainly bulked up on machines. Spending on equipment and software hit an all-time high in the third quarter of 2011. "Huge advances in technology have allowed businesses to do more with less," vaporizing jobs for everyone from steelworkers to travel agents, President Barack Obama warned in December.

So are robots getting all the good jobs? Most economists, cheered by 540,000 hires in the last quarter of 2011, say technology inevitably destroys some jobs even as it ultimately creates new ones. But with more than 20 million Americans still jobless or underemployed, others worry that something fundamental has changed.

Economists including James D. Hamilton say there's nothing new about machines replacing people. In 1900, 41 percent of Americans worked on farms. Today, thanks to labor-saving tractors and combines, the figure is less than 2 percent. Yet ex–farm workers found new jobs. And as manufacturing grew leaner in recent decades, factory workers—or their children—migrated to finance, health care, computers, and other growing industries.

"In 2005 the average U.S. worker could produce what would have required two people to do in 1970, what would have required four people in 1940, and would have required six people in 1910," Hamilton writes in an e-mail. "The result of this technological progress was not higher unemployment but instead rising real wages. The evidence from the last two centuries is unambiguous—productivity gains lead to more wealth, not poverty."

Americans have worried about a robot-controlled future since the first industrial robot (called "Unimate") started work at a General Motors plant in Ewing Township, N.J., in 1961. Chris Matthews, host of MSNBC's *Hardball*, recently mentioned on air about the increasing number of automated kiosks (at airports, for parking, etc.) as well as the replacement of "seven or eight cameramen" on his program with machines. "Everywhere we go, it's robots," he said.

Technology is not just revolutionizing the assembly line. Paralegals can't match software in accurately searching thousands of documents for specific words or patterns. New software apps can do a better job at covering a sports event than your ordinary sportswriter can with pen and paper. "The era we're in is one in which the scope of tasks that can be automated is increasing rapidly, and in areas where we used to think those were our best skills, things that require thinking," says David Autor, a labor economist at Massachusetts Institute of Technology.

Technology is sorting workers into winners and losers. Over the past three decades job growth has been fastest among high- and low-skill jobs, while mid-skill job growth has slowed, according to economists Jaison Abel and Richard Deitz. Although the economy created nearly 50 million new nonfarm positions in that period, technology decreased jobs in areas such as machine operators, by more than half.

While there are concerns that technology and machines can replace workers, at the same time, revolutionary technologies can also spawn unimagined new businesses and jobs.

*The bottom line:* Although machines may appear to get all the good jobs, there's nothing wrong with the labor market that resurgent demand for goods and services wouldn't fix.

## DID YOU READ IT?

1) According to the article, what happened to the U.S. production possibilities between 1999 and 2011? What are the reasons behind this change?

2) How does technology "sort" workers into winners and losers?

## WHAT DO YOU THINK?

1) If an economy has high unemployment, or many workers are "underemployed," how is this shown in a production possibilities frontier model?

2) Can you think of situations in which technology has replaced people in the workplace? What about situations in which technology has made people more productive in the workplace?

EXCERPTED FROM www.businessweek.com/printer/magazine/its-a-man-vs-machine-recovery-01052012.html

# Ellen Hughes-Cromwick

### Chief Economist at Ford

**Why did you choose to study economics?**

My husband and I went into the Peace Corps, and we got very interested in political development (the study of progress in poorer nations). When I returned, I started graduate courses, and I got very interested in economics because I thought the economic solutions were very attractive and very productive. So from there I got interested in graduate school and economics.

**When did you take your first economics course?**

I did not have economics in high school. The first course that I took in economics was in university and I was not an economics major, undergrad. I was a political science major. So, my first exposure was an international political economy course. That particular course gave us a very good introduction to international political economy. I got interested at that point.

**Tell us about the role of economics in your life. Has it been beneficial?**

Oh, absolutely. The economic way of thinking is an important knowledge base, especially in terms of understanding incentives and also being grounded in factors that determine supply and demand for a variety of goods and services. It is particularly rewarding. When you think about "what do you want to do in life?" you really want to make sure you lead a self-examined life and also, this sounds very philanthropic, but how can you give back over time? The economic body of knowledge gives

people a tremendous capacity to do that.

**You started in the Peace Corps and now you are the chief economist at Ford. Can you tell us a little bit about how that took place?**

Well, it was a journey. When we were towards the end of our education, my husband and I were offered positions in Washington, DC. He was at the Department of Health and Human Services, and I was at the Council of Economic Advisers. It was an outstanding experience because it was an opportunity to use what I had learned in the classroom in an applied setting and in a setting that helped to inform policy making. I saw that intersection as being so exciting. After the Council, I taught at Trinity College (Hartford, CT) for some time before I was recruited by Mellon Bank as a senior economist covering Latin markets. I stayed there six years before joining Ford.

**What do you love the most about your job at Ford?**

It is a dream job for an economist. Ford operates in so many countries with assembly facilities as well as other activities, and really what we do is meet the demand that folks have when they get to a stage of economic development when they want to have private transportation services. They want to own their own cars. We have to understand the nature and evolution of economic development in countries and be able to gauge how demand will materialize, and for what types of products. So, fundamentally, there are so many economic tools that we apply.

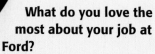

### What tools do you use?

From the standpoint of opportunity cost, when a family reaches a certain level of income in a country, they make a decision about what they want to purchase. But there are always tradeoffs, right? So, if they get to the point where they want to purchase a new vehicle, essentially they are making a tradeoff; they realize that the new vehicle will generate some services they need to maybe get to work or to help with their family's activities. That income they are devoting to the purchase and operation of the vehicle cannot be spent somewhere else. So, we have to be cognizant of what those tradeoffs are for the individuals reaching the middle-income level.

### What advice do you have for students of economics, even if they might be interested in careers outside of economics?

Economics is a very solid grounding for many different career paths, and we often do a terrible job explaining that to young people. They don't know what an economist is. Economics provides a firm grounding for many different careers. What it does for a high school student is it keeps all options open. It isn't a narrow field. And I think if you have an economics background your chances of being successful . . . and happy . . . are higher than some other professions. So, I think it is a very fulfilling and opportunistic science to pursue.

# CHAPTER 1 REVIEW AND SELF-ASSESSMENT

## REVIEW

### Points to Remember

#### MODULE 1: WHAT IS ECONOMICS?

1. **Economics** is the study of choice under conditions of scarcity.

2. **Scarcity** exists if we desire more of something than we can have.

3. You make a **tradeoff** when you give up one thing to get something else.

4. The **opportunity cost** of a choice is the value of the next-best alternative given up when that choice is made.

5. A **society** is a collection of people who share a common bond, such as those living in a city, a country, or even the entire world.

6. **Needs** are minimal requirements of things such as food, water, and shelter that are necessary for survival.

7. **Wants** are things that are desired but are not essential to life.

8. An **economy** is a system for coordinating the production and distribution of goods and services.

9. **Goods** are physical items produced in an economy, such as jeans, tennis rackets, popcorn, cars, and homes.

10. **Services** are activities produced in an economy, such as education, entertainment, and health care.

11. **Resources** are the basic elements from which all goods and services are produced.

12. **Land** is anything drawn from nature for use in the production of goods and services.

13. **Labor** is the time and effort people contribute to the production process.

14. **Capital** is anything long lasting that is created by humans for use in production.

15. **Physical capital** is any long-lasting good that is used to make other goods or services.

16. **Human capital** refers to the skills and knowledge of workers.

17. **Entrepreneurship** is the willingness of people to organize, operate, and assume the risks involved with business ventures.

18. **Inputs** include the four types of resources—land, labor, capital, and entrepreneurship—along with anything created from these resources that is then used to make something else, such as cement, steel, lumber, and plastic.

#### MODULE 2: PRODUCTION POSSIBILITIES FOR A NATION

19. A **model** is a simplified representation of reality. Models help you focus on a few aspects of the real world by stripping away nonessential details.

20. A **production possibilities frontier**, or **PPF**, is a curve that shows the maximum quantity of one good that can be produced for each possible quantity of another good produced.

21. The **law of increasing opportunity cost** states that the opportunity cost of a good rises as more of the good is produced.

22. An economy is **efficient** if there is no opportunity to make someone better off without making at least one person worse off.

23. **Economic growth** is an increase in the ability to produce goods and services over time.

#### MODULE 3: THE WORLD OF ECONOMICS

24. **Microeconomics** is the study of how people make decisions and how those decisions affect others in the economy.

25. **Macroeconomics** is the study of the economy as a whole.

26. **Positive economics** is the study of what the world is like and why it works the way it does.

27. **Normative economics** is the study of the way things should be rather than the way things are.

28. In economics, a **market** is not a place but a collection of buyers and sellers, wherever they may be.

## SELF-ASSESSMENT

The following questions are the type your teacher might ask you on a quiz or a test. Practice with these in order to improve your performance in class on tests.

### Multiple-Choice Questions

1. To an economist, the cost of going to a movie on Friday night would include

   a. the price of the ticket.

   b. the price of snacks while watching the movie.

   c. the value of the activity you could have done if you did not go to the movie.

   d. all of the above.

*Use the figure provided to answer the following four questions.*

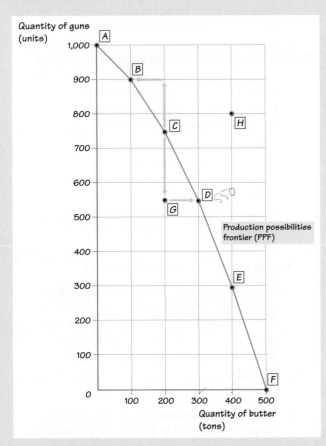

2. The opportunity cost of increasing the production of butter from 300 tons to 400 tons is

   a. 100 tons of butter.

   b. 250 guns.

   c. 300 guns.

   d. 400 tons of butter.

3. Point *G* on the graph

   a. is impossible to obtain given the current amount of resources available.

   b. represents an efficient level of production of guns and butter.

   c. is a combination of guns and butter production that would result if some resources were not being used.

   d. indicates the opportunity cost of butter.

4. Point *H* on the graph is

   a. possible to obtain given the current amount of resources available.

   b. an inefficient level of production of guns and butter.

   c. a combination of guns and butter production that would result if all resources were being used to the fullest.

   d. a combination of guns and butter production that is impossible given the current amount of resources available.

5. Points like *A*, *B*, *C*, *D*, *E*, and *F* represent combinations of guns and butter that are

   a. made using all available resources.

   b. the minimum amounts that can be produced.

   c. better than other points on the frontier.

   d. impossible to produce with scarce resources.

6. Which of the following would **not** be considered one of society's resources?

   a. entrepreneurship

   b. money

   c. land

   d. labor

7. Economic growth could be represented on a production possibilities frontier model by showing

   a. a rightward shift of the production possibilities frontier.

   b. a leftward shift of the production possibilities frontier.

   c. a movement from a point under (or inside) the production possibilities frontier to a point on the production possibilities frontier.

   d. a movement from one point on the production possibilities frontier to another point on the production possibilities frontier that is more desirable.

8. As used in economics, which of the following is an example of capital?

    a. stocks and bonds
    b. a sandwich
    c. a bulldozer
    d. money in your savings account

9. Which of the following is a positive economic statement?

    a. Soft drinks should not be sold in high school lunchrooms.
    b. The price of health care should be lowered by federal law to make it more affordable.
    c. Decisions made by businesses to raise prices on consumer goods that are necessities should not be allowed by the government.
    d. Every choice made by a consumer has an opportunity cost.

10. Which of the following is an example of a macroeconomic question?

    a. How much will an increase in the price of crude oil affect gasoline prices?
    b. What effect does the deficit have on the economy?
    c. What will happen to food prices if another natural disaster, like a flood, hits the United States?
    d. What will be the effect of an advanced degree on my lifelong earnings?

## Constructed Response Questions

1. Use the information in the table below to construct a production possibilities graph. Be certain to correctly label your graph.

| QUANTITY OF CORN (BUSHELS) | QUANTITY OF COMPUTERS |
|---|---|
| 2,000 | 0 |
| 1,600 | 250 |
| 1,200 | 450 |
| 400 | 700 |
| 0 | 800 |

2. Consider the following production combinations. For each combination listed in a–e, determine which of the following classifications (I, II, or III) best describes the combination:

    I. The combination is feasible and efficient: the combination is on the production possibilities frontier.
    II. The combination is feasible but inefficient: the combination is inside the production possibilities frontier.
    III. The combination is not feasible: the combination is outside the production possibilities frontier.

    a. 300 bushels of corn; 1,200 computers
    b. 450 bushels of corn; 1,400 computers
    c. 500 bushels of corn; 600 computers
    d. 725 bushels of corn; 600 computers
    e. 250 bushels of corn; 1,600 computers

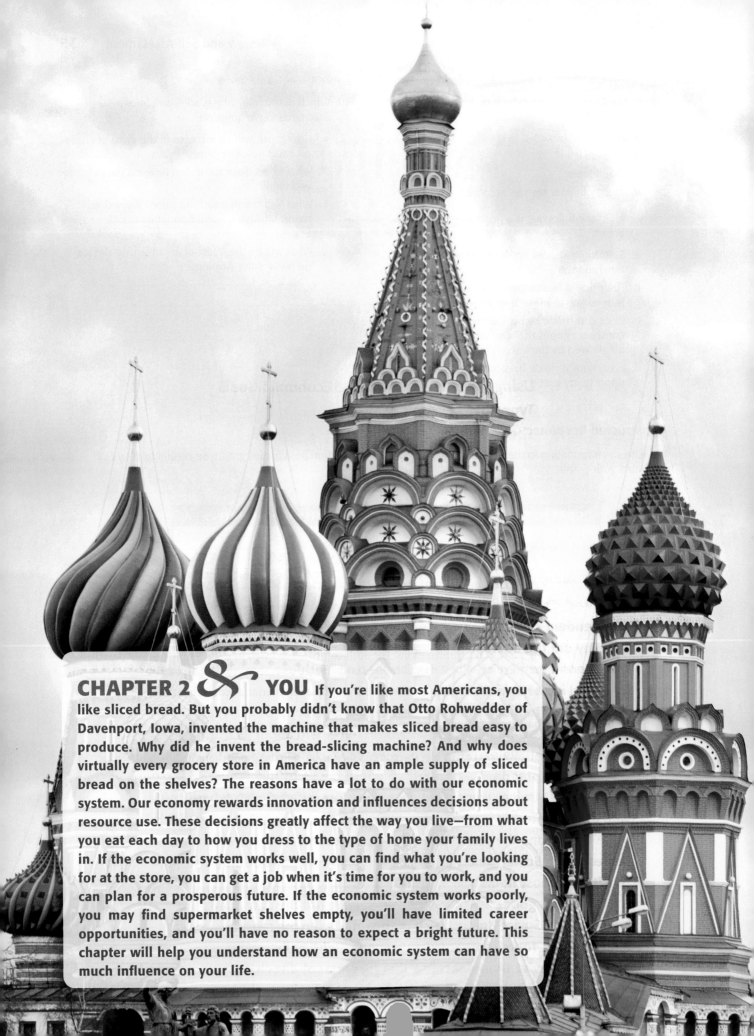

**CHAPTER 2 & YOU** If you're like most Americans, you like sliced bread. But you probably didn't know that Otto Rohwedder of Davenport, Iowa, invented the machine that makes sliced bread easy to produce. Why did he invent the bread-slicing machine? And why does virtually every grocery store in America have an ample supply of sliced bread on the shelves? The reasons have a lot to do with our economic system. Our economy rewards innovation and influences decisions about resource use. These decisions greatly affect the way you live—from what you eat each day to how you dress to the type of home your family lives in. If the economic system works well, you can find what you're looking for at the store, you can get a job when it's time for you to work, and you can plan for a prosperous future. If the economic system works poorly, you may find supermarket shelves empty, you'll have limited career opportunities, and you'll have no reason to expect a bright future. This chapter will help you understand how an economic system can have so much influence on your life.

# Comparing Economic Systems

**MODULE 4:** **Using Resources to Achieve Economic Goals**

**MODULE 5:** **Types of Economic Systems**

**MODULE 6:** **The Modern Market Economy**

## BACK IN THE SOVIET UNION

In 1991, the Soviet Union—one of the most powerful countries in the world—collapsed. The territory that made up the Soviet Union was broken into 15 independent countries, including today's Russia—the largest of the 15.

Why did the Soviet Union fail? One reason is that it could not deliver the goods and services its citizens wanted. Suppose, for example, that you lived in the Soviet Union and you wanted to buy a car. You first would have needed to place your name on a list and wait up to five years before a car became available. Then you would have paid about as much money as you would have earned in two years for a car that was not very good by American standards. Similarly, if you wanted to buy a pair of jeans in the Soviet Union, you would have been out of luck (unless you could find a visiting foreigner who was willing to sell you a pair), because jeans were not among the goods that the Soviet government chose to produce. Stores in the Soviet Union offered very little variety in clothing, sneakers, music, and most items you would be interested in buying.

Consumer goods, like cars and jeans, were not the only goods in short supply in the Soviet Union. Much of the time, even the most basic goods—shoes, meat, forks, notebook paper, and light bulbs—were difficult to buy in the Soviet Union because the government directed production. A plan detailed what would be produced and how it would be produced.

In the Soviet Union, people sometimes had to stand in line for hours to get bread and cheese.

Sometimes the plan worked well. The military was well supplied with advanced equipment because having a strong military was a priority. The Soviet Union launched the world's first satellite and was able to put a man in outer space before the United States. But the government did a poor job producing the goods that consumers were looking for. People sometimes had

to wait in line for hours just to buy a loaf of bread. In the United States, by contrast, popular goods like jeans were available when people wanted to buy them.

Why did the economies of the Soviet Union and the United States produce such different results for their citizens? The main reason is that the two countries had very different *economic systems*. In this chapter, you will learn what an economic system is and how these systems affect day-to-day life.

## BOTTOM LINE
**The economic system of a country affects the way its economy serves its citizens.**

# MODULE 4

# Using Resources to Achieve Economic Goals

**KEY IDEA:** **Every society must determine how to use its resources to achieve its economic goals.**

### OBJECTIVES

- **To explain the three basic economic questions.**
- **To identify five economic goals that societies pursue.**
- **To describe tradeoffs made among the five goals.**

## Haves and Have-Nots

Have you ever wondered why some countries are rich and others are poor? Or why the people in some countries have a great deal of freedom in their daily lives, while in other countries there are strict limits on individuals' choices? Even countries with very similar resources can have very different levels of wealth and freedom. For instance, the average citizen of North Korea earns less than $2,000 a year and faces severe restrictions on everything from travel to Internet use. Across the border in South Korea, the average citizen earns more than $30,000 a year and enjoys considerable freedom of choice. These differences relate to the economic systems in each country and the way scarce resources are distributed—or as economists like to say, *allocated*—within those systems. This module focuses on the three fundamental questions at the heart of resource allocation.

## THE THREE BASIC ECONOMIC QUESTIONS

Some countries with few resources have achieved great prosperity, while some countries with abundant resources have failed to prosper. Clearly what a country does with its resources can be more important than the resources it has to begin with. The choices countries must make about their resources can be summarized by three basic questions:

1.  What should be produced?

2.  How should it be produced?

3.  For whom should it be produced?

Let's consider each of these questions about resource allocation more fully.

## What Should Be Produced?

We know that tradeoffs are unavoidable. Because resources are limited, decisions must be made about which goods to produce. If more of some goods are

*Choices must be made about what is produced, how it is produced, and who gets it.*

produced, less of others must be produced. If more cars are produced, less material and labor are available to produce fighter jets. If more land is used to grow corn, less land is available to grow wheat. If more corn is used for ethanol, less corn is available for corn chowder. These tradeoffs force decisions within each country of *what* to make with the scarce resources available.

### How Should It Be Produced?

The "How?" question involves choosing which combination of resources to use in the production of each good and service. For example, a guitar can be made by many workers who shape and assemble the parts by hand, using a small number of jigsaws, sanders, and other machines. Or a manufacturer can use industrial robots to shape the parts and put them together, using just a few workers to program and control the robots. Should the

*This craftsman has chosen to make a guitar with a limited amount of machinery. The question of how to produce something is one of the three basic economic questions.*

guitar company use many workers and few machines or many machines and few workers? Each time a company plans to produce a product, it faces this question of "How?"

As another example, consider the many different ways to produce electricity. It can be generated from fuels such as coal, oil, ethanol, or nuclear material. Electricity can also be generated using flowing water, wind, or sunlight. For almost any product you can imagine, there is more than one way to produce it, and different ways use different combinations of resources. Thus, the question of "How?" arises.

### For Whom Should It Be Produced?

After the questions of "What?" and "How?" are answered, the "For whom?" question remains. In every society, choices must be made about who gets the limited supply of jeans and cars and electric guitars. Should each person get the same amount of each good? Or should some people get two pairs of jeans while others have none? If everyone doesn't get exactly the same things, how do we decide who gets more and who gets less? Should people who work harder than others receive more goods? Should we reward workers who are able to complete more challenging tasks, such as inventing new products or lifting large loads, because they are smarter or stronger or faster than the average person? What about people who are not as productive because they are ill or elderly? They may need more of certain goods and services, such as health care, than the average person. Because people don't agree about what is fair and what is best, the "For whom?" question creates frequent and heated public debates.

**DID YOU GET IT?**

**What are the three basic economic questions?**

## ECONOMICS IN ACTION

# The Three Basic Economic Questions and the U.S. Health Care Debate

A rapid rise in health care spending has led to an ongoing debate in the United States. We can use the three economic questions to help understand the issues. First, some background. The United States uses a greater percentage of its resources for health care than almost any other country. These resources are used to produce medicine and medical equipment, as well as health care services such as health screenings and surgeries. In 1970, about 7 percent of our resources were used for health care. By 2011, the percentage had risen above 18 percent, and it continues to grow. The government pays a large share of the health care costs in the United States through programs for low-income, elderly, and disabled citizens. Because these programs are funded with taxes, growing health care costs have many taxpayers worried.

Let's look at the health care debate from the perspective of our three questions.

*What should be produced?* Many people feel that a smaller percentage of our resources should be used for health care or that we should at least slow down the growth in medical expenditures. They believe that society would be better off if we avoided the least beneficial health care spending, such as large expenditures to keep terminally ill patients alive for a few more days. Instead, they would like to see more money and resources devoted to the most beneficial alternatives, which might include education, care for the elderly, and crime prevention.

*How should it be produced?* Here, too, we find many opinions. Most economists agree that we do not produce health care efficiently in the United States. By this they mean that we use more resources than necessary for what we receive. This happens, in part, because of how patients pay for health care. Most Americans have health insurance from private insurance companies or the government. If your doctor

wants to perform a test or procedure, you are likely to agree, because you trust your doctor and because your health insurance company or the government will pay for it. By contrast, in many other countries where the government pays for everyone's health care, the government restricts doctors' choices. If two treatments have roughly similar results, but one treatment requires more resources and money, that treatment will not be allowed. In the United States, the government is less restrictive, leaving more decisions to doctors and their patients. As a result, U.S. citizens have more medical goods and services available to them, and U.S. doctors tend to use more expensive procedures than doctors in other countries.

Inefficiency in health care production can also result from the frequent lawsuits against doctors. *Malpractice* occurs when a doctor harms a patient with irresponsible or unprofessional conduct. For example, if a doctor fails to test a patient for an

*The rising cost of health care leads to debates over what health care to provide, how to provide it, and who should receive it.*

ailment that turns out to be a problem, that failure can be the basis for a malpractice lawsuit. To reduce the chance of a malpractice lawsuit, doctors may order an excessive number of expensive tests and procedures to address illnesses the patient is unlikely to have.

*For whom should it be produced?* This third basic economic question is possibly the most controversial of all. Many Americans feel that everyone should have access to quality health care, regardless of their ability to pay for it. Others argue that trying to provide everyone with quality care would be too expensive. In recent years debate over health care has engulfed citizens, doctors, presidents, Congress, and the Supreme Court. The topic remains controversial, in part because when it comes to health care, people cannot agree on how to answer the question, "For whom?"

# SOCIETY'S ECONOMIC GOALS

Five key goals form the basis for judging any economic system: *economic growth, efficiency, equity, economic security,* and *economic freedom.* Weak performance in any of these areas can make life difficult for the people involved. Attempts to remedy weaknesses and maintain strengths in these areas are a primary focus of economic policy. We will consider each of the five goals in turn and mention several other goals that will be addressed later in the book. In the next module we will evaluate the ability of several economic systems to achieve these goals.

The **standard of living** is a measure of comfort in terms of the goods and services available.

*A society with a high standard of living can meet everyone's basic needs and many of their wants.*

## Economic Growth

Recall from Module 2 that economic growth is an increase in the amount of goods and services an economy can produce over time. Production in some economies increases by leaps and bounds. In China, for example, production has grown by around 10 percent per year for more than a decade. In other countries, production isn't going anywhere fast. Spain, for example, has experienced economic growth of between negative 1.5 percent and 1.5 percent every year for the past decade. With the population of most countries growing all the time, economic growth is important for the maintenance of a country's *standard of living*. The **standard of living** is a measure of the wealth of goods and services available to help people in the country live comfortably. Do people enjoy plenty of goods and services, including things like secure homes and reliable cars that make life more enjoyable? Or do people have a hard time meeting their basic needs for food and housing, not to mention wants for transportation and entertainment? Societies generally seek a standard of living that will place all of their citizens' needs, along with some of their wants, within reach.

Without economic growth, as populations grow, the same amount of goods and services would have to be divided among more and more people. There would therefore be less for the average person, and the standard of living would fall. An increase in the standard of living is only possible if a country's economy can grow faster than its population.

© CORBIS RF / ALAMY

In Chapter 1 we saw that innovation is an important source of economic growth. New products and processes, such as electronic stethoscopes, advanced robots, cloud computing, and laser surgery, allow workers to make more and better goods and services. An economic system that encourages innovations like these will lead to relatively more economic growth and a relatively high standard of living.

Economic growth comes from far more than an increase in manufacturing. In fact, *services* make up the majority of production and the majority of growth in the U.S. economy. Societies can have a higher standard of living without more manufacturing if they use their resources to increase the production of things like health care, education, police protection, art, cancer research, music lessons, national parks, and hazardous waste cleanups.

**DID YOU GET IT?**
**Describe why economic growth is necessary to support a high standard of living.**

## Efficiency

You learned in Module 2 that an economy is efficient if it takes every opportunity to make some people better off without making anyone worse off. The achievement of efficiency depends on how the three basic economic questions are answered. Consider the question of what to produce. If the goods and services that are produced differ from what society wants or needs, the allocation of resources is inefficient. For example, nearly half of the residents of India are vegetarians—they do not eat meat. If most of the farms in India produced only meat, and some of that meat went to waste, the allocation of resources would be inefficient. By producing less meat and more of the types of food that are in high demand, some people could be made better off without making anyone worse off. Likewise, if the question of how to produce is answered with a production method that wastes resources, production is inefficient. And if the question of

*Economic growth doesn't always come from growth in manufacturing. It can come from growth in services like medical research to find a cure for cancer.*

for whom to produce is answered with the wrong people—if meat lovers are getting fruit and fruit lovers are getting meat—then the distribution of goods is inefficient. The tools of economics help societies address the three basic questions as they work toward the goal of efficiency.

## Equity

The standard of living is one measure of how well-off society is as a whole, but it tells us nothing about **equity**, the quality of being fair and just. A high standard of living indicates that a lot of goods and services are produced relative to the size of the population, but are those goods and services distributed among people in a fair and just way? Do a lot of people receive the goods and services, or do a small number of people reap the benefits of the country's productivity?

To complicate the matter, people have differing views of what is "fair," "just," and "equitable." Some people believe a society should provide *equality of outcome*. By this they mean that each member of society should share equally in what the economy produces. If there are groups of people who have more than others, then outcomes are unequal and the economy falls short of that ideal. Other people argue for *equality*

**Equity** is the quality of being fair and just.

*of opportunity.* They believe that everyone in a society should have the same opportunities in life. The idea is that if there are equal opportunities for quality education and jobs and yet people end up with unequal outcomes, it is the fair and just result of the choices individuals make. For example, some people choose to attain less education than others, take more leisure time, or work for charities or other organizations that pay comparatively low wages.

As you can see, opinions differ about whether a society's efforts toward equity should lean more toward equal outcomes or equal opportunities. Nevertheless, almost everyone agrees that some form of equity is an important economic goal.

*Most people agree that a society should offer an equal opportunity for education to all of its members.*

A **social safety net** is any form of government assistance for those with financial needs.

**DID YOU GET IT?**
What are two different ways of looking at the goal of equity?

## Economic Security

When it comes to money, "easy come, easy go!" Or so they say. When putting food on the table, paying bills, financing college, fixing the roof, and insuring the car, money seems to go a lot faster than it comes. In fact, financial problems are among the leading causes of stress, divorce, and depression. Citizens with **economic security** have confidence in their ability to support themselves and their families.

One source of economic security is an ample number of well-paying jobs.

Citizens with **economic security** have confidence in their ability to support themselves and their families.

The wages earned from jobs pay those pesky bills, and the availability of jobs reduces stress because those who lose their jobs can be hopeful about finding work again soon. When jobs are scarce, competition for openings gets fierce, and people can seek work for a year or more without success. For a household without a paycheck, wants are seldom satisfied. Scariest of all, it can be hard to meet basic needs including food, shelter, and health care. When jobs are hard to come by, even those fortunate enough to have one must live with the fear of job loss and the hardships that follow.

A second source of economic security is a **social safety net**, which can be any form of government assistance for those with financial needs. There are several different forms of assistance available in the United States. Unemployment insurance helps those who have lost their jobs, workers' compensation helps victims of work-related injuries, Social Security assists retired and disabled citizens, and Supplemental Nutrition Assistance is available to help put food on the table in low-income households. Most social safety nets offer incomplete protection from financial loss, but they make the worst-case scenario something people can live with, however uncomfortably.

**DID YOU GET IT?**
What are two sources of economic security?

## Economic Freedom

You have seen that economics is about making the best choices in the face of scarcity. The benefits from making the best choices are lost when people are not free to make those choices. If you've ever received ugly pajamas from Aunt Betty for your birthday, you've felt the burden of limited choices. Economists see cash as a great gift, because the recipient can choose whatever he or she wants to buy with it. Some economic systems severely restrict the choices individuals can make and leave a lot of decisions to leaders who may or may not have better ideas than your Aunt Betty.

With **economic freedom**, people can make economic decisions for themselves. Most people would prefer to live in a country where they are free to choose where to live, what goods and services to buy, and what type of work to perform. And most entrepreneurs would prefer to open a business in a country where they can choose what to produce and what prices to charge.

The Heritage Foundation and the *Wall Street Journal* rank the economic freedom of countries on the basis of 10 related types of freedom. These include *trade freedom*, the freedom to trade goods and services with other countries; *monetary freedom*, stable prices without government price controls; and *business freedom*, the freedom to open and close a business without government-imposed costs or delays. In 2012, the United States ranked tenth out of 179 countries for economic freedom. Table 4.1 shows the 5 countries that ranked the highest and the lowest in 2012.

Economic freedom has been built into the economic system of the United States since the beginning. The opening words of the Declaration of Independence and the Constitution of the United States emphasize the importance of *liberty*, another word for freedom. It is easy to take economic freedom for granted when you have grown up with it. Later in this chapter you will learn about the standard of living in countries that have failed to achieve this goal.

## Other Goals

The previously mentioned goals begin the list of what most societies want their economic system to promote.

Societies have many other goals. Module 41 discusses the goal of having enough jobs for those who want to work. Module 42 discusses the goal of stable prices. Beyond economic growth and a high standard of living, people want a high *quality of life*, the recipe for which includes goods and services but also friends and family, mental and physical health, leisure time, and various other personal goals. Beyond economic security, people want personal security—we value secure schools, violence-free streets, and a safe food supply. And beyond economic freedom, people want many other types of freedom, including freedom of speech and freedom of religion.

Among the other goals is **sustainability**, which is the ability to continue actions indefinitely. A society with a pleasing level of production would at least like to sustain that production and the standard of living it supports.

**Economic freedom** gives people the ability to make economic decisions for themselves.

**Sustainability** is the ability to continue actions indefinitely.

| Table 4.1 **Economic Freedom** | | | |
|---|---|---|---|
| **TOP TEN** | | **BOTTOM TEN** | |
| 1. Hong Kong | 6. Canada | 170. Equatorial Guinea | 175. Eritrea |
| 2. Singapore | 7. Chile | 171. Iran | 176. Libya |
| 3. Australia | 8. Mauritius | 172. Democratic Republic of Congo | 177. Cuba |
| 4. New Zealand | 9. Ireland | 173. Burma | 178. Zimbabwe |
| 5. Switzerland | 10. United States | 174. Venezuela | 179. North Korea |

SOURCE: *2012 Index of Economic Freedom*, the Heritage Foundation, and the *Wall Street Journal*, www.heritage.org/index.

However, even current production levels are unsustainable if resources are being used up faster than they become available. If farmers overwork their land, for instance, nitrogen and other nutrients in the soil are depleted, and crop production falls. The goal of sustainability is to allow current generations to live comfortably without preventing future generations from doing the same. Concerns that economic activity is causing global climate change, exhausting supplies of key resources such as oil, and creating an unhealthy environment highlight the importance of that goal. By targeting sustainability now, societies are more likely to dodge the bullet of lost resources and a compromised standard of living later.

To make citizens as well-off as possible, societies would like to achieve each of the five economic goals, as well as many broader goals. Unfortunately, there are choices to be made, because more success in achieving one goal can come at the expense of achieving another. Next we'll look at these tradeoffs among goals.

*Vending machines that rent movies increase productivity at the expense of jobs for store clerks.*

**DID YOU GET IT?**
What are five key economic goals that societies strive to achieve?

# TRADEOFFS AMONG GOALS

You know that life involves tradeoffs: to have more of one good you must give up some of another. Likewise, achieving one economic goal can mean sacrificing another. Remember Robin Hood? He took money from the rich and gave it to the poor to achieve equity. But Robin Hood's favorite pastime erodes the economic security of people whose money is taken. Transferring money from the rich to the poor can also create incentive problems. Perhaps at some point you've earned a tip for a job well done. What if you weren't allowed to keep that tip? You probably wouldn't work as hard the next time. So you can understand that if workers can't keep the rewards of their hard work, they might not work as hard. This would decrease economic growth and the standard of living.

Among other tradeoffs, a high level of economic growth today can deplete resources, thereby reducing economic growth in the future. And while vending machines that rent movies and sell iPods promote economic growth and jobs for vending machine companies, they take away jobs and economic security for store clerks.

The necessary tradeoffs force societies to prioritize among economic goals. Naturally, the tradeoffs people prefer depend on what they have to gain or lose. Vending machine manufacturers and others whose skills serve a rapidly changing economy may prefer to see change even if it reduces equity. People whose livelihoods are threatened by economic change—bookstore clerks, for example—tend to value the economic security of keeping things as they are more than growth. When the gains from change exceed the losses, it is possible to achieve an improved standard of living without neglecting the goals of equity and economic security. One solution is to make the change and then direct some of the gains from change into financial assistance and training for the clerks and other workers in the declining industries. Over time, this will help them transition into new occupations in the expanding industries.

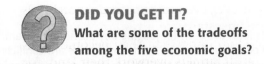

**DID YOU GET IT?**
What are some of the tradeoffs among the five economic goals?

# MODULE 4 REVIEW AND ASSESSMENT

## Summing Up the Key Ideas: Match the following terms with the correct definition.

A. Standard of living
B. Equity
C. Efficiency
D. Economic security

E. Social safety net
F. Economic freedom
G. Allocated
H. Equality of outcome

I. Equality of opportunity
J. Economic growth

___B___ 1. The quality of being fair and just.

___A___ 2. A measure of the wealth of goods and services available to help people live comfortably.

___H___ 3. Each member of society shares equally in what the economy produces.

___F___ 4. The ability for people to make economic decisions for themselves.

___D___ 5. The confidence of citizens in their ability to support themselves and their families.

___I___ 6. Each member of society has the same opportunities in life.

___C___ 7. Achieved when an economy takes every opportunity to make some people better off without making anyone worse off.

___G___ 8. The way that scarce resources are distributed in an economic system.

___E___ 9. Any form of government assistance for those with financial needs.

___J___ 10. An increase in the amount of goods and services an economy can produce over time.

## Analyze: In the process of allocating scarce resources, countries answer questions about **what**, **how**, and **for whom to produce**. Identify which of these three basic questions is answered by each of the following decisions.

|  | QUESTION |
|---|---|
| 1. The government enacts workplace safety regulations. | What |
| 2. Medicare provides health care for senior citizens. | for whom |
| 3. Online downloads replace CDs as the most popular form of music. | what |
| 4. Technology innovation assists firms with better productivity. | what / how? |
| 5. Goods go to those who are willing to pay the most for them. | for whom |
| 6. Machines increasingly replace workers in factories. | what |
| 7. E-books become more popular than hardcover books. | what |

**Apply:** Five key goals form the basis for judging any economic system: *economic growth, efficiency, equity, economic security,* and *economic freedom.* Sometimes there are conflicts between society's economic goals. For the following pairs of goals, determine whether they are conflicting or complementary. If they are conflicting, identify a potential necessary tradeoff. Then explain the conflicting or complementary relationship between the two goals.

| | TRADEOFF OR NO TRADEOFF | EXPLAIN |
|---|---|---|
| 1. economic security and equity | tradeoff | Give up equity for economic security |
| 2. economic growth and efficiency | no tradeoff | |
| 3. economic growth and a high standard of living | no tradeoff | |
| 4. economic freedom and economic security | no tradeoff | |

# MODULE 5

# Types of Economic Systems

**KEY IDEA:** A country's economic system determines how well it can achieve each economic goal.

**OBJECTIVES**

- **To explain what an economic system is and how incentives play a role.**
- **To describe the features of a traditional economy, a command economy, a market economy, and a mixed economy.**

## Questions and Answers behind the Scenes

When you got dressed this morning, you probably didn't think about all the resources that went into making your clothes. But the three basic economic questions were asked and answered over and over as resources from around the world came together to make the clothing you're wearing right now. For example, before your shirt could be made, someone in a place like North Carolina or Egypt had to answer the "What should be produced?" question with "Cotton!" rather than "Broccoli!" or "Hub caps!" The cotton farmer had to answer the "How should it be produced?" question to determine how the cotton would be grown and harvested.

*Even something as simple as a T-shirt requires a complex set of coordinated activities that an economic system provides.*

Finally, with guidance from your behavior as a consumer, the "For whom should it be produced?" question was answered with your name.

Suppose the cotton was sold to a textile company in Thailand. The same three questions were answered as the textile company turned the cotton into fabric. The fabric was then dyed, which required another company to answer the "What?" question with "Dye!" The questions were answered again when the fabric was cut and sewn into T-shirts by some combination of people and machines. They were answered when the T-shirts were transported by ship or air to a warehouse, when they were distributed to stores by trucks or trains, and when a store offered the shirt to you in exchange for money.

As with shirts, there are many stages in the production process for most goods, and the three questions must be answered at each stage. Multiply the many stages by the millions of different goods produced in a typical economy and the importance of the three key questions becomes clear. How, exactly, are these questions answered? In this module you'll see that it all depends on the *economic system* in place.

# ECONOMIC SYSTEMS AND INCENTIVES

An **economic system** is an organizational structure for addressing what, how, and for whom to produce.

In a **traditional economy**, decisions about resources are made by habit, custom, superstition, or religious tradition.

An **incentive** is the prospect of a reward or punishment that influences a decision or motivates greater effort.

An **economic system** is an organizational structure for addressing what, how, and for whom to produce. The way an economic system answers these questions deeply influences people's lives. As you saw in this chapter's opening story, the economic system of the former Soviet Union allocated relatively few resources to the satisfaction of citizens' wants, which made life in the Soviet Union dramatically different from life in the United States. Economic systems come in three main forms: *traditional economies*, *command economies*, and *market economies*. Most economies are influenced by more than one of these forms, the result being a *mixed economy*.

If economic research shows one thing, it is that *incentives* shape human behavior. An **incentive** is the prospect of a reward or punishment that influences a decision or motivates greater effort. We encounter incentives in our lives every day. Consider the following examples:

- The reward of wages gives people an incentive to work. Higher wages motivate people to work more.

- The fear of a parking ticket provides an incentive to park legally.

- The desire for good grades is an incentive for you to do your homework.

- The prospect of a better job is an incentive for you to stay in school and graduate.

It's not that people necessarily dislike their work, and you know how much fun school is! But every activity has an opportunity cost. By choosing to do one activity, you are foregoing the opportunity to do any other activity. In any given hour you can choose from hundreds of things you like to do or should do. It is often incentives that determine which activity you pick.

In this module we examine how each type of economic system answers the three basic economic questions. And we look at how well the incentives created within each system address the five key economic goals.

**DID YOU GET IT?**
What is an economic system, and what role do incentives play?

# TRADITIONAL ECONOMIES

In a **traditional economy**, decisions about resources are made by habit, custom, superstition, or religious tradition. For a traditional economy, the answers to the three basic economic questions might be summed up with the response "We do it the way we've always done it." For the question "What should be produced?" participants in a traditional economy answer, "What has *always* been produced." For the question "How should it be produced?" participants in a traditional economy answer, "The same way we've *always* produced it." And for the question "For whom should it be produced?" the answer is "For the people who have received our products in the past." These decisions require very little planning. People in traditional economies just do what is expected, which is the same as what has always been expected.

Although traditional economies are rare in the twenty-first century, they still exist in remote parts of Africa and the islands of Oceania in the southwest Pacific. For example, the Melanesian clans of Papua New Guinea, an island located north of Australia, live in traditional agricultural villages much as they have for thousands of years. Within the United States, the Amish—a religious group that emphasizes simple living—operate something close to a traditional economy. Many of the Amish drive horse-drawn buggies instead of cars; some do not have electricity in their homes; and they tend to work at farming, carpentry, baking, and other traditional occupations.

## Incentives in a Traditional Economy

In a traditional economy, the incentives include social approval for performing well at a traditional role and disapproval for rebelling against traditions or performing poorly. Serious violations might be met with punishment or even banishment from the community. But because traditional values are instilled early in life, and exposure to outsiders is often limited, much of the behavior in a traditional economy is determined by established patterns.

## Advantages of Traditional Economies

Traditional economies tend to provide economic security. Every person has an economic role to play. Unless there is a natural disaster like an earthquake or a flood, there are no dramatic changes in the economy, so people don't have to worry about losing their jobs. Traditional economies also tend to be sustainable because they grow very slowly, if at all. And they can achieve a relatively equitable distribution of goods and services, at least according to the traditional standards of the community.

## Disadvantages of Traditional Economies

As for disadvantages, traditional economies rarely achieve the goals of economic freedom, economic growth, and a high standard of living. Equity can also be a problem if the standards of the community are unfavorable to certain groups, such as women. Some traditional societies resist the adoption of new technologies, such as electricity or the Internet, that contribute to education, health, comfort, and the satisfaction of other needs and wants. As a result, living standards generally remain low. If you lived

*The Amish people have a traditional economy.*

in a traditional economy, your freedom would be limited because your future would be largely determined by your family or by the judgment of the village elders. If you were expected to be a hunter or a chicken farmer, you could not start a business or become a musician.

**DID YOU GET IT?**
**What are the characteristics of a traditional economy?**

# COMMAND ECONOMIES

In a **command economy**, central planners make the important decisions about what, how, and for whom to produce. *Communist* and *socialist* economies are examples of command economies. Under **communism**, legislators from a single political party—the Communist Party—establish wages, oversee production, and allocate goods according to what they judge to be the needs of their citizens. Under **socialism**, citizen groups known as *general assemblies*, along with councils of workers and consumers, are the primary economic decision makers. These groups sometimes work in cooperation with a centralized government. Socialist economies distribute goods in proportion to the work contributions of citizens. In each type of command economy, key resources and businesses are owned by groups of workers or by the government, rather than by private individuals.

In a **command economy**, central planners make the important decisions about what, how, and for whom to produce.

**Communism** is a political-economic system under which all resources and businesses are publicly owned and economic decisions are made by central authorities.

**Socialism** is an economic system under which most resources and businesses are publicly owned and economic decisions are made by groups of workers and consumers.

Command economies require tight control over economic decisions and activities. Insufficient production of one good can disrupt the production of many other goods and cause the entire plan to fail. If a mine fails to produce the required amount of iron ore, then steel factories that use the iron ore will fall short of their required production. Without enough steel, producers of cars, ovens, and tanks will not be able to meet their own requirements. To maintain control, central planners assign production levels called *quotas* for factories. If central planners want one million cars to be produced this year, they will issue a quota of one million cars to manufacturers. They will then assign people to work in car factories and issue similar quotas and worker assignments to producers of steel, aluminum, and other inputs needed to make cars.

Until the end of the 1980s, dozens of countries had command economies. Examples included the former Soviet Union, China, Poland, East Germany, Bulgaria, and Albania. All these countries considered themselves to be *communist*. Their systems featured a combination of central planning, public ownership of key resources and businesses, and *authoritarian* political control, meaning that political power was held tightly by a small number of government authorities who demanded strict obedience. These systems were not successful. Today, almost all the former Communist countries have abandoned public ownership and central planning. China, North Korea, Cuba, and Vietnam are among those that retain authoritarian political control.

## PEOPLE IN ECONOMICS

# Karl Marx and Communism

The idea of communism was made famous by Karl Marx (1818–1883), a German economist and political activist. Marx analyzed economic systems through the lens of history. He argued that private ownership of resources caused wealth and power to become concentrated in the hands of a small number of people. In *The Communist Manifesto* he predicted that all economic systems would be replaced by communism, which he idealized as a classless society.

Under communism as Marx saw it, all resources would be owned by everyone jointly, rather than by a government or individuals. Marx was not very specific about how communal ownership would work or how resources would be allocated under common ownership.

In the decades after Karl Marx wrote about communism, the term came to have a second meaning. *Communism* described the real-world economic and political systems put in place by governments influenced by Marx's ideas. The Communist countries had command economies with key resources owned by the government. Politically, the system was authoritarian. The "Communist Party" ran the government and made all political decisions. Newspapers and TV stations were run by the government, and people could be arrested for saying anything against the Communist Party. In a nutshell, *communism* came to mean central planning, public ownership, and authoritarian political control.

Today, only Cuba and North Korea retain all three features of the former Communist countries: central planning, public ownership of key resources and businesses, and strict authoritarian political control. All the others have abandoned central planning and public ownership. China's government still calls itself communist, because the old Communist Party continues to run the government, but the label no longer describes its economic system.

## Incentives in a Command Economy

The incentives in a command economy come from the government. To ensure fulfillment of the plan, rewards and punishments are given to the managers of factories, transportation systems, schools, and other key enterprises. Those who meet their production quotas might be rewarded with better jobs, nicer apartments, or access to luxury goods such as cars or vacation homes. Those who fall short may be demoted or transferred to less desirable locations. Anyone caught using government-owned resources for personal gain is likely to receive a stiff prison sentence. These incentives are designed to ensure that production goes as planned in each industry and to avoid glitches and delays that can have a domino effect across industries and cause the central plan to fail.

## Advantages of Command Economies

Command economies can provide economic security. The central planners guarantee employment by assigning every person to a job that is part of the plan. No safety net is needed, because everyone works for, and is paid by, the government, and many basic needs such as housing, education, and medical care are provided by the government without charge. As long as the country has reached a level of production high

enough to provide basic goods and services for everyone, a command economy can make great strides in eliminating hunger, homelessness, illiteracy, and extreme poverty. The Soviet Union and many other command economies eventually managed to satisfy the most basic needs of their citizens during the first half of the twentieth century.

Command economies also have the ability to adjust rapidly to changing circumstances. If the government decides that more computers, more bridges, or more missiles are needed, it can quickly shift resources away from other types of production into these industries. This flexibility enabled many command economies to grow rapidly in the first half of the twentieth century, when resources were shifted away from consumer goods like food and clothing toward the production of physical capital, such as farm machinery, factories, highways, and harbors. At first, living standards fell dramatically because of shortages of consumer goods. Living standards rose again as the capital stock grew and production increased.

## Disadvantages of Command Economies

Overall, command economies have had a poor economic track record and have failed to meet several important economic goals. Economic freedom is sacrificed to ensure that every part of

**Rationing** is the placement of limits on the amount of goods each person can purchase.

the central plan is obeyed. People cannot start a business or change jobs in a command economy without government permission, if at all. The standard of living in command economies is low despite an abundance of jobs. To understand why, remember that the businesses are not privately owned. Since those who run the businesses don't get to keep the money they earn, there are few incentives to work hard, to innovate, or to use resources efficiently. This incentive problem generally leads to weak economic growth.

In practice, the decision makers in command economies have chosen to allocate a large portion of their scarce resources to the production of military goods and physical capital, such as roads, bridges, dams, and power plants. As a result, citizens face shortages of consumer goods, and the government must resort to *rationing*. **Rationing** refers to the placement of limits on the amount of goods each person can purchase. For instance, in Cuba, which still has a command economy, people want more cars than are available, so cars are rationed. The next Economics in Action box describes rationing under Castro's communist rule in Cuba.

When the goods consumers want aren't available in adequate quantities, illegal "underground" markets flourish. Those lucky enough to get rationed goods will often resell them secretly,

## ECONOMICS IN ACTION

# Rationing in a Command Economy

*As a small boy, author Ernesto Mestre-Reed lived in Cuba under Fidel Castro's communist government. In the following passage, he describes the imbalance of products in Cuba as compared with the United States and what it's like to experience rationing.*

In the Cuba of my childhood, *nisperos* and *mammees* (Caribbean fruits) were so abundant

we ate them in every way we could imagine: on the side at breakfast, lunch and dinner, pulped and made into shakes with coconut milk as an afternoon snack. In a country where milk, cigarettes, coffee and pork chops were marked off on a ration card—with only so much allotted to each family and only so much in the store (so that my grandmother awoke before dawn to go stand in line with her card)—the fruit trees offered rare abundance.

In America, where we are surrounded by abundance, it's easy to lose awareness of it, even to forget about it. In New York, where I live, I can go down the street at 3 a.m. to the 24-hour market and get as much milk or coffee or as many cigarettes or pork chops as I want. For a few months every summer, I can even buy *nisperos* and *mammees* at the delis in the Latino areas along Fifth Avenue in Brooklyn.

SOURCE: Ernesto Mestre-Reed, "A Spitting Image of Cuba," *New York Times*, July 28, 2004.

at a price much higher than what they paid. The Soviet Union had a very active underground market in many consumer goods, including, believe it or not, burnt-out light bulbs. The reason was that central planners never produced enough light bulbs for household use. So in order to have a ready supply of bulbs at home, people stole working light bulbs from the factories and offices where they worked. To hide the theft, they would replace the good bulbs with burnt-out bulbs purchased in the underground market.

Lastly, in spite of the promises of their governments, most countries with command economies have failed to achieve acceptable levels of equity. High officials, top bureaucrats, and military officers typically fare better in a command system. They get special treatment such as better housing, medical care, and access to special stores stocked full of consumer goods that the rest of the population cannot buy.

The disadvantages of command economies explain why this type of economic system has been abandoned by almost every country that experimented with it. Instead, these countries have moved to the third type of economic system—the market economy.

**DID YOU GET IT?**
**What are the features of a command economy?**

## PEOPLE IN ECONOMICS

# Friedrich von Hayek

Friedrich August von Hayek (1899–1992) was an Austrian-born economist and political philosopher. He was awarded the Nobel Prize in 1974 and also received several high honors from the governments of the United States and United Kingdom.

After serving in an artillery regiment in World War I, Hayek attended the University of Vienna, where he studied law, economics, and psychology. The horrors of war and the difficulties of postwar Europe inspired Hayek to look for ways to improve social and economic conditions.

At a time when socialism was on the rise, Hayek described

the problems with creating a centrally planned economy. His famous book *The Road to Serfdom* (1944) warned that central planning could lead to oppression. While advocates of a planned economy believed that they could take all the available data about the economy and create a system that would work better than the free market, Hayek believed that no planner could possibly account for the vast amount of local and specialized knowledge that goes into everyday economic decisions. Today, Hayek's ideas about the importance of the free market continue to influence economists and policy makers, and many of his articles and books are still widely studied.

# MARKET ECONOMIES

In a market economy, most key economic decisions are made by business owners and consumers. Business owners are free to choose what to produce and how to produce it, and businesses sell their products to whoever chooses to buy them. Market economies operate under a **capitalist system**, which means that most resources and businesses are *privately owned*. Individuals can use, rent, or sell the resources they own as they see fit, with relatively little governmental interference. For example, because individuals own their own labor in market economies, they can "rent" it to employers in exchange for a wage or salary. Land-owners can rent their property to a farmer or a business owner or sell the land to a development company that wants to build on it. Entrepreneurs can start a business and succeed or fail on their own merits.

A key feature of market economies is that exchanges of resources or goods for money take place *voluntarily* between parties. No one is forced to buy or sell resources or goods. Because a market economy is based on *voluntary exchange* and gives people so much freedom to start businesses and decide how their resources are used, it is also called a **free-enterprise system**.

The United States is a primary example of a country with a market economy. Other countries with successful market economies include Canada, England, France, Germany, Japan, and Singapore. As discussed later in this module, most market economies contain elements of other economic systems as well. The label *market economy* applies whenever private ownership and voluntary exchange play a major role.

## Incentives in a Market Economy

The incentives in a market economy are the gains and losses that follow from the economic choices of business owners and consumers. Any exchange in a market economy must benefit both sides, or else it wouldn't be carried out voluntarily. An exchange can also be called a *trade*. When buyers and sellers benefit from trade, economists say that there are *gains from trade*. To enjoy these gains, each participant in a trade has an incentive to ensure that the trade satisfies the other party. For example, a car dealer can't motivate a voluntary purchase without offering a car that satisfies the buyer. And the buyer can't motivate the voluntary sale of a car without offering enough money to satisfy the seller. The need to please others in order to enjoy personal gain is a driving force in all market economies.

## Advantages of Market Economies

When you want to buy running shoes, jeans, soda, or almost anything else in a market economy, you usually can, thanks to a strong set of incentives. Store owners are rewarded with more customers and higher profits if they stock the goods people want to buy. Manufacturers that ship goods rapidly to stores will rapidly make more money than manufacturers that are slow to respond to orders. The prospect of financial rewards for satisfying the needs and wants of others keeps individuals and businesses "on their toes" and helps ensure that goods are available when people want them. The availability of desirable goods is one reason market economies create higher living standards than traditional economies or command economies.

Efficient production methods are another reason for high living standards in market economies. In a market economy, business owners have to pay for the inputs they use, so they have an

*In a market economy, businesses have a strong incentive to satisfy customer desires.*

---

In a **market economy**, most key economic decisions are made by business owners and consumers.

In a **capitalist system**, most resources and businesses are privately owned.

A **free-enterprise system** is an economic system based on private (individual or business) ownership of resources and voluntary exchange.

incentive to avoid waste. For example, if a soda company can reduce its electricity costs by conserving energy, the company has a strong incentive to do so. Less money spent on electricity means more money to keep or to invest in the business. In the bigger picture, the soda company's decision to use less electricity frees up more electricity for the production of shoes, jeans, and other goods and services that people want. So when businesses respond to market-economy incentives to produce more efficiently, the standard of living goes up.

Market economies also tend to have rapid economic growth, largely because they encourage discovery and innovation. Inventors of useful products or processes can reap tremendous financial rewards. Consider Henry Ford, whose innovative use of the assembly line made automobiles cheap and Ford wealthy. Larry Page and Sergey Brin, the entrepreneurs who started Google, along with eBay founder Pierre Omidyar and Facebook founder Mark Zuckerberg, are billionaires. By satisfying millions of consumers and helping the economy grow, they made themselves rich.

Finally, a market economy allows more freedom for consumers and businesses than traditional or command economies. People are free to make their own choices about where to work and what to buy with the money they earn. Businesses can decide what to produce and how to produce it. Indeed, freedom for individuals to make choices is the defining characteristic of a market economy.

## Disadvantages of Market Economies

Like traditional and command economies, market economies have their disadvantages. One problem is equity, especially when viewed as equality of outcome rather than equality of opportunity. The prospect of multibillion-dollar rewards for the most successful entrepreneurs—while a spur to innovation and growth—leads to highly unequal economic outcomes. In the United States, for example, one-fifth of all households earned less than $20,500 in 2009, while the average income among the richest 1 percent was about $960,000. In 2012, members of a group known as Occupy Wall Street held rallies across the United States to protest perceived inequities. The participants felt that some corporations charged consumers prices that were too high, paid workers wages that were too low, or in other ways contributed to unfair economic outcomes.

Economic security can also be a problem in a market economy. There are no central plans or strong traditions to ensure everyone has a job. It is up to each individual to plan for the future and find work. When a market economy is booming, people who want jobs can generally find them. But market economies also go through rough periods—sometimes lasting years—in which many people lose their jobs and it is difficult to find work. One such period began in late 2007, when tens of millions of people in market economies around the world lost their jobs.

Resource conservation is another challenge for market economies. When individuals decide how to use resources, they may overlook the effects of their decisions on the environment and on future generations. For example, consumers in the United States generate about 30 million tons of plastic waste per year, including billions of single-use plastic bags. Most plastic comes from oil, which is limited in supply, and only 7 percent of plastic waste is currently

A market economy rewards innovation by entrepreneurs like Mark Zuckerberg, the founder of Facebook.

recycled. Market economies may provide too few incentives to conserve resources and adopt renewable alternatives such as polylactic acid—a plastic substitute made from corn.

Finally, the powerful incentives in market economies can lead to behavior that goes against society's goals. There are incentives for drug companies to rush new medicines to market without adequate testing. There are incentives for businesses to grow so large that they can take control of markets, restrict the availability of goods, and inflate prices. And there are incentives for advertisers to mislead consumers about the benefits or costs of their products. To avoid problems such as these, governments can intervene with laws for the protection of society. When government involvement in a market economy becomes substantial, society has a new concoction called a *mixed economy*.

**DID YOU GET IT?**
**What are the features of a market economy?**

# MIXED ECONOMIES

A **mixed economy** combines a market economy with significant government involvement and elements of tradition.

Banana splits are a favorite dessert because they contain the advantages of fruit, ice cream, and chocolate syrup without too much of any one thing. Mixed economies are the banana splits of economic systems and every bit as popular. A **mixed economy** combines a market economy with significant government involvement and elements of tradition. All modern market economies are mixed economies. For example, in the United States, while most decisions about resources are still made by individuals and most resources are privately owned, government agencies make key decisions about public services including national defense, education, and police protection. The government also regulates activities that could present harm to society if left unchecked,

like drug sales, food production, child labor, the use of smoke detectors, and the release of pollution.

Government involvement in market economies has evolved over time. In the novel *Oliver Twist*, British author Charles Dickens described the food ration in a nineteenth-century house for the working poor this way: "Three meals of thin gruel a day, with an onion twice a week and half a roll on Sundays." It's no wonder that young Oliver, the central character in the novel, famously asks for more. Countless reports of the mistreatment of women and children during the Industrial Revolution led governments to enact new laws for their protection. In England, the Factory Act of 1802 restricted the number of working hours for young apprentices to no more than 12 hours a day. Employers were also required to treat their young workers more humanely by providing clothing; instruction in reading, writing, and arithmetic; and at least one bed for every two apprentices. By today's standards, this doesn't sound very appealing, but conditions were so poor at the time that the Factory Act was a major improvement.

Over time, governments in market economies have expanded their roles in the pursuit of equity, economic security, and sustainability. Because government oversight limits freedom but assists with other goals, there is much debate over just how involved government should be. In the United States, for example, some people think the government has overstepped its bounds. Others think the government should do more. We'll look more closely at the role of government and other features of modern market economies in Module 6.

Figure 5.1 summarizes the differences among the three economic systems in their purest forms.

**DID YOU GET IT?**
**What are the strengths and weaknesses of a mixed economy?**

Traditional Economy

| TRADITIONAL ECONOMY | |
| --- | --- |
| **Primary incentives** | |
| Social approval and disapproval | |
| **Economic goal** | |
| Efficiency | Low |
| Economic growth | Varying |
| Equity | High |
| Economic security | High |
| Economic freedom | Low |

Command Economy

| COMMAND ECONOMY | |
| --- | --- |
| **Primary incentives** | |
| Government rewards and punishments | |
| **Economic goal** | |
| Efficiency | Varying |
| Economic growth | Low |
| Equity | Medium |
| Economic security | High |
| Economic freedom | Low |

Market Economy

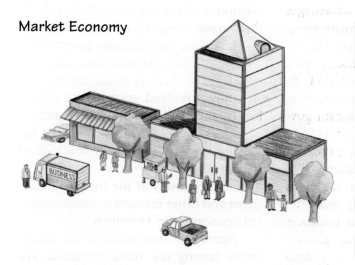

| MARKET ECONOMY | |
| --- | --- |
| **Primary incentives** | |
| Private gains and losses from voluntary exchange | |
| **Economic goal** | |
| Efficiency | High |
| Economic growth | High |
| Equity | Low |
| Economic security | Low |
| Economic freedom | High |

**Figure 5.1** Economic Systems and Economic Goals
The performance of each economic system in meeting the five key economic goals is graded low, medium, or high.

# MODULE 5 REVIEW AND ASSESSMENT

**Summing Up the Key Ideas:** Match the following terms with the correct definition.

A. Economic system    E. Communism      I. Capitalist system
B. Traditional economy    F. Socialism      J. Free-enterprise system
C. Incentive      G. Rationing      K. Mixed economy
D. Command economy    H. Market economy

_**G**_    1. The placement of limits on the amount of goods each person can purchase.

_**B**_    2. Decisions about resources are made by habit, custom, superstition, or religious tradition.

_**J**_    3. Exchanges of resources or goods for money take place voluntarily between parties.

_**I**_    4. Most resources are privately owned.

_**A**_    5. An organizational structure for addressing what, how, and for whom to produce.

_**C**_    6. The prospect of a reward or punishment that influences a decision or encourages greater effort.

_**K**_    7. Combines a market economy with significant government involvement.

_**F**_    8. Citizen groups known as *general assemblies*, along with councils of workers and consumers, are the primary decision makers.

_**E**_    9. Legislators from a single political party—the Communist Party—establish wages, oversee production, and allocate goods according to the needs of citizens.

_**D**_    10. Central planners make the important decisions about what, how, and for whom to produce.

_**H**_    11. Most key decisions are made by business owners and consumers.

**Analyze:** Over time, economies have used different systems to answer the three basic economic questions. For each of the following, identify if the system described is a **traditional economy**, a **command economy**, a **market economy**, or a **mixed economy**.

ECONOMIC SYSTEM

1. Production techniques are handed down to family members from generation to generation.    _traditional_

2. The goods and services available for consumption are determined by the voluntary interaction of producers and consumers.    _market_

3. Wages and distribution system are controlled by government planners.    _mixed_

4. Profit motive drives sellers; self-interest drives buyers.    _market_

5. All decisions involving production and consumption of goods and services are made by the government.    _mixed+_

6. No central planning occurs.    _command?_

7. The right to make production and distribution decisions is based on political power.    _mixed+_

8. Change comes slowly, often with opposition.    _mixed_

9. The system uses the same production methods used in the past and produces the same or similar products as in the past.

*traditional*

10. Most decisions about what goods and services are produced are made by voluntary exchange, even though there are many regulations on acceptable production techniques determined by the government.

*market*

**Apply:** Identify and explain the **type of economic system** that would work best to accomplish the goals set out for each of the following.

| | TYPE OF ECONOMIC SYSTEM | EXPLANATION |
|---|---|---|
| 1. An economy is concerned with growing rapidly, achieving a high standard of living, and efficiently using its scarce resources. | *market* | |
| 2. An economy aims to achieve equity, sustainability, and economic security. | *command* | |
| 3. An economy is concerned only with producing goods and services that are of a certain type and making sure that the distribution of them does everything possible to promote economic security. | *traditional* | |

# MODULE 6

# The Modern Market Economy

**KEY IDEA:** In modern market economies, government participation can support market exchanges and improve economic performance.

### OBJECTIVES

- To explain the relationship among households, firms, and markets in a market economy.
- To explain the government's role in a market economy.
- To describe how the government fits into the circular flow model of the economy.
- To describe the tradeoffs different countries make in designing social safety nets.

## Bridge for Sale

George Parker sold New York City's Brooklyn Bridge early in the 1900s. In fact, he sold it about twice a week for several years. He also sold the Statue of Liberty, the Metropolitan Museum of Art, and Grant's Tomb. The trouble is, Parker never owned any of these landmarks—he was a con man. When a few sellers get away with scams like these, honest sellers suffer because buyers don't know whom to trust and are reluctant to make purchases. Sellers similarly become wary of making sales when some buyers pay their bills with bad checks or false promises. One role of government is to limit these and other pitfalls that could deter business transactions. By establishing and enforcing laws against sellers who don't deliver and buyers who don't

pay, the government can help promote mutually beneficial sales. To that end, Parker spent the last eight years of his life behind bars.

In Module 5 you learned that modern market economies that receive substantial government influence are called *mixed economies*. In this module we'll look at how households, business firms, and the government interact in a market economy and learn three meaningful forms of government involvement. While government policy can fix problems in a market economy, governments can also cause problems and make mistakes. In Chapter 9 you will learn about sources of government failure.

*Before there was adequate law enforcement to prevent it, people would get away with "selling" the Brooklyn Bridge, even though they didn't own it.*

## HOUSEHOLDS, FIRMS, AND MARKETS

The two most important categories of decision makers in a market economy are *households* and *firms*. A **household** consists of an individual or a group of people who live together and share income, such as you and your family. Households participate in a market economy in two ways:

1. Households purchase goods and services from businesses.

2. Households provide land, labor, capital, and entrepreneurship from which goods and services are produced.

In economics, a **firm** is what people generally refer to as a business—a privately owned organization that produces goods or services and sells them to others. Microsoft, McDonald's, Ford, and ExxonMobil are all firms. There are also millions of small firms with names you've never

*Restaurants hire their workers from households.*

heard of. They include everything from farms to stores to businesses owned by self-employed hairdressers, architects, and lawyers. To produce goods and services, firms must either purchase or rent resources from households. For example, McDonald's rents labor from households every time it hires workers for one of its restaurants.

## THE SIMPLE CIRCULAR FLOW

As households buy goods and services from firms, and firms buy or rent resources from households, a circular, give-and-take relationship is formed. We've just seen that the government also plays a role, but to begin with, let's look only at the economic relations between firms and households—the main actors in market economies. We'll add the government later.

A **circular flow diagram** illustrates the interactions between key players in the economy. Figure 6.1 is a simple version of the circular flow diagram that includes only households and firms. The upper half of the diagram shows the exchange of goods and services for money that takes place in **product markets**. Recall that the word *market* has a special meaning in economics; it refers to a collection of buyers and sellers of something, wherever they may be. The exchanges in a single market may take place in many different locations, including online. In a product market, households are the buyers and firms are the sellers. As a buyer of jeans, for example, you are a participant in the product market for jeans. The blue arrows in the diagram represent the flow of goods and services from firms like Nike to households like yours, by way of the product markets. As illustrated by the green arrows, payments for goods and services flow in the opposite direction; they leave households, pass through the product markets, and are received as *revenue* by firms like Nike.

A **household** consists of an individual or a group of people who live together and share income, such as you and your family.

A **firm** is a privately owned organization that produces goods or services and sells them to others.

A **circular flow diagram** illustrates the interactions between key players in the economy.

**Product markets** are where goods and services are exchanged for money.

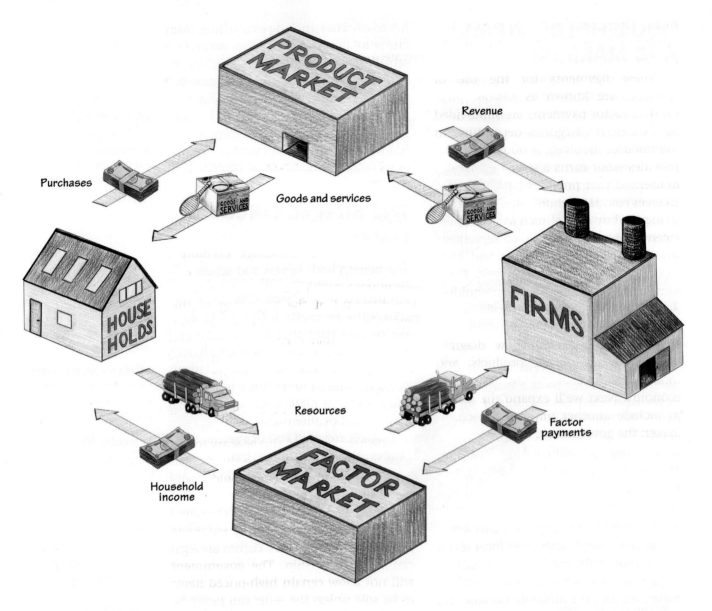

**Figure 6.1** The Simple Circular Flow

*What goes around comes around! Households exchange money for goods and services in the product markets. The money flows back to households as payments for resources by way of the factor markets.* **DID YOU GET IT?** *Where do the factors of production sold in the factor markets come from?*

> ⚠️ **Markets Are More Than Supermarkets**
>
> It's tempting to think of a market as a physical place, such as your local supermarket. But remember that *market* has a special meaning in economics; it refers to a group of buyers and sellers of a specific product or resource. The exchanges in a single market may take place in many different locations, including online.

**Factor markets** are where resources are exchanged for money.

Resources are also known as *factors of production*, and resources are exchanged for money in **factor markets**. If you've ever taken a job, you've been a seller in one example of a factor market, the *labor market*. The red arrows in the lower half of Figure 6.1 show the flow of resources through the factor markets, starting from the households that own them and ending at the firms that use them. The green arrows show the flow of money from firms to households to pay for the resources.

These payments for the use of resources are known as **factor payments**. Factor payments are subdivided into different categories depending on the resource involved. A household that provides labor earns a *wage* or *salary*. A household that provides land to a firm receives *rent*. Households that lend firms money to buy capital such as machinery receive *interest*. And the entrepreneurs who risk their own money and time to build a business receive *profit*. These four factor payments to households—wages, rent, interest, and profit—make up *household income*.

The simple circular flow diagram clarifies how resources, products, and money are exchanged in a market economy. Next we'll expand the model to include another important decision maker: the government.

# GOVERNMENT'S ROLE IN A MARKET ECONOMY

In the United States, government agencies at the federal, state, and local levels touch your daily life in a multitude of ways. If you know the amount of fat in a frozen burrito, it's probably because the federal government requires nutrition labels on food. State and local governments maintain the roadways that take you to soccer games and the mall. If you attend a public high school, the government uses tax collections to pay your teachers' salaries and to help pay for those thawed burritos served in the cafeteria. Even while you sleep, your local government provides police protection for your neighborhood and the federal government provides military protection for U.S. interests around the world.

A government can contribute to a market economy in several ways:

**1.** A government can establish and enforce rules that improve market performance.

**2.** A government can provide important goods and services that private individuals tend not to purchase.

**3.** A government can help improve economic security, equity, and sustainability.

We'll consider each type of contribution in turn.

## Improving Market Performance

A broad collection of government rules are designed to encourage exchanges that benefit both buyers and sellers and discourage exchanges that cause harm. As discussed at the beginning of this module, the Brooklyn Bridge has been "sold" more than once by con men who never really owned it. You can imagine how hesitant buyers would be to pay hard-earned money for things like homes, cars, farmland, and oil wells if they couldn't be sure the sellers were the true owners. It would also be scary to pay a lot for something, even to the rightful owner, if another person could easily come along and take it away.

Our government improves the safety of buying expensive goods by enforcing *property rights*. **Property rights** are legal claims of ownership. The government will not allow certain high-priced items to be sold unless the seller can prove he or she is the true owner. For example, a car *title* is a certificate issued by the state government to identify the owner of a car. When a car is sold, the seller must present the title as proof of ownership. The buyer's name is then recorded as the new owner on the title and in government records.

These restrictions on trade actually make it easier for trades to take place. Without government-enforced property rights, you could pay for a car, a home, or—for that person who has everything—a bridge, and not really become the owner! This would make people reluctant to buy things and there would be much less economic activity. By enforcing property rights, the government helps more mutually

**Factor payments** are payments for the use of resources.

A **property right** is a legal claim of ownership.

beneficial exchanges take place and thereby improves market performance.

The government also assists markets by enforcing contracts. Imagine you sign a contract to pay for a good or service but fail to do so. You have violated the contract and can be sued in a court set up by the government. For example, if you sign a contract to pay someone $500 to fix a dent in your car and then do not pay, the repair person can sue you for the $500 you owe. Contracts also help protect buyers. If you pay $500 in advance and the work is not completed, you can sue the repair person. Without a government to help enforce contracts, many buyers and sellers would pass up mutually beneficial exchanges such as these out of fear that the other party wouldn't honor the agreement.

*Regulations* are rules of conduct passed by federal, state, or local governments. Regulations can help consumers trust sellers more and increase their willingness to buy goods and services. For example, the Federal Trade Commission limits dishonesty in advertising. The Food and Drug Administration requires pharmaceutical companies to test the safety and effectiveness of new drugs before offering them for sale. At the state and local levels, government agencies require workers in certain occupations—hairdressers and doctors, for example—to obtain licenses that demonstrate some degree of expertise. Enforcement

of these regulations can give consumers greater confidence that they will receive the quality of goods and services they expect. In this way, regulations—like laws that protect property rights and enforce contracts—can help markets function effectively.

## Providing Public Goods

When you buy things like M&M's, coffee mugs, and dental care, other people can't share them, at least not at the same time. Some goods and services you might buy—posters, pet lizards, guitar lessons—can be enjoyed by many people at once, but as the owner you can exclude other people from using them if you want to. But what about street lights, parks, and police protection? These things are very useful, so let's examine why you've never bought any of them yourself.

A good or service that can be consumed by many people at once and that other people can't be prevented from using is called a **public good**. Examples of public goods include national defense, snow removal from roadways, and fireworks displays. People tend not to buy public goods because they'd rather enjoy the benefits of someone else's purchase, and they can't be prevented from doing so. In order for citizens to enjoy the benefits of public goods in a market economy, the government usually needs to provide them.

Take the example of national defense. Private firms make the guns, jets, and battleships that help protect the United States, but no firm tries to sell national defense to private individuals. If national defense were sold in stores, rather than rushing out to buy it, consumers would hope to benefit from the purchases of others. The poor incentives for voluntary payments would leave national defense lacking. The government, however, can attain adequate levels of national defense because it has the power to tax people. By requiring everyone to contribute to cover the costs, the government provides this and other valued public goods.

A **public good** is a good or service that can be consumed by many people at once and that other people can't be prevented from using.

By establishing and enforcing property rights, the government helps assure that when you buy something, you get to keep it.

© FSTOP / ALAMY

*Because you can enjoy a fireworks display without paying for it, and no one can prevent you from watching it, it is a public good.*

## Promoting Economic Security, Equity, and Sustainability

The three goals that market economies have the greatest difficulty achieving are equity, economic security, and sustainability. This is why, in market economies around the world, governments help shape the decisions about what, how, and for whom to produce in efforts to better satisfy these goals.

In pursuit of equity, governments fund education. High school and college diplomas give workers access to better jobs, and education for all promotes equality of opportunity. The government of the United States funds public education for everyone through  the twelfth grade. For those who choose to go on to college, the government operates state and community colleges that are less expensive than private colleges and provides grants and loans to help pay tuition and other college-related expenses. Notice that by funding education, the government influences *what* the economy produces. By running public schools, the government determines *how* it is produced. And by deciding who qualifies for free education and who receives financial assistance, the government influences *for whom* education is produced.

To advance economic security, most governments provide a social safety net to assist people who have difficulty supporting themselves. In the United States, for example, *Medicare* and *Medicaid* pay most medical expenses for people 65 and older, those with certain disabilities, and the poor. In 2010, the federal government expanded the safety net further by requiring all Americans to purchase health insurance while covering part of the cost for families with low earnings.

As concern for the environment has grown, so have government efforts to improve the sustainability of economic activities. For instance, the U.S. Environmental Protection Agency limits the use of dangerous substances, including lead in gasoline, arsenic in drinking water and treated lumber, sulfur dioxide released from coal-fired power plants, and mercury released from cement plants. These actions have successfully reduced the pollution levels in the air of most major cities and in rivers and lakes across the country.

 **DID YOU GET IT?**
**What is the government's role in the economy?**

*Government policies have made the air in our cities cleaner than it used to be.*

# GOVERNMENT IN THE CIRCULAR FLOW

The simple circular flow diagram focused on households and firms and left the government out, but now we've seen how the government fits into the picture. In the process of enforcing rules, providing public goods, and working toward the goals of society, the government takes in money, products, and resources. The circular flow diagram in Figure 6.2 includes the government as a key player. Let's explore some details about how government activity reaches into the circular flow.

## Buying Goods and Services in Product Markets

To provide public goods and enforce laws and regulations, governments do their own shopping for products made by private firms. For example, in the United States, governments at various levels go to the product markets to buy firetrucks, police cars, and fuel for these vehicles; computers, furniture, and supplies for public schools; and airplanes, uniforms, and food for the military. Look at the blue arrow in the top half of Figure 6.2 that starts at the product markets and ends at sythe government. This represents government purchases. The green arrow that goes from the government to the product markets represents government spending on these purchases, which flows from the product markets to firms as revenues.

## Producing Goods and Services

In addition to buying products, governments produce goods and services for use by households and firms. This is shown by the blue arrows that extend outward from the government in Figure 6.2. To make these goods and services, governments use resources just as private firms do. For example, to produce the service of national defense, the U.S. government buys and rents land for military bases and hires the labor of soldiers. To maintain roads and bridges, the government hires crews to repair them. And to make and enforce regulations, the government hires labor to work in regulatory agencies such as the Environmental Protection Agency. With about two million civilian employees, the federal government is the largest employer in the United States. In all of these cases, the government buys resources in the factor markets, as shown by the red arrow going from the factor markets to the government. In exchange, the government makes factor payments, as shown by the green arrow

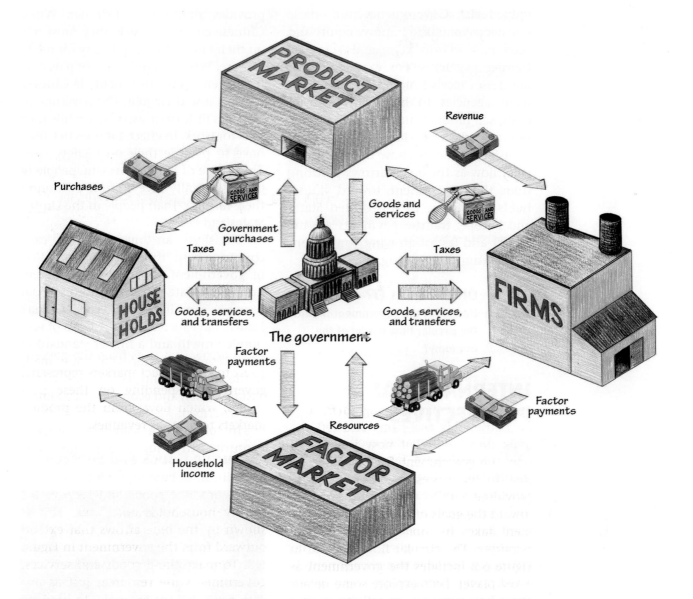

**Figure 6.2** Government in the Circular Flow

As a buyer of resources, goods, and services, and as a provider of transfers, goods, and services, the government is another key player in the economy. **DID YOU GET IT?** After the government collects taxes, where does the money go?

extending from the government to the factor markets. These payments end up as income for the households that supplied the resources.

## Collecting Taxes and Making Transfer Payments

Buying firetrucks, building military bases, and healing the poor takes a lot of money. To fund their activities, governments collect taxes from households and firms, as shown by the green arrows

pointing toward the government. Some tax revenue is spent in product markets on things like firetrucks, some is spent in factor markets on things like military personnel, and the rest is spent on *transfer payments* to households and businesses. **Transfer payments** are expenditures for which the government receives no good, service, or resource in return. The majority of transfer payments are made as part of the social safety net to support disadvantaged

**Transfer payments** are expenditures for which the government receives no good, service, or resource in return.

individuals. Governments use these transfer payments to improve equity and economic security. Firms also receive transfer payments. For example, some businesses receive money from government agencies to help with start-up costs, sell products in foreign countries, or hire workers who have lost their jobs. Transfer payments show up in the circular flow as the green arrows pointing from the government toward households and firms. In the United States and Europe, transfer payments are the largest and fastest growing component of government spending.

**DID YOU GET IT?**
How does the government fit into the circular flow model of the economy?

# INTERNATIONAL PERSPECTIVES

All modern market economies rely on assistance from their governments, but the degree and type of assistance varies. The governments of Sweden and Denmark, for example, play a relatively large role in their economies. Transfer payments are higher, but so are tax payments. The large transfer payments in Sweden and Denmark go toward generous social safety nets, including payments to the unemployed of about 80 percent of their previous earnings for a full year. By comparison, payments to unemployed workers in the United States are typically about half of a worker's previous earnings and last for six months.

Now consider China, which has transitioned in recent decades from a command economy toward a market economy. China's government still owns vast quantities of resources and owns large numbers of firms. Among other remnants of the command economy are limits on economic and other types of freedom. The government does not let people live wherever they choose and even restricts the number of children families can have. China's government

provides almost no safety net. When Chinese citizens get sick, they must rely on their family's savings to pay for medical care. When a family cannot pay, doctors often refuse treatment. If Chinese workers lose their jobs, the government provides little or no assistance while they look for work. In effect, families in China have to provide their own safety nets. This is one of the reasons why people in China typically save a larger portion of their earnings than people in the United States and Europe.

Decisions are made within each country about the size and intention of government involvement. Different priorities create different choices about resource use. In recent years, China's leaders have focused on the goals of economic growth and a higher standard of living. For this, sacrifices have been made in the areas of equity, economic security, sustainability, and economic freedom, as just described.

In contrast, the leaders of European countries strive for greater equity and

*The social safety net in Sweden is more generous than that in the United States, but the tax rate in Sweden is higher. Decisions about resource allocation are never easy due to the necessary tradeoffs.*

economic security and are willing to sacrifice some economic growth to achieve it. European citizens pay relatively high taxes to support a generous safety net. Higher taxes reduce the rewards for innovation and new discoveries and have the potential to slow economic growth.

The safety net in the United States, while much more generous than China's, is not as generous as that in most European countries. The United States and Europe address the tradeoffs differently: the United States has less equity and economic security, but its economy grows more rapidly over time. Of course, there is disagreement within every country about how the government and the economy should be run. Some of the most heated debates in the United States are between those who think we should move closer to a European-style market economy—with a larger role for government—and those who want to maintain the more limited government of the United States or shrink the government's role further.

**DID YOU GET IT?**
Rank the safety nets of the United States, Europe, and China from highest to lowest.

# MODULE 6 REVIEW AND ASSESSMENT

**Summing Up the Key Ideas:** Match the following terms with the correct definition.

A. Household
B. Firm
C. Circular flow diagram
D. Product market
E. Factor market
F. Factor payment
G. Property right
H. Public good
I. Transfer payment
J. Regulation

__I__ 1. An expenditure for which the government receives no good, service, or resource in return.

__B__ 2. A privately owned organization that produces goods and services and sells them to others.

__H__ 3. A good or service that can be consumed by many people at once and that other people can't be prevented from using.

__G__ 4. A legal claim of ownership.

__E__ 5. A market in which resources are exchanged for money.

__A__ 6. Consists of an individual or a group of people who live together and share income, such as you and your family.

__C__ 7. Models the interactions between key players in the economy.

__D__ 8. A market in which goods and services are exchanged for money.

__J__ 9. A rule of conduct passed by federal, state, or local governments.

__F__ 10. A payment for the use of a resource.

**Analyze:** Identify whether each of the following transactions occur in the **Product Market** or the **Factor Market**.

| | PRODUCT MARKET OR FACTOR MARKET |
|---|---|
| 1. workers paid in California to make Levi's jeans | product |
| 2. Levi's jeans bought at a mall store | product |
| 3. payment made for Levi's jeans | factor |

4. rent paid for the use of land _____ *factor*

5. interest paid for the use of capital _____ *factor*

6. profit paid to an entrepreneur _____ *product*

**Apply:** Use Figure 6.2 in the text to describe the following as they relate to the **circular flow diagram**. In your description, indicate where the money or factor comes from, where it goes, what path it takes, and what it is given in exchange for.

*on laptop*

**DESCRIPTION OF FLOW**

1. money spent on private good and services
*from the gov, going to the firms in exchange for taxes*

2. production of public goods and services _____

3. labor provided in the production of private good and services _____

4. labor provided in the production of public good and services _____

5. monetary payment for capital used in the production process _____

6. monetary payment for labor used in the production of private good and services _____

7. taxes paid by individuals for the production of public goods and services _____

8. taxes paid by businesses for the production of public goods and services _____

## AN INTERVIEW WITH Jan Švejnar

### Professor of International and Public Affairs;
### Director, Center for Global Economic Governance

In this chapter you learned about the differences between command and market economies. You also learned about communism, which combines a command economy with a government controlled by the Communist Party. The life experience of Professor Jan Švejnar illustrates how these economic and political systems affect daily life and how they can shape one's perspective on politics and economics.

Professor Švejnar came from the country of Czechoslovakia, which has since split into the Czech Republic and Slovakia. After the fall of communism in 1989, he led an economic education program in the Czech Republic and advised that country's president, Vaclav Havel. In 2008 he ran for president of the Czech Republic and lost by 30 votes.

**Where did you grow up?**
I was born in 1952 and grew up in Prague, Czechoslovakia, during the harsh Stalinist regime of the 1950s and early 1960s and then the political thaw of the mid-to-late 1960s. I left Czechoslovakia in 1970 for Switzerland and then the United States in large part because I might have faced discrimination because the communist leaders did not look favorably on me or my parents.

**How did living in a centrally planned economy compare with living in the market-based system in the United States?**
For a young boy it was not all that different, in that the usual activities like going to school, playing soccer, and going to the movies seemed (and in most respects were) quite standard. The noticeable differences then were the shortages of many consumer products, ranging from domestically produced meat to imported tropical fruit. It was during my teenage years, when I

started thinking seriously about public issues and politics, that I became aware of differences. Parents would usually not share their critical political views with their children until the children were mature; the teenage years were the age of political awakening. For many, this was also the time of rude awakening to the fact that if your parents were not from the working class or were not members of the Communist Party, you might not be allowed to study at the senior high school or college level.

**When did you first take a course in economics?**
I took my first course in economics as a college freshman. It was an eye-opener for me and I immediately liked the subject because it provided both personal enrichment and a means to change things in the real world.

**What is the most important first step for formerly Communist countries to take in their move toward a market-based economic system?**
The first key step is to establish a system of laws and institutions that are conducive to the functioning of markets. Under central planning, courts were primarily a means of keeping the population and [business] enterprises under control rather than institutions settling commercial disputes.

**How has economics helped you in your political career?**
First and foremost, economics teaches you a logical way of thinking. It also gives you a very useful framework in which you can interpret events and formulate sensible approaches to problem solving. As such, it constitutes a valuable background for entering politics and striving to improve the life of people around you.

**CNNMoney.com**

# Why Amish Businesses Don't Fail

Want to find America's most successful entrepreneurs? Skip Silicon Valley and Manhattan; head to the rural Amish enclaves. Amish businesses have an eye-popping 95% success rate at staying open at least five years, according to author Erik Wesner's new book, *Success Made Simple: An Inside Look at Why Amish Businesses Thrive.* It's a statistic drawn in part from survey data from a 2009 report by sociology professor Donald Kraybill. Studying several Amish settlements, Kraybill found failure rates ranging from 2.6% and 4.2%. Compare that to the average five-year survival rate for new businesses across the United States, which hovers just under 50%. So what's the secret?

Wesner, who worked in business management and sales before immersing himself in all things Amish, thinks it lies in the culture, which emphasizes "qualities like hard work and

cooperation." Networking through Facebook doesn't exactly have the same community-building pull as teaming up with neighbors to build a barn, and few Americans these days can point to a childhood where they awoke regularly at dawn to milk the cows.

Another key advantage is that Amish business owners tend to stick with what they know. "Everything about the Amish says things like 'rustic,' 'traditional,' 'handmade,' so they tend to play to those strengths," Wesner says. "Would consumers trust an Amish cell-phone dealer or an Amish computer repair guy to know what he's doing? It'd be a pretty big mental and marketing hurdle to get over."

Kraybill estimates that there are at least 9,000 Amish business owners across the U.S, which he divides into two groups: "caretakers" and "entrepreneurs." "Caretakers generally

have smaller, at-home or near-home businesses with five or fewer employees, and they don't want to grow, but simply sustain income for themselves and a small number of employees," Kraybill says. "The entrepreneurs are a different breed. They have larger businesses and somewhat want to grow, and they are more aggressive in marketing, trying new ideas, and are willing to take risks."

Risks like buying a failing business and trying to turn it around. Two years ago, in Glen Rock, Penn., Ben Riehl purchased a flagging food stand at Markets at Shrewsbury, a gathering spot for Amish vendors. He turned to entrepreneurship as a way out of what he calls "somewhat of a dead-end job," working in the metalworking and machine shop at a plastics company. Riehl renamed the shop the Country Style Deli and enlisted his wife, Mary, and their two sons to help him work the stand, which sells local and imported cheeses, homemade breads, and subs and sandwiches. They also employ four other people part-time.

## Clinging to values

While Amish business owners face more restrictions than your typical entrepreneur, modern touches are creeping into the business scene. Some Amish retailers use electricity in their shops, more as a nod to customers who expect air-conditioning and credit-card machines. They're often fueled with alternative energy sources, like solar and wind power. In his field research, Wesner found some Amish entrepreneurs conducting business using cell phones, fax machines and even e-mail. It's still a sensitive topic—not because the Amish believe it's unethical to use these devices, but because they can have a subtle, adverse impact on the entrepreneur. "The smarter you get, and the more technology you use for your business, the more impact it has on families," he says. "For instance, there was a time the farmer would be in the parlor milking cows, and everyone was there, singing songs, and it was work, but it was also family time. Now, an Amish farmer is likely to be milking forty cows, and the children are at school. That's practical living, and you've got to keep up. But at the same time, it takes away from that balance, and you have to ask yourself, 'How far do you let technology affect your business?'"

## DID YOU READ IT?

1) What does the article suggest are reasons for the success rate of businesses in the Amish community?

2) According to the article, what are some examples of market forces that have influenced the way Amish businesses operate?

## WHAT DO YOU THINK?

1) Is the U.S. economy mainly organized by the traditional system described by this article? Or are there elements of all three types of systems—traditional, command, and market—in the U.S. economy? Think of some examples to support your argument.

2) What are some of the problems that the traditional system faces in today's electronic, technically advanced world?

EXCERPTED FROM http://money.cnn.com/2010/05/04/smallbusiness/amish_business_success/index.htm.

# CHAPTER 2 REVIEW AND SELF-ASSESSMENT

## REVIEW

### Points to Remember

#### MODULE 4: USING RESOURCES TO ACHIEVE ECONOMIC GOALS

1. A country's **standard of living** is a measure of the wealth of goods and services available to help people in the country live comfortably.

2. **Equity** is the quality of being fair and just.

3. Citizens with **economic security** have confidence in their ability to support themselves and their families.

4. A **social safety net** is any form of government assistance for those with financial needs.

5. **Economic freedom** means that people can make economic decisions for themselves.

6. **Sustainability** is the ability to continue actions indefinitely.

#### MODULE 5: TYPES OF ECONOMIC SYSTEMS

7. An **economic system** is an organizational structure for addressing what, how, and for whom to produce.

8. In a **traditional economy**, decisions about resources are made by habit, custom, superstition, or religious tradition.

9. An **incentive** is the prospect of a reward or punishment that influences a decision or motivates greater effort.

10. In a **command economy**, central planners make the important decisions about what, how, and for whom to produce.

11. Under **communism**, all resources and businesses are publicly owned and economic decisions are made by central authorities.

12. Under **socialism**, citizen groups known as *general assemblies*, along with councils of workers and consumers, are the primary economic decision makers.

13. **Rationing** is the placement of limits on the amount of goods each person can purchase.

14. In a **market economy**, most key economic decisions are made by business owners and consumers.

15. Under a **capitalist** system, most resources and businesses are *privately owned*.

16. Because a market economy is based on *voluntary exchange* and gives people so much freedom to start a business and decide how their resources are used, it is also called a **free-enterprise system**.

17. A **mixed economy** combines a market economy with significant government involvement and elements of tradition.

**MODULE 6: THE MODERN MARKET ECONOMY**

18. A **household** consists of an individual or a group of people who live together and share income, such as you and your family.

19. A **firm** is what people generally refer to as a business—a privately owned organization that produces goods or services and sells them to others.

20. A **circular flow diagram** is a model of the interactions between key players in the economy.

21. The **product markets** are where goods and services are exchanged for money.

22. Resources are also known as *factors of production*, and resources are exchanged for money in **factor markets**.

23. **Factor payments** are payments for the use of resources.

24. A **property right** is a legal claim of ownership.

25. A good or service that can be consumed by many people at once and that other people can't be prevented from using is called a **public good**.

26. **Transfer payments** are expenditures for which the government receives no good, service, or resource in return.

27. Government's role in the economy includes establishing and enforcing rules to improve market performance, such as guaranteeing **property rights**; providing **public goods and services**; and helping improve economic security, equity, and sustainability.

## SELF-ASSESSMENT

The following questions are the type your teacher might ask you on a quiz or a test. Practice with these in order to improve your performance in class on tests.

### Multiple-Choice Questions

1. Which of the following is **not** one of the *three basic questions* every economy must address?

   a. What should be produced?
   b. How should it be produced?
   c. When should it be produced?
   d. For whom should it be produced?

2. Society's economic goals include all of the following **except**

   a. equity.
   b. sustainability.
   c. economic growth.
   d. economic justice.

3. People respond to incentives because

   a. incentives act as rewards that encourage people to behave in certain ways.
   b. incentives exploit opportunities to make people better off.

   c. incentives exploit opportunities to make people worse off.
   d. incentives discourage the use of free time.

4. The concept of equity focuses on

   a. how to produce the maximum possible output from a given amount of resources.
   b. how government can intervene to make markets work better.
   c. the issue of fairness.
   d. the buildings and equipment an employer owns.

5. Which of the following is considered to be the main advantage of a market economy?

   a. equity
   b. sustainability
   c. economic security
   d. efficiency

6. If an economy makes all decisions based on custom and history, which of the following systems must be in effect?

   a. entrepreneurial economy system
   b. traditional economy system
   c. command economy system
   d. market economy system

7. Government's role in a market economy would include all of the following **except**

   a. establishing and enforcing rules that improve market performance.
   b. providing important goods and services that private individuals tend not to purchase.
   c. shaping market outcomes to improve economic security, equity, and sustainability.
   d. providing complete equality of outcome for every individual.

8. A typical circular flow diagram would include

   a. stocks and bonds.
   b. households and businesses.
   c. command and market economies.
   d. the role of incentives.

9. The market in which resources are exchanged for monetary payments is called the

   a. factor market.
   b. goods market.
   c. services market.
   d. public goods market.

10. Which of the following correctly matches a *factor* of production with the corresponding *factor payment*?

   a. capital and interest
   b. money and interest
   c. labor and profit
   d. land and wages

## Constructed Response Questions

1. Economic systems have been used throughout history for addressing what, how, and for whom to produce goods and services.

   a. List and briefly describe the three types of economic systems.
   b. What is the role of incentives in each of the economic systems?
   c. List and explain one advantage of each economic system.
   d. List and explain one disadvantage of each economic system.
   e. The U.S. economy, among others, has been identified as a *mixed economy*. Define the mixed nature of this type of economy.

2. Discuss how a circular flow diagram demonstrates the features of a modern market economy.

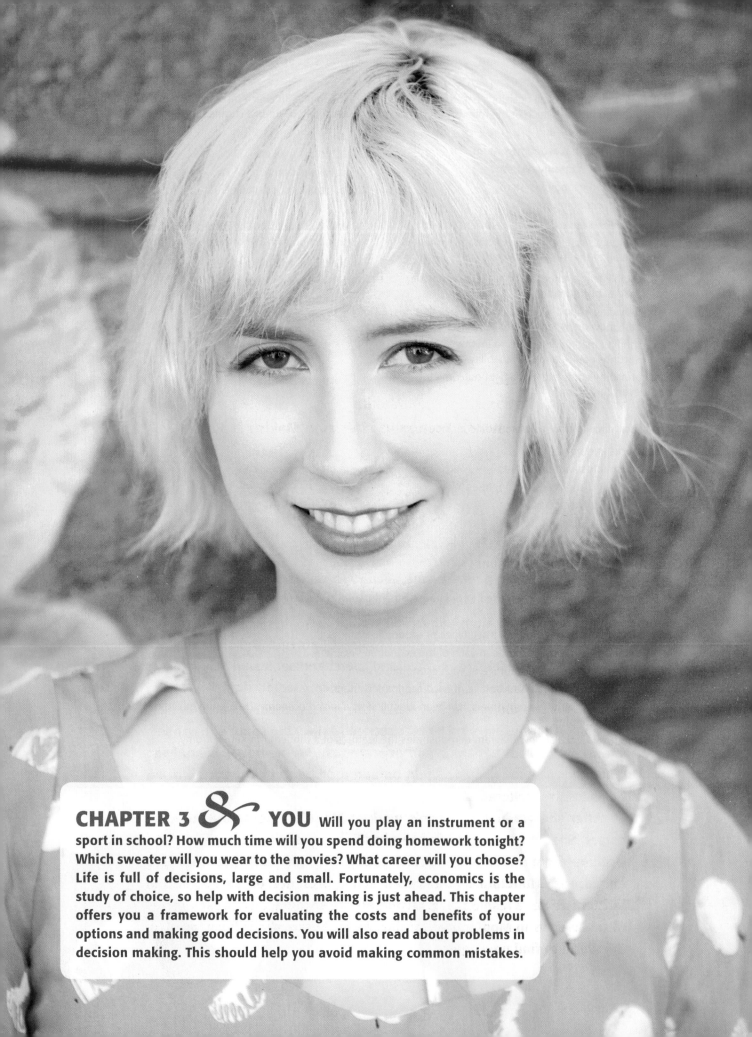

**CHAPTER 3 & YOU** Will you play an instrument or a sport in school? How much time will you spend doing homework tonight? Which sweater will you wear to the movies? What career will you choose? Life is full of decisions, large and small. Fortunately, economics is the study of choice, so help with decision making is just ahead. This chapter offers you a framework for evaluating the costs and benefits of your options and making good decisions. You will also read about problems in decision making. This should help you avoid making common mistakes.

# Making Economic Decisions

**MODULE 7:** **Understanding Costs and Benefits**

**MODULE 8:** **Rational Decision Making**

**MODULE 9:** **Behavioral Economics: Decision Making in Practice**

## SUSAN AND BEN'S BIG DECISIONS

Susan Gregg Koger, pictured here, always loved shopping in thrift stores for vintage clothing. At the age of 17, she and her boyfriend (now husband) Eric Koger founded ModCloth to sell vintage clothing online. Before long the business outgrew Susan's dorm room at Carnegie Mellon University, which lacked space for an office and merchandise. Susan struggled to find enough time for school and work. She considered dropping out of school, but she did not. With careful time management Susan was able to balance her business and her education. To find the space she needed, she moved out of the dorm and into a house. By staying in school she gained more knowledge to build on and a degree to fall back on if her business ever faltered.

After she graduated, Susan's work at ModCloth became a full-time career. She and Eric expanded the business by adding vintage-inspired clothing from modern designers. Today, the company has over 275 employees. ModCloth maintains an active presence on Facebook and Twitter and has a fashion blog. Customers are encouraged to post pictures of themselves in ModCloth's clothing. As for Susan, she is busy traveling the world to find new items.

Ben Kaufman approached a similar decision in a different way. Ben always had big ideas and a passion for business. At the age of 14 he started his first company, producing videos and designing websites for high-profile clients. Two weeks before his high school graduation he started his second company, Mophie, which produced and sold the Song Sling, an iPod carrying case worn around the user's neck. It was so successful that Ben expanded the business to include other innovative iPod accessories, like armbands and clips. His product line won Best in Show at the 2006 Macworld Conference and Expo. Before long, investors offered him $2 million to help expand the company.

Ben was busy running Mophie when he enrolled in Champlain College in Vermont. Having a college degree was important to him. But taking classes and studying for exams took too much time away from his business. He faced a difficult choice between finishing college and devoting himself full time to Mophie. After weighing the benefits and costs, Ben decided to drop out of college. Just a year later, *Inc.* magazine named him top U.S. entrepreneur under the age of 30. More recently, Ben started Quirky, which offers inventors an online community of people eager to help them design their products. If a product succeeds, everyone who influenced the design shares in the profits.

In deciding to leave college, Ben Kaufman joined a number of entrepreneurs who never graduated, including Microsoft cofounder Bill Gates, Dell computers founder Michael Dell, and Facebook founder Mark Zuckerberg. For them, the benefit of finishing college was less than the cost. Many other entrepreneurs—Amazon.com founder Jeff Bezos, Berkshire Hathaway CEO Warren Buffett, and Google cofounders Larry Page and Sergey Brin—shared Susan Gregg Koger's decision that the benefits of finishing college exceeded the cost of any delay in their business careers. Good decision making can lead people with similar choices in different directions. Why? Because they value the costs and the benefits of their choices differently.

This chapter is about decision making. Making wise decisions requires that you understand how to measure the costs and benefits as they apply to *you* and that you take both costs and benefits into careful consideration.

## BOTTOM LINE
Learning how to compare costs and benefits can improve your decision making throughout life.

# MODULE 7

# Understanding Costs and Benefits

**KEY IDEA:** To make a good decision you need to weigh all the costs against all the benefits.

**OBJECTIVES**

- **To identify the opportunity costs of decisions you make.**
- **To describe the tradeoffs necessitated by budget constraints.**
- **To explain why sunk costs should not affect decisions.**

If they'd rather be hiking, they've made an unfortunate decision to be in the car instead.

### Where They'd Really Rather Be

It's a bit strange for people to drive around with a bumper sticker that says they'd rather be hiking. If they would really rather be hiking, why aren't they? Why did they pick a less satisfying activity? Perhaps they mean to say that they enjoy hiking, but the things they would give up to go hiking at the moment are more valuable than hiking. After all, hiking may be free of charge, but it's not without opportunity costs. The time spent on a hike could otherwise be spent earning money, going to school, or completing important chores. Wise decisions come from careful comparisons of the costs and benefits of each option. For those who choose not to hike, a more accurate bumper sticker might read, "I love to hike, but I love having a job even more."

In Chapter 2 we saw that in a market economy, individuals are responsible for making decisions well beyond whether to be at work or in the woods. For example, buyers decide what to buy and sellers decide what to sell. But how do buyers and sellers know if they're doing the right thing? It takes a good understanding of the costs and benefits of the options. In this module we will take a closer look at how to evaluate costs and benefits.

## THE TRUE COST OF DECISIONS: OPPORTUNITY COST

Chapter 1 explained that the true cost of a decision is its opportunity cost, which is the value of what you give up for that decision. If you decide to go see a football game, the ticket price is part of the opportunity cost, but so is the value of the time spent traveling to the stadium and watching the game. If you do not see the game, you can spend the money and time on something else, such as buying your own football and playing a game with your friends.

Let's apply the principal of opportunity cost to Ben Kaufman's decision about college. What would his true cost—the opportunity cost—of staying in college have been? Tuition would have been part of the cost, but not the largest part. His best alternative was to spend his time operating and expanding his successful business. By staying in college, Kaufman would have delayed the growth of his business. He would have sacrificed the income he could have earned during those years. Those forgone earnings would have been part of the opportunity cost of going to college.

### Opportunity Cost and Tradeoffs

If you had unlimited time and unlimited amounts of money to spend, the opportunity cost of any decision would be zero. You would not have to give up anything to get something else. You could

have it all! But Chapter 1 explained that because of scarcity, you can't always have as much of most things as you might want. Both time and money are generally scarce. There are more things we'd like to do with our time than we can fit in, so the decision to do one activity means sacrificing another. There are also more things we'd like to buy than we can afford, so the decision to buy one good means we cannot buy another. If you have only $1 to spend at the Dollar Store, where everything costs $1, you have a tough decision to make. If you buy the

## ECONOMICS IN ACTION

# Opportunity Cost Doesn't Always Mean Dollars Paid Out

People often confuse the opportunity cost of a decision with the direct dollar cost of that decision. If you've ever missed a sports practice to take a make-up exam after school, you've experienced an opportunity cost that doesn't involve money at all. And even if you're not Ben Kaufman, the opportunity cost of attending college includes more than the cost of tuition. College students also give up the best alternative to attending college, which is typically going straight to work. Suppose you would earn $25,000 a year in the best available job right after high school. Then the opportunity cost of attending college would be the tuition cost plus the forgone income of $25,000 for each of four years, or $100,000. Although it isn't actually paid out, that money you would have earned is part of the cost, too.

The first step in making good decisions is to understand that the true cost of any decision is the opportunity cost, and not just the amount of money spent as a result of the decision. This applies to life's big decisions, such as whether to attend college, and to everyday decisions, such as whether to make up an exam.

*The opportunity cost of attending college is the tuition and the forgone income that you would have earned had you been working instead.*

Coca-Cola dinner plate, the opportunity cost is that you cannot buy the stuffed purple gorilla. If you buy the stuffed gorilla, you can't buy the dinner plate. And even if you brought $100 to the Dollar Store, every purchase of one thing would have the opportunity cost that you couldn't buy something else. This is why your choice at the store—and your choices in general—necessarily involve tradeoffs.

## Budgets and the Budget Line

When you have a certain amount of money available to spend, such as $1 at the Dollar Store, we say you have a *budget*. Because your budget is limited, you are forced to make a tradeoff (the plate or the gorilla, not both). Let's look at another example of how a limited budget leads to tradeoffs.

Suppose you have a budget of $25 for school lunches for the week. You can choose some combination of sandwiches, which cost $5 each, and pizza slices, which cost $2.50 each. If you spend your entire budget on sandwiches, you can have $25 ÷ $5 = 5 sandwiches. If you spend your entire budget on pizza, you can have $25 ÷ $2.50 = 10 slices. Of course, you don't have to buy only sandwiches or only pizza; you can have some of both.

You can see the tradeoffs in Figure 7.1, which shows every possible way to spend your budget. The quantity of pizza slices is shown on the horizontal axis and the quantity of sandwiches is shown on the vertical axis. The *budget line* on the graph goes through every point that represents a quantity of pizza slices and a quantity of sandwiches that would cost $25. That is, the budget line shows the combinations of the two items that you can afford if you spend your budget. Suppose you choose to buy 2 sandwiches and 6 pizza slices; you can afford this combination because it is on the budget line, represented by point *A*. You cannot buy another sandwich, however, without giving up some pizza slices. If you want a third sandwich, you have

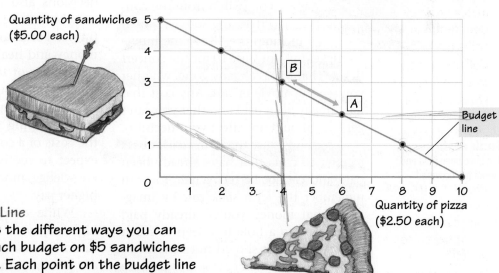

**Figure 7.1** The Budget Line
This budget line shows the different ways you can spend a weekly $25 lunch budget on $5 sandwiches and $2.50 pizza slices. Each point on the budget line represents a combination of sandwiches and pizza slices that you can afford if you spend the entire budget. For example, moving from point *A* to *B* gives you 3 sandwiches rather than 2, but for each additional sandwich, you give up 2 pizza slices. Similarly, if you want more pizza, you can move rightward along the budget line, giving up 1 sandwich for every 2 pizza slices.

to give up 2 pizza slices, because a sandwich costs twice as much as a slice of pizza. Buying the third sandwich would move you from point *A* to point *B* on the budget line. This move illustrates the tradeoff you face: the opportunity cost of buying another sandwich is 2 pizza slices. If you want more pizza, you can move in the other direction along the budget line, giving up 1 sandwich for every 2 pizza slices.

## SUNK COSTS

Suppose your friend talks you into going to hear a new band in concert at the local community center. Tickets to the concert cost $10 each. As the band begins to play, you and your friend decide that you don't like the music. If you leave you can watch the new Will Ferrell movie instead. Movie tickets cost $8. What is the opportunity cost of seeing the Will Ferrell movie? In considering this, be careful to ignore costs that are now inescapable, such as the $10 you paid for the concert ticket. The opportunity cost of seeing the movie is only what you have to give up if you switch from the concert to the movie, which includes the $8 for the movie ticket but not the $10 for the concert ticket. That $10 is already gone, whether you see the movie or not. Any cost that has already been paid and that you can't get back should not affect your decision.

Economists use the term **sunk costs** to refer to costs that have already been paid and cannot be recovered. You can remember the term *sunk cost* by imagining that money you've already paid has sunk into a hole too deep to reach into. A sunk cost should not be a factor in decision making because it is paid no matter what you decide. The only costs that matter when making a decision are those that come with the decision you make. The $10 you already spent on the concert is not relevant. So if the movie is worth at least $8 plus the value of the time it will take you to watch it, then

**Sunk costs** are costs that have been paid and cannot be recovered.

you should go to the movie. You will pay an additional $8, not an additional $18, for the movie ticket. If you say to yourself, "I'm not going to spend $18 to see one movie!" you might decide not to see it even though it is worth more to you than its true opportunity cost. To make good decisions, it is important to recognize the difference between the costs that matter and the costs that don't matter because they are sunk.

Understanding how to evaluate costs is just one part of making good decisions. Costs must be weighed against benefits, as we'll see in the next section.

**? DID YOU GET IT?**
**What are sunk costs, and why should they be disregarded when you make a decision?**

## BENEFITS ARE IN THE EYE OF THE BEHOLDER

We've seen that decisions come with opportunity costs that should not be neglected and, in some cases, sunk costs that should be ignored. Hopefully decisions also come with *benefits* that somehow make life better now or in the future. For example, ice cream has its money and health costs, but it also has the benefit of tasting delicious! On the other hand, cough medicine tastes bad and costs money, but it provides the benefit of helping you feel better. And for the costs of a college education, one can expect to receive the benefits of more knowledge, more job opportunities, and higher pay.

While everyone would agree that higher pay is a benefit and college tuition is a cost, other benefits and costs are personal and depend on the tastes and preferences of the person making the decision. For example, if you're the type of person who enjoys learning new things, then furthering your education will provide the additional benefit of allowing you to learn. If you have a brother who hates to learn new things, education will have a higher cost for him than for you. Likewise, some people wake up at 5:00 a.m. to enjoy a jog before school, and other people only run when being chased. Clearly, one person's benefit can be another person's cost. In the next chapter we'll see how information on benefits and costs is used to make good decisions.

**DID YOU GET IT?**
How can the benefits of the same activity be different for different people?

# MODULE 7 REVIEW AND ASSESSMENT

**Summing Up the Key Ideas:** Match the following terms with the correct definition.

A. Budget
B. Budget line
C. Sunk cost

___B___ 1. Represents the combinations of the two items that you can afford if you spend your budget.

___A___ 2. A certain amount of money that you have available to spend.

___C___ 3. Cost that is already paid and that cannot be recovered.

**Analyze:** List one opportunity cost for each of the following decisions.

OPPORTUNITY COST

1. You decide to stay in school and complete a degree program.  *work experience*

2. You decide not to go on vacation this summer but to stay at home and work instead.  *relaxation*

3. You decide to drop out of school and go to work.  *education*

4. You decide to join a club at your school.  *homework time*

5. You decide to cook your meals at home instead of going out to a restaurant.  *better food?*

6. You decide to buy some new clothes rather than a birthday gift for your mother.  *love*

7. You decide to take a nap rather than study for your economics test.  *good grades*

**Apply:** Use Figure 7.1 to answer the following questions.

1. In terms of pizza slices, what is the opportunity cost of the first sandwich?  *2*

2. In terms of sandwiches, what is the opportunity cost of the first slice of pizza?  *0.5*

3. If your budget decreased to $10, at what quantity would the budget constraint meet the axis that measures the quantity of pizza?  *2 ?*

# MODULE 8

# Rational Decision Making

**KEY IDEA:** To make rational decisions, people must compare the costs and benefits of each option and choose the one that best serves their interests.

**OBJECTIVES**

- To explain the requirements of rational decision making.
- To identify key types of decisions.
- To apply the concept of marginal analysis to real-world situations.

## Decisions, Decisions

Many days are filled with an endless flurry of questions. When? How? Which one? Who should you spend time with? Where should you go? What should you wear, eat, bring, or buy? Later in your life you will face important decisions about family, health, education, and career. It would be nice to make these decisions wisely. In this module we will look at some specific methods for making good decisions.

*Today's forecast: windy with flurries of heavy questions.*

## COMPARING BENEFITS AND COSTS TO MAKE RATIONAL DECISIONS

**A rational decision** benefits the decision maker as much as possible.

A **rational decision** benefits the decision maker as much as possible. To make a rational yes-or-no decision, you should compare all your benefits to all your costs and say yes only if the benefits outweigh the costs.

Consider a decision you make every time you get into a car: whether or not to wear a seat belt. The major benefit of wearing a seat belt is that it helps you avoid injury or death in the event of an accident. Most states have laws requiring seat belt use, so wearing your seat belt also eliminates the risk of paying a fine for not wearing one. What are the costs of wearing a seat belt? Some people find seat belts uncomfortable. It can take

**A self-interested** individual makes decisions for his or her own benefit.

a moment to buckle up, and it may be considered "uncool." With more than six million car accidents occurring in the United States every year, most people decide that the substantial benefits of seat belt use outweigh the costs, which makes it rational to wear one.

Most economic models rest on the assumption that people are **self-interested**, meaning that they make decisions for their own benefit. This doesn't imply that people don't care about others. Most people do! Your interests may well include helping others and seeing them succeed. Rational, self-interested decision makers make choices to further their objectives, whatever those objectives may be. When

©DRBIMAGES/iSTOCKPHOTO.COM

you care about others, it is in your self-interest to help them because their benefit is your benefit.

The idea of rational decision making has become widely accepted and used in disciplines beyond economics. Political scientists apply rational decision making to explain how voters select one candidate over another by weighing the benefits and costs associated with each candidate. Sociologists apply rational decision making to explain mob behavior and participation in protest demonstrations and terrorism. And demographers apply it to explain dating and marriage decisions. In each case, the assumption is the same: that people weigh the benefits and costs of their options to make decisions that best serve their objectives.

People who engage in rational decision making do not always make the right decisions. Instead, rational decision making leads people to make the best decisions possible given what they know at the time. For example, suppose

# ECONOMICS IN ACTION

# *Freakonomics* and Rational Decision Making

The popular book *Freakonomics* by Steven Levitt and Stephen Dubner explains that rational decision making is the source of many behaviors that seem odd. In one striking example, the authors use rational decision making to explain the performance of sumo wrestlers. Sumo is a style of wrestling that originated in Japan. In a sumo wrestling tournament, every participating wrestler competes in 15 matches. A wrestler must win at least 8 matches to stay in the top league. Levitt and Dubner studied the final matches. A wrestler going into the final match with 7 wins and 7 losses obviously had a strong incentive to win; if he wins the final match he advances to the top league. A wrestler going into the final match with 8 wins and 6 losses knows that he has already made it into the top league. Since he has little to gain by winning, he has an incentive to take it easy in the final match. He might even intentionally lose to help the other fighter advance to the top league.

Levitt and Dubner confirmed that the wrestlers used rational decision making to determine their strategy. They found that in a matchup of a 7–7 wrestler against an 8–6 wrestler, the 7–7 wrestler wins approximately 80 percent of the time. You would expect an 8–6 wrestler to be stronger and more skilled than a 7–7 opponent. Even if they were equally matched, the 8–6 wrestler would win 50 percent of the time. But because a 7–7 wrestler benefits more from winning than his 8–6 opponent, the 7–7 wrestler tries harder and usually wins.

*Sometimes it may be a rational decision not to try your hardest.*

you buy a bag of apples from a fruit stand. When you get home and slice the apples for your apple pie, you realize that most of the apples are rotten inside. Buying those apples turned out to be an unfortunate decision. But you made a rational decision to buy the apples if—based on your knowledge at the time—you could not identify another decision that would better serve your interests. Sometimes employers, sports teams, and people looking for a date get a bad apple, too.

Rational decision makers don't always get things right, but they learn from their mistakes. It would be irrational to buy apples again and again from the fruit stand with rotten apples.

**DID YOU GET IT?**
**What is a rational decision?**

# TWO TYPES OF DECISIONS

Comparisons of costs and benefits are part of all rational decision making. But the best approach depends on what type of decision you are making. There are two broad types of decisions. The first involves a choice among different options. For example, deciding whether to go to a movie, a play, or a party is a choice among different options. The second type of decision involves how much of something to do. Decisions such as how much ice cream to buy, how much pizza to eat, and how much time to devote to studying are all decisions of how much of something to do. Next we'll examine the appropriate way to make each type of decision.

## Deciding Which One

When you go to the store to buy breakfast cereal you usually have dozens of options to choose from. As consumers,

our challenge is to determine which option is best—which breakfast cereal, which car, which house, which college, and which combination of ice cream flavors.

Suppose you are choosing among three used cars. Table 8.1 gives information about the benefits and costs that will help you make a rational decision. Column 1 lists the three cars you can choose from. Column 2 indicates how you feel about each car. You would prefer the Toyota to the Ford and the Ford to the Hyundai. Column 3 translates your feelings about each car into dollars. That may seem strange to you: how can a "feeling" be measured in dollars? All you have to do is ask yourself, "What is the most I would I be willing to pay for each car if I had to?" The answer you give for each car is what that car is worth to you. Economists do this sort of analysis all the time. It allows us to directly compare a choice's benefits with its costs.

Naturally, the better you feel about a car, the greater the dollar measure of its benefits to you. Column 3 indicates that you would pay up to $6,000 for the Toyota, so from this dollar measure of the benefits, we know that the Toyota is worth $6,000 to you. You don't like the Ford quite as much; the most you'd pay for it is $4,000. The Hyundai is your least favorite among these cars, and you'd pay at most $2,500 for it. The costs of buying the cars are entered in column 4.

Choose among these cars using the information provided. If you react emotionally and think only about how much you like each car, you'll fail to consider the costs and choose the Toyota. If you think only about avoiding high costs, you'll choose the Hyundai because it is the least expensive. Neither of those choices would make you as well off as you could be. A rational decision maker will consider both benefits and costs. These are combined into a measure called *net benefit*. The **net benefit** of a choice is the benefit of the choice (measured in dollars) minus its cost. It provides a dollar measure of the gain from that choice.

The **net benefit** of a choice is the benefit of the choice (measured in dollars) minus the cost of the choice.

## Table 8.1 Using Rational Decision Making to Choose a Car

| (1) CAR | (2) HOW YOU FEEL ABOUT THE CAR | (3) BENEFIT (MEASURED IN DOLLARS) | (4) COST OF CAR (DOLLARS) | (5) NET BENEFIT (BENEFIT − COST) |
|---|---|---|---|---|
| 2006 Toyota Corolla | Love it! | $6,000 | $8,000 | −$2,000 |
| 2005 Ford Taurus | Like it | $4,000 | $3,000 | $1,000 |
| 2002 Hyundai Sonata | It's OK | $2,500 | $2,000 | $500 |

Column 5 shows how net benefit is calculated for each car. The Toyota's benefit is $6,000, but its cost is $8,000, so its net benefit is $6,000 − $8,000 = −$2,000. The net benefit is negative because the car costs more than it is worth to you. A rational decision maker would never choose an option with a negative net benefit.

The net benefits received from the other two cars are positive. That tells us that either choice would make you better off than not buying a car. But which choice is best? A rational decision maker will make the choice that provides the greatest net benefit. The Ford has a net benefit of $1,000, while the Hyundai has a net benefit of $500. So the best choice is the Ford.

To see why the Ford is best, let's take a closer look at the idea of net benefit. Suppose the Ford cost $4,000 instead of $3,000. Then the net benefit would be $4,000 − $4,000 = 0. If you did buy it for $4,000, you wouldn't be better off, because you'd be giving up $4,000 to get something worth exactly $4,000 to you. There would be no net benefit from doing that! But if you buy a Ford worth $4,000 to you for a price of $3,000, you come out $1,000 ahead.

Now consider the Hyundai. You'd be willing to pay $2,500 for it, but you can actually buy it for $2,000, so by choosing the Hyundai you come out $500 ahead. A net benefit of $500 is better than nothing. However, the Ford's net benefit is greater. A rational decision maker who values the cars as shown in the table will choose the Ford.

The *net benefit rule* of choosing the option with the greatest net benefit applies to any choice among different options. It will help you choose your classes in school, your running shoes, your activities on a Saturday night, and your career. The benefit you would get from each choice is personal—it depends on your own preferences and personality. But if you translate the personal benefit into dollars by asking yourself, "What is the most I would be *willing* to pay for this benefit?" and then subtract the cost, you get the net benefit from that choice. The best choice is the one that offers the highest net benefit.

> ### ⚠ The Value of Benefits
>
> When placing a dollar value on the benefits you would receive from a good, be sure to think about the largest amount you would be willing to pay if you had to, not what you would like to pay. From a buyer's perspective, the ideal price for anything would be zero, and paying less is always better than paying more, but that has nothing to do with the value of the good. When you think you've identified the most you'd be willing to pay, check your number by asking yourself if you'd buy it if the price were a bit higher. If you would, the product is worth more to you than you've estimated.

## Deciding How Much

In addition to making decisions among options, we also make decisions about how much of something to do or buy. For example, when you travel somewhere for vacation, you have to decide how many days to spend there. When you go  to a cookie store at the mall, you have to decide how many cookies to buy. And whatever you do—shower, study, work out, practice the trumpet, or go for a walk—you have to decide how much time to spend on that activity. Similarly, firms have to decide things like how much labor to hire, and governments have to decide things like how long to fight in a war.

A "How much?" decision can be viewed as a question of how far to go along a series of steps. The decision to buy each unit of the good or activity—a single cookie, a day of vacation—is a step. Every time you take a step, you must decide whether to take another step. For example, at the cookie store,

your first step is the decision to buy one cookie rather than none. If that first cookie would make you better off, you buy it. Then you consider the next step: buying a second cookie. If taking that step would make you even better off, you buy another cookie. You continue in this way, one step at a time, taking those steps that make you better off. If a step happens to make you neither better nor worse off, you are torn between taking it or not and might as well flip a coin to decide. When you finally reach a step that would make you *worse* off, you stop without taking that step. For example, if the fourth cookie would make you worse off than buying just three, you don't buy that cookie. The step before that—buying the third cookie—is the last one you should take.

The question of whether each step makes you better off involves *marginal* comparisons. *Marginal* has a special meaning in economics. Note that the margin of a sheet of notebook paper is the section along the edge of the paper, often marked with a red vertical line that defines the boundary of the writing area. The margin is the area beyond the writing area. Likewise, in economics, the word *marginal* is used when we're looking a bit beyond where we are now, at the effects of taking another step—buying another cookie, vacationing for another day, studying for another hour.

When deciding how much of something to do, a rational decision maker

*You should continue to buy cookies only as long as the marginal benefit from another cookie will exceed the marginal cost.*

compares the *marginal benefit* of the action with the *marginal cost* at each step along the way. The **marginal benefit** is the additional benefit of taking the next step and doing something one more time. The **marginal cost** is the additional cost of taking the next step and doing something one more time.

If the marginal benefit is greater than the marginal cost, the next step should be taken. If the marginal benefit is less than the marginal cost, then the next step should not be taken. Next we'll consider an example of how this is done.

**DID YOU GET IT?**
What are the two types of decisions, and how should each type of decision be made?

## AN EXAMPLE OF MARGINAL ANALYSIS: REPLACING WORN TIRES

When we decide how much or how many by comparing the marginal benefit and the marginal cost at each step, we are conducting *marginal analysis*. Let's see how marginal analysis can guide a car seller named Lin to a good decision. Lin's goal is to get as much money as possible for her car after subtracting the cost of any improvements she decides to make. The four tires on the car vary in condition from being in terrible shape to being almost brand new. Before selling the car, Lin needs to decide which, if any, tires to replace with new ones that cost $100 each.

Table 8.2 lists the tires in order of their condition from worst to best, along with the marginal benefit, marginal cost, and net benefit of replacing each tire with a new one. The marginal benefit of a new tire is the increase in the resale price of the car that would result from the installation of that tire. If Lin replaces the worst tire with a new one, the improved quality and appearance of the car will allow her to sell it for $200 more. Thus, the marginal benefit of the first new tire is $200. The net benefit is the marginal benefit minus the marginal cost: $200 − $100 = $100. If she replaces the second-worst tire, the resale price of the car will increase by $150. The $150 marginal benefit of the second new tire is less than the $200 marginal benefit of the first new tire because the tire being replaced doesn't detract as much from the quality and appearance of the car as the worst tire did. The net benefit of the second new tire is $150 − $100 = $50. The marginal benefit of the third new tire is $90, again less than the one before it, because the used tire replaced by the third new tire is in relatively good shape. The net benefit is $90 − $100 = −$10. The marginal benefit of the fourth new tire is just $10 because it would replace a tire that is practically new. The net benefit is $10 − $100 = −$90.

*Tires in bad condition are dangerous and unattractive. Lin will get a better price for her car if she replaces some tires, but how many should she replace?*

**Marginal benefit** is the additional benefit of doing something one more time.

**Marginal cost** is the additional cost of doing something one more time.

**Table 8.2 Comparing Marginal Benefit and Marginal Cost**

| TIRE REPLACED | MARGINAL BENEFIT (MEASURED IN DOLLARS) | MARGINAL COST (DOLLARS) | NET BENEFIT (BENEFIT − COST) |
|---|---|---|---|
| 1. Tire in worst condition | $200 | $100 | $100 |
| 2. Tire in second-worst condition | 150 | 100 | 50 |
| 3. Tire in second-best condition | 90 | 100 | −10 |
| 4. Tire in best condition | 10 | 100 | −90 |

The marginal cost of replacing each tire with a new one is $100, regardless of how many tires are replaced. In this situation, Lin would choose to replace the first two tires, because the marginal benefit of replacing each of them exceeds the marginal cost. That is, there is a positive net benefit of $100 from replacing the worst tire and $50 from replacing the second-worst tire. The $90 marginal benefit of replacing the third tire is less than the $100 marginal cost, so Lin should stop buying tires without taking that step.

In this module you have learned a lot about rational decision making. Whether you face a choice among different options or a decision about how much of something to buy or do, comparisons of costs and benefits will assist you in making choices that serve your interests well. The table below summarizes five lessons for rational decision making.

In addition to learning the process of making good choices, you should also be aware of some decision-making mistakes that lead people into bad choices. Module 9 discusses common mistakes and how to avoid them.

 **DID YOU GET IT?**
**What is marginal analysis, and why is it useful?**

## Five Lessons for Rational Decision Making

 **1.** Consider the benefits and costs of each choice.

 **2.** Don't neglect opportunity costs.

 **3.** Approach "which one" questions by choosing the option with the greatest net benefit.

 **4.** Consider "how much" and "how many" decisions one step at a time.

 **5.** Take steps with a marginal benefit that exceeds the marginal cost.

# MODULE 8 REVIEW AND ASSESSMENT

**Summing Up the Key Ideas:** Match the following terms with the correct definition.

A. Rational decision      D. Marginal benefit
B. Self-interested        E. Marginal cost
C. Net benefit

_____B_____  1. When people make decisions for their own benefit and to further their objectives.

_____A_____  2. When a decision maker's goals are advanced as much as possible, given the limited money and time available.

_____E_____  3. The additional cost of taking the next step and doing something one more time.

_____D_____  4. The additional benefit of taking the next step and doing something one more time.

_____C_____  5. The benefit of a choice (measured in dollars) minus its cost; provides the dollar measure of the gain from a choice.

**Analyze:** Each of the following decisions violates several of the lessons for rational decision making. Indicate one of the lessons that is violated.

LESSON VIOLATED

1. Kim decides to go to a concert without considering the high price of tickets.

   _____

2. Maya gets $5 worth of satisfaction out of soup and $3 worth of satisfaction out of salad. Soup costs $4 and salad costs $1. Maya decides to buy soup.

   _____

3. Darius runs 10 miles because the total benefit of the exercise exceeds the cost, although the last mile does more harm than good.

   _____

4. Rondi decides to spend a weekday at the beach because it gives her $40 worth of fun. The day off causes her to lose $60 worth of earnings.

   _____

**Apply:** Use the table below to answer the following questions.

1. Calculate the **net benefit** for each of the following types of jackets.

| JACKET | APPEAL | BENEFIT (MEASURED IN DOLLARS) | COST (DOLLARS) | NET BENEFIT (DOLLARS) |
|--------|--------|-------------------------------|----------------|-----------------------|
| Cloth | Low | $35 | $40 | -5 |
| Nylon | Medium | 55 | 50 | 5 |
| Microfiber | High | 75 | 65 | 10 |
| Leather | High | 95 | 90 | 5 |

2. Which type of jacket should you choose? Why?

micro fiber       high net benefit

# MODULE 9

# Behavioral Economics: Decision Making in Practice

**KEY IDEA:** Recognizing six common decision-making mistakes can help you make better choices.

**OBJECTIVES**

- **To explain why decision making is often less than fully rational.**
- **To identify common decision-making mistakes.**
- **To present guidelines for avoiding irrational behavior.**

## Nobody's Perfect

Economists typically assume that people make rational decisions. Models based on this assumption yield many useful insights into how the economy works. For example, at least 30 U.S. cities have considered a tax on soda. Economists can use models to estimate how an increase in the cost of soda would affect the quantity demanded. In response to the higher cost of soda, some people might buy an irrationally low quantity, and others might mistakenly buy too much for their own good. But as long as the response of consumers resembles rational behavior on average, the predictions of economic models built on the assumption of rationality will hold true.

*Sometimes our emotions get in the way of rational decision making.*

Nonetheless, it is important to acknowledge irrational behavior. After all, we are all human! We care about things like fairness, we get impatient, and we are influenced by the way things are presented to us. These are among the many things that get in the way of rational decision making. In this module you will see how economists use ideas from the study of psychology to achieve a better understanding of the decision-making process. You will also learn how to avoid the pitfalls of irrational behavior as you make your own decisions.

## WHAT IS BEHAVIORAL ECONOMICS?

**Behavioral economics** is the branch of economics that uses ideas about decision making from psychology to explain economic behavior.

Rational decisions help people move toward their goals and get more satisfaction out of life. However, people do not always make rational decisions. Sometimes we make mistakes and take actions that are not in our best interests. The field of psychology has much to say about how people make decisions—and mistakes—and economists have applied ideas from psychology to improve their own studies of decision-making behavior. The branch of economics that merges psychology into explanations of economic behavior is called **behavioral economics**. Lessons from behavioral economics can help you understand and avoid some common mistakes that people make.

Why do people make irrational decisions? One explanation is that as human beings, emotions sometimes cloud our judgment about costs and benefits. For example, suppose you are going to a movie. You decide in advance that you will not buy popcorn, because the cost of popcorn is greater than the benefit you expect to receive from it. Perhaps you realize that the opportunity cost of buying popcorn is that you can't use that money to buy Junior Mints, which you prefer. Or maybe you realize that eating popcorn would make you thirsty and that you would want to buy an expensive soft drink as well. But after entering the theater, the smell of popcorn overtakes you, causing a momentary lapse of judgment. You forget about the costs and benefits and buy the popcorn. That is an irrational decision. You haven't changed your mind about the costs and benefits—you're just not taking them into account.

As a student of economics and as a decision maker, it's important for you to recognize the behaviors that call rationality into question. In the next section we'll look at six common mistakes in decision making.

**DID YOU GET IT?**
What is the difference between a rational decision and an irrational decision?

# MISTAKES PEOPLE MAKE

In some circumstances, mistakes are predictable. People tend to stray from rational decision making in six common ways:

**1.** Allowing the presentation or *framing* of options to affect decisions

**2.** Letting sunk costs matter

**3.** Being too impatient

**4.** Making errors due to overconfidence

**5.** Avoiding change even when things could be better

**6.** Devoting time and energy to punish people who treat them unfairly even when it is not in the punisher's self-interest

Let's examine each of these types of mistakes more closely.

## Mistake 1: Letting Framing Affect Decisions

We have seen that rational decision making involves comparing benefits and costs. Yet sometimes people let the way choices are presented, or *framed*, affect their decision. For example, when choosing among similar items, shoppers are more likely to select an item that is made out to be a good deal, even if it isn't. Suppose two stores sell jackets that are equally attractive to you. One jacket is priced at $80 every day. The other is advertised as a $160 jacket that is on sale for $80. Which one would you prefer to buy? If you'd lean toward the jacket that is $80 on sale, framing affects your decisions. You're not alone. Because shoppers love to feel like they're getting a deal, promotions claiming "sales" and "special prices" are far more common than true bargains. If it were just prices and not framing that mattered, stores would stick with signs indicating the prices of goods without emphasizing "price cuts," "clearance

*Sometimes it's not a bargain but just a matter of how the price is framed.*

## ECONOMICS IN ACTION

# Sweden Uses Behavioral Economics to Make People Healthier

As long as behavioral economics is going to influence people to change their behavior, it might as well be used to promote beneficial behavior. That was the reasoning of the government of Sweden when it set out to fight obesity. The Odenplan subway station in Stockholm, Sweden, was the site for a successful experiment. To get up to the street level, commuters arriving at the station have a choice between taking the escalator or using the stairs. Most people took the escalator. To encourage subway riders to get some exercise, the options were framed differently. The stairs were redesigned to look like giant piano keys that produced real musical tones. When people looked up the stairway, they faced what looked like a fun musical game rather than an exhausting march up concrete stairs. Of course, the physical exertion of the climb was the same either way. As a result of this framing, more people took the stairs and got some exercise.

*Would you take the stairs instead if framing made it seem more fun?*

sales," "discounts," and "specials." And if framing didn't matter, stores would simply charge prices like $20 rather than $19.99. Although the penny difference has little effect on our budget, it has a significant effect on the way we see things.

### Mistake 2: Letting Sunk Costs Matter

Have you ever heard the old expression "Don't cry over spilled milk"? It warns against the common decision-making mistake of letting sunk costs matter. As you learned earlier in this chapter, sunk costs are irrelevant to your decisions because they are already paid and you can't escape them regardless of your choice. What's done is done, or as economists say, sunk costs are sunk. Nonetheless, people do cry over spilled milk, and they are swayed by sunk costs.

Think about all the times you've purchased a meal and then decided you didn't really like the food. If the food doesn't have a benefit to you, the rational thing to do is discard it because its cost is sunk. But many people continue to eat food they don't like because they have spent hard-earned money on it. The money is gone either way, so we should all spare ourselves the punishment of lousy food. The same goes for lousy concerts, vacations, books, clothing, ballet lessons, hockey games, and anything else.

### Mistake 3: Being Too Impatient

There are good reasons to want benefits sooner rather than later. As John Maynard Keynes pointed out, "In the long run, we are all dead." And, as will be explained in Module 37, the sooner you have money, the sooner you can put it in the bank to earn interest. But people who are overeager for immediate satisfaction can make irrational decisions that sacrifice too much in the future for too little today.

Consider the shocking fact that many students don't study enough for exams. Time spent preparing for exams has the opportunity cost of getting in the way of other activities, like watching *American Idol*. You know that if you study

## ECONOMICS IN ACTION

# Impatience and the Adjustable-Rate Mortgage Crisis

*Mortgages* are loans for the purchase of a home. The borrowers are required to pay back the loans, plus interest, over time. While the housing market was booming in the mid-2000s, banks began to offer mortgages to people who previously could not afford to buy homes. New types of loans were offered, including some with monthly payments that started out low and then were adjusted to become more expensive over time. These *adjustable-rate mortgages* enabled more people to buy homes, but the increasing payments were hard to keep up with. Many borrowers were impatient and too focused on the present. They accepted these loans, sometimes not paying attention to how much their payments would rise. They also didn't take the time to understand the terms of their loans. Some lenders also misled borrowers about how much interest they would have to pay. Many families lost their homes as a result.

Consider the case of Justino Mendoza Cortez, a farm worker in Watsonville, California. In 2004, Mr. Cortez took out a $695,000 adjustable rate mortgage to buy the house of his dreams for his wife and six children. The monthly payments were fixed at $2,722 for the first three years. In May of 2007, the required payment jumped to $4,054 a month, a sum he could not afford. As a result, Mr. Cortez lost his house in a *foreclosure*, which means that he was forced out of the house and the bank took ownership. Millions of others found themselves in the same situation as Mr. Cortez.

*When buying a home it's important to take the time to know what your monthly payments will be and to make sure you can afford them.*

more you will learn more and get better grades. The payoff in the future will include access to better colleges, more satisfying jobs, improved productivity, and higher pay. But when swept up by peer pressure and alluring advertising, one can *too* heavily discount the future benefits of studying and decide to watch amateur acts struggle for stardom on television, even when the future benefits of studying are well worth the immediate costs.

Sometimes people borrow money at high interest rates in order to buy things they don't really need. In this case it is future costs that might be discounted too heavily. When it's time to repay the money, they often wonder why the purchase seemed like a good idea at the time. Consumers with the patience to limit borrowing and purchase only what they can afford end up spending less on interest payments and credit card fees. Over time, that allows them to spend more money on the goods and services that give them satisfaction.

## Mistake 4: Being Overconfident

**Status quo bias** is the tendency to keep things the way they are.

Many decisions involve unavoidable uncertainty. If you decide to run for class president, you must commit time and resources to a campaign without knowing the outcome. The decision to invest in a business comes with uncertainty about whether the business will succeed. And if you decide to buy your own home, there is no guarantee that the value of the property will stay the same or rise; it could fall. Uncertainty forces people to estimate outcomes and decide how sure they are about those estimates. If you feel sure that you will win the election or that a business investment will pay off, the rational decisions—to run for office and invest heavily in the business—are very different than if you feel quite unsure about the outcomes.

Psychologists have found that when people can't know something for sure, they tend to overestimate their ability to forecast what will happen. This *overconfidence* can lead to irrational optimism and bad decisions. For example,

many people are too optimistic about how their investments will turn out. Studies find that the average investor expects to receive a 5 percent higher payoff than is typically earned. Overconfidence about future earnings causes people to save too little as they prepare to buy a house, pay for college, or retire. Overconfidence can also lead people to put too much money into a small number of risky investments or to drop out of school with the false hope that their new business idea will make them the next Ben Kaufman. In reality, the majority of new businesses fail within five years. To make rational decisions when the outcome is uncertain, it is important to be realistic about all the possible consequences of your choices.

## Mistake 5: Sticking to the Status Quo

Sometimes people react to uncertainty by resisting change. To avoid making a mistake, many of us are tempted to keep doing the same thing, even if it's not in our best interest to do so. Economists call this inclination to keep things the way they are **status quo bias**.

Life presents many options that involve some degree of uncertainty and risk—trying new foods, asking someone to a dance, moving to a new town, exploring new careers. On one hand, excessive risk taking can lead to painful losses. On the other hand, the old saying holds true: no guts, no glory. Sticking with the status quo and shying away from making new choices can slow the advancement of your interests. When you are presented with a new set of options, you should take a rational approach: compare the costs and benefits of each option and select the best one.

## Mistake 6: Worrying Too Much about Fairness

Suppose you have a sister who wants to go to Simply Salads for dinner and you want to go to Simply Pasta, although you'd rather eat at Simply Salads than at home. What would you do if your parents let you decide between two options:

the whole family goes to Simply Salads, or the whole family eats at home? If your goal is to eat as well as possible, then fairness should not weigh into your decision, and you should go to Simply Salads. If you are distracted by the unfair omission of Simply Pasta from the restaurant options, you might choose to eat at home. The key is to avoid being so concerned about fair treatment that it prevents you from making the best decision.

We all like to be treated fairly. Sometimes insisting on fair treatment can be in your self-interest. For example, by calling attention to the unfair eating options, you might be granted the choice of restaurants next time to balance things out. But sometimes people go too far, insisting on fairness or punishing unfair behavior even when it makes them worse off.

Would you give up money to punish unfair treatment? Daniel Kahneman, Jack Knetsch, and Richard Thaler have examined the struggle between self-interest and fairness. They ran experiments in which one person—"the divider"—received money to divide between herself and another person—"the recipient." After a division

| Table 9.1 | **Six Guidelines for Making Rational Decisions** | |
|---|---|---|
| **MISTAKE TO AVOID** | **DESCRIPTION** | **GUIDELINES** |
| 1. Being swayed by the way a decision is framed | Framing is the way a product or deal is presented. It can make options seem better than they really are. | Consider the costs and benefits of the decision, which most often have nothing to do with how they are framed. |
| 2. Letting sunk costs matter | A sunk cost is a cost that is irrelevant to new decisions because it has already been paid. | Recognize that sunk costs are unrecoverable. They should not be counted among the costs of new options. |
| 3. Letting impatience lead to unfortunate decisions | Impatience can cause people to discount future benefits and costs too heavily and focus too much on immediate benefits and costs. | Pay appropriate attention to benefits and costs that will come in the future, even though they may seem a long way off. |
| 4. Letting overconfidence lead to bad decisions | Overconfidence leads people to believe they know more about what will happen in the future than is possible given the information available. This leads to excessive risk taking. | Be realistic about the ability to predict future events and consider all the possible consequences of a choice. |
| 5. Sticking to the status quo when better alternatives exist | Status quo bias is a tendency to avoid making changes, even when a change is likely to be beneficial. | Actively consider options for change by considering their benefits and costs, and don't be afraid to try new things that seem likely to provide a net benefit. |
| 6. Focusing too much on fairness rather than happiness | People sometimes punish others for unfair behavior, even if it makes the punisher worse off. | Recognize that life is sometimes not fair! It is often in your interest to ignore fairness and base your decision on an evaluation of benefits and costs. |

was proposed, the recipient could either accept the money offered by the divider or reject it, in which case neither side got anything. A rational recipient with the goal of gaining as much money as possible would accept any amount of money, even a penny, because some money is better than the alternative of no money. However, hundreds of trials revealed that fairness has a strong influence on decision making. The typical recipient rejected anything less than about one-quarter of the money to be divided, and the average divider offered almost half of the money to the recipient. Accepting a small amount of money in the economists' *ultimatum game* is a lot like accepting the option of going to Simply Salads in the eating-out dilemma—it is better than the alternative unless fair treatment weighs on the decision.

Fair treatment affects shoppers, too. Some people will walk out of a store when they don't like the way a sales clerk treats them. They want to punish the bad behavior. But if the item they seek is hard to find elsewhere, then walking out will make the shoppers worse off. Someone who makes a habit of punishing others regardless of the costs and benefits will walk out of a lot of stores and give up a lot of benefits. Rational decision makers focus on their goals and will not let knee-jerk responses to unfairness get in the way of the decisions that best serve their interests.

## HOW TO AVOID MISTAKES IN DECISION MAKING: A SUMMARY

To make a rational decision, you have to compare benefits and costs. Rational decision makers also avoid the influences of framing, sunk costs, impatience, overconfidence, status quo bias, and excessive concerns about fairness. Table 9.1 (on the previous page) summarizes the mistakes discussed in this module and offers advice on how to avoid them.

**DID YOU GET IT?**
What are six common decision-making mistakes, and how can you avoid them?

---

# MODULE 9 REVIEW AND ASSESSMENT

**Summing Up the Key Ideas:** Match the following terms with the correct definition.

A. Behavioral economics
B. Framing
C. Status quo bias
D. Sunk cost bias
E. Impatience
F. Overconfidence
G. Worry over fairness

_C_ 1. The inclination to keep things the way they are.

_F_ 2. The tendency to overestimate the ability to forecast what will happen.

_A_ 3. The branch of economics that merges psychology into explanations of economic behavior.

_B_ 4. The way choices are presented.

_G_ 5. The tendency to respond to fairness rather than self-interest.

_D_ 6. The inclination to let irrelevant costs be part of a decision.

_E_ 7. A feeling or a desire for immediate satisfaction.

**Analyze:** Identify each of the following decisions as being guilty or not guilty of the **status quo bias**.

| | GUILTY | NOT GUILTY |
|---|---|---|
| 1. I decided to get pizza and fries again today for lunch at school and not try the "healthy lunch" option because that is what I have always done. | ✓ | ✓ |
| 2. I decided to buy the cotton shorts rather than the nylon shorts because the cotton ones had a higher net benefit. | ✓ | ✓ |
| 3. I did not sign up for the 401(k) plan at work because I have not done so in the past and reading and understanding it required a lot of time. | ✓ | ✓ |

**Apply:** Recall the six mistakes to avoid, summarized in Table 9.1. In each of the following scenarios, indicate if the decision was a rational decision or an irrational decision. If it was an irrational decision, indicate in the second column which of the six common mistakes was made.

| | RATIONAL OR IRRATIONAL | MISTAKE MADE (IF ANY) |
|---|---|---|
| 1. I bought the advertised special because it was "on sale." | irrational | framing |
| 2. I bought the "generic brand" because it was less expensive than the "name brand." | rational | |
| 3. I really did not like the concert and was thinking about walking out but decided to stay because I paid a lot for the ticket. | irrational | sunk costs |
| 4. I like to scuba dive and many of my friends like to scuba dive. I am sure that I can make money by opening a scuba diving supply shop in the Midwest. I think I will drop out of school and give the scuba shop business a try; it can't fail. | irrational | overconfident |
| 5. I am never going to shop at that store again. I just don't like the way they treat people. I don't care that they have the lowest prices around. | irrational | impatience |

# Burger King Tries Home Delivery

BY BRUCE HOROVITZ, USA TODAY

The door-to-door Whopper may soon be on the menu. Burger King, the No. 2 burger chain, has quietly begun testing home delivery of its burgers, fries and other sandwiches since fall at four of its restaurants in the greater Washington, D.C., area, with an eye on expanding beyond that.

Should home delivery catch on for the burger giants—as it has for the pizza kingpins—it could be an industry changer. But it runs counter to long-held consumer perception that fast-food burgers and fries travel poorly—and don't warm up well in the microwave. It also would require millions of hungry folks to change their at-home eating habits. "There are some real food-quality issues here," says Ron Paul, president of research firm Technomic. "But there's no question that consumer expectation for having things delivered has risen."

In some markets, Amazon can deliver books the same day they're ordered. Groceries are increasingly being delivered. And retail giants, including Sears and Target, even offered home delivery of fresh-cut Christmas trees. In an electronic age of instant everything—when millions of consumers expect to get what they want at the click of a button—the logic may seem sound. But what about those soggy fries and limp burgers that folks fear go hand-in-hand with home delivery?

Well, Burger King has developed a "proprietary thermal packaging technology," says Jonathan Fitzpatrick, chief brand and operations officer for Burger King, "which ensures the Whopper is delivered hot and fresh, and the french fries are delivered hot and crispy." There's a $2 delivery fee.

And depending on the store (three in Maryland and one in Virginia), minimum orders vary from $8 to $10.

The stores try to deliver within 30 minutes of the time a phone or online order is received. Delivery customers must live within a 10-minute drive of the store. All soft-drink orders are in bottles. And breakfast items are not delivered. Delivery times are 11 a.m. to 10 p.m.

McDonald's has two restaurants in Manhattan that offer delivery only to businesses. But there are no plans to expand the service, spokeswoman Ashlee Yingling says.

And Domino's, whose business is 70% delivery, is watching—with a smile. "We wish them luck," spokesman Tim McIntyre says. "There is a reason that not all pizza places deliver: It isn't easy."

## DID YOU READ IT?

1) **What kinds of economic decisions are discussed in this article?**

2) **What factors do you think influenced Burger King's decision to test a home delivery service?**

## WHAT DO YOU THINK?

1) **Is it rational for consumers to choose to order delivery service from Burger King?**

2) **Why do you think Domino's would claim that delivery service "isn't easy"? What do you think this means in economic terms?**

EXCERPTED FROM www.usatoday.com/money/industries/food/story/2012-01-12/burger-king-delivery/52604104/1

# CHAPTER 3 REVIEW AND SELF-ASSESSMENT

## REVIEW

### Points to Remember

**MODULE 7: UNDERSTANDING COSTS AND BENEFITS**

1. A **budget** is a certain amount of money that you have to spend.

2. The **budget line** shows the combinations of the two items that you can afford if you spend your budget.

3. **Sunk costs** are costs that have been paid and cannot be recovered.

**MODULE 8: RATIONAL DECISION MAKING**

4. A **rational decision** benefits the decision maker as much as possible.

5. A **self-interested** individual makes decisions for his or her own benefit.

6. The **net benefit** of a choice is the benefit of the choice (measured in dollars) minus the cost of the choice.

7. **Marginal benefit** is the additional benefit of doing something one more time.

8. **Marginal cost** is the additional cost of doing something one more time.

**MODULE 9: BEHAVIORAL ECONOMICS: DECISION MAKING IN PRACTICE**

9. **Behavioral economics** is the branch of economics that uses ideas about decision making from psychology to explain economic behavior.

10. People tend to **stray from rational decision making** in six common ways.

11. **Status quo bias** is the tendency to keep things the way they are.

## SELF-ASSESSMENT

The following questions are the type your teacher might ask you on a quiz or a test. Practice with these in order to improve your performance in class on tests.

### Multiple-Choice Questions

1. A rational decision benefits the decision maker as much as possible. To make a rational yes-or-no decision you should pick the option that has

   a. the highest benefit.
   b. the lowest cost.
   c. benefits that outweigh the costs.
   d. costs that outweigh the benefits.

2. Thinking like an economist would lead you to believe that for a gifted college football player, the most significant cost of remaining in college for another year rather than entering the NFL draft is

   a. tuition.
   b. books.
   c. housing.
   d. lost wages.

3. A student operating on her budget line for shoes and shirts

   a. would not be able to buy more shirts.
   b. would not be able to buy more shoes.
   c. would not be able to buy more shoes without buying more shirts.
   d. would not be able to buy more shoes without buying fewer shirts.

4. Which of the following would be considered a sunk cost?

   a. money you will spend to repair your car
   b. money you already spent to buy your car
   c. insurance premiums on your car for the coming six months
   d. the cost of gasoline to operate your car

5. The net benefit of a choice is
   a. the benefit of the choice plus the cost of the choice.
   b. the benefit of the choice minus the cost of the choice.
   c. the benefit of the choice times the cost of the choice.
   d. the benefit of the choice divided by the cost of the choice.

6. The decision-making rule for making a rational choice is best described by which of the following?
   a. Always buy the item with the lowest cost.
   b. Always buy the item with the highest benefit.
   c. Always buy the item with the lowest net benefit.
   d. Always buy the item with the highest net benefit.

7. The table below lists the benefit and cost of four different vacation destinations. Based on the information in the table, a rational consumer would pick
   a. Six Flags because it is the least expensive.
   b. the Grand Canyon because it has the highest net benefit.
   c. Disney World because it has the highest benefit.
   d. New Orleans because it has the lowest net benefit.

8. Which of the following accurately describes the concept of marginal benefit?
   a. the total benefit derived from consuming all units of a good
   b. the total benefit derived from consuming all units of a good minus the total cost of consuming all units of the good
   c. the additional benefit of consuming the next unit of a good
   d. the net benefit of consuming the next unit of a good

9. All of the following are mistakes to avoid in making rational decisions **except**
   a. letting sunk costs matter.
   b. focusing exclusively on fairness.
   c. making purchases using net benefit analysis.
   d. sticking to the status quo.

10. The branch of economics called behavioral economics combines economics and
    a. psychology.
    b. history.
    c. sociology.
    d. accounting.

| VACATION DESTINATION | BENEFIT (MEASURED IN DOLLARS) | COST (DOLLARS) | NET BENEFIT (DOLLARS) |
|---|---|---|---|
| Disney World | $3,000 | $4,000 | -1000 |
| Grand Canyon | 2,000 | 1,500 | 500 |
| New Orleans | 1,250 | 1,000 | 250 |
| Six Flags | 200 | 100 | 100 |

## Constructed Response Questions

1. James and Lauren are trying to decide if they should go on vacation or cancel the trip. James argues that they cannot afford to cancel the trip since they paid for part of the trip with a nonrefundable deposit. Lauren argues that they should cancel the trip because the additional cost of the trip outweighs the additional benefit of the trip and the nonrefundable deposit should not factor into the decision-making process. Who is correct? Explain.

2. Siblings Austin and Ally are on a camping trip. One afternoon they have the options of going canoeing, playing tennis, or staying at their campsite. Austin's favorite activity is canoeing and his least favorite activity is staying at the campsite. However, when Ally won't go canoeing, Austin refuses to play tennis. That way, he reasons, Ally won't get to do her favorite activity either. Which of the common mistakes is Austin making?

**CHAPTER 4 & YOU** When you buy music online, you probably consider the price. If the price of music doubles, you might decide to download far fewer songs. The story is different for some other goods. For example, if the price of bubble gum, flu shots, or salt doubles, you might respond with only a small change in your purchases. This chapter will help you understand why price has a strong influence on some buying decisions and a weak influence on others. You will also see how factors such as tastes and income affect decisions of how much to buy.

# The Demand for Goods and Services

MODULE 10: **Determining Demand**
MODULE 11: **Shifts of the Demand Curve**
MODULE 12: **Elasticity of Demand**

## SEEING THE LAW OF DEMAND THROUGH NEW LENSES

During the mid-2000s the company that makes Acuvue brand contact lenses, Johnson & Johnson, figured out a way to produce lenses more cheaply and lowered its prices. The price of a pair of popular Acuvue contact lenses fell from about $24 in 2004 to under $18 in 2008. Largely because of the drop in price, purchases of contact lenses nearly doubled over this period.

This example illustrates the relationship economists expect between price and quantity: when the price of a good falls, people usually buy more of it. Likewise, when the price of a good rises, people usually buy less of it. In this chapter you will learn how price and other key factors determine the quantities of goods and services that customers are prepared to purchase.

## BOTTOM LINE
The demand curve illustrates how prices and other factors influence the amount of a good or service people are willing and able to buy.

## MODULE 10

# Determining Demand

**KEY IDEA:** When the price of a good or service increases, consumers buy less of it for two reasons: (1) they substitute the good with other goods whose prices haven't increased, and (2) their income will buy less of the good at the higher price.

**OBJECTIVES**

- **To describe the law of demand and the role of the substitution effect and the income effect.**
- **To explain what economists mean by "all else equal."**
- **To show the relationship between a demand schedule and a demand curve.**

### The Demand for Information on Demand

U.S. firms spend about $16 billion a year on information about consumer demand. Why is this information so valuable? Because it helps firms understand what consumers like you want to buy. Firms also use information on demand to predict what would happen if they offered new products or changed their prices. Governments care about demand, too. It tells them, for example, whether a tax on unhealthy food would cause consumers to buy a little less or a lot less. That's just the beginning of what an understanding of demand means to participants in the economy. At the core of that understanding is the *law of demand*.

*Information on demand indicates whether a price increase will cause consumers to buy a little less or a lot less.*

## THE LAW OF DEMAND

In the opening story you read that purchases of Acuvue contact lenses rose when the price fell. It's also true that when the price of contact lenses rises, purchases fall because some consumers are unwilling or unable to pay the higher price. This illustrates a central principle of economics: a change in the price of a good affects the *quantity demanded* of that good.

In economics, the term **quantity demanded** has a special meaning. It is the amount of a good that consumers are *willing and able* to purchase at a *particular* price over a given period of time. Notice that the quantity demanded is not just how much of the good you want. You have to be willing and able to buy that quantity. For example, if

you love going to concerts, you might want to attend a dozen or more every month. But because your income is limited and concert tickets are expensive, you might be unwilling or unable to buy more than one every few months. Your quantity demanded at a particular price is the number of tickets you are willing to pay for and can actually afford at that price. So even if you love live music, your quantity of concert tickets demanded is zero at every price you can't afford to pay.

As illustrated in Figure 10.1, a rise in the price leads to a fall in the quantity demanded, and a fall in the price leads to a rise in the quantity demanded. This is one of those commonly observed

The **quantity demanded** is the amount of a good that consumers are willing and able to purchase at a particular price over a given period of time.

Price     Demand

As price goes up. . .

quantity demanded goes down.

As price goes down. . .

quantity demanded goes up.

**Figure 10.1** The Law of Demand
When the price goes up, consumers buy less, and when the price goes down, consumers buy more. That's the law of demand in action!

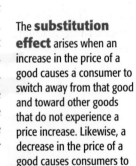

behaviors that economists call "laws," like the law of increasing opportunity cost you learned about in Chapter 1. The tendency for the price and the quantity demanded to move in opposite directions is known as the **law of demand**.

There are two distinct reasons why a consumer buys less of a good after its price increases: the *substitution effect* and the *income effect*.

## The Substitution Effect

Suppose your meals consisted of a combination of $1 tacos and $2 burritos. The opportunity cost of each burrito would be 2 tacos, because the $2 spent on a burrito could otherwise buy 2 tacos for $1 each. If the price of burritos rose to $3, you would then have to give up 3 tacos for each burrito. At the same time, the price rise for burritos would lower the opportunity cost of tacos: instead of giving up a burrito for every 2 tacos, you would give up a burrito for every 3 tacos. The higher burrito price would thus give you reason to substitute more tacos, whose opportunity cost has fallen, for some burritos, whose price and opportunity cost have risen.

The tendency for consumers to switch away from a good whose price has risen and toward other goods that have become relatively less expensive

is known as the **substitution effect**. This effect helps explain why a rise in the price of movie tickets causes consumers to buy fewer tickets and instead rent more DVDs or download more movies. The substitution effect also explains why some commuters switch to public transportation—buses and trains—when a rise in the price of gasoline makes it more expensive to drive a car. The substitution effect always causes consumers to buy less of a good whose price has increased and more of a good whose price has decreased. This is one of the reasons why consumer purchases follow the law of demand.

### DID YOU GET IT?
Why does a price increase cause a substitution effect?

The **law of demand** is the tendency for the price and the quantity demanded to move in opposite directions.

The **substitution effect** arises when an increase in the price of a good causes a consumer to switch away from that good and toward other goods that do not experience a price increase. Likewise, a decrease in the price of a good causes consumers to switch toward that good.

When the price of gasoline goes up, so does the popularity of trains and buses.

The **income effect** is the change in consumption that occurs when a price increase causes consumers to feel poorer or when a price decrease causes them to feel richer.

## The Income Effect

Income has *purchasing power*, meaning that it gives people the power to buy things. When prices are low, a given amount of income will buy more things—it has greater purchasing power—than when prices are high. For example, with an income of $100 per week, you can purchase 100 music downloads for $1 each. But if the price rises to $1.25, your income will have the power to buy only 80 downloads. This leads us to the second reason why a price increase causes a decrease in the quantity demanded: because a price increase lowers the overall purchasing power of consumers' income.

Suppose that you currently spend half of your income on music downloads and the other half on food, clothing, and other goods. If the price of downloads suddenly doubles, you will essentially be poorer because your income will purchase less than it did before. After the price rises, you will not be able to afford the same combination of music and other goods as before. You will have to do some belt tightening and cut back on one or more of the goods you buy, most likely including music downloads. The change in consumption that results from the diminished purchasing power of your income is called the **income effect**. This effect is the same as if your income actually decreased and the prices stayed the same. There is an income effect in the other direction if the price falls: you will feel richer and you are likely to buy more of one or more goods.

The income effect and the substitution effect have one thing in common: each can be a reason why consumers buy less of a good when its price rises. So each plays a role in explaining why consumers follow the law of demand. It is important to distinguish between these two effects. The substitution effect of a price increase is the switch to other goods that have become a relatively good deal. The income effect of a price increase is the change in consumption that results from the decrease in the purchasing power of consumers' income. Module 11 explains that a *normal good* is one that you buy less of when your income decreases. Figure 10.2 summarizes how each effect works when the price of a normal good rises or falls and how the two effects combine to help explain the law of demand.

 **DID YOU GET IT?**
Why does a price increase cause an income effect?

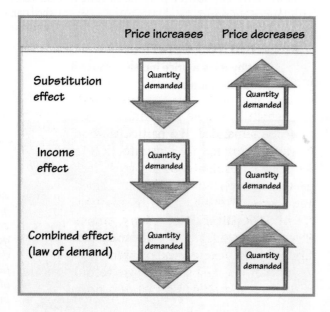

**Figure 10.2** Income and Substitution Effects
When the price of a good rises, consumers tend to switch away from that good and buy more of other goods that have become relatively less expensive. This is known as the *substitution effect*. *The income effect* of a price increase is the change in consumption that results from the diminished purchasing power of income. Both the substitution effect and the income effect help explain why a consumer buys less of a good or service when the price rises.

## THE LAW OF DEMAND AND THE "ALL ELSE EQUAL" ASSUMPTION

Imagine the price of chocolate rises. We would expect a fall in the quantity demanded. But what if at the same time new research reveals surprising health benefits from eating chocolate? The price rise will discourage chocolate consumption, but the research will make people want to eat more chocolate. The net result could be either an increase or a decrease in the quantity of chocolate people buy.

According to the law of demand, when the price of a good goes up, the quantity demanded goes down, and when the price of a good goes down, the quantity demanded goes up. This relationship applies only when we assume that other influences on the quantity demanded, such as peoples' tastes for a good, are "held constant" or unchanged when the good's price changes. If the price changes and other influences change at the same time, then the law of demand might not hold.

Economists use the Latin term *ceteris paribus*, meaning "all else equal," to indicate that they are looking only at a specified relationship, such as the one between price and quantity demanded. Ceteris paribus means that all other factors that might affect that relationship are held constant. In the real world, of course, everything else is not held constant. The price of a good may increase and consumer tastes may change at the same time, as in our chocolate example. This does not strike down the law of demand. It just means that in the real world, price is not the only force affecting purchasing decisions. Nonetheless, understanding how price affects the quantity demanded, without interference from other factors, is quite useful.

In case the "all else equal" assumption gives you a headache, let's seek clarification and relief by thinking about aspirin. We know that aspirin can reduce a fever—that is, if other influences on body temperature are held constant. If you start running around after taking an aspirin, your fever might actually rise. Even so, it is useful to isolate the effect of aspirin on body temperature by saying that, all else equal, taking aspirin reduces your temperature. Knowing this is important to those treating a fever. In the same way, it is important to isolate the effect of price changes on the quantity demanded. It helps us understand how markets work and how different policies and events are likely to influence a market.

## THE DEMAND SCHEDULE AND THE DEMAND CURVE

As you've seen, the price of a good plays a central role in the quantity that consumers demand. Think of all the times you've said to yourself, "I'd buy one of those if they weren't so expensive," or "What a great deal—I'm going to buy a lot of these!" Economists use a *demand schedule* and a *demand curve* to summarize the relationship between the quantity of a product demanded and its price.

Let's start with the **demand schedule**, which is a table that indicates the quantity demanded of a particular good at various prices. To illustrate how a demand schedule is constructed, let's imagine interviewing a driver named Alicia about her purchases of gasoline. We can ask Alicia, "How many gallons of gasoline would you purchase each month if the price per gallon were $2?" If she answers, "20 gallons," we record in the demand schedule that at a price

A **demand schedule** is a table that relates the quantity demanded of a particular good to its price.

of $2 per gallon, the quantity demanded is 20 gallons. Then we can ask Alicia how much gasoline she would buy if the price increased to $2.50 per gallon and nothing else changed. If her response is "15 gallons," we record in the demand schedule that at a price of $2.50, the quantity demanded is 15 gallons. We could continue to ask about the quantity she would purchase at different prices and record her answers. The table in Figure 10.3 displays Alicia's demand schedule for gasoline. Notice that as the price of gas goes up, the quantity of gas Alicia demands goes down. High gas prices might motivate Alicia to use public transportation, take fewer unnecessary trips, ride her bike more, and carpool with friends.

 **DID YOU GET IT?**
**What is a demand schedule?**

### The Individual Demand Curve

> A **demand curve** is a graphical representation of the demand schedule for a good, showing the quantity demanded at each price.

The **demand curve** is a graphical representation of the demand schedule, showing the quantity demanded at each price. Although it is called a "curve," it is sometimes a straight line. Each price

and quantity in the demand schedule is represented by a point on the demand curve. Let's draw Alicia's demand curve for gasoline using the information from the demand schedule in Figure 10.3. In the first row of the demand schedule, we see that at a price of $2, Alicia buys 20 gallons of gasoline per month. This is represented by the point on the far right on the graph. The price of $2 is measured on the vertical axis (also called the *y-axis*), and the quantity of 20 gallons is measured on the horizontal axis (also called the *x-axis*).

As you can see from the graph in Figure 10.3, Alicia's demand curve slopes downward and to the right, which means that the lower the price, the more gasoline she buys. For example, if the price falls from $3 to $2, Alicia's quantity demanded rises from 10 gallons to 20 gallons. This change in the quantity demanded is represented as a *movement along the demand curve*. We call this a movement along the curve because, to illustrate what happened, we can simply slide a pencil along the curve, moving from the point representing $3 and 10 gallons to the point representing $2 and 20 gallons. The curve

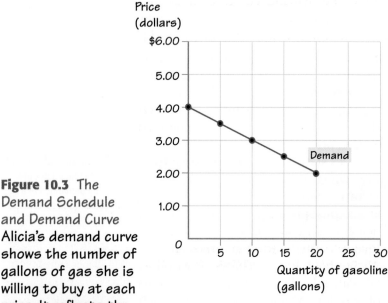

**Figure 10.3** The Demand Schedule and Demand Curve Alicia's demand curve shows the number of gallons of gas she is willing to buy at each price. It reflects the law of demand: as the price of gas goes up, Alicia purchases less gas.

| **Alicia's Demand Schedule for Gasoline** | |
|---|---|
| **PRICE (DOLLARS)** | **QUANTITY OF GAS DEMANDED (GALLONS)** |
| $2.00 | 20 |
| 2.50 | 15 |
| 3.00 | 10 |
| 3.50 | 5 |
| 4.00 | 0 |

itself does not change position. All that changes when the price changes is the point on the curve that indicates the quantity Alicia purchases at the current price. When the price changes, we move along the demand curve; this is the law of demand in action.

**DID YOU GET IT?**
What is a demand curve, and why does it slope downward?

## The Market Demand Curve

We started our study of demand by looking at the behavior of a single consumer, Alicia, in Figure 10.3. The people who run businesses and make economic policy, however, are often interested in the demand curve of all the consumers of a good combined. The **market demand curve** is a graphical representation of the quantity of a good demanded by *all* consumers in the market at each price.

To see how the market demand curve is drawn, let's suppose that there are two consumers in the market for gasoline: Fred and Alicia. Fred's demand for gasoline, like Alicia's, can be summarized in a demand schedule. The first three columns of Table 10.1 repeat Alicia's demand schedule and provide Fred's. Notice that at each price, Fred demands more gasoline than Alicia. Why? Fred might have a longer ride to work each day. Or he might drive a big car because he has a large family, while Alicia drives a hybrid car that gets better gas mileage. Notice that regardless

of their differences, Fred and Alicia *each* demand less gasoline at a higher price than they do at a lower price.

We calculate the market demand—the demand of all consumers in the market combined—by adding together Fred's and Alicia's quantity demanded at each price, as shown in the fourth column of the Table 10.1. For example, at a price of $2, Alicia demands 20 gallons and Fred demands 30 gallons, so the quantity demanded in the market is 50 gallons. At a price of $2.50, Alicia demands 15 gallons and Fred demands 25 gallons, so the quantity demanded in the market is 40 gallons. We continue in this fashion, combining the quantities demanded at each price, to complete the table.

The graph in Figure 10.4 shows the market demand curve drawn from the demand schedule in the table. Like the individual demand curves, the market demand curve slopes downward: as the price falls, the quantity demanded collectively by Alicia and Fred rises. The law of demand thus applies to the market demand curve as well as to the individual demand curve of each consumer.

From now on in this book, we will focus on market demand curves rather than the demand curves of individual consumers. So when you see the term *demand curve*, it will refer to the market demand curve.

The **market demand curve** for a good is a graphical representation of how the quantity demanded by *all* consumers in the market varies with the price.

**DID YOU GET IT?**
How is the market demand curve found?

| Table 10.1 **The Market Demand Schedule** | | | |
|---|---|---|---|
| **PRICE (DOLLARS)** | **ALICIA'S DEMAND (GALLONS)** | **FRED'S DEMAND (GALLONS)** | **MARKET DEMAND (GALLONS)** |
| $2.00 | 20 | 30 | 50 |
| 2.50 | 15 | 25 | 40 |
| 3.00 | 10 | 20 | 30 |
| 3.50 | 5 | 15 | 20 |
| 4.00 | 0 | 10 | 10 |

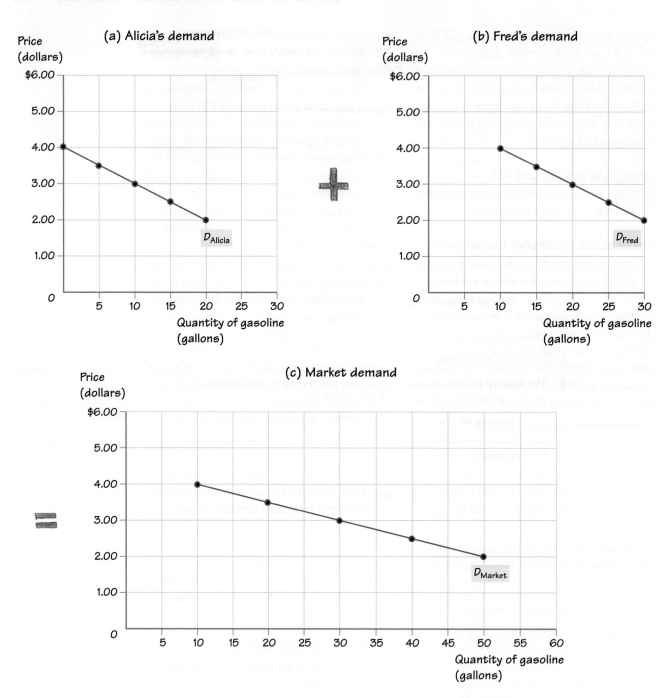

**Figure 10.4** The Market Demand Curve
The market demand curve is a graphical representation of the quantity of a good demanded by all the consumers in the market at each price. If Alicia and Fred are the only two people in a market, we find the market demand curve by adding their individual demand curves together.

# MODULE 10 REVIEW AND ASSESSMENT

**Summing Up the Key Ideas:** Match the following terms to the correct definitions.

A. Substitution effect
B. Income effect
C. Law of demand
D. Market demand curve

E. Demand schedule
F. Demand curve
G. Quantity demanded
H. Ceteris paribus

_____ 1. A graphical representation of a demand schedule.

_____ 2. The amount of a good that consumers are willing and able to purchase at a particular price over a given period of time.

_____ 3. The tendency for consumers to switch away from a good whose price has risen and toward other goods that have become relatively less expensive.

_____ 4. A term used to mean "all else equal."

_____ 5. A table that indicates the quantity of a particular good demanded at various prices.

_____ 6. The change in consumption that occurs when a price increase causes consumers to feel poorer or when a price decrease causes them to feel richer.

_____ 7. The tendency for the price and the quantity demanded to move in opposite directions.

_____ 8. A graphical representation of the quantity of a good demanded by all consumers in the market at various prices.

**Analyze:** Assume that shoes are a normal good. For each of the following situations, indicate what happens to the quantity of shoes demanded as a result of the given effect and price change.

QUANTITY DEMANDED

1. Effect: the substitution effect
   Change: The price of shoes increases.                          _____

2. Effect: the income effect
   Change: The price of shoes increases.                          _____

3. Effect: the substitution effect
   Change: The price of shoes decreases.                          _____

4. Effect: the income effect
   Change: The price of shoes decreases.                          _____

## Apply:

1. Suppose Randy, Jessica, and Mark are the only buyers in the market for oranges. Complete the demand schedule for oranges by calculating the market demand for oranges.

| PRICE (DOLLARS) | RANDY'S QUANTITY DEMANDED | JESSICA'S QUANTITY DEMANDED | MARK'S QUANTITY DEMANDED | MARKET DEMAND FOR ORANGES |
|---|---|---|---|---|
| $1.00 | 5 | 8 | 4 | |
| 1.25 | 4 | 6 | 3 | |
| 1.50 | 3 | 5 | 2 | |
| 1.75 | 2 | 3 | 1 | |
| 2.00 | 1 | 1 | 0 | |

2. Draw the market demand curve for oranges using the information in the demand schedule from question 1. Be sure to label the axes.

# MODULE 11

# Shifts of the Demand Curve

**KEY IDEA:** The demand curve for a good can shift due to changes in tastes, income, the prices of related goods, expectations about the future, and the number of buyers in a market.

**OBJECTIVES**

- **To identify what shifts the demand curve to the left and what shifts it to the right.**
- **To distinguish between the terms *quantity demanded* and *demand*.**
- **To explain how goods are categorized as normal goods, inferior goods, substitutes, and complements.**

## The Changing Story of Demand

The demand curve tells the story of how much consumers will buy at every price. That story can change. For example, the demand for umbrellas changes when it rains. The demand for sports cars changes when incomes rise. And the demand for orange juice changes when we're persuaded to have a healthy dose of vitamin C every day. Changes in demand typically cause the price of the good and the quantity sold to change as well, as we'll investigate later. This module explores the reasons for changes in demand and the demand-curve shifts that result.

*When it rains there is a shift of the demand curve for umbrellas.*

## SHIFTS OF THE DEMAND CURVE

Module 10 explained that a change in the price of a good causes a movement along the demand curve for that good. Consider the movement from point A to point B in the graph, which shows that for $1, consumers would buy 100 oranges, but if the price changed to $0.75, consumers would buy 200 oranges. As we look at how changes in price cause movements along the demand curve, we assume that all other influences on the purchase of oranges do not change.

Now suppose that a successful advertising campaign makes people more aware of the health benefits of eating

oranges. This will change people's tastes for oranges. At any particular price, people will be willing to buy more oranges

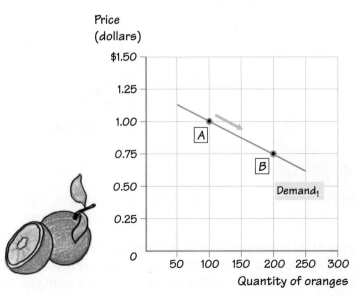

than before. Looking at panel (b) of Figure 11.1, we see that this causes the entire demand curve to shift to the right, from Demand₁ to Demand₂. Consider the quantity demanded at a price of $1. Previously, people were willing to buy 100 oranges for $1, as shown by point A. Now they are willing to buy 150 oranges at a price of $1 at point C. While the effect of a price change was illustrated by sliding a pencil along the existing demand curve, the effect of a change in tastes is illustrated by picking up the pencil and drawing a new curve.

A **shift of the demand curve** means that at every price, the amount people are willing and able to buy has changed. In Figure 11.1, you saw an example of a rightward shift of the demand curve. Figure 11.2 illustrates another possible shift of the demand curve for oranges, this time to the left. What would cause a leftward shift? Suppose the price of apples decreases. Many people are content with either apples or oranges. So when apples become less expensive, more people will choose apples over oranges. At a price of $1, for example, people

are now willing to buy only 50 oranges as shown by point D, instead of the 100 they were buying before at point A. The quantity of oranges people are willing to buy decreases at other prices, too, shifting the demand curve to the left.

## The Language of Demand
Let's take another look at terms with precise meanings in economics. We've seen that *quantity demanded* refers to a particular quantity that people want to buy at a specific price, while *demand* refers to the relationship between price and quantity demanded, as represented by the entire demand curve. The proper use of these terms helps us distinguish between a movement along a demand curve and a shift of the demand curve. When we move along a demand curve, we call the resulting change in the quantity that consumers want to buy a **change in the quantity demanded**. For example, in panel (a) of Figure 11.1, the drop in price from $1 to $0.75 caused a movement along demand curve Demand₁ and an *increase in the quantity demanded* from 100 to 200 oranges.

A **shift of the demand curve** represents a change in the amount people are willing and able to buy at every price.

A movement along a demand curve caused by a price change is called a **change in the quantity demanded**, not to be confused with a change in demand.

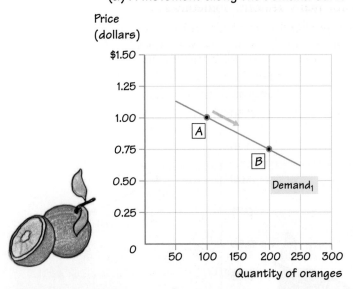
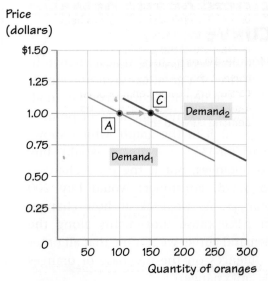

**Figure 11.1** Movement along the Demand Curve versus a Shift of the Demand Curve
Panel (a) shows a movement along the demand curve. When the price of oranges changes from $1 to $0.75, consumers are willing to buy 100 more oranges. Panel (b) shows what happens if people want to purchase more oranges at every price; the entire demand curve shifts to the right.

When the demand curve shifts, we call the change in consumers' willingness to buy the product a **change in demand**. For example, in panel (b) of Figure 11.1, the change in tastes in favor of oranges caused an *increase in demand*, shown as a shift from demand curve Demand₁ to the entirely new demand curve Demand₂.

If you are asked, "What happens to the demand for running shoes when there is a citywide sale and prices are marked down?" the correct answer is "Nothing." *Demand* refers to the entire demand curve, and a change in price does not cause the demand curve itself to change. The sale on running shoes causes a movement along the demand curve. But this is an increase in the *quantity demanded*, not an increase in demand. If the announcement of a new race led to an increase in the quantity of running shoes consumers were willing to buy at any given price, that would constitute an increase in *demand*.

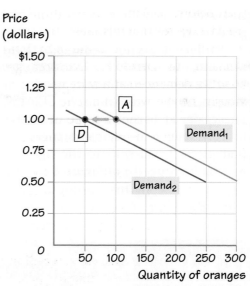

Price (dollars)

**Figure 11.2** A Leftward Shift of the Demand Curve When the quantity of oranges demanded goes down at every price, the demand curve shifts to the left.

A shift of the demand curve is called a **change in demand**, not to be confused with a change in the quantity demanded.

---

## WHAT CAUSES THE DEMAND CURVE TO SHIFT?

You've learned that price changes cause a change in the quantity demanded, and changes in some other factors cause the demand curve to shift. But what are these factors that shift the demand curve? The five emphasized by economists—because they play a central role in many markets—are tastes, income, the prices of related goods, expectations, and the number of buyers. Let's explore each of these in turn.

### Tastes

Particular styles of goods, including clothing, jewelry, music, cars, and computers, rise and fall in popularity. Depending on the year, for example, the jeans in fashion might have straight, flared, or bootcut legs, and they might be low-rise, stonewashed, distressed, baggy, or tight. Tastes change and styles go in and out of favor for many reasons. Sometimes the wardrobes of famous people influence the tastes of the broader population, as when the styles of first ladies and royalty cause buying frenzies. Firms try to influence tastes by hiring advertising agencies to promote new products and styles. A successful ad campaign convinces

*Tastes change the demand for certain fashions. These teenagers in the 1980s bought different clothes from teenagers today.*

customers to be willing to buy more of a good or service at every price.

Earlier you saw how a change in tastes can shift the demand curve for oranges by changing the quantity demanded at every price. Likewise, if a style of jeans, music, or car becomes more attractive to consumers, the demand curve for that product will shift to the right, as we saw in panel (b) of Figure 11.1. If a good becomes less popular or attractive, the demand curve will shift to the left, as we saw in Figure 11.2.

### Income

The amount of money people earn affects the amount they are willing and able to spend. A rise in income means there is more money to spend on consumption. A fall in income generally

# ECONOMICS IN ACTION

# Creating Demand for Diamonds

*The world's largest diamond company, De Beers, has managed to change people's tastes for diamond engagement rings around the globe. The company's ad campaign caused the demand curve for diamonds to shift to the right, so that more could be sold at each price. Indeed, the following news article argues that the demand for diamonds was "invented" by advertising executives.*

The diamond invention—the creation of the idea that diamonds are rare and valuable, and are essential signs of esteem—is a relatively recent development in the history of the diamond trade.

The campaign to internationalize the diamond invention began in earnest in the mid-1960s. The prime targets were Japan, Germany, and Brazil. . . . De Beers brought in the J. Walter Thompson agency, which had especially strong advertising subsidiaries in the target countries, to place most of its international advertising. Within ten years, De Beers succeeded beyond even its most optimistic expectations, creating a billion-dollar-a-year diamond market in Japan. . . .

Until the mid-1960s, Japanese parents arranged marriages for their children through trusted intermediaries. . . . There was no tradition of romance, courtship, seduction, or prenuptial love in Japan; and none that required the gift of a diamond engagement ring. . . . J. Walter Thompson began its campaign by suggesting that diamonds were a visible sign of modern Western values. It created a series of color advertisements in Japanese magazines showing beautiful women displaying their diamond rings. . . .

The campaign was remarkably successful. Until 1959, the importation of diamonds had not even been permitted by the postwar Japanese government. When the campaign began, in 1967, not quite 5 percent of engaged Japanese women received a diamond engagement ring. . . . By 1981, some 60 percent of Japanese brides wore diamonds. . . . Japan became the second largest market, after the United States, for the sale of diamond engagement rings.

SOURCE: Edward Jay Epstein, "Have You Ever Tried to Sell a Diamond?" *Atlantic Monthly*, February 1982, http://www.theatlantic.com/magazine/archive/1982/02/have-you-ever-tried-to-sell-a-diamond/4575/.

 **DID YOU GET IT?**
How did De Beers change the demand curve for diamonds?

causes people to cut back on the quantity of goods they buy. What would happen to your purchases of clothing if your income fell because you lost your after-school job? Chances are they would fall.

If the demand for a particular good rises when income rises and falls when income falls, we call it a **normal good**. Most goods are normal goods. For example, when people have more income, they tend to buy more newspapers, cars, fruit juice, televisions, and restaurant meals.

Not all goods are normal goods, however. For the goods known as **inferior goods**, a rise in income actually leads to a fall in demand. An example of an inferior good is intercity bus transportation. Buses are popular among students and others with relatively low incomes. A rise in income leads people to take buses less frequently and instead drive or take a plane between cities. In developing countries such as India and China, bicycles are an inferior good. As people become wealthier, they tend to buy more cars and fewer bicycles. Canned meat and processed cheese are other examples of inferior goods.

For a normal good, a rise in income causes a rightward shift of the demand curve. When income rises, people want to buy more of the normal good at every price. For an inferior good, a rise in income causes the demand curve to shift to the left. At every price, people want to buy less of the inferior good when income is high than when income is low.

**DID YOU GET IT?**
What is the difference between a normal good and an inferior good?

## The Prices of Related Goods

Earlier we saw that when the price of apples fell, people ate more apples and fewer oranges. This shifted the demand curve for oranges. In other words, a change in the price of one good can shift the demand curve for *another* good.

*Many people in developing countries, such as this Chinese porter in the Sichuan province, still rely on bicycles to transport goods.*

The demand for a **normal good** increases when income rises and falls when income decreases.

The demand for an **inferior good** decreases when income rises and increases when income falls.

Consider the demand curve for hot dogs. What would happen if the price of hamburgers increased? We would expect some consumers to switch from eating hamburgers to eating hot dogs to avoid the new, higher price of hamburgers. This would shift the demand curve for hot dogs to the right. The price of hamburgers affects the demand for hot dogs because hot dogs and hamburgers are *substitutes* for each other—one can take the place of the other. When two goods are **substitutes**, an increase in the price of one leads to an increase in demand for the other. The opposite is true as well: a decrease in the price of a substitute encourages some customers to switch to that good, which decreases demand for the other. DVDs are a substitute for movie downloads, tea is a substitute for coffee, and Burger King burgers are a substitute for McDonald's burgers.

Some pairs of goods go well together. For example, buns and hot dogs are complements—when people buy one of these goods, they are likely to also buy the other. When two goods are

Two goods are **substitutes** if an increase in the price of one of the goods leads to an increase in the demand for the other.

## ECONOMICS IN ACTION

# Conspicuous Consumption and the Demand for Goods

The economist Thorstein Veblen (1857–1929) coined the phrase *conspicuous consumption* to convey the idea that wealthy people purchase certain luxury goods as a signal that they have a high social standing. A $50 Timex brand watch, for example, tells time about as well as a $5,000 Rolex brand watch. But many people buy the more expensive brand. Likewise, Veblen saw purchases of unnecessarily expensive designer clothing, jewelry, and silver utensils as efforts to display wealth and social status.

Conspicuous consumption remained just an interesting idea for more than a century. But in 2005, Ori Heffetz of Cornell University developed a way to test Veblen's idea. He reasoned

*Conspicuous consumption?*

that goods must be visible to be conspicuous. So his first step was to develop a measure of product visibility by asking people how long it would take them to notice their neighbors' spending on various goods. Clothing, cars, and jewelry were among the most visible products on Heffetz's list, while underwear, home insurance, life insurance, and car insurance were the least visible.

Using his measure of product visibility and information on families' spending habits, Heffetz found that conspicuous (or highly visible) goods make up a greater share of the consumption budget in wealthier families. For example, as a household's overall income rises, so does the percentage of the household's budget that is spent on cars and jewelry—two highly visible items. Conversely, spending on household electricity and water—inconspicuous goods— falls as a percentage of the budget as income rises. Ultimately, Professor Heffetz found that increases in family income cause the demand for highly visible goods to increase by more than the demand for goods that are not very visible. In other words, he showed that Veblen was right.

---

Two goods are **complements** if, because they are consumed together, an increase in the price of one of the goods leads to a decrease in the demand for the other good.

**complements**, an increase in the price of one of the goods leads to a decrease in the demand for the other. Suppose the price of buns increases. Eating a hot dog on a bun will now be more expensive, so people will buy fewer hot dogs at every price for hot dogs. The demand for hot dogs decreases, and the demand curve for hot dogs shifts leftward.

Similar complementary relationships between goods are common. If the price of maple syrup rises, a meal of pancakes with syrup becomes more expensive, so the demand curve for pancakes will shift to the left. If the price of gasoline rises, the demand curve for SUVs will shift to the left. And if the price of tennis balls rises, the demand curve for tennis racquets will shift to the left. These effects work in reverse as well: if the price of gasoline falls, it will become less expensive to drive an SUV and the demand curve for SUVs will shift to the right.

**DID YOU GET IT?**
**What is the difference between goods that are substitutes and goods that are complements?**

## Expectations

Your expectations about the future price of a good can influence your demand for that good today. If you think the price of a good will fall in the future, you are likely to postpone your purchase of that good until the price is lower. Because expectations about future prices affect the quantity you demand at every price, they cause demand curves to shift. For example, there is a leftward shift in the demand curve for Macy's clothing in the days before a major sale.

Expectations that the price of a good will rise in the future lead people to buy more of it today. For example, suppose consumers expect the price of gasoline to increase soon, perhaps due to a new conflict in oil-producing countries. Many are likely to buy more gasoline now, even if their gas tanks are far from empty. This increase in the quantity of gasoline demanded at every price shifts the demand curve for gasoline to the right.

A similar situation occurs when consumers know that a change in sales taxes is coming up. Many states temporarily suspend the sales tax on clothing and other items for a week before school starts each year to encourage families to go shopping, especially for back-to-school items. If it is late August and people know there will be no sales tax in a week or two, they will probably postpone some of their purchases. The future opportunity for tax-free purchases causes people to buy less clothing at every price today, which shifts the demand curve for clothing to the left. This is a shift in the demand curve and not a movement along it because people buy less clothing even though the price did not change.

*If consumers expect to have a week without sales taxes, they will delay some of their purchases until that tax-free week. This shifts the current demand curve to the left.*

Like changing expectations about prices, changing expectations about future income affect the demand for goods today. Rather than waiting for an anticipated increase in income to arrive before spending some of it, consumers like to spread out their expenditures. If new information about a job offer or a raise brings you to expect a higher income in the future, your consumption of normal goods is likely to increase now; you might buy a new outfit or upgrade your laptop. When the economy as a whole shows strong signs of improvement, many people expect higher incomes in the future, and the demand curves for many normal goods shift rightward. Going in the other direction, if there is a forecast of lower incomes in the future, people start spending less immediately and the demand curves for many normal goods shift leftward.

## The Number of Buyers

The fifth and final factor that can shift a demand curve is the number of buyers in the market. Remember that to draw the market demand curve, we add together the quantities demanded by each of the individual consumers at every price. If the number of consumers in a market

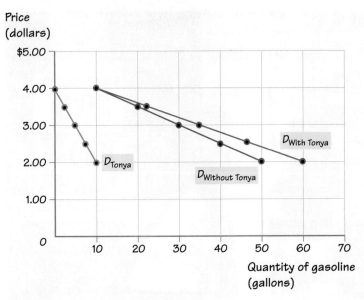

**Figure 11.3** The Number of Buyers
Adding buyers to the market shifts the demand curve to the right.

increases—say because the population grows—then the market demand curve shifts to the right. Figure 11.3 takes the market for gasoline from Figure 10.4 and adds a third consumer, Tonya. At each price, we add Tonya's quantity demanded to Alicia's and Fred's to find the quantity demanded in the market. The blue demand curve represents the original market demand before Tonya joined the market; the red market demand curve represents demand with Tonya in the market. The shift from the blue curve to the red curve illustrates how the addition of buyers shifts the market demand curve to the right.

## YOUR TURN

### Is It a Movement along the Curve or a Shift of the Curve?

**Directions:** For each of the following situations, indicate whether the change would cause a movement along an existing demand curve or a shift of the demand curve for the product mentioned. Also indicate whether any movements are upward or downward and whether any shifts are to the left or to the right.

1. The price of jeans decreases.
2. Additional consumers find vitamin-enriched bottled water pleasant tasting.
3. John enjoys steaks and expects his income to double within the next two years.
4. Dress shirts and ties are complements. The price of shirts increases. What happens in the tie market?
5. The birth rate in a country falls. What happens in the disposable diaper market?
6. Soft drink companies launch a successful advertising campaign.
7. You expect the price of orange juice to increase next week.

**Answers:** 1. downward movement along the existing demand curve; 2. demand curve shifts right; 3. demand curve shifts right (assuming steaks are a normal good); 4. demand curve shifts left; 5. demand curve shifts left; 6. demand curve shifts right; 7. demand curve shifts right.

# MODULE 11 REVIEW AND ASSESSMENT

**Summing Up the Key Ideas:** Match the following terms to the correct definitions.

A. Change in the quantity demanded
B. Change in demand
C. Normal goods
D. Expectations

E. Substitutes
F. Complements
G. Conspicuous consumption
H. Taste

I. Inferior goods
J. Income

_____ 1. The demand for this type of good rises when income rises and falls when income falls.

_____ 2. A desire for a specific good or service.

_____ 3. Movement along a demand curve.

_____ 4. The idea that wealthy people choose to purchase certain luxury goods to signal to others that they have high social standing.

_____ 5. Good A and good B are this type of good if an increase in the price of good *A* leads to a decrease in the demand for good *B*.

_____ 6. A shift of a demand curve.

_____ 7. The amount of money people earn and which affects the amount they are willing and able to spend.

_____ 8. Good A and good B are this type of good if an increase in the price of good *A* leads to an increase in the demand for good *B*.

_____ 9. The demand for this type of good rises when income falls and falls when income rises.

_____ 10. Thinking about the future price of a good that can influence your demand for that good today.

**Analyze and Explain:** In the following situations, identify if the **demand** or the **quantity demanded** changes. Explain the reason for the change.

| | DEMAND OR QUANTITY DEMANDED? | EXPLANATION |
|---|---|---|
| 1. Holly gets a raise at work and decides that she will buy more music downloads. | _____ | _____ |
| 2. David notices that the price of coffee has increased, so he buys less coffee. | _____ | _____ |
| 3. George decides not to buy new tires now since he expects tire prices to fall next month. | _____ | _____ |
| 4. Eric notices that the price of Coke is higher and as a result buys more Pepsi. | _____ | _____ |
| 5. As the population ages, more people buy hearing aids. | _____ | _____ |
| 6. James decides to buy more peanut butter as a result of jelly going on sale. | _____ | _____ |
| 7. Madeline does not need to buy diapers anymore for her three-year-old son. | _____ | _____ |

**Apply:** Indicate what would happen to the current **demand** for pencils as a result of each of the following changes.

DEMAND FOR PENCILS

1. Pencil consumers experience an increase in income. (Pencils are considered a normal good.) _____

2. The price of pens (a substitute for pencils) increases. _____

3. The price of paper (a complement for pencils) decreases. _____

4. Pencil consumers experience an increase in income. (Pencils are considered an inferior good.) _____

5. The number of consumers in the pencil market increases. _____

6. The price of pencils falls. _____

7. The price of pencils is expected to decline next month. _____

# MODULE 12

# Elasticity of Demand

**KEY IDEA:** An important aspect of demand is how sensitive quantity demanded is to price changes.

**OBJECTIVES**

● **To explain how economists measure the sensitivity of quantity demanded to price changes.**

● **To identify what makes the demand for a good more or less sensitive to changes in its price.**

● **To show the connection between price sensitivity and the total revenue of firms in a market.**

## Changing the Price of Chocolate

In 2011, the Hershey Company raised its chocolate prices by about 10 percent. The law of demand tells us that a price increase such as this will cause the quantity demanded to fall. What the Hershey Company really wants to know is *how much* it will fall. Can Hershey raise the price and sell almost as much chocolate as before? Or will the price hike cause a lot of customers to switch to Nestlé or Cadbury chocolate? That depends on how sensitive consumers are to the price change by Hershey. In this module you will learn how economists measure this important type of sensitivity.

*When the Hershey Company considers a change in the price of its chocolate, it wants to know how the price change would affect the quantity demanded.*

## WHAT IS ELASTICITY?

Economists use the **elasticity of demand** to measure how strongly consumers respond to a change in price. When consumers are very sensitive to the price, such that they respond to a price increase with a relatively large decrease in quantity demanded, demand is **elastic**. When consumers are not so sensitive to the price, so that a price increase leads to a relatively small decrease in quantity demanded, demand is **inelastic**. When consumers respond to a price increase by decreasing the quantity demanded by the same percentage, demand is **unit-elastic**. As it raises its prices, Hershey would prefer to face inelastic demand, so that its higher prices will cause only a relatively small decrease in the quantity sold.

## WHAT MAKES DEMAND MORE OR LESS ELASTIC?

When prices change, why does the quantity demanded change by a lot for some goods and by just a little for other goods? Or to put it another way, why is demand for some goods elastic and for other goods inelastic? Economists have identified five factors that make the demand for a good more or less sensitive to price changes.

### Necessities versus Luxuries

Goods that people cannot do without have an inelastic demand. For example, people with diabetes usually purchase the medication their doctor prescribes whether the price is low or high.

**Elasticity of demand** is a measure of how strongly consumers respond to a change in the price of a good, calculated as the percentage change in the quantity demanded divided by the percentage change in price. Demand is **elastic** if consumers respond to a change in price with a relatively large change in the quantity demanded and it is **inelastic** if consumers respond to a change in price with a relatively small change in the quantity demanded. Demand is **unit-elastic** if consumers respond to a change in price by changing the quantity demanded by the same percentage.

Likewise, goods that satisfy basic needs, such as the first few units of food, water, and shelter a person purchases, have an inelastic demand. After enough units of these items are purchased to assure survival, we only buy additional units if the price is reasonably low, and demand becomes elastic.

Goods that people can easily do without are considered "luxuries." They include the latest electronic gadgets, the second car, and vacation travel. When prices rise, these goods can be given up, so demand tends to be elastic. If the price of a trip to Florida is too high, people will stay home. The same holds for an expensive new television. After all, it's possible to keep the old television for another year or two.

## The Availability of Close Substitutes

Another factor that affects the elasticity of demand for a particular good is whether there are close substitutes for that good. A close substitute, being very similar to another good, can easily take the other good's place. For example, for most people, oranges are a close

substitute for tangerines. If the price of tangerines rises, consumers can easily switch to oranges. The demand for a good with close substitutes tends to be elastic, because a rise in the price of that good causes people to buy much less of it and redirect their dollars toward a substitute.

Sometimes goods are *perfect substitutes* for each other, such as red carpet pad and blue carpet pad. Since carpet pad goes under carpet and the color cannot be seen, even a slight increase in the price of, say, red carpet pad above the price of blue carpet pad would cause rational consumers to stop buying the more expensive red carpet pad. In the extreme case when any increase in the price of a good will lead consumers to reduce their consumption to a quantity of zero, demand is *perfectly elastic* and the demand curve is horizontal as shown in Figure 12.1.

When close substitutes are not available, there are no products to switch to if the price rises. Customers must either pay the higher price or go without. This makes demand relatively unresponsive to price changes and thus inelastic. For example, the demand for broad categories of goods with few close substitutes, such as shoes, computers, and light bulbs, is generally inelastic. However, the demand for particular brands of shoes, computers, and light bulbs is more elastic because competing brands are close substitutes. If the price of Diesel brand shoes increases, you can easily switch to Nine West brand shoes.

## The Share of Income Spent on the Good

The elasticity of demand for a good also depends on how much of consumers' income is devoted to that good. Expenditures on goods such as salt, envelopes, and bubble gum probably make up a very small part of your budget. As a result, your response to a change in the price of one of these items is likely to be small. In general, the demand for goods that are inexpensive and purchased infrequently is inelastic.

*A trip to Disney World is a luxury, which makes the demand for it very elastic.*

Price

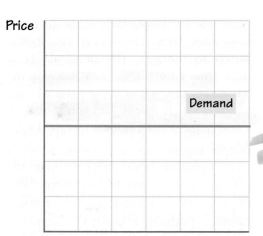

Demand

Quantity

**Figure 12.1** Perfectly Elastic Demand
When demand is perfectly elastic, the demand curve is horizontal.

Demand is elastic for goods like breakfast cereal and cheese that are purchased with greater frequency, because price changes are more noticeable and take a bigger bite out of a consumer's budget. Demand also tends to be elastic for expensive goods, even if they are only purchased once in a while. Products such as refrigerators or automobiles make up a large portion of a consumer's budget. And because of their high prices, even a small percentage increase in price can mean paying hundreds of dollars more. Faced with the extra expense, many consumers might decide to wait to replace their refrigerator or car until their old one breaks down. This makes the demand for these goods elastic.

## Time

Demand is typically less elastic over a shorter time span than over a longer one. To see why, suppose the price of gasoline rises and stays very high. Initially, people may not be able to cut back much on their purchases of gasoline. They can cancel nonessential trips, but if

they commute by car to work or school, they will have to buy gasoline for that purpose until alternatives can be found. Therefore, the demand for gasoline will initially be inelastic.

Over a longer time period, say many months or a year, some consumers will replace gas-guzzling cars with cars that get better gas mileage. Others will join car pools, and some might even move closer to their jobs to save on gasoline. These responses cause the quantity of gasoline demanded to fall more over time than it did initially. So the demand for gasoline becomes more elastic over a longer time period than over a shorter time period.

## Who Pays the Bill

Think about how you select a restaurant when you go out to dinner with your family. If your parents are paying the bill, you probably don't think too much about the restaurant's prices. The elasticity of demand is smaller when someone else is paying, or helping pay, for a good. Insurance coverage creates many situations in which buyers aren't paying the full cost of their purchases. If you have health insurance that covers the entire cost of a doctor's checkup, then even if the price of a checkup increases, it won't increase for you. Your payment will still be zero, so the price increase will not cause you to go less often. Your quantity demanded will stay the same regardless of the price. When there is no response to a price change, demand is *perfectly inelastic* and the demand curve is vertical as shown in Figure 12.2.

Sometimes employees make decisions about purchases that are paid for by their employers. When the administrators at your school purchase desks, chairs, and whiteboards, they are not spending their own money, so they might not be as responsive to price changes as they would be if the money came out of their own pockets. And when a company sends a salesperson to another city to make a sales pitch, the traveler will be relatively

**Figure 12.2** Perfectly Inelastic Demand
**When demand is perfectly inelastic, the demand curve is vertical.**

unconcerned about the price of hotels, meals, and rental cars, because the company is paying the bill. If the price at the most convenient hotel has increased by $20 since the last trip, the salesperson will probably stay there anyway. This makes the demand for business-related expenses inelastic.

## PREDICTING ELASTICITY

Each of the factors we've discussed helps determine a good's elasticity of demand. Knowing about these factors can help you predict whether demand for a good is more likely to be elastic or inelastic. However, demand for a good can be affected by several of these factors at the same time. So if you are trying to predict the elasticity of demand, you have to take account of several factors at once.

Consider the example of cars. Many people regard cars as necessities rather than luxuries. This suggests that the demand for cars would be inelastic. But buying a car is also a large part of many families' budgets, a factor that tends to make demand elastic. The actual elasticity of demand for cars at any time is influenced by both of these factors and others, too.

In some cases, however, one of the factors has a larger influence on elasticity than the others. This allows us to make a good guess—based on that factor alone—about the elasticity of demand. Table 12.1 lists determinants of the elasticity of demand. For each determinant, the table lists a good for which demand is predictably elastic or inelastic due to the influence of that determinant.

**DID YOU GET IT?**
**What five factors tend to make demand elastic?**

---

**Table 12.1 Determinants of the Elasticity of Demand**

| DETERMINANT | ELASTICITY | EXAMPLES |
| --- | --- | --- |
| The good is a necessity. | Inelastic | Open heart surgery |
| The good is a luxury. | Elastic | Cashmere sweaters |
| There are few close substitutes. | Inelastic | Drinking water |
| There are many close substitutes. | Elastic | Dasani brand water |
| Expenditures on the good are a small share of income. | Inelastic | Bubble gum |
| Expenditures on the good are a large share of income. | Elastic | Yachts |
| There is a short time horizon. | Inelastic | Emergency room visit |
| There is a long time horizon. | Elastic | Plastic surgery |
| Someone else pays much of the bill. | Inelastic | Health care covered by insurance |
| The customer pays the bill. | Elastic | Backpacks |

## MEASURING ELASTICITY

Elasticity of demand—consumers' sensitivity to a price change—can be measured numerically. To calculate the elasticity of demand for a good, we divide the percentage change in the quantity demanded by the percentage change in the price. For example, if a 10 percent rise in the price of a chocolate bar causes the quantity demanded to fall by 20 percent, then the elasticity of demand is 20 percent ÷ 10 percent = 2.0. Technically, the elasticity of demand is a negative number, because a rise in price (a positive percentage change) causes a drop in the quantity demanded (a negative percentage change). But to keep things simple, economists usually ignore the negative sign when discussing elasticity of demand. That is why the elasticity for the chocolate bars in our example is 2.0, instead of −2.0.

To see how the elasticity of demand can be calculated using information from a demand graph, read the Show Me the Numbers! box.

# SHOW ME THE NUMBERS!

# Calculating the Elasticity of Demand

Figure 12.3 shows two demand curves for large chocolate bars in a small city. In both graphs, the price per chocolate bar is measured on the vertical axis, and the quantity of bars demanded per month is measured on the horizontal axis. Both demand curves obey the law of demand: a rise in price from $2 to $2.50 causes the quantity demanded to decrease. But in response to this price increase, demand is more elastic in panel (a) than in panel (b). This means that people are more sensitive to the change in price in panel (a). Let's show this by calculating elasticities using the information in the graph.

We start with the formula for elasticity of demand, which is defined by the following equation:

elasticity  = percentage change in quantity demanded / percentage change in price
= (100 × change in quantity demanded ÷ original quantity demanded) ÷
(100 × change in price ÷ original price)

We'll first work with the demand curve in panel (a). As we move from point $A$ to point $B$ along that demand curve, the price of chocolate rises from $2 per bar to $2.50. This causes the quantity demanded to fall from 20,000 to 10,000 bars. We can calculate the elasticity of demand in three steps.

**1.** Calculate the percentage change in the quantity demanded:

$$\frac{(10{,}000 - 20{,}000)}{20{,}000} \times 100 = -50 \text{ percent}$$

**2.** Calculate the percentage change in the price:

$$\frac{(\$2.50 - \$2)}{\$2} \times 100 = 25 \text{ percent}$$

**3.** Divide the percentage change in the quantity demanded by the percentage change in the price and drop the negative sign:

$$\frac{50 \text{ percent}}{25 \text{ percent}} = 2.0$$

So the elasticity of demand for chocolate when moving from point A to point B has the value of 2.0. If you do a similar calculation in panel (b), you will find that the percentage change in the price is the same as in panel (a) but the change in quantity from 20,000 to 18,000 is only a 10 percent change. So the elasticity of demand in panel (b) will be smaller as well, with a value of 0.4. This tells us that demand is more price sensitive—more "elastic"—between point A and point B in panel (a) than between point A and point C in panel (b).

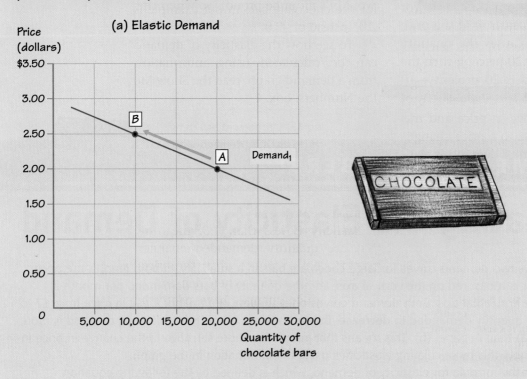

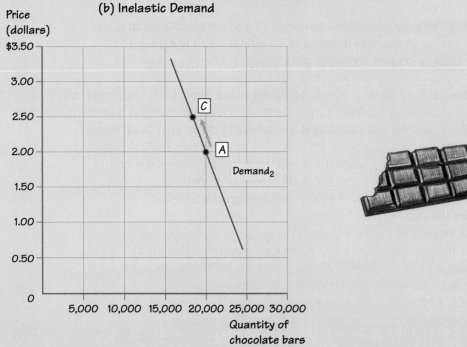

**Figure 12.3** Calculating the Elasticity of Demand for Chocolate Bars

# COMPARING ELASTICITIES

By calculating the value of elasticity, economists can categorize the demand for goods according to how sensitive consumers are to price changes. Remember that the elasticity of demand is equal to the percentage change in the quantity demanded divided by the percentage change in the price. So the larger the elasticity, the greater the percentage change in quantity demanded relative to the percentage change in price and the stronger the response to a price change. We can specify whether demand is elastic, inelastic, or unit elastic, depending on the value of elasticity.

## Don't Let Elasticity Intimidate You

Although *elasticity* has a special meaning in economics, don't let the term intimidate you. It's simply about responsiveness. Later in this book we'll mention the elasticity of labor demand in addition to the elasticity of consumer demand for a good. These terms merely refer to how responsive labor demand is to changes in the wage and how responsive consumer demand is to changes in the price of a good. If the response is large, the elasticity is large. If the response is small, the elasticity is small.

## Elastic Demand

If the elasticity of demand for a good is greater than 1.0, meaning that the quantity demanded changes by a larger percentage than the price, then demand is elastic. When demand is elastic, consumers are particularly responsive to a change in price. In our earlier example, a 10 percent rise in the price of chocolate bars caused a 20 percent drop in the quantity demanded, and the elasticity of demand was 20 percent ÷ 10 percent = 2.0. Since 2.0 is greater than 1.0, the demand for chocolate bars is elastic.

One of the reasons why demand can be elastic is that there are many substitutes for the good. With the many alternatives to chocolate in the grocery aisle, an increase in the price of chocolate causes many customers to switch to licorice, caramel, or maybe even a banana (wouldn't mom be proud). So when the price changes by a small percentage, the quantity demanded changes by a large percentage.

### DID YOU GET IT?
If the demand for a good is elastic, would a 10 percent rise in price cause quantity demanded to rise by more than 10 percent, less than 10 percent, or exactly 10 percent?

## Inelastic Demand

If elasticity is less than 1.0, meaning that the quantity demanded changes by a smaller percentage than the price, demand is inelastic. When demand is inelastic, price changes have relatively little effect on the quantity demanded. Goods that are hard to do without, like medicine and heating oil, often have inelastic demand. The price can change a lot for these goods, but the quantity demanded will change very little. For those who are addicted to chocolate—and you know who you are—the demand for chocolate will be inelastic, too.

If a 10 percent rise in the price caused only a 5 percent drop in the quantity demanded, then the elasticity of demand would be 5 percent ÷ 10 percent = 0.5. Since 0.5 is less than 1.0, the demand for chocolate bars would be inelastic.

An extreme case occurs if the elasticity is 0. In this case, a change in the price has no effect on the quantity demanded—the percentage change in quantity demanded is 0. When the price of life-saving surgery increases or decreases, for example, consumers will probably not change the quantity of surgeries they demand.

## Unit-Elastic Demand

The quantity demanded could change by the same percentage as the price. In that case, the elasticity would be equal to 1.0, and demand would be unit-elastic. Demand that is unit-elastic is an "in-between" case, in which demand is neither elastic (with an elasticity greater than 1.0) nor inelastic (with an elasticity less than 1.0). Table 12.2 summarizes the different categories of demand elasticity.

**DID YOU GET IT?**
What elasticity values define the demand for a good as elastic, inelastic, and unit-elastic?

### Table 12.2 **Summary of the Elasticity of Demand**

| TYPE OF DEMAND | MEANING | EXAMPLES | ELASTICITY VALUE | WHY ELASTICITY HAS THIS VALUE |
|---|---|---|---|---|
| Elastic | Demand is very sensitive to price changes. | Airline tickets for vacation travel | Greater than 1.0 | percentage change in quantity > percentage change in price |
| Unit-elastic | Demand is moderately sensitive to price changes. | Soft drinks | Equals 1.0 | percentage change in quantity = percentage change in price |
| Inelastic | Demand is *not* very sensitive to price changes. | Medicine, heating oil | Less than 1.0 | percentage change in quantity < percentage change in price |

## ELASTICITY, TOTAL SPENDING, AND TOTAL REVENUE

One way that economists and business owners use the elasticity of demand is to predict the effect of price changes on the amount of money spent to purchase a good. The total amount consumers spend on a good is also the **total revenue** received by firms. For example, U.S. consumers spent about $25 billion on video games in 2010. Each dollar spent by consumers on video games is a dollar of revenue for the firms that make and sell games and consoles. So in 2010, these firms received about $25 billion in total revenue from selling the games in the United States—the same amount that consumers spent on them.

We can use information on the demand curve for a good to calculate the total revenue that would be received for that good, or equivalently, the total

**Total revenue** is all the money consumers spend on a good, and firms receive for a good, during a particular period of time: it is the price of the good multiplied by the quantity of the good sold.

spending on the good at any price. To find the total revenue at a particular price, we multiply that price by the quantity that would be purchased at that price. That is

total revenue = price × quantity.

Figure 12.4 shows hypothetical demand curves for slices of pie, potted plants, and bottles of soda. At point *A* in each panel, the price is $4 and 100 units are demanded. The total revenue received for each good at a price of $4 is $4 × 100 = $400. This total revenue is represented by the area of the green rectangle in each graph. The area of a rectangle is height times width. So to find the area, we take the height of the rectangle, which is $4, and multiply by the width, which in this case is 100 units. This gives a total revenue of $4 × 100 = $400.

What happens to total revenue when price rises by, say, 25 percent? On the one hand, the rise in price means

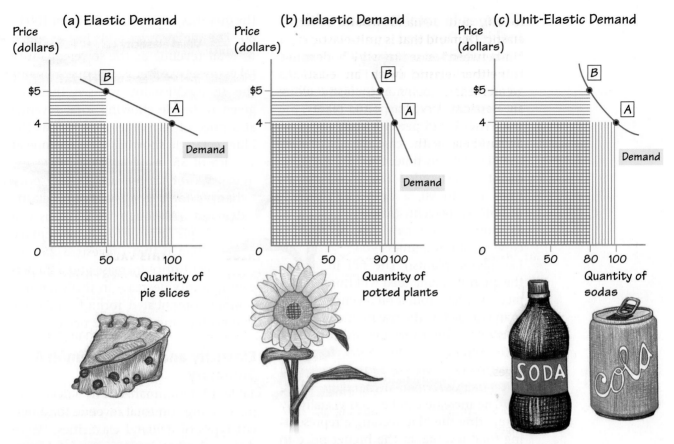

**Figure 12.4** Spending, Revenue, and Elasticity

On a demand graph, the rectangle with the current price as its height and the current quantity demanded as its width shows the size of total revenue. We can see the effect of a price change by comparing the new, blue total revenue to the old, green total revenue in each figure. Panel (a) shows that when demand is elastic, a price increase leads to a decrease in total revenue. Panel (b) shows that when demand is inelastic, a price increase leads to an increase in total revenue. Panel (c) shows that when demand is unit-elastic, a price increase has no effect on total revenue.

that people will spend more on each unit that they buy. If the quantity demanded stayed the same, this would cause total revenue to rise along with the price. On the other hand, with the higher price, people will buy less. The drop in quantity demanded takes away from total revenue. So the 25 percent rise in price could make total revenue rise or fall. Which is it? The answer, as you are about to see, depends on the elasticity of demand for the product.

## Changes in Total Revenue with Elastic Demand

Let's start by considering how a price increase affects total revenue when demand is elastic. Consider panel (a) of

Figure 12.4, where the demand for pie is elastic. As we move from point A to point B, the price of a slice of pie rises by 25 percent from $4 to $5. The quantity demanded falls by 50 percent from 100 slices to 50 slices. What happens to total revenue? The relatively large drop in the quantity demanded will take more away from total revenue than the rise in price adds, so total revenue will fall. It falls from $4 × 100 = $400, as represented by the green rectangle, to $5 × 50 = $250, as represented by the blue rectangle. As expected, because demand is elastic, the rise in price makes total revenue fall.

## Changes in Total Revenue with Inelastic Demand

What if demand is inelastic? We can see this effect in panel (b) of Figure 12.4. As we move from point A to point B along the demand curve for potted plants, the price rises by 25 percent from $4 to $5, as in the case of the pie. But this time, the quantity demanded falls from 100 to 90, a drop of only 10 percent. (After all, potted plants have few close substitutes, unless you like plastic plants!) The fall in the quantity demanded will thus take away less from total revenue than is added by the rise in price. This brings total revenue up from $4 × 100 = $400 to $5 × 90 = $450. Total revenue always increases as the result of a price increase when demand is inelastic. The increase can be seen visually by comparing the blue rectangle representing total revenue at the higher price to the green rectangle representing total revenue at the lower price.

## Constant Total Revenue with Unit-Elastic Demand

What if demand is unit-elastic? Panel (c) of Figure 12.4 shows a unit-elastic demand curve for soda. As we move from point A to point B along the demand curve, the price rises from $4 to $5, and the quantity demanded falls from 100 to 80. The higher price adds just as much to total revenue as the lower quantity takes away, so total revenue remains the same. Visually, we see that the green rectangle showing total revenue at a price of $4 is the same size as the blue rectangle showing total revenue at a price of $5. As always, total revenue remains unchanged when the price changes for a good with unit-elastic demand. (Although we have used a simple formula for the percentage change that suggests a 25 percent price increase and a 20 percent quantity decrease in this example, a more complicated formula indicates that both changes are 22.2 percent.)

## Elasticity and Total Revenue: A Summary

Table 12.3 summarizes the effect of a price change on total revenue for different types of demand elasticities. We've discussed what happens to total revenue when the price rises, which is summarized in the second column of the table. The third column of the table tells us what happens when the price *falls*. Notice that for each type of elasticity, total revenue changes in the opposite direction when price falls compared to when price rises. For example, when demand is inelastic, a drop in price won't increase quantity demanded by much, so total revenue will fall.

| Table 12.3 **Elasticity and Total Revenue** | | |
|---|---|---|
| **TYPE OF DEMAND** | **EFFECT OF PRICE RISE ON TOTAL REVENUE** | **EFFECT OF PRICE DROP ON TOTAL REVENUE** |
| Elastic | ↓ | ↑ |
| Inelastic | ↑ | ↓ |
| Unit Elastic | No change | No change |

# ECONOMICS IN ACTION

# Lowering the Price of TV Downloads

In early 2010, Apple wanted to lower the price it charged on iTunes for downloading TV shows from $1.99 to $0.99 per episode. But Apple first needed permission from the TV networks that supplied the shows. Apple's managers believed that lowering the price would cause so many more people to download shows that total spending on the shows—and the total revenue of the TV networks—would rise. If they were right, the TV networks would come out ahead, and so would Apple, which kept a portion of the sales revenue for itself.

The managers at the TV networks weren't so sure. They agreed that lowering the price would increase the number of downloads, but each download would bring in less money than before. The TV executives worried that the rise in quantity demanded might not make up for the fall in price and that their total revenue would decrease.

Who was right, the managers at Apple or those at the TV networks? In making their case, the Apple managers were essentially arguing that the demand for downloaded TV shows was elastic. If that were true, then the rise in the quantity demanded would more than make up for the lower price, causing an increase in total spending on downloads and the total revenue for the networks and for Apple.

The TV networks, by contrast, were concerned that the demand for downloaded TV shows might be inelastic. If they were right, then the quantity demanded would not rise by enough to make up for the price drop, and total revenue would fall.

In February 2010, the TV networks decided to dip their toes in the water. They gave Apple permission to charge $0.99 for certain shows only, on an experimental basis. Their goal was to determine if demand was elastic or inelastic. Based on the results, they would decide whether to allow Apple to lower the price of all TV shows. Because the networks didn't announce the revenue for specific shows, no one knows for sure how the experiment turned out. But we can make a good guess about the results, because six months after the experiment began, the networks were still charging the higher $1.99 price on almost all their shows. This suggests that the demand for TV downloads was inelastic and that the revenue from the experimental shows fell when the price fell.

*The demand for TV downloads is inelastic. That is, a price change leads to a relatively small change in the quantity of downloads demanded.*

# MODULE 12 REVIEW AND ASSESSMENT

**Summing Up the Key Ideas:** Match the following terms to the correct definitions.

A. Elasticity of demand    C. Inelastic demand    E. Unit-elastic demand    G. Luxury

B. Elastic demand    D. Necessity    F. Total revenue    H. Close substitute

_____ 1. When consumers respond to a given percentage change in price with a smaller percentage change in the quantity demanded, meaning that the elasticity of demand is less than 1.0.

_____ 2. A good that satisfies basic needs.

_____ 3. A measure of how strongly consumers respond to a change in the price of a good, calculated as the percentage change in the quantity demanded divided by the percentage change in price.

_____ 4. A good that people can easily do without.

_____ 5. The price of a good multiplied by the quantity of the good sold.

_____ 6. When consumers respond to a given percentage change in the price with an equivalent percentage change in the quantity demanded, meaning that the elasticity of demand equals 1.0.

_____ 7. When consumers respond to a given percentage change in the price with an even larger percentage change in the quantity demanded, meaning that the elasticity of demand is greater than 1.0.

_____ 8. One good that is very similar to another.

## Analyze and Explain:

1. Using the list of determinants in Table 12.1 indicate whether the demand for each item is likely to be **elastic** or **inelastic**. Then explain your choice.

| | ELASTIC OR INELASTIC? | EXPLANATION |
|---|---|---|
| a. ball point pen | _____ | _____ |
| b. Crest toothpaste | _____ | _____ |
| c. a gallon of water | _____ | _____ |
| d. sugar | _____ | _____ |
| e. a luxury holiday vacation | _____ | _____ |
| f. refrigerator | _____ | _____ |
| g. life-saving medical treatment | _____ | _____ |
| h. diamond ring | _____ | _____ |

2. What does a perfectly elastic demand curve look like?

3. What does a perfectly inelastic demand curve look like?

**Apply:** Based on the following information, determine if the demand in each case is **elastic**, **inelastic**, or **unit-elastic**.

ELASTICITY

1. A grocery store owner finds that her total revenue increases when she lowers the price of fresh produce.

   _____

2. A corner gas station owner finds that his total revenue decreases when he lowers the price of gas.

   _____

3. A music store owner realizes that when the price of CDs increases by 20 percent, there is a 40 percent decline in sales.

   _____

4. A movie theater owner finds that her total revenue stays the same when she raises the price of tickets.

   _____

5. A car dealership owner finds that when he lowers the price of new cars by 10 percent, he experiences a 5 percent increase in sales.

   _____

# PEOPLE IN ECONOMICS

AN INTERVIEW WITH **Jeff Bezos**

*Perhaps more than anyone else, Jeff Bezos, the founder and head of Amazon, can lay claim to having invented e-commerce. Amazon started out as an Internet bookseller and quickly spread into other consumer products. In the following interview, Mr. Bezos explains how economics has influenced his thinking and helped Amazon succeed.\**

**Did you ever take a class in economics?**

The only economics class that I ever took was Econ 101 in college. I did find it very helpful

and very interesting. Economics is sort of a point of view. Do you know the Alan Kay quote "A new point of view is worth 80 IQ points"? Economists have a certain way of thinking about the world. They are able to come to interesting conclusions, sometimes because they can view the world through that particular lens.

For example, you can add scarcity to a customer review system. Right now we let customers give as many five-star reviews as they want, but what if we said that you could give only one gold star per month? That limitation would cause people to behave differently because you've introduced scarcity into the system. That way of thinking can lead to new kinds of inventions.

**Have you studied how the price of goods sold on Amazon affects the quantity that consumers buy?**

We don't like to do active experiments in pricing because that requires charging different prices for the same item at the same time, which erodes trust. But we do look at demand elasticities because prices do change over time, and, if we can figure out ways of holding other variables constant, we can get a certain understanding of customer responses to price changes.

I can tell you that every single time we have done a price elasticity study, it tells us to raise prices—and we never do! It is a very interesting problem because we haven't yet figured out how, in a practical way, to do long-term studies of demand elasticities. So the studies that we are able to do are really measuring short-term customer responses, and we've taken it as an article of faith that the long-run elasticity is bigger than the short-run elasticity, but we can't demonstrate it for sure. Our belief is that offering the lowest price earns trust with customers and generates good business results for us in the long term.

**What determines how much Amazon sells of the various products it offers?**

The big drivers for us are having the lowest price, biggest selection, and fastest, most reliable delivery system. The reason we like to put energy into those three things is because we know they will be true ten years from now. Sometimes I get asked the question "What is going to change in the next ten years?" That

is indeed an interesting question. You can spend some time thinking about that and discussing it. Rarely do I get asked the question "What is *not* going to change in the next ten years?" That second question is actually more important than the first, because you can build a strategy around it.

The things that I know will not change tend to be focused on customer needs. So I know that customers will want low prices ten years from now. I know that they will still want fast delivery. I know that they will still want vast selection.

It's impossible to imagine a scenario where ten years from now customers will say, "I love Amazon, but I just wish they delivered a little more slowly."

We put a lot of energy into having a low-cost structure so that we can offer low prices to customers and a lot of energy into building fulfillment centers and reducing cycle times inside those fulfillment centers so that we can deliver reliably and quickly.

**One thing you didn't mention was advertising. I presume advertising is useful for showing the range of selection. But is advertising an important aspect of what gets sold and what people buy?**

There are different kinds of advertising, of course. Most of our advertising budget is spent on very measurable forms of advertising—online advertising, in particular. We also do some broad-scale advertising. Instead of giving the money to the television networks or other advertising venues, we are giving the money to our customers. An example of that would be *free super saver shipping*. Offering day-in and day-out free shipping is a kind of advertising. It's an expensive program for us, but it is a kind of marketing. Our goal is to ensure that the marginal benefit of each form of advertising exceeds its marginal cost; if not, we would cut back.

## The Economist

# Chevrolet's Centenary

From 0 to 100

### WHY YOU CAN STILL "SEE THE USA IN YOUR CHEVROLET"

Chevrolet, which celebrated its centenary on November 3, 2011, is as woven into the fabric of American culture as Coca-Cola. Not all of its birthdays have been happy, but as it reaches its 100th its prospects are on the up. In the July to September quarter, a record 1.2m cars and pickups with the Chevy "bow-tie" badge on their bonnets were sold worldwide.

In 1911, when William Durant, GM's founder, was [removed] by the company's bankers, he joined forces with Louis Chevrolet, a Swiss-born racing driver, to set up a new carmaker (later folded into GM, when Durant briefly regained control). At $2,150, their first car, the Classic Six, looked pricey next to Henry Ford's $490 Model T. So in 1915 Durant met his rival head on with a model called the 490 and costing the same. Then Chevrolet really started motoring.

By the 1960s, the era of the fabulous, bullet-shaped Corvette Stingray, Chevrolet accounted for about half of GM's 60% share of America's car market. Then the road got bumpy. In the 1970s, its reputation, along with the quality and design of its cars, went into a long tailspin, ending with a bump in GM's bankruptcy and bailout in 2009, when Chevy's market share was just 12.7%. It then dawned on GM's bosses, as Durant realised in 1915, that Chevrolet needed to do better at the smaller end of the market—this time against foreign brands, not local rivals.

Since then a steady stream of attractive small cars has begun to restore Chevrolet's fortunes, such as the Cruze, now America's best-selling compact. Improvements in quality and finish have also been seen across Chevrolet's whole range. But its revamped small-car range is the key to cracking Chevrolet's biggest American challenge: as with its Detroit rivals Ford and Chrysler, its cars sell well in the Midwest but poorly in the coastal cities, especially among the young: Chevy's market share is 23% back home in Michigan but just 6% in California.

Drivers' perceptions may not yet have caught up with the quality of Chevrolet's new line-up. Consumer behaviour research suggests it can take ten years for buyers to respond to such improvements. Most customers quickly narrow their choices down to a shortlist of just three models, though there may be 15 that meet their requirements. A good brand image is what gets a car onto such shortlists.

Although Chevrolet is now cruising along, America's car market is stalling. The Japanese marques may have lost some shine but Chevy faces ever tougher competition at home from Korean and, soon, Chinese small cars.

IFCAR/WIKIMEDIA COMMONS

Fortunately it is now making 60% of its sales outside America—they are growing especially strongly in China and Europe. As Chevrolet enters its second century, it will have to dodge some potholes at home while keeping its foot on the gas elsewhere.

# CHAPTER 4 REVIEW AND SELF-ASSESSMENT

## REVIEW

### Points to Remember

#### MODULE 10: DETERMINING DEMAND

1. The **quantity demanded** is the amount of a good that consumers are willing and able to purchase at a specific price over a given period of time.

2. The **law of demand** is the tendency for the price and the quantity demanded to move in opposite directions. The law of demand applies when the price of a good changes, but all other influences on demand—such as income or tastes—are held constant.

3. **Consumer demand** for goods comes from the consumers' preferences. Consumer demand for goods is limited by their income and the price of goods.

4. A change in the price of a good leads to a **substitution effect** and an **income effect**. The **substitution effect** causes consumers to switch to other goods and reduce the quantity demanded of a good whose price has increased. The **income effect** arises because a consumer feels poorer when the price of a good increases and therefore tends to consume less of all normal goods.

5. A **demand schedule** is a table that shows the quantity of a good that a consumer will buy at various possible prices. A **demand curve** is a graphical summary of the relationship between a good's price and the quantity demanded.

6. We find the **market demand curve** or **schedule** by adding together the quantity demanded by all participants in a market at each particular price. The demand curve slopes downward because of the law of demand: at a higher price, consumers buy less of a good or service.

#### MODULE 11: SHIFTS OF THE DEMAND CURVE

7. Factors other than price affect demand. These factors include tastes, income, the price of related goods, expectations, and the number of buyers in a market. A change in any one of these factors causes a **shift of the demand curve** either to the right or to the left.

8. A **change in demand** for a good refers to a shift of the entire demand curve when something other than the price of the good changes. A **change in the quantity demanded** refers to a *movement along a demand curve*, which occurs when the price of the good changes.

9. An increase in income causes the demand curve to shift to the right for a **normal good** and to the left for an **inferior good**. If the demand curve shifts to the right, more of the good is demanded at every price than was the case before, and if it shifts to the left, less is demanded at every price.

10. **Substitutes** are goods that can take the place of one another, such as tea and coffee. **Complements** are goods that are consumed together, such as hamburgers and hamburger buns. If the price of a substitute good falls, then the demand curve for the other good shifts to the left. If the price of a complement falls, then the demand curve for the other good shifts to the right.

## MODULE 12: ELASTICITY OF DEMAND

11. The responsiveness of the quantity demanded to a change in the price is summarized by the concept of **elasticity of demand**. When elasticity is larger than 1.0, demand is **elastic**, and quantity demanded is more sensitive to price changes. When elasticity is less than 1.0, demand is **inelastic**, and quantity demanded is less sensitive to price changes.

12. In general, demand tends to be **less elastic** (it has a lower elasticity) if the good is a necessity, if it has no close substitutes, if it is inexpensive and purchased so infrequently that consumers don't react to price changes, if the time frame is short, or if it is paid for partly by others.

13. If demand is elastic, a decrease in the price will cause the **total revenue** of sellers to increase. If demand is **inelastic**, a decrease in the price will cause **total revenue** to decrease.

## SELF-ASSESSMENT

The following questions are the type your teacher might ask you on a quiz or a test. Practice with these in order to improve your performance in class.

### Multiple-Choice Questions

The accompanying table provides the demand schedule for movie tickets in a small town. Answer the first three questions based on this table.

| PRICE (DOLLARS) | QUANTITY DEMANDED |
|---|---|
| $5.00 | 10 |
| 4.50 | 15 |
| 4.00 | 20 |
| 3.50 | 25 |
| 3.00 | 30 |
| 2.50 | 35 |

1. As the price of movie tickets falls from $4.50 to $4.00,

   a. the quantity of movie tickets demanded increases from 15 to 20.

   b. the quantity of movie tickets demanded decreases from 20 to 15.

   c. the demand for movie tickets increases.

   d. the demand for movie tickets decreases.

2. When the price changes from $5.00 to $4.50, total revenue

   a. increases from 10 to 15.

   b. decreases from $5.00 to $4.00.

   c. increases from $50.00 to $67.50.

   d. remains the same.

3.  In the price range from $3.00 to $2.50, the demand for movie tickets is

    a.  inelastic.
    b.  unit-elastic.
    c.  elastic.
    d.  unable to be determined from the information given.

4.  If the price of meat rises and consumers purchase more potatoes, then the two goods must be

    a.  substitutes.
    b.  complements.
    c.  inferior.
    d.  normal.

5.  Folklore tells us that pregnant women like to eat ice cream with pickles. If they were the only consumers of both goods, an increase in the price of pickles would

    a.  decrease the demand for pickles.
    b.  increase the demand for ice cream.
    c.  increase the demand for pickles.
    d.  decrease the demand for ice cream.

6.  When the transit authority raises subway fares by 10 percent, ridership falls by 5 percent. What is the price elasticity of demand for subway rides?

    a.  1.0
    b.  0.5
    c.  2.0
    d.  5.0

7.  If a good has many close substitutes, its price elasticity of demand will be

    a.  constant.
    b.  more inelastic than if there existed few close substitutes.
    c.  more elastic than if there existed few close substitutes.
    d.  unit-elastic.

8.  If people eat more restaurant meals when their income increases, meals prepared at home are

    a.  a normal good.
    b.  an inferior good.
    c.  a complement of food eaten at home.
    d.  an exception to the law of demand.

9.  Which of the following correctly describes the substitution effect?

    a.  When the price of a good decreases, consumers buy less of it because they substitute other goods whose prices haven't decreased.
    b.  When the price of a good increases, consumers buy less of it because they substitute other goods that have become relatively less expensive.
    c.  When the price of a good decreases, consumers buy the same amount of it because they ignore the prices of other goods.
    d.  When the price of a good increases, consumers buy more of it because they substitute other goods whose prices haven't increased.

10. Which of the following will increase the demand for economics textbooks?

    a.  a decrease in the price of economics textbooks
    b.  a decrease in the incomes of economics textbook consumers
    c.  a decrease in the number of students taking economics classes
    d.  a decrease in tuition for economics classes, a complementary good for economics textbooks

## Constructed Response Question

1.  Draw a market demand curve for oranges based on the following demand schedule. Be certain to correctly label your graph.

    a.  How does your graph support the law of demand? Explain.
    b.  Suppose you expect that the price of oranges will decrease in the near future. What effect does this have on your graph?

c.  Calculate the total revenue when the price of oranges is $1.50.

d.  Is the demand for oranges elastic, inelastic, or unit-elastic in the price range of $1.50 to $1.75? Explain.

| PRICE PER POUND OF ORANGES (DOLLARS) | POUNDS OF ORANGES DEMANDED |
|---|---|
| $1.00 | 4,000 |
| 1.25 | 3,500 |
| 1.50 | 3,000 |
| 1.75 | 2,500 |
| 2.00 | 2,000 |

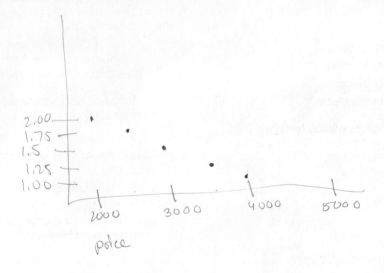

**CHAPTER 5** & **YOU** Perhaps you already supply services such as baby-sitting, yard work, or lifeguarding. In the future you may supply goods or services as the owner of your own business. In each case you must decide how much to supply. How do the suppliers of everything from soap to dog food decide how much of their products to supply? Price is a key consideration. It's helpful to understand the connection between the price of a good and the quantity suppliers offer for sale. If the price increases, it's likely that suppliers will make more available for you to buy. Sometimes it's better to have *less* of something available for sale. If you want to save endangered elephants, you want lower ivory prices, which will lead to less poaching by elephant hunters. And if you ever manage a business, you'll benefit from knowing how prices can inform decisions about how much of your product to put up for sale in order to earn as much profit as possible.

# The Supply of Goods and Services

## THE *P*'S AND *Q*'S OF HOW THE GARDEN GROWS

Popcorn has been a popular snack food since long before Columbus came to America. Corn is also fed to cattle and pigs for beef and pork production. Increasingly, corn is also used to produce ethanol, an additive to gasoline and an alternative fuel for cars. Farmers in every state except Alaska and Hawaii grow large quantities of corn.

Between 2005 and 2008, something big happened with corn: its price tripled from about $2 per bushel to more than $6. As a result, farmers found it more profitable to grow corn than other crops. Many farmers stopped growing wheat and instead planted corn. Some plots of land that were not being used to grow crops were planted with corn seed. In addition, farmers applied more fertilizer to existing corn fields and used better seeds to increase their yields. All these efforts caused the quantity of corn supplied in the market to increase by 25 percent in just a few years.

This chapter explains how the price, along with things such as improved production methods, affects the availability of a good.

## BOTTOM LINE

Firms strive to make as much profit as possible. To do so, they adjust the quantity of the good or service they produce in response to changes in either the price at which it can be sold or the cost of producing it.

(C)ISTOCKPHOTO /THINKSTOCK

# MODULE 13

# Understanding Supply

**KEY IDEA:** Producers respond to price changes, offering more goods for sale when prices increase and fewer goods when prices decrease.

**OBJECTIVES**

- To explain the concept of supply and the law of supply.
- To explain the relationship between a supply schedule and a supply curve.
- To identify the factors that cause the quantity supplied to be more or less responsive to price changes.

## The Draw of High Coffee Prices

As the price of fancy coffee drinks has increased, so has their availability. The caffeine craze fueled by Starbucks has brought in Caribou Coffee, Gimme Coffee, Biggby Coffee, and hundreds of others. Even McDonald's and Dunkin' Donuts now sell premium coffee. Low prices have the opposite effect. For example, as the prices paid for homes fall, so does the quantity supplied by construction companies. To examine the relationship between prices and the quantity offered for sale is to study *supply*. In this module we explore the supply decisions of firms.

## THE QUANTITY SUPPLIED

**Profit** is the total revenue a firm receives from selling its product minus the total cost of producing it.

The owners of most firms want to make as much *profit* as possible. **Profit** is the total revenue a firm receives from selling its product minus the total cost of producing it. We're going to see how managers can maximize profit by using information on price and production costs to determine how much of their product to put up for sale. Initially we'll make the assumption that production costs remain unchanged and focus on how price changes influence the *quantity supplied*.

The **quantity supplied** is the amount of a good that firms are willing to supply at a particular price over a given period of time.

To economists, the **quantity supplied** means the quantity of a good or service that firms would be willing to sell at a particular price over a given period of time, such as a day. The quantity supplied of bottled drinking water, for example, is the number of bottles firms would make available for sale each day at a particular price. The quantity supplied is measured in physical units, which could be bottles, gallons, bushels, slices, or pounds, depending on the good.

**? DID YOU GET IT?**
What do economists mean by the *quantity supplied?*

## THE LAW OF SUPPLY

In general, as shown in Figure 13.1, if the price of a good rises, the quantity supplied by firms will increase. If the price falls, the quantity supplied by firms will decrease. This tendency for the price and the quantity supplied to

TIM BOYLE/GETTY IMAGES

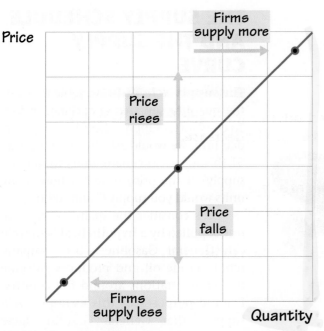

**Figure 13.1** The Law of Supply
The tendency for the price and the quantity supplied to move in the same direction is known as the law of supply.

move in the same direction is known as the **law of supply**. For example, at a price of about $2 per bottle, firms in the United States produce and sell about 85 million bottles of water each day. If they could receive $3 per bottle, they would be willing to produce more—perhaps 100 million bottles.

Why are firms willing to produce more of a good when its price rises? Because as production increases, the cost of making each additional unit generally rises, so it takes a higher price to cover the higher cost of making additional units. Imagine you're in the business of making skateboards by hand. You can produce more skateboards each day by spending more of your time making them. As you devote more time to production, the opportunity cost of your time increases because you must give up increasingly important activities in your day. You can make one skateboard in the time you would otherwise spend watching TV reruns. Making a second skateboard would take up your study time. Making a third would cause you to lose several hours of sleep. You might make one skateboard for a low price, but

you would require a higher price in exchange for the higher opportunity costs of making the second and third skateboards. Later in this chapter we'll discuss why the cost of making additional units of a good tends to rise even if new workers are hired to carry out the production.

## When Does the Law of Supply Apply?

Soon you'll see that many factors affect the supply of a good. These factors include input costs, government policies, and production methods. Like the law of demand, the law of supply applies under the *ceteris paribus* condition that these other influences remain unchanged when the price of the good changes. If there are changes in these other influences, you might mistakenly think you see violations of the law of supply all the time. Suppose, for example, you observe that the price of skateboards is higher this year than last year, and yet fewer skateboards are available for sale this year. This would not be a violation of the law of supply if the price

According to the **law of supply**, an increase in the price of a good leads to an increase in the quantity supplied.

The law of supply holds when only the price of the good changes. So if plywood prices rise substantially, an increase in the price of skateboards might not correspond with an increase in the quantity of skateboards supplied.

The **supply schedule** for a good is a table listing the quantity of the good that will be supplied at specified prices.

of plywood increased over the same period or if new government regulations required costly safety inspections of each skateboard, thus increasing the cost of production. The law of supply applies in the hypothetical situation in which the price of skateboards changes but there is no change in the price of plywood, the existence of regulations, or any other influence on supply.

# THE SUPPLY SCHEDULE AND THE SUPPLY CURVE

The **supply schedule** is a table that lists the quantity supplied at specified prices. To construct a supply schedule for a particular firm, we would ask, "If the price were $1 this week, how many units would you supply? If the price were $2, how many units would you supply?" and so on.

Let's consider the quantity of gasoline supplied by a hypothetical firm we'll call General Gasoline. This company refines crude oil and produces gasoline for service stations around the country. For the purposes of this example we'll suppose that General Gasoline faces many competitors selling identical gasoline. The table in Figure 13.2 is a supply schedule for General Gasoline. At a price of just $1.50 per gallon, the firm is unwilling to produce any gasoline; it would rather shut down its refinery. At a price of $2.00, however, General Gasoline is willing to produce and sell 5,000 gallons of gasoline per week. If the price were to rise to $2.50, it would be willing to sell 10,000 gallons, and so on. The

**Figure 13.2** The Supply Schedule and the Supply Curve for General Gasoline
The supply schedule indicates the quantity supplied at various prices. The supply curve is a graphical representation of the supply schedule.

## Supply Schedule for General Gasoline

| PRICE (DOLLARS) | QUANTITY OF GASOLINE SUPPLIED (GALLONS) |
| --- | --- |
| $1.50 | 0 |
| 2.00 | 5,000 |
| 2.50 | 10,000 |
| 3.00 | 15,000 |
| 3.50 | 20,000 |

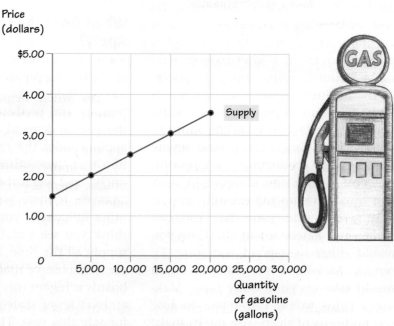

The Supply Curve for General Gasoline

supply schedule lists the amount of gasoline the company would offer for sale at various prices.

### The Firm's Supply Curve

The **supply curve** for a firm is a graphical representation of the supply schedule, showing the quantity supplied at each price. Next to the supply schedule in Figure 13.2 we display the supply curve based on the same information. In this example, the supply "curve" is a straight line, but as with the demand curve, the supply curve can be straight or curved.

The vertical axis of the supply curve graph indicates the price of each unit of the good. In this example it measures the price per gallon of gasoline. The horizontal axis indicates the quantity of the good—the gallons of gasoline in this case. The supply curve shows the amount the producer is willing to sell at each price. Notice that the supply curve slopes upward from left to right. The upward slope of the supply curve is a graphical representation of the law of supply that you learned about earlier: at a higher price, the company is willing to supply more gasoline.

**DID YOU GET IT?**
What is a firm's supply schedule? How does a supply schedule relate to a supply curve?

## THE MARKET SUPPLY CURVE

So far we have considered the supply curve of just one firm, General Gasoline. However, as in most cases, many firms supply the same good. The **market supply curve** is a graphical representation of the quantity supplied at various prices by all firms in the market. To determine the market supply schedule and draw the associated market supply curve, we add up the quantity supplied by each firm in the market at each price. As a simple example, imagine there are just two firms supplying gasoline: General Gasoline and National Gasoline. Figure

13.3 provides the supply schedules for each firm. The supply curves based on these schedules are illustrated in panels (a) and (b) of Figure 13.3.

At a price of $2.50, General Gasoline would supply 10,000 gallons, as shown by point *A* in panel (a). At the same price, National Gasoline would supply 12,000 gallons, as shown by point *B* in panel (b). The total quantity supplied to the market at a price of $2.50 would thus be 10,000 + 12,000 = 22,000 gallons, as indicated by point *C* on the market supply curve in panel (c).

Notice that the market supply curve—just like the supply curve for each individual firm—obeys the law of supply. That is, when the price rises, the quantity supplied to the market rises. For example, as the price rises from $2.00 to $2.50 per gallon, the quantity supplied to the market rises from 11,000 to 22,000 gallons. As with the demand curve, a rise in the price does not cause the supply curve itself to move. Instead, it causes a movement *along* the supply curve, to a new point on the same curve.

**DID YOU GET IT?**
What is the market supply curve?

## MARKETS WITH SUPPLY CURVES

Some types of markets have no supply curve because the relationship between the price and the quantity supplied changes when demand changes. For example, this is the case for a *monopoly* as discussed in Chapter 8. Supply schedules and curves as discussed in this module exist under conditions of *perfect competition*. There is **perfect competition** among firms in a market when four conditions are met:

**1.** Every unit of the good sold in the market is identical, regardless of which firm is selling it.

**2.** The good is produced by many firms, none of which is large enough to influence the price of the good.

A firm's **supply curve** is a graphical representation of the supply schedule, showing the quantity the firm will supply at each price.

The **market supply curve** is a graphical representation of the quantity supplied at various prices by all firms in the market.

There is **perfect competition** in a market when there are many firms selling identical goods, firms are free to enter and exit the market, and consumers have full information about the price and availability of goods.

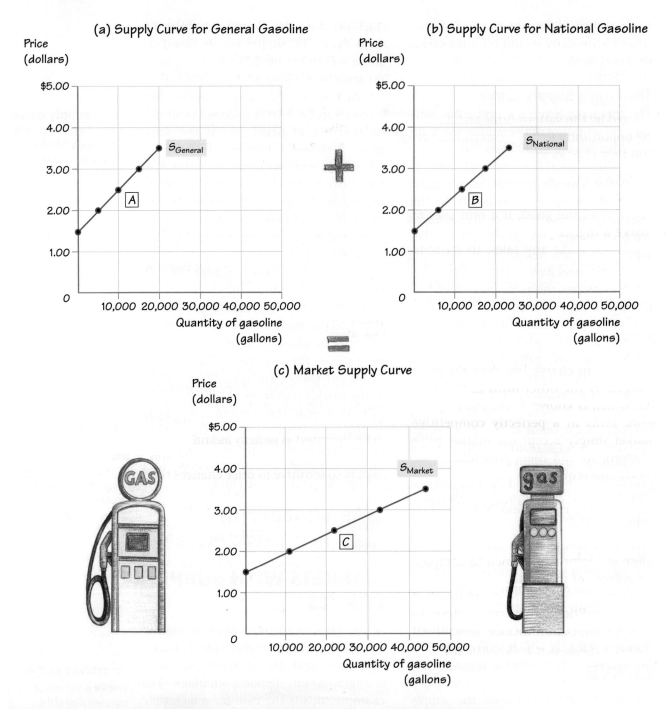

(a) Supply Curve for General Gasoline

(b) Supply Curve for National Gasoline

(c) Market Supply Curve

| PRICE (DOLLARS) | QUANTITY OF GASOLINE SUPPLIED (GALLONS) | QUANTITY SUPPLIED BY NATIONAL GASOLINE (GALLONS) | MARKET QUANTITY SUPPLIED (GALLONS) |
|---|---|---|---|
| $1.50 | 0 | 0 | 0 |
| 2.00 | 5,000 | 6,000 | 11,000 |
| 2.50 | 10,000 | 12,000 | 22,000 |
| 3.00 | 15,000 | 18,000 | 33,000 |
| 3.50 | 20,000 | 24,000 | 44,000 |

**Figure 13.3** The Market Supply Curve
The market supply is found by adding the quantity supplied by each firm at each price.

**3.** New firms that want to supply the good are free to enter the market, and existing firms that want to stop supplying it are free to exit the market.

**4.** Consumers are aware of the price charged by the various firms and have the opportunity to buy from whichever firm they choose.

When perfect competition exists, individual firms have no control over the price of the good. If a firm tries to charge a higher price than other firms, it will not make any sales. Its customers will buy from the competitors who sell the exact same good at a lower price. Perfect competition drives the price down until a lower price would prevent the firms from covering their costs. This removes any temptation for a firm to charge less than the price charged by the other firms in the market, which is known as the *market price*. Since firms in a perfectly competitive market simply accept the market price as given, we call them *price takers*. The conditions required for perfect competition are simplifications of reality—few markets truly meet them. Yet they permit us to make useful economic models that resemble reality and provide a reference point from which to compare other types of markets.

Examples of goods that are supplied under conditions that come close to perfect competition include agricultural products, such as wheat, corn, and cotton. These goods are similar regardless of which farm supplies them, and they are produced by thousands of farms.

**DID YOU GET IT?**
**What conditions are required for perfect competition among firms?**

# ELASTICITY OF SUPPLY

In Chapter 4, you learned that the elasticity of demand measures how responsive consumers are to price changes. Likewise, the **elasticity of supply** measures how responsive firms are to price changes. Specifically, the elasticity of supply is the percentage change in the quantity supplied divided by the percentage change in the price.

Sometimes the quantity supplied is not very sensitive to price changes. For example, if you have little else to do on a Friday night, you might be willing to supply about the same number of baby-sitting hours whether you are paid $7 an hour or $12 an hour. When the quantity supplied changes by a smaller percentage than the price, the elasticity of supply is less than 1.0 and supply is considered to be *inelastic*.

Panel (a) of Figure 13.4 shows a hypothetical inelastic supply curve for pizza. A 50 percent rise in the price, from $10 to $15, causes only a 25 percent rise in the quantity supplied, from 100 to 125. The elasticity of supply for this price change is 25 percent ÷ 50 percent = 0.5. Because this elasticity value is less than 1.0, pizza supply is inelastic. The most extreme case of inelastic supply is a vertical supply curve, which has a supply elasticity of 0 and is described as *perfectly inelastic*.

For many goods the quantity supplied is so sensitive to price changes that it changes by a *larger* percentage than the price. In these cases the elasticity of supply is greater than 1.0 and supply is *elastic*. Elastic supply is illustrated in panel (b) of Figure 13.4. Along that supply curve, the same 50 percent rise in the price of pizza from $10 to $15 causes the quantity supplied to rise by 100 percent, from 100 to 200. The elasticity of supply here is 100 percent ÷ 50 percent = 2.0.

The **elasticity of supply** is a measure of the responsiveness of the quantity supplied to price changes, calculated by dividing the percentage change in the quantity supplied by the percentage change in price.

*The market for corn is very competitive because many farms sell corn and all corn is pretty much the same.*

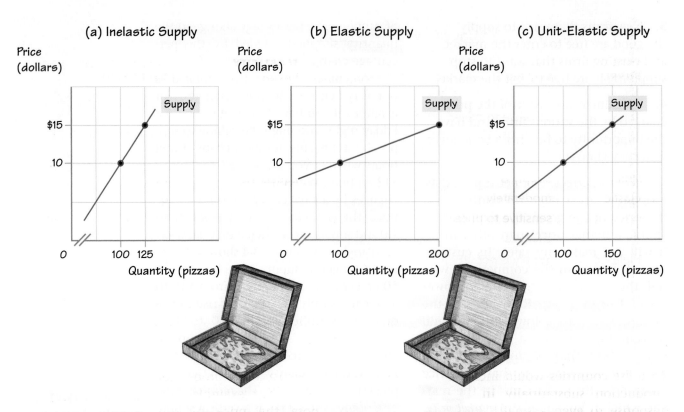

**Figure 13.4** Elasticity of Supply
If the quantity supplied doesn't change very much when the price changes, as in panel (a), supply is inelastic. If the quantity supplied is very responsive to price changes, as in panel (b), supply is elastic. If the quantity supplied changes by the same percentage as the price, supply is unit-elastic.

Because the elasticity is greater than 1.0, supply is elastic. The most extreme case of elastic supply is a horizontal supply curve, which has an infinite supply elasticity and is described as *perfectly elastic*.

If the quantity supplied is moderately sensitive to price changes, such that the percentage change in the quantity supplied is the same as the percentage change in the price, the elasticity of supply is 1.0 and supply is *unit-elastic*. Panel (c) of Figure 13.4 illustrates unit-elastic supply. Here, the 50 percent rise in price from $10 to $15 causes the quantity supplied to rise by 50 percent, from 100 to 150. The elasticity of supply in panel (c) is 50 percent ÷ 50 percent = 1.0, so supply is unit-elastic. Table 13.1 summarizes the various types of supply elasticity.

**DID YOU GET IT?**

What is the elasticity of supply? What does it mean for supply to be elastic? Inelastic? Unit-elastic?

## Production Costs and the Elasticity of Supply

What determines the elasticity of supply? In large part, it depends on how costly it is for firms to increase production. When it is difficult or expensive to make more of something, even a large price increase will not cause the quantity supplied to increase by very much. The supply of gold, for example, is inelastic because it is very costly for firms to find and extract more gold. If the price of gold rises by 10 percent, the quantity of gold supplied will rise by less than 10 percent.

In contrast, the supply of T-shirts is elastic because it is cheap and easy to produce more T-shirts. Firms in countries around the world, including India, Sri Lanka, Mexico, Turkey, and China, have the equipment needed to produce T-shirts by the truckload. They also have plenty of cotton, the key input for making T-shirts. Firms

**Table 13.1 Elasticity of Supply Summary Table**

| TYPE OF SUPPLY | MEANING | EXAMPLE | ELASTICITY VALUE | WHY ELASTICITY HAS THIS VALUE |
|---|---|---|---|---|
| Elastic | Supply is very sensitive to price changes | T-shirts, cookies | Greater than 1.0 | Percentage change in quantity supplied > percentage change in price |
| Unit-elastic | Supply is moderately sensitive to price changes | Fresh fish | Equals 1.0 | Percentage change in quantity supplied = percentage change in price |
| Inelastic | Supply is *not* very sensitive to price changes | Gold, houses | Less than 1.0 | Percentage change in quantity supplied < percentage change in price |

in these countries would increase production substantially in response to even a small rise in price. If the price of T-shirts rose by 10 percent, the number of T-shirts supplied to the market would rise by more than 10 percent.

## Time and the Elasticity of Supply

Time is another factor that determines the elasticity of supply. When the price of a good rises, firms can increase their production by more after they have time to adjust their production facilities. For example, suppose the price of running shoes increases. Over time, firms that make running shoes can expand their factories and install new assembly lines to increase their production. But factory space and assembly lines cannot be adjusted right away. So we generally expect supply to become more elastic as time passes after the price change. Figure 13.5 summarizes the influences on supply elasticity.

**Figure 13.5** Interpreting the Elasticity of Supply
Supply is inelastic when additional output is much more costly to produce. This is often the case when firms have little time in which to respond to a price change. Supply is elastic when additional output doesn't cost much more to produce. This is more likely when firms have a long period of time to respond to price changes.

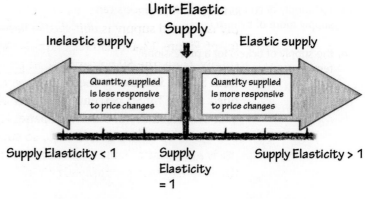

# MODULE 13 REVIEW AND ASSESSMENT

## Summing Up the Key Ideas: Match the following terms to the correct definitions.

A. Profit
B. Quantity supplied
C. Unit-elastic supply
D. Elastic supply

E. Supply schedule
F. Supply curve
G. Market supply curve
H. Elasticity of supply

I. Law of supply
J. Inelastic supply
K. Perfect competition

_____ 1. A condition that exists when every unit of the good sold in the market is identical, the good is produced by many firms, new firms are free to enter the market, existing firms are free to exit the market, and consumers are aware of the prices charged by the various firms.

_____ 2. The tendency for the price and quantity supplied to move in the same direction.

_____ 3. When the quantity supplied is moderately sensitive to price changes, such that the percentage change in the quantity supplied is the same as the percentage change in the price.

_____ 4. A graphical representation of the supply schedule, showing the quantity supplied at each price.

_____ 5. The total revenue a firm receives from selling its product minus the total cost of producing it.

_____ 6. Measures how responsive firms are to price changes.

_____ 7. When the quantity supplied is so sensitive to price changes that it changes by a larger percentage than the price.

_____ 8. A table that lists the quantity supplied at specified prices.

_____ 9. A graphical representation of the quantity supplied by all firms in the market at various prices.

_____ 10. The quantity of a good or service that firms would be willing and able to sell at a particular price over a given period of time.

_____ 11. When the quantity supplied changes by a smaller percentage than the price.

## Analyze and Explain: In the following situations, identify if the supply is **elastic** or **inelastic** and then provide an explanation for your answer.

| | ELASTIC OR INELASTIC? | EXPLANATION |
|---|---|---|
| 1. the supply of houses | _____ | _____ |
| 2. the supply of a service such as car washing | _____ | _____ |
| 3. the supply of computers, which producers can supply more of by next year | _____ | _____ |
| 4. the supply of tickets for a professional tennis match | _____ | _____ |

**Apply:** In each of the following, determine if the good is being supplied in a **perfectly competitive** market or not.

PERFECT COMPETITION OR NOT?

1. Every unit of the good sold in the market is identical, regardless of which firm is selling it.

    _____

2. New firms that want to supply the good are not allowed to enter the market, and existing firms that want to stop supplying are not allowed to exit the market.

    _____

3. Many firms produce the good.

    _____

4. Consumers find it difficult to obtain information about the prices being charged by various firms in the market and therefore have great difficulty shopping.

    _____

5. No one firm that has any influence over the price of the product.

    _____

6. Consumers have the opportunity to buy the product from any seller they choose.

    _____

# MODULE 14

# Shifts of the Supply Curve

**KEY IDEA:** The supply curve can shift because of changes in the cost of inputs, government policies, the number of firms, technology, weather, and expectations about future prices.

## OBJECTIVES

- **To differentiate between a movement along the supply curve and a shift of the supply curve.**
- **To explain how changes in factors other than price cause the supply curve to shift.**
- **To recognize which types of changes cause the supply curve to shift to the left or to the right.**

## Shaking Up the Supply Curve

In the 1950s, Ray Kroc sold milkshake machines that allowed one worker to make five milkshakes at once. These machines reduced the cost of making milkshakes by allowing restaurants to hire fewer workers. Among Kroc's customers were Dick and Mac McDonald, who used eight of his machines at their hamburger stand. Kroc became so impressed with Dick and Mac's business that he bought it for himself and started a worldwide restaurant chain. If you visit one of the McDonald's restaurants that are his legacy, you'll see many more examples of cost-saving devices. One is a computer that makes french fries so easy to cook that almost anyone can do it—while taking an order from the drive-through window at the same time! In this module we'll explore how changes such as these innovations in the production process affect the supply curve.

## WHEN OTHER FACTORS CHANGE

A **shift of the supply curve** is the result of a change in the quantity supplied at every price, not to be confused with a movement along the supply curve, which is the result of a change in the price.

We've seen that an increase in the price of pizza from, say, $10 to $15, causes the quantity supplied to increase. That is a movement along the pizza supply curve, as from point *A* to point *B* in Figure 14.1. In that case, only the price and the quantity offered for sale change. When we look at how price changes affect the quantity supplied, we make the *ceteris paribus* assumption that everything else that could influence the quantity supplied remains the same.

But sometimes pizza shops become willing to supply more pizzas for $10 than before, and more for $15 than before, and more at every other price than before. If the quantity firms are willing to supply changes at every price, there is a **shift of the supply curve**. This is represented by the shift from Supply₁ to Supply₂ in Figure 14.1. A shift of the supply curve is always the result of something other than a change in the price of the good, such as a change in production costs. Depending on the situation, the supply curve can shift to the left or to the right. After shifting, the supply curve

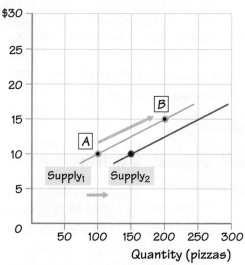

**Figure 14.1** Movement along the Supply Curve versus a Shift of the Supply Curve A change in the price causes a change in the quantity supplied. This is represented by a movement along the supply curve, as from point A to point B. A change in the quantity firms are willing to supply at every price causes the supply curve to shift, as from Supply₁ to Supply₂. The result is a change in supply.

will continue to slope upward because a higher price will still cause firms to supply more of their good to the market.

When the supply curve shifts, we call the corresponding change in the amount firms are willing to supply at every price a **change in supply**. If it is necessary to pick up your pencil and draw another supply curve to the right or left of the initial one to illustrate a particular change, there has been a change in supply. By contrast, when the price changes, you can illustrate the change by sliding the point of your pencil along the original supply curve—up the curve in the case of a price increase and down the curve in the case of a price decrease. This movement *along* the supply curve represents a **change in the quantity supplied** but not a change in supply.

## FACTORS THAT SHIFT THE SUPPLY CURVE

In this section, we consider the factors that can cause a change in supply—a shift of the entire supply curve. These factors include the cost of inputs, government policy, the number of firms supplying the good, technological change, natural disasters and bad weather, and expectations about a good's future price.

### The Cost of Inputs

To produce goods, firms must pay for inputs such as raw materials and workers. If the costs of these inputs change, there will be a change in supply. The cost of inputs can change for many reasons, including new discoveries of raw materials, changes in the rental costs of buildings and equipment, tax changes, wars, and modified production techniques. Higher input costs shift supply curves to the left, because when it becomes more expensive to produce a good, firms will supply fewer units at any given price. When inputs become less expensive, supply curves shift to the right, because firms will supply more units at any given price.

For example, if workers at gasoline refineries are successful in negotiating higher wages, the supply curve for gasoline will shift to the left. This decrease in supply is shown in panel (a) of Figure 14.2. The original supply curve is labeled *Supply₁*, and the new supply curve is labeled *Supply₂*. At every price, firms are willing to supply a lower quantity because it now costs them more to hire each worker. We can see an example of this by comparing point *A* on the original supply curve to point *B* on the new supply curve. At point *A* on *Supply₁*, 300 million gallons of gasoline are supplied

When the supply curve shifts, this is called a **change in supply**.

When there is a movement along the supply curve, this is called a **change in the quantity supplied**.

at a price of $3.50 per gallon, but at point *B* on *Supply₂*, only 200 million gallons are supplied at the same price.

Suppose that instead of wages rising, they fall as a result of a large number of unemployed workers desperate for jobs. This lowers input costs and causes the supply curve for gasoline to shift to the right. This increase in supply is shown in panel (b) of Figure 14.2. Again, the original supply curve is labeled *Supply₁* and the new supply curve is labeled *Supply₂*. At every price, more is supplied because the cost of producing gasoline has gone down. For example, at point *A* on *Supply₁*, firms supply 300 million gallons at a price of $3.50 per gallon. After the shift to *Supply₂*, point *B* shows that 400 million gallons will be supplied at the same price.

## Government Policies

Government policies can change the cost of producing a good, or they can change the amount of money that suppliers receive for selling their goods. In either case, the government's actions can cause supply curves to shift. Government policies include taxes, regulations, and subsidies.

**Figure 14.2** Shifts of the Market Supply Curve **(a)** Higher wages cause input costs to rise and shift the supply curve to the left. **(b)** Lower wages cause input costs to fall and shift the supply curve to the right.

## Taxes

Government raises tax revenue to pay for national defense, schools, roads, and other vital goods and services. Taxes can cause a shift of the supply curve. Suppose that the government collects a tax of 40 cents per pack from suppliers of gum. If a pack of gum is sold for $1, the government gets 40 cents and gum suppliers keep only 60 cents. Because of the tax, the company receives less revenue from selling gum at any given price. The added expense of the tax causes the supply curve for bubble gum to shift to the left, much like the supply curve for gasoline shifted to the left in panel (a) of Figure 14.2.

## Regulations

Regulations place restrictions on firms and individuals. For example, regulations require that children's sleepwear be made of flame-resistant material. This prevents firms from using lower-cost material that might endanger children who come too close to a candle, match, lighter, or fireplace. These regulations—while helping avoid injuries and death—also raise the cost of producing children's sleepwear and shift the supply curve to the left.

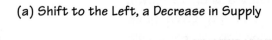

### (a) Shift to the Left, a Decrease in Supply

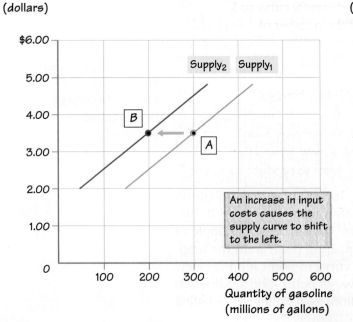

An increase in input costs causes the supply curve to shift to the left.

### (b) Shift to the Right, an Increase in Supply

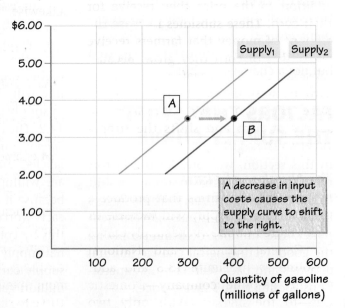

A decrease in input costs causes the supply curve to shift to the right.

## ECONOMICS IN ACTION

# How Wars Shift Supply Curves

Wars that involve oil-producing countries, including the Iran-Iraq War in the 1980s, the Persian Gulf War in the early 1990s, and the Iraq War in the 2000s, tend to disrupt shipments of crude oil and cause its price to rise. Crude oil is the main input used to make gasoline. When crude oil prices rise, input costs rise for gasoline suppliers. This causes the supply curve for gasoline to shift to the left.

But crude oil is an important input for many other goods besides gasoline. For example, plastic is made from oil. When the price of oil rises, so does the cost of making plastic products, such as grocery bags, soda bottles, and the interior panels on cars. When wars cause oil prices to soar, these goods become more expensive to produce, so the supply curves for these and other plastic products shift to the left.

*War can decrease the supply of oil.*

## Subsidies

A *subsidy* is a payment made by the government to support a particular activity or good. For example, the federal government subsidizes the production of corn in a variety of ways, including paying some farmers a subsidy in addition to the price they receive for their corn. These subsidies increase the amount of money that farmers receive per bushel of corn they grow. Because subsidies raise the profit that farmers earn from supplying corn at a given price, the corn subsidy increases the supply of corn and shifts the supply curve to the right.

## The Number of Firms

If the number of firms that produce a good increases, supply will increase as well. Figure 14.3 shows the supply curves for General Gasoline and National Gasoline as in Figure 13.3 and adds a third gasoline company—Domestic Gas—to the market. With only two suppliers, the market supply curve was $S_{\text{Without Domestic}}$. The new market supply curve is found by adding the quantity supplied at each price by Domestic Gas to the quantity supplied by the other two firms. The result is a rightward shift of the market supply curve to $S_{\text{With Domestic}}$. Likewise, if the number of firms producing a good decreases, the supply curve will shift to the left.

## Technological Change

*Technology* refers to the methods used to create goods and services from inputs. The discovery of a new production method that enables firms to produce more goods from the same inputs—or from new, less costly inputs—is called *technological progress*. When technological progress occurs, firms' costs decrease and production becomes more profitable. At any price for the good, firms will want to produce more than before. This causes the supply curve to shift rightward.

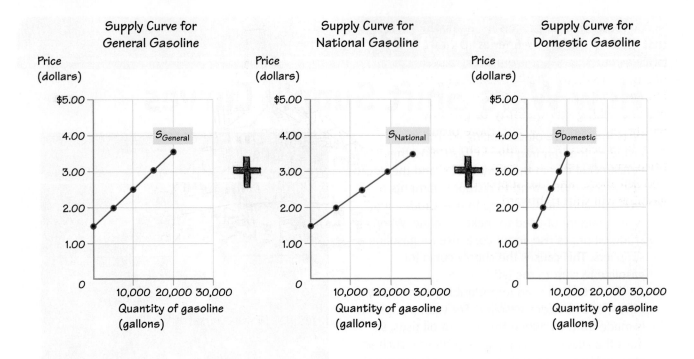

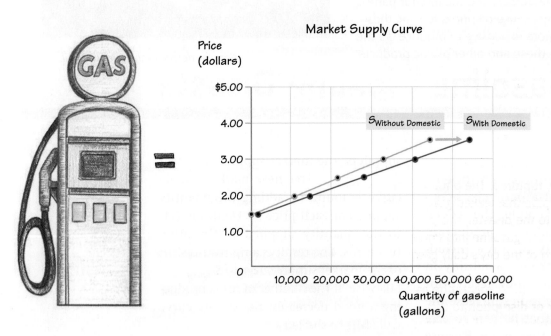

**Figure 14.3** Market Supply with Three Firms
When new firms enter the market, supply increases and
the supply curve shifts to the right.

Suppose that a process is invented that enables gasoline refineries to make twice as much gasoline from every barrel of crude oil as before while using the same amount of all other inputs. Then producing and selling any quantity of gasoline will become less costly, and more profitable, than before. As a result, at any given price, gasoline firms will want to produce and sell more, and the supply curve for gasoline will shift rightward.

**DID YOU GET IT?**

**Why does technological progress cause a shift of the supply curve? In what direction does the supply curve shift because of technological progress?**

*"Yes, the business has become bigger, but Fred still likes to work at home"*

## ECONOMICS IN ACTION

# The Gasoline Pipeline Disaster in Arizona

On July 30, 2003, a major gasoline pipeline to Phoenix, Arizona, ruptured. The photograph shows the burst pipe that leaked gasoline into the desert. Prior to the disaster, this pipeline fed 2.2 million gallons of gasoline into Phoenix every day—about a third of the city's daily gasoline consumption.

We can think of this catastrophe as a temporary *shock* or disruption to technology. Why? After the rupture, gasoline suppliers could no longer use the pipeline. Instead, they trucked gas into Phoenix. Moving gas required the use of more inputs—trucks, diesel fuel for the trucks, and labor. Due to the added expense of delivering gas, the quantity suppliers would supply at each price decreased. As a result, the pipeline rupture led to a decrease in supply and the supply curve for gas in Phoenix shifted leftward. As you'll see in the next chapter, the pipeline disaster had a major impact on the market for gasoline in Phoenix.

*A break in a major gasoline pipeline to Phoenix, Arizona, disrupted the supply and caused the gasoline supply curve to shift to the left.*

*The earthquake and tsunami that hit Japan in 2011 caused catastrophic damages that shifted the supply curve leftward for many products.*

**Inventory** consists of goods that are held in temporary storage.

### Natural Disasters and Weather

Natural disasters and unusually bad weather have the opposite effect of technological progress. These events require some types of firms to use *more* inputs to produce any given quantity of their goods and thus cause the supply curve to shift to the *left*. For example, during a drought, orange growers will have to pay for greater amounts of water to irrigate their groves. Because the cost of producing each orange has increased, growers will want to produce fewer oranges at any given price. So the supply curve for oranges shifts to the left as a result of a drought.

Similarly, natural disasters make it more costly to produce some types of goods, thereby shifting their supply curves leftward. The earthquake and tsunami that struck Japan in 2011 disrupted rail and highway transportation and cut off the supply of electricity to many homes and businesses. Some Japanese firms used more expensive power generators to replace electricity from power utilities. The transportation of inputs and goods became more costly as firms followed longer travel routes to bypass the affected areas. The disasters even caused the Toyota Motor Corporation to temporarily close several factories. This reduced the quantity of cars supplied to the United States by more than 40,000 units. In 2005, Hurricane Katrina caused similar spikes in transportation and energy costs in the United States, crippling many businesses. And massive floods in Australia in 2011 shifted the supply curve for the global steel market leftward, as floods disrupted the supply of Australian coal and raised the cost of this important input for steel production.

### Expectations about Future Prices

Unlike perishable goods such as tomatoes and milk, goods such as light bulbs and dishwashers can be stored over time. For storable goods, the seller has a choice between selling the good now or in the future. Light bulb manufacturers will be reluctant to sell now if they think bulb prices will rise in the near future. Instead, they will find it more profitable to store some of the light bulbs they have made in **inventory**, or temporary storage, until the price increases. But remember, the supply curve for a good tells us how much is offered for sale *now*. So expectations that the price will rise in the future cause *today's* supply curve to shift to the left.

The opposite is true if sellers expect prices to fall in the near future: they will be eager to sell now. So when the light bulb price is expected to fall, the supply curve for light bulbs will shift to the right. The effect of future prices on supply occurs mainly for goods that can be stored in inventory for some time. For goods that cannot be stored because they would spoil—for example, yogurt, bananas, and cakes—expectations about future prices make little difference.

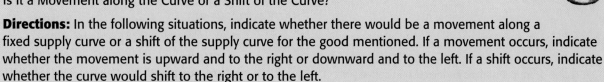

## YOUR TURN

Is It a Movement along the Curve or a Shift of the Curve?

**Directions:** In the following situations, indicate whether there would be a movement along a fixed supply curve or a shift of the supply curve for the good mentioned. If a movement occurs, indicate whether the movement is upward and to the right or downward and to the left. If a shift occurs, indicate whether the curve would shift to the right or to the left.

1. The wage rate for workers who make cell phones decreases.
2. The price of jeans doubles.
3. Wheat farmers face an increase in the cost of farm tractors.
4. The number of sellers of plywood increases.

5. Advancements in technology lower the cost of manufacturing watches.
6. Producers expect the price of bedroom furniture to increase in the near future.
7. The price of MP3 players falls.

**Answers: 1.** The supply curve shifts to the right. **2.** There is a movement rightward along the supply curve. **3.** The supply curve shifts to the left. **4.** The supply curve shifts to the right. **5.** The supply curve shifts to the right. **6.** The supply curve shifts to the right. **7.** There is a movement leftward along the supply curve.

# MODULE 14 REVIEW AND ASSESSMENT

**Summing Up the Key Ideas:** Match the following terms to the correct definitions.

A. Change in supply
B. Technological progress
C. Change in the quantity supplied
D. Inventory
E. Subsidy

_____ 1. Movement along a supply curve.

_____ 2. Payment made by the government to support a particular activity or good.

_____ 3. Temporary storage.

_____ 4. A shift of a supply curve.

_____ 5. The discovery of a new production method enabling firms to produce more goods from the same inputs or from new, less costly inputs.

**Analyze and Explain:** In the following situations, identify whether the **supply** or just the **quantity supplied** changes for the good mentioned. In your explanation, indicate the direction of the change.

| | CHANGE IN SUPPLY OR CHANGE IN THE QUANTITY SUPPLIED? | EXPLANATION |
|---|---|---|
| 1. A coffee producer notices an increase in coffee prices and responds by increasing coffee production. | _____ | _____ |
| 2. A local bakery is able to obtain ingredients for making baked goods at a lower cost. | _____ | _____ |
| 3. The government collects a new tax from firms on each unit of output produced. | _____ | _____ |
| 4. A new technology is discovered that enables firms to produce more output from the same quantity of an input. | _____ | _____ |
| 5. The government gives firms a subsidy for each unit of a good that is produced. | _____ | _____ |
| 6. Book publishers have an expectation that e-book sales will surge in the next year and prices will rise. | _____ | _____ |
| 7. The price of oil decreases. | _____ | _____ |
| 8. Favorable market conditions bring more sellers into the market. | _____ | _____ |

**Apply:** Indicate whether each of the following will **increase**, **decrease**, or have **no effect** on the supply of pencils.

| | SUPPLY OF PENCILS |
|---|---|
| 1. Pencil producers expect an increase in the price of pencils in the near future. | _____ |
| 2. The number of pencil producers decreases. | _____ |
| 3. The government subsidizes the production of pencils. | _____ |
| 4. The price of pencils increases. | _____ |
| 5. A technological innovation lowers the cost of producing pencils. | _____ |
| 6. The government taxes producers of pencils. | _____ |
| 7. Wage rates for workers who make pencils increase. | _____ |

# MODULE 15

# Production, Cost, and the Profit-Maximizing Output Level

**KEY IDEA:** Firms can maximize their profit by producing the quantity that equates marginal revenue and marginal cost.

### OBJECTIVES

- **To explain the components of total cost.**
- **To identify the condition for profit maximization.**
- **To explain how a profit-maximizing entrepreneur decides whether to open a new firm and whether to shut down an existing firm.**

*When capital, land, labor, and entrepreneurship come together in the production process, big things can happen.*

### Bringing It All Together

In the production process, entrepreneurs bring together capital, labor, and land to produce goods and services. To build a skyscraper, cranes and construction workers join forces on a patch of land to create a city in the sky. To make a latte, an espresso machine, a worker known as a *barista*, and coffee beans intermingle with piping-hot water to form a beverage with a jolt of caffeine. In this module we'll discuss the costs of production. We'll also explore the decision of how much to produce of anything from big buildings to little shots of espresso.

# UNDERSTANDING PRODUCTION

The law of supply tells us that a firm wants to produce and sell more of a good when its price rises. But how does a firm decide exactly how much to produce and sell? We'll answer that question soon. Our starting point is the relationship between the amount of various inputs a firm uses and its *output*, the amount of a good or service the firm produces.

If a coffee shop wants to sell more lattes, it will need to use more inputs. But should it hire more baristas or buy more espresso machines? And how much more of each input should it buy? As you're about to see, that depends on

the nature of the inputs themselves and on how much time the firm has to make adjustments.

### Fixed and Variable Inputs

The amounts of some types of inputs can't be adjusted quickly. In Module 13 we discussed how it takes a long time to expand factories and assembly lines. As another example, consider a construction company that wants to expand its business. It can take several months of planning and negotiation before the company can complete the purchase of heavy equipment like cranes and bulldozers. The same is true if a company wants to downsize and sell some of the equipment it already owns. So over a time period that can last several months or more, the construction company is stuck with the fixed quantity of cranes and bulldozers it happens to have on hand.

Economists define the **short run** as the period of time during which the quantity of at least one input is fixed. The **long run** is the period of time in which the quantities of all inputs are variable. There is no set period of time that distinguishes the short run from the long run; this is determined by the time it takes to acquire new inputs in particular industries. If, in the construction industry, the quantities of all inputs could be adjusted in as few as three months, then the short run in that industry is a period of three months. If, in the education industry, it takes two years to add classroom space to a school building, then the short run in that industry is a period of two years.

A *fixed input* is an input like cranes and classroom space, the quantity of which cannot be changed in the short run. This means that in the short run, the quantities of fixed inputs remain the same no matter how much output the firm decides to produce.

The amount of a *variable input* can be adjusted up or down. A construction company can quickly increase or decrease its orders of plywood, cement, or copper pipes, so these are variable inputs. Labor, too, can often be adjusted rapidly. In the construction industry, it might take just a few days to find additional workers, and these workers can be laid off with very short notice if they are not needed. So even in the short run, a construction company's labor and materials are variable inputs. In the short run, as in the long run, firms use more of their variable inputs when they produce more output and less of their variable inputs when they produce less output.

In the long run, a firm can adjust the quantities of *all* its inputs.

It can acquire a larger or smaller factory than it has now. It can get new equipment or sell the equipment it has. What were fixed inputs in the short run thus become variable inputs in the long run. That is, in the long run, all inputs are variable inputs.

> ### ⚠ Short Run versus Long Run
>
> Don't be confused by the terms *short run* and *long run*. It boils down to this: in the short run, the quantity of at least one input is fixed, whereas in the long run the quantities of all inputs are variable. The inputs with fixed quantities in the short run are called fixed inputs. In the long run, even fixed inputs become variable inputs.

*In the short run, the quantity of capital, such as bulldozers, is fixed. The quantity of labor is variable. All inputs are variable in the long run.*

### The Production Schedule

A firm's *production schedule* indicates the inputs needed to produce different quantities of output. Let's look at a production schedule for a fictional lawn mowing company we'll call Blade Runner Lawn Mowing. The table in Figure 15.1 contains a production schedule for Blade Runner for a typical week.

The table shows that Blade Runner uses two inputs: mowers and workers. Notice that the number of mowers is

---

The **short run** is the period of time during which the quantity of at least one input is fixed.

The **long run** is the period of time in which the quantities of all inputs are variable.

**Figure 15.1** The Production Schedule and Production Function for Blade Runner Lawn Mowing Company
A production schedule indicates the inputs needed to produce different quantities of output. A production function is a graphical depiction of a production schedule.

The Production Function for Blade Runner Lawn Mowing Company

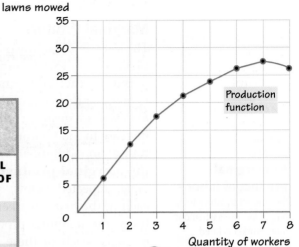

### The Production Schedule for Blade Runner Lawn Mowing Company

| QUANTITY OF MOWERS | QUANTITY OF WORKERS | TOTAL OUTPUT (LAWNS MOWED PER DAY) | MARGINAL PRODUCT OF LABOR |
|---|---|---|---|
| 2 | 0 | 0 | – |
| 2 | 1 | 6 | 6 |
| 2 | 2 | 12 | 6 |
| 2 | 3 | 17 | 5 |
| 2 | 4 | 21 | 4 |
| 2 | 5 | 24 | 3 |
| 2 | 6 | 26 | 2 |
| 2 | 7 | 27 | 1 |
| 2 | 8 | 26 | −1 |

fixed at 2. We are looking at Blade Runner's production options in the short run, which in this case is several weeks because that is the amount of time it would take Blade Runner to acquire more of its fixed input—mowers—or sell the mowers it has. Labor, however, is a variable input. Blade Runner can quickly increase or decrease the quantity of workers it employs.

Total output is measured by the quantity of lawns Blade Runner can mow per day. This is shown in the third column for each number of workers that Blade Runner could employ. With 2 employees, Blade Runner could mow 12 lawns each day, with 3 it could mow 17, with 4 it could mow 21, and so on.

The information in Blade Runner's production schedule is also displayed graphically in Figure 15.1. The curve on this graph is called the *production function*. Moving rightward on the graph corresponds to hiring more workers. Moving upward on the graph corresponds to mowing more lawns. The upward slope

of the production function up to a quantity of 7 workers shows that more lawns are mowed as each of the first 7 workers is hired. When the eighth worker is hired, total output decreases from 27 to 26. The eighth worker causes output to decrease by achieving nothing except getting in the way, as discussed later in this module. Our advice: don't be that eighth worker.

*With only two lawn mowers to work with, a third worker can't contribute as much to productivity as the first and second worker.*

## Marginal Product

The last column of the production schedule in Figure 15.1 reports the *increase* in output for each additional worker hired. Remember that economists use the word *marginal* to mean "additional." So the increase in total output that results from hiring an additional worker is called the **marginal product of labor**. The table, repeated below, shows that for each of the first 2 workers Blade Runner hires, the marginal product of labor is 6 lawns—each of these workers adds 6 lawns to the total output of the firm. But following that last column down, you can see that after the second worker, each additional worker has a smaller marginal product than the previous worker. The marginal product is 5 lawns for the third worker, 4 lawns for the fourth worker, 3 lawns for the fifth worker, and so on. Let's explore why marginal product behaves this way.

The **marginal product of labor** is the amount by which total output increases when one more worker is hired.

## Diminishing Marginal Product

As more and more of a variable input like labor is added to the unchanging quantity of a fixed input like lawn mowers, congestion and redundancy cause the marginal product of labor to decline. Because Blade Runner has exactly two lawn mowers in the short run, the first and second workers can use a lawn mower full time. The third worker has the disadvantage of having to share a lawn mower with the other two workers. The third worker can mow lawns only while someone else is on break but might be useful for fetching gasoline and removing rocks and branches from lawns before they are mowed. So the marginal product of the third worker is substantial at 5, but not as high as the marginal product of 6 for the previous workers.

As more workers are added, the mowers are spread even more thinly. More time is spent on breaks or less productive work. Each additional worker contributes less to total output than the worker before because additional workers have less equipment to work with. When the marginal product decreases as the quantity of the variable input increases, we say there is **diminishing marginal productivity**. You can also see the effect of diminishing marginal productivity on the graph. As the number of workers increases, total output rises by less and less with each additional hire.

**Diminishing marginal productivity** describes the decrease in the marginal product of a variable input, such as labor, as more and more of it is combined with a fixed input, such as equipment.

**Figure 15.1** (repeated)

### The Production Schedule for Blade Runner Lawn Mowing Company

| QUANTITY OF MOWERS | QUANTITY OF WORKERS | TOTAL OUTPUT (LAWNS MOWED PER DAY) | MARGINAL PRODUCT OF LABOR |
|---|---|---|---|
| 2 | 0 | 0 | – |
| 2 | 1 | 6 | 6 |
| 2 | 2 | 12 | 6 |
| 2 | 3 | 17 | 5 |
| 2 | 4 | 21 | 4 |
| 2 | 5 | 24 | 3 |
| 2 | 6 | 26 | 2 |
| 2 | 7 | 27 | 1 |
| 2 | 8 | 26 | −1 |

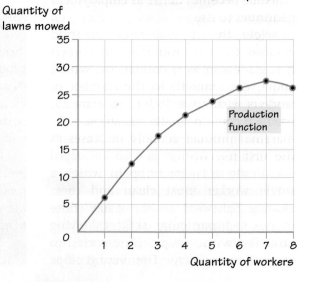

The Production Function for Blade Runner Lawn Mowing Company

## ECONOMICS IN ACTION

# Diminishing Marginal Productivity in Military Battles

Economists Ralph Rotte and Christoph Schmidt applied some ideas about production to military battles. Instead of being used to produce goods and services, the inputs in a military battle are used to increase the likelihood of victory on the battlefield. Using data from the Army Concepts Analysis Agency, Rotte and Schmidt classified 625 battles from the seventeenth to twentieth centuries according to whether the invading or defending side won. A variety of factors, including the size of the forces, troop morale, and leadership skills, was used to analyze which side won. They found that having more soldiers than the opponent remained a significant determinant of victory, even as military technology went through major changes. For example, they credit Napoleon's crushing 1815 defeat at Waterloo in part to the fact that he was greatly outnumbered: Napoleon had 68,000 men to oppose a combined English and Prussian force of 137,000 men.

As in production, however, the marginal productivity of soldiers declines. Given the strength of an enemy, each time another soldier is added to fight them, the chances of victory increase—the marginal product of a soldier is positive. But as more and more soldiers are added, the chances of victory rise by *less and less* each time—there is diminishing marginal productivity. Therefore, to raise the chances of victory by a lot—say, to near certainty—it is necessary to add so many soldiers that the enemy is completely overwhelmed. This is often called the Powell Doctrine, after the retired soldier and statesman Colin Powell.

This is why the graph of the production schedule becomes flatter as employment continues to rise.

Note that the marginal product does not decrease until the third worker is hired. There were enough mowers to allow some growth in the number of workers without a decline in marginal productivity. In many situations the marginal product actually increases as the first few workers are added. Consider a dry-cleaning shop in which a single worker must clean and press clothes. This worker will not have time to develop particular skills in either task. But with two workers, each can specialize in a task and get very good at it. Because of their increased skills and focus, marginal product will increase. However, when some inputs are fixed, sooner or later we can expect the other inputs to display diminishing marginal productivity. According to the **law of diminishing returns**, as more of a variable input is used in combination with a fixed input, the marginal product will eventually decrease.

It is even possible that past a certain point, additional workers would cause total output to decrease, meaning that marginal product is negative. With too many workers and only two lawn mowers, additional workers won't spend much time mowing lawns. They will just

According to the **law of diminishing returns**, there is a general tendency for total output to increase at a decreasing rate when additional amounts of an input are used in production, holding the amount of other inputs constant.

get in the way and distract other workers who would otherwise be productive. This causes total output to decrease. Looking back at Figure 15.1, we see that as Blade Runner expands from 7 to 8 workers, the marginal product is negative because total output declines from 27 lawns to 26 lawns. There would be no reason to hire an eighth worker who causes total output to decline!

**Fixed cost** is the cost of inputs that do not vary with the amount of output produced.

**Variable cost** is the cost of inputs that do vary with the amount of output produced.

**DID YOU GET IT?**
What is the marginal product of labor? Why does Blade Runner have a diminishing marginal product of labor in our example?

---

⚠️ **Diminishing versus Negative Marginal Product**

It's easy to confuse *diminishing* marginal product with a *negative* marginal product, but they are very different. When marginal product is decreasing but still positive, hiring additional workers causes total output to rise. But when marginal product is negative, employing more workers actually causes total output to fall.

---

## THE COST OF PRODUCTION

What you've learned about production involves inputs and outputs. The inputs (mowers and workers) and the output (lawns mowed) are all measured as quantities. But firms are in business to make *profit*, which is measured in dollars. In this section, we'll begin to translate our knowledge about production into dollars. The first step is to understand how much it costs to produce different amounts of output.

### Fixed Cost versus Variable Cost

Firms face two different kinds of cost: fixed cost and variable cost. **Fixed cost** is the cost of a firm's fixed inputs—those inputs whose quantity cannot be changed as the output level changes in the short run. Typical sources of fixed cost include the rent paid for buildings, the cost of equipment, and fees for operating licenses. In the long run, when the quantity of all inputs is variable, there is no fixed cost. Firms can spend more or less on buildings, equipment, licenses, and other inputs to best suit their level of production.

**Variable cost** is the cost of the firm's variable inputs. Variable cost changes with the number of units of output produced. Typical sources of variable cost include payments for wages, electricity, and raw materials.

**DID YOU GET IT?**
How does variable cost differ from fixed cost?

### Fixed and Variable Cost at Blade Runner

Table 15.1 illustrates the various types of cost for the Blade Runner Lawn Mowing Company. The first two columns repeat

*To minimize costs, firms try to hire only the workers needed to get the job done.*

RAINER ELSTERMANN/THINKSTOCK

| Table 15.1 | **Output, Cost, Revenue, and Profit for Blade Runner Lawn Mowing Company** | | | | | | | |
|---|---|---|---|---|---|---|---|---|
| (1) QUANTITY OF WORKERS | (2) OUTPUT PER DAY | (3) FIXED COST (DOLLARS) | (4) VARIABLE COST (DOLLARS) | (5) TOTAL COST (DOLLARS) | (6) MARGINAL COST (DOLLARS) | (7) PRICE PER LAWN MOWED (DOLLARS) | (8) TOTAL REVENUE (DOLLARS) | (9) PROFIT (DOLLARS) |
| 0 | 0 | $80 | $ 0 | $80 | — | $20 | $0 | −$80 |
| 1 | 6 | 80 | 60 | 140 | $10 | 20 | 120 | −20 |
| 2 | 12 | 80 | 120 | 200 | 10 | 20 | 240 | 40 |
| 3 | 17 | 80 | 180 | 260 | 12 | 20 | 340 | 80 |
| 4 | 21 | 80 | 240 | 320 | 15 | 20 | 420 | 100 |
| 5 | 24 | 80 | 300 | 380 | 20 | 20 | 480 | 100 |
| 6 | 26 | 80 | 360 | 440 | 30 | 20 | 520 | 80 |
| 7 | 27 | 80 | 420 | 500 | 60 | 20 | 540 | 40 |
| 8 | 26 | 80 | 480 | 560 | — | 20 | 520 | −40 |

the worker and output information from the production schedule in Figure 15.1. Column 3 shows Blade Runner's fixed cost, which is $80 per day ($40 per lawn mower per day). The fixed cost includes the expense of renting and storing the two lawn mowers. Recall that a firm's fixed cost does not increase as output increases. Thus, the fixed cost is $80 regardless of the number of lawns that are mowed.

Column 4 shows Blade Runner's variable cost, which is what it must pay its workers. This cost does increase as output increases, because the company must hire more workers in order to mow more lawns. In Table 15.1, the daily wage of each worker is $60, so the variable cost is $60 × (the number of workers hired). For example, to mow 21 lawns, Blade Runner hires 4 workers, so the variable cost is $60 × 4 = $240. To keep things simple we will suppose that any other variable costs, such as the cost of gasoline for the lawn mowers, are insignificant.

## Total Cost

A firm's **total cost** is the entire amount the firm must spend to produce a specified amount of output, found by adding the firm's fixed cost to its variable cost. Blade Runner's total cost is reported in

column 5 of Table 15.1. For example, the total cost of mowing 24 lawns is $80 fixed cost + $300 variable costs = $380.

**DID YOU GET IT?**
What is total cost? Which two numbers are added to find total cost?

## Cost Minimization

Firms that want to earn the highest possible profit will seek the cheapest way to produce a given quantity of output. Otherwise, they would be wasting money that could otherwise contribute to their profit. A firm that selects its inputs in order to produce its desired level of output at the lowest cost possible is called a *cost minimizer*.

A firm can only adjust variable inputs to minimize cost. In the long run, all inputs are variable, and Blade Runner could sell all its mowers and change the quantity of any other input. But in the short run, Blade Runner can vary only the number of workers it hires to mow lawns. So minimizing cost in the short run comes down to mowing lawns using as few workers as possible. The costs in Table 15.1 are the minimum costs for mowing each number of lawns. For example, Blade Runner cannot mow

**Total cost** is fixed cost plus variable cost.

17 lawns with fewer than 3 workers, so the lowest possible variable cost of mowing 17 lawns is 3 × $60 = $180.

In the long run, mowers become a variable input for Blade Runner. Then, cost minimization involves selecting the cheapest combination of mowers and workers to mow any given number of lawns. But for now we are considering the firm's cost in the short run, when Blade Runner cannot adjust the number of mowers.

**DID YOU GET IT?**
What does it mean for a firm to be a cost minimizer?

### Marginal Cost

Chapter 3 explained that *marginal cost* is the additional cost of doing something one more time. In the context of production, marginal cost is the additional cost of producing one more unit of output. For most goods, the cost of making another unit rises at some point as more is produced. This occurs because of the law of diminishing returns: if each worker adds less to output than the previous worker, then the expenditure on labor to produce each additional unit of output will rise, as it takes more and more workers (or more time from a particular worker) to produce the additional output.

Column 6 of Table 15.1 shows the marginal cost at various levels of production for Blade Runner. Marginal cost is calculated as the change in total cost divided by the change in output. For example, if Blade Runner increases its output from 12 to 17 lawns, an increase of 5 lawns, total cost rises from $200 to $260, an increase of $60. So the marginal cost per additional lawn is $60 ÷ 5 = $12.

Notice that as you look down column 6, the marginal cost increases as output increases. For example, as we just calculated, the marginal cost is $12 to increase output to 17 lawns. But when Blade Runner increases output from 17 to 21 lawns, the marginal cost rises to $15, and a further increase to 24 lawns raises the

marginal cost to $20. It becomes increasingly costly to mow additional lawns as the total number of lawns mowed increases.

**DID YOU GET IT?**
What typically happens to marginal cost as output rises? How does the law of diminishing returns help explain this?

## PROFIT MAXIMIZATION AND MARGINAL ANALYSIS

You've seen that total revenue is the money a firm receives from selling goods or services and that profit is total revenue minus total cost. Profit is also the firm owner's source of income. The lure of profit is a major reason why entrepreneurs start businesses. And once a business is in operation, its owners will generally strive to make the largest possible profit. In this section we'll examine how that is done.

### The Profit-Maximizing Output Level

The amount of output that gives a firm as much profit as possible is called the firm's **profit-maximizing output level**. How does the firm find this output level? One approach begins with a calculation of the firm's total revenue, which is the price charged multiplied by the quantity sold, at each output level. Table 15.1, repeated on the next page, presents Blade Runner's total revenue in column 8. For example, when Blade Runner mows 17 lawns for $20 each, its total revenue is 17 × $20 = $340.

We are now ready to calculate Blade Runner's profit at each output level, as shown in column 9. The profit earned at a particular level of output is simply the total revenue at that output level (column 8) minus the total cost at that output level (column 5). For example, when Blade Runner mows 17 lawns, its total revenue

The **profit-maximizing output level** is the amount of output that gives a firm as much profit as possible.

is $340, while its total cost is $260. Thus, Blade Runner earns a profit of $80 if it mows 17 lawns, which is the total revenue of $340 less the total cost of $260.

Once the profit is calculated for each output level, we can find the profit-maximizing output level, or levels, very easily. If you run your finger down column 9, you'll see that profit increases up to a quantity of 21 lawns, remains the same for 24 lawns, and then decreases for higher quantities of lawns. So Blade Runner can earn its maximum profit of $100 per day by mowing either 21 or 24 lawns.

**DID YOU GET IT?**

How are a firm's total revenue and profit calculated?

## Marginal Analysis

In Chapter 3 you learned that individuals can make good decisions by taking actions that provide a marginal benefit that exceeds the marginal cost. The same type of marginal analysis guides firms to their profit-maximizing output level.

Because profit is measured in dollars, so is the "marginal benefit" of producing and selling more output. The additional revenue a firm receives from selling another unit of output is called the firm's **marginal revenue**. For price-taking firms like Blade Runner in perfectly competitive markets, the price is the same no matter how much output they produce, and the marginal revenue is simply the price of each unit. That is, Blade Runner's marginal revenue is $20, no matter how many lawns it mows. Chapter 8 explains that marginal revenue falls below the price for monopolies and other firms that must lower their price in order to sell more.

Firms compare the marginal revenue with the marginal cost when deciding whether to increase production. Suppose a firm is considering a new, higher output level. If the marginal revenue exceeds the marginal cost for that increase in production, then the additional output will add more to total revenue than to total cost, and profit will rise. By contrast, if the marginal revenue is less than the marginal cost, profit will decline as output increases. This suggests a simple rule for the firm: increase production as long as marginal revenue is greater than marginal cost; do *not* increase production if marginal revenue is less than marginal cost.

Let's see how this logic works at Blade Runner. If output rises from 0 to 6 lawns, the marginal revenue is $20 (the price for each lawn), while the marginal cost is $10. So profit rises as output increases to 6 lawns. As you can verify in Table 15.1, the marginal revenue of $20

**Marginal revenue** is the additional revenue a firm receives from selling another unit of output.

| Table 15.1 | **Output, Cost, Revenue, and Profit for Blade Runner Lawn Mowing Company** | | | | | | | |
|---|---|---|---|---|---|---|---|---|
| (1) QUANTITY OF WORKERS | (2) OUTPUT PER DAY | (3) FIXED COST (DOLLARS) | (4) VARIABLE COST (DOLLARS) | (5) TOTAL COST (DOLLARS) | (6) MARGINAL COST (DOLLARS) | (7) PRICE PER LAWN MOWED (DOLLARS) | (8) TOTAL REVENUE (DOLLARS) | (9) PROFIT (DOLLARS) |
| 0 | 0 | $80 | $ 0 | $80 | — | $20 | $0 | −$80 |
| 1 | 6 | 80 | 60 | 140 | $10 | 20 | 120 | −20 |
| 2 | 12 | 80 | 120 | 200 | 10 | 20 | 240 | 40 |
| 3 | 17 | 80 | 180 | 260 | 12 | 20 | 340 | 80 |
| 4 | 21 | 80 | 240 | 320 | 15 | 20 | 420 | 100 |
| **5** | **24** | **80** | **300** | **380** | **20** | **20** | **480** | **100** |
| 6 | 26 | 80 | 360 | 440 | 30 | 20 | 520 | 80 |
| 7 | 27 | 80 | 420 | 500 | 60 | 20 | 540 | 40 |
| 8 | 26 | 80 | 480 | 560 | — | 20 | 520 | −40 |

continues to exceed the marginal cost for all increases in output up to 21 lawns, so Blade Runner will hire at least the 4 workers needed to mow 21 lawns.

When Blade Runner hires the fifth worker to increase output from 21 to 24 lawns, the marginal revenue and the marginal cost are equal at $20. For this move, each additional lawn adds the same amount to revenue as it adds to cost, so profit will not change. Blade Runner will be indifferent about increasing output from 21 to 24 lawns. The owners might as well flip a coin to decide between these quantities. To simplify our view of these situations, we can assume that the firm does go ahead and produce the last unit (or units) for which marginal revenue equals marginal cost.

Now consider the option to hire a sixth worker and increase output from 24 to 26 lawns. For this change, the marginal revenue of $20 is *less* than the marginal cost of $30, so profit falls. Blade Runner should *not* make this change.

In general, the profit-maximizing output level can be found where the marginal revenue and the marginal cost are equal. At that output level, all changes for which marginal revenue exceeds marginal cost have been exploited. If the marginal revenue never equals the marginal cost, profit is maximized at the largest quantity for which the marginal revenue exceeds the marginal cost. Blade Runner's marginal cost and marginal revenue are equal at an output of 24 lawns per day. Thus, Blade Runner will maximize profit by mowing 24 lawns and earning $100 in daily profit. The information for this quantity of output is bold in Table 15.1. You can see for yourself that no quantity of output provides a higher level of profit for Blade Runner than 24 lawns per day.

**DID YOU GET IT?**
What is meant by the term *marginal revenue*? If a firm's marginal revenue exceeds its marginal cost, what will happen to the firm's profit if it increases output?

## Price, Profit, and Supply

Marginal analysis helps us understand the logic behind the firm's supply curve discussed earlier in this chapter. Marginal cost is the cost of producing another unit, and marginal revenue is the revenue gained from selling another unit. In a perfectly competitive market, the marginal revenue is the price of the good. If the price is greater than the marginal cost, the firm's profit will rise as it produces more. If the price is below the marginal cost, the firm will earn higher profit by producing less. The fact that marginal cost rises as output increases means that a profit-maximizing firm will produce more output only if the price rises. This explains the law of supply.

**DID YOU GET IT?**
If the price of a good exceeds the marginal cost of production, does profit increase or decrease if the firm increases output? Why?

## To Be or Not to Be in Business?

What makes an entrepreneur decide to start a firm? The answer is profit. If an entrepreneur thinks a firm can make a profit at some level of output, she or he will have an incentive to take the necessary risks and make the necessary investments to start the firm. We can see from Table 15.1 that Blade Runner's total revenue exceeds its total cost at output levels between 12 and 27, so Blade Runner is profitable. An entrepreneur with the information in Table 15.1 would decide to go into business supplying lawn mowing services.

Entrepreneurs may be hit by unexpected events after going into business. The price of their product could fall or their costs could rise. For some period of time, these events can cause profit to turn negative, even when the firm is producing the best possible output level. When a firm faces a loss, the entrepreneur must decide whether to keep operating or shut down until conditions change.

How should the entrepreneur make this critical decision? If the firm's total revenue is below its *variable* cost, the entrepreneur is wise to shut the firm down. Why? Because a firm's variable cost is paid only if the firm stays open. If the variable cost that can be avoided by shutting down is larger than the revenue to be gained by staying open, losses are minimized by shutting down. For instance, if the price received is $9 per lawn, Blade Runner would have to pay its workers more than it received from customers. If it hired the 5 workers needed to mow 24 lawns, for example, its variable cost would be $60 x 5 = $300, and its total revenue would be $9 × 24 = $216. Thus, it would lose less by not mowing any lawns.

But what if total revenue covers the variable cost but not the fixed cost? In this case, the firm should stay open. Remember that the firm must pay its fixed cost regardless of whether it produces output or not. So if a firm's total revenue is above its variable cost, even if there are losses, it is better for the firm to remain open and pay off some of the unavoidable fixed cost, rather than shutting down and not earning any revenue to put toward the fixed cost. In the long run, when it is possible to get out of rental contracts and avoid other sources of fixed cost, the firm will stay open only if there are no losses.

Notice that the decision to start a business and the decision to shut down are based on different criteria. The decision to go into business hinges on the ability to make profit, which occurs if total revenue exceeds total cost. This decision takes both fixed and variable cost into account, because total cost is the sum of fixed and variable cost. But a

*The decision to start a business and the decision to close a business are based on different criteria.*

firm should shut down if it cannot cover its variable costs. As a result, some firms that are incurring losses will continue producing in the short run, because their total revenue exceeds their variable cost. Many automakers, for example, have remained in business even after months or years of being unprofitable. Automakers have very large fixed costs associated with their factories and equipment. But during those periods their total revenue exceeded their variable cost, so it made sense for them to stay in business.

**DID YOU GET IT?**
**Under what conditions should an entrepreneur go into business to supply a product? Under what conditions should an entrepreneur shut a firm down?**

# MODULE 15 REVIEW AND ASSESSMENT

**Summing Up the Key Ideas:** Match the following terms to the correct definitions.

A. Short run
B. Marginal product of labor
C. Long run

D. Marginal revenue
E. Law of diminishing returns
F. Fixed cost

G. Variable cost
H. Profit-maximizing output level
I. Total cost

J. Output
K. Diminishing marginal productivity
L. Cost minimization

_____ 1. A period of time in which the quantity of at least one input is fixed.

_____ 2. The decrease in the marginal product of a variable input, such as labor, as more and more of it is combined with a fixed input, such as equipment.

_____ 3. The cost of inputs that vary with the amount of output produced.

_____ 4. A period of time in which the quantities of all inputs are variable.

_____ 5. Fixed cost plus variable cost.

_____ 6. The additional revenue a firm receives from selling another unit of output.

_____ 7. The cost of inputs that do not vary with the amount of output produced.

_____ 8. The amount of output that gives a firm as much profit as possible.

_____ 9. Selecting inputs in order to produce a desired level of output at the lowest cost possible.

_____ 10. The general tendency for output to increase at a decreasing rate when additional amounts of an input are used in production, holding the amount of other inputs constant.

_____ 11. The amount by which total output increases when one more worker is hired.

_____ 12. The amount of a good or service a firm produces.

**Analyze and Explain:** Firms face two different kinds of costs: fixed cost and variable cost. Analyze each of the following and determine if it is a **fixed cost** or a **variable cost**. Explain your decisions.

| | FIXED OR VARIABLE COST? | EXPLANATION |
|---|---|---|
| 1. the fee paid for your business license | _____ | _____ |
| 2. the rent paid for your office space | _____ | _____ |
| 3. the amount paid for electricity to operate production machinery | _____ | _____ |
| 4. the amount paid in wages to production workers | _____ | _____ |
| 5. the amount paid for raw material | _____ | _____ |
| 6. the amount paid for computers and cell phones in the firm | _____ | _____ |

**Apply:** Analyze each scenario and make a recommendation about whether the firm should increase production, decrease production, or shut down. Explain your decision.

|  | RECOMMENDATION | EXPLANATION |
|---|---|---|
| 1. A sporting goods store owner finds that her marginal revenue exceeds her marginal cost. | _____ | _____ |
| 2. A corner gas station owner finds that his total revenue is less than his variable cost. | _____ | _____ |
| 3. A movie theater owner finds that her total revenue is less than her total cost but is above her variable cost, and her marginal revenue equals her marginal cost. | _____ | _____ |
| 4. A bicycle dealership owner finds that his marginal cost exceeds his marginal revenue. | _____ | _____ |

## The Economist

# Orangonomics

## A War Effort Gone Wrong
### JANUARY 11, 2012

Analysis of swings in commodity prices usually involves sage pronouncements on the Chinese economy, geopolitics or the rise of resource nationalism in developing countries. But recent gyrations in orange-juice prices have far more to do with the usual supply factors such as the weather in southern Florida or the ravages of blossom blight and black-spot disease on Brazil's crop. The price of frozen-concentrated-orange-juice futures has leapt by around 25% since the start of the year to a 34-year high, mainly on concerns that Brazil, an important source of American imports, may have used banned fungicides which could result in an import ban.

Frozen orange-juice concentrate was developed by the Florida Citrus Commission and the United States Department of Agriculture as part of America's effort to bring the savour of fresh fruit to struggling allies in the second world war.

More recently, Americans lost some of their thirst for orange juice: sales fell by nearly 9% in December compared with a year ago. And juice made from frozen concentrate has been losing ground to tastier fresh juices in recent year. But trees in Florida are disappearing faster, not least because many orange groves were turned into housing developments during the property boom. As a result, citrus output (which includes grapefruit) dropped by nearly 40% between 1996 and 2010.

Thus, potential for problems with Brazilian imports, coupled with a recent cold snap in Florida that might have done some damage to the orange crop, has added extra volatility to a market whose small trading volumes are already reason enough for barely explicable rapid price movements.

### DID YOU READ IT?

1) **What are some important factors affecting the supply, and thus the price, of frozen orange juice concentrate?**

2) **Draw the supply curve for frozen orange juice concentrate. Using the graph, show how the factors you discussed in question 1 affect the supply curve.**

### WHAT DO YOU THINK?

1) **What other suppliers might suffer from the same problems the orange juice market is experiencing?**

2) **Since the U.S. orange juice industry is having difficulties, how can orange juice producers try to boost demand for their orange juice? Why might this benefit U.S. orange juice producers?**

EXCERPTED FROM www.economist.com/blogs/schumpeter/2012/01/orangonomics

# CHAPTER 5 REVIEW AND SELF-ASSESSMENT

## REVIEW

### Points to Remember

#### MODULE 13: UNDERSTANDING SUPPLY

1. **Profit** is the total revenue a firm receives from selling its product minus the total cost of producing it.

2. The **quantity supplied** is the amount of a good that firms are willing to supply at a particular price over a given period of time.

3. There is **perfect competition** in a market when there are many firms selling identical goods, firms are free to enter and exit the market, and consumers have full information about the price and availability of goods.

4. According to the **law of supply**, an increase in the price of a good leads to an increase in the quantity supplied.

5. The **supply schedule** for a good is a table listing the quantity of the good that will be supplied at specified prices.

6. A firm's **supply curve** is a graphical representation of the supply schedule, showing the quantity the firm will supply at each price.

7. The **market supply curve** is a graphical representation of the quantity supplied by all firms in the market at various prices.

8. The **elasticity of supply** is a measure of the responsiveness of the quantity supplied to price changes, calculated by dividing the percentage change in the quantity supplied by the percentage change in price.

#### MODULE 14: SHIFTS OF THE SUPPLY CURVE

9. A **shift of the supply curve** is the result of a change in the quantity supplied at every price. This is not to be confused with a movement along the supply curve, which is the result of a change in the price.

10. When the supply curve shifts, this is called a **change in supply**.

11. When there is a movement along the supply curve, this is called a **change in the quantity supplied**.

12. **Inventory** consists of goods that are held in temporary storage.

#### MODULE 15: PRODUCTION, COST, AND THE PROFIT-MAXIMIZING OUTPUT LEVEL

13. The **short run** is the period of time during which the quantity of at least one input is fixed.

14. The **long run** is the period of time in which the quantities of all inputs are variable.

15. The **marginal product of labor** is the amount by which total output increases when one more worker is hired.

16. **Diminishing marginal productivity** describes the decrease in the marginal product of a variable input, such as labor, as more and more of it is combined with a fixed input, such as equipment.

17. According to the **law of diminishing returns**, there is a general tendency for output to increase at a decreasing rate when additional amounts of an input are used in production, holding the amount of other inputs constant.

18. **Fixed cost** is the cost of inputs that do not vary with the amount of output produced.

19. **Variable cost** is the cost of inputs that do vary with the amount of output produced.

20. **Total cost** is fixed cost plus variable cost.

21. The **profit-maximizing output level** is the amount of output that gives a firm as much profit as possible. This level is achieved by producing every unit for which marginal revenue exceeds (or equals) marginal cost.

22. **Marginal revenue** is the additional revenue a firm receives from selling another unit of output.

## SELF-ASSESSMENT

The following questions are the type your teacher might ask you on a quiz or a test. Practice with these in order to improve your performance on class tests.

### Multiple-Choice Questions

| PRICE (DOLLARS) | QUANTITY SUPPLIED |
|---|---|
| $5.00 | 100 |
| 4.50 | 90 |
| 4.00 | 75 |
| 3.50 | 55 |
| 3.00 | 30 |
| 2.50 | 0 |

1. As the price falls from $4.50 to $4.00,

    a. the quantity supplied decreases from 90 to 75.
    b. the quantity supplied increases from 75 to 90.
    c. the supply increases.
    d. the supply decreases.

Answer the following four questions based on the production function for juice at Jimmy's Juice Joint, shown in the following table:

4. The marginal product of the seventh worker is

    a. 0.
    b. 4.
    c. 50.
    d. 250.

5. The marginal product of the third worker

    a. is equal to that of the second worker.
    b. is less than the marginal product of the second worker.
    c. is greater than the marginal product of the second worker.
    d. cannot be compared to the marginal product of the second worker.

6. If Jimmy must pay $50 per day for each worker, and he has a fixed cost of $200, what is the cost of producing 40 ounces of juice?

    a. $50
    b. $200
    c. $250
    d. $400

2. When a perfectly competitive firm shuts down in the short run, there is still the obligation to pay

    a. all the variable costs, but not the fixed cost.
    b. no costs at all.
    c. the variable costs.
    d. the fixed costs.

3. Which of the following correctly defines *profit*?

    a. marginal revenue minus marginal cost
    b. fixed cost minus variable cost
    c. marginal revenue minus marginal product
    d. total revenue minus total cost

| WORKERS | JUICE PRODUCED (IN OUNCES) |
|---|---|
| 0 | 0 |
| 1 | 10 |
| 2 | 22 |
| 3 | 32 |
| 4 | 40 |
| 5 | 46 |
| 6 | 50 |
| 7 | 50 |
| 8 | 45 |

7. At what point did diminishing returns set in at Jimmy's Juice Joint?

    a. when the first worker was hired
    b. when the third worker was hired
    c. when the seventh worker was hired
    d. when the eighth worker was hired

8. Firms seeking to maximize profits in perfectly competitive markets will set marginal revenue

a. equal to marginal cost.

b. equal to the variable cost.

c. above the price.

d. below the price.

9. Which of the following will **not** increase the supply of a good?

a. an increase in the price of the good

b. a decrease in the cost of inputs for the good

c. an increase in the number of firms producing the good

d. a government subsidy granted to the producers of the good

10. There are diminishing returns to an input because

a. as you add more and more of a variable input to less and less of the fixed input, total product decreases.

b. as you add more and more of a variable input to the fixed input, total product decreases.

c. as you add more and more of a variable input to the fixed input, the marginal product of the last unit of the variable input will decrease.

d. as you add more and more of a variable input to less and less of the fixed input, the marginal product of the last unit of the variable input will decrease.

## Constructed Response Questions

1. Complete the blank spaces in this table of costs and revenue for a typical firm:

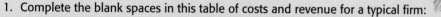

| NUMBER OF WORKERS | TOTAL PRODUCT | MARGINAL PRODUCT PER WORKER | FIXED COST (DOLLARS) | VARIABLE COST (DOLLARS) | TOTAL COST (DOLLARS) | MARGINAL COST (DOLLARS) | PRODUCT PRICE (DOLLARS) | TOTAL REVENUE (DOLLARS) | PROFIT (DOLLARS) |
|---|---|---|---|---|---|---|---|---|---|
| 0 | 0 | 0 | 200 | — | $200 | | $10 | 0 | -200 |
| 1 | 20 | 20 | | $60 | 260 | 3 | 10 | 200 | -40 |
| 2 | 50 | 30 | 60 | 120 | 320 | 2 | 10 | 500 | 180 |
| 3 | 70 | 20 | 60 | 180 | 380 | 3 | 10 | 700 | 320 |
| 4 | 80 | 10 | 60 | 240 | 440 | 6 | 10 | 800 | 360 |
| 5 | 85 | 5 | 60 | 300 | 500 | 12 | 10 | 850 | 350 |
| 6 | 88 | 3 | 60 | 360 | 560 | 20 | 10 | 880 | 320 |
| 7 | 90 | 2 | 60 | 420 | 620 | 30 | 10 | 900 | 280 |
| 8 | 91 | 1 | 60 | 480 | 680 | 60 | 10 | 910 | 230 |

2. Answer these questions using the data in the chart:

a. How much are the fixed costs for this firm?

b. In what type of market does this firm sell its product? Explain.

c. What is the marginal product of the fifth worker?

d. At what point (if any) do diminishing returns set in? Explain.

e. What is the profit-maximizing output level for this firm? Explain.

f. At the profit-maximizing output level, how much profit does this firm earn?

**CHAPTER 6** & **YOU** Why do you pay more for a steak than for a hamburger? Why does an avocado sell for a higher price than an apple? Why must you pay more for a diamond, which isn't necessary for survival, than for a pint of water, which you cannot live without? The answer to all these questions is supply and demand. In fact, the price of nearly everything you might buy—shoes, computers, cars, tennis balls—is determined by supply and demand. Familiarity with supply and demand will help you understand why some goods are expensive and others are cheap. It will help you predict whether the price of something you are thinking about buying will rise or fall in the next few months. Knowing how supply and demand determine prices will help you understand how the economy works. It may even help you become a savvier shopper!

# Prices and Quantities: Putting Supply and Demand Together

## SUPPLY AND DEMAND FROM THE MOUTH OF A VOLCANO

On April 15, 2010, a volcano in Iceland erupted. The volcano's name is *Eyjafjallajokull*. (If you'd like a challenge, try to pronounce it. Most newscasters at the time could not.) For the first few hours after the eruption began, the world's attention was focused on the thick black cloud of smoke rising from the volcano. But as the hours passed, a new concern arose: the ash particles from the volcano were quickly spreading to the continent of Europe. Airline safety experts believed that the particles could clog jet engines and even bring down a plane. As a result, two dozen countries grounded all flights and closed down their airports. In some countries, airports remained closed for more than a week. Thousands of flights were canceled.

*The 2010 eruption of Eyjafjallajokull left more than a million passengers stranded when their flights were canceled.*

The airport closings had some immediate effects. The most direct impact was on the tourists and business travelers who could not take trips or who were stranded and unable to return home. But the volcano also had indirect effects on prices for goods and services around the world. For example, within days, the price of salmon in China and Japan skyrocketed, even though both countries were untouched by the ash from the volcano. And in the global market for jet fuel, the price dipped.

Why did prices change in these markets? Before the volcano erupted, the supply and demand for jet fuel and salmon were in balance. After the volcano erupted, the balance changed. In the market for jet fuel, the cancellation of flights caused a sharp drop in demand. This decrease in demand caused the price of jet fuel to fall.

In the case of salmon, because most of the fresh salmon sold in Asia is caught in Norway and delivered by jet, the salmon could not be delivered. So there was a sharp drop in the supply of salmon, which caused the price to rise.

When either supply or demand changes, the price and quantity adjust as well. This chapter considers how the forces of supply and demand interact to determine the price that a good sells for and how much of it is bought and sold.

## BOTTOM LINE

The price of nearly everything you buy is determined by the interaction of supply and demand. Supply and demand also determine the quantity of goods and services that are bought and sold in a market.

# MODULE 16

# Supply and Demand

**KEY IDEA:** The interaction of supply and demand determines the price at which a good is sold in the market and the quantity of the good that is exchanged between buyers and sellers.

**OBJECTIVES**

- To demonstrate how supply and demand work together to determine the price and quantity of a good.

- To explain why market equilibrium occurs when the quantity supplied equals the quantity demanded.

- To recognize how market forces cause the market price and quantity to adjust to equilibrium.

### Determining Price

In Chapter 4, you learned that the market demand curve tells us how much of a good buyers want to buy at each possible price. In Chapter 5, you learned about the market supply curve, which tells us the quantity firms will offer for sale at each price. But what determines the price that will actually be charged in the market? For example, why do the shorts at the mall cost around $30 rather than $5 or $90? To answer this question, we must think about both sides of the market—supply and demand—at the same time.

## PUTTING SUPPLY AND DEMAND TOGETHER: MARKET EQUILIBRIUM

As we explore the crossroads of supply and demand, our first step is to define the market we are talking about. We know that a market is a collection of people who could potentially buy or sell a good during a particular time period. A market could be as small as the people in one particular neighborhood, or it could be all the people in the global economy, depending on where buyers and sellers of the good in question are located. For our example, we'll use the entire U.S. market for cotton shorts, consisting of all buyers and sellers in the United States. We'll imagine that the offerings by each firm are the same and that the market is perfectly competitive.

Our next step in determining the market price is to combine the supply and demand curves in the same graph, as shown in Figure 16.1. We can combine the two curves because the separate supply and demand graphs each have price on the *y*-axis and quantity on the *x*-axis. Notice that the *x*-axis, which is labeled "Quantity of shorts (millions of pairs)," represents either the quantity demanded or the quantity supplied, depending on which curve we are looking at.

The purpose of putting the two curves together is to find the point of *equilibrium* in the market. At the market **equilibrium**, point *E* on the graph, the quantity of shorts firms are willing to supply equals the quantity of shorts consumers are willing to buy. You can think of the equilibrium point as the "point of rest" in the market, resulting

*Supply and demand determine the prices you pay for clothing and most other things.*

The market **equilibrium** is the point at which the quantity supplied equals the quantity demanded.

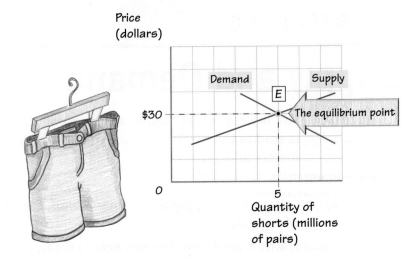

**Figure 16.1** Market Equilibrium
The equilibrium point lies at the intersection of supply and demand. At that point, the quantity supplied equals the quantity demanded.

from a balance of forces. A seesaw is in equilibrium when two people of equal weight are on the opposite sides. In equilibrium, there is no tendency for either side of the seesaw to rise or fall. In a similar way, a market has reached its equilibrium point when there is no tendency for the price or quantity to change, because the forces of supply and demand are in balance.

### Equilibrium on a Graph

On a supply and demand graph, the equilibrium is represented by the point where the two curves intersect. For example, the equilibrium in Figure 16.1 occurs at the point labeled *E* for equilibrium. At this point, the price is $30 per pair of shorts. The price that equates the quantity supplied and the quantity demanded is called the **equilibrium price**.

At point *E*, the quantity demanded and the quantity supplied are both equal to 5 million pairs of shorts. The quantity supplied and demanded at the equilibrium price is called the **equilibrium quantity**. Because the quantity demanded equals the quantity supplied at point *E*, we know that every pair of shorts that firms want to sell will have a willing buyer. With this balance, there is no tendency for the equilibrium price or quantity to change unless something causes the supply curve or the demand curve to shift.

In the markets for most goods and services, powerful forces move the price and quantity toward their equilibrium values. We can explore these forces by asking what happens when the price is below or above the equilibrium price.

### What Happens When Price Is Below Equilibrium?

Figure 16.2 shows what would happen if the market price started out at $20 per pair, which is below the equilibrium price of $30. At $20 per pair, consumers would want to buy 7 million pairs of shorts, as shown by point *A* on the demand curve. But firms would supply only 2 million pairs, as shown by point *B* on the supply curve. When the quantity demanded is larger than the quantity supplied, the difference between them is called **excess demand**. In Figure 16.2, the excess demand for shorts amounts to 5 million pairs, as represented by the horizontal distance between the supply and demand curves at a price of $20.

When there is excess demand, the price will not remain where it is for long. Some consumers will be unable to purchase all the shorts they want to buy at the market price. Rather than going without, they would gladly pay more to get what they want. At the same time, firms will see shorts disappearing from store shelves, lines forming, and consumers willing to pay higher prices. In response,

---

The **equilibrium price** is the price that equates the quantity supplied and the quantity demanded.

When the quantity demanded is larger than the quantity supplied, the difference between them is called **excess demand**.

The **equilibrium quantity** is the quantity that is supplied and demanded at the equilibrium price.

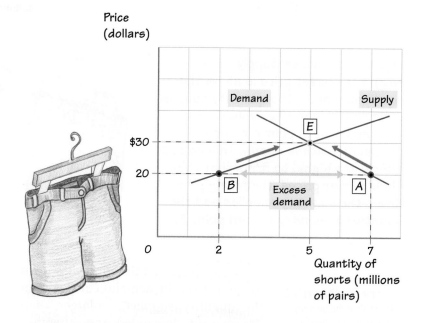

## Figure 16.2 Excess Demand
When the market price is below the equilibrium price, the quantity demanded exceeds the quantity supplied. The gap between points A and B represents excess demand. The excess demand is a signal to firms that they can raise the price. The rising price drives the quantity demanded and the quantity supplied toward point E.

firms will raise the price of shorts above $20 per pair.

What happens next is even more interesting. As the price of shorts rises, the quantity of shorts demanded will decrease. This follows the law of demand that you learned about in Chapter 4. The result is a leftward movement along the demand curve, away from point *A* and toward point *E*. At the same time, the rising price causes the quantity supplied to increase. This follows the law of supply, which you learned about in Chapter 5. The increase in the quantity supplied is seen as a rightward movement along the supply curve, from point *B* toward point *E*. These movements along the two curves shrink the gap between them. So as the price rises, the excess demand for shorts gets smaller.

When will the price stop rising? Only when it reaches the equilibrium price of $30, at point *E*. Until the price hits $30, the excess demand continues to exert upward pressure on the price. But at $30, with no gap between the supply and demand curves, there is no more excess demand to push the price higher. At point *E*, with the price at $30, the quantity demanded and the quantity supplied

are both 5 million pairs. There are enough shorts for every consumer to buy as many as desired at the market price.

## What Happens When Price Is above Equilibrium?
Similar market forces are at work whenever the market price is above the equilibrium price. Figure 16.3 illustrates the case of a $40 price for shorts. At this price, firms are willing to supply 8 million pairs, as shown by point *G* on the supply curve. But consumers only want

*When there is excess demand for a good because of low prices, customers have to wait in long lines and might not get what they want.*

Price
(dollars)

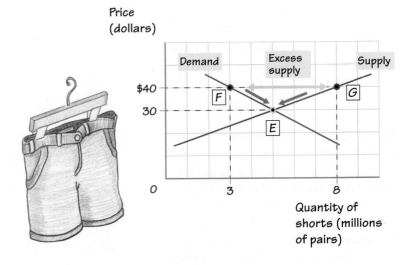

**Figure 16.3** Excess Supply
When the market price is above the equilibrium price, the quantity supplied exceeds the quantity demanded. The gap between points *F* and *G* represents excess supply. This excess supply is a signal to firms that they should lower prices. The falling price drives the quantity supplied and the quantity demanded toward point *E*.

When the quantity supplied is larger than the quantity demanded, the difference between them is called **excess supply**.

3 million pairs at this price, as shown by point *F* on the demand curve. When the quantity supplied is larger than the quantity demanded, the difference between them is called **excess supply**. In the figure, the horizontal distance

between the supply and demand curves at a price of $40 represents the excess supply of 5 million pairs of shorts.

An excess supply causes sellers to be frustrated, because they cannot sell all the 8 million pairs of shorts they are producing. As firms compete with each other to find customers, they will offer shorts at lower and lower prices. So the market price of shorts—which started at $40 per pair—will fall. As the price falls, the quantity demanded rises, causing a movement along the demand curve from point *F* toward point *E*. At the same time, the quantity supplied falls, resulting in a movement along the supply curve from point *G* toward point *E*. These movements cause the excess supply of shorts to shrink like cotton in a hot dryer. Finally, when the price falls to $30, the excess supply is gone. The price stops falling. With the quantities of shorts supplied and demanded now equal, producers can sell every pair they produce.

## Getting to Equilibrium: A Summary

You've just learned that whenever the market price is different from the equilibrium price, market forces move the price toward its equilibrium value. Figure 16.4 summarizes how this happens. When the market price is higher than the equilibrium price, there is excess supply and the market price falls. When

**How Prices Reach Equilibrium**

**Market price > Equilibrium Price**

⬇

**Quantity supplied > Quantity demanded**

⬇

**Excess supply**

⬇

**Market price falls**

**Market price < Equilibrium price**

⬇

**Quantity supplied < Quantity demanded**

⬇

**Excess demand**

⬇

**Market price rises**

**Figure 16.4** How Prices Reach Equilibrium
When the market price is higher than the equilibrium price, there is excess supply and the market price falls. When the market price is lower than the equilibrium price, there is excess demand and the market price rises.

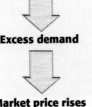

the market price is lower than the equilibrium price, there is excess demand and the market price rises. In both cases, unless something like government price controls prevents the market price from fully adjusting, it will keep moving until it reaches the equilibrium price.

**? DID YOU GET IT?**
**Why can we expect the price of a good to reach the equilibrium price?**

## SCARCITY AND PRICES

Now that you understand how a market reaches equilibrium, you can see that both the supply curve and the demand curve influence the price of a good. The supply and demand curves work like the two blades of a pair of scissors. Just as both blades are necessary to cut through a piece of paper, both curves work together to determine the equilibrium price and quantity in a market.

The interaction of supply and demand also explains why some prices are high and others are low. The *relative scarcity* of a good—meaning the size of

Even though no one really needs the latest electronic gadget, prices tend to be high when long lines of customers form for gadgets that are in short supply.

demand relative to supply—is the key to price determination. When there is a lot of demand for something that is in short supply, like gold, Super Bowl tickets, and Picasso paintings, the relative scarcity causes the good to be expensive even though no one really "needs" it to survive. The same idea explains why many goods that are very important to us—such as food and clothing—are available at much lower prices. For these goods, prices are low because supply is high relative to demand.

## ECONOMICS IN ACTION

# The Diamond-Water Paradox

Why are diamonds expensive while water is cheap? After all, water is essential for survival, whereas diamonds are a luxury good used mainly in jewelry. This presents a paradox, or seeming contradiction: how can something as important as water have a lower price than something unessential like diamonds?

This question, known as the *diamond-water paradox*, was posed by Adam Smith in his book *The Wealth of Nations*, back in 1776. Smith did

not provide a satisfactory answer, but another English economist, William Stanley Jevons (1835–1882), did.

Jevons pointed out that people are willing to pay a very high price for water when they don't have very much. But because water is not very scarce—the supply is large relative to the demand—people don't *have* to pay a high price. The plentiful supply moves the equilibrium point very far down along the market demand curve, driving down the equilibrium price. Any seller who asks a high price—say $20—for a pint of water will not be able to attract a buyer, even for a fancy bottle of Evian water.

Diamonds, by contrast, are found in only three U.S. states and a small number of countries, making the available quantity relatively small. Some buyers are willing to pay several thousand dollars for a diamond. They would pay even more for the first few pints of water needed to stay alive, but they don't have to because

water is plentiful. For diamonds, buyers do have to pay a high price, because the limited supply leaves the equilibrium point in the diamond market higher up on the demand curve.

**DID YOU GET IT?**

Why are some goods that nobody needs more expensive than some goods that are essential to life?

# MODULE 16 REVIEW AND ASSESSMENT

## Summing Up the Key Ideas: Match the following terms to the correct definitions.

A. Equilibrium
B. Equilibrium price
C. Equilibrium quantity
D. Excess demand
E. Excess supply

_____ 1.    When the quantity supplied is larger than the quantity demanded.

_____ 2.    The quantity that is supplied and demanded at the equilibrium price.

_____ 3.    The point at which the quantity supplied equals the quantity demanded.

_____ 4.    The price that equates the quantity supplied with the quantity demanded.

_____ 5.    When the quantity demanded is larger than the quantity supplied.

## Analyze and Explain: Use the graph provided to answer the following questions.

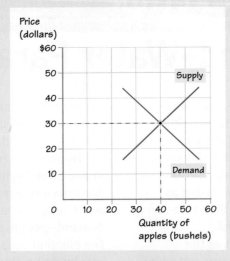

1.    What is the equilibrium price and equilibrium quantity of apples?

2.    Describe the condition when the price is $20. What will happen in the market to return to the equilibrium price and quantity?

3. Describe the condition when the price is $40. What will happen in the market to return to the equilibrium price and quantity?

**Apply:** For each of the following scenarios, indicate whether price would increase, decrease, or remain the same. Explain your answer.

|  | PRICE | EXPLAIN |
|---|---|---|
| 1. Currently the quantity demanded is 10 and the quantity supplied is 20. | _____ | _____ |
| 2. Currently the quantity demanded is 15 and the quantity supplied is 15. | _____ | _____ |
| 3. Currently the quantity demanded is 25 and the quantity supplied is 5. | _____ | _____ |

# MODULE 17

# Changes in Supply and Demand

**KEY IDEA:** A change in supply or demand, as shown by a shift of the supply or demand curve, causes the equilibrium price and quantity to change in a predictable way.

**OBJECTIVES**

- To explain how a change in supply affects the equilibrium price and quantity.
- To explain how a change in demand affects the equilibrium price and quantity.
- To explain what is known and what is unknown about the effect of a simultaneous change in both supply and demand.

## How Things Change

In the preceding module we saw that when a market is in equilibrium, there is no tendency for the price or quantity to change. But we also know from Chapters 4 and 5 that the demand curve and the supply curve can shift. These shifts cause the equilibrium price and quantity in the market to change.

For example, many teenagers like to wear the latest fashions. The popularity of particular types of clothing—whether soccer jerseys, leggings, or board shorts—changes from year to year. These and similar changes in tastes affect the demand for trendy goods and services. When an article of clothing becomes fashionable, the demand curve for that article shifts to the right, the excess demand causes the price to rise, and suppliers respond by increasing the quantity supplied.

Similarly, changes in technology and disruptions in transportation cause the supply curves for some goods to shift. In the chapter-opening story, for example, we saw that the eruption of the Icelandic volcano in 2010 disrupted the supply of salmon to Asia. Thus, in the Asian market for salmon, the supply curve shifted to the left, the price rose, and buyers responded by decreasing the quantity demanded.

Some of the most important questions you will encounter in economics involve predicting how a shift of the supply curve or demand curve will affect a market. In this module, we consider what happens to price and quantity when the supply curve shifts, when the demand curve shifts, and when both curves shift at the same time.

Our first step in exploring these changes is to recall the different types of events that can change supply or demand and thus shift the supply or demand curve. Table 17.1 summarizes the causes of shifts you learned in Chapters 4 and 5.

*Fashion changes from year to year, and with it the demand for particular articles of clothing.*

| Table 17.1 **A Review of the Factors That Shift the Demand Curve or the Supply Curve** | |
| --- | --- |
| **DEMAND SHIFTERS** | **SUPPLY SHIFTERS** |
| Tastes | The cost of inputs |
| Income | Government policies |
| The prices of related goods (complements or substitutes) | The number of firms |
| The number of buyers | Technology |
| Expectations about the future | Natural disasters and weather |
| | Expectations about future prices |

# CHANGES IN DEMAND

When demand changes, the price consumers pay and the quantity purchased change as well. Next we'll examine the reasons for these potentially important changes in equilibrium price and quantity.

## An Increase in Demand

Let's consider the market for spinach. Some people really like to eat spinach, but it takes a backseat to potatoes, lettuce, tomatoes, carrots, and even celery in terms of popularity. Suppose new research reveals unexpected health benefits from eating spinach. News of these benefits would increase people's preference for spinach. What would happen to the price and quantity of spinach?

To answer this question, let's first consider the equilibrium in the spinach market before the new research is announced. Figure 17.1 shows the market supply and demand curves for spinach. The initial equilibrium, indicated by point $E_1$, is determined by the intersection of the original demand curve, *Demand*$_1$, and the supply curve, *Supply*$_1$.

You may have noticed something different about this graph: there are no numbers along the axes. Rather than being labeled with specific numbers, the equilibrium price is labeled $P_1$ on the *y*-axis and the equilibrium quantity is labeled $Q_1$ on the *x*-axis. It is often useful to illustrate a market with a *generic supply and demand graph* like this, which does not indicate actual numbers for prices or quantities. The generic graph is just a simplified version of the supply and demand graphs we've been discussing. Generic graphs make it easy to see how equilibrium is determined and how it changes after a shift. In the generic graph, $P$ stands for price, and the number 1 indicates that $P_1$ is our first or initial equilibrium price, before the shift in demand. Similarly, $Q$ stands for quantity, and $Q_1$ is our initial equilibrium quantity.

Now let's consider the effect of the new research finding on the spinach

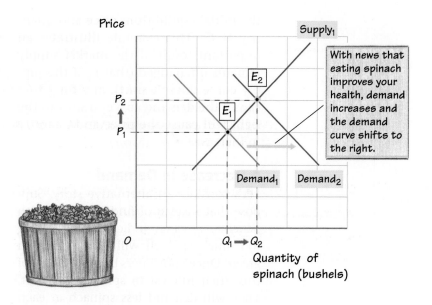

With news that eating spinach improves your health, demand increases and the demand curve shifts to the right.

**Figure 17.1** The Demand Curve Shifts Right

market. Knowing that spinach is especially healthy, at any given price consumers will demand more spinach than before. This change in tastes causes an increase in demand, represented by a rightward shift of the demand curve from *Demand*$_1$ to *Demand*$_2$.

When the demand curve shifts to the right, the price will not stay at $P_1$. After the shift, the quantity of spinach demanded at the old price of $P_1$ is greater than the quantity supplied. There is an excess demand for spinach, and some buyers cannot get the spinach they desire, so the price rises. In fact, the price keeps rising until the quantities supplied and demanded are equal again. This occurs at the new equilibrium point, $E_2$, where the new demand curve, *Demand*$_2$, intersects the original supply curve, *Supply*$_1$.

At the new equilibrium price of $P_2$, the quantity supplied and the quantity demanded are both equal to $Q_2$, the new equilibrium quantity of spinach. Because supply and demand are back in balance, there will be no tendency for the price to rise or fall.

Note what has happened to the price and quantity. Because of the change in tastes and the resulting increase in demand, the new equilibrium price and quantity at $E_2$ are both higher than the initial equilibrium price and quantity at $E_1$. This example illustrates an important result: if the market supply remains unchanged (that is, if the supply curve doesn't shift), anything that causes the demand curve to shift to the right will cause the price and quantity to increase.

### A Decrease in Demand

Let's consider an alternative story. Suppose that instead of finding new health benefits, research indicates that eating too much spinach will turn your skin green! Once consumers become aware of this, their interest in spinach will wilt. They will demand less spinach at each price, as illustrated by a leftward shift of the demand curve.

Figure 17.2 illustrates what happens in this case. As before, the initial equilibrium at point $E_1$ is determined by the intersection of the original demand curve, $Demand_1$, and supply curve, $Supply_1$. The initial equilibrium price is $P_1$ and the initial equilibrium quantity is $Q_1$. The new revelation about spinach causes the demand curve to shift leftward to the demand curve labeled $Demand_2$. There is excess supply at the initial price, which leads to a price decrease. The new equilibrium is at point $E_2$, where the new demand curve,

$Demand_2$, intersects the original supply curve, $Supply_1$. At the new equilibrium price of $P_2$, the quantity supplied and the quantity demanded are both equal to $Q_2$, which is the new equilibrium quantity of spinach.

As a result of the decrease in demand, the new equilibrium price and quantity are lower than the initial price and quantity. This example illustrates another important result: if market supply remains unchanged, any factor that causes the demand curve to shift to the left will cause the price and quantity to fall.

## CHANGES IN SUPPLY

Like changes in demand, changes in supply influence the equilibrium price and quantity in important ways. Let's explore how that happens.

### A Decrease in Supply

Consider what happens when supply decreases, as represented by a leftward shift in the supply curve. We'll use the example of the ruptured gasoline pipeline in Phoenix, Arizona, first discussed in Chapter 5. As a result of this disaster, the quantity of gasoline available for sale in Phoenix decreased at every price. Now we can consider how this event affected the equilibrium price and quantity of gasoline in Phoenix.

Figure 17.3 provides hypothetical supply and demand curves for the gasoline market in Phoenix. In the month before the pipeline broke, the market for gasoline in Phoenix was in equilibrium at point $E_1$, where the original supply curve, $Supply_1$, and the original demand curve, $Demand_1$, intersect. The equilibrium price was \$2.50 per gallon and the equilibrium quantity was 4 million gallons.

After the pipeline broke, firms were willing to supply less gasoline at each price. This shifted the supply curve for gasoline leftward to $Supply_2$. At the original price of \$2.50 per gallon, the quantity demanded exceeded the quantity supplied. The resulting excess demand pushed the price up to the level at which the new supply curve, $Supply_2$, crossed the

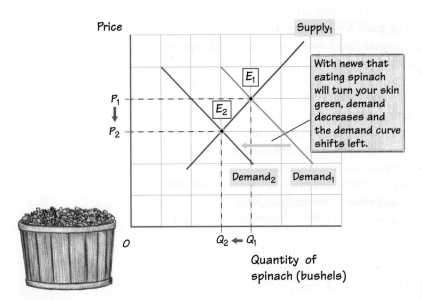

**Figure 17.2** The Demand Curve Shifts Left

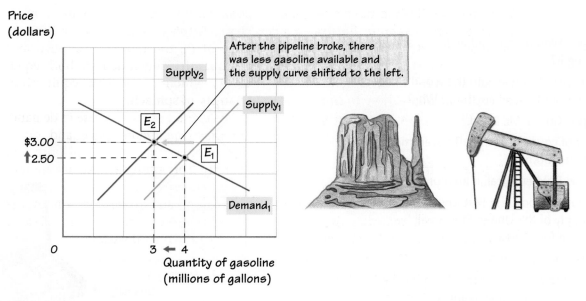

Price
(dollars)

After the pipeline broke, there was less gasoline available and the supply curve shifted to the left.

Supply₂

Supply₁

$E_2$

$E_1$

$3.00

↑2.50

Demand₁

0    3 ← 4

Quantity of gasoline
(millions of gallons)

**Figure 17.3** The Supply Curve Shifts Left

original demand curve, *Demand*₁. At the new equilibrium point, $E_2$, the price was $3.00 per gallon and the equilibrium quantity was 3 million gallons. As you would expect, drivers in Phoenix were not very happy about the 50-cent price increase. Their wallets felt the effects of the gasoline pipeline rupture.

## YOUR TURN

What do you think happened to the price and quantity of gasoline in Phoenix after the pipeline was *fixed*? Hint: think about what would have happened to the supply curve once the pipeline was repaired.

# ECONOMICS IN ACTION

# Supply and Demand in a James Bond Movie

In the 1964 movie *Goldfinger*, the spy James Bond discovers "Operation Grand Slam," a plan devised by arch villain Auric Goldfinger. Goldfinger, who has already amassed a sizable quantity of gold, plans to break into the U.S. gold depository at Fort Knox, which contains $15 billion in gold. At first, Bond cannot understand Goldfinger's motivation. Bond and Goldfinger have the following conversation:

**Bond:** You disappoint me, Goldfinger. You know operation Grand Slam won't work. . . . At the most you are going to have two hours before the Army, Navy, Air Force, and Marines move in and make you put it back.

**Goldfinger:** Who mentioned anything about removing it?

**Bond:** You plan to break into the world's largest bank, but not to steal anything? Why?

**Goldfinger:** Go on, Mr. Bond.

**Bond:** But of course, [a foreign] government has given you a bomb.

**Goldfinger:** I prefer to call it an atomic device.

**Bond:** If you explode it in Fort Knox, the entire gold supply of the United States will be radioactive for 57 years.

**Goldfinger:** 58, to be exact.

**Bond:** I apologize, Goldfinger, it is an inspired deal. They get what they want—economic chaos in the West—and the value of your gold increases many times.

**Goldfinger:** I conservatively estimate 10 times.

**Bond:** Brilliant.

Goldfinger's plan—to remove much of the gold supply from the market by making it radioactive—was designed to make gold even more scarce than it was already. The price would then have to rise to bring supply and demand back into balance, as shown in Figure 17.4. Those who already owned gold, such as Goldfinger himself, would see the value of their holdings increase. The economic logic of the plan was sound. Fortunately, James Bond prevented it from being carried out.

FROM *Goldfinger*, Dir. Guy Hamilton, United Artists, 1964.

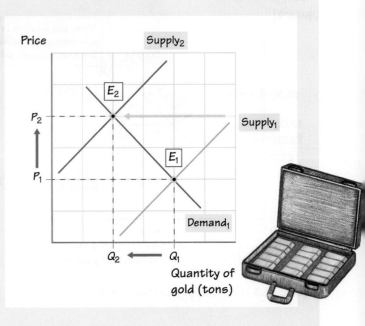

**Figure 17.4** The Shift Goldfinger Wanted Goldfinger wanted to shift the supply curve for gold to the left. As a seller of gold, this would allow him to charge a higher price.

## AN INCREASE IN SUPPLY

A supply curve can also shift in a rightward direction, indicating an increase in supply. Consumers like this much better. Figure 17.5 provides a simplified version of what happened in the Florida strawberry market between 2010 and 2011. In the spring of 2010, the market for Florida strawberries was in equilibrium at point $E_1$, where the original supply curve, $Supply_1$, and the original demand curve, $Demand_1$, intersect. The

price of a pound of strawberries was $3.50, and the quantity sold was 205 million pounds.

In the spring of 2011, strawberry producers found that their fields were producing far more strawberries than in 2010 because of an unusual combination of sunshine and rain. An abundance of fruit made producers willing to supply more strawberries at each price. Supply increased, and the supply curve shifted rightward from $Supply_1$ to $Supply_2$. This shift caused an excess supply at the initial price. As a result, the price fell and

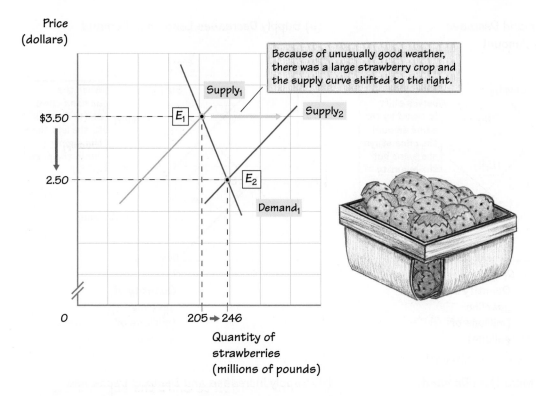

Price
(dollars)

Because of unusually good weather, there was a large strawberry crop and the supply curve shifted to the right.

Supply₁

Supply₂

$3.50 ‒ ‒ ‒ E₁

2.50 ‒ ‒ ‒ E₂

Demand₁

0    205 → 246

Quantity of
strawberries
(millions of pounds)

**Figure 17.5** The Supply Curve Shifts Right

the market moved to a new equilibrium at point $E_2$, the intersection of the new supply curve, $Supply_2$, and the original demand curve, $Demand_1$. At the new equilibrium, the price was $2.50 per pound, a $1.00 decrease from the initial price per pound. The equilibrium quantity rose from 205 million pounds to 246 million pounds. Buyers were delighted with the lower price at the new equilibrium. They were left with more money in their wallets to buy additional goods, including more strawberries.

**DID YOU GET IT?**

Why does an increase in the supply of a good result in a change in the equilibrium price and quantity of that good?

# CHANGES IN BOTH SUPPLY AND DEMAND

Sometimes simultaneous changes in supply and demand cause both the supply curve and the demand curve to shift at the same time. For example, the supply curve for gasoline could shift because of a pipeline accident, and by coincidence, at the same time the demand curve for gasoline could shift because of the introduction of a popular new electric car. In this example, both the supply curve and the demand curve would shift to the left. In other cases, the curves both shift to the right, or they shift in opposite directions. In this section we consider how shifts of both the demand curve and the supply curve affect the market.

Panel (a) of Figure 17.6 shows the initial equilibrium point in the gasoline market, $E_1$, at the intersection of the original demand curve, $Demand_1$, and the original supply curve, $Supply_1$. At $E_1$, the price is $P_1$ per gallon and the quantity of gasoline supplied and demanded is $Q_1$. The pipeline accident causes the supply curve to shift to the left. At the same time, the popular new electric car reduces the use of gasoline, so the demand curve shifts to the left.

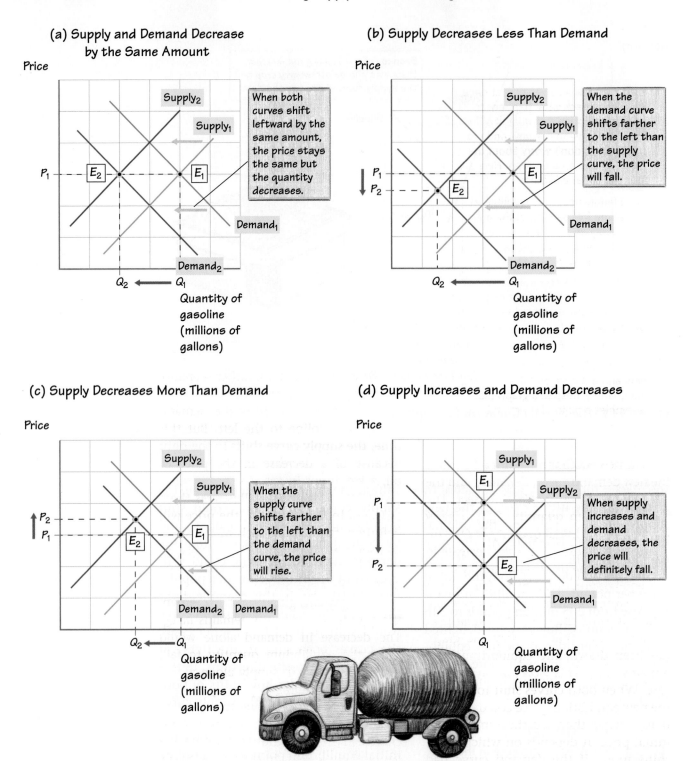

**Figure 17.6** Shifts of Both the Supply Curve and the Demand Curve
When the supply curve and the demand curve shift at the same time, the effect on equilibrium depends on the relative sizes of the shifts. Panel (a) shows that when supply and demand both decrease by the same amount, the equilibrium quantity decreases but the equilibrium price stays the same. Panel (b) shows that when supply decreases by less than demand, both the equilibrium quantity and the equilibrium price decrease. Panel (c) shows that when supply decreases by more than demand, the equilibrium quantity decreases but the equilibrium price increases. Panel (d) shows that when supply increases and demand decreases, the equilibrium price decreases. As drawn, the equilibrium quantity stays the same, but it could increase or decrease depending on the relative size of the shifts.

## Don't Be Intimidated by Double Shifts!

Even when two curves shift at once, it's easy to track what happens to equilibrium price and quantity. The key is to focus on the new and old equilibrium; don't worry about the mess of lines on the graph. Here are four steps that will help:

1.  Identify the initial equilibrium at the intersection of the initial supply and demand curves.
2.  Label the corresponding price and quantity as $P_1$ and $Q_1$.
3.  Identify the new equilibrium at the intersection of the new supply and demand curves.
4.  Label the corresponding price and quantity as $P_2$ and $Q_2$.

It will then be easy to compare the new and old price and the new and old quantity, despite a graph that resembles a plate of spaghetti!

*An increase in the use of electric cars could reduce the demand for gasoline and shift the demand curve to the left. At the same time, a pipeline accident could shift the supply curve for gasoline to the left. The result would be a double shift, meaning a shift in both the supply curve and the demand curve.*

The new equilibrium point is $E_2$, where the new demand curve, $Demand_2$, and the new supply curve, $Supply_2$, intersect. The new equilibrium quantity, $Q_2$, is clearly lower than the initial quantity of $Q_1$. This makes sense because both the decrease in demand and the decrease in supply cause the equilibrium quantity to fall, so the combination of these two decreases will definitely lower the equilibrium quantity.

But notice that the way the graph has been drawn, the equilibrium price remains at $P_1$. This won't always be the case. When both curves shift to the left, the new equilibrium price could be lower than, higher than, or the same as the initial price. It depends on which curve shifts more. If the demand curve had shifted leftward by more than the supply curve, the price would have fallen. If the supply curve had shifted more, the price would have risen. These two possibilities are illustrated in panels (b) and (c) of Figure 17.6. Look at the figures closely and make sure you understand why the price in this example can stay the same, rise, or fall depending on the size of the supply shift relative to the demand shift.

Now let's consider another scenario. Suppose once again that the new electric car is introduced, shifting the demand curve for gasoline to the left. But this time, the supply curve shifts to the right because of a decrease in the price of oil, a key input in gasoline production. Panel (d) of Figure 17.6 illustrates these changes. In this situation, the price will definitely fall because each of the shifts by itself contributes to a drop in price, so the two shifts combined are guaranteed to bring the price down.

The way this graph has been drawn, the equilibrium quantity remains at $Q_1$. The decrease in demand alone would cause the equilibrium quantity to fall, and the increase in supply alone would cause the equilibrium quantity to rise. In this particular case, the two changes balanced each other out, resulting in no change in the equilibrium quantity. If the demand curve had shifted a bit more to the left, the equilibrium quantity would have fallen. If, instead, the supply curve had shifted a bit more to the right, the equilibrium quantity would have risen.

### DID YOU GET IT?
**If the supply curve and the demand curve both shift to the left, how can you tell what happens to the equilibrium price?**

**Table 17.2** **Summary of Price and Quantity Changes**

| SHIFTS | | CHANGES IN MARKET EQUILIBRIUM | |
|---|---|---|---|
| Supply | Demand | Price | Quantity |
| 1. Decrease (shift to the left) | Unchanged | ⬆ | ⬇ |
| 2. Increase (shift to the right) | Unchanged | ⬇ | ⬆ |
| 3. Unchanged | Increase | ⬆ | ⬆ |
| 4. Unchanged | Decrease | ⬇ | ⬇ |
| 5. Decrease | Increase | ⬆ | ? |
| 6. Increase | Decrease | ⬇ | ? |
| 7. Decrease | Decrease | ? | ⬇ |
| 8. Increase | Increase | ? | ⬆ |

# CHANGES IN SUPPLY AND DEMAND: A SUMMARY

Table 17.2 summarizes how various changes in supply and demand affect the equilibrium price and quantity of a good. For example, if supply decreases and demand is unchanged, then the equilibrium price must increase and the equilibrium quantity must decrease. Remember that for both supply and demand, a rightward shift represents an increase and a leftward shift represents a decrease.

## YOUR TURN

Draw a graph of the market for cheesecake and label the supply curve, the demand curve, the equilibrium price, and the equilibrium quantity. Show how a popular new diet that forbids cheesecake consumption would affect the curves and the equilibrium price and quantity.

# MODULE 17 REVIEW AND ASSESSMENT

## Summing Up the Key Ideas: Match the following terms to the correct definitions.

A. An increase in demand    C. An increase in supply

B. A decrease in demand    D. A decrease in supply

_____ 1.    A rightward shift of the supply curve.

_____ 2.    A leftward shift of the demand curve.

_____ 3.    A leftward shift of the supply curve.

_____ 4.    A rightward shift of the demand curve.

## Analyze and Explain: Determine whether each of the following scenarios shifts the **demand curve** or the **supply curve** and indicate the direction of the shift. Then identify the effect of the shift on **equilibrium price** and **quantity**. You might find it helpful to draw the graphs.

| | DEMAND OR SUPPLY SHIFT? | EQUILIBRIUM PRICE | EQUILIBRIUM QUANTITY |
|---|---|---|---|
| 1. The cost of production rises in the computer market. | _____ | _____ | _____ |
| 2. Wearing blue jeans becomes more fashionable among consumers. | _____ | _____ | _____ |
| 3. Favorable weather conditions allow for a greater-than-normal crop of avocados in California. | _____ | _____ | _____ |
| 4. In search of profit, 10 new firms enter the market for electric cars. | _____ | _____ | _____ |
| 5. A freeze destroys a good portion of the coffee crop and raises the price of coffee. How does this affect the market for tea, a substitute for coffee? | _____ | _____ | _____ |

6. People become aware that drinking orange juice helps prevent heart disease.

_____  _____  _____

7. Consumers are convinced that cell phones will be cheaper during the next holiday season.

_____  _____  _____

**Apply:** Predict what will happen to **equilibrium price** and **equilibrium quantity** in each of the following sets of conditions. First think about the change in demand and/or supply and then determine the change in the price and quantity. You might find it helpful to draw the graphs.

|  | EQUILIBRIUM PRICE | EQUILIBRIUM QUANTITY |
|---|---|---|
| 1. Consumers' incomes rise and steaks are a normal good. The supply of beef cattle has fallen recently due to a harsh winter in the western United States. | _____ | _____ |
| 2. Consumer information that there is a shock hazard with hair dryers becomes available. Workers who produce hair dryers have signed a wage agreement that cuts their paycheck by 10 percent. | _____ | _____ |
| 3. Consumers' taste for American cars fades. Simultaneously, automakers must pay more for their workers' health insurance. | _____ | _____ |
| 4. Ten new sellers of athletic shoes enter the market, as there is a surge of demand for athletic shoes. | _____ | _____ |

# MODULE 18

# Shortages, Surpluses, and the Role of Prices

**KEY IDEA:** Equilibrium prices provide benefits that are lost when forces prevent markets from reaching their equilibrium price.

**OBJECTIVES**

- **To show how price ceilings and floors cause shortages and surpluses.**
- **To explain the important incentives prices create.**
- **To identify problems with rationing as a way of allocating goods and services.**

## Lasting Imbalance

When farmers produced more milk than consumers demanded in 2009, milk prices fell by 30 percent. The lower price made farmers less eager to produce milk and lured more consumers into buying it. These changes nudged the market toward equilibrium. Then in 2011, with growing demand from China and elsewhere, the quantity of milk supplied fell short of the quantity demanded, and the price of milk rose to new heights. The higher price encouraged production and discouraged consumption, again leading the market toward a new equilibrium. In the milk market, as in all the markets we've discussed so far, changes in the price serve to bring supply and demand into balance. Most markets work this way most of the time: they are either in equilibrium or heading toward it.

But sometimes a market will remain out of equilibrium for a long time. The price does not adjust upward or downward as needed to bring about equilibrium. We'll discuss the reasons for this a bit later. But first, let's explore what happens if a price does not adjust to its equilibrium level.

*Rising prices can eliminate an excess demand for milk. But sometimes there is no moovement in prices.*

## SHORTAGES AND SURPLUSES

Figure 18.1 shows the market for milk. A price below the equilibrium price of $3, such as $2, creates an excess demand for milk: 35 million gallons are demanded but only 15 million are supplied. The existence of buyers who are willing to pay more than the current price ordinarily causes the price to rise until it reaches the equilibrium price. But what happens if, for some reason, the price does *not* rise? Then the excess demand will not go away. Consumers will continue trying to buy more milk than is available.

When an excess demand for a product persists for a significant period of time—weeks, months, or even years—we call it a **shortage**. Shortages create many problems. For instance, consumers sometimes find it necessary to spend time standing in long lines at stores to increase their chances of getting the product. After the earthquake and nuclear accident in Japan in 2011,

A **shortage** exists when an excess demand for a product persists for a significant period of time.

THINKSTOCK

**Figure 18.1** A Shortage or Surplus
When price remains below the equilibrium price for a significant period of time, there is a shortage. The size of the shortage can be found as the horizontal distance between the quantity supplied and the quantity demanded at the current price. When price remains above the equilibrium price for a significant period of time, there is a surplus equal to the horizontal distance between the quantity demanded and the quantity supplied.

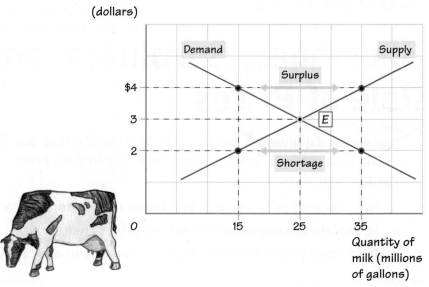

A **surplus** exists when an excess supply persists for a significant period of time.

*Consumers in Hong Kong line up for milk after the 2011 nuclear accident in Japan. Because the price of milk was below the equilibrium price, the quantity demanded exceeded the quantity supplied, and a shortage occurred.*

consumers in Hong Kong feared that supplies of milk from Japan would be limited or contaminated. Shoppers lined up at stores to buy milk from safe sources. Because the price of milk was below the equilibrium price, the quantity demanded exceeded the quantity supplied, and many consumers went home disappointed.

The opposite situation occurs when a price stays too high. Figure 18.1 shows that a price of $4 per gallon creates an excess supply of milk: 35 million gallons are supplied but only 15 million are demanded.

Ordinarily, an excess supply makes the price of a good fall. But if, for some reason, the price does not fall, sellers will continue trying to sell more than consumers want to buy.

When an excess supply persists for a significant period of time, we call it a **surplus**. Sellers become frustrated with a surplus, because they cannot find enough buyers. For example, there was a surplus in the U.S. housing market in 2009 and 2010. More homes were offered for sale than people wanted to buy at the prices sellers were asking. Although prices did fall during those years, they did not fall enough to bring supply and demand into balance. The resulting housing surplus lasted for more than two years.

Moving forward, we will look at the primary causes of shortages and surpluses. You'll learn that the government sometimes causes shortages or surpluses with policies that impose *price ceilings* and *price floors*. You'll also see that the behavior of buyers and sellers themselves can cause shortages and surpluses. We'll use these insights to understand how prices help the economy accomplish some important goals.

---

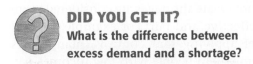

**DID YOU GET IT?**
What is the difference between excess demand and a shortage?

# PRICE CEILINGS

A **price ceiling** is a government-imposed limit on the highest price firms can charge in a market. For example, New York State has a law that prevents milk prices from exceeding an amount considered to be "unconscionably excessive." Sellers cannot charge a price above $4.37 a gallon. However, the equilibrium price of milk is seldom above that boundary. If they would charge, say, $4.10 in the absence of the law, the price ceiling is *ineffective*—it makes no difference. In contrast, a price ceiling that is set below the equilibrium price has an effect on the market because it prevents the price from reaching equilibrium. If the price ceiling for milk were $3.50, that would be an *effective* price ceiling because it would have the effect of forcing sellers to charge less than the equilibrium price.

Several cities, including New York City, impose rent controls that prevent some landlords from charging more than a certain amount for an apartment. Figure 18.2 illustrates the effect of this price ceiling in the market for apartments subject to rent control. In the absence of rent control, the equilibrium would occur at point $E$, with the quantity supplied and the quantity demanded both equal to $Q_e$ and the price equal to $P_e$. However, rent control prevents the price from reaching its equilibrium value. The price is set at $P_{Ceiling}$, which is below $P_e$. At the price of $P_{Ceiling}$, $Q_2$ apartments are demanded. Landlords, however, are willing to provide only $Q_1$ apartments for people to rent. The quantity of apartments supplied is not only smaller than the quantity demanded, $Q_2$, but it is also smaller than $Q_e$, the quantity that would be supplied without the price ceiling. This is because the lower rent decreases the incentive to make apartments available. Because the price ceiling limits the earnings of apartment landlords, fewer new apartment buildings are built. Some existing apartment buildings are converted into hotels or office buildings. And with potential renters clamoring for the low-rent apartments, there is little incentive to keep rent-controlled apartments attractive or in good repair, so the apartment buildings tend to become rundown.

The most direct impact of rent control is that those people who do manage to rent apartments pay less than they would without rent control. However, for reasons we'll explore next, most economists do not believe that price ceilings such as rent control are the best way to help consumers.

## Problems with Price Ceilings

One problem with price ceilings is that, although they are usually designed to help the poor, the beneficiaries are sometimes the rich. With the simplest form of rent control, for example, everyone pays the lower rent, including those who are very well off. Some renters may even be wealthier than the landlords who own the apartments. In these cases, a wealthier renter benefits at the expense of a less wealthy landlord who must charge a lower rent.

A **price ceiling** is a government-imposed limit on the highest price firms can charge in a market.

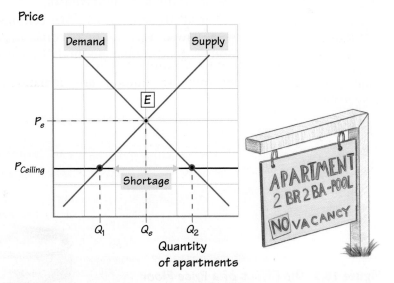

**Figure 18.2** The Effect of a Price Ceiling
Rent control serves as a price ceiling in the market for apartments. When a price ceiling holds the price below the equilibrium price, the quantity supplied falls below the quantity demanded. This creates a shortage in the market, as shown by the horizontal distance between $Q_1$ and $Q_2$.

Another problem with price ceilings is that—because they create shortages—some people who want a good at the current price cannot get it. Or they may have to waste valuable time trying to find a willing seller. Even those who *do* get the good might end up paying more than the equilibrium price. For example, with a price ceiling on milk, some people would buy a lot of milk and sell it for a price above the price ceiling—illegally—to people who could not find it in the stores. This type of illegal market is called a *black market*. Because milk would be so scarce, the price in the black market could be higher than the equilibrium price.

The same types of problems occur with rent control. Apartment hunters have to spend more time looking for an apartment than they otherwise would. Some will have to pay real estate agents to help them find one. Others may bribe a building superintendent or a current resident to give them a heads up when an apartment is about to become available. Taking into account the opportunity cost of the extra search time and the payments to real estate agents or building superintendents, it may end up costing as much or more to rent an apartment than it would without the rent control.

For all these reasons, price ceilings are a flawed way to help consumers afford a good. Other methods that do not create shortages are considered more effective and fair. For example, instead of applying rent controls, many cities now help people with low incomes pay for apartments or homes. This allows cities to target assistance to the people who need it most. These policies also allow landlords to charge the equilibrium rent, thereby avoiding a shortage of apartments among other problems.

**DID YOU GET IT?**
What is one problem created by an effective price ceiling?

# PRICE FLOORS

Price ceilings are intended to assist buyers of things like apartments and milk, but what about the sellers? Policies are made with them in mind, too. For example, in an effort to help dairy farmers, the U.S. government does not allow the price of nonfat dry milk to fall below $0.80 per pound. Instead, the government establishes a *price floor* for dry milk. A **price floor** is a government-imposed limit below which prices cannot fall.

Figure 18.3 shows the effect of a price floor on the market for milk. Without the price floor, the equilibrium price would be $P_e$ and the equilibrium quantity would be $Q_e$. The price floor is set at $P_{Floor}$, which is greater than $P_e$. This creates a

A **price floor** is a government-imposed limit below which prices cannot fall.

**Figure 18.3** The Effect of a Price Floor
When a price floor holds the price of dry milk above the equilibrium price, the quantity demanded remains below the quantity supplied. This creates a surplus in the market, as shown by the horizontal distance between $Q_2$ and $Q_1$.

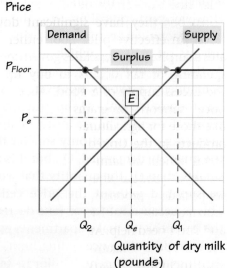

surplus: at $P_{Floor}$, the quantity demanded, $Q_2$, is less than the quantity supplied, $Q_1$. Because the price floor is above the equilibrium price, it is an *effective* price floor—it makes a difference. A price floor below the equilibrium price would make no difference because market forces would bring the price even higher than the ineffective price floor. That is, if the equilibrium price were $0.75 per pound of nonfat dry milk and the government said the price cannot fall below $0.50, the price floor wouldn't make any difference because firms wouldn't charge less than $0.50 anyway.

The government uses two methods to keep the price of milk from falling below $P_{Floor}$. First, it provides incentives for dairy farmers to produce a smaller quantity than $Q_1$, which is the quantity farmers would like to supply at the price of $P_{Floor}$. Second, when an excess supply exists at $P_{Floor}$, the government buys up the excess milk itself. Both of these methods are designed to avoid a surplus of milk in the market and the resulting downward pressure on the price.

Price floors have been used in the United States to support the prices for milk, cheese, butter, peanuts, sugar, and many other agricultural products. They exist to make the incomes of farmers—who receive the elevated prices as revenue—higher than they would be without the floors.

## Problems with Price Floors

Price floors are created with good intentions, but they have significant downsides. An effective price floor either creates a surplus or necessitates government spending of tax dollars to buy up the excess supply of a good. Also, price support programs like those for agricultural products in the United States benefit *all* farmers who produce the supported products, even if they are wealthy and don't need help. At the same time, consumers, including many  low-income families, have to pay more for products like milk, peanut butter, and sugar. Some of the farmers helped by the price floors are better off than the average consumer who buys their products. For all these reasons, economists generally do not favor price floors as a way to help farmers.

**DID YOU GET IT?**
What is one problem created by an effective price floor?

## STICKY PRICES

In many markets, shortages and surpluses have nothing to do with price floors or ceilings. Instead, they are caused by **sticky prices**, which are prices that move to their equilibrium values very slowly. When prices are sticky, it can take weeks, months, or longer for a market to reach equilibrium. In the meantime, if the price is below its equilibrium value there will be a shortage, and if the price is above its equilibrium value there will be a surplus.

**Sticky prices** are prices that move to their equilibrium values very slowly.

Prices can be sticky for a number of reasons. Habits, customs, and traditional arrangements with suppliers sometimes prevent prices from changing. For example, when demand is unexpectedly high for tickets to a new movie, theaters generally do not raise the ticket price for that movie. People who want to see the movie may not be able to get tickets for days as the result of a shortage. Why don't theaters raise the price, which would give them more profit and eliminate the shortage? The reason is partly that movie studios pressure theater owners to be consistent with ticket prices. Also, theater owners have traditionally charged the same price for every movie showing at a particular time. Breaking that custom could upset customers, who might not come back to a theater that seems to charge unfair prices.

Prices can also be sticky because it is costly to change them. Restaurants have to print up new menus when they raise or lower prices, and hotels have to change their advertising on billboards, in magazines, and on the Internet. When the demand or supply curve shifts, some businesses may prefer to wait for some time before incurring the cost of changing prices. They want to be sure that the new equilibrium is going to last.

Finally, sticky prices can occur because of stubbornness or due to disbelief among sellers that the equilibrium price has dropped substantially from a long-standing value. For example, the housing surplus in 2009 and 2010 arose when the equilibrium price of homes fell dramatically, but many sellers refused to lower their asking price enough to bring supply and demand back into balance.

Sticky prices can delay a movement to equilibrium, but prices do not remain sticky forever. Even Motel 6, a motel chain named after its practice of charging $6 per room, eventually had to break with its tradition due to increases in the equilibrium price. As long as prices are allowed to move up and down, sooner or later, firms tend to make adjustments toward the equilibrium price. As the housing surplus continued, for example, more and more home sellers realized

they would have to accept a lower price if they wanted to sell. And as prices moved toward equilibrium, the housing surplus began to shrink.

*It was hard for Motel 6 to break with tradition and charge more than $6 per room, but prices don't stay sticky forever.*

## ECONOMICS IN ACTION

# Lessons from Super Bowl Sunday

You can learn a lot about economics just by studying the price of Super Bowl tickets. Here are two lessons that one of your authors, Alan Krueger, learned from attending Super Bowl XXXV with his father.

*Lesson 1. If the price remains below the equilibrium price, there will be a shortage.* For example, the face value listed on Super Bowl tickets in 2001 was $325. This price was much too low to balance demand with the limited supply. The National Football League held a lottery for 500 pairs of tickets and was flooded with 36,000 applications—the odds of being

admitted to Princeton University are better. On game day, hundreds of frustrated fans gathered outside the stadium and displayed "Ticket Wanted" signs that offered $1,500 and up for a ticket.

*Lesson 2. If the price remains below the equilibrium price, a secondary market will develop to bring supply and demand into balance.* A secondary market is one in which previously purchased goods are resold. The secondary market for Super Bowl tickets involves scalpers, licensed ticket brokers, and online auctions like those on StubHub.com.

About half of the states regulate the resale of sports tickets in some way. And as shown in Figure 18.4, the official price of Super Bowl tickets has risen considerably over time. Still, tickets are often resold, because the price remains far below the equilibrium price. A week before the Super Bowl, tickets on Yahoo! Auctions traded for $1,500 to $3,500 each.

ADAPTED FROM Alan B. Krueger, "Economic Scene," *New York Times*, February 1, 2001.

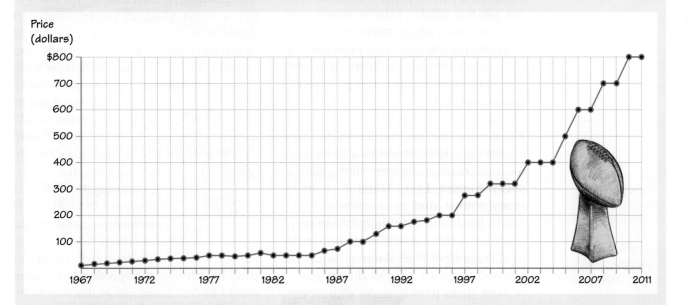

**Figure 18.4** The Price of a Super Bowl Ticket
This figure shows the lowest official price (face value) for a Super Bowl ticket in every year since the Super Bowl began. Although the official price has risen substantially, it is still below the equilibrium price, and scalpers resell tickets for thousands of dollars each.

**YOUR TURN**
Why do you think the National Football League does not charge a high enough price to eliminate the shortage of Super Bowl tickets?

## THE IMPORTANCE OF PRICES

Wouldn't it be nice if the goods you like to consume were free? You might think so. But bringing the price of a good to zero can create serious problems and make everyone worse off. To see why, let's conduct a thought experiment.

### A Thought Experiment: Free Clothes

Suppose the government announced that from now on, it would distribute clothing to households free of charge. To prevent any shortages, the government would have to either produce the clothing itself or buy it from private businesses. What would happen?

First, the quantity of clothing demanded by you and everyone else would skyrocket. After all, since you don't have to pay for it, why not fill your closets to the brim? Why not turn a spare bedroom or garage into a closet and fill that, too? In fact, why do laundry? After you wear a shirt once, you could just throw it away and get a new one. Fashions would probably change quickly due to the rapid turnover of clothing. When a skirt or a pair of pants fell out of fashion, you'd replace it with the latest style. And why buy paper towels or napkins when you could just use free T-shirts to wipe up spills? In short, without a price, you and everyone else would overconsume clothes.

Now let's consider the supply side of the market. To avoid a shortage, production would have to increase dramatically to match the huge increase in demand. More and more resources would be shifted into the production of clothing. Land currently used to grow food crops would be used to grow cotton

*If clothing were free, people wouldn't wear 245 shirts at once like this man, but they would go overboard with their consumption!*

instead. More and more labor would be shifted to the tasks of manufacturing, transporting, and distributing clothes. While we would all have plenty of clothes, they would come at the sacrifice of other valued goods and services: we would have less food, entertainment, education, health care, and so on. If enough clothing were produced to keep

up with demand at a price of zero, we would overproduce it.

Despite the clothing being free, households would feel the effects in their pocketbooks. To fund the expanding "Department of Clothing" that would buy (or produce) and distribute free clothes, households would have to pay a larger share of their incomes in taxes. And households would have to pay higher prices for other goods and services. Why? Because with increasing amounts of resources being used for clothing, firms in other industries would have to pay more for the increasingly scarce land, labor, and capital not used to make clothing. As their costs rose, these firms would have to charge higher prices. For example, with so much farmland shifted into cotton production, there would be less farmland available for the production of wheat, and the price of farmland would rise. This would increase the cost of growing wheat, among other food crops, and cause food prices in general to rise.

Due to the effects on the typical household's pocketbook, "free" clothes would not really be free at all. Through tax dollars and higher prices for other goods, we would still pay for our clothing indirectly. Because enormous quantities of clothes would be produced, we would pay a lot! These problems with giving things away force us to consider better ways to allocate clothing and other goods.

## Rationing

To prevent the indirect cost of free clothes from getting out of control, the government would have to limit the supply. But when there is limited availability of a free good, shortages cause problems. For example, when a Shell gas station in Virginia offered free gasoline at a customer appreciation event in 2011, the line of cars waiting for gas was so long that several cars ran out of gas before they reached the station. And in 2008 a Walmart employee in New York was trampled to death by a crowd rushing into a store to buy goods at particularly low prices. Likewise, there would be long lines and the potential for chaos if distribution centers offered a limited quantity of free clothing on a first-come, first-served basis. To prevent problems, the government could *ration* clothes.

To **ration** a good is to give a fixed quantity to each person. For example, the policy might be "Each year, every person will get 10 pairs of pants, 15 T-shirts, 20 pairs of socks, and a winter coat." People would receive government-issued coupons for their clothing allotments, and no one would be permitted to get clothing without a coupon. With rationing, the government could reduce production while avoiding long lines and empty-handed consumers.

Many countries have used rationing when distributing goods for free or when trying to cut production without letting prices rise to the new equilibrium level. For example, during World War II, the U.S. government wanted to free up resources for military production by decreasing the production of consumer goods. To deal with the resulting shortages, the government issued coupons to ration butter, sugar, and many other basic goods. The United States also rationed gasoline during the 1970s when supply suddenly decreased due to a rise in oil prices. And during the milk shortage of 2011, some stores in Hong Kong rationed dry milk.

## Rationing and the Achievement of Goals

Rationing provides a way to allocate goods when the price is below the equilibrium price, as happens when there is a price ceiling or the price is zero. But unlike equilibrium prices that keep demand and supply in check, a policy of limiting production and relying on rationing does a poor job of accomplishing three important goals: finding the best level of production, keeping costs low, and achieving consumer satisfaction.

### Finding the Best Level of Production

Production always involves tradeoffs: the opportunity cost of making more of one good is that less of other goods can be made. Government officials don't have complete information on everyone's needs and desires. Therefore, they can't find the best level of production for consumers. And production decisions must be made over and over again as market conditions change. For example, if tastes changed and certain clothing items became more desirable, it would be appropriate for clothing production and individual rations to rise. Or if bad weather destroyed much of the cotton crop, it would make sense to reduce production and individual rations. The government would have a hard time keeping up with complex market conditions such as these.

### Keeping Costs Low

Rationing free clothes would be costly. The government would have to set up new agencies to buy and distribute clothing and issue coupons. Consumers might try to pressure or bribe agency workers to get extra coupons, and

To **ration** a good is to provide each person with a fixed quantity.

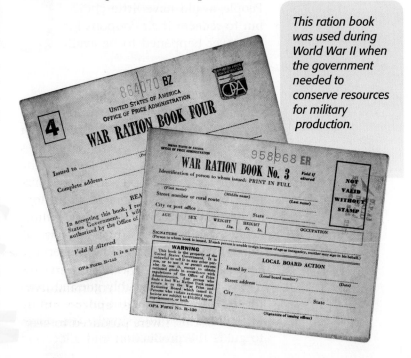

*This ration book was used during World War II when the government needed to conserve resources for military production.*

producers might try to pressure or bribe government workers to buy their clothes at artificially high prices. To prevent corruption, the government would have to catch and prosecute agency workers who broke the rules. It would also have to prevent clothing from "leaking" out of government warehouses into the black market, where it could be sold for a profit. All these government activities would use up resources and add to the government's cost.

### Achieving Consumer Satisfaction

If clothing were rationed, it would be poorly allocated among households. People who really love clothes would want to consume more than their yearly allotment. Others with full closets or little interest would receive additional clothing that gave them little happiness. Getting the clothes to those who value them most would involve added expenditures of time and money to set up online auctions, yard sales, and flea markets. There would also be problems with the clothes themselves. With limits on prices and production, firms would have little incentive or ability to produce high-quality, fashionable attire. People would have little choice but to redeem their coupons for whatever happened to be available.

### What Prices Accomplish

Imagine that a society rations free clothing but grows tired of the problems just discussed. The government announces a contest: a big prize will go to the designer of the best system for organizing clothing production and allocation. To win the prize, the new system must achieve the goals obstructed by rationing, while at the same time preventing shortages.

As you have probably guessed from the title of this section, the prize-winning idea would be quite simple: use prices to guide the production and allocation of clothing. Let's consider how prices would do the trick.

### Prices Guide the Economy to the Best Level of Production

When a good is free, people have no incentive to be careful about how much they use. They demand too much, and if production levels are set to match the quantity demanded, too much is produced. By contrast, when people have to pay for a good, they think twice before consuming it. They limit their consumption to amounts that are "worth it" for them. For example, if the price of a pair of jeans is $30, you will not throw your jeans away just because they need laundering—that convenience isn't worth the price of a new pair. Positive prices help avoid wasteful overconsumption and thereby avoid wasteful overproduction.

Prices serve as a *signal* to change consumption in the appropriate direction when market conditions change. If bad weather ruins the cotton crop, the cost of making jeans and thus the market price of jeans will increase. The consumers who place a relatively low value on jeans will respond to the higher price by decreasing their quantity demanded. Likewise, if new loom technology makes it less expensive to weave jeans, prices will fall and consumers will appropriately purchase more of the now easier-to-make product.

Prices also serve as a direct signal to firms to change production in the right direction when market conditions change. For example, if many people suddenly want more clothing, the increase in demand will cause the market price to rise. The higher price indicates to firms that people want more clothing. To earn higher profits, firms will increase production. The next section explains more about how prices guide production to desirable levels.

## Prices Help Keep Costs Low

The influence of prices eliminates the need for a costly government rationing program. Instead, the government can play a supportive role by establishing and enforcing laws that allow buyers and sellers to trade, protecting their rights and ensuring that no one is harmed by their activities. Unless the market has special problems that require more direct government involvement as discussed in Chapter 9, the government can stay mostly in the background and let prices do the work.

## Prices Help Achieve Consumer Satisfaction

Unlike a rationing system, a market driven by prices allows people to buy as much or as little of each good as they want at the market price. Those who are willing to pay the market price for a large quantity of clothing buy more than those who place little value on clothing. No buyer ends up with a lot of a disfavored good, as they might if the good were rationed. And because production and prices are not restricted, firms will aim to make more of the goods that provide the most value to consumers relative to the cost of providing them.

## Prices Help Prevent Shortages

As you've learned, when prices can adjust freely, they settle at their equilibrium values, where supply and demand are in balance. Every buyer can find a seller, and every seller can find a buyer. Even when a price is sticky, it tends to move to its equilibrium value over time. Equilibrium prices eliminate shortages without any need for rationing.

## How Prices Prevent Overproduction and Underproduction

How much of a good *should* the economy produce? And how do we know that prices will guide us to the right quantity of output?

One approach to answering these questions is based on the *gains from voluntary exchange*. If you are willing to voluntarily pay for a good, either you're nuts, or you see some benefit from the purchase. If the owner of a firm is willing to voluntarily sell the good to you, either the owner is nuts, or the owner is made better-off by the sale. Thus, under the assumption of rationality (that is, assuming neither you nor the firm owner is nuts), every voluntary sale is a win-win situation for the two of you. Except when goods create benefits or costs not felt by the buyer or the seller as discussed in Chapter 9, we want more units of a good to be made and sold as long as each unit creates this type of win-win outcome.

We can identify the units of a good that make both buyers and sellers better off on a graph of supply and demand. Consider the market for laptop computers depicted in Figure 18.5. In this market, each of the first 800 laptops produced in a week would create gains for both the buyer and the seller. To see why, let's zero in on one of these laptops—the 400th. The height of the demand curve at the quantity of 400 tells us that some consumer—let's call her Laura—would buy the 400th laptop if the price were $1,000 or less. The 400th laptop must be *worth* $1,000 to Laura, because that is the most she would pay for it.

By contrast, the height of the supply curve at a quantity of 400 laptops is only $200. This tells us that some business—let's call it Ace Laptops—would produce the 400th laptop if it could get $200 or more for it. The 400th laptop must cost Ace $200 to produce, because that is the least Ace would accept in exchange for making it.

Now let's summarize what we know. The 400th laptop is worth $1,000 to Laura but would cost Ace $200 to produce. If this laptop were produced and exchanged for any amount of money between $200 and $1,000, both Laura and Ace would benefit. For example, if the price were $700, Ace would benefit by getting $700 for a laptop that costs

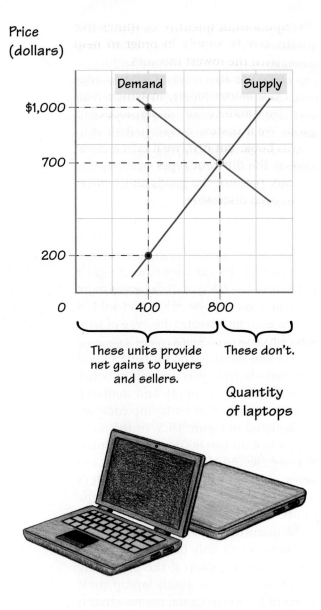

Price (dollars)

$1,000

700

200

0   400   800

These units provide net gains to buyers and sellers.

These don't.

Quantity of laptops

**Figure 18.5** Gains from Voluntary Exchange
For the first 800 laptop computers, the additional benefit consumers receive from each additional computer exceeds the additional cost of making it. The additional benefit from any laptops beyond 800 is below the additional cost. So the equilibrium price brings about the voluntary production of every laptop that provides a net gain to society.

laptops would cost more to make than it is worth to a consumer.

Now consider what happens when we let the market determine the price and quantity of laptops. The equilibrium price is $700 and the equilibrium quantity is 800. All the laptops that can provide gains to both buyer and seller—and only those laptops—are produced and consumed. The equilibrium price automatically brings about the proper level of production and consumption. This important result follows from a simple fact: when buyers and sellers can trade freely, they will naturally make all the exchanges—and only those exchanges—that make both the buyer and the seller better off.

## When Prices Are Not Enough
You've seen that prices accomplish a great deal for consumers, firms, and the economy as a whole. But they do not solve every problem. The price signal for market production is based on buyers' willingness to pay for a good and producers' willingness to supply it. But what consumers are willing and able to pay depends not just on their desire for a good but also on their income. Those with the lowest incomes thus have relatively little influence on the goods provided in markets.

Consider the money pharmaceutical companies devote to finding cures for baldness and wrinkled skin. The same money could instead be used to fight deadly diseases like malaria and tuberculosis that kill millions of

$200 to produce. And Laura would benefit by paying only $700 for a laptop that is worth $1,000 to her.

We can apply the same logic to *any* of the first 800 laptops in this market. For each of those first 800 units, the demand curve lies above the supply curve, so the laptop is worth more to some buyer than it would cost some seller to make. To take advantage of *all* such opportunities for a buyer and a seller to gain, production should continue until firms have made every laptop for which the demand curve lies above the supply curve, or 800 laptops per week.

The 801st laptop and all of those beyond it should not be produced. For these units, the supply curve lies above the demand curve, so each of these people every year in developing countries. Why bother with baldness and wrinkles? Because people in developed (relatively rich) countries are willing and able to pay more for cures for those problems than individuals in developing countries can possibly pay to save their own lives. The guidance of market prices alone may not address this concern in a satisfactory way. Society must therefore decide how much more than the equilibrium quantity of things like health care to supply in order to help those with the lowest incomes.

There are also cases of what economists call *market failure*, in which markets overproduce or underproduce a good. We'll discuss market failure later in this book. But first, we'll take a closer look at the different types of firms that actually produce the goods and services we've been discussing.

# MODULE 18 REVIEW AND ASSESSMENT

## Summing Up the Key Ideas: Match the following terms to the correct definitions.

A. Shortage
B. Black market
C. Price ceiling
D. Price floor

E. Sticky prices
F. Rationing
G. Market failure
H. Surplus

_____ 1.  When an excess demand persists for a significant period of time.

_____ 2.  A government-imposed limit below which prices cannot fall.

_____ 3.  Condition when markets overproduce or underproduce a good.

_____ 4.  Giving a fixed quantity to each person.

_____ 5.  A government-imposed limit on the highest price firms can charge in the market.

_____ 6.  Prices that move to their equilibrium values very slowly.

_____ 7.  When an excess supply persists for a significant period of time.

_____ 8.  Illegally selling a good for a price above the price ceiling to people who could not find it in the stores.

## Analyze and Explain: Identify and explain the effect of each of the following on the **market price**.

| | EFFECT ON MARKET PRICE | EXPLANATION |
|---|---|---|
| 1. The government sets a price floor below the equilibrium price. | _____ | _____ |
| 2. The government sets a price ceiling below the equilibrium price. | _____ | _____ |
| 3. The government sets a price ceiling at the equilibrium price. | _____ | _____ |
| 4. The government sets a price floor above the equilibrium price. | _____ | _____ |

**Apply:** Determine if each of the following would lead to a **shortage** or a **surplus**.

SHORTAGE OR SURPLUS?

1. In spite of rising demand for her merchandise, a storeowner keeps prices the same.

   _____

2. As fall approaches, a beachfront bathing suit vendor continues to raise prices as he did during the hot summer months.

   _____

3. Even though the demand for flu shots continues to rise, the government will not allow companies to raise the price they charge for flu shots.

   _____

4. The government sets the price of gas at a level below the equilibrium price.

   _____

5. A government farm program requires that the price of farm commodities be set above the equilibrium price.

   _____

6. A shoe store puts all its merchandise on sale at 20 percent off previous prices.

   _____

# AN INTERVIEW WITH Jeff Fluhr of StubHub

*Jeff Fluhr was a cofounder of StubHub, an Internet trading website for buying and selling tickets to sporting and entertainment events. He attended Morristown High School in Morristown, New Jersey. Although he didn't take an economics class in high school, economics has had a big impact on his life. In 2007, he sold StubHub to eBay for $310 million and looked for other ventures to start.*

**When did you think of the idea for StubHub?**

I was a first-year student getting my MBA in business school in 2000 when I started the company. Prior to this, I had the uncomfortable experience of buying and selling tickets in parking lots before basketball games or concerts when I needed an extra ticket or when I had an extra ticket I couldn't use. After reflecting on these personal experiences, a friend and I came up with the idea for StubHub at business school and then started the company.

**What did you learn about economics that was useful in starting up and running StubHub?**

The lessons of economics were extremely valuable in my work at StubHub. In fact, the entire business model was built on the laws of supply and demand. StubHub is a marketplace where fans buy and sell tickets and the prices of the tickets are based on supply and demand. Understanding the fundamental economics of supply and demand was the key to developing the StubHub business model.

**How, exactly, does supply and demand work at StubHub?**

Concert promoters often sell tickets at less than the equilibrium price, for a variety of reasons. So there's an excess demand for tickets. Some people would prefer to pay a higher price rather than not go. And at higher prices, some people with tickets would prefer to sell them, because they have better things to do with the money. The higher price brings supply and demand back into balance. StubHub provides a market to create that balance.

**Can you give an example?**

For the Miley Cyrus concert tour that began in October 2007, tickets were first sold by Ticketmaster at $65—far below the equilibrium price. People were not permitted to buy more than four tickets each, but all the tickets sold out within minutes anyway. Many devoted fans— even if they were willing to pay more—would have been unable to go. So they turned to StubHub, where the average price was about $200. At that price, ticketholders who didn't think the tickets were worth $200 could sell them to others who did.

**How did you get the funding to start StubHub?**

Within a few months after starting the company in 2000, I pitched the StubHub business model to many executives from the sports, entertainment, and financial industries. I also spoke to friends, family, and former colleagues about the idea. Many of these contacts resulted in interest in investing in our company. So we raised the initial money from these folks, and with this funding we were able to launch the first version of StubHub. As the company grew, we raised more capital in subsequent rounds of financings.

**Do you have any advice for high school students who might want to become entrepreneurs?**

My advice is to get a great education and a few years of work experience before taking the plunge.

# AP

# "Sneakerheads" Hype Shoes for Credit and Profit

CHICAGO—They are lined up in the freezing rain, waiting patiently, stubbornly. All night. All for a few pairs of shoes. Sean Rivera is among the 60 or so die-hards on this sidewalk along Chicago's Magnificent Mile shopping district. He looks a little crazy, smiling and squinting through fogged glasses.

It's all part of the life of "sneakerheads," people who spend hundreds, even thousands of dollars on shoes, many of which carry the name of professional basketball stars, past and present. Chicagoans proudly point out that it started here with Michael Jordan and his Nike Air Jordan brand.

Jesus Estrella, a blogger who has become a self-made sneaker guru on YouTube, filmed one recent melee outside a mall in Orlando, Florida. "This shoe game officially has gone bananas," Estrella, who is known as

"JStar" in the sneakerhead community, said as he watched police arrive and then begin sending people home.

You don't always know which shoe is going to be "the shoe" of the ones that are released, Estrella says. But often, the shoes that go the quickest are those that are "reissued"—new versions of old standards, including Air Jordans and the Nike "Mag" sneakers worn by the character Marty McFly in the movie "Back to the Future." Consignment shops and online auctions have seen some of those shoes resell for thousands of dollars, while others sit on shelves longer and sell for less. A pair of original Air Jordans in good condition—bought by the most serious collectors—can sell today for $4,000 to $5,000. "Back to the Future" Mags, originally released to raise money for the Michael J. Fox

Foundation and Parkinson's research, go for that much, or more.

Often, sneakerheads are young men in their teens, 20s and 30s, many of whom now use the Internet to show off their "kicks." And companies like Nike are using that instant, word-of-mouth communication to their benefit, marketing experts say.

Limiting the supply—a tactic sometimes called "artificial scarcity"—also fuels the demand in an age when young people are bombarded with products and looking for ways to stand out. "It's harder and harder to make yourself different and distinct. Everybody has access to the same stuff," says Gary Rudman, president of California-based GTR Consulting, which tracks the habits of young people.

For sneakerheads, it's all about showing off your shoes to gain credibility with your peers. Dina Mayzlin, an associate professor of marketing at Yale University, refers to this dynamic as "social signaling"—associating yourself with a hard-to-get brand to build status. So companies are, in turn, limiting access to a product or service to create a buzz and reputation of coolness. She and her colleagues have, for instance, studied Google and Spotify, an online music service—both of which have initially made some services available to consumers by invitation only.

"It's a bit of a puzzle—why would the company early on try to slow down the adoption of their product?" she says. She found that the goal for Google, with Google+, or Spotify was to eventually draw in even more members who wanted what the initial members had. Michael Carberry, marketing professor at American University in Washington, says when you factor in what it costs to design and promote the limited edition shoes, Nike may not make as much money on them as it would if they were mass produced, but the publicity they generate is priceless. "The buzz is what works for them and it just enhances the aura of Nike," he says—and, in turn, generates more overall shoe sales to those who might not be able to afford a limited edition pair, but still want to attach themselves to the brand.

Because of the chaos it has created, some have questioned whether Nike has gone too far with its limited edition shoes and hyped releases. A Nike spokesman did not respond to questions about whether the company is looking for ways to avoid the mayhem created by recent shoe releases. But in February, the company did issue a statement stressing the importance of "consumer safety and security." To cut back on crowds, some stores already hand out a limited number of tickets to consumers before a shoe release. Without a ticket, you can't enter the store.

## DID YOU READ IT?

1) What factor(s) influence the demand for "reissued" sneakers? What factor(s) influence the demand for new limited edition sneakers?

2) How does "artificial scarcity" affect the price of these sought-after limited edition or "reissued" sneakers? Explain why.

## WHAT DO YOU THINK?

1) Is the market for "reissued" or new, limited-edition sneakers influenced by the market for mass-produced sneakers from companies like Converse or Nike? How do you think these markets are related?

2) What would happen to the market for "reissued" sneakers if a large number of sneakerheads decided to sell off their collections? Use a demand and supply diagram to explain your answer.

EXCERPTED FROM www.delawareonline.com/viewart/20120321/BUSINESS06/120320046/-Sneakerheads-hype-shoes-credit-profit

# CHAPTER 6 REVIEW AND SELF-ASSESSMENT

## REVIEW

### Points to Remember

#### MODULE 16: SUPPLY AND DEMAND

1. The market **equilibrium** is the point at which the quantity supplied equals the quantity demanded.

2. The **equilibrium price** is the price that equates the quantity supplied and the quantity demanded.

3. The **equilibrium quantity** is the quantity that is supplied and demanded at the equilibrium price.

4. When the quantity demanded is larger than the quantity supplied, the difference between them is called **excess demand**.

5. When the quantity supplied is larger than the quantity demanded, the difference between them is called **excess supply**.

#### MODULE 17: CHANGES IN SUPPLY AND DEMAND

6. When a demand curve shifts to the right, that shift is called an **increase in demand**.

7. When a demand curve shifts to the left, that shift is called a **decrease in demand**.

8. When a supply curve shifts to the right, that shift is called an **increase in supply**.

9. When a supply curve shifts to the left, that shift is called a **decrease in supply**.

#### MODULE 18: SHORTAGES, SURPLUSES, AND THE ROLE OF PRICES

10. A **shortage** exists when an excess demand for a product persists for a significant period of time.

11. A **surplus** exists when an excess supply persists for a significant period of time.

12. A **price ceiling** is a government-imposed limit on the highest price firms can charge in a market.

13. A **floor price** is a government-imposed limit below which prices cannot fall.

14. **Sticky prices** are prices that move to their equilibrium values very slowly.

15. To **ration** a good is to provide each individual with a fixed quantity.

## SELF-ASSESSMENT

The following questions are the type your teacher might ask you on a quiz or a test. Practice with these in order to improve your performance on class tests.

### Multiple-Choice Questions

The accompanying demand and supply schedules represent the current conditions in a particular market. Answer the first three questions based on this table:

| PRICE (DOLLARS) | QUANTITY DEMANDED | QUANTITY SUPPLIED |
|---|---|---|
| $2.50 | 150 | 0 |
| 3.00 | 100 | 30 |
| 3.50 | 90 | 55 |
| 4.00 | 75 | 75 |
| 4.50 | 55 | 90 |
| 5.50 | 30 | 100 |

1. If the price currently being charged is $3.00, which of the following is true?

   a. There is an excess supply of 70 in the market.
   b. The market has achieved equilibrium.
   c. A surplus will result if prices do not fall.
   d. A shortage will result if prices do not rise.

2. To be effective, a price floor would need to be set at

   a. $2.50.
   b. $3.00.
   c. $4.00.
   d. $4.50.

3. The market equilibrium exists when the

   a. equilibrium price is $4.50 and the equilibrium quantity is 90.
   b. equilibrium price is $4.50 and the equilibrium quantity is 55.
   c. equilibrium price is $4.00 and the equilibrium quantity is 75.
   d. equilibrium price is $3.50 and the equilibrium quantity is 55.

4. Equilibrium in the fish market is disturbed by two different events: (1) a report by the American Medical Association announces that increased consumption of fish is associated with lower heart disease, and (2) fishermen are banned from fishing in environmentally sensitive areas that previously were important sources for their catch. In the market for fish,

   a. equilibrium price will increase and equilibrium output will decrease.
   b. both equilibrium price and output will increase.
   c. both equilibrium price and output will decrease.
   d. equilibrium price will increase but we don't have enough information to determine the change in equilibrium output.

5. Which of the following explains why some things that are relatively useless are expensive and some things that are essential for life are cheap?

   a. rationing
   b. the diamond-water paradox
   c. price ceilings
   d. price floors

6. The government might impose a price ceiling in the market for a good if it believed that the price in the market was

   a. too high for the consumer of the good.
   b. too low for the consumer of the good.
   c. too high for the producer of the good.
   d. too low for the producer of the good.

7. Goods can be allocated based on a system of rationing or by using prices. Which of the following is **not** an advantage of using prices as a resource allocation device?

   a. keeping costs low
   b. achieving consumer satisfaction
   c. finding the best level of production
   d. creating shortages

8. Which of the following could lead to a shortage?

   a. an increase in demand when prices are sticky
   b. an increase in supply when prices are sticky
   c. a decrease in demand when prices are flexible
   d. a decrease in supply when prices are flexible

9. Price floors and price ceilings

   a. both cause shortages.
   b. both causes surpluses.
   c. cause the demand and supply curves to shift until equilibrium is established.
   d. interfere with the rationing function of prices.

10. Which of the following is true?

   a. If an excess demand persists, it can lead to a shortage.
   b. If an excess supply persists, it can lead to a shortage.
   c. Effective price ceilings always lead to a surplus.
   d. Effective price floors always lead to a shortage.

## Constructed Response Questions

Draw a correctly labeled graph of supply and demand based on the demand and supply schedules below.

| PRICE (DOLLARS) | QUANTITY DEMANDED | QUANTITY SUPPLIED |
|---|---|---|
| $4.00 | 1,200 | 0 |
| 5.00 | 1,000 | 200 |
| 6.00 | 800 | 400 |
| 7.00 | 600 | 600 |
| 8.00 | 400 | 800 |
| 9.00 | 200 | 1,000 |

1. What is the equilibrium price and equilibrium quantity?
2. Identify a price on your graph that would result in an excess supply.
3. If a price of $5.00 persists for an extended period of time, what economic problem would result?
4. If the government were to establish an effective price floor, where would that price floor be?
5. An increase in demand for the product would have what effect on the equilibrium price and equilibrium quantity?
6. A decrease in supply for the product would have what effect on the equilibrium price and equilibrium quantity?
7. If the government sets a price of $8.00, what action would they need to take to alleviate the condition created?

**CHAPTER 7 & YOU** Have you ever thought about starting your own business? What type of business would you start? Maybe instead you'd like to work for a large corporation like General Motors or Disney. This chapter compares the different types of business firms and looks at the advantages and disadvantages of each type. It also describes the role of businesses in the U.S. economy and examines some controversial issues related to business practices and behaviors. Most workers in the United States are employed by one of the 30 million privately owned businesses. More than half a million businesses are born each year, and in each case, entrepreneurs make key decisions about how to organize their firm. Whether you'll make those decisions for your own firm someday or help guide an existing firm toward greater success, it's important to know how firms are structured. This chapter will help you understand the businesses that might provide your next job or investment opportunity.

# Business Organizations

## STARTING APPLE

Steve Jobs, the co-founder of the Apple Computer Company and Pixar Animation Studios, is an American success story. His genius for organizing businesses and his willingness to take chances were a big part of the reason for his success. Born to a single mom in San Francisco, he was put up for adoption when he was just a week old. Jobs graduated from Homestead High School in Cupertino, California, and then attended Reed College in Oregon. He dropped out after just one semester but credited a course in calligraphy (artistic handwriting) as the inspiration for the innovative fonts that Apple products use.

After working for a computer game company and traveling, Jobs and his friend Steve Wozniak started the Apple Computer Company. He was just 21 years old at the time. They started as a partnership in 1976. In 1980, the company changed from a partnership to a different type of business: a publicly traded company. This means that the company raised money by selling shares of stock and bringing in new owners. Steve Jobs became an instant millionaire, and the company continued to grow, using the funds it raised to develop new products.

Apple president John Sculley talks with co-founders Steve Jobs and Steve Wozniak about the Apple IIc in 1984. The company's first portable computer had only 128 KB of memory!

The company later introduced the Mac computer, the iPod, the iPhone, and the iPad. It also introduced some products that were not a commercial success, such as the Apple Lisa computer, about 2,700 of which were reportedly dumped by Apple in a Utah landfill in 1989. In 2012, Apple Inc. was the most valuable company in the world.

In this chapter we'll explore why businesses like Apple Inc. exist, how they are organized, and how they grow. We'll also touch on trends and issues related to the behavior of businesses in the United States.

## BOTTOM LINE

In a market economy such as the United States, numerous types of privately owned, for-profit businesses produce most of the goods and services we buy and enjoy. Before starting a business, it is important to know the advantages and disadvantages of each type of business.

# MODULE 19

# Businesses and the Economy

**KEY IDEA:** The lure of profits motivates entrepreneurs to take risks and start businesses.

**OBJECTIVES**

- **To describe how the workings of a business firm differ from the workings of a market.**
- **To explain why and how entrepreneurs start businesses.**
- **To discuss the risks and rewards of running a business.**

## The Birth and Death of Firms

Business firms take on a life of their own. The opening of a new firm is called a *firm birth*. When a firm closes, it is a *firm death*. Over 600,000 new firms are born in the United States in a typical year. Firms don't have parents, but they do have entrepreneurs who create them and try to give them the care they require. That's not so easy. Unlike humans, only half of new firms survive the first five years after birth. Given the likelihood of an early firm death, it takes the possibility of profits to motivate entrepreneurs to take the necessary risks. About 1 in 30 small business owners earn more than $1 million a year. Although most entrepreneurs can't expect to become millionaires, all hope to master the care and feeding of their firms well enough to successfully nurture them through many birthdays. In this module we will discuss the reason for firms' existence and the role of entrepreneurs in firm birth and survival.

*Entrepreneurs do their best to nurture new firms to health and success.*

## WHY ARE THERE BUSINESS FIRMS?

In earlier chapters you learned how the market brings buyers and sellers together. The market determines what is produced, how it is produced, and who gets it. One place where the market plays almost no role, however, is within a company. If you ever work for a business firm, you will see that each person has a well-established set of tasks to perform. Once you accept a job at a certain wage and become an employee, you will be expected to do your job without further negotiations. Your boss will not say, "I'll pay you $25 if you call a customer this morning." Instead, he or she will assign you the task of calling the customer. And your employer will not ask you how much money you must be paid to go to a staff meeting. You will be required to attend staff meetings, the likely alternative being that you lose your job. Within a business, the price signals that drive markets are replaced by direction from management and established expectations.

Nobel laureate Ronald Coase asked why we have business firms at all. Why not dispense with firms and let the forces of supply and demand take over the decisions currently made within firms? After careful analysis he concluded that it is more efficient to use commands to allocate resources within a firm. Imagine if every time you had to go through an intersection, motorists stopped to negotiate a price for who can go through first. Following the rules established by law—obeying traffic signals and stop

*It would be inefficient to use negotiations between drivers to determine who can cross an intersection first. Within firms, rules and commands work like traffic signals to simplify decision making and avoid the need for negotiations.*

signs—makes it much easier to get across town. Similarly, workers can't negotiate every work-related decision instead of obeying the boss. The opportunity cost of time spent on unnecessary negotiations can be large. Rules and commands provide a more cost-effective way to allocate labor and other resources within a business firm. Before the efficiencies of a firm can be realized, however, it takes an entrepreneur to create the firm.

**DID YOU GET IT?**
**How does decision making in firms differ from decision making in markets?**

## THE ROLE OF ENTREPRENEURS

In 2003, no one had a Facebook page. In 2012, more than 500 million people around the world had one. What accounts for this dramatic difference? The answer is simple: in 2003, Facebook did not exist. No one had created it yet. In order for Facebook to exist, someone had to play the role of entrepreneur.

An entrepreneur is an innovator and risk taker who creates new products, figures out new ways of producing things, or starts a business for profit. Entrepreneurs have the vision to see business opportunities that may not occur to others and the courage to start a new venture. They transform promising ideas into profitable business enterprises.

In the case of Facebook, the entrepreneur was Mark Zuckerberg, a Harvard student. When he created the first version of Facebook he did not have a new business venture in mind. But he soon realized that he had a good business idea. In early 2004, Zuckerberg began the hard work of developing his idea into a business. He spent a month writing the computer code for a new, more interactive website. He assembled a team to help him market the new service. Within a few months, Facebook was operating on a dozen college campuses. Over the next few years, it spread rapidly to colleges, then high schools, and finally to anyone in the world who wanted a Facebook page. By 2009, large corporations were offering billions of dollars to buy the company. Zuckerberg and his co-owners refused to sell.

Zuckerberg, like Steve Jobs decades earlier, created a new product and a new company where none had existed before. But the employees of an existing company can be entrepreneurs, too, when they develop a new product or a new way of doing business. An example of such a product is the Kindle, a device for reading books downloaded from the Internet. It was one of many innovations developed by employees of Amazon.com, long after the company was established.

Employees at many large companies play the role of entrepreneur. For example, Stephanie Kwolek was a research chemist at DuPont when she discovered Kevlar, the synthetic material used to make bulletproof vests. But small businesses are a major source of innovations, too. For example, you might be familiar with the chocolate chip cookie, which was invented in 1937 by Ruth Wakefield in a tourist lodge called the Toll House Inn. Table 19.1 lists other examples of products created from entrepreneurial activity at small businesses.

**DID YOU GET IT?**

**What do entrepreneurs do?**

*Mark Zuckerberg, the entrepreneur who started Facebook.*

**Table 19.1 A Sample of Small Business Innovations during the Twentieth Century**

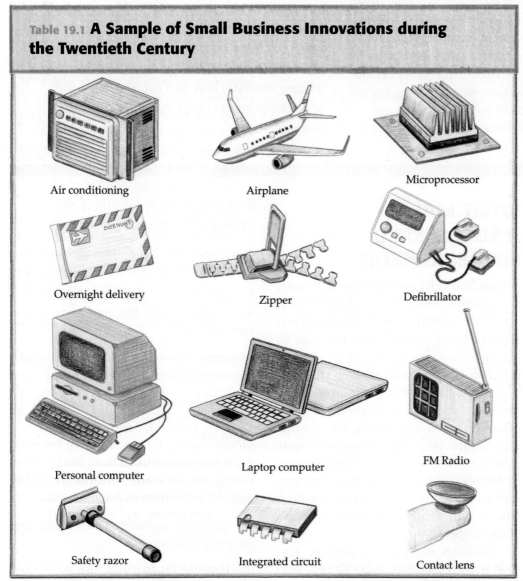

SOURCE: U.S. Small Business Administration, Office of Advocacy. *The Small Business Economy: 2005* (Washington, DC: United States Government Printing Office, 2005), 186.

# ECONOMICS IN ACTION

# Going Green Makes Cents

The world suffers from a variety of environmental problems. Headlines warn us of impending crises related to climate change, rising energy prices, mountains of trash, and other environmental ills. What does this have to do with business firms? The answer is simple—there's money to be made in protecting our planet.

Entrepreneurs have a knack for discovering profitable business opportunities. In recent years, forward-looking entrepreneurs have created environmentally friendly technologies, called *green technologies*, to address environmental problems. Airtricity is a global leader in one type of green technology—wind farms. Wind farms use a network of windmills to produce electricity. Wind farms are considered "green" because wind produces no hazardous by-products or pollutants, and it can never be used up like some other energy sources,

such as oil. The downside is that many people consider them to be eyesores and they can pose a threat to migratory birds.

Airtricity was started by Eddie O'Connor, an engineer and entrepreneur, in 1997. During the early 2000s the company built wind farms in England, Ireland, Scotland, Wales, and elsewhere. In 2008, it was sold to another British company, which continues its operations today. The founding of Airtricity, and other firms in the renewable energy industry, illustrates how high demand for a good or service prompts entrepreneurs to create new businesses.

## WHAT MAKES A SUCCESSFUL ENTREPRENEUR

It takes a special type of person to start a successful business. The person must have the initiative and organizational skills to bring many inputs together to produce a good or service. It takes stamina to work long hours to keep the business alive. It takes wisdom to make good decisions about firm location, product offerings, prices, advertising, and the hiring of employees. An entrepreneur must have the ability to raise the large amount of money needed to launch a business. And an entrepreneur must face the high risk of firm death within the first few years of operations.

Although everyone is unique, successful entrepreneurs share similar personal characteristics. An entrepreneur is typically

- visionary—sees a business opportunity when others may not;

- innovative—transforms ideas into new products, processes, or businesses;

- willing to take risks—puts savings and reputation on the line by starting a new venture;

- optimistic—is realistic but confident of business success;

- self-motivated—is disciplined and persistent, willing, and able to solve problems;

- attentive—learns from experts, colleagues, and customers and recognizes and adapts to market conditions; and

- organized—coordinates and manages resources efficiently.

How entrepreneurial are you? Consider this question carefully before you decide to start a business of your own.

# IMAGINE YOU'RE AN ENTREPRENEUR

Perhaps you have what it takes to be an entrepreneur. How would you go about it? In most cases, you'd start with an idea for a product or business. It might begin something like this:

One day, you are musing about the students at your school. You've noticed that some of them do not perform well in certain classes. They could do much better if they had someone to help them study. Many of these students—or their parents—would be willing to pay for that help. It also occurs to you that people who do well in those same subjects—at your high school and the local college—might want to earn some extra money.

That's when it hits you: you could create a business to connect the students who need help with those who can provide it. The idea intrigues you. But is it realistic? Could *you* make money performing this service? Maybe it's worth thinking about some more.

You take out a sheet of paper and write at the top "The Tutor Shop," a possible name for your new business. Then you list some questions to answer:

**1.** How would you earn revenue?

**2.** Would you collect a fee from the tutor after each session with a student?

**3.** Would you charge the tutors a one-time fee when you first connect them to each student?

**4.** How would you find and recruit good tutors?

**5.** How would you inform those who need tutors about the service?

Once you begin trying to answer these questions, you are in the early stages of

Catherine and Dave Cook founded their popular social networking site, MyYearbook, when they were high school students.

planning a business. You have become an entrepreneur.

If you go through with your idea and build a successful business, you will be a living example of Adam Smith's "invisible hand," discussed in Chapter 1. Your main motive may be to earn profit for yourself. But to earn it, you will be providing a valuable service to society. Students who need help will have an easier time connecting to the right tutor. And potential tutors will have an easier time finding work and earning income. You will make other people, as well as yourself, better off.

We'll leave it to you to think about how you could solve these specific puzzles and turn The Tutor Shop into a profitable business. In the next module we will consider another decision you'll have to make: the *form* of the business you will create.

**DID YOU GET IT?**
What are some of the questions that an entrepreneur must answer when starting a new business?

# MODULE 19 REVIEW AND ASSESSMENT

## Summing Up the Key Ideas: Match the following terms to the correct definitions.

A. Visionary               D. Optimistic            G. Organized
B. Innovative              E. Self-motivated        H. Entrepreneur
C. Willing to take risks   F. Attentive

_____ 1.    Coordinates and manages resources efficiently.

_____ 2.    Learns from experts, colleagues, customers; recognizes and adapts to market conditions.

_____ 3.    An innovator and risk taker who creates new products, figures out new ways of producing things, or starts a business for profit.

_____ 4.    Is disciplined and persistent; willing to solve problems.

_____ 5.    Sees a business opportunity when others may not.

_____ 6.    Puts savings and reputation on the line by starting a new business venture.

_____ 7.    Is realistic but confident of business success.

_____ 8.    Transforms ideas into new products, processes, or businesses.

## Analyze and Explain: In the following situations, identify if each is **entrepreneurial** in nature and then explain your answer.

|  | YES OR NO? | EXPLANATION |
|---|---|---|
| 1. operating a hot-dog stand that you own | _____ | _____ |
| 2. teaching in a public school | _____ | _____ |
| 3. being an active-duty member of the military | _____ | _____ |
| 4. running your lawn-mowing service | _____ | _____ |

## Apply: Suppose someone was interested in opening a new pizza restaurant. Using your own reasoning combined with what you've learned in this module, provide an example of the type of problem that might arise if the entrepreneur lacked each of the following characteristics:

1. willing to take risks

2. optimistic

3. self-motivated

4. organized

# MODULE 20

# Types of Businesses

**KEY IDEA:** Entrepreneurs consider the advantages and disadvantages of different organizational types before they form a new business.

## OBJECTIVES

- **To identify the important features of sole proprietorships, partnerships, and corporations.**
- **To evaluate the advantages and disadvantages to the owners of each form of business organization.**
- **To assess the importance of each form of business organization to the economy.**
- **To explain other ways to organize a business.**

## The Choice of Business Type

Most businesses in the United States are organized as a sole proprietorship, a partnership, or a corporation. Which form of organization would be best for The Tutor Shop or any other particular business concept? That depends. Before you can make a choice, you should understand each type of business and the associated advantages and disadvantages. In this module we will assess the various ways to organize a business.

*Seven out of every ten businesses in the United States are sole proprietorships.*

## SOLE PROPRIETORSHIPS

A **sole proprietorship** is a business firm owned by one person, the proprietor. Seven out of every ten businesses in the United States are organized as sole proprietorships. Most sole proprietorships are small firms. They are especially common in industries such as health care, real estate, retail trade, agriculture, and the arts. Professionals such as doctors, dentists, lawyers, and accountants are often sole proprietors.

### How to Start a Sole Proprietorship

A sole proprietorship is the easiest and least expensive type of business to organize. To start a sole proprietorship, you have four important tasks:

**1. Register the name of your business.** Unless you name your business after yourself (such as "Lori Stanton's Tutor Shop"), you will have to register your business's name ("The Tutor Shop") with a state, county, or local agency.

**2. Check and conform to regulations.** As the owner of a sole proprietorship, you'll have to comply with federal, state, and local regulations. For example, almost all cities have *zoning regulations* that restrict the types of businesses that can operate in different neighborhoods. There may also be regulations involving health and safety, as with restaurants, or training and certification, as with hair stylists and plumbers.

**3. Obtain any necessary licenses and permits.** For most businesses, you'll need a general business license from your

A **sole proprietorship** is a business firm owned by one person, the proprietor.

THINKSTOCK IMAGES

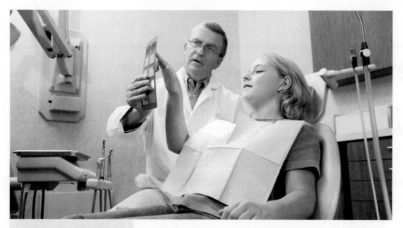

*Many professionals, like this dentist, are sole proprietors.*

state and local government. You may also need a permit verifying that you've conformed to any special state and local regulations. It is generally necessary to pay a small fee for licenses and permits.

4. **Keep records and prepare tax forms.** Because you will have to pay taxes on your profit, you will have to keep records of all your costs and revenue. And if you hire employees, there are some additional tax forms you'll need to fill out when you start the business.

## Advantages of Sole Proprietorships

Is a sole proprietorship the right choice for The Tutor Shop? Let's consider some of the advantages.

1. **Easy start-up.** As you've just seen, setting up a sole proprietorship is easy and inexpensive. You can do all the paperwork yourself, without hiring a lawyer or an accountant. The fees for licenses and permits are low.

2. **Ease of decision making.** As a sole proprietor, you have no boss. You make all the decisions yourself. You don't need anyone's approval or agreement if you want to try something new. For example, if you wanted to advertise The Tutor Shop by putting fliers on cars at high school sporting events, you could just do it. This freedom of action enables sole proprietors to respond rapidly to changing market conditions.

3. **Ownership of profits.** As a sole proprietor, all the profits of the business—after you pay taxes—belong to you. It is up to you how much of each year's profit you invest back into the business. The rest you are free to spend or save as you desire.

4. **Tax benefits.** A sole proprietorship has certain tax benefits over a corporation—another form of business that we'll discuss a bit later. The profits of a corporation are taxed twice: once as corporate profits and again as income for the owners. But as a sole proprietor, your profits are considered part of your ordinary income. Each dollar of profit is taxed only once, when you pay income taxes.

5. **Intrinsic rewards.** Aside from the financial advantages, many people enjoy the freedom of being their own boss and the feeling of accomplishment from building a successful business.

## Disadvantages of Sole Proprietorships

While a sole proprietorship has many advantages, there are disadvantages, too.

1. **Burden of responsibility.** As a sole proprietor, all the responsibility of ownership falls on you. Even if you have employees, it is likely that they will look to you for guidance and expect you to make the tough decisions. If you fall ill, the business may suffer. When you take a vacation, you can never fully escape your responsibilities. Imagine relaxing at the beach and getting a frantic call from one of your employees informing you that half of your tutors have suddenly quit.

2. **Difficulty raising funds.** It takes money to start a new business, and sole proprietors sometimes have trouble finding the financial resources they need. Banks may not want to lend money to a new sole proprietor,

because the business might fail, and there is no business property the bank could claim if the loan is not paid back. Many sole proprietors have to fund their start-up with their own savings or by borrowing from friends or family.

**3.   Unlimited liability.** A sole proprietor is personally responsible for all the debts and other obligations of the business. If you own a sole proprietorship that fails, or if someone sues your business, you will have to use your personal wealth to pay back any debts or to settle or fight the lawsuit. You may even have to sell your house and other personal possessions.

**? DID YOU GET IT?**
**What are a pro and a con of organizing The Tutor Shop as a sole proprietorship?**

# PARTNERSHIPS

Suppose you've been operating The Tutor Shop for a while as a sole proprietorship. Things are going well, and you are making money. You have dozens of tutors serving hundreds of students. You've even hired a few employees to help you manage the business. But being responsible for all the big decisions is hard. You find yourself wishing you had a partner—someone who cared about the business as much as you did. Now you are thinking of changing the form of your business to a partnership.

A **partnership** is a for-profit business firm owned by two or more people, called partners, each of whom has a financial interest in the business. Like sole proprietorships, most partnerships are small firms. Many stores, restaurants, and contractors operate their small businesses as partnerships. But many larger businesses are organized

as partnerships, too. These include large law firms, medical practices, and business consulting firms.

## How to Create a Partnership

Partnerships, like sole proprietorships, are fairly easy to organize. The initial steps are the same as for a sole proprietorship. To make The Tutor Shop a partnership, you would register the name of your business, check and conform to regulations, obtain any necessary licenses or permits, and deal with accounting and tax forms.

Forming a partnership, however, usually involves one additional step—creating a partnership agreement. While a partnership agreement is not required under the law, it is highly recommended for all partnerships.

A *partnership agreement* is a written document that identifies the roles, responsibilities, and obligations of partners. Much of the agreement deals with the what-ifs of the business. What if profits soar or if revenues plummet? What if there is a serious dispute among partners? What if one or more partners want to dissolve the business? The partnership agreement states, in advance, a process for addressing these types of questions. Partnerships usually hire lawyers, accountants, or other experts to help them draft a workable partnership agreement. This is the main reason that forming a partnership is a bit more complex and expensive than forming a sole proprietorship.

The partnership agreement also identifies which partners are *general partners* and which are *limited partners*. The general partners share full financial and decision-making responsibility. Every partnership must have at least one general partner. A limited partner invests money in the partnership but does not share decision-making or full financial responsibility.

*Ben and Jerry's began as a partnership. It is now part of the Unilever Corporation.*

A **partnership** is a for-profit business firm owned by two or more people, called partners, each of whom has a financial interest in the business.

### Advantages of Partnerships

Would a partnership be a good choice for a business like The Tutor Shop? Let's first consider the upsides. A partnership has many of the same advantages as a sole proprietorship, but these advantages are a bit weaker with a partnership. For example, while a partnership is relatively easy to set up, it has that one extra step of forming a partnership agreement. The partners own all the profits of the business. But each partner gets only *part* of the profits, because they must be shared with the other partners. Each partner's profits are taxed as ordinary household income, just as in a sole proprietorship.

Partnerships, however, have some special advantages over sole proprietorships:

**1. Larger pool of financing.**
In a partnership, each partner can contribute funds to start the business. Banks may be more willing to provide loans, because they can collect from more than one person if the business fails. Organizing The Tutor Shop as a partnership would permit the business to grow, because it would give you access to more funds, which you could spend on increased advertising, recruiting, equipment, or office space.

**2. Shared decision making.**
Recall that one of the disadvantages of sole proprietorships is the burden of responsibility for all decision making. In a partnership with more than one general partner, this burden can be shared. If you are ill or go on vacation, you know that your partner will take care of things in your absence. Also, each general partner may have different skills and talents. For example, at The Tutor Shop, you might be especially good at recruiting and managing new tutors, while one of your partners might do a better job dealing with the parents of students. A partnership can exploit these different abilities to create better decisions and a more successful business.

### Disadvantages of Partnerships

Before deciding to start a business as a partnership, you'd need to consider the downsides, too. The two most significant disadvantages are as follows:

**1. Unlimited liability for general partners.** Each general partner shares personal responsibility for all the debts and other obligations of the business. If the business fails, or if someone sues the business, each general partner will have to use his or her personal wealth to pay back any debts or address the lawsuit. This means that errors by one partner—if they lead to lost business or lawsuits—can cause devastating losses to all the general partners. Limited partners, by contrast, can only lose the funds they have invested in the partnership.

**2. Disagreements among partners.** Decision making requires the agreement of all general partners. When everyone agrees, it's fine. But disagreement can cause major conflict. Suppose you were sure that The Tutor Shop could increase its profit if you hired a full-time receptionist to handle phone calls. But your partner wanted to limit contacts to e-mails and thought a receptionist would be a waste of money. You might argue endlessly, each trying to change the other's mind. Bad feelings might result. While some partnerships go smoothly, others are so conflict ridden that they eventually dissolve or blow up into battles over who is to blame and who owns what. Remember the advice about forming a partnership agreement in advance to help avoid such issues!

 **DID YOU GET IT?**
What are a pro and a con of organizing The Tutor Shop as a partnership?

## CORPORATIONS

Suppose you've been running The Tutor Shop as a sole proprietorship or a partnership for some time. The business has been successful. But you are ambitious and see an opportunity for even greater profit: to start connecting students with tutors at *other* high schools, as well as junior high schools and colleges. To run the business on such a large scale, you'll need to hire several employees. You'll need workers to spend more time recruiting tutors and advertising to students and parents. You'll need an accountant to handle the higher volume of business. You'll want to design a better website and maybe even have an office with a classy sign to lend more respectability to your business. All of this will require money.

You could grow the business gradually, one school at a time. But you are worried that if you wait, someone will beat you to it. You need a burst of new financing. In this situation, you (and your partners, if any) might want to reorganize your business as a *corporation*.

## What Is a Corporation?

The most complicated form of business is a *corporation*. A **corporation** is a business firm that is itself a legal entity. This means that the law treats a corporation similarly to how it treats an individual human being. The corporation has certain rights and obligations, just as people do. For example, a corporation can own property, enter into contracts with people or other businesses, and bring lawsuits (or be sued by others).

The corporation itself is owned by its *stockholders*. One becomes a stockholder by purchasing *shares of stock*, which represent partial ownership of the corporation. A certain number of shares are issued, and the percentage of the total shares owned by each stockholder is the proportion of the corporation that he or she owns. For example, suppose a corporation issues 100,000 shares of stock. One investor, Bill, purchases 10,000 of these shares. Because 10,000 is 10 percent of 100,000, Bill owns 10 percent of all the shares. That means he owns 10 percent of the corporation. If Bill owned all 100,000 shares, he would own the entire corporation.

When one person (or a small group of people) owns all of a corporation's shares, the business is a *private corporation*. By contrast, the shares of a *public corporation* are held by many people and can be freely bought and sold. Almost all the large corporations that you've heard of are public corporations, including ExxonMobil, Microsoft, Walmart, and Google. You can buy shares in these businesses and become a stockholder.

## Creating a Corporation

A corporation—especially a public corporation—is the most expensive type of business to organize. Because a public corporation uses other people's money to get started, safeguards are needed to protect the investors. The federal government and the government of the state in which the corporation starts have regulations that help ensure that people

A **corporation** is a business firm that is itself a legal entity.

*A corporation, like Amazon.com, has certain legal rights and obligations, just as people do.*

## Organizational structure of a public corporation

Stockholders

Board of directors

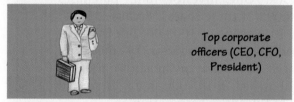

Top corporate officers (CEO, CFO, President)

Vice presidents

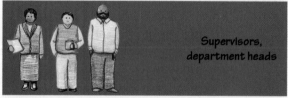

Supervisors, department heads

Rank and file employees

**Figure 20.1** Organizational Structure of a Public Corporation

aren't cheated or misled. Compliance with these regulations takes time, legal advice, and money.

To form a corporation, you may need a lawyer to help you complete a *corporate charter*, or *certificate of incorporation*, from the state government. The writing of a corporate charter will involve substantially more work for you, or a lawyer, than is needed for a partnership agreement. The corporate charter must state how the company will raise money to finance start-up costs. It sets an upper limit on the number of shares of stock that can be sold to investors. And it will include details about the organizational structure of the corporation.

## Organizational Structure

Figure 20.1 shows the typical structure of a large, public corporation. Stockholders take the top spot because they own the corporation, and they elect the board of directors. The stockholders are rarely directly involved in the operation of the company. The board of directors establishes the corporation's goals and priorities. The board also hires the firm's officers, including the chief executive officer, or CEO, who runs the company from day to day and reports to the board. Other officers ordinarily include a chief financial officer (CFO) and a company president. One person may wear more than one hat. For example, it is common for the same person to hold the position of CEO and company president.

Beneath the top officers is a layer of vice presidents, each in charge of a different aspect of the company's business. Different categories of supervisors and, finally, the rank-and-file employees complete the corporation's organizational structure.

A small, privately held corporation typically has a similar, but often simpler, structure. The board of directors can be one or a few people, and the same person or small group can hold all or most of the top officer positions.

## Advantages of Corporations

A corporation—especially a large, public corporation—has several advantages over the other business types:

**1. Limited liability for stockholders.** Unlike the owners of a sole proprietorship or a partnership, the stockholders of a corporation enjoy *limited liability*. This means that the stockholders' losses are limited to what they paid to buy their shares. If the corporation goes bankrupt and owes more funds than it can pay or if someone sues it, no one can go after the stockholders' personal wealth. The protection of personal wealth is one reason a sole proprietor or general partner might prefer to form a corporation and become a stockholder instead.

**2. Ability to raise funds by issuing shares.** A corporation is the only business type that can raise funds by selling shares of stock. The limited liability of stockholders makes them more willing to buy and hold the shares, even when they don't personally know anyone at the firm. After all, the most they can lose is what they've paid for the shares.

**3. Ability to raise funds by issuing bonds.** A corporation is the only type of business that can borrow money directly from the public by issuing and selling *bonds*. A **corporate bond** is a contract between a corporation and whoever currently owns the bond. The contract obligates the corporation to pay the bond's owner a certain amount of money in the future, usually with periodic *interest payments*. For example, a bond issued by a corporation might promise to pay $1,000 in interest every year for five years and $20,000 at the end of the five years. If the corporation sells this bond to someone for $20,000, it is effectively borrowing $20,000 for five years and paying $1,000 in annual interest on the loan. Issuing bonds often allows corporations to borrow at lower interest rates than they would pay on bank loans.

**4. Rapid growth.** A corporation, if successful, can gain access to large amounts of money and grow rapidly. As it grows larger, it may gain several advantages over smaller firms organized as sole proprietorships or partnerships. A large firm can often take advantage of *economies of scale*, which means that the cost per unit falls as output rises, thanks to major costs being spread over a growing quantity of output. For example, the developer of a cell phone app might spend $5,000 on a computer, training, and the time it takes to create the app. If only one person buys the app, the developer's fixed cost per unit is $5,000. If 5,000 people buy the app, the developer's fixed costs are spread across those 5,000 units, and the cost per unit is only $1.

A large firm can also attract and hire managers with specialized talents and training. If The Tutor Shop grows into a large, nationwide corporation, it can move from advertising with fliers to hiring a professional marketing manager.

The manager could design an advertising campaign that promotes The Tutor Shop on Facebook, billboards, and Super Bowl commercials.

## Disadvantages of Corporations

As with the other forms of business, organizing a firm as a corporation involves tradeoffs. Some of the downsides apply to any corporation, while others apply especially to large corporations. The issues to contend with include the following:

**1. Expensive start-up costs.** As we've discussed already, forming a corporation involves higher legal fees than forming other business types. The substantial up-front expense means you must be as sure as possible that your business will succeed as a corporation before starting down that road.

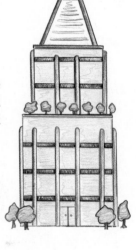

A **corporate bond** is a contract between a corporation and the owner of the bond that obligates the corporation to pay the bond's owner a certain amount of money in the future.

**2. Delays in decision making.**
In a large corporation, layers of decision makers can make it difficult to move fast as market conditions change. Minor decisions can take time as they work their way through the bureaucracy, and major decisions can take even longer. For example, at a large corporation, decisions about advertising—while handled with greater expertise—may have to be approved by the departments of marketing, human resources, accounting, and legal affairs, along with the corporation's leaders. By the time a decision is made, the competitive landscape may have changed and opportunities for profits might have been sacrificed.

**3. Low nonmonetary rewards.**
The feeling of satisfaction from owning and running your own business will be diluted in a large public corporation. The owners are now stockholders, who have nothing to do with the day-to-day operation of the firm. And the managers function within a hierarchy. Unlike in a sole proprietorship, no one person in a corporation can take pride in the business's success as a personal achievement.

**4. Divided ownership of profits.**
Corporate profits are divided among stockholders, who are entitled to a portion of the profits, and the company, which reinvests some profits back into the company. Decisions about how to divide the profits are made by the corporation's managers who, in turn, are responsible to the board of directors. In a large public corporation, stockholders as individuals have very little control over how the company's profit is allocated.

**5. Tax treatment.** In most cases, each dollar of corporate profits is taxed twice. First, the corporation faces a special tax, called the corporate profits tax. Any profits paid to stockholders are taxed again, as income, when stockholders pay personal income tax.

**6. More reporting requirements.**
Corporations face more regulations than other business types. In some cases they face stricter health, safety, and environmental rules, and they are more closely monitored for compliance. And corporations—especially public ones—must provide additional financial information to the government each quarter. This information is provided to current and potential stockholders to help them make better investment decisions.

**DID YOU GET IT?**
What is a pro and a con of organizing The Tutor Shop as a corporation?

# THE THREE MAJOR BUSINESS TYPES: AN OVERVIEW

Table 20.1 summarizes our discussion of the advantages and disadvantages of each business type. We compare the experience of being a sole proprietor, a general partner in a partnership, or a stockholder of a large public corporation. In the table, a star indicates an advantage of that type of business; two stars means an even stronger advantage. No star indicates a disadvantage compared to one or both of the other business types.

This table highlights the tradeoffs involved in any choice of business type. How do entrepreneurs respond to these tradeoffs? More specifically, how many entrepreneurs choose each type of business organization? And how important is each type in the economy? Figure 20.2 shows the common types of business organizations in the United States. As you can see in (a), most businesses are organized as sole proprietorships. This is not surprising, because a sole proprietorship is easy and inexpensive to set up. Only about one in five U.S. businesses is organized as a corporation. And only about one

| Table 20.1 **A Summary of Advantages and Disadvantages** | | | |
|---|---|---|---|
| | **SOLE PROPRIETORSHIP (SOLE PROPRIETOR)** | **PARTNERSHIP (GENERAL PARTNER)** | **CORPORATION (STOCKHOLDER)** |
| Ease of starting | ★ ★ | ★ | |
| Rapid decision making | ★ ★ | ★ | |
| Tax treatment | ★ ★ | ★ ★ | |
| Ability to raise funds | | ★ | ★ ★ |
| Ability to take time off | | ★ | ★ ★ |
| Safety of personal wealth (limited liability) | | | ★ ★ |
| Ownership and control of profit | ★ ★ | ★ | |

in ten is a partnership. So in terms of numbers of businesses, sole proprietorships lead the pack.

But now look at (b). It shows the total *revenue* earned by businesses of each type. As you can see, even though they are fewer in number, corporations earn the lion's share of all business revenue. They also earn most of the profit (not shown). Why? Because virtually all the largest businesses organize as corporations. For a very large business, the advantages of being a corporation far outweigh the disadvantages.

# OTHER TYPES OF BUSINESS ORGANIZATIONS

While sole proprietorships, partnerships, and corporations are the three main types of businesses, they are not the only types. As you are about to see, some businesses combine the features of the three main types. Others create a system of independently owned firms that look to the parent company for guidance. And some businesses do not seek to earn profit at all. Let's consider some of the common examples.

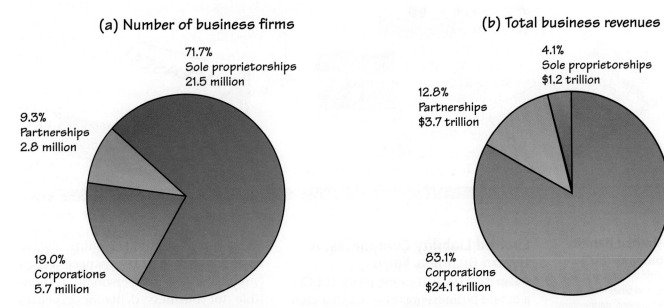

**(a) Number of business firms**

71.7%
Sole proprietorships
21.5 million

9.3%
Partnerships
2.8 million

19.0%
Corporations
5.7 million

**(b) Total business revenues**

4.1%
Sole proprietorships
$1.2 trillion

12.8%
Partnerships
$3.7 trillion

83.1%
Corporations
$24.1 trillion

**Figure 20.2** Comparing the Common Types of Business Organizations
Most business firms are sole proprietorships, but most business revenues go to corporations.

SOURCE: U.S. Census Bureau, *Statistical Abstract of the United States: 2009*, Table 722.

# ECONOMICS IN ACTION

# How Long Does It Take to Start a Corporation?

Some countries require those wishing to start a new corporation to cut through a lot of "red tape" in the form of paperwork and approvals. Other countries have very few requirements. The list in Table 20.2 shows the average amount of time it takes to open a moderate-sized corporation in 9 countries.

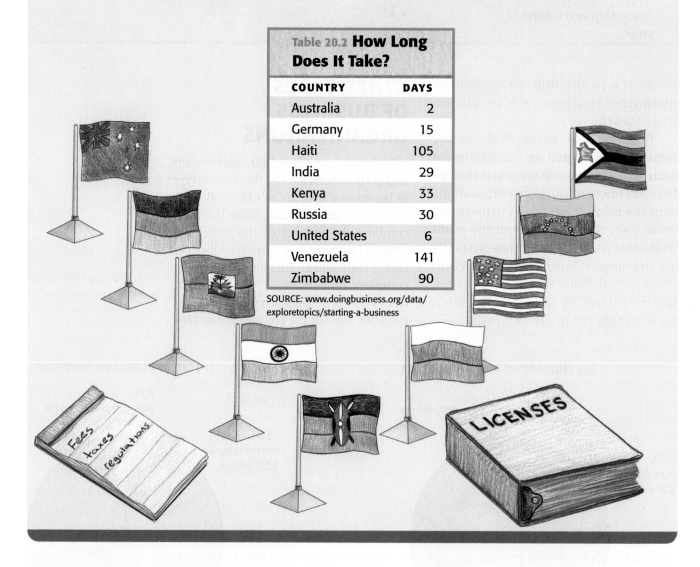

### Table 20.2 **How Long Does It Take?**

| COUNTRY | DAYS |
| --- | --- |
| Australia | 2 |
| Germany | 15 |
| Haiti | 105 |
| India | 29 |
| Kenya | 33 |
| Russia | 30 |
| United States | 6 |
| Venezuela | 141 |
| Zimbabwe | 90 |

SOURCE: www.doingbusiness.org/data/exploretopics/starting-a-business

A **limited liability company (LLC)** is a hybrid business organization that combines features of corporations, partnerships, and sole proprietorships.

## Limited Liability Companies: A Hybrid Business Form

A **limited liability company (LLC)** is a hybrid business organization that combines features of corporations, partnerships, and sole proprietorships. Like the stockholders who own corporations, the owners of an LLC enjoy *limited liability*. That is, LLC owners, called "members," are not personally responsible for business debts or expenses related to lawsuits. Instead, members' maximum financial loss is limited to the amount of money they invested in the LLC. Their personal assets, such as their homes and cars, are protected from creditors.

An LLC has two advantages over a corporation. First, forming an LLC is far easier than forming a corporation. Second, like the owners of a sole proprietorship or partnership, the owners of an LLC avoid the double taxation of profit. An LLC's profit is taxed just once as the personal income of its members. Examples of LLCs include Century 21 Real Estate LLC and EZ Lube LLC. For many entrepreneurs, the advantages of forming an LLC outweigh its key disadvantage: an LLC cannot raise funds by selling shares of stock to the general public.

## Business Franchises

A **business franchise** consists of a parent company and numerous associated businesses that sell a standardized good or service. The parent company, called the *franchisor*, owns a recognized brand name or trademark, such as 7-Eleven or Dunkin' Donuts. As owner of the brand name or trademark, the franchisor has exclusive rights to the product. This means the franchisor is the only company that can legally produce the product or grant permission to other companies to do the same.

To see how this works, imagine that you want to expand The Tutor Shop to other high schools, but you'd prefer that your business not manage or take the risks of investing in these other branches. You could instead enter into a legal business relationship with students who would run the operations at the other schools. Your business, The Tutor Shop, would be the parent company or franchisor. The business operations at the other schools would be your *franchisees*.

To open a new location of The Tutor Shop, a franchisee would pay you a *franchise fee*. In return, the franchisee would have the exclusive right to offer your service at the new location under your brand name, "The Tutor Shop." Your franchisees might also receive your help setting up their businesses. For example, you could offer a training program on how the business works, provide them with signs and

*A Japanese franchisor called Seven & i Holdings Company owns the 7-Eleven brand name.*

software, and give them tips on how to solve common problems. On top of the initial fees, there are typically ongoing fees figured as a percentage of the franchisees' revenues or profits. The fees support advertising and other services provided by the parent company. The remainder of the profits of each local Tutor Shop would belong to the franchisee.

McDonald's, a public corporation, is a leading example of a business with franchisees. The parent company has its corporate headquarters in Oak Brook, Illinois. The local McDonald's where you buy a hamburger is a franchisee. In all, McDonald's has more than 34,000 franchisees in about 120 countries. McDonald's has tight control over the products offered by each franchisee, how they are made, their prices, and other aspects of the business.

Many people who want to run a business choose to become franchisees rather than starting from scratch. They prefer to avoid the risk of charting their own course with an untested business idea. As franchisees, they get training and support from the parent company, and they can sell a known brand with proven appeal. However, the fee to become a franchisee can be high, even hundreds of thousands of dollars. So a franchisee risks losing a substantial sum if the operation isn't successful.

A **business franchise** consists of a parent company and numerous associated businesses that sell a standardized good or service.

**DID YOU GET IT?**
**What sorts of things do franchisees receive in exchange for their franchise fees?**

# ECONOMICS IN ACTION

## Business Franchises versus Other Chain Businesses

The media often reports on the sales performance of "franchise chains," "chain stores," "hotel chains," "supermarket chains," and other "chain" businesses. Although these enterprises are often lumped into a single category, there is a major difference between franchise chains and other chain businesses. A *franchise chain* is a network of independently owned businesses selling the same brand of a product. The parent company, or franchisor, helps manage this network under the terms outlined in the franchise contract. The franchisee retains some independence in running the business. Examples include Subway, KFC, Domino's Pizza, and Sonic Drive-In Restaurants.

A *chain business* is a single company, run by a single management team at the firm's corporate headquarters. Some minor decisions are delegated to local managers, but there is no franchisee who owns the local store. Chain restaurants like Starbucks and chain stores like Walmart operate nearly identical stores and provide a standardized shopping experience at thousands of locations. Other chain businesses include Home Depot, Lowe's, Target, Barnes & Noble, and In-N-Out Burger.

*Franchise chains like Domino's are a network of independently owned businesses selling the same brand of a product.*

## Cooperatives

A **cooperative**, or co-op, is a business owned by its members and operated to supply members and others with goods and services. Some co-ops earn profits, but this is not the primary purpose of the businesses. Co-ops share certain core principles, which center on democratic decision making, active participation by members, and concern for the well-being of other co-ops and local communities.

A **cooperative**, or co-op, is a business owned by its members and operated to supply members and others with goods and services.

According to the National Cooperative Business Association (NCBA), co-ops in the United States serve 120 million members.

Some co-ops produce and sell goods. Most of these are agricultural co-ops. Examples include Ocean Spray, Welch's, Sunkist, Sun-Maid, and Land O'Lakes. Other co-ops *purchase* goods and services for their members. Many cities have local food co-ops. They purchase their goods in bulk at low prices and enable their members to buy them at a considerable savings.

## Nonprofit Organizations

A **nonprofit organization**, also called a *nonprofit*, is a legal entity formed to carry out a "not-for-profit" mission. This mission might involve charity, education, scientific discovery, religion, health care, public safety, or the arts. Some nonprofits are large, such as Amnesty International, Doctors Without Borders, Feed The Children, the Metropolitan Museum of Art, the Red Cross, Veterans of Foreign Wars, and the World Wildlife Fund. Many other nonprofits are small and deal with local issues. Some nonprofits, such as nonprofit hospitals and private schools, charge money for the goods or services they provide. Rather than distributing any profits to owners, the earnings of nonprofits are used to further the mission of the organization.

In all, the U.S. Internal Revenue Service (IRS) recognizes more than 1.5 million nonprofits in the United States. Nonprofits can be organized as corporations, cooperatives, or limited liability companies, among other types of firms. Most nonprofits choose to become corporations and are thus called *nonprofit corporations*.

Small nonprofit organizations often rely on volunteer labor. Large nonprofit corporations typically hire employees. They raise funds by soliciting donations from private individuals, businesses, governments, or private foundations set up to grant money to charities and other nonprofits. Unlike their for-profit cousins, nonprofit corporations are prohibited from raising funds through the sale of corporate stocks or bonds to investors.

Nonprofit corporations, like other nonprofit organizations, enjoy tax-exempt status. That is, nonprofits do not pay federal or state income taxes. This tax exempt status is one way the government supports the work of nonprofits. The government also allows donors, such as individuals and corporations, to deduct contributions to nonprofits from their income taxes.

A **nonprofit organization** is a legal entity formed to carry out a "not-for-profit" mission.

*Ocean Spray is a cooperative owned by more than 600 growers of cranberries and grapefruit.*

# MODULE 20 REVIEW AND ASSESSMENT

## Summing Up the Key Ideas: Match the following terms to the correct definitions.

A. Sole proprietorship     D. Corporate bond     G. Limited liability company

B. Partnership     E. Business franchise     H. Cooperative

C. Corporation     F. Nonprofit organization

_____ 1. A legal entity formed to carry out a "not-for-profit" mission.

_____ 2. A for-profit business firm owned by two or more people, each of whom has a financial interest in the business.

_____ 3. Consists of a parent company and numerous associated businesses that sell a standardized good or service.

_____ 4. A business firm owned by one person, the proprietor.

_____ 5. A business firm that is itself a legal entity.

_____ 6. A hybrid business organization that combines features of corporations, partnerships, and sole proprietorships.

_____ 7.    A business owned by its members and operated in order to supply members and others with goods and services.

_____ 8.    A contract between a corporation and the owner of the bond that obligates the corporation to pay the bond's owner a certain amount of money in the future.

## Analyze and Explain:
Indicate whether organization as a **sole proprietorship**, **partnership**, or **corporation** would best match each of the following items. Then determine whether each item represents an advantage or a disadvantage for the firm.

| | FORM OF ORGANIZATION | ADVANTAGE OR DISADVANTAGE? |
|---|---|---|
| 1. safety of personal assets | _____ | _____ |
| 2. satisfaction in knowing that your efforts are rewarded | _____ | _____ |
| 3. more reporting requirements | _____ | _____ |
| 4. not having to share (after-tax) profits with anyone | _____ | _____ |
| 5. difficulty raising money to start and operate a business | _____ | _____ |
| 6. shared decision making and easy to start-up | _____ | _____ |

## Apply:
For each of the following business ventures, indicate what **type of business** organization (sole proprietorship, partnership, or corporation) you would recommend.

TYPE OF BUSINESS ORGANIZATION

1. A new start-up company wants to launch a national chain of health-food stores.

_____

2. A recent cooking-school graduate wants to start a national chain restaurant.

_____

3. An author decides to write a sequel to her latest best-selling book.

_____

4. A group of friends decides to start a business without going through a lengthy legal process.

_____

5. A group of farmers want to save money on fertilizer, seeds, and other related materials by buying them in bulk and dividing the cost among the members of the group.

_____

6. A handyman decides to quit his job in a factory and start his own home repair business. He is very concerned about protecting his home and personal assets from being exposed to any business-related liability.

_____

# MODULE 21

# How Businesses Grow

**KEY IDEA:** Business organizations have many avenues for growth.

**OBJECTIVES**

- **To explain how firms can grow by reinvesting profits.**
- **To identify sources of outside funding used for business growth.**
- **To recognize the role of mergers and acquisitions in business growth.**

## Starting Small

What do Amazon, Apple, Disney, Google, Harley-Davidson, Hewlett-Packard, Lotus Cars, Maglite, Mattel, and Yankee Candle Company have in common? They all started out in a garage. Almost all large businesses began as operations so small that almost no one could imagine their ultimate size. Steve Jobs and Steve Wozniak began the Apple Computer Company by tinkering in their garage. Neither they nor their friends believed their initial efforts would lead to one of the largest and most successful corporations in the world.

How do small companies grow into large ones? And how do so many large companies continue to grow even larger? Mostly by expanding the market for their product and increasing their capacity to produce for that growing market. To expand the market, a business will have to increase spending on advertising and other forms of marketing. To expand productive capacity, it will have to purchase new capital equipment, hire more workers, increase factory and office space, and find ways to distribute its product on a broader scale. In other words, the future growth of a business depends on its present investments in all these areas. Where can businesses get the funds needed to prepare for growth? In this module we will explore the possibilities.

*Several of the world's largest corporations started out in a garage. This is the garage where the first Apple computers were made.*

## GROWTH FROM REINVESTING PROFITS

One way that any profitable company can grow is by reinvesting some of its profits back into the business. To understand how this works, it helps to understand the *income statement* for a business. The income statement lists a business's revenue, expenses, and profit over some time period. To comply with tax laws, most businesses must construct an income statement each quarter.

As an example, let's consider The Tutor Shop in its early phase as a small business. We'll look at information for a three-month period known as a *quarter* because it is a quarter of a year. The business experiences the following receipts and payments in a quarter:

- $5,000 in revenue, collected from student clients;

- $450 in costs for materials and services, including paper and printing costs for advertising fliers;

- $900 in wages and salaries for tutors and a part-time assistant you've hired;

- $50 in quarterly interest payments, for a long-term loan you obtained from an uncle to buy a computer and set up your business;

- $0 for rent, because you are operating out of your family's home; and

- $100 in depreciation for your computer.

That last item, depreciation, requires some explanation. Suppose your computer cost $800 and you expect it to last two years. After that you will need to replace it. In two years there are eight quarters, so in each quarter, one eighth of the $800 value of your computer—100 dollars' worth—is effectively "used up." The dollar value of capital used up due to aging and wear in this way is called *depreciation*. For an ongoing business, depreciation must be thought of as an expense. Even if you don't use these funds to buy new equipment this quarter, you will have to do so eventually.

We will assume that any funds you set aside for depreciation are kept within the business.

Your business's income statement would contain all these transactions as shown in Table 21.1.

The Tutor Shop's profit (revenue minus expenses) is $3,500. After paying taxes of $1,000, its *net* or *after-tax profit* is $2,500. The business could grow by reinvesting some of this profit. For example, the advertising budget could be increased or better software could be purchased to enable the business to handle more tutors and clients.

One of the arrows in Table 21.1 shows that The Tutor Shop has decided to pay out $500 in profit to the firm's owner(s). If The Tutor Shop is a sole proprietorship, you are the only owner

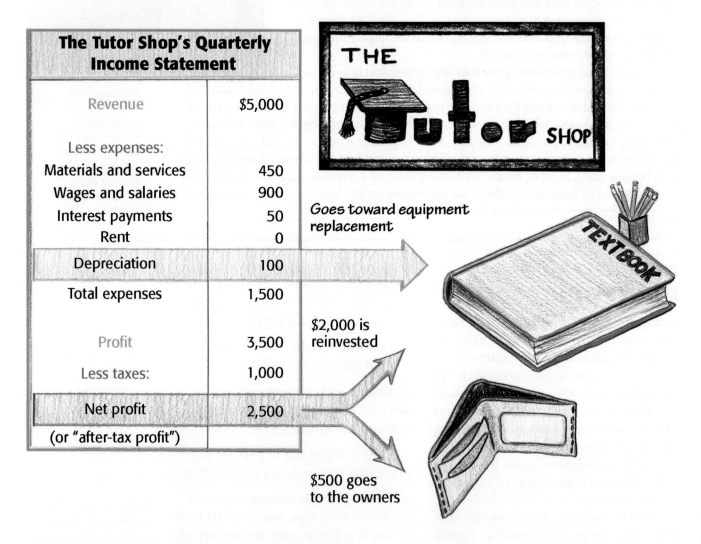

**The Tutor Shop's Quarterly Income Statement**

| | |
|---|---|
| Revenue | $5,000 |
| Less expenses: | |
| Materials and services | 450 |
| Wages and salaries | 900 |
| Interest payments | 50 |
| Rent | 0 |
| Depreciation | 100 |
| Total expenses | 1,500 |
| Profit | 3,500 |
| Less taxes: | 1,000 |
| Net profit (or "after-tax profit") | 2,500 |

Goes toward equipment replacement

$2,000 is reinvested

$500 goes to the owners

**Table 21.1** The Tutor Shop's Quarterly Income Statement

and that $500 goes to you. If it is a partnership, you and your partner(s) share the $500. If it is a corporation, the $500 is divided among the many stockholders. The remaining $2,000 of net profit is reinvested in the firm. This is the type of reinvestment that will make the business grow.

While the $100 depreciation expense is also reinvested in the business, it does not contribute to growth. Rather, it just covers the replacement of capital lost to depreciation, so it prevents the business from shrinking. If you don't replace your capital as it wears out, you will eventually be left with none at all.

**DID YOU GET IT?**
What is depreciation and why doesn't expenditure on depreciation contribute to the growth of a firm?

## GROWTH FROM OUTSIDE FUNDING

One drawback to growth by reinvesting profits is that the available profits might be inadequate for important investment opportunities. A business with good prospects might want to spend more than it earns. If it grows more slowly, relying on the slow growth of profits, a competitor might take over part of its market.

When a business wants to invest more in growth than it earns in current profits, it can obtain funding from outside sources. For a sole proprietorship or partnership, the funds might come from personal savings of the owners. Funds could also come from a bank loan. A corporation can also borrow from a bank, but it has two additional options: it can borrow funds by issuing and selling bonds, or it can raise funds by issuing and selling new shares of stock.

For example, in 2004, Google had ambitious plans to expand its Internet search and advertising business. To do so, it needed to hire more researchers,

*At Google, it took bigger buildings to support faster growth, and the sale of stock made that possible.*

programmers, marketers, and managers. It also needed more servers to handle the growth in daily searches and more buildings to house the new servers and employees. Over the next few years, Google wanted to invest much more money than it could earn in profit. But as a privately held corporation, it was not allowed to issue shares of stock to outsiders.

So in 2004, Google became a public corporation. In August of that year, it issued millions of shares of new stock and sold them for $85 each. This gave it an instant $1.7 billion in new funding. Outsiders were happy to buy the stock, because they wanted to own a share of Google's future profits.

## MERGERS AND ACQUISITIONS

A third way that a business can grow is through *mergers* and *acquisitions*. A **merger** occurs when two firms legally join together to form a single, larger firm. In some cases, the merger involves two firms of comparable size that agree to combine their business operations. The world's largest company, ExxonMobil, was created in 1999 through the merger of two firms, Exxon Chemical Company and Mobil Chemical Company.

In other cases, a merger is the result of an **acquisition**—the purchase by one firm of a controlling interest in

A **merger** occurs when two firms legally join together to form a single, larger firm.

An **acquisition** is the purchase by one firm of a controlling interest in another firm.

another firm. To gain a controlling interest, the acquiring firm must generally purchase at least 51 percent of the shares of stock in the "target" firm.

Some acquisitions are *friendly*, meaning the owners and managers of the target firm are content about being acquired. Others are *hostile*, meaning some stockholders or managers of the target company resist being acquired. An example of a friendly acquisition was The Walt Disney Company's 2006 purchase of Pixar Animation Studios for $7 billion. An example of a hostile takeover was the move by Kraft Foods to acquire the candy maker Cadbury in 2010.

## Horizontal Mergers versus Vertical Mergers

Imagine that one day, you discover a student at another high school has started a business just like yours, called "The Tutor Connection." You are immediately suspicious of your competitor. On the other hand, you are curious and want to meet the owner.

You make contact and agree to meet for lunch on neutral territory: at a diner located between your two schools. At the lunch, you are pleasantly surprised to find that the two of you could *help* each other. You could learn from each other's mistakes and exchange tips on management and marketing. And then it occurs to you: you might *both* make more profit if you combined your two companies into one. You could share software and computer equipment, and avoid unnecessary duplication. Each of you could specialize in the management areas in which you excel. You could have one person manage a single website, instead of having two people managing separate sites. Economists call the combination you are considering a *horizontal merger*.

A **horizontal merger** combines two firms that produce the same type of product. An example occurred in 2007, when Whole Foods Market, a company that owns a chain of natural food stores, acquired its rival, Wild Oats, for $565 million. An even larger horizontal merger occurred in 2002, when the pharmaceutical company Pfizer acquired the pharmaceutical company Pharmacia for about $60 billion.

Horizontal mergers are often controversial. On the one hand, they have the potential to lower costs by combining operations and creating new efficiencies in production. On the other hand, they can reduce competition and lead to higher prices for consumers. For example, suppose one motive for merging The Tutor Shop and The Tutor Connection is to avoid competition that might lower the fees each of you charge for your service. Then the merger would be harmful to your customers.

For this reason, horizontal mergers between large corporations are almost always investigated by the government agencies that must approve them. In the United States, the Federal Trade Commission reviews proposed mergers to determine the likely effects on competition and prices. If competition is threatened, the merger might be blocked. For example, the Federal Trade Commission first tried to prevent Whole Foods from acquiring Wild Oats.

A **horizontal merger** combines two firms that produce the same type of product.

In 2007, Whole Foods Market acquired its rival Wild Oats for $565 million. This was a horizontal merger.

© ERIK FREELAND/CORBIS

In the end, the merger was approved, but only under conditions designed to maintain competition in the market for natural foods.

A **vertical merger** combines firms that operate at different stages in the production of a good. For example, if a firm that makes greeting cards merged with a firm that makes paper, this would be a vertical merger. Vertical mergers can increase a firm's control over the production and distribution of its product, leading to greater efficiencies and lower costs. Vertical mergers are generally less controversial than horizontal mergers, unless they are perceived as reducing competition in one of the stages of production.

In the early days of automobile manufacturing, Henry Ford pushed the idea of vertical control to the extreme. His company owned firms at almost every stage of car production and distribution, from the iron ore mines that supplied steel producers to the dealerships where cars were sold. In recent times, such extremes of control are rare, but vertical mergers are still common. In 2009, Boeing purchased a manufacturer of parts for its new jet, the 787 Dreamliner. And at the end of that year, the cable company Comcast—a distributor of entertainment

A **vertical merger** combines firms that operate at different stages in the production of a good.

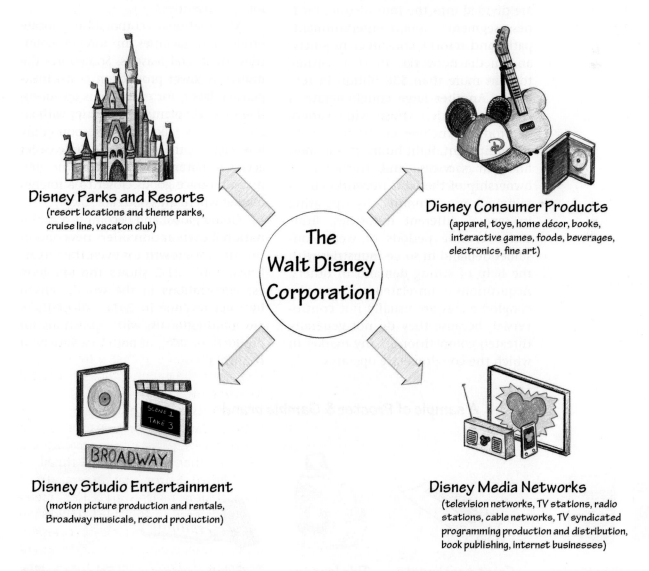

**Disney Parks and Resorts**
(resort locations and theme parks, cruise line, vacaton club)

**Disney Consumer Products**
(apparel, toys, home décor, books, interactive games, foods, beverages, electronics, fine art)

**The Walt Disney Corporation**

**Disney Studio Entertainment**
(motion picture production and rentals, Broadway musicals, record production)

**Disney Media Networks**
(television networks, TV stations, radio stations, cable networks, TV syndicated programming production and distribution, book publishing, internet businesses)

**Figure 21.1** The Walt Disney Company
The Walt Disney Company is an example of a conglomerate.

programs—announced that it would try to acquire NBC—a creator of entertainment programming.

**DID YOU GET IT?**
What is the difference between a vertical merger and a horizontal merger?

### Conglomerates

A **conglomerate** is a single business enterprise formed by combining firms from unrelated industries. As shown in Figure 21.1 on the previous page, the Walt Disney Company is an example of a conglomerate. Broadly speaking, Disney is in the business of entertainment. The company's vast holdings, however, are divided into the four distinct business segments: studio entertainment, parks and resorts, consumer products, and media networks. In 2010 Disney took in more than $38 billion in revenues. Another large conglomerate is General Electric, whose wide variety of products include electricity, medical equipment, light bulbs, jet engines, financial services, and (through its ownership of the NBC network) entertainment programming. By operating in several different industries, firms can overcome periods of weak consumer demand in some industries with the help of strong demand in others. Acquisitions of unrelated businesses by conglomerates are usually not controversial, because they do not generally threaten competition in any market in which the conglomerate operates.

> A **multinational corporation** is a company that operates in more than one country.

> A **conglomerate** is a single business enterprise formed by combining firms from unrelated industries.

## GOING GLOBAL

Many corporations grow larger by expanding internationally and becoming *multinational corporations*. A **multinational corporation** is a company that operates in more than one country. The corporate headquarters will be in one country, but it will operate branches for production or distribution in other countries. An example is Procter & Gamble (P&G), a conglomerate with its headquarters in the United States. You probably use some of P&G's products every day, under brand names such as Crest, Tide, Folgers, Gillette, and Duracell. But did you know that more than half of P&G's employees are located in foreign countries?

Multinational corporations locate production facilities in foreign countries for several reasons. Sometimes the motive is lower production costs. Inexpensive labor, for example, is an incentive to locate plants in countries with an abundance of labor and correspondingly low wages. Other motives include easier access to natural resources and the ability to produce goods closer to a foreign market where the goods are sold.

Going global and becoming a multinational corporation offers new opportunities for growth for even the largest firms. Table 21.2 shows the ten largest corporations in the world, ranked by total revenue in 2011. All of them are multinationals, with operations for production, sales, or both in a variety of countries.

### A sample of Procter & Gamble brands

**Duracell batteries**

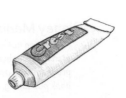
**Crest toothpaste**

**Tide laundry detergent**

**Gillette razors**

**Folger's coffee**

Table 21.2 **Top Ten Companies in the Global Economy in 2011 (Ranked by Business Revenues)**

| 2011 RANK | COMPANY | HEADQUARTERS COUNTRY | TOTAL REVENUES (BILLIONS OF DOLLARS) | NUMBER OF EMPLOYEES |
|---|---|---|---|---|
| 1 | Walmart Stores | United States | 422 | 2,100,000 |
| 2 | Royal Dutch Shell | Netherlands | 378 | 97,000 |
| 3 | Exxon-Mobil | United States | 355 | 103,700 |
| 4 | BP | United Kingdom | 309 | 79,700 |
| 5 | Sinopec Group | China | 273 | 640,535 |
| 6 | China National Petroleum | China | 240 | 100,007 |
| 7 | State Grid | China | 226 | 100,031 |
| 8 | Toyota Motor | Japan | 222 | 317,716 |
| 9 | Japan Post Holdings | Japan | 204 | 233,000 |
| 10 | Chevron | United States | 196 | 62,196 |

SOURCE: http://money.cnn.com/magazines/fortune/global500/2011/snapshots/2255.html

# MODULE 21 REVIEW AND ASSESSMENT

## Summing Up the Key Ideas: Match the following terms to the correct definitions.

A. After-tax profit
B. Acquisition
C. Income statement

D. Horizontal merger
E. Vertical merger
F. Depreciation

G. Conglomerate
H. Multinational corporation

_____ 1.   Revenue minus expenses and taxes.

_____ 2.   The dollar value of capital used up due to aging and wear.

_____ 3.   It combines firms that operate at different stages in the production of a good.

_____ 4.   The purchase by one firm of a controlling interest in another firm.

_____ 5.   A single business enterprise formed by combining firms from unrelated industries.

_____ 6.   A company that operates production facilities or sells products in more than one country.

_____ 7.   It combines two firms that produce the same type of product.

_____ 8.   Lists a business's revenue, expenses, and profit over some time period.

## Analyze: Consider the Tutor Shop's income statement as shown in Table 21.1. By how much will the Tutor Shop's profit increase or decrease in each of the following scenarios?

EFFECT ON PROFIT

1. The word gets out that the Tutor Shop offers great services, and revenue increases to $6,000.   _____

2. Employees get a raise, which increases expenditures on wages, and salaries increase to $1,200.   _____

3. The firm decides to rent office space for $500.   _____

## Apply: Determine if each of the following describes a **horizontal** or **vertical merger**.

DETERMINATION

1. A business owner decides that the best way to make more money is to eliminate the competition by buying out the firms with whom she is competing.   _____

2. A textbook company merges with a paper company.   _____

3. A business decides to buy the firm that supplies it with raw materials and the trucks used to deliver the finished product to market.   _____

# MODULE 22

# Business Ethics

**KEY IDEA:** Increasingly, businesses are expected to pursue not only profits but the ethical treatment of workers, consumers, communities, and the environment.

## OBJECTIVES

- **To explain two viewpoints in the controversy over corporate responsibility.**
- **To describe how public scrutiny of business behavior has increased in modern times.**
- **To identify ways in which firms can make decisions about questionable behavior.**

## Grappling with Right and Wrong

What constitutes acceptable business behavior? That question is as old as business itself. But a recent string of questionable business decisions and expanding global markets highlight its importance. One concern is that firms, eager to maximize profits, might jeopardize the health and safety of workers, customers, and other members of society. Almost all production involves tradeoffs between the creation of profits and the creation of pollution, which forces corporate leaders, consumers, and governments to grapple with the ethical responsibilities of firms. This module addresses some of the relevant issues to assist you with your own debates and decisions about business ethics.

"Our core values statement is now official."

## THE VALUE OF "DOING RIGHT"

In the early 2000s a new wave of corporate scandals shook consumer confidence in American businesses. The allegations involved accounting firms misrepresenting profits, pharmaceutical companies selling dangerous medicines, airlines putting off aircraft maintenance, government contractors overcharging taxpayers, and assorted acts of bribery, theft, fraud, dishonesty, and abuse. These scandals, and the hardships caused by this corporate mischief, brought the topic of business ethics out of the shadows and into the headlines.

**Business ethics** is the examination of standards for "right" and "wrong" behavior by firms. When companies pursue right actions their behaviors are considered ethical. When companies pursue wrong actions their behaviors are considered unethical. But what is right and what is wrong in the conduct of business? There is still considerable disagreement on this question.

Perceptions of right and wrong business behaviors have evolved over time. During much of America's economic history, it was right for a business to focus almost exclusively on building a profitable enterprise and rewarding investors with high earnings. The damage caused by unsafe working conditions or damage

**Business ethics** is the examination of standards for "right" and "wrong" behavior by firms.

*In 2011, a group called Corporate Accountability International called for McDonald's to stop using Ronald McDonald to market unhealthy food to children. Is this group correct in asserting that this business behavior is wrong?*

to the natural environment was not a pressing concern. In this type of business environment, the clearly wrong business actions were decisions, policies, or practices that interrupted the flow of profits to investors.

In modern times, it is more common to consider the impact of a business on many stakeholders in the economy—workers, consumers, investors, other businesses, and local communities. It is also better understood that a healthy environment is vital to all of those stakeholders and to the supply of natural resources that are inputs into production. That is, if trees couldn't grow, there would be no paper to print this book on.

There is a growing consensus that right business actions, or ethical behaviors, can support profitable business enterprises and, at the same time, promote the well-being of other people and the environment. Wrong actions, or unethical behaviors, are business actions that pursue profits without regard to the other stakeholders or society at large.

Society's laws and regulations have kept pace with this changing view of business ethics. Many practices that were once considered close to unethical but legal are today illegal. For example, in 1970, the U.S. Congress created the Occupational Safety and Health Administration (OSHA). OSHA required employers to protect the health and safety of their workers in specific ways, such as limiting exposure to toxic fumes and deafening noise. Similarly, the Clean Air Act and the Clean Water Act, originally passed by Congress in the early 1970s, limit the amount of pollution that factories, mills, mines, and other businesses can release into the environment.

## Business Ethics in the 2000s

In the first decade of the 2000s, two events renewed the public's interest in business ethics. The first was the wave of corporate scandals mentioned earlier. Corporate corruption toppled leaders in several major U.S. corporations, including Adelphia, Enron, and WorldCom. The corruption took different forms, but a common theme was apparent—unethical business practices that had crossed the line into illegal behavior. Top corporate executives took actions to enrich themselves at the expense of other stakeholders, especially employees and stockholders. The business leaders spent company funds for personal pleasures, devised or encouraged fraudulent accounting practices, supplied false and misleading information to investors, and lied to federal investigators. After years of litigation, the unethical behaviors of many top executives earned them stiff prison sentences and hefty fines.

The second event that spurred public debate about business ethics was the financial crisis of 2008. This time, the problem was irresponsible behavior and excessive risk taking by managers and employees of financial institutions. Their collective behavior brought the world's financial system to the brink of collapse. While an actual collapse was prevented, the crisis caused vast amounts of harm. Households around the world lost trillions of dollars of wealth. Millions of jobs were destroyed. Many economists believed that the entire structure of incentives in the financial system had encouraged irresponsible behavior and actually punished those trying to act responsibly.

In 2009, governments around the world—including the U.S. government—responded. They began to explore ways to reorganize financial markets and financial institutions to prevent a repeat of the 2008 crisis. Before the year was out, initial steps had already been taken. In the United States, the Federal Reserve—one of the agencies that regulates banks—cracked down on hidden charges and misleading information for consumers who held checking accounts and credit cards. Congress began the creation of an entirely new government agency, the Consumer Financial Protection Bureau.

It would be empowered in 2011 to issue regulations and standards to protect consumers from misleading information and other unethical behavior by banks, credit card companies, investment advisors, mortgage brokers, and others offering financial services to the public.

*The Starbucks Global Responsibility Report states, "We have found that we're able to serve a great cup of coffee while helping to improve the lives of farmers and protect the planet."*

## BUSINESS ETHICS AT THE FIRM

These efforts by the government illustrate one way to decrease unethical behavior: by making it illegal. But beyond the law, how does a company encourage ethical business behaviors by its workers, from top executives to rank-and-file employees? Philosophers, business leaders, government officials, and others have opinions on this goal. A national professional association, the Ethics and Compliance Officer Association (ECOA), has even been formed to help corporations address sticky ethical issues in the workplace. There is no "one glove fits all" blueprint for creating an ethical corporation. Ethical business behaviors are encouraged when businesses do the following:

- develop a clear vision of company values and mission;
- publish a "code" of business conduct;
- conduct ethics training programs;
- reward employees who exhibit ethical behaviors; and
- obey national and international laws.

Ethical business practices make good business sense. First, ethical businesses are able to attract and retain honest and motivated employees. Second, ethical businesses develop reputations that can help them survive and prosper in the long run. And an ethical business can avoid costly litigation and government fines. After all, the dividing line between behavior that is legal but unethical and behavior that is outright illegal is easy to cross. By encouraging ethical behavior, a business can prevent its employees from getting too close to that line and decrease the chances they will cross it.

There are questions employees can ask themselves to guide ethical behavior. Suppose that when staffing The Tutor Shop, you could hire less knowledgeable tutors who aren't qualified to teach and pay those tutors lower wages. You can apply the *Front Page of the Newspaper* test by asking yourself whether you would want the action you are contemplating to appear in a newspaper headline. Would you want to read "Tutor Shop Tutors Are Faking It!" on the front page of the paper? If not, you shouldn't cut corners in that way.

Other helpful questions include the following:

- Would society be worse off if everyone did the sort of thing I'm about to do?
- Would I want to be treated the way I'm treating others?
- What would the business leader I most respect do in this situation?
- What does my conscience tell me about whether this is right or wrong?

Similar questions are useful for guiding individual decisions as well.

## CORPORATE SOCIAL RESPONSIBILITY IN THE GLOBAL ECONOMY

As more firms do more business in more places, there is an expanded range of opportunities to do right or wrong. **Globalization** is the broadening access to products, people, businesses, technology, ideas, and money across national borders to create a more integrated and interdependent global economy. Globalization has created business opportunities and jobs for millions of people through expanded trade and business relationships among countries. But it has also intensified some of the ongoing debates about how business firms should behave. For example, should firms relocate to countries with lower standards for the treatment of workers and the environment? Issues of business ethics come to the forefront as we struggle with such questions.

**Corporate social responsibility (CSR)** refers to the duties and obligations corporations have to different stakeholders. Discussions about corporate social responsibility spark heated controversies. Much of the debate about CSR deals with a basic question: to whom is a corporation responsible? With globalization, the number of people affected by corporate decisions has grown. A new medicine with dangerous side effects could affect customers around the world. A multinational corporation with unsafe working conditions could affect employees around the world. And a firm that releases toxic pollution could affect communities and wilderness areas around the world.

One viewpoint is that corporations are socially responsible if they focus on production and profit maximization. Within the context of free enterprise, advocates of this view seek fair treatment for workers, rewards for investors, and compliance with existing laws in domestic and foreign markets. They believe the government, not businesses, should attend to broader social issues such as human rights, environmental decay,

The mission of the Hard Rock Café is to "do well by doing good" in local and global communities.

and the conditions for people in affected communities. These broader issues are viewed as distinct from the corporation's real mission—to earn profits for investors. Profitable companies, in turn, supply goods to consumers, create jobs for workers, and invest in new technologies and capital goods. Profitable companies also pay taxes to support government programs, including programs that protect the environment and support the needy. Supporters of this viewpoint argue "a rising tide raises all boats"—that the success of many individual firms raises everyone's living standards.

A second viewpoint is that corporations are socially responsible if they actively pursue *two* goals: business profits and a broader vision of good corporate citizenship. Advocates of this view say that to be good corporate citizens, firms should actively support the rights of workers, the safety of consumers, human rights, and respect for communities and the environment.

Over the last decade, many corporations have moved closer to this second viewpoint. Today, most large corporations have a *corporate code of conduct* or a similar document that defines how the firm's policies and practices promote good corporate citizenship. The

*Some firms relocate to countries where environmental standards are lower, which decreases production costs. Is that ethical?*

BOTTOM LEFT: © DIPTENDU DUTTA/AFP/GETTY IMAGES; TOP RIGHT: © RICHARD T. NOWITZ/CORBIS

Google Corporate Code of Conduct emphasizes the phrase "Don't be evil," which the company says is about serving customers well but also "doing the right thing more generally—following the law, acting honorably and treating each other with respect." Walmart has a Corporate Statement of Ethics that speaks of "leading with integrity" in the workplace, in the marketplace, and in communities. And the basic principles listed among McDonald's Standards of Business Conduct include not only "We grow our business profitably" but also "We operate our business ethically" and "We give back to our communities."

# MODULE 22 REVIEW AND ASSESSMENT

## Summing Up the Key Ideas: Match the following terms to the correct definitions.

A. Business ethics    B. Globalization    C. Corporate social responsibility

_____ 1.   Refers to the duties and obligations corporations have to different stakeholders.

_____ 2.   The examination of standards for *right* and *wrong* behavior by firms.

_____ 3.   The broadening access to products, people, businesses, technology, ideas, and money across national borders to create a more integrated and interdependent global economy.

## Analyze: Analyze each of the following statements and determine if it **encourages** or **discourages** ethical business behavior.

|  | ENCOURAGES | DISCOURAGES |
|---|---|---|
| 1. A business decides to develop a clear vision of company values and mission. | _____ | _____ |
| 2. A business owner decides to pursue the maximum profit potential for his company and ignore what he considers unnecessary government regulations. | _____ | _____ |
| 3. Workers are pressured to take risks that border on unethical behavior and are rewarded for this behavior. | _____ | _____ |
| 4. A business decides to publish a "code" of business conduct. | _____ | _____ |
| 5. A business hosts guest speakers for presentations at worker seminars on reaching ethical goals and doing the right thing. | _____ | _____ |
| 6. A business in the United States decides it will obey all U.S. laws but ignore international agreements and international laws. | _____ | _____ |

**Apply:** Suppose you earn $80 a day as a bookstore sales clerk. One day you wake up with strep throat, a highly contagious illness that causes considerable throat pain. You have enough energy to work, but you must consider the ethics of working and exposing many people to your illness. Discuss your answer to each of the questions this module describes as being helpful for guiding ethical decision. The questions are repeated here for your convenience:

1. Would I want the decision I'm contemplating to appear in a newspaper headline?

2. Would society be worse off if everyone did the sort of thing I'm about to do?

3. Would I want to be treated the way I'm treating others?

4. What would the business leader I most respect do in this situation?

5. What does my conscience tell me about whether this is right or wrong?

## HEADLINE ECONOMICS

# THE WASHINGTON POST

# Be an NFL Owner: Green Bay Packers to Sell Stock for $250, Giving Fans Chance to Buy into Team

MILWAUKEE—Want to own a piece of the Green Bay Packers? The Super Bowl champions of 2010 are about to give you a chance. The Packers, the NFL's only publicly owned team, announced details Thursday about their first stock sale in 14 years and fifth in team history. The money will help pay for $130 mil-lion in renovations at historic Lambeau Field in Green Bay. Own just one share and technically you're a team owner. However, be aware that Packers stock isn't like regular stock. The value doesn't go up, there are no dividends and it has virtually no resale value. Stockholders do get voting rights, along with invitations to attend annual meetings where they can meet Packers executives, tour the Packers Hall of Fame and stick around for the kickoff of training camp.

Each share will cost $250 plus a handling charge and will be offered for only a limited time. Stock can only be purchased by individuals, not businesses, and there's a 200-share cap, a figure that includes any stock purchased during the last sale in 1997. Newly purchased shares can be given as gifts. However, once ownership is established, a share can only be transferred within the immediate family.

Staughton Wade, 29, of Fort Wayne, Ind., said $250 was a reasonable price to pay for a Packers share. His favorite team is the winless Indianapolis Colts (0–11), and he said he welcomed a chance to buy into the league's only undefeated team, the Packers (11–0). "It's a completely unique item," Wade said of the stock. "You can't get this anywhere else, and who knows when the next opportunity will be?"

While being a shareholder might come with some perks, it won't help you move up on the season-ticket waiting list, which has more than 81,000 names.

All the money raised in the stock sale will go toward stadium renovations. The Packers plan to add thousands of seats and other amenities in time for the 2013 season. While other teams often ask taxpayers to help pay for building upgrades, the Packers will foot the entire bill themselves through the stock sale and private financing. That's part of the reason that Joel Tchao, 38, a San Francisco 49ers fan from Fremont, Calif., said he would "definitely" buy a share next week. "It's showing my appreciation for how they're run as a team," he said.

The Packers have been a publicly owned nonprofit corporation since 1923. The team held its first stock sale that year, followed by sales in 1935 and 1950 that helped keep the franchise afloat even as other small-markets teams were sinking.

There's been at least one complaint about the price this year. Michael Constantine, a Wisconsin native who now lives in Washington, had planned to buy a share this year when the rumored price was $200. When he found out the actual price Thursday, he said $250 was just over the edge of affordability. "For me living in Seattle, I could spend $250 on tickets to go back to Wisconsin and go to a Packers game," said Constantine, 26. "For that price I'd be looking at other Packers-related activity I could use that money for."

## DID YOU READ IT?

1) **What form of organization best describes the Green Bay Packers? Why are the Green Bay Packers selling stock in their team?**

2) **What is the difference between being an owner of a share of stock in a traditional corporation and being an owner of a share of stock in the Green Bay Packers?**

## WHAT DO YOU THINK?

1) **What factors influence the price of a share of Green Bay Packers stock?**

2) **Most professional sports teams are not publicly owned and therefore do not sell shares of stock. How can concepts from the chapter help explain this?**

EXCERPTED FROM www.washingtonpost.com/business/industries/fans-can-be-nfl-owners-for-250-as-publicly-owned-green-bay-packers-announce-5th-stock-sale/2011/12/01/gIQA0vchHO_print.html

## AN INTERVIEW WITH
# Jeff Bezos, Part II

*When you read books about entrepreneurship, Jeff Bezos, the founder of Amazon, is likely to be listed as one of the most successful and important entrepreneurs of all time—and you may well be reading the book on one of his devices, the Kindle. Bezos grew up in Texas and was always fascinated by inventions. The company that started in his garage in 1995 is now valued at around $90 billion. In the following interview, Mr. Bezos, who remains CEO, president, and chairman of the board of Amazon, describes how he became an entrepreneur and his approach to business.*

**Is it true that you came up with the business plan for Amazon after you studied various mail order catalogues and discovered that there would be a comparative advantage for selling books online, because a printed catalogue would be too large to contain all the books that were available?**

That's exactly right. I made a list of twenty different products and ultimately picked books as the first, best product to sell online. At that time, this was back in 1994 or 1995, there were 3 million books active and in print at any given time globally. The largest physical book superstores had about 150,000 titles. So online, where you had no shelf space constraints, you could build a true book superstore with universal selection. And that became the founding vision for Amazon—a bookstore with universal selection.

**How did you write the business plan for Amazon and start the company?**

I typed up the business plan while my wife was driving our car from Texas to Seattle in July 1994. I called a lawyer and incorporated the company from my cell phone. I initially called the company *Cadabra*—as in "abra cadabra"—and the lawyer in Seattle exclaimed, "Cadaver?" The name got changed to Amazon a few months later.

In addition to me, the team that started Amazon included four people working for the company, software engineers primarily. The company was started in a garage of my house in Bellevue, Washington, just outside of Seattle. The garage didn't have enough electricity so we had to siphon electricity from the rest of the house to the garage with big orange extension cords.

**What advice would you have for high school students who are thinking about starting a business someday?**

Make sure you get work experience first. There are a lot of famous examples of very successful entrepreneurs who didn't do that, so it's clearly not a prerequisite. But I think you increase your odds dramatically if you work for ten years, or some reasonable period of time. You just learn so much. Then you should find an idea you believe in, that you have conviction for, and the idea should be so compelling to you that you would worry that if you didn't try it that when you're eighty years old you would always regret it. That's how I would propose making the decision on something like that. It needs to be something that you are passionate about.

**Did you expect when you were in high school or college that you would become an entrepreneur?**

I had thought about it from time to time. It wasn't a primary driver for me. In high school I wanted to be a physicist. In fact, I went to college to study physics and ended up in electrical engineering and computer science.

I was always attracted to the idea of invention. My heroes were Thomas Edison and Walt Disney and people like that. I wasn't as focused on business as I was idea focused.

**Speaking of inventions, Amazon not only sells products that others produce, but it also invented and manufactures the Kindle. How did the idea for the Kindle come about?**

We had been selling e-books for more than a decade, and you needed an electron microscope to find the sales. They were that small! We worked on the Kindle for three years before it went on the market. There were a whole bunch of pieces that we had to assemble. We looked at the technologies that were available and sort of thought, "Well, if we combine 3G wireless with electronic ink, then the 3G wireless gives us this ability to think of a book and then be reading it in sixty seconds, and that will follow you around anywhere you are."

The vision for Kindle was that every book ever printed in every language—all available within sixty seconds. That fit in with the idea of a free 3G wireless. We also wanted the device to be something that disappeared. Whenever we looked at physical books…when you analyze the physical books as an object, an invention, one of the most elegant things about it is how it disappears while you are reading. You enter the author's world and you forget about the ink and the paper, the glue and the stitching, none of that is important. We wanted Kindle to have that same characteristic, that when you enter the author's world Kindle disappeared.

**What has been your strategy for Amazon?**

We are, for better and for worse, the company that likes inventing, pioneering, and going down unknown alleyways to see if there is a broad avenue at the end. We try to be knowledgeable about what our competitors are doing, but it is not the focus. We are really focused on how we can improve the experience for our customers. My own belief is that our approach is better, especially in a fast-moving industry where close following tends not to work that well anyway, and I can assure you that our approach is more fun.

**While running Amazon is more than a full-time job, I'm curious what you like to do outside of work?**

I have four kids, age 6 to 11, which certainly keeps me busy outside of work and I enjoy that a great deal.

I'm also very interested in long-term thinking. So with a group of people, I am helping to build a 10,000-year clock that is a symbol for long-term thinking in West Texas.

I also read on my Kindle. I am a big reader and I have been since I was a little kid. I read science fiction. I read literary fiction. My favorite authors are Kazuo Ishiguro and Cormac McCarthy. On the science fiction side I really like Iain Banks and Neal Stephenson.

# CHAPTER 7 REVIEW AND SELF-ASSESSMENT

## REVIEW

### Points to Remember

**MODULE 19: BUSINESS AND THE ECONOMY AND MODULE 20: TYPES OF BUSINESSES**

1. A **sole proprietorship** is a business owned by one person, the proprietor.

2. A **partnership** is a for-profit business firm owned by two or more people, called partners, each of whom has a financial interest in the business.

3. A **corporation** is a business firm that is itself a legal entity.

4. A **corporate bond** is a contract between a corporation and the owner of the bond that obligates the corporation to pay the bond's owner a certain amount of money in the future.

5. A **limited liability company (LLC)** is a hybrid business organization that combines features of corporations, partnerships, and sole proprietorships.

6. A **business franchise** consists of a parent company and numerous associated businesses that sell a standardized good or service.

7. A **cooperative**, or co-op, is a business owned by its members and operated to supply members and others with goods and services.

8. A **nonprofit organization**, also called a *nonprofit*, is a legal entity formed to carry out a "not-for-profit" mission.

**MODULE 21: HOW BUSINESSES GROW**

9. A **merger** occurs when two firms legally join together to form a single, larger firm.

10. An **acquisition** is the purchase by one firm of a controlling interest in another firm.

11. A **horizontal merger** combines two firms that produce the same type of product.

12. A **vertical merger** combines firms that operate at different stages in the production of a good.

13. A **conglomerate** is a single business enterprise formed by combining firms from unrelated industries.

14. A **multinational corporation** is a company that operates production facilities or sells products in more than one country.

**MODULE 22: BUSINESS ETHICS**

15. **Business ethics** is the examination of standards of "right" and "wrong" behavior by firms.

16. **Globalization** is the broadening access to products, people, businesses, technology, ideas, and money across national borders to create a more integrated and interdependent global economy.

17. **Corporate social responsibility (CSR)** refers to the duties and obligations corporations have to different stakeholders.

## SELF-ASSESSMENT

The following questions are the type your teacher might ask you on a quiz or a test. Practice with these in order to improve your performance on class tests.

### Multiple-Choice Questions

Answer the first two questions based on the income statement to the right.

1. The dollar value of capital used up due to aging and wear for this business is

   a. $10,000.

   b. $5,200.

   c. $2,800.

   d. $1,100.

| Revenue | $10,000 |
|---|---|
| Less expenses: | |
| Raw materials | $1,500 |
| Wages | $1,400 |
| Rent | $1,200 |
| Depreciation | $1,100 |
| **Total expenses** | **$5,200** |
| **Profit** | **$4,800** |
| Less taxes | $2,000 |
| **Net (or after-tax) profit** | **$2,800** |

2. What amount of money does this business have available for reinvestment and growth?

   a. $10,000
   b. $5,900
   c. $4,800
   d. $2,800

3. Which of the following common expressions would be used by someone opposed to the concept of a conglomerate and in favor of a vertical merger?

   a. "Jack of all trades, master of none."
   b. "You can lead a horse to water, but you can't make him drink."
   c. "Don't put all of your eggs in one basket."
   d. "That is water under the bridge."

4. Which of the following is NOT a characteristic of an entrepreneur?

   a. self-motivated
   b. reluctant to take risks
   c. innovative
   d. organized

5. Which of the following is a *disadvantage* of the corporate form of business organization?

   a. limited liability for the owners
   b. ability to raise money by issuing stock
   c. ability to raise money by issuing bonds
   d. extra reporting requirements

6. In the United States, corporations

   a. are more numerous than sole proprietorships and partnerships.
   b. produce more business revenue than sole proprietorships and partnerships.
   c. are more numerous and produce more revenue than sole proprietorships.
   d. are more numerous and produce more revenue than partnerships.

7. If you own your own business that is part of a parent company with numerous associated businesses that sell a standardized good or service, your business is a

   a. cooperative.
   b. franchise.
   c. nonprofit organization.
   d. limited liability company.

8. A business that owns and operates a number of different firms in completely unrelated product lines is described as

   a. having completed a diagonal venture.
   b. having gone through a vertical merger.
   c. having gone through a horizontal merger.
   d. a conglomerate.

9. Those opposed to the notion that corporations have a social responsibility believe

   a. that the government should attend to social goals and that the real mission of a corporation is to operate within the law and maximize profit.
   b. that the government and business in partnership should attend to social goals and that the real mission of a corporation is not to just make a profit.
   c. that businesses should attend to social goals and that the real mission of a corporation is to earn a profit and be a good corporate citizen.
   d. in a *corporate code of conduct*.

10. A contract between an individual and a corporation that pays back a loan over a specified period of time with interest is

    a. a corporate charter.
    b. a stock certificate.
    c. a corporate bond.
    d. a conglomerate.

## Constructed Response Question

1. There are three distinct forms of business organization.

   a. List the three types.
   b. Identify the most numerous type in the United States.
   c. Identify the type that generates the most revenue in the United States.
   d. List and explain one advantage and one disadvantage of each type of business organization.

**CHAPTER 8 & YOU** If you've ever bought a soda at a ball park, you probably paid more than you would at a convenience store. Of course, the soda at ball parks doesn't contain more expensive ingredients. The higher prices at ball parks result largely from a lack of competition. Convenience stores compete with other stores nearby, so relatively high prices at one convenience store would cause customers to go elsewhere for lower prices. But all the concession stands at a ball park are typically owned by the same firm. The model of perfect competition does not apply in this situation because the firm faces little or no competition. Since thirsty baseball fans must buy their soda from a concession stand, the firm can raise its prices without losing customers to a competitor. In this chapter you'll learn how the nature of competition among firms affects more than just the price you pay for a Coke as you watch your favorite team hit home runs.

# Market Structure

## MARKET POWER IN THE POWER MARKET

The Enron Corporation was a major energy supplier that was caught in a web of scandals in the early 2000s. Enron, the seventh-largest company in the United States at the time, supplied electricity and natural gas to its customers. The firm built and operated power plants and pipelines around the world and organized a market for buying and selling energy. The firm had few competitors, so the model of perfect competition introduced in Module 13 did not apply to Enron.

Enron used its influence on the power industry in California to drive up electricity prices there. As you've learned, a decrease in supply results in an increase in price. Enron reduced the supply of electricity in California by closing power plants that served the state. By cutting supply, Enron caused the price of electricity to rise and that increased its profit. An incident on the afternoon of January 16, 2001, illustrates Enron's strategy. An Enron employee was recorded on tape telling an operator of a 50-megawatt power plant, "We want you guys to get a little creative and come up with a reason to go down." The next day,

THINKSTOCK

267

the plant stopped supplying electricity and one million customers in California were hit by blackouts. The cut in supply caused the price of electricity to surge. This created a handsome profit for Enron—until these and other questionable practices were revealed, the company went bankrupt, and its top officers went to prison.

This chapter considers how price and quantity are determined in markets that are not perfectly competitive.

*Sometimes powerful companies in the energy industry produce too little power, and the result is a blackout.*

## BOTTOM LINE
In markets with little competition among firms, less output is produced than in perfectly competitive markets, and firms charge higher prices.

# MODULE 23

# Monopoly

**KEY IDEA:** **A monopoly is a market with just one firm that can earn continual profit if competitors have difficulty entering the market.**

**OBJECTIVES**

- **To explain the concept of market structure.**
- **To describe the characteristics of a monopoly.**
- **To explain the effects of *price discrimination*.**

## Size and Influence

Chapters 4, 5, and 6 discussed perfectly competitive markets in which many consumers and firms buy and sell goods. In a perfectly competitive market, no single buyer or seller can influence the price, because each market participant is small relative to the market. In some ways a perfectly competitive market is like a beach, with each grain of sand representing a firm. If you stood on the beach and one grain of sand shifted below you, it would make no difference to you because it is such a small part of the beach. Likewise, the actions of one out of thousands of carrot sellers would have no significant influence on the market for carrots. If instead you stood on a large bolder, a shift in the bolder would have a dramatic effect on you. Similarly, in this module you will learn about firms that are large enough to influence an entire market with their actions.

*A perfectly competitive firm has no influence on a market, like a grain of sand has no influence on a beach. In contrast, some firms are like boulders—they're large enough to make a real difference.*

## MARKET STRUCTURE

An exploration of markets with differing amounts of competition is an exploration of *market structure*. **Market structure** is the term economists use to describe the nature of competition within a market. The spectrum of market structures is shown in Figure 23.1. At the top, with the most firms, is perfect competition, the result of a great many firms supplying the same product. At the bottom is *monopoly*, the case of only one firm supplying a product that has no close substitutes. In between we find the intermediate market structures of *monopolistic competition* and *oligopoly*. In every market that isn't perfectly competitive there is *imperfect competition*. **Imperfect competition** arises when there is not enough competition among firms to prevent individual firms from raising their price above the equilibrium level determined by supply and demand. In this module we will take a closer look at monopoly.

### Defining a Product Market

Before we can classify the market structure for a good, we must identify the group of products that compete in the *product market* for that good. The **product market** for a good includes all of those products that consumers consider to be close substitutes. For example, the product market for headache medicine consists of Bayer aspirin,

**Market structure** describes the nature of competition within a market.

**Imperfect competition** arises when there is not enough competition among firms to prevent individual firms from raising their price above the equilibrium level determined by supply and demand.

The **product market** for a good includes all those products that consumers consider to be close substitutes for that good.

**More firms**

**Perfect Competition**
Many farmers selling the same type of apples.

**Monopolistic Competition**
Many restaurants selling a variety of types of food.

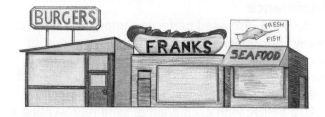

**Oligopoly**
A few manufacturers selling cars and trucks.

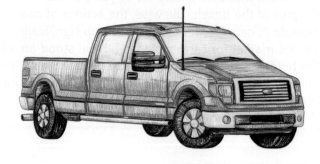

**Monopoly**
The only power plant serving a region.

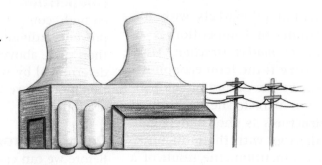

**Fewer firms**

**Figure 23.1** Four Types of Market Structure
Market structures range from perfect competition, with many firms selling the same good, to monopoly, with one firm selling a good not offered by competitors.

CVS aspirin, generic aspirin, Tylenol, Advil, Aleve, and many other brands of pain relievers. Some of the products in this market are identical—all brands of aspirin have the same active ingredient—while others are different. For most consumers, these products are close substitutes. When two goods are substitutes, a rise in the price of one of the goods causes consumers to switch to the other good. If the price of Tylenol rises, many consumers will shift to Aleve, so Aleve and Tylenol are in the same product market.

Geography also affects the makeup of a product market. Suppose a town has both a movie theater and a community theater in the downtown area. If people consider the movies and plays at these theaters to be close substitutes, the movies and plays share the product market for local entertainment. On the other hand, even two movie theaters are not in the same product market if they are 100 miles apart. If a town has only one theater and there isn't another theater around for miles, the one theater doesn't need to worry about losing customers to competitors. The movie theaters in other towns are not close substitutes for the local theater, so the product market for movies in that town would consist of the movies shown by that one theater.

*There are so many choices in the product market for headache medicine, trying to pick one could cause a headache!*

charge more for tickets than it could if there were a theater across the street competing for its customers. However, a monopolist must be careful in setting its price because as the price increases, the quantity demanded decreases. If the movie theater tried to charge $50 per ticket, its customers might all stay home.

Recall from Module 13 that in a perfectly competitive market, every unit of the good is the same, there are many firms, firms can enter or exit the market easily, and consumers are aware of the prices charged at each firm. Monopoly is at the other end of the market structure continuum from perfect competition. Whereas firms in a perfectly competitive market have many competitors, a monopolist has none. This results in a difference in *market power*. It is **market power** that allows individual firms to influence the market price. Firms in a perfectly competitive market have no market power. They are *price takers*, meaning that they must take the market price as given. Imagine a town with many theaters showing the latest James Bond movie for the market price of $10 per ticket. If one theater tried to raise its price to $12, it would lose its customers to the

**Market power** is the ability of a firm to change the market price of a good or service.

A **monopoly** is a product market served by only one firm.

The one supplier in a monopoly is called a **monopolist**.

**?** **DID YOU GET IT?**
What is a product market?

## WHAT IS A MONOPOLY?

Monopoly literally means "one seller." A **monopoly** is a product market served by only one firm. The sole supplier to a monopoly market is called a **monopolist**. By avoiding the forces of competition, a monopolist can enjoy sustained profit. Consider that movie theater we just mentioned that has no competitors within a reasonable driving distance. As a monopolist, the theater can

**Table 23.1 Perfect Competition and Monopoly Compared**

| | PERFECT COMPETITION | MONOPOLY |
|---|---|---|
| Number of firms | Many | One |
| Market power of firms | Price takers | Set their own price |
| Entry of new firms | Free | Restricted |

**Barriers to entry** are obstacles that prevent firms from entering particular markets.

A **natural monopoly** is a market in which high start-up costs make it prohibitively expensive for more than one firm to operate.

The **average cost** is the total cost of production divided by the quantity of output.

*Most cable service providers are monopolists because high start-up costs prevent several firms from sharing a market.*

competition. Table 23.1 compares the market structures of monopoly and perfect competition.

Some monopolists can earn considerable profit, and competitors are attracted to profit like ants to a picnic. For a monopolist to maintain its market power there must be a **barrier to entry**, which is something that prevents other firms from entering the market and competing for the monopolist's customers and profit. There are four general types of barriers to entry that allow a firm to maintain a monopoly: start-up costs, exclusive access to a critical input, government protection, and unfair practices. These four sources of monopoly power are not mutually exclusive. Some firms gain and maintain monopoly status for more than one reason.

## Start-Up Costs

Think about what it was like when your local cable TV service provider wanted to start offering service. It had to set up an extensive system of cables connecting homes with TV networks. Since then, as more homes have needed cable connections, that firm has been able to hook them up easily because it has cables running down every street. On the other hand, it would cost a fortune for a new competitor that hasn't laid any cables to set up a system and compete with the existing firm. As a consequence of the high start-up cost of providing cable TV service, about 90 percent of towns have only one cable service provider.

A cable service provider is an example of a monopolist in a *natural monopoly*. A **natural monopoly** is a market in which high start-up costs make it prohibitively expensive for more than one firm to operate. By serving the whole market, a single firm can produce a large quantity and spread the high start-up costs across many units of output. Most power plants operate in natural monopolies. It costs hundreds of millions of dollars to build a power plant. Once the plant is built, however, the marginal cost of producing additional electricity is very low. As the plant produces and sells more electricity, the high start-up costs are spread across more kilowatt-hours of output.

Firms earn a profit if the price of their good or service exceeds the *average cost* of producing it. The **average cost** is simply the total cost divided by the quantity. For a power plant and other natural monopolies, the average cost falls dramatically as output grows and the large start-up costs are divided among large quantities of output. Decreasing average cost gives the first power plant in a region an important advantage over other plants that might enter the market. By serving the whole market, the first plant has many customers and produces electricity at a lower cost per kilowatt-hour than a new plant could. This cost advantage

enables the first producer to charge less than potential competitors would need to charge to cover their costs and thereby discourages competitors from entering the market.

Economists have a special term for the source of this cost advantage. If, in the long run, an increase in output lowers a firm's average cost, the firm is experiencing **economies of scale**. Most firms enjoy economies of scale at low levels of output. Because start-up costs are a large part of the total cost for a natural monopoly, increases in output cause average cost to decrease for relatively high levels of output as well. In other words, a natural monopoly is in the unique situation of experiencing economies of scale at every relevant output level.

When the production process results in a natural monopoly, it is inefficient for more than one supplier to serve the market. That's because one monopolist can supply the whole market at a lower cost than two or more firms. We will see, however, that the desire to maximize profit gives monopolists an incentive to supply less than the efficient quantity of output.

## Exclusive Access to a Critical Input

When a firm has exclusive access to a critical input, it creates a barrier to the entry of other firms. For example, the U.S. Steel Corporation is the world's largest producer of steel. Iron ore is a critical input into steel manufacturing, and U.S. Steel owns many iron ore mines. In the past, control over critical iron ore gave U.S. Steel a monopoly position in the market for steel. New firms could not enter the market unless they could find their own source of iron ore.

## Government Protection

Sometimes government protection enables a firm to become a monopoly. This can be achieved by granting a patent, copyright, or trademark that legally prohibits other firms from producing the same good. Patents reward inventors with the ability to make more profit than competition would allow. A patent prevents competitors from using the invention

for 20 years unless the patent holder grants permission. For example, Thomas Alva Edison was awarded patent number 223,898 for the electric light bulb in 1880, which gave his firm a monopoly in light bulb sales. He subsequently made many improvements to the light bulb and applied for patents for these improvements. Only after Edison's patents expired could competitors enter the market and eliminate the light bulb monopoly.

The government can protect monopolies in other ways as well. For example, it can exempt firms from *antitrust regulations* that are designed to keep markets competitive. Congress has given Major League Baseball such an exemption by saying it can exclude new teams from entering the league. Normally, antitrust regulation would not permit an organization or group of organizations to prevent others from entering a market. If baseball did not have an antitrust exemption, large cities such as New York, Los Angeles, and Chicago would have many more teams than the one or two each has now. Japan does not permit its baseball league to have a monopoly. Tokyo, Japan's largest city, is home to 6 of the country's 12 professional baseball teams.

**Economies of scale** exist if, in the long run, an increase in output results in a decrease in average cost.

*If Congress did not exempt Major League Baseball from antitrust regulation, large cities such as Chicago might have more than two teams.*

# ECONOMICS IN ACTION

# Sewing Barriers to Entry

United States Patent and Trademark No. 1,139,254 is not much to look at: a pentagon surrounding a childlike drawing of a seagull in flight.

But the design for a Levi's pocket, first used 133 years ago, has become the biggest legal battleground in American fashion.

Levi Strauss claims that legions of competitors have stolen its signature denim stitches—two intersecting arcs and a cloth label—for their own pockets, slapping them on the seats of high-priced, hip-hugging jeans that have soared in popularity.

So Levi's is becoming a leader in a new arena: lawsuits. The firm, once the undisputed king of denim . . . has emerged as the most litigious in the apparel industry when it comes to trademark infringement lawsuits, firing off nearly 100 against its competitors since 2001.

The legal scuffles offer a rare glimpse into the sharp-elbowed world of fashion, where the line between inspiration and imitation is razor thin. After all, clothing makers' trade secrets are hung on store racks for all to see, and designs can be quickly copied with small changes to exploit a hot trend.

The lawsuits, which Levi's says it is compelled to file to safeguard the defining features on its jeans, are not about the money— one settled for just $5,000 in damages. Instead, the firm says, they are about removing copycats from stores.

SOURCE: Michael Barbaro and Julie Creswell, *The New York Times*, January 29, 2007 (see www.nytimes.com/2007/01/29/business/29jeans .html?_r=1).

**DID YOU GET IT?**

What do you think would happen to the price of Levi's if competitors were allowed to sell jeans that are similar to Levi's?

## Unfair Practices

There are also some firms that create barriers to entry using unfair practices that prevent others from competing. For example, several large retailers have been accused of lowering their prices below their own costs to drive competitors out of business. And the radio giant Clear Channel was once accused of trying to monopolize the concert industry by threatening to only play music by bands that signed up with its concert promotion company, Live Nation.

In the 1990s, a popular web browser from Netscape helped fuel that firm's spectacular growth. Microsoft, the world's largest software supplier, soon introduced its own browser called Internet Explorer. Explorer was provided together with Microsoft's widely used Windows operating system at no extra cost. As a result,

anyone with Windows—which was nearly everyone with a computer—had no need to buy a separate web browser.

Netscape dwindled under the fierce competition from Microsoft. The U.S. Department of Justice (DOJ) alleged that Microsoft's practice was illegal. The DOJ argued that Microsoft used its dominant position in the computer software market to unfairly restrict competition from other web browsers like Netscape. In its defense, Microsoft argued that Internet Explorer represented a feature of its operating system and that it was not a separate product.

The legal battle threatened not only to force Microsoft to stop bundling Explorer with Windows but to break up the firm. The first judge to hear the case ruled that Microsoft was in fact a monopoly and recommended that the firm be split in two:

| Table 23.2 **The Four Main Sources of Market Power** | |
|---|---|
| Natural monopoly | The average cost of production declines as output rises. |
| Exclusive input | No other firm has everything needed to produce the good. |
| Government protection | Government action prevents competitors from providing the same good or service. |
| Unfair practices | Unjustified actions by existing firms thwart entry by new firms. |

one firm would sell Windows and the other would sell the various other Microsoft products. After a long appeals process, however, Microsoft avoided severe punishment. It received a reduced penalty but was not broken up and could still package programs including Explorer with its Windows operating system.

Critics of the lawsuit argued that if the government prevents firms from developing market power, it will discourage firms from spending on research and innovation. Others argued that Microsoft was let off too lightly.

Table 23.2 summarizes the four main sources of monopoly power.

**DID YOU GET IT?**
Name four ways in which a firm can gain a monopoly position.

**YOUR TURN**
Should the government intervene to create more competition when a firm amasses considerable market power?

## Threats to a Monopolist

A monopoly can be undone by the introduction of competition. The primary threats to monopolists include the following:

**1. Technological change.**
Technological change enables new firms to produce goods that are close substitutes for a monopoly's product.

This is happening in the market for cable TV, for example. Because satellite TV is a close substitute for cable TV, in communities where both are available, they must compete for the same customers.

**2. The entry of international firms.** Sometimes international firms enter into markets formerly monopolized or dominated by domestic firms. For example, the European company Airbus provides competition for the U.S. airplane manufacturer Boeing. And Korean and Japanese steel manufacturers have weakened the monopoly position of U.S. Steel.

**3. The end of government protection.** We noted earlier that patents expire after 20 years. Copyrights, which create a monopoly in the sale of an author's work,

*Competition from international firms has weakened the market power of Boeing.*

generally last for the life of the author plus 70 years. After that time, competitors can enter the market and sell the formerly protected good. Sometimes government protection ends due to a policy change. For example, in the 1970s, the U.S. government weakened regulations that limited competition in the trucking and airline industries, among others.

**DID YOU GET IT?**
What are three threats to a monopolist's position?

# WHAT DO MONOPOLISTS DO?

You've learned that in a perfectly competitive market, the price is determined by supply and demand. Recall also that the firms in a perfectly competitive market are price takers, because there is an equilibrium price that no firm can influence by its individual actions. The demand curve for an individual firm in a perfectly competitive market is simply a horizontal line at the equilibrium price. If a firm in such a market asked for more than the equilibrium price, its customers would switch to buying from competitors. And a firm in a perfectly competitive market can sell as much as it wants at the equilibrium price, so it has no reason to charge less than the equilibrium price.

A monopolist, however, has no competitors. Anyone who wants the monopolist's product must buy it from the monopolist. This advantage affects the monopolist's behavior. Because it does not face competition, the monopolist has the power to raise its price without necessarily losing all its customers. This power is limited by what consumers are willing and able to pay. If the product is something people need or want very much, people may be willing to pay a very high price. A monopolist may also choose to lower its price in order to attract more customers.

## Monopolists as Price Makers

The monopolist's power to set the price means the monopolist is a *price maker*. A monopolist is interested in choosing the combination of price and quantity that will maximize its profit. It does so recognizing that the demand for the monopolist's product is the entire market demand. According to the law of demand, a higher price causes customers to buy less of the product. So a monopolist faces a tradeoff. If it raises its price, it will lose some sales. There is also a tradeoff if a monopolist wants to sell more of its product: it must lower its price.

Suppose the software development industry is monopolized by a firm called MONOPOLE. Table 23.3 shows a revenue and cost schedule for this fictional firm. MONOPOLE can produce up to 8 units of a computer operating system called WindowShade. The fixed cost of MONOPOLE's operation is $5 and its marginal cost—the cost of producing an additional unit of WindowShade—is $3. MONOPOLE sells WindowShade to all its customers for the same price, which is chosen to maximize profit as explained in the next section. The total revenue that MONOPOLE receives is the price times the quantity sold, as reported in column 3 of Table 23.3. For example, the total revenue received by MONOPOLE if 3 units are produced and sold at a price of $7 is $21. Because it is a monopoly, the demand for MONOPOLE's product is the market demand curve, which is downward sloping. Whenever a firm faces a downward-sloping demand curve, it must lower its price to sell more. So MONOPOLE must lower the price of WindowShade if it wants to sell more units.

In Module 15 we explained that *marginal revenue* is the change in the total revenue a firm receives when it sells one more unit of output. Comparing columns 2 and 4 in Table 23.3, we see that after the first unit, the marginal revenue for a monopoly is less than the price. This is because when MONOPOLE lowers its price to sell another unit, the change in total revenue is not simply the price

## Table 23.3 Revenue and Cost Schedule for MONOPOLE

| (1) QUANTITY (Q) | (2) PRICE (P) (DOLLARS) | (3) TOTAL REVENUE (P × Q) (DOLLARS) | (4) MAR-GINAL REVENUE (DOLLARS) | (5) MARGINAL COST (DOLLARS) | (6) TOTAL COSTS ($5 FIXED COST + MARGINAL COST FOR ALL UNITS) | (7) PROFIT (TOTAL REVENUE − TOTAL COST) |
|---|---|---|---|---|---|---|
| 1 | $9 | $9 | $9 | $3 | $8 | $1 |
| 2 | 8 | 16 | 7 | 3 | 11 | 5 |
| 3 | 7 | 21 | 5 | 3 | 14 | 7 |
| 4 | 6 | 24 | 3 | 3 | 17 | 7 |
| 5 | 5 | 25 | 1 | 3 | 20 | 5 |
| 6 | 4 | 24 | -1 | 3 | 23 | 1 |
| 7 | 3 | 21 | -3 | 3 | 26 | -5 |
| 8 | 2 | 16 | -5 | 3 | 29 | -13 |

MONOPOLE

it receives for that last unit. Instead, it is the price minus the decrease in revenue on all the other units that could be sold for more if the price weren't lowered to sell the last unit. For example, to sell the second unit, MONOPOLE must lower its price from $9 to $8. Its marginal revenue from selling the second unit is the new price of $8 minus the $1 it loses on the first unit by lowering the price from $9 to $8. So marginal revenue is $8 − $1 = $7.

**DID YOU GET IT?**
Why does a monopolist face a downward-sloping demand curve?

## Maximizing Profit

A monopolist, like other types of firms, is interested in maximizing profit, not revenue. MONOPOLE's profit is reported in column 7 of Table 23.3. To find profit in this case we started with total revenue, subtracted the fixed cost of $5, and subtracted the marginal cost of each of the units produced. By comparing the profit numbers in the table you can see that MONOPOLE maximizes its profit by producing either 3 or 4 units of output. But what if you didn't have a nice table telling you the profit for each quantity? The same marginal analysis that Blade Runner used to maximize profit in the perfectly competitive market described

in Module 15 applies to other types of markets as well: any type of firm can maximize profit by producing up to the quantity at which the marginal revenue equals the marginal cost. If they are never equal, it will produce the largest quantity for which the marginal revenue exceeds the marginal cost. Employing this marginal analysis, MONOPOLE would produce 4 units, which we know to be a profit-maximizing quantity of output.

### Firms Maximize Profit, Not Revenue

One might think that firm owners seek to take in as many dollars as possible—to maximize revenue. However, a sizable portion of revenue is spent to cover costs, and firm owners really seek to maximize what remains after deducting costs from revenue, which is profit. Suppose a firm could increase its revenue by spending recklessly on all sorts of advertising. If $100,000 worth of advertising led to $75,000 in additional revenue, the increase in revenue would come at the cost of a decrease in profits of $100,000 − $75,000 = $25,000, and the firm owners would have that much less money to keep for themselves or reinvest in the firm. So what owners seek to maximize is profit, not revenue.

Maximizing profit isn't all about choosing the right quantity. The monopolist must also choose the right price. Fortunately, that's even easier than choosing the right quantity. To maximize profit, the monopoly chooses the highest price at which it can sell the profit-maximizing quantity. The first two columns in Table 23.3 provide a demand schedule of the quantity that would be sold at each price. We can see that the highest price at which 4 units could be sold is $6.

**DID YOU GET IT?**
Why does a monopolist choose the quantity of output that equates marginal revenue and marginal cost?

# MONOPOLY: USING THE GRAPH

We can review the profit-maximizing practices of a monopolist with the aid of Figure 23.2. To maximize profit, a monopolist chooses the quantity of output at which the marginal cost of production is equal to the marginal revenue gained from selling another unit. We have drawn the marginal cost curve as a flat line, consistent with the assumption that the marginal cost is $3, regardless of how much output is produced. For other monopolists, the marginal cost curve could be rising or falling, and it often resembles the Nike swoosh!

To simplify the situation, we'll assume that software can only be sold in whole units, so the lines between the dots in Figure 23.2 are just connectors that don't represent options to sell partial units of WindowShade. Marginal revenue and marginal cost are equal at a quantity of 4 units. This equality marks the profit-maximizing quantity of output. To find the highest price MONOPOLE can charge for 4 units, we look at the height of the demand curve at a quantity of 4 units. Follow the dashed line in Figure 23.2 up from a quantity of 4 to the demand curve, and then left from the demand curve to the vertical axis to find the profit-maximizing price of $6.

## Supply and the Monopolist

You may have noticed that we did not mention a supply curve in discussing how price and quantity are determined in a market controlled by a monopolist. This is because the quantity supplied by a monopolist depends on more than the price—it also depends on the demand curve. Under the same cost conditions, two monopolists with different demand curves would supply different quantities. As price makers, monopolists will charge more for a given quantity if the demand

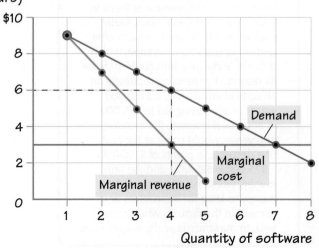

**Figure 23.2** *The Monopoly Graph*
*The profit-maximizing quantity of output is always found directly below the intersection of marginal revenue and marginal cost.*

is high than if the demand is low. Thus it is impossible to use a supply curve to determine the quantity a monopolist would supply at each price.

**DID YOU GET IT?**
Why can't we define a monopolist's supply curve?

# THE INEFFICIENCY OF MONOPOLY

Monopolies earn profits for their owners, but they result in an inefficient allocation of resources. In Figure 23.2, note how the market demand curve is above the marginal cost curve until the two curves intersect. Since the height of the demand curve shows us the amount consumers are willing and able to pay for each unit, we can conclude that every unit up to the seventh is worth more to consumers than the cost of making it. It is thus an efficient use of resources to make all those 7 units.

In a perfectly competitive market, the supply curve is based on marginal cost. You've learned that the intersection of supply and demand determines the market quantity. So a perfectly competitive market facing the same marginal cost as the monopoly in Figure 23.2 would produce 7 units of output.

Because a monopoly restricts the quantity of output to 4, the monopolist's quantity of output is inefficiently small. Consumers would be willing to purchase additional units of output for a price that exceeds the cost of producing those units. Let's examine the inefficiently low output of a monopoly by considering specifics about MONOPOLE's demand and output. We'll assume that consumers buy 1 unit of the software if the price is right, but no customer needs more than one.

Good software is important, but consumers are only willing to pay so much for it. If you are in the market for something, the highest price you would pay is known as your **reservation price**. In Chapter 4 we saw how the height of the demand curve at each quantity represents the most a consumer is willing to pay for that unit—the reservation price for that unit.

Table 23.4 lists the reservation prices of MONOPOLE's 8 potential customers for its WindowShade software product, in descending order. We have already seen that the firm's profit-maximizing quantity is 4 and its profit-maximizing price is $6. Notice that for $6, only Adrian, Brie, Cody, and Deshawn would buy the software. If the price fell to $5, Evan would also buy the software, so a total of 5 units would be sold. But the monopolist is unwilling to produce and sell the fifth unit even though it costs $2 less to produce than Evan is willing to pay. Why would MONOPOLE forego this apparent gain from trade and cause inefficiency by preventing Evan from receiving software that is worth more to him than the marginal cost? Because if MONOPOLE were to lower its price to $5 in order to sell the fifth unit, it would receive a dollar less from Adrian, Brie, Cody, and Deshawn, who were all willing to pay at least $6. MONOPOLE's revenue from the first 4 units would fall by $4, and Evan would pay $5 for the fifth unit, so the marginal revenue would only be $1. MONOPOLE is wise to keep the price at $6 rather than paying the marginal cost of $3 to gain $1 in revenue.

**DID YOU GET IT?**
Why does the refusal to sell the fifth unit lead to an inefficient allocation of resources?

A consumer's **reservation price** for a product is the highest price he or she is willing to pay to own one more unit of the product.

**Table 23.4 Reservation Prices of Eight MONOPOLE Customers**

| CUSTOMER | RESERVATION PRICE (DOLLARS) |
|---|---|
| Adrian | $9 |
| Brie | 8 |
| Cody | 7 |
| Deshawn | 6 |
| Evan | 5 |
| Fernando | 4 |
| Greg | 3 |
| Holly | 2 |

# PRICE DISCRIMINATION

So far we've assumed that MONOPOLE has to charge all its customers the same price. We saw that charging a lower price to Evan would require the monopolist to charge a lower price to Adrian, Brie, Cody, and Deshawn as well. Lowering the price to get Evan's business would decrease the firm's profit. Therefore, MONOPOLE passed up the opportunity to sell to Evan.

Now let's explore the possibility that MONOPOLE does not have to charge everyone the same price. In that case, the firm could raise its profits by charging each customer his or her reservation price—assuming that price could be determined. MONOPOLE would charge Adrian $9, Brie $8, Cody $7, and so on, all the way down to Greg. MONOPOLE would not sell a unit to Holly, because her reservation price of $2 is below MONOPOLE's marginal cost of $3.

MONOPOLE receives more profit by price discriminating than by charging all customers the same price. We know this because with price discrimination, Adrian, Brie, and Cody pay more than the $6 they would pay if the firm charged a single price, Deshawn pays the same amount as before, and Evan and Fernando contribute to profit as well by buying units for a price that exceeds marginal cost. Thus firms with market power prefer to charge customers their reservation prices if they can.

The practice of charging different customers different prices for the same good is called **price discrimination**. Four conditions must be met before a firm can price discriminate:

**1.** Some customers must have higher reservation prices than others for the same good.

**2.** The firm must be able to distinguish between customers with higher and lower reservation prices.

**3.** It cannot be possible for customers to resell the good. If the resale of

WindowShade were possible, for example, Evan would buy 5 units at his reservation price of $5 and resell them to Adrian, Brie, Cody, and Deshawn, who have higher reservation prices and thus are charged more by MONOPOLE.

**4.** The firm must have market power. Under perfect competition, competitors would enter and drive the price down to the marginal cost of production.

It is easiest for firms to distinguish between whole groups of customers. For example, price discrimination is often practiced between younger and older age groups. When individual customers are charged their reservation price, this is called *perfect price discrimination*.

> **DID YOU GET IT?**
> **What is price discrimination? What conditions make it possible?**

## Perfect Price Discrimination and Efficiency

Have you ever gone car shopping with your family? If so, you may have heard people at the car dealership ask questions that help them learn your family's reservation price. Sometimes they ask direct questions like "How much would you like to spend for a car today?" They may also ask questions about where you live, what your family members do for a living, and what type of car your family owns now. This information helps the seller guide your family to a car, and a price, that matches your reservation price and maximizes the seller's profit.

Perfect price discrimination removes the inefficiency that arises when a firm charges all customers the same price. Recall that Evan has a reservation price of $5 for WindowShade, and MONOPOLE can produce another unit of WindowShade for $3. If it had to charge everyone the same price, MONOPOLE wouldn't sell Evan the software for $5 because it would lose more money by lowering its price for other buyers than it would gain by selling

**Price discrimination** is the practice of charging different customers different prices for the same good.

a unit to Evan. The lost opportunity to sell a unit that is worth more to a buyer than it costs a seller to make causes inefficiency. But price discrimination prevents MONOPOLE from having to lower the price on other units in order to sell one more. With perfect price discrimination, MONOPOLE would sell a unit of Window-Shade to everyone willing to pay at least as much as the $3 marginal cost of making a unit. This includes Evan, who would pay $5, Fernando, who would pay $4, and Greg, who would pay $3.

To maximize profit, a price-discriminating monopolist will increase output until the marginal cost is equal to the reservation price of the last customer. That brings the firm to produce every unit for which the reservation price exceeds the marginal cost. Price discrimination thus results in an efficient level of production.

Despite the favorable output level, price discrimination is not without its problems. Think about your own buying experiences. You're happiest with purchases when the price you pay is well below your reservation price. For example, suppose you're thinking of buying some red paint to fix up an old skateboard that you're going to sell. If you're convinced that the price you could fetch for the skateboard would be $10 higher if it had a new paint job, the most you would pay for the paint is $10. The real gain from a purchase comes from paying less for a good than it is worth to you. If the paint cost $10, there would be little point in buying it. If you paid $6 for it, your benefit would exceed the price, so you would have reason to feel good about the purchase. Likewise, if every customer had to pay his or her reservation price for a good, the customers would be indifferent between buying it or not. Their net gain from the purchase would be zero. By tailoring the price to equal the reservation price, the firm manages to extract all the gains from trade. No wonder firms look for ways to price discriminate!

**DID YOU GET IT?**

**Why is price discrimination attractive to firms?**

## Price Discrimination in Practice

Many familiar pricing schemes are actually versions of price discrimination. Let's look at three examples.

You may know that airlines charge different prices for the same seat on the same flight. These pricing policies are designed so that people with higher reservation prices pay higher ticket prices. For example, business travelers, whose employers pay for their tickets, typically have higher reservation prices than vacationers, who must pay for their own tickets. To distinguish business travelers from vacationers, airlines note that vacationers usually plan their trips further in advance and are more likely to travel over weekends. To benefit from this, the airlines charge more for tickets when the departure date is near and for trips that do not include a Saturday-night stay.

Another familiar example of price discrimination takes place in movie theaters. You probably remember that when you were under the age of 12, you received a discount on movie tickets. Because children have a lower reservation price than adults, a movie theater can use age to separate its customers and charge more to those with a higher willingness to pay.

Finally, many restaurants give discounts to senior citizens. Why? Because senior citizens generally have a lower willingness to pay for eating out. By giving senior citizens a discount, restaurants can gain more customers while charging more to those who are willing to pay more. Many movie theaters, grocery stores, and vacation destinations price discriminate with senior discounts as well.

Notice that none of these examples of price discrimination constitutes perfect price discrimination. Rather than charging each individual his or her reservation price, the prices are assigned to whole groups that include members with

*Adults have a higher reservation price for movie tickets than kids, so movie theaters price discriminate by charging adults more for tickets.*

differing reservation prices. Real estate agents and car dealers often come closer to achieving perfect price discrimination. Their one-on-one interactions with buyers allow them to assess each buyer's interests and ability to pay. They may size up buyers by observing their clothing and jewelry, seeing how eager they are to make a purchase, and asking about their occupation and financial situation. This helps them negotiate a price that approximates the buyer's reservation price. So when you go out to purchase a home, don't wear your most expensive clothes and don't say you're so in love with the house that you'd pay an arm and a leg for it, or you might.

## MONOPOLIES AND INNOVATION

Innovative new products improve our standard of living and promote economic growth. Investments in research and product development are the fuel of innovation. But while we know that monopolies charge higher prices and produce smaller quantities, the effect of monopoly on innovation is less clear. Due to contrasting influences, it turns out that monopoly power can either advance innovation or get in its way.

The relatively high profits conferred by monopoly power can be invested in research and development projects. This supports innovation. For example, when AT&T was still a monopoly, the research budget of its Bell Laboratories exceeded the entire research budget of the Japanese Ministry of Industry and Trade. The inventions made at Bell Laboratories included the transistor, a critical component in TVs, computers, cell phones, cars, and hundreds of other products.

On the other hand, we have seen that monopolists have an interest in protecting their monopoly power by thwarting would-be competitors who might offer better products. Some of the profit that could be spent on innovation might be spent on barriers to entry. For example, monopolists can use some of their profit to lobby politicians for protection along the lines of extended patents, limits on competition from other countries, or stricter licensing requirements for competitors. Even that great defender of free markets, Adam Smith, worried that powerful merchants and manufacturers, pursuing their own self-interest, would seek to use government regulation to their advantage. George Washington was so concerned by this potential problem that in his farewell address he warned, "Even our commercial policy should hold an equal and impartial hand: neither seeking nor granting exclusive favors or preferences." Such defensive posturing by monopolists can slow the pace of technological improvement.

**DID YOU GET IT?**
How might a monopoly speed up or slow down the pace of innovation?

# MODULE 23 REVIEW AND ASSESSMENT

**Summing Up the Key Ideas:** Match the following terms to the correct definitions.

A. Imperfect competition    D. Monopoly    G. Barriers to entry    J. Economies of scale

B. Market structure    E. Monopolist    H. Natural monopoly    K. Reservation price

C. Product market    F. Market power    I. Average cost    L. Price discrimination

_____ 1. The market for a good that includes all the products that consumers consider to be close substitutes for that good.

_____ 2. A product market served by only one firm.

_____ 3. Obstacles that prevent firms from entering particular markets.

_____ 4. This exists if, in the long run, an increase in output results in a decrease in average cost.

_____ 5. The practice of charging different customers different prices for the same good.

_____ 6. Arises when there is not enough competition among firms to prevent individual firms from raising their price above the equilibrium level determined by supply and demand.

_____ 7. A market in which high start-up costs make it prohibitively expensive for more than one firm to operate.

_____ 8. The sole supplier to a monopoly market.

_____ 9. The total cost of production divided by the quantity of output.

_____ 10. Allows individual firms to have an influence on the market price.

_____ 11. Describes the nature of competition within a market.

_____ 12. The highest price a person is willing to pay to own one more unit of the product.

**Analyze and Explain:** Determine whether each of the following promotes or deters competition within a market. Explain your answers.

|  | PROMOTES OR DETERS? | EXPLANATION |
| --- | --- | --- |
| 1. The average cost of producing another unit of output falls dramatically as output levels grow larger. | _____ | _____ |
| 2. Firms enjoy the protection of patents or copyrights. | _____ | _____ |
| 3. Economies of scale do not exist. | _____ | _____ |
| 4. A critical input in the production process is owned by one firm. | _____ | _____ |

**Apply:** Determine whether each of the following is a characteristic of **perfect competition** or **monopoly**.

|  | PERFECT COMPETITION OR MONOPOLY? |
| --- | --- |
| 1. Firms are price makers. | _____ |
| 2. Suppliers are free to enter and exit the market. | _____ |
| 3. There is only one firm. | _____ |
| 4. Firms are price takers. | _____ |

# MODULE 24

# Oligopoly and Monopolistic Competition

**KEY IDEA:** When there are many firms in a market, they can gain market power if they can differentiate their products. When there are only a few firms in a market, they might be able to work together to reduce output below the perfectly competitive level, charge a relatively high price, and raise their profits.

## OBJECTIVES

- To describe what characterizes oligopolies and how they operate.
- To explain why it is difficult for a small number of firms to enforce an agreement that restricts output.
- To analyze how firms in markets characterized by monopolistic competition behave with regard to pricing, advertising, product development, and quality of service.

## More Than One but Fewer Than Many

Many industries are dominated by a small number of firms. For example, of the 1,149,700 video game consoles purchased in the United States in April of 2010, 185,400 were the Xbox 360 made by Microsoft, 718,000 were the DS or Wii made by Nintendo, and 246,300 were the PS3 or PSP made by Sony. Those three firms supply the entire U.S. market for game consoles. That is, there are multiple firms but they are not price takers. This module considers two types of market structure that involve both competition and market power.

The competition among makers of game consoles is as intense as the competition among users of game consoles.

## OLIGOPOLY: A SMALL NUMBER OF FIRMS

An **oligopoly** is a market with a small number of firms.

An **oligopolist** is a firm in an oligopoly.

A market with a small number of firms is called an **oligopoly**. The name comes from the Greek word *oligos*, meaning "few." Each firm in the market is called an **oligopolist**. Although the names sound strange, oligopolistic firms are all around you. Four firms—Kellogg's, General Mills, Post, and Quaker Oats—make more than 83 percent of breakfast cereal purchased in the United States. And four automakers—General Motors, Ford, Toyota, and Chrysler—produce 74 percent

of the cars sold in the United States. An industry in which the largest four firms account for more than 40 percent of sales is generally considered to be an oligopoly.

When a small number of firms account for a large proportion of the sales, we say that an industry is *highly concentrated*. Table 24.1 reports the share of sales made by the 4 largest firms in 10 industries that are highly concentrated.

Any market like these with a small number of influential firms is an oligopoly. These include the industries

## Table 24.1 **Ten Highly Concentrated Industries**

| INDUSTRY | TOP FOUR COMPANIES' SHARE OF SALES | TOP FOUR COMPANIES |
|---|---|---|
| Batteries | 88% | Duracell, Energizer, Rayovac, Panasonic |
| Dog food | 86 | Iams, Pedigree, Purina One, Friskies |
| Washing machines | 85 | Kenmore, Maytag, Whirlpool, GE |
| Chocolate | 84 | Hersheys, Nestle, Russell Stover, Masterfoods |
| Breakfast cereal | 83 | Kelloggs, General Mills, Post, Quaker Oats |
| Automobiles | 74 | GM, Ford, Toyota, Chrysler |
| Tires | 73 | Goodyear, Michelin, Bridgestone, General |
| Sneakers | 72 | Nike, Reebok, New Balance, Adidas |
| Toilet paper | 68 | Charmin, Quilted Northern, Angel Soft, Cottonelle |
| Cookies | 65 | Nabisco, Keebler, Pepperidge Farm, Parmala |

listed in the table and many others such as airlines, soft drink companies, bike manufacturers, and textbook companies. Clearly, many of our favorite goods come from oligopolies. An oligopolist can decide to work together with other firms in its industry or to compete against them. Let's analyze these strategies.

**DID YOU GET IT?**
**What is an oligopoly?**

## Collusion among Oligopolists

Oligopolists face a dilemma. Because their products are not identical and because competitors are not as numerous as in a perfectly competitive market, one oligopolist can charge a bit more or less than another. This is clear from the varying prices for things such as game consoles, breakfast cereals, cars, and airline flights. But the firms in an oligopolistic market can also decide to work together, which is known as *collusion*. Acting together, the firms can collude to restrict output and raise prices. If they limit their combined output to the

quantity that a monopolist would produce and charge the price a monopolist would charge, they can earn the profit a monopolist would earn. A group of firms that collude to monopolize a market is called a **cartel.**

The most famous cartel is the Organization of the Petroleum Exporting Countries, or OPEC for short. OPEC assigns its member countries production limits called *quotas*. By restricting the output of oil, the quotas drive up the price and therefore the profit for each member of the cartel. In most countries it is illegal

A **cartel** is a group of firms that agree to work together and act like a monopoly.

*To increase profit, the Organization of Petroleum Exporting Countries assigns its member countries production limits called quotas.*

for firms to form a cartel. OPEC sidesteps these laws, however, because the members of the cartel are oil-producing countries, not firms.

A group of oligopolists has an incentive to form a cartel or act like a cartel; if they agree to restrict output, they will maximize profit. At the same time, individual cartel members face an incentive to cheat. After all, if the supply in the market is restricted, a member who breaks the agreement can sell more at a price that exceeds marginal cost and raise its own profits. This practice of cheating on the cartel by producing more than the quota amount is called *chiseling*. If enough oligopolists chisel, the market price tumbles and the cartel falls apart.

The actual behavior of firms in an oligopoly is hard to predict. At times, for example, OPEC has been able to enforce quotas, while at other times some member states have chiseled their production to undermine the cartel. Also, many oil-producing countries have not entered OPEC, so its power to restrict worldwide oil output is not absolute.

Airlines provide another example of the difficulty of predicting oligopolists' behavior. If one airline raises its price for a particular travel route in an effort to raise its profit, other airlines may or may not match the price increase. If they do not, the original airline will suffer, losing passengers to competitors. If the other airlines follow suit, the airlines may all enjoy more profit.

In a market characterized by **monopolistic competition**, many firms supply similar but not identical goods.

The key to understanding oligopoly behavior is to remember that oligopolists have a *collective* incentive to collude. *Individually*, however, they have an incentive to produce more than the quantity that is in the collective interest of the oligopoly. This tension makes it hard to know exactly how much oligopolists will decide to produce. Although the oligopolists may not enforce a perfect cartel and act as if they were one big monopoly, they are likely to supply the market with a lower quantity—and use their market power to charge a higher price—than would be the case under perfect competition.

**DID YOU GET IT?**
Why would an oligopolist want to collude with other oligopolists to restrict output? Why would an oligopolist want to break from a collusive agreement and produce more output?

## MONOPOLISTIC COMPETITION

At the sprawling Mall of America near Minneapolis, hungry shoppers can choose among dozens of fast-food restaurants, including A&W, Arby's, Burger King, Burger Zone Express, McDonald's, Pizza Hut, Sbarro, Taco Bell, and Villa Pizza. These restaurants offer similar but not identical service and food. Although there are many restaurants, they are not price takers as under perfect competition, because each restaurant enjoys some degree of customer loyalty for its slightly different brand of food. A *brand* is a type of product offered by a particular firm under a particular name. For example, Yum! Brands is a corporation that offers fast food under the brand names of A&W, KFC, Long John Silver's, Taco Bell, and Pizza Hut. Although Pizza Hut is one of three pizza brands sold in the Mall of America, the pizza prices differ across these brands because customers do not see the products as identical.

In the fast-food market there is *monopolistic competition*. Under **monopolistic competition**, many firms sell similar but not identical products. These **differentiated products** are goods and services with distinguishing characteristics that set them apart. There are several sources for product differentiation. These include quality, as in Swiss watches; design, as in Abercrombie clothing; availability, as in 7-Eleven stores, and promotion, as in advertisements that use lizards and ducks to sell insurance.

When a firm offers a differentiated product, it can act in some ways like a small monopolist. The firm faces a downward-sloping demand curve like a monopolist. And the absence of a perfect substitute gives it some ability to be a price maker rather than a price taker. For example, Levi's will not lose all its customers if it raises the price of jeans by a small amount, because some customers prefer Levi's to other brands of jeans, even at a slightly higher price.

**DID YOU GET IT?**
What is monopolistic competition?

## Building Brand Loyalty

Customer loyalty gives firms some market power, which enables them to increase their profits. Not surprisingly, firms invest a great deal of money in product differentiation and the development of *brand loyalty*, which gives customers reasons to buy their product instead of similar products offered by competitors. Monopolistic competitors prefer to compete with claims of better products, rather than lower prices, because price-based competition cuts directly into profits.

Advertising is key when it comes to cultivating brand loyalty. TV commercials plant slogans in our heads, making it hard to shake the notion that Avis tries harder, Coke is the real thing, KFC is finger lickin' good, and Gillette is the best a man can get. Notice that these commercials do not advertise products like rental cars or chicken in general but a particular brand of the product.

Another strategy is to compete over the quality of service offered. Firms including Macy's and Southwest Airlines seek to differentiate their products and develop brand loyalty through superior customer service. McDonald's keeps careful track of how long customers have to wait in line before their order is taken, because customers who have to wait for a long time are less likely to come back.

Yet another way to develop brand loyalty is to issue loyalty cards that provide discounts to regular customers. Loyalty card promotions are common at bookstores, coffee shops, and grocery stores. Similarly, airlines promote brand loyalty with frequent flyer programs, and hotel chains cultivate a loyal customer base with frequent-stay programs.

*Customers exhibit brand loyalty when they bypass other cafes to stand in line at Starbucks.*

## Free Entry

Unlike a pure monopoly, a monopolistically competitive industry has free entry: no substantial barrier prevents another firm from entering the market and selling a similar good. Free entry has two important effects. First, a firm in a monopolistically competitive industry can earn profit in the short run, but not in the long run. If a firm is making profit, others will eventually enter the market and produce a similar product, taking away some of the original firm's customers until that firm's profit falls to zero. Second, monopolistic competitors will continually try to differentiate their products from others, so product development and the introduction of new variations of old products are frequent occurrences. If you haven't been to McDonald's lately, they probably have something on the menu that wasn't there the last time you visited.

## Monopolistic Competition versus Perfect Competition and Monopoly

Monopolistic competition differs from perfect competition because each monopolistic competitor is a price maker, not a price taker. It is similar to perfect competition, however, in that there are many firms that supply a similar good. This competitive aspect of monopolistic competition limits the amount by which a firm can raise its price. If Levi's raises its price too much above that of other jeans makers, some customers will switch over to jeans made by the Gap, Wrangler, Old Navy, and Lucky Brand. With perfect competition, if Levi's were to raise its price by even a small amount above the competition, it would lose all its customers.

Table 24.2 summarizes the differences between perfect competition, monopolistic competition, and monopoly. Monopolistic competition and perfect competition involve competition with other firms for customers that is absent in the case of a monopoly. And unlike monopolists and perfectly competitive firms, monopolistically competitive firms invest resources to build brand loyalty. In markets with monopolistic competition and perfect competition there is free entry into the markets, whereas barriers to entry are the source of sustained monopoly power and of the monopolist's ability to earn profit in the long run.

### DID YOU GET IT?
How does monopolistic competition differ from perfect competition? How does it differ from monopoly?

## Price, Marginal Cost, and Profit
Because firms in monopolistically competitive industries have some market power, they will set the price above their marginal cost to maximize their profit. This practice leads to inefficiency, as we saw in the case of monopoly, because some units that provide benefits in excess of their marginal cost will nonetheless not be offered for sale. The profit earned by monopolistically competitive firms is reduced, however, by the need to spend money on advertising, product development, and other means of creating brand loyalty. And in the long run, free entry invites

| Table 24.2 **Features of Perfect Competition, Monopolistic Competition, and Monopoly** | | | |
|---|---|---|---|
| | **PERFECT COMPETITION** | **MONOPOLISTIC COMPETITION** | **MONOPOLY** |
| Earns profit in the long run | | | X |
| Invests in brand loyalty | | X | |
| Has downward-sloping demand curve | | X | X |
| Has competitors | X | X | |
| Price maker | | X | X |

competition that eliminates profits in both monopolistically competitive and perfectly competitive firms.

We know that relative to a monopoly, a perfectly competitive market provides more output at a lower price. Monopolistic competition has both pros and cons from the consumer's perspective. On the pro side, consumers in monopolistically competitive markets are offered a wider range of products than in the other market structures, and firms compete to distinguish themselves for the quality of service they provide. As for cons, consumers pay a higher price for products sold under monopolistic competition than they would for an undifferentiated good under perfect competition. Also, under monopolistic competition firms produce an inefficiently low quantity of output. We will explore this in Module 25.

# MODULE 24 REVIEW AND ASSESSMENT

## Summing Up the Key Ideas: Match the following terms to the correct definitions.

A. Oligopoly
B. Oligopolist
C. Cartel

D. Monopolistic competition
E. Highly concentrated
F. Collusion

G. Differentiated products
H. Quotas
I. Chiseling

_____ 1. A firm in an oligopoly.

_____ 2. A small number of firms account for a large proportion of the sales.

_____ 3. Goods and services with distinguishing characteristics that set them apart.

_____ 4. A group of firms that collude to monopolize a market.

_____ 5. A market with a small number of firms.

_____ 6. The practice of cheating on a cartel by producing more than the quota amount.

_____ 7. A market in which many firms supply similar, but not identical, goods.

_____ 8. When firms in an oligopolistic market decide to work together to set price and quantity.

_____ 9. Production limits agreed to by cartel members to drive up price.

## Analyze and Explain: Determine whether each of the following is a characteristic of an **oligopoly** or a **monopolistically competitive** market.

|  | OLIGOPOLY OR MONOPOLISTIC COMPETITION? |
|---|---|
| 1. A few influential firms compete. | _____ |
| 2. The many firms use advertising to build brand loyalty. | _____ |
| 3. The industry is highly concentrated. | _____ |
| 4. The firms face a collective incentive to collude and form a cartel. | _____ |

**Apply:** Determine whether each of the following apply to a **perfectly competitive** market, a **monopolistically competitive** market, or a **monopoly**. In some cases the correct answer could be all three market structures; in other cases the correct answer can be only one of the three market structures.

TYPE OF MARKET

1. Firms are price takers. _____

2. Firms invest in fostering brand loyalty. _____

3. Firms face a downward-sloping demand curve. _____

4. Firms are price makers. _____

5. Firms face competition. _____

6. Firms can earn economic profit in the long run. _____

# MODULE 25

# Regulating Market Power

**KEY IDEA:** Antitrust regulations are designed to limit the inefficiencies brought about by imperfectly competitive markets.

**OBJECTIVES**

- **To analyze the effects of market structure on efficiency.**
- **To discuss the pros and cons of price controls.**
- **To explain the purpose of antitrust policy and how it is enforced.**

## Monopolies and Muckraking

Concerns over market power are nothing new. In the early 1900s, newspaper and magazine writers known as *muckrakers* published stories about the abusive practices of large firms in the transportation, energy, and steel industries, among others. Ida Tarbell's *History of the Standard Oil Company* (1904), for example, exposed John D. Rockefeller's drive to create an oil monopoly. Eventually, the muckrakers' revelations caused public outrage, particularly because the high cost of rail transport increased the cost of many other goods. The result was the adoption of government regulations meant to make society better off by promoting competition among firms. In this module we'll recap the efficiency of each market structure and discuss old and new ways of dealing with problems created by market power.

*Over 100 years ago Ida Tarbell, pictured here, was among the business watchdogs called muckrakers, who raised concerns about market power.*

## MARKET STRUCTURE AND EFFICIENCY

In Module 23 we saw that it is best for society if production increases until the cost of making another unit would exceed the highest price consumers would pay for it. When the price equals marginal cost, consumers can purchase every unit that is worth at least as much to them as the cost of making it. When the price exceeds the marginal cost, the quantity of output is inefficiently small. Additional units of the good are worth more to consumers than the cost of making them, and yet they are not made. Whenever competition is imperfect, as in a monopoly, an oligopoly, or a monopolistically competitive market, this sort of inefficiency arises.

### Perfect Competition, Monopoly, and Efficiency

Perfect competition results in the efficient level of production. This results from a condition for efficiency hidden within our model of supply and demand.

The supply curve indicates the marginal cost of production, and, as you know, the equilibrium price is determined by the intersection of the supply and demand curves. Since the price comes from a point along the supply curve (at the intersection with demand), and the supply curve tells us the marginal cost, we know that the price equals the marginal cost in a perfectly competitive market. The resulting efficiency explains why economists are fond of competition.

Monopoly, on the other hand, represents an extreme form of imperfect competition. A monopolist selects the output level that equates marginal revenue and marginal cost, and chooses its price by going *up* from the intersection of marginal revenue and marginal cost to the demand curve. The price therefore exceeds the marginal cost, and the monopoly produces an inefficiently small quantity of output. If a monopolist can employ perfect price discrimination, charging each customer his or her reservation price, then the inefficiency of monopoly is eliminated. Price discrimination can be difficult to implement, however, because it is hard to estimate consumers' reservation prices. Remember also that the gains from perfect price discrimination go entirely to firms, not to consumers. The consumers are charged a price that equals their benefit from the good, so they are indifferent between buying the good or not.

**Price controls** are policies by which the government sets the prices in an industry.

**DID YOU GET IT?**
Why is perfect competition more efficient than monopoly?

### Monopolistic Competition, Oligopoly, and Efficiency

An oligopoly is always one collusive step away from being a monopoly. Firms in an oligopoly have a joint incentive to act like a monopolist and set the price above the marginal cost.

But they have individual incentives to compete with each other by undercutting one another's prices. An oligopoly is unlikely to be as inefficient as a monopoly, but it is also unlikely to be as efficient as perfect competition.

Finally, monopolistic competition results in some inefficiency because each supplier has market power due to brand loyalty and therefore can set its price above the marginal cost. Yet monopolistic competition yields some benefits for consumers as well. Firms have an incentive to invest in product development and product differentiation, which results in greater product variety for consumers. Monopolistic competition thus has some benefits for consumers compared with the case of a pure monopoly.

**DID YOU GET IT?**
Are oligopoly and monopolistic competition likely to be as inefficient as monopoly? Why or why not?

## DIRECT REGULATION: PRICE CONTROLS

**Price controls** are limits established by the government on prices for a product or service in a particular industry. Price controls are not common today, but during the course of U.S. history, many natural monopolies were subject to price controls. Examples have included cable TV, airlines, and trucking. Price controls still exist, for instance, in the markets for public utilities, including water and electricity.

The goal in setting price controls is to bring about the efficient quantity of the good. As you have learned, this means setting the price equal to the marginal cost. There is an interesting exception in the case of natural monopolies. The marginal cost is below the average cost for a natural monopoly, so a price equal to the marginal cost would result in losses for the firm. Instead, the price can be set equal to the average cost, which is as low as the price can go without eventually putting the firm out of business.

Price controls have lost favor among many economists and policy makers due to the difficulty of pinpointing the price that will achieve efficiency. It is difficult for the government to accurately assess firms' marginal cost and consumers' willingness to pay. And if the factors that determine cost should change, the marginal cost becomes a moving target. Consumer preferences also change over time, which causes the efficient quantity to change. Monitoring these changes in market conditions is difficult if not impossible. So price regulation introduces its own set of problems. This does not necessarily mean that regulation is undesirable, but it does mean that the benefits should be weighed against the costs.

**DID YOU GET IT?**
What are price controls?

## ANTITRUST POLICY

A large body of law has evolved to prevent firms from unfairly acquiring or using market power. Together, this set of laws forms our government's **antitrust policy**. A *trust* is a combination of corporations formed for the purpose of reducing competition and controlling prices in an industry. Antitrust policy places regulations on business practices to encourage competition. Even in a market economy, laws are important to ensure adequate rivalry on a level playing field.

As an early landmark of antitrust policy, the U.S. Congress passed the Sherman Antitrust Act in 1890 to eliminate restraints on trade and competition. This was followed by the Clayton Antitrust Act of 1914, which strengthened and clarified the Sherman Act. The Sherman and Clayton Acts apply to firms that do business in more than one state. Most states have comparable laws that apply to firms that operate only in one state.

Antitrust laws promote competition by making it illegal for firms to engage in a conspiracy to fix prices at an agreed-upon level. They also block firms from merging together if the merger is likely to reduce competition and harm consumers. And they prohibit *predatory acts* that achieve or maintain market power, such as temporarily cutting prices to drive competitors out of business.

Bear in mind that the mere existence of a monopoly is not illegal. It is illegal, however, to gain or exploit a monopoly position by improper conduct. For example, the Clayton Act prevents a practice known as *tying*, in which a customer who wants to buy a product from a firm is required to buy other products from the same firm. The maker of your school's copy machine, for instance, can't require the school to buy its paper and ink as well. The Clayton Act also prohibits firms from having *interlocking directorates*, meaning that one person serves on the corporate boards of two competing firms at the same time, which could reduce the competition between those firms.

To learn more about the history and current activities of the Antitrust Division of the Department of Justice and the Federal Trade Commission, you can visit their websites: www.usdoj.gov/atr and www.ftc.gov.

**DID YOU GET IT?**
What is antitrust policy?

**Antitrust policy** is a set of laws designed to promote competition in the marketplace.

# John D. Rockefeller, 1839–1937

In 1867, John D. Rockefeller (1839–1937) and a handful of partners formed an oil-refining firm by merging five smaller refineries into one big one. In 1870, Rockefeller reorganized the firm as the Standard Oil Firm of Ohio, which pursued a strategy of buying up the competition. By 1878, Standard Oil controlled about 90 percent of the oil-refining capacity in the United States. In 1882, the firm was reorganized as the Standard Oil Trust, with Rockefeller at the helm.

Rockefeller obtained favorable shipping rates from railway firms. He also arranged for the railroads to refuse to ship competitors' oil. At times he lowered Standard Oil's price to drive competitors into bankruptcy and then bought those firms at bargain prices. Rockefeller was able to prevent competitors from entering because he cut costs and controlled the distribution network.

Although Standard Oil was a visible and aggressive monopolist, the steel and railroad industries, among others, also lacked competition in the late nineteenth century. In response to growing concerns over market power, Congress passed the Sherman Antitrust Act in 1890 to rein in the activities of monopolists and foster competition.

In a historic 1911 ruling, the U.S. Supreme Court broke up Standard Oil into many smaller firms, including Standard Oil of New Jersey (which later became Exxon), Standard Oil of New York (which later became Mobil), Standard Oil of Ohio, Standard Oil of Indiana (now Amoco, part of BP), and Standard Oil of California (now Chevron). The court also paved the way for new firms, such as Gulf and Texaco, to enter the market.

In recent years, competition in the oil industry has diminished again. In 1984, Chevron acquired Gulf in what was then the largest corporate merger in U.S. history. In the 1990s, Exxon merged with Mobil. Two other former Standard Oil firms, Amoco and Standard Oil of Ohio, merged to form BP Amoco. The three largest oil firms now control almost as much of the oil market as the Standard Oil Trust did 100 years ago.

*In the late nineteenth century, the railroad industry was one among many that engaged in unfair practices.*

## YOUR TURN

Why do you think that, years after the Standard Oil Trust was broken up, many of the oil firms merged again?

## The Enforcement of Antitrust Policy

Antitrust laws are enforced primarily by two agencies of the federal government: the Antitrust Division of the Department of Justice and the Federal Trade Commission. These two agencies can investigate practices that restrict competition, and they can bring a lawsuit against a firm that they believe has violated the law in an effort to exert monopoly power.

The Department of Justice and the Federal Trade Commission keep a watchful eye on potential mergers of firms and proposed acquisitions of one firm by another. If two firms in an industry were to merge—for example, the office supply giants OfficeMax and Staples—the combined firm would have greater market power, which might hurt consumers and other competitors. With the advice of many economists, the government has developed a set of guidelines to assist decisions about whether a merger should be challenged.

If an antitrust agency's experts believe that the merger of two firms will raise the product price by 5 percent or more, the agency will generally challenge the proposed move in court. A judge then decides whether the merger would indeed harm consumers.

A number of other federal and state regulatory agencies also have jurisdiction over aspects of anticompetitive practices in specific industries. For example, the Securities and Exchange Commission monitors the financial industry and the Federal Communications Commission regulates the broadcast TV and radio industries. It is important for the managers of a firm to know who their regulators are and to avoid participation in any improper anticompetitive practices.

**DID YOU GET IT?**
Which two agencies are primarily responsible for enforcing antitrust laws?

---

# ECONOMICS IN ACTION

# The Federal Trade Commission Clips Merger of Staples and Office Depot

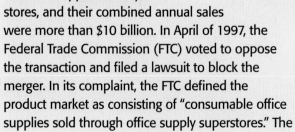

On September 4, 1996, Staples and Office Depot announced that they planned to merge. At the time, each office supply chain had approximately 500 stores, and their combined annual sales were more than $10 billion. In April of 1997, the Federal Trade Commission (FTC) voted to oppose the transaction and filed a lawsuit to block the merger. In its complaint, the FTC defined the product market as consisting of "consumable office supplies sold through office supply superstores." The

commission identified 42 geographic markets in which it predicted a lack of competition that would mean consumers would see price increases.

Figure 25.1 reproduces a key piece of evidence that the FTC presented to the court. The graph shows an index of average office supply prices at Staples depending on the amount of competition it faced in a geographic area. In some areas, such as St. Louis, Staples had competition from Office Depot and OfficeMax, while in others it faced less intense competition.

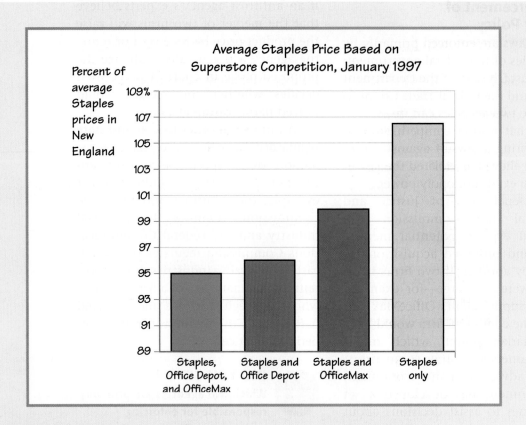

**Figure 25.1** Staples: Prices Are Higher with Less Superstore Competition
A little competition has a big effect on the prices you pay at the store.

In markets where Staples had no other superstores to compete with (shown in orange), prices were substantially higher than in markets where Staples and Office Depot both had stores.

The FTC won an injunction against the merger in U.S. District Court in June of 1997. Subsequently, Staples and Office Depot abandoned the proposed merger.

**DID YOU GET IT?**
Why do you think prices were lowest in markets where Staples had two competitors?

TO READ MORE about the economics of the Staples/Office Depot case, see Orley Ashenfelter, et al., "Econometric Methods in Staples," www.irs .princeton.edu/wpframe.html, April, 2004.

# MODULE 25 REVIEW AND ASSESSMENT

**Summing Up the Key Ideas:** Match the following terms to the correct definitions.

A. Price controls          C. Tying                E. Interlocking directorates
B. Trust                   D. Antitrust policy     F. Predatory acts

_____ 1. A set of laws designed to prevent firms from unfairly acquiring or using market power.

_____ 2. Requiring a customer who wants to buy a product from a firm to buy other products from the same firm.

_____ 3. A combination of corporations formed for the purpose of reducing competition and controlling prices in an industry.

_____ 4. The practice of having one person serving on the corporate boards of two competing firms at the same time.

_____ 5. Limits on prices established by the government for a product or service in a particular industry.

_____ 6. Practices such as temporarily cutting prices to drive competitors out of business.

**Analyze and Explain:** Analyze the situations described and determine if each is a likely target for the enforcement of antitrust policy. Explain why or why not.

|  | LIKELY TARGET? | EXPLANATION |
|---|---|---|
| 1. The last two remaining firms in the U.S. market attempt a merger. | _____ | _____ |
| 2. A farmer in Iowa decides to buy the neighboring farm. | _____ | _____ |
| 3. The largest and fifth-largest banks in the United States announce a merger. | _____ | _____ |
| 4. Coca-Cola plans to buy PepsiCo. | _____ | _____ |
| 5. Staples buys a small office supply store in a small town. | _____ | _____ |
| 6. Ford Motor Company decides to stop making the Ford F-150 pickup truck. | _____ | _____ |

**Apply:** Determine whether each of the following situations leads to an **efficient** or an **inefficient** level of output.

|  | EFFICIENT OR INEFFICIENT? |
|---|---|
| 1. Price equals marginal cost. | _____ |
| 2. Firms enjoy market power due to brand loyalty by consumers. | _____ |
| 3. A firm is the sole producer of a particular product. | _____ |
| 4. Price exceeds marginal cost. | _____ |
| 5. Firms engage in collusion. | _____ |
| 6. Firms practice price discrimination. | _____ |

## Bloomberg Businessweek®

# A Google Monopoly Isn't the Point

BY MATHEW INGRAM

Despite howls of outrage at Google's size and power in the search market, the fact remains that—for the purposes of U.S. antitrust law, at least—being a monopoly isn't illegal. What is illegal is either acquiring that monopoly by nefarious or anticompetitive means or using that dominant position in a way that harms the market for those services.

Antitrust expert Thomas Barnett, a former head of the Justice Dept.'s antitrust division and now an adviser to Expedia, summed up the case against Google with these four points: First, search is the critical gateway by which users navigate the web. As a Google executive has noted: "[S]earch is critical. If you are not found, the rest cannot follow." Second, Google dominates search and search advertising. Third, Google is expanding its dominance into a broadening range of search-dependent products and services, which also protect and reinforce

its search dominance. And fourth, as one company gains control over access to further products and services on the Internet, consumers can expect to face higher prices and reduced innovation.

The first three of Barnett's points are fairly obvious. Barnett notes that Google clearly has a "dominant position" in search and search advertising—true, given a market share estimated at 65 percent for search and 80 percent for search advertising. The hard part comes when Barnett says Google's dominance in these areas affects consumers because they face higher prices and reduced innovation. This is the core of an antitrust case. It's not enough that a company such as Google has a dominant or even monopolistic market position. It's not even enough to argue that a company with a monopoly is using its position unfairly. It has to be proven that consumers or the marketplace

as a whole are being harmed by that behavior, either through higher prices, reduced choice, or both.

The problem with a company such as Google is that users don't pay for the vast majority of Google's products and services. I'm not paying any more to use Google Maps than I would for a competing service, nor am I paying more to use Yelp because it has somehow been disadvantaged by Google's attempts to "scrape" its content for local recommendations.

How does Google affect prices? Barnett tries to answer this with the argument that, since Google controls a majority of the market for search advertising, it influences prices in that market, causing advertisers to pay more. The higher prices are then passed on to consumers. That's an interesting argument, though it will be tough to make the case. For one thing, Google's ad prices are set by open auction, so how are Barnett or antitrust officials going to prove they are higher than they should be? What's the actual market value of a click on an ad? Even if a court accepts the argument that prices are higher because Google controls the market, it's not clear that the end user or consumer has to pay more for a particular product or service simply because advertising it on Google searches costs a penny or two more than it might otherwise cost.

Even arguing that innovation is being reduced is a tough sell. Has Google's move into mobile with Android, or into local recommendations or travel, or any other new market caused innovation in that market to decline and thus affected consumers or choice? There are few tangible signs of it.

Being big is not illegal and no one (or at least no one credible) seems to be arguing that Google achieved its market size through nefarious means. Simply being unfair to competitors isn't against the law, either. This leaves it to the government to prove that the company is somehow harming consumers by its behavior.

**DID YOU READ IT?**

1) **Why do consumers dislike monopolies?**

2) **How easy is it for the U.S. government to prove a firm is harming consumers?**

**WHAT DO YOU THINK?**

1) **Can you think of examples of firms that do use their dominant position in a way that harms the market?**

2) **Why might Google want to innovate? What might discourage them from innovating?**

EXCERPTED FROM www.businessweek.com/printer/technology/a-google-monopoly
-isnt-the-point-09232011.html

# CHAPTER 8 REVIEW AND SELF-ASSESSMENT

## REVIEW

### Points to Remember

#### MODULE 23: MONOPOLY

1. **Market structure** describes the nature of competition within a market.

2. **Imperfect competition** arises when there is not enough competition among firms to prevent individual firms from raising their price above the equilibrium level determined by supply and demand.

3. The **product market** for a good includes all those products that consumers consider to be close substitutes for that good.

4. A **monopoly** is a product market served by only one firm.

5. The sole supplier to a monopoly market is called a **monopolist**.

6. It is **market power** that allows individual firms to influence the market price.

7. **Barriers to entry** are obstacles that prevent firms from entering the market and competing for the monopolist's customers and profit.

8. A **natural monopoly** is a market in which start-up costs make it prohibitively expensive for more than one firm to operate.

9. The **average cost** is the total cost of production divided by the quantity of output.

10. **Economies of scale** exist if, in the long run, an increase in output lowers a firm's average cost.

11. A consumer's **reservation price** for a product is the highest price he or she is willing to pay to own one more unit of the product.

12. **Price discrimination** is the practice of charging different customers different prices for the same good.

#### MODULE 24: OLIGOPOLY AND MONOPOLISTIC COMPETITION

13. An **oligopoly** is a market with a small number of firms.

14. An **oligopolist** is a firm in an oligopoly.

15. A **cartel** is a group of firms that collude to monopolize a market.

16. In a market characterized by **monopolistic competition**, many firms supply similar but not identical products.

17. **Differentiated products** are goods and services with distinguishing characteristics that set them apart.

**MODULE 25: REGULATING MARKET POWER**

18. **Price controls** are limits on prices established by the government for a product or service in a particular industry.

19. An **antitrust policy** is a set of laws designed to prevent firms from unfairly acquiring or using market power.

## SELF-ASSESSMENT

The following questions are the type your teacher might ask you on a quiz or a test. Practice with these in order to improve your performance on class tests.

### Multiple-Choice Questions

1. Which of the following is NOT an example of price discrimination?

   a. A cell phone company that charges different rates for weekday and weekend service.

   b. An amusement park that charges higher prices for adults than for senior citizens.

   c. A college that charges different tuitions (when financial aid and scholarships are included) to different students.

   d. Different movie theaters that charge different ticket prices for the same movie.

2. Antitrust policies in the United States make each of the following illegal, **except**

   a. companies meeting and agreeing to charge a particular price.

   b. oligopolies merging to form a monopoly.

   c. companies deciding to produce different products than their competitors.

   d. companies meeting and agreeing to limit production to a certain level.

3. A market that is characterized by a large number of sellers facing a downward-sloping demand curve is a(n)

   a. perfectly competitive market.

   b. monopoly.

   c. oligopoly.

   d. monopolistic competitor.

4. The marginal revenue curve for a monopolist always

   a. lies above the demand curve.

   b. equals the demand curve.

   c. lies below the demand curve.

   d. exceeds the price.

5. Which of the following lists market structure from least to most competitive?

   a. monopoly, oligopoly, monopolistic competition, perfect competition

   b. monopoly, monopolistic competition, oligopoly, perfect competition

   c. monopolistic competition, oligopoly, perfect competition, monopoly

   d. perfect competition, monopolistic competition, oligopoly, monopoly

6. Which of the following describes *economies of scale*?

   a. An increase in output results in an increase in average cost.

   b. An increase in output results in a decrease in average cost.

   c. An increase in output results in an increase in average revenue.

   d. An increase in output results in a decrease in average revenue.

Answer the next two questions based on the following table:

| QUANTITY SOLD | PRICE (DOLLARS) |
|---|---|
| 1 | $10 |
| 2 | 9 |
| 3 | 8 |
| 4 | 7 |
| 5 | 6 |
| 6 | 5 |

7. What is the total revenue if this firm sells 4 units?
   a. $4
   b. $7
   c. $28
   d. $34

8. What is the marginal revenue from selling the sixth unit?
   a. $30
   b. $5
   c. $0
   d. $–1

## Constructed Response Question

1. The Frankfort Faucet Water Works is the only seller of bottled water from a special spring in Illinois believed to have medical benefits. The following table shows the demand for gallons of Frankfort Faucet water per month. The company has no fixed costs and its marginal cost is constant at $4 per gallon.

| PRICE OF WATER (DOLLARS) | QUANTITY OF WATER (GALLONS) | TOTAL REVENUE (DOLLARS) | MARGINAL REVENUE (DOLLARS) |
|---|---|---|---|
| $10 | 0 | | |
| 9 | 1,000 | | |
| 8 | 2,000 | | |
| 7 | 3,000 | | |
| 6 | 4,000 | | |
| 5 | 5,000 | | |
| 4 | 6,000 | | |
| 3 | 7,000 | | |
| 2 | 8,000 | | |
| 1 | 9,000 | | |

a. In what market structure does Frankfort Faucet Water Works operate? Explain.
b. Complete the table by calculating the total revenue and the marginal revenue.
c. Using a correctly labeled graph, with price per gallon on the vertical axis and gallons of water on the horizontal axis, graph and label the following:
   i. the demand curve
   ii. the marginal revenue curve
   iii. the marginal cost curve
d. What is the profit-maximizing price and output for Frankfort Faucet Water Works?
e. How much profit will Frankfort Faucet Water Works earn at the profit-maximizing level of output?

**CHAPTER 9** & **YOU** Sometimes markets do not work well. For example, if a company dumps poisonous waste in a reservoir that supplies water to your community, the market has failed to adequately serve you and your neighbors. A situation like this can literally be a matter of life and death. When markets produce undesirable results, the government can take steps to improve the allocation of resources. In this chapter you will learn to identify factors that prevent markets from producing the best results for society. We will look at what the government and communities can do to prevent or fix undesirable results. We will also see that other problems can arise when the government plays an active role in the economy. Once you understand the limitations of both the market and government policy, you will be in a better position to understand the issues involved in policy debates.

# Market Failure and Government Failure

**MODULE 26: When the Invisible Hand Is All Thumbs: Market Failure**
**MODULE 27: The Heavy Hand of Government: Government Failure**

## ECONOMICS TO THE RESCUE

Brooktrout Lake in upstate New York, as its name suggests, was once teeming with fish. In the 1980s, the fish all died as a result of acid rain. The acid rain was caused by pollution from power plants located as far away as Chicago and Cleveland. The power plants spewed sulfur dioxide into the air, and when it rained, the sulfur dioxide mixed with water to create the sulfuric acid concoction known as acid rain. The acid rain fell down on Brooktrout Lake and large parts of the Northeastern United States, harming the environment. The people who came to the lake to fish, swim, and boat suffered as a result of the pollution.

Although there would be no pollution in an ideal world, society wouldn't want to do away with businesses and activities that cause pollution because almost all manufacturing, motorized transportation, and construction creates pollution, and the benefits of some pollution exceed the costs. Without some pollution, we could have no schools, hospitals, cars, or computers. The market forces of supply and demand can bring about too much pollution, however, because pollution causes problems for people who were not involved in the decisions to buy or sell the products

*Government incentives to reduce sulfur dioxide emissions helped restore Brooktrout Lake to a place where fish could live.*

that caused the pollution. The power plants did not compensate the people who visited Brooktrout Lake for their lost recreational opportunities or pay a price for the damage acid rain caused to trees and buildings.

The Brooktrout Lake story has a happy ending for the fish and people who want to enjoy the lake. In 1990, the government tightened restrictions on sulfur dioxide emissions for power plants in the Midwest. It did this by using economics! The plants were required to pay for the sulfur dioxide they produced. This policy encouraged the firms to use technology that produced less pollution. In 2006, trout were reintroduced into Brooktrout Lake, and so far they are doing well.

This story illustrates what economists call a *negative externality*, or an undesirable spillover from the decisions of some people that affects the well-being of others. This chapter explains how externalities, among other problems, cause markets to fail to achieve the best outcome for society. You will learn how the government can guide markets toward better outcomes. And you will learn reasons why the government might fail to produce the best result as well.

## BOTTOM LINE

Under some circumstances markets fail to produce the best results possible. Government action sometimes improves outcomes and other times fails in the quest for efficiency.

## MODULE 26

# When the Invisible Hand Is All Thumbs: Market Failure

**KEY IDEA:** Market outcomes can be inefficient if there are spillover effects from the production or use of goods, if some consumers cannot be excluded from consuming a good, if information is imperfect, or if firms have market power (as discussed in Chapter 8).

### OBJECTIVES
- To define market failure.
- To explain the concepts of public goods, externalities, and imperfect information.
- To identify possible solutions to the sources of market failure.

## Evaluating Market Performance

Market outcomes can be evaluated along two lines: efficiency and equity. In Chapter 1 you learned that efficiency has to do with getting the most out of available resources. A market is efficient if no one can be made better off without making someone else worse off. Chapter 2 introduced equity as the quality of being fair and just. An economy can be efficient without being fair. For example, if Ebenezer Scrooge owned all the goods in an economy and everyone else lived in poverty, this unfair allocation could nonetheless be efficient if there were no opportunities to make someone better off without making someone else worse off.

There are several paths to efficiency under the right conditions. For example, in Chapter 8 we saw that both perfect competition and perfect price discrimination (the practice of charging each consumer his or her reservation price) result in an efficient allocation of resources. This is true even though monopolists capture all the gains from trade with perfect price discrimination, while firms earn no profit in the long run under perfect competition. But under the wrong conditions, even these paths don't lead to efficiency due to *market failure*.

*Markets can be evaluated in terms of equity and efficiency, which don't always go hand-in-hand. If Ebenezer Scrooge owned all the goods in the economy, this unfair allocation could be efficient.*

## EFFICIENCY AND MARKET FAILURE

Why should you care about efficiency? Because in an inefficient market, it is possible to make someone better off without making anyone worse off. For example, if the Ebenezer Scrooge–style market is inefficient, it would be possible to make Bob Cratchit better off without making Ebenezer or anyone else worse off. If someone can be made better off without harming anyone else, society has missed an opportunity to improve the well-being of its members.

If a market is inefficient, in principle, it is possible to make everyone better off. Remedies may initially make some firms or consumers worse off, even if society as a whole is better off. But inefficiency exists only if the gains from shifting to an efficient outcome exceed the losses.

*Ads for Eggo brand frozen waffles feature customers saying "Leggo my Eggo" to people trying to steal their waffles. Because we can generally prevent others from eating our Eggos, waffles are excludable, one of the two characteristics of a private good.*

Some of the gains from efficiency could be used to compensate those who don't benefit from the change, making it a win-win situation.

Suppose there is an inefficiently small quantity of solar panels because each one costs $500 more to install than it saves on electricity bills, but each panel prevents $1,000 worth of pollution damage. A $501 government subsidy for each solar panel, paid for with a tax on the beneficiaries of cleaner air, would make society better off by $1,000 − $501 = $499 per panel and consumers better off by $501 − $500 = $1 per panel. Win-win!

This module considers reasons why a market, left to its own devices, might miss opportunities to make someone better off without harming anyone. The inability to achieve an efficient market outcome is known as **market failure**. We have already seen that market power, the ability of individual firms to set prices, can cause market failure. Chapter 8 explained, for example, that a monopoly is inefficient because the price charged to consumers is greater than the firm's marginal cost of production, meaning that additional units could be made for less than their value to consumers. The exercise of market power is one cause of market failure, but there are others.

## PRIVATE GOODS AND PUBLIC GOODS

Most of the goods that you encounter every day—breakfast cereal, gym shorts, mystery books, and so on—are *private goods*. **Private goods** can be used by only one person at a time. In fact, private goods are so common that we usually just call them "goods," without mentioning that they're "private." You probably take it for granted that if you buy a bike helmet, a

necklace, or a calculator, you will be the only user of it. Even if you lend it to a friend, it's still a private good because only one person can use it at a time.

Private goods have two defining qualities: they are *excludable* and *rival*. If a good is **excludable**, it is possible to prevent others from consuming it. The owner of a private good, such as a waffle, can prevent other people from consuming that particular good. The enforcement of laws makes many goods excludable. If someone tries to use your bike without permission, you can call the police and have them arrested for theft. To prevent others from eating your waffle, you may need to run fast or eat in the closet. A good is **rival** if one person's consumption of the good makes it impossible for others to consume it at the same time. For example, if I eat your waffle, you can't because it's all gone. Keep your eyes on your Eggo.

A **public good** is the opposite of a private good: it is neither excludable nor rival. For example, a forecast from the National Weather Service is a public good. Each day, the National Weather Service makes forecasts about weather conditions in every part of the country. If you look up the weather forecast for your region at the service's web page (www.nws.noaa.gov), you do not reduce the opportunity for someone else to look up the same forecast. For this reason, weather forecasts are nonrival; there is no limit on the number of people who can consume the same weather forecast at the same time. In addition, weather forecasts are nonexcludable because once they are announced, anyone can use them. Other

---

A good is **excludable** if it is possible to prevent others from consuming it.

**Market failure** is the inability of a market to achieve an efficient outcome.

A good is **rival** if one person's consumption of the good makes it impossible for others to consume it.

A **public good** is nonrival and nonexcludable.

**Private goods** can be used by only one person at a time.

examples of public goods include national defense, police and fire protection, public radio, Global Positioning Satellite (GPS) signals, and street signs.

Weather forecasts and public radio are pure public goods because they remain nonexcludable and nonrival. But most public goods do become rival at some point. For example, one fire station's crew can be on the alert to serve hundreds of residents and has plenty of trucks and water to save your house if it catches fire. But if all the houses on your block caught fire at the same time, the station's resources would be stretched pretty thin. Likewise, parks and roads are public goods when they are uncongested and open to all but become rival when enough people use them at the same time.

In some cases it is also possible to exclude people from enjoying a public good. Parks can be fenced and roads can be barricaded to shut users out. In Obion County, Tennessee, fire protection extends only to households that have paid the $75 annual fee for it. Others are left to fend for themselves if their house catches fire. Despite a few exceptions and qualifications, the distinction between public and private goods is a useful one.

**DID YOU GET IT?**
What is the difference between a public and a private good?

## The Underprovision of Public Goods

From the standpoint of economic efficiency, public goods pose a problem: firms have little incentive to supply them because consumers have little incentive to pay for them. The market will thus provide an inefficiently small quantity of public goods.

Suppose you wanted to start a business that installed street signs. Although many people would benefit from additional street signs, and their combined willingness to pay for these signs might exceed your marginal cost of installing them, it is difficult to get anyone to pay for a street

sign because of what is called the *free-rider problem*. The **free-rider problem** is that people consume public goods without paying for them, and this destroys market incentives for firms to provide public goods. Since you can't exclude anyone from reading a street sign, consumers have an incentive to benefit from that public good without paying for it. Even if some people pay for public goods, not everyone will, and the market will provide too few. If everyone free rides, then the public good will not be provided at all. That is a serious market failure—imagine a city without street signs or police protection!

**DID YOU GET IT?**
What is the free-rider problem? Why are public goods underprovided?

## The Drop-in-the-Bucket Problem

The free-rider problem is worse when there are many consumers of a public good and the required contribution of each consumer is tiny—just a "drop in the bucket"—compared with the total cost of providing it. If only a few people consume a public good, then each person might be embarrassed by not contributing something toward its provision. If there are many anonymous consumers, however, it is harder to collect from each one. The **drop-in-the-bucket problem** arises when no one person's payment is essential, which diminishes each person's incentive to contribute.

Suppose your community wants to erect a new statue of a local hero using donations from community members. The statue will go in a square that is open to the public, so enjoyment of the statue will be nonexcludable. Since many people can

The **free-rider problem** is that people take advantage of the nonexcludable and nonrival nature of public goods to avoid paying for them.

The **drop-in-the-bucket problem** arises when no one person's payment for a good is essential, which diminishes each person's incentive to contribute.

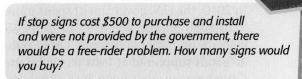

*If stop signs cost $500 to purchase and install and were not provided by the government, there would be a free-rider problem. How many signs would you buy?*

gaze at a statue at once, it will also be nonrival. In a small community with only a few members, the financial contribution of each member would clearly be important, and attempts to free ride would be obvious. But if the community has tens of thousands of members, each feels more anonymous, giving rise to the drop-in-the-bucket problem. Even people who would receive great pleasure from the statue would be tempted not to contribute to its cost. With the thousands of potential donors, it seems that one more donation would make little difference.

The free-rider and drop-in-the-bucket problems have many applications. Suppose your teacher offered to give every student in the class an A if at least *half* of the students in the class handed in an extra homework assignment. Each student would have an incentive to free ride, hoping that other students would do the extra homework. The incentive to free ride would be stronger in a larger class than in a smaller one, because with more people involved, each person's contribution has less effect and it is easier to be anonymous. How do you think the students' incentives for free riding would change if the teacher promised an A to every student if only one student handed in the homework, as opposed to half of the students?

**DID YOU GET IT?**
What is the drop-in-the-bucket problem? How does it worsen the underprovision of public goods?

## Providing Public Goods

Because of the free-rider problem, the task of providing public goods usually falls to the government. The most obvious technique is for the government to purchase them directly. For example, the largest single item in the federal government's budget is national defense, a public good. In 2010, the U.S. government spent more than $660 billion, about $1 in every $5 it spent, on national defense. Other public goods supported at least partly by the federal government include the National

Weather Service, National Public Radio, the National Parks, and the National Aeronautics and Space Administration. State and local governments also provide public goods such as police and fire protection, roads, street signs, parks, lifeguards at public beaches and swimming pools, and voting booths around election time.

In some cases, the government subsidizes the private sector to provide public goods. For example, citizens can receive a tax break if they make a contribution to an eligible charity because many charities, like the Red Cross, provide public goods. The government can also ensure the provision of a public good by allowing a private party to make it excludable. For example, free riding on the use of a park could be prevented by granting a private firm the right to charge admission and exclude anyone who doesn't pay. Some states have turned over their highways—another public good—to private firms that collect tolls from drivers who use the highways.

If you write a song, copyright protection keeps others from using it to make money without your permission. The government grants copyrights to make songs, books, artwork, photographs, and other creations excludable. Module 23 explained that patents serve a similar purpose for inventions such as pharmaceutical drugs. If creations and inventions were nonexcludable, the free-rider problem would result in too few of them, because the incentive to innovate and create new products would be diminished.

Due to the importance of this topic, more discussions of the provision of public goods are coming up. In the next chapter we explain how the government uses taxes to pay for public goods. In Module 27 of this chapter we discuss problems encountered when the government provides public goods.

**DID YOU GET IT?**
What are three methods used by the government to help make public goods available? Why does the government provide public goods?

## The Tragedy of the Commons

A *common* is an area of land that is open for members of the community to use. For example, the Boston Common is a 50-acre park once used by many families as a cow pasture. A problem arose at the Boston Common, as is common at commons around the world, because farmers bought too many cows, and the land was overgrazed. Open access makes the common nonexcludable, but unlike a public good, it is rival because there is only so much grass for the cows to eat. The **tragedy of the commons** refers to the problem that nonexcludable-but-rival goods become overused.

Consider ocean fishing. In many parts of the ocean it is difficult to prevent people from catching fish, so the fish are nonexcludable. But if you catch a fish, no one else can, so fish are rival. Individual fishers have little incentive to limit their catch, because each fisher receives the full benefit of the fish in his or her net. But the damage from overfishing is shared by fishers around the world. The result of this tragedy of the commons is that more than one quarter of the world's fish stocks are harvested more rapidly than they can reproduce. Similar problems arise in regard to logging in national parks, littering in public restrooms, irrigating farms with river water, and emitting car exhaust into the air.

The **tragedy of the commons** is that nonexcludable but rival goods become overused.

### YOUR TURN

Think of an example of the tragedy of the commons that you have observed in your school or community.

---

## ECONOMICS IN ACTION

# The Tragedy of the Sturgeon

Caviar, which is fish eggs, is a delicacy to many consumers. The most highly prized caviar comes from the beluga species of sturgeon. The largest supply of sturgeon is in the Caspian Sea, a body of water between Europe and Asia, bordered by Russia, Iran, and Kazakhstan, among other countries. A good day's catch of sturgeon could sell for $50,000, which exceeds the lifetime income of many people in the region. Not surprisingly, the Caspian Sea attracts many sturgeon fishermen, even though it is illegal to catch sturgeon, because they are threatened with extinction.

As sturgeon become scarcer, prices rise, giving fishermen a stronger incentive to overfish sturgeon. To make matters worse, the large size of the Caspian Sea makes exclusion a real challenge. Attempts to enforce the ban are further hindered by corruption, with fishermen bribing the police to allow them to fish. You might say the problem is one of overfishing the commons. Each individual fisherman has an incentive to catch as many sturgeon as possible, even though the fishermen's collective actions are causing the species to go extinct. As a result of this tragedy, beluga caviar may become a thing of the past.

    **DID YOU GET IT?**
How does the tragedy of the commons apply to caviar?

# EXTERNALITIES

An **externality** is an effect felt beyond those whose decisions caused the effect.

If you've ever been helped or harmed by someone else's decision, you've experienced an *externality*. An **externality** is any effect felt beyond those whose decisions caused the effect. For example, suppose the Anaheim Steel Company contracts with Disneyland to provide steel beams for a new amusement ride. Suppose further that in the process of producing the steel beams, the Anaheim Steel Company releases pollution into the air. The pollution creates a negative externality for people who breathe the polluted air, because they were not involved in the decision to produce the steel and pollute the air. Other sources of negative externalities include disruptions to the class when one student misbehaves, secondhand smoke, and greenhouse gases released by the burning of fossil fuels. In each of these cases, people are harmed by decisions they didn't make. In the case of the misbehaving student, when weighing the costs and benefits of acting up, the class clown might consider the likelihood of detention and a phone call home but probably doesn't include the costs of slowing your progress or distracting the teacher.

An externality can be positive as well as negative. A positive externality occurs, for example, if your neighbors put a fresh coat of paint on their house. This makes it more pleasant to look at. Although you were not involved in the decision to paint their house, it makes you better off because you get to see a freshly painted house when you look out your window.

On the other hand, if they decide to fill their front yard with piles of junk, you may have a negative externality to deal with, depending on your tastes.

Because externalities can be positive or negative, you can see them as benefit or cost spillovers that are not taken into account by those causing the spillover effects. For example, when you get a flu shot, health benefits spill over to other people who don't get the flu because they don't catch it from you, creating a positive externality. When you leave sweaty clothes in your locker for two weeks, offensive odors spill over to affect other people, causing a negative externality.

A competitive market will produce too little of a positive externality and too much of a negative externality. Consider the example of positive externalities from attractively painted houses and negative externalities from ugly ones. Many of those who want to paint their homes an attractive color will decide not to, because the cost of repainting exceeds their willingness to pay. But in some of those cases the benefit to *society*, including the owner's willingness to pay and the external benefit received by neighbors and passersby who enjoy the view, will exceed the cost. Since the homeowners only consider their own cost and benefit, there will be too few attractively painted houses.

Likewise, there will be those with unusual tastes who decide to paint their homes a shocking shade of orange or purple because the cost of repainting is less than the homeowners' willingness to pay. But in some of those cases the cost

*The decisions of your neighbors can improve or destroy your view, thus creating positive or negative externalities.*

BOTTOM RIGHT: THINKSTOCK; BOTTOM LEFT: THINKSTOCK

to society, including the cost of painting and the cost imposed on shocked neighbors and passersby, will exceed the benefit. Because the homeowners disregard the cost imposed on others, an excess of purple paint will be splashed around.

**DID YOU GET IT?**
What is a negative externality? What is a positive externality? Are goods with negative externalities overproduced or underproduced in competitive markets?

## Solving the Externality Problem: Taxes and Subsidies

Negative externalities cause inefficiency because their cost is not reflected in the amount spent on the associated goods and services. For example, think about what happens when we drive our cars with engines that run on gasoline. The burning of fossil fuel contributes to

pollution problems, our cars contribute to road congestion, and our consumption of gasoline increases the country's dependence on foreign oil. As serious as these problems are, they are externalities because drivers bear only a fraction of the cost. For that reason, drivers tend to travel an inefficiently large number of miles.

One way to handle negative externalities is to place a tax on the goods that cause them. The tax can be collected from either firms or consumers, because either way the tax will reduce the quantity of the good that is causing the externality. First consider a gasoline tax paid by consumers. The lines labeled *Supply* and *Demand*$_1$ in Figure 26.1 represent the supply and demand curves for gasoline before the tax. The equilibrium without a tax occurs at point $E_1$, where the supply and demand curves intersect. Without a tax, the equilibrium price is $P_1$ and the equilibrium quantity is $Q_1$.

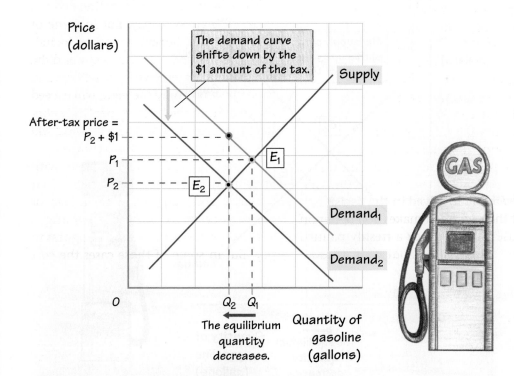

**Figure 26.1** A Tax on Consumers
Before a tax is imposed on gasoline, the demand curve is Demand$_1$. With a tax of $1 per gallon paid by consumers, the demand curve shifts down by $1 to Demand$_2$. The equilibrium quantity falls from $Q_1$ to $Q_2$. So the tax reduces the use of gasoline, which is a source of negative externalities.
**DID YOU GET IT?** If the tax were $1.25 per gallon instead, would consumption fall by more or less? Why?

To reduce gasoline consumption, the government can impose a tax of $1 per gallon that buyers must pay in addition to the price of gasoline. We know that $Demand_1$ shows the most consumers would pay for each gallon of gasoline. The need to pay $1 per gallon in tax to the government decreases the amount consumers are willing to pay firms by $1 per gallon. This shifts the demand curve faced by firms down by $1 to $Demand_2$. For example, if the most a consumer would pay for the fiftieth gallon of gasoline is $5, with a $1 tax per gallon, the most a consumer would pay a firm for the fiftieth gallon is $5 − $1 = $4.

The supply curve is unchanged because the tax is paid by consumers. The new equilibrium, $E_2$, occurs at a lower price, $P_2$, and a lower quantity, $Q_2$, than before the tax. The *after-tax price* for consumers is $P_2$ plus the tax of $1. Even though the price paid to firms falls

due to the shift in demand, the after-tax price of $P_2$ + $1 is higher than $P_1$. Note that the burden of the tax is shared by consumers and firms: consumers pay more than they did before the tax, and firms receive less. Since consumers pay an after-tax price above the original price and firms receive a price below the original price, the tax decreases both the quantity demanded and the quantity supplied.

Figure 26.2 illustrates the situation if the tax is imposed on firms instead of consumers. Supply curve $Supply_1$ shows the smallest amount of money firms would accept for each gallon. When firms have to pay a $1 tax in addition to their marginal cost for each gallon, the supply curve shifts up by $1. For example, if the marginal cost of producing the fiftieth gallon of gasoline is $2, with a $1 tax per gallon on top of their marginal cost, the least a firm would accept for the fiftieth gallon is $2 + $1 = $3.

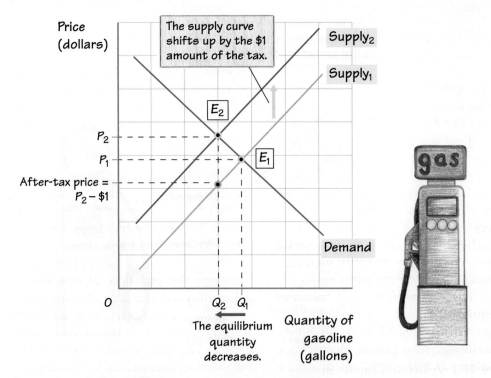

**Figure 26.2** A Tax on Firms
The supply curve without a tax is $Supply_1$. After a tax of $1 per gallon is imposed on firms, the supply curve shifts up by $1 to $Supply_2$. The equilibrium quantity falls from $Q_1$ to $Q_2$. Like a tax on consumers, a tax on firms reduces gasoline use and the associated negative externalities.
**DID YOU GET IT?** Why do you think the supply curve shifted upward?

The supply shift causes the equilibrium quantity to fall to $Q_2$, the same quantity that resulted from a tax on consumers. The new equilibrium price for consumers, $P_2$, is the same as the after-tax price paid by consumers in Figure 26.1, $P_2 + \$1$. And the after-tax price that firms receive, $P_2 - \$1$, is the same as the price firms received with the tax in Figure 26.1, $P_2$. So the tax on firms has the same effect as the tax on consumers, including the intended result that quantity falls and negative externalities decline.

If the tax paid per unit equals the cost of the negative externality per unit, then the price of the good reflects the cost of the good to society, which leads consumers to purchase the efficient quantity of the good. In the United States, the combined federal and state tax on gasoline differs across states, but the average is about 40 cents per gallon. Economists Ian Parry and Kenneth Small estimate that the 40-cent tax is too small compared with the size of the negative externalities caused by gasoline consumption. They advise that the optimal tax to encourage the efficient amount of gasoline consumption, taking account of the negative externalities, would be close to $1 per gallon.

Just as the government can prevent negative externalities from causing market failure by taxing goods that are overproduced, the government can promote positive externalities by subsidizing goods that would otherwise be underproduced. When consumers receive a subsidy for purchasing a good, the demand curve shifts upward and the equilibrium quantity increases. Likewise, a subsidy for firms shifts the supply curve downward and increases the equilibrium quantity. For example, the government subsidizes flu shots, tree seedlings, solar panels, electric cars, education, and the arts, all of which provide positive externalities.

**DID YOU GET IT?**
How can a tax on gasoline help solve the problem of negative externalities from driving?

*The government subsidizes the purchase of tree seedlings because trees provide the positive externalities of clean air and beauty.*

## Creating a Market for Negative Externalities

We know that when the full cost of a good isn't paid by those who buy or sell that good, the market outcome is inefficient. The goal of taxing negative externalities is to have their cost reflected in the marketplace. Another approach to the same goal is to create a market for negative externalities. One ingenious application of this idea is the creation of *tradable permits*, each granting the right to emit a particular amount of pollution. Since tradable permits were instituted under the Clean Air Act of 1990, sulfur dioxide emissions have fallen by more than 60 percent.

Here's an example of how tradable permits work: power plants produce sulfur dioxide as a byproduct of producing electricity. Sulfur dioxide causes acid rain, which erodes buildings and damages the environment. Power plants receive a set number of permits, each allowing the emission of one ton of sulfur dioxide. The total amount of sulfur dioxide emissions across all plants is capped by the amount of permits issued. The plants can trade the permits among themselves. For example, if Plant A has permits to emit 1,000 tons of sulfur dioxide but can cut its emissions to 800 tons, it can sell the permits for the remaining 200 tons to Plant B, which may be older and thus less able to reduce its emissions.

Tradable permits create a market for pollution emissions.

Emissions trading programs provide three particular benefits:

**1. They allow flexibility and creativity.** Each firm can reduce emissions in the most feasible and affordable way, based on the firm's particular situation.

**2. They allocate emissions rights to those who value them the most.** Newer firms with better systems for emissions reduction can sell their permits to firms that would have a harder time reducing their emissions.

**3. They provide an incentive to minimize emissions.** The ability to sell unused permits gives firms a reason to keep reducing their pollution level even when they are below the level stipulated by regulations.

With a market in place for sulfur dioxide emissions, there is no longer an externality. The cost of the pollution to those not involved in the decision is now part of the marginal cost of producing electrical power. As a consequence, if the efficient number of permits is granted, the market does not overproduce sulfur dioxide emissions. The solution of tradable permits has also been applied, for example, to phosphorus, nitrogen, and sediment releases into waterways in the United States, carbon dioxide and nitrogen oxide emissions in Europe, salt mining in Australia, and car use in Singapore.

An alternative to tradable permits is a *command-and-control* approach to environmental regulations, which sets out blanket standards for how much sulfur dioxide each plant can emit or what type of equipment each plant can use. Unlike such inflexible regulations, tradable permits harness the power of market incentives to reduce pollution. Firms that develop new ways to reduce emissions save money on their permits, which motivates innovation. Tradable permits yield a higher rate of compliance with pollution reduction goals than command-and-control standards. And there is evidence that tradable permits have been more cost-effective for the firms involved.

## IMPERFECT INFORMATION

Have you ever paid one price at a shop in a tourist area, only to find lower prices for the same thing just a few blocks away? In such cases a lack of information prevents competition from keeping

THINKSTOCK

prices in check. Buyers and sellers must have access to information in order for markets to function efficiently.

A problem of **asymmetric information** arises if one side of a market—either buyers or sellers—has better information than the other. As a classic example, sellers of used cars are better informed about the quality of the cars than the potential buyers. Regardless of their appearance, some cars are good and others are "lemons," likely to break down in the near future. If you own a car, you are more likely to put it up for sale if it is a lemon than if it is a dependable vehicle. You are also more likely than the buyer to know whether your car is a lemon or not.

How does this information asymmetry affect the used-car market? Nobel Prize–winning economist George Akerlof examined just this problem in his 1970 article "The Market for Lemons." Akerlof reasoned that the seller of a used car is more likely to know whether it is a lemon than the buyer. This state of affairs should make buyers very wary. If someone wants to sell you a car and that person knows more about it than you do, you might think that, chances are, he is trying to unload a lemon. Other buyers probably feel the same way and would only buy the car for less than the price of a reliable car. In the extreme, the asymmetric information problem could cause the market to unravel: if buyers refuse to pay the price of a reliable car, only car owners with lemons will offer their cars for sale. Since no one wants to buy a lemon, the whole used-car market could shut down. To avoid this type of market failure, *lemon laws* assist buyers who find that they've purchased a lemon, and reports on the repair and accident history of cars are available to help car shoppers avoid lemons.

Asymmetric information also causes market failure when the buyer has better information than the seller. This problem is common in the market for insurance, particularly health insurance, fire insurance, and life insurance. Suppose a health insurance company offered an insurance plan that charged the same price to all buyers. Unfortunately for the company, the people with the worst health and the greatest need for medical expenditures would be the ones most likely to buy the insurance plan. This tendency would hurt the insurance company's ability to earn profit because people in poor health make particularly large health care expenditures. This is a problem of *adverse selection*. In the insurance market, **adverse selection** occurs when those with the greatest need for a particular type of insurance are the ones most likely to buy it. More generally, adverse selection arises whenever an individual's decision depends on asymmetric information in a way that places uninformed market participants at a disadvantage.

A common solution to the problem of adverse selection in the health insurance industry is to sell insurance to groups of people that are unlikely to be in particularly poor health. For example, most Americans get their health insurance through their place of employment. Because most of the employees in a large business participate in the health insurance plan, the problem of adverse selection is greatly reduced. For those who are not insured as part of a group, perhaps because they are self-employed or unemployed, the problem remains. In these cases, the least healthy are more likely to buy insurance than the healthiest people. The high cost of insuring relatively unhealthy customers necessitates high insurance prices. Because of these high prices, adverse selection makes it more difficult for healthy people to afford insurance.

Adverse selection is not a problem in the market for car insurance, because the government mandates that every car be insured to some minimum extent against losses from an accident. Both bad drivers and good drivers are required to buy insurance, so there is no adverse selection based on accident risk.

**Asymmetric information** is an imbalance of information between parties, meaning that one party knows things that the other does not.

When there is **adverse selection**, people with the greatest need for a particular type of insurance are the ones most likely to buy it.

In the absence of imperfect information and the other sources of market failure, we can expect markets to be efficient. Table 26.1 summarizes the conditions that lead to market efficiency.

**DID YOU GET IT?**
Explain two ways in which market failure can result from asymmetric information.

| Table 26.1 **A Summary of Conditions for Market Efficiency** |
| --- |
| **FIVE CONDITIONS REQUIRED FOR A PRIVATE MARKET TO BE EFFICIENT** |
| 1.  Rational decision makers |
| 2.  Perfect competition |
| 3.  Goods that are excludable and rival |
| 4.  No externalities |
| 5.  Sufficient information |

# MODULE 26 REVIEW AND ASSESSMENT

## Summing Up the Key Ideas: Match the following terms to the correct definitions.

A. Market failure
B. Private good
C. Excludable

D. Rival
E. Public good
F. Free-rider problem

G. Drop-in-the-bucket problem
H. Tragedy of the commons

I.  Externality
J.  Asymmetric information
K. Adverse selection

_____ 1.  Can only be used by one person at a time.

_____ 2.  When no one person's payment for a good is essential, which diminishes each person's incentive to contribute.

_____ 3.  An effect felt beyond those whose decisions caused the effect.

_____ 4.  Occurs when the people with the greatest need for a particular type of insurance are the ones most likely to buy it.

_____ 5.  The inability of a market to achieve an efficient outcome without government intervention.

_____ 6.  When it is possible to prevent others from consuming a good.

_____ 7.  An imbalance of information between parties, meaning that one party knows things that the other does not.

_____ 8.  A good that is nonrival and nonexcludable.

_____ 9.  Occurs when nonexcludable but rival goods become overused.

_____ 10.  When people take advantage of the nonexcludable and nonrival nature of public goods to avoid paying for them.

_____ 11.  If one person's consumption of a good makes it impossible for others to consume it.

## Analyze and Explain: Analyze the following activities and explain if each is more likely to be provided as a public good or a private good.

| | PUBLIC OR PRIVATE? | EXPLANATION |
|---|---|---|
| 1. the haircut you got at your local salon | | |
| 2. snow removal on a public street | | |
| 3. repairs made to your roof after it was damaged by hail | | |
| 4. police and fire protection for a town | | |
| 5. a flood-control project on the Mississippi River | | |
| 6. snow removal from your driveway | | |
| 7. a subscription to a radio service | | |

## Apply: In the following situations, determine if each involves a **positive** or **negative externality**.

| | POSITIVE EXTERNALITY OR NEGATIVE EXTERNALITY? |
|---|---|
| 1. One homeowner on your block decides to completely relandscape his yard, including the parkway in front of his house. | |
| 2. A driver decides to throw his trash from a fast-food restaurant out the window of the car rather than take it home and throw it in the trash. | |
| 3. A customer in a crowded restaurant decides to light a cigarette immediately after finishing her dinner. | |
| 4. The large factory in town sells products around the world but is polluting the air with a dangerous level of carbon dioxide. | |
| 5. A new resident in your community decides to plant trees in the boulevard, install solar panels on her house, and purchase an electric car. | |
| 6. Your neighbor replaces his old, smoky, gasoline-powered lawn mower with a new, state-of-the-art electric lawn mower. | |

# MODULE 27

# The Heavy Hand of Government: Government Failure

**KEY IDEA:** The government can create problems of its own when it tries to prevent market failure.

**OBJECTIVES**

- To explain the meaning of government failure.
- To identify six reasons for government failure.
- To explain influences that can reduce government failure.

## Good Intentions Sometimes Go Badly

In the battle against market failure caused by market power, public goods, externalities, or information asymmetries, government action can promote efficiency. Yet when the government steps in to fight market failure, the government, too, might fail. **Government failure** is the inability of government to achieve an efficient outcome. Sometimes government intervention causes problems that are worse than those the intervention was intended to defeat. For example, Module 18 explained how government rent controls cause shortages in the market for apartments. In this module we'll explore more examples of how well-intended policy actions, and not-so-well-intended actions by government officials, can result in government failure.

*Despite the watchful eyes of the Supreme Court, Congress, and the president, among other checks and balances, the government has its share of failures.*

Fortunately, there are some safeguards against government failure. The U.S. Constitution places checks and balances on the government by spreading government power across the judicial, legislative, and executive branches: the Supreme Court, Congress, and the presidency. The ability of people to "vote with their feet" by moving across areas further limits the potential for government inefficiency. If a local, state, or national government should get out of hand, people can move to a different city, state, or even country.

**Government failure** is the inability of government to achieve an efficient outcome.

## SIX REASONS FOR GOVERNMENT FAILURE

The government has its fingerprints all over the economy. It affects economic activity by taxing income and consumption, regulating safe work conditions and business transactions, and providing goods and services such as schools, hospitals, and national defense. In these and other ways, the various branches of the U.S. government reach into virtually every market. Given the size and scope of government activity, you should recognize the possibility of government failure.

There are six main reasons for government failure:

1. Electoral pressures and interest group politics

2. Regulatory capture, or the tendency for those who are being regulated to twist regulations in their favor

3.  Rent seeking, or the tendency for individuals and organizations to expend resources in efforts to increase their slice of the government pie

4.  Missing input from buyers and sellers on the values they place on goods and services provided by the government

5.  Undesirable incentive effects of government intervention

6.  Unintended consequences of government action

ELECTORAL PRESSURES
REGULATORY CAPTURE
RENT SEEKING
MISSING VALUATIONS
INCENTIVE EFFECTS
UNINTENDED CONSEQUENCES

Let's consider each of these reasons in turn.

## Electoral Pressures and Interest Group Politics

Most politicians are concerned about getting reelected or being appointed to a higher position. These personal goals make politicians responsive to their constituents' desires, especially near election time. Sometimes this motivates politicians to do what is best for society, but other times politicians can yield to pressure from certain constituents to take actions that are less than ideal. Relatively small groups of voters with similar interests, known as *interest groups*, seek a large influence on government policies. Examples of interest groups include farmers, gun owners, environmentalists, restaurant owners, and workers in the ready mix concrete industry. Interest groups are the most effective in exerting pressure when they are well organized, well funded, widely represented geographically, or represented by popular leaders. The influence of interest groups can be a problem if their goals diverge from what is best for society.

Consider farm subsidies. The governments of the United States, the European Union, and Japan spend large sums of money to subsidize farmers. The intent is to help stabilize prices and income for vulnerable farmers. These farm subsidies turn out to be detrimental to poor farmers in developing countries who must compete with subsidized farm products. The subsidies are also expensive for taxpayers, and

when farm policies include price supports (various forms of price floors as discussed in Module 18), shoppers pay higher prices.

As an example, U.S. sugar beet policy has involved a mix of subsidies, price supports, regulations that limit production, and import quotas that limit foreign competition. These supports and limits help maintain the price of sugar above the market equilibrium price. This helps sugar beet farmers. Unfortunately, it hurts those in the candy, baking, and breakfast cereal industries who must purchase a lot of sugar, it is costly to the government, and it forces those buying products made with sugar to pay higher prices. The combined costs of this program may well exceed the benefits, but the price supports and quotas remain because sugar beet farmers are a small, well-organized group that has effectively lobbied Congress for support.

More generally, when an interest group is small but highly focused on a particular issue and represented in many states, it can often influence the government to intervene to its advantage. Interest groups sometimes succeed at the expense of overall economic efficiency. This problem is compounded when legislators **logroll** on issues, which means they trade votes to help each other enact their favored policies. A senator from a state that produces sugar beets, for example, might agree to vote for policies that support corn farmers in exchange for a vote by a senator from a corn-producing state in favor of sugar beet import quotas. Logrolling thereby brings about more potentially inefficient policies than would exist if each policy were evaluated on its merits.

To **logroll** is to work toward the passage of legislation by trading votes with other legislators.

### DID YOU GET IT?
How can logrolling lead to reduced economic efficiency?

Another problem that results from electoral pressures on economic decisions is **short-termism**, a tendency to place too

**Short-termism** is a tendency to place too much weight on immediate benefits and not enough weight on longer-term benefits and costs.

# ECONOMICS IN ACTION

# Electoral Pressures Influence Disaster Spending

Although the declaration of a natural disaster should be clear-cut and above politics, the Federal Emergency Management Agency (FEMA) legislation gives the president much discretion to decide whether a disaster qualifies for government assistance. Upon receiving a request from a state's governor, the president may declare a "major disaster" if a natural catastrophe "causes damage of sufficient severity and magnitude to warrant major disaster assistance."

Presidents tend to declare more disasters in years when they face reelection. Mary W. Downton of the National Center for Atmospheric Research and Roger A. Pielke Jr. of the University of Colorado, for example, looked at the flood-related disasters declared over a 32-year period. Even after accounting for the amount of rainfall and flood damage each year, they found that the average number of flood-related disasters declared by the president was 46 percent higher in election years than in other years.

The tendency to declare more disasters during election years is not limited to floods. Former president Bill Clinton set a record by declaring 73 major disasters in 35 states and the District of Columbia in 1996, the year he was up for

reelection. When George W. Bush faced reelection in 2004, he declared 61 major disasters in 36 states—10 more than he declared in 2003 and tied for the second most declarations ever. The increase from 2003 to 2004 was particularly sharp in the 12 battleground states in which the election was decided by 5 percent or less; these states accounted for 90 percent of the increase.

SOURCE: Adapted from Alan B. Krueger, "At FEMA, Disasters and Politics Go Hand in Hand," *New York Times*, September 15, 2005.

 **DID YOU GET IT?**
**Why do you think more disasters are declared in years when the president is up for reelection than in other years?**

*Is it considered a major disaster? That may depend on whether it occurred in an election year.*

much weight on immediate benefits and not enough weight on longer-term benefits and costs. In the United States, members of the House of Representatives are up for reelection every two years, senators face an election every six years, and presidents serve four-year terms, as do most state and local government politicians. The frequency of elections places pressure on elected officials to deliver benefits in a short period of time. It also creates

pressure to shift the burden of paying for those benefits into the future, when it falls on the elected officials' successors.

## Regulatory Capture

We saw in Chapter 8 that the exercise of market power, as by a monopolist, reduces efficiency compared to perfect competition. Antitrust policy is designed to reduce that inefficiency by restricting the ways in which firms can exercise their market power. For example, the Federal Trade Commission can prevent two firms from merging together if their merger would result in a monopoly. However, there is some concern that regulatory agencies may be "captured" by the firms they are supposed to regulate. To maximize profits, firms that are subject to regulation have an incentive to manipulate the regulatory apparatus to preserve their market power. For example, if existing firms were able to convince the regulatory agency to block new firms from entering the market, the existing firms would benefit from less competition. Other regulatory agencies, such as those enforcing health and safety laws, can also be pressured to serve the interests of those who should be regulated.

An example highlights this concern. In 2005, an advisory panel of the Food and Drug Administration decided, by majority vote, that a pain reliever called Bextra was safe enough to remain on the market. The panel made this recommendation despite mounting evidence that taking the medication raised the risk of having a heart attack. It turns out that 10 of the 30 experts on the advisory panel had previous financial ties to Pfizer, the company that sells Bextra. Without those 10 experts, the panel would have voted to ban sales of the drug. This is an example of **regulatory capture**—the control of a regulatory agency by the industry it is supposed to regulate.

Regulatory capture diverts policy makers from the goal of maximizing efficiency for society. Because of this possibility, citizens should question whether regulatory agencies are truly acting to serve the public or advancing the interests of those they are supposed to regulate. If a regulatory agency becomes captured by an interest group, the resulting government regulation can cause more severe market failure than in the absence of regulation.

**DID YOU GET IT?**
What problem does regulatory capture create?

## Rent Seeking

Interest groups often try to extract as much help from the government as possible. If there is a chance that the government will intervene on their behalf, individuals, firms, and organizations have an incentive to devote resources to seek governmental support. For example, the insurance industry spent $157.7 million on lobbying efforts in 2010, as it tried to obtain favorable treatment from government agencies.

The time and money spent lobbying policy makers could often be used more productively elsewhere in the economy. The hundreds of millions of dollars that the pharmaceutical industry spends lobbying Congress for such things as higher Medicare reimbursements, for example, could be spent developing new cures for deadly diseases.

Table 27.1 shows the lobbying expenditures of the 10 highest-spending industries in 2010. A total of $3.5 billion was spent on lobbying in that year alone. Note that these expenditures go toward things like boosting the price support for

**Regulatory capture** is the control of a regulatory agency by the industry it is supposed to regulate.

| Table 27.1 **Spending on Lobbying Congress and Federal Agencies: Top Ten Industries** | |
|---|---|
| **INDUSTRY** | **SPENDING (DOLLARS)** |
| Pharmaceuticals/health products | $242,132,934 |
| Electric utilities | 191,344,085 |
| Business associations | 171,246,733 |
| Insurance | 157,713,658 |
| Oil and gas | 145,892,043 |
| Misc. manufacturing and distributing | 128,491,948 |
| Computers/internet | 121,053,773 |
| TV/movies/music | 111,127,528 |
| Hospitals/nursing homes | 107,209,978 |
| Securities and investment | 101,073,730 |

SOURCE: Center for Responsive Politics, www.opensecrets.org/lobby/top.php?showYear=2010&indexType=i.

**Rent seeking** is the pursuit of profit by shifting existing gains rather than by creating new gains for society.

sugar, which effectively transfers money to farmers and away from the makers and buyers of chocolate, among others. An effort to shift financial gains around, without creating new gains for society, is called **rent seeking**. In the process of rent seeking, resources are expended in order to increase one group's slice of the economic pie, without increasing the size of the pie itself. Some economists worry that the United States is becoming a "rent-seeking society" because more and more resources are being used for persuasive efforts rather than productive efforts.

**DID YOU GET IT?**
What is rent seeking? Why is it a problem?

## Missing Valuations

One of the advantages of leaving economic decisions to the market is that market-based outcomes reflect the values buyers and sellers place on using and making a good. Buyers decide whether to buy based on the market-determined price and sellers decide whether to sell at that price. Hopefully, these decisions are based on rational considerations. When it comes to externalities like pollution, however, there is no market-determined price. The problem with externalities is that the party that produces the externality does not trade with the party that is affected by it. Because there is no market for an externality, it is harder for policy makers to determine how much people value the harm it causes or the benefit it provides. For example, perhaps you would be willing to pay up to a certain amount each year to breathe clean air rather than polluted air. That information would not be observable by others the way a market price is. A similar problem arises with public goods. It is not clear how much people would be willing to pay for them because there is no market for public goods.

*What is a robin worth to you? With no market for wild birds, it is difficult for policy makers to place an accurate value on them.*

According to the **law of unintended consequences**, intervention in a complex system can have surprising and undesirable consequences.

Without market prices to indicate value, economists and policy makers are forced to assess value in alternative ways. A common technique is to ask people how much they would be willing to pay, for example, to eliminate an externality. This raises another important question: Are responses to survey questions good indications of value? Sometimes questions can be posed in ways that elicit honest and meaningful answers. In other cases the results aren't so revealing. One study asked people how much money they would be willing to pay for a program that would save 2,000 birds and asked another group how much they would be willing to pay for a program that would save 200,000 birds. The average answer to each question was about the same, even though the number of birds saved was 100 times higher in the second case. Inevitably, when market-determined prices are unavailable, policy makers must make decisions about costs and benefits on the basis of imperfect information.

## Incentive Effects

Government intervention in the economy inevitably changes incentives. If the government wishes to provide a public good, for example, it must raise the funds to pay for it. It is most obvious to turn to taxes for these funds, but it's not so easy. Most taxes create disincentives for productive activities. A tax on income, for instance, reduces workers' take-home pay and therefore reduces the incentive for people to join the workforce. Since the incentive effects of taxes deserve more attention, we'll address them further in Chapter 10.

## Unintended Consequences

According to the **law of unintended consequences**, intervention in a complex system—such as the economy—can have surprising and undesirable consequences. Let's explore the unintended consequences of government actions with several examples.

Since medieval times, governments have tried to help the poor by setting maximum prices (price ceilings) for bread. When the French government did so between 1945 and 1980, bakers responded by finding new ways to make bread as cheaply as possible. Inferior ingredients went into the dough and the dough-rising times were cut. These short-cuts made the bread tough and flavorless. In Zimbabwe, the government instituted price controls for bread in 2005, only to create a severe bread shortage because the price ceiling was so low that most bakers couldn't cover their costs. As with the rent controls discussed earlier, any price ceiling below the equilibrium price will reduce the quantity supplied, increase the quantity demanded, and result in a shortage.

Sometimes governments set up barriers to imports as a way to support domestic manufacturers. This can set off a trade war, because when we set up barriers, our trading partners tend to set up barriers in retaliation. Restrictions on imports decrease supply and cause domestic prices to be higher for consumers. And when domestic firms can't sell their goods overseas, they earn less profit. Some economists point to this type of *protectionism* as a factor that worsened the Great Depression.

The Americans with Disabilities Act of 1990 requires firms to make accommodations for workers with a disability. These might include the addition of special ramps, drinking fountains, elevators, bathrooms, doors, and telephones. The result is an increase in the cost of hiring a disabled worker, which has caused some firms to hire fewer disabled employees. Of course, this was an unintended consequence of the act, the purpose of which was to make it easier for disabled people to work, not to reduce their employment opportunities.

The final example stems from government-mandated insurance. The purpose of insurance is to reduce the cost of unfortunate events, although that can have unintended consequences. Someone with car insurance bears less than the full cost of auto repairs in the event of an accident. Similarly, flood insurance and unemployment insurance reduce the cost of floods and being laid off. That's good if you're the insured victim of misfortune. The bad news is that insurance reduces the incentive to *avoid* unfortunate events like car accidents, flooding, and unemployment. People with insurance can more safely take risks. A driver with car insurance, for example, has less incentive to drive slowly and take other precautions when driving than an uninsured driver. Car insurance can thus have the unintended consequence of causing more accidents.

*If there are injuries involved, the damage caused by a car accident can run into the millions of dollars. Would you drive more carefully if you didn't have insurance and had to pay the full cost of an accident yourself?*

## YOUR TURN

Can you think of ways in which theft insurance and earthquake insurance might have unintended consequences?

**? DID YOU GET IT?**
What is the law of unintended consequences?

## VOTING WITH YOUR FEET: A CHECK ON GOVERNMENT FAILURE

Individuals have an important check on government failure: they can pick up and move to another location. This is especially true at the local and state government levels. If government failure in a particular town reaches a high level, more and more people will leave. The government will be forced to respond. Otherwise, the town and the government's ability to collect taxes to support itself will dwindle.

*In response to people voting with their feet, Cleveland is becoming a better place to live.*

This check on government failure was applied in the city of Cleveland. In 1960, Cleveland was the eighth largest city in the United States, with a population of 876,000. Today, Cleveland's population is about half as large as it was in 1960. People moved out of Cleveland because of high taxes, crime, inferior schools, and a lack of parks and other public goods. The opportunity for citizens to "vote with their feet" creates a form of competition among states, cities, and towns to provide the public goods and policies that people want. To stem its dwindling population and attract more people, Cleveland has been providing a better mix of public goods and lower taxes.

### Should the Government Ever Intervene?

The ability to vote with your feet, like other checks on government actions, has only a limited effect on government failure. But the fact that government

*Opinions differ, but it is clear that market failure and government failure are both too important to ignore.*

failure occurs is not an argument against government intervention in all cases. Sometimes there is no better alternative. For example, it is essential for our government to provide police protection, fire protection, and national defense, among other public goods. In other cases, the cost of government failure must be weighed against the cost of market failure in the absence of government intervention. For example, most states have concluded that car insurance is desirable despite the fact that it has the unintended consequence of more accidents.

Not surprisingly, reasonable people can disagree about the desirability of government intervention and about the best course of action should the government choose to intervene. Disagreements are unavoidable for several reasons. Valuations placed on public goods and externalities are hard to estimate. Opinions vary about the importance of unintended consequences from specific policies. And people have differing views about how much we should rely on private markets to solve society's problems. Regardless of where you stand on these issues, an understanding of the reasons for market failure and government failure should help you formulate your views and evaluate the many arguments on each side.

## MODULE 27 REVIEW AND ASSESSMENT

**Summing Up the Key Ideas:** Match the following terms to the correct definitions.

A. Government failure
B. Interest groups
C. Logroll
D. Short-termism
E. Regulatory capture
F. Rent seeking
G. Missing valuations
H. Law of unintended consequences

_____ 1. The control of a regulatory agency by the industry it is supposed to regulate.

_____ 2. A principle that holds that intervention in a complex system can have surprising and undesirable consequences.

_____ 3. To work toward the passage of legislation by trading votes with other legislators.

_____ 4. Relatively small groups of voters with similar interests who seek to influence government policies.

_____ 5. The lack of a market-determined price that causes policy makers to ask what is the value of some action.

_____ 6. The pursuit of profit by shifting existing gains rather than creating new gains for society.

_____ 7. The tendency to place too much weight on immediate benefits and not enough weight on longer-term benefits and costs.

_____ 8. The inability of government to achieve an efficient outcome.

## Analyze and Explain: Analyze each of the following to determine if a **market failure** or a **government failure** is being described.

MARKET FAILURE OR
GOVERNMENT FAILURE?

1. Shortly after imposing rent controls, New York City noticed a shortage of rental housing developments.

_____

2. In the process of making goods worth $2 million, a factory releases toxins into a lake that cause $3 million worth of losses to the fishing industry and lakeside resorts.

_____

3. Due to a law that bans construction near the habitat of endangered species, developers kill and hide endangered species found on their land.

_____

4. Knowing that he can benefit from streetlights whether or not he helps pay for them, a resident refuses to contribute to his neighborhood association's streetlight fund.

_____

## Apply: Analyze each of the following and determine the **type of government failure** described.

TYPE OF GOVERNMENT FAILURE

1. Senators from two neighboring states agree to trade votes for legislation that would provide additional funding to each state.

_____

2. The Over-the-Road Truck Drivers Association manages to get some of its members on the National Transportation Safety Board.

_____

3. The nation's largest oil producer spends $10 million every year urging Congress to pass laws favorable to their business interests.

_____

4. A new tax on personal income causes people to think twice about working at all.

_____

5. In an effort to create jobs, the government imposes new taxes on businesses. These new taxes force some businesses to lay off employees to save money.

_____

6. In an election year, a governor declares twice as many counties disaster areas as he did in the three previous years combined, even though the weather remained fairly consistent over that four-year period.

_____

# End of Ethanol Subsidy Will Raise the Price of Gas

BY CHRIS WOODYARD

Gasoline could cost 4.5 cents a gallon more starting as early as this week, and it's not because of rising oil prices. It's because Congress declined to renew the 30-year-old federal subsidy for ethanol, letting it expire Sunday. Ethanol, denatured grain alcohol used as a proven smog-cutting ingredient, currently makes up 10% of most gasoline-based motor fuel for general use, so-called E-10. In a few areas, E-85 fuel, 85% ethanol, also is available. E-85 can be burned only by vehicles equipped for "flex fuel."

How much the end of the subsidy could add to gas prices, and how soon, is yet to be seen. Ethanol blenders got a 45-cents-a-gallon tax credit, which amounts to 4.5 cents for the amount blended into each gallon of E-10 fuel. It's hard to calculate the immediate impact. Oil prices and ethanol stocks are in flux.

And unknown is the impact of another move by Congress: dropping the 54-cents-per-gallon tariff on ethanol imports. Brazil is a leading global producer of ethanol made mostly from sugar cane. In the United States, ethanol primarily is made from corn. That has made the ethanol subsidy controversial because of allegations that it raised food prices. The estimated $6 billion annual cost of the subsidy also has added to the federal deficit. The end of the subsidy, however, has caused barely a ripple among ethanol backers or corn producers. Corn prices remain high because of healthy exports, especially to China. E-10 is now standard, and more demand for ethanol is guaranteed by an escalating federal alternative fuel mandate requiring more use of it.

Gas prices averaged $3.28 for a gallon of regular (E-10) nationwide Monday, up from $3.07 a year ago. E-85 ethanol averaged $2.95. But because cars can't squeeze as much mileage out of every gallon of ethanol, the price when adjusted to equal the mileage of a gallon of regular was $3.88.

### DID YOU READ IT?

1) The article mentions at least three different ways the U.S. government influences the price of a gallon of E-10 gasoline. List these three policies the government uses to influence the price of E-10.

2) Voters often think that the U.S. government can directly control the price we pay for a gallon of gasoline. To what extent is this true?

### WHAT DO YOU THINK?

1) How are the markets for corn and gasoline related?

2) Is this article about the failure of a market or the failure of the government?

EXCERPTED FROM www.usatoday.com/money/industries/energy/story/2012-01-03/ethanol-subsidy-gas-prices/52355056/1.

HEMERA/THINKSTOCK

# CHAPTER 9 REVIEW AND SELF-ASSESSMENT

## REVIEW

### Points to Remember

**MODULE 26: WHEN THE INVISIBLE HAND IS ALL THUMBS: MARKET FAILURE**

1. **Market failure** is the inability of a market to achieve an efficient outcome.

2. **Private goods** can be used by only one person at a time.

3. A good is **excludable** if it is possible to prevent others from consuming it.

4. A good is **rival** if one person's consumption of the good makes it impossible for others to consume it.

5. A **public good** is nonrival and nonexcludable.

6. The **free-rider problem** is that people take advantage of the nonexcludable and nonrival nature of public goods to avoid paying for them.

7. The **drop-in-the-bucket problem** arises when no one person's payment for a good is essential, which diminishes each person's incentive to contribute.

8. The **tragedy of the commons** is that nonexcludable but rival goods become overused.

9. An **externality** is an effect felt beyond those whose decisions caused the effect.

10. **Asymmetric information** is an imbalance of information between parties, meaning that one party knows things that the other does not.

11. When there is **adverse selection**, people with the greatest need for a particular type of insurance are the ones most likely to buy it.

**MODULE 27: THE HEAVY HAND OF GOVERNMENT: GOVERNMENT FAILURE**

12. **Government failure** is the inability of government to achieve an efficient outcome.

13. To **logroll** is to work toward the passage of legislation by trading votes with other legislators.

14. **Short-termism** is a tendency to place too much weight on immediate benefits and not enough weight on longer-term benefits and costs.

15. **Regulatory capture** is the control of a regulatory agency by the industry it is supposed to regulate.

16. **Rent seeking** is the pursuit of profit by shifting existing gains rather than by creating new gains for society.

17. According to the **law of unintended consequences**, intervention in a complex system can have surprising and undesirable consequences.

## SELF-ASSESSMENT

The following questions are the type your teacher might ask you on a quiz or a test. Practice with these in order to improve your performance on class tests.

### Multiple-Choice Questions

1. Which of the following is an example of a positive externality?

   a. the greenhouse gases that are caused by the burning of fossil fuel

   b. the benefit to your neighborhood when you landscape your yard

   c. secondhand smoke when someone smokes in public

   d. a driver going 25 miles per hour over the speed limit to get to work on time

2. If the supplier of a good cannot prevent people who don't pay for the good from consuming it, we say that the good is

   a. excludable.

   b. nonexcludable.

   c. rival in consumption.

   d. nonrival in consumption.

3. A good that benefits people whether or not they have paid for it and whose benefits to any one individual do not depend on how many others also benefit is a(n)

   a. private good.
   b. public good.
   c. common resource.
   d. artificially scarce good.

4. The *tragedy of the commons* occurs when goods are

   a. nonexcludable and rival.
   b. nonexcludable and nonrival.
   c. excludable and rival.
   d. excludable and nonrival.

5. Which of the following is a source of *market failure*?

   a. asymmetric information
   b. positive externalities
   c. negative externalities
   d. all of the above are sources of market failure

6. If the government wanted to correct for a negative externality by imposing a tax on producers, the result would be

   a. a lower price and a lower quantity.
   b. a lower price and a higher quantity.
   c. a higher price and a lower quantity.
   d. a higher price and a higher quantity.

7. If the government wanted to correct for a positive externality, it would

   a. impose a tax.
   b. limit production.
   c. limit consumption.
   d. create a subsidy.

8. Which of the following is a source of *government failure*?

   a. logrolling
   b. short-termism
   c. rent seeking
   d. all of the above are sources of government failure

9. Which of the following is an example of a negative externality?

   a. A late-season hurricane destroys the grapefruit crop in Florida.
   b. The government imposes a tax in the market for grapefruit.
   c. Fertilizers used in the production of grapefruits are believed to be adversely affecting wildlife in Florida.
   d. Many Florida grapefruit growers go bankrupt because of an increase in imported grapefruit.

10. If one person's consumption of a good prevents others from consuming it at the same time, we say that the good is

    a. excludable.
    b. nonexcludable.
    c. rival in consumption.
    d. nonrival in consumption.

## Constructed Response Question

1. Use the information in the table to answer each of the following:

| PRICE (DOLLARS) | QUANTITY DEMANDED | QUANTITY SUPPLIED |
|---|---|---|
| $4.00 | 1,200 | 0 |
| 5.00 | 1,000 | 200 |
| 6.00 | 800 | 400 |
| 7.00 | 600 | 600 |
| 8.00 | 400 | 800 |
| 9.00 | 200 | 1,000 |

a.  Draw a correctly labeled market graph for movie tickets.

b.  Identify the equilibrium price for movie tickets.

c.  Identify the equilibrium quantity of movie tickets.

d.  The government imposes a tax on movie theaters of $2.00 per ticket sold. Identify the equilibrium price paid by consumers after the imposition of the tax.

e.  Identify the equilibrium quantity after the imposition of the tax.

f.  Would a ticket tax like this be appropriate if watching movies created a positive externality? Explain.

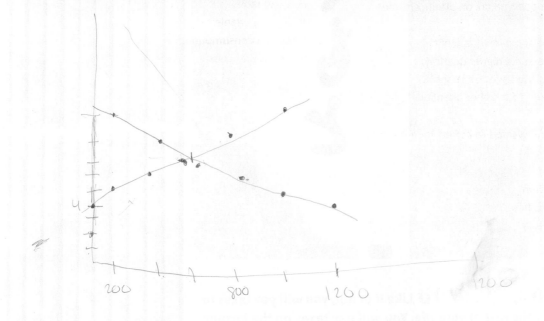

**CHAPTER 10 & YOU** Like it or not, you will pay taxes to the government for the rest of your life. You will pay taxes on the income you earn, on the returns from your saving and investing, and on most of the items you buy. In exchange, you are likely to receive education; health care; retirement benefits; unemployment insurance; access to a justice system; police, fire, and military protection; and a host of other public goods ranging from roads to research on disease control. This chapter will help you understand the various types of taxes you will pay and why they are necessary. You will learn how taxes are likely to change your behavior and how they alter the workings of the economy.

CHAPTER **10**

# Taxes: The Price of a Functioning Government

## TAXING CHOPSTICKS

A *tax* is a required payment to the government. In 2006, China placed a 5 percent tax on the sale of disposable wooden chopsticks. The reason for this tax was concern that chopstick production was destroying forests in China. The tax hit Japan hard; Japanese restaurants and consumers buy nearly 25 billion pairs of wooden chopsticks from China each year. Laid end to end, that's enough chopsticks to stretch back and forth to the moon 10 times. The price of chopsticks in Japan increased because of the tax. Restaurants in Japan reacted in a predictable way: they offered reusable plastic chopsticks and gave discounts to customers who brought their own chopsticks.

This sticky episode reveals some interesting lessons about taxation. First, people and businesses change their behavior in response to taxes. Second, taxes distort economic activity and usually make some people worse off. Restaurant customers in Japan, for example, probably felt a little worse off because they were given plastic chopsticks instead of wooden

THINKSTOCK

ones. Third, although the primary motivation for most taxes is to raise revenue for the government, sometimes taxes can be used to advance other goals, such as preventing deforestation.

Module 28 discusses the reasons for taxation and the kinds of taxes that are collected in the United States. Module 29 addresses the question of who pays for taxes. Although the answer may seem obvious, the person who pays a tax to the government is not always the one who bears the ultimate burden of the tax. Module 30 considers how taxes affect economic welfare and whether taxes are fair.

*After a tax in China raised the price of wooden chopsticks, many consumers changed their habits and purchased plastic chopsticks instead.*

## BOTTOM LINE

Although necessary to support government activities, most taxes cause people to change their behavior and have the potential to make some people worse off.

THINKSTOCK

# MODULE 28

# Why and How Are We Taxed?

**KEY IDEA:** The primary goal of the tax system is to raise enough money for the government to function effectively while doing so as fairly and efficiently as possible.

## OBJECTIVES

- **To explain the need for taxes.**
- **To identify taxes that discourage undesired behavior and taxes that encourage desired behavior.**
- **To describe several important taxes used in the United States.**

## Death and Taxes

Benjamin Franklin once quipped, "The only things certain in life are death and taxes." People tend to put off both for as long as possible. Having delayed the inevitable, millions of Americans rush to file their income tax returns before the mid-April deadline. To assist them, many post offices stay open late to accept mailed returns. The popular option to submit returns online helps last-minute filers avoid a penalty for being late. But what are taxes all about and why do we go through the trouble of paying them? This module explains the purposes of taxation and the most common types of taxes.

*Many post offices stay open late on tax day to help taxpayers beat the midnight deadline for mailing their income tax returns. Because tax payments are the price of a functioning government, it's better late than never.*

## WHY TAX?

**Taxes** are required payments to the government. They have three main purposes. First and foremost, taxes raise revenue for the government. Second, taxes can discourage unfavorable behavior such as drinking alcohol and smoking. Third, tax breaks can encourage favorable behavior such as the opening of new firms in a town that needs to create more jobs. Let's explore each of these purposes.

## Raising Revenue

"The fundamental purpose of our tax system," said the President's Advisory Panel on Tax Reform in 2005, "is to raise revenues to fund government." Taxes are necessary to fund the essential provisions of government, such as national defense, elections, and public education. Imagine your town without the things paid for with taxes—things like public schools, roads, traffic signals, streetlights, police and fire departments, city hall, the courthouse, the health department, sewers, bridges, snowplows, health inspectors, animal control, libraries, and parks. It wouldn't be the same, nor would your quality of life. The primary goal of tax policy, therefore, is to raise enough money for the government to function effectively. At the same time, policy makers seek to raise the required revenue while being as fair as possible and disrupting the economy as little as possible.

**Taxes** are required payments to the government.

TIM BOYLE/GETTY IMAGES

### Discouraging Undesirable Activity

Beyond raising revenue, the objective of some taxes is to discourage undesirable behavior. The chapter-opening story explained how a tax on disposable wooden chopsticks eased problems with forest destruction in China. And we saw in Chapter 9 that a gasoline tax can help limit pollution and other negative externalities. Similar taxes have been imposed in some areas to reduce the use of high-sulfur heating oil, plastic shopping bags, substances that damage the earth's protective ozone layer, and the volume of trash.

The government also imposes taxes on goods such as alcohol and tobacco products that are harmful to human health. These taxes are given the colorful name of **sin taxes** because they are meant to discourage undesired behavior. Taxes on "sins" can be win-win solutions, because they raise revenue for the government *and* motivate healthier living. Sin taxes have also been considered to address the overconsumption of fatty foods, soft drinks, and other sources of obesity.

**Sin taxes** discourage undesired behavior, such as the use of tobacco products.

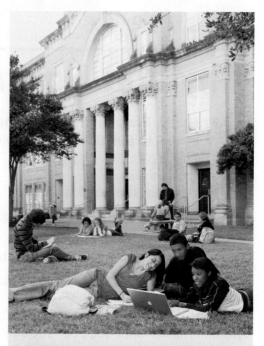

*Tax incentives make it less expensive to go to college.*

**YOUR TURN**

The average American consumes over 50 gallons of soft drinks per year. Do you think a soft drink tax would be appropriate? For what other goods would you recommend sin taxes?

### Encouraging Desirable Activity

Some tax policies are designed to encourage desirable types of spending by taxing them at a lower rate than others, or not at all. For example, the government makes it easier to buy a house by giving a tax break to people who pay interest on home loans. It also provides tax breaks for people who pay college tuition or donate to charity. And the government encourages employers to provide health insurance and retirement

The **tax base** for a particular type of tax is the value of the activities or assets subject to the tax.

benefits to workers by excluding the cost of these benefits from a firm's taxable income. Such provisions are called *tax expenditures* because they cause the government to lose tax revenues as if the money had been spent.

**? DID YOU GET IT?**
Identify three reasons for taxes.

## WHAT IS TAXED AND WHO DOES THE TAXING?

For each particular type of tax, the **tax base** is the value of the activities or assets subject to the tax. There are five main tax bases: the income individuals earn from all sources, the payments firms make to workers, the sales made by firms, the value of property such as your house, and the profits that corporations earn. The taxes on these sources are appropriately called the *income tax*, the *payroll tax*, the *sales tax*, the *property tax*, and the *corporate income tax*.

It is a combination of the tax base and the *tax rate* that determines the amount of revenue collected from a particular type of tax. The **tax rate** is a specific percentage of the tax base that is paid in taxes. For example, the sales tax rate in Michigan is 6 percent. So if you purchased a pair of shoes in Michigan for $100, you would pay 6 percent of that amount, $6, for the sales tax.

Taxes are charged by the federal, state, and local governments. The degree of reliance on particular types of taxes varies with the level of government. Local governments, like your city or township, primarily use property taxes to fund their activities. Most state governments rely heavily on income taxes and sales taxes to fund their activities. And the federal government uses the income tax, various payroll taxes, and corporate taxes to collect revenue.

**DID YOU GET IT?**
If your local government pays the expenses at your school, what type of tax is likely to provide those funds?

## The Federal Income Tax

The federal income tax, which applies to the income that individuals earn from their jobs and investments, raises about $1 trillion in a typical year. This exceeds the amount raised by any other tax. To put this in perspective, note that the amount paid in federal income taxes in the United States exceeded the total size of the economy in all but 13 countries in the world in 2011, including Australia, Turkey, and Taiwan! Figure 28.1 shows the revenue from the federal income tax on individuals among other sources of federal tax revenue in 2011.

Payment of the federal income tax begins with the completion of a form known as a **tax return**. Tax returns are provided by, and returned to, the *Internal Revenue Service (IRS)*, which is the government agency responsible for collecting federal income taxes. The IRS is a branch of the U.S. Treasury Department, whose other services include the production of all U.S. coins and currency. Income taxes normally are due by April 15 of each year. Taxpayers can now pay their taxes and receive any refund they might be owed online.

The laws governing the income tax have become so complicated that more than half of all taxpayers hire a firm such as H&R Block to help them prepare their taxes. About a quarter of taxpayers use a software program such as TurboTax to prepare their tax returns. Whether you seek help or go it alone, as a taxpayer you will need to save information on your various forms of income over the year to feed into your tax calculation. The average person spends 26 hours a year preparing his or her taxes.

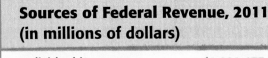

To encourage accuracy, the IRS conducts *audits*, which are examinations of tax records to make sure an individual or a firm paid the correct amount of taxes. Errors or fraudulent information can result in financial penalties. The possibility of an audit makes it important to keep good records to support the information in your tax return. In Module 29 you will see that the federal income tax plays an especially important role in influencing people's behavior.

**DID YOU GET IT?**
How does the IRS motivate people to pay the correct amount of taxes?

The **tax rate** is a specific percentage of the tax base that is paid in taxes.

A **tax return** is a form you will complete and submit to the government when you pay your income taxes. It contains the information used to determine the amount of taxes you owe.

| Sources of Federal Revenue, 2011 (in millions of dollars) | |
|---|---|
| Individual income tax | $1,091,473 |
| Payroll tax | 818,792 |
| Corporate income tax | 181,085 |
| Sales and excise tax | 72,381 |
| Other | 139,735 |
| Total revenue | 2,303,466 |

SOURCE: www.whitehouse.gov/sites/default/files/omb/budget/fy2013/assets/hist.pdf

**Figure 28.1** *Sources of Federal Revenue, 2011*
*Individual income taxes provide the largest share of federal tax revenue, followed by payroll taxes, corporate income taxes, sales and excise taxes, and other taxes.*

## ECONOMICS IN ACTION

# The Origins of the Federal Income Tax

*16ᵗʰ*

*The Congress shall have power to lay and collect taxes on incomes, from whatever source derived, without apportionment among the several States, and without regard to any census or enumeration.*

*The following passage describes the history of the income tax in the United States. You may be surprised to learn that the income tax, as a permanent source of money for the government, did not begin until the twentieth century and that only very rich Americans were required to pay taxes at first.*

For much of its history the United States did not have an income tax. Except for a brief period during and immediately after the Civil War, the nation relied almost exclusively on tariffs—taxes on imported goods—to support government functions. A lively constitutional debate, including a decision by the Supreme Court in 1895, weighed against the creation of an income tax.

But in 1913, the Sixteenth Amendment was ratified, ending all debate about whether an income tax was constitutional. A few months later, Congress enacted an income tax. At its inception, less than 1 percent of Americans paid the individual income tax. Most Americans were exempt from paying the tax because their income did not exceed a relatively high threshold, and even those who were subject to the tax paid at modest rates. By the 1920s, tax rates had

increased and a majority of government revenue came from income taxes that helped fund what was still a small federal government.

World War II created a pressing need for greater government revenues, and the income tax was greatly expanded to fill the shortfall. The threshold for paying taxes was dramatically reduced, subjecting millions of families to the income tax for the first time . . . . By the end of World War II, almost 75 percent of Americans were subject to the income tax, compared with only 5 percent in 1939. The income tax had been transformed from a "class tax" on the wealthiest Americans into a "mass tax" paid by most Americans to fund what had become a substantially larger federal government.

**DID YOU GET IT?**
On what type of tax did the U.S. government rely for much of its early history?

QUOTED FROM The President's Advisory Panel on Tax Reform, November 2005, Final Report, http://govinfo.library.unt.edu/taxreformpanel/final-report/index.html p. 12.

---

### Payroll Taxes

A **payroll tax** is a tax collected from employers on the basis of the wages and salaries paid to workers.

Second in size to the federal income tax is a series of *payroll taxes*. A **payroll tax** is a tax collected from employers on the basis of the wages and salaries paid to workers. The largest payroll tax is the Social Security tax, which funds retirement benefits. The Social Security tax rate in 2012 was 10.4 percent of a worker's earnings up to $110,100 and 0 percent for earnings beyond that amount. The tax payment is paid partly by employees and partly by employers. In 2012, employees paid 4.2

percent and employers paid 6.2 percent. The self-employed paid 10.4 percent. Other payroll taxes are collected to pay for Medicare (health insurance, mostly for those 65 and over), disability insurance, and unemployment insurance.

Payroll taxes differ from income taxes in that they only apply to wage and salary earnings; they do not apply to income earned from savings in a bank account or from the sale of stocks or bonds, for example. Another difference is that the money raised from payroll taxes is dedicated to a particular use, such as funding Social Security benefits, rather than going into a pool of money for more general use, as is the case for income taxes. The pay stub in Figure 28.2 includes the employee's share of Social Security and Medicare payroll taxes as well as federal and state income taxes.

**DID YOU GET IT?**
What is the purpose of the largest U.S. payroll tax?

## Corporate Taxes

Recall that a corporation has a legal status that relieves the firm's shareholders from personal responsibility to pay the firm's debts. The tax on corporate profit, known as the **corporate income tax**, is paid directly by the corporation. Although there are many accounting adjustments that complicate the story, in principle, corporations pay a tax that is equal to 35 percent of their profit.

The share of all tax revenue that comes from the corporate income tax has declined over time. In 1960, for example, 23 percent of all federal government revenue came from the corporate income tax. In 2008, the corporate income tax contributed only 12 percent of federal revenue. In part, the corporate tax's contribution has fallen because changes in tax rules have made it easier for corporations to deduct investment expenses from revenue, thereby lowering the tax base for the corporate income tax.

**DID YOU GET IT?**
In recent years, what has happened to the contribution to the federal government's revenue made by the corporate income tax?

## Property Taxes

A **property tax** is a required payment made by the owners of property, such as land, buildings, boats, and cars. The size of the property tax is typically based on the value of the property. For example, in 2012, the owners of a house that was estimated to be worth $200,000 in

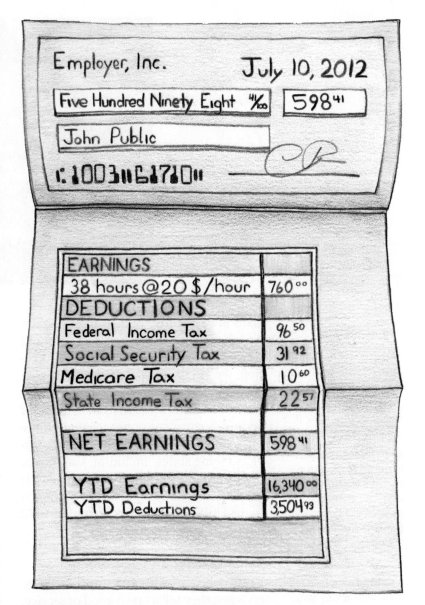

**Figure 28.2** Pay Stub with Tax Deductions
This pay stub, which came attached to the employee's paycheck, shows the employee's share of payroll taxes and the estimated income taxes that have already been deducted from his pay.

Minneapolis, Minnesota, paid a property tax of about $3,500 per year. The owners of a house worth $400,000, also in Minneapolis, paid a higher property tax of around $7,000 per year.

Local governments set the property tax rate. The property tax varies considerably across cities. If that $400,000 house were in Morristown, New Jersey, instead of Minneapolis, for example, the owners would have a property tax of around $10,000 per year. Property

A **corporate income tax** is a tax on corporate profit that is paid directly by the corporation.

A **property tax** is a required payment made by the owners of property, such as land, buildings, boats, and cars.

A neighborhood filled with expensive homes represents a large tax base for the property tax.

An **excise tax** applies to specific goods, such as cigarettes or gasoline, and is typically assessed as a certain amount of money per unit, rather than a percentage of the price.

A **sales tax** is collected from consumers by firms when a taxed good or service is purchased. The tax is then passed on to the government.

taxes are typically used to pay for public schools and other local government services, such as fire and police protection. Property taxes vary because government services are more expensive to provide in some areas than in others and because some areas prefer to spend more on schools and other government services. Some states, including California, limit the amount that can be charged for property tax. In 2010, local governments in the United States raised a total of $472 billion from property taxes.

### Sales Taxes

Firms collect a **sales tax** from consumers when they sell a taxed good or service. This is passed on to the government. The next time you buy something at a store, look carefully at your receipt. It will list the amount of sales tax that you paid. Sales taxes are generally a percentage of the price of the taxed item. The sales tax rate—the percentage paid—is set by state and local governments, so it can vary from state to state and city to city. The states of Alaska, Delaware,

```
*============*
   The Bagel Spot
*============*
*============*
1 Sesame w/    $1.75
cream cheese
2 Poppy w/     $3.50
hummus
1 Iced tea     $2.00
1 Coffee       $1.50
            --------
Subtotal       $8.75
Sales Tax      $0.77
@8.75%
            --------
Total          $9.52
```

The price of a good and the amount you actually pay for it differ by the amount of the sales tax, which is listed separately on the receipt.

Montana, New Hampshire, and Oregon have no state sales tax. In 2011, a total of $462 billion was raised by state and local governments from sales taxes.

Sales taxes apply broadly to goods and services, with exceptions that can include groceries, prescription medication, farm machinery, and solar panels, depending on the state. An **excise tax** is a variation on a sales tax that applies more narrowly to specific goods, such as cigarettes or gasoline. Excise taxes are typically set at a certain amount per unit, such as $2 per pack of cigarettes, rather than being a percentage of the price of the good.

**DID YOU GET IT?**
What is the difference between a sales tax and an excise tax?

### Miscellaneous Taxes

The taxes described so far—the federal income tax, payroll taxes, corporate income taxes, property taxes, and sales taxes—account for most of the revenue raised by federal, state, and local governments. Assorted other taxes are also used, however. For example, some states place a tax on luxury items, such as expensive cars or yachts. Many states charge licensing fees for hunting, fishing, and driving, which closely resemble a tax. And the federal government will collect a gift tax from you if you receive a gift worth more than $13,000. Most

Istockphoto/Thinkstock

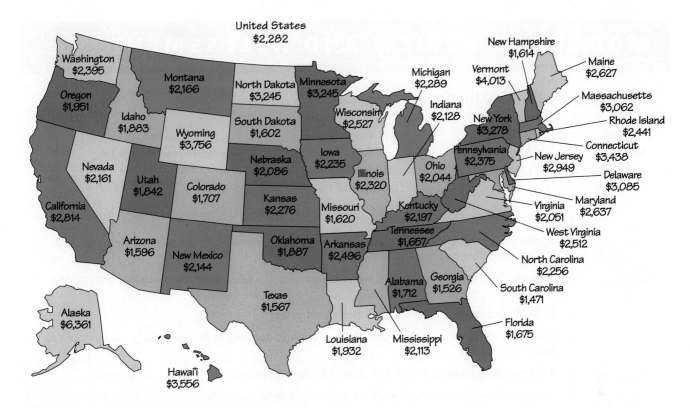

**Figure 28.3** State Taxes per Capita
States differ in the taxes they collect. In 2010, people in Alaska and Vermont paid the most in state taxes on a per-person basis, while people in South Carolina and Georgia paid the least.

SOURCES: www.census.gov/govs/statetax/; http://2010.census.gov/2010census/data/

states and some large cities also raise revenue by imposing their own income tax, which taxes people's earnings from work and other sources. Figure 28.3 shows the average amount of taxes paid per person in each state, including sales taxes, income taxes, and miscellaneous taxes and fees.

## Comparisons with Other Countries

Although it is common for Americans to express concern about paying high taxes, the United States has relatively low taxes compared with other wealthy countries. For 30 well-off countries, the Organization for Economic Cooperation and Development (OECD) calculated the percent of each country's *gross domestic product* (*GDP*)—the value of goods and services produced within the country—that is paid in taxes. Table 28.1 reports the figures for the five highest-taxed countries and the five lowest-taxed countries in 2009. By this measure, the United States has the third

lowest taxes out of all these countries. The taxes Americans pay represent 24.1 percent of GDP. Mexico has the lowest taxes, which account for 17.4 percent of GDP, and Denmark has the highest taxes, which account for 48.1 percent of GDP.

**Table 28.1** **Tax Revenue as a Share of GDP**

| THE FIVE HIGHEST-TAXED COUNTRIES | |
|---|---|
| Denmark | 48.1% |
| Sweden | 46.7 |
| Italy | 43.4 |
| Belgium | 43.2 |
| Norway | 42.9 |
| **THE FIVE LOWEST-TAXED COUNTRIES** | |
| Korea | 25.5% |
| Turkey | 24.6 |
| United States | 24.1 |
| Chile | 18.4 |
| Mexico | 17.4 |

# MODULE 28 REVIEW AND ASSESSMENT

## Summing Up the Key Ideas: Match the following terms to the correct definitions.

A. Taxes
B. Sin tax
C. Tax base
D. Tax rate

E. Tax return
F. Payroll tax
G. Corporate income tax

H. Property tax
I. Sales tax
J. Audit
K. Internal Revenue Service

L. Excise tax
M. Federal income tax

_____ 1. Required payments to the government.

_____ 2. A form that contains information used to determine the amount of taxes owed, to be completed and submitted to the government when taxes are paid.

_____ 3. Collected from consumers by firms with the purchase of a taxed good or service and then passed on to the government.

_____ 4. A specific percentage of the tax base that is paid in taxes.

_____ 5. The examinations of tax records to make sure an individual filer or firm paid the correct amount of taxes.

_____ 6. A tax on corporate profit that is paid directly by the corporation.

_____ 7. The government agency responsible for collecting federal income taxes.

_____ 8. Discourages undesired behaviors, such as the use of tobacco products.

_____ 9. A tax on the income individuals earn from their jobs and investments.

_____ 10. Applies to specific goods, such as cigarettes or gasoline, and is typically assessed as a certain amount of money per unit rather than a percentage of the price.

_____ 11. A required payment made by the owners of property such as land, buildings, boats, and cars.

_____ 12. A tax collected from employers on the basis of the wages and salaries paid to workers.

_____ 13. The value of taxed assets or of economic activity subject to the tax.

## Analyze and Explain: Analyze each of the following and determine if the change would **encourage** or **discourage** the economic activity that is being taxed. Explain your answers.

| | ENCOURAGE OR DISCOURAGE? | EXPLANATION |
|---|---|---|
| 1. The government imposes a $0.10 tax on nonreusable bottles and cans. | _____ | _____ |
| 2. The government increases the amount of charitable contributions that can be deducted from income when calculating income taxes. | _____ | _____ |
| 3. The government decreases the deduction allowed for home loan interest on federal income taxes. | _____ | _____ |
| 4. The government lowers the payroll tax on employers. | _____ | _____ |
| 5. The government imposes a sin tax on foods containing high levels of fat and extremely high levels of sodium. | _____ | _____ |

6. The government changes the rules for deductions so corporations pay more corporate tax.

_____    _____

7. The government removes the sales tax on the purchase of new cars.

_____    _____

8. The government lowers the property tax rate for new factories.

_____    _____

## Apply: Determine the **type of tax** that applies in each of the following situations.

TYPE OF TAX

1. Employers are required to pay a percentage of their employees' wages to the government.

_____

2. People who own houses, boats, cars, and buildings are required to pay a percentage of the value of what they own to the government.

_____

3. The government decides to tax only certain goods at a set amount when those goods are purchased.

_____

4. Corporations are required to pay a percentage of their profits to the government.

_____

5. Employees are required to pay a portion of their earnings as tax to federal, state, and local governments.

_____

MODULE 29

# Responding to Taxes

**KEY IDEA:** People respond to taxes because a tax changes the cost of a particular activity.

**OBJECTIVES**

- **To explain how buyers and sellers respond to taxes.**
- **To show how the burden of paying a tax can shift from one party to another.**
- **To explain the difference between the average tax rate and the marginal tax rate.**

## The Window Tax

In the seventeenth century, England, France, Belgium, and other countries raised tax revenue with what is known as a *window tax*—a tax based on the number of windows in the taxpayer's house. The window tax had several advantages. It was easy to count windows, even from the outside of a house. Wealthier people, who could afford to pay higher taxes, generally had more windows. And a window was easy to define. Yet there was one serious drawback to the window tax: it was not very difficult to remove a window by covering the space with boards or bricks. Indeed, people responded to the tax by reducing the number of windows in their homes. This led to

*The tax on windows caused the occupant of this house in Bruges, Belgium, to fill in his windows with bricks and a drawing over 300 years ago. Evidently, the response to some taxes has a lasting effect.*

darker, drearier dwellings, but people were willing to make that tradeoff for lower taxes.

The window-tax story illustrates how taxes can change people's behavior. In many other situations, people respond to the imposition of a tax by altering their behavior. Taxes raise the prices of certain goods, services, and activities, and from the law of demand we know that people respond to higher prices by cutting back on the quantity demanded. In this module you'll see how taxes cause people to cut back on a lot more than the number of windows on their homes. We'll look more closely at the influence of taxes on buyers and sellers, and at how the tax burden is shared, regardless of who pays the tax.

## HOW BUYERS AND SELLERS RESPOND TO A TAX

As a buyer of movie tickets, you're only willing to pay so much for a ticket. If you have to pay a tax on movie tickets, that reduces the amount you would be willing to pay to the movie theater. That is, a tax affects your demand for movie tickets. Similarly, sellers of movie tickets have a minimum price they would accept for tickets. If sellers have to pay a tax for every ticket sold, the lowest price they would accept for tickets is increased by the amount

of the tax. So a tax affects the supply of movie tickets. In Module 26 you learned that whether a sales (or excise) tax is collected from consumers or firms, it reduces consumption by the same amount. Next we'll revisit how a tax affects the supply or demand curve for a good, and we'll see where the burden of the tax really falls.

### A Tax on Buyers

Recall from Module 28 that an excise tax can apply to a particular good, say hamburgers. Suppose you would pay at most $3.00 for a hamburger. If buyers had to pay a $0.50 tax on every hamburger, what

Alamy

is the highest price you would pay a seller for a hamburger in addition to the $0.50 tax? You'd be willing to pay a seller at most $2.50, because that plus the tax comes to a total of $3.00. If you paid, say, $2.55 to the seller, after paying the tax, you would end up shelling out $2.55 + $0.50 = $3.05 for a hamburger that is only worth $3.00 to you! Let's consider how this excise tax on hamburgers would affect the entire market demand for hamburgers.

In Figure 29.1, the light blue demand curve labeled $D_{Before\ tax}$ shows the market demand curve for hamburgers before there is a tax. Once the $0.50 tax is added to the price, from the standpoint of the consumers, each hamburger becomes more expensive. The added cost of the tax shifts the demand curve downward by $0.50. This is shown by the dark blue demand curve labeled $D_{After\ tax}$ that lies below the original demand curve. At each quantity, the height of the new demand curve is below the height of the old demand curve by $0.50, reflecting the cost of the tax.

The downward shift of the demand curve in Figure 29.1 illustrates the response to an excise tax that is placed on consumers. Consumers respond to the tax by being willing to pay less to firms for any given quantity. Notice that the shift of the demand curve also means consumers want to purchase fewer hamburgers at any given price. That is, a downward shift of demand has the same effect as a leftward shift. To see this, place your finger at any price along the vertical axis and move it rightward to meet the after-tax demand curve. Your finger will be above a lower quantity than if you went all the way to the before-tax demand curve. This shows us that at each price consumers are cutting back on the quantity they demand.

## A Tax on Sellers

Now suppose that the firms, not the consumers, are required to pay the tax. Some taxes work that way: the firms must pay the government a certain amount per unit sold. To explore this possibility, suppose a state requires hamburger

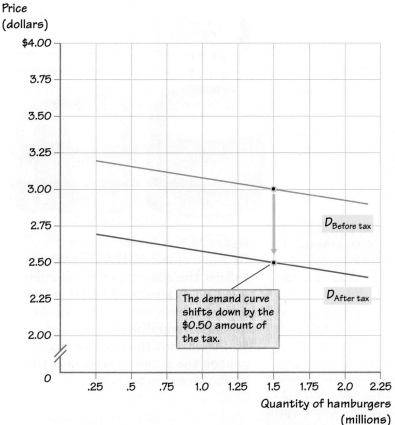

**Figure 29.1** A Tax on Buyers Because of the $0.50 tax, the quantity of hamburgers demanded at a price of $2.50 is the same as the quantity that would have been demanded at a price of $3.00 without the tax. The tax causes the entire demand curve to shift downward by $0.50.

restaurants to pay $0.50 for each hamburger sold. The situation without a tax is illustrated in Figure 29.2 by the light red supply curve labeled $S_{\text{Before tax}}$. Once the tax is subtracted from the price, the sale of each hamburger brings in less money. The after-tax price that the firms receive is $0.50 lower than the price charged. At a price of $3.50, the amount a firm actually gets to keep is $3.00—the $3.50 price minus the $0.50 tax. So with the tax in place, firms supply the same quantity of hamburgers at a price of $3.50 as they did without the tax at a price of $3.00. The added cost of the tax thus shifts the supply curve upward by $0.50, as shown by the dark red supply curve labeled $S_{\text{After tax}}$ that lies above the original supply curve. The shift in the supply curve also means that firms are willing to supply fewer hamburgers at any given price.

## Who Really Pays the Tax?

Several states have considered a tax on fast food, including hamburgers. In 2011, the government of Hungary adopted a "hamburger tax" to be collected from

manufacturers of a wide variety of foods the authorities regard as unhealthy. How do taxes like these affect the price and quantity of hamburgers? And who really pays these taxes? We can extend our analysis of hamburger supply and demand to find the answers.

Let's first consider the case of a tax on buyers of hamburgers. We know that the tax causes demand to fall and the demand curve to shift downward. Figure 29.3 shows how this shift in demand causes the equilibrium price of hamburgers to fall. Initially, the price is $3.00, because that is the price at which the supply and demand curves intersect. If the price stayed at $3.00, the customers would have to pay a total of $3.50 per hamburger after paying the $0.50 tax.

With the tax, however, the demand curve shifts downward while the supply curve remains unchanged. Figure 29.3 shows that the new demand curve intersects the supply curve at a price of $2.60. The equilibrium price has thus fallen from $3.00 to $2.60. The customers must also pay the $0.50 tax,

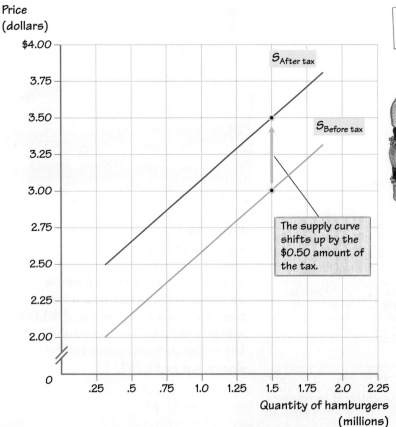

**Figure 29.2** A Tax on Sellers
Because of the $0.50 tax paid by sellers, the quantity of hamburgers supplied at a price of $3.50 is the same as the quantity that would have been supplied at a price of $3.00 without the tax. The tax causes the entire supply curve to shift upward by $0.50.

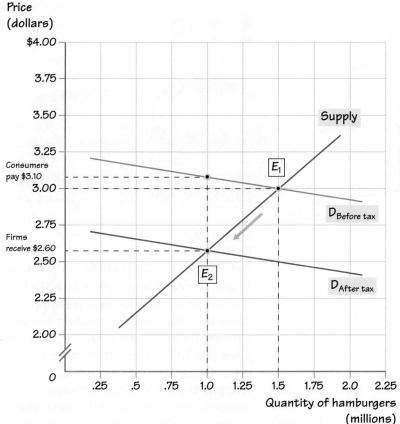

**Figure 29.3** A Tax on Buyers Is Partially Shifted to Sellers

Before the tax, the equilibrium point is $E_1$ and the equilibrium price is $3.00. The tax on consumers causes the demand curve to shift downward, creating a new equilibrium at $E_2$ and a new equilibrium price of $2.60. The consumers also have to pay the $0.50 tax, but the $0.40 drop in price shifts most of the tax burden to the firms. Compared to the original equilibrium price, consumers pay $0.10 more and firms receive $0.40 less.

bringing the after-tax price (the price including the tax) to $3.10, but that is a lot better than paying the original $3.00 price plus the $0.50 tax. So the customers are better off than first appeared. The cost to the customers has only increased by $0.10. Firms, however, make only $2.60 per hamburger after the tax is in place, $0.40 less than the $3.00 they received before the tax. The equilibrium quantity of hamburgers falls from 1.5 million to 1.0 million.

We just saw a surprising result: a $0.50 excise tax placed on hamburger consumers ended up being felt mostly by firms. The important point is that much of the burden of a tax can be shifted to another party. In this case, the seller bears most of the burden of the tax even though the tax is actually collected from the buyers, because the sellers end up charging a lower price than before. In other cases, depending on the shapes of the supply and demand curves, it might be the buyers who bear most of the burden. In general,

tax shifting is the result of adjustments in the equilibrium price that offset some or all of the cost of a tax for the party being taxed and place that cost on someone else.

What if the tax is on firms, as in Hungary? We know that a sales or excise tax on firms shifts the supply curve upward, as was shown in Figure 29.2. To see what happens to the equilibrium price, look at Figure 29.4, where we've put the supply shift together with the unchanged demand curve. Because of the shift in supply, the equilibrium price of hamburgers rises by $0.10, from $3.00 to $3.10. The equilibrium quantity of hamburgers falls from 1.5 million at $E_1$ to 1.0 million at $E_2$, as before.

Notice that the final result for the firms is the same regardless of whether the tax is placed on the firms or the consumers. When the tax was on the consumers, the firms ended up receiving just $2.60 per hamburger. Now that the firms pay the tax, the price increases to $3.10, but the firms have to pay $0.50 in taxes

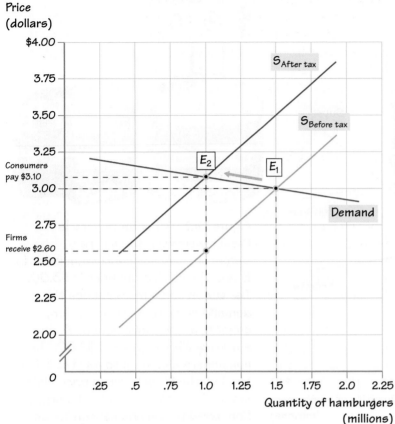

**Figure 29.4** A Tax on Sellers is Partially Shifted to Buyers
Before the tax, the equilibrium point is $E_1$ and the equilibrium price is $3.00. The tax on firms causes the supply curve to shift upward, creating a new equilibrium at $E_2$ and a new equilibrium price of $3.10. After receiving that price, firms have to pay the $0.50 tax, but the $0.10 price increase shifts some of the tax burden to the consumers. Compared to the original equilibrium price, consumers pay $0.10 more and firms receive $0.40 less.

for each hamburger sold, so the firms still end up receiving $2.60 per hamburger after paying the tax.

Likewise, the situation for consumers is the same regardless of whether the tax is placed on them or the firms. If the consumers pay the tax, the price is $2.60 plus the $0.50 tax, so the after-tax price is $3.10 per hamburger. And if the firms pay the tax, the equilibrium price is $3.10 per hamburger. So we have another surprising result: it doesn't matter whether the consumers or the firms are required to pay the tax. Either way, the amount consumers end up paying for a hamburger is the same, the amount firms keep after selling a hamburger is the same, and the equilibrium quantity is the same.

 **DID YOU GET IT?**
**Does it matter whether the buyer or the seller is responsible for paying a tax? Why or why not?**

# RESPONDING TO THE INCOME TAX

The income tax is more complicated than a sales or excise tax and affects many decisions in a taxpayer's life. In 2012, a single adult could earn up to $9,750 without paying income tax. The threshold for income being taxable is lower for people, such as children, who depend on other taxpayers for support and higher for people such as parents who have dependents of their own. Income above the threshold amount is taxed according to a schedule. The 2012 tax rate schedule in Table 29.1 indicates that the first $8,700 of a single person's taxable income was taxed at a rate of 10 percent. The next $26,650—that is, the amount earned from $8,700 to $35,350—was taxed at a 15 percent rate. The tax rate increased in this fashion until it reached the highest rate, which was 35 percent of income earned over $388,350.

The income tax affects people's incentive to work. Suppose Saul, a single nurse, is deciding whether to accept a part-time job. The income tax reduces the amount

| Table 29.1 **The 2012 Federal Income Tax Schedule for Single Individuals** | |
| --- | --- |
| **TAX RATE (PERCENT)** | **TAXABLE INCOME (DOLLARS)** |
| 10% | $0–8,700 |
| 15 | 8,700–35,350 |
| 25 | 35,350–85,650 |
| 28 | 85,650–178,650 |
| 33 | 178,650–388,350 |
| 35 | Over 388,350 |

The tax rate in the left column applies only to the taxable income between the two values in the right column. For example, if you earned taxable income of $10,000, you would only pay 15 percent of the amount above $8,700. For the first $8,700 you would pay only 10 percent.

of money Saul keeps if he takes the job, so if the decision is tough to begin with, the tax may discourage him from joining the workforce. If the job paid $30,000 a year, for example, the income tax would have left him with only $27,397. At that level of income, Saul might have decided that it was not worthwhile to work.

### Average and Marginal Tax Rates

As a worker you will probably have some flexibility in the amount of time you can spend working. The options might include working full-time or part-time, taking two or more jobs, or picking your own work hours as a self-employed worker. Given flexibility, you will make decisions about how much to work by asking yourself, "Should I work a bit more?" over and over until the answer is "No." This is decision making *on the margin*, meaning you weigh the cost and benefit of changing your work effort bit by bit.

*Income taxes can affect the decision of whether, and how much, to work.*

## ECONOMICS IN ACTION BOX

# Why Do People Pay Taxes?

It is everyone's civic duty to pay taxes. This obligation clearly motivates some people to be honest taxpayers. Others, however, are motivated because they fear hefty penalties or time served in prison. Economists have confirmed that people respond to incentives when it comes to paying their taxes. Indeed, 68 percent of the respondents to a survey said they paid their taxes honestly because they had little choice—their income was already reported to the IRS by their employer so they would be in trouble if they underreported. Many also said they feared an IRS audit that would reveal any cheating.

So how much cheating takes place? A careful review of 46,000 tax returns by the IRS found that the average American underpaid his or her taxes by $1,000. This amount was not spread evenly

across all people. Actually, most people did not cheat at all. Those who were most likely to underpay were self-employed, perhaps because they had more ability to hide some of their income from the government. Many people seem to consider the cost and benefit of cheating on their taxes, taking into account the odds of getting caught.

**YOUR TURN**
Would you pay your taxes honestly if you thought you would not get caught if you didn't pay them?

Thinkstock

The **marginal tax rate** is the portion of an additional dollar of income that is paid in taxes.

The **average tax rate** is the proportion of a taxpayer's total taxable income that is paid in taxes.

The effect of the income tax on decisions to work a little more or a little less depends on the **marginal tax rate**, which is the portion of an additional dollar of income that is paid in taxes. If the marginal tax rate increases, you will keep less of each additional dollar earned, so you might decide to work less. Likewise, if the marginal tax rate decreases, you will keep more of each additional dollar of income and you might decide to work more. All the tax rates in Table 29.1 are marginal tax rates because, for each range of income, they tell us the portion of each additional dollar of income that goes to taxes.

It is important to distinguish the marginal tax rate from the *average tax rate*. The **average tax rate** is the proportion of your total taxable income that is paid in taxes. It is found by dividing total taxes paid by total taxable income:

$$\text{average tax rate} = \frac{\text{total taxes paid}}{\text{total taxable income.}}$$

If you earned the same score on every test in school, let's say a 95, your average test score would be 95 as well. The same is true for marginal and average tax rates. Suppose you face the tax schedule in Table 29.1 and your taxable income is less than $8,700. Since your tax rate is 10 percent on every dollar, your marginal tax rate and your average tax rate are both 10 percent. More realistically, just as your score on the next test might not equal your average test score, the tax rate on an additional dollar earned by most workers is different from their average tax rate. For example, suppose you've already earned $8,700 this year. Table 29.1 indicates that the marginal tax rate for incomes between $8,700 and $35,350 is 15 percent, so if you earn another dollar, you will have to pay another $0.15 in taxes. In this case your average tax rate is 10 percent because that's the rate you've paid on every dollar earned so far. But your marginal tax rate is 15 percent because that is the rate you will pay on your next dollar. The marginal tax rate, not the average tax rate, determines how much of your additional income you would pay in taxes and how much you would get to keep. So when it comes to decisions about whether to work more, it is the marginal tax rate that matters. Read the Show Me the Numbers! box for another example of the difference between marginal and average tax rates.

## SHOW ME THE NUMBERS!

# Marginal and Average Tax Rates

Consider a single individual named Terri who earned $14,600 in taxable income in 2012. Recall that the first $8,700 of taxable income is taxed at a 10 percent rate and the next $26,650 is taxed at a 15 percent rate. So Terri paid 10 percent of her first $8,700 in taxes and 15 percent of her remaining $5,900 in taxes. Her total tax bill was

$$(10\% \times \$8,700) + (15\% \times \$5,900) = \$1,755.$$

As a percentage of her total taxable income, Terri's taxes were

$$\$1,755 \div \$14,600 = 0.12 \text{ or } 12\%.$$

This is her average tax rate. While her average tax rate was 12 percent, Terri's marginal tax rate was 15 percent. Why? Because the percent of the last dollar Terri earned that went to taxes was 15 percent. If Terri earns one more dollar, she will have to pay $0.15 more in taxes, not $0.12.

An increase in the marginal tax rate could affect Terri's decision to work more or fewer hours. For example, if her marginal tax rate changed from 15 percent to 25 percent, Terri would be able to keep $0.75 rather than $0.85 out of each additional dollar of earnings for herself. If Terri is like most workers, a higher marginal tax rate that lowered her after-tax earnings would cause her to supply fewer hours of labor.

*Would you work less if your marginal tax rate rose from 15 percent to 25 percent?*

# MODULE 29 REVIEW AND ASSESSMENT

**Summing Up the Key Ideas:** Match the following terms to the correct definitions.

A.  Marginal tax rate
B.  Average tax rate

_____     1.   The fraction of an additional dollar of income that is paid in taxes.
_____     2.   The proportion of total taxable income that is paid in taxes.

**Analyze and Explain:** Analyze each of the following and determine if the change in the tax described would increase or decrease the equilibrium **price** and **quantity** of the good. Explain your answer.

| | PRICE | QUANTITY | EXPLANATION |
|---|---|---|---|
| 1. an increase in a tax on producers | _____ | _____ | _____ |
| 2. a decrease in a tax on consumers | _____ | _____ | _____ |
| 3. an increase in a tax on consumers | _____ | _____ | _____ |
| 4. a decrease in a tax on producers | _____ | _____ | _____ |

**Apply:** For each of the following levels of taxable income, use the information in Table 29.1 to determine the marginal tax rate and the average tax rate.

| TAXABLE INCOME | MARGINAL TAX RATE | AVERAGE TAX RATE |
|---|---|---|
| 1. $0 | _____ | _____ |
| 2. $5,000 | _____ | _____ |
| 3. $30,000 | _____ | _____ |

# MODULE 30

# Evaluating Taxes

**KEY IDEA:** **Taxes are evaluated along two lines: whether they are fair and whether the same amount of money could be raised with less harm to the economy.**

**OBJECTIVES**

- **To explain the concepts of efficiency as it relates to taxes.**
- **To define two measures of tax fairness: vertical equity and horizontal equity.**
- **To evaluate proposals for tax reform.**

## Seeking Equity and Efficiency in Taxation

Recall that the primary purpose of taxes is to raise enough money to pay for the government's activities and programs. The success of the tax system can be judged on two additional criteria: equity and efficiency. Module 4 described equity as the quality of being fair and just. Taxpayers around the world tend to let it be known with angry protests when they don't feel a tax policy meets these standards. Module 2 explained that efficiency is about taking all opportunities to make someone better off without making anyone worse off. Efficiency is important in the context of taxes because although policy makers want to collect the tax revenue needed to provide beneficial government programs, they also want to minimize the tax burden on society. Let's consider both efficiency and equity in more detail, and then consider proposals for tax reform in light of these goals.

*Tax collections allow the government to purchase essential goods and services, but an efficient tax system minimizes the burden of paying those taxes.*

## EFFICIENCY

An efficient economy produces the greatest possible net gains for society. Taxes are part of an efficient economic system because they allow the government to provide public goods such as national defense and fire protection, the benefits of which exceed the costs. However, the collection of taxes imposes costs beyond the actual amount paid to the government. The added costs of sales and excise taxes come in the form of lost gains from trades between buyers and sellers that would otherwise take place but are discouraged by taxation. The goal is to set up a tax system that collects a given amount of revenue at the lowest possible cost to society. If the lost gains from trade are larger than necessary, the tax system is not efficient.

The hamburger tax discussed in Module 29 provides an example of how taxes can reduce the gains from trade. We saw that a tax on sellers causes the supply curve to shift upward, raising the equilibrium price. Because the price is higher, the quantity demanded falls. By cutting back on the quantity demanded, the tax eliminates the sale of hamburgers that cost less to make than the value they provided to customers. In this way, the tax reduces the gains from trade.

Any time the quantity of output differs from that which would maximize the gains from trade, the resulting harm is a loss of efficiency. Just as sales and excise taxes reduce the quantity of goods below the efficient level, income taxes reduce the quantity of labor below the efficient level. No wonder

Thinkstock

Americans have complained about taxes since at least as far back as the Molasses Act of 1733, which imposed taxes on molasses, sugar, wine, and other imported goods.

## Improving Tax Efficiency

Taxes are generally more efficient if they cause people to change their behavior relatively little. An exception was noted in Chapter 9, where we saw that taxes on activities that cause negative externalities such as pollution can increase economic efficiency by causing a significant change in people's behavior. Three additional points should be considered to improve tax efficiency:

**1.  All similar goods should be taxed at the same rate.** This will prevent people from substituting one good for another just because of the differential tax treatment. Suppose, for example, that hamburgers were taxed at the grocery store but not at fast food restaurants. This tax policy would be inefficient because some people would be swayed to drive to a fast food restaurant to buy a burger instead of grilling one at home. It is wasteful to drive to a restaurant if one would rather eat at home, so the change in behavior caused by the tax reduces efficiency.

**2.  A low marginal tax rate changes people's behavior less than a high marginal tax rate.** It is rational for people to make decisions on the basis of marginal benefits and marginal costs. If the marginal tax rate on income, for example, is relatively high, the marginal benefit of working another hour is relatively low. As a result, more people will choose to work less than if a lower marginal tax rate were applied.

**3.  Simple can be better.** A tax system that makes it easy to calculate and pay taxes reduces unproductive taxpayer effort. The U.S. tax system is so complex that nearly $150 billion is spent by families, businesses, and

the government each year to make sure that the right amount of taxes is paid and collected. A federal tax panel noted that this is more than the amount spent each year on TVs, household electricity, or breakfast cereal.

 **DID YOU GET IT?**
How can the efficiency of a tax system be improved?

# TAX FAIRNESS

Economists use two standards to evaluate fairness: *vertical equity* and *horizontal equity*. **Vertical equity** means that those who have a greater ability to pay taxes make a larger tax payment. **Horizontal equity** means that those with the same ability to pay taxes make the same tax payment. Let's explore how these standards of fairness are measured and achieved.

## Vertical Equity

Income serves as an available measure of people's ability to pay taxes, so we can measure vertical equity by looking at what happens to the amount of taxes people pay as their income increases. A tax is **progressive** if people with a higher income pay a higher share of their income in taxes. An example of a progressive tax is the U.S. federal income tax. Those with higher incomes generally pay a higher share of their income in taxes.

*Taxes have long caused a stir. The Boston Tea Party was a protest against a change in tea taxes in 1773 that helped spark the American Revolution.*

**Vertical equity** means that those who have a greater ability to pay taxes make a larger tax payment.

**Horizontal equity** means that those with the same ability to pay taxes make the same tax payment.

A tax is **progressive** if people with a higher income pay a higher share of their income in taxes.

Nathaniel Currier

A tax is **regressive** if people with a higher income pay a lower share of their income in taxes.

A tax is regressive if people with a higher income pay a lower share of their income in taxes. An example of a regressive tax is a sales tax on groceries. Suppose Jenna earns $1 million per year, 100 times as much income as Neil, who earns $10,000 per year. If they each bought the same amount of groceries each year and paid $1,000 in sales taxes, that would represent one tenth of one percent of Jenna's income, but 10 percent of Neil's income. People with high incomes tend to spend relatively more on groceries, but their expenditures typically do not increase in proportion to their income. That is, it's unlikely that Jenna would buy 100 quarts of milk for every one that Neil buys. So the sales tax on groceries is regressive.

A tax is **proportional** or **flat** if everyone pays the same share of their income in taxes, regardless of their level of income

A tax is **proportional** or **flat** if everyone pays the same share of their income in taxes, say 10 percent, regardless of their level of income. No U.S. tax is truly proportional, although a few come fairly close. Expenditures on property increase more or less in proportion to income, so a property tax can resemble a proportional tax. And a payroll tax is proportional up to the income limit beyond which the payroll tax is not collected.

Progressive taxes provide the highest degree of vertical equity because not only do people with higher incomes pay more in taxes, they pay a higher share of their income in taxes. Proportional taxes achieve vertical equity because they require higher payments from people with higher incomes, but everyone pays the same *share* of their income. Regressive taxes may or may not provide vertical equity. For example, in the case of the sales tax on groceries, people with higher incomes devote a relatively low *percentage* of their income to groceries, but they still spend relatively more on groceries and thus pay more for the tax. A tax on something that lower-income people spend more money on than higher-income people, such as used cars, would be so regressive that it would not achieve vertical equity. Instead, the people with the lowest

ability to pay would end up paying the largest amount in taxes because they spend more on used cars.

**DID YOU GET IT?**
What is vertical equity?

## Horizontal Equity

Horizontal equity requires that people who have the same level of income pay the same amount in taxes. The basis for this idea is straightforward: you probably would not think it was fair if someone who made just as much money as you paid less in taxes than you did.

The U.S. tax system is sufficiently complicated that people with the same income often do, in fact, pay different amounts in taxes. Most importantly, some different sources of income are taxed at different rates. For example, investment income that is received in a special, tax-free savings account is not taxed at all, while investment income that is received from an ordinary bank account is taxed at a taxpayer's ordinary income tax rate. Thus two people who have the same amount of investment income but have their savings invested in different types of accounts will pay different amounts in income taxes. As a taxpayer, you will want to seek untaxed accounts for your savings if possible.

As another example in which horizontal equity fails, consider the effect of state income taxes. Some states have higher income tax rates than others. Several states, including Florida and Washington, have no income tax. Citizens in high-tax states with the same income as those in low-tax or no-tax states pay different amounts in taxes. In some cases this horizontal inequity affects where people choose to live.

**DID YOU GET IT?**
What is horizontal equity?

## Tax Fairness in Practice

The recipe for the perfect tax is not obvious. The progressive taxes offer vertical equity, but taxes that are very progressive may lead people to work less than they would under less progressive taxes. And the goal of horizontal equity conflicts, for example, with the goal of letting each state choose its own income tax rate. Whether a tax is considered "fair" depends on judgments about the importance of vertical and horizontal equity. Tax fairness also depends on how the tax burden is shifted from one party to another.

Figure 30.1 shows estimates of the percent of income that people with various income levels pay in federal taxes. It is clear from the figure that the federal income tax is progressive. The highest-earning 20 percent of families paid 23.2 percent of their income in taxes. By contrast, the lowest-earning 20 percent of families paid 1 percent of their income in taxes. In terms of dollars, the bottom 20 percent had an average income of $23,500 and paid $235 in taxes, while the top 20 percent had an average income of $223,500 and paid $51,852 in taxes.

## YOUR TURN

Do you think the sizes of the tax payments just mentioned are fair? Do you think the poor should pay more or less in taxes? Do you think the wealthy should pay more or less?

# THE FUTURE DIRECTION OF TAXES

The United States has a problem: the federal government is spending more money than it collects in taxes. As a result, it is likely that major changes will be made to tax policy in the near future. These changes could have a dramatic effect on you and your family, so they are worth following in the news. Some proposed reforms include broadening the tax base, replacing the income tax with a sales tax, and replacing the progressive income tax with a flat tax. Let's explore each type of tax reform.

## Broadening the Tax Base

This is the least radical change. In 2005 a federal commission recommended an expansion of the tax base by including employer-provided health insurance and interest payments on home loans (called *mortgages*) in taxable income. In 2011 the Obama Administration also proposed reductions in the tax breaks for mortgage interest payments for high-income taxpayers. Currently, these payments are not taxed. Broadening the tax base in these ways would increase horizontal equity because, as it is now, two people who receive the same total compensation but receive different shares of their compensation as health insurance or pay different

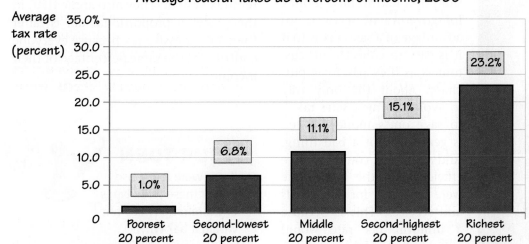

**Average Federal Taxes as a Percent of Income, 2009**

Average tax rate (percent)

- Poorest 20 percent: 1.0%
- Second-lowest 20 percent: 6.8%
- Middle 20 percent: 11.1%
- Second-highest 20 percent: 15.1%
- Richest 20 percent: 23.2%

Family income

**Figure 30.1** Average Federal Taxes as a Percent of Income, 2009 Families with more income pay a higher portion of their income in federal taxes.

SOURCE: Congressional Budget Office

*The Obama administration proposed a broadening of the tax base for high-income taxpayers.*

amounts in mortgage interest pay different amounts in taxes.

These changes would also increase vertical equity. Higher-income people tend to receive more of their income in nontaxed forms of compensation such as health insurance, so taxing those types of compensation would cause a relatively large increase in the amount that higher-income people pay in taxes. Taxing all forms of compensation and expenditure equally could also increase efficiency, because differential treatment causes people to substitute expenditures that receive preferential tax treatment for those that do not, as discussed in the previous section. The difficulty with expanding the tax base, however, is that interest groups, such as home builders and insurance companies, are opposed to it. In addition, many people have gotten used to the tax breaks in our current tax system and oppose change.

## A Nationwide Sales Tax

*Many European countries use a national sales tax to help fund government services.*

Many European countries use a sales tax (also called a consumption tax) to raise money for government services. An advantage of a sales tax is that it is easy to collect from customers as they pay for a purchase. About the only way to avoid paying a sales tax is to save one's money, which is generally not a bad thing. And a sales tax could improve efficiency if the same rate were charged for all goods and services. This is because a uniform tax rate would avoid incentives for people to

substitute items with low tax rates for items with high tax rates, such as the switch from hamburgers from grocery stores to hamburgers from restaurants, as mentioned earlier.

A possible disadvantage of a nationwide sales tax is that the poor would pay the same tax rate as the rich. In fact, the poor would pay a larger share of their income in taxes than the rich, because the poor spend a larger share of their income on consumption than the rich. For example, someone who earns $10,000 a year is likely to spend all of it on consumption, so that person would pay taxes on $10,000 worth of purchases. In contrast, someone who earns $1,000,000 a year is unlikely to spend it all. If $100,000 of the $1,000,000 is spent on consumption, that person would pay a sales tax on one tenth of her income. Because people with low incomes pay taxes on a larger share of their income than people with high incomes, a sales tax is regressive.

## A Flat Tax

A flat tax requires all tax payers to pay a constant percentage of their income—say 20 percent—in taxes. The flat tax, being proportional, would move America away from its baseline of a progressive income tax. Nevertheless, supporters of the flat tax argue that it would improve the efficiency of the tax system because the marginal tax rate would be lower for high-income people than under the current tax system. They also argue that, in their view, a proportional tax is fairer than a progressive tax because everyone contributes the same percentage of their income.

**YOUR TURN**

If you were to choose one of these three types of tax reform, which one would it be? Why?

# MODULE 30 REVIEW AND ASSESSMENT

## Summing Up the Key Ideas: Match the following terms to the correct definitions.

A. Vertical equity
B. Horizontal equity
C. Progressive tax

D. Regressive tax
E. Proportional tax

_____ 1. Means that those with the same ability to pay taxes make the same tax payment.

_____ 2. If everyone pays the same share of their income in taxes, regardless of their level of income.

_____ 3. If people with a higher income pay a lower share of their income in taxes.

_____ 4. If people with a higher income pay a higher share of their income in taxes.

_____ 5. Means that those who have a greater ability to pay taxes make a larger tax payment.

## Analyze and Explain: Indicate whether the following changes would **improve** or **reduce tax efficiency** and explain your answers.

|  | EFFICIENCY: IMPROVED OR REDUCED? | EXPLANATION |
|---|---|---|
| 1. The tax code is simplified, making it much easier for people to complete their own tax returns. | _____ | _____ |
| 2. The government imposes taxes on economic activity with negative externalities and subsidizes economic activity with positive externalities. | _____ | _____ |
| 3. Marginal income tax rates are significantly increased. | _____ | _____ |

## Apply: Determine if each of the taxes listed below is **progressive**, **proportional**, or **regressive**.

PROGRESSIVE, PROPORTIONAL, OR REGRESSIVE?

1. a tax of $100 on each resident of a town _____

2. an income tax of 10% on every taxpayer _____

3. a tax of $1,000 on a person earning $10,000 and a tax of $1,500 on a person earning $20,000 _____

4. a tax of 10% on the first $50,000 of income, 20% on the next $50,000 of income, 30% on the next $50,000, and 40% on all income over $150,000 _____

## Bloomberg Businessweek®

# Both Parties Misunderstand Taxes

STEPHEN L. CARTER

SEPTEMBER 01, 2011

Taxes are in bad political odor these days. True, there has been no era in which taxation was popular, but we seem to have reached a moment of particular confusion. We have one major party dedicated to the bizarre principle that nothing that is not taxed now should ever be taxed again, and another dedicated to the equally bizarre principle that taxes are a magical elixir that will eliminate the nation's indebtedness while touching only those who happen to own private jets. I would like to say a word or two in defense of taxation, and then to suggest that each party is on the track of an important truth. Taxes will inevitably go up. The Democrats are right about that much. Alas, they get the reason wrong every time they try to explain. The reason taxes must rise is not that millionaires and billionaires have too much money, or that corporations aren't paying their fair share. It's that the federal government, under the joint leadership of the two parties, has fallen so deeply into debt that its need has grown desperate. Under no

plausible scenario are we going to grow ourselves out of the remarkable hole we have dug.

The Republicans, too, are wrong, in their opposition to any increase in any taxes for any reason. But they are right to criticize the Democrats' constant chatter about asking the rich to sacrifice—this makes it sound as if taxes are the punishment one suffers for success. And they are right in admitting, in their unguarded moments, that the tax base is too narrow.

The progressive tax structure rests upon the notion that those who earn more should be taxed at a higher rate. But progressivity is merely one factor in working out tax rates. It isn't the reason taxes exist. They exist to raise revenue, to be used to pay back the government's debt and to fund important services the government must provide. These are points easily forgotten in the rhetoric of the day. And there isn't nearly enough income in the upper bracket to make a serious dent in the nation's debt.

A vast majority of Americans should be willing to pay taxes. All but the very poorest should contribute financially to the great American experiment. The shared sacrifice should certainly be progressive, but it should also be shared. When almost half of households pay no federal income taxes, the concept of shared sacrifice vanishes, and America becomes not that to which we contribute but that from which we receive.

Taxes are in themselves neither good nor evil, and both parties should stop talking as though they are. They are simply one among many ways of raising revenue. There was a time when the federal government relied almost entirely on import duties for its income. Lately its addiction has been to borrowed money. Perhaps a future generation will discover some other magical means for supporting the state. In the meanwhile, if indeed we need to sacrifice, let's at least sacrifice together.

---

**DID YOU READ IT?**

1) Why are taxes necessary?

2) What does it mean to have a "progressive" tax system?

**WHAT DO YOU THINK?**

1) Do you agree with the author of the article that the tax burden in the United States should be shared? If so, how should it be shared?

2) What are the costs of taxation?

EXCERPTED FROM www.businessweek.com/news/2011-09-01/both-parties -misunderstand-taxes-stephen-l-carter.html

# CHAPTER 10 REVIEW AND SELF-ASSESSMENT

## REVIEW

### Points to Remember

#### MODULE 28: WHY AND HOW ARE WE TAXED?

1. **Taxes** are required payments to the government.

2. **Sin taxes** discourage undesired behaviors, such as the use of tobacco products.

3. The **tax base** for a particular type of tax is the value of taxed assets or economic activity subject to the tax.

4. The **tax rate** is a specific percentage of the tax base that is paid in taxes.

5. A **tax return** is a form you complete and submit to the government when you pay your income taxes. It contains the information used to determine the amount of taxes you owe.

6. A **payroll tax** is a tax collected from employers on the basis of the wages and salaries paid to workers.

7. A **corporate income tax** is a tax on corporate profit that is paid directly by the corporation.

8. A **property tax** is a required payment made by the owners of property, such as land, buildings, boats, and cars.

9. A **sales tax** is collected from consumers by firms when a taxed good or service is purchased and then passed on to the government.

10. An **excise tax** applies to specific goods, such as cigarettes or gasoline, and is typically assessed as a certain amount of money per unit, rather than a percentage of the price.

#### MODULE 29: RESPONDING TO TAXES

11. The **marginal tax rate** is the fraction of an additional dollar of income that is paid in taxes.

12. The **average tax rate** is the proportion of a taxpayer's total income that is paid in taxes.

#### MODULE 30: EVALUATING TAXES

13. **Vertical equity** means that those who have a greater ability to pay taxes make a larger tax payment.

14. **Horizontal equity** means that those with the same ability to pay taxes make the same tax payment.

15. A tax is **progressive** if people with a higher income pay a higher share of their income in taxes.

16. A tax is **regressive** if people with a higher income pay a lower share of their income in taxes.

17. A tax is **proportional** or **flat** if everyone pays the same share of their income in taxes, regardless of their level of income.

## SELF-ASSESSMENT

The following questions are the type your teacher might ask you on a quiz or a test. Practice with these in order to improve your performance on class tests.

### Multiple-Choice Questions

1. The government imposes a tax of $1,000 per household to fund a new program. This tax is a

   a. progressive tax.
   b. proportional tax.
   c. regressive tax.
   d. flat tax.

2. The largest source of revenue for the federal government has as its base

   a. sales.
   b. property.
   c. wealth.
   d. income.

Answer the next two questions based on the following table.

| INCOME (DOLLARS) | TAX PAID (DOLLARS) |
|---|---|
| $10,000 | $1,000 |
| 20,000 | 2,000 |
| 40,000 | 4,000 |
| 80,000 | 8,000 |

3. This tax is

   a. progressive.
   b. proportional.
   c. regressive.
   d. none of the above.

4. If numbers in the Tax Paid column were doubled,

   a. the tax would become progressive.
   b. the tax would become regressive.
   c. the tax would become vertical.
   d. the progressive, regressive, or proportional nature of the tax would be unchanged.

5. A tax system in which individuals with the same ability to pay taxes make the same tax payment would rank high on

   a. vertical equity.
   b. horizontal equity.
   c. progressivity.
   d. regressivity.

6. Which of the following is **not** considered a reason to tax?

   a. a way for the government to raise revenue
   b. a way for the government to encourage desirable activity
   c. a way for the government to redistribute income
   d. a way for the government to discourage undesirable activity

7. A flat tax is

   a. a progressive tax.
   b. a regressive tax.
   c. a proportional tax.
   d. none of the above.

Answer the next two questions based on the following table.

| INCOME (DOLLARS) | TAX RATE (PERCENT) |
|---|---|
| $0–10,000 | 0% |
| 10,001–40,000 | 10 |
| 40,001–100,000 | 20 |
| 100,001–250,000 | 30 |
| 250,001 and up | 40 |

8. What is the marginal tax rate paid by a person whose income increases from $100,000 to $125,000?

   a. 0%
   b. 10%
   c. 20%
   d. 30%

9. The average tax rate for a person earning $175,000 would be

   a. 0%.
   b. less than 30%.
   c. 30%.
   d. greater than 30%.

## Constructed Response Question

For each of the following taxes or fees, indicate who directly pays it, what the tax base is, and what level of government collects it.

| TAX | WHO PAYS? | TAX BASE | LEVEL OF GOVERNMENT |
|---|---|---|---|
| Individual income tax | | | |
| Payroll tax | | | |
| Corporate income tax | | | |
| Property taxes | | | |
| Sales tax | | | |
| Excise tax on alcohol | | | |
| Driver's license fee | | | |
| Gift tax | | | |

**CHAPTER 11 & YOU** You may already choose to participate in the labor market as a part-time worker. When your school days are over you will have more decisions to make about whether to work, where to work, and how much to work. These decisions will help determine what you can afford to buy, your quality of life, and where you spend your time. Later in life you may find yourself in the role of deciding how many workers to hire. In this chapter you will learn more about the job market, including what you can do to get a better job and why some workers are paid considerably more than others. The information in this chapter might also bring you closer to figuring out which job is best for you.

# Labor Markets

MODULE 31: **Labor Demand**

MODULE 32: **Labor Supply and Labor Market Equilibrium**

MODULE 33: **The Skills of Workers and the Quality of Jobs**

## HITTING THE JACKPOT

Working at a meat processing plant is challenging. So what would you do if you worked at such a plant and suddenly won millions of dollars? That is the dilemma that Dun Tran, a 34-year-old refugee from Vietnam, and seven of his coworkers faced in 2006. Mr. Tran bought the winning $365 million Powerball ticket, one of the largest lottery prizes in U.S. history, on behalf of himself and his lucky coworkers from the ConAgra meat processing plant in Lincoln, Nebraska. Mr. Tran said he planned to use his winnings to stop working and spend more time with his wife and young son, and "play a little again." Most of the other winners also planned to use their bounty to retire.

The lucky workers at the ConAgra plant are not alone. Research shows that workers who win large lottery jackpots or receive large monetary gifts from relatives are less likely to work than others who win small prizes or do not receive monetary gifts. The fact that many people work less when they have plenty of money suggests that payday is a primary motivation for those who do work. But people work for many reasons apart from money; for example, it helps them make friends, feel good about themselves, avoid boredom, develop skills, and gain experience. Remember that economics is the study of choices involving scarcity, so the scarcity of friends, self-esteem, excitement, skills, and experience

*After eight meat packing workers in Nebraska shared a $365 million lottery jackpot, most of them decided to retire. How would wealth affect your decision to work?*

puts all these benefits under the umbrella of economic decision making. Tradeoffs among these benefits can also explain such things as why people do volunteer work; it might give them good experience and make them feel they are making a contribution to society. It can also explain why some people continue in a job they find boring; it may pay so well that they are willing to tolerate the boredom.

Economic reasoning can help us understand the amount of time people spend working, the number of workers firms hire, and the amount of money people earn from their jobs. Module 31 explores the demand for labor and the sensitivity of labor demand to changes in the wage. Module 32 discusses the supply of labor, the determination of wage and employment levels, and implications for policies such as minimum wage laws. Module 33 considers additional factors that influence workers' wages. These include education, dangerous working conditions, discrimination, labor unions, and requirements for work-related licenses.

## BOTTOM LINE

Employment levels and wages are determined by supply and demand in the labor market, with the additional influence of government policy and institutions such as labor unions.

# MODULE 31

# Labor Demand

**KEY IDEA:** The demand for labor is determined by how much workers contribute to the revenue firms receive.

**OBJECTIVES**

- **To describe the market for labor.**
- **To explain how a profit-maximizing firm determines the quantity of labor to hire.**
- **To describe how the demand for labor is derived from the demand for goods and services.**

*The decisions of how many cooks to hire and how much to pay them are guided by economic principles.*

## The Puzzles of Staffing

There are some 23,500 restaurants in New York City. The owners of each restaurant must decide how many workers to hire as cooks, managers, cashiers, wait staff, and dishwashers. And then there's the issue of how much to pay each type of worker. Economic guidelines assist with these daunting tasks. The highest wage an owner should be willing to pay a worker depends on the worker's contribution to revenue. If another cook would increase a restaurant's revenue by $50 per hour, the owner would pay a new cook no more than $50 as an hourly wage. This module explains how such reasoning underpins the demand curve for labor. You'll also learn that, when there are many buyers and sellers of labor, the wage paid by individual employers is largely determined by supply and demand in the labor market.

## THE LABOR MARKET

Module 6 explained that labor, the time and effort people put into the production process, is known as a factor of production and sold in a factor market appropriately called the *labor market*. The labor market is not a place, but a collection of workers interested in selling their services and firms interested in hiring them. Separate markets for capital and other factors of production function in similar ways. Firms purchase or rent the services of factors of production in order to produce output. In the case of labor, this typically amounts to firms paying workers an annual salary or an hourly wage in exchange for their work.

When the amount of time each person works is standard—perhaps 40 hours per week or 8 hours per day—we can measure the quantity of labor in terms of the number of workers hired. To handle situations in which some workers work more than others, an alternative is to measure the number of hours that workers spend working for the firms that hire them. One hour of work by one worker is called a *labor hour*.

To simplify matters, we first treat all workers as if they were identical. That is, we assume that any worker would produce the same quantity of output if he or she worked for the same employer under the same circumstances using the same amount of capital. When hired, workers are also known as *employees*, and the firms hiring them are also known as *employers*.

## A Perfectly Competitive Labor Market

You learned in Module 13 that a perfectly competitive product market is made up of many firms and consumers, and that no individual firm can influence the market price. The story is similar for a perfectly competitive labor market: there are many firms and workers, and no individual firm can influence the market wage. Rather, the wage is determined by the equilibrium of supply and demand in the labor market. As a small fish in a big ocean of employers, each firm is powerless and must take the market wage as given. For example, if a restaurant tried to hire dishwashers in a perfectly competitive labor market for less than the wage paid at other restaurants, the workers would head for one of the many other restaurants that pay more. Only by matching the market wage can the restaurant attract the dishwashers it needs.

There are plenty of situations in which some firms could pay lower wages than others. For instance, a restaurant with particularly comfortable working conditions or relatively attractive health insurance benefits could pay dishwashers less than other restaurants. However, these situations violate the conditions for perfect competition. In a perfectly competitive labor market, all firms are identical.

Another condition for perfect competition in a labor market is that workers must be able to move freely from one job to another when a better opportunity arises. This is called *costless mobility*. Dishwashers in New York City may be able to walk across the street to find better work. If contract restrictions prevent basketball players like Kobe Bryant of the Los Angeles Lakers from easily moving to another team, then there is not costless mobility in the labor market for professional basketball players. Costless mobility is also prevented by *noncompete clauses* that prevent workers from joining competing firms. For example, an accounting firm may require an employee to sign a noncompete clause saying she will not work for another accounting firm in the same city for at least two years. These barriers to changing jobs would not exist in a perfectly competitive labor market.

In a perfectly competitive labor market, the wage is determined by the equilibrium of supply and demand. Because supply equals demand at the equilibrium wage, we know that the number of labor hours workers want to provide at that wage equals the number of labor hours firms want to purchase. In other words, each employer can hire all the workers he or she desires at the equilibrium wage, and anyone who wants to work for the equilibrium wage can find a job.

Some of the conditions for perfect competition in the labor market may seem unrealistic. We will see that in some cases the model works well, and in others, adjustments in the model lead to satisfying accuracy. The key question for economists is whether the model provides useful predictions of behavior in the actual labor market. For labor markets that come close to meeting the conditions of perfect competition, it does.

*In a perfectly competitive labor market, workers can easily switch between employers. Restaurant workers can often find similar work just down the street. Kobe Bryant's nearly $90 million contract with the Los Angeles Lakers creates barriers to such a switch.*

## A Commonsense View of Hiring

Before we delve more deeply into the demand for labor, let's consider the basic logic of the hiring decision. It stands to reason that a firm will only hire you if the value of what you produce is more than the amount the firm must pay to hire you. Likewise, if the value of what an existing employee produces falls below the cost of employing him or her, perhaps because the price of the firm's product falls, then the firm will let the employee go.

As with all good *"How much?"* decisions, profit-maximizing employers decide how many workers to hire by hiring more and more until the marginal benefit of another worker falls to equal the marginal cost. Next we'll examine what the marginal benefit of another worker is, why it falls, and what the marginal cost of hiring another worker is. We'll do this by exploring the hiring decisions of a familiar, fictional firm.

**DID YOU GET IT?**
What is the labor market?

## HOW MANY WORKERS SHOULD BLADE RUNNER HIRE?

Let's revisit good old Blade Runner, the lawn mowing firm introduced in Chapter 5. Table 31.1 provides Blade Runner's

**NOW HIRING**

*The best hiring decisions are made on the basis of marginal analysis: does the marginal benefit of another worker exceed the marginal cost?*

production schedule when the firm has three lawn mowers for its workers to share. The first three workers hired have full use of a mower and the productivity it allows. Because the number of lawn mowers is fixed in the short run, after the third worker is hired, each additional worker necessitates more sharing of mowers and thus contributes less to output than the previous worker. That is, the *marginal product of labor*—the additional output produced by the last worker hired—eventually decreases as more workers are hired. Recall from

**Table 31.1  Blade Runner's Production Schedule**

| QUANTITY OF WORKERS | NUMBER OF LAWNS MOWED | MARGINAL PRODUCT (MP) | VALUE OF MARGINAL PRODUCT (VMP = MP × PRICE) |
|---|---|---|---|
| 1 | 12 | 12 | 480 |
| 2 | 24 | 12 | 480 |
| 3 | 36 | 12 | 480 |
| 4 | 45 | 9 | 360 |
| 5 | 53 | 8 | 320 |
| 6 | 60 | 7 | 280 |
| 7 | 66 | 6 | 240 |
| 8 | 71 | 5 | 200 |
| 9 | 75 | 4 | 160 |
| 10 | 78 | 3 | 120 |
| 11 | 80 | 2 | 80 |
| 12 | 81 | 1 | 40 |
| 13 | 80 | -1 | -40 |

Module 15 that this tendency for the marginal product to decrease as more of a variable input (labor) is used in combination with a fixed input (mowers) is known as the *law of diminishing returns*. We will soon see that the demand curve for labor is downward sloping due to this characteristic decrease in the additional output gained by hiring more and more workers.

The first column of Table 31.1 shows the various quantities of workers that Blade Runner could employ. The second column shows the total output of those workers in a week. For example, 7 workers could mow 66 lawns and 8 workers could mow 71 lawns. The third column shows the marginal product of labor. For example, the eighth worker causes the number of lawns mowed to increase from 66 to 71, so the marginal product of the eighth worker is 71 − 66 = 5 lawns. The fourth column shows the **value of the marginal product** of labor, which is the marginal product of labor multiplied by the $40 price that Blade Runner charges per lawn. The value of the marginal product tells us the increase in Blade Runner's revenue as the result of each additional worker hired and thus indicates the dollar value of each worker's contribution to output. The value of the marginal product of the eighth worker is 5 lawns × $40 per lawn = $200.

As a profit maximizer, Blade Runner tries to hire the quantity of workers that will result in the highest profit possible. If the weekly wage for its workers is $200, Blade Runner will make a profit on the first 7 employees and break even on the eighth employee, because the value of the marginal product of each of the first 7 workers is greater than $200 and the value of the marginal product of the eighth worker is exactly $200. If Blade Runner hires a ninth worker, its profit will fall because the wage of $200 exceeds the value of the additional output the ninth worker produces, $160. So the firm would maximize profit by hiring 8 workers (assuming it hires the eighth worker on which it breaks even).

The **value of the marginal product** of an input, such as labor, is the marginal product of that input multiplied by the price of the output being produced. This value indicates the additional revenue gained from hiring one more unit of that input.

## A Rule for Choosing the Right Number of Workers

This hiring story illustrates an important rule: a profit-maximizing employer in a competitive labor market hires workers up until the value of the marginal product of labor equals the wage. Why? Because the difference between these values is the net gain an employer receives from each worker hired. As the gap between the value of the marginal product and the wage disappears, so does the reason to hire another worker. If the value of the marginal product of the last worker hired is less than the wage, the firm is paying more to that worker than it gains from hiring him or her, and the firm will have a higher profit if it does not hire that worker.

*Hiring rule for a profit-maximizing employer in a perfectly competitive labor market:*

*Hire more workers until*

*Wage = Value of Marginal Product of Labor =*

*Marginal Product of Labor × Price.*

**DID YOU GET IT?**
Up until what point does an employer hire workers in a perfectly competitive labor market?

## Blade Runner's Labor Demand Curve

To better understand how Blade Runner makes its hiring decisions, we want to look at the firm's *labor demand curve*, which indicates how much labor the employer would hire at each wage. The rule that firms hire until the wage equals the value of the marginal product of labor is the key to our quest for the labor demand curve. As the wage rises or falls, Blade Runner will adjust the quantity of labor it demands so that the value of the marginal product stays equal with the wage. Another clue about the shape of the labor demand curve comes from the law of diminishing returns, which says that the marginal product of labor will eventually fall as more labor is hired, and thus the value of the marginal product will fall as well.

Assembling the pieces of this puzzle, we know that when the wage is high, a relatively small quantity of workers will produce output that is worth more than the wage. With diminishing returns, additional workers will add less to total revenue than the workers before them, so they will be hired only if the wage is low enough to fall below the lower value of their contribution to output. The firm's desire to hire more workers at a lower wage results in a downward-sloping labor demand curve.

Table 31.1 demonstrates the connection between labor demand and the value of the marginal product for Blade Runner. We saw that if the wage is $200 a week, Blade Runner will hire 8 workers. This is because the wage is less than or equal to the value of the marginal product for the first 8 workers. The ninth worker would add only $160 to total revenue, which is less than the wage of $200. If the weekly wage increased to $240, Blade Runner would not employ the eighth worker either, because that worker's contribution of $200 worth of output doesn't justify a wage of $240. So Blade Runner would cut back to 7 workers if the weekly wage increased to $240.

All this means that the labor demand curve isn't hard to find: it is traced out by the value of the marginal product schedule. This is shown in Figure 31.1 for Blade Runner. The figure displays the wage on the vertical axis and the number of workers hired on the horizontal axis. The demand curve indicates the number of workers hired at each wage. Its height at each quantity of labor is the value of the marginal product of that unit of labor. The demand curve is downward sloping as a result of diminishing marginal productivity. The result of that downward slope is that more workers are hired when the wage falls, and fewer are hired when the wage rises.

## The Derived Demand for Labor

The labor demand is built on the value of worker contributions to output. So labor demand rises and falls with the two things that affect that value of the

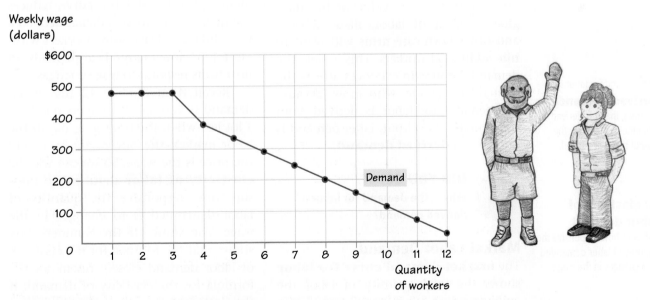

**Figure 31.1** Blade Runner's Labor Demand Curve

Blade Runner's demand for labor is determined by the value of the marginal product of labor. A firm will hire workers as long as the wage rate is less than or equal to the value of the marginal product.

**DID YOU GET IT?** Why does the demand curve for labor slope downward?

marginal product of labor: the productivity of workers and the selling price of whatever they make. If technological advancements cause worker productivity to increase, the value of the marginal product will increase and drive up the demand for labor. And if the price of the product they make goes up, the value of the workers' output rises, again driving up the demand for labor. Similarly, labor demand falls if worker productivity decreases or if the price of output falls. What determines that price? Other things being equal, the price of a good rises and falls with the demand for that good.

Let's examine the links between the demand for mowed lawns and the demand for workers. If more customers want their lawns mowed, the increase in consumer demand will cause the equilibrium price of lawn mowing to increase. As a result, the value of people's work mowing lawns will also rise, because lawn mowing services can be sold for a higher price. With a higher value of the marginal product of labor, Blade Runner and other lawn-care firms will want to hire additional workers. This is how the demand for mowing services affects the demand for people who mow. Because the demand for labor is derived from the demand for output, labor demand is known as a **derived demand**.

*The demand for employees who mow lawns is derived from the demand for mowing services.*

The demand for labor is a **derived demand**, meaning that it is derived from the demand for the output being produced.

The **elasticity of labor demand** indicates how responsive the quantity of labor demanded is to changes in the wage.

The **market demand curve for labor** shows the total quantity of labor the employers in a labor market would hire at each wage.

we find the market demand curve for labor by adding together the labor demand curves for all the individual firms.

Figure 31.2 shows how points on the market labor demand curve are found by adding up the quantities of labor demanded by all the firms at each wage. For simplicity we assume that this market contains only two employers: Blade Runner and Grass Cutter. To find the market labor demand at a wage of $160 per week, for example, we add together the 9 workers that Blade Runner would hire and the 4 workers that Grass Cutter would hire for a total of 13. The remainder of the market demand curve is found by repeating this exercise for each wage.

**DID YOU GET IT?**
How is a market demand curve for labor found?

# HOW FIRMS RESPOND TO WAGE CHANGES

Most workers think of higher wages as a good thing, but be careful what you wish for. The labor demand curve shows that when the wage increases, the movement upward along the curve reduces the quantity of workers demanded. So a wage hike can leave some workers without a job. How many? That depends on how firms respond to wage changes.

Recall from Module 12 that when demand is very elastic, buyers purchase a lot less when the price goes up. In the labor market, the buyers are firms and the price is the wage. So we can use the **elasticity of labor demand** to measure how responsive the quantity of labor demanded is to changes in the wage. The Show Me the Numbers! box shows that the formula for the elasticity of labor demand closely resembles the formula for the elasticity of demand. If the elasticity is low, wage changes have a relatively small effect on the quantity of labor demanded. If the elasticity is high, wage changes have a relatively large effect on hiring.

**DID YOU GET IT?**
Why is the demand for labor a derived demand?

## Market Labor Demand

The **market demand curve for labor** shows the total quantity of labor the employers in a labor market would hire at each wage. In Module 10 we found the market demand curve for goods by adding together the demand curves for all the individual consumers. In similar fashion

THINKSTOCK

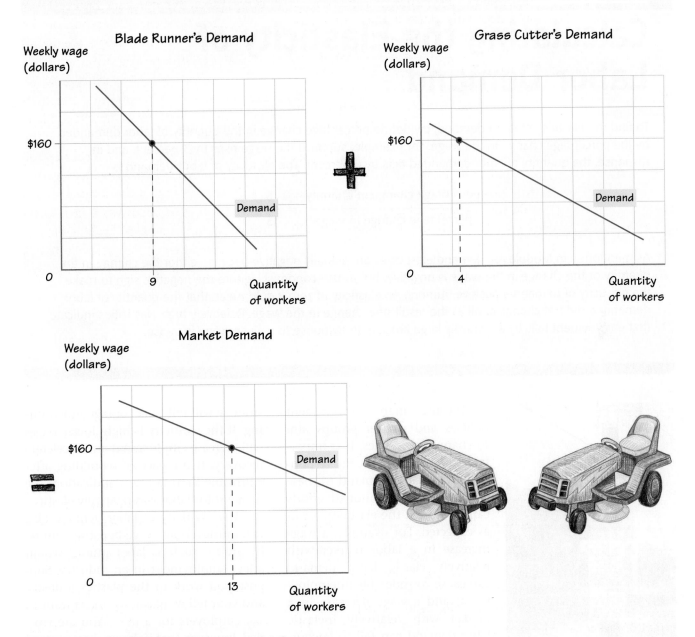

**Figure 31.2** The Market Labor Demand Curve
In this market there are only two employers, Blade Runner and Grass Cutter.
To find the market labor demand for employees to work mowing lawns, at each
wage we add together Blade Runner's and Grass Cutter's demand for labor.

# SHOW ME THE NUMBERS!

# Calculating the Elasticity of Labor Demand

To find the elasticity of labor demand, divide the percentage change in the quantity of labor demanded by the percentage change in the wage. For example, suppose the wage rises by 3 percent, and in response, the quantity of labor demanded falls by 6 percent. The elasticity of labor demand is

$$\frac{\text{percentage change in quantity}}{\text{percentage change in wage}} = \frac{6}{3} = 2$$

As mentioned in Module 12, demand elasticities are actually negative because either the change in the quantity or the change in the wage is negative, but most economists ignore the negative sign to make the elasticity of demand a positive number. An elasticity of zero would mean that the quantity of labor demanded did not change at all as the result of a change in the wage. Relatively high elasticities indicate that employment falls by a relatively large amount in response to a given wage increase.

The effect of policies to rebuild Louisiana after Hurricane Katrina depended on the elasticity of labor demand.

Because many government policies and worker groups aim to change wage rates, it is important to look closely at the responsiveness of labor demand to these changes. Well-intentioned efforts can go afoul if the elasticity is not as expected. For example, a wage increase in a labor market with relatively elastic labor demand can cause considerable unemployment, and a wage decrease in a market with relatively inelastic labor demand can fail to encourage the desired increase in employment. Consider the Davis-Bacon Act of 1931. This law requires that workers on federally funded construction projects be paid at least the prevailing market wage. After Hurricane Katrina struck in 2005, President Bush suspended the Davis-Bacon Act in affected areas so that contractors could pay lower wages. The goal of the suspension was to encourage contractors to hire more construction workers than would be employed at higher wages. If labor demand is inelastic, this type of strategy will fail to encourage much hiring. If the elasticity is high, lower wages will increase employment and accelerate recovery. If the pace of rebuilding after Hurricane Katrina is any indication, the demand for labor was relatively elastic.

The elasticity of labor demand also determines how wage-boosting efforts by groups such as labor unions would affect employment in an industry. Suppose you work in the plastics industry and your fellow plastics workers want to ask employers for a raise. You are worried, however, that if the workers succeed in negotiating a higher wage, plastics employers might hire fewer workers and you might lose your job. The lower the elasticity of demand for labor, the smaller the chance that you will lose your job. Workers have more ability to bargain for higher wages without jeopardizing their jobs in industries with a relatively low elasticity of demand for labor.

 **DID YOU GET IT?**
How does the elasticity of demand for labor influence the effect of higher wages in an industry?

## ECONOMICS IN ACTION

# How High Is the Elasticity of Labor Demand?

The elasticity of labor demand tells us by what percentage employment will fall if the wage increases by one percent. A study by David Card, an economist at the University of California at Berkeley, estimated the elasticity of labor demand by studying various union contracts. Unions negotiate contracts for wages on behalf of workers. The wages under some union contracts are automatically adjusted for inflation, which means that following a broad increase in the prices of items like housing, food, and gasoline, employees' wages increase as well. In other contracts, wages are not adjusted for inflation. From an employer's perspective, workers become more expensive to hire during periods of high inflation if wages are adjusted for inflation than if wages are not adjusted for inflation.

Professor Card examined how employment and wages changed during periods of high and low inflation in firms with these two types of contracts. He concluded that the elasticity of labor demand was 0.5. This estimate was similar to previous estimates by other economists. An elasticity of demand for labor of 0.5 means that a 1 percent increase in wages causes a 0.5 percent decrease in employment. To take an example, in 2011 there were about 140 million employees in the United States and the average wage was about $21 an hour. An increase in the wage by 1 percent, or 21 cents, would cause employment to decline by 0.5 percent, or by 700,000 jobs (0.5% × 140,000,000 = 0.005 × 140,000,000 = 700,000).

**DID YOU GET IT?**
How do differences in the way contracts handle inflation make it possible for economists to study the elasticity of labor demand?

## MODULE 31 REVIEW AND ASSESSMENT

**Summing Up the Key Ideas:** Match the following terms to the correct definitions.

A. Value of the marginal product
B. Labor market
C. Derived demand
D. Labor hour

E. Marginal product of labor
F. Market demand curve for labor
G. Elasticity of labor demand

H. Perfectly competitive labor market

_____ 1. The additional output produced by the last worker hired.

_____ 2. Shows the total quantity of labor the employers in a labor market would hire at each wage.

_____ 3. One hour of work by one worker.

_____ 4. There are many firms and workers, and no individual firm can influence the market wage, which is determined by supply and demand in the labor market.

_____ 5. It is the marginal product of an input multiplied by the price of the output being produced. This value indicates the additional revenue gained from hiring one more unit of that input.

_____ 6. Indicates how responsive the quantity of labor demanded is to changes in the wage.

_____ 7. Demand for labor that is derived from the demand for the output being produced.

_____ 8. A collection of workers interested in selling their services and firms interested in hiring them.

## Analyze and Explain: Determine whether the demand for labor would **increase**, **decrease**, or **remain unchanged** in each of the following situations and explain your answer.

| | EFFECT ON THE DEMAND FOR LABOR | EXPLANATION |
|---|---|---|
| 1. The price of a good produced by the labor in question increases. | _____ | _____ |
| 2. The wages paid for labor increase. | _____ | _____ |
| 3. The marginal product of labor decreases. | _____ | _____ |
| 4. The price of a good produced by the labor in question decreases. | _____ | _____ |

## Apply: For each of the following scenarios, indicate whether the change would best accomplish the stated goal if the demand for labor were relatively **inelastic** or relatively **elastic**.

INELASTIC OR ELASTIC?

1. The federal government seeks to increase the number of teachers hired in public schools by providing a subsidy that lowers the portion of teacher wages paid by local school systems.   _____

2. A labor union wants to negotiate higher wages for its members without causing much of a decrease in the quantity of labor demanded.   _____

3. The state of Nevada wants to increase the quantity of labor demanded by allowing firms to pay workers lower wages.   _____

# MODULE 32

# Labor Supply and Labor Market Equilibrium

**KEY IDEA:** The supply of labor by workers and the demand for labor by firms establish wages and employment levels in labor markets just as supply and demand determine prices and quantities in markets for goods.

## OBJECTIVES

- **To identify factors that influence how the quantity of labor supplied responds to changes in the wage.**
- **To describe the labor market supply curve.**
- **To explain how the forces of supply and demand work together to determine wages and employment levels in a competitive labor market.**

*Work-related decisions depend on each individual's situation in life. Some people would choose not to work even if the wage were very high. Other people want to work so badly they would accept almost anything as compensation.*

## Signs of the Times

The inside scoop on labor demand is only half the story about labor markets, the wages workers receive, and the employment levels achieved in each industry. The other half is about labor supply. When labor supply and labor demand aren't in equilibrium, you can see signs of it around town—literally. If there is a shortage of labor, "Help Wanted" signs show up in the windows of firms. If there is a surplus of labor, some unemployed workers may carry signs advertising a desire to work. You've seen how price changes can eliminate a shortage or surplus in the market for a good. Likewise, wage changes can remedy a shortage or surplus in the market for labor. In this module we'll explore how changes in wages affect the quantity of labor supplied, sometimes in surprising ways. Then we'll put supply and demand together to examine equilibrium in the labor market.

## DECISIONS ABOUT WORK

Every adult faces two fundamental decisions about labor force participation. The first is whether to work at all. If the answer is yes, the worker must decide how much to work. These decisions are complicated by the tug-of-war between interests in money and in leisure time.

### To Work or Not to Work?

If you currently choose not to work, you could probably imagine a wage that would change your mind. Maybe you don't want to take time away from friends and studies to work for $8 an hour, but you would make the sacrifice for $50 an hour. Your decision of whether to accept a job comes down to a comparison of the wage offered with your *reservation wage*. A worker's **reservation wage** is the lowest wage a worker would accept for a job. If the wage offered is greater than or equal to the reservation wage, then the worker will accept the job. If the wage is less than the reservation wage, the worker

A worker's **reservation wage** is the lowest wage a worker would accept for a job.

would rather spend time doing other things, which might include searching for a job that pays more.

Workers have different reservation wages depending on their situations and preferences. One worker may have a low reservation wage because her elderly mother is in a nursing home and relies on her to cover the cost. Another worker may have a high reservation wage because he is married to a wealthy movie star who pays for all his expenses. Reservation wages have a lot to do with the workers' options for spending time and paying the bills. Table 32.1 shows the percentage of men and women of working age who participate in the labor force in 10 countries.

## How Much to Work?

In our Blade Runner example we assumed that all workers worked full time. In reality, many work options are available.

There are full-time and part-time jobs, one worker can hold multiple jobs, and many jobs offer a flexible number of work hours. When it comes to the choice of how much to work, it may seem obvious that higher wages will lead workers to work more. However, the "How much?" decision isn't always predictable. Module 10 explained how a change in the price of a good triggers a substitution effect and an income effect. These same effects have opposing influences on the quantity of labor a worker chooses to supply after the wage changes.

Recall that the opportunity cost of something is whatever must be given up to get it. In the context of labor supply, the *substitution effect* is the quantity of labor supplied as a result of a change in the opportunity cost of leisure time. Suppose you can work any number of hours baby-sitting for $8

Table 32.1 **The Percentage of Men and Women Age 16 or Older in the Labor Force, 2011**

|  | MEN | WOMEN |
|---|---|---|
| United States | 63.9% | 53.2% |
| Canada | 66.6 | 58.5 |
| Australia | 69.5 | 56.8 |
| Japan | 67.6 | 45.6 |
| France | 56.1 | 46.4 |
| Germany | 61.5 | 50.2 |
| Italy | 54.2 | 34.7 |
| The Netherlands | 65.7 | 55.4 |
| Sweden | 64 | 56.6 |
| United Kingdom | 63.6 | 52.8 |

SOURCE: U.S. Bureau of Labor Statistics

an hour. To get an hour of leisure, you must give up the $8 you could earn baby-sitting for that hour. When the wage increases, so does the opportunity cost of leisure time. If the wage for baby-sitting increased to $12 an hour, you would give up $12 for every hour of leisure. Higher wages will encourage you to substitute away from spending time on leisure activities and toward spending more time working.

When workers earn more, they increase their consumption of normal goods as discussed in Module 11. Leisure is a normal good, so people demand more of it as their income increases. Someone who receives a higher income can afford to take more days off, to take longer vacations, and perhaps to retire early. In the context of labor supply, an *income effect* is any such change in the quantity of labor supplied as a result of a change in income. Higher wages allow people to earn more income and trigger the income effect. For example, if your wage for baby-sitting increased from $8 to $12, your income would increase, and the income effect would lead you to increase your consumption of normal goods, including leisure. Notice that the income effect of a wage increase pushes you to work less, while the substitution effect pushes you to work more. Next we'll see how these conflicting influences could play out for a factory worker.

## Income and Substitution Effects in Practice

Suppose a worker named Charlie works in a chocolate factory. Charlie's wage is $10 an hour and he chooses to work 30 hours a week. His weekly earnings are thus $300. Now suppose Charlie received a $5 raise so that his wage became $15 an hour. How would this affect the number of hours he wanted to work? On the one hand, Charlie would find leisure more costly, because each hour he spent carousing around candy shops or hanging out with his grandparents would cost him $15 of foregone earnings instead of $10. This realization

would cause Charlie to want to substitute time away from leisure and toward work.

If Charlie keeps his 30-hour schedule with the higher wage, he will be making $450 a week, which is a lot more than the $300 he was making before. Even though the opportunity cost of leisure time has increased, Charlie will feel richer and able to afford more of the pleasures of leisure time. The substitution effect and the income effect will create a conflict for Charlie. The substitution effect pushes him to want to work more while the income effect pushes him to want to work less. For people like Charlie, who are already working, the net effect of a wage increase could go either way; they might want to work more hours or fewer. In most cases the substitution effect is larger than the income effect and a higher wage will lead to more work. For a person who is not working initially, there is no option to work less, so a wage increase can either cause the person to start working (if his or her reservation wage is met) or have no effect.

*If Charlie's wage increases, will he spend more or less time with his family? The income and substitution effects pull him in opposite directions.*

**DID YOU GET IT?**
**What is the difference between the substitution effect and the income effect as they apply to labor supply?**

# THE MARKET LABOR SUPPLY CURVE

Imagine an auction in which an employer calls out a wage offer to workers, who indicate how many hours they would work at that wage, if at all. The employer first offers $7 an hour, then $8, then $9 and so on. The workers with the lowest reservation wages will be the first to accept a job in this auction. As the wage increases, it will exceed the reservation

wage of more workers, so growing numbers of workers will offer their time. As workers see that they could earn a higher income at the higher wages, the income effect will work against the substitution effect. Some workers will eventually supply fewer hours as the wage increases, even as other workers with different preferences will work more. If we added together all the hours offered by workers at each wage and plotted the wages and hours on a graph, we would have the *market labor supply curve*. The **market labor supply curve** shows the total number of hours workers would be willing to supply at each wage.

The **market labor supply curve** shows the total number of hours workers would be willing to supply at each wage.

Figure 32.1 provides an example of a market labor supply curve. In the graph, the wage is on the vertical axis. The horizontal axis indicates the quantity of labor supplied, measured as the number of hours that people would be willing to work at each wage. Notice that the labor supply curve in this example is upward sloping: at a higher wage people are willing to work more hours, and at a lower wage people will work fewer hours. This is usually the case.

Economists have observed that the amount of time people are willing to spend working increases very little when the wage rises. The reason for the weak response to a higher wage is that the income effect tends to offset much of the substitution effect for most workers. This explains why the labor supply curve in Figure 32.1 is very steep. If the income effect exactly offset the substitution effect, the labor supply curve would be vertical, and an increase in the wage would not lead workers to supply any additional hours of labor.

Unlike most other supply curves, the market labor supply curve does not have to slope upward. As discussed in the previous section, when the wage increases, the substitution effect causes workers to work more and the income effect causes workers to work less. If the wage is high enough, workers may feel so rich that the income effect is larger than the substitution effect. This causes the labor supply curve to bend backward as in Figure 32.2. Perhaps you know a dentist, a doctor, or another professional who takes a day off midweek. When workers

Wage

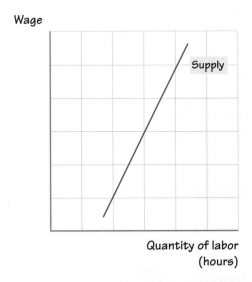

Quantity of labor
(hours)

**Figure 32.1** The Market Labor Supply Curve
The market labor supply curve in this example is upward sloping and very steep. People are typically willing to work more hours as the wage increases because they substitute work for leisure. However, the increase in the quantity of labor supplied is not large, because the income effect of wanting to consume more leisure as income increases offsets some of the substitution effect.

Wage

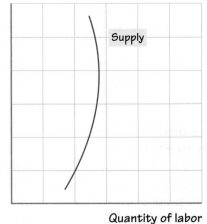

Quantity of labor
(hours)

**Figure 32.2** The Backward-Bending Labor Supply Curve
If the wage rises high enough, workers may feel so rich that the income effect becomes larger than the substitution effect. This causes the labor supply curve to bend backward. In the backward-bending section of the labor supply curve, a wage increase can cause a worker to work less.

with high wages work fewer hours than workers with lower wages, this may be the result of a backward-bending labor supply curve.

**DID YOU GET IT?**
Why is the market supply curve typically steep?

## ECONOMICS IN ACTION

# Labor Supply and the Demise of the Feminine Mystique

The rise in the employment of American women in the last century was nothing short of revolutionary. Figure 32.3 shows that in 1948, only 31.3 percent of women over the age of 16 worked, but by 2000 that figure had nearly doubled to 58 percent.

The rise in employment was particularly rapid for women with children. Ask your mother and grandmother if they worked full time when they were in their early 30s. Chances are that your grandmothers did not work but your mother did. Just as dramatic as the increase in

the employment of women has been the shift in the types of jobs held by women. In 1940, more than 70 percent of the college-educated, working women in their early 30s were employed as teachers, nurses, librarians, social workers, or secretaries. By 2000, almost half of college-educated, working women in their early 30s were employed as doctors, lawyers, managers, professors, or scientists.

Harvard economist Claudia Goldin attributes much of women's rise in employment since the 1940s to an increase in the substitution effect

**Figure 32.3** *Percent of Men and Women Age 16 or Older Employed Each Year*

and a reduction in the income effect. Recall that the substitution effect leads people to substitute work for leisure when their wage increases, and the income effect causes people to reduce their work hours if they become wealthier. Professor Goldin concluded that the growing availability of part-time work

in the 1940s and 1950s increased women's substitution toward more work hours. This was reinforced by the growing availability of modern household appliances. As more families could afford washing machines, dryers, dishwashers, and other time-saving devices, the reservation wage for women decreased. Meanwhile, women's wages were on the rise, all of which led to a large increase in the quantity of labor they supplied.

*Since the 1950s, women have made a large substitution of paid work for housework.*

**DID YOU GET IT?**
**What made it easier for women to commit more time to work outside the home starting in the middle of the last century?**

# EQUILIBRIUM IN A PERFECTLY COMPETITIVE LABOR MARKET

In a perfectly competitive labor market, the equilibrium wage and quantity of labor are determined by the intersection of the market labor supply curve and the market labor demand curve. Figure 32.4 shows the equilibrium in the market for

day-care workers. The hourly wage for day-care workers is measured on the vertical axis, and the quantity of labor (in thousands of hours) is measured on the horizontal axis. In this case, the equilibrium wage is $15 and the equilibrium quantity of labor is 50 thousand hours.

**DID YOU GET IT?**
**How is the equilibrium wage determined?**

**Figure 32.4** Equilibrium in the Labor Market

In a perfectly competitive labor market for day-care workers, there are many small day-care centers and many potential day-care workers. The hourly wage rate for day-care workers is shown on the vertical axis, and the quantity of labor (in thousands of hours) is shown on the horizontal axis. At the equilibrium of supply and demand, the wage is $15 and the quantity of labor is 50 thousand hours.

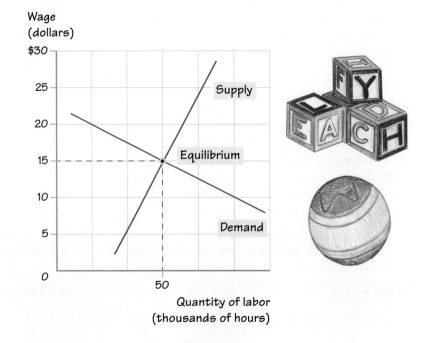

## Labor Market Boundaries

If all workers and jobs were identical, and workers could flow effortlessly between jobs, then there would be one big labor market with a single equilibrium wage. That is not the case. Different labor markets exist for workers with different sorts of skills and qualifications. For example, the labor market for electrical engineers is separate from the labor market for manicurists. There is no free flow of workers between these markets because the relevant skills and qualifications are very different. Manicurists cannot easily become electrical engineers, and electrical engineers cannot easily become manicurists. The wages and quantities of labor in these markets thus differ as the result of differing supply and demand curves for each type of worker.

Another consideration is geography. Some labor markets are national in scope, while others are local. An example of a national labor market is the market for school superintendents. School systems tend to search all over the country for good candidates, and superintendents move all over to find jobs. Car mechanics, by contrast, have a much more localized labor market. Repair shops don't search for mechanics in distant states because there are generally good candidates nearby. The supply and demand of qualified workers in the relevant geographic region—the nation for superintendents and the local area for mechanics—determines the wage and employment level in a perfectly competitive labor market.

## Shifts of Labor Supply and Labor Demand

As in the markets for goods and services, shifts in the supply and demand curves for labor cause the labor market equilibrium to change. Figure 32.5 illustrates how the equilibrium wage and quantity of labor are affected by each possible shift of labor supply or labor demand.

Consider the effect of a nationwide increase in educational attainment. This would increase the supply of highly educated workers and decrease the supply of

less educated workers. Other things being equal, the result would be a decrease in the equilibrium wage for highly educated workers as in panel (b) of Figure 32.5 and an increase in the equilibrium wage of less educated workers as in panel (a). As another example, about one quarter of U.S. chemists are immigrants from other countries. If such immigration increased, the larger supply of chemists would shift their labor supply curve to the right and decrease their wages.

In Module 31 you learned that labor demand is determined by the value of the marginal product of labor, which depends on the marginal product of labor and the price of output. Changes in either of those items on a broad scale shift the labor demand curve. For example, if a surge in the popularity of wind energy decreased the demand for coal, the price of coal would decrease and so would the demand for coal miners. The labor demand curve in the coal market would shift leftward and the equilibrium wage would decrease as in panel (d) of Figure 32.5. If, instead, new coal mining technology made coal miners more productive, the demand curve for coal miners would shift to the right and the equilibrium wage would increase as in panel (c).

If both curves shift at the same time, the result depends on the direction and relative sizes of the shifts. For example, if both labor supply and labor demand increase, the equilibrium quantity of labor definitely increases, and the equilibrium wage may either increase or

*A movement toward wind energy and away from coal energy would decrease the price of coal and thus the demand for coal miners. The resulting leftward shift in the demand curve for coal miners would lower the equilibrium wage for miners and the quantity of mining labor hired.*

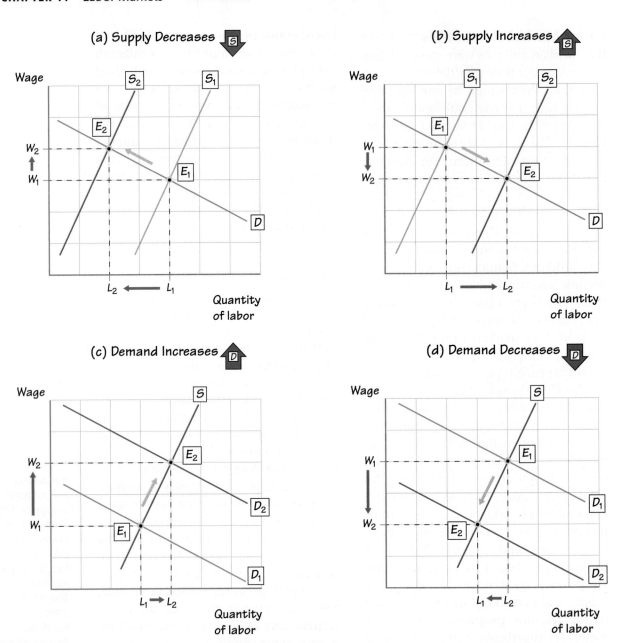

**Figure 32.5** Shifts of Labor Supply and Demand
Panel (a) shows that a decrease in labor supply leads to an increase in the equilibrium wage and a decrease in the equilibrium quantity of labor. In panel (b) we see that an increase in labor supply leads to a decrease in the equilibrium wage and an increase in the equilibrium quantity of labor. Panel (c) shows that an increase in labor demand raises both the equilibrium wage and the equilibrium quantity of labor. Panel (d) shows that a decrease in labor demand lowers both the equilibrium wage and the equilibrium quantity of labor.

decrease, depending on whether the increase in demand or the increase in supply is relatively large.

## A Minimum Wage in a Perfectly Competitive Labor Market

A **minimum wage** is a price floor for labor that is set by the government, below which wages are not allowed to

fall. The federal minimum wage in the United States as of 2012 was $7.25 per hour. Some states have their own minimum wage. For example, the minimum wage in California in 2012 was $8.00 per hour. The supply-and-demand model will help us see the effect of a minimum wage on employment in a perfectly competitive labor market. To have any effect,

A **minimum wage** is a price floor for labor that is set by the government, below which wages are not allowed to fall.

the minimum wage must be set above the equilibrium wage level. This situation is illustrated in Figure 32.6.

The horizontal black line in Figure 32.6 indicates a minimum wage of $8.00, which is above the equilibrium wage of $6.00. This is a price floor for labor—employers are not permitted to pay a wage below $8.00. When a minimum wage is in place, employers decide whether to hire more labor by comparing the value of the marginal product of another hour of labor to the minimum wage, rather than to the equilibrium wage. The value of the marginal product exceeds the minimum wage until the intersection of the horizontal minimum wage line and the demand curve at point $E_M$. Thus 650 hours of labor will be hired. Without the minimum wage, 1,000 hours of labor would be hired, as determined by the intersection of the supply and demand curves at point $E_C$. On the basis of the supply-and-demand model for a perfectly competitive market we would therefore predict that a minimum wage that exceeds the equilibrium wage will result in a decrease in the quantity of labor hours hired.

We would expect an increase in the minimum wage to cause a further decrease in the quantity of labor hired. This is shown by the green horizontal line at a height of $9 in Figure 32.6. The

intersection of the higher minimum wage line at point $E_H$—farther to the left along the demand curve—means that fewer labor hours would be hired. In this example, 450 hours of labor are hired at a wage of $9. As discussed in Module 31, the decrease in hiring that results from a higher wage in a perfectly competitive labor market can be large or small, depending on the elasticity of labor demand.

 **DID YOU GET IT?**
How does a minimum wage affect the quantity of labor hired in a perfectly competitive market?

# THE MINIMUM WAGE IN PRACTICE

Most of the recent research suggests that modest minimum wage increases have little effect, if any, on employment. A landmark study compared the employment growth of fast food workers in New Jersey and nearby Pennsylvania before and after New Jersey raised its state minimum wage from $4.25 to $5.05 per hour in April 1992. Pennsylvania's minimum wage remained at the federal level of $4.25 throughout this period. With a perfectly competitive labor market and a downward-sloping demand curve, employment in New Jersey would have

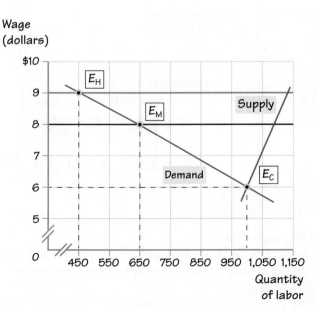

**Figure 32.6** A Minimum Wage
This graph shows a perfectly competitive labor market that is in equilibrium at a wage of $6 per hour. A minimum wage of $8 per hour causes a decrease in the quantity of labor demanded from 1,000 to 650 hours. A higher minimum wage of $9 results in a lower quantity demanded of 450 hours.

fallen relative to that in Pennsylvania. Figure 32.7 shows employment in both states over time based on the payroll tax records of fast food restaurants. Fast food restaurants are among the most likely employers to pay the minimum wage. Yet there is no evidence that employment fell in New Jersey relative to Pennsylvania in the first few years after the New Jersey minimum wage increased.

In another study, economists compared the effect of a higher federal minimum wage on low-wage states and high-wage states. The national minimum wage increased from $4.25 to $4.75 per hour in October 1996 and then to $5.15 in September 1997. Many workers in low-wage states saw their wage rise when the minimum wage increased. Fewer workers in high-wage states received a wage boost from the higher minimum wage. The percentage of teenage workers who earned wages between the old minimum ($4.25) and the new one ($5.15) just before the minimum wage increased in 1996 ranged from 11 percent in Hawaii to 73 percent in Mississippi. In a competitive labor market with a downward-sloping labor demand curve, one would

expect job growth to be hindered in states with more wage growth, other things being equal. Yet the percentage of workers with higher wages due to the minimum wage hikes appeared unrelated to job growth. Perhaps employment would have grown even faster in the low-wage states had it not been for the minimum wage increase. The findings also suggest that many labor demand curves may be inelastic, or that many labor markets may lack competitiveness. Even so, the model of a perfectly competitive labor market provides a useful starting point for thinking about the minimum wage and has been helpful in predicting labor market developments such as the effect of technological change on employment.

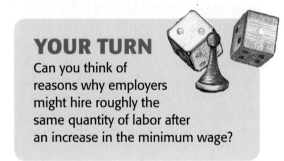

**YOUR TURN**

Can you think of reasons why employers might hire roughly the same quantity of labor after an increase in the minimum wage?

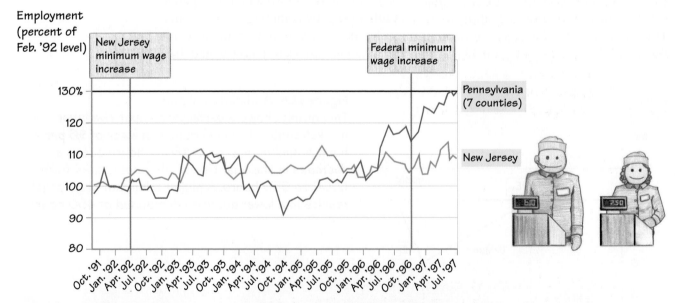

**Figure 32.7** Fast Food Employment in New Jersey and Pennsylvania
When New Jersey raised its minimum wage from $4.25 to $5.05 per hour, Pennsylvania's minimum wage remained at $4.25. There is no evidence that employment fell in New Jersey relative to Pennsylvania in the first few years following New Jersey's minimum wage increase.

# MODULE 32 REVIEW AND ASSESSMENT

**Summing Up the Key Ideas:** Match the following terms to the correct definitions.

A. Reservation wage
B. Market labor
   supply curve

C. Substitution effect
D. Minimum wage
E. Income effect

_____ 1. A price floor for labor that is set by the government, below which wages are not allowed to fall.

_____ 2. Any change in the quantity of labor supplied as a result of a change in income.

_____ 3. Shows the total number of hours workers would be willing to supply at each wage.

_____ 4. The quantity of labor supplied as a result of a change in the opportunity cost of leisure time.

_____ 5. The lowest wage at which a worker would accept a job.

**Analyze and Explain:** Analyze each of the following, determine the effect on the **equilibrium wage**, and then explain your answer.

|  | EQUILIBRIUM WAGE | EXPLANATION |
|---|---|---|
| 1. The value of the marginal product of labor increases. | _____ | _____ |
| 2. Workers value leisure time less and less. | _____ | _____ |
| 3. Workers become more productive as a result of attaining increased job skills. | _____ | _____ |
| 4. The price of the good produced by labor decreases. | _____ | _____ |

**Apply:** In each of the following situations, is the substitution effect **larger**, **smaller**, or the **same** size as the income effect? Explain your answer.

|  | LARGER, SMALLER, OR THE SAME? | EXPLANATION |
|---|---|---|
| 1. Dixie works less when her wage increases. | _____ | _____ |
| 2. Joe works more when his wage increases. | _____ | _____ |
| 3. Andreas works the same amount when his wage increases. | _____ | _____ |

## MODULE 33

# The Skills of Workers and the Quality of Jobs

**KEY IDEA:** Workers can earn higher wages by investing time and money in the development of new skills that make them more valuable to employers.

**OBJECTIVES**

- **To analyze the decision to invest in education.**
- **To describe how workers choose jobs.**
- **To explain how perfect competition can thwart employer discrimination.**
- **To explain the roles of unions and occupational licensing in the labor market.**

### Human Capital

Why do people go to college? It's expensive and challenging, and probably not as much fun as traveling in Europe, but it's a great investment of time and money. By advancing their education, workers become eligible for jobs in labor markets that pay relatively high wages and offer relatively comfortable working conditions. These perks, along with personal satisfaction, are among the big rewards for education. You learned in Module 1 that education and training develop a worker's *human capital*—the skills and knowledge that make people more productive members of society. Employers value investments in human capital because workers with more human capital are better able to contribute to the output of firms. In this module we'll discuss human capital as one reason among many why wages differ across people and jobs.

## INVESTING IN HUMAN CAPITAL

As with any wise decision about how much of something to do, marginal analysis leads workers to the appropriate amount of education. Rational workers will invest in education until the marginal cost of investment equals the marginal benefit. The cost of education is chiefly the opportunity costs of a student's time spent attending classes, doing homework, and studying for tests rather than working for pay or enjoying leisure. The cost of tuition is also substantial, and then there are fees and expenses for books and supplies.

Investments in education tend to lead to higher incomes, which justifies the cost. Figure 33.1 shows that education is highly valued in the labor market. For example, in 2011, the *median* full-time worker with a professional degree such as a law or medical degree—the one right in the middle of the pack if they were lined up from lowest to highest earnings—received $1,665 a week. Meanwhile the median full-time worker who dropped out of high school earned just $451 a week.

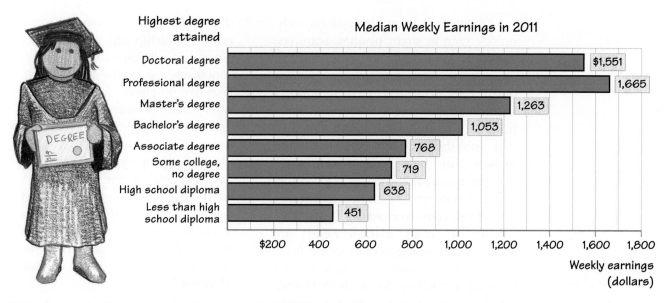

Highest degree attained

Median Weekly Earnings in 2011

| Highest degree attained | Median weekly earnings |
| --- | --- |
| Doctoral degree | $1,551 |
| Professional degree | 1,665 |
| Master's degree | 1,263 |
| Bachelor's degree | 1,053 |
| Associate degree | 768 |
| Some college, no degree | 719 |
| High school diploma | 638 |
| Less than high school diploma | 451 |

Weekly earnings (dollars)

**Figure 33.1** Median Earnings by Educational Attainment
Education pays. The more degrees you earn in school, the more money you are likely to earn later on.

Looking at this sort of data, economists initially couldn't be sure the difference in pay resulted from the education itself. Another possibility was that the type of people who attain more education also have other things about their background or genetics that help them earn more. To standardize the types of people involved, they studied identical twins with different education levels. Again, they found large differences in earnings between those with high and low levels of education. So the earnings advantage associated with higher educational attainment does not appear to result from family-background or genetic advantages. Instead, it appears that as they progress in school, individuals gain more skills and credentials that employers value.

**DID YOU GET IT?**
What are the economic benefits of education? What are the costs? When should someone stop investing in education?

## Trends in Today's Labor Markets
New technologies help shape the types of human capital most in demand. Growing Internet use has created new jobs for people skilled in areas such as web design and computer programming. Competition from Internet services has

also reduced the need for people with the skills to be travel agents, newspaper journalists, and postal workers. Other types of technology have replaced jobs in industries that include farming, banking, retail sales, and manufacturing. This places a premium on workers with the human capital needed to develop and use the latest technology, such as mobile devices, data security systems, and social media.

The skills in demand also depend on what goods and services are produced in this country. Module 58 explains that other countries are increasingly the source of manufactured goods purchased in the United States. That makes U.S. manufacturing jobs harder to come by. At the same time, U.S. specialization in service industries has created millions of jobs. The U.S. Bureau of Labor Statistics projects considerable job growth in careers that include financial analysis, insurance sales, plumbing, social work, software development, truck driving, and many areas of health care. When there aren't enough U.S. workers with the human capital to fill job openings, the growing mobility of workers makes it possible for employers to hire workers from an international job market. For example, about one quarter of the doctors practicing in the United States received their education in another country.

*"An investment in knowledge always pays the best interest."*
—Benjamin Franklin

Advances in communications technology such as smart phones, scanners, and teleconferencing systems make it easier for workers to *telecommute*, which means they work at home or in another location that is not a traditional workplace. For example, although the firm that published this textbook is located in New York, heavy use of technology allowed the book's authors and editors to collaborate while working in different states from coast to coast.

Not all labor market trends are related to technology. For example, firms are now hiring more *temporary workers* who fill a position for a short period. Temporary workers can be less expensive than permanent workers, and they give firms the flexibility to expand production when demand picks up for a brief time. With more temporary jobs and rapidly changing labor markets, it is likely that people in your generation will change jobs more often than people in your parents' generation.

# COMPENSATING WAGE DIFFERENTIALS

The typical forest ranger doesn't earn as much money as the typical engineer, and yet many people prefer to be forest rangers. This is because earnings aren't the only thing that matters to workers. Jobs differ in terms of other important aspects, including working conditions, hazards, prestige, difficulty, and fringe benefits. For example, working in an air-conditioned office is considered more pleasant by most workers than is working underground in a dark, damp, and often dangerous coal mine. Likewise, some jobs offer generous benefits such as health insurance plans that cover the costs of injuries or illness, and other jobs offer very few or no fringe benefits.

In a competitive labor market, the wage that workers are paid is adjusted to compensate for the desirability or undesirability of working conditions and fringe benefits. As Adam Smith put it in 1776,

A **compensating wage differential** is a premium paid to persuade someone to work in undesirable circumstances.

[T]he wages of labor vary with the ease or hardship, the cleanliness or dirtiness, the honourableness or dishonourableness of the employment. Thus in most places . . . a journeyman tailor earns less than a journeyman weaver. [The tailor's] work is much easier. A journeyman weaver earns less than a journeyman smith. [The weaver's] work is not always easier, but it is much cleanlier. . . . The most detestable of all employments, that of public executioner, is, in proportion to the quantity of work done, better paid than any common trade whatever.

Suppose a high school science teacher is considering job offers from two schools, which we will call School A and School B. In School A, the students are well behaved, respectful, and polite. In School B, the students are poorly behaved, disrespectful, and sometimes threatening. If the two jobs paid the same salary, the teacher would prefer to work in School A, and School B would have a rough time filling the position. To persuade the teacher to accept their job, School B will have to offer a higher salary than School A. This is the type of wage adjustment Adam Smith was talking about.

More generally, to motivate workers to accept jobs with undesirable working conditions, they must be paid extra. The premium paid to persuade someone to work under objectionable circumstances is called a **compensating wage differential**.

**DID YOU GET IT?**
What is a compensating wage differential?

## Matching Workers and Jobs

People have different tastes. The types of working conditions you find distasteful may be desirable to others. Some people like to lift heavy objects and go out of their way to pump iron in the gym after work, while others detest all physical activity. Some like to work alone and others enjoy talking to people while working. Some do not mind working in confined quarters and others are claustrophobic. There is reason to celebrate these differences—they mean that some people are content in jobs that you and many others would hate.

Labor markets help sort people into the jobs they most prefer and match them with the employers who most value their skills and tolerances. Workers who like a particular work environment are eager to apply for and accept jobs that offer such an environment, and those who dislike that environment steer clear of those jobs. Consider, for example, jobs that involve strenuous physical activity such as building or road construction. All else being equal, people who like physical activity will seek jobs that require it, and those who prefer to sit at a desk will apply for jobs that entail just that. If employers with physically demanding jobs cannot find enough workers who are happy to fill them, they will offer a wage premium—that is, higher pay—for jobs that require physical activity. Similar matching of workers and jobs occurs on the basis of work that involves blood, mathematics, being outside, travel, danger, and many other such factors.

## YOUR TURN
In what type of work environment would you like to work? How much pay would you be willing to give up to work in your favored environment?

## DISCRIMINATION

While human capital and compensating wage differentials can lead to higher wages for some workers, *discrimination* has the opposite effect. **Employment discrimination** occurs if workers who are equally productive are treated differently because of characteristics

unrelated to their job performance. If brown-eyed and green-eyed workers were equally productive but employers paid less to brown-eyed workers because they have a preference for green-eyed workers, there would be discrimination against brown-eyed workers. In addition to pay, discrimination can affect the chances of being hired or fired, opportunities for promotion, and other subtle aspects of the work environment, such as the provision of encouragement and mentoring.

Here's another remarkable result of competition: a perfectly competitive market drives discrimination out of existence. To see why, suppose that some employers indeed have a preference for green-eyed workers over brown-eyed workers even though both groups of workers are equally productive. Other employers do not care about the color of workers' eyes and only value workers for their economic contributions. The discriminating employers will try to hire from the subset of the workforce with green eyes. Having fewer workers to choose from—that is, facing a smaller labor supply—means the discriminating employers must pay higher wages. Beyond that, if workers were not equally productive, the discriminators would be at a further disadvantage: by driving away brown-eyed workers with exclusion or lower wages, those employers will not have

*Firefighting is a job that you probably wouldn't take unless you received a compensating wage differential to reward you for working under dangerous or unpleasant conditions.*

**Employment discrimination** exists if workers who are equally productive are treated differently because of characteristics unrelated to their job performance.

equal access to all the best workers. In a perfectly competitive environment, firms with higher wage costs or less productive workers are put out of business by firms with lower costs or more productive workers. Discrimination would thus be driven out of a perfectly competitive market.

 **DID YOU GET IT?**
**What is employment discrimination? Why can't it persist in a perfectly competitive market?**

### Evidence of Discrimination

The preceding logic suggests that discrimination could persist only in imperfectly competitive markets. Research bears out this prediction. One study of discrimination against female bank employees found that banks that had a monopoly in their town were less likely to hire female employees. That is, banks that faced little or no competition from other banks in their area were more likely to discriminate against female employees. In areas where banks faced steeper competition, however, they were less likely to discriminate against women workers.

Discrimination against black workers persisted in the United States for centuries with only gradual improvement. For example, in 1940 the average black male earned about $0.40 for every dollar earned by the average white male. In 1990 that figure had risen to $0.75 and has remained roughly the same to this day. For most of this country's history, a system of racial exclusion and separate, unequal schools perpetuated discrimination. Those resistant to change prevailed until the federal government and society as a whole took steps to address racial discrimination. The greatest progress in closing the black-white wage gap came with the passage of the Civil Rights Act of 1964, which outlawed discrimination based on race, sex, or national origin. Competition in the United States, imperfect as it was, could not eradicate discrimination on its own.

### Not All Disparities Are Discrimination

The United States has seen meaningful progress in racial and gender equality in the last century. Discrimination is a far less potent and blatant fact of life than it used to be. And it is important to bear in mind that the differences in economic circumstances that we currently observe between racial groups and men and women may not be entirely or even mainly due to discrimination. The gap in earnings between the average black and average white worker may result, for example, from differences in past schooling opportunities and have nothing to do with discrimination in the labor market. The influence of factors that include family life, culture, and education, as well as discrimination, is an area of active debate among economists.

## LABOR UNIONS

A **labor union** is a group of workers who bargain over the terms and conditions of employment, including pay, work hours, vacation time, pensions, health insurance, and grievance procedures. Local unions are often affiliated with a national or international union. For example, the United Automobile, Aerospace and Agricultural Implement Workers of America (UAW) is an international union made up of 390,000 active members who belong to 750 local unions.

Unions existed in the American colonies before the Revolutionary War. Early unions consisted mainly of local associations of skilled crafts workers, such as carpenters, cabinet makers, and printers. In 1869 the Knights of Labor emerged as a national union that combined skilled and unskilled workers. The Knights broke up over infighting between skilled and unskilled workers. The American Federation of Labor (AFL), a coalition of skilled crafts unions headed by a former cigar maker named Samuel Gompers, succeeded the Knights in 1886. The Congress of Industrial Organizations (CIO), a group of unions representing industrial

> A **labor union** is a group of workers who bargain collectively with employers over the terms and conditions of employment.

# ECONOMICS IN ACTION

# What's in a Name? A Test of Labor-Market Discrimination

To test whether employers discriminate against black job applicants, Marianne Bertrand of the University of Chicago and Sendhil Mullainathan of Harvard University conducted an unusual experiment. They selected 1,300 help-wanted ads from newspapers in Boston and Chicago and submitted multiple resumes from phantom job seekers. The researchers were deliberate in their selection of names for the resumes, sometimes using names common among blacks and sometimes using names common among whites.

Nine names were selected to represent each category: black women, white women, black men, and white men. Last names common to the racial group were also assigned. Four resumes were typically submitted for each job opening. For example, fictional candidates Kristen, Tamika, Brad, and Tyrone applied for the same jobs and had equivalent resumes. Nearly 5,000 applications were submitted from mid-2001 to mid-2002. Professors Bertrand and Mullainathan kept track of which candidates were invited for job interviews.

Apart from their names, applicants had the same experience, education, and skills, so employers had no reason to distinguish among them. The results are disturbing. Applicants with white-sounding names were 50 percent more likely to be called for interviews than were those with black-sounding names. Interviews were requested for 10.1 percent of applicants with white-sounding names and only 6.7 percent of those with black-sounding names. At the low end, the interview-request rate was 2.2 percent for Aisha, 3.8 percent for Keisha, and 5.4 percent for Tamika, compared with 9.1 percent for Kenya and Latonya and 10.5 percent for Ebony.

Their most alarming finding was that the likelihood of being called for an interview rose sharply with an applicant's credentials—like experience and honors—for those with white-sounding names but much less for those with black-sounding names. A grave concern is that this phenomenon may dampen the incentives for blacks to acquire job skills, producing a self-fulfilling prophecy that perpetuates prejudice and discrimination.

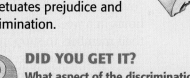

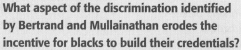

**DID YOU GET IT?**
What aspect of the discrimination identified by Bertrand and Mullainathan erodes the incentive for blacks to build their credentials?

EXTRACTED FROM "Sticks and stones can break bones, but the wrong name can make a job hard to find," by Alan B. Krueger, *New York Times*, December 12, 2002.

workers, split from the AFL in 1935. Union organizing got a boost after the passage of the National Labor Relations Act in 1935, which gave workers a legal right to unionize. The AFL and CIO reunited in 1955, forming the AFL-CIO. In 2005 unions representing about a third of the AFL-CIO's members, including service workers and truck drivers, split from the AFL-CIO, creating a new organization called the Change to Win Federation, with the goal of organizing additional labor unions.

The National Labor Relations Act of 1935 (also known as the Wagner Act, for its chief sponsor, Senator Robert Wagner of New York) set forth procedures for the formation of a union. The act requires that a union election be held if 30 percent or more of employees in a work unit sign

Although the UAW began as a union representing autoworkers, its members now come from industries as diverse as aerospace, higher education, and farm tools.

Workers picket outside a Verizon store.

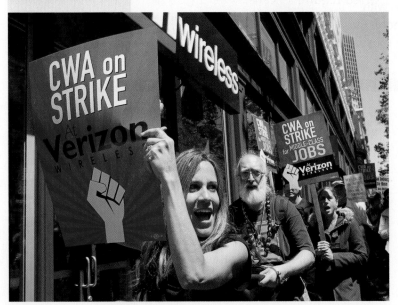

a card showing interest in a union. If the union receives a majority of the votes in the election, the employer is obligated to bargain with the union.

Unions negotiate with employers on behalf of their members. Local unions may also represent workers if they have a grievance against their employer. And national unions play an active role supporting or opposing legislation that affects workers. Unions, for example, supported legislation requiring that an extra 50 percent of the normal wage be paid for any "overtime hours" worked in excess of 40 hours in a week. Unions collect dues from their members to support their activities.

To press their agenda with employers, a labor union can go *on strike* against a firm, which means asking the workers

to collectively stop working. When workers go on strike, they often carry signs in front of their workplace to discourage other workers from returning to work and to discourage customers from doing business there. Strikes are much less common today than they used to be. Have you ever seen workers on strike outside a firm?

In 2010, 14.7 million workers, or 11.9 percent of the workforce, were union members. Unions represented 6.9 percent of workers in the private sector and 36.2 percent in the public (government) sector. The union membership rate in the private sector has fallen since the 1950s. Among occupational groups, teachers, librarians, firefighters, and police officers have the highest rates of union membership. In many European countries, unions negotiate with firms at the industry or regional level, whereas in the United States they typically negotiate with individual firms.

Harvard economist Richard Freeman argues that labor unions have two faces. One face is to provide workers a voice in the workplace. For example, unions give workers a way to voice their concerns to management. The other face is to act as a monopolist and negotiate for higher wages than would result under perfect competition in the labor market. In the next section we'll see the effects of such a *monopoly union* on a graph.

**DID YOU GET IT?**
What is the purpose of a union?

## MODELING IMPERFECT COMPETITION IN THE LABOR MARKET

As you've just learned, the labor market is not always perfectly competitive. Factors such as labor unions, government regulation, discrimination, and efforts by employers to pay less than the value of workers' marginal product interfere with competition. A common view of labor markets is that supply and demand play a major role in determining pay and employment, as was emphasized previously, but noncompetitive forces also matter. Let's explore how some of these forces affect labor market graphs.

## A Monopoly Union

Figure 33.2 illustrates the monopoly face of unions as described by Freeman. Without a union, workers would be paid the equilibrium wage, indicated by $W_C$. As usual in a perfectly competitive market, the wage is determined by the intersection of the labor supply curve and the labor demand curve at point $A$. A union, however, can act as a monopoly and restrict supply. Remember, a monopoly is a single seller. A *monopoly union* is a union made up of most or all of the workers in an industry. And as the representative of that body of workers, the monopoly union can act as the single seller of labor in that industry. Unions can exercise their monopoly power by threatening to strike or by restricting the availability of workers in other ways. As a result, unions can negotiate a wage that is higher than the competitive equilibrium wage. Available evidence suggests that unions typically raise wages by 10 to 15 percent above the equilibrium level.

In Figure 33.2, the horizontal line at $W_U$ indicates the wage that the union negotiates with employers. Employment is now determined by the intersection of the union-negotiated wage and the labor demand curve, at point $B$. Notice that employment is lower at point $B$ than at point $A$. This occurs because, while the union can negotiate a higher wage than the competitive equilibrium wage, the employer has the right to choose the number of workers to employ. If the wage is raised by a union acting like a monopoly, employers will respond by reducing employment.

**DID YOU GET IT?**

**How does a union act like a monopoly?**

## Occupational Licensing

Workers in a growing number of occupations in the United States must have a license to perform their job, which is one more thing that restricts the supply of workers and brings about a relatively high equilibrium wage. Doctors, dentists, accountants, and lawyers have long been required to pass a certification test and to complete a specified course of study to practice their profession. Occupational licenses are now required in many states to work as a massage therapist, manicurist, barber, librarian, or beekeeper. Overall, nearly one in three workers is employed in an occupation that requires a license. Do any of the occupations you have considered require a license?

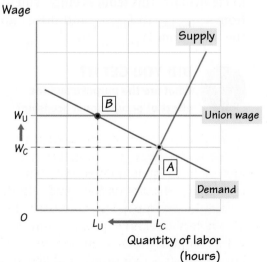

**Figure 33.2** A Monopoly Union Without a union, workers would be paid the equilibrium wage rate, $W_C$. The horizontal line at $W_U$ indicates the wage negotiated by the union. Fewer workers are employed at the union wage, but those who are employed are better off. Do you consider that a good tradeoff?

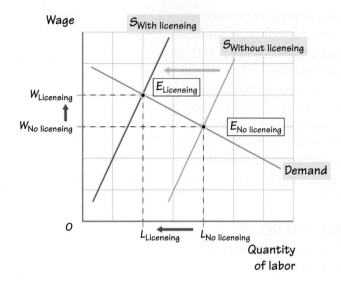

**Figure 33.3** The Effect of Occupational Licensing on Labor Supply

Occupational licensing helps protect consumers from unqualified workers. It can also restrict supply, which reduces employment from $L_{\text{No licensing}}$ to $L_{\text{Licensing}}$ and drives up the wage from $W_{\text{No licensing}}$ to $W_{\text{Licensing}}$.

A rationale for occupational licensing is that it protects consumers from unqualified workers. Requiring workers to pass a test of competency and to have completed relevant education prevents unqualified workers from entering the profession. No one wants to be examined by a doctor who does not know the difference between his ankle and his elbow. Likewise, teacher certification and licensing requirements are intended to prevent unqualified teachers from working in the classroom. But there are always tradeoffs: occupational licensing requirements are a barrier to perfect competition in the labor market. A worker cannot freely move from one occupation to another because of licensing requirements. For example, the authors of this textbook would not be able to teach an economics course at most public high schools without going through the costly certification process.

Many economists question whether occupational licensing has gone too far. After all, consumers have some information about the quality of the people from whom they buy services. For example, if you get a bad haircut from a particular barber or stylist, you can easily avoid that person in the future. Reviews on websites such as AngiesList.com allow consumers to share information about good and bad service providers. Beyond protecting customers, occupational licensing may serve as a way of restricting supply in some cases. Because only people who have passed the certification requirements are allowed to work in the occupation, supply is limited. As shown in Figure 33.3, this reduces employment from $L_{\text{No licensing}}$ to $L_{\text{Licensing}}$ and drives up the wage from $W_{\text{No licensing}}$ to $W_{\text{Licensing}}$.

 **DID YOU GET IT?**
What are the purpose and the effect of occupational licensing?

# MODULE 33 REVIEW AND ASSESSMENT

**Summing Up the Key Ideas:** Match the following terms to the correct definitions.

A. Compensating wage differential        B. Employment discrimination        C. Labor union

_____ 1. A premium paid to persuade someone to work in undesirable circumstances.

_____ 2. A group of workers who bargain collectively with employers over the terms and conditions of employment.

_____ 3. Exists if workers who are equally productive are treated differently because of characteristics unrelated to their job performance.

**Analyze and Explain:** For each of the following, determine whether **employment discrimination** is involved and explain your answer.

| | DISCRIMINATION OR NO DISCRIMINATION? | EXPLANATION |
|---|---|---|
| 1. Two workers are hired at the same time in two different states doing the same job and are paid different wages. | _____ | _____ |
| 2. Workers are hired in a perfectly competitive labor market. | _____ | _____ |
| 3. Professional women basketball players playing in the WNBA earn lower wages than professional men basketball players playing in the NBA. | _____ | _____ |
| 4. Mary and Diego have the same experience and qualifications and perform the same job for the sole coal mining company in a small town. Mary is paid a lower wage than Diego. | _____ | _____ |

**Apply:** In each of the following situations there is a wage difference described. Analyze each and determine if the difference in wages is due to **compensating wage differentials**.

| | COMPENSATING WAGE DIFFERENTIAL OR NOT? |
|---|---|
| 1. A chemical engineer and a mechanical engineer at the same factory receive different wages and fringe benefits. | _____ |
| 2. A security guard at Disney World is paid less than a security guard at a maximum security federal prison. | _____ |
| 3. An economics professor at a local college is paid more than a psychology professor at the same college. | _____ |
| 4. The secretary working in the office at a garbage collection service is paid less than the worker who drives the truck and lifts the garbage containers into the truck. | _____ |

## Bloomberg Businessweek®

# As Work Goes Global, Will Holidays Disappear?

**With more and more business conducted across borders, workers find it increasingly difficult to rest on national or religious holidays**

BY STACEY HIGGINBOTHAM

As the Internet and a more global economy erase the nine-to-five workday, will they also erode the sense of holidays? Employees are now based around the world and may always be connected, so it's no longer enough to juggle time zones; you have to juggle differing national and religious holidays, too.

Recently I received two requests for a briefing on Thanksgiving from companies in Israel and the UK, respectively. In the same week, my husband, who works for a company based in India, had to deflect his superiors when they tried to schedule a U.S. data center tour for Wednesday and Thursday. In each case, when the holiday was explained, both parties backed off, but clearly there are cases when postponing doesn't work, such as when a major trade show falls on a national holiday or your bosses

expect you to be available for a deal's closing. Will requests such as these pile up to make taking time off during holidays more difficult?

For an employee, it's difficult to defend against the expectations of bosses and clients who don't understand or even know today is a day off. Sure, an employee can communicate that, but a manager doesn't have to listen, and it's not as if the employee/boss relationship is completely even. Plus, in a global economy, it's becoming harder to shut down (or expect a slowdown) during what in the Western world were traditionally dull times in August or the week between Christmas and New Year's.

Given that some workers don't take their vacation days, and those naturally slow times in the business might be the sole respite that hardworking or important employees get, is there any reason to hope employees will be diligent defending their holidays? This year, for example, several big stories were announced in August, indicating that bankers, lawyers, and executives were putting off vacations and keeping analysts, reporters, and other folk on their toes. Given the growing economic power of China, the Chinese New Year pads what might be a traditionally dull quarter for some companies, but it also means the week between Christmas and New Year's requires production lines to run and companies to do business.

### DID YOU READ IT?

1) What are some of the problems for workers and businesses of "work going global" in the United States?

2) If eliminating vacation time does not cause workers to quit, how might it affect the labor supply curve?

### WHAT DO YOU THINK?

1) Should the government set a minimum for the amount of vacation time workers receive? What reasons might the government give to support a minimum amount of vacation time?

2) How would eliminating vacation time affect the demand curve for tourism?

EXCERPTED FROM www.businessweek.com/printer/technology/as-work-goes-global-will
-holidays-disappear-11232011.html.

# CHAPTER 11 REVIEW AND SELF-ASSESSMENT

## REVIEW

### Points to Remember

#### MODULE 31: LABOR DEMAND

1. The **value of the marginal product** of an input, such as labor, is the marginal product of that input multiplied by the price of the output being produced. This value indicates the additional revenue gained from hiring one more unit of that input.

2. The demand for labor is a **derived demand**, meaning that it is derived from the demand for the output being produced.

3. The **market demand curve for labor** shows the total quantity of labor the employers in a labor market would hire at each wage.

4. The **elasticity of labor demand** indicates how responsive the quantity of labor demanded is to changes in the wage.

#### MODULE 32: LABOR SUPPLY

5. A worker's **reservation wage** is the lowest wage at which that worker would accept a job.

6. The **market labor supply curve** shows the total number of hours workers would be willing to supply at each wage.

7. A **minimum wage** is a price floor for labor that is set by the government, below which wages are not allowed to fall.

#### MODULE 33: THE SKILLS OF WORKERS AND THE QUALITY OF JOBS

8. A **compensating wage differential** is a premium paid to persuade someone to work in undesirable circumstances.

9. **Employment discrimination** exists if workers who are equally productive are treated differently because of characteristics unrelated to their job performance.

10. A **labor union** is a group of workers who collectively bargain with employers over the terms and conditions of employment.

## SELF-ASSESSMENT

The following questions are the type your teacher might ask you on a quiz or a test. Practice with these in order to improve your performance on class tests.

### Multiple-Choice Questions

1. There will be an increase in the demand for blueberry pickers if there is
   a. an increase in the demand for blueberries.
   b. a decrease in the demand for blueberries.
   c. a decrease in the price of blueberries.
   d. a decrease in the amount of land available for blueberry production.

2. A police officer in a crime-ridden inner city earns more than a police officer in the suburbs because of
   a. employment discrimination.
   b. monopoly power.
   c. compensating wage differentials.
   d. the minimum wage.

Answer the next three questions based on the short-run production function for organic jelly at Jim's Jelly Joint, as shown in the following table.

| QUANTITY OF WORKERS | JELLY PER DAY (IN JARS) |
|:---:|:---:|
| 0 | 0 |
| 1 | 10 |
| 2 | 22 |
| 3 | 32 |
| 4 | 40 |
| 5 | 46 |
| 6 | 50 |

3. If Jim sells his jelly for $10 per jar, what is the value of the marginal product of the fourth worker?

a. $10
b. $80
c. $100
d. $400

4. Jim sells his jelly for $10 per jar and currently has 3 employees but is considering hiring a fourth worker. Jim should hire the fourth worker as long as his workers do not earn more than

a. $30 per day.
b. $50 per day.
c. $60 per day.
d. $80 per day.

5. Jim sells his jelly for $10 per jar and pays his workers $50 each per day to produce jelly. How many workers should Jim hire to maximize profits?

a. 3
b. 4
c. 5
d. 6

6. Which of the following would lead to the largest increase in employment for a particular group within society?

a. a decrease in the substitution effect and an increase in the income effect
b. a decrease in the substitution effect and a decrease in the income effect
c. an increase in the substitution effect and a decrease in the income effect
d. an increase in the substitution effect and an increase in the income effect

7. Which of the following would result in an increase in the equilibrium wage and an increase in the equilibrium quantity of labor?

a. a decrease in the demand for labor
b. an increase in the demand for labor
c. a decrease in the supply of labor
d. an increase in the supply of labor

8. When the demand for an input, like labor, is determined by the demand for the good being produced, this is referred to as

a. inelastic demand.
b. elastic demand.
c. derived demand.
d. backward-bending demand.

9. When a person with two job offers takes the job they find less desirable because it pays more than the other job, they are

a. making an irrational decision.
b. a victim of the minimum wage.
c. experiencing employment discrimination.
d. motivated by a compensating wage differential.

10. Occupational licensing

a. increases supply and decreases wages.
b. decreases supply and increases wages.
c. increases demand and increases wages.
d. decreases demand and decreases wages.

## Constructed Response Question

1. Lauren's Licorice Lounge sells licorice for $2.50 each; her daily production function is shown in the following table. Lauren pays each of her workers $50 per day.

| QUANTITY OF WORKERS | TOTAL PRODUCT | MARGINAL PRODUCT | VALUE OF THE MARGINAL PRODUCT |
|---|---|---|---|
| 0 | 0 | | |
| 1 | 95 | | |
| 2 | 180 | | |
| 3 | 255 | | |
| 4 | 320 | | |
| 5 | 375 | | |
| 6 | 420 | | |
| 7 | 455 | | |
| 8 | 480 | | |
| 9 | 495 | | |
| 10 | 500 | | |

   a. Calculate the marginal product and the value of the marginal product of labor for Lauren's Licorice Lounge.
   b. Using a correctly labeled graph, draw Lauren's labor demand curve.
   c. How many workers will Lauren hire? Explain.
   d. If the price of licorice rises to $5, how many workers will Lauren hire?
   e. What would happen if the price of licorice was still $2.50, but Lauren doubled her workers' pay?

**CHAPTER 12 & YOU** As you become more responsible for your own finances you will need to address a new set of questions. Should you pay for your groceries with a debit card or a credit card? Can you upgrade your cell phone plan and pay for car insurance and still have enough money left over to join the health club? As exciting as it is to gain independence and support yourself, it is equally important to make responsible decisions about managing your money, making big purchases, accepting risk, and saving for the future. This chapter will help you make sense of these and other financial decisions.

# Personal Finance: Managing Your Money

## A TALE OF TWO BUDGETS

For 70 years, Oseola McCarty made her living washing and ironing other people's clothing in Hattiesburg, Mississippi. Ms. McCarty did not earn much money, but she started saving every week when she was young. She budgeted her money wisely and lived well within her means, never even buying a car or an air conditioner. Ms. McCarty made national news in 1995 when she decided to donate $150,000 of her life savings to the University of Southern Mississippi to help needy students. "I'm giving it away," she said, "so that the children won't have to work so hard, like I did." The fact that Ms. McCarty amassed so much money and generously gave it away inspired many others, and she was honored with the Presidential Citizens Medal.

By contrast, William "Bud" Post III died penniless in 2006. He had won $16.2 million in the Pennsylvania lottery in 1988. Born in Erie, Pennsylvania, Mr. Post had been poor most of his life. He drifted from job

to job and never owned a house. He told reporters that he was down to $2.46 in his bank account on the day he won the lottery. He pawned a ring to raise the $40 that he used to buy lottery tickets, one of which contained the winning number. However, in the first two weeks after becoming a millionaire he spent $300,000, and within three months he was $500,000 in debt. By 1998 he had spent almost all the money, gone bankrupt at one point, and landed in jail. After his release, he was reported to have been living on $450 per month in disability payments.

*No matter how much money you make, you will end up penniless if you make poor financial decisions.*

These two stories illustrate the importance of spending your money wisely and staying within a budget. No matter how much money you make—even if you win millions of dollars in the lottery—you will wind up in trouble if you make poor financial decisions. This chapter explains the basics of personal finance, including how to find a job, how to manage a budget, and what to consider when spending and investing your money.

## BOTTOM LINE

To successfully manage your personal finances, you need to budget your spending, carefully consider options to borrow or invest, save for the future, and be prepared for unexpected losses.

# MODULE 34

# Finding a Job

**KEY IDEA:** The secrets to finding a great job are research and preparation.

**OBJECTIVES**

- To explain the importance of researching different careers before applying for jobs.
- To identify the key elements of a resume.
- To explain how to prepare for an interview.

## The Tradeoffs of Career Choice

It's never too soon to think about careers that might interest you. It's likely that you'll face tradeoffs between your most favored job, your most favored income, and your most favored place to live, among other things. For example, would you rather earn an annual salary of $38,000 as a park ranger or $64,000 as a coal miner? To earn a high salary you may need to tolerate a relatively unpleasant workplace, stressful conditions, long work hours, or other challenges. If one of your strengths is being a good student, remember that education and training will give you access to more jobs that pay well. As you contemplate your future career, you may find inspiration in the community, where a good teacher, a successful parent, or a local leader can spark your imagination. In this module we'll discuss ways to learn more about careers and conduct a successful job search.

*Every job has its pros and cons. For example, jobs in great places may not pay great salaries. Focus your ambition on the career that best fits your skills and priorities.*

## THE RIGHT JOB FOR YOU

Most Americans of working age who do not have a disability rely on a job to support themselves and their families. Recognizing what jobs you might be qualified for and how much they pay is a first step in planning for your economic future. The prospect of working for a living can be daunting. But finding your first "real" job is exciting as well as challenging. When you are ready to start looking for a job, your teachers, family, and mentors will be good sources of information. Talk to them about career opportunities and keep an eye on the newspaper for stories about jobs that interest you. The Internet provides a wealth of additional information.

Research is essential to any job hunt. What kinds of skills and educational degrees are required for the jobs that interest you? Will you have to get a special license? Do you have to live in a certain part of the country? What are the prospects for employment? Is the number of jobs growing or shrinking in that field? In the process of doing research on one occupation, you might learn about another that might be an even better, more realistic fit for your background and interests.

### How to Learn about Jobs

The Internet is bursting with job information. One of the best online sources is the Bureau of Labor Statistics website at BLS. gov. Among the wealth of information on the site, you will find employment and

*The Internet offers many sources of information about jobs.*

*"Choose a job you love, and you will never have to work a day in your life."*
—Confucius

wage estimates for over 800 occupations under the "subject areas" tab. The *Occupational Outlook Handbook* under the "publications" tab provides detailed descriptions of hundreds of occupations and forecasts of the future demand for workers in those occupations.

Another source is O*Net Online, an occupational information network that contains detailed descriptions of over 800 occupations, including the types of skills required and what the job entails. Don't fail to consider more traditional ways to explore job opportunities as well. Watch for career fairs where employers set up booths to share information about their firms. The want ads in the newspaper indicate the types of jobs available nearby. It never hurts to ask people in your community who have interesting jobs to discuss the pros and cons of their work situations. Even better, arrange to spend a day with a worker in a job that you want to learn more about. It will be easier to make contact with workers and employers if you develop a network of working friends ahead of time. Be active in your community, join clubs, do volunteer work, and attend social events. When the time comes to seek a job, let your friends know what you're looking for and they may be your greatest resource.

## THE RESUME AND COVER LETTER

**A resume** is a brief document that summarizes your education, work experience, and skills.

A **resume** is a brief document that summarizes your education, work experience, and skills. A resume is sometimes referred to as a *curriculum vitae* or *CV*, which is Latin for "course of one's life."

The purpose of a resume is to convey your relevant background information, qualifications, and skills to potential employers who are deciding whether to give you a job interview. Along with a *cover letter*, your resume is usually the first piece of information that potential employers have about you, so it must look professional and portray your experiences accurately. You should be able to find sample resumes in the guidance office at your school and, of course, on the Internet. Here are some basic guidelines:

**Education**

Boyle County High School, Boulder, CO
2009 - 2013

**Experience**

Newspaper Carrier
2008 - Present
• Delivered newspapers to 100 homes.

Child Care
2010 - 2012
• Cared for several children for two evenings each week.

**Achievements**

• National Honor Society member, 2013
• All-A Honor Roll, 2011-2013
• 4H Leadership Award, 2012

**Volunteer Work**

• English as a Second Language Program
• Boulder Animal Shelter
• Math Tutoring Program

**Activities**

• Boyle County High School Marching Band
• Varsity Cross Country Team
• Spanish Club

**Skills**

• Proficient with Microsoft Excel, PowerPoint and Word
• Experience with Macintosh and PC computing
• Fluent in conversational Spanish

Alexandra Lathrop
42 Old Bridge Road
Boulder, CO 80302
home: 555-465-9211
cell: 555-821-7315
email: ally@boyleschools.com

• Include your full name, address, and all contact phone numbers.

• Divide your resume into sections labeled "Education," "Experience," "Achievements," "Volunteer Work," "Activities," and "Skills."

• Present the information in reverse chronological order, so that the first items listed under "Education" and "Experience" are the most recent.

• Check your grammar and spelling carefully and ask someone else to proofread it for you. Also use the active voice rather than the passive voice. For example, you might write, "Delivered newspapers to 100 homes," rather than, "Newspapers for 100 homes were delivered by me."

• Present yourself in the best light possible but do not exaggerate. Never misrepresent your past accomplishments. Employees can be fired and embarrassed if they are later discovered to have lied on their resume.

### DID YOU GET IT?
**What is a resume?**

A *cover letter* should accompany your resume when you apply for a job. A **cover letter** is a short note that tells the potential employer how you heard about the job, why you are interested in it, and why he or she should look at your resume and invite you for an interview. You should use the cover letter to direct the employer's attention to certain elements of your background and experience that qualify you for the job.

## THE INTERVIEW

After submitting a well-crafted resume and cover letter, if you are sufficiently qualified, the employer may invite you to visit for a job interview. Again, preparation is key. This is your opportunity to impress the interviewer and convince him or her that you are *the* person for the job. In addition to presenting yourself in a neat and professional way, you must go to the interview informed about what the firm does. Study the employer's website and any recent news stories about the firm or industry, and incorporate what you learn into some of your answers. For example, if you are asked why you would like to work for Company X, you might say, "I've read that Company X is experimenting with new batteries for laptop computers that aren't made from lithium, which interests me because

I understand that lithium is in short supply. It would be exciting to help create a new battery to serve the company and its customers."

You should also have a few questions of your own to ask the interviewer about the job. This will make you appear more confident and genuinely interested in the position. However, don't ask about the amount you will be paid. Remember that the interview is a time for the employer to see what type of person you are, so if you're prompt, professional, and enthusiastic, that's the image you will leave them with. If you're tardy, sloppy, and uninformed at the interview, the employer will assume that's the type of employee you would be.

*During an interview, employers make important judgments quickly. Be prepared and look your best.*

### DID YOU GET IT?
**Why should you prepare for an interview?**

## WHAT NEXT?

If all goes well, the employer will offer you a job. The employer will typically state the terms of the position—how much it pays, how many vacation days you get, whether you receive health insurance, and so on. Depending on the situation, there may be some opportunity to negotiate over the terms. For example, if you've received a better offer from another employer, you might say, "Company Y has offered me a wage of $10 per hour. Would you be able to match that offer?" Never try to negotiate before you have a job offer. And if you do negotiate, be respectful and frame the conversation as a joint effort to determine what is fair for both you and the employer. Your long-term employment prospects depend on whether hiring you turned out to be beneficial for both you and the firm.

If you are not offered a job after applying to a particular company, do not feel discouraged. Job searching takes

A **cover letter** is a short note that tells a potential employer how you heard about the job, why you are interested in it, and why he or she should look at your resume and invite you for an interview.

THINKSTOCK

persistence. It can take months or longer to find a job, especially if you have little previous work experience. There are many qualified applicants for most positions and all but one must be rejected. The labor market is also plagued by imperfect information, and success can hinge on being in the right place at the right time. One of the authors of this textbook managed to get his foot in the door for the most important job in his life because he happened to sit next to the right person on an airplane!

If you find it difficult to obtain interviews after applying for many jobs, reconsider whether you are applying for jobs that match your qualifications. You may need to start at a lower level and work your way up the corporate ladder, or you may need to seek additional training in your field of interest. Also, keep in mind that the Internet can be a source of information about you for potential employers. Be careful not to post anything on the web or on a social networking site that might hurt your chances of getting a job in the future.

# MODULE 34 REVIEW AND ASSESSMENT

## Summing Up the Key Ideas: Match the following terms to the correct definitions.

A. Resume            B. Cover letter            C. Curriculum vitae

_A_ 1. A brief document that summarizes your education, work experience, and skills.

_C_ 2. Another name for a resume, Latin meaning "course of one's life."

_B_ 3. A short note that tells a potential employer how you heard about the job, why you are interested in it, and why he or she should look at your resume and invite you for an interview.

## Analyze: Analyze each of the following statements and determine if they belong in a resume or a cover letter.

### RESUME OR COVER LETTER?

1. a listing of your education, experience, achievements, and skills

_resume_

2. a note that tells your potential employer how you heard about the job

_cover letter_

3. a list of volunteer work and other activities

_resume_

4. an explanation about why you are interested in the job

_cover letter_

## Apply

1. What are some good ways to learn about jobs that might be available to you?

_Internet, newspaper_

2. Give two examples of work or activities that you would put on your resume.

_volunteer, internships_

3. What are two good things for you to bring up during a job interview?

_questions, background knowledge about the company_

# MODULE 35

# Creating a Budget

**KEY IDEA:** **If you get into the habit of creating and following a budget, you will find it much easier to manage your money and meet your financial goals.**

### OBJECTIVES

- **To explain why a budget is important.**
- **To show how a budget is created.**
- **To explain the importance of saving.**
- **To explain the basics of borrowing.**

## It's Better to Budget

We saw in Chapter 3 that as people pursue happiness, they are constrained by a budget that defines what they can afford. Sometimes it is possible to get a loan that allows you to spend money before you earn it. But sooner or later, those who spend more than they can afford run into serious problems. For example, they may be forced to sell their home or car. They may also reach the state of financial ruin called *bankruptcy*, which means they cannot pay their debts and will have great difficulty getting any sort of loan or credit card for many years. In this module we'll discuss approaches to money management that will help you avoid that fate.

*A budget will help you steer clear of financial trouble.*

## WHY CREATE A BUDGET?

The term *budget* has several meanings. Your town might *budget* (allocate) $10 million for a new city hall. You can buy a *budget* (inexpensive) cell phone plan. The U.S. federal government had a *budget* (amount of money to spend) of $3.8 trillion in 2011. And you can manage your money wisely by creating a **budget** (specific plan for spending money). It is this last type of budget that we'll explore here.

The thought of making and following a budget may not be at the top of your mind. But training yourself to ask questions like "How much should I spend on restaurant meals each month?" and "Do I really need the newest video game?" is extremely important to your future financial health. Unfortunately, many adults never develop the habit of

adhering to a budget. That's partly because it's hard to follow a budget after other spending habits have been established and partly because many people do not want to accept the realities of their financial situation. Some people say that ignorance is bliss, but such bliss can end with bankruptcy. In the first half of 2012, more than 601,000 individuals filed for bankruptcy in the United States. To ward off that fate, start the habit of following a budget early on, before you become overwhelmed with rent, student loan bills, and credit card balances.

Next we'll see how simple it is to create a budget for your money. If you haven't already, you can use the same

A **budget** is a specific plan for how to spend your money.

skills to budget your *time* by writing down how you plan to spend your time on homework, chores, and after-school activities.

**DID YOU GET IT?**
What is a budget?

# CREATING YOUR OWN BUDGET

Making a budget is essentially an exercise of listing income from all sources, listing expenses of all sorts, and making adjustments as needed so that the expenses do not exceed the income. Success with a budget requires accuracy. If your income isn't as large as planned, or your expenses are larger than expected, things can get ugly. That makes careful budget planning important.

As you prepare your budget, note that the amount of income specified in your employment contract is not the amount you will have to spend. You must adjust for the taxes that will be taken out of that income before you can spend it. The amount you earn before taxes are deducted is called your **gross income**. The income you are left with after subtracting taxes is called your **net income** or *disposable income* or *after-tax income*. If you work as an employee for a firm, a large portion of your income taxes will most likely be deducted from your pay automatically. You might also have to pay additional income taxes in April of each year, depending on your situation and income level.

Once you have a good idea of your net income for a given period—say, a month—write it down and identify its source as in the top section of Table 35.1. If possible, do this using

Your **gross income** is the total amount of money you make.

Your **net income** is the income that you are left with after paying taxes.

a spreadsheet software program such as Microsoft Excel that will facilitate number crunching. Then make a list of every expense you expect to incur. You can estimate monthly expenditures on each item, including clothing, food, your cell phone, insurance, entertainment, gasoline, gifts, and so on, as in the bottom section of Table 35.1. Once you have a complete list, compare the total amount you expect to spend to your net income. If you will spend more money than you make with the existing budget, you will need to adjust your spending plans or look for additional sources of income, such as working overtime or taking a second job.

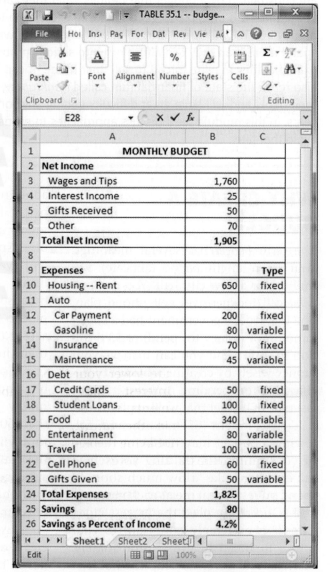

| MONTHLY BUDGET | | |
|---|---|---|
| **Net Income** | | |
| Wages and Tips | 1,760 | |
| Interest Income | 25 | |
| Gifts Received | 50 | |
| Other | 70 | |
| **Total Net Income** | **1,905** | |
| | | |
| Expenses | | Type |
| Housing -- Rent | 650 | fixed |
| Auto | | |
| Car Payment | 200 | fixed |
| Gasoline | 80 | variable |
| Insurance | 70 | fixed |
| Maintenance | 45 | variable |
| Debt | | |
| Credit Cards | 50 | fixed |
| Student Loans | 100 | fixed |
| Food | 340 | variable |
| Entertainment | 80 | variable |
| Travel | 100 | variable |
| Cell Phone | 60 | fixed |
| Gifts Given | 50 | variable |
| **Total Expenses** | **1,825** | |
| **Savings** | **80** | |
| **Savings as Percent of Income** | **4.2%** | |

In reviewing your budget, it is useful to distinguish between expenses that normally stay the same every month and those that vary from one month to the next. Your rent, car payment, and insurance payment are examples of **fixed expenses** because they remain about the same unless you move or buy a new car. Expenditures on gasoline, food, and entertainment represent **variable expenses** because they can change frequently at your discretion. By recognizing the difference, you will know how to cut costs quickly (decrease variable expenses) and which cuts—when possible—will generate the longest-lasting savings (cuts in fixed expenses).

Given our unlimited wants and limited earnings, planned expenditures tend to exceed net income in the early stages of budget making. If that happens to you, and if working more isn't what you have in mind, then it's time to eliminate some planned expenditures. That's the hard part, but it doesn't have to be that hard. With the list of expenses in front of you, it becomes easier to identify the least painful cuts. If it would be difficult to change some types of consumption, such as eating out, think outside of the pizza box and you may find better solutions. Over time you can reduce your fixed expenses and have a long-term effect on your budget. Consider ways to cut down on fixed expenses—switching to a cheaper cell phone plan, driving a less expensive car, or renting a more modest apartment. The more of your debt that you pay off now, the lower your interest payments will be in the future. Delaying big-ticket purchases also saves you money. Try getting a few more months out of your old refrigerator, dryer, and phone before replacing them. Drive your used car another year or two before trading up. Make that trip to Europe next year and vacation closer

to home this year. These are all ways to stay ahead in the money game. The box below summarizes the steps to making a budget.

**Fixed expenses** are expenses that remain about the same from month to month.

---

### Four Steps to Making a Monthly Budget

 **1.** Identify your monthly net income from every source.

 **2.** Create a list of your fixed and variable monthly expenses.

 **3.** Compare the totals of monthly income and expenses.

 **4.** If expenses exceed income, look for unnecessary spending and missed opportunities to increase your income.

---

 **DID YOU GET IT?**

How does gross income differ from net income? What are two fixed expenses and two variable expenses that your family paid last month?

**Variable expenses** can change frequently at your discretion.

## SAVING

Many people spend all their income each month. That's understandable for someone just starting out. The large expenses of establishing a home and paying off school and car loans far exceed most starting incomes. But it is important to establish a pattern of saving for your future, and the sooner the better. If you can set aside just a few dollars each week even in the beginning, it will help you form the essential habit of saving.

Why save? There are two main reasons. First, you will want to have some money tucked away in a *rainy day fund*

for those unforeseen expenses that often arise. When you least expect it, you might need extra money for a new laptop, a smart-phone, car repairs, or travel. Second, even for anticipated expenses, when it rains, it pours: some of the largest expenses come all at once and would overwhelm your budget for any given year. These include expenditures for college, a house, a wedding, raising a family, retirement, and end-of-life care. The *least* expensive of these items, a wedding, typically costs between $20,000 and $30,000.

The budget example in Table 35.1 includes savings of $80, which is 4.2 percent of net income. More would be better. Many financial advisors suggest saving 10–15 percent of net income, which is easier said than done. For perspective, Figure 35.1 shows the average percentage of net income that was saved by Americans between 1959 and 2011. Saving, like studying and dieting, takes self-discipline. And as with other challenges, there are tricks that make it easier. One approach is to "pay yourself first," meaning that you set aside a certain amount of money for your own saving each month before paying other people for their products and services. This practice forces budget discipline

that may be hard to maintain otherwise. To accomplish this, deposit the amount you can afford into a savings account or your favored type of investment each month upon receiving your paycheck. Most banks can even set up an automatic withdrawal so that the planned amount is whisked out of the account that receives your paycheck and deposited into your savings account without any effort from you. Whichever method you choose, be sure to stick with it. By securing your financial health you will avoid a lot of headaches.

**DID YOU GET IT?**
**What is a good way to begin saving?**

## BORROWING

Usually people need the most money when they have the least. The expense of college comes when most people have little money. The expense of starting a business comes before the first item is sold. And the expense of a first home comes early in life before much wealth can be acquired. It is normal to borrow money to pay for these big-ticket items. Particular care must be taken when spending other people's money because of the responsibility you have to the lenders. But if you are confident that you will have extra money in the future for repayment, then borrowing can make sense.

**Figure 35.1** Personal Saving as a Percentage of Net Income, 1959–2011

After you borrow money and start enjoying your new acquisitions, you will need to pay back what you have borrowed, typically a bit at a time. In addition, you will have to pay an extra amount known as *interest*. Interest is the fee you pay for borrowing and it is what makes lending worthwhile for the lender. The amount of interest owed on a loan is usually quoted as an **annual percentage rate** or APR, which is the percentage of the borrowed amount that you would pay in interest if you had the loan for exactly one year, taking into account how frequently interest is compounded. APR is larger than the quoted rate if interest is compounded more than once a year. The standard of stating an annual rate makes it easier to compare the rates on loans from different lenders. The actual percentage of the loan amount that you pay in interest will be smaller than the APR if your loan is for less than a year and larger than the APR if your loan is for more than a year. For example, if you borrow $20,000 for a car and the APR is 5 percent, you would be required to pay the lender 5% × $20,000 = $1,000 per year in interest for the privilege of borrowing the $20,000, in addition to repaying the $20,000 itself. If you borrowed the $20,000 for half a year, you would pay 1/2 × 5% × $20,000 = $500, or 2.5 percent of the amount borrowed. If you borrowed the $20,000 for two years, you would pay 2 × 5% × $20,000 = $2,000, or 10 percent of the amount borrowed. For simplicity, these figures assume that you borrow the $20,000 for the full period of the loan. If you pay back some of the $20,000 each month, as is common, then the amount you pay in interest will decrease.

Money can be borrowed from a variety of sources, including banks, credit unions, and credit card companies. By making a purchase with a credit card, you can borrow money for a short period of time without paying interest. However, if you don't pay your entire balance by the due date, the credit card company will charge you an interest fee

in addition to the amount of your original purchase. To avoid these substantial fees, it is beneficial to pay off your credit card debt without delay. Many people run into financial trouble by owing money to credit card companies. As the amount they owe grows, so do their monthly fees and the hole they've dug themselves into.

In May of 2009, President Obama signed into law major new legislation called the Credit Card Accountability, Responsibility, and Disclosure (CARD) Act. The law has helped consumers by eliminating many credit card practices that cost customers extra money. For example, credit card companies can no longer offer enticingly low "teaser" interest rates on credit cards and hike them up immediately once the card is issued; the new rules require low introductory rates to be in effect for at least six months. In addition, if you're under 21, you must have an adult cosign or show proof that you are able to pay. Since 2011, the Consumer Financial Protection Bureau (CFPB) has been responsible for administering the CARD Act.

If you decide to borrow money, bear two things in mind. First, the interest rate varies widely among lenders. Credit card companies often charge relatively high

The **annual percentage rate** is the percentage of the borrowed amount that you would pay in interest if you had the loan for one year.

*Interest is the fee you pay for borrowing money.*

interest fees. The Economics in Action box describes another source of loans known as *payday lenders*. These lenders usually charge rates even higher than the credit card companies. You should seek to borrow from the source with the lowest available rate, other things being equal. Often people can improve their financial situation by borrowing from lower-cost lenders such as banks and credit unions to pay off debt owed to higher-cost lenders such as credit card companies.

Second, remember that there is no such thing as a free lunch. A common mistake is to be too impatient when it comes to consumption, failing to appreciate that money borrowed today will have to be paid back—and then some—in the future. When a sizable portion of your income goes to paying back loans, it becomes harder to buy goods and services. So use caution to avoid taking out loans you might regret later on.

**DID YOU GET IT?**
What two things should you be aware of if you decide to borrow money?

# ECONOMICS IN ACTION

# Payday Lending

*The following article from* The Wall Street Journal *describes the practice of payday lending and discusses its pros and cons.*

Payday lenders are so named because they provide short-term cash advances that are often due when borrowers receive their next paycheck. A typical borrower takes out a two-week loan and pays around $15 for every $100 he borrows, or the equivalents of a 390% annual interest rate. Lenders say this structure is necessary to cover costs, offset higher default rates, and still turn a profit. Critics say the rates are exorbitant and often trap financially strapped borrowers in a cycle of paying additional "rollover" fees to renew the same amount of principal.

About 13 states have effectively banned payday lending; the other 37 regulate the practice to varying degrees. But demand for small, short-term loans appears to be soaring, and just about every state is debating whether the accessibility and comparative ease of payday loans outweigh the risk for consumers of falling further into debt. The industry, which generates roughly $40 billion in loans each year, is regulated at the state level.

*Payday lenders provide short-term loans at relatively high interest rates.*

Since this article was written, the federal government has gotten involved. The Consumer Financial Protection Bureau (CFPB), mentioned in Chapter 7, now helps to enforce federal laws that require all payday lenders to provide better information to potential borrowers. The CFPB also works to avoid excessive interest rates and fees.

SOURCE: Christopher Conkey. *The Wall Street Journal*, February 21, 2007.

**DID YOU GET IT?**
Why do critics oppose payday lending? Do you find their arguments convincing?

## PEOPLE IN ECONOMICS

# Alexa von Tobel, LearnVest.com

When she graduated from Harvard College, Alexa von Tobel realized that although she was about to start a job on Wall Street, she did not feel comfortable managing her own money. In fact, she had never taken a personal finance class and wasn't sure how to deal with credit cards, insurance, and taxes. It occurred to her that many young women must be in a similar situation.

A few years later, in 2008, von Tobel took a leave of absence from Harvard Business School (to which she had since returned) to start LearnVest.com. Her goal was to explain personal finance in clear and understandable ways, and to provide tools that would help women manage their financial situation. LearnVest offers features for tracking expenditure and budgeting, as well as tutorials on saving money and reducing debt. Users can also pay to receive advice from financial experts and enroll in online finance courses. Alexa von Tobel believes that financial planning is something that everyone should be able to do and that taking control of your finances can help you achieve your dreams.

## MODULE 35 REVIEW AND ASSESSMENT

**Summing Up the Key Ideas:** Match the following terms to the correct definitions.

A. Budget
B. Bankruptcy
C. Net income
D. Fixed expenses
E. Variable expenses
F. Annual percentage rate
G. Interest
H. Payday lenders
I. Gross income
J. Rainy day fund

_____I_____ 1. The total amount of money you earn before taxes.

_____C_____ 2. The income you are left with after paying taxes, also called disposable income.

_____J_____ 3. Money for unforeseen expenses that should be saved.

_____F_____ 4. The percentage of the borrowed amount that you would pay in interest if you had the loan for one year.

_____D_____ 5. Expenses that remain about the same from month to month.

_____H_____ 6. Fee paid for borrowing, and what makes lending worthwhile for the lender.

_____B_____ 7. Condition in which one cannot pay their debts and will have great difficulty getting any sort of loan or credit card for many years.

_____A_____ 8. A specific plan for how to spend your money.

_____E_____ 9. Expenses that can change frequently at your discretion.

_____G_____ 10. Provide short-term cash advances that are often due when borrowers receive their next paycheck.

## Analyze and Explain: Imagine you have started your career and own a home. Indicate whether each of the following changes would have a positive or negative effect on your budget. Explain your answer.

| | EFFECT ON BUDGET | EXPLAIN |
|---|---|---|
| 1. Your furnace breaks down. | negative | how |
| 2. You decide to purchase a new car. | neg | |
| 3. Your boss raises your salary. | pos | |
| 4. You make an unexpected visit to the emergency room. | neg | |
| 5. Gas prices jump. | neg | |
| 6. You take a second job. | pos | |

## Apply: Categorize each of the following as a fixed expense or a variable expense.

| | FIXED EXPENSE OR VARIABLE EXPENSE? |
|---|---|
| 1. movie tickets | variable |
| 2. rent | fixed |
| 3. insurance payments | fixed |
| 4. music downloads | variable |
| 5. going out to eat | variable |
| 6. going on vacation | variable |
| 7. car payments | fixed |
| 8. gift giving | variable |

# MODULE 36

# Essential Elements of Personal Finance

**KEY IDEA:** Before depositing or spending your hard-earned money, you should weigh the pros and cons of different alternatives.

## OBJECTIVES

- **To describe how to use a checking account.**
- **To explain approaches to funding your college education.**
- **To discuss decisions to be made when buying a car.**
- **To explain how to protect yourself from identity theft and what to do if you become a victim.**

*Depending on how you manage your checking account, it can be a great convenience or a dangerous money pit.*

## Check, Cash, or Charge?

Now that we've discussed ways to earn and budget money, it's time to explore ways to spend it. Cash works, but if you carry around a lot of cash you risk loss and theft. There is also an opportunity cost of holding cash because it could otherwise be deposited in accounts that earn interest. Module 35 mentioned credit cards. These are popular but can be difficult for young people to obtain on their own and often involve high fees. Checking accounts are more accessible and, if properly managed, are inexpensive or free. In this module we'll evaluate these options, discuss major purchases, and explain how to protect your money from identify theft.

# CHECKING ACCOUNTS AND ELECTRONIC BANKING

As you begin to earn sizable amounts of money, you probably won't want to carry it all around or stash it in your room. It's nice to have a place to put it where it won't be lost or stolen but where you have easy access to it. A checking account is essentially a safe holding area for money until it is spent. Let's explore how checking accounts work.

## Why a Checking Account?

A checking account holds money you intend to spend soon and offers several easy ways to pay for things. Clearly, one option is to write a check. Beyond the convenience, checks provide a record of payment. After the recipient exchanges a check for cash at his or her bank, the check is returned to your bank, where you can obtain a copy if needed to dash any doubt that the payment was made.

As the holder of a checking account, you can usually also apply for a *debit card* that you can use to make purchases. A debit card is like a credit card, except that rather than receiving a monthly bill for your expenditures, the money for debit card purchases is withdrawn directly from your bank account.

The payment of monthly bills can take time and money for stamps. To avoid this, most banks allow you to

*A debit card is like a credit card except that the money for purchases is withdrawn directly from your bank account.*

set up an *automatic check handling* (ACH) withdrawal. By giving the firm you are paying some basic information about your account, they will be able to tap directly into your checking account for your monthly payment. This requires no additional effort from you, except to make sure there is enough money in your account at the right time and that the charges are correct. If you don't, the resulting fees will make you regret it.

Although checking accounts do not pay as much interest as savings accounts and some other types of accounts and investments, they offer easier access to your money when you need it. Another benefit of establishing a checking account is that lenders and credit card companies see them as a sign of financial stability, which might help you get a loan or a credit card later on.

## Questions to Ask Your Banker

Many banks compete for your business. Take your time and select a bank only after asking the following questions:

**1.  What free services do you provide?** These might include debit and credit cards, car and home loans, direct deposit so that your paycheck goes directly from your employer to your bank, multilingual tellers, free checks, drive-up windows, and ATMs.

**2.  Are you FDIC insured?** The Federal Deposit Insurance Corporation (FDIC) is an independent agency of the federal government established to insure bank deposits. The FDIC guarantees that if your bank closes down, you will get your deposits back, up to a limit of $250,000. This insurance is provided by the government to give depositors confidence and help stabilize the economy during an economic crisis.

**3.  What are your fees?** You need a clear picture of the costs of doing business at a particular bank because bank fees are expensive, and you don't want to discover a lot of hidden charges later on. Find out if there are any monthly fees, fees for opening an account, or ATM fees. Also ask about fees for overdrawing your account (that is, bouncing a check, as discussed in the next section), debit or credit cards, checks, money orders, foreign currency conversion, and any other services you might use.

**4.  Is there a minimum balance?** A deposit of a certain amount may be required to open an account. For most checking accounts the requirement is modest, perhaps $50 or $100. Some banks charge a fee for each month during which your *balance*—the amount of money in your account—falls below a minimum. Be sure to find out what that minimum is and choose a bank with a minimum you can stay above.

**5.  Does the account pay interest?** Some checking accounts pay interest and some don't. For those that do, they usually require larger minimum balances. Especially if you plan to hold a serious amount of money in that account, be clear on how much interest you'll receive. Don't be lured in by a high interest rate on an account with fees and other aspects that aren't so great, because the interest rate may fall and the fees may not.

**6.  Can I access my account online?** The more banking you can do online, the more time you will save on trips to the bank. Most banks allow customers to at least check their balances and make transfers online, but you should check on the details.

**7.  Where are the ATMs I can use for free (if any)?** Most banks allow you to access your account at ATMs all over the world, but there is typically a fee to use ATMs that are not provided by your particular bank. Some large banks have thousands of ATMs from coast to coast. Others have a few around town. With ATM fees rising, it's worth asking about the locations of free ATMs in the cities where you expect to spend time.

## Avoiding Added Costs

Checking accounts that could be cheap or free can become terribly expensive if you don't keep tabs on your balance. If you spend money you don't really have by writing a check for more than your balance, the check will *bounce*, meaning that your bank will send (*bounce*) the check back to the store with a big stamp on it saying "insufficient funds." The store is likely to charge you a fee in the vicinity of $30 for their trouble in collecting payment for your check. Then the bank will charge you its own fee, maybe $35, for their trouble in returning the check to the store. The bank's fee is deducted from your account, which can lead more checks to bounce. Your own trouble is compounded if you have a check-bouncing problem because check verification services such as ChexSystems share lists of frequent offenders with banks, which can make it difficult to open a new account.

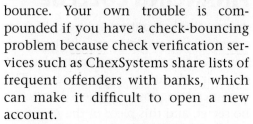

The moral of the check-bouncing story is that you really need to *balance your checkbook*. Here's how: The provider of your checks will give you a little book in which to record your checking account transactions. If you prefer, you can do this on your computer or with a phone app. Begin by recording your initial deposit into the account. Then record each subsequent deposit and withdrawal, being careful to include any automatic payments, fees, or credits to your account.

Each month, by mail or e-mail, you will receive a *statement* that reports all your transactions. Compare the items in your statement with your records to be sure nothing is missed. When you can keep enough money in your checking account to assure nothing will bounce, you can worry less about balancing your checkbook. Until that time, be vigilant!

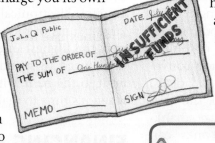

There's an old joke about a woman whose husband wanted to be buried with the $100,000 he had amassed over his career. The woman obeyed his wishes, sort of, by writing him a check for $100,000 and placing it in his casket. This is a clever approach because the money transferred by a check is only withdrawn from the check writer's account when the check is presented for payment at the bank. The woman in this story can safely assume that the check to her husband won't reach her account. Read the neighboring Caution Box for warnings about checks that only *look* like they will never show up.

---

> ⚠️ **Keep Your Balance**
>
> Don't rely on your monthly statement to determine your account balance. Keep your own record. After you write a check, there's no telling how long it will take for the payment to be withdrawn from your account. The recipient of the check might lose it, only to find it months later. So the balance reported on your statement may be $200, but then, even if you haven't written a check recently, fall to zero when a long-forgotten $200 check finally clears your account. If you put reliance on the $200 balance and write another check, it will be a *rubber check* that will bounce.
>
> On the other hand, don't assume it will take a while for a check to clear your account. The digital age has brought links between stores and banks that allow clearing to occur almost instantaneously in some cases. Thus don't plan to deposit money tomorrow to cover a check written today. You must have the money in your account before the check is written.

As an added precaution, your bank probably offers *overdraft protection*, which is essentially a very expensive automatic loan triggered by a check that would otherwise bounce. If you sign up for overdraft protection, your bank will use its own money to cover the check that overdraws your account. The fees for overdraft protection can be significant but are generally lower than what you would pay for a bounced check. You can also arrange overdraft protection by setting up a direct link between your checking and saving accounts.

### Banking Online

Since the 1970s, *automatic teller machines* (ATMs) have made it possible to deposit and withdraw money without entering a bank. With online banking you can now

*Technology has changed the face of the banking industry.*

do most of your banking from home in your pajamas. The Internet allows banks to serve you without erecting a handsome building on Main Street or hiring a single teller. This can be good and bad.

The pros of online banking include convenience and good deals. By saving on the cost of face-to-face banking, online banks can offer lower fees and pay higher interest rates on deposits. Online you can quickly request bill payments and transfers or set up an automatic alert that will tell you when your account is running low. Some banks even allow customers to deposit a check by submitting a photo of it with a phone app. As the opportunity cost of your time grows, so does the value of taking care of banking chores from home.

On the con side, online banking isn't so easy when you need personal attention or when you must deal with cash or paperwork requiring signatures. At a neighborhood bank you can walk in and ask questions or resolve problems with

the help of a living, breathing, perhaps even smiling teller. Online banks tend to test customers' patience with the navigation of automated phone systems. With an online bank you can deposit checks through the mail and deposit cash or checks at an ATM, although you may have to pay an ATM fee of several dollars. Before you open an account, find out whether the bank will reimburse you for the cost of using ATMs outside of their network. There are also limits on the amount you can withdraw from an ATM each day.

A common solution to the "local or online?" banking dilemma is to dabble in both. It is usually free to open a bank account, so you can open one account at a local bank that will give you personal attention and unlimited access to your cash, and another at an online bank that might pay more interest on your deposits and allow you to accomplish more of your banking in your pajamas. Most local banks offer some online services. By transferring money between your accounts electronically, you can put your largest sums of money in the bank that pays the highest interest rate when you don't need to spend it and then transfer it to the bank with the easiest access when it's time to make a big purchase.

## FINANCING COLLEGE

As you think about attending college or a professional program after high school, you need to consider one essential aspect of your education—paying for it. The ever-increasing cost of higher education is no secret, and this piece of the American dream often seems out of reach. But there are sources of financial aid for students who qualify, and there are cost-cutting strategies for students who don't. Here's some information that will help you navigate the process of paying for college.

### FAFSA

The *Free Application for Federal Student Aid*, or *FAFSA*, is a part of your college application that your parents or guardians need to fill out. Filling out the form and its worksheets takes some time, but the information provided will determine how much you and your family can afford to pay toward college. This is known as the *Expected Family Contribution* or *EFC*. The EFC is the starting point for determining the financial aid package that colleges can offer you upon admission. For a preview of the amount that colleges will determine your family can afford, you can go to http://apps .collegeboard.org/fincalc/efc_welcome .jsp and try out the EFC calculator.

Remember, the basis of this calculation is not income alone. Assets such as stocks, savings accounts, and real estate are included, as are other expenses, such as a brother or sister already in college. Many financial aid counselors recommend completing the FAFSA early, rather than waiting until tax returns are completed. If your parents are divorced, you only need to report income for the parent you lived with for more than half of the year.

The universities to which you apply will be your best source of additional information on financing options. Based on your family's need, the universities that offer you admission will provide a *financial aid package* that covers the difference between your estimated cost and your family's ability to pay. That package will include one or more of the funding sources described in the next section.

**DID YOU GET IT?**
What is the purpose of the FAFSA?

## Student Loans

Federally sponsored student loans include Stafford loans and Perkins loans. Stafford loans are available directly from the U.S. Department of Education under the Federal Direct Student Loan Program (FDSLP) or privately through a bank under the Federal Family Education Loan Program (FFELP). If you demonstrate need, you will qualify for a subsidized loan. This means that the federal government will pay the interest due on your loan for as long as you attend school at

least half time and for the first six months after you graduate.

Stafford loans are still available if you do not demonstrate need. However, you are responsible for the interest payments on your loan even while in school. The amount of money you may borrow varies, depending on whether you borrow directly from the federal government or from a private lender and whether your loan interest is subsidized or not. In 2011, the maximum lifetime amount for a Stafford loan was $138,500, of which the maximum amount that could be subsidized was $65,500. The amount you may borrow in any given year depends on how many years of school you have completed.

Perkins loans are only available directly from the U.S. Department of Education. They differ from Stafford loans in that only those students with demonstrated need can qualify. The interest rate charged is lower, and the grace period after college before interest must be paid is longer: nine months. In addition, students who choose careers in teaching and other public-service professions may qualify for their loans to be canceled or postponed. The maximum amount undergraduates may borrow under this program is $20,000.

Student loans are also available from banking institutions and other private lenders. Another option is a PLUS loan. PLUS loans are available to parents of students. Parents are responsible for interest immediately and repayment ultimately.

*College is a good but expensive investment. Explore your financing options now.*

**DID YOU GET IT?**
What loans are available to students who demonstrate financial need?

### Grants

Pell grants to assist with education costs are available from the federal government. Eligibility is based on need. The average Pell grant in 2010 was $3,593. The award is based entirely on the expected family contribution (EFC) determined through the FAFSA application process. *Grants* are scholarships that do not require any repayment. In addition to the federal Pell Grant Program, many states, universities, and other institutions have scholarship programs for which you may be eligible. Many local organizations and employers offer scholarships to students and children of employees. Your high school guidance counselor can help you discover these opportunities.

When something **depreciates**, its value falls.

### Work-Study

Taking a part-time job while in college is another way to help fund your education. And a full-time summer job may go a long way toward covering costs such as living expenses and books. As part of a financial aid package, you may qualify for a job in the school's *work-study program*. These are part-time jobs in the university itself, with 80 percent of the payments coming from the federal government.

### Finish On Time

A college education is a large undertaking—one that many students take more than the targeted four years to complete. One way to keep the cost of your education down is to stay focused and finish your degree in four years. Not only will you avoid paying tuition and fees for additional semesters, but you will be available to work and earn an income that much sooner.

# BUYING A CAR

You probably don't need a car while in high school, but car ownership is likely to be in your not-so-distant future. Few purchases summon so much excitement and fear. Thanks to the Internet, there is considerable competition among car sellers because buyers can compare cars of every make and model, new and used, for purchase or lease, from all over the country. What follows are some guidelines that will hopefully make the process straightforward and successful for you.

### Buying Used

It's no surprise that buying a used car is cheaper than buying the same car new. What's important to understand is that a new car loses value rapidly during the first few years of ownership. In fact, the value of a car will **depreciate**, or drop, by about one third over the first three years after the car's purchase. Thus, unlike a home and other investments that may hold their value well when the economy is strong, you are very unlikely to sell your car for more than you paid for it. That means a car is best seen as an expense rather than an investment, and you should minimize your cost of ownership. Buying a used car is often the best way to save money on this purchase.

There are, however, certain precautions you should take when you buy a used car. Using the *vehicle identification number* or *VIN* for the car, you can obtain a vehicle history report online at sites such as CARFAX.com for about $30. Although some activities may go under the radar, these reports include useful information on accidents, repairs, service, use, and ownership. The report might tell you that the car was in a serious accident, was well maintained, was a rental car, or had four previous owners—all important things to know. Check the car's odometer and determine how many miles the car has been driven per year. Mileage in excess of 15,000 per year is a sign that the car has faced higher-than-average wear and tear. It is also wise to have a mechanic look the car over to see if there are any detectable problems.

You should be able to negotiate a better price if you buy a car from the current owner rather than a used car dealer because you are cutting out the middleman. The owner should also have access to the car's service history, which indicates the age of the tires, the repairs the car has received, and whether the car has received regular oil changes. Ask the seller for records showing that the car was taken in for all manufacturers' *recalls*, which request that the car be brought in to fix a significant problem.

Buying from a dealer has advantages, too. Many dealers perform rigorous checks on the cars they purchase, and they have a wide variety of cars in one location. Dealers are required by federal law to post a Buyer's Guide on used cars that states, among other things,

- whether the vehicle is being sold "as is" or with a warranty;

- what portion of the repair costs a dealer will pay under the warranty;

- that you should get all promises in writing because verbal promises are hard to enforce; and

- that you should ask to have the car inspected by an independent mechanic before purchasing it.

The price of a car must be negotiated, which makes for a game of tug of war. After asking a high price, the seller might bolster his or her bargaining position by claiming that another very interested customer is coming by later to get the car if you do not. You can improve your own bargaining position by keeping any strong interest you have in the car to yourself and by pointing out options you have to purchase similar cars elsewhere for reasonable prices. To simplify the negotiations, come armed with an estimate of the car's value from the online *Kelley Blue Book*, which provides estimates particular to the car's location, make, model, year, and other detailed characteristics. This can serve as the basis for a fair price. You can also get an idea of the appropriate price range for the car by looking at newspaper and online ads for similar cars.

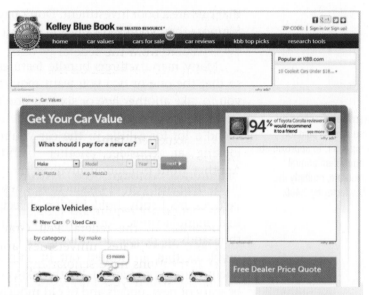

When you make an offer, the seller is likely to suggest that the amount is too low. You can get a better idea of the truth by walking away and saying you're going to look around. The seller might then take you up on the offer. If the seller lets you leave, that's an indication that your offer was on the low side, and you can always go back and make a higher offer.

After you've agreed on a price, make sure everyone is clear that everything is included in that price, and you won't be asked to pay more at a later stage of the game.

*Arrive at price negotiations armed with good estimates of the car's value.*

**DID YOU GET IT?**

What are some of the precautions you should take when buying a used car?

## Buying New

Some buyers really want a brand new car. That's fine, as long as they're in a position financially to pull it off. There are advantages to a new car. You don't have to worry that it's a known lemon that someone is trying to get rid of. It may not require much maintenance for several years. It probably carries features that were not available when older models came out. Safety seems to improve with each model year as automakers try to meet or exceed federal standards and offer more than their competitors. And there's that new car smell! As for fancy extras, remember that cars are a poor investment. Don't pay for more than you need—or can comfortably afford—in a new car.

Many manufacturers bundle features so that the one or two you want require you to take another five or six you don't want. If this tactic would force you to spend a lot for a little in the car you're looking at, consider another brand. Another word of caution involves models in their first year of production. These vehicles frequently hold hidden defects that manufacturers don't uncover until thousands of people are driving them—problems that are ironed out in subsequent years of production. For this reason, be wary of new models and of old models that have just gone through a major redesign. Finally, just because you can pay for a car doesn't mean you can afford it. The purchase price is just one of many costs of car ownership. You must also pay for insurance, oil changes, fuel, license fees, and maintenance expenses. Consider all of these costs before deciding to buy a car.

## Leasing

A new car can be prohibitively expensive. To ease people into driving a new car, dealers offer lease plans. Think of a lease as a long-term rental. The lease will give you the car for two, three, or even five years. Then you return the car to the dealer. Lease agreements have some features in common with rental contracts, such as mileage limitations and requirements that the car be returned in good condition. Any violation of these terms and conditions will cost you extra. Leases often require a large payment in the beginning, called a *down payment*, and then monthly payments for the duration of the lease.

Two key numbers to look at in a lease agreement are the *residual value* and the *money factor*. The **residual value** is the value assigned to the car at the *end* of the lease. In effect, this is the portion of the car's price that you are not paying for under a lease. And this is the main reason why the cost of a lease is less than the cost of a loan for the same car. For example, if

> A **money factor** or *lease rate* is paid for leasing a car. To approximate the equivalent annual interest rate, multiply the money factor by 2,400.

> A **residual value** is the value assigned to a car at the end of its lease period.

you lease a $30,000 car with a $20,000 residual value, you are only paying for $10,000 or one third of the value of the car. If you take out a loan to buy a $30,000 car, you are paying for the full value of the car.

The **money factor** or *lease rate* is like an interest rate paid for leasing a car, but there's a difference, so don't be fooled by low money factors. A money factor is roughly equivalent to an annual interest rate of the money factor multiplied by 2,400. For example, a money factor of 0.0025 is roughly equal to an annual interest rate of 0.0025 × 2,400 = 6 percent. Some leasing agents will state a money factor of 0.0025 as "2.5," which sounds like a low interest rate but isn't so low after the appropriate conversion to 6 percent.

For the three-year period of a typical lease, with equivalent down payments and interest rates, it is cheaper to lease a car than to take out a three-year loan and buy the same car. This is because when you lease, you are not paying for the full value of the car—you are only paying for the depreciation in the value of the car down to the residual value. The benefit of buying a car comes at the end of the three-year period because you own the car, and if you had leased it you would not. From that point on, you have no monthly payments, so you will generally end up paying less over the long term by buying. The specific savings depend on how long you drive the car and on the fees, down payments, finance charges, and other details of the options available to you.

You can compare the payments you would make on a lease or loan in your specific situation using online estimates from the likes of edmunds.com, cars.com, or bankrate.com. To find such sites, search the Internet for "car lease calculator" or "car loan calculator."

**DID YOU GET IT?**

What are two key numbers to look at in a lease agreement?

## Dealing with Dealers

When you walk into a car dealer's showroom, you will receive more attention from a salesperson than you ever have at a convenience store. That's because there's a lot of money at stake. If you have not done your homework in advance, you will open yourself to manipulative sales tactics, pressure, and confusion. Remember, you are spending your money, and you should do it on your terms. The following tips may help:

1. **Do your homework.** Always collect as much information as you can about relevant prices and alternatives before going to a dealership. Most everything you need is available online. Cars.com, edmunds.com, and other automotive websites offer direct price comparisons between cars with the features you choose. After prioritizing and narrowing your choices, find out what the dealer paid for the car. It is better to start with the dealer's cost and make the salesperson try to negotiate upward, rather than starting with the *manufacturer's suggested retail price*, or *MSRP*, and trying to negotiate downward. You can get a rough idea of the dealer's cost by looking up the *invoice price* on an automotive website. However, the dealer often receives behind-the-scenes incentives, rebates, and "holdbacks" that ultimately reduce the dealer's cost for the car. Closer estimates of the true dealer cost include the Consumer Reports Bottom Line Price available at consumerreports.org. Edmunds.com offers a True Market Value Price, which is the average sales price for a particular car in a particular region. As you negotiate, remember that there is money to be earned on any trade-in, financing, and extended warranty handled by the dealer. So if the salesperson suggests that you're not offering enough profit for the dealer, think about whether that's true in light of all the ways the dealer will benefit from your purchase.

2. **Think clearly about financing.** Once you have settled on the car of your choice, you must decide how to pay for it. Most manufacturers offer financing from their own finance company. Attractive interest rates may be available on specific models. Remember your options to borrow at your bank, savings and loan, or credit union as well, and look into the interest rates available from these institutions. When you have a conversation with someone from the dealer's finance department, take your time and ask a lot of questions.

3. **Don't yield to pressure.** Don't succumb to pressure tactics. The ever-present option to walk away gives you the upper hand in any negotiation with a salesperson. Don't fall for the *bait-and-switch* trick of advertising a bargain to get you into the dealership and then trying to sell you a more expensive car instead. If you feel tricked or hurried, or if the salesperson is unwilling to negotiate, head for the door. There are many dealers out there, and the more willing you are to shop around and develop your options, the stronger your bargaining position will be.

4. **Get the most out of a trade-in.** If you have a car to sell to the dealer at the time when you buy your new car, this is called a *trade-in*. The dealer is not likely to offer you as much for your trade-in as you would receive if you sold the car directly to another individual, but the dealer will save you the hassle of doing so. An alternative is to donate your old car to a charity such as the United Way or the Salvation Army. The charity will arrange to pick up the car and send you documentation of the value of your donation. Depending on your tax situation, you may be able to deduct the value of your car from your income when you calculate your taxes.

*Don't yield to pressure from a salesperson. When spending your money, you should do so on your terms.*

THINKSTOCK

## Paying Cash

To buy a car with "cash" doesn't mean that you bring a big bag of money to the dealer to pay for the car. It means that, rather than borrowing money to buy the car, you pay with a check or some other form of direct payment. Paying cash for something as expensive as a car is difficult for most people, and especially for young people starting out on their own. However, if you are able to pay with cash, there are advantages. If you limit yourself to cash, you will have a clear boundary on exactly how much you can spend. The ability to pay cash is a good indication that you can afford the price of the car.

Paying with cash also simplifies the transaction because there's no need to fill out all the paperwork for a loan and go through the loan-approval process. Unless you get a particularly good deal on a loan, the fees and interest on it are likely to exceed the interest you would lose by removing your own money from the bank to pay for the car. And paying cash gives you immediate *title to* (ownership of) the car. In contrast, while you are paying off a car loan, the lender will place a *lien* on the title that prevents you from taking full ownership until you have paid off the loan.

# IDENTITY THEFT

**Identity theft** is any crime involving the wrongful acquisition and use of another person's personal information. The information is used without the knowledge of the victim to commit fraud and other crimes. For example, a thief could use your information to open a checking account in your name and then bounce a series of checks—with you getting the blame. Your Social Security number, bank account number, and credit card number can all be used by imposters for their personal gain. Recovering from identity theft and restoring your credibility with lenders can take years and an unfortunate amount of your money.

## How to Protect Yourself from Identity Theft

Identity theft is a complex crime that goes far beyond stealing your wallet or purse. Thieves find identity information in many places, including electronic files, mailboxes, and trash cans. Proper care on your part will go a long way to reduce the risks. Here are some suggestions:

• Make a habit of shredding documents containing sensitive information before throwing them away. Thieves are known to sort through trash hoping to find preapproved credit card applications, credit card bills, bank statements, and numbers used for identification.

• Keep your Social Security card at home in a safe place; never carry it in your wallet. Never include your Social Security number on a check, and only give it out if absolutely necessary.

• When choosing a password, make it hard to guess. Do not choose your birth date, name, telephone number, "password," or "123456."

• Do not give out personal information on the phone or Internet unless you are certain with whom you are doing business. Criminals often try to trick people into revealing valuable information by sending e-mails that appear to be from banks, people in trouble, employers, or the IRS. Do not click on links in e-mails from unknown sources and use up-to-date antivirus software to protect your computer.

• When using an ATM, be careful to enter your password in such a way that no one else can see it. By shielding the keypad with one hand while entering numbers with the other you can deter potential thieves from looking over your shoulder or photographing you from a distance to acquire your access code.

• Thieves can overhear your phone conversations, so never give out your credit card number on the phone in a public place.

- While away on vacation, have your mail held at the post office so that bills are not stolen from your mailbox.

**DID YOU GET IT?**
What are two ways to reduce the risk of identity theft?

## Check Your Bills and Credit Report

Whether bills and financial statements arrive in the mail or online, it is important to check them carefully for accuracy. Check bills for unexpected amounts or items you did not purchase. Tell the sender if your bill does not arrive. And watch for bills from companies that you don't do business with. They may be fake companies trying to get your money, or they may be legitimate companies collecting for purchases made by someone who has stolen your identity.

*Shredding keeps sensitive information out of the hands of thieves.*

Be suspicious if you are denied credit unexpectedly, which is another clue that someone is acting as you. The law requires each of the three major consumer reporting companies—Equifax, TransUnion, and Experian—to give you a free copy of your *credit report* each year if you request it. Your **credit report** shows all the credit-card accounts and

A **credit report** shows all the credit card accounts and loans you have, the balances, and whether your bills are paid on time.

## ECONOMICS IN ACTION

# Identity Theft Is Now a Federal Offense

In one pivotal case of identity theft, the criminal incurred more than $100,000 of credit card debt, obtained a federal home loan, and bought homes, motorcycles, and handguns in the victim's name. But that's not all: the criminal also called his victim to taunt him, saying that he could continue to pose as the victim for as long as he wanted because identity theft was not a federal crime at that time. While the victim and his wife spent more than four years and $15,000 of their own money to restore their credit and reputation, the criminal served a brief sentence for making a false statement to buy a firearm. The criminal made no restitution to his victim for any of the harm he caused. This case, and others like it, prompted Congress in 1998 to pass the Identity Theft and

Assumption Deterrence Act. This act makes it a federal crime to "knowingly transfer or use, without lawful authority, a means of identification of another person with the intent to commit, or to aid or abet, any unlawful activity that constitutes a violation of Federal law, or that constitutes a felony under any applicable State or local law."

**YOUR TURN**
What steps do your parents take to protect themselves from identity theft?

loans you have, the balances, and whether your bills are paid on time. By checking any of these reports you can see whether anyone else has received a credit card in your name. Report any suspicious activity to the credit card company.

**DID YOU GET IT?**
What is a credit report?

## What to Do If You Become a Victim

If you suspect that your identity has been stolen you should immediately file a police report. Creditors will need to know that you are the victim of a crime. Any account that has been opened in your name and any of your own accounts that have been compromised should be closed right away. You will find a number to call in such emergencies on your credit card bill and on the back of your credit card.

You should follow up on your call with a written notification. Your credit card company will have a process by which you can dispute any charges you did not make. Keep a record of every call you make about the theft and save copies of the written correspondence.

Place a "Fraud Alert" on your credit reports to prevent any new accounts from being opened in your name. Calling Equifax (1-888-766-0008), TransUnion (1-800-680-7289), or Experian (1-888-397-3742) will place a 90-day fraud alert with all three of these credit-reporting companies. They will give you immediate access to free copies of your credit reports so that you can check carefully for any other unexpected activity. For further assistance, the Federal Trade Commission offers a toll-free telephone hotline for victims of identity theft: 1-877-ID THEFT (438-4338).

# MODULE 36 REVIEW AND ASSESSMENT

**Summing Up the Key Ideas:** Match the following terms to the correct definitions.

A. Depreciate
B. Checking account
C. Residual value
D. Money factor

E. Grants
F. Identity theft
G. FDIC
H. Debit card

I. Credit report
J. Direct deposit
K. Overdraft protection
L. Check

___I___ 1. Shows all the credit-card accounts and loans you have, the balances, and whether your bills are paid on time.

___B___ 2. Holds the money you intend to spend soon and offers several easy ways to pay for things like writing a check or using a debit card.

___C___ 3. The value assigned to a car at the end of its lease period.

___G___ 4. Independent agency of the federal government established to insure bank deposits up to $250,000.

___L___ 5. A paper form of payment that withdraws money from your checking account.

___D___ 6. The amount paid for leasing a car, also referred to as the lease rate.

___F___ 7. Any crime involving the wrongful acquisition and use of another person's personal information.

___A___ 8. To fall in value.

___E___ 9. Scholarships that do not require any repayment.

___H___ 10. Used to buy goods and services, the money is withdrawn directly from your bank account.

___J___ 11. This banking feature allows paycheck funds to go directly into your checking account.

___K___ 12. An automatic loan triggered by a check that would otherwise bounce.

## Analyze and Explain: Determine whether each of the following car-buying tactics is generally a good idea or a bad idea and explain your answer.

| | GOOD OR BAD IDEA? | EXPLANATION |
|---|---|---|
| 1. taking money out of a savings account to pay cash for a car rather than financing the purchase with a typical car loan | *bad* — | |
| 2. buying a used car at a dealership relying exclusively on the honesty, integrity, and knowledge of the salesperson | *bad* | *do research* |
| 3. taking the financing offer by the car salesperson without comparing interest rates available from other lending institutions, believing all lenders are likely to charge about the same rate anyway | *bad* | *research* |

## Apply: Determine whether it would be appropriate for each of the following customers to buy a new car, buy a used car, or lease a car.

| | NEW, USED, OR LEASE? |
|---|---|
| 1. a person with little mechanical knowledge who doesn't want to be surprised with unexpected repair bills and has a large down payment available | *new* |
| 2. a person who has very little money going into the deal, drives few miles per year, and wants to know up front how much the car will cost each month | *used* |
| 3. a person who does not like to see their purchase depreciate rapidly and feels comfortable doing research on car reliability | *lease* |

# MODULE 37

# Investing and Personal Financial Planning

**KEY IDEA:** There are many ways to save and invest, but it is important to know which strategies and financial instruments are best suited for your goals.

**OBJECTIVES**

- To describe the risks and benefits of various investment options.
- To distinguish among savings accounts, certificates of deposit, and other financial products, such as stocks, bonds, and mutual funds.
- To understand the difference between active and passive investment management.

### Your Money Can Take Many Paths

Saving and investing should be two of the most important concerns facing young people starting out on their own. You are probably already familiar with savings accounts and some types of investment. When you were young, you and your parents might have opened a savings account at a local bank. Or you might have received government savings bonds from your grandparents on a big occasion. If you are interested in becoming an active investor, you might even have explored buying stocks or mutual funds with your savings. This module explores the paths and pitfalls you should be aware of as you chart the course for your hard-earned money.

*If you decide to invest in stocks, your money will probably flow through the U.S. Stock Exchange.*

## COMMON WAYS TO SAVE

**Risk tolerance** is the ability to accept and absorb losses.

Savings accounts and the many investment options carry varying degrees of risk and reward. Typically, larger rewards come with greater risks. It is important to know how much risk is involved and whether the reward is in line with the risk. Your saving and investment decisions will hinge on your **risk tolerance**—your ability to accept and absorb losses. If you couldn't handle large losses, you shouldn't take large risks. Knowledge of the amount of risk that makes sense for you will guide you through tough calls on where to put your money. Let's start by looking at saving.

**DID YOU GET IT?**
What will guide your saving and investment decisions?

# ECONOMICS IN ACTION

## Don't Miss a Good Deal

Many companies offer their employees an incentive to save by matching every dollar the employee places in a special retirement savings account, known as a *401(k) plan*, with their own contribution. If an employee puts away $50 a month, for example, the company will also deposit $50 a month in that employee's account. Sound like a good deal? It is. But far too many workers do not choose to participate. They may not understand the great opportunity they're missing.

To promote employees' savings, some companies automatically enroll their employees in a saving program. This changes the default option, so that unless employees take the step of filling out a form to opt out of the program, a certain amount of their pay is automatically deposited into the savings account with an equal contribution from the employer. A study of one company that switched to such an automatic enrollment plan found dramatic results. Before the plan, only 37 percent of new employees chose to participate in the savings plan. After the switch to an automatic enrollment plan in which 3 percent

of an employee's pay was automatically deposited into a savings account with an equal contribution from the employer, 86 percent of new employees participated and only 14 percent chose to opt out.

The lesson of this example should be clear: pay attention to the saving plans that are available to you and choose the one that offers the best deal. It may be necessary for you to fill out a little paperwork to take advantage of a good deal. Invest the time to prepare for a prosperous future.

SOURCE: Based on Brigitte C. Madrian and Dennis F. Shea, "The Power of Suggestion: Inertia in 401(k) Participation and Saving Behavior," *Quarterly Journal of Economics*, November 2001.

### YOUR TURN

Ask some workers you know what type of retirement plan is available at their place of employment.

## Savings Accounts

The interest rates paid on savings accounts are relatively low, but depositors are offered one of the safest ways to save money. You can open a savings account at several types of financial institutions that have slightly different missions:

- Commercial banks are the banks you see around town. In their efforts to gain profits, commercial banks offer checking and savings accounts, a wide variety of loans, and a full complement of services, such as foreign currency exchange, safe deposit boxes, credit cards, and money orders.

- Credit unions carry out most of the functions of commercial banks but operate on a not-for-profit basis to serve their members—the depositors and lenders—all of whom share ties to a particular employer, community, university, or other organization.

*Commercial banks are the banks you see around town.*

A **mutual fund** is a collection of investments, such as stocks, bonds, or money-market instruments, selected by a fund manager in accordance with the goals of the particular fund.

A **passbook savings account** is a savings account that typically has a low or zero minimum balance requirement, pays a relatively low interest rate, and offers easy access to funds.

**Demand deposits** are deposits that the depositor is free to withdraw, or "demand," at any time.

A **money-market fund** is a mutual fund made up entirely of money-market instruments.

A **certificate of deposit**, or CD, documents a deposit into a financial institution that promises to pay a fixed interest rate for a specified period of time. CDs require a minimum balance and represent *time deposits* rather than demand deposits because you cannot withdraw your money before a stated maturity date without paying a penalty.

**Principal** refers to the amount of a deposit or, in the case of a loan, the amount of the loan before any interest is paid.

With **principal protection**, every dollar put in will be available to take out.

A **bond** represents a loan to the bond's issuer in exchange for specified payments to the bond purchaser over time.

• Savings and loan associations are for-profit institutions that specialize in holding savings deposits and making loans for homes, cars, and other purchases by individuals.

The most common type of savings account is a **passbook savings account**, characterized by a low or zero minimum balance requirement, a relatively low interest rate, and easy access to funds. Deposits in passbook savings accounts are called **demand deposits** because depositors are free to withdraw, or "demand," those funds at any time. Other types of savings "instruments" include *certificates of deposit*, or *CDs*. A **certificate of deposit** documents a deposit into a bank or other financial institution that promises to pay a fixed interest rate for a specified period of time. CDs require a minimum balance and represent *time deposits* because you cannot withdraw your money prior to a stated maturity date without paying a penalty. In exchange for the restriction of not being able to withdraw your deposits at any time, the interest rate is typically higher than on a demand-deposit account.

Savings accounts are considered safe because in most cases the deposits (up to $250,000) are insured by the FDIC. Savings accounts and CDs are also *principal protected*. The term **principal** refers to the amount of the deposit or, in the case of a loan, the amount of the loan before any interest is paid. **Principal protection** means that every dollar put in will be available to take out. In that sense there is no risk of loss from depositing money in accounts such as these. If you have very low or no risk tolerance, these accounts are advisable because your money is secure and you will earn a return based on the stated rate of interest.

 **DID YOU GET IT?**
Why are CDs a good savings instrument for people with low risk tolerance?

## Mutual Funds

If you have some tolerance for risk, you can usually earn a higher return by investing in a *mutual fund*. A **mutual fund** is made up of a collection of smaller investments selected by a fund manager in accordance with the goals of the particular fund. The money comes from a large group of investors like yourself. The investments might include stocks, bonds, and various money-market instruments with fancy names like "commercial paper" and "U.S. Treasury Bills" that are essentially promises to repay money at some time in the future. A **money-market fund** is one type of mutual fund made up entirely of money-market instruments. A money-market fund does not carry FDIC insurance. Losses to principal are quite rare because a money-market fund manager is expected to maintain the funds' invested principal even if he or she has to draw from other funds to do so.

While the risk of loss is remote in the world of money-market funds, losses are common for mutual funds created with investments in *stocks* and *bonds*, particularly over a short period of time. Glance at the prices for mutual funds in the newspaper or online and you'll probably see that some prices have increased since the day before and some have decreased. If you own shares of the funds whose prices have decreased, you have lost money over the last day. As compensation for the risk of loss, the riskier mutual funds generally offer a higher rate of return over time.

 **DID YOU GET IT?**
Why is there risk involved in money-market accounts?

## Bonds

A **bond** represents a loan to the bond's issuer in exchange for specified payments to the purchaser of the bond over time. By issuing bonds, corporations, governments, and other entities can pay for things like new factories or courthouses over a period of many years. The issuer is obligated to pay the investor the promised amount, which includes the purchase price or *face value* of the bond and payments of interest known as *coupon payments*. Other things being equal, bond prices move in the opposite direction of the interest rates paid on other investments. For example, bond prices go down when interest rates go up, until the rate of return on bonds at the current price makes bonds competitive with other investments. Among other determinants of bond prices is the risk that the issuer will fail to make the promised payments. In order to lure investors, companies and governments that are relatively likely to default on these payments must sell their bonds at a relatively low price.

*Bond funds* are a type of mutual fund made up of investments in—you guessed it—bonds. Bonds and bond funds come in a range of risk levels, from U.S. Treasury bonds, which are among the safest investments, to "investment grade" bonds with little to moderate risk, to "junk bonds" with high risk. Like U.S. Treasury bonds, most bonds from large, established corporations offer a relatively safe investment and a moderate rate of return. Bonds and bond funds come in a variety of classes, such as government bonds, corporate bonds, and municipal bonds (issued by city governments), each with its own unique characteristics and risk factors.

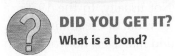

**DID YOU GET IT?**
What is a bond?

## Stocks

The investments we've looked at so far are all *fixed-income investments* because they provide a specified payment or rate of return. A share of **stock** represents partial ownership of a company. Companies sell shares of stock to raise money that can be used for expansion and increased profitability. Stock purchases do not come with a promise to repay invested funds, and stock prices can fluctuate widely. If the company goes out of business or enters bankruptcy, the stock value becomes zero or close to it.

To reduce their exposure to risk, many investors buy *stock mutual funds*. A share in a stock mutual fund represents

ownership in a collection of stocks issued by many different companies. This diversification reduces the risk because poor performances by some companies can be balanced by strong performances by others. These funds do fluctuate in value, but with less volatility than individual stocks. As with stocks, there is no principal protection for stock market funds, so if you're unlucky you might end up selling your shares for less than you paid for them.

Purchasing shares of stock in one company is a risky way to invest. The price of shares is subject to many risk factors, and in the event of bankruptcy, the entire investment can become worthless. But shares of stock also represent the greatest potential for appreciation. No doubt you've heard of companies whose shares skyrocket in value after the company brings a hugely successful product to market. Google and Apple are recent examples of this phenomenon. So for individual stocks, the risk of loss goes hand-in-hand with the potential for reward.

**DID YOU GET IT?**
Why is it risky to invest in shares of just one company?

## ASSET ALLOCATION

An **asset** is anything of value that is owned or controlled with the expectation that it will provide benefits in the future. An asset can be a financial instrument, such as a savings account or a stock or bond; a physical object, such as a work of art; or some form of real estate, such as

*The sale of bonds helps corporations and governments pay for things like factories and schools over a period of many years.*

*A share of stock represents partial ownership of a company.*

A share of **stock** represents partial ownership of a company.

An **asset** is anything of value that is owned or controlled with the expectation that it will provide benefits in the future.

**Active investing** is carried out with the goal of outperforming the market.

The **life-cycle approach** to asset allocation is to make riskier investments with higher expected returns early in life and then turn to safer investments with lower returns later in life.

The **passive investing** strategy is to duplicate the components of a benchmark index, such as the Dow Jones Industrial Average, and then receive the same returns as the index (less some minimal expenses).

*The best investment strategy depends on your stage of life.*

land or a building. The assets you acquire as an investor should be selected with a few basic criteria in mind. The first is your investment objective: Are you investing to fund a future purchase or to make a down payment on a home? Are you saving for college or for retirement? The most important aspect of your investment objective is its time horizon. If you will need the funds in the near future, then safe investments that are easily converted to cash, such as savings account deposits, are the most appropriate. If you are looking to pay for something several years in the future, such as a home or retirement, you might decide to accept more risk in return for the potential for higher rewards. This is because your investment has time to recover from any short-term losses. For long-term objectives, investments such as bonds, stocks, and real estate are the most appropriate.

**DID YOU GET IT?**
What are assets?

## Stages of Life

Many financial advisors recommend a **life-cycle approach** to asset allocation. This approach holds that young investors with long-term objectives should buy high risk/high expected return assets such as stocks, long-term bonds, or real estate. Middle-aged investors face the more immediate expenses of homes and college educations for their children. At this stage of life, investors should own assets that are fairly safe and can be converted to cash at the appropriate times.

These include short-term bonds, stock funds, and CDs. Finally, retirees have the short-term objective of paying for daily living expenses by selling assets. At this stage, investments should be almost entirely in assets that are safe and comparatively *liquid*, meaning that they can quickly be converted to cash. Examples include money-market funds and savings accounts.

# INVESTMENT STRATEGIES AND THE EFFICIENT MARKET HYPOTHESIS

Investors and fund managers who feel they have insights about investments can try to earn higher returns than the overall market for stocks, bonds, or another type of investment. This strategy of trying to outperform the market is called **active investing**. Success in active investing is gauged by the ability to beat a *benchmark index*. For example, the Dow Jones Industrial Average, the NASDAQ Composite Index, and the Standard & Poor's (S&P) 500 Index all measure the performance of a sampling of stocks and serve as benchmark indexes for the stock market. In the early 1900s, active investing was the norm.

Can fund managers really outperform the market? Not usually. In the 1970s, a new outlook grew out of the finding that a majority of fund managers do worse than the targeted benchmark. On top of that, fund managers who beat the benchmark in one year were not more likely than others to beat it the next year, which suggests that a lot of luck was involved. These findings gave rise to an investment management approach that is passive. The **passive investing** strategy is to simply assemble investments that match the components of a benchmark index and then watch the investments deliver the same returns as the index (less some minimal expenses). For example, the Dow Jones Industrial Average is a benchmark index made up of stocks from 30 companies that include Walt Disney, Microsoft, McDonald's, and Home Depot. If your investments mirror those in the benchmark index, so will your

returns. Initially the investment community was reluctant to accept this strategy and few fund management companies adopted it. One that did was told the strategy was "un-American" by an advertising agency that had been invited to run an ad campaign for the "indexed" fund.

**DID YOU GET IT?**
What is the difference between active investing and passive investing?

The passive strategy is based on the principle that all information about a stock or bond is reflected in its price almost instantaneously. The idea is that any special knowledge about a stock or bond would prompt action by investors that would cause the investment's price to adjust to reflect that information. For example, if available information showed that the price of a stock was too low, those with the information would keep buying it until their purchases bid the price up to where it should be. On this basis, the **efficient market hypothesis** holds that markets respond to information so efficiently that it is not possible to predict whether the prices of stocks or bonds will rise or fall without *inside information*, meaning information that is not shared with the public.

The efficient market hypothesis spawned investment funds that are called **index funds** because they are replicas of the benchmark indexes. The passive investment strategy of purchasing shares of these funds has several advantages:

- Investors know exactly what they are getting, which is not the case when investing in actively managed funds whose holdings are only disclosed every three months.

- The fees are lower. For example, companies that offer index funds charge fees of as little as 0.2 percent of the value of assets under management while actively managed funds typically charge 2 percent or more—10 times as much as index funds.

- Except for the fees they charge, you don't need to worry much about who is managing an index fund because their investment practices are clear: they mimic a published index. In contrast, the loss of a successful fund manager for an actively managed fund can cause the performance of the fund to weaken.

A corollary of the efficient market hypothesis holds that, because the financial markets are efficient—with prices that reflect all available information at all times—one cannot use past price

An **index fund** is a mutual fund that duplicates the investments in a benchmark index, such as the S&P 500 Index.

The **efficient market hypothesis** holds that markets respond to information so efficiently that it is not possible to predict whether the prices of stocks or bonds will rise or fall without inside information.

## ECONOMICS IN ACTION

# *A Random Walk Down Wall Street*

*Can a monkey or an ape pick stocks as well as the pros?*

Can blindfolded monkeys pick stocks as well as financial market professionals? Yes, they can, according to Princeton University professor Burton Malkiel. He discusses this claim in his landmark book, *A Random Walk Down Wall Street*. The book's central theory is that stock prices follow a random path and cannot be predicted on the basis of past trends or other publicly available information. One upshot of this theory is that

THINKSTOCK

a blindfolded monkey throwing darts at a newspaper's stock tables could pick stocks that performed as well as any professional investor.

Widely questioned when introduced in 1973, the theory is now widely taught, and its acceptance drives the popularity of index funds. To test the result about blindfolded dart throwers, the *Wall Street Journal* held a series of contests between 1988 and 2002 that pitted professional stock fund managers against amateurs throwing darts. The feature's first volunteer dart thrower was Professor Malkiel himself.

In each widely followed round of the contest, three or four high-powered managers submitted their picks to go up against the stocks hit by the darts. After watching the performance of the stocks for a few months, the *Wall Street Journal* declared the winners. Ultimately, over the course of the 142 contests, the performance of the stocks picked by the fund managers edged out that of

the dart throwers. Although the results fail to back up Professor Malkiel's theory, the fact that most fund managers can't pick stocks that outperform benchmark indexes indicates the difficulty of predicting stock prices. And the contest's popularity demonstrated the high level of intrigue in the efficient market hypothesis.

## YOUR TURN

Using the listings in a newspaper or on a website such as finance. yahoo.com, see if you can pick a stock whose price increases by more than the Dow index between today and tomorrow.

movements to predict future price movements. Like the efficient market hypothesis, this theory has supporters and critics, and the Economics in Action box that follows sheds some light on the controversy. To the extent that this theory is true, there is no advantage to be gained by buying stocks when the market *appears* to be poised to rebound or selling stocks when the market *appears* to be ready to tumble, because the true path of stock prices is unpredictable.

# MODULE 37 REVIEW AND ASSESSMENT

**Summing Up the Key Ideas:** Match the following terms to the correct definitions.

A. Risk tolerance
B. Passbook savings account
C. Demand deposit
D. Certificate of deposit

E. Principal
F. Principal protection
G. Mutual fund
H. Money-market fund

I. Bond
J. Stock
K. Asset
L. Life-cycle approach
M. Active investing

N. Passive investing
O. Efficient market hypothesis
P. Index fund

_____C_____ 1. Deposits that the depositor is free to withdraw, or "demand," at any time.

_____G_____ 2. A collection of investments, such as stocks, bonds, or money-market instruments, selected by a fund manager in accordance with the goals of the particular fund.

_____F_____ 3. Refers to the fact that every dollar put into an account will be available for withdrawal.

_____P_____ 4. A mutual fund that duplicates the investments in a benchmark index, such as the S&P 500 Index.

_N_ 5. An investment strategy used to duplicate the components of a benchmark index, such as the Dow Jones Industrial Average, and then receive the same returns as the index (less some minimal expenses).

_B_ 6. A savings account that typically has a low or zero minimum balance requirement, pays a relatively low interest rate, and offers easy access to funds.

_H_ 7. A mutual fund made up entirely of money-market instruments.

_E_ 8. Refers to the amount of a deposit or, in the case of a loan, the amount of the loan before any interest is paid.

_I_ 9. Represents a loan to the bond's issuer in exchange for specified payments to the bond purchaser over time.

_K_ 10. Anything of value that is owned or controlled with the expectation that it will provide benefits in the future.

_A_ 11. The ability to accept and absorb losses.

_L_ 12. An approach to asset allocation that makes riskier investments with higher expected returns early in life and then turns to safer investments with lower returns later in life.

_M_ 13. Carried out with the goal of outperforming the market.

_J_ 14. Represents partial ownership of a company.

_D_ 15. Documents a deposit into a financial institution that promises to pay a fixed rate for a specified period of time.

_O_ 16. Holds that markets respond to information so efficiently that it is not possible to predict whether the prices of stocks or bonds will rise or fall without inside information.

## Analyze and Explain: Analyze each of the following and determine if a **stock** or a **bond** investment would best suit the investment goals in each case.

STOCK OR BOND?

1. a person with very little risk tolerance — _bond_

2. a person looking for a fixed return — _bond_

3. a person willing to assume some risk and looking for a higher-than-average potential for return — _stock_

## Apply: In each of the following situations a potential saver is considering a **passbook savings account, a demand deposit account**, or a **certificate of deposit** account. Analyze each investment goal and make a recommendation as to the appropriate type of savings instrument to accomplish the stated goal.

TYPE OF ACCOUNT

1. a saver who wants complete access to the principal while at the same time earning interest — _demand deposit_

2. a saver who wants to know in advance the amount of interest that will be paid for the duration of the investment — _certificate of deposit_

3. a saver who needs to have instant access to the principal and needs to use the principal to pay bills by mail — _demand deposit_

4. a saver who is willing to sacrifice access to the principal to earn a higher rate of return — _passbook savings_

## TIME

# Living to 100: As It Becomes Common, Money Regrets Follow

**We're on track for a population with 600,000 folks over the age of 100 by 2050. Yet almost nobody is planning for it financially.**

BY DAN KADLEC

The longevity revolution is a blessing. We shouldn't view it any other way. Medical breakthroughs and new understanding of health and wellness have lengthened life expectancy at birth in the United States from 49 years in 1900 to 78 years today, and this extra time can be both happy and productive. But these bonus years may also be filled with regrets, a Merrill Lynch survey suggests.

The likelihood of living to 78 only hints at the full story. If you are already 65, odds are you'll live to 84. A 65-year-old couple has a 31 percent chance of at least one of them making it to 95. And get this: The Census Bureau estimates that the number living to 100

rose by a factor of 35 from 2,300 in 1950 to 80,000 in 2010. Centenarians will exceed 600,000 by 2050.

The Merrill Lynch Affluent Insights Survey found that 58 percent have a positive view of living to 100. They see longevity as a bonus, not as a prolonged period of feebleness. That's good. In my book *The Power Years* (with Ken Dychtwald), we describe these bonus years (roughly spanning ages 65 to 85) as "middlescence," a new period of productivity and self-discovery that previous generations did not enjoy.

But to get the most of these middlescent years your money has to last, and that is where the regrets come

into play. Despite all the evidence that we are living longer, most people still do not account for the extra years in their financial plan. In the Merrill survey, 75 percent said they would approach money management differently if they were certain they would live to 100. They said they would:

- Work at least part-time during retirement (39 percent).

- Re-evaluate their savings and investment strategies (37 percent).

- Invest in a lifetime income product, like an annuity (32 percent).

- Contribute more to a 401(k) or other retirement savings vehicle (32 percent).

- Purchase long-term care insurance (29 percent).

- Retire closer to 85 than 65 (25 percent).

These days almost no one targets a certain age for retirement. In the survey, just 14 percent of those over 50 said they had a date in mind. For a great many, retirement will be a function of opportunity (when they are confident they have sufficient resources) or necessity (their health or the health of a family member dictates leaving the office).

Most would prefer to work longer than to cut their lifestyle. But if they had to cut costs, here's how they would do it:

- Trim day-to-day expenses (38 percent).

- Purchase fewer personal luxuries (35 percent).

- Limit budgets for vacations (32 percent).

- Keep the same car longer (27 percent).

- Leave less of an inheritance (25 percent).

- Downsize their home (24 percent).

Here's the thing: most folks would benefit from living like this anyway. Cutting costs is one of the things you can control. Meanwhile, a lot of folks are going to live to 100. So why not just plan to work longer, save more and secure a guaranteed income stream for life? In the survey, 73% viewed retirement as time for a second act. Yet they are not doing what it takes to realize that vision.

EXCERPTED FROM http://moneyland.time.com/2012/02/28/living-to-100-as-it-becomes-common-money-regrets-follow/#ixzz1uZCCVG3A

## DID YOU READ IT?

1) **What factors influence a person's decision to retire?**

2) **How can people save or prepare for retirement?**

## WHAT DO YOU THINK?

3) **What markets will be influenced by the fact that people are now living longer?**

4) **How do you save? What are you saving for?**

# PEOPLE IN ECONOMICS

## AN INTERVIEW WITH Laura Adams

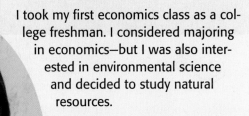

*Laura Adams is a personal finance expert who writes and hosts the Money Girl podcast at http://moneygirl quickanddirtytips.com. Laura has a passion for educating people on how to manage money, build wealth, and achieve their potential. Her book,* Money Girl's Smart Moves to Grow Rich, *won the prestigious Excellence in Financial Literary Education award for 2011.*

**Have you always been interested in finance? When you were in high school did you think you might have a career in finance?**

I was always very interested in money and good at math in high school, but I didn't consider working in finance until much later.

**When did you take your first economics course? Was it an important part of your journey toward becoming Money Girl?**

I took my first economics class as a college freshman. I considered majoring in economics—but I was also interested in environmental science and decided to study natural resources.

**Why did you decide to pursue an MBA?**

I decided to get an MBA at the University of Florida while I was working as a consultant for DuPont. They were willing to pick up about a third of the tab and I knew it would help me excel in my job, plus open the doors to many future opportunities.

**How did you become Money Girl?**

My husband gave me an iPod in 2005 as a graduation present after I got my MBA. I got hooked on audio podcasts and decided to start my own. The first show I created had marginal success—but I got noticed by the Quick and

Dirty Tips media network (www.quickanddirty tips.com). They invited me to write and produce a weekly podcast and blog called Money Girl as a paid host starting in 2008. Later that year, Macmillan offered me a book deal and *Money Girl's Smart Moves to Grow Rich* was published in 2010. Being an author and getting covered in the national media opened up many new opportunities, like freelance writing, being a spokesperson, and speaking.

### What do you do in a typical day as Money Girl?

A typical day for me includes writing about personal finance for book projects, my podcast, various blogs, newsletters, and live presentations. I spend time marketing what I create and the services I provide. I also connect with Money Girl blog readers and podcast listeners by answering their questions on e-mail and social media.

### Do you have any advice about finance for high school students? Should they be concerned about their financial future?

I believe that everyone should be concerned about their financial future—especially high school students. If I knew then what I know now—I'm sure I would already be retired! If I could have three financial do-overs, I would

1. Negotiate wages and salary more aggressively—because employers always start with a low offer and you're usually worth more than you think.
2. Participate in a retirement plan at work sooner—you can always take 100 percent of your money with you if you leave a job for any reason.
3. Never spend more than you make—buying an item you can't afford using a credit card typically makes it cost double or triple what you originally paid.

# CHAPTER 12 REVIEW AND SELF-ASSESSMENT

## REVIEW

### Points to Remember

#### MODULE 34: FINDING A JOB

1. A **resume** is a document that summarizes your education, work experience, and skills.

2. A **cover letter** is a short note that tells a potential employer how you heard about the job, why you are interested in it, and why he or she should look at your resume and invite you for an interview.

#### MODULE 35: CREATING A BUDGET

3. A **budget** is a specific plan for how to spend your money.

4. Your **gross income** is the total amount of money you make.

5. Your **net income**, also called after-tax income or disposable income, is the income that you are left with after paying taxes.

6. **Fixed expenses** are expenses that remain about the same from month to month.

7. **Variable expenses** can change frequently at your discretion.

8. The **annual percentage rate** is the percentage of the borrowed amount that you would pay in interest if you had the loan for one year.

#### MODULE 36: ESSENTIAL ELEMENTS OF PERSONAL FINANCE

9. When something **depreciates**, its value falls.

10. A **residual value** is the value assigned to a car at the end of its lease period.

11. A **money factor** or *lease rate* is paid for leasing a car. To approximate the equivalent annual interest rate, multiply the money factor by 2,400.

12. **Identity theft** is any crime involving the wrongful acquisition and use of another person's personal information.

13. A **credit report** shows all the credit card accounts and loans you have, the balances, and whether your bills are paid on time.

#### MODULE 37: INVESTING AND PERSONAL FINANCIAL PLANNING

14. **Risk tolerance** is the ability to accept and absorb losses.

15. A **passbook savings account** is a savings account that typically has a low or zero minimum balance requirement, pays a relatively low interest rate, and offers easy access to funds.

16. **Demand deposits** are deposits that the depositor is free to withdraw, or "demand," at any time.

17. A **certificate of deposit** (CD) documents a deposit into a financial institution that promises to pay a fixed interest rate for a specified period of time. CDs require a minimum balance and represent *time deposits* rather than demand deposits because you cannot withdraw your money before a stated maturity date without paying a penalty.

18. **Principal** refers to the amount of a deposit or, in the case of a loan, the amount of the loan before any interest is paid.

19. With **principal protection**, every dollar put in will be available to take out.

20. A **mutual fund** is a collection of investments, such as stocks, bonds, or money-market instruments, selected by a fund manager in accordance with the goals of the particular fund.

21. A **money-market fund** is a mutual fund made up entirely of money-market instruments.

22. A **bond** represents a loan to the bond's issuer in exchange for specified payments to the bond purchaser over time.

23. A share of **stock** represents partial ownership of a company.

24. An **asset** is anything of value that is owned or controlled with the expectation that it will provide benefits in the future.

25. The **life-cycle approach** to asset allocation is to make riskier investments with higher expected returns early in life and then turn to safer investments with lower returns later in life.

26. **Active investing** is carried out with the goal of outperforming the market.

27. The **passive investing** strategy is to duplicate the components of a benchmark index, such as the Dow Jones Industrial Average, and then receive the same returns as the index (less some minimal expenses).

28. The **efficient market hypothesis** holds that markets respond to information so efficiently that it is not possible to predict whether the prices of stocks or bonds will rise or fall without inside information.

29. An **index fund** is a mutual fund that duplicates the investments in a benchmark index, such as the S&P 500 Index.

## SELF-ASSESSMENT

The following questions are the type your teacher might ask you on a quiz or a test. Practice with these in order to improve your performance on class tests.

### Multiple-Choice Questions

1. Which of the following is a good strategy when trying to find a job?
   a. include a cover letter and a curriculum vitae
   b. include a curriculum vitae but not a cover letter
   c. negotiate for your wage and fringe benefit package **before** you get the actual job offer
   d. exaggerate your accomplishments to present yourself in a better light

2. Which of the following is considered good practice in developing a budget?
   a. basing your budget on gross income
   b. basing your budget on net income
   c. ignoring fixed expenses in your budget
   d. ignoring variable expenses in your budget

3. Which of the following is a variable expense?
   a. gift giving
   b. insurance
   c. rent
   d. loan payments

4. For most Americans, the relationship between actual savings and "ideal savings" is that
   a. actual savings is significantly above "ideal savings."
   b. actual savings is slightly above "ideal savings."
   c. actual savings is about equal to "ideal savings."
   d. actual savings is below "ideal savings."

5. Checking accounts
   a. usually pay higher interest rates than savings accounts.
   b. are easily linked to ACH payments.
   c. are riskier than cash.
   d. are easy to use and a wise choice of payment for those who find record keeping tedious and something they do not want to do.

6. A good strategy to follow when using credit wisely is to
   a. pay back a loan over a long period of time to keep monthly payments and interest charges low.
   b. get a loan from the most convenient source, since all lenders are regulated by the government and charge about the same rate of interest.
   c. keep down payments low to save money on finance charges.
   d. make as large a down payment as you can afford to save money on finance charges.

7. Which of the following is true?
   a. It is always better to buy a used car.
   b. It is always better to buy a new car.
   c. It is always better to lease a car.
   d. The decision to buy a used car, buy a new car, or lease a car depends on your individual situation.

8. Which of the following is true?

   a. 401(k) plans are very risky and most people should avoid putting money in them.

   b. Certificates of deposit typically pay higher interest rates than open passbook accounts.

   c. Money-market funds, mutual funds, certificates of deposit, and open passbook accounts are all insured by the FDIC.

   d. Stock purchases, bond purchases, and mutual fund purchases are all equal in their risk exposure to the investor.

9. Which of the following is **not** sound investment advice?

   a. Save early; save often.

   b. Don't be in a hurry to begin saving.

   c. Savings goals change over time.

   d. Relatively small rewards should come with relatively low risks.

10. Which of the following is true?

    a. Time deposits pay higher interest than demand deposits.

    b. Mutual funds and money-market funds are principal protected.

    c. The dividends on a stock are set in advance, whereas the interest paid on a bond varies with the profitability of the issuing company.

    d. Belief in the efficient market hypothesis would lead a person to rely on their own ability to predict the market and make profitable decisions on a short-term basis.

## Constructed Response Question

1. For each of the following savings alternatives, list one benefit and one drawback.

   a. open passbook savings account

   b. certificate of deposit

   c. checking account

**CHAPTER 13 & YOU** This chapter begins our exploration of macroeconomics—the study of the economy as a whole. When the economy is in good shape, there are more new stores opening up downtown, more new homes going up in the neighborhoods, and relatively few people who are fed up about their financial situation. If the economy is healthy when you complete your education, it will be easier for you to find a job or start a business. When the economy is trending downward, you see more factories and stores closing and fewer homes being built, and workers express more concern about their employment prospects. As a consumer, homeowner, and worker, your own life is affected by the state of the economy. That makes it important to know how to take the pulse of the economy and to understand the forces that send it, and so many things connected to it, up or down.

# Macroeconomic Performance

## GROWTH MATTERS

In 1800, Argentina was richer than the United States. The amount of goods and services produced by the average person each year—called *output per person*—was greater in Argentina than in the United States. Over the next two centuries, however, Argentina's economy didn't keep pace with the United States. By 1900, output per person in the United States was about twice that of the average Argentinean. And in 2011, output per person in the United States was about three times that in Argentina. Not surprisingly, as the production gap widened, so did the income gap between Americans and Argentineans. In 2011, the average income per person was $48,100 in the United States compared to just $17,400 in Argentina. The United States became a superpower because of its strong economic growth, while Argentina lagged behind. Why did this production and income gap develop over the past 200 years? The widening gap can be explained by different rates of economic growth in the United States and Argentina because of different economic policies that the countries pursued. In this chapter we will explore several key factors that influence economic growth.

## BOTTOM LINE

Decisions made by consumers, managers, and policy makers affect how fast living standards rise over the long run and how well the economy performs in the short run.

# Measuring National Output and Income

**KEY IDEA:** **Gross domestic product, a measure of the value of goods and services produced in the economy each year, is the most widely used gauge of economic activity.**

**OBJECTIVES**

- **To explain what gross domestic product is and how it is measured.**
- **To identify what is not included in gross domestic product.**
- **To discuss the difference between real and nominal values.**
- **To explain why real gross domestic product is the most useful measure of a country's total output.**

## The Knowledge Gap

In the early 1930s, the United States' economy was in crisis. All around the country, factories were shutting down and businesses and banks were failing. Millions of people were losing their jobs, and many were driven into sudden poverty. By 1933, one out of every four Americans who wanted to work could not find a job. Many countries in Europe were having a similar crisis. This downward economic spiral of the 1930s is commonly called the Great Depression.

In 1932, the U.S. Congress invited leading economists to answer some basic questions about the state of the economy. How much output was the country producing? How rapidly was production falling? How much income were Americans earning? How much were they spending? To the surprise of everyone present, none of the economists could provide answers. The information was simply not available! The most recent measurement of the country's total output and income had been made in 1929, and even that measurement had been incomplete.

To fix the knowledge gap, the U.S. government set up a *national income accounting system* to measure the country's production and income in a timely manner. Once the system was in place in the United States, it was rapidly copied by other countries. Today, almost every country in the world uses this accounting system to measure economic performance. At the center of this accounting system is a measure of a country's production called *gross domestic product.*

*During the Great Depression the U.S. Congress lacked adequate measures of economic performance.*

# GROSS DOMESTIC PRODUCT DEFINED

A country's **gross domestic product** (GDP) is the total dollar value of all final goods and services produced within the country's borders in a given year. Let's dissect this definition of GDP to better understand its five important features: dollar value, goods and services, final products, within a country's borders, and in a given year.

## Dollar Value

In order to measure the country's production, we need a common unit with which to measure everything produced. We could, in theory, use any common unit. For example, we could measure production in pounds. In that case, GDP would be the total weight of the country's production. But that wouldn't be a very useful measure. A pound of tortilla chips would count the same as a pound of computer chips, even though the computer chips are much more costly to produce and have greater value to people. Instead, GDP takes a more sensible approach: it measures production in dollars. Earlier chapters explained that the price of a good is determined by a combination of the cost of producing it as reflected by the supply curve and consumers' willingness to pay for it as reflected by the demand curve. A good with a higher price (a computer chip) will contribute more to GDP than a good with a lower price (a tortilla chip). Each good or service enters GDP at its *dollar price,* so a pair of running shoes that you buy for $100 contributes $100 to that year's GDP.

## Goods and Services

*Production* doesn't only refer to making goods like baseball bats and hamburgers. Production includes *services,* such as the work performed by plumbers, airline pilots, truck drivers, and doctors. Once a service is performed, there may be no physical trace left to look at or hold. Still, services are critical to our well-being and make up a large part of our production. To take just one example, imagine that the economy continued to produce goods but stopped producing transportation services. Unless you lived very close to a farm, you would not be able to buy food.

## Final Products

To measure GDP, we include only *final* goods and services, not *intermediate products*. What's the difference? **Final goods and services** are those that are sold to their final users. A household such as your family is a final user, as is a government agency like the U.S. Army. A firm such as Delta Airlines is a user when it purchases airplanes and other capital. By contrast, **an intermediate product** becomes part of a final good or service, or is used up in the production process. Examples of intermediate products include raw materials like lumber and semifinished goods like the computer chip in your cell phone. Coal is an intermediate product that is burned in the production of electricity. Capital goods such as buildings and machinery are not intermediate products because they do not become part of the final good and they are not used up in the production process.

Many goods can be either a final good or an intermediate product, depending on how they are used. For example, the flour your family buys to cook with is a final good, whereas the flour used to make hamburger buns for McDonald's is an intermediate product. Intermediate products are not counted in GDP because they are *already* included in the dollar value of the final good. When you buy a cell phone (a final good), the price you pay includes the value of all the intermediate products used to make the phone, including the computer chip, the display screen, the plastic casing, and the software. If we counted these intermediate products in GDP as well, we'd be double counting them.

A nation's **gross domestic product** (GDP) is the total dollar value of all final goods and services produced within the country's borders in a given year.

A **final good or service** is one that is sold to its final user, rather than to a firm that will use it to make something else.

An **intermediate product** is a product that becomes part of a final good or service, or is used up in the production process.

*Computer chips are intermediate products, the sales of which are not counted directly as part of GDP to avoid double counting. The value of the chip is included in the price of the electronic device built with the chip.*

**Investment** is business spending on physical capital, new homes, and inventories.

## Within a Country's Borders

GDP measures production that takes place in the country, regardless of the citizenship of those who produce it. Hence, the U.S. GDP includes all production by firms that operate in the United States, even if they are foreign owned. Production that takes place in other countries is not counted as part of U.S. GDP even if it occurs in firms owned by U.S. citizens.

## In a Given Year

GDP includes only final goods and services produced in a single calendar year, from January 1 to December 31. It does not include the sale of items left over from the previous year. However, those items that are made in one year and sold in the next are counted in GDP in the year in which they are made.

## THE EXPENDITURE APPROACH

The **expenditure approach** to calculating GDP is to add up the spending on everything included in GDP.

**Exports** are goods, services, and intermediate products bought by people in other countries.

GDP can be calculated in more than one way. The most direct method is called the **expenditure approach**, which is to add up the spending on everything included in GDP. To apply this approach, we first divide the economy into four basic sectors: the household sector, the business sector, the government sector, and the foreign sector. We then label final goods and services according to the sector that buys them, as shown in Figure 38.1

Household purchases are called *consumption* and are represented by the letter *C*. This is the largest component of GDP. It includes almost every good or service that your family buys during the year: food, clothes, furniture, movie tickets, dry-cleaning services, gasoline, and so on. But there is one big exception: houses. When new houses are built, they enter GDP as an *investment* by the construction company, which puts them in the expenditure category explained next. To avoid double counting, the value of houses is not counted again when they are purchased by household members.

In the context of measuring GDP, **investment** (*I*) is business spending on final goods of three types: (1) physical capital including equipment, software, and buildings; (2) new homes; and (3) any goods produced but not sold during the year. When goods are produced but not sold, they go into business inventories and the businesses that produced them are considered the final users for that year. For example, suppose Ford builds a car worth $25,000 in one year but doesn't sell it. The value of the car is counted in GDP as an investment in inventory by Ford. Then when the car is sold to a consumer the next year, the value of Ford's investment in inventory decreases by $25,000 and consumption increases by $25,000, so these two components of GDP balance out—the sale has no effect on GDP.

Goods and services bought by any level of government are called *government purchases* (*G*). Examples include purchases of military equipment, highways, police and fire department services, and public schools. Not included in GDP is government spending on transfer payments such as Social Security payments, welfare payments, and other government grants of money. These payments are excluded from GDP because they are not made in exchange for goods or services.

Finally, goods, services, and intermediate products bought by people in other countries are called **exports** (*X*). In a typical year the United States exports over $1 trillion worth of goods such as agricultural products, pharmaceuticals, and aircraft, as well as services such as movies, software, and banking services. For example, the United States exports about 30 million metric tons of wheat to other countries each year.

### Correcting for Imports

If we tried to find GDP by adding together the spending on consumption, investment, government purchases, and exports, we'd have a little problem. Some of the spending in each of these categories was for goods produced in other countries. Even many of the goods

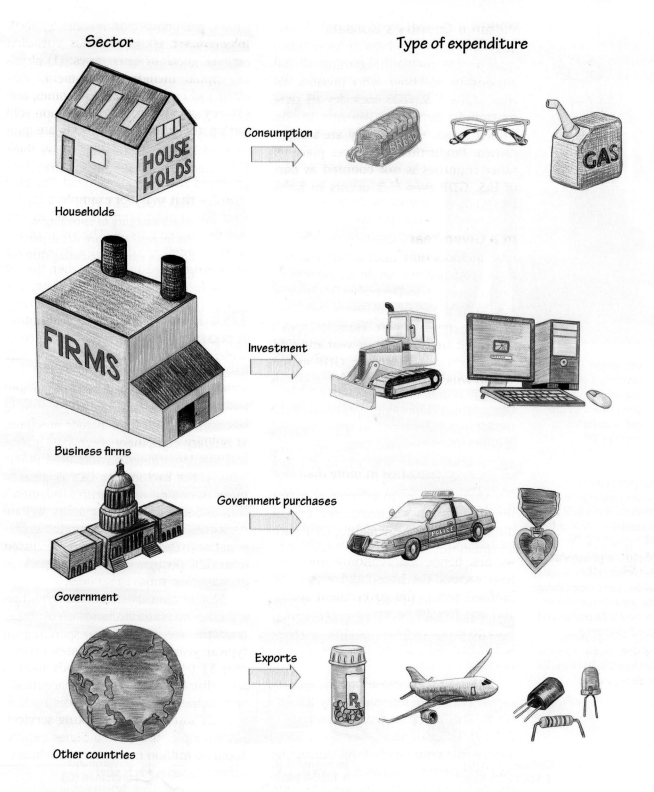

**Figure 38.1**  The Four Basic Sectors

The expenditure approach to calculating GDP entails adding up expenditures on consumption by households, investment by business firms, purchases by the government, and net exports.

*Our many purchases of goods imported from other countries are not included as part of GDP.*

**Imports** are goods, services, and intermediate products produced in other countries.

The **income approach** to calculating GDP is to add up all the income earned during the year by people who are involved in the production of goods and services.

that come out of U.S. factories have some components that were produced abroad. For example, the book you are holding was written, printed, assembled, and shipped in the United States. All that production is part of U.S. GDP. But the paper for the book is an intermediate product that might have come from Finland, India, or some other country. If so, the value of the paper should *not* be counted in U.S. GDP.

Goods, services, and intermediate products produced in other countries are called **imports** (*M*). The value of these imports is not included in U.S. GDP, which represents production in the United States only. So when we add together the four types of spending, we must subtract out imports to get the proper measure of U.S. GDP.

After making this correction for imports, we can summarize the expenditure approach to calculating GDP with an equation:

$$GDP = C + I + G + (X - M).$$

The last part of this equation, $X - M$, represents net exports. A country that exports more than it imports, such as China, will have positive net exports. A country that imports more than it exports, such as the United States, has negative net exports. In 2011, U.S. exports totaled $2,094 billion while U.S. imports were $2,662 billion. So U.S. net exports in 2011 were $2,094 billion − $2,662 billion = −$568 billion. Figure 38.2 shows these four categories of spending for 2011.

**DID YOU GET IT?**
Which category of spending is the largest? Why are net exports negative when calculating GDP for the United States?

## THE INCOME APPROACH

A second way to calculate GDP is less direct. The **income approach** is to add up all the income earned during the year by people involved in the production of goods and services. This includes the wages paid to workers who supply their labor; the rent paid to property owners who supply land, buildings, or equipment; the interest paid to individuals who supply their personal savings for loans; and the profit earned by business owners who provide entrepreneurship.

Note that every dollar you spend on a final good or service ends up as someone's income. So the total spending on

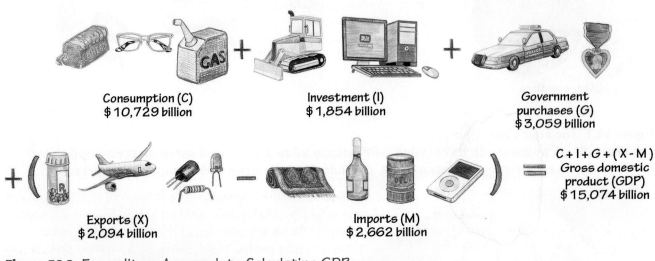

Consumption (C)
$ 10,729 billion

Investment (I)
$ 1,854 billion

Government purchases (G)
$ 3,059 billion

Exports (X)
$ 2,094 billion

Imports (M)
$ 2,662 billion

C + I + G + ( X - M )
Gross domestic product (GDP)
$ 15,074 billion

**Figure 38.2** Expenditure Approach to Calculating GDP

AP PHOTO/BEN MARGOT

final goods and services found using the expenditure approach is roughly equal to the total income earned by everyone involved in producing those goods and services. In practice, some adjustments are needed to equate the total of all income with GDP. For example, sales taxes are part of what consumers pay for goods and services, but they are not part of what firms pay out as income, so their value must be added to the amount received as income to arrive at GDP.

To understand the expenditure and income approaches better, look at Figure 38.3. The arrows labeled *consumption*, *investment*, *government purchases*, and *received for exports* show the flow of spending from households, financial institutions (which lend savings to firms to finance investments), government agencies, and foreigners to the U.S. firms that sell final goods. When this spending is added together, and imports are deducted (as represented by the arrow from business firms to other countries), we find GDP using the expenditure approach. In 2011, this was $15.1 trillion. Where did this $15.1 trillion in spending go? As shown by the arrow pointing leftward from business firms to households, the spending becomes income for the households that supplied the resources for all that production.

The income approach is to add the four main categories of income—wages, rent, interest, and profit—to calculate GDP. Economists often summarize the income approach with the formula

GDP = wages + rent + interest + profit.

Later in this chapter you'll see that the equality of a country's GDP and its total income can help explain why economies sometimes experience serious downturns.

 **DID YOU GET IT?**
How does the income approach calculate gross domestic product?

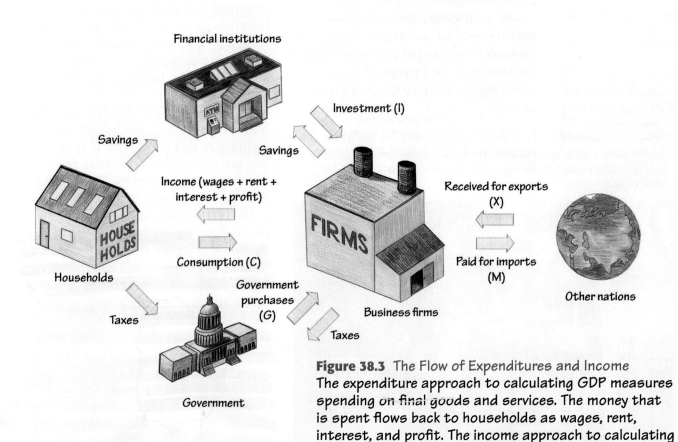

**Figure 38.3** The Flow of Expenditures and Income
The expenditure approach to calculating GDP measures spending on final goods and services. The money that is spent flows back to households as wages, rent, interest, and profit. The income approach to calculating GDP is to add up those four types of income.

## WHAT'S NOT INCLUDED IN GDP?

GDP is meant to include the total value of the final goods and services produced in an economy each year. Economic activities other than domestic production are *not* included in GDP. You've already learned about two types of transactions excluded from GDP:

- foreign production

- transfer payments such as Social Security payments

Other economic activities excluded from GDP include the following:

- Unpaid work. You know those household chores that you always wished you were paid for but you weren't? The (high, we're sure!) value of that work isn't included in GDP. The same goes for volunteer work, as for civic or religious organizations.

- Purely financial transactions, such as the purchase of corporate stocks, bonds, gold, or real estate. In these transactions, the ownership of existing property is exchanged for money. But the money is not a payment for new goods and services, so it is not included in GDP.

- The sale of used goods, such as secondhand cars, furniture, or homes. These were already counted in GDP

The **underground economy** represents business activity conducted without the knowledge of the government.

*Sales of used goods and any sales not reported to the government are not counted as part of GDP.*

when they were first produced and sold. When they are resold as used goods, they are not counted again.

- Production in the *underground economy*. The **underground economy** represents business activity conducted without the knowledge of the government, such as the sale of items by unlicensed street vendors, or barter exchanges of services, such as when an auto mechanic fixes a plumber's car in exchange for the plumber fixing his sink.

**DID YOU GET IT?**
What types of transactions are not included in gross domestic product?

## NOMINAL AND REAL GDP

The most important reason we measure GDP is to monitor changes in production over time. But because GDP is measured in dollars, we have a problem: the *prices* of the goods and services that make up GDP are constantly changing. For example, suppose 10 million cars are made in the United States this year and the average price of a car is $25,000. Then 10 million × $25,000 = $250 billion worth of car production will be included in this year's GDP. If 10 million cars are made once again next year, but the average price rises to $30,000, then next year's GDP will include 10 million × $30,000 = $300 billion worth of car production. The dollar value of car production will have risen even though the number of cars produced hasn't changed at all. Changing prices present a similar problem when tracking any measurement in dollars over time, such as wages, government purchases, or savings. Economists deal with this problem by creating a second, adjusted version of every dollar-based measurement. The adjusted version removes the effects of price changes. As a result, economic measurements based on dollars always have two versions.

Thinkstock

The first, unadjusted version of a dollar-based measure is called a *nominal* value. A nominal value uses each year's actual dollar values with no modifications for price changes. **Nominal GDP**, for example, values each good at the dollar price it actually sold for in the year in which it was produced. Nominal GDP is sometimes called *current dollar* GDP. For any given output level, a general rise in prices causes nominal GDP to rise. This is why nominal GDP is not a good way to judge what is happening to total output over time.

The second version of any dollar-based measure is called a *real* value. The real value is adjusted to remove the effects of price changes. It answers a hypothetical question: What would our dollar measure be if prices never changed? For example, **real GDP** measures total production in dollars after removing the distorting effect of changing prices.

To obtain real values, economists choose an arbitrary *base year*, such as 2005. The real dollar value in any year is calculated using the prices in the base year. For example, the figure for real GDP in 2010 tells us what the dollar value of total production would have been in 2010 if the price of every good had remained at its 2005 level. Real values are often called *constant-dollar* values. For example, in tables of economic information it is common to see that real GDP is measured in "2005 dollars." This tells us that when creating the tables, every year's real GDP was calculated using 2005 prices. Real GDP is immune to the effects of rising prices. It rises only when production actually rises, which is the goal for a true gauge of productivity.

Figure 38.4 shows both nominal GDP and real GDP (in 2005 dollars) in the United States from 2005 to 2011. Notice that both measures are the same

**Nominal GDP** values each good at the dollar price it actually sold for in the year in which it was produced.

**Real GDP** measures total production in dollars after removing the distorting effect of price changes.

Real and nominal GDP (billions of dollars)

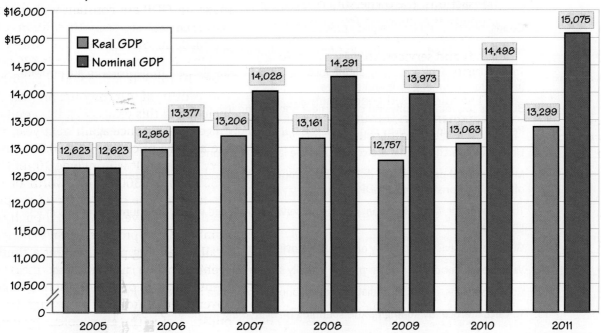

**Figure 38.4** Real and Nominal GDP in the United States

The change in nominal GDP from one year to the next reflects both the change in output and the change in prices. The change in real GDP reflects only the change in output. For this reason, sometimes we see nominal GDP increase while real GDP decreases.

SOURCE: Bureau of Economic Analysis, www.bea.gov/national/index.htm.

in 2005. For that year, both versions are calculated using 2005 prices. In other years, while real GDP is calculated using 2005 prices, nominal GDP is based on the actual prices in the given year. So a change in nominal GDP could be caused by a change in output, a change in prices, or a combination of price and output changes. A change in real GDP always indicates a change in output. The differences between real GDP and nominal GDP are apparent in Figure 38.4. For example, when output decreased and prices increased between 2007 and 2008, real GDP fell, but nominal GDP rose because prices increased by more than output decreased.

When economists track any dollar-based measure over time, they use the real value, not the nominal value. This practice is so common that often, the term *real* will just be assumed, rather than stated. So, for example, when you hear a news report about "GDP growth," it probably means real GDP growth.

# MODULE 38 REVIEW AND ASSESSMENT

**Summing Up the Key Ideas:** Match the following terms to the correct definitions.

A. Gross domestic product (GDP)
B. Final good or service
C. Intermediate product
D. Expenditure approach
E. Consumption
F. Investment
G. Government purchases
H. Exports
I. Imports
J. Income approach
K. Underground economy
L. Nominal GDP
M. Real GDP

_____ 1. A product that is itself used to make a final good or service.

_____ 2. Goods, services, and intermediate products produced in other countries.

_____ 3. Sold to its final user, rather than to a firm that will use it to make something else.

_____ 4. To calculate GDP by adding up all the income earned during the year by people who are involved in the production of goods and services.

_____ 5. Business spending on physical capital, new homes, and inventories.

_____ 6. Represents business activity conducted without the knowledge of the government.

_____ 7. Household purchases that are counted as the largest component of GDP.

_____ 8. Measures total production in dollars after removing the distorting effect of price changes; this is often called constant dollar GDP.

_____ 9. The total dollar value of all final goods and services produced within the country's borders in a given year.

_____ 10. Goods and services bought by any level of government.

_____ 11. Values each good at the dollar price it actually sold for in the year in which it was produced.

_____ 12. Goods, services, and intermediate products bought by people in other countries.

_____ 13. To calculate GDP by adding up the spending on everything included in GDP.

## Analyze and Explain:
Analyze each of the following and then determine if it would be counted in the calculation of U.S. GDP as **consumption spending** (C), **investment spending** (I), **government spending** (G), **exports** (X), or **imports** (M).

C, I, G, X, OR M?

1. A new home is constructed in Texas. _____

2. Your city buys a new fire truck. _____

3. You buy some chocolate made in Germany. _____

4. The U.S. government agency NASA contracts with a firm in Alabama to provide parts for the space station. _____

5. You get a haircut at the shop in your neighborhood. _____

6. You buy a new Chevy truck made in Michigan. _____

7. A Japanese boy buys a new toy made in Ohio. _____

8. You enjoy a makeover at the local spa. _____

9. You buy lipstick that was made in France. _____

10. Apple Computer builds a new factory in Missouri. _____

11. You buy a new BMW made in South Carolina. _____

## Apply:
In the following situations, determine if each of these items would be **included** or **not included** in the count of GDP.

INCLUDED OR NOT INCLUDED?

1. the purchase of a new tractor by a farmer _____

2. the purchase of a used tractor by a farmer _____

3. income from cashing in a U.S. savings bond _____

4. services of a mechanic in fixing the radiator on his own car _____

5. a Social Security check received by a retired store clerk _____

6. an increase in business inventories _____

7. government purchases of parts for a submarine for the Navy _____

8. the income of the barber who cuts your hair _____

9. income received from redeeming coupon payments on an AT&T bond _____

10. purchase of a Van Gogh painting by an art dealer _____

# MODULE 39

# Economic Growth

**KEY IDEA:** Economic growth—when it arises from growth in productivity—raises living standards, although some countries have had great difficulty achieving this kind of growth.

### OBJECTIVES

- **To explain what economic growth is and how it is measured.**
- **To compare economic growth in countries across the globe.**
- **To identify the four factors that cause growth in productivity.**
- **To evaluate some of the controversies over economic growth.**

## What Growth Brings

If a time machine could take you back to be a typical working American in 1900, you would work about 60 hours per week and earn about 15 cents an hour. Prices would be lower, but your hourly wage would buy you less than what $3 buys today. You could not expect to live past your late 40s. If you fell seriously ill at any age, your doctor would be of little help, because most of the medicine and medical techniques we have today would not exist. Most of your "free" time would be spent doing household chores—without the assistance of a vacuum cleaner, a microwave oven, or anything made of plastic. And for your evening entertainment, you'd be without a TV, computer, or radio, but perhaps your Uncle Max could tell you his favorite joke one more time.

Today, the typical American worker has a higher **standard of living** than in the past, meaning more goods and services and more wealth to purchase them with. He or she works about 35 hours per week, and the average hourly wage is about $21, plus *fringe benefits* such as health insurance and paid vacations. The average worker today can expect to live until the age of about 80. Thanks to dishwashers, laundry machines, microwaves, and other automated devices, there is more free time to spend on recreation and relaxation. And the entertainment choices are seemingly endless, including hundreds of cable radio and TV stations, movies by mail, YouTube, digital downloads of shows and music, and travel by car or jet to entertainment venues all over the world.

What is responsible for these dramatic changes in the average worker's standard of living? The answer is growth in real GDP per person. In the United States, as in many other countries, the annual production of goods and services has increased faster over time than the population has grown. As a result, the average worker today can afford more food, clothing, health care, and other items than the average worker of the 1900s. Moreover, growth has led to the development of entirely new goods and services that people in the 1900s could not have imagined.

The **standard of living** is the level of material wealth as measured by the consumption of goods and services.

# ECONOMIC GROWTH DEFINED

**Economic growth** is a sustained increase in real GDP over time. Economic growth is about trends in productive capacity over years, rather than short-term ups and downs in the economy. Figure 39.1 shows economic growth in the United States over the last four decades. You can see that the general, long-run trend in real GDP is upward. There are also shorter periods over which real GDP decreased, but these downturns were outweighed by prolonged periods of rising output.

Since the beginning of the Great Depression in 1929, real GDP in the United States has grown by more than 3 percent per year on average. The rate at which real GDP increases is called the *economic growth rate*. While a 3 percent growth rate may not sound very impressive, it propels the overall real GDP to striking new heights over time. This is illustrated by the *Rule of 70*. To calculate the real GDP's approximate doubling time, simply divide 70 by the economic growth rate. If real GDP grows by 3 percent per year, it should double every 70 ÷ 3 = 23.3 years. That is a good approximation of the real GDP doubling time in the United States. For countries like Dominica and Iran, whose economic growth rates hover closer to 1 percent, it will take about 70 ÷ 1 = 70 years for real GDP to double unless the growth rates change substantially. A relatively high economic growth rate over the last century made the United States the world's largest economy.

**DID YOU GET IT?**
If the country produced more output this month than last month, would that constitute economic growth?

# TRACKING LIVING STANDARDS

Real GDP tells us how fast the entire economy is growing. But it cannot, by itself, tell us whether living standards

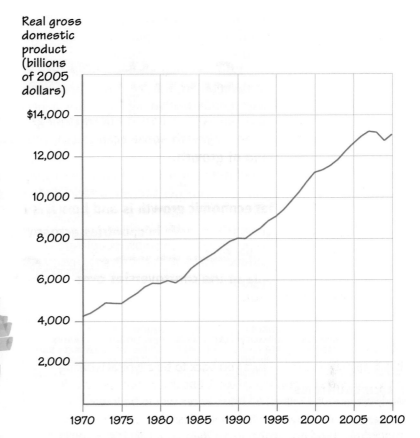

**Figure 39.1** Real GDP, 1970–2010
Economic growth is a sustained increase in real GDP over time. The United States has enjoyed economic growth over most of the past four decades.

are improving. That's because in most economies, the population is growing, too. Over time, a country's output must be divided among more and more people. The standard of living is determined by **real GDP per capita**, or output per person, which is the real GDP divided by the total population. In 2011, the real GDP in the United States (measured in 2005 dollars) was $13,299 billion, while

**Economic growth** is a sustained increase in real GDP over time.

**Real GDP per capita** is output per person, calculated as real GDP divided by the total population.

*One of the most pressing economic goals is to find a solution to persistent poverty.*

the population was about 312 million. So real GDP per capita was $13,299 billion ÷ 312 million = $42,625.

Economists use real GDP per capita as the main indicator of a country's average standard of living. It is not a perfect indicator. A bit later in this chapter, you'll learn some problems with this measure. But in spite of the problems, large differences in real GDP per capita among countries are important signals about living conditions for the people in those countries. Where real GDP per capita is very low, most people are poor. Where real GDP per capita is high, people generally live more comfortable lives.

The connection between real GDP per capita and economic well-being is illustrated in Figure 39.2. It provides data for a few countries that are considered "rich" because they have a high real GDP per capita and a few countries considered "poor" because they have a low real GDP per capita. In the third column, the *under-5 mortality rate* tells us how many children die before the age of 5. This mortality rate is consistently low in the rich countries but at least ten times higher in the poor countries. The column for life expectancy shows that people in rich countries live considerably longer, on average, than those in poor countries. The next column shows the high percentages of people in the poorest countries who live in extreme poverty, meaning they have less than $1.25 to spend per day. The final column shows that rich countries provide basic education to virtually every citizen. In the poor countries, a large fraction of the population cannot even read.

# GROWTH IN GDP PER CAPITA: INTERNATIONAL COMPARISONS

 Almost all the countries that were relatively rich 20 years ago have continued to enjoy economic growth, with only a few short-lived downturns. These countries have benefited from remarkable improvements in their living standards. But what about the poorest countries? Their experience has been mixed.

Figure 39.3 shows real GDP per capita for a sample of countries between 1991 and 2010. These figures are in 2000 dollars, the base year chosen by the creator of the data. The United States and France are examples of two countries that started out with relatively high living standards

| | GDP PER CAPITA* (DOLLARS) | UNDER 5 MORTALITY* (PER 1,000 LIVE BIRTHS) | LIFE EXPECTANCY AT BIRTH* (YEARS) | PERCENT OF POPULATION LIVING ON < $1.25 PER DAY | ADULT LITERACY RATE (PERCENT) |
|---|---|---|---|---|---|
| **RICH COUNTRIES** | | | | | |
| United States | $42,078 | 7.5 | 78.2 | <0.1%** | >99%** |
| France | 29,483 | 4.2 | 81.4 | <0.1** | >99** |
| Japan | 30,965 | 3.2 | 82.9 | <0.1** | >99** |
| Germany | 33,414 | 4.1 | 80 | <0.1** | >99** |
| **POOR COUNTRIES** | | | | | |
| Pakistan | 2,410 | 73.7 | 65.2 | 21† | 56† |
| Cambodia | 1,968 | 46 | 62.5 | 22.8† | 78† |
| Sierra Leone | 741 | 188.8 | 72.4 | 53.4‡ | 41§ |
| Niger | 650 | 130.9 | 54.3 | 43.6† | 29** |

*2010   †2008   §2009
**2005   ‡2003

**Figure 39.2** Some Indicators of Economic Well-Being in Rich and Poor Countries
**Key indicators of well-being vary widely between rich and poor countries.**

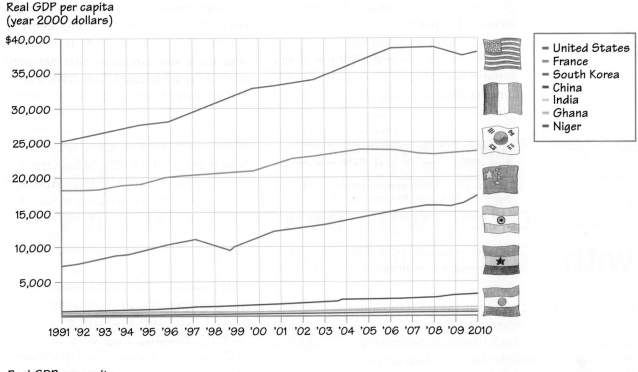

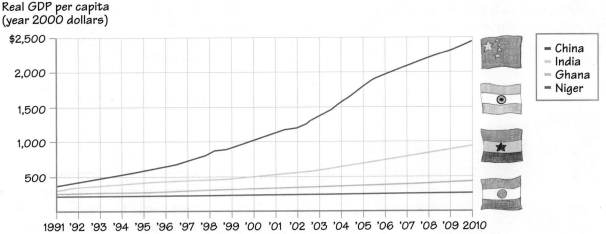

**Figure 39.3** Growth in GDP per Capita in Selected Countries
Some countries have shown impressive growth in real GDP per capita; others have made little progress. Economists study the reasons for these differences.

in 1991. Their real GDP per capita has continued to grow, and living standards have risen further over time. South Korea is an example of a country that started out poor but, through rapid growth, is fast approaching the living standards of the rich countries. Other formerly poor countries (not shown in the graph) that have become rich countries include Singapore, Taiwan, and Hong Kong.

The lower graph in Figure 39.3 expands the scale for the poorer countries to make comparisons easier. China began to separate from the pack in the 1990s and India followed in the 2000s. While they are still far behind, they are making progress. Finally, the two poorest countries in the graph, Ghana and Niger, continue to be very poor. Ghana has had some healthy growth in recent years but still remains among the world's poorest countries. And Niger shows no signs of escaping poverty. Its real GDP per capita—a few hundred dollars per year—has been flat for decades.

The examples in the figure show us that a country that was once poor can become rich. But not all countries manage to escape poverty. To understand why, let's take a closer look at the causes of economic growth.

## ECONOMICS IN ACTION

# U.S. States Renamed for Countries with Similar GDP

We often forget just how large the U.S. economy is compared to the economies of most other countries. Professor Mark J. Perry of the University of Michigan designed the following map of the United States, with each state renamed for a country with a very similar GDP. To get the GDP of the United States, you would have to add together the GDPs of every country on the map.

If we designed a similar map using U.S. metropolitan areas, we would see some equally interesting comparisons. For example, the output of the New York metropolitan area (including New York City, Northern New Jersey, and Long Island) is equal to the entire GDP of India. And the output of the St. Louis metropolitan area is the same as New Zealand's.

SOURCE: *Carpe Diem*, Professor Mark J. Perry's Blog for Economics and Finance, http://mjperry.blogspot.com/2007/12/update-americas -ridiculously-large.html, posted December 11, 2007.

**Figure 39.4** U.S. States Renamed for Countries with Similar GDP
Professor Mark J. Perry of the University of Michigan designed this map by renaming each state for a country with a very similar GDP.

# SEARCHING FOR SOURCES OF ECONOMIC GROWTH

An economy can grow for many different reasons. But which reasons are the most important? Not the ones you might think. Consider, for example, the discovery of new natural resources, such as lumber, oil, silver, or copper. This would seem to be a primary basis for economic growth. It is true that newly discovered resources sometimes create a temporary spurt of economic activity. For example, oil discoveries in the North Sea in the 1970s helped increase real GDP in Norway, England, and several other countries. But newly available natural resources are not a key determinant of long-term growth. Many countries grow for decades or longer without significant new discoveries of natural resources. Being rich in natural resources can help explain a high real GDP. But it cannot explain a continually growing real GDP. In fact, some countries with only small quantities of natural resources—such as South Korea or Japan—have grown rapidly and become rich. And some countries with ample supplies of natural resources—such as Belize and Nigeria—have remained poor.

Another possible source of growth is a rising population. It is true that with more people, a country can produce more goods and services. But a rising population does not provide the type of growth economists are looking for. A rising population causes real GDP to grow, but it does not cause real GDP *per capita* to grow. Remember that it is real GDP per capita that determines a country's standard of living because that is the measure of how much output is available for the average person. For real GDP per capita to rise, the average person in the economy must produce more output. Simply having more people does not make output per person grow.

## The Central Role of Productivity

If natural resource discoveries and rising population don't explain rising living standards, then what does? Economists who study economic growth focus on one key factor: *productivity*. Sometimes called *labor productivity*, **productivity** is the amount of output the average worker can produce in an hour. It is calculated by dividing a country's total output of goods and services by the total number of hours it takes to produce it. For example, suppose the United States produces $14 trillion of real GDP in a year (measured

**Productivity** is the amount of output the average worker can produce in an hour.

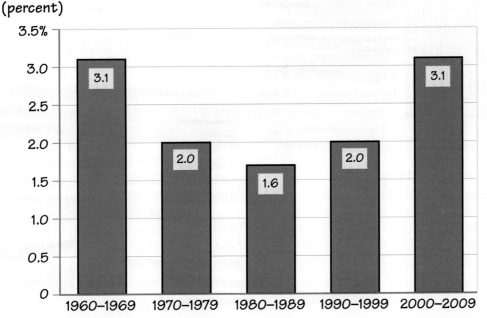

Annual change (percent)

**Figure 39.5** U.S. Average Annual Productivity Gains by Decade, 1960–2009

A country's **capital stock** is the total amount of physical capital in the country.

**Capital deepening** is an increase in a country's capital per worker.

in 2005 dollars) using 350 billion labor hours. Then U.S. productivity is $14 trillion ÷ 350 billion = $40. As long as people continue to work the same number of hours, an increase in productivity (output per worker per hour) will cause an increase in real GDP per capita (output per person per year).

In growing countries, productivity rises year after year, but its rate of increase can vary. Figure 39.5 shows the average annual increases in U.S. productivity, by decade, from 1960 to 2009. During the 1980s, for example, growth in labor productivity averaged just 1.6 percent per year, compared to the much higher 3.1 percent yearly growth in productivity during the 2000s. In the countries that remain impoverished, productivity growth tends to remain low and dips frequently into the negative numbers.

**DID YOU GET IT?**
Identify and define the key source of economic growth.

## The Four Pillars of Economic Growth

Growth in productivity is critical to the advancement of living standards. But what makes productivity rise? Improvements in any of four areas can lead to higher productivity. Think of them as the *four pillars of economic growth*: physical capital, human capital, technological change, and sound governance.

Physical Capital | Human Capital | Technological Change | Sound Governance

### Pillar 1: Physical Capital

Have you ever tried to dig a hole without a shovel? Or write a research paper without a computer? Like you, workers are more productive when they have the right tools, electronic devices, buildings, vehicles, and other forms of physical capital to work with. The total amount

of physical capital in a country is called its **capital stock**. What matters for productivity is not the capital stock itself but the average amount of capital available per worker. An increase in a country's capital per worker is called **capital deepening**.

To better understand how capital deepening can raise productivity, imagine you and two friends start a tree-planting business in your neighborhood, which has you digging a lot of holes. If you have just one shovel for the group, the three of you will have to share it. Your business has just one third of a shovel per worker. You can take turns using the shovel, but output per hour (including the hours spent waiting to use the shovel) will be relatively low. If you get a second shovel, your capital per worker rises and the group is more productive. With three shovels, you each have your own, and productivity (output per worker per hour) is higher still. Even a fourth shovel would increase productivity, because you could use it when one of the others breaks or becomes dull. Up to a point, the more capital you have per worker, the greater your output per hour. The same applies in almost any job and for the economy as a whole.

In order to increase the amount of capital per worker, a country's capital stock must increase more rapidly than its workforce. To see why, imagine that your tree-planting business went from having three shovels to having six. And suppose that at the same time you brought on three more friends to work with you, so you had six shovels for six workers. With twice the capital and twice the labor, you would end up with the same amount of capital per worker as before: one shovel. But if your capital stock doubled from three shovels to six and the number of workers less than doubled—say, it increased from three to five—then capital per worker would rise. There would then be one and one third shovel per worker. Likewise, if a country can increase its capital stock at a faster rate than its workforce, it can achieve capital deepening.

## Investment and the Capital Stock

The meaning of *investment* depends on the context, but it usually involves foregoing current benefits for future growth. In our discussion of personal finance in Chapter 12 we saw how investments in stocks and bonds can help your wealth grow. Module 38 explained that in the context of macroeconomics, investment is primarily spending on physical capital, which helps the economy grow. This includes investment by firms on things like cranes, delivery trucks, computer systems, office cubicles, and assembly lines. It also includes spending on **economic infrastructure**, which is physical capital that provides a basic foundation that users share for many types of economic activity. Economic infrastructure includes communication systems, such as satellites and fiber-optic cable lines; power systems, such as power grids and electricity generation plants; financial systems, such as banks, stock exchanges, and markets for goods and services; and transportation systems, such as railways, highways, bridges, airports, and seaports. Spending on infrastructure includes elements of both private investment and government spending.

In order to increase the capital stock, investment spending must be greater than *depreciation*, which is the amount of capital that is used up each year. For example, if a computer is expected to last three years, then one third of the computer's productive life is "used up"

each year. If one new computer is purchased every three years, the capital stock will not increase because investment is just keeping pace with depreciation.

For a given amount of depreciation, more investment spending means more growth in the capital stock. In 2011, investment in the United States topped $2.1 trillion. This represented about 16 percent of GDP that year. Of the total, firms spent about $1.7 trillion, and federal, state, and local governments spent the remaining $400 billion. In almost all years, U.S. investment spending exceeds depreciation, so the capital stock rises. And although the population is growing at the same time, the capital stock grows faster, resulting in an increase in the capital per worker. This increase in the availability of capital puts more shovels and computers and delivery cars at the disposal of each worker, which explains why investment helps raise productivity. Figure 39.6 shows that more than half of the private sector's investment dollars was spent on business equipment and software in 2011. The rest is divided between business structures and residential structures. But where do the funds for all this investment come from?

*A strong economy relies on investments in economic infrastructure, including power systems, communication systems, and transportation systems.*

**Economic infrastructure** is physical capital, such as communications systems and power systems, that provides a basic foundation that users share for many types of economic activity.

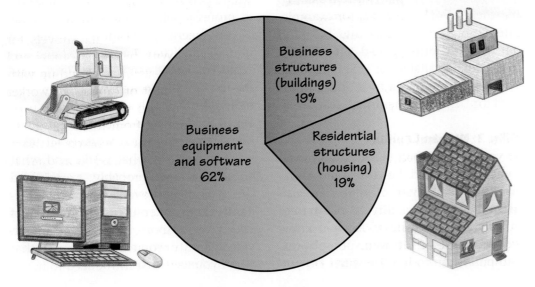

Business structures (buildings) 19%

Business equipment and software 62%

Residential structures (housing) 19%

**Figure 39.6** U.S. Private Sector Investment, 2011

### The Role of Saving

Business investment is largely funded with *domestic savings*—that portion of a country's total income that is not paid in taxes or spent by households on consumption goods. These savings represent a pool of funds available for investment purposes. Domestic savings flow into financial institutions such as banks where they can be loaned out to firms. You saw an illustration of this flow of savings in Figure 38.3.

In a simple world, income would be divided among consumption, taxes, and saving; the government would spend just the amount collected in taxes; and the amount available for business investment would equal the amount saved. Our world is not that simple. To begin with, governments often spend more than they collect in taxes. When that occurs, the government must borrow funds to fill the gap. The government then competes with firms for the pool of available savings, reducing the amount available for private investment.

As a second complication, the foreign sector affects the amount of savings available for business investment in a country. For example, Americans make some of their savings available to foreign borrowers. But foreigners make even more of their savings available to American borrowers. Because the U.S. economic and legal systems are so stable, foreigners have traditionally found the United States to be a good place to put their savings. In 2011, for example, international flows of savings into and out of the country added $467 billion to the total available for U.S. borrowers. This was more than a fifth of the funds used for U.S. investment that year.

### Pillar 2: Human Capital

So your tree-planting business borrowed some money and bought some shovels. The productivity of your crew also depends on your ability to plant trees quickly and successfully. Do you know what mixture of nitrogen, phosphorus, and potassium to fertilize with? Do you know the correct diameter and depth for the hole? Are you experienced with the shoveling posture and grip that will minimize injuries and maximize performance? These are examples of the productivity-enhancing competencies that comprise *human capital*.

Chapter 1 introduced human capital as the knowledge and skills of workers. Human capital is gained through education, experience, and training, and is a vital determinant of productivity. The more skills a car mechanic has, the less time it takes to diagnose and fix a car that won't run. The more skills a lawyer has, the faster he or she can prepare for a case. If human capital makes a difference when planting trees, you can imagine how it affects productivity when designing software or performing brain surgery.

In the richer *developed countries* where it is widely available, and to a lesser extent in the relatively poor *developing countries* where offerings are limited, public education provides a basic foundation of human capital. The private sector also serves up many opportunities for human capital acquisition. Private training at places like the Second City Training Center for sketch comedy, Le Cordon Bleu College of Culinary Arts, and the UTI Automotive Technology Training Program can turn workers with much potential but little human capital into comedians, cooks, and NASCAR mechanics. Many students attend private colleges, and some go on to professional programs in such fields as engineering, business administration, or medicine. Human capital is also acquired on the job, both through on-the-job training programs and through trial and error. This is why more experienced workers tend to be more productive than newly hired workers—it takes a while to learn what works and what doesn't. You've probably experienced this type of improvement in skills first-hand. Compare your current mastery of your favorite sport, musical instrument, video game, or topic in school with that when you were first introduced to it.

One way for a country to increase the level of human capital per worker is to increase the average number of years that citizens attend school. Figure 39.7 shows that the high school and college completion rates in the United States have increased dramatically in recent history. For example, in 1960, only 41 percent of Americans over the age of 25 had a high school education. Today, 87 percent do. Over the same period, the percentage of people with a college education shot up from 8 percent to 30 percent. This has contributed to the higher level of human capital per worker and thus to rising productivity.

Even if the years of schooling remained constant, human capital per worker and productivity could still rise over time as the result of increases in productivity in the field of education. Your teachers use instructional methods and technology that were not available to teachers in the past. Think about how you have used the Internet in your high school classes to gather information and learn about the world. When your parents went to high school, they did not learn how to use the Internet because (gasp) there *was* no Internet.

The computer skills you are learning will make you more productive than earlier generations could imagine.

## Pillar 3: Technological Change

You've just learned that new discoveries affect productivity by increasing the level of human capital per worker. But they also affect productivity more directly as part of the third pillar of economic growth: *technological change*. Productivity enhancements follow technological change in two circumstances. First, technological innovation can change how goods and services are produced. For example, industrial robots now assemble cars, package food, and fill bottles with juice. Most of these robots did not exist a few decades ago, and even better robots are in development. Recently, a new type of robot was invented to increase productivity in the premade salad industry. These robots use photo imagery to find insects sitting on lettuce leaves and then blow them off with a puff of air. With the help of the robot, productivity in salad-packaging plants has increased.

*Has technological change made you more productive?*

People older than 25 with high school or college education (percent)

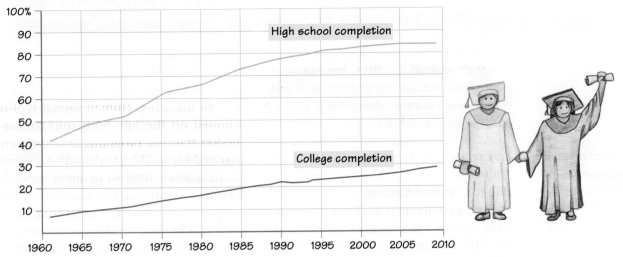

**Figure 39.7** Education Trends
High school and college completion rates in the United States have increased dramatically over the past 50 years.

istockphoto

# ECONOMICS IN ACTION

## "Creative Destruction" Yesterday and Today

In a growing, changing economy, new products made by new firms replace older products and firms. Nearly a century ago, the car replaced the horse and buggy as the primary means of transportation in the United States. A few decades ago, the personal computer replaced the typewriter. More recently, the Internet replaced most of the ticket-sales and trip-planning services formerly supplied by travel agents. And in large cities, e-mail has replaced the services of bicycle messengers who used to deliver important documents and letters. These changes in the marketplace are a natural feature of capitalism.

Economists use the term *creative destruction* to describe this process of dynamic change. The term was coined by economist Joseph A. Schumpeter in his famous book, *Capitalism, Socialism, and Democracy*, published in 1942. Schumpeter argued that capitalist economies are built on innovation. Over time, in irregular spurts, innovation and entrepreneurship increase productivity by creating new products, businesses, and jobs. But as new products and

production methods are created, older products and methods become obsolete. People who used to produce the old goods and services must often go through difficult adjustments to find different lines of work. This is one of the costs of economic growth.

In today's information-based economy, the pace of creative destruction has quickened. Innovations, particularly those in the field of information and communications technologies (ICTs), have changed entire industries with lightning speed. Consider what has happened to the music industry in recent years. In the 1990s, the CD largely replaced record albums and tapes. Over the last ten years or so, iPods and similar devices for downloading music have been replacing CDs. Ten years from now, you may find yourself trying to explain to a young child what a CD player was. There won't be many around.

### DID YOU GET IT?
What is an example of creative destruction?

---

**Firms conduct research and development** activities to discover or improve products or procedures.

The second way that technological change can enhance productivity is by allowing new types of goods and services to be made. For example, in a typical year the manufacture of computers and related electronics makes up about $300 billion of U.S. real GDP (in 2005 dollars), and computer systems design and related services make up another $170 billion. On top of that, broadcasting and telecommunications add $380 billion. It was technological change over the past several decades that placed these industries among the largest in the country.

Although there is always an element of luck involved in new discoveries, the pace of technological change depends heavily on *research and development* (R&D) expenditures. Firms conduct **research and development** activities to discover or improve products or procedures. Pharmaceutical companies, for example, spend tens of billions of dollars each year in the quest for new drugs that cure whatever ails us. In 2010, total R&D spending in the United States reached $399 billion, or 2.9 percent of GDP. As a proportion of GDP, this exceeded the R&D spending of most developed countries, the exceptions being Israel, Japan, Sweden, Finland, and South Korea. In terms of total R&D spending, the United States is the world's leader. Figure 39.8 shows the main funding sources for R&D in the United States in 2009.

Inventor Thomas Alva Edison, an early R&D pioneer, designed America's first research laboratory in the late 1800s. In his research lab, then called an "invention factory," Edison created an orderly system for inventing new goods. Edison's handiwork included an improved telephone transmitter, the phonograph, the incandescent light bulb, and hundreds of other inventions.

### Pillar 4: Sound Governance

The fourth pillar of economic growth is *sound governance*, meaning that the economy is well managed by competent and ethical authorities. An essential element of sound governance is respect for the **rule of law**—the principle that no person is above the law. That is, all people must follow the same rules and regulations regardless of their wealth or position. Sound governance also requires that public officials administer the government responsibly. A result of sound governance is that entrepreneurs and others in the economy feel confident that the government will treat them fairly. Without sound governance, people spend time and effort protecting

themselves from corrupt officials and arbitrarily applied laws rather than on productive activities.

A number of systems support sound governance:

• **A fair legal system**. The legal system consists of laws and methods of law enforcement, including government agencies, the courts, and the police. When the system works well, it helps people protect the money and other rewards they have received for productive activities. It does so by fighting theft, protecting property rights, and enforcing contracts. The legal system also protects the right to profit from *intellectual property*—new

*Thomas Alva Edison was a pioneer of research and development. He invented hundreds of products including the incandescent light bulb.*

The **rule of law** is the principle that no person is above the law.

R&D spending
(billions of dollars)

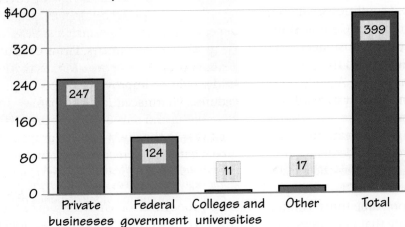

**Figure 39.8** U.S. Funding for Research and Development in 2009

*Without the legal system's protection of intellectual property, someone else might have received the roughly $1 billion J. K. Rowling earned for conjuring up Harry's magic.*

ideas or discoveries—with patents, trademarks, and copyrights. For example, author J. K. Rowling owns the copyright for the Harry Potter books. Anyone wishing to use her material or make movies from her books must get permission and pay for the legal right to use her work. The protections of a fair legal system create incentives for entrepreneurs, workers, investors, and property owners to contribute to economic growth. When the rewards for hard work are unprotected, the incentives for such work are weak.

• **A fair regulatory system**. A variety of government agencies work to protect people and natural resources from harm by making and enforcing regulations. In the U.S. economy, for example, the Occupational Safety and Health Administration (OSHA) enforces regulations to protect workers from dangerous working conditions. The Consumer Product Safety Commission (CPSC) aims to protect consumers from unsafe products. And the Environmental Protection Agency (EPA) oversees regulations meant to ward off environmental problems.

Like most things, the creation of regulations involves tradeoffs. Regulations that limit risk taking are a constraint on productivity. For example, pharmaceutical companies must conduct tests to demonstrate that new drugs are

safe and effective. If regulations didn't require those tests, it would be easier to introduce new drugs but more likely that some of the drugs would cause harm. Likewise, environmental regulations that limit toxic emissions make production more expensive. But they also help prevent environmental disasters that would harm people and natural resources critical to the normal functioning of an economy. It is therefore appropriate for regulators to weigh the costs of regulations against the benefits and to adopt those regulations that do more good than harm.

• **A fair tax system**. The government must collect taxes from individuals and firms in a reasonable and consistent manner. A failed tax system cannot support the legal and regulatory systems that you just learned are vital to economic growth, not to mention the construction of roads, bridges, and other infrastructure. If taxes are not collected, or if they are siphoned off by corrupt public officials, these needs will go unfulfilled and productivity will suffer. In the other extreme, unfairly high tax rates can dissuade people from working and again harm productivity. For example, in 2011, Italy's largest labor union threatened to go on strike (have workers stop working) in

*Regulatory demands for extensive drug testing slow productivity but limit the danger of deadly side effects. A fair regulatory system strikes the right balance between too many demands and too little safety.*

response to tax increases approved by the Italian government. In the United States, the Internal Revenue Service ensures that individuals and businesses comply with tax laws. The Government Accountability Office, among other government agencies, oversees how taxpayer dollars are used.

**DID YOU GET IT?**
How does sound governance help foster productivity growth?

# BENEFITS OF ECONOMIC GROWTH

When economic growth is based on increases in productivity rather than increases in population, it increases living standards in developed and developing countries alike. In developing countries, such as China and India, that have begun to grow rapidly, hundreds of millions of people have escaped extreme poverty. But in Africa and elsewhere, roughly one billion people continue to live below the threshold of extreme poverty: a budget of $1.25 per day. Economic growth can help these people obtain the food, shelter, and health care they need to survive.

Why is economic growth so important in a developed country like the United States? Don't we produce enough already? In one sense, yes. In another sense, no. We certainly produce enough goods and services in the United States for everyone to survive, and the average American lives quite comfortably relative to the average citizen in many developing countries. But it is part of human nature to always want more. The United States was considered a developed country in 1960, too, but few people would want to go back in time and live the shorter lifespans in the smaller homes with the precomputer technology and the lower wages of that period. (Not to mention the hairdos!) Fifty years from now, a high school economics textbook—assuming books still exist—might make the same point about going back in time to our era. And students in the future may shudder

at the thought of having to live like you do now. ("You mean they couldn't even travel at the speed of light?")

Even if the average American got over the desire to have more, economic growth would still serve the important purpose of helping those below-average Americans who don't have enough. In 2011, an American family of four was officially considered to live in poverty if its annual income was below $22,811. Using this definition, 15.9 percent of the U.S. population—about 48.5 million people—were living in poverty.

There are several options for what the government or private charitable organizations could do with resources that could become available with more economic growth. Possible approaches, all of which are controversial, include the following:

• providing additional direct financial assistance to the poor, so that they have more money to spend

• supporting job training programs so that adults who lack marketable skills can become candidates for good jobs

• carrying out work projects, such as building new highways or retrofitting old buildings with energy-saving windows, in order to create jobs while improving the capital stock

• providing more support to schools and colleges so that children from poor families (among others) can receive a better education

*With economic growth comes growth in the size of homes. In the United States, the average size of new, single-family homes was about 1,200 square feet in 1960 and 2,400 square feet in 2010.*

These solutions involve tradeoffs because they require the use of resources that could otherwise be used for other purposes. As long as real GDP per capita is growing, we can divert more resources to solve social problems such as poverty without reducing the goods or services available to others. There is more to go around.

Finally, productivity growth can give us more free time. When productivity rises, real GDP per capita rises if we all work the same number of hours. But instead we could work fewer hours and keep our real GDP per capita the same. That is, productivity growth can be used to give the average person more goods, more leisure, or more of both. Even if we felt we had enough goods, more free time would still be desirable. Productivity growth is the only way to increase leisure without sacrificing goods and services.

# MODULE 39 REVIEW AND ASSESSMENT

## Summing Up the Key Ideas: Match the following terms to the correct definitions.

A. Standard of living
B. Economic growth
C. Rule of 70

D. Real GDP per capita
E. Productivity
F. Capital stock

G. Capital deepening
H. Economic infrastructure
I. Rule of law

J. Research and development
K. Depreciation
L. Intellectual property

_____ 1. The total amount of physical capital in the country.

_____ 2. Physical capital, such as communication systems and power systems, that provides a basic foundation that users share for many types of economic activity.

_____ 3. The level of material wealth as measured by the availability of goods and services.

_____ 4. An increase in a country's capital per worker.

_____ 5. The principle that no person is above the law.

_____ 6. A sustained increase in real GDP per person over time.

_____ 7. The amount of output the average worker can produce in an hour.

_____ 8. Activities to discover or improve products or procedures.

_____ 9. Output per person, calculated as real GDP divided by the total population.

_____ 10. A calculation that shows the number of years it takes for an economy's real GDP to double.

_____ 11. The amount of capital that is used up each year.

_____ 12. New ideas and discoveries.

Economic Growth 467

**Analyze and Explain:** Analyze each of the following, determine if each would **contribute to** economic growth or **detract from** economic growth, and explain your answer.

| | CONTRIBUTE TO OR DETRACT FROM? | EXPLANATION |
|---|---|---|
| 1. In an effort to reduce the unemployment rate, the government of a country passes a law making it illegal to use machinery in the production of certain goods. | _____ | _____ |
| 2. A country implements a project to increase the average number of years that its citizens attend school. | _____ | _____ |
| 3. An economy experiences "creative destruction" at an increasing rate. | _____ | _____ |
| 4. An economy suffers from corrupt public officials and an arbitrarily applied legal system. | _____ | _____ |
| 5. Investment exceeds depreciation in an economy. | _____ | _____ |

**Apply:** Apply the **Rule of 70** to each of the following to determine how long it would take real GDP per capita to double.

|  | TIME TO DOUBLE |
|---|---|
| 1. a growth rate of 1 percent | _____ |
| 2. a growth rate of 2 percent | _____ |
| 3. a growth rate of 7 percent | _____ |

# MODULE 40

# Business Cycles

**KEY IDEA:** Economies go through ups and downs as the result of changes in the overall, or *aggregate*, supply and demand for goods and services in the economy.

**OBJECTIVES**

- **To describe the business cycle.**
- **To explain the general causes of economic expansions and contractions.**
- **To identify the specific causes of the recession of 2007–2009.**

## The Great Recession

In December of 2007, the economies of countries around the world, including the United States, began to spiral downward. In just 12 months, U.S. real GDP fell by almost 4 percent. That may not sound like much of a drop, but even a one-percent decrease in real GDP causes more than 1 million Americans to lose their jobs. During this economic storm, the worst of which lasted until June of 2009, some countries fared even worse than the United States. Total production dropped by 5 percent in Europe and by more than 8 percent in Japan.

Workers who lost their jobs weren't the only victims of the economic downturn. Young people looking for their first full-time job after graduating from high school or college suddenly found almost no employers hiring. And many families lost large portions of their life savings when the value of their investments plummeted. In the United States, the value of household wealth declined by about $14 trillion. That number is roughly equal to the total income earned by all Americans in a year. Worldwide, the decline in wealth over the worst year and a half of this episode has been estimated at $40 trillion or more.

Why did this happen? And why have similar (although much milder) economic downturns occurred in the United States once or twice every decade? The answer starts with an exploration of business cycles.

*The Charging Bull statue on Wall Street in New York represents the prosperity of upward phases of the business cycle. Downward phases of the business cycle are symbolized by a bear.*

## WHAT ARE BUSINESS CYCLES?

**Business cycles** are alternating periods of rising and falling real GDP.

An **expansion** is a phase of the business cycle during which real GDP rises.

**Business cycles** are alternating periods of rising and falling real GDP. They refer to the ups and downs in total output observed over relatively short time periods—for example, several months or even a few years. Between 1945 and 2010, the United States experienced 12 distinct business cycles.

## Phases of the Business Cycle

Although no two business cycles are alike, they are all characterized by the same two phases: *expansions* and *contractions*, as illustrated in Figure 40.1. During the **expansion** phase of the business cycle, real GDP rises. Generally, rising real GDP is accompanied by a number of favorable conditions. For example, income levels are on the rise, and firms hire more employees, making it easier for people to find jobs.

Real GDP

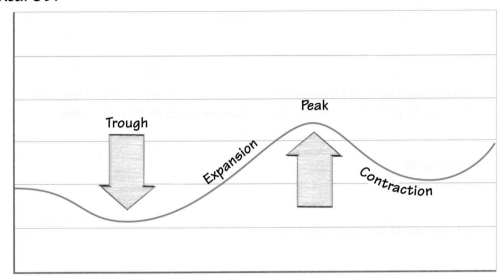

Time

**Figure 40.1** Phases of the Business Cycle

During the **contraction** phase, real GDP falls. Economic contractions make life more difficult. Many people have less money to spend, firms hire fewer workers, and more firms go out of business than during an expansion. When a contraction is severe enough to last several months or longer and have widespread effects on production, real income, employment, and sales across the economy, it becomes a **recession**. There is no consensus on the exact criteria for a recession, but in the United States the Business Cycle Dating Committee of the National Bureau of Economic Research (NBER) has the final say of whether a contraction has become a recession.

### Peaks and Troughs

Figure 40.1 shows the wave-like appearance of the business cycle. When an expansion is ending and the economy will proceed into a contraction, the business cycle is at a *peak*, as shown by the highest point in each cycle on the diagram. The lowest point in a cycle, where a contraction ends and an expansion begins, is called a *trough*. Putting this terminology together, we can say that an expansion starts at a trough and continues until the next peak, while a contraction starts at a peak and ends at the next trough.

Actual business cycles come in all sizes, and expansions usually last much longer than contractions. Since World War II, the average contraction has lasted about 11 months, while the average expansion has continued for 5 years. The very serious recession of 2007–2009, however, lasted an unusually long 18 months. Figure 40.2 shows the five business cycles in the U.S. economy since 1980. The shaded periods are contractions; the unshaded periods are expansions.

## WHAT CAUSES BUSINESS CYCLES?

Why does the level of economic activity fluctuate? That is the subject of debate. But economists agree that business cycles can be caused by two types of events: changes in *aggregate demand* or changes in *aggregate supply*.

### Aggregate Supply

*Aggregate supply* is an economy-wide version of supply, the level of which depends on an economy-wide version of a price. When the prices of goods and services

A **contraction** is a phase of the business cycle during which real GDP falls.

A **recession** is a contraction severe enough to last several months or longer and have widespread effects on production, real income, employment, and sales across the economy.

Real GDP
(trillions of 2005 dollars)

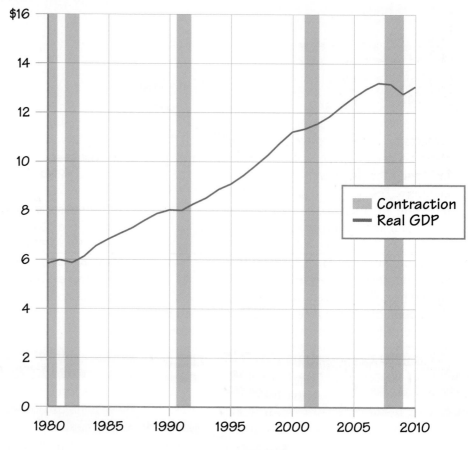

**Figure 40.2** Contraction and Expansions since 1980 There have been five business cycles in the United States since 1980. The shaded periods are contractions and the unshaded periods are expansions.

**Aggregate supply** is the total output a country's firms are willing and able to produce, contingent on the price level.

across the economy go up or down, we call this a change in the *price level*. **Aggregate supply** is the total output the country's firms are willing and able to produce, contingent on the price level. In the short run, when the price level rises and wages and other input prices don't have time to catch up, firms can increase their profits by selling more. So the level of aggregate supply generally increases with the price level in the short run. In the long run, an increase in the price level leads the sellers of inputs to demand a corresponding increase in wages and other input prices, which eliminates the incentive to produce more at the higher price level. Likewise, price level decreases typically cause the level of aggregate supply to decrease in the short run but have no effect on aggregate supply in the long run.

As with the supply for a particular good, an *increase in aggregate supply* means that firms are willing to supply more at any given price level, and a *decrease in aggregate supply* means that firms are willing to supply less at any given price level. Aggregate supply is based on the cost of production, which varies with the prices and availability of labor and other inputs, and of technology, human capital, and other determinants of productivity.

Changes in aggregate supply can cause expansions or contractions. Rather than resulting from decisions by the country's households or firms, many changes in aggregate supply arise from *external shocks*, which are uncontrollable events or decisions made in other countries. The results can be negative or positive. For example, when an earthquake and tsunami hit Japan in 2011, tens of thousands of people were killed, power plants were destroyed, and ports, roads, bridges, and factories shut down. On the other hand, the influx of capital that came with China's 2010

## ECONOMICS IN ACTION

# Recession or Depression—What's the Difference?

A recession is a serious economic decline, characterized by falling real GDP, significant job loss, and other unfavorable developments in the economy. The official beginning and end of a recession are identified by a committee within the National Bureau of Economic Research (NBER).

A **depression** is an extremely serious recession. Although the National Bureau of Economic Research decides when a contraction should be called a recession, it makes no official declaration of when a recession is serious enough to be considered a depression. Still, a depression is commonly understood to be an episode during which real GDP falls significantly (say, 10 percent

or more) and that is not over until real GDP returns to normal levels. By this definition the economy can still be in a depression or recession even if GDP has begun to rise.

Economists commonly refer to the entire decade of the 1930s as the *Great Depression*. From 1929 to 1933, real GDP fell by more than 25 percent. By 1933, one in four workers was jobless. After 1933, real GDP had some ups and downs, but the economy did not recover fully until 1940.

**DID YOU GET IT?**
How does a recession differ from a depression?

---

investments in Argentina, Brazil, Chile, and Venezuela provided a positive external shock in Latin America. In the United States, key changes in aggregate supply that have caused or contributed to expansions and contractions include weather changes, changes in the price of oil, and technological changes.

### Weather Changes

While relatively few Americans work in farming today, the influence of the agricultural sector is still strong. A single crop, such as corn, for example, is used as an input in thousands of final goods. These goods range from the obvious—canned corn, corn flakes, popcorn, and corn oil—to the less obvious—diapers, latex paint, animal feed, soft drink sweeteners, and biofuels. When the weather is particularly good for growing corn, production rises and the price of corn drops. This makes firms willing and able to produce more final goods

that use corn. Favorable weather can do the same for scores of crops used in millions of products, thereby increasing aggregate supply and fueling an expansion. Poor weather can have the opposite effect, decreasing aggregate supply. For example, floods and droughts can cause a contraction by destroying crops and thereby making it more difficult to produce goods that contain those crops.

A **depression** is an extremely severe recession.

*Coke is sweetened with corn syrup, which puts it among the many products affected when changes in the weather alter the cost of farming.*

Alamy

**Aggregate demand**
is the total amount of domestic output purchased by all sectors of a country's economy, contingent on the price level.

### Changes in the Price of Oil

Many of the inputs used by U.S. firms come largely from abroad. One of the most important is oil. While we produce a lot of oil in the United States, about 60 percent of our oil comes from other countries. Much of our electricity comes from oil, and we use oil-based fuels to transport virtually every raw material, intermediate product, and final good.

When the global price of oil declines, it costs U.S. firms less to manufacture goods and bring them to market. Hence, they are willing and able to produce more output at any given price level, and aggregate supply increases.

A variety of events can cause oil prices to rise. These include increased demand for oil by other countries, decisions by foreign governments to cut oil exports, and disruptions of supplies caused by war or other threats. Higher oil prices cause a decrease in the quantity of output firms will supply at any given price level, thus decreasing aggregate supply. The result can be a contraction.

**? DID YOU GET IT?**
Why do changes in the price of oil cause a change in aggregate supply?

### Technological Changes

Earlier in this chapter you learned that steady technological change is one force behind long-run economic growth. When the change is especially rapid, it can lead to a rapid increase in aggregate supply and set off the expansion phase of the business cycle. Remember that technological change increases productivity or output per worker per hour. When labor is more productive, firms find it less costly and more profitable to increase production. Rapid productivity gains from the Internet, for example, contributed to the eight-year expansion during the 1990s.

### Aggregate Demand

Just because firms are willing and able to produce a certain amount of output doesn't mean they will actually produce it. After all, a firm will produce only what

it thinks it can sell. Therefore, the total output firms *actually* produce depends not just on aggregate supply but also on *aggregate demand*—the total output that people want to buy.

More specifically, **aggregate demand** is the total amount of domestic output purchased by all sectors of the country's economy, contingent on the price level. Higher price levels lead to lower levels of aggregate demand and vice versa. When you buy a hamburger, you are contributing to aggregate demand. Likewise, when Delta Airlines purchases a passenger jet from Boeing, or when government agencies build new roads or hire more economists, they, too, are contributing to aggregate demand.

Let's explore how changes in aggregate demand contribute to business cycles. Suppose aggregate demand increases—that is, some combination of households, firms, and the government begins to spend more than usual on final goods and services at any given price level. Just as an increase in the demand for hot dogs causes the price of hot dogs to increase, an increase in aggregate demand causes the price level to rise. The higher price level motivates firms to make and sell more, thus increasing real GDP, and an expansion is born.

But that's not the end of the story. For firms to produce more output, they hire additional workers, who therefore have more income to spend. The spending of these additional workers causes aggregate demand—and real GDP—to rise further. This leads to still more hiring and spending, and so on. This virtuous cycle of higher spending and production increases real GDP and extends the expansion phase of the business cycle.

On the flip side, when households, firms, or the government *decrease* their spending at any given price level, aggregate demand falls, as does the price level, and firms respond by producing less output. It takes fewer workers to produce the diminished real GDP, so firms reduce hiring and lay off some of their current employees. The newly unemployed workers have less income, so their spending drops, too, which leads to further decreases in aggregate demand. The opposite of the virtuous cycle of expansion is thus a vicious cycle of contraction.

What causes aggregate demand to change in the first place? Three of the leading causes are changes in household wealth, changes in confidence, and government policy.

### Changes in Household Wealth

A person's **wealth** (sometimes called *net worth*) is the value of everything the person owns minus what the person owes to others. You may own real estate, artwork, cars, financial assets like shares of stock or bank accounts, and assorted other items of value. You may owe money for debts that include bank loans, student loans, and mortgage loans used to purchase a home. People naturally spend more when they have more wealth. Suppose, for example, you own an old car that you could sell for $5,000 and you have a bank account with $1,000 in it. You also *owe* your parents $2,000 that they lent you to buy the car. Your wealth would be $5,000 + $1,000 − $2,000 = $4,000. Now suppose your old car becomes a hot collector's item and the *Vintage Car Guide* estimates its value at $70,000. Your wealth increases dramatically to $70,000 + $1,000 − $2,000 = $69,000. Even if the income you're receiving wearing a chicken suit to advertise fried chicken stays the same, you will probably spend more than before, starting with a party to celebrate your incredible luck. The same thing happens across the country when there are widespread increases in wealth. For example, when housing or stock prices rise, the many people who own them are wealthier, so they increase their spending and boost aggregate demand. But when housing or stock prices fall, their owners are less wealthy. They cut back on their spending, and aggregate demand falls.

### Changes in Confidence

People spend less when they are less confident about the future. Have you ever asked your parents to buy something for you and received the answer "This is not a good time to spend money" or "Not in *this* economy"? They might have been worried about the future and the possibility of a pay cut or job loss. People with these concerns usually prefer to save more than usual, just in case. But saving more means spending less. The same is true of firms: if they become less confident about future sales, they will be reluctant to invest in new capital, hire new workers, or expand their inventories of goods. The consequence is a decline in spending by firms. If enough people or firms lose confidence in the economy at the same time, aggregate demand can drop significantly. Likewise, confidence that the economy is doing well leads people to buy more consumer goods and firms to invest more in preparation for growing sales, all of which increases aggregate demand. Note that in these ways, thoughts about the economy guide reality: fear about a weak economy weakens the economy, and confidence about a strong economy strengthens the economy.

### Government Policy

In later chapters you will learn about two types of policies that can change aggregate demand: fiscal policy carried out by the government and monetary policy carried out by the *central bank*. (You will learn about the central bank in Chapter 17.) When successful, these policies can *smooth out* the business cycle and prevent wide swings in real GDP. Sometimes, however, these policies miss their mark due to delays in implementation. For example, if a policy is meant to slow down an expansion but it doesn't have its effect until after the economy has slowed down on its own, it can cause a contraction instead. And if a policy that is meant to boost the economy takes effect after the economy is already flying high, it can send the expansion out of control and cause prices to rise rapidly.

A person's **wealth** is made up of everything the person owns minus what the person owes to others.

*When the value of what you own changes, so do your wealth and your attitude toward spending.*

# THE RECESSION OF 2007–2009

Earlier in this module we briefly discussed the serious recession of 2007–2009. By some measures, it was the worst recession since the Great Depression. What caused it? Much of what you've just learned about business cycles was part of the story. Some economists believe that an external shock—a decrease in aggregate supply—helped to make the economy vulnerable. In late 2007 and early 2008, oil became increasingly scarce because China, India, and other rapidly growing countries were demanding much more oil than before. Oil prices rose dramatically, from less than $70 per barrel in 2007 to more than $140 per barrel by mid-2008. Firms in the United States responded by producing fewer goods that involve oil in some stage of production or transportation, thus decreasing aggregate supply.

The decrease in aggregate supply by itself might have caused a recession, although certainly not the deep one we experienced. But powerful changes in aggregate demand started around the same time. To understand why aggregate demand fell so much and so fast, we have to go back to the years preceding the recession and look at the housing bubble.

## The Housing Bubble

In the context of economics, a **bubble** is a rapid and unsustainable increase in the price of homes, gold, corporate stocks, or some other *asset*. An **asset** is anything of value that is owned or controlled with the expectation that it will provide benefits in the future. Bubbles arise from a circular logic as illustrated in Figure 40.3. Everyone wants to buy the asset because they think its price will continue to rise. All this buying causes the price to rise—just as was predicted! As prices rise, new potential buyers want to get in on the action, making the price rise further. This continues until the bubble bursts, meaning that the prices that were rising skyward suddenly start falling back to earth.

From the late 1990s to 2006, the United States (and many other countries) experienced a housing bubble. What caused all the demand for homes that set off the bubble in the first place? That's the subject of heated debate, but likely contributors include

- inadequate government regulation of financial institutions that were providing risky home loans,

- low interest rates that made home loans temporarily cheap, and

- speculation by investors that housing prices would only go up.

Figure 40.4 on page 476 shows the bubble's effect on real housing prices in the United States from 1975 to 2010. The right end of the figure shows the rise in housing prices that began in 1997. Over the next nine years, the *median* price of a home (the price of the home in the middle if you arranged them from least to most expensive) in 2011 dollars rose sharply, from $143,629 to $266,889. Although new homes were built each year, the demand for new homes rose faster than the construction industry could supply them. So prices continued to rise.

Homes are an important part of the typical family's wealth. As home prices rose, homeowners felt richer. They saved less and spent more, causing an increase in aggregate demand. As spending rose, firms increased production and hired more workers, providing them with more income. This caused still more rounds of spending. In these ways, the housing bubble helped fuel the economy's expansion from 2001 to 2007.

## The Housing Bust

Just like a soap bubble, an asset bubble can grow only so large before it will burst. If nothing else stops it, the price of the asset eventually rises so high that few new buyers find it appealing or affordable. Without enough buyers, the price stops rising. People begin to find the asset less attractive, and some begin to sell it. Then the price begins to fall, so

A **bubble** is a rapid and unsustainable increase in the price of certain assets, such as homes, gold, or stocks.

An **asset** can be anything of value that is owned or controlled with the expectation that it will provide benefits in the future.

*more* people want to sell, and the downward tumble of prices continues.

The burst of the housing bubble was hastened by another thorny situation. In 2007, after five years of rising interest rates caused the size of mortgage (home loan) payments to rise, an unusually large number of homeowners were not making their payments. This made banks and other financial institutions reluctant to provide new loans for home purchases. Once it became harder to get a loan, the home-buying frenzy that created the bubble began to fizzle. Housing prices stopped rising, and as in the standard story of an economic bubble bursting, more and more people wanted to sell their homes and few

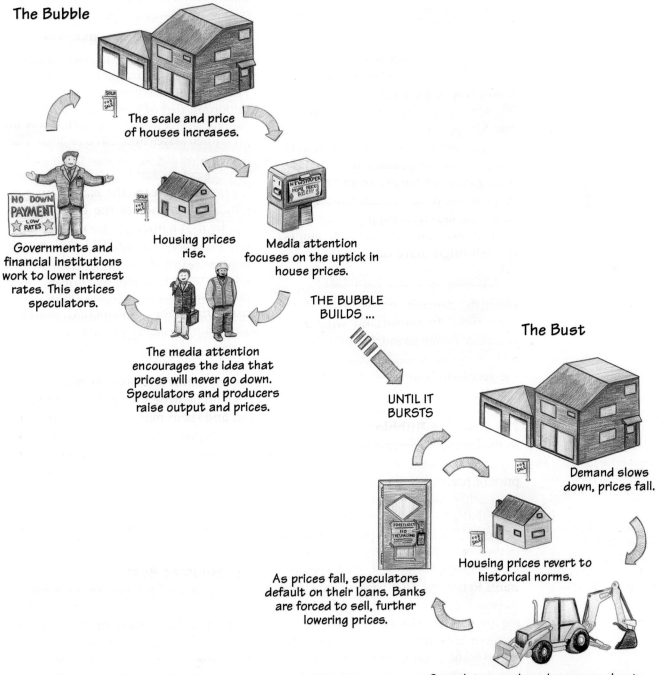

**The Bubble**

The scale and price of houses increases.

Housing prices rise.

Media attention focuses on the uptick in house prices.

Governments and financial institutions work to lower interest rates. This entices speculators.

The media attention encourages the idea that prices will never go down. Speculators and producers raise output and prices.

THE BUBBLE BUILDS ...

UNTIL IT BURSTS

**The Bust**

Demand slows down, prices fall.

Housing prices revert to historical norms.

As prices fall, speculators default on their loans. Banks are forced to sell, further lowering prices.

Speculators and producers are slow to respond to demand changes, believing conditions will improve. Production exceeds demand, pushing prices down.

**Figure 40.3** The Origin of a Bubble

wanted to buy one. Figure 40.4 shows the dramatic drop in home prices that began in 2007. In some cities in California, Nevada, and Florida, home prices ended up lower than before the bubble began.

As house prices fell, millions of homeowners around the country suddenly had less wealth. As you've learned, decreases in wealth lead to decreases in spending. Aggregate demand declined significantly. This was a major cause of the recession that began in late 2007 and continued for the next 18 months. But it was not the only cause.

**DID YOU GET IT?**

What causes an asset bubble to burst?

## Other Factors behind the Recession of 2007–2009

Once the housing bubble burst and the recession began, several related events made the recession worse by causing further decreases in aggregate demand:

- **A financial crisis**. While the housing bubble existed, many banks and other financial institutions had invested heavily in housing or lent money to others to buy homes. When housing prices fell, these institutions lost trillions of dollars. Some went bankrupt, and those that survived had difficulty performing the normal financial functions needed to keep an economy running. For example, before the crisis began, many households and firms had plans to borrow money. After the crisis, they were unable to borrow and had to cancel their plans for spending the money. You'll learn more about the financial system—and how the financial crisis evolved—in Chapter 16.

- **Plunging stock prices**. Chapter 16 also details how shares of *stock* represent partial ownership in a corporation. These shares, like homes, are an important part of wealth for many people. As the recession took hold, stock prices fell as well. This often happens during a recession, because falling production brings down profits and makes it less valuable to own part of a corporation. But in the recent recession, stock prices fell even more than usual. From late 2007 to early 2009, stock market wealth fell by more than 40 percent. This downfall was driven by the growing realization that the recession itself would be unusually deep and long and the fact that financial companies needed to sell stocks to stay afloat.

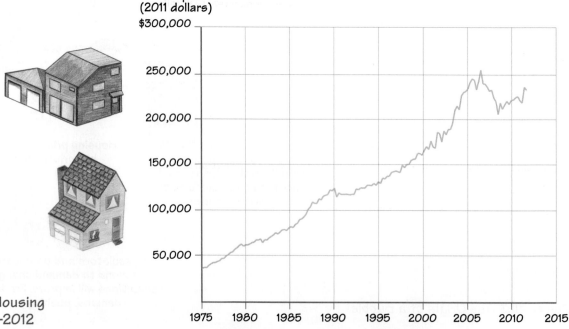

**Figure 40.4** Housing Prices, 1975–2012

- **Loss of confidence**. The recession of 2007–2009 destroyed household and business confidence more than any since the Great Depression. Every month, hundreds of thousands of jobs were lost. News media delivered nonstop bad news—bank failures, business closures, massive layoffs, and further drops in home prices. TV commentators—and even some government officials—warned of the possibility of another Great Depression. Those who had jobs, worried that they might be laid off, cut back further on their spending. And business firms, uncertain about the economy's future, canceled planned spending on new capital equipment.

There are many more questions about the recession of 2007–2009 still to be explored: What did the government do to fight the recession? Why did the recession last so long? What did we learn from the experience? You'll discover some answers to these and other questions over the next several chapters.

# MODULE 40 REVIEW AND ASSESSMENT

## Summing Up the Key Ideas: Match the following terms to the correct definitions.

| | | | |
|---|---|---|---|
| A. Business cycle | E. Depression | I. Aggregate supply | M. Bubble |
| B. Expansion | F. Peak | J. External shocks | N. Asset |
| C. Contraction | G. Trough | K. Aggregate demand | |
| D. Recession | H. Change in price level | L. Wealth | |

_____  1. The total output a country's firms are willing and able to produce, contingent on the price level.

_____  2. Made up of everything a person owns minus what that person owes to others.

_____  3. Anything of value that is owned or controlled with the expectation that it will provide benefits in the future.

_____  4. Alternating periods of rising and falling real GDP.

_____  5. A rapid and unsustainable increase in the price of certain assets, such as homes, gold, or stocks.

_____  6. A phase of the business cycle during which real GDP falls.

_____  7. An extremely severe recession.

_____  8. The total amount of domestic output purchased by all sectors of a country's economy, contingent on the price level.

_____  9. A contraction severe enough to last several months or longer and have widespread effects on production, real income, employment, and sales across the economy.

_____ 10. A phase of the business cycle during which real GDP rises.

_____ 11. When the prices of goods and services across the economy go up or down.

_____ 12. Where an expansion ends and a contraction begins.

_____ 13. Uncontrollable events, or decisions made in other countries.

_____ 14. The lowest point of a business cycle.

**Analyze:** Analyze each of the following and then determine if each would increase or decrease **aggregate supply** or **aggregate demand**.

| | AGGREGATE SUPPLY OR AGGREGATE DEMAND? | INCREASE OR DECREASE? |
|---|---|---|
| 1. Manufacturing technology improves. | _____ | _____ |
| 2. The government lowers income tax rates on consumers. | _____ | _____ |
| 3. The agricultural sector of an economy experiences a period of favorable weather over an entire year. | _____ | _____ |
| 4. Consumers become increasingly confident about the future direction of the economy. | _____ | _____ |
| 5. Corporate and other business taxes increase. | _____ | _____ |
| 6. The stock market surges and people find themselves feeling wealthier. | _____ | _____ |
| 7. The price of oil increases significantly. | _____ | _____ |

**Apply:** Explain how each of the following contributed to the recession of 2007–2009.

1. stock prices falling

2. firms uncertain about the economy's future

3. continuous news coverage on the worsening state of the economy

4. lack of demand for goods and services from those who held jobs

5. a surge in home buying and house prices rising

6. a government policy that allowed banks to make home loans to more risky borrowers

## The Economist

# Downturn, Start Up

### The Effects of Recessions on Entrepreneurs and Managers Run Deep

JANUARY 7, 2012

The list of famous companies founded during economic downturns is long and varied. It includes General Motors, AT&T, Disney, and MTV, all founded during recessions. A 2009 study found that over half of Fortune 500 companies got their start during a downturn or a bear market. A recession, it seems, may not be an entirely bad time to start a company.

Some argue that recessions speed up the process of productive economic churn—what Joseph Schumpeter called "creative destruction." The destruction part is easy to see: downturns kill businesses, leaving boarded-up windows on the high street as their gravestones. But recessions may also spur the creation of new businesses. When people suddenly have less money to spend, clever entrepreneurs may see an opportunity to set up businesses that give them what they want more

cheaply or efficiently. Downturns may also swell the ranks of potential firm creators, because many who might otherwise have sought a stable salary will reinvent themselves as entrepreneurs. A recent study by Robert Fairlie of the University of California, Santa Cruz found that the proportion of Americans who start a new business each month is on average about half as high again in metropolitan areas where unemployment is in double digits as in those where it is under 2%.

A recession is a difficult time to start a company, of course. Credit is scarce. Would-be entrepreneurs are further handicapped by falling asset prices, since they might want to use their homes as collateral for a start-up loan. Whether downturns on balance help or hurt entrepreneurs depends therefore on the relative strength of these opposing sets of forces.

A shrinking economy makes it hard for young firms to take root and grow. Young companies, typically responsible for the bulk of U.S. job creation, added only 2.3 million jobs in 2009, down from about 3 million a year earlier. Research suggests that recessions have lasting effects on how executives manage businesses. John Graham of Duke University and Krishnamoorthy Narasimhan of PIMCO, a bond manager, have found that chief executives who lived through the Depression tended to run companies with lower debt levels. Bosses whose careers began in a recession also tend to be so concerned about cost-effectiveness that the companies they go on to run spend less on research and development. They may thus be too conservative: firms with bosses whose professional baptism came in a weak economy have lower returns on assets than those run by other managers.

Downturns also funnel people into different jobs from those they might otherwise have entered. A 2008 study by Paul Oyer of Stanford University found that Stanford MBAs disproportionately shunned Wall Street during a bear market. This may seem unsurprising—who wants a job in finance when the market is tanking? But there are reasons to believe that these choices make a difference well into the future. Those who begin their careers in a bust are less footloose than their boom-time equivalents.

The pool of candidates for top jobs in a particular industry reflects the choices that people make early on in their working lives. Yet these choices are the result not only of managers' preferences and abilities, as you might expect, but also of the economic circumstances that prevailed at the time they began working. Whether they were set up during a boom or a bust, today's firms are deeply affected by the economic fluctuations of the past.

**DID YOU READ IT?**

1) Why are recessions sometimes a bad time to start a business? Why are recessions sometimes a good time to start a business?

2) How might a manager's decisions be affected by his or her business experience during a downturn?

**WHAT DO YOU THINK?**

1) How does a recession influence the labor market? How does it affect the decisions of both job seekers and those who are employed?

2) What industries might do well during a recession? What industries might be particularly hard hit during recessions?

EXCERPTED FROM www.economist.com/node/21542390

# CHAPTER 13 REVIEW AND SELF-ASSESSMENT

## REVIEW

### Points to Remember

**MODULE 38: MEASURING NATIONAL OUTPUT AND INCOME**

1. A nation's **gross domestic product** (GDP) is the total dollar value of all final goods and services produced within the country's borders in a given year.

2. A **final good or service** is one that is sold to its final user, rather than to a firm that will use it to make something else.

3. An **intermediate product** is a product that is itself used to make a final good or service.

4. The **expenditure approach** to calculating GDP is to add up the spending on everything included in GDP.

5. **Consumption** is the largest component of GDP and includes all the household purchases of consumers.

6. **Government purchases** are the goods and services bought by any level of government.

5. **Investment** is business spending on physical capital, new homes, and inventories.

6. **Exports** are goods, services, and intermediate products bought by people in other countries.

7. **Imports** are goods, services, and intermediate products produced in other countries.

8. The **income approach** to calculating GDP is to add up all the income earned during the year by people who are involved in the production of goods and services.

9. The **underground economy** represents business activity conducted without the knowledge of the government.

10. **Nominal GDP** values each good at the dollar price it actually sold for in the year in which it was produced.

11. **Real GDP** measures total production in dollars after removing the distorting effect of price changes.

**MODULE 39: ECONOMIC GROWTH**

12. The **standard of living** is the level of material wealth as measured by the availability of goods and services.

13. **Economic growth** is a sustained increase in real GDP over time.

14. **Real GDP per capita** is output per person, calculated as real GDP divided by the total population.

15. **Productivity** is the amount of output the average worker can produce in an hour.

16. A country's **capital stock** is the total amount of physical capital in the country.

17. **Capital deepening** is an increase in a country's capital per worker.

18. **The Rule of 70** is a calculation that shows the number of years it takes for an economy's real GDP to double.

19. **Economic infrastructure** is physical capital, such as communication systems and power systems, that provides a foundation for economic activity.

20. Firms conduct **research and development** activities to discover or improve products or procedures.

21. The **rule of law** is the principle that no person is above the law.

**MODULE 40: BUSINESS CYCLES**

22. **Business cycles** are alternating periods of rising and falling real GDP.

23. An **expansion** is a phase of the business cycle during which real GDP rises.

24. A **contraction** is a phase of the business cycle during which real GDP falls.

25. A **recession** is a contraction severe enough to last several months or longer and have widespread effects on production, real income, employment, and sales across the economy.

26. A **depression** is an extremely serious recession.

27. **Aggregate supply** is the total output a country's firms are willing and able to produce, contingent on the price level.

28. **Aggregate demand** is the total amount of domestic output purchased by all sectors of a country's economy, contingent on the price level.

29. A person's **wealth** is made up of everything the person owns minus what the person owes to others.

30. A **bubble** is a rapid and unsustainable increase in the price of certain assets such as homes, gold, or stocks.

31. An **asset** can be anything of value that is owned or controlled with the expectation that it will provide benefits in the future.

## SELF-ASSESSMENT

The following questions are the type your teacher might ask you on a quiz or a test. Practice with these in order to improve your performance on class tests.

### Multiple-Choice Questions

1. Which of the following most likely contributed to the growth of the housing bubble that burst in 2007?

    a. high interest rates
    b. speculation by investors that housing prices would rise
    c. regulations that prevented banks from making risky loans
    d. low demand for homes

2. As used in the context of GDP calculation, *investment* would include

    a. consumer spending on stocks, bonds, and savings accounts.
    b. government spending on infrastructure.
    c. business spending on financial capital, stocks, and bonds.
    d. business spending on physical capital, new homes, and inventories.

Answer the next two questions based on the following nominal figures for an economy:

| | |
|---|---|
| Consumer spending on new goods | $900 |
| Consumer spending on used goods | 700 |
| Government spending | 500 |
| Investment spending | 100 |
| Exports | 50 |
| Imports | 40 |

3. Nominal GDP for this economy is

   a. $2,290.
   b. $1,510.
   c. $1,500.
   d. $1,410.

4. If all the numbers in the table remain the same for two years in a row, even though the economy experiences an increase in the price level,

   a. real GDP will increase from the first year to the second year.
   b. nominal GDP will increase from the first year to the second year.
   c. real GDP will decrease from the first year to the second year.
   d. nominal GDP will decrease from the first year to the second year.

5. Which of the following is considered a contributing factor to economic growth?

   a. a high savings rate
   b. rapid technological change
   c. adherence to the idea of rule of law and sound governance
   d. All of the above would contribute to economic growth.

6. The phase of the business cycle where output and employment are increasing is

   a. a contraction.
   b. an expansion.
   c. a recession.
   d. a depression.

7. Which of the following is not one of the pillars of economic growth?

   a. human capital
   b. technological change
   c. sound government
   d. the business cycle

8. Aggregate demand would increase as a result of

   a. an increase in aggregate supply.
   b. a decrease in household wealth.
   c. an increase in consumer confidence.
   d. a widespread fear of an impending recession.

9. If an economy has been expanding for a long period of time and begins to contract, we can conclude that the economy has passed through a

   a. peak.
   b. trough.
   c. recession.
   d. depression.

10. Which of the following would have a positive effect on U.S. GDP?

   a. production from a foreign-owned factory located in Kentucky
   b. production from an American-owned factory located in Canada
   c. a foreign-made good purchased by an American citizen
   d. an increase in sales at garage sales and flea markets

**Constructed Response Question**

1. Answer the following questions about gross domestic product (GDP).

   a. Explain the difference between *nominal GDP* and *real GDP*.

   b. Explain each of the following in the context of real GDP:

      i. a peak

      ii. a trough

      iii. a contraction

      iv. an expansion

   c. Explain why final goods and services are included in GDP and intermediate goods are not.

   d. In the formula for the expenditure approach to calculating GDP, what do *C*, *I*, *G*, *X*, and *M* stand for?

**CHAPTER 14** & **YOU** Unemployment and inflation are two of the biggest threats to our economy. This chapter offers you a framework for understanding why. You will learn about the unemployment rate that influences your prospects for getting a job, the types of unemployment, and the trouble unemployment brings. You will discover the causes and costs of inflation and the dangers of deflation. And you will learn how unemployment and inflation might affect you, your family, and the overall economy.

# Unemployment and Inflation

**MODULE 41: Unemployment**

**MODULE 42: Inflation**

**MODULE 43: Unemployment, Inflation, and the Business Cycle**

## DO NOT PASS GO

The failure of the highly respected global investment bank Lehman Brothers on September 15, 2008, stunned not only the financial world but most of its employees as well. Two young employees were especially surprised: Edouard D'Archimbaud, age 24, from Paris, France, and Adonis Watkins, age 20, from Queens, New York City.

Eduoard's first day on the job was also his last. Edouard arrived at Lehman's offices in the Canary Wharf section of London on Monday morning for his first day of work but did not even make it to his desk. The company had just declared bankruptcy, and upon reaching the office, he discovered that he and all his coworkers no longer had jobs. Unable to pay his London rent, Edouard headed back to Paris.

Adonis Watkins did not even make it to his first day on the job. Having worked as an intern for three summers at Lehman Brothers in New York, he had accepted a full-time job with the company, to start after his graduation in May 2009. His position disappeared along with Lehman Brothers.

Because Edouard and Adonis were young and had no families to support, they managed to adjust to unexpected unemployment. Both had to curtail spending but eventually found good jobs. For older employees with families to support, however, job loss can be catastrophic. To make

MARIO TAMA/GETTY IMAGES

*Firm death can leave even the best and most-experienced workers without a job.*

matters worse, when many people become unemployed at the same time, the negative consequences of job loss to individuals and families are multiplied many times over. In 2008 and 2009, the problem of unemployment became worse around the country. By September 2009, 15 million people were unemployed—twice as many as were jobless just two years earlier. When many people are out of work, spending on goods and services declines, causing a downward spiral: decreased spending leads to lower national output, which leads to further unemployment. Unemployment and inflation are painful but often solvable problems. Unfortunately, as we'll explain in this chapter, solutions to either of these problems tend to lead to more of the other problem, at least in the short run. In Module 41 you will learn about unemployment. In Module 42 you will learn about inflation. In Module 43 you will explore the link between unemployment and inflation.

## BOTTOM LINE
Unemployment and inflation are two of the biggest concerns of economists today.

*It's a recession when your neighbor loses his job;*
*it's a depression when you lose yours.*
—Harry S. Truman, president of the United States, 1945–1953

# MODULE 41

# Unemployment

**KEY IDEA:** High unemployment is costly to the economy.

**OBJECTIVES**

- To explain how unemployment is measured.
- To explore the types of unemployment and what causes each type.
- To identify the economic costs of unemployment.

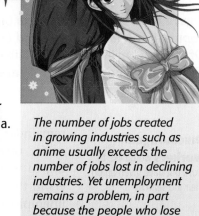

The number of jobs created in growing industries such as anime usually exceeds the number of jobs lost in declining industries. Yet unemployment remains a problem, in part because the people who lose their jobs don't always have the skills needed to perform the new jobs.

## Jobs Lost and Found

Back in 2006, Whirlpool's plant in Fort Smith, Arkansas, employed 4,500 workers who made refrigerators, ice makers, and trash compactors. Over the six years that followed, the plant slowed production and laid off most of its workers. The plant closed in 2012, leaving its last 917 employees out of work. Stories of job loss are common. Fortunately, so are stories of job creation. For example, Crunchyroll started up in 2006 as an online provider of Japanese-style anime cartoons headquartered in San Francisco, California. By 2012, Crunchyroll had a large staff and its website listed openings for workers in nine different work areas. Overall, the number of jobs created by growing industries like anime usually exceeds the number of jobs lost in declining industries like home appliance manufacturing. So why does the problem of unemployment persist? One reason is that the people who lose their jobs often don't have the skills required for the new jobs—laid-off refrigerator makers may not know much about producing anime. Even people with the right skills spend time unemployed as they search for the right job in the right place. And in the worst of times for the economy, the number of jobs created falls short of the number lost. In this module we'll look more closely at the types, causes, and costs of unemployment.

## EMPLOYMENT AND UNEMPLOYMENT

Deciding whether someone is *employed* is easy. If the person works for pay, he or she is employed. It doesn't matter whether the work is full time or part time. **Total employment** in an economy is the total number of employed workers. The definition of *unemployment* is not so obvious. Many people without jobs are not considered unemployed. If you have grandparents who are retired, or younger siblings who are too young to work, they are not among the unemployed. That label is reserved for people who are 16 or older and actively looking for work but not actually working. **Total unemployment** in an economy is the number of these job seekers.

If we add together the total number of employed and unemployed workers, we get the **labor force**. Figure 41.1 provides a breakdown of the U.S. civilian (nonmilitary), noninstitutional (not in a prison, mental hospital, or nursing home) population aged 16 and over for December 2011. At that time, 64 percent of that population of 240 million people participated in the labor force, the

**Total employment** in an economy is the total number of employed workers, whether they work part time or full time.

**Total unemployment** in an economy is the number of workers who are actively seeking jobs but not actually working.

The **labor force** is the combination of the employed workers and the unemployed workers, excluding those in the military or in prison.

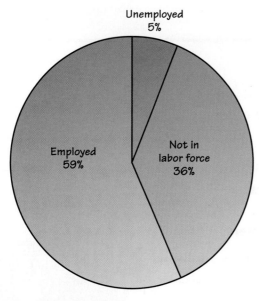

Unemployed
5%

Employed
59%

Not in
labor force
36%

**Figure 41.1** Breakdown of the Civilian, Noninstitutional Population Aged 16 Years and Older
*Of the 240 million people eligible to work in December 2011, 64 percent chose to participate in the labor force.*

**Discouraged workers** would like to work but have given up on their job search.

**Underemployed** workers would like to work more hours or prefer a job that better matches their skills.

The **unemployment rate** is the percentage of the labor force without a paid job.

remainder being retired, discouraged, or for other reasons unable or unwilling to work. Of the 154 million workers in the labor force, 13.1 million were unemployed, which is 8.5 percent of that whole population.

How does the government know whether people are unemployed? They ask them! Since 1940, the federal government has conducted monthly surveys to estimate how many Americans are employed and unemployed. Government workers will contact thousands of households across the country and ask about changes in employment. They then use this data to summarize the current employment situation in the United States.

## The Unemployment Rate

The *unemployment rate* is the most basic gauge of America's employment situation. The **unemployment rate** is the percentage of the labor force without a paid job. Economics in Action, "Calculating the Unemployment Rate" shows the simple process of calculating the unemployment rate.

## Issues in Measuring Unemployment

The official unemployment rate published by the Bureau of Labor Statistics can be used to measure changes in the economy's performance over time, but it is not the only measure of underutilized labor. The unemployment rate leaves out workers who desire a job but have given up searching for one. To be counted as unemployed, a worker must have searched for a job in the previous four weeks. People who give up and stop looking for work are called **discouraged workers**. The unemployment rate also does not include **underemployed** workers, who would like to work more hours or prefer a job that better matches their skills.

Another complication is that some workers hide their employment from government surveyors in an effort to avoid paying taxes. Those members of the underground economy who claim to be looking for work are counted among the unemployed; those who

*To measure the unemployment rate in the United States, the U.S. Department of Labor's Bureau of Labor Statistics surveys 60,000 households every month.*

## ECONOMICS IN ACTION

# By the Numbers: Calculating the Unemployment Rate

The U.S. Department of Labor calculates the monthly unemployment rate as follows:

*Step 1*: Divide the number of unemployed workers by the number of workers in the labor force.

*Step 2*: To obtain the rate as a percentage, multiply by 100.

For example, we would calculate the unemployment rate for 2011 as follows:

$$\frac{13.1 \text{ million (number of unemployed)}}{154 \text{ million (size of labor force)}} \times 100 = \text{unemployment rate for 2011}$$

$$.085 \times 100 = 8.5 \text{ percent}$$

Hence in 2011, the unemployment rate in the U.S. economy was 8.5 percent.

**DID YOU GET IT?**
In May 2008, the total number of unemployed workers was 8.5 million, and the labor force was made up of 154.4 million workers. Calculate the unemployment rate for May 2008.

don't claim to be looking are counted as not being in the labor force. Both types of hidden employment cause the official unemployment rate to be overstated.

**DID YOU GET IT?**
Why is the unemployment rate sometimes not an accurate measure of unemployment in the economy?

## TYPES OF UNEMPLOYMENT AND THEIR CAUSES

Some types of unemployment cause extreme hardship for workers and their families and have negative repercussions on the economy. Other types of unemployment are a normal part of a healthy economy. When we lump all the unemployed together, we can lose sight of these important distinctions. So let's

*When someone with an advanced degree works as a clerk at McDonald's, the worker is underemployed because another job would better match his or her skills.*

**Seasonal unemployment** occurs when workers lose their jobs due to a change of seasons.

**Frictional unemployment** is short-term unemployment that occurs while workers search for the jobs best suited for their skills and interests.

consider how economists classify unemployment into different types depending on its cause.

## Frictional Unemployment

**Frictional unemployment** is short-term unemployment that occurs while workers search for the jobs best suited for their skills and interests. The frictionally unemployed include people who have left one job to search for another, perhaps to earn a higher wage or to find a better place to live. Also included are new labor-force entrants, such as students graduating high school or college, and *reentrants*, such as a parent who left the labor force to raise a child and now wants to work again. These workers may not want to take the first job that comes along, and so they remain unemployed while searching.

Frictional unemployment is a necessary, even healthy type of short-term unemployment. It is a sign that people are spending some time looking for the right job and that employers are spending some time looking for the right workers. The result is a better match between the skills of a particular worker and the skills needed for a particular job.

**DID YOU GET IT?**

Why is frictional employment necessary for a well-functioning economy?

## Seasonal Unemployment

**Seasonal unemployment** occurs when workers lose their jobs due to seasonal changes. During the winter season, for example, job loss is common in the construction industry, landscaping, crop agriculture, and beach resorts. Once the winter is over, many workers are rehired to fill these jobs again. Because seasonal unemployment is predictable and lasts for only a few months, it is usually not considered a serious problem. In some industries such as construction, workers are paid extra while on the job to compensate for the predictable unemployment they will suffer in the off-season.

## Seasonal Adjustment

Because the unemployment rate changes predictably in different months due to special seasonal factors, government economists "seasonally adjust" the official unemployment rate before they report it. That is, they remove the typical and predictable changes in unemployment from each month's unemployment numbers. This helps avoid mistakes in the interpretation of labor market conditions. For example, every June, many high school students begin looking for summer jobs. While they are looking, they are frictionally unemployed. If the government just reported actual unemployment in June, it would look like joblessness worsens among typical workers every June. By removing the *normal* rise in unemployment from its June report, the government tries to provide a number that more accurately reflects changing conditions for U.S. workers.

*Some people are frictionally unemployed because they left one job to find another job in a place where they would be happier.*

THINKSTOCK

## ECONOMICS IN ACTION

# The Grapes of Wrath: Migrant Farmworkers and Seasonal Unemployment

Migrant workers are an important part of the U.S. agricultural economy and a classic example of seasonal workers. Migrant workers move from place to place harvesting crops such as grapes, sweet potatoes, and tobacco. Although most migrant workers are married, a majority of men who are migrants do not live with their families. Because crops are seasonal, migrant workers accept unemployment during the off-season as a way of life. The average migrant is unemployed for a full 14 weeks each year.

The Department of Labor conducts periodic surveys on the status of migrant workers. A 2002 survey revealed some surprising statistics. Migrant workers make up about 42 percent of all farmworkers. Most migrant workers are foreign born with Spanish as their native language. A majority of migrants are not able to read English. Fully 38 percent of them were newcomers to the United States who had been in the country less than a year when they were interviewed. And almost none of these newcomers were authorized to work legally in this country.

Migrant workers perform the crucial task of harvesting crops within the brief window of time between when they are not yet ripe and when they are rotten. Many farmers actually report a shortage of workers to tend and harvest their crops. But why are so many migrant workers immigrants? Because being a migrant worker is a tough job that few native-born Americans want to perform.

Even when migrants are working, their pay is low. In the 2002 survey, migrants reported receiving on average $7.25 per hour, and only 23 percent reported having any form of health insurance. Despite hard work, the typical migrant worker makes only about $13,500 per year. A full 30 percent of migrant workers earn incomes below

the official U.S. poverty line. Not so much has changed since John Steinbeck wrote his classic novel, *The Grapes of Wrath* (1939), about migrant workers during the Great Depression—migrant workers remain one of the poorest groups in the American economy. Yet as unattractive as these jobs are, they offer better pay and employment prospects than most of these workers could find in their countries of origin, most often Mexico or other Latin American countries.

**DID YOU GET IT?**
Why are few native-born Americans interested in jobs as migrant workers?

*Migrant workers harvesting crops in California.*

## Structural Unemployment

**Structural unemployment** arises from a mismatch between job seekers and the types of jobs available.

**Structural unemployment** arises from a mismatch between job seekers and the types of jobs available. One cause of structural unemployment is a mismatch of skills. For example, suppose firms in a particular city have 500 job openings, and 500 people there are looking for jobs. At first, this doesn't sound like a problem. But suppose the available jobs are for accountants, physician assistants, and other professionals with advanced degrees, while the 500 unemployed workers are not qualified for these jobs. The unemployed will remain jobless for some time—say, until they acquire the skills needed for the available jobs or else move to another place with jobs for which they are qualified. In the meantime, they will be structurally unemployed.

Skill mismatches become more serious during periods when technology or patterns of consumer spending change rapidly. For example, in the early 2000s, the ability to download music from the Internet destroyed the jobs of many sales clerks in stores that sold CDs. It also created new jobs at Apple and other companies for web page designers, software engineers, and designers of digital music players. But music store clerks lacked the skills to perform most of these new high-tech jobs.

Most recently, a large skill mismatch developed in 2008 and 2009 due to changes in consumer spending. An oversupply of housing and uncertainty about future housing prices made people hesitant to buy new homes, and the construction of new homes plummeted. Hundreds of thousands of construction workers lost their jobs. These construction workers did not have the skills needed for jobs in expanding sectors, such as health care or education.

Structural unemployment can also be caused by a *geographical* mismatch between workers and jobs. This occurs when the available jobs are far away from those who would like them. For example, in 2008 and 2009, when car factories were slowing production and laying off workers in the Detroit area, solar-cell factories in California and Massachusetts were hiring. Although unemployed automobile workers may have the skills for solar-cell manufacturing, they may not want to uproot their families to move far away. For this reason, they may remain unemployed for a long time.

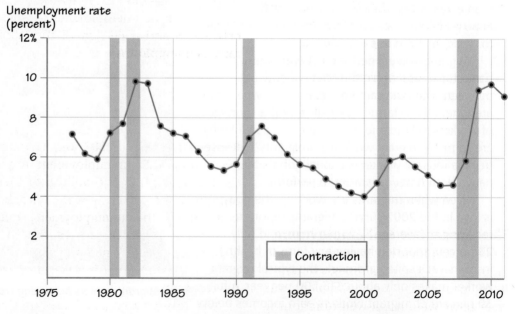

**Figure 41.2** Unemployment Rates and Contractions, 1977–2011
A high unemployment rate tends to linger for a while even after a contraction has ended.

## Cyclical Unemployment

**Cyclical unemployment** is joblessness caused by an economic contraction. Recall that during a contraction, production (measured as real GDP) declines. As production falls, fewer workers are needed. The unemployment rate rises because many firms lay off workers. It rises further because firms cut back on hiring, making it harder for new labor-force entrants such as recent high-school and college graduates to find jobs.

Figure 41.2 shows the unemployment rate from 1977 through 2011. The green-colored bands represent contractions. As the economy recovers from a contraction, the unemployment rate falls. But it can remain high for some time even after the contraction is over, in what is called a *jobless recovery*. During a jobless recovery, output begins to rise, but the unemployment rate remains high. Firms are often cautious about hiring new workers as a recovery begins. Many firms will wait to expand their workforce until they are confident the economy has really improved. At first they will increase the hours of their current workers, and only later will they begin to hire new workers. In Figure 41.2 you can see that the recovery from several contractions—including the most recent recession—was a jobless recovery. Even after the recession ended in June 2009, the unemployment rate continued to climb for several months and remained higher than normal through 2011.

 **DID YOU GET IT?**
Why does the unemployment rate rise during contractions? Why does it often remain high even after the contraction is over?

## The Concept of Full Employment

Since unemployment is costly for individuals and their families, wouldn't it be great if the unemployment rate were zero? Well, no. A well-functioning economy will always have *some* unemployment. Even when the economy is doing well, people will spend some time

searching for jobs and be frictionally unemployed until they are hired. Some workers will still be seasonally unemployed in the off-season for their industries. And because technology and spending patterns are always changing, there will always be some structural unemployment for those whose skills are no longer in demand. You can see why the unemployment rate should not, and could not, be zero.

In fact, economists describe a *natural rate of unemployment* for a healthy economy. The **natural rate of unemployment** is the unemployment rate in the absence of cyclical unemployment, around which the actual unemployment rate fluctuates. The achievement of **full employment** does not mean that everyone in the labor force is employed but that unemployment in the economy is at its natural rate. Although no one knows that exact number, most experts believe the U.S. economy has achieved full employment—and thus reached the natural rate of unemployment—when between 5 and 6 percent of the labor force is unemployed.

## THE COSTS OF UNEMPLOYMENT

Between December 2007 and October 2009, total U.S. unemployment more than doubled, from 7.6 million to 15.4 million unemployed people. At the same time, the unemployment rate rose from 5 percent to 10 percent. Most of this rise in unemployment was cyclical, meaning that it was caused by the recession.

Job loss creates problems for the unemployed and their families. In addition to losing household income, many unemployed workers lose health

*The rise of iTunes led to the loss of many jobs for sales clerks in music stores.*

**Cyclical unemployment** is joblessness caused by an economic contraction.

The **natural rate of unemployment** is the unemployment rate in the absence of cyclical unemployment, around which the actual unemployment rate fluctuates.

**Full employment** is the level of employment when there is no cyclical unemployment. Due to the existence of other types of unemployment, the achievement of full employment does not mean that every worker is employed.

insurance that had been provided by their employers. Families with no other wage earner are forced to use their savings for food, clothing, and shelter, which leaves them unprepared for unplanned expenditures on things such as health care, car repairs, or recovery from storm damage. Research has shown that family financial problems can also contribute to children having difficulty in school, family separation, and even crime.

Unemployment is costly not only to households but also to the national economy. Unemployment represents the underuse of an important resource—labor. When labor resources are not used efficiently, the total output of goods and services falls below the economy's potential. Unemployment also has a negative impact on the federal budget. High unemployment forces the government to spend more money on social programs such as unemployment insurance and the Supplemental Nutrition Assistance Program, which helps low-income households put food on their dinner table. At the same time, the government's tax revenues fall because unemployed workers and struggling firms pay relatively little in taxes. The lower tax revenues make it especially difficult for the government to cover its higher expenditures.

## How the Costs of Unemployment Are Distributed

The burden of unemployment is not distributed equally among groups or locations within the country. Even when the overall unemployment rate is low, some types of workers may find it difficult to find a job. A lack of work experience, a lack of opportunity, a lack of job skills, and discrimination are among the factors that complicate the job search in some cases. Table 41.1 shows that the

**Table 41.1** Unemployment Rates by Race, Age, and Educational Attainment, September 2012
The factors that cause unemployment rates to vary across groups include work experience, opportunities, and discrimination.

* Educational attainment for workers 25 years old and over

| GROUPS | UNEMPLOYMENT RATE |
|---|---|
| **Race/Ethnicity** | |
| All workers | 7.8% |
| White | 7.0 |
| Black | 13.4 |
| Hispanic | 9.9 |
| **Age** | |
| All teenagers | 23.7 |
| White teenagers | 20.8 |
| Black teenagers | 38.1 |
| Hispanic teenagers | 27.8 |
| **Educational Attainment*** | |
| No high school diploma | 11.3 |
| High school graduate (no college) | 8.7 |
| Some college | 6.5 |
| Bachelor's degree or higher | 4.1 |

unemployment rate is relatively high for minorities and teenagers for reasons such as these.

The unemployment rate also varies considerably across states. Figure 41.3 shows the rates across the country in December 2011. Nevada had the highest unemployment rate, 12.6 percent. Nevada had a severe unemployment problem because the state's economy relied heavily on jobs in the tourism, hospitality, and construction industries. In the weak economy leading up to 2011, these industries were hit hard because vacations, gambling activities, and new home purchases are easy to put off during a recession. The major Las Vegas hotels and casinos laid off thousands of workers during the recent recession, and many employers stopped filling jobs vacated by retiring and departing workers. Like the federal government, the governments in states with high unemployment rates suffer declining tax revenues and may be forced to cut spending on education and other programs. These cuts create more layoffs and further hardship.

**DID YOU GET IT?**
Name two states with unemployment rates below the national average of 8.5 percent. Name two states with unemployment rates above the national average.

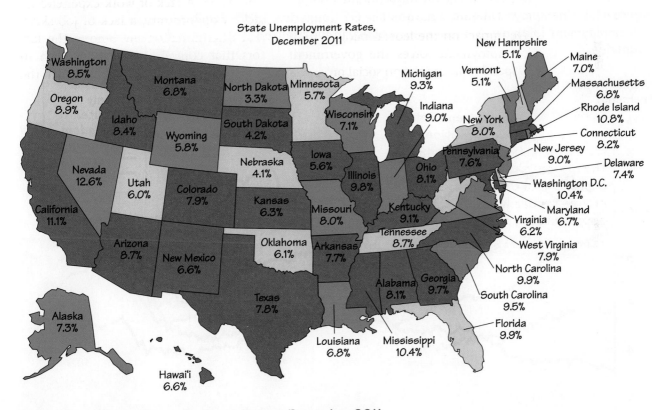

**Figure 41.3** State Unemployment Rates, December 2011
The unemployment rate varies considerably across states. The highest unemployment rates generally appear in states whose major industries are in decline.

# ECONOMICS IN ACTION

# Unemployment around the World: How Does the U.S. Stack Up?

Although unemployment rose dramatically during the recession of 2007–2009, U.S. unemployment rates over the past few decades have been relatively low compared to many advanced economies. Figure 41.4 shows the unemployment rates for the *Group of 7* (G7) countries: Canada, France, Germany, Italy, Japan, the United Kingdom, and the United States. The U.S. rates were among the lowest before the recession and then leaped up to be among the highest during and after the recession.

Significant job creation in the U.S. economy drove America's success with employment in the 1990s. From 1989 to 2008, the number of employed workers jumped by about 29 million—an average increase of about 1.5 million employed

**Figure 41.4** Unemployment Rates across the G7 Countries, 1995–2010
Full employment is an elusive goal even in highly industrialized countries.

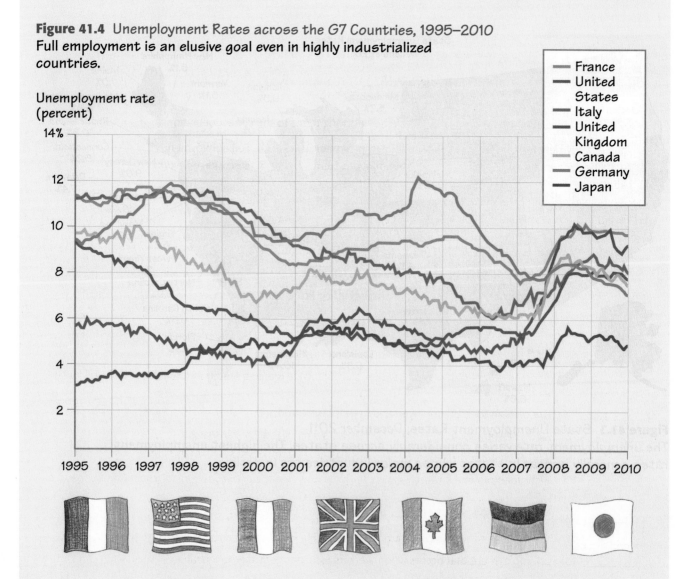

workers each year. Job growth has consistently been more rapid in the United States than in other G7 countries.

Many economists believe that inefficient or poorly designed regulations can make it harder for unemployed workers to find jobs. Labor market regulations include rules that affect the hiring and firing of workers, the terms and conditions of work, and the resolution of work-related disputes. Labor-market regulations in the United States are less restrictive than those in most European countries. For example, in some European countries it can be very difficult to lay off workers. While this provides security to those who already have jobs, it can make employers hesitant to hire in the first place.

 **DID YOU GET IT?**

How does the U.S. unemployment rate compare with that in other countries? How has the unemployment rate changed for the G7 countries over the past two decades?

# MODULE 41 REVIEW AND ASSESSMENT

**Summing Up the Key Ideas:** Match the following terms to the correct definitions.

A. Total employment
B. Total unemployment
C. Labor force
D. Unemployment rate
E. Frictional unemployment

F. Seasonal unemployment
G. Structural unemployment
H. Cyclical unemployment
I. Natural rate of unemployment

J. Full employment
K. Discouraged workers
L. Underemployed
M. Jobless recovery

_____ 1. The percentage of the labor force without a paid job.

_____ 2. The total number of employed workers, whether they work part time or full time.

_____ 3. The unemployment rate in the absence of cyclical unemployment, around which the actual unemployment rate fluctuates.

_____ 4. Workers who would like to work more hours or prefer a job that better matches their skills.

_____ 5. Unemployment caused by an economic contraction.

_____ 6. Unemployment that is short-term and occurs while workers search for the jobs best suited for their skills and interests.

_____ 7. The combination of employed and unemployed workers.

_____ 8. Workers who would like to work but have given up on their job search.

_____ 9. Unemployment that arises from a mismatch between job seekers and the types of jobs available.

_____ 10. High unemployment that persists after an economy enters the expansion phase of the business cycle.

_____ 11. The level of employment when there is no cyclical unemployment.

_____ 12. The number of workers who are actively seeking jobs but not actually working.

_____ 13. Unemployment that occurs when workers lose their jobs due to a change of seasons.

**Analyze and Explain:** Determine whether each of the following people is **unemployed** or **not unemployed**. Explain your answer.

| | UNEMPLOYED OR NOT UNEMPLOYED? | EXPLANATION |
|---|---|---|
| 1. a 15-year-old high school student who is looking for an after-school job and unable to find one | | |
| 2. a retired person | | |
| 3. a mother seeking work after her children are all old enough to be in school | | |
| 4. a factory worker who lost her job due to an economic contraction and has given up looking until the economy recovers | | |
| 5. an out-of-work construction worker who is looking for any type of employment until the home-building industry recovers | | |
| 6. a factory worker who lost his job when the factory closed and has entered a trade school to learn new skills | | |
| 7. a new college graduate who is looking for that dream job | | |

**Apply:** Determine whether each of the following people would be considered **frictionally unemployed**, **seasonally unemployed**, **structurally unemployed**, or **cyclically unemployed**.

| | TYPE OF UNEMPLOYMENT |
|---|---|
| 1. a high school graduate who is looking for work after graduation | |
| 2. a factory worker who is laid off due to slow sales throughout the economy | |
| 3. a chef at a summer resort who loses her job when summer is over | |
| 4. a recent graduate with a degree in information technology who is interviewing for a number of prospective employers but has not yet accepted any of the jobs offered | |
| 5. a department store Santa Claus during the summer months | |
| 6. a construction worker laid off during a recession | |
| 7. a new nursing graduate who is ready to work but has not found the job he wants | |
| 8. a worker who finds that the job skills he possesses are no longer needed in the current job market | |

# MODULE 42

# Inflation

**KEY IDEA:** Inflation reduces the purchasing power of money.

**OBJECTIVES**

- **To explain how inflation is measured.**
- **To explain what causes inflation and why high inflation is a problem.**
- **To identify the dangers of deflation.**

*Prices seldom stay the same for long.*

## Inflation and Deflation

In 1950—around when your grandparents might have been in high school—prices were much lower than they are today. In that year, a can of Coke cost a nickel and a movie cost about 50 cents. College tuition at private universities averaged under $500 per year. Tuition at state colleges was even lower—well under $100 per year. In fact, the price of most goods was a lot lower in 1950 than today. Of course, incomes were lower, too—and so was the weekly allowance of the typical high school student. But the fact remains that prices, on average, have increased almost every year since 1950 and in most of the years before 1950, too.

To understand how and why prices change, it's useful to establish some terminology. We've already seen that the *price level* is a broad measure of the prices for goods and services in the economy, not a measure of the price of one particular item. We'll discuss specific ways to measure the price level in the next section. A rise in the price level is called **inflation**. The **inflation rate** is the annual percentage increase in the price level. The opposite of inflation is **deflation**, which is a decline in the price level. When there is deflation, the inflation rate is negative.

As you're about to see, inflation and deflation can create serious problems for the economy. But before we discuss these problems, let's look at how the government actually measures inflation.

## MEASURING INFLATION

To determine the inflation rate, the government must first measure the price level. There are several different ways of measuring the price level that can result in somewhat different measures of inflation. For many purposes, including those of the U.S. government, the *consumer price index* is the favored price-level gauge.

### The Consumer Price Index

The **Consumer Price Index** (CPI) measures the overall level of prices faced by a typical consumer. To construct the CPI, the government first determines a *market basket*—a bundle of goods that an average consumer might buy. Then the government tracks the cost of this market basket over time. If the price of the market basket rises by 10 percent over some time period, the CPI will rise by 10 percent as well.

Of course, every consumer buys different goods and even different brands of the same goods. So the market basket is actually a hypothetical bundle of goods that is broadly representative of typical purchases. For example, suppose the average American family buys five boxes of breakfast cereal each month. The Jones family might buy mostly Cheerios,

**Inflation** is a rise in the price level.

The **inflation rate** is the annual percentage increase in the price level.

**Deflation** is a decline in the price level.

The **Consumer Price Index (CPI)** is a measure of the overall price level faced by a typical consumer.

while the Smith family might buy Apple Jacks, and so on. To help the CPI reflect the variety of consumer purchases, the market basket includes many different types of popular cereals. The same is done for other goods and services—gasoline, bananas, dresses, car repairs, and so on.

The government regularly conducts a survey of urban households to learn what goods people actually buy, so it can update the market basket to mirror changes in purchasing patterns. The eight main categories of consumer goods included in the market basket for December 2010, along with each category's share of the total basket's cost, are shown in Figure 42.1.

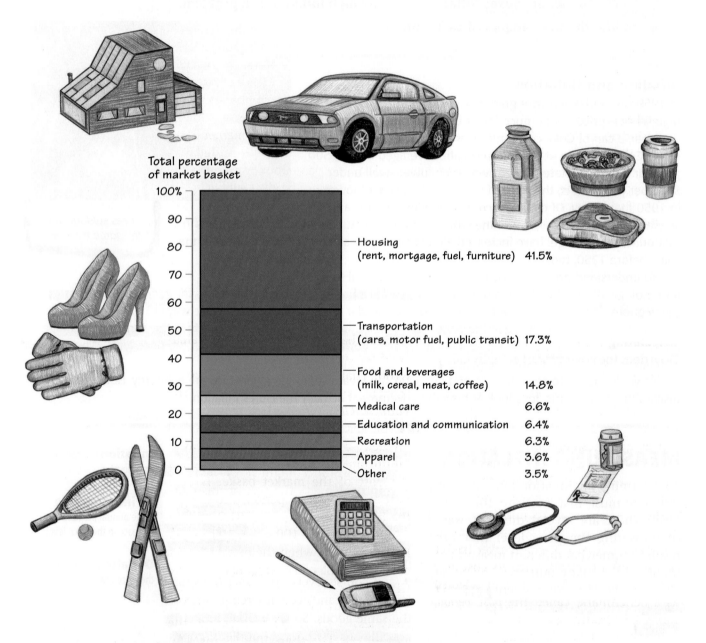

Total percentage of market basket

Housing (rent, mortgage, fuel, furniture)   41.5%

Transportation (cars, motor fuel, public transit)  17.3%

Food and beverages (milk, cereal, meat, coffee)   14.8%

Medical care   6.6%

Education and communication   6.4%

Recreation   6.3%

Apparel   3.6%

Other   3.5%

**Figure 42.1** The Market Basket of Consumer Goods, December 2010
To determine the price level, the Bureau of Labor Statistics has people go shopping to check the prices for 84,000 popular goods.

# ECONOMICS IN ACTION

# Shopping for America

When Margaret Humphrey goes shopping, she shops for the nation. Margaret works for the U.S. Bureau of Labor Statistics, the government agency that produces the CPI. She is one of many economic assistants who gather price data for the market basket that is used in the calculation of the CPI. Her job is to travel to corner stores, superstores, and all other types of retail outlets to record prices that will be transformed into the CPI. She and her trusty laptop have spent hundreds or even thousands of hours shopping together.

If you think her job is easy, think again. Before an economic assistant is let loose on the aisles, she must take a training course in Washington, DC, complete dozens of hours of homework, and go through extensive on-the-job training. Finding the exact item that is required for the market basket requires diligence and persistence. To ensure consistency in the index, the exact same items must be compared each time the CPI is calculated. So if a notebook is part of the market basket, each time the price is recorded it is important to find a notebook with the same number of pages, type of binding, ability to remove pages, and even the same narrow or wide spacing between the lines. Shopping for the Bureau of Labor Statistics is serious business.

## Calculating the CPI

How does the government actually calculate the CPI? Each month, the Bureau of Labor Statistics sends out "shoppers" like Margaret Humphrey to gather 84,000 prices for the goods and services that the typical urban resident might buy. Urban residents make up about 87 percent of the U.S. population. The prices the shoppers gather are used to determine the cost of the market basket for that month. To determine the CPI, the government compares the cost of the market basket in the current month with its cost at a time in the past that has been selected as a benchmark, called the *base period*. More specifically, the CPI is calculated using the following formula:

$$\text{CPI in a given month} = \frac{\text{cost of market basket in the given month}}{\text{cost of market basket in base period}} \times 100$$

Notice that when the CPI is calculated for the base period itself, its value is 100. That's because when the "given month" and the base period are the same, the CPI formula becomes the cost of the market basket in the base period divided by itself—which is always 1—multiplied by 100. For example, if the cost of the market basket is $1.2 million in the base period, the CPI for the base period would be ($1.2 million ÷ $1.2 million) × 100 = 1 × 100 = 100. For any month when the market basket costs more than in the base period, the CPI will be greater than 100. Likewise for any month when the market basket costs less than in the base period, the CPI will be less than 100. Changes in the CPI tell us how prices are changing. When most prices are rising, the cost of the market basket increases, so the CPI rises. A rise in the CPI is an indicator of inflation. When prices are falling, the cost of the market basket decreases, so the CPI falls. A fall in the CPI is an indicator of deflation.

The current base period for CPI calculations is the three years from 1982 to 1984. So the denominator (bottom part) of the formula for the CPI is the average cost of the market basket from 1982 to 1984. In March 2006, the CPI had a value of 199.8. This tells us that the market basket cost almost twice as much in that month as its average cost during the 1982–1984 base period. By late 2012 the CPI had reached 230.

### Other Price Indexes

The CPI is just one among many measures of the price level. Another is the *Producer Price Index* (PPI), which measures the cost of a basket of goods and services bought by producers rather than by consumers. Changes in the PPI normally show up before changes in the CPI because producers experience price changes for raw materials and intermediate goods before consumers feel changes in retail prices. Because producers will eventually pass higher costs on to wholesalers and retailers, economists look for changes in the PPI as a predictor of changes in the CPI.

The *GDP Deflator* or *GDP Price Index* is another price index that, like the CPI, is used to measure the prices of final goods. It is calculated indirectly, using the difference between nominal GDP (GDP measured at current prices) and real GDP (GDP measured with the prices of a base period). While the CPI tracks only the prices of goods purchased by consumers, the GDP deflator tracks the prices of every good that is part of GDP. This includes government purchases as well as investment purchases by firms. For example, the government buys fighter jets and farmers buy tractors, but the typical consumer does not. So these items are included in calculations for the GDP deflator but not for the CPI.

Besides the CPI, the PPI, and the GDP deflator, the government uses several other measures of the price level to monitor inflation. Because each price index is different, each one gives us a somewhat different measure of the inflation rate. But the inflation rate that comes from the CPI is the most widely used and most widely reported among them.

# THE COSTS OF INFLATION

*Price stability* exists when the inflation rate is very low—say, less than 2 or 3 percent per year. With such minimal inflation, changes in the price level from one year to the next are hardly noticeable. The prices of individual goods may rise or fall a great deal, but the overall price level is fairly stable.

Unfortunately, the U.S. economy has not always enjoyed price stability. Inflation has been a problem over several periods in the past century. Our most recent bout with high inflation occurred during the late 1970s and early 1980s, as shown in Figure 42.2. More recently, inflation rates have been modest.

### The Inflation Myth

Why does price stability matter to consumers? Why is inflation bad? You might think it's because inflation reduces the number of goods we can buy with each dollar that we earn, and that makes us poorer. The first part of this statement is true. The second part, that it makes us poorer, is not necessarily true. Let's see why.

Inflation does reduce the purchasing power of every dollar you earn. If prices double, the purchasing power of each dollar you earn is cut in half. For example, if candy bars cost 50 cents each and you earn one dollar, your dollar will get you two candy bars. But if the price of candy bars doubles to $1, your dollar can only get you one candy bar. Your purchasing power over candy bars is half of what it used to be. Now let's consider the second part of the statement about inflation and see why it's false. Inflation *can* make you poorer, but there's a good chance it won't. Inflation definitely makes you poorer if you continue to earn the same number of dollars. But

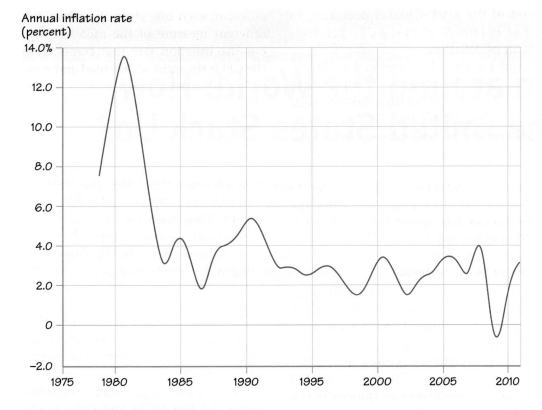

Annual inflation rate (percent)

**Figure 42.2** U.S. Inflation Rates, 1978–2011
The United States sometimes fails to achieve price stability.

in periods of rapidly rising prices, most people also earn more dollars. This is because inflation tends to raise all prices. If you make your living selling furniture, the price you charge for furniture will probably rise along with the prices of the things you buy. If you make your living as a lawyer or an accountant, the price you can charge for your services will probably rise with inflation. Wage earners, too, tend to get bigger raises when prices are rising. So yes, the purchasing power of each dollar you earn falls during periods of inflation, but your earnings will probably increase!

The overall effect of inflation on your purchasing power depends on how the increase in your earnings compares with the increase in the price level. Some workers end up poorer during periods of inflation because their earnings increase by less than the inflation rate. Some end up richer because their raises exceed the inflation rate. And some maintain the same purchasing power because their earnings increase at the same rate as the price level. But you can see that inflation, by itself, does not automatically make everyone poorer.

## The True Costs of High Inflation

Even though inflation, by itself, does not automatically decrease the purchasing power of everyone's income, inflation can be costly for society in other ways. Let's explore a few.

### Shoe Leather Costs

When inflation is high, it becomes costly to hold money in your wallet or at home because the purchasing power of cash declines as prices rise. Instead, people prefer to keep their money in the bank where it can earn interest. This is especially true during periods of very rapid inflation, known as **hyperinflation**, which can leave a country's currency virtually worthless. Indeed, during the German hyperinflation described in an upcoming Economics in Action box, firms would employ people whose sole job was to take their cash to the bank many times a day in

**Hyperinflation** is very rapid inflation.

# ECONOMICS IN ACTION

# Inflation around the World: How Does the United States Stack Up?

The developed countries of the world have achieved price stability over most of the past two decades. Figure 42.3 shows the average U.S. inflation rate compared to other Group of 7 (G7) countries from 1993 to 2002 and from 2003 to 2011. The G7 consists of some of the world's largest and most advanced economies. The average inflation rate was fairly low and stable for all the countries. If we compared inflation during either period with inflation in the 1970s, we would see an improvement from troubling double-digit rates to low, single-digit rates.

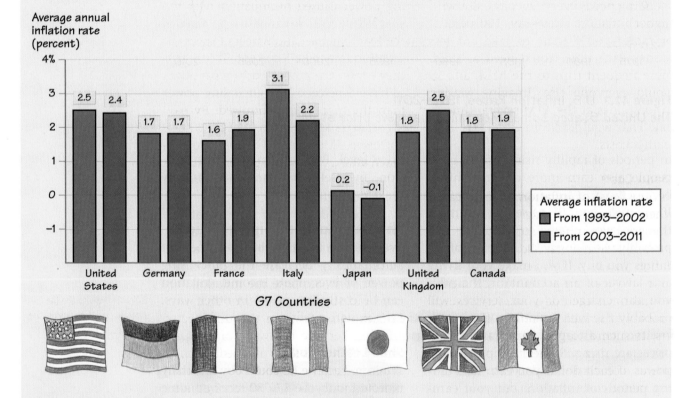

**Figure 42.3** Inflation Rates of G7 Countries, 1993–2011
The highly industrialized G7 countries have experienced low and stable inflation in recent years. Which economy experienced deflation recently?

order to invest it in something that would hold its value or exchange it for a more stable currency such as the U.S. dollar. The term **shoe leather costs** was coined to reflect the cost of the time and effort involved in running to the bank—and wearing out the soles of shoes—to avoid holding cash.

In modern times, with ATMs so readily available as a source of cash when you need it, shoe leather costs may not seem that serious. Even if the inflation rate rose to 10 or 20 percent per year, it would be easy to leave most of your money in the bank, where it can earn interest that would prevent any decline in its purchasing power. You could withdraw just enough money to cover your spending needs every few days. But with higher inflation rates—say, 100 percent or more—you'd want to take out less money each time. You'd need to make more frequent trips to the ATM, and so would everyone else. Imagine waiting in long lines at the ATM several times a day. That would add up to serious shoe leather costs.

## Menu Costs

Another cost of inflation arises because when inflation is high, firms must change their prices more often. For example, during the German hyperinflation in the 1920s, restaurants sometimes changed the prices on their menus several times each day. The term **menu costs** was coined to reflect the costly inputs such as labor, paper, and printing services used by restaurants whose menus constantly had to be updated. But menu costs apply to other industries as well. For example, when inflation is high, grocery stores must change the prices of every item more frequently. Even if the store uses bar codes and optical scanners, someone has to spend time updating the prices in the computer. When prices change, advertising brochures,

billboards, and sales contracts must be updated. All these efforts use resources that could otherwise be put to better use.

## The Costs of Unexpected Inflation

Inflation—when unexpected—can create winners and losers in a way that is unfair to the losers and costly for the economy. Suppose an entrepreneur named Barbara borrows $1,000 from her friend Michael to start a new real estate business. Michael agrees to lend Barbara the $1,000 for one year in exchange for a payment of $1,080 at the end of the year. Thirty dollars of this payment is to compensate Michael for being unable to use his $1,000 for the year. Fifty dollars of this payment is to compensate for the erosion of purchasing power caused by inflation over the year. Why $50? Because at the time of the loan, Michael and Barbara expect the inflation rate to be 5 percent. This means they expect the money Barbara pays back to have 5 percent less purchasing power than the money she borrowed. By paying an extra $50—5 percent of the $1,000 borrowed—Michael will be able to buy as much after a year with 5 percent inflation as he could with $1,000 at the beginning of the year.

Nobody knows for sure what the inflation rate will be in the future, and it is very possible that Michael and Barbara will be wrong about their predicted rate of 5 percent. Suppose the inflation rate turns out to be 7 percent for that year. Barbara will gain from this unexpected inflation because the value of her payment will be less than planned. Michael will lose, because he could buy less than expected with the $1,080 received after a year. It will take 7 percent more than the $1,000, which is $1,070, for Michael to buy as much at the end of the year as he could have at the beginning of the year. That leaves only $1,080 − $1,070 = $10 as compensation for being unable to use his money for the year.

**Shoe leather costs** are the costs of time and effort involved in frequent trips to the bank or ATM to avoid holding much cash during periods of high inflation.

**Menu costs** are the costs of updating prices due to inflation.

In general, people who borrow money benefit when inflation turns out to be higher than expected. But people who lend money lose from higher-than-expected inflation. The opposite occurs when inflation is lower than expected: borrowers lose and lenders gain because the value of the money to be paid back is higher than expected.

The possibility of unexpected inflation makes borrowing and lending more risky. No one knows in advance whether they will be a winner or a loser. The added uncertainty of unstable prices can make lenders hesitant to lend and borrowers hesitant to borrow. The result is

less lending and borrowing in the economy and fewer prosperous businesses such as Barbara's Real Estate.

**? DID YOU GET IT?**
What are three costs to the economy of inflation? Who are the winners and losers from unexpected inflation?

## DEFLATION AND ITS EFFECTS

You've learned that inflation—especially high inflation—is costly to society. But what about *deflation*—a decrease in the

---

## ECONOMICS IN ACTION

# Hyperinflation in Germany and Zimbabwe

Germany's economic nightmare began shortly after World War I ended in 1918. The German economy was severely weakened by four long years of war. Complicating Germany's economic recovery were mandated payments from Germany to France, the United Kingdom, and other victorious countries. By the early 1920s Germany was unable to pay its bills, and the cash-poor government resorted to printing more of its national currency, the mark. The flood of new currency into the German economy had an immediate impact on the prices of goods and services—prices increased, fast! Germany's hyperinflation reached its height in October of 1923, when prices rose by 29,525 percent and many workers were paid once or twice *every day*. Workers often received large bundles of marks, and on breaks during the work day, they ran to stores to buy food and other necessities. Panicky consumers often carried stacks of money in wheelbarrows when they shopped. Prices changed every few minutes. By 1923 the price

of a postage stamp hit 50 billion marks, and the price of a loaf of bread 200 billion marks. By November 1923, it cost 726 billion German marks to buy what had cost one mark in July 1914. People's savings in banks and the fixed retirement pensions of the elderly were made worthless.

As bad as Germany's hyperinflation was, several countries have had even higher inflation rates. Zimbabwe experienced hyperinflation during the mid- and late 2000s. Zimbabwe's worst month was November 2008, when its price level rose by 79,600,000,000 percent. This means prices in Zimbabwe more than doubled every day. By the end of 2008, most stores refused to accept the national currency, the Zimbabwean dollar. Instead, they insisted on payment in U.S. dollars, Euros, or other foreign currencies.

price level? You might think that falling prices are cause for celebration. After all, wouldn't you want to pay *less* for products as time goes on? But even moderate rates of deflation, say 1 percent or 2 percent per year, can cause serious problems for an economy.

One problem with deflation is that it causes consumers to reduce spending. Why? Because a period of deflation can make people expect *more* deflation in the future. As a result, consumers who have money in the bank will postpone certain purchases, especially of big-ticket items such as homes or cars. Why spend $250,000 on a home today if the same or similar home can be purchased next year for $50,000 less? When large numbers of people postpone major purchases, aggregate demand decreases. The drop in aggregate demand causes a contraction and leads anxious sellers to reduce prices, leading to still more deflation.

Another problem with deflation is that it is not just dollar prices that fall but also dollar incomes. Debts, on the other hand, do not fall. Suppose you owe $100,000 to a bank for a loan you took out to buy a home. You have to pay back a certain number of dollars on this loan each month. If there is deflation, your income falls, but the monthly payments on your loan remain the same. You will have a harder time making those payments out of your shrinking income.

What is true for homeowners applies to any individual or firm that owes money. As prices and incomes fall, it becomes more and more difficult to make payments. Some individuals and firms may reach the state of financial ruin called *bankruptcy*, which means they cannot make their payments. Bankruptcies result in more losses for banks and other lenders. If the losses are great enough, these lenders may themselves go bankrupt, because they count on loan repayments from others to help them make payments of their own. As bankruptcy spreads throughout the economy, lending—even for short periods of time—becomes riskier. Economic activity slows down and spending decreases. Once again, the result is a contraction and possibly a recession or depression.

The United States suffered a serious bout of deflation during the recession of the early 1920s, but the worst deflation occurred during the early years of the Great Depression, when average prices dropped 9 percent in 1931, 9.9 percent in 1932, and 5.1 percent in 1933. Deflation during this period led to waves of bankruptcies throughout the economy, a reduction of lending and borrowing, and a decrease in spending. In short, deflation worsened the depression and made it last longer.

**DID YOU GET IT?**
How might expectations of deflation weaken people's demand for some products? How does deflation affect a recession?

# MODULE 42 REVIEW AND ASSESSMENT

## Summing Up the Key Ideas: Match the following terms to the correct definitions.

A. Inflation
B. Inflation rate
C. Deflation

D. Consumer price index
E. Market basket
F. Base period

G. Producer price index
H. Hyperinflation

I. Shoe leather costs
J. Menu costs

_____ 1. A decrease in the price level.

_____ 2. A measure of the overall price level faced by a typical consumer.

_____ 3. The costs of updating prices due to inflation.

_____ 4. A bundle of goods that an average consumer might buy.

_____ 5. The annual percentage increase in the price level.

_____ 6. A period of very rapid inflation.

_____ 7. A rise in the price level.

_____ 8. A period in the past used as a benchmark for comparisons.

_____ 9. A measure of the cost of a basket of goods and services bought by producers.

_____ 10. The costs of time and effort involved in frequent trips to the bank or ATM to avoid holding much cash during periods of high inflation.

## Analyze and Explain: Determine if the person described in each of the following situations would be **helped** by inflation or **hurt** by inflation and then explain your answer.

|  | HELPED OR HURT? | EXPLANATION |
|---|---|---|
| 1. a retired worker with a fixed pension during a time of inflation | _____ | _____ |
| 2. a lending bank that expected the inflation rate to be 7 percent when the actual rate of inflation for the duration of the loan turned out to be 4 percent | _____ | _____ |
| 3. a landscape contractor who negotiated a three-year landscaping agreement for a set fee with a major university (after the agreement was signed, the inflation rate was much higher than expected) | _____ | _____ |
| 4. a grocery store that must update its product database when prices change | _____ | _____ |

## Apply: Suppose that Year 1 is the base year and recall that the CPI in the base year is 100. Indicate whether there was inflation, deflation, or neither between Year 1 and Year 2 in each of the following scenarios.

| CPI IN YEAR 2 | INFLATION, DEFLATION, OR NEITHER? |
|---|---|
| 1. 100 | _____ |
| 2. 80 | _____ |
| 3. 120 | _____ |

# MODULE 43

# Unemployment, Inflation, and the Business Cycle

**KEY IDEA:** Changes in unemployment and inflation are caused by changes in aggregate demand and aggregate supply.

### OBJECTIVES

- **To explain how changes in aggregate demand and aggregate supply affect both unemployment and inflation.**
- **To discuss the short-run tradeoff between unemployment and inflation.**
- **To describe stagflation.**

## Ties between Inflation and Unemployment

We have discussed inflation and unemployment separately. But inflation and unemployment often move at the same time and are sometimes linked. Changes in the economy that reduce unemployment sometimes increase inflation, and efforts to reduce inflation sometimes create more unemployment. Why should these two problems be related? We'll address that question toward the end of this module. Our first step is to understand why the economy almost always has at least some inflation and some unemployment.

*During downturns in the business cycle, inflation is seldom a problem, but the search for jobs becomes particularly competitive.*

## ONGOING INFLATION AND UNEMPLOYMENT

A certain amount of unemployment and inflation can be considered part of the normal workings of the economy. You've already learned why the unemployment rate can never drop to zero. As long as the economy is growing and changing, there will always be some frictional, seasonal, and structural unemployment. So even when the economy is performing well, some unemployment remains.

The same is true of inflation. Even when the economy is performing well, there is usually some inflation. This ongoing inflation arises from our past experience of inflation. The process works like this: When prices have been rising at a certain rate, employers and workers come to expect inflation to continue at the same rate in the near future. As a result, workers want their wages to grow at least at that rate, in order to maintain the purchasing power of their incomes. Although higher wages mean higher costs for firms, the firms are generally willing to pay the higher wages. Why? Because they expect to be able to raise their prices in the coming year, giving them more revenue from which to pay the higher wages. As wages rise and prices rise to cover higher costs, the expected inflation becomes a reality.

Ongoing inflation can be a *self-fulfilling prophecy*, which occurs when a prediction comes true primarily because people believe it will. In this case, inflation often continues as in the past because everyone believes it will and acts accordingly. Their actions bring about the inflation they predicted. But what causes unemployment or inflation to change? The most important cause is the business cycle, which is most often driven by changes in aggregate demand.

 **DID YOU GET IT?**
How does inflation in the past create inflation in the future?

# HOW AGGREGATE DEMAND AFFECTS UNEMPLOYMENT AND INFLATION

In the last chapter you learned that a drop in aggregate demand is a common cause of economic contractions. When aggregate demand declines, firms don't sell as many goods and services, so they produce less. Production is too low to justify employing everyone who wants a job. The unemployment rate rises above the natural rate brought about by frictional, seasonal, and structural unemployment. Now we have cyclical unemployment as well, and we have entered a contraction caused by a decrease in aggregate demand.

Changes in aggregate demand can also cause the unemployment rate to fall. As aggregate demand rises and people buy more goods and services, firms increase production and hire more workers. The unemployment rate drops and we enter an expansion.

This is familiar ground from the last chapter. Now let's move to a relationship you did *not* learn in the last chapter: changes in aggregate demand typically also change the inflation rate. To understand the relationship between aggregate demand and inflation, it helps to understand the concept of *potential output*. The economy's **potential output** is the level of real GDP that is produced when there is full employment. Remember that full employment does not

imply the absence of unemployment. Rather, full employment exists when there is no *cyclical* unemployment, so that the unemployment rate is equal to the natural rate of unemployment. In other words, reaching full employment, achieving the natural rate of unemployment, and producing at the potential output level all describe the same situation in the economy. Which expression we use depends on whether we want to focus on employment, unemployment, or production.

What happens if an increase in aggregate demand causes real GDP to rise above potential output? Then, by definition, unemployment will fall below its natural rate. With few unemployed workers, firms will have difficulty hiring the labor they need for their higher-than-normal production level. Employers around the country will offer higher wages in an effort to attract new workers and to prevent their current workers from being lured to other firms.

In a situation like this—with real GDP exceeding potential output—we say that the economy is *overheated*. The added demand for goods places upward pressure on prices, and the scarcity of available workers places upward pressure on wages. We have seen that wages usually rise anyway, because everyone expects some inflation. In an overheated economy, wages rise more rapidly, because—in addition to expected inflation—there is the added factor of very few unemployed workers. With wages rising more rapidly, firms' costs rise more rapidly as well, causing them to raise their prices more rapidly. The elevated demand for goods and the rising cost of workers thus bring the inflation rate above its previous level.

The opposite happens when a decrease in aggregate demand brings real GDP below potential output. In that case, the weakened demand for goods places downward pressure on prices. Unemployment rises above its natural rate, and jobless workers have difficulty finding jobs. Competition among workers for scarce jobs means that employers

The economy's **potential output** is the level of real GDP that is produced when there is full employment.

can pay lower wages to the smaller number of workers they need. With lower wages, firms' costs fall, allowing them to charge lower prices as they compete for customers. The lower demand for goods and the decrease in costs thus cause the price level to fall.

Finally, when real GDP is equal to potential output, the unemployment rate is equal to its natural rate. In that case, the unemployment rate is neither artificially high nor artificially low, and wages need not rise or fall as the result of a shortage or surplus of available labor. At the same time, there is no upward or downward pressure on the price level as would result from a change in aggregate demand that caused real GDP to differ from potential output. So there is no reason for the inflation rate to change.

# THE LINK BETWEEN UNEMPLOYMENT AND INFLATION

It is the effects of changes in aggregate demand that send unemployment and inflation in opposite directions. Figure 43.1 summarizes this relationship. An increase in aggregate demand causes unemployment to fall and the price level to rise, resulting in inflation. The lower unemployment comes from a heightened need for workers to keep up with the higher demand for goods and services. Inflation occurs for two reasons: First, the increase in aggregate demand causes the real GDP demanded to exceed the real GDP supplied at the original price level, and this excess demand places upward pressure on

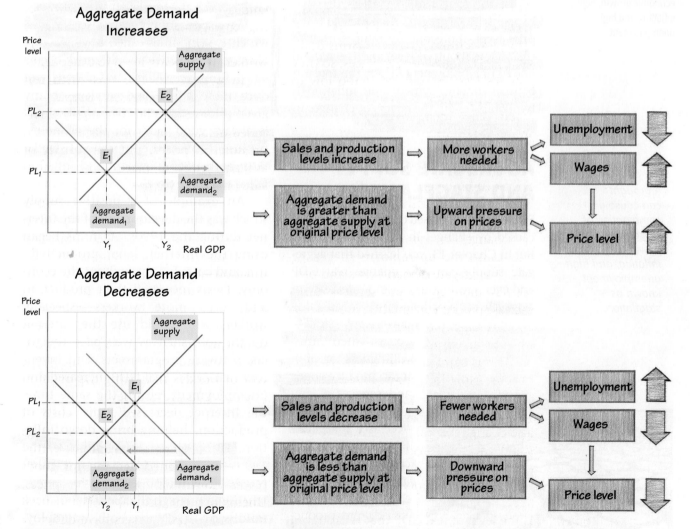

**Figure 43.1**  *Changes in Aggregate Demand*
Changes in aggregate demand send unemployment and price level in opposite directions.

prices. Second, with fewer unemployed workers, firms have to pay more to attract additional workers and must charge higher prices to cover the higher costs.

In the opposite direction, a decrease in aggregate demand causes unemployment to rise and the price level to fall, resulting in deflation. The rise in unemployment results from the decreased number of workers needed to satisfy the weakened demand for goods and services. Deflation occurs for two reasons: First, the decrease in aggregate demand brings the real GDP demanded below the real GDP supplied at the original price level. This creates a glut of goods and places downward pressure on prices. Second, with more unemployment, competition among workers for jobs causes wages to rise more slowly or even to decrease, and lower labor costs for firms allow lower prices for customers.

In the long run, regardless of what happens to aggregate demand and the price level, the economy returns back to the potential output level and the natural rate of unemployment. Thus, the tradeoff between unemployment and inflation is temporary, as are the effects of changes in aggregate demand on real GDP.

**Stagflation** is a combination of sluggish economic growth, high inflation, and high unemployment.

# AGGREGATE SUPPLY AND STAGFLATION

So far, we've discussed changes in real GDP caused by changes in aggregate demand. But in Chapter 13, you learned that aggregate supply can also change real GDP and even create a recession. A decrease in aggregate supply—sometimes called a *negative supply shock*—occurs when firms' willingness or ability to produce goods and services at any given price level decreases. Negative supply shocks can be caused by increases in oil prices, wars that destroy capital and disrupt production, or bad weather that destroys crops.

*A drought can cause a combination of sluggish economic growth, high inflation, and high unemployment known as stagflation.*

When a negative supply shock hits, output falls, and fewer workers are needed. This causes unemployment to rise. At the same time, the negative supply shock raises production costs for firms around the country. For example, when oil prices rise, every firm must pay more for its energy, for plastic (which is made using oil), and for transportation services. With higher costs, firms raise prices more than usual, and the inflation rate rises. The rise in inflation occurs at the same time as the rise in unemployment.

Notice that with a negative supply shock, unemployment and inflation no longer move in opposite directions. Instead, they have a positive relationship. When the economy is sluggish and unemployment and inflation rise together, the economy is said to experience **stagflation**. The term is a combination of *stagnation* (because GDP is stuck at a low level) and *inflation*.

Aggregate supply can also *increase*, which is sometimes called a *positive supply shock*. A positive supply shock occurs when firms are willing and able to produce more goods and services at any given price level. A positive supply shock is always good news for the economy, because it causes the opposite of stagflation: both unemployment and inflation fall at the same time.

An example of a positive supply shock was the development of the Internet during the 1990s. As firms began using the Internet, labor productivity rose and costs fell throughout the economy. Firms increased their production and hired more workers—especially workers who could use the Internet on the job, such as web page designers, software programmers, and inventory managers. Real GDP increased and unemployment fell. At the same time, the Internet decreased firms' costs of production, helping bring down inflation. The positive supply shock of the 1990s—from the Internet and other causes—is a major reason why people who lived through that period look back fondly on it. When both unemployment and inflation fall together, people feel very good about the economy.

# MODULE 43 REVIEW AND ASSESSMENT

**Summing Up the Key Ideas:** Match the following terms to the correct definitions.

A. Potential output
C. Negative supply shock
B. Stagflation
D. Positive supply shock

_____ 1.  Occurs when firms' willingness or ability to produce goods and services at any given price level decreases.

_____ 2.  A period of sluggish economic growth, high inflation, and high unemployment.

_____ 3.  The level of real GDP that is produced when there is full employment.

_____ 4.  Occurs when firms are willing and able to produce more goods and services at any given price level.

**Analyze and Explain:** Indicate whether each of the following statements is true or false and explain your answers.

|  | TRUE OR FALSE? | EXPLANATION |
|---|---|---|
| 1. Expectations of inflation lead to inflation. | _____ | _____ |
| 2. When real GDP exceeds potential output there is downward pressure on wages. | _____ | _____ |
| 3. A negative supply shock causes inflation. | _____ | _____ |

**Apply:** Determine the effect of each of the following on **unemployment** and **inflation**.

|  | EFFECT ON UNEMPLOYMENT | EFFECT ON INFLATION |
|---|---|---|
| 1. a decrease in aggregate demand | _____ | _____ |
| 2. a decrease in aggregate supply | _____ | _____ |
| 3. an increase in aggregate demand | _____ | _____ |
| 4. an increase in aggregate supply | _____ | _____ |

# US News and World Report

## Teenagers without Jobs May Be Missing Out on Job Skills, Future Wages

BY DANIELLE KURTZLEBEN

The youngster who takes movie tickets, scans groceries, or walks neighborhood dogs is doing much more than earning extra cash. She is investing in her future.

Yet nearly one in four Americans age 16 to 19 were unemployed in February, according to the latest numbers from the Labor Department. Even as the overall jobless rate held firm at 8.3 percent, the teen rate climbed from 23.2 to 23.8 percent. That number has far to fall before it is in healthy territory. In the mid-2000s, the rate hovered between 14 and 18 percent. For much of the late 1990s and early 2000s, it held at or below 15 percent.

"It's a huge problem," says Heidi Shierholz, a labor market economist at the Economic Policy Institute, a liberal Washington-based think tank. The teen jobless rate is in part a function of the larger national jobs crisis, she says. "It shoots up higher during recessions . . . it pretty much tracks the overall unemployment rate at a much higher level."

The problem has proven persistent, even since the Great Recession ended. The national teen unemployment rate has been above 20 percent since mid-2008. And it is disproportionately affecting certain minorities. The February unemployment rate for Hispanics age 16 to 19 was 27.5 percent, and for blacks it was more than one-third, at 34.7 percent.

Beyond the effect on a teenager's wallet, the high unemployment rate among teens foreshadows economic problems for these youth as they reach adulthood. "Many of those first-time jobs, even before a career begins, are very formative from some very basic standpoints," says Paul Conway, president of Generation Opportunity, a conservative organization aimed at young Americans. "They teach the basics of how to operate in a workplace—simple things like arriving on time, working on a team, feeling as though you are being compensated for work that you do."

The effects of youth employment go beyond responsibility and how to behave in a professional work environment. Research suggests that, if work doesn't cut into a teen's education, it can boost future earnings. He points to a 1995 National Bureau of Economic Research working paper that shows that high school seniors employed 20 hours per week were, 6 to 9 years later, expected to earn approximately 11 percent more annually than their counterparts who did not work.

While a 1995 Labor Department study on teen employment found only a short-lived wage boost, the study's author also suggested that the experience could boost job-seeking skills "by teaching [young workers] how to locate good employment opportunities and communicate effectively with potential employers."

**DID YOU READ IT?**

1) What are some of the potential long-term problems with persistently high teenage unemployment?

2) What skills does a teenager learn from having a job?

**WHAT DO YOU THINK?**

1) Why is the teenage unemployment rate much higher than the overall unemployment rate, especially during a recession?

2) What other age or demographic groups in the economy are more likely to suffer from very high unemployment during a recession?

EXCERPTED FROM www.usnews.com/news/articles/2012/03/15/
high-teen-unemployment-could-hurt-future-job-growth_print.html

## AN INTERVIEW WITH Laurence Meyer

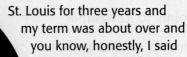

**Did you take an economics class when you were in high school?**

I did and I guess it was influential. The fact that I had taken it and enjoyed it was certainly a motivation for me to take introductory economics as a freshman. Although, I would have done it anyway, I'm sure.

**What was it that you loved about the subject?**

For one, I saw it as a fantastic way, and this is the way I taught it, to increase problem-solving ability, analytical ability. Now you certainly can do that in math and the sciences, perhaps with greater difficulty. Economics constantly was testing you with things that you had to figure out, and I loved that. It's kind of a puzzle to be figured out.

**Why is the study of economics important to students in high school?**

What I tell students is that you will have choices. But you'll be rewarded if you choose a career that is meaningful to you—where you think you're making a contribution; where you are adding to a social network. [An understanding of economics helps you make better choices.]

**Why did you start Macroeconomics Advisors?**

I had been chairman of the economics department at Washington University in St. Louis for three years and my term was about over and you know, honestly, I said to myself, "What do you want to do with the rest of your life?" I said, I have to make a difference; that was my kind of temperament, and I thought that given the relative quality of people who were in economic consulting and forecasting versus academics, well that's the place I felt I would have a real ability to contribute. What was exciting about that in part was the ability or the necessity to be entrepreneurial. Macroeconomic Advisors was an idea-driven business.

**What is economic forecasting? What does Macroeconomic Advisors do and who are your clients?**

We love models: models of the economy, models of the macroeconomy. How is it used? It's used by businesses that have to make projections of their sales, and their sales depend on the overall economy. It's used by governments that want to make projections of the economy that underpin their budget and policies. For me now, I'm working principally with large financial firms, hedge funds and the like. I'm working with people for whom interest rates matter a lot.

GETTY IMAGES

# CHAPTER 14 REVIEW AND SELF-ASSESSMENT

## REVIEW

### Points to Remember

#### MODULE 41: UNEMPLOYMENT

1. **Total employment** in an economy is the total number of employed workers, whether they work part time or full time.

2. **Total unemployment** in an economy is the number of workers who are actively seeking jobs but not actually working.

3. The **labor force** is the combination of the employed and the unemployed workers.

4. The **unemployment rate** is the percentage of the labor force without a paid job.

5. **Frictional unemployment** is unemployment that occurs while workers are searching for a job.

6. **Seasonal unemployment** occurs when workers lose their jobs due to a change of seasons.

7. **Structural unemployment** arises from a mismatch between job seekers and the types of jobs available.

8. **Cyclical unemployment** is joblessness caused by an economic contraction.

9. The **natural rate of unemployment** is the unemployment rate in the absence of cyclical unemployment, around which the actual unemployment rate fluctuates.

10. **Full employment** is the level of employment when there is no cyclical unemployment.

11. **Discouraged workers** would like to work but have given up on their job search.

12. **Underemployed** workers would like to work more hours or prefer a job that better matches their skills.

#### MODULE 42: INFLATION

13. **Inflation** is a rise in the price level.

14. The **inflation rate** is the annual percentage increase in the price level.

15. **Deflation** is a decline in the price level.

16. The **Consumer Price Index** (CPI) is a measure of the overall price level faced by a typical consumer.

17. **Hyperinflation** is very rapid inflation.

18. **Shoe leather costs** are the costs of time and effort involved in frequent trips to the bank or ATM to avoid holding much cash during times of high inflation.

19. **Menu costs** are the costs of updating prices due to inflation.

#### MODULE 43: UNEMPLOYMENT, INFLATION, AND THE BUSINESS CYCLE

20. The economy's **potential output** is the level of real GDP that is produced when there is full employment.

21. **Stagflation** refers to a time of sluggish economic growth, high unemployment, and high inflation.

## SELF-ASSESSMENT

The following questions are the type your teacher might ask you on a quiz or a test. Practice with these in order to improve your performance on class tests.

### Multiple-Choice Questions

1. The number that is published by the federal government for the unemployment rate is expressed as a percentage of

   a. the population.
   b. those employed.
   c. those unemployed.
   d. the labor force.

2. The type of unemployment that would be zero when the economy is at "full employment" is

   a. frictional unemployment.
   b. seasonal unemployment.
   c. cyclical unemployment.
   d. structural unemployment.

Answer the next two questions based on the following numbers for the Consumer Price Index (CPI):

| YEAR | CPI |
|------|-----|
| 1 | 90 |
| 2 | 100 |
| 3 | 120 |
| 4 | 138 |
| 5 | 160 |

3. The base year for this CPI is year

   a. 1.
   b. 2.
   c. 3.
   d. 4.

4. If something cost $10 in year 2, how much would we expect it to cost in year 5?

   a. $10
   b. $12
   c. $16
   d. $20

5. Shoe leather costs are the highest when there is

   a. deflation.
   b. hyperinflation.
   c. no menu cost.
   d. an unchanging CPI.

6. Which of the following would lead to a simultaneous decline in unemployment and inflation?

   a. an increase in aggregate demand
   b. a decrease in aggregate demand
   c. an increase in aggregate supply
   d. a decrease in aggregate supply

7. The most widely used and widely reported measure of inflation is the

   a. GDP Deflator.
   b. Consumer Price Index.
   c. Producer Price Index.
   d. GDP Price Index.

8. If actual inflation turned out to be less than anticipated inflation,

   a. lenders would benefit and borrowers would be hurt.
   b. borrowers would benefit and lenders would be hurt.
   c. borrowers and lenders would both benefit.
   d. borrowers and lenders would both be hurt.

9. *Stagflation* is a time period in which

   a. a recession turns into a depression.
   b. hyperinflation occurs.
   c. deflation occurs.
   d. the economy is sluggish, and unemployment and inflation are high.

**Constructed Response Question**

1. See how specific you can be in answering the following questions.

   a. Define the unemployment rate.
   b. List and explain the four types of unemployment.
   c. Define the natural rate of unemployment.
   d. How does the actual unemployment rate in the United States currently compare with the natural rate of unemployment?
   e. How would an increase in aggregate demand affect the actual unemployment rate?
   f. Define *inflation*.
   g. Define *deflation*.

**CHAPTER 15 & YOU** You play many roles in the economy—consumer, taxpayer, worker, saver, investor, and voter. How the federal government manages *fiscal policy* by adjusting its tax rates and spending levels affects you in each of these roles. In turn, your reaction to economic policies as a voter can affect the election of policy makers. The more you understand about fiscal policy, the better you will be able to make wise choices in all these roles.

# Fiscal Policy

## JUMP-STARTING THE ECONOMY

If someone gave you $400, how would you spend it? Or would you save it? That was a question economists asked in 2009 when President Barack Obama signed into law the American Recovery and Reinvestment Act, which, among other things, provided a $400 tax credit for more than 100 million American workers. The purpose of the tax credit was to jump-start the economy, which had fallen into a recession. However, there was uncertainty about whether the larger paychecks would spur the economy. It was possible that the recipients would save the money rather than spend it.

Three economists, David Johnson, Jonathan Parker, and Nicholas Souleles, tested that theory with data from rebates averaging $480 to taxpayers in 2001. They found that the rebates did provide a boost to the economy. About two thirds of the 2001 rebate checks were spent within six months of when taxpayers received them. Within the first three months, households spent $51 more than normal on food and $179 more on *nondurable goods*, meaning items that last for less than three years. That is, people in general did not use the money to buy dishwashers and TVs; instead they bought items such as clothes and cell phones. Households with lower incomes tended to spend more of their rebate than high-income households.

AP PHOTO/MATT ROURKE

*Most American households buy nondurable goods with their tax rebate checks, using the extra cash to update their wardrobe or get the latest cell phone.*

The added expenditures of $51 and $179 per taxpayer household may not seem like much, but they translated into a 2.7 percent increase in spending on food and a 3.2 percent increase in spending on nondurable goods. Overall, the three economists concluded that the rebates were an important factor in bringing an end to the recession in the fourth quarter of 2001. Spending of the 2001 rebates foreshadowed spending of a similar 2008 tax rebate, which was again largely on nondurable goods and food.

This chapter explores how the federal government uses policies such as tax rebates and government spending to affect the nation's economy. In Module 44, you will learn how the federal government uses the money it collects and borrows. Module 45 discusses why the federal government borrows money and the effects of the *national debt*. Module 46 looks at why and how the federal government attempts to moderate the business cycle.

## BOTTOM LINE

Policies on government spending, tax collections, and transfer payments have a sizable influence on most individuals and on the economy as a whole.

# MODULE 44

# Government Revenue and Spending

**KEY IDEA:** The government uses tax collections to fund its operations and programs. About two thirds of federal government spending is mandated by law.

### OBJECTIVES

- **To identify the sources of federal government revenue.**
- **To specify how the federal government spends its revenue.**
- **To explain the difference between mandatory and discretionary spending.**

## Burdens and Benefits

Taxes are a necessary burden. Tax revenues allow the government to relieve citizens of other burdens. The government protects our borders, monitors contagious diseases, offers student loans, and provides health care for the elderly and disabled. Tax revenues fund the construction of most roads, schools, prisons, and sewer systems, and pay the salaries of most teachers, air traffic controllers, trash collectors, and police officers. In this module we'll examine the federal budget for a closer look at how the government spends its revenues and how those spending decisions are made.

*Public schools are funded with tax revenues.*

## SOURCES OF GOVERNMENT REVENUE

All levels of government raise revenue through taxation. Some taxes are in the form of *user fees*. For example, if you have a dog, the local government where you live may charge a fee for a dog license. If you go camping at a national park, the federal government will collect a camping fee. Such fees are effectively taxes. Chapter 10 explained that individual income taxes bring in the largest share of revenue for the federal government—47 percent in 2011. Close behind are payroll taxes, the source of 36 percent of federal tax revenues. The third-largest portion of federal taxes, 8 percent, comes from corporate income taxes. Smaller amounts of revenue come from federal sales and excise taxes—3 percent. Other taxes, including estate taxes, gift taxes, and import taxes, combine to provide 6 percent of federal tax revenues.

When the government spends more than it takes in as revenues, it borrows to make up the difference. It does so by selling *government securities* of various types, which represent a promise to repay a certain amount of money over time. These include *Treasury bills*, *Treasury notes*, and *Treasury bonds*. The prices for these securities are determined at auction. **Treasury bills (T-bills)** sell for less than the amount to be repaid. The amount to be repaid is called the *face value* or *par value*. The Treasury bills are repaid after a specified period of 4, 13, 26, or 52 weeks. For example, you might pay $97 today for a T-bill with a face value of $100 to be repaid in 26 weeks. This would provide you with $100 − $97 = $3 as compensation for putting off the use of your money for half a year and for any decrease in your money's purchasing power due to inflation.

**Treasury notes (T-notes)** are government securities that are repaid in 2, 3, 5, or 10 years, and **Treasury bonds (T-bonds)** are repaid in 30 years. Every

A **Treasury bill (T-bill)** is a security issued by the U.S. Treasury that matures in 4, 13, 26, or 52 weeks.

A **Treasury note (T-note)** is a U.S. Treasury security that pays interest in the form of coupon payments and matures in 2, 3, 5, or 10 years.

A **Treasury bond (T-bond)** is a U.S. Treasury security that pays interest in the form of coupon payments and matures in 30 years.

six months, buyers of T-notes and T-bonds receive *coupon payments*, which are payments of a small percentage of the face value of their securities. Because of these coupon payments, the purchase price for a security is sometimes greater than the face value. For example, you might be willing to pay $101 for a T-bond with a face value of $100 in order to receive coupon payments of $2 every six months for 30 years. Investors around the world buy these securities because, although other investments offer higher returns on average, U.S. government securities involve very little risk.

 **DID YOU GET IT?**
**Which forms of government securities offer coupon payments?**

## THE FEDERAL BUDGET

The **federal budget** is a plan for how the federal government will spend money in a particular year. The budget applies to the **fiscal year**, which begins on October 1 and ends on September 30. The fiscal year is named for the year in which it ends, so fiscal 2012 ended in September of 2012. The crafting of the budget begins with the Office of Management and Budget (OMB), a component of the Executive Office of the President, working to align the requests of federal agencies with the president's priorities. Then the Congressional Budget Office (CBO) reviews the budget, congressional committees hold hearings, and Congress develops its own version of the budget.

The budget appears back on the president's desk not as a single document but as 13 separate spending bills known as *appropriations bills*. If the president signs all the bills, they become law. If the president *vetoes* some of them, Congress must override the vetoes with a two-thirds majority in both the House of Representatives and the Senate in order for the bills to become law.

The **federal budget** is a plan for how the federal government will spend money over the coming fiscal year.

The **fiscal year** for the federal government is the period over which the federal budget applies. It begins on October 1 and ends on September 30.

*Sometimes the federal budget is adjusted with emergency spending bills in the wake of disasters such as Hurricane Irene in 2011.*

If an appropriations bill has been held up beyond the beginning of the new fiscal year, Congress must pass—and the president must sign—a continuing resolution. This enables the agencies to fund operations based on the previous year's funding. If a continuing resolution were not approved, the agencies would have to shut down. Continuing resolutions were needed in 8 of the 11 years between 2001 and 2011.

The process for preparing, reviewing, and approving the federal budget is summarized in Figure 44.1. Once

---

**Federal agencies submit budget requests to the OMB**
(February to December)
The OMB works with the agencies to align the requests with the president's priorities.

**The president and the OMB prepare the final budget request**
(December to February)
The OMB prepares the final budget based on direction from the president and revised requests from the federal agencies.

**Congress reviews the budget and develops revisions**
(March to October)
The CBO reviews the budget, congressional committees hold hearings, and Congress develops a budget as the basis for 13 major appropriations bills.

**Congress sends the appropriations bills to the president**
(by October 1st)
The appropriations bills are sent to the president to sign or veto. If a bill is vetoed, a two-thirds majority in each house of Congress may override the veto. Otherwise, Congress must revise the bill and send it back to the president.

**Congress passes a continuing resolution**
(after October 1st)
If an appropriations bill has been held up beyond the beginning of the new fiscal year, Congress must pass—and the president must sign—a continuing resolution to fund operations.

**Figure 44.1** Steps in the Federal Budget Process
The budget-creation process involves input from federal agencies, Congress, and the president.
**DID YOU GET IT?** What happens if the 13 major appropriations bills are not passed by October 1?

MARILEE CALIENDO/FEMA

approved, the budget becomes the primary source of public policy for the nation.

The budget is more than a spending plan. It is also a political document. The budget submitted to Congress declares the president's priorities for the nation. These may or may not be the same as Congress's. If both houses of Congress are led by the president's political party, then the priorities are likely to be similar. However, if either or both houses are not led by the president's political party, the president's budget may see many changes before congressional approval. This was not always true. The presidency was a much weaker office until the administrations of Franklin Roosevelt in the 1930s and

1940s. Since then, presidents have used the budget to exercise considerable influence on national policies.

During the year, Congress may submit emergency spending bills to the president to cover the cost of wars, relief efforts for natural disasters, and other unplanned events. For example, in 2011 a group of senators proposed $7 billion in emergency spending to assist victims of Hurricane Irene and Tropical Storm Lee, as well as past disasters dating back to Hurricane Katrina in 2005.

Figure 44.2 shows the federal budget for fiscal year 2012. You learned in Module 4 that economic security is one of society's six economic goals. This priority is reflected in the budget. The Social Security program that assists retired and

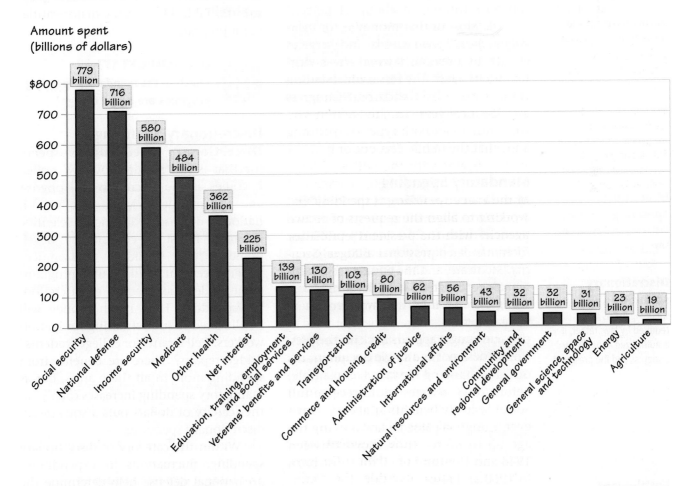

**Figure 44.2** *Federal Government Spending, 2012*
Total spending by the federal government in fiscal year 2012 was $3.7 trillion.
**DID YOU GET IT?** Where does net interest rank among the costs?

SOURCE: Analytical Perspectives, Budget of the United States Government, Fiscal Year 2013. Office of Management and Budget, www.gpo.gov/fdsys/pkg/BUDGET-2013-PER/pdf/BUDGET-2013-PER.pdf.

disabled workers with economic security makes up the largest spending category. And the third-largest category is income security, which includes unemployment insurance, workers' compensation for injured workers, and other programs that provide economic security. Broader priorities for national security and health are clear from the budget allocations as well. Among the top five spending categories are national defense, health, and Medicare, which assists a growing number of older citizens with health care expenditures.

# HOW THE FEDERAL GOVERNMENT SPENDS OUR MONEY

The federal budget for fiscal year 2012 was $3.7 trillion, or about 24 percent of GDP. Most of that money is for *mandatory spending* on goods and services chosen by previous lawmakers as written into the law. The rest is for spending choices made by the current Congress and the president. In this section you will learn about both types of spending and what the public gets out of it.

## Mandatory Spending

**Mandatory spending** is spending that is required by existing law. About two thirds of the federal budget is set aside for such mandated programs as Social Security, Medicare, and the Children's Health Insurance Program (CHIP). These programs were set up to continue from year to year so that Congress does not have to pass new laws to maintain the benefits. Congress can modify these programs only by changing the law. For example, before 2003, retirees could receive full Social Security benefits at age 65. However, Congress passed a law moving the age up to 66 for those born between 1943 and 1960 and to 67 for those born in 1960 and after.

Programs that fall under the mandatory spending category are known as **entitlement programs** because people are entitled by law to receive

benefits if they meet the eligibility requirements. For example, to receive payments under the Disability Insurance program of the Old Age, Survivors, and Disability Insurance (OASDI) system, a worker must be unable to work due to a disability. Age and past contributions are the only eligibility requirement for Social Security recipients, the other part of OASDI. The story is different for Medicaid and the Supplemental Nutrition Assistance Program, commonly referred to as *food stamps* (that name came from the stamps used to disburse benefits before the current electronic card-based system). Both programs are **means-tested**, meaning that eligibility for benefits depends on the prospective recipients' income. These and other government-provided benefits that are not in exchange for goods or services are known as **transfer payments.** Table 44.1 lists the major entitlement programs.

 **DID YOU GET IT?**
Which of the mandatory spending programs are based on age?

## Discretionary Spending

**Discretionary spending** is spending that is not required by law; rather, it comes at the discretion of Congress and the president. Most spending on national defense, education, scientific research, housing, community development, farm subsidies, environmental enforcement, and similar programs come under the heading of discretionary spending. How much money will be allocated to job retraining for laid-off workers? Pell Grants for college students? Bridge repairs? There are benefits from spending more in all these areas, but as mandatory spending increases each year, the scarcity of dollars puts a squeeze on discretionary spending.

Within the category of discretionary spending, fluctuations in expenditures on national defense help determine the amount available for other purposes. In the 1990s, thanks to the improved relationship between the United States and the former Soviet Union that

---

Eligibility for **means-tested** programs depends on the prospective recipients' income.

**Transfer payments** are payments for which the government receives no goods or services in return.

**Mandatory spending** is spending that is required by existing law.

**Discretionary spending** is government spending that is not required by law; rather, it is authorized annually by Congress and the president.

**Entitlement programs** are programs that people are entitled to by law if they meet certain qualifications.

## Table 44.1  The Major Federal Government Entitlement Programs

| PROGRAM | DESCRIPTION | BENEFICIARIES |
|---|---|---|
| Social Security | • Compulsory program for most workers (federal government civilian employees and the military are not covered) that makes payments to retirees based on their average earnings over their lifetime<br>• Not means-tested | • Persons 62 or older who have paid into the system<br>• Widows, widowers, and dependent children of deceased workers |
| Disability Insurance | • Payments to workers with disabilities that make it impossible for them to work<br>• Eligible after six months | • Workers with disabilities who are no longer able to work |
| Medicare | • Part A: Compulsory hospital insurance that helps pay for inpatient hospital services, nursing care, hospice care, and some home health care<br>• Part B: Voluntary medical insurance that pays for such services as doctor visits and lab tests<br>• Part D: Voluntary plan that helps pay for prescription drugs | • People 65+ who have paid into the system and those with disabilities<br><br><br>• People eligible for Part A who pay a monthly fee<br>• People eligible for Part A who pay a monthly fee |
| Medicaid | • Joint program between the federal government and the states<br>• Pays the cost of medical care for low-income persons | • Families and individuals whose incomes fall below a certain level<br>• Includes elderly, the blind, and those with disabilities |
| Supplemental Nutrition Assistance Program ("food stamps") | • Federal program delivered through the states to counties and cities<br>• Supplements incomes to encourage the purchase of nutritionally adequate diets | • Low-income households |
| Temporary Assistance for Needy Families | • Federal and state program<br>• States determine eligibility (within federal guidelines) and benefit levels | • Families that need temporary assistance while becoming self-sufficient. |
| Unemployment Insurance | • Federal and state program<br>• The federal government deducts the money from workers' paychecks and holds the money in the Treasury<br>• States set weekly benefits and eligibility requirements, which vary from state to state<br>• Federal government sets the number of weeks a worker may receive benefits | • Workers (full-time and, in many states, part-time) who are laid off or terminated |

*Most government spending on scientific research is discretionary spending because it is made at policy makers' discretion rather than being mandated by law.*

ended the Cold War, defense spending declined. Beginning in late 2001 with the invasion of Afghanistan and continuing in 2003 with the invasion of Iraq, spending on national defense rose sharply. By 2009, defense spending had outpaced spending on Social Security. More than half the nation's budget for discretionary spending was being used for national defense.

The budget can only be cut so much. Mandatory spending is, well, mandatory, and the public expects certain government services and programs to continue. Discretionary spending is easier to adjust year to year. Each year the president and Congress attempt to align the budget with their priorities for the nation and to be responsible with taxpayers' money. They add to some programs, trim others, and cut still others. The process is difficult because every cut hurts the people who were receiving the money, even as it may help others. Imagine being a politician from a state where cuts are proposed. Reelection may depend on your ability to protect funds that are flowing to the voters you represent. The existence of many worthwhile projects and reluctance to cut programs or raise taxes lead to government expenditures that far exceed revenues.

## ECONOMICS IN ACTION

# How Do State and Local Governments Spend Their Money?

State and local governments spend their revenue for many of the same things as the federal government: education, health services, and support for the poor. Actually, some of the funding for state and local spending comes from the federal government. In 2010, the federal government provided $624 billion to state and local governments. In the process of this *intergovernmental spending*, money is transferred from one level of government to another in the form of *grants-in-aid* to fund programs. Medicaid, unemployment insurance, highway construction and repairs, and education are among the state and local programs for which the federal government provides some funding. For example, the federal government's contribution to elementary and secondary education is about 8

percent of the total cost in any given year. In 2010, local governments spent $566 billion to fund elementary and secondary education, and the states spent $8 billion.

In total, state and local governments took in $3.17 trillion in revenue from all sources in 2010. Table 44.2 shows how they spent it. What it does not show is the amount of debt that state and local governments carried. In 2010, the average amount owed by state governments per resident—the average per capita debt—was $3,600. Between 1999 and 2008, state and local debt as a percentage of GDP rose from 12.8 percent to 15.5 percent. The longer the recession that began in December 2007 lasted, the higher the debt as a percentage of GDP climbed, as tax revenues fell and demands on government social services increased.

## Table 44.2 State and Local Government Spending, Fiscal Year 2010

| CATEGORY | STATE GOVERNMENTS (MILLIONS OF DOLLARS) | LOCAL GOVERNMENTS (MILLIONS OF DOLLARS) |
| --- | --- | --- |
| Intergovernmental | $486,025 | $13,998 |
| Elementary/secondary education | 7,892 | 566,137 |
| Higher education | 202,964 | 39,765 |
| Other education including libraries | 43,655 | 11,575 |
| Public welfare | 404,331 | 52,377 |
| Hospitals | 58,708 | 84,147 |
| Health services | 40,065 | 41,433 |
| Employment security | 5,109 | 48 |
| Veterans services | 793,609 | 0 |
| Highways and roads | 93,097 | 62,773 |
| Airports | 1,724 | 21,404 |
| Parking facilities | 7,436 | 1,672 |
| Sea and inland port facilities | 1,245 | 4,084 |
| Fire protection for local government only and police | 12,376 | 125,746 |
| Corrections and other law enforcement | 46,095 | 26,844 |
| Natural resources, parks, and recreation | 24,275 | 45,116 |
| Housing and community development | 10,715 | 42,777 |
| Sewage and solid waste management | 3,399 | 72,263 |
| Governmental operations including judicial and legal, finance, building maintenance | 47,044 | 50,963 |
| Utilities | 23,507 | 182,678 |
| Unemployment insurance, employee retirement; workers' compensation for states only | 321,204 | 38,590 |
| Interest on debt | 45,297 | 60,424 |

SOURCE: www.census.gov/govs/estimate.

**DID YOU GET IT?**
Which takes the larger share of state spending: health services or public welfare? Which takes the largest share of local spending: natural resources, parks and recreation, or police and fire protection? How does the amount that state and local governments spend on housing and community development compare?

# MODULE 44 REVIEW AND ASSESSMENT

## Summing Up the Key Ideas: Match the following terms to the correct definitions.

A. Treasury bill
B. Treasury note
C. Treasury bond
D. Face value

E. Coupon payments
F. Government security
G. Fiscal year
H. Federal budget

I. Mandatory spending
J. Entitlement programs
K. Means-tested
L. Transfer payments

M. Appropriation bills
N. Discretionary spending

_____ 1. The period of time over which the federal government budget applies; begins on October 1 and ends on September 30.

_____ 2. Programs that people are entitled to by law if they meet certain qualifications.

_____ 3. A security issued by the U.S. Treasury that pays interest in the form of coupon payments and matures in 2, 3, 5, or 10 years.

_____ 4. Government spending that is not required by existing law; rather, it is authorized annually by Congress and the president.

_____ 5. A plan for how the federal government will spend money over the coming fiscal year.

_____ 6. Eligibility for these programs depends on the prospective recipients' income.

_____ 7. A document that represents government's promise to repay a certain amount of money over time.

_____ 8. A security issued by the U.S. Treasury that pays interest in the form of coupon payments and matures in 30 years.

_____ 9. The amount of money to be repaid to the holder of a security; also called the par value.

_____ 10. Payments for which the government receives no goods or services in return.

_____ 11. Payments of a small percentage of the face value of a security.

_____ 12. Spending that is required by law.

_____ 13. A security issued by the U.S. Treasury that matures in 4, 13, 26, or 52 weeks.

_____ 14. Separate spending bills that are part of the budgeting process.

## Analyze: Do the following characteristics apply to **Treasury bills**, **Treasury notes**, or **Treasury bonds**? Indicate each type of security to which each characteristic applies. (There may be more than one answer for each characteristic.)

T-BILL, T-NOTE, OR T-BOND?

1. Its price is determined at auction.   _____

2. Coupon payments are an incentive to purchase.   _____

3. Its price may be greater than its face value.   _____

4. Its face value is repaid in one year or less.   _____

5. It is always sold at a discounted price.   _____

**Apply:** In the following situations, determine if the type of spending described is **mandatory** or **discretionary**.

MANDATORY OR DISCRETIONARY?

1. Social Security payments to retirees _____

2. job retraining for unemployed workers _____

3. Medicare payments for a covered patient _____

4. repair and replacement of bridges and roads _____

5. national defense spending _____

6. Children's Health Insurance Program payments _____

# MODULE 45

# Deficits and the National Debt

**KEY IDEA:** When the federal government spends more than it receives in revenues, it runs a deficit for the year and adds to the national debt.

## OBJECTIVES

- **To identify the difference between an annual deficit and the national debt.**
- **To explain how deficits and debt are related.**
- **To analyze the effects of the national debt on individuals and firms.**

## A History of Deficit Spending

Little did the framers of the Constitution know that granting the federal government the power to borrow money "on the credit of the United States" would someday add up to a debt in excess of $16 trillion. Beginning with the Great Depression, the size and programs of the federal government have shown marked growth. The government has come to rely on **deficit spending**—spending in excess of revenues—as a way to fund program expansion that outpaces revenue expansion. As a result, the federal government has spent more money than it received in all but four years since 1969. However, borrowing is not new to Americans. The nation's founders financed the American Revolution with deficit spending. The next major round of borrowing by the federal government occurred during the Civil War.

*It is difficult for the government to collect enough in taxes to pay for its expenses, especially in times of war and recession.*

**Deficit spending** is spending in excess of revenues.

**A budget deficit or budget surplus** is the difference between the amount of government payments and the amount of government revenues in a particular year. It is a deficit when the payments exceed the revenues and a surplus when the revenues exceed the payments.

**The national debt** is the amount of money that the federal government has borrowed over time to fund annual budget deficits and has not yet repaid.

## DEBT, DEFICITS, AND SURPLUSES

To explain the effects of government borrowing, it is first necessary to distinguish between annual *budget deficits* and the *national debt*. An annual **budget deficit** is the difference between the amount the government pays out and the amount it collects in revenues in a particular year. Figure 45.1 shows the budget deficits between 1980 and 2011. Notice that in four of those years, 1998 through 2001, the line rises into positive territory. This indicates an annual **budget surplus**, which occurs when government revenue is greater than outlays in a particular year. The booming economy of the 1990s led to higher incomes and profits, and thus to higher tax collections. Cuts

in government programs and reductions in the size of the federal government also contributed to the budget surpluses.

The **national debt** is the amount of money that the federal government has borrowed over time to fund annual budget deficits and has not yet repaid. The national debt also includes the amount of interest paid to investors who lent the government money to cover the debt by purchasing U.S. Treasury securities. When there is an annual budget deficit, the national debt grows. An annual budget surplus can be used to pay off some of the debt.

The national debt consists of two kinds of debt: money owed to investors and money the government owes to itself. The investors are individuals, banks, pensions (retirement) fund managers, insurance companies, and similar firms, both domestic and foreign. These investors lend money to the government by purchasing U.S. Treasury securities. The money that is owed to investors is called **public debt**. The public debt is a meaningful measure of debt as far as the economy is concerned because it reflects borrowing from investors who might invest elsewhere in the economy if the public debt were reduced. The government also borrows from its own programs such as Social Security, Medicare, and federal employee pensions. For example, if the Social Security program collects money it won't need for several years, the money can be lent to other government agencies. Money the government owes to itself is known as **intragovernmental debt**. As of December 7, 2012, the public debt was $11.575 trillion and the intergovernmental debt was $4.790 trillion. Figure 45.2 shows the public debt from 1980 to 2011.

The **public debt** is the money owed to investors by the federal government.

The **intragovernmental debt** is the money the federal government owes to government programs such as Social Security and Medicare.

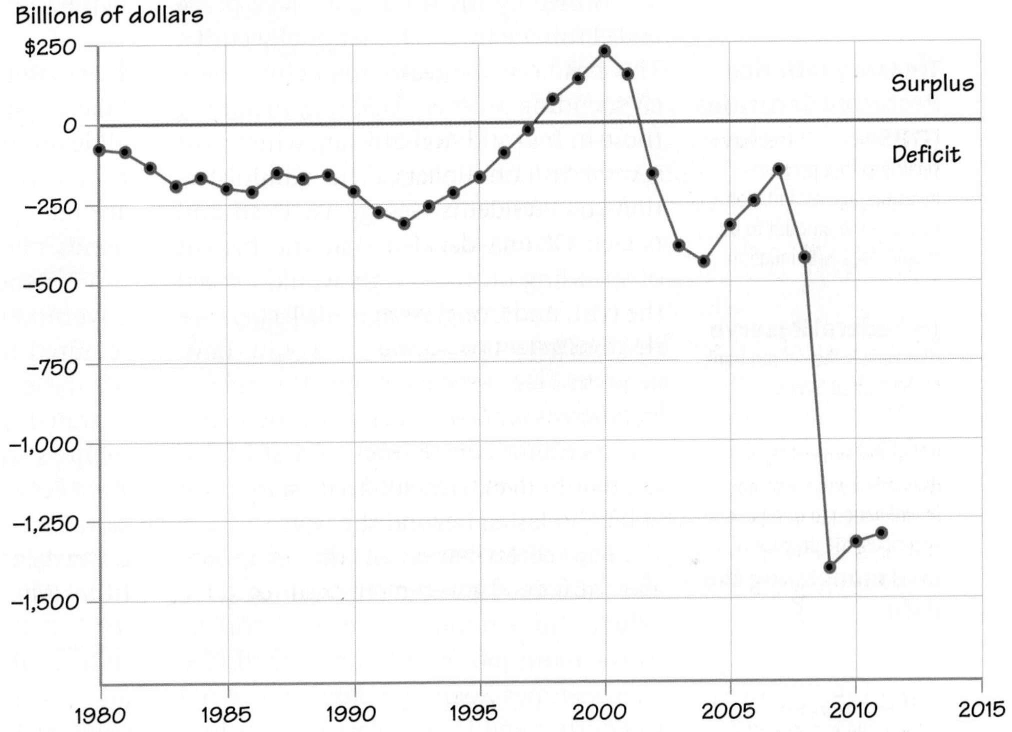

**Figure 45.1** Budget Deficits and Surpluses, 1980–2011

If the government takes in more money than it spends in a particular year, the result is a budget surplus. If the government spends more than it takes in, there is a budget deficit. The size of budget surpluses and deficits fluctuates considerably as economic conditions change.
**DID YOU GET IT?** Between which two years was there a transition from a budget surplus to a budget deficit?
SOURCE: Office of Management and Budget.

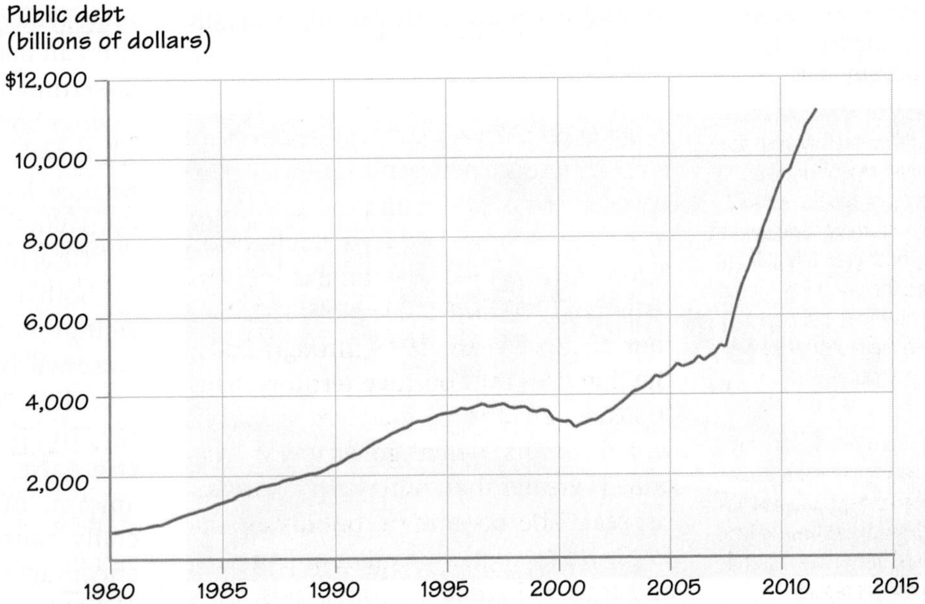

Billions of dollars

**Figure 45.2** Public Debt, 1980–2011

The public debt is the accumulation of annual deficits and surpluses of the past. When there is an annual budget deficit, the public debt grows.
**DID YOU GET IT?** In which five-year period did the public debt increase the most? In which five-year period did the public debt increase the least?
SOURCE: U.S. Department of the Treasury.

Public debt (billions of dollars)

A **balanced budget** is a budget designed to equate expected revenues with planned expenditures.

**Treasury Inflation-Protected Securities** (**TIPS**) are U.S. Treasury securities that protect investors against inflation because the amount to be repaid rises with inflation.

The **Federal Reserve** (the Fed) is the central bank of the United States.

When the Federal Reserve uses money that was not in circulation to purchase securities, the practice is called **monetizing the debt**.

*The National Debt Clock keeps track of the money owed by the federal government.*

A **balanced budget** is a budget designed to equate expected revenues with planned expenditures. If the budget is successfully balanced, no change occurs in the national debt.

## Reasons for Annual Deficits

Most annual budget deficits are planned. As attractive as it sounds to balance the budget, it is often argued that borrowing now will have worthwhile payoffs later on. When the country is at war, the burden of debt on future generations can be justified by the need to achieve peace and eliminate threats to national security. This has been the reasoning behind deficit spending on every U.S. war, including those in Iraq and Afghanistan, which cost several trillion dollars. The administrations of Presidents George W. Bush and Barack Obama decided that the benefit of spending on these wars would exceed the cost, and Congress agreed. To balance the budget, tax increases would have been needed to accompany the spending increases. Taxes were not raised, and the spending contributed to a string of annual budget deficits that started in 2002 and lasted beyond the wars.

The performance of the economy also affects the need to run deficits. When the economy weakens, workers worry about job security and spend less. As consumer spending falls, firms sell less output and lay off workers or reduce their work hours. Because individuals and firms are both earning less, the government receives less in tax revenue. At the same time, government outlays for social services such as food stamps, unemployment insurance, and Medicaid rise, because more people need assistance. Also, as discussed earlier in this chapter, the government may try to jumpstart the economy with added spending and tax rebates. These measures add to annual deficits and the national debt. But as with expenditures on national security, the benefits of measures that help end a recession can make it worthwhile to run a deficit.

## Borrowing to Fund Deficits

Like most individuals, governments at all levels borrow money so that at times they can spend more money than they are taking in. The sale of U.S. Treasury bonds, bills, and notes generates money to fund deficit spending by the federal government. The government is then required to pay back the purchase price of these securities and interest over a stated period of time. The government also sells **Treasury Inflation-Protected Securities** (**TIPS**), which as their name implies, protect investors against inflation. The protection comes from adjustment of the amount repaid for inflation using the Consumer Price Index. TIPS are issued in terms of 5, 10, and 30 years and are offered with a par value of $100. Like T-notes and T-bonds, they are sold at auction and offer interest payments every six months. Investors can make smaller investments in the government by buying series E, EE, and I savings bonds, which start at $25 or $50. All these government securities serve to finance deficit spending, including interest payments on the national debt.

Government securities are purchased by both private investors and the U.S. central bank, known as the **Federal Reserve** (the Fed). When the Fed creates new money to purchase securities, the practice is called **monetizing the debt**. The resulting increase in the amount of money in circulation generally causes interest rates to fall and encourages business and consumer

*If the debt limit is reached midyear, Congress must raise it, or nonessential government operations will shut down.*

spending to rise. The Fed chose this course of action during the financial crisis that began in 2007, with several rounds of security purchases, including a $600 billion dollar purchase of Treasury bonds that began in 2010.

## The National Debt Limit

Credit cards have limits and so does the national debt. The national debt ceiling, or **debt limit**, is the highest amount that the national debt can reach, as authorized by Congress. When the government is in danger of reaching this debt limit, Congress must raise it, or the government will no longer be authorized to borrow. If the government cannot borrow to fund its operations in this situation, it will run out of money and shut down. Between 1940 and 2012, the national debt limit rose from $45 billion to $16.4 trillion.

The national debt is seldom far below the debt limit. To gain perspective on the size of the debt and its limit, it is useful to compare the debt to GDP. In 1980, the national debt was about 33 percent of GDP and the portion owed to the public was about 25 percent of GDP. By 2011 the national debt had risen to equal GDP and the public debt was about 65 percent of GDP. Figure 45.3 shows how the public debt-to-GDP ratio changed over that period. Although the public debt grew between 1995 and 1999, GDP grew faster, lowering the public debt-to-GDP ratio. The wars that started in Afghanistan in 2001 and in Iraq in 2003 weighed heavily on the debt-to-GDP escalation. Wars are costly, and spending during wars has outpaced government revenues throughout the nation's history. Typically, the ratio of debt to GDP decreases when a war ends. In addition to the wars, there were major tax cuts in 2001 and 2003. Then in 2007, the economy experienced a dramatic downturn

as problems in the banking and real estate sectors, the collapse of the stock and bond markets, and a run-up in oil prices dragged down economic activity and ushered in the worst financial crisis since the Great Depression.

The **debt limit** is the highest amount that the national debt can reach, as authorized by Congress.

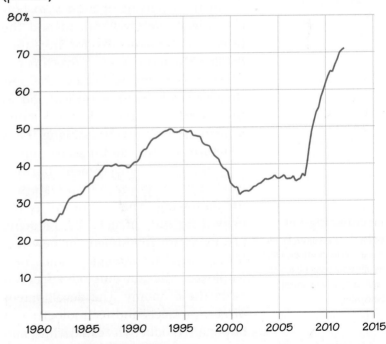

**Public Debt-to-GDP ratio (percent)**

**Figure 45.3** Public Debt as a Percentage of GDP, 1980–2012
**DID YOU GET IT?** How can the debt-to-GDP ratio decrease while debt and GDP are both increasing?
SOURCE: Department of the Treasury and Office of Management and Budget.

*Corporations such as McDonald's compete with the government for investor dollars. If the government borrows too much, it can crowd out investment in the private sector.*

**Dividends** are payments made out of a corporation's profits to owners of its stocks.

The payment of interest on the national debt is called **servicing the debt.**

The **crowding-out effect** is the constraint on private sector borrowing that results from higher interest rates due to government borrowing.

# THE EFFECTS OF THE NATIONAL DEBT

We've discussed several reasons for increasing the national debt. Weighing against them are some undesirable consequences of debt, which can include higher interest rates, a burden for future generations, and vulnerability due to foreign debt ownership.

## Interest Rates

With corporations selling stocks and bonds and the government selling its own securities, investors face choices about where to put their money. Investors seek a high return on their investment. To appeal to investors, most corporations such as McDonald's or Apple periodically give payments known as **dividends** to the owners of their stocks. Similarly, the federal government makes interest or *coupon* payments to the owners of its T-notes, T-bonds, and TIPS. The government offers a competitive rate of return and a lower level of risk than investments in corporations.

In their pursuit of money to borrow, the federal government and the private sector compete for investors' dollars. The more money investors put into government securities, the less they have to invest in firms. And as the federal government borrows more, firms must give investors higher rates of return to compete for scarce funds. At some point, government borrowing begins to squeeze out private sector borrowing. This is known as the **crowding-out effect.** By reducing private sector investment in new factories, new technologies, and new employees, the crowding-out effect can harm the economy. The development of new products and technologies can be put off. Productivity can decline, and workers' incomes can suffer. Crowding-out is much less likely to occur when the economy is weak and interest rates are low.

## The Burden on Future Generations

Like everyone who borrows, the federal government must pay interest on its loans. This is called **servicing the debt.** By 2011, the annual interest on the national debt had grown to $454 billion. Each year that the government runs a deficit and borrows more money, the size of the interest payment grows. Were it not for the debt, this money could be used to fund government programs or reduce tax payments.

Besides losing the potential for current programs, future programs are also endangered because future tax payments must go toward servicing the debt. As the national debt grows, interest payments take a larger and larger chunk of the annual federal budget. The 1993 interest payment was $292 billion, or an average of $1,123 for every U.S. citizen. In 2011, it was $454 billion, or $1,457 for every U.S. citizen. In order to pay off the entire 2012 national debt, U.S. citizens would have to pay an average of $50,172 each.

## The Risk of Foreign Investment

Another concern about the national debt is the amount owed to foreign investors. This amount grew from $650.3 billion in 1993 to more than $5.1 trillion in 2012. However, it would be more expensive for the U.S. government to raise this amount of money at home in addition to what it already raises through taxation and selling Treasury securities. The downside is that the interest payments on this foreign-owned debt end up in the foreign individuals' or companies' homelands, rather than in the U.S. economy. On the other hand, the U.S. economy benefits from this foreign investment. Without it, the government would have less to spend, and government spending helps boost the economy.

The dependence of the United States on foreign investment became a critical concern during the worldwide economic downturn beginning in

2007. China is a principal buyer of new U.S. debt, and because of China's own financial problems, there were fears that it would decrease, or even end, its purchase of U.S. Treasuries. China did not end up making any big changes in its investment strategies during the recession.

## Some Good News about the National Debt

A large debt poses the types of problems we have discussed, but there is some good news. While persistent debt can only spell trouble for an individual, the U.S. government can stomach debt in ways no individual can. For starters,

## ECONOMICS IN ACTION

# What Is the Future of Social Security?

The ability of the Social Security Administration to keep sending out checks depends on a mix of demographics, economics, and politics. The Old Age, Survivors, and Disability Insurance (OASDI) program, better known as Social Security, was created in 1935. At that time, the average life expectancy in the United States was 61. Today, people who reach 65 can expect to live another 20 years or more.

The population was also only 127 million in 1935, compared with over 315 million today. In 2008, the 70 million people in the "baby boomer" generation born between 1946 and 1964 began to retire. Over time, this enormous number of people will put a strain on the Social Security funds, because there is not a similarly large population of young workers following them. Instead of 2.9 workers paying into the Social Security system for every one person receiving benefits as there were in 2011, there will be only 2.0 workers by 2035.

Workers' contributions to Social Security are deducted from their paychecks or paid on a quarterly basis if the worker is self-employed. This money goes into the Social Security trust fund and is invested on a daily basis in securities called "special issues" of the U.S. Treasury.

Some people fear that the Social Security system will run out of money as the large number of baby boomers become eligible for benefits. There are many options available to keep the

*Social Security checks help people cover their expenses during retirement. As the number of retired people increases, policy changes might prevent the program from running out of money.*

program going. For example, in 2013 workers paid social security tax only on the first $113,700 of their income. If that amount were raised, the Social Security program would receive more revenue. The retirement age has already been increased, and further increases would reduce the cost of maintaining the program. A third option would be to decrease the amount of benefits given to retirees.

### DID YOU GET IT?

**Why do some people think that the Social Security system will run out of money? What changes are being considered for the Social Security system?**

*The United States relies heavily on China to finance its national debt.*

our government can collect taxes and it will not retire, so it can continue collecting taxes indefinitely. The government can also print money, although printing large amounts of money to pay down the debt would cause inflation. None of these advantages provides an easy fix for the national debt, but they, along with lenders' confidence in the government's ability to repay loans, will allow the debt to continue into the foreseeable future.

What about the size of the debt? In absolute terms, it is as large as it ever has been, but so is the gross domestic product. Growth in output and income increases the government's ability to collect taxes and service a growing debt. As a percentage of GDP, our debt is not at a historical high. During World War II, the debt was as high as 122 percent of GDP, whereas in 2011 the debt was about 100 percent of GDP. The national debts of Singapore, Belgium, and Ireland are also roughly equivalent to their GDPs, and the national debt of Japan is about twice as large as its GDP. The economy's ability to withstand a prolonged debt explains why policy makers don't necessarily place debt reduction ahead of competing national priorities, such as national security and the end of recessions.

# MODULE 45 REVIEW AND ASSESSMENT

## Summing Up the Key Ideas: Match the following terms to the correct definitions.

A. Deficit spending
B. Budget deficit
C. Budget surplus
D. National debt
E. Balanced budget
F. Treasury Inflation-Protected Securities
G. Federal Reserve
H. Monetizing the debt
I. Debt limit
J. Public debt
K. Intragovernmental debt
L. Dividends
M. Crowding-out effect
N. Servicing the debt

_____*E*_____ 1. A budget designed to equate expected revenues with planned expenditures.

_____ 2. Spending in excess of revenues.

_____ 3. U.S. Treasury securities that protect investors against inflation because the amount to be repaid rises with inflation.

_____ 4. The constraint on private sector borrowing that results from higher interest rates due to government borrowing.

_____ 5. The highest amount that the national debt can reach as authorized by Congress.

_____ 6. The Central Bank of the United States, known as the Fed.

_____ 7. Payments made out of a corporation's profits to owners of its stock.

_____ 8. The difference between the amount of government payments and the amount of government revenues in a particular year when payments exceed the revenues.

_____ 9. The practice of having the Federal Reserve create new money to purchase securities.

_____ 10. The money owed to investors by the federal government.

_____ 11. The amount of money that the federal government has borrowed over time to fund annual budget deficits and has not yet repaid.

_____ 12. The money the federal government owes to government programs such as Social Security and Medicare.

_____ 13. The difference between the amount of government payments and the amount of government revenues in a particular year when revenues exceed the payments.

_____ 14. The payment of interest on the national debt.

## Analyze and Explain: Determine whether each of the following situations would lead the federal government toward a **budget surplus** or a **budget deficit.** Explain your answer.

|  | BUDGET SURPLUS OR DEFICIT? | EXPLANATION |
|---|---|---|
| 1. Defense spending to fund a war increases, but tax rates are not increased. | | |
| 2. A recession begins, and demands for assistance from the federal government escalate. | | |
| 3. Consumer spending falls, and workers are laid off. | | |
| 4. A prolonged period of peacetime economic prosperity significantly increases the incomes of all Americans. | | |
| 5. A series of national disasters plagues the United States, and demands for federal assistance increase. | | |

## Apply: Indicate how each of the following events would affect the **federal deficit** or **surplus** and the **national debt.**

|  | DEFICIT OR SURPLUS? | DEBT |
|---|---|---|
| 1. There is an unexpected surge in government revenue due to an upturn in the economy. | Surplus | decrease |
| 2. An aging population places increasing demands on Social Security, Medicare, and Medicaid. | deficit | increase |
| 3. The federal government increases its expenditures on the military. | deficit | increase |

# MODULE 46

# Managing the Business Cycle

**KEY IDEA:** The federal government has several tools that sometimes help smooth out contractions and expansions in the economy.

**OBJECTIVES**

- To explain the difference between contractionary and expansionary fiscal policies.
- To analyze the problems associated with economic forecasting.
- To convey the difference between discretionary fiscal policies and automatic stabilizers.

## Fiscal Policy

When few shoppers are in the malls and many workers need jobs, you may hear suggestions that the government should do something about it. To attempt such a fix, the government can use its *fiscal policy* toolbox. **Fiscal policy** is the use of government spending and taxation to pursue the macroeconomic goals of economic growth, full employment, and price stability. The government can lower tax rates or increase its spending to encourage more people to go shopping and lead more employers to make new hires. During an economic expansion, higher tax rates and less government spending can keep prices from rising too rapidly. These fiscal policies are in addition to *automatic stabilizers*, such as the decrease in income tax payments when incomes decrease during a recession, that are built into the economy.

*Economic downturns can leave shopping malls empty.*

*The business of America is business.*
—Calvin Coolidge, president of the United States, 1923–1929

**Fiscal policy** is the use of government spending and taxation to pursue economic growth, full employment, and price stability.

**Macroeconomic equilibrium** occurs when aggregate supply equals aggregate demand.

## LOOKING FOR MACROECONOMIC EQUILIBRIUM

We have seen that the economy has its ups and downs in the form of recurring business cycles during which real GDP expands and contracts. During expansions, real GDP rises. Compared to the state of the economy during a contraction, consumers spend more money, firms make more output and investments, the inflation rate is high, and the unemployment rate is low. During contractions, real GDP falls. Consumers pull back on spending, firms make less output and fewer investments, prices rise more slowly or decline, and good jobs are harder to

come by. The result may be a short, mild recession or a long, deep depression. The federal government seeks to smooth out both extremes of economic activity. The goals are to promote economic growth, stable prices, and full employment.

Figure 46.1 illustrates the economy at **macroeconomic equilibrium**, which is where aggregate supply equals aggregate demand. Directly below this equilibrium on the horizontal axis you will find the equilibrium level of real GDP labeled *Y*. To the left of the macroeconomic equilibrium on the vertical axis you will find the equilibrium price level labeled *PL*.

Fiscal policy can affect the macroeconomic equilibrium by changing aggregate demand. A little more than two thirds of

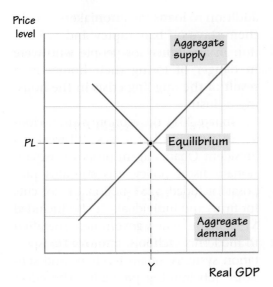

Price level (vertical axis), Real GDP (horizontal axis). Aggregate supply and Aggregate demand curves cross at Equilibrium, with PL on the vertical axis and Y on the horizontal axis.

**Figure 46.1** Macroeconomic Equilibrium
The intersection of the aggregate demand curve and the aggregate supply curve marks the macroeconomic equilibrium. Directly below this equilibrium on the horizontal axis you will find the equilibrium level of real GDP labeled Y. To the left of the macroeconomic equilibrium on the vertical axis you will find the equilibrium price level labeled PL.
**DID YOU GET IT?** What two things can you determine by starting at macroeconomic equilibrium and looking to the axes?

the nation's aggregate demand is made up of consumer demand, which is influenced by the amount of **disposable income**—income after taxes have been removed—available to households. By altering tax policy or transfer payments, fiscal policy can directly affect disposable income. The other type of fiscal policy, government purchases, are themselves part of aggregate demand, which gives the government even more direct influence on the macroeconomic equilibrium.

## Expansionary Policies

When a country is on the brink of recession, the federal government can use **expansionary fiscal policy** to give the economy a boost. This can be any

combination of lower taxes and more government spending on purchases or transfer payments. If successful, the result is a rightward shift of the aggregate demand curve as shown in Figure 46.2. After this shift, aggregate demand exceeds aggregate supply at the beginning price level, $PL_1$. Just as a shortage of orange juice tends to send orange juice prices upward until a new market equilibrium is achieved, a shortage of real GDP tends to send the price level upward until a new macroeconomic equilibrium is reached at a higher level of real GDP. In Figure 46.2, this occurs at a price level of $PL_2$ and a real GDP level of $Y_2$.

As an example of expansionary fiscal policy, the 2009 American Recovery and Reinvestment Act dedicated $787 billion

**Disposable income** is income after taxes have been removed.

**Expansionary fiscal policy** is any combination of government spending and tax cuts meant to spur the economy.

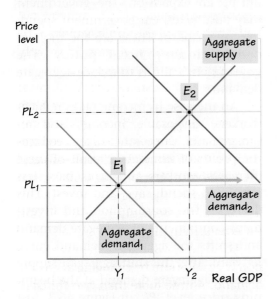

Price level (vertical axis), Real GDP (horizontal axis). Aggregate supply curve with Aggregate demand₁ shifting right to Aggregate demand₂. Equilibrium moves from $E_1$ at ($Y_1$, $PL_1$) to $E_2$ at ($Y_2$, $PL_2$).

**Figure 46.2** Expansionary Fiscal Policy
The government can carry out expansionary fiscal policy by increasing government spending or lowering taxes. The result is a rightward shift of the aggregate demand curve. This causes an increase in real GDP from $Y_1$ to $Y_2$ and an increase in the price level from $PL_1$ to $PL_2$.
**DID YOU GET IT?** Suppose the graph shows what happened when temporary tax cuts went into effect during the last recession. Once they expired, what would you expect to see happen to the aggregate demand curve, *Aggregate demand₂*?

to a combination of changes in tax policy and increases in government spending. Tax breaks for firms and individuals amounted to $287 billion. Payroll taxes were reduced for a majority of workers. First-time home buyers and new car buyers received tax credits. Existing tax credits increased for families and individuals at certain income levels who were paying for a college education. Unemployed workers receiving unemployment benefits no longer had to pay federal income tax on the first $2,400 of benefits. Tax policy was also used to lower the cost of commuting to work, stimulate investment in renewable energy, and make homes more energy efficient.

Beyond the benefits of supporting valued activities and vulnerable individuals, the tax cuts were intended to stimulate the economy. With more money in their pockets, consumers would visit stores to buy more goods, thus decreasing store inventories. The stores would then order replacement goods, which would cause manufacturers to buy more raw materials and hire more workers. In the meantime, firms all along the chain of supply—trucking companies, oil companies, railroads, farmers, food processors, textile mills, advertising agencies, and so on—would benefit from this renewed consumer spending. In these ways, fiscal policy's effect on aggregate demand is expanded by additional rounds of spending by individuals and firms.

The American Recovery and Reinvestment Act also included increases in spending by the federal government. It provided $192 billion in direct aid to states to help them pay for Medicaid, increase unemployment benefits, and expand and upgrade the Medicaid and Medicare offerings. In addition, the federal government provided $308 billion for programs such as job training, highway and bridge construction and repair, modernization of the energy grid, expansion of rural Internet access, extension of food stamp provision, and support for programs that help the poor find housing. This stimulus was the largest such government spending program since the Great Depression. It came in

addition to loans for automakers to help them stave off bankruptcy and $75 billion in assistance for people who were in danger of losing their homes as a result of the ongoing crisis in the housing industry.

In late 2011 the economy was no longer in recession but it was still weak, so President Obama again proposed expansionary fiscal policy. His stimulus proposal included $253 billion in tax cuts for firms and individuals. It also included $194 billion in new government spending to modernize schools, improve transportation systems, retain teachers, and subsidize job training programs. The effect of such government spending is similar to that of tax cuts, although it generally takes longer to affect the economy, as discussed later in this module. New projects create demand for workers and materials, which cuts unemployment, elevates business profits, and spurs investment by firms. More workers making more output means more income and more consumer spending on goods and services. Congress passed a scaled-down version of the president's request.

## Contractionary Policies

The danger of an expanding economy is that it can heat up too quickly and cause inflation. The overall level of prices for goods and services shoots upward as aggregate demand rises faster than aggregate supply. To slow the economy during an expansion, the government may raise taxes, cut government spending, or do both. These are the tools of **contractionary fiscal policy**. The government's aim is to reduce aggregate demand.

An increase in income taxes reduces workers' disposable income, and an increase in corporate taxes reduces the profits of firms. As a result of these increases, workers and firms have less money to spend, save, and invest. This decreases the consumption and investment components of aggregate demand and shifts the aggregate demand curve leftward. After this shift, aggregate supply exceeds aggregate demand at the beginning price level, $PL_1$ in Figure 46.3. Just

**Contractionary fiscal policy** is any combination of government spending cuts and tax increases meant to slow the economy down.

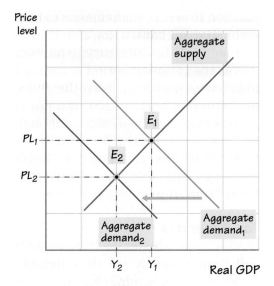

Price level

Aggregate supply

$E_1$

$PL_1$

$E_2$

$PL_2$

Aggregate demand$_2$

Aggregate demand$_1$

$Y_2$    $Y_1$

Real GDP

**Figure 46.3** Contractionary Fiscal Policy
The government can carry out contractionary fiscal policy by decreasing government spending or raising taxes. The result is a leftward shift of the aggregate demand curve. This causes a decrease in real GDP from $Y_1$ to $Y_2$ and a decrease in the price level from $PL_1$ to $PL_2$.
**DID YOU GET IT?** What effect does a decrease in government spending have on aggregate demand, the price level, and real GDP?

as a surplus of orange juice sends orange juice prices downward until a new market equilibrium is achieved, a surplus of real GDP sends the price level downward until a new macroeconomic equilibrium is reached at a lower level of real GDP. In Figure 46.3, this occurs at a price level of $PL_2$ and a real GDP level of $Y_2$.

A reduction in government spending has a similar effect. The federal government employs several million people, hires thousands of outside contractors, and buys billions of dollars' worth of goods and services. When the government cuts its spending by a few billion dollars here and there, the suppliers of goods and services and their employees feel the effects. The government spending component of aggregate demand falls, and as the former beneficiaries of government spending sell less and earn less, they spend less as well, all of which causes a leftward shift in aggregate demand.

If the government cuts spending or raises taxes too much, there is danger that efforts to tame an expansion will result in a contraction. Likewise, excessive spending increases or tax cuts during a contraction could spur problematic inflation. It thus takes great care to forecast the effects of fiscal policy and push just hard enough on the economy to work out the kinks without causing new ones—which is easier said than done.

# DISCRETIONARY FISCAL POLICIES

The tax changes and spending programs we have discussed so far are *discretionary fiscal policies*. The president and Congress must pass new laws to make them happen. Increasing the period over which unemployed workers receive unemployment insurance benefits is another discretionary fiscal policy that can be used to combat a recession. Unemployment insurance benefits typically last 26 weeks. Extending the number of weeks the jobless receive benefits during a prolonged recession has two advantages. It helps those in need and it adds purchasing power to the economy. For example, in the midst of the recession that began in 2007, President Bush and Congress extended jobless benefits for an additional 13 weeks. This added an estimated $850 million to the economy in New York State alone. In 2010, President Obama and Congress extended the duration of jobless benefits to up to 99 weeks and made more unemployed workers eligible for them.

Discretionary fiscal policy has also been used to form *public works programs*. For example, during the Great Depression, President Franklin Roosevelt proposed and Congress passed legislation creating a number of government-funded programs that put people to

*During the Great Depression, the Works Progress Administration created jobs for artists, among other workers. Their artwork was displayed in schools, hospitals, and libraries.*

work. Among them were the Civilian Conservation Corps and the Works Progress Administration.

Naturally, policies that increase taxes or cut spending are less popular with the public, but they have been used to fight inflation. President Lyndon Johnson and Congress approved a 10 percent tax surcharge in 1968, a risky move in an election year. Similarly, President Jimmy Carter proposed a $50 billion tax increase during a period of high inflation shortly before the 1980 election. Despite the political risks, these presidents considered it necessary to get the inflation rate down.

# AUTOMATIC STABILIZERS

In addition to discretionary fiscal policies, the economy has a set of existing programs that work as **automatic stabilizers** to help moderate the economy. As the term implies, neither the president nor Congress has to act in order to set these forces in motion. Two of these stabilizers—tax revenues and transfer payments—are already part of existing laws. Although it is not a fiscal policy, a third automatic stabilizer—personal savings—varies according to whether the economy is experiencing a contraction or an expansion.

The function of automatic stabilizers is to smooth out the business cycle and help prevent a slide into a recession or inflationary period. However, as the troughs and peaks of the business cycle show, the automatic stabilizers are not always successful in evening out economic growth. If they were, the government would never need to step in with discretionary fiscal

policies. However, thanks in part to the automatic stabilizers—imperfect tools as they may be—the nation has not relived the Great Depression or the high inflation of the 1970s. Even the severe recession that began in 2007 was not as deep as the Great Depression, although by some measures the financial shock that caused the recession was larger than the one that precipitated the Great Depression.

## Tax Revenues

During an expansion, households and firms generally see their incomes increase. Higher earnings lead to higher tax payments. For firms, higher tax payments reduce the ability to raise wages, invest in new facilities and technologies, and initiate new research and development. Higher tax payments also reduce the amount of additional disposable income available to individuals as the result of a pay raise. Because of the dampening effect taxes place on new expenditures, the expansion of aggregate demand is slowed, as is the rise in the price level.

The opposite occurs when the economy is contracting. Firms and households earn less money, so they pay less in taxes. As a result, firms and households have more money to spend, save, and invest than they would if their taxes stayed the same. The effect is to slow the drop in aggregate demand, and thus slow recessionary tendencies in the economy.

**Automatic stabilizers** are changes in taxation and transfer payments that moderate changes in GDP and do not require authorization from the government.

*During an expansion, higher tax payments have a dampening effect on consumer spending. During a contraction, lower tax payments leave consumers with more to spend than if taxes stayed the same.*

THINKSTOCK

## Transfer Payments

Module 44 introduced government spending on transfer payments that stem from entitlement programs. Among them, unemployment insurance is both a discretionary fiscal tool and an automatic stabilizer. A worker who is laid off can apply for a weekly unemployment insurance payment. The availability of this payment is automatic for 26 weeks once a person demonstrates eligibility. The discretionary aspect of unemployment insurance comes from the option to extend payments for a longer period, which requires action from Congress and the president.

Other transfer payments affected by a recession include Temporary Assistance to Needy Families (TANF) and food stamp benefits. Benefits do not rise, but as with unemployment insurance, more people become eligible to receive these benefits as the economy weakens and people lose income. The increase in transfer payments is also one reason why the federal budget deficit increases during a recession. As more people receive food stamps, for example, the amount of money needed to fund the program increases. As the economy improves again, the rising incomes of many recipients make them no longer eligible for TANF and food stamps.

As a result of the additional money pumped into the economy through transfer payments in bad economic times, aggregate demand—and thus real GDP—do not decline as dramatically as they would without transfer payments. Likewise, the decline in transfer payments in good economic times has a moderating effect on the rise in aggregate demand and real GDP.

## Supply-Side Policy

Policy designed to stabilize or stimulate the economy by changing aggregate demand is called **demand-side policy**. As an alternative, **supply-side policy** aims to stimulate the economy by increasing aggregate supply. We have seen that aggregate supply increases when the cost of producing goods and services decreases. If lower taxes on firms or less government regulation decreases the cost of production, the resulting increase in aggregate supply can boost real GDP and decrease the price level.

Supply-side policies became popular in the 1980s with the embrace of President Ronald Reagan, among others. Supply-side advocates sought to increase the incentives for work by lowering tax rates for individuals and firms. They argued that when workers pay lower taxes they keep more of their earnings and should be willing to work more. As a result, they earn more money to spend, save, and invest. In the long term, this should raise economic activity. In practice, the effects have been mixed.

The downside of lower taxes can be a decrease in tax collections and an increase in the national debt. The hope for supply-side policies was that lower taxes would stimulate so much new economic activity that tax collections would actually increase. President Reagan lowered taxes substantially in 1981, as did President George W. Bush in 2001. When adjusted for inflation, however, tax collections decreased after both these tax cuts. Yet there are merits to the supply-side goals. Whether they consider themselves supply-siders or demand-siders, most policy makers would like to create more incentives for hard work and to eliminate regulations for which the cost exceeds the benefit.

## THE LIMITS OF FISCAL POLICY

The ability of fiscal policy to smooth out the business cycle is limited. To begin with, expenditures on mandatory programs are hard to fine-tune in response to changes in the economy. Other limits involve the time required for solutions to take effect. The influence of politics on fiscal policy presents yet more limits.

**Demand-side policy** is policy meant to stabilize or stimulate the economy by changing aggregate demand.

**Supply-side policy** is policy meant to stimulate the economy by increasing aggregate supply.

## Mandatory Spending

The government may want to decrease spending when inflation is a problem, but much of its spending is inflexible. Changing the spending level on mandatory programs requires changes in the law. Entitlement programs are important to large numbers of voters, which means that proposed changes also face considerable resistance. This makes Congress reluctant to amend the laws. The government is left with limited options. Cuts could be made in military spending, environmental protection enforcement, or medical research, but each of these valued programs has strong advocates and armies of lobbyists working against reductions. For cuts within a budget year, often the best the government can do is to put a hold on authorized funding for some programs. It is easier for the government to cut taxes or increase spending during a recession than to raise taxes or cut spending in an inflationary period.

## Inside Lags

An **inside lag** is a delay between the onset of a problem and the implementation of a solution. Two types of lags make up an inside lag. First, there is the **recognition lag**, which is the time it takes economists and government officials to realize that the economy is experiencing a problem. Economists use models to forecast future inflation and economic downturns, but the forecasts can be inaccurate and there may be disagreement about how to interpret the available information. Even if there is consensus, it takes time for policy makers to be sure that the automatic stabilizers are not enough to turn the economy around.

Between the recognition of a problem and the decision about how to address it there is an **implementation lag**. It can take the president and Congress months to agree on whether to pass a special spending bill or provide tax rebates in a recession, or whether to put a hold on

authorized spending for certain programs or raise taxes to curb rising inflation.

## Outside Lags

Once a policy is enacted, there is an **outside lag** between the policy action and the resulting effect on the economy. An example is the lag time between enactment of the economic stimulus package in early 2008 and its effect on the economy. By the summer of 2008, the economy seemed to be slowing even more and there were fears of a deepening recession. The last stimulus checks had been mailed on July 11. By the following week, Democrats, some Republicans, the presidential candidates, Wall Street, and some economists were calling for another stimulus package. President Bush's response was, "We ought to see how the first one works. Let it run its course. I'm an optimist." He was acknowledging the outside lag of fiscal policy.

## Unintended Consequences

Inside and outside lags present the risk that policy actions will have undesirable effects. If expansionary policy doesn't have its effect until after the economy is out of a recession, it can send the economy into an inflationary period. For example, suppose spending programs proposed during a downturn don't get enacted and implemented until a recovery has begun. The resulting increases in income and subsequent rounds of consumer spending might come after the economy is expanding and add to inflationary pressures.

In the same way, contractionary policy could come too late to affect the inflation it was meant to correct, take effect after the targeted inflationary period has ended, and create unneeded downward pressure on the economy. Fiscal policy needs to be planned carefully and designed to provide the right amount of stimulus before it's too late. Poorly timed efforts can push the economy in the opposite direction of what is intended.

An **outside lag** is the time between a policy action and the resulting effect on the economy.

An **inside lag** is a delay between the onset of a problem and the implementation of a solution.

A **recognition lag** is the time it takes economists and government officials to realize that the economy is experiencing a problem.

An **implementation lag** is the time between the recognition of a problem and the decision about what to do about it.

## PEOPLE IN ECONOMICS

# John Maynard Keynes

**Classical economics**, the school of economic thought that supports minimal government intervention, provided the dominant economic theory from the early 1800s to the 1930s. Then, the inability of the economy to turn itself around during the Great Depression led to new interest in *Keynesian* policies inspired by British economist John Maynard Keynes (1883–1946). A major difference between the two schools of thought is the role of government in overseeing the economy. Classical economists believe the economy will regulate itself over time if left alone. Keynesian economists believe the government needs to step in at times with fiscal policy to help the economy in the short term.

In his popular book, *The General Theory of Employment, Interest and Money*, Keynes argued that when left alone, the economy can fail to steer itself out of a rut for a painfully long time. The recommended remedy was government intervention. The 1936 publication of this message was well timed, as it came on the tail of the Great Depression. The economy's prolonged failure during the Great Depression highlighted the thrust of Keynes's arguments, which became known as **Keynesian economics**. The recession-fighting fiscal policy measures of Presidents Bush and Obama reflect belief in the principles of Keynesian economics.

**DID YOU GET IT?**
What is the central concept of classical economics? How does this differ from the central concept of Keynesian economics?

**Classical economics** is the school of economic thought, dominant from the 1700s to the 1930s, that favors policies with minimal government intervention.

**Keynesian economics** is the school of economic thought, named after British economist John Maynard Keynes, that advocates fiscal policy to mend problems with the economy.

# MODULE 46 REVIEW AND ASSESSMENT

## Summing Up the Key Ideas: Match the following terms to the correct definitions.

A. Fiscal policy
B. Macroeconomic equilibrium
C. Disposable income
D. Expansionary fiscal policy
E. Contractionary fiscal policy
F. Discretionary fiscal policy
G. Automatic stabilizers
H. Demand-side policy
I. Supply-side policy
J. Inside lag
K. Recognition lag
L. Implementation lag
M. Classical economics
N. Keynesian economics
O. Outside lag

_____ 1. A delay between the onset of a problem and the implementation of a solution.

_____ 2. The time between the recognition of a problem and the decision about what to do about it.

_____ 3. Changes in taxation and transfer payments that moderate changes in GDP and do not require authorization from the government.

_____ 4. Income after taxes have been removed.

_____ 5. The school of economic thought named after British economist John Maynard Keynes that advocates fiscal policy to mend problems with the economy.

_____ 6. Any combination of government spending and tax cuts meant to spur the economy.

_____ 7. Taxation and government spending that comes about as a result of new laws.

_____ 8. The school of economic thought dominant from the 1700s to the 1930s that favors laissez-faire policies with minimal government intervention.

_____ 9. Occurs when aggregate supply equals aggregate demand.

_____ 10. Aims to stimulate the economy by increasing aggregate supply.

_____ 11. The time it takes economists and government officials to realize that the economy is experiencing a problem.

_____ 12. The time between a policy action and the resulting effect on the economy.

_____ 13. Designed to help the economy by increasing or decreasing aggregate demand.

_____ 14. The use of government spending and taxation to pursue economic growth, full employment, and price stability.

_____ 15. Any combination of government spending cuts and tax increases meant to slow the economy down.

## Analyze and Explain:

1. Explain the purpose of expansionary fiscal policy.

2. Explain the purpose of contractionary fiscal policy.

3. Determine if the event described in each of the following situations would cause a **recognition lag**, an **implementation lag**, or an **outside lag**.

TYPE OF LAG

a. The president and Congress spend months debating whether to increase spending or cut taxes to help the economy out of a recession. _____

b. There is a debate among economists and government officials about the severity of the problems facing the economy. _____

c. Even after expansionary policy actions have been taken by the government, the economy is slow to come out of the recession. _____

**Apply:** Indicate whether each of the following describes **discretionary fiscal policy**, **mandatory spending**, or an **automatic stabilizer**.

DISCRETIONARY, MANDATORY, OR AUTOMATIC?

1. Income tax revenues decline during a recession because workers earn less income. _____

2. Congress votes to expand the interstate highway system. _____

3. Tax rates for small businesses are lowered. _____

4. Congress decides to increase personal income taxes to slow down inflation. _____

5. Every month, millions of Americans receive Social Security benefits. _____

6. Congress votes to change the age at which individuals can receive Social Security benefits. _____

7. The federal government decides to extend unemployment benefits during a prolonged recession. _____

# THE NEW YORK TIMES

# Governments Move to Cut Spending, in 1930s Echo

BY DAVID LEONHARDT, JUNE 29, 2010

The world's rich countries are now conducting a dangerous experiment. They are repeating an economic policy out of the 1930s—starting to cut spending and raise taxes before a recovery is assured—and hoping today's situation is different enough to assure a different outcome.

In effect, policy makers are betting that the private sector can make up for the withdrawal of stimulus over the next couple of years. If they're right, they will have made a head start on closing their enormous budget deficits. If they're wrong, they may set off a vicious new cycle, in which public spending cuts weaken the world economy and beget new private spending cuts.

The private sector in many rich countries has continued to grow at a fairly good clip in recent months. In the United States, wages, total hours worked, industrial production and corporate profits have all risen significantly. And unlike in the 1930s, developing countries are now big enough that their growth can lift other countries' economies.

On the other hand, the most recent economic numbers have offered some reason for worry, and the coming fiscal tightening in this country won't be much smaller than the 1930s version. From 1936 to 1938, when the Roosevelt administration believed that the Great Depression was largely over, tax increases and spending declines combined to equal 5 percent of gross domestic product.

Back then, however, European governments were raising their spending in the run-up to World War II. This time, almost the entire world will be withdrawing its stimulus at once. From 2009 to 2011, the tightening in the United States will equal 4.6 percent of GDP, according to the International Monetary Fund. In Britain, even before taking into account the recently announced budget cuts, it was set to equal 2.5 percent. Worldwide, it will equal a little more than 2 percent of total output.

Today, no wealthy country is an obvious candidate to be the world's growth engine, and the simultaneous moves have the potential to unnerve consumers, businesses and investors, says Adam Posen, an American expert on financial crises now working for the Bank of England. "The world may be making a mistake, and it may turn out to make things worse rather than better," Mr. Posen said.

---

**DID YOU READ IT?**

1) What does "fiscal tightening" mean? Why does a government sometimes need to do this?

2) What is the difference between the spending cuts proposed for 2009–2011 and those cuts made back in the 1930s?

**WHAT DO YOU THINK?**

1) If a government stops spending, how will the economy keep growing? What will be the source of needed spending?

2) How easy is it for a government to cut spending?

EXCERPTED FROM www.nytimes.com/2010/06/30/business/economy/30leonhardt.html?_r=3&ref=economy&pagewanted=print

## AN INTERVIEW WITH Peter R. Orszag

Peter R. Orszag has served as the director of the Congressional Budget Office (CBO) and Director of the Office of Management and Budget (OMB). He left the government in 2010 and now is a vice chairman of Global Banking at Citigroup.

### What does the director of CBO do?

The CBO's job is to estimate how proposed legislation will affect the budget and the economy, project future spending and tax trends, and issue papers on a wide range of economic topics. While I was at CBO, some of the topics covered income trends among low-income families with children, the impact of immigration reform on the budget, and the cost of ongoing military operations in Iraq and Afghanistan.

My typical week involved lots of interaction with CBO analysts, members of Congress and congressional staff; reviewing and editing drafts of CBO publications; congressional testimony (I have been averaging one almost every other week); and interviews with the media.

### What does the director of OMB do?

The OMB job is significantly different than the CBO one. At OMB, the director is a member of the president's cabinet but also on the White House staff and has both external and internal responsibilities. OMB is much more operational and much less analytical. I spent much less of my time at OMB writing and reviewing analyses than I did at CBO; much more of my time was spent in meetings with other administration officials.

### What did you do in your government jobs that you are most proud of?

I focused a lot of my attention on the important issue of health care, which was

receiving less attention than seemed warranted. At CBO, for example, we created a new Panel of Health Advisers and a new health intern program, and we shifted roughly 20 more people into the health area. At OMB, we helped enact landmark legislation on health care.

### How did you get into this line of work?

I have been interested in public policy since high school, but economic policy did not interest me that much until college, where I took an introductory economics course and ended up majoring in economics. I even took some classes with the author of this textbook! The rest has followed from that.

### What is involved in estimating the effects of taxes and public policies?

Estimating budget effects is like being an economic detective: you have to figure out what proposed legislation would do and then figure out what impact that would have on the budget.

Sometimes the estimates are simple and straightforward, and sometimes they are complex and controversial. For example, CBO's cost estimate of a recent immigration bill was over 40 pages long and considered how the bill's provisions would affect the number of new immigrants, their role in the labor market, their use of government benefits, and how much taxes they would pay.

### What did you learn from economics that was most useful in your jobs in government?

Economics often emphasizes the role of incentives in affecting people's behavior, and that basic insight has proven to be useful in a wide variety of settings. Another key insight emphasized by economics is that correlation need not imply causation. In addition, the growing work in the field of behavioral economics—which examines the various biases that arise because real people don't process information effortlessly and perfectly—is proving to be quite useful in applications such as retirement saving.

**When you were in high school, what type of work did you think you would do?**

Once I got past the obviously unrealistic notion that I would play professional basketball, I wanted to become some sort of government official. In my dreams (high school students should aim high!), I wanted to become the secretary of defense—and wrote a paper my senior year in high school about how to reorganize the Joint Chiefs of Staff.

**How did economics help you in your roles in government?**

A big part of my job at CBO was translating economics into language that members of Congress and Senators could relate to. In addition, an economics background was extremely helpful because it provided insight into most of the issues we faced at both CBO and OMB—from health care to unemployment to the trajectory of government spending and tax revenues.

**Do you have any advice for high school students who are interested in public policy? What are the most important policy issues for their future?**

The five most important economic policy issues for the future, in my opinion, are the rate of productivity growth in the United States, the increasing integration of economies across the globe, the rate at which health care costs grow relative to income, the trend in income disparities, and climate change. Students who focus on any of those topics should be plenty busy in the future!

**How has studying economics and working at high levels in the government affected your work at Citigroup?**

I do two things at Citigroup. First, I advise CEOs of major corporations on their strategic challenges. Second, I interact with investors and provide insight into macroeconomic and other trends. Both of these activities are significantly informed by my economics background.

# CHAPTER 15 REVIEW AND SELF-ASSESSMENT

## REVIEW

### Points to Remember

**MODULE 44: GOVERNMENT REVENUE AND SPENDING**

1. A **Treasury bill** (**T-bill**) is a security issued by the U.S. Treasury that matures in 4, 13, 26, or 52 weeks.

2. A **Treasury note** (**T-note**) is a U.S. Treasury security that pays interest in the form of coupon payments and matures in 2, 3, 5, or 10 years.

3. A **Treasury bond** (**T-bond**) is a U.S. Treasury security that pays interest in the form of coupon payments and matures in 30 years.

4. The **federal budget** is a plan for how the federal government will spend money over the coming fiscal year.

5. The **fiscal year** for the federal government is the period over which the federal budget applies. It begins on October 1 and ends on September 30.

6. **Mandatory spending** is spending that is required by law.

7. **Entitlement programs** are programs that people are entitled to by law if they meet certain qualifications.

8. Eligibility for **means-tested** programs depends on the prospective recipients' income.

9. **Transfer payments** are payments for which the government receives no goods or services in return.

10. **Discretionary spending** is government spending that is not required by existing law; rather, it is authorized annually by Congress and the president.

**MODULE 45: DEFICITS AND THE NATIONAL DEBT**

11. **Deficit spending** is spending in excess of revenues.

12. A **budget deficit** is the difference between the amount of government payments and the amount of government revenues in a particular year when the payments exceed the revenues.

13. A **budget surplus** is the difference between the amount of government payments and the amount of government revenues in a particular year when the revenues exceed the payments.

14. The **national debt** is the amount of money that the federal government has borrowed over time to fund annual budget deficits and has not yet repaid.

15. A **balanced budget** is a budget designed to equate expected revenues with planned expenditures.

16. **Treasury Inflation-Protected Securities** (**TIPS**) are U.S. Treasury securities that protect investors against inflation because the amount to be repaid rises with inflation.

17. The **Federal Reserve** (the Fed) is the central bank of the United States.

18. When the Federal Reserve creates new money to purchase securities, the practice is called **monetizing the debt**.

19. The **debt limit** is the highest amount the national debt can reach, as authorized by Congress.

20. The **public debt** is the money owed to investors by the federal government.

21. The **intragovernmental debt** is the money the federal government owes to government programs such as Social Security and Medicare.

22. **Dividends** are payments made out of a corporation's profits to owners of its stock.

23. The **crowding-out effect** is the constraint on private sector borrowing that results from higher interest rates due to government borrowing.

24. The payment of interest on the national debt is called **servicing the debt**.

**MODULE 46: MANAGING THE BUSINESS CYCLE**

25. **Fiscal policy** is the use of government spending and taxation to pursue economic growth, full employment, and price stability.

26. **Macroeconomic equilibrium** occurs when aggregate supply equals aggregate demand.

27. **Disposable income** is income after taxes have been removed.

28. **Expansionary fiscal policy** is any combination of government spending and tax cuts meant to spur the economy.

29. **Contractionary fiscal policy** is any combination of government spending and tax increases meant to slow the economy down.

30. **Automatic stabilizers** are changes in taxation and transfer payments that moderate changes in GDP and do not require authorization from the government.

31. **Demand-side policy** is policy meant to stabilize or stimulate the economy by changing aggregate demand.

32. **Supply-side policy** is policy meant to stimulate the economy by increasing aggregate supply.

33. An **inside lag** is a delay between the onset of a problem and the implementation of a solution.

34. A **recognition lag** is the time it takes economists and government officials to realize that the economy is experiencing a problem.

35. An **implementation lag** is the time between the recognition of a problem and the decision about what to do about it.

36. An **outside lag** is the time between a policy action and the resulting effect on the economy.

37. **Classical economics** is the school of economic thought, dominant from the 1700s to the 1930s, that favors laissez-faire policies with minimal government intervention.

38. **Keynesian economics** is the school of economic thought, named after British economist John Maynard Keynes, that advocates fiscal policy to mend problems with the economy.

## ASSESSMENT

The following questions are the type your teacher might ask you on a quiz or a test. Practice with these in order to improve your performance on class tests.

### Multiple-Choice Questions

1. The practice of solving macroeconomic problems with the active use of fiscal policy is referred to as

   a. macroeconomic equilibrium.
   b. classical economics.
   c. Orszag economics.
   d. Keynesian economics.

2. The type of federal government spending that is decided on every year by Congress and the president is

   a. entitlement program spending.
   b. discretionary spending.
   c. deficit spending.
   d. surplus spending.

Answer the next two questions based on the following numbers for the federal government:

| YEAR | REVENUE | | EXPENDITURES |
|------|---------|------|--------------|
| 1 | $90 | 30 | $120 |
| 2 | 100 | 20 | 120 |
| 3 | 120 | 0 | 120 |
| 4 | 138 | -8 | 130 |
| 5 | 160 | -20 | 140 |

3. Assume the government has no debt before year 1. At the end of the five-year period shown, the debt for the federal government is

   a. $20.
   b. $22.
   c. $120.
   d. $140.

4. During year 4, the federal government experienced a

   a. budget surplus of $8.
   b. budget deficit of $8.
   c. debt of $8.
   d. budget deficit of $42.

5. The lowering of private investment spending due to higher interest rates caused by federal government borrowing is known as

   a. deficit spending.
   b. supply-side economics.
   c. the crowding-out effect.
   d. Keynesian economics.

6. Which of the following would be considered an example of mandatory spending for the federal government?

   a. space exploration
   b. environmental protection programs
   c. Medicare
   d. national defense

7. Which of the following would have an expansionary effect on an economy?

   a. an increase in taxes
   b. an increase in transfer payments
   c. an increase in the federal government budget surplus
   d. a decrease in the national debt

8. The time it takes economists and government officials to realize that the economy is experiencing a problem is known as

   a. a recognition lag.
   b. an inside lag.
   c. an outside lag.
   d. an implementation lag.

9. Which of the following are considered potential problems associated with an increasing national debt?

   a. the crowding-out effect
   b. servicing the debt
   c. the amount owed to foreign investors
   d. all of the above

10. Which of the following actions by the federal government would have the most contractionary effect on an economy?

   a. increase taxes and increase spending
   b. decrease taxes and decrease spending
   c. increase taxes and decrease spending
   d. decrease taxes and increase spending

## Constructed Response Question

1. At some point in the future, you might find yourself in charge of creating macroeconomic policies. Answer each of the following as a policy maker.

   a. Your economy finds itself in macroeconomic equilibrium. Draw a correctly labeled aggregate supply and aggregate demand diagram of that equilibrium.
   b. On your graph for part *a*, demonstrate the effect of a decrease in consumer spending caused by fears of a coming recession. Identify the new price level and real GDP that would result.
   c. What discretionary fiscal policy measures could you offer to offset the effects shown in part *b*?
   d. What effect would the discretionary fiscal policy measures you identified in part *c* have on the budget and the debt?

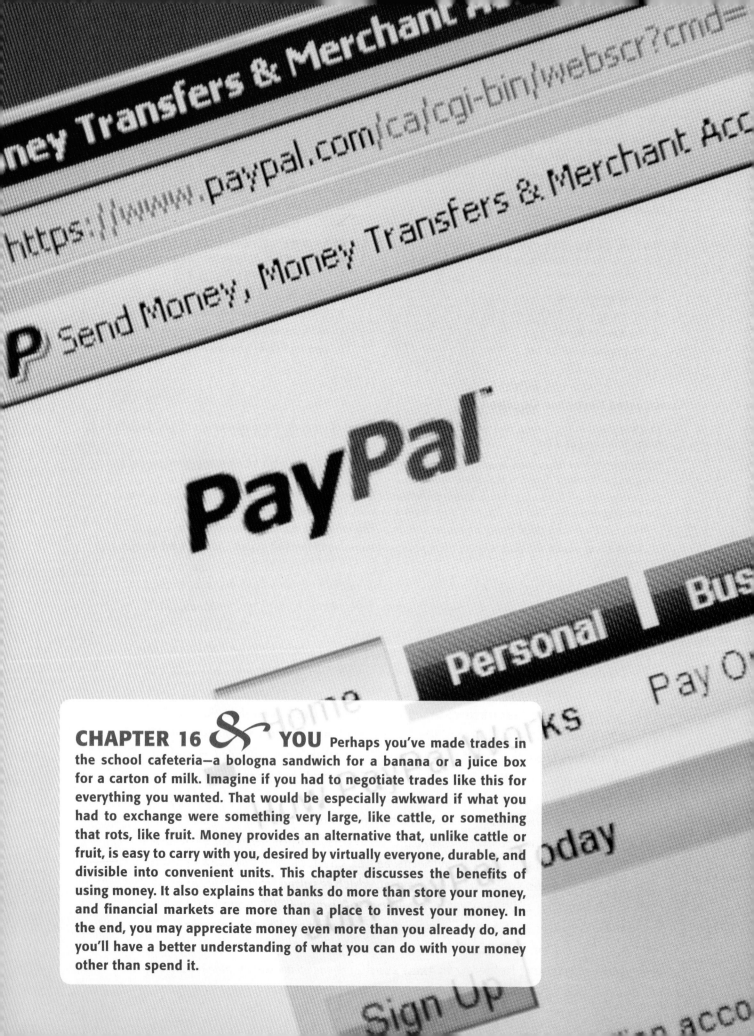

**CHAPTER 16 & YOU** Perhaps you've made trades in the school cafeteria—a bologna sandwich for a banana or a juice box for a carton of milk. Imagine if you had to negotiate trades like this for everything you wanted. That would be especially awkward if what you had to exchange were something very large, like cattle, or something that rots, like fruit. Money provides an alternative that, unlike cattle or fruit, is easy to carry with you, desired by virtually everyone, durable, and divisible into convenient units. This chapter discusses the benefits of using money. It also explains that banks do more than store your money, and financial markets are more than a place to invest your money. In the end, you may appreciate money even more than you already do, and you'll have a better understanding of what you can do with your money other than spend it.

# Money, Banking, and Financial Markets

**MODULE 47: What Is Money?**

**MODULE 48: The Banking System**

**MODULE 49: The Role of Financial Markets in the Real Economy**

## PAYPAL: HOW A NEED LED TO INNOVATION

New technologies have delivered a burst of innovation over the past two decades: video game consoles, cell phones, digital cameras, MP3 players, GPS navigation systems, and the list goes on. The birth of the Internet fundamentally changed the way people communicate and do business. Since the mid-1990s, more and more firms have connected to their employees and customers online.

One of the first businesses to make use of the Internet as its sole link to customers was Amazon, the online retailer. Another was eBay, which revolutionized the auction business by setting up a way for people to auction goods online. As the Internet flourished, entrepreneurs saw it as a great vehicle for sales but struggled with how sellers would be paid. Companies could take credit card payments over the Internet, but was it safe? As can happen with innovations, several groups came up with ideas that would make online payments easier, cheaper, and potentially safer.

One of those ideas became PayPal, which resulted from a merger of two rival firms in 2000. PayPal is a *person-to-person (P2P)* payment service, meaning that it allows one person to send money directly to another. To use PayPal, an individual or firm must register and open a PayPal account online. Account holders can then send and receive money electronically.

They can also hold funds in their accounts for future transactions. PayPal is easy to use, inexpensive, reportedly safer than other P2P payment systems, and can be used for electronic money transfers as well as purchases. PayPal also provides money market accounts and debit cards.

*If you're a fan of websites like eBay and Amazon, you may often need to pay or receive money from people you've never met.*

By 2002, PayPal had become so popular that eBay shut down its own P2P payment business and bought PayPal for $1.4 billion. Many of PayPal's other competitors have gone out of business, too. In 2012, PayPal had operations in 190 global markets, accepted 25 currencies, and managed 117 million active accounts. During 2011, it handled $118.7 billion in transactions.

In the United States, PayPal is considered a money transmitter, not a bank. As a result, it is not regulated by the federal government but is licensed individually by the states. However, PayPal is liable under federal consumer protection laws. Even though money held in PayPal accounts is not directly insured by the Federal Deposit Insurance Corporation (FDIC), the banks where PayPal deposits users' money are insured. Therefore, should a bank holding PayPal money fail, PayPal users would recover their money from the bank, not PayPal. In Europe, PayPal is licensed and regulated as a bank.

This chapter explains the functions and characteristics of money. You will learn how the banking system and financial markets have changed with technological innovations such as e-commerce and online banking. You will also discover the role of the federal government in the banking system and the financial markets after the financial crisis that began in 2007.

## BOTTOM LINE
Money, the banking system, and the financial markets are integral to the smooth functioning of the economy.

*Money speaks sense in a language
all nations understand.*
—Aphra Behn, The Rover,
Part II, Act III, Scene I

# MODULE 47

# What Is Money?

**KEY IDEA:** Money is a medium of exchange, a store of value, and a unit of account.

**OBJECTIVES**

- To identify the functions of money.
- To describe the characteristics of money.
- To explain the sources of money's value.
- To describe the money supply.

## What Makes It Money?

**Money** can be anything that is widely accepted in exchange for goods and services. The coins in your pocket and the bills in your wallet are money in the form of **currency**. Deposits in checking accounts, known technically as *demand deposit accounts*, are another form of money. Before currency and checking accounts existed, a variety of items such as shells and spices served as money. More recently, in places such as prisons where money is not allowed, prisoners have used cigarettes or other scarce objects as money. *ATM cards* and *debit cards* are not money, but like checks, they give you access to the money in your bank account. Credit cards aren't money either, but they assist with transfers of money from buyers to sellers. The same is true of new apps such as Google Wallet that allow purchases using smart phones. It's been said that the best things in life are free, but in more ways than one, money makes it a lot easier to get the things that are not. In this module you'll learn all about the role of money.

*Bills and coins are money, but so are checking deposits and, in some cases, cigarettes, shells, and spices.*

## THE FUNCTIONS OF MONEY

It wouldn't be much fun to live with only the goods and services you can create for yourself. People in every society benefit from trade by making purchases and sales. Before money, people used a system of **barter** to exchange goods and services for other goods and services. A person who made baskets would exchange a basket for, say, a piglet from a farmer who needed a basket. If the farmer didn't need a basket but did need fence repair from a worker who needed a basket, you can see how the series of necessary trades would become complicated.

Bartering still goes on today, especially in the rural areas of developing countries. However, most people pay for goods and services with money. Money simplifies business transactions by serving as a *medium of exchange*, a *store of value*, and a *unit of account*.

### Money as a Medium of Exchange

Money is what you usually give to get whatever good or service you want. As a generally accepted form of payment for virtually anything buyers seek, money serves as a **medium of exchange**. Stones, gold, silver, tea, salt, ivory, furs, and tobacco have all served as money in the past. Over time, money has evolved

**Money** can be anything that is widely accepted in exchange for goods and services.

**Currency** is paper money and coins.

**Barter** is the exchange of goods or services for other goods or services without the use of money.

A **medium of exchange** is something people acquire for the purpose of payment for goods and services.

THINKSTOCK

*Some coins are easier to carry around as a medium of exchange than others.*

A **unit of account** is a standard measure used to set prices and make economic calculations.

A **store of value** is something that can be saved and will hold its value relatively well over time.

into the more convenient forms of currency we use today. It is much easier to carry around a few dollar bills and some coins than, for example, the large stones used as money on Yap Island pictured above. And it is far easier to find a seller who wants to exchange a T-shirt for money than it is to find a seller who wants to barter a T-shirt for a chicken.

## Money as a Store of Value

An ice cream manufacturer or a tomato farmer can create products with a great deal of value, but someone who wants to hold on to that value wouldn't want to hold on to ice cream or tomatoes—they do not store value well! Money, as a **store of value**, can be saved and will hold its value relatively well over time. When you work and save part of the money you earn, you are storing the value of your efforts for later use. When you decide to spend your savings, you are making use of the stored purchasing power of your money. The stored value of your money won't change very much over short periods of time: one dollar next week will still be able to buy about what one dollar buys today.

Over long periods of time, it is likely that some of the value stored in money will be lost due to inflation. As prices

rise during periods of inflation, the purchasing power of money decreases. For example, between 1987 and 2011, the price level in the United States doubled. If enough money to buy two pizzas were placed into a piggy bank in 1987 and taken out in 2011, it would only have bought one pizza in 2011. Fortunately, there are places to put money for long periods that offer interest or returns to help keep up with inflation, such as interest-bearing checking accounts and the various types of investments discussed in Chapter 12.

## Money as a Unit of Account

When you go into a store, tags or signs listing prices in a standard **unit of account**—dollars and cents in the United States—make it easy to see how much each item costs. Without the accounting units that money provides, posting of prices would be an awkward endeavor. Sellers would need to indicate the variety of nonstandard payments they would accept for their goods. A cup of coffee might be offered for a pound of flour, a gallon of gasoline, three packs of gum, or a pair of socks. Using a single standard means that all parties to a business transaction have the same understanding of the price involved.

A single measure of value also makes it possible for a buyer to compare prices easily. Similarly, in deciding which of two after-school jobs to take, the first thing you probably compare is the hourly wage. If prices and wages were listed in nonstandard ways—perhaps in eggs in one place and in seashells in another—comparisons would be difficult.

**DID YOU GET IT?**
Explain each of the three functions of money. Use an example in your explanations.

# CHARACTERISTICS OF MONEY

Given the functions that money must serve, most things don't make the cut. To be considered useful as modern money, an object must be

- durable,
- portable,
- uniform,
- divisible,
- in limited supply, and
- accepted for payment.

Many of the items used in earlier societies as money would not meet these standards. For example, would you want to carry around a stack of furs in your backpack to pay for lunch or a movie? Gems such as diamonds seem to have greater potential as money. They are durable, small enough to carry, and in limited supply. In fact, gems have been accepted as payment in some societies. However, they are not uniform in size or quality and are not easy to divide into smaller units. Early forms of money made of precious metals such as gold and silver do fit these characteristics of modern money.

## Durable and Portable

The currency that we carry around as money would be of little use if it were not small and light enough to be portable. And because it is passed from hand to hand and lives in cramped quarters in our wallets and purses, it needs to be durable. The U.S. Department of the Treasury, which oversees the printing of money, estimates that $1 bills wear out about every 21 months, whereas $100 bills have a life cycle of about 89 months. Worn bills are collected, shredded, and replaced with new bills printed by the federal Bureau of Engraving and Printing. The U.S. Mint produces some 20 billion coins a year, valued at more than $2 billion. Like worn bills, badly worn or bent coins are collected and returned to the Mint. They are then melted down and recycled into new coins.

## Uniform and Divisible

A dollar is a dollar is a dollar, and any dollar will buy any good or services priced at a dollar. If money were not uniform in value, there would be awkward uncertainty about what each unit would buy. Imagine, for example, if money came in the form of distinct pieces of art. More attractive pieces would fetch more in the market, but how much more would have to be worked out between buyers and sellers.

Money must also be divisible so that consumers can pay the exact price for each purchase. Suppose instead that money came only in the form of $10 bills and lunch cost $5.87. Without the divisibility of U.S. money into smaller bills and coins, you would either lose $4.13 or go without lunch. Many early forms of money were divisible. For example, Spanish gold coins were called "pieces of eight" because they could be cut into eight equal pieces in order to pay exact purchase prices. Marks dividing the coins into eight sections were etched into the coins when they were made.

Other forms of early money were also divisible but not necessarily uniform in value. For example, blocks of tea could be cut into smaller portions in order to pay for

*Dollar bills wear out about every 21 months. Replacements are printed by the federal Bureau of Engraving and Printing.*

a good or service. However, there was always the possibility that the new piece was not exactly as large as it was supposed to be. One could always shave a bit off.

### Limited in Supply and Accepted for Payment

As with most things, an increase in the availability of money causes it to lose value. For this reason, among others, the nation's central bank—the *Federal Reserve*—keeps close tabs on the amount of money in circulation. If the money supply grows too large, the Federal Reserve has ways of mopping up some of the excess money, as explained in Chapter 17.

Perhaps the most important characteristic of money is that people accept it as payment for goods and services. You accept your paycheck in dollars and cents from your summer job because you are confident that the bank will accept that check as a deposit. In time, you can withdraw money from your account and you know that it will be accepted at a store in exchange for something you want.

 **DID YOU GET IT?**
**What are the six characteristics of money? Explain how U.S. currency satisfies each characteristic.**

---

## ECONOMICS IN ACTION

# Weighed Down by Wampum

Wampum, which was made from seashells, was a form of money used by Native Americans in parts of what is today New England. The word *wampum* means "white shell beads" and comes from the Narragansett language. There was also purple-black wampum, which was more valuable. The color depended on the kind of shell used to fashion the wampum bead. Wampum had a variety of uses in addition to money. The designs on wampum belts, headbands, and bracelets were used as mnemonic devices to remind groups of their histories and traditions. Wampum was also exchanged when treaties were made between groups.

After the arrival of Europeans, wampum became a formal medium of exchange between Native Americans and Europeans. The use of European tools to cut the hard shells increased the quantity of wampum in circulation. By the 1700s, Europeans in the colonies were manufacturing wampum because there was so little European currency available. Counterfeiters even tried their hand at making wampum using glass beads.

Wampum, like all forms of money, was also a store of value and a unit of account. Six feet of a single strand of purple wampum was equal in value to 20 shillings in English money, but the same length of white wampum was only valued at 10 shillings. As coins and paper money became more common in the colonies, wampum declined in use.

 **DID YOU GET IT?**
**Why did Europeans in the colonies manufacture wampum?**

*Native Americans used shell beads called wampum as money.*

# THE BASIS OF MONEY'S VALUE

In the past, many of the items accepted as money have had other uses as well. These include precious metals and gems that can be made into jewelry, furs that can become clothing, and tea, dried fish, and even cattle that can become beverages and food. These items are examples of **commodity money** because they have value apart from their use as money. This value helped assure acceptability. Things like fish, furs, and precious metals had important uses, so they were unlikely to be turned down. The value of commodity money could also present problems. For example, when coins were made of silver or gold, some people would shave off the edges of the coins, melt down the shavings, and sell them. Most forms of commodity money do not meet the standards for money in modern societies. For example, dried fish are not particularly durable, portable, uniform, or divisible.

Unlike commodity money, **representative money** has no value of its own, but can be exchanged for something of value. Representative money is in limited supply because it represents a claim to some scarce resource such as gold or silver. On and off between the late 1700s and 1971, the United States used representative money in the form of gold or silver certificates that could be redeemed at a bank for gold or silver. To prepare for a sudden loss of faith in U.S. money that could lead to a large-scale exchange of currency for these commodities, the government maintained large reserves of gold and silver. The question of whether the government should use representative money tied to precious metals created many debates and political problems for the nation.

Since the United States stopped issuing representative money, it has issued **fiat money**, which is money that has value not because it is a commodity or is tied to a commodity but because the government declares that it shall have value. People accept the *Federal Reserve notes*, which we call bills, because they have faith in the United States government and its order that they be accepted as *legal tender*, or money. The government's *fiat*, or order, gives people the confidence to accept the notes as well as government-issued coins in payment of goods and services.

## DID YOU GET IT?

How is fiat money different from commodity money and representative money?

# THE MONEY SUPPLY TODAY

The money in your pocket and in your checking account is part of the economy's **money supply**, the amount of money

**Commodity money** is money that has value apart from its use as money.

**Fiat money** has value because the government has ordered that it be accepted in payment of debts.

**Representative money** has no value of its own but can be exchanged for something of value.

The **money supply** is the amount of money available for the purchase of goods and services.

*Most early U.S. currency was representative money like this silver certificate, which could be redeemed for precious metal.*

*Today our bills are Federal Reserve notes that serve as fiat money: they have value because the government says they do.*

available for the purchase of goods and services. The Federal Reserve tracks several versions of the money supply, including *M1* and *M2*.

## M1

**M1** is the smaller of the two measures of the money supply because it includes only the forms of money that are readily available to spend. M1 consists of

1.   **Currency in circulation**. This is the currency that individuals and firms have on hand to spend, not the currency that is held by the Federal Reserve or in bank vaults.

2.   **Deposits in checking accounts**. This includes other types of accounts from which checks are used to withdraw money. Other *checkable deposits* include *negotiable orders of withdrawal* (NOW) accounts, *automatic transfer service* (ATS) accounts, and *share draft accounts* at credit unions that are similar to checking accounts at banks.

3.   **Traveler's checks.** You can purchase *traveler's checks* at most banks as an alternative to carrying large sums

of cash while traveling. Traveler's checks are safer than cash because if one is lost or stolen, the company that sold the check will refund the value of the check. Unlike the checks you write on your checking account, traveler's checks are a form of money.

In October of 2012, M1 amounted to $2.4 trillion. Figure 47.1 shows how M1 grew between 1998 and 2011.

## M2

**M2** includes M1 as well as assets that are less *liquid*, meaning that they are less easily converted to cash. M2 contains the following:

1.   M1 as described previously

2.   Deposits in savings accounts

3.   Time deposits under $100,000, such as certificates of deposit, as explained in Chapter 12

4.   Money market deposit accounts, which are similar to savings accounts, but typically pay higher interest rates and limit the number of monthly transactions

---

**M1** is a measure of the money supply that includes only the forms of money that are readily available to spend: cash, checking account deposits, and traveler's checks.

**M2** is a measure of the money supply that includes M1 along with forms of money that are less easily converted to cash.

---

**Figure 47.1**

*Comparison of M1 in 1998 and 2012\**

*M1 contains only the forms of money that are readily available to spend.*

**DID YOU GET IT?**

**Which component of M1 got smaller between 1998 and 2012?**

*\*July 1998 and October 2012; seasonally adjusted figures.
SOURCE: www.federalreserve .gov/releases/h6/hist/h6hist2 .htm.*

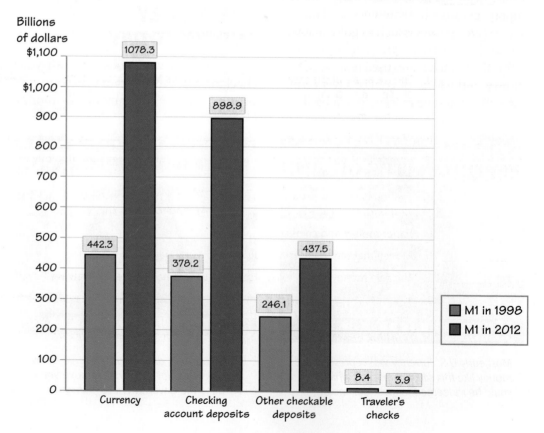

Billions of dollars

Legend: ■ M1 in 1998   ■ M1 in 2012

| Category | M1 in 1998 | M1 in 2012 |
|---|---|---|
| Currency | 442.3 | 1078.3 |
| Checking account deposits | 378.2 | 898.9 |
| Other checkable deposits | 246.1 | 437.5 |
| Traveler's checks | 8.4 | 3.9 |

**5.** Balances in retail money market mutual funds as explained in Chapter 12. Unlike deposits in money market accounts, investments in money market mutual funds are usually made through brokerage companies and are not insured by the FDIC.

In October of 2012, M2 was $9.6 trillion. Until 2006, the Federal Reserve also tracked a broader measure of money called *M3*, made up of M2 plus assets that are even more difficult to convert into cash. Among these are time deposits of more than $100,000, money market funds designed for large corporations and other institutions, and *repurchase agreements* or *repos*, which combine the sale of securities with an agreement to buy the securities back at a later date. An accurate account of the money supply is critical to monetary policy decisions, but the Federal Reserve found that tracking M3 added little useful information to the story.

**DID YOU GET IT?**
What characteristic distinguishes the types of money that are only part of M1 from the types of money that are added to form M2?

# MODULE 47 REVIEW AND ASSESSMENT

**Summing Up the Key Ideas:** Match the following terms to the correct definitions.

A. Money
B. Currency
C. Liquid assets
D. Barter

E. Medium of exchange
F. Store of value
G. Unit of account
H. Repurchase agreements (repos)

I. Commodity money
J. Representative money
K. Fiat money
L. Money supply

M. M1
N. M2

_____ 1. The role money serves when it is used as a standard measure to set prices and make economic calculations.

_____ 2. The exchange of goods or services for other goods or services without the use of money.

_____ 3. The amount of money available for the purchase of goods and services.

_____ 4. The measure of the money supply that includes M1 along with forms of money that are less easily converted to cash.

_____ 5. The role money serves when it is used as a form of payment.

_____ 6. Money that has no value of its own but can be exchanged for something of value.

_____ 7. Agreements that combine the sale of securities with an agreement to buy the securities back at a later date.

_____ 8. The measure of the money supply that includes only the forms of money that are readily available to spend: cash, checking account deposits, and traveler's checks.

_____ 9. Paper money and coins.

_____ 10. Money that has value apart from its use as money.

_____ 11. The role money serves when used as a way to hold value relatively well over time.

_____ 12. Money that has value because the government has ordered that it be accepted in payment of debts.

_____ 13. Anything that is widely accepted in exchange for goods and services.

_____ 14. Assets that are easily converted to cash.

## Analyze and Explain:

A. Analyze each of the following situations and determine if money is being used as a **medium of exchange**, a **store of value**, or a **unit of account**.

USE OF MONEY

1. A customer uses money to buy fruit at the local market. _____

2. The prices of items in a store are assigned in terms of dollars and cents. _____

3. A banana farmer sells her crop and deposits the money she receives into a checking account for future use. _____

B. The module explains that money must be **durable**, **portable**, **uniform**, **divisible**, **limited in supply**, and **accepted for payment**. List the characteristics among these that apply to each of the following items. Then explain why these items would or would not serve well as money.

| | CHARACTERISTICS | EXPLANATION |
|---|---|---|
| 1. pebbles from the beach | | |
| 2. pieces of chalk | | |
| 3. diamonds | | |
| 4. gold and silver | | |

## Apply: Determine if these financial assets are part of **M1 only**, **M2**, or **neither**.

M1 ONLY, M2, OR NEITHER?

1. deposits in checking accounts _____

2. money market funds for large corporations and institutions _____

3. money market accounts including funds in retail money market mutual funds _____

4. share draft accounts in savings and loans _____

5. the smaller of the two measures _____

6. currency in circulation _____

7. ATS accounts _____

8. time deposits more than $100,000 _____

9. repurchase agreements _____

10. certificates of deposit under $100,000 _____

11. traveler's checks _____

12. deposits in savings accounts _____

13. currency in vault of the Federal Reserve _____

## MODULE 48

# The Banking System

**KEY IDEA:** **The varied depository institutions in our banking system don't just hold money; they create money, but not by making new currency.**

### OBJECTIVES

- **To compare and contrast different types of depository institutions.**
- **To explain how depository institutions create money in the economy.**
- **To describe key aspects of the regulatory system for depository institutions.**

### Many Places to Bank

People use the term *bank* loosely to describe the financial institution—or ceramic pig—that holds their money when it is not in use. People may actually be doing their "banking" at credit unions, savings banks, or savings and loan associations. Any place that obtains money mainly through client deposits falls into the broader category of a **depository institution**. In this module you will learn about the roots of the banking industry and the importance of banks and other depository institutions.

## THE BANKING INDUSTRY

The banking industry is composed of four types of depository institutions: commercial banks, savings banks, saving and loan associations, and credit unions. Figure 48.1 provides a timeline of U.S. banking history. In the early days of banking, each type of depository institution offered specialized services or served specific groups of customers. For example, commercial banks offered services only to large businesses, and savings and loans were set up primarily to offer mortgage loans to workers. However, today, the missions of the various depository institutions overlap.

### Commercial Banks

Your neighborhood bank is a branch of a *commercial bank.* Although they once provided loans and other services only to businesses, **commercial banks** now offer a wide variety of financial services to individuals as well. Among these are savings accounts, checking accounts, mortgages, consumer loans for things such as cars, certificates of deposit (CDs), and various investment opportunities.

Before 1999, when Congress changed the Glass-Steagall Act of 1933, banks were barred from selling investments such as stocks. As banks began to offer investment services, the banking industry changed considerably. Large banks began buying up smaller banks. One acquisition led to another until a small number of giant banking corporations made up most of the banking industry. Although the ownership of many banks changed, most customers noticed little difference other than a change in the corporate logo printed on their checks and the availability of an expanded list of financial services.

*A bank is more than just a safe place to keep money.*

A **depository institution** is a financial institution that obtains money mainly through deposits from clients.

A **commercial bank** accepts deposits from individuals and firms, and provides them with loans in addition to a wide variety of other services.

THINKSTOCK

First Bank of the United States
Philadephia, PA

Second Bank of the United States
Philadephia, PA

**1781**
The first U.S. commercial bank, the Bank of North America, is chartered.

**1791-1811**
The First Bank of the United States is established to hold the federal government's money, issue paper money and provide credit to the government. Members of Congress question the bank's constitutionality, and state banks oppose it as a competitor. Congress does not renew the 20-year charter of the bank.

**1811-1816**
Without a central bank to oversee other banks, a period of chaos in U.S. banking follows. State-chartered banks issue their own notes, and not all banks have sufficient gold and silver to back their deposits. Many banks fail.

**1816-1836**
The Second Bank of the United States is established. President Andrew Jackson questions the bank's constitutionality and removes federal funds from the bank, placing them in state banks.

**1836-1860**
In this free banking era, some 8,000 state-chartered banks each issue their own currencies. There are no federal banking regulations.

The Confederate States of America Dollar

The United States of America Dollar
Known as a "greenback"

The Federal Reserve Banks
Boston, New York, Philadelphia, Cleveland, Richmond, Atlanta, Chicago, St. Louis, Minneapolis, Kansas City, Dallas, San Francisco

**1861**
To fund the Civil War, the Union prints the first greenbacks, fiat money backed only by the "full faith and credit of the United States." The Confederacy prints its own notes backed by the value of cotton. The notes become worthless after the war.

**1863-1864**
The National Banking Acts of 1863 and 1864 create a national banking system and a national currency.

**1900**
The Gold Standard Act makes gold the only metal for which bills can be exchanged and assigns a value of 0.048 troy ounces of gold per dollar.

**1907**
Problems in the banking industry and stock market spark the Panic of 1907. Depositors overwhelm banks in an effort to withdraw their money. Word that some banks have no money fuels more "runs" on banks as desperate depositors clamor for their savings, large portions of which have been lent out to others.

**1913**
The Federal Reserve Act is passed as a result of the Panic of 1907, establishing the Federal Reserve System as the nation's central bank.

**1914**
The First Federal Reserve Notes, the nation's current currency, are issued.

The Federal Deposit Insurance Corporation
Since the establishment of the FDIC no depositor has ever lost a single penny of FDIC-insured funds.

**LINCOLN**
**SAVINGS AND LOAN**

Lincoln Savings and Loan
In the aftermath of this S&L's collapse, it is revealed that several senators squashed early investigations into improper conduct at the bank, resulting in losses for depositors and a grand political scandal.

**1933**
Congress passes the Glass-Steagall Act to regulate banks and establish the Federal Deposit Insurance Corporation (FDIC).

**Late-1970s**
Lobbied by financial institutions, Congress begins a series of deregulations of the banking industry.

**1980s**
The savings and loan (S&L) crisis unfolds. The rescue of collapsing S&Ls costs taxpayers billions of dollars. Congress brings S&Ls under FDIC regulation.

**1999**
In response to aggressive lobbying, Congress ends the Glass-Steagall Act's ban on the sale of investments by banks.

**2007**
A worldwide financial crisis begins, caused largely by the mortgage lending practices of many banks and mortgage companies.

**2008**
Banks and investment companies experience huge losses on their investments in mortgages and mortgage-backed securities. The Treasury Dept. and Federal Reserve inject money into major banks and begin reregulation of the banking and securities industries.

**2010**
The Dodd-Frank Act establishes the Financial Stability Oversight Committee and creates new levels of oversight for financial institutions.

**Figure 48.1** A Timeline of U.S. Banking

Commercial banks are *chartered*, which means they are given the right to exist, by either the federal government or a state government. Federally chartered banks are called national banks, and state-chartered banks often have *state* in their names. National banks account for about one-third of all commercial banks and are members of the Federal Reserve System, the nation's central bank, as discussed in the next chapter.

Because the regulation of depository institutions is the topic of heated debate, and both too much and too little regulation has been blamed for recent economic crises, we will mention the agencies that regulate each type of institution. The Office of the Comptroller of the Currency was established in 1863 as the federal agency that regulates national banks. State banks are regulated by their state's banking department. Many state banks are also members of the Federal Reserve System. All federal banks and most state banks are insured by the Federal Deposit Insurance Corporation (FDIC).

## Saving Banks

A **savings bank** is a depository institution that specializes in loans for the purchase of homes and other real estate. Some savings banks are corporations owned by stockholders, while others are *mutual savings banks* (MSBs) that do not issue stock and are owned by depositors. The profits of an MSB are distributed to depositors on the basis of the amount of business they do with the bank.

Savings banks were founded in the early 1800s to encourage working-class Americans to be thrifty and save. Like savings and loans and credit unions, savings banks are known as **thrifts.** Originally, the savings that customers deposited in savings banks were used to fund long-term loans, especially home mortgages. Today, in addition to savings accounts and mortgages, savings banks offer checking accounts, CDs, credit cards, and a broad set of loans for businesses and consumers.

## Savings and Loan Associations

**Savings and loan associations (S&Ls)** are depository institutions similar to savings banks that originated in the early nineteenth century to encourage workers to save their money and to help them buy homes. Unlike savings banks, S&Ls were initially insured by the Federal Savings and Loan Insurance Corporation (FSLIC) rather than the FDIC. This changed in 1989 when the FSLIC ran out of funds during a wave of S&L failures. Today, the significant differences between savings banks and S&Ls have evaporated, and S&Ls are insured by the FDIC. Both savings banks and S&Ls are chartered and regulated either by the federal government's Office of the Comptroller of the Currency (OCC) or by state banking departments.

True to their mission to support the construction, purchase, and improvement of homes, some S&Ls were actually called "building and loan associations," and in some states, they could only make loans for home buying. Initially, all S&Ls were similar to mutual savings banks because they were owned by their depositors. In 1981, new legislation allowed S&Ls to issue stock to raise funds. The profits of S&Ls that issue stock are distributed on the basis of stock ownership, in the way other corporations pay dividends. Savings and Loan Associations were not allowed to offer checking accounts until the 1970s. Now, like savings banks, S&Ls may offer a variety of financial services, including savings accounts, checking accounts, CDs, and loans for businesses and consumers.

## Credit Unions

**Credit unions** are not-for-profit depository institutions owned by their *members*, who are also their customers. These members share a common bond—they may work in the same company or industry, belong to the same labor union, or live in the same community. The *not-for-profit* status of credit unions means that they operate for the purpose of serving their members, rather than to maximize profits. Any surplus

**Savings and loan associations** (S&Ls) are depository institutions, similar to savings banks, that specialize in loans for the purchase of homes.

A **savings bank** is a depository institution that specializes in loans for the purchase of homes and other real estate.

A **credit union** is a not-for-profit depository institution owned by its members, who are also its customers.

A **thrift** is a depository institution established to encourage saving and can be a savings and loan association, a credit union, or a savings bank.

of earnings is used to improve services, lower member costs, or in some other way aid the members.

The credit union idea was developed in Europe in the mid-nineteenth century. The first U.S. credit union was organized in New Hampshire in 1908. Originally, credit unions took deposits and lent money to members at low interest rates for short-term needs rather than for home mortgages. Today, credit unions continue to offer short-term loans but also offer a wider range of banking services. Most provide mortgage loans, issue credit cards, and offer share draft accounts that serve as checking accounts.

Every credit union is chartered by either the federal government through the National Credit Union Administration (NCUA) or a state government through its banking department. Federal credit unions are regulated by the NCUA and insured by the National Credit Union Share Insurance Fund (NCUSIF). Most state-chartered credit unions are also insured by the NCUSIF and regulated by the NCUA.

*A credit union is a not-for-profit depository institution owned by its customers. A student at Fossil Ridge High School in Texas makes a deposit at the first student-run credit union, started in 2011.*

# THE FUNCTIONS OF DEPOSITORY INSTITUTIONS

Depository institutions have three primary functions in common: storing money, lending money, and issuing credit cards. Without depository institutions, where would you put your money? Would you put it under your mattress? Besides not being very safe, putting your money under the mattress would prevent you from earning interest on your deposit. Module 37 explained that most depository institutions provide a safe place to keep your money, principal protection, and interest payments. The amount of interest you will receive depends on where you put your money. Certificates of deposit (CDs) typically offer the highest interest rates among standard types of deposits, followed by money market deposit accounts, savings accounts, and checking accounts.

Depository institutions earn the money used to pay interest on deposits from their second function: lending money. Banks and thrifts provide a variety of types of loans, from home mortgages to car loans to student loans. They also provide loans to home and business owners through *lines of credit*, which differ from other loans in that money can be borrowed and repaid over and over. A line of credit works this way: An individual or firm receives money from the depository institution using the line of credit. Usually, the borrower later repays the money and the agreed upon amount of interest. However, the borrower's home or business has been designated as the *collateral*, or guarantee, for the money. If the loan isn't paid back, the lender gets the collateral. If the loan is paid back, the borrower can use the same line of credit to withdraw money again.

Banks and thrifts also issue credit cards. These handy plastic cards, sometimes known simply as "plastic," allow cardholders to borrow money from the

## ECONOMICS IN ACTION

# How Safe Is Your Money?

In 1933, during the Great Depression, depositors worried that if their banks failed, their deposits might be unrecoverable. The federal government established the Federal Deposit Insurance Corporation (FDIC) as an independent government agency to insure bank deposits. The FDIC presently insures individual checking, savings, and retirement accounts held by banking institutions up to $250,000. The FDIC does not insure stocks, bonds, mutual funds, life insurance policies, annuities, or government securities that are sold by banks through their investment divisions. The FDIC also does not insure the contents of the safe deposit boxes offered by many financial institutions.

The Securities Investor Protection Corporation (SIPC)

*To help protect your money, the Federal Deposit Insurance Corporation (FDIC) insures bank deposits and the Securities Investor Protection Corporation (SIPC) provides insurance on brokerage accounts.*

provides insurance on brokerage accounts held in SIPC member firms up to $500,000. This includes up to $250,000 for claims of missing cash. The SIPC is an organization of member firms that sell securities. However, not all brokerage firms are SIPC members. Having SIPC coverage means that if a brokerage firm goes out of business, clients will receive their original investment in stocks, bonds, and mutual funds plus cash up to the designated limits. The SIPC does not cover investors against losses because of changes in the market.

Credit union deposits are insured through the National Credit Union Share Insurance Fund of the National Credit Union Administration. Like the FDIC, the NCUA insures individual savings accounts and share draft accounts up to $250,000.

### DID YOU GET IT?
If an investor loses $50,000 in the value of his account with a stock broker due to changes in stock prices, can he be reimbursed by the SIPC? What agency insures retirement accounts at banks?

---

depository institution to pay for goods or services. Once a month, the cardholders are billed for these purchases. If the balance owed on the card is not paid off each month, the cardholder pays a finance charge that is typically a percentage of the balance. The finance charges for credit card debt can be very high. It is wise to avoid these charges by paying off credit card balances each month. Credit card issuers also collect fees and a percentage of each purchase amount from the stores accepting the cards.

## FRACTIONAL RESERVE BANKING AND THE RESERVE REQUIREMENT

The United States has a **fractional reserve banking system**, which means that banks must hold on to a fraction of their deposits and may lend out the rest. As mentioned previously, this lending allows banks and thrifts to earn the interest payments that keep them up and running. The Federal Reserve sets **reserve requirements** that specify the percentage of deposits that banks

In a **fractional reserve banking system**, banks must hold on to a fraction of their deposits and may lend out the rest.

A **reserve requirement** specifies the percentage of deposits that banks must hold as reserves.

must hold as *reserves*. This helps avoid the bank panics that can occur when banks run out of money for withdrawals. In the next chapter we will see that reserve requirements also function as a monetary policy tool. Counted among reserves is money held in a bank's vault and money the bank has on deposit with the Federal Reserve. The current reserve requirements range from 0 to 10 percent, depending on the types of deposits and the total holdings of the depository institution. Any reserves that exceed the required reserves are considered *excess reserves* and can be loaned out. The fractional reserve banking system makes it possible for banks and thrifts to actually create money, as we'll see next.

## HOW DEPOSITORY INSTITUTIONS CREATE MONEY

Depository institutions accomplish the feat of money creation in the process of making loans such as mortgage loans, business loans, student loans, and consumer loans for items such as cars and home repair. Here's how lending expands the money supply:

• Suppose $100,000 of new money is introduced into the banking system— for example, because the Federal Reserve (the Fed) purchases $100,000 worth of T-bonds from a commercial bank.

• The reserve requirement does not apply to money received from bond sales. The bank then has $100,000 of excess reserves, which it lends out to Person A for the purchase of a home.

• Person A buys the home from Person B, who deposits the $100,000 in her checking account.

• Given a reserve requirement of 10 percent, Person B's bank must hold $10,000 of the $100,000 deposit in its vault. The remaining $90,000 can be lent out.

• Person B's bank loans $90,000 to Person C. Now Person B has $100,000 and Person C has $90,000, for a total of $190,000 that did not exist before the Fed's purchase.

• Person C spends the $90,000 on a commercial coffee-roasting system from Person D, who deposits the money in his checking account.

• Person D's bank must hold $9,000 as required reserves but lends out the remaining $81,000 to Person E.

• There is now $100,000 + $90,000 + $81,000 = $271,000 in the money supply that did not exist before the Fed's purchase.

• This process continues until no more money can be lent out.

Suppose individuals deposit all cash receipts into bank or thrift accounts, and these depository institutions loan out all excess reserves. The cycle of loans and deposits will continue until the entire $100,000 from the bond purchase is held as required reserves. At that point the Fed's introduction of $100,000 into the money supply will have caused the money supply to increase by $1,000,000. This increase is found by dividing the initial increase in the money supply ($100,000) by the reserve requirement (10 percent, or 0.1). Less money is created if the reserve requirement is higher, if people hold cash, or if banks hold excess reserves. Figure 48.2 illustrates the money creation process.

**DID YOU GET IT?**
If Person E deposited the $81,000 loan into his checking account, what next step would continue the money creation process?

## REGULATION AND CRISES IN DEPOSITORY INSTITUTIONS

Because depository institutions are central to the smooth functioning of the economy, when depository institutions are in

**Figure 48.2** The Money Creation Process

Money is created in the banking system by a cycle of loans and deposits, ending when there are no more excess reserves to loan out. In the example illustrated here, a $100,000 bond purchase by the Fed results in loans of $100,000 + $90,000 + $81,000 = $271,000. If no money is held as cash and all excess reserves are loaned out, the money supply will eventually increase by a total of $1,000,000 as the result of the bond purchase.

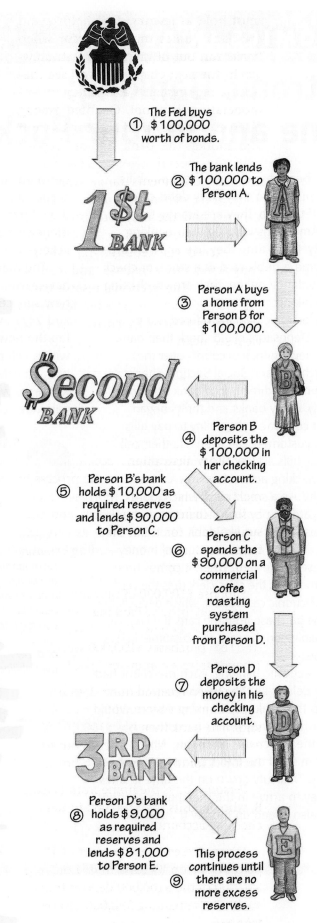

① The Fed buys $100,000 worth of bonds.

② The bank lends $100,000 to Person A.

③ Person A buys a home from Person B for $100,000.

④ Person B deposits the $100,000 in her checking account.

⑤ Person B's bank holds $10,000 as required reserves and lends $90,000 to Person C.

⑥ Person C spends the $90,000 on a commercial coffee roasting system purchased from Person D.

⑦ Person D deposits the money in his checking account.

⑧ Person D's bank holds $9,000 as required reserves and lends $81,000 to Person E.

⑨ This process continues until there are no more excess reserves.

crisis, the economy is in crisis. Firms need loans to start up and grow; individuals need loans to purchase homes, cars, and college educations. And everyone needs a reliable place to store their money. The importance of depository institutions has led policy makers to seek just the right amount of oversight—not too little and not too much. The result, over the past century, has been regulation, deregulation, and reregulation. The next two sections describe two of the costly crises of recent decades and their connections to regulatory issues.

## The Savings and Loan Crisis

The Federal Reserve oversees several types of regulation that became law during the Great Depression. Among them, the Federal Home Loan Acts of 1932 and 1933 provided additional money to state S&Ls for home loans. These acts also established federally chartered S&Ls. In 1933, Congress passed the Glass-Steagall Act to separate banks from investment services. Banks could no longer sell stocks and bonds, with the exception of government bonds, and the brokerages that sold stocks could not own banks. This law was meant to end what Congress considered some of the abuses that led to the Great Depression.

Beginning in the 1970s, the banking industry lobbied Congress for deregulation. In order to become more profitable,

# ECONOMICS IN ACTION

# Electronic Banking: Online and in Your Pocket

Do the members of your household pay bills using a computer? Do they carry debit cards? ATM cards? If they do, they are among the millions of Americans who do their banking electronically. Every time they use an ATM card to get cash, swipe a debit card at a store, or check an account balance online, they are conducting electronic banking.

At first, electronic banking offered just a few services. Depositors could check their bank balances by viewing their accounts over the Internet. Paychecks and Social Security checks could be deposited directly into bank accounts. More recently, many banks and thrifts began offering their customers the ability to pay bills online. Now, customers can even use their cell phones to pay bills and receive notices about overdrawn checking accounts.

You might use a *smart card*, which looks like a credit card, to pay for lunch in your school cafeteria. These cards act like debit cards, but they are preloaded with a certain amount of money upon purchase of the card. When it comes time to pay for something, the sales clerk runs the card through an electronic card reader, which deducts the amount of the purchase from the card. If there is a balance remaining on the card, the customer keeps it for later use.

Before electronic banking, each merchant had to physically deliver all the checks received from customers to the bank. The banking system would then transfer the money from the customers' accounts to the merchants' accounts. Now merchants can send the information on the check electronically. This cuts down on the time it takes for the money to arrive in the merchant's account. Debit cards also speed up money transfers between customers and merchants. A customer swipes the debit card in a machine that sends the information to the customer's bank, and the money is transferred to the merchant's account lickety-split.

The many advantages of electronic banking have revolutionized the banking industry with new services, convenience, speed, efficiency, and 24/7 availability. And now customers can tap the new services and constant availability with a cell phone while visiting family in Egypt, with an ATM machine on a street corner in Rome, or with a computer while wearing pajamas at home.

**DID YOU GET IT?**
How have electronic banking services changed in recent times?

*Electronic banking has revolutionized the banking industry with new services, convenience, speed, and 24/7 availability.*

depository institutions wanted Congress to remove restrictions on the services they could provide. For example, they wanted more flexibility in the types of loans and investments they could offer. They also wanted the ceiling lifted on the interest rates they could charge for loans. Meanwhile, investment companies saw the value of owning banking institutions and sought a repeal of the Glass-Steagall Act. The first wave of deregulation removed interest rate ceilings and allowed S&Ls to offer services such as checking accounts and consumer and business loans.

A contraction of the economy in the 1980s along with bad loans, mismanagement, and corruption in the S&L industry resulted in a savings and loan crisis in the 1980s. More than 700 S&Ls collapsed. Because of the central role that depository institutions play in the economy, there was concern that an even larger collapse could follow. The federal government stepped in to bail out the industry and to reregulate it. The Resolution Trust Corporation (RTC) was established to buy up the bad loans of S&Ls to keep the whole S&L industry from collapsing. The cost to taxpayers is estimated at $500 billion.

## The Financial Crisis of the New Century

The repeal of the Glass-Steagall Act in 1999 was one of the last steps in the deregulation process. It allowed banks to sell investments and insurance. Banks also sold mortgage loans to companies such as the Federal Home Loan Mortgage Corporation (Freddie Mac) and the Federal National Mortgage Association (Fannie Mae), both government-sponsored entities. These companies bundled together the mortgage loans for large numbers of homes and sold them as investments known as *mortgage-backed securities* (MBSs). Buyers of these securities received a share of the mortgage loan payments from borrowers. At the same time, the U.S. housing market soared and the value

of homes rose dramatically. The value of the mortgages in the MBSs soared along with home values.

However, the bubble of high prices in the housing market began to deflate in 2007. The economy was weakening and home prices were falling. Banks had been approving a growing number of relatively risky home loans known as *subprime mortgages* for people who did not have a good track record for repaying loans. The interest rates on many of these mortgages rose every six months, creating growing mortgage payments. Rising numbers of people with subprime mortgages fell behind on their payments in 2007 and 2008. When the loan payments were not received, the lenders took legal possession of the homes through the process of *foreclosure*. As the economy continued to weaken, other people began to miss mortgage payments as they lost their jobs. Home foreclosures rose even more. Many people owed more for their home loans than the homes were worth. Some of these borrowers became *walkaways*, meaning that they simply left their homes and let the banks have them.

By the summer of 2008, the United States faced a crisis in the financial industry. Several of the largest investment companies and their banking units were

*Rising interest rates and falling incomes make it difficult for homeowners to make loan payments. When lenders don't receive their payments, they can take legal possession of the homes through the process of foreclosure.*

in danger of collapsing. Freddie Mac and Fannie Mae were also in trouble. The Treasury Department and the Federal Reserve stepped in. At their request, Congress passed the Emergency Economic Stabilization Act of 2008 (EESA), which authorized a $700 billion bailout package known as the Troubled Asset Relief Program (TARP). By the time its authority had expired, TARP had disbursed $412 billion in loans and relief to banks, investment companies, the auto industry, AIG (a large insurance company), and even homeowners. However, by December 2012, $372 billion, or 90 percent of these payments, had been recovered. In 2010, the federal government tightened regulations governing financial institutions with the passage of the Dodd-Frank Wall Street Reform and Consumer Protection Act. The Act includes major changes to the United States financial regulatory system to improve oversight and supervision of banks and other financial institutions. It also set up an agency called the Consumer Financial Protection Bureau (CFPB) to protect consumers' rights in the market for financial products and services.

# MODULE 48 REVIEW AND ASSESSMENT

## Summing Up the Key Ideas: Match the following terms to the correct definitions.

A. Depository institution
B. Commercial bank
C. Bank charter

D. Savings bank
E. Thrifts
F. Savings and loan associations

G. Credit union
H. Lines of credit
I. Collateral
J. Smart card

K. Fractional reserve banking system
L. Excess reserves
M. Reserve requirement

_____ 1. A depository institution that accepts deposits from individuals and firms, and provides them with loans in addition to a wide variety of other services.

_____ 2. The percentage of deposits that banks must hold as reserves.

_____ 3. A depository institution established to encourage saving, which can also be a savings and loan association, a credit union, or a savings bank.

_____ 4. A depository institution that obtains money mainly through deposits from clients.

_____ 5. Any reserves that exceed the required reserves and can be loaned out.

_____ 6. A not-for-profit depository institution owned by its members, who are also its customers.

_____ 7. A depository institution that specializes in loans for the purchase of homes and other real estate.

_____ 8. A real asset, such as a home or business, that is the guarantee for the money that has been borrowed.

_____ 9. A banking function that provides loans to home and business owners using the home or the business as collateral.

_____ 10. A depository institution similar to a savings bank that specializes in loans for the purchase of homes.

_____ 11. A system where banks must hold on to a fraction of their deposits and may lend out the rest.

_____ 12. Acting like a debit card, these cards are preloaded with an amount of money and then purchases are deducted from the card balance.

_____ 13. A document issued by federal or state government that gives a commercial bank the right to exist.

**Analyze:** Determine whether each of the following characteristics fits a **commercial bank**, a **savings bank**, a **savings and loan association**, or a **credit union**. Some characteristics might apply to more than one type of depository institution.

| | COMMERCIAL BANKS | SAVINGS BANKS | SAVINGS AND LOAN ASSOCIATIONS | CREDIT UNIONS |
|---|---|---|---|---|
| 1. deposits covered by FDIC | | ✓ | ✓ | |
| 2. not-for-profit institutions | | | | ✓ |
| 3. can be members of the Federal Reserve System | ✓ | | | |
| 4. originally only funded long-term loans | | ✓ | | |
| 5. most owned by stockholders and pay dividends | | ✓ | | ✓ |
| 6. deposits covered by NCUSIF | | | | ✓ |
| 7. provide savings and checking accounts, CDs, mortgages, consumer loans, and investment opportunities | ✓ | ✓ | ✓ | ✓ |
| 8. owned by members who are customers | | | | ✓ |
| 9. chartered by state or federal government | ✓ | ✓ | ✓ | ✓ |
| 10. can be owned by stockholders or depositors | | | | ✓ |
| 11. offer short-term and mortgage loans, issue credit cards, and offer share draft accounts | | | | ✓ |

**Apply:** In a paragraph, explain how loans made to the customers of commercial banks expand the money supply.

## MODULE 49

# The Role of Financial Markets in the Real Economy

**KEY IDEA:** Savings fuel a country's economic growth. Financial markets assist with the flow of savings from savers to borrowers.

### OBJECTIVES

- **To explain the role of savings in the nation's financial system.**
- **To discuss how bonds are bought and sold.**
- **To describe the role of stocks in the economy.**
- **To explain how various indexes measure stock market performance.**

*Businesses grow using the surplus funds of savers like you.*

### The Engine of Economic Growth

In Chapter 12 we discussed financial markets from the investor's point of view. We examined options for investing your money when you're not using it. The term *real economy* in the title of this module refers to the side of the economy that produces goods and creates jobs. In this module we explore the financial markets from the perspective of entrepreneurs seeking *financial capital*—the money of savers like you—to fuel their endeavors to build firms and contribute goods and services to the economy.

---

*A penny saved is a penny earned.*

*—Benjamin Franklin*

A **financial intermediary** is an institution that channels money between savers and borrowers.

## THE FINANCIAL SYSTEM

Suppose you have invented the greatest piece of technology since computer chips. How do you get the money needed to start a company and produce your invention? Unless you're fabulously wealthy, you borrow your start-up financial capital from a bank. Where does the bank get the money? It gets it from the deposits of customers' savings.

Savings are the engine of economic growth. Without savings, there would be no financial capital for investments in new businesses or for the expansion of existing ones. Savings invested in government securities also provide the money for government expenditures when tax revenues are not enough to

fund programs. Savers and borrowers are two components of the financial system that are critical to the workings of the economy.

The **financial intermediaries** that channel money between savers and borrowers are the third component of a financial system. As illustrated in Figure 49.1, several types of institutions make up this category of financial go-betweens. The banking institutions—commercial banks, savings and loan associations, savings banks, and credit unions—take in customers' savings, which represent surplus income, and lend it to others. Banks charge interest on the money they lend and pay a part of that interest to depositors for the use of their money. The rest of the money is used to fund banks' own operations and pay their stockholders.

## Nondepository Financial Institutions

Notice that Figure 49.1 lists more than just banking institutions among the types of financial intermediaries. There are also *nondepository financial institutions*. They receive their money from savers in differing ways, but none accept deposits, and all share the same goal: to invest that money in a profitable way.

In Module 37 we saw that the managers of a *mutual fund* assemble a portfolio of investments that might include stocks, bonds, and T-bills, depending on the objectives of the fund. The payback comes in the form of dividends for stock funds and interest for bond funds. The mutual fund acts as a financial intermediary. Money from the sale of shares, called *units*, of the mutual fund is funneled to the firms and governments issuing the various securities.

*Real estate investment trusts* (REITs) invest in real estate, either by owning and managing property like shopping malls or by owning mortgages on property. The return on an investment in a REIT is based on the profit earned by the REIT. Like mutual funds, REITs make money by investing money in other operations, not by producing goods and services directly.

Insurance companies earn profit by collecting *premiums*, which are the payments for the life insurance policies they issue. These premiums may amount to hundreds of millions of dollars a year for the biggest companies. Rather than sitting on the premiums until it's time to pay out insurance claims, they seek to earn more money with this money. The premiums are invested in corporate and government bonds, among other securities, which provide financial capital for the issuers of these securities.

A number of firms, usually large corporations, have *pension plans* that pay workers a percentage of their former salaries after they have retired. The firm contributes

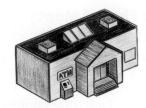

**Financial Intermediaries**

Commercial banks
Savings and loans
Savings banks
Credit unions
Life insurance companies
Real estate investment trusts
Mutual funds
Pension funds
Finance companies

**Figure 49.1** Financial Intermediaries
A variety of financial go-betweens help get savers' money into the hands of borrowers for mutual gain.

an amount for each working employee, and depending on how the plan is set up, employees may also contribute. The firm invests the funds that accumulate in the pension fund in assorted securities. The goal is to offer a return on investment that will increase the financial resources available to employees in their retirement.

*Finance companies* are lending institutions that get their funds not by accepting deposits but by borrowing from banks and other lending institutions. Some finance companies make loans with relatively high interest rates to individuals who have trouble getting loans from depository institutions. Others make loans to small manufacturers and wholesalers. These small firms often borrow to pay their bills while waiting to collect payments for goods. A third type of finance company purchases consumer loans owed to car dealers and other merchants and then collects the payments from the customers. By giving merchants their money right away and taking the risk that the loans won't be repaid, these finance companies provide speed and certainty to merchants in exchange for a discount on the purchase price of the loans.

**DID YOU GET IT?**

What is an example of a financial intermediary?

## The Circular Flow of Money

Figure 49.2 shows that households and firms—as savers—place their surplus funds in banking institutions and nondepository institutions. Those institutions then lend that money to firms and the government, largely for investment in physical capital. Also, some of the money goes to households for their own purchases. The flow of money enables savers and financial intermediaries to generate income on savings while helping firms expand and governments fund programs. This additional income may be spent by individuals or saved in the accounts of financial intermediaries to generate still more lending and more income to continue the flow of funds.

Note that the arrows from left to right in Figure 49.2 represent the flow of savings. One set of arrows flows through the financial intermediaries, but the top arrow connects savers directly with borrowers. Individuals may buy and sell corporate bonds directly on the bond market and may buy government bonds directly from the Treasury. However, most financial transactions that involve borrowing are performed with the assistance of financial intermediaries.

## Raising Financial Capital

**Equity financing** occurs when corporations sell stock to raise financial capital. Like the government, corporations can also sell bonds and take out other types of loans, which is called **debt financing**. The amount of money savers make available for loans depends on the interest rates, also known as coupon rates in the case of bonds, offered to compensate the savers. The

**Equity financing** is getting money by selling stock.

**Debt financing** is getting money by borrowing.

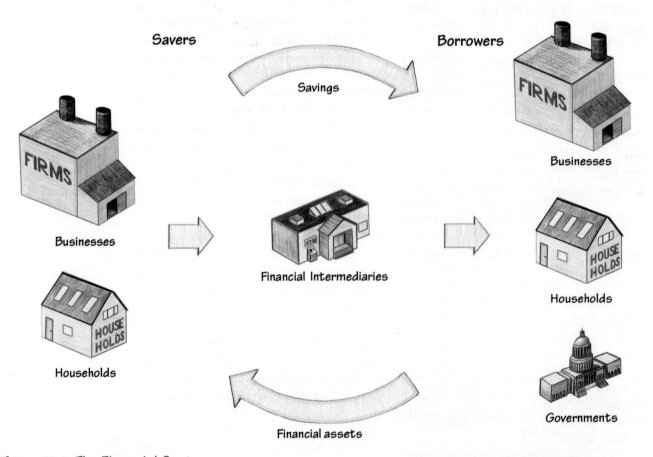

**Figure 49.2** The Financial System
Households and businesses can lend their savings directly to borrowers in exchange for financial assets such as bonds, or they can lend indirectly through financial intermediaries.

interest rates quoted in bank advertisements or by the government for bonds are **nominal interest rates.** They indicate what the saver will receive for depositing money in the bank or buying the government bond. The higher the nominal interest rate, the more savings will grow.

However, it is the **real interest rate**—the nominal interest rate minus the expected rate of inflation—that is central to the decisions of savers and borrowers. Suppose a corporation is contemplating an investment that would require a $100,000 loan with a 5 percent nominal interest rate for one year. To weigh the costs and benefits of the investment, the corporation will consider the real interest rate that must be paid for the loan. If the rate of inflation is expected to be 2 percent, the expected real interest rate is found by subtracting the 2 percent expected inflation rate from the 5 percent nominal interest rate: 5 percent − 2 percent = 3 percent. The corporation will take out the loan if the expected real interest rate is less than the expected real return on the investment, which is what they get out of it after adjusting for inflation.

Inflation erodes the purchasing power of the money, including both the principal and the interest, that must be paid back after a loan. Suppose the corporation takes out the $100,000 loan. If inflation is 2 percent as expected, the $105,000 the corporation will pay back in one year will only buy as much as about $103,000 would buy today. If inflation is higher than expected, the amount that must be paid back will be worth less than expected, which is good for the borrower and bad for the lender. For example, if the inflation rate turns out to be 4 percent, the $105,000 paid back in one year will only buy as much as about $101,000 would buy today. On the other hand, if inflation

turns out to be only 1 percent, that will be good for the lender and bad for the borrower. In that case the $105,000 paid back in one year will buy as much as about $104,000 would buy today, so in real terms the loan will cost the corporation more than expected.

**DID YOU GET IT?**
What is the difference between nominal interest rates and real interest rates?

# BUYING AND SELLING BONDS

Let's summarize what you've learned about bonds and then add some important insights. Bonds are a type of loan and are thus a form of debt for the corporation or government that issues them. Bond sales are used to fund business expansions and government programs like highway construction. The borrower promises to pay a specific coupon (interest) rate for a specific period of time and to repay the face value of the bond on its maturity date. Bonds are sold directly by the government and some corporations, and indirectly through financial institutions, including banks and online trading companies such as E*TRADE.

The price of bonds is determined at auction and can be higher or lower than the face value. If the coupon rate for bonds is high relative to the rate of return on alternative investments of comparable risk, such as the interest rate on CDs, then investors will prefer to put their money into bonds. This preference for bonds will lead investors to bid up the price of bonds to exceed their face value. On the other hand, if the coupon rate for bonds is low relative to the rate of return on alternative investments, disinterest in bonds will cause them to sell for less than their face value. The result

The **nominal interest rate** is the actual rate of interest that a saver will receive and a borrower will pay.

The **real interest rate** is the nominal interest rate minus the expected rate of inflation.

is an inverse relationship between bond prices and interest rates on alternative investments, as illustrated in Figure 49.3.

If the price of a bond equals its face value—for example, if a $1,000 bond sells for $1,000—then the rate of return on the bond will equal the coupon rate. In that case, for example, if the coupon rate is 10 percent, then the rate of return on the bond is 10 percent. If the price of a bond differs from its face value—say, if a $1,000 bond sells for $900—then the rate of return on the bond will differ from its coupon rate. To see why, we will focus on one of several ways to measure the return on a bond: the *current yield*.

Consider that bond with a $1,000 face value and a coupon rate of 10 percent sold for $900. The discounted price results in a higher rate of return. The **current yield** is the annual coupon payment (10 percent of $1,000, or $100) divided by the price: $100 ÷ $900 = 0.11 or 11 percent. If instead the bond sold for $1,110, the current yield would be $100 ÷ $1,110 = 0.09 or 9 percent. Notice that the current yield moves in the opposite direction of the price of the bond as illustrated in Figure 49.4.

Bond purchases also carry the risk that the issuer will run out of money and be unable to repay the loan or make the coupon payments. To make good decisions about which bonds to buy and at what price, investors need information about the company or government issuing the bonds. Bond-rating agencies such as Standard & Poor's and Moody's make it easier to find out this information. Their analysts investigate the finances of the issuer—past and present—to determine if it can be expected to make coupon payments over the life of the bond and repay the face value of the bond at maturity.

Table 49.1 lists the ratings that each company uses to assign risk to bonds. AAA or Aaa bonds are the least risky, but they also offer lower rates of return than the other bonds. The higher the risk, the higher the rate of return required to compensate investors for taking the risk.

The **current yield** is the annual coupon payment divided by the price.

**DID YOU GET IT?**
**Which of Moody's bond ratings indicates that bonds are generally not desirable?**

## TYPES OF BONDS

Corporations and various levels of government issue bonds to fund long-term projects. Low risk and exemption from income taxes make government bonds especially attractive to investors.

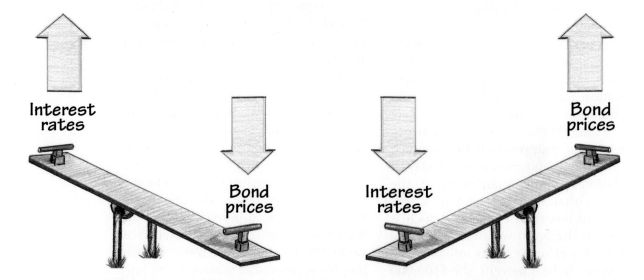

**Figure 49.3** The Inverse Relationship between Interest Rates and Bond Prices Higher interest rates lead to lower bond prices, and lower interest rates lead to higher bond prices.

### Table 49.1 Bond Ratings

| STANDARD & POOR'S | | MOODY'S | |
| --- | --- | --- | --- |
| **Rating** | **Description** | **Rating** | **Description** |
| AAA | Highest investment grade | Aaa | Best quality |
| AA | High grade | Aa | High quality |
| A | Upper medium grade | A | Upper medium grade |
| BBB | Medium grade | Baa | Medium grade |
| BB | Lower medium grade | Ba | Possesses speculative elements |
| B | Speculative | B | Generally not desirable |
| CCC | Vulnerable to default | Caa | Poor; possibly in default |
| CC | Repaid after other debt-rated CCC | Ca | Highly speculative, likely in, or very near, default |
| C | Repaid after CC debt | C | Typically in default; little prospect for recovery of principal or interest |
| D | Bond in default | D | Interest and principal payments in default |

## Municipal Bonds

State and local governments issue bonds when their current expenses exceed their available tax revenues. A state may issue bonds to build a new superhighway, a school district may issue bonds to build a new high school, and a government-owned transit system may issue bonds to build a tunnel. With the exception of bonds issued by the federal government, government-issued bonds are called *municipal bonds*, or *munis*. The earnings on these bonds are exempt from federal income taxes and are generally exempt from state and local income taxes for residents of the state. The bonds are rated as generally safe investments because governments have an ongoing revenue stream from taxes with which to cover their debts. The terms

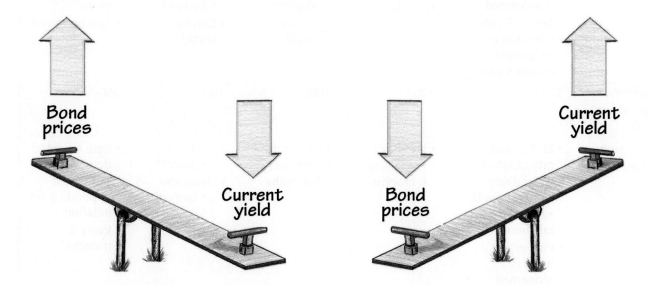

**Figure 49.4** The Inverse Relationship between Bond Prices and Current Yields
Higher bond prices result in lower current yields, and lower bond prices result in higher current yields.

of municipal bonds vary based on their purposes but are usually long—20, 30, or even 40 years.

## Federal Government Borrowing

Table 49.2 provides an overview of the variety of bonds issued by the federal government as introduced in previous chapters. They vary in term, yield, and minimum investment. Treasury bonds, notes, bills, and TIPS are sold at auction, where bidding sets the price. With the exception of an August 2011 credit-rating downgrade to AA+ by Standard & Poor's, financial assets backed by the federal government have received the highest ratings and are considered the safest investments available. Because there is so little risk to compensate for, these securities offer a lower rate of return than most other investments.

On the bright side for investors, the income on federal government securities is exempt from state and local income taxes.

**DID YOU GET IT?**

Which is the only kind of government debt that cannot be sold without a penalty?

## Corporate Bonds

Corporations sell bonds to finance the expansion of their operations. They might want to acquire other firms, build new factories, or develop new technologies. Unlike government-issued bonds, the income on corporate bonds is taxed by all levels of government. However, corporate bonds tend to offer higher rates of return than government bonds because they are considered riskier investments.

---

**Table 49.2  Types of Government Bonds**

| | U.S. SAVINGS BONDS: SERIES EE/E SERIES I* | TREASURY BONDS (T-BONDS) | TREASURY NOTES (T-NOTES) | TREASURY BILLS (T-BILLS) | TREASURY INFLATION-PROTECTED SECURITIES (TIPS) |
|---|---|---|---|---|---|
| Price | Sold at face value | Set at auction | Set at auction | Set at auction | Set at auction |
| Term | • EE/E: Penalty if redeemed before 5 years<br>• I: Penalty if redeemed before 5 years | • 30 years<br>• Can be resold | • 2, 3, 5, 7, or 10 years<br>• Can be resold | • 4, 13, 26, or 52 weeks<br>• Can be resold | • 5, 10, or 30 years<br>• Can be resold |
| Minimum purchase ($) | $25 | 100 | 100 | 100 | 100 |
| Coupon Rate | • EE/E: Fixed rate of return<br>• I: Fixed rate combined with adjustment for inflation<br>• Paid when bond is redeemed | • Fixed rate<br>• Paid every 6 months | • Fixed rate<br>• Paid every 6 months | • Sold at a discount**<br>• Depends on term of T-bill | • Rate adjusted downward or upward depending on inflation<br>• Every 6 months |

*THE rate for Series I bonds takes into consideration the rate of inflation and tends to be higher than that of Series EE/E bonds. Because of the built-in inflation factor, I bonds are considered a good way to save for college.

**T-BILLS are sold at a discount, or less than their face value. This difference between the purchase price and the face value is interest ($950 purchase price of a $1,000 T-Bill equals $50 in interest). In addition, the T-bill pays a stated rate of interest.

Most large corporations have favorable bond ratings, but even well-regarded firms can have their bond ratings downgraded. A firm may make some bad decisions that affect its revenue, or an economic downturn may weaken the firm's prospects for continued success. Both can cause the firm to have difficulty making coupon payments on its bonds and perhaps to fail to repay the principal as well. Sensing this danger, the rating agency will downgrade the firm's bond rating, thus making it harder for the firm to sell bonds. To attract buyers, the firm may offer higher coupon rates. As the firm's earnings' outlook improves, its ability to cover its debts also improves, and rating agencies will upgrade its bond ratings.

Bonds that Standard & Poor's rates BB or lower are considered **junk bonds**. These are high-risk investments, and as such, they offer high rates of return. The bond issuer might be a young corporation that has yet to gain solid financial footing, a financially troubled firm that has no alternatives for raising financial capital except to issue junk bonds, or a firm that needs to raise funds quickly to finance a risky takeover of another firm. Investors buy junk bonds not for safe and steady returns over the long term, but for the possibility of quick, high returns.

**DID YOU GET IT?**
**Why do corporations sell bonds?**

# FINANCIAL ASSET MARKETS

Financial assets such as stocks, bonds, CDs, and shares of money market mutual funds are bought and sold in *financial asset markets*. These can be either *capital markets* or *money markets*, depending on the period of time over which the asset is held. The markets can also be either *primary markets* or *secondary markets*, depending on whether the asset is being sold for the very first time.

## Capital and Money Markets

In **capital markets**, money is lent for one year or more. U.S. savings bonds, T-notes, T-bonds, and TIPS, as well as municipal bonds and corporate bonds with maturities of a year or more, fit in this category. T-bills that mature in one year and CDs with maturities of one year or longer are also sold in capital markets. In **money markets**, money is lent for less than one year. Short-term CDs, T-bills with 4-, 13-, and 26-week maturities, and money market mutual funds fit in this category.

## Primary and Secondary Markets

In **primary markets**, new assets are sold by their issuers. For example, new securities are sold by the governments or corporations issuing them. The issuers receive the proceeds of this first sale. In the case of a new stock, this initial sale is called an *initial public offering*. Subsequent sales of these assets occur on *secondary markets*.

In **secondary markets**, investors buy and sell financial assets that have already been purchased at least once. Corporate stocks and bonds, municipal bonds, T-bonds, T-notes, T-bills, and TIPS are all traded on secondary markets. The proceeds of these sales go to the investors who sold the assets. Stock exchanges such as the New York Stock Exchange were formed primarily to bring buyers and sellers of stocks together for secondary-market sales. Today, most investors take advantage of online services such as Ameritrade.com to buy and sell financial assets of all sorts.

# THE SCOOP ON STOCKS

We've seen that corporations can issue stock to raise money for operations and growth. The purchase of stock gives the

A **capital market** is a market in which money is lent for one year or more.

A **money market** is a market in which money is lent for less than a year.

In a **primary market**, new assets are sold by their issuers.

A **junk bond** is a high-risk, high-interest-rate corporate bond.

In **secondary markets**, investors buy and sell financial assets that have already been purchased at least once.

investor *equity*, or a share of ownership in the corporation. There are two classes of stock: common and preferred. Owning common stock gives an investor an active role in the management of the corporation. Shareholders with common stock exercise their voting rights at the company's annual shareholders' meeting. They vote on the board of directors and may also be asked to vote on one or two other issues, such as proposals to merge with another firm or change the structure of the firm's leadership. Owners of preferred stock generally do not have voting rights, but they receive higher dividends at more regular intervals. They also receive preferential treatment when it comes to distributing payments from a corporation that cannot cover all its obligations.

Not all stocks pay dividends. Some corporations, especially those in the technology sector such as Amazon.com, Apple,

*The purchase of stock gives an investor a share of ownership in the corporation.*

## ECONOMICS IN ACTION

# What Are Futures and Options?

*Futures contracts* are agreements that an investor will buy a specific quantity of an item now at a specific price but receive that quantity on a specified date in the future. The item may be rice, cattle, gold, government bonds, or currency, among other commodities and assets. Investors buy futures with the idea that the price they pay now will be less than the price they can sell the item for when it is delivered. The difference is profit. Sellers have the opposite idea—that the price will be lower in the future—or prefer to dodge the risk of falling prices and have money now rather than later for, say, corn that they are growing for future harvest.

*Option contracts* do not place an obligation on the buyer the way futures contracts do. An option gives an investor the right to buy a specific stock at a certain price during a specific time period in the future. However, the investor may choose not to exercise that option and is not penalized. An option contract for the right to buy a stock is a *call option*. An option contract for the right to sell a stock is a *put option*.

PORK BELLIES

Some corporations reward employees by granting them options to buy the firm's stock at a discounted price within a certain time period. For example, a worker who comes up with a time-saving production process could be awarded 1,000 stock options that enable her to buy the firm's stock for $25 a share within one year, even though it is currently valued at $35 a share on the stock market. Suppose the worker exercises the option to buy the stock and holds the stock until its value reaches $50 a share. The worker makes a profit of $25 on each share. The benefit to the firm is twofold: it has created an incentive for workers to contribute innovative ideas, and it can put the $25 × 1,000 = $25,000 investment from the worker to use. Technology start-ups, which typically do not have much money, often use options to attract talented employees.

**? DID YOU GET IT?**

What is the major difference between futures and options?

FINE GOLD 999.9 1 KILO

THINKSTOCK

Dell, and Google, normally do not pay stock dividends. Instead, they take the money they would otherwise use to pay dividends and reinvest it in their business. The value of their stock grows as their business expands. Investors reap the benefit of investing in these stocks, known as growth stocks, when they sell their shares. For example, in the late 1990s, Apple stock sold for around $20 per share. By 2011, it had jumped to more than $400 per share.

Stocks are not rated the way bonds are. However, there are market research companies that analyze the performance of stocks and issue their findings. If analysts at a firm such as Morningstar advise investors to sell a particular stock because of a low earnings forecast by the corporation, many stockholders will think seriously about selling their shares.

 **DID YOU GET IT?**
The owners of preferred stock do not have voting rights. What do they receive that owners of common stock do not?

## Measuring Stock Market Performance

During the financial crisis that started in 2007, many Americans with daytime access to the Internet checked the *Standard & Poor's 500 Stock Index*, the *Dow Jones Industrial Average*, and the *NASDAQ Composite Index* over and over throughout the day. By midyear in 2007, all three indexes had reached record highs. However, by the end of the summer, bad news from the housing and financial industries began to affect certain parts of the economy. By October 2008, all three indexes had reached lows not seen in many years. The nation was in a recession, and economists were predicting that it might be a year before the economy improved. Stock prices reflected the lowered growth expectations of corporations as they laid off workers, and consumers scaled back their spending to prepare for the worst. People saw their retirement investments and stock and bond portfolios drop in value by as much as 45 percent, depending on their asset allocations.

The stock indexes measure how the stock market is performing minute by minute and reflect the general health of the economy. We will outline the three most widely known and followed U.S. stock indexes. However, there are many other indexes that track stocks and bonds in the United States. Other countries also have indexes that follow their own financial markets, such as the Nikkei Index in Japan and the FTSE Index in the United Kingdom.

## The Standard & Poor's 500 Stock Index

The *S&P 500*, as the Standard & Poor's stock index is known, follows a list of 500 stocks that are traded on the New York Stock Exchange (NYSE), the National Association of Securities Dealers Automated Quotation (NASDAQ) Stock Market, or the over-the-counter (OTC) market. The list is divided into 90 industry groupings to represent 4 major sectors of the economy: the industrial sector, the utilities sector, the financial sector, and the transportation sector. The stocks chosen are generally those of industry leaders in the various sectors. The list changes from time to time as declining companies are replaced with new leaders in their sectors. Of all the indexes, the S&P 500 provides the broadest look at the overall performance of the stock market. Figure 49.5 shows the S&P 500 values from 1950 through 2011.

## The Dow Jones Industrial Average

The *Dow*, on the other hand, tracks only 30 stocks, and the majority of these are traded only on the NYSE. These 30 stocks represent large corporations with good performance in their industries, such as AT&T, Coca-Cola, Microsoft, Verizon, and Disney. Like those on the S&P 500, the stocks on the Dow also change from time to time to reflect industry performance.

## The NASDAQ Composite Index

The NASDAQ Composite tracks the stocks of U.S. and foreign corporations traded on the NASDAQ Stock Market.

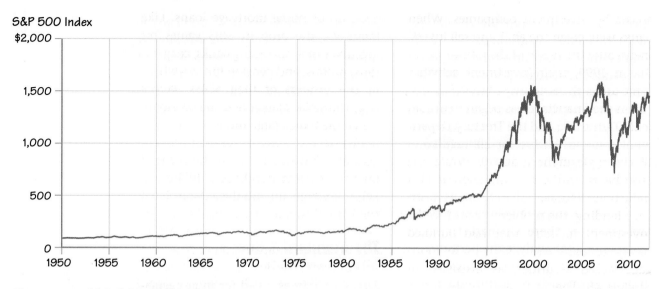

**Figure 49.5** *S&P 500, 1950–2011*

In general, companies that are listed on the NASDAQ Composite are growth stocks. Among these are technology-based companies such as Amazon.com and real estate investment trusts (REITs) such as Kilron Realty. The NASDAQ Composite is much larger than the S&P 500 and the Dow, with a list of more than 3,000 stocks in its index. The NASDAQ Composite also adds and drops stocks over time.

A **bear market** is characterized by rapidly declining stock prices.

### Bear and Bull Markets

During the late 1990s, when Amazon.com, among other high-tech companies, was attracting investors and losing money at the same time, the country was experiencing steady economic growth. Firms were hiring more and more workers, and consumers were spending more and more money. The stock market reflected this growth. This type of steady rise in stock prices over a period of time is known as a **bull market**.

A **bull market** is characterized by steady growth in stock prices.

The rapid rise of Internet-based firms between 1995 and 2000 was known as the *dot-com bubble* because so many of the firms had names that ended with ".com." In 2000, the dot-com bubble burst. Many

firms failed, such as online grocer Webvan.com and pet-supply retailer Pets.com. Others, such as Amazon.com and eToys.com, were wounded but eventually recovered. The economy slowed and the nation entered a short-lived recession. Between 2001 and 2003 stock prices fell sharply. During a period of rapidly declining stock prices such as this, we experience a **bear market**. In spring of 2003 the markets then swung upward again, beginning another bull market.

One of the sharpest stock market drops since the Wall Street Crash of 1929 occurred in October of 2008, when all three indexes fell day after day. By the end of the month, the NASDAQ Composite had lost 45 percent of its value since the height of the bull market a year earlier. Over that period, its index value fell from above 2,800 points to 1,552.

## REGULATING FINANCIAL MARKETS

The stock and bond markets are regulated by the federal Securities and Exchange Commission (SEC), which was established in 1934 during the Great Depression. Its mission was to protect investors from abuses by investment companies. When banks were given the ability to sell investments after the repeal of the Glass-Steagall Act in 1999, their investment activities came under the authority of the SEC, too.

As the financial crisis began to unfold in 2007, the SEC and the Treasury Department came under fire for lax regulation of the investment industry. While the crisis began in the housing and banking industries because of subprime mortgage lending, the problems spread to the investment industry that had bundled mortgage loans and sold them as mortgage-backed securities, as discussed in Module 48. The crisis also hit the insurance industry, which had provided a form of insurance on MBSs called credit-default swaps. When home prices plummeted so did the values of MBSs, because they are made up of home mortgage loans. Like dominoes, the drop in MBS values hit MBS investors—including banks, corporations, unions, and pension funds—which hit the insurers of their MBSs. Before long, the stock market and the economy as a whole took a large hit.

As we discussed in Module 48, the Treasury Department and the Federal Reserve disbursed hundreds of billions of dollars through the Troubled Asset Relief Program (TARP) to rescue banks, investment companies, the auto industry, AIG (a large insurance company), and homeowners. But before the dust had settled, politicians and citizens called for more regulation of financial markets. The Dodd-Frank Wall Street Reform and Consumer Protection Act of 2010 was a partial response to these calls.

## ECONOMICS IN ACTION

# Spending Money to Make Money: Amazon.com

Profit can be a long time coming. Some firms spend millions of dollars of investors' money before they turn a profit. The old saying "You have to spend money to make money" was certainly true in the case of Amazon.com. Jeff Bezos, the founder of Amazon.com, had a vision of selling books online—no brick-and-mortar stores. Today, that doesn't seem so revolutionary, but it was in 1994 when Bezos founded Amazon.com. However, he was not alone in thinking that the Internet could provide a fast and easy way to order goods. Armed with money from a few venture capitalists—the folks who fund start-up businesses—Bezos set to work.

Fast and easy ordering was not the only requirement for an online store. Amazon.com would have to ship goods quickly and relatively cheaply to lure people away from their local bookstores where they could walk out with what they wanted. Bezos hired people who shared his ideas to build a computer-operated system for moving books in and out of Amazon.com's warehouses quickly. The warehouses were custom-built to facilitate the system. Bezos also experimented with different formulas for charging shipping and handling costs. By 2002, he had settled on a policy to eliminate these charges for orders of $25 or more.

Once Amazon.com had built a reputation for fast, easy, and cheap book sales, Bezos moved into other products. In 1998, Amazon.com began selling music and movies, and in 1999, small electronics and toys. In 1999, Amazon.com also opened an auction site to compete with eBay.

In 1997, to gain more capital, Amazon.com had issued stock for the first time. Eager investors snapped up its first $54 million in stock and continued buying stock in later offerings. Loyal investors kept Amazon.com stock even during downturns for the company and the economy.

However, Amazon.com did not turn a quarterly profit until 2002. The company's first annual profit did not appear until 2004. In the meantime, Bezos and Amazon.com were criticized for the company's free spending ways as Amazon.

com built customers and product lines. The company's slogan was "Get Big Fast." But investors who shared Bezos's belief in the Internet as a business tool held Amazon.com stock despite its policy not to pay dividends. And they were rewarded—it was a healthy growth stock, gaining value over time as you can see from Figure 49.6.

**DID YOU GET IT?**
Why did investors hold Amazon.com stock even though it didn't pay dividends?

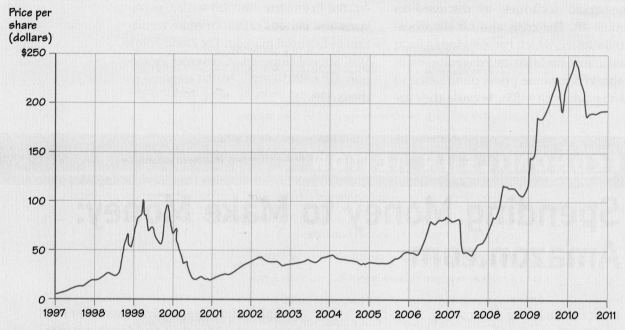

**Figure 49.6** Amazon.com Stock Performance, 1997–2011

# MODULE 49 REVIEW AND ASSESSMENT

**Summing Up the Key Ideas:** Match the following terms to the correct definitions.

A. Financial capital
B. Financial intermediaries
C. Equity financing
D. Debt financing

E. Nominal interest rate
F. Real interest rate
G. Current yield
H. Municipal bonds
I. Corporate bonds

J. Junk bond
K. Capital market
L. Money market
M. Primary market
N. Secondary market

O. Common stock
P. Preferred stock
Q. Bull market
R. Bear market

_____ 1. A market in which money is lent for one year or more.

_____ 2. An institution that channels money between savers and borrowers.

_____ 3. A market that is characterized by rapidly declining stock prices.

_____ 4. The annual coupon payment divided by the price.

_____ 5. Gives shareholders voting rights and may pay dividends.

_____ 6. A market that is characterized by steady growth in stock prices.

_____ 7. The corporate practice of obtaining financial capital by selling stock.

_____ 8. A market in which new assets are sold by their issuers.

_____ 9. The nominal interest rate minus the expected rate of inflation.

_____ 10. A market in which investors buy and sell financial assets that have already been purchased at least once.

_____ 11. Shareholders have no voting rights but receive higher dividends at more regular intervals.

_____ 12. Sold by corporations to finance expansion of their operations—acquiring other firms, building new factories, or developing new technologies.

_____ 13. The corporate practice of obtaining financial capital by borrowing.

_____ 14. A market in which money is lent for less than a year.

_____ 15. A high-risk, high-interest-rate corporate bond.

_____ 16. The actual rate of interest that a saver will receive and a borrower will pay.

_____ 17. The money of savers to fuel endeavors to build firms and contribute goods and services to the economy.

_____ 18. Government bonds issued by state and local governments for public works projects exempt from federal income taxes.

## Analyze:

A: Determine if the nondepository financial institution described in each of the following situations would be a **mutual fund**, a **real estate investment trust**, an **insurance company**, or a **finance company**.

TYPE OF INSTITUTION

1. A type of lending institution that gets funds not by accepting deposits but by borrowing from banks and other lending institutions. It makes loans with relatively high interest rates to individuals who have trouble getting loans from depository institutions or makes loans to small manufacturers and wholesalers.

_____

2. A type of financial institution that makes money by owning and managing property, like shopping malls, or by owning mortgages on properties. It makes money by investing money in other institutions, not by producing goods and services directly.

_____

3. A type of financial institution that makes money by charging premiums. This type of institution then invests the premiums it collects in corporate and government bonds, among other securities, which provide capital for the issuers of these securities.

_____

4. A type of financial institution that assembles a portfolio of investments that might include stocks, bonds, or T-bills. This type of institution sells units to investors who profit by receiving dividends or interest.

_____

B: Read each of the facts described here and determine if it applies to the **Dow Jones Industrial Average**, the **S&P 500 Stock Index** or the **NASDAQ Composite Index**.

NAME OF INDEX

1. tracks 30 stocks traded on the NYSE in its index
_____

2. tracks U.S. and foreign stocks
_____

3. provides the broadest look at the overall performance of the stock market
_____

4. tracks 500 stocks on the NYSE, NASDAQ, and over-the-counter market
_____

5. represents the largest corporations with good performance in their industries
_____

6. lists more than 3,000 stocks in its index
_____

**Apply:** Analyze each of the following and then determine if the type of bond being described is a **municipal bond**, a **federal government bond**, or a **corporate bond**.

TYPE OF BOND

1. issued by a state or local government
_____

2. offers the highest degree of safety for the purchaser
_____

3. exempt from state and local income tax
_____

4. the riskiest of all three types
_____

5. terms are 20, 30, or 40 years
_____

6. offers the highest potential return to the investor but is subject to federal, state, and local income tax
_____

7. exempt from federal income tax
_____

8. sold to finance public work projects    _____

9. sold to finance business expansion and operation    _____

10. some have coupon rates that are adjusted for inflation    _____

11. generally exempt from state and local income taxes
for residents of state    _____

12. one type in this category cannot be resold    _____

## HEADLINE ECONOMICS

# THE NEW YORK TIMES

# Battered by Economic Crisis, Greeks Turn to Barter Networks

BY RACHEL DONADIO

Volos, Greece—The first time he bought eggs, milk and jam at an outdoor market using not euros but an informal barter currency, Theodoros Mavridis, an unemployed electrician, was thrilled. "I felt liberated, I felt free for the first time," Mr. Mavridis said in a recent interview at a cafe in this port city in central Greece. "I instinctively reached into my pocket, but there was no need to."

Mr. Mavridis is a co-founder of a growing network here in Volos that uses a so-called Local Alternative Unit, or TEM in Greek, to exchange goods and services—language classes, baby-sitting, computer support, home-cooked meals—and to receive discounts at some local businesses. Part alternative currency, part barter system, part open-air market,

the Volos network has grown exponentially in the past year, from 50 to 400 members.

"Ever since the crisis there's been a boom in such networks all over Greece," said George Stathakis, a professor of political economy and vice chancellor of the University of Crete. In spite of the large public sector in Greece, which employs one in five workers, the country's social services often are not up to the task of helping people in need, he added. "There are so many huge gaps that have to be filled by new kinds of networks," he said.

Here in Volos, the group's founders are adamant that they work in parallel to the regular economy, inspired more by a need for solidarity in rough times than a political

push for Greece to leave the euro zone and return to the drachma. The group's concept is simple. People sign up online and get access to a database that is kind of like a members-only Craigslist. One unit of TEM is equal in value to one euro, and it can be used to exchange goods and services. Members start their accounts with zero, and they accrue credit by offering goods and services. They can borrow up to 300 TEMs, but they are expected to repay the loan within a fixed period of time. Members also receive books of vouchers of the alternative currency itself, which look like gift certificates and are printed with a special seal that makes it difficult to counterfeit. Those vouchers can be used like checks. Several businesspeople

in Volos, including a veterinarian, an optician and a seamstress, accept the alternative currency in exchange for a discount on the price in euros. There is a system of ratings so that people can describe their experiences using TEM, in order to keep transparent quality control.

The group also holds a monthly open-air market that is like a cross between a garage sale and a farmers' market, where Mr. Mavridis used his TEM credit to buy the milk, eggs and jam. Those goods came from local farmers who are also involved in the project. "We're still at the beginning," said Mr. Mavridis, who lost his job as an electrician at a factory last year. In the coming months, the group hopes to have a borrowed office space where people without computers can join the network more easily, he said.

As she bustled around her sewing table in her small shop in downtown Volos, Angeliki Ioanniti, 63,

said she gave discounts for sewing to members of the network, and she has also exchanged clothing alterations for help with her computer. "Being a small city helps, because there's trust," she said. In exchange for euros and alternative currency, she also sells olive oil, olives and homemade bergamot-scented soap prepared by her daughter, who lives in the countryside outside Volos.

Similar initiatives have been cropping up elsewhere in Greece. In Patras, in the Peloponnese, a network called Ovolos, named after an ancient Greek means of currency, was founded in 2009 and includes a local exchange currency, a barter system and a so-called time bank, in which members swap services like medical care and language classes. The group has about 100 transactions a week, and volunteers monitor for illegal services, said Nikos Bogonikolos, the president and a founding member.

**DID YOU READ IT?**

1) **In what way(s) has the introduction of this new informal currency called TEM helped the people of Volos?**

2) **What protections are in place to ensure that the TEM will be accepted in exchange for goods and services?**

**WHAT DO YOU THINK?**

1) **What will happen to the TEM once the Greek economy has recovered from its economic crisis?**

2) **Why is economic cooperation important in times of economic crisis?**

EXCERPTED FROM www.nytimes.com/2011/10/02/world/europe/in-greece-barter-networks-surge.html?pagewanted=all&_r=0

# AN INTERVIEW WITH Michael Lewis

**You majored in art history yet have written several important books with an economics focus, including *Liar's Poker*, *Moneyball*, and *The Big Short*. When did you first become interested in economics? What was the first course you took in economics, and what do you remember most from it?**

I was actively hostile to economics before I became interested in it. My freshman year in college I watched vast numbers of my otherwise-promising fellow students vanish into the economics department, not because they had any interest in economics but because they believed a degree in economics was a ticket to a job on Wall Street. No one even pretended to enjoy it or be interested in it. My senior year, consumed with a thesis to complete my degree in art history, I took an introductory course in microeconomics, taught by an inspired lecturer named Uwe Reinhardt. And I remember thinking two things: (1) why didn't anyone ever tell me this stuff was so interesting? and (2) the adult world is a conspiracy of people who understand it.

**Did you realize that economics would influence your life when you first took an economics course?**

Though I had those thoughts I didn't pursue them in any practical way, at least not at first.

**Why did you decide to get a degree in economics after all?**

I failed to get a job on Wall Street.

**Why are you so drawn to write about topics with an economics slant?**

I did indeed earn a master's degree from the London School of Economics, but I'm obviously not a professional economist. And I don't think of myself as writing about topics with an economic slant, though I can understand why I am accused of doing so. I simply write about what interests me, and what often interests me touches in one way or another with the question of value, and that question is at the heart of economics. Why are some baseball players paid more than others? What are the forces in the world that affect the value of this poor black kid living on the streets of the Memphis ghetto? Why would any Wall Street firm pay me huge sums of money to offer financial advice?

**What are the two or three main economic themes from *Moneyball*, particularly as they relate to the labor market?**

The biggest point is that markets can do a surprisingly poor job of valuing people. A baseball player has been performing a job that has been performed in more or less the same way for a century. He has statistics attached to every move he makes on the field. Millions of people watch him do what he does: if he can be misvalued, who can't be?

**Neoclassical economics says that workers are paid based on the value of their marginal product. From your first-hand observations of finance and baseball, do you think this is true? If not, why don't competition and the forces of supply and demand push us to an equilibrium where workers are paid based on their contributions to output? (The last part is hard, so you don't have to answer completely; I couldn't.)**

I do not think this is true. Here's a question I would love for some economics student to answer: in 2007, the big Wall Street firms shelled out the most in their history in bonus payments to their employees. That same year these same firms lost huge sums of money—to the point where most of them probably would have gone bust if the government had not bailed them out—and sunk massive amounts of capital in unproductive investments. How does one explain this using the tools and assumptions of neoclassical economics?

**How would you advise high school students to think about economics even if they are interested, as the vast majority will be, in careers that are not economics-related in nature at all?**

As a tool in a toolkit. Everyone should have some facility with the ideas in introductory econ courses. If you don't, you are at a disadvantage in the world.

**What does it feel like to see one of your books turned into a movie?**

Warm and fuzzy. Writing books is essentially an individual sport; making movies is essentially a team sport. It's nice to get a chance to see one's individual efforts find a home in a team.

# CHAPTER 16 REVIEW AND SELF-ASSESSMENT

## REVIEW

### Points to Remember

#### MODULE 47: WHAT IS MONEY?

1. **Money** can be anything that is widely accepted in exchange for goods and services.

2. **Currency** is paper money and coins.

3. **Barter** is the exchange of goods or services for other goods or services without the use of money.

4. Money serves as a **medium of exchange** when it is used as payment for goods and services.

5. Money as a **store of value** can be saved and will hold its value relatively well over time.

6. Money serves as a **unit of account** when it is used as a standard measure used to set prices and make economic calculations.

7. **Commodity money** is money that has value apart from its use as money.

8. **Representative money** has no value of its own but can be exchanged for something of value.

9. **Fiat money** has value because the government has ordered that it be accepted in payment of debts.

10. The **money supply** is the amount of money available for the purchase of goods and services.

11. **M1** is a measure of the money supply that includes only the forms of money that are readily available to spend: cash, checking account deposits, and traveler's checks.

12. **M2** is a measure of the money supply that includes M1 along with forms of money that are less easily converted to cash.

#### MODULE 48: THE BANKING SYSTEM

13. A **depository institution** is a financial institution that obtains money mainly through deposits from clients.

14. A **commercial bank** is a depository institution that accepts deposits from individuals and firms, and provides them with loans in addition to a wide variety of other services.

15. A **savings bank** is a depository institution that specializes in loans for the purchase of homes and other real estate.

16. A **thrift** is a depository institution established to encourage savings and can be a savings and loan association, a credit union, or a savings bank.

17. **Savings and loan associations** (S&Ls) are depository institutions, similar to savings banks, that specialize in loans for the purchase of homes.

18. A **credit union** is a not-for-profit depository institution owned by its members, who are also its customers.

19. In a **fractional reserve banking system**, banks must hold on to a fraction of their deposits and may lend out the rest.

20. A **reserve requirement** specifies the percentage of deposits that banks must hold as reserves.

#### MODULE 49: THE ROLE OF FINANCIAL MARKETS IN THE REAL ECONOMY

21. A **financial intermediary** is an institution that channels money between savers and borrowers.

22. Corporations can sell stocks to raise financial capital, which is called **equity financing**.

23. Corporations can sell bonds and take out other types of loans to raise financial capital, which is called **debt financing**.

24. The **nominal interest rate** is the actual rate of interest that a saver will receive and a borrower will pay.

25. The **real interest rate** is the nominal interest rate minus the expected rate of inflation.

26. The **current yield** is the annual coupon payment divided by the price.

27. A **junk bond** is a high-risk, high-interest-rate corporate bond.

28. A **capital market** is a market in which money is lent for one year or more.

29. A **money market** is a market in which money is lent for less than a year.

30. In a **primary market**, new assets are sold by their issuers.

31. In **secondary markets**, investors buy and sell financial assets that have already been purchased at least once.

32. A **bull market** is characterized by steady growth in stock prices.

33. A **bear market** is characterized by rapidly declining stock prices.

## SELF-ASSESSMENT

The following questions are the type your teacher might ask you on a quiz or a test. Practice with these in order to improve your performance on class tests.

### Multiple-Choice Questions

1. Each of the following would be included in the M1 definition of money **except**

   a. coins and currency.
   b. deposits in checking accounts.
   c. deposits in savings accounts.
   d. traveler's checks.

2. The type of relationship that exists between bond prices and interest rates is best described by which of the following?

   a. When interest rates rise, bond prices fall.
   b. When interest rates rise, bond prices rise.
   c. When interest rates fall, bond prices fall.
   d. When interest rates fall, bond price may rise or fall.

3. When money is used to purchase goods or services, it is being used as a

   a. unit of account.
   b. store of value.
   c. legal tender.
   d. medium of exchange.

Answer the next two questions based on the following scenario.

Bank #1 receives a $20,000 deposit from a customer. Bank #1 then loans out all its excess reserves of $18,000, which are deposited into Bank #2. Bank #2 loans out all its excess reserves, as does Bank #3, and so on.

4. The reserve requirement for the banks described previously is

   a. 1 percent.
   b. 10 percent.
   c. $18,000.
   d. $20,000.

5. If the process described previously continues throughout the banking system until all excess reserves are loaned out, the total change in the money supply resulting from the $20,000 deposit would be

   a. $18,000.
   b. $20,000.
   c. $38,000.
   d. $200,000.

6. The type of money that has value apart from its use as money is

   a. commodity money.
   b. fiat money.
   c. representative money.
   d. paper money.

7. The amount by which actual reserves exceed required reserves is called

   a. fractional reserves.
   b. excess reserves.
   c. deficit reserves.
   d. the reserve requirement.

8. The relationship that exists in the bond market between risk and return is best described by which of the following?

   a. A bond with a higher yield usually has a lower risk.
   b. A bond with a higher yield usually has a higher risk.
   c. A bond with a lower yield usually has a higher risk.
   d. A bond with a lower yield risk is just as likely to have a higher or lower risk.

9. Which of the following is **not** considered a type of depository institution?

   a. commercial bank

   b. credit union

   c. finance company

   d. savings and loan association

10. Which of the following contributed to the financial crisis of 2007–2009?

   a. deregulation of the banking system that allowed collateralized debt obligations and credit default swaps to be sold

   b. a decrease in the number of subprime mortgages issues by banks

   c. a decrease in the number of home foreclosures

   d. increased scrutiny of banks by the Federal Reserve

## Constructed Response Questions

1. Identify one problem that arises under a barter system.
2. Why would raspberries be a poor choice as a medium of exchange?
3. Give an example of each of the following:

   a. commodity money

   b. representative money

   c. fiat money

4. Why are credit cards not considered part of the money supply?
5. Describe the difference between nominal interest rates and real interest rates.

**CHAPTER 17 & YOU** The Federal Reserve System influences the money supply, interest rates, and the availability of loans. What does this mean for the average citizen? The Fed's actions may influence the car you drive, the house you live in, and even the college you attend. The payments most families make on car, home, and student loans depend on the interest rates established by the Federal Reserve. Lower interest rates mean lower loan payments for fast cars, comfortable homes, and tuition at respected colleges. Interest rates and the money supply also affect how much consumers spend and how much businesses invest, both of which influence the availability of jobs. In these and other ways, the Federal Reserve plays a key role in setting the pace of overall economic activity in the country.

# The Federal Reserve System and Monetary Policy

## A FORCE IN DIFFICULT TIMES

It's not easy being the Federal Reserve System, the U.S. central bank known as the *Fed* by friends and foes. Fed policy is often the subject of debate. For example, congressman and 2012 presidential candidate Ron Paul wrote a book titled *End the Fed*. A spin-off of the 2011 Occupy Wall Street movement that calls itself Occupy the Fed Now seeks a "complete dissolution" of the Fed. And monetarist economists including Milton Friedman and Anna Schwartz have blamed the Fed for allowing an economic downturn to spiral into the Great Depression of the 1930s. Speaking as a governor of the Fed in 2002, current Fed chairman Ben Bernanke agreed, saying to Friedman and Schwartz, "You're right, we did it. We're very sorry. But . . . we won't do it again." Bernanke spent much of his career studying the causes and consequences of the Great Depression and is determined to make the Fed a positive force in difficult times.

The **Federal Reserve System** is the U.S. central banking system.

*Responsible and timely actions by the Fed help prevent economic crises, like a recurrence of the Great Depression of the 1930s.*

This chapter describes the structure and functions of the Federal Reserve System and how the actions of the Fed affect the economy. Module 50 sheds light on why the Federal Reserve System was created and describes its organization. In Module 51 you will learn about the traditional monetary policy tools of the Fed. Module 52 outlines the unusual powers summoned by the Fed to combat the financial crisis that began in 2007.

## BOTTOM LINE

The Federal Reserve regulates the nation's banking institutions and carries out monetary policy, which affects the health of the economy.

# MODULE 50

# The Federal Reserve System

**KEY IDEA:** As the nation's central bank, the Federal Reserve acts to maintain the safety of the banking system and the stability of the economy.

## OBJECTIVES

- **To explain why the Federal Reserve System was created.**
- **To identify the structure of the Federal Reserve System.**
- **To describe the functions of the Federal Reserve System.**
- **To explain the role of the Federal Reserve System in formulating and executing monetary policy.**

*Did you ever wonder why Alexander Hamilton's portrait is on the ten dollar bill? As the first secretary of the Treasury, Hamilton was instrumental in establishing the nation's first central bank.*

## Central Banks in Times of Crisis

Central banks oversee banking systems and try to stabilize economies. For example, as several European countries struggled with debt problems in 2012, the European Central Bank increased the money supply and lowered interest rates to help governments and banks find their financial footing. In 1790, secretary of the Treasury Alexander Hamilton wrote *Report on a National Bank* in an effort to persuade Congress to establish a central bank for the new United States. He was a strong believer in the value of a central banking authority, but Hamilton could not have foreseen the role that a national bank would play 200 years later. After the September 11 terrorist attacks of 2001, the Federal Reserve System moved quickly to reassure financial markets. It lent money to keep banks open as the country recovered from the tragedy. In 2008, the Fed took steps to calm the crisis coming out of the housing and financial markets. The severity of this crisis motivated the use of escalated powers to prop up collapsing banks and make credit available from cash-strapped lending institutions. The Fed had been established in response to a series of similar economic disasters almost a century earlier. In this module we explore the system that serves these and other purposes.

## THE PURPOSE AND ORGANIZATION OF THE FEDERAL RESERVE SYSTEM

The Federal Reserve is not one big bank; it is a central banking system with major banks in 12 districts and 24 branch banks. The Fed's duties differ considerably from those of the commercial banks discussed in Module 37. The Federal Reserve System has four major areas of responsibility:

**1.** Conducting the nation's monetary policy with the goals of maintaining full employment and price stability, both of which promote economic growth.

**2.** Regulating, supervising, and examining the nation's banks to ensure the safety of the banking system.

**3.** Maintaining the stability of the financial system and containing "systemic risk that may arise in the financial markets."

**4.** Providing financial services to the federal government and serving as the "bankers' bank" for commercial banks

THINKSTOCK

The **Board of Governors** of the Federal Reserve is made up of seven members appointed by the president and manages the operations of the Federal Reserve.

and other depository institutions. This includes holding cash reserves for them, processing checks, and providing electronic payments.

When the economy is misbehaving, Fed action in several of these areas may be needed to work toward a fix.

 **Don't Confuse Central Banks with Commercial Banks**

Central banks such as the Federal Reserve are very different from commercial banks. Unlike commercial banks, central banks operate within the government. Rather than operating with the goal of profits, central banks seek to stabilize the economy. And unlike commercial banks, central banks do not set up accounts for individuals. Instead, central banks set up accounts for commercial banks and the government. So don't try to open a checking account at the Federal Reserve, and don't expect a commercial bank to conduct monetary policy.

The Federal Reserve is an independent body within the federal government. When Congress established the Fed, it created this independence so that the Fed's policies would not be swayed by political considerations. As an added buffer between the government and the Fed, Congress made the Fed self-supporting. The Fed's operating income comes from the services it provides, not from the federal government. The largest source of Fed income is the interest it receives on government securities, such as T-bills, which it buys through the Federal Open Market Committee. This interest amounted to $84.5 billion in 2011. Member banks pay the Fed for services such as check clearing and pay interest on money they borrow from the Fed. The excess of the Fed's income over its expenses—$75.4 billion in 2011—is provided to the U.S. Treasury.

The **Federal Reserve Banks** implement Federal Reserve policies and provide services to member banks and federal government agencies.

## The Board of Governors

The **Board of Governors** of the Federal Reserve meets in Washington, D.C., to manage the operations of the Fed. The seven governors are appointed by the president for 14-year terms. The terms are staggered so that a new member joins the board on February 1 of each even-numbered year. Although resignations can increase the frequency of appointments, it is unlikely that even a two-term president would be able to appoint a full Board of Governors. This system limits the influence of politics on monetary policy.

Governors may serve only one full term. The board has a chair and a vice chair who are chosen from among the seven governors on the board. They are nominated by the president for four-year terms and must be confirmed by the Senate. The chair leads board meetings, manages the board's staff, and acts as the spokesperson for board policies. The chair reports twice a year to Congress on monetary policy and testifies as requested at congressional hearings.

The most important function of the Board of Governors is to set monetary policy. The board approves changes in interest rate targets and serves as 7 of the 12 members on the Federal Open Market Committee. The board oversees the workings of the Federal Reserve Banks. The board also writes banking regulations and supervises the compliance of member banks and bank holding companies. Under the guidance of the board, Fed staff members prepare reports on economic trends and issues such as housing and e-commerce.

## The Federal Reserve Banks

The 12 **Federal Reserve Banks** are both bankers' banks and the federal government's banks, in that they provide services to commercial banks and to federal government agencies in their districts. Figure 50.1 shows the 12 Fed districts, the location of each Federal Reserve Bank, and the system's 24 branch banks. Each district has a 9-member board of directors that oversees operations at the district level.

The Federal Reserve Banks are the operating arm of the Federal Reserve. They implement the Fed's policies and the laws passed by Congress that relate to the banking industry. These Federal Reserve Banks also monitor the economic health of their regions and report back to the Fed. Each region is made up of a mix of industrial sectors—agricultural, manufacturing, and service—and geographic areas—urban, metropolitan, and rural. By reviewing economic activity across these sectors and geographic areas, each Federal Reserve Bank provides information to help the Federal Open Market Committee determine national monetary policy.

In addition to their monetary policy responsibilities, Federal Reserve Banks have several other responsibilities, including

- holding the cash reserves of depository institutions, including banks, credit unions, and savings and loans;

- making loans to depository institutions;

- acting as an agent for the federal government in a variety of transactions, including issuing and redeeming government securities such as savings bonds;

- supervising and acting as bank examiner for member banks of the Federal Reserve System.

## The Member Banks

Module 48 explained that banks in the United States are chartered either by the federal government or a state government. All federally chartered banks must be **member banks** of the Federal Reserve System, and state-chartered banks may join if they meet certain requirements. About 38 percent of the slightly more than 8,000 banks in the United States are member banks.

**Member banks** of the Federal Reserve System include all nationally chartered banks and many state-chartered banks. They are stockholders in their district bank and help elect the district's board of directors.

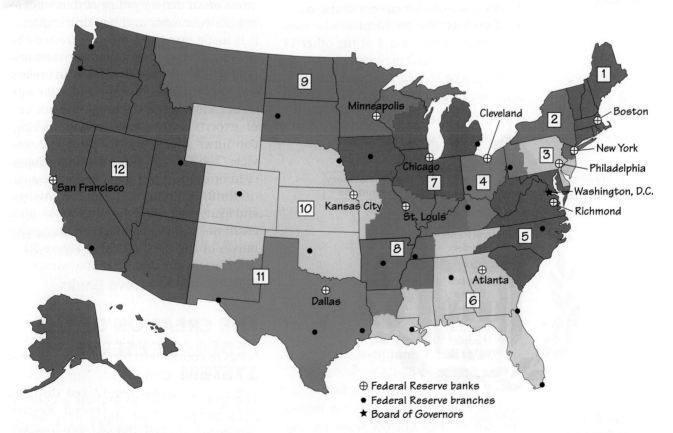

- ⊕ Federal Reserve banks
- ● Federal Reserve branches
- ★ Board of Governors

**Figure 50.1** The 12 Federal Reserve Districts
**The Federal Reserve System has a bank in each of 12 districts.**
**DID YOU GET IT?** In which Federal Reserve district do you live?

Member banks must place 3 percent of their financial capital in the Federal Reserve Bank in their district to help finance its operations. In exchange for this, the member banks are considered stockholders in the district bank and receive an annual dividend of up to 6 percent of their investment. As stockholders, member banks elect six of the nine directors of their district's board of directors. The other three directors are appointed by the Board of Governors at the federal level.

Whether or not a bank joins the Federal Reserve System, it can use the financial services offered through the Federal Reserve Bank in its district. These include check clearing, electronic funds transfers, and the distribution of currency.

## The Federal Open Market Committee

The **Federal Open Market Committee** (FOMC) is the body that actually creates monetary policy. It has 12 voting members and 7 nonvoting participants. The voting members are the 7 members of the Board of Governors, the president of the New York District Bank, and 4 of the other 11 Federal Reserve Bank presidents on a rotating basis. The Federal Reserve Bank presidents who are not serving on the FOMC

The **Federal Open Market Committee** is the group within the Federal Reserve that creates monetary policy.

still attend the committee's meetings as nonvoting participants and provide their views on monetary policy and the condition of the economy from their region's point of view.

The FOMC exercises one tool of monetary policy: it carries out open-market operations to manipulate the cost and availability of money in the economy as explained in the next module. In addition to its principal role in monetary policy, the FOMC oversees the Fed's operations in foreign exchange markets and helps oversee the U.S. securities market. The New York District Bank implements the FOMC's policies in these markets, which is why it is a permanent member of the FOMC.

## The Federal Advisory Committees

In addition to receiving updates on economic conditions and issues from the 12 district banks, the Board of Governors receives reports and advice from three advisory committees known as *councils*. The *Federal Advisory Council* has expertise on economic and banking matters. It is made up of one member from each reserve district. The *Consumer Advisory Council* advises the board on issues relating to consumers and the financial services industry. This council is made up of experts with a background in law, consumer affairs, and the financial services. The *Thrift Institutions Advisory Council* informs the board about matters related to thrift institutions, including savings and loans associations, savings banks, and credit unions. The members are representatives of the thrift industry. Figure 50.2 summarizes the organizational structure of the Federal Reserve.

## THE CREATION OF THE FEDERAL RESERVE SYSTEM

The initial efforts to launch a central bank in the United States were not a smashing success. Alexander Hamilton's First National Bank operated for only 20 years. When its charter came due for renewal in 1811, Congress

**Figure 50.2** The Organizational Structure of the Federal Reserve
The Federal Reserve is managed by its Board of Governors, with direction from the Federal Open Market Committee and advice from three federal advisory committees.

## ECONOMICS IN ACTION

# Why a Few Words by the Fed Chairman Make a Big Difference in the Financial Markets

Chairman Bernanke

The following are actual newspaper headlines:

*"Markets Will Look for Hints in Bernanke's Words"*

*"Bernanke's Speech Sends Stocks Higher"*

*"Markets Close Higher on Bernanke Speech"*

*"Bernanke Speaks, and Markets Inch Higher"*

"Bernanke" is Ben Bernanke, the chairman of the Federal Reserve System. The news stories are about how the stock market responds to his public pronouncements. If he speaks of good news about the economy, the demand for stocks rises, as do stock prices. If the news isn't so rosy, stock prices fall. Why are one man's words so important?

While Bernanke is an experienced and respected economist, this isn't why investors, corporations, banks, and other nations take notice when he speaks. The opinions the chairman delivers are not his alone. When the chairman testifies at Congressional hearings and speaks to business groups, he represents the Federal Reserve Board of Governors.

Bernanke's words reflect the Fed's perspective on the economy. Fed policy hinges on that perspective. With its monetary policy tools, the Fed affects the availability of money and credit in the economy. When the Fed lowers interest rates, loans for the expansion of businesses and for the purchase of cars and homes become cheaper. When the Fed raises rates, money for expansions and purchases is harder to come by. So the Fed's decisions, as conveyed by the chairman, affect businesses and thus the value of corporate stocks. That's why stock market investors listen carefully to the Fed chairman's words.

**DID YOU GET IT?**
Why is the chairman's role as spokesman for the Fed so important?

refused to reauthorize it. Farm owners in the southern and western states opposed it because they felt it catered to bankers and business people in the North. As detailed in the timeline of U.S. banking in Chapter 16, the Second National Bank was chartered in 1816 as a new attempt at a central bank, but its charter was allowed to expire as well. From the late 1800s until the early 1900s, the nation lurched from one financial crisis to another. Recessions in 1873 and 1907 and a depression in 1893 convinced many Americans that the nation needed a stable financial system. A central bank once again appeared to be the answer.

### The Federal Reserve Act of 1913

The appropriate structure and oversight for a national banking system was long under debate, both inside and outside the federal government. Conservatives wanted a banking system that was privately owned and not regulated by the government. Reformers known as progressives wanted the opposite—a banking system owned and regulated by the federal government.

**Foreign reserves** are deposits of foreign currencies held by central banks.

The resulting Federal Reserve Act of 1913 was a compromise. The nation's banks remained privately owned but were to be regulated by the Federal Reserve Board. The members of the board, known as *governors*, were to be appointed by the president of the United States. The nation was divided into 12 districts with a Federal Reserve Bank in each district to oversee the banks in its region. The 12 Federal Reserve Banks were given a great deal of authority to make decisions. Over the century since its inception, the Federal Reserve System has gone through considerable change and expansion.

## ECONOMICS IN ACTION

# The European Union's Central Bank

The European Central Bank (ECB) is the central bank for the 17 countries that have adopted the euro, as shown in blue in Figure 50.3. These countries retain their own national central banks (NCBs), which work in cooperation with the ECB to set and carry out monetary policy for the Eurozone. All 27 European Union (EU) countries are connected through the European System of Central Banks.

Some of the principal tasks of the European Central Bank are to

• develop monetary policy for member national central banks;
• authorize the issuance of euro currency by member NCBs;
• intervene in the foreign exchange markets;
• facilitate international and European cooperation on monetary matters; and

• manage **foreign reserves**, which are deposits of foreign currency held by the ECB and NCBs.

The European Central Bank has three decision-making bodies: the Executive Board, the Governing Council, and the General Council. The day-to-day operations of the ECB are overseen by the Executive Board. The board implements monetary policy decisions made by the Governing Council and monitors and provides guidance to the NCBs on how to carry out the policies.

The Governing Council's main responsibility is to develop monetary policy for the Eurozone. Among its other duties are setting foreign exchange rates for the Eurozone, ensuring compliance with ECB guidelines, authorizing the issuance of euro currency, and establishing standard accounting and reporting practices for NCBs.

The General Council is considered a "transitional body" that will act until all EU countries adopt the euro and then will cease to exist. It reports progress toward adopting the euro by the non-Eurozone countries, providing technical assistance to these countries in their efforts to meet the requirements and overseeing foreign exchange rates between Eurozone and non-Eurozone EU countries.

The national central banks of the Eurozone carry out the monetary policies developed by the European Central Bank. They also manage the foreign reserves of the European Central Bank as well as their own foreign reserves and issue euro currency in conjunction with the ECB.

And national central banks conduct a variety of functions within their own countries, such as supervising their own financial institutions, providing credit, and operating the payment system that moves money around within their banking systems.

**DID YOU GET IT?**

Explain one way in which the responsibilities of the European Central Bank differ from those of the Federal Reserve.

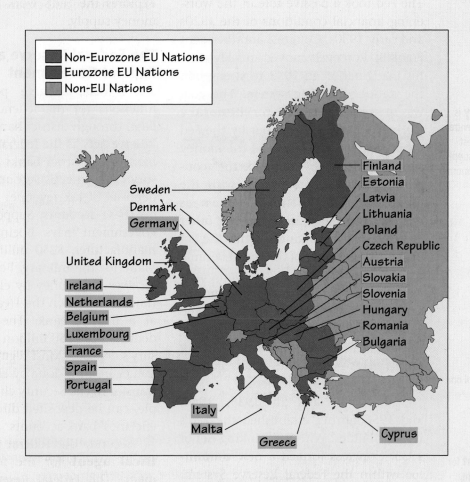

**Figure 50.3** Map of the EU and Eurozone Nations

*Congress and President Franklin Roosevelt took action in 1933 in an effort to shore up the nation's banking system.*

## The Great Depression and Reforms to the Fed

The Fed took a passive role in the worsening financial conditions of the 1920s and early 1930s. Congress and President Franklin Roosevelt moved quickly after his inauguration in 1933 to strengthen the nation's banking system. The goal was to improve the tools for **monetary policy**, which is carried out by the Fed to manage interest rates and the money supply, and thereby influence the economy. The first change came with the Glass-Steagall Act, formally known as the Banking Act of 1933. Among other changes to the banking system, the act expanded the duties of the Fed. It became responsible for *open market operations*, which allow the Fed to alter the money supply as explained later in this chapter. The Fed was also assigned to examine the accounting books of **bank holding companies**—companies that control banks—to watch for problems.

Additional laws in 1935, 1946, and 1956 further established the Fed's responsibilities. With the Banking Act of 1935, Congress formed a new committee within the Federal Reserve System, the *Federal Open Market Committee*, to carry out monetary policy. The Employment Act of 1946 had the Fed focus its monetary policy on the objectives of full employment, price stability, and economic growth. And the Bank Holding Company Act of 1956 made the Fed responsible for regulating bank holding companies in addition to acting as their bank examiner.

**Monetary policy** is actions taken by the central bank to manage interest rates and the money supply in pursuit of macroeconomic goals.

**Bank holding companies** are companies that control one or more banks.

As the **fiscal agent** for the federal government, the Fed sells, redeems, and pays interest on government securities.

# THE CENTRAL BANK IN ACTION

Its service as the central bank and the "bankers' bank" brings the Federal Reserve to a crossroads with both the federal government and the country's financial institutions. Meanwhile the Fed holds the purse strings for the money supply, which makes the Fed's work all the more relevant to us all. In this section we'll take a closer look at what the Fed actually does for the government and the commercial banks. Module 51 explores the Fed's work to control the money supply.

## The Federal Reserve and the Federal Government

The Federal Reserve performs three functions for the federal government. First, through district banks, the Federal Reserve acts as the federal government's bank. The district banks hold the Treasury Department's accounts and process deposits of tax revenues and payments on these accounts. Suppose the federal government pays Boeing, an aircraft manufacturer, $250 million for an airplane for the military. Boeing's account receives the money by electronic funds transfer drawn on the Treasury's account at a district bank. The district bank deducts the $250 million from the Treasury's deposits. Most regular federal payments are now done by electronic funds transfer. Social Security checks, for example, can be deposited directly into beneficiaries' bank accounts.

Second, the Federal Reserve is the **fiscal agent** for the federal government. The Federal Reserve Banks sell and redeem government securities—the Treasury notes, bills, bonds, and TIPS you read about in previous chapters. The Federal Reserve Banks also pay out the interest on these securities to investors.

Third, the Federal Reserve puts newly printed paper currency and newly minted coins into circulation. The Treasury arranges for the production of the currency, but the Federal Reserve Banks

*The Federal Reserve puts newly minted coins into circulation.*

are responsible for getting the money out to the commercial banks and ultimately to the public. The Federal Reserve Banks also remove old, worn bills and coins from circulation.

## The Federal Reserve and Financial Institutions

In addition to being the federal government's banker, the Fed is the banker for the commercial banks. Through the Federal Reserve Banks in Cleveland and Atlanta, the Fed operates a *check-clearing* system as shown in Figure 50.4. **Check clearing**

is the process of removing money from the bank account of the person who wrote the check—the *payer*—and delivering it to the account of the check's recipient—the *payee*. The check-clearing system processes millions of checks between payer and payee banks every day, 24 hours a day.

Since the Check 21 Act (also known as the Twenty-first Century Act) went into effect in 2004, banks have not had to physically ship checks from bank to bank. Instead, checks can be scanned and sent electronically, which makes the process more efficient, less costly, and more secure. The process is principally the same as before: money is still withdrawn (or *debited*) from payer accounts and deposited (or *credited*) to payee accounts. But instead of receiving used paper checks back with the monthly statement, the payer receives a *substitute check*, which is a high-quality paper reproduction of both

**Check clearing** is the processes of removing money from the bank account of the person who wrote the check—the *payer*—and delivering it to the account of the check's recipient—the *payee*.

**Figure 50.4** Check-Clearing Process

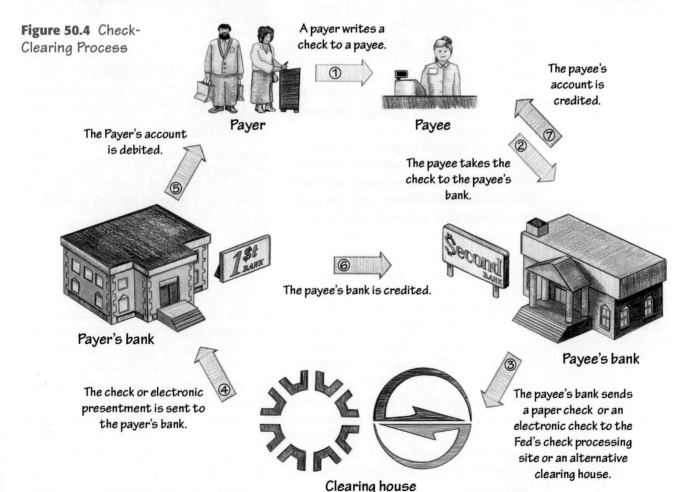

A payer writes a check to a payee.

① 

**Payer**

The Payer's account is debited.

⑤

The payee's account is credited.

② ⑦

**Payee**

The payee takes the check to the payee's bank.

**Payer's bank**

⑥ The payee's bank is credited.

**Payee's bank**

④ The check or electronic presentment is sent to the payer's bank.

③ The payee's bank sends a paper check or an electronic check to the Fed's check processing site or an alternative clearing house.

**Clearing house**

sides of the check. However, a payer may still request the return of paper checks—usually for a service charge—if the payer needs them as evidence that a payment has been made.

The Federal Reserve Banks provide two additional types of service through the Fed's nationwide electronic payment system. *Fedwire* provides a secure communications network for transmitting large payments between Federal Reserve Banks for business customers. Suppose a corporation in one city wants to transfer 5 million dollars from its account in that city to the account of a company in a city in another Federal Reserve district. The two district banks carry out the payment transaction over Fedwire.

**ACH (automated clearing house) transfers** are transfers between payers' and payees' accounts carried out without the use of checks on a secure electronic funds-transfer network.

The *automated clearing house* (ACH) system carries out relatively small **ACH transfers** between the accounts of payers and payees without the use of checks. For example, ACH transfers are used for the direct deposit of Social Security checks, payroll deposits, and electronic bill payment. Payments using smart cards, debit cards, and the Internet are not part of the federal electronic funds transfer network, but the Fed is involved in developing standards for the safety and accessibility of these electronic forms of payment.

The Fed plays another role in relation to financial institutions: regulator. The Fed monitors and regulates financial institutions and activities with the goals of ensuring the safety of the banking system and the stability of financial markets. Through the district banks, the Fed supervises U.S. bank holding companies, financial holding companies, and state member banks. In addition, the Fed supervises the foreign activities of these organizations and the U.S. activities of foreign banking organizations.

As part of regulating banks, the Fed writes rules and guidelines for financial institutions under its supervision. These include protections for borrowers and depositors. The district banks examine the records of commercial banks in their districts and assess their financial stability. If a commercial bank is found to have violated a law or a safe banking practice, the district bank has a variety of enforcement actions, including the imposition of fines, that it can take against the bank. The supervision of banking institutions provides the Fed with a close-up view of financial conditions in the country, which aids the development of monetary policy.

The Fed is also the "lender of last resort" for financial institutions. Under ordinary financial conditions, the Federal Reserve Banks frequently lend money to banks for short-term needs. Under unusual conditions, such as a recession, the Fed may need to lend money to banks to enable them to continue operating. You will read more about this and other policy tools of the Fed in Modules 51 and 52.

# MODULE 50 REVIEW AND ASSESSMENT

**Summing Up the Key Ideas:** Match the following terms to the correct definitions.

A. Federal Reserve System
B. Monetary policy
C. Bank holding companies
D. Foreign reserves
E. Board of Governors
F. Federal Reserve Banks
G. Member banks
H. Federal Open Market Committee
I. Fiscal agent
J. Check clearing
K. ACH (automated clearing house) transfers

_____ 1. Deposits of foreign currencies held by central banks.

_____ 2. The process of removing money from the bank account of the person who wrote the check—the payer—and delivering it to the account of the check's recipient—the payee.

_____ 3. Seven members who manage the operations of the Federal Reserve, appointed by the president and approved by the Senate for 14-year terms.

_____ 4. An independent body within the federal government which serves as the central banking system in the United States.

_____ 5. Transfers between payers' and payees' accounts carried out without the use of checks on a secure funds-transfer network.

_____ 6. The responsibility the Fed has when it sells, redeems, and pays interest on government securities.

_____ 7. Includes all nationally chartered banks and many state-chartered banks. They are stockholders in their district bank and help elect the district's board of directors.

_____ 8. Actions taken by the central bank to manage interest rates and the money supply in pursuit of macroeconomic goals.

_____ 9. The group within the Federal Reserve that creates monetary policy.

_____ 10. They implement Federal Reserve policies and provide services to member banks and federal government agencies.

_____ 11. Companies that control one or more banks.

**Analyze and Explain:** Analyze each of the following and then determine in each case if the problem described would fall **inside** or **outside** the realm of responsibility of Federal Reserve Banks.

INSIDE OR OUTSIDE?

1. holding cash reserves of banks, credit unions, and savings and loans

_____

2. acting as an agent for corporations in a variety of transactions, including buying their bonds and supporting the price of their stocks

_____

3. supervising and acting as bank examiner for member banks of the Federal Reserve System

_____

4. making loans to depository institutions

_____

5. making home loans to individuals and businesses

_____

6. acting as an agent for the federal government in a variety of transactions, including issuing and redeeming government securities

_____

**Apply:** In the following situations, determine if the duty described would be one the Fed is **responsible** or is **not responsible** to enforce.

RESPONSIBLE OR NOT RESPONSIBLE?

1. to provide opportunities for individuals and businesses to open checking accounts

   _____

2. to write rules and guidelines for financial institutions under its supervision

   _____

3. to be the lender of "last resort" for financial institutions

   _____

4. to conduct the nation's monetary policy with the goals of maintaining full employment and price stability

   _____

5. to transmit large payments through Fedwire

   _____

6. to regulate and supervise the stock market to provide stability and security to individual investors

   _____

7. to supervise bank holding companies and state member banks

   _____

8. to make loans to businesses who want to expand their operations

   _____

9. to operate the check-clearing system for the nation

   _____

10. to provide financial services to the federal government and serve as the "bankers' bank" for commercial banks and other depository institutions

    _____

11. to serve as the fiscal agent of the U.S. government

    _____

12. to place printed paper currency and newly minted coins into circulation

    _____

# The Federal Reserve and Traditional Monetary Policy

**KEY IDEA:** Monetary policy is one of the tools available to the Fed to help stabilize the economy.

### OBJECTIVES

- **To identify the goals of the Federal Reserve's monetary policy.**
- **To describe the Federal Reserve's monetary policy tools.**
- **To explain the issues involved in implementing monetary policy.**
- **To analyze an alternative way for the Federal Reserve to minimize inflation.**

## The Fed Fights Inflation

In 1989 Alan Greenspan, the chairman of the Federal Reserve System at that time, declared that "the central focus of what we are doing at the Fed is to keep inflation from accelerating." The nation was recovering from the 1987 stock market crash, and the Fed under his chairmanship was working to make sure the economy did not grow too quickly and fuel inflation. Controlling inflation is one goal of the Federal Reserve's monetary policy, the actions the Fed takes to influence the availability and cost of money and credit.

*Alan Greenspan, Chairman of the Federal Reserve from 1987 to 2006, saw accelerating inflation as the primary enemy of the Fed.*

## THE GOALS OF MONETARY POLICY

The primary function of the Fed is to carry out monetary policy in pursuit of the macroeconomic goals of "maximum employment, stable prices, and moderate long-term interest rates." The accomplishment of these goals promotes consistent economic growth. Monetary policy is meant to moderate the peaks and valleys—*expansions* and *contractions*—of business cycles.

The Fed monitors economic indicators closely and changes monetary policy in response to shifts toward inflation or recession. But it is tricky to steer the economy in a particular direction. If the Fed fights inflation too soon or too vigorously, instead of just heading off the inflation, it can set the economy on the path to recession. And if the Fed tries too hard to provide an expansionary boost, it can push the economy into a bout with inflation.

### The Money Market

Monetary policy involves manipulations of the money supply. We can see the effects of these changes with a look at the market for money. The money market looks a lot like the markets for goods and services, with two exceptions, as illustrated in Figure

When the Fed achieves its goals of consistent economic growth, low inflation, and full employment, relatively more workers have jobs to go to.

51.1. First, the "price" of money isn't a dollar amount but an interest rate. The opportunity cost of holding that money you have in your pocket is the interest rate you could earn if you invested it instead. There are a variety of interest rates paid on various types of investments, deposits, and loans. For simplicity, in this discussion we will speak as if there is a single interest rate. That interest rate is the price for money measured on the vertical axis of the money market graph.

The second difference between the money market and the market for, say, baby-sitting or brownies, is that in the short run, the money supply is fixed. A higher price for baby-sitting services or brownies will increase the quantity supplied, but the money supply as determined by the Fed isn't responsive to the interest rate. The fixed amount of money that is available regardless of the interest rate results in a vertical money supply curve as shown by $MS_1$ in Figure 51.1.

Changes in prices or income affect the demand for money. When the price level rises, people need more money to buy goods and services, so the demand for money increases. As prices decline, less money is needed, and the demand for money decreases. With higher incomes, people have more money to spend, and their demand for money increases. Likewise, when incomes are lower, people have less money to spend, so their demand for money is lower.

Changes in interest rates have a different effect. The demand curve for money indicates the quantity demanded at each interest rate. As shown in Figure 51.1, $700 billion is demanded at an interest rate of 6 percent and $900 billion is demanded at an interest rate of 2 percent. Because the demand curve itself captures the effect of a change in the interest rate, it is not appropriate to shift the money demand curve to show the result of a new interest rate. Rather, changes in the interest rate cause movements along the money demand curve.

As the interest rate rises, so does the opportunity cost of holding money. A high interest rate makes investments in CDs, bonds, and similar savings instruments more attractive. If people hold their money rather than investing it, they fail to gain the benefit of the higher interest rate, so the quantity of money demanded

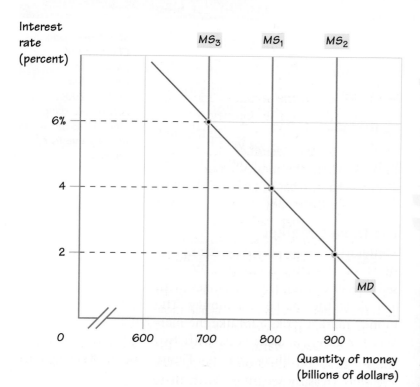

**Figure 51.1** Money Supply and Demand The price in the money market is the interest rate. The supply curve for money is vertical because there is a fixed amount of money available regardless of the interest rate.

decreases. When the interest rate falls, the lower opportunity cost of holding money leads to an increase in the quantity of money demanded. This inverse relationship between the interest rate and the quantity of money demanded results in a downward-sloping money demand curve.

Now we're ready to see how the Fed can spur or rein in the economy by increasing or decreasing the money supply. Notice that an increase in the money supply from $MS_1$ to $MS_2$ lowers the equilibrium interest rate from 4 percent to 2 percent. With this lower interest rate, loans become cheaper for retailers who want to open new stores, schools that want to invest in computers, drug companies that want to expand their research and development efforts, and families that want to buy new homes. As more of these and other investments are made, the economy expands.

Going in the other direction, if the Fed decreases the money supply to $MS_3$, the interest rate increases to 6 percent. Higher interest rates make investments in new buildings, machines, and various other projects less attractive. So the result of a decrease in the money supply and the corresponding rise in the interest rate is that the economy contracts. Next we'll see how the Fed goes about changing the money supply.

**DID YOU GET IT?**
What happens to the interest rate when the money supply increases?

# TRADITIONAL MONETARY POLICY TOOLS

Traditionally, the Fed has influenced the economy by using three major tools: open market operations, the discount rate, and reserve requirements. When the economy is slowing, the Fed adopts an **easy money policy**, which means it increases the money supply. As we have seen, this lowers the interest rate and

encourages new investments in physical capital, among other things. Because this helps the economy expand, this is also called *expansionary monetary policy*.

When the economy is growing, prices are rising, and inflation seems likely, the Fed shifts to a **tight money policy**, which means it decreases the money supply. This causes an increase in the interest rate and discourages new investment projects. The result is a smaller economy, so this is also called *contractionary monetary policy*.

## Open Market Operations

Open market operations are the Fed's primary monetary policy tool. As you read in Module 50, the Federal Open Market Committee (FOMC) determines the policy, and the Federal Reserve Bank of New York executes it. The actual "operations" entail the Fed buying or selling Treasury securities on the open market, meaning from securities brokers and dealers rather than directly from the Treasury.

If the FOMC determines that the economy is slowing and needs an infusion of money, the Federal Reserve will buy Treasury securities. With these purchases, money that had not been in circulation is exchanged for securities that, you will recall, are just promises to repay some money at some time in the future. The Fed holds on to the securities and sends the new money on its journey into the economy. This journey begins in the bank accounts of the securities dealers and brokers, where the money creates excess reserves that the banks can lend out. This lending sets the money creation process in motion—loans that lead to deposits that lead to more loans, and so on, as discussed in Chapter 16. The increase in the money supply brought about by the purchase of securities gives the economy a boost by lowering interest rates and making more investment projects worthwhile.

If the FOMC wants to tighten the money supply to ward off inflation, the Fed sells Treasury securities. With these

**Tight money policy**
decreases the money supply.

**Easy money policy**
increases the money supply.

sales, the Fed takes in money that had been in circulation and exchanges it for securities that do not constitute money. The securities dealers and brokers receive the securities and the Fed debits their bank accounts. The bank reserves used to pay the Fed are removed from the banks' books and from the money supply. With decreased reserves, the banks make fewer loans. This reverses the money creation process and decreases the money supply even more. The decrease in the money supply brought about by the Fed's sale of bonds causes interest rates to rise and cools the economy by making investment projects less attractive. Figure 51.2 summarizes these open-market operations.

The New York Federal Reserve Bank doesn't buy and sell securities as it pleases. At its meetings, the FOMC sets a target for the **federal funds rate**, which is the interest rate that commercial banks charge one another for

short-term loans. In inflationary times, the FOMC wants to tighten the money supply, so it raises the federal funds target rate. The New York Federal Reserve Bank is then instructed to sell Treasury securities to decrease the money supply and force the short-term interest rate upward. When the commercial banks have to pay a higher federal funds rate to borrow money, they pass the additional cost on to their customers by raising the interest rates on their various business, mortgage, and personal loans.

If the Fed forecasts recessionary tendencies in the economy, it will lower the federal funds target rate. The New York Federal Reserve Bank will be instructed to buy government securities to increase the money supply and push the short-term interest rate downward. When it costs banks less to borrow money, they are willing to offer customers lower interest rates on their loans.

The **federal funds rate** is the interest rate that commercial banks charge one another for short-term loans.

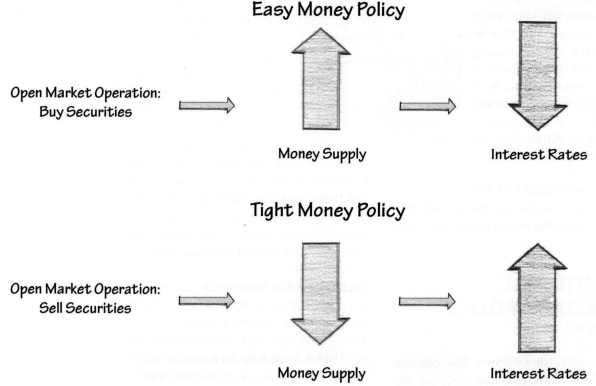

**Figure 51.2** Monetary Policy in Action
When the Fed buys Treasury securities, the money supply increases and interest rates fall. This gives the economy a boost by encouraging new investments. When the Fed sells Treasury securities, the money supply decreases and interest rates rise. This cools the economy by discouraging some investment projects.

Figure 51.3 shows the federal funds target rate from 2001 to 2011. The Fed's response to the recession that started in 2007 is a good example of how the FOMC works to stabilize the economy. At the beginning of 2007, before problems in the housing market began to affect the economy, the federal funds rate was 5.25 percent. The Fed cut the federal funds target rate six times in six months between late 2007 and early 2008. By December of 2008, the target rate was reduced to a target range of between 0 and 0.25 percent, which remained through 2012. Each time the Fed cut the federal funds rate, the stock market went up. The easing of interest rates also resulted in a small upswing in housing sales in 2009. However, as you will read in Module 52, the Fed needed more than interest rate cuts to stabilize the economy and nudge it upward.

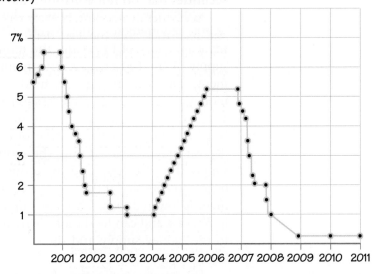

**Figure 51.3** The Federal Funds Rate, 2001–2011
When a recession hit in 2007, the Fed responded by cutting the federal funds target rate six times in six months.

## The Discount Rate

The Fed's monetary policy toolbox also contains the **discount rate**, which is the interest rate that the Federal Reserve Banks charge financial institutions for short-term loans. Usually, commercial banks use these loans to meet their reserve requirements. As you learned in Chapter 16, banks are required to hold a fraction of their customer's demand deposits either in their own vault or at the district's Federal Reserve Bank.

By raising or lowering the discount rate, the Fed can influence the activities of banks. Increasing the discount rate makes it more expensive for banks to borrow from the Fed. As with the cost of a higher federal funds rate, the cost of a higher discount rate is passed on to individuals and firms through higher interest rates. The result is the same—fewer loans for business expansions and other investments are worthwhile to borrowers, and the economy slows down. The opposite is also true: lowering the discount rate results in less costly borrowing for banks and thus for bank customers.

In practice, banks do not often borrow from the Fed. Banks must exhaust all other sources of borrowing before turning to the Fed's "discount window," as this source of lending is known. The provision of the discount window is an example of how the Fed acts as the "lender of last resort," as mentioned in Module 50.

Changes in the discount rate are infrequent. When the Fed does change the discount rate, investors and businesspeople see it as a signal of how the Fed views the economy and what the Fed might do next. For example, if the discount rate is lowered, that might mean the beginning of a period of easy money policy. Seeing this, a firm wanting to borrow money might wait, anticipating lower interest rates in the near future.

The **discount rate** is the interest rate that the Fed charges financial institutions for short-term loans.

## Reserve Requirements

As discussed in Chapter 16, the Federal Reserve sets the reserve requirements that specify the percentage of demand deposits that banks must keep on hand. For example, as of 2013 the reserve requirement for banks with demand deposits of over $79.5 million is 10 percent, so a bank with $100 million in demand deposits must place $10 million in reserves. The Fed seldom changes reserve requirements. In practice, the Fed uses the reserve requirement more to ensure stability in the banking system than as a tool of monetary policy.

When the Fed does raise or lower reserve requirements, the change affects the availability of loans and the money supply. If the Fed raises reserve requirements, banks are required to hold more money in reserves and have less to lend. The money creation process is diminished because a smaller portion of each deposit may be loaned out. The money supply thus decreases and the economy begins to contract. If the reserve requirement is lowered, banks hold less money in reserves and can lend more. This adds to the money supply and the economy begins to expand.

The reserve requirement has a strong effect on the money creation process. In Module 48 we saw that with a reserve requirement of 10 percent, the introduction of $100,000 of new money into the economy led to a $1,000,000 increase in the money supply. Now imagine the reserve requirement is 20 percent instead of 10 percent. In this case a $100,000 deposit would initially create $80,000 in excess reserves that could be loaned out, rather than $90,000. Likewise, each subsequent loan will be smaller because more of each deposit must be held as required reserves. In the end, the total growth in the money supply as a result of the initial $100,000 increase will be $500,000 rather than $1,000,000.

# FACTORS AFFECTING MONETARY POLICY

A variety of factors limit the success of Federal Reserve policies. As with the government, the Fed faces the problem of time lags between the beginning of a problem and the response to policies meant to resolve the problem. It takes time for the Fed to identify problems, select a policy response, and implement it. The time lags between policy changes and their effect vary. For example, the stock and bond markets react quickly to changes, whereas financial institutions, firms, and consumers react more slowly.

There is also the problem of pessimism. Suppose the Fed acts to halt a slowing economy by buying Treasury securities, which adds to the money supply. Banks now have more money to lend, but having lost money on bad loans in the past, they may hesitate to make new loans. They may continue to be concerned for a long time about the reliability of those seeking loans. Firms may hesitate for some time to borrow money and expand because they are not sure there is demand for their products. Consumers may hesitate to spend or to borrow because they are still concerned about their jobs even as the economy shows improvement. So after the Fed expands the money supply, confidence must be restored before banks, firms, and consumers will be eager to tap

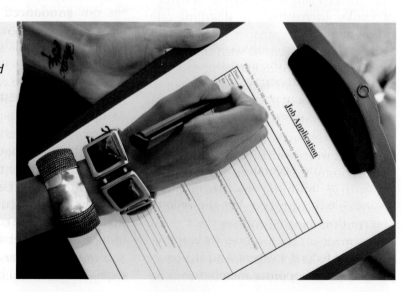

*The ability of monetary policy to create jobs is limited by expectations of a weak economy. Pessimistic firms are hesitant to fill job openings, and pessimistic consumers are reluctant to spend money.*

into the additional money to increase demand and production, and therefore reduce unemployment.

The Fed must take all these factors into consideration when deciding on a course of action and then fine-tune its policy after studying its effects. However, few policies work as wonderfully in practice as they sound in theory. In other words, the Fed's power over the economy is limited. Sometimes even a concerted application of monetary and fiscal policy cannot fix what ails the economy, and recovery comes only with additional influences such as changes in governance, optimism, and time.

## ADVANTAGES OF MONETARY POLICY

Despite the limitations, there are good reasons to consider monetary policy. The ability to adjust policy decisions quickly is one of the advantages of monetary policy. The FOMC meets about every six weeks to review the state of the economy and deliberate on the best course of action. Depending on whether the FOMC decides to refine its policy or hold steady, the Federal Reserve Banks can move immediately to implement new policies.

Monetary policy also allows for flexibility. It does not tell firms or individuals what to do. The policy contracts or expands the economy, but individuals and firms make their own decisions about spending cuts or increases. That way, cuts can be made where they will cause the least harm, and expansions can be made where they will do the most good.

The third advantage of monetary policy is the lack of political influence on the decision makers. Unlike fiscal policy, which is influenced by partisan politics, lobbyists, and donors to political campaigns, the Federal Reserve is independent of both political parties. It is responsible to Congress, but the Federal Reserve does not depend on the federal government for its revenue. Its employees are not federal workers. And although the president appoints members of the

*The central bank of the United Kingdom, the Bank of England, develops monetary policy with an inflation target in mind.*

Board of Governors, the terms of board members are staggered so that only two scheduled openings arise during each presidential term.

## INFLATION TARGETING

 As an alternative focus for monetary policy, some central banks target the inflation rate. Under **inflation targeting**, the central bank sets a target rate—or range—of inflation for some time in the future and develops monetary policy with that goal in mind. About two dozen nations, both industrialized and developing, have adopted inflation targeting since the 1990s. Examples include the United Kingdom, Canada, Brazil, Mexico, Israel, and New Zealand. The Federal Reserve typically has not announced a formal inflation rate target, although in January of 2012 it announced an inflation target of 2 percent.

To stay close to an inflation rate target, a central bank must remain focused on inflation and be willing to compromise other potentially conflicting goals, such as full employment. Economists refer to inflation targeting as being "future focused" because the central bank must be proactive rather than reactive in dealing with economic conditions that can lead to inflation. Once inflation is chosen as the target, there are three steps for the central bank to take:

Under **inflation targeting**, the central bank sets a target rate–or range–of inflation for some time in the future and develops monetary policy with that goal in mind.

1. Set inflation targets for future time periods.

2. Establish an inflation forecasting model based on a variety of inflation indicators.

3. Provide a regular process for adjusting policy in response to forecasts in order to hit the targets.

Studies show that inflation targeting is most useful in countries with high annual rates of inflation. It is also useful in countries with persistent difficulty in maintaining a stable, low rate of inflation. The highest rates of inflation are generally found in developing countries. After adopting inflation targeting, these countries have shown the greatest declines in average annual inflation rates—as much as 6 percentage points. Industrialized countries tend to experience smaller declines but generally have lower inflation rates to begin with.

# ECONOMICS IN ACTION

# Inflation Targeting and the Canadian Economy

Transparency and predictability assist in the success of inflation targeting. In this context, *transparency* means full disclosure of information. The central bank states its target so that firms and consumers are aware of it and can plan for slow price increases based on a stable and low rate of inflation. *Predictability* refers to the consistent policy of the central bank in naming a target and sticking to it. Both of these characteristics build confidence in the economy.

Consider Canada's central bank, the Bank of Canada (BoC), which adopted inflation targeting in 1991. The current target is 2 percent inflation, with an "inflation-control target range" of 1 to 3 percent. This target is reset every five years. To stay within the target range, the BoC reviews monetary policies bimonthly based on forecasts of future conditions. Before 2000, reviews and announcements of policy decisions were not made on a regular schedule. Changing from an unpredictable decision-making system to a system of scheduled announcements has decreased uncertainty in the stock and bond markets. In addition, the BoC regularly publishes "Monetary Policy Report Updates" on the current state of inflation and the outlook for the future. These reports have added to the public's sense of trust in the system.

Canada held its inflation rate within the target range for most of its first 20 years of inflation targeting. From month to month, the inflation rate ranged from about −1 percent to 5 percent, but these large fluctuations were short-lived. Over the same 1991 to 2011 period, unemployment declined from a high of 12 percent in 1992 to a low of 6 percent in 2008. In that year, unemployment began to rise again as the worldwide recession hit the Canadian economy. Canada's GDP has also shown positive growth for most years since 1991. Officials of the BoC contend that while the BoC has not targeted either employment or GDP, inflation targeting has aided both.

**DID YOU GET IT?**
Describe how the policies of the BoC illustrate the core characteristics of inflation targeting: transparency and predictability.

# MODULE 51 REVIEW AND ASSESSMENT

**Summing Up the Key Ideas:** Match the following terms to the correct definitions.

A. Money market
B. Easy money
C. Tight money

D. Open market operations
E. Federal funds rate
F. Discount rate

G. Inflation targeting

_____ 1. A tool of monetary policy that entails the Fed buying or selling Treasury securities.

_____ 2. A policy that decreases the money supply, also called contractionary monetary policy.

_____ 3. The process of the central bank setting a target rate—or range—of inflation for some time in the future and developing monetary policy with that goal in mind.

_____ 4. The interest rate that the Fed charges financial institutions for short-term loans.

_____ 5. The interest rate that commercial banks charge one another for short-term loans.

_____ 6. A policy that increases the money supply, also called expansionary monetary policy.

_____ 7. The market in which the equilibrium of supply and demand determines the equilibrium interest rate and quantity of money.

**Analyze and Explain:** Determine whether it would be appropriate for the Federal Reserve to **increase** or **decrease** the money supply in the following situations. Explain your answer.

| | INCREASE OR DECREASE? | EXPLANATION |
|---|---|---|
| 1. The U.S. economy enters a period of rapid inflation. | _____ | _____ |
| 2. The unemployment rate in the U.S. economy is much higher than normal. | _____ | _____ |
| 3. Real GDP decreases from one year to the next. | _____ | _____ |

**Apply:** Suppose the Fed chooses to address the following situations using monetary policy. Indicate the type of open market operations (**buy** or **sell bonds**), the discount rate change (**increase** or **decrease**), and the adjustments in the reserve requirement (**increase** or **decrease**) that would be appropriate in each case.

| | OPEN MARKET OPERATIONS | DISCOUNT RATE | RESERVE REQUIREMENT |
|---|---|---|---|
| 1. The economy falls into a recession. | _____ | _____ | _____ |
| 2. The FOMC orders a tight money policy. | _____ | _____ | _____ |
| 3. The economy enters a period of high inflation. | _____ | _____ | _____ |
| 4. The FOMC decides to adopt easy money policy. | _____ | _____ | _____ |

# MODULE 52

# Extraordinary Times, Extraordinary Tools

**KEY IDEA:** In addition to its traditional powers, the Federal Reserve has special powers for severe economic emergencies.

**OBJECTIVES**

- To explain how the Federal Reserve reacted to the Great Recession.
- To identify when and how the Federal Reserve may use its "unusual powers."
- To discuss lessons learned from the Great Recession.

## Testing the Fed's Unusual Powers

In 2000, Ben Bernanke wrote that "the economic repercussions of a stock market crash depend less on the severity of the crash itself than on the response of economic policymakers, particularly central bankers." He said these words long before the financial crisis that began in 2007, which would test policy makers, including him. By March of 2008, the Fed was calling on its "unusual and exigent" powers, established by Section 13(3) of the Federal Reserve Act, which was added in 1932 in the midst of another financial crisis. Section 13(3) states that the Federal Reserve in "unusual and exigent circumstances" may provide funds to "any individual, partnership or corporation"

provided the borrower "is unable to secure adequate credit accommodations from other banking institutions." The Federal Reserve typically lends money to commercial banks and other depository institutions. It had not lent money to other types of financial companies since the 1930s. In this module we'll look into the events that sent the Federal Reserve into emergency mode.

## THE BEGINNING OF THE PROBLEMS

You've been introduced to several aspects of the "Great Recession" of 2007–2009. Here we'll examine those troublesome times from the Fed's point of view. By May of 2007, the crisis in the housing market was beginning to affect U.S. lending institutions as more and more mortgage holders were unable to make their payments. Because many loans weren't being repaid, banks didn't have as much

money to lend and new loans became relatively hard to come by.

 In August 2007, a similar *credit crisis* hit Europe for the same reasons: the housing boom was collapsing and there was a diminishing availability of loans. With these crises came fear that lending institutions would go bankrupt. By mid-September, worried depositors staged a run on Northern Rock Bank in the United Kingdom, asking for their deposits back. The bank was heavily invested in mortgages. To raise financial capital to lend out, it had bundled those mortgages as securities and sold them on the international financial markets. As loanable funds began to dry up on a global scale, Northern Rock had trouble borrowing from those same markets and asked the Bank of England for emergency funding. The request sparked the run on Northern Rock. Depositors, worried that the bank would collapse, lined up for blocks to withdraw their money. The Bank of England stepped in with a **bailout**, which is an infusion of money, usually in the form of loans or stock purchases, to keep a firm from failing. The bailout provided over $43 billion in loans to save Northern Rock from collapse. Unfortunately, the damage was done. Depositors and investors had lost confidence in Northern Rock, and the British government was forced to purchase the bank six months later to keep it afloat. In saving Northern Rock, the government demonstrated that it was taking action to stop any wider damage to the economy.

## The Fed's Initial Reactions

When the Federal Reserve stepped in to prop up U.S. financial institutions, it took the same approach as the Bank of England. The Fed's goal—in coordination with the Bush administration, and later the Obama administration and the Treasury Department—was to stabilize the economy and get money flowing to businesses and consumers.

In 2007 and early 2008, the Fed focused on its traditional monetary policy tools. It cut the federal funds rate sharply in September of 2007 and twice more before the end of that year. In August of 2007, the Federal Reserve also began cutting the discount rate, which the Fed usually does not touch. This lowered the interest rate that financial institutions had to pay the Federal Reserve Banks for short-term loans. Remember that the Fed's discount window is the last resort for financial institutions that cannot get a loan elsewhere. The situation became so desperate for some banks that the Fed ended up cutting the discount rate four times in 2007 and eight times in 2008. The rate was held steady in 2009 and raised slightly in 2010. It remained unchanged at 0.75 percent through 2011.

A **bailout** is an infusion of money, usually in the form of loans or stock purchases, to keep a firm from failing.

### DID YOU GET IT?
**What were the Fed's initial efforts to address the financial crisis?**

# CHANGING POLICIES TO MEET CHANGING ECONOMIC REALITIES

Despite the Fed's early response to the crisis, the credit markets were freezing up—banks were not lending enough money. Indeed, they had less and less money to lend. As the housing market collapsed, so did the value of banks' holdings of mortgages and mortgage-backed securities, and the value of their stock. The weak financial state of the banks made it all the more difficult for them to raise financial capital.

*The Great Recession had global consequences. The Bank of England and the British government had to rescue banks like Northern Rock as depositors lined up to withdraw their money.*

The Fed's traditional policy tools were not working in this environment. The problem wasn't one that could be solved by simply easing the money supply and lowering interest rates, which were already about as low as they could go. The problem was a lack of confidence in the credit markets. Would borrowers be able to pay back loans? How many more investors would desert the stocks of big commercial banks, driving down their value even more? To maintain operations, banks were saving their cash and granting relatively few loans. The Fed needed to create new tools to deal with this problem.

### New Programs

In December of 2007, the Fed established the *Term Auction Facility* (TAF). Under this temporary program the Fed provides loans with terms of either 28 or 84 days. The interest rates on these loans are determined at auction. The bidders are depository institutions, such as commercial banks and thrifts. To secure a loan, institutions provide **collateral**—an asset that is forfeited to the lender if the loan is not paid back. In this case, the collateral can be any of a variety of financial instruments, including risky mortgage-backed securities. The TAF allows financial institutions to borrow money at interest rates below the discount rate.

The *Term Securities Lending Facility* (TSLF) was established in March of 2008. Also an auction program, it lends Treasury securities to *primary dealers*—investment banks and securities firms authorized to deal directly with the Fed, such as Banc of America Securities and Cantor Fitzgerald—for 28 days. Like the depository institutions borrowing through the TAF, the primary dealers can use mortgage-backed securities as collateral for TSLF loans. Student loans, car loans, and credit card debt are also among the acceptable collateral. In that way, primary dealers overloaded with high-risk assets can temporarily obtain low-risk Treasury assets that are more liquid and serve as more acceptable collateral for other types of loans. In the

**Collateral** for a loan is an asset that must be forfeited to the lender if the loan is not paid back.

first month of the program, the Fed pumped $200 billion into the economy with the TSLF.

The Fed also established the *Primary Dealer Credit Facility* (PDCF) in March of 2008 to increase the total supply of financial reserves in the banking system. The PDCF lent money to primary dealers at the *primary credit rate*—the discount rate paid by the most financially sound financial institutions—at the New York Federal Reserve Bank. A loan taken out through the PDCF was for one day only, but a new one-day loan could be taken out the next day. After 45 days, a primary dealer was assessed a frequency fee for using the PDCF. Mortgage-backed securities were again accepted as collateral for these loans. This facility was closed in 2010.

The goal of all three programs was to make loans available and add money to the economy. As mortgage foreclosures skyrocketed and the overall economy weakened, depository institutions had become increasingly unwilling or unable to lend. The lack of credit was affecting the ability of companies to finance regular business transactions, such as paying for goods or buying new equipment. Businesses were laying off workers and cutting back on production, which only deepened the recession. With the TAF, the TSLF, and the PDCF, the Fed was trying new ways to help financial institutions make loans.

### Rescuing a Brokerage Firm

The Fed's "unusual powers" in the face of crisis continued to unfold in 2008. Instead of dealing only with depository institutions like banks and savings and loans, it intervened in the dealings of a brokerage firm called Bear Stearns.

In March, the Fed approved a $30 billion line of credit to help the banking corporation JPMorgan Chase buy Bear Stearns. The Fed promised to protect JPMorgan from some of the bad assets it received when it acquired Bear Stearns. Bear's stock had been valued at $170 in 2007. The crisis had gotten so bad that JPMorgan was able to buy it for $10 a share. The Fed's goal was to prevent Bear, which was in need of money, from selling off its vast holdings of mortgage-backed securities. It feared that if Bear dumped these securities, the country's—and possibly the world's—financial markets might collapse. Already, the recession that had begun in the United States and moved to Great Britain had become global.

**DID YOU GET IT?**
Why did the Fed feel it was important to save Bear Stearns?

## Bailing Out AIG

As the housing crisis worsened, the Fed faced yet another problem: the deteriorating condition of American International Group (AIG), the world's largest insurer operating in 130 countries. As you read in Chapter 16, lending institutions insured themselves against losses on bundles of mortgage loans by taking out a type of insurance called *credit default swaps*. As the major provider of credit default swaps, AIG was facing collapse because of losses on this insurance and due to investors' lack of confidence in the value of AIG's own stock.

The government decided that AIG's size and the global scope of its investors made it "too big to fail." As a result, in September 2008, the Federal Reserve arranged an $85 billion line of credit for AIG to be repaid in two years. In intervening to save AIG, the Fed cited the power given to it under Section 13(3) of the Federal Reserve Act.

AIG's financial condition continued to deteriorate. By the following May, the Federal Reserve and the Treasury Department had provided another $96.5 billion to AIG in the form of an extended line of credit and purchases of mortgage-backed assets. By the fall of 2009, the company was more stable. On January 27, 2010, Treasury secretary Timothy F. Geithner told a congressional panel that had AIG failed, "thousands of more factories would have closed their doors" and "millions more Americans would have lost their jobs."

Under government monitoring, AIG began selling off small units of the company and selling stock to repay the

*The government decided that AIG was too big to let fail.*

assistance from taxpayers. In early 2011, AIG repaid its loan from the Fed and Chief Executive Officer Robert Benmosche was optimistic about repaying the Treasury, saying, "We will work to make sure that the U.S. taxpayer will get back all of its money with a healthy profit." By September of 2012, the Treasury had recovered all its funds, with a net gain of almost $1 billion, and still owned 15.9 percent of AIG's assets.

## Intervention in the Housing Market

The Federal Home Loan Mortgage Corporation (Freddie Mac) and the Federal National Mortgage Association (Fannie Mae) are stockholder-owned corporations chartered by Congress to help make home loans available to low- and middle-income families. Together, they own or guarantee about half of all U.S. home mortgages. As the recession deepened, high default rates plagued the mortgage loan industry. Investors were selling Fannie's and Freddie's stock and the companies were losing value.

In July of 2008, in an effort to bolster confidence in Freddie Mac and Fannie Mae, both companies were allowed to begin borrowing money from the Fed. The government determined that like AIG, Freddie and Fannie were too important to the financial system to be allowed to fail. However, the two continued to lose value, and in September the Treasury Department took control of both companies.

In November of 2008, the Fed took another unprecedented step—into the housing market. The Fed proposed a $600 billion program for mortgage lenders. The goals were to ease the availability of credit and help stabilize the housing market, which continued its decline. The Fed proposed to buy up debt and troubled mortgages guaranteed by Fannie Mae and Freddie Mac. This program was also extended to the government-owned provider of mortgage-backed securities, the Government National Mortgage Association (Ginnie Mae).

### Intervention in Consumer Debt

On the front line of the battle against the woes of recession were the consumers and small business owners, who had crushing debt problems of their own. So in late 2008, the Fed announced its first direct intervention into the consumer debt market. The *Term Asset-Backed Securities Loan Facility* (TALF) was established to make one-year loans to financial institutions that give car loans, student loans, and credit card loans. TALF also provided money for business loans guaranteed by the Small Business Administration. The $200 billion program was supported with $180 billion from the Fed and $20 billion from the Treasury Department.

### Glimmers of Hope

By the summer of 2009, the financial crisis seemed to be easing slightly. Unemployment continued to rise, but the American Recovery and Reinvestment Act passed in February (as described in Chapter 15) seemed to have raised business and consumer confidence. After the various interventions by the Treasury Department and the Fed, the banking system was more stable and loans were increasingly available. However, as the country learned in the 1930s, reducing interventions and tightening the money supply too soon can lead to another downturn.

With that lesson in mind, the Fed continued its efforts. In June 2009, the Fed announced a program to encourage commercial real estate lending. The idea was to prevent defaults by owners of malls and other commercial real estate by making credit available to investors. Investors would be able to borrow money from the Fed to buy securities backed by commercial real estate loans. The program was to be administered under the TALF. Rather than offering short-term loans as under the other new programs, the Fed provided five-year loans.

**? DID YOU GET IT?**
Why didn't the Fed cut back on its interventions when it saw business and consumer confidence rising in 2009?

## RETRACTING THE SAFETY NET FOR THE ECONOMY

By the fall of 2009, the economy was recovering and the recession was officially over. The unemployment rate was still near 10 percent and would remain high for several years as firms regained strength and confidence. Because the economy was improving, the Fed slowly removed some of the financial supports erected under Section 13(3) of the Federal Reserve Act. In August the Fed began phasing out TALF support for consumer debt, which ended in early 2010. In September, the Fed began slowing its purchase of mortgage-backed securities. Experts estimated that the Fed was buying about 80 percent of all new mortgage-based securities at the time. Funding for the TAF and TSLF programs was also curtailed.

## LESSONS FROM THE FED'S EXPERIENCE

The Fed's actions had mixed results. On one hand, the country emerged from the recession and did not face the feared "double dip" of a second recession on the tail end of the first. Inflation remained in check despite the Fed's injections of money into the economy, and stock markets rebounded from the deep lows of early 2009. The recession was less deep and shorter in the United States than in Europe, in large part because of the Fed's aggressive actions. On the other hand, the unemployment rate remained near 9 percent through 2011, leaving 14 million people out of work and straining budgets of households and governments at every level.

Some of the Fed's policies received acclaim. The TALF program, for example, supported nearly 3 million auto loans, 1 million student loans, and 900,000 small business loans when private credit markets were frozen. The Fed's unconventional bond-buying program maintained low interest rates and yielded a profit for the Treasury, but with interest rates near zero, the Fed was left with few options if further action was needed.

The Fed's efforts to rescue the economy inevitably led it to support the financial industry and raised concerns that some of its funds ended up in undeserving hands. In 2011, protesters in the Occupy Wall Street movement raised questions about the corporate leaders who fared well financially despite heading up firms that contributed to the financial crisis and received aid from the Fed. Additionally, the bailouts led by the Fed and Treasury raised the risk of "moral hazard" problems down the road, meaning that financial companies might take excessive risks with the expectation that the government would bail them out if their failure threatened the economy.

There is a sobering lesson from the Fed's experience in the Great Recession. Despite mighty tools that grant it power over the money supply, interest rates, and credit markets, even the Fed cannot move the economy from a deep recession to a period of prosperity in a short period of time. The business climate often hinges on the attitudes of many players and on economic conditions around the world. During the Great Depression, the economist John Maynard Keynes used the term "animal spirits" to describe the emotions that affect human behavior. Optimism and pessimism drive business decisions to hire or fire, to increase or decrease investment, and to produce more or less output. The same emotions motivate consumers to spend or save. Monetary policy can accomplish much, but it has limited ability to temper animal spirits in boom times or to reverse the fear and lethargy that rule markets in difficult times.

**DID YOU GET IT?**
What drives business hiring and production decisions in difficult times?

*Occupy Wall Street protesters raised concerns that some Fed money ended up in undeserving hands.*

# MODULE 52 REVIEW AND ASSESSMENT

## Summing Up the Key Ideas: Match the following terms to the correct definitions.

A. Bailout       B. Collateral       C. Credit default swaps

_____ 1. An infusion of money, usually in the form of loans or stock purchases, to keep a firm from failing.

_____ 2. A type of insurance to protect against losses on bundles of mortgage loans given by financial institutions.

_____ 3. The term for an asset that must be forfeited to the lender if the loan is not paid back.

## Analyze: Determine whether each of the following falls within the **usual** or **unusual** powers of the Fed.

USUAL OR UNUSUAL?

1. buying and selling bonds through the Federal Open Market Committee to affect the federal funds rate

   _____

2. intervention in the home loan industry by allowing Fannie May, Freddie Mac, and later Ginnie Mae to borrow money from the Fed

   _____

3. setting up the Primary Dealers Credit Facility to increase the total supply of financial reserves in the banking system

   _____

4. making one-year loans to financial institutions that give car loans, student loans, and credit card loans through the Term Asset-Backed Securities Loan Facility

   _____

5. operating the discount window at the Fed

   _____

6. rescuing firms "too big to fail"

   _____

7. lowering the reserve requirement on bank deposits

   _____

8. establishing the Term Auction Facility

   _____

## Apply

A. Describe one lesson from the Fed's experience in attempting to aid the economy during the Great Recession.

B. Explain the term "animal spirits" as used by John Maynard Keynes.

## USA TODAY

# Fed to Pull Back Curtain on Members' Interest-Rate Forecasts

BY TIM MULLANEY

The Federal Reserve will begin disclosing the interest-rate forecasts of its policymaking committee members after this month's meeting, a move economists say will let everyone from consumers to corporate treasurers make financial plans with a clearer view of the future. The change means the Fed will disclose members' forecasts for its key federal funds rate in the fourth quarter and coming years, according to the minutes of the Fed's November meeting released Tuesday. That rate—what banks charge one another for overnight loans—influences rates on bank loans and deposits. It has been kept near zero since December 2008, and the Fed said as recently as last month (December 2011) that economic conditions are likely to warrant "exceptionally low" rates through at least mid-2013.

The new policy will take effect with the FOMC's Jan. 24–25 meeting. On a practical level, the decision means that a consumer can make smarter decisions about whether to buy a car or when to refinance a mortgage, while a corporate treasurer might be able to choose whether to finance operations with short-term commercial paper or lock in long-term bond financing, said Allen Sinai, chief economist at New York consulting firm Decision Economics. "This is a little deal by itself, but part of a bigger picture," said Sinai, noting that Fed Chairman Ben Bernanke has been gradually moving the central bank toward more complete and faster disclosure of its deliberations. "If I know, for example, that the Fed

forecasts that interest rates will be very low for a long time, that helps me make decisions."

More openness may also translate into less volatility in the economy, and on Wall Street, as people don't have to guess so much about the Fed's next moves, said University of Oregon economist Tim Duy, author of the blog *Tim Duy's Fed Watch*. For example, more transparency about how dire the Fed believed the economy was in 2008, combined with more insight into how far the central bank was willing to go to slash interest rates and pump credit into banks, might have cut the impact of the financial crisis on the Main Street economy, Duy said.

PHOTO VIA NEWSCOM

### DID YOU READ IT?

1) What does FOMC stand for and what does this group do?

2) Why are interest rates important in an economy?

### WHAT DO YOU THINK?

1) What does it mean to have a more "transparent" Fed? Why does the Fed think that being more "transparent" about its policy decisions will be good for the economy?

2) What are some examples of interest rates that might directly affect high school or college students?

EXCERPTED FROM www.usatoday.com/money/economy/fed/rates/story
2012-01-03/fed-regularly-forecast-interest-rate-changes/52360890/1

# CHAPTER 17 REVIEW AND SELF-ASSESSMENT

## REVIEW

### Points to Remember

#### MODULE 50: THE FEDERAL RESERVE SYSTEM

1. The **Federal Reserve System** is the U.S. central banking system.

2. **Monetary policy** is actions taken by the central bank to manage interest rates and the money supply in pursuit of macroeconomic goals.

3. **Bank holding companies** are companies that control one or more banks.

4. **Foreign reserves** are deposits of foreign currencies held by central banks.

5. The **Board of Governors** of the Federal Reserve is made up of members of the Federal Open Market Committee and manages the operations of the Federal Reserve.

6. The **Federal Reserve Banks** implement Federal Reserve policies and provide services to member banks and federal government agencies.

7. **Member banks** of the Federal Reserve System include all nationally chartered banks and many state-chartered banks. They are stockholders in their district bank and help elect the district's board of directors.

8. The **Federal Open Market Committee** is the group within the Federal Reserve that creates monetary policy.

9. As the **fiscal agent** for the federal government, the Fed sells, redeems, and pays interest on government securities.

10. **Check clearing** is the process of removing money from the bank account of the person who wrote the check—the payer—and delivering it to the account of the check's recipient—the payee.

11. **ACH (automated clearing house) transfers** are transfers between payers' and payees' accounts carried out without the use of checks on a secure electronic funds-transfer network.

#### MODULE 51: THE FEDERAL RESERVE AND TRADITIONAL MONETARY POLICY

12. **Easy money policy** increases the money supply.

13. **Tight money policy** decreases the money supply.

14. The **federal funds rate** is the interest rate that commercial banks charge one another for short-term loans.

15. The **discount rate** is the interest rate that the Fed charges financial institutions for short-term loans.

16. Under **inflation targeting**, the central bank sets a target rate—or range—of inflation for some time in the future and develops monetary policy with that goal in mind.

#### MODULE 52: EXTRAORDINARY TIMES, EXTRAORDINARY TOOLS

17. A **bailout** is an infusion of money, usually in the form of loans or stock purchases, to keep a firm from failing.

18. **Collateral** for a loan is an asset that must be forfeited to the lender if the loan is not paid back.

## SELF-ASSESSMENT

The following questions are the type your teacher might ask you on a quiz or a test. Practice with these in order to improve your performance on class tests.

### Multiple-Choice Questions

1. The duties of the Fed include all the following **except**

   a. conducting monetary policy to maintain full employment and price stability.

   b. maintaining the stability of the financial system and containing "systemic risk that may arise in the financial markets."

   c. maintaining the stability of financial markets to assure there are minimal fluctuations in stock and bond prices.

   d. regulating, supervising, and examining the nation's banks to ensure the safety of the banking system.

2. If the Federal Reserve wanted to reverse an economic slowdown, it would

   a. sell bonds.
   b. buy bonds.
   c. raise the reserve requirement.
   d. raise the discount rate.

Answer the next two questions based on Figure 51.1 in the book.

3. Movement from $MS_1$ to $MS_2$ could be caused by

   a. an increase in the reserve requirement.
   b. an increase in the discount rate.
   c. an increase in interest rates.
   d. the purchase of bonds by the FOMC.

4. Starting at $MS_1$ and $MD$, if the Fed pursued an easy money policy, the result would be

   a. an interest rate of 2 percent and a quantity of money of $900 billion.
   b. an interest rate of 4 percent and a quantity of money of $800 billion.
   c. an interest rate of 6 percent and a quantity of money of $700 billion.
   d. an interest rate of 6 percent and a quantity of money of $900 billion.

5. The Federal Reserve is

   a. a branch of the federal government.
   b. an independent body within the federal government funded by the federal government through the U.S. Treasury.
   c. self-supporting but under the direct control of the U.S. Treasury.
   d. an independent body within the federal government and completely self-supporting.

6. The Federal Reserve operates through its

   a. system of district banks, with one in each of the 50 states.
   b. system of 12 districts.
   c. system of 24 districts.
   d. system of one central district.

7. The tools of monetary policy include

   a. the reserve requirement.
   b. the discount rate.
   c. open market operations.
   d. all of the above.

8. If the Federal Reserve wanted to slow down the rate of inflation, it would

   a. increase the money supply by selling bonds in the open market.
   b. increase the money supply by buying bonds in the open market.
   c. decrease the money supply by selling bonds in the open market.
   d. decrease the money supply by buying bonds in the open market.

9. The federal funds rate is

   a. the rate of interest the Fed charges the federal government on loans.
   b. the rate of interest that commercial banks charge one another for short-term loans.
   c. the rate of interest the federal government charges the Fed on loans.
   d. the rate of interest the Fed charges commercial banks for short-term loans.

10. If the Federal Reserve followed an easy money policy, it would

   a. increase the money supply to lower interest rates.
   b. increase the money supply to raise interest rates.
   c. decrease the money supply to lower interest rates.
   d. decrease the money supply to raise interest rates.

## Constructed Response Question

1. The United States enters a recession.

   a. What could the Fed do with the reserve requirement to help the economy?
   b. What could the Fed do with the discount rate to help the economy?
   c. What could the Fed do to open market operations to help the economy?
   d. Use a correctly labeled graph of money supply and demand to show the combined effect of parts *a*, *b*, and *c*. On your graph, be sure to show what would happen to the money supply and the interest rate.

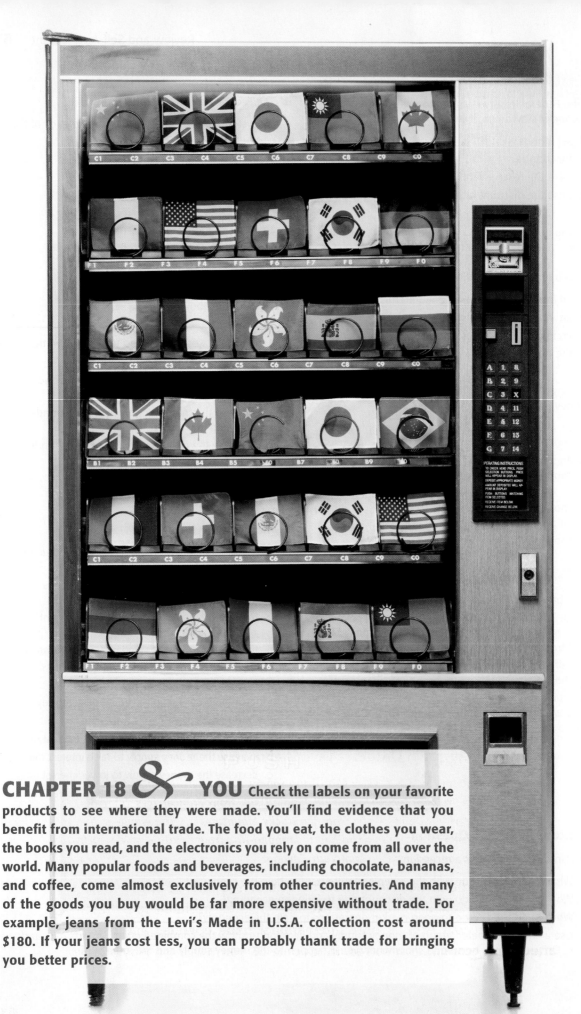

**CHAPTER 18 & YOU** Check the labels on your favorite products to see where they were made. You'll find evidence that you benefit from international trade. The food you eat, the clothes you wear, the books you read, and the electronics you rely on come from all over the world. Many popular foods and beverages, including chocolate, bananas, and coffee, come almost exclusively from other countries. And many of the goods you buy would be far more expensive without trade. For example, jeans from the Levi's Made in U.S.A. collection cost around $180. If your jeans cost less, you can probably thank trade for bringing you better prices.

# Trade and the Global Economy

## CONSUMPTION IN A SMALL WORLD

International trade has broadened our consumption horizons since well before Dr. Martin Luther King Jr. spoke so eloquently of global commerce:

*When we rise and go to the bath, a cake of soap is handed us by a Frenchman, a sponge is handed us by a Pacific Islander, a towel by a Turk, our underclothes by an American or Englishman. We go down to breakfast, our tea is poured out by a Chinese. Our toast we accept at the hands of an English speaking farmer, not to mention the baker. We are indebted to half of the world before we finish breakfast.*

Similarly, John Maynard Keynes remarked in 1919,

*The inhabitant of London could order by telephone, sipping his morning tea in bed, the various products of the whole earth, in such quantity as he might see fit, and reasonably expect their early delivery upon his doorstep.*

And in 1858, Abraham Lincoln remarked about a young American,

*Look at his apparel, and you shall see cotton fabrics from Manchester and Lowell; flax-linen from Ireland; wool-cloth from [Spain;] silk from France; furs from the Arctic regions, with a buffalo-robe from the Rocky Mountains . . . The whale of the Pacific furnishes his candle-light; he has a diamond-ring from Brazil; a gold-watch from California; and a Spanish cigar from Havana.*

Trade has flourished since prehistoric hunters journeyed across what is now the U.S.-Canadian border to exchange furs for obsidian spearheads. This chapter will explore how international trade operates and how it affects the economies involved. In Module 53 you will learn why people

in different countries trade with each other and the factors that affect trade. Module 54 discusses barriers to trade, how trade wars are created, and free trade. Module 55 explores how foreign exchange rates work, the balance of trade between countries, and the effects of trade deficits.

*Americans have been trading since they first settled here, when they traded with Native Americans for food, clothing, and weapons.*

## BOTTOM LINE

Global trade affects the goods that we can buy and the prices that we pay for them.

# MODULE 53

# The Benefits of International Trade

**KEY IDEA:** Differing opportunity costs of production allow countries of all sizes to benefit from trade with each other.

**OBJECTIVES**

- **To identify reasons for international trade.**
- **To explain the determinants of what each country produces and trades.**
- **To analyze how international trade works in the real world.**

## Voluntary Exchange Creates Win-Win Situations

To feed its expanding economy, China demands more oil, coal, lumber, and other raw materials than are available within its borders. China also demands goods and services beyond what it produces, including electronic components, machinery, plastics, organic chemicals, and college educations. The solution is international trade. In a typical year, China buys $1 trillion worth of goods, services, and resources from other countries, including oil from Canada, coal from Australia, and lumber from the United States. This *voluntary exchange* benefits both the people of China and the sellers around the globe, who can use the money to satisfy their own desires, which include over $1 trillion in purchases of everything from apparel to steel from China.

China spends about $1 trillion on goods and services from other countries in a typical year.

The uneven distribution of resources among the world's nearly 200 countries is one reason for trade. The resources, or *factors of production*, held by a particular country position it to **specialize** in certain products by producing a disproportionate amount of those products for consumption and trade. Canada's relative abundance of oil and natural gas, for example, lead it to specialize in those products while other countries specialize in apparel, electronics, and machinery for trade with countries like Canada. In this module we'll explore how advantages in access to factors of production, among other things, result in opportunities for mutually beneficial trade.

*China's rapidly growing demand for raw materials is driving a boom in the oil sands of northern Alberta [Canada]. Chinese firms and the Chinese government are very concerned about securing long-term supplies of oil, and the massive potential of the oil sands is drawing a great deal of investing in and importing from the region.*

*—Paul S. Ciccantell, Western Michigan University*

To **specialize** in a good is to produce a disproportionate amount of that good for consumption and trade.

# FACTORS THAT AFFECT TRADE

Why do countries trade? To begin with, the availability of land, labor, capital, and technology affects a country's ability to produce particular goods and services. Climate also matters, which explains why, for example, coffee beans aren't grown on the mainland of the United States and downhill ski lessons aren't available in Jamaica. Every country has some land, labor, and capital, but by specializing in goods made with the most abundant factors of production and trading for goods made by other countries with differing advantages, each country can become better off.

## Land

Module 1 explained that land is more than surface area. Land as an economic resource includes anything drawn from nature for use in the production of goods or services. Figure 53.1 illustrates the uneven distribution of one form of land: the world's oil reserves. To heat homes, power factories, and transport things like apparel and steel, not to mention 1.3

| RANK | NATION | PROVEN OIL RESERVES (BILLIONS OF BARRELS) |
|---|---|---|
| 1 | Saudi Arabia | 267.0 |
| 2 | Venezuela | 211.2 |
| 3 | Canada | 173.6 |
| 4 | Iran | 151.2 |
| 5 | Iraq | 143.1 |
| 6 | Kuwait | 104.0 |
| 7 | United Arab Emirates | 97.8 |
| 8 | Russia | 60.0 |
| 9 | Libya | 47.1 |
| 10 | Nigeria | 37.2 |
| 11 | Kazakhstan | 30.0 |
| 12 | Qatar | 25.4 |
| 13 | United States* | 20.7 |
| 14 | China | 20.4 |
| 15 | Brazil | 14.0 |
| 16 | Algeria | 12.2 |
| 17 | Mexico | 10.2 |
| 18 | Angola | 9.5 |
| 19 | India | 8.9 |
| 20 | Ecuador | 7.2 |
| | World Total | 1,523.2 |

**Figure 53.1** *Proven Oil Reserves of the Top 20 Nations, 2012* **The availability of oil, among other resources, varies considerably across countries.**

* U.S. estimate is from 2009

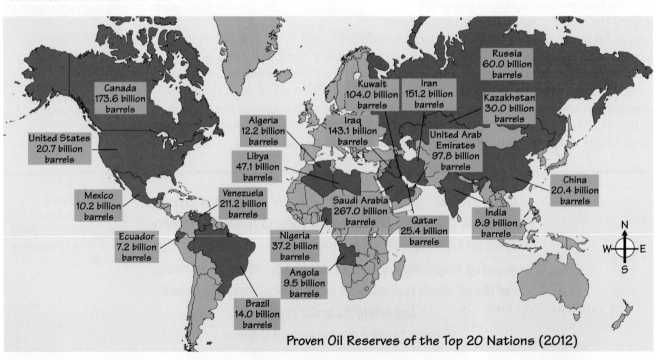

Proven Oil Reserves of the Top 20 Nations (2012)

billion people, China needs more than the roughly 190 million tons of oil it produces each year. So China must **import** about 55 percent of the oil it consumes, meaning that it buys the oil from other countries. Canada and other countries with rich oil reserves **export** oil, meaning that they sell some of their oil on the global market to countries such as China.

The production of most goods at the lowest possible cost requires a long list of natural resources. It is unusual for any one country to have ample supplies of everything on the list. The production of the shoes on your feet, for example, may have required leather for the uppers, rubber for the soles, aluminum for the eyelets, cotton for the laces, plastic for the decoration, coal to power the sewing machines, and oil to bring the shoes to market. As we shall see, the hands-on process of shoe assembly will have steered the manufacturer to a country with abundant supplies of another resource: labor. But that country probably imported a lot of the other resources to make the shoes before exporting the shoes to the United States for your use.

## Labor and Human Capital

The availability of labor varies considerably across countries, and where the supply of labor is relatively large, wages tend to be lower. It is thus natural for manufacturing processes like shoemaking that require a lot of labor to end up in countries like China that have a lot of labor. Indeed, your favorite shoe company may not make any of its shoes in the United States.

Another factor of production, *human capital*, refers to the education and skills of a country's labor force, as explained in Module 1. A country in which many people can't read is likely to specialize in the types of farming that don't require a formal education. Some of the agricultural products will then be exported, and the country will import relatively large quantities

of manufactured goods. For example, Guatemala spends 2.6 percent of its GDP on education, which gives it a ranking of 154th out of nearly 200 countries in spending on education. Almost one in three Guatemalans cannot read. Half the labor force is engaged in agriculture, and most of Guatemala's major exports are food: coffee, sugar, bananas, fruits and vegetables, and cardamom, a spice. The country's major imports are fuels, machinery and transportation equipment, construction materials, grain, fertilizers, and electricity. GDP per capita in Guatemala is $5,200.

In contrast, South Korea spends 4.6 percent of its GDP on education and ranks eighty-fifth in education spending among the world's countries. The literacy rate is 97.9 percent. Only 7.2 percent of the labor force is engaged in agriculture. The top exports from South Korea are semiconductors, wireless telecommunications equipment, motor vehicles, computers, steel ships, and petrochemicals. Its major imports are machinery, electronics and electronic equipment, oil, steel, transport equipment, organic chemicals, and plastics. A sizable portion of these imports is used by South Korean firms to produce more manufactured goods for export. South Korea's GDP per capita is $30,000.

## Physical Capital

The availability of physical capital—any long-lasting good used to make other goods—also sets the stage for most types

> To **import** goods is to purchase them from sellers in another country.

> To **export** goods is to sell them to buyers in another country.

> *Countries with high literacy rates tend to specialize in manufactured goods such as televisions, while those with lower literacy rates are more likely to specialize in agricultural goods such as bananas.*

*Countries with more physical and human capital can help supply it to those with less. This photo shows China-Africa Development Fund president Chi Jianxin (second from left) and Gabonese prime minister Paul Biyoghe (second from right) at the announcement of new investment projects.*

of production. For example, without factories and sewing machines, it's hard to make a lot of shoes, and without drilling rigs and oil refineries, it's hard to make a lot of gasoline. An examination of the economic development of sub-Saharan Africa reveals how insufficient physical capital can limit countries' production options. In the nineteenth and early twentieth centuries, for example, Britain, France, and Belgium controlled the governments of many African countries. Raw materials from Africa were sent to factories in Europe, which used them to manufacture goods, some of which were sold back to the African colonies. There was little investment in physical capital for the African colonies or in education for the native Africans.

When the African countries gained their independence in the second half of the twentieth century, they had little in the way of factories, machines, equipment, and other physical capital for industrialization. They were also limited in terms of human capital: there was not a large, educated labor force ready to program computers and design transportation networks. As a result, African countries continued to be primarily exporters of **commodities**— standardized raw materials such as copper and agricultural products such as coffee beans—and importers of finished goods such as cell phones and cars.

**Commodities** are standardized raw materials and agricultural products.

The economic landscape in Africa is now changing, largely as a result of non-Africans investing in African countries. China in particular is devoting large amounts of money and technical expertise to development projects in sub-Saharan Africa. If all goes as planned, the China-Africa Development Fund will have invested $2 billion in Africa by around 2013. Chinese companies currently operate mines in several African countries and oil fields in Angola.

## Climate

What did the city of Lulea, Sweden, have to offer Facebook, Inc.? A five-acre data center where Facebook stores the digital images for your Facebook page. The facility is located so close to the Arctic Circle because of the favorable *climate*— the prevailing weather conditions in the region. Computers generate heat, and five acres of computers generate so much heat that it would cost a fortune to keep them cool in the climate of California where Facebook is based. However, northern Sweden is a really cool place, which gives it an advantage in the global market for data-center hosting.

A country's climate affects both what it exports and what it imports. For example, Italy's Mediterranean climate—hot, sunny, dry summers and mild, rainy winters—is well suited for growing olives. Northern countries such as Canada and Sweden are eager to import olive oil because their colder climates aren't so kind to olives. The vast tropical rainforest of Brazil's Amazon basin, which is hot and rainy year round, is harvested for hardwoods that are cherished imports in countries with more moderate climates like the United

## ECONOMICS IN ACTION

# The Red Sea: Gateway to Trade

There is nothing new about the quest to import and export goods. Indeed, Christopher Columbus came upon the Americas while seeking a western trade route to Asia, where Europeans could purchase things like spices and silk. Until late in the nineteenth century, sea travel to the East from Europe required a long detour around Africa or a launch east of Africa in the Red Sea.

The Red Sea connects Egypt to the Gulf of Aden, which allows passage to the Indian Ocean and the Pacific Ocean. Trading expeditions sailed south through the Red Sea as early as 2500 BCE. Both Darius I of Persia in the sixth century BCE and Alexander the Great 200 years later investigated the waterway's potential for long-distance trade. After the Romans conquered Egypt in 30 BCE, the Roman Empire became part of the growing network of trade. The Red Sea was so important to this trade that in the first century CE, a guidebook was written describing the various water routes to Asia through the Red Sea. The kingdom of Axum in northern Ethiopia controlled Red Sea trade from the second to the eighth century. By the fifteenth century, Muslim merchants had gained control of the Red Sea.

Over the millennia, everything from ostrich feathers to weapons to slaves traversed the Red Sea. Goods traveling west from Asia made their way to the northwest end of the Red Sea and then followed overland routes across Egypt to the Mediterranean Sea, which takes ships to the southern shores of European countries from Spain to Turkey.

In 1859, the French began building the Suez Canal to connect the Red Sea to the Mediterranean Sea. It took 10 years to complete the 102-mile canal. Between 1976 and 1980, the canal was deepened for modern oil tankers. Now, close to 20,000 ships bring their cargo through the canal each year to serve importers and exporters in the East and West.

**DID YOU GET IT?**
Why is the Suez Canal important to trade between Europe and Asia?

Red Sea Region (2012)

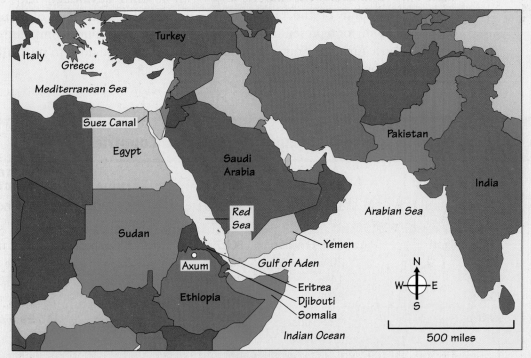

States. And much of the United States has a favorable climate for grain crops, which farmers export to countries with tropical climates, like the Central African Republic. What one country would have difficulty producing because of climate, it can import from others.

## Technology

The technology available in a country also affects what it produces—and therefore what it exports and imports. Cell phones are popular imports in countries like Sierra Leone that have lacked the technology for traditional telephones because cell phones do not rely on the absent phone wires and wall jacks. Countries with high levels of technology are relatively good at producing, among other things, more high-tech goods. Japan and South Korea are examples of countries that use their available technology to manufacture a vast array of electronic and telecommunications equipment. A country that has made less investment in technology, such as Tajikistan in central Asia, cannot match the type, quantity, or quality of goods produced in Japan and South Korea. Table 53.1 summarizes the imports and exports, and some of the factors that determine them, for representative countries in North America, South America, Asia, and Europe.

**DID YOU GET IT?**
1. Which country has the largest percentage of its labor force engaged in (a) agriculture? (b) industrial production? (c) services?
2. Does there seem to be any relationship between literacy rate and the types of work that a labor force does?

## THE KEY TO MUTUALLY BENEFICIAL TRADE

There are many ways in which a country can be "better" at producing something than another country. For example, a country can produce a good faster, with a lower environmental impact, or at a lower cost. We will assume that every unit of a particular good or service is identical regardless of where it comes from—for instance, oil from Iraq and Canada will be considered the same—and focus on who can produce more of it and who can produce it at a lower opportunity cost. Economists refer to these two ways of being "better" as having an *absolute advantage* and having a *comparative advantage*. It turns out that an absolute advantage helps a country have a higher standard of living with or without trade, but a comparative advantage opens the door to mutually beneficial trade.

Table 53.1 **A Comparison of Resource Distribution in Selected Countries***

|  | UNITED STATES | BRAZIL | CHINA | INDIA | UNITED KINGDOM |
|---|---|---|---|---|---|
| **GDP per capita** | $49,000 | $11,900 | $8,500 | $3,700 | $36,600 |
| **Labor force:** | 153.6 million | 100.9 million | 807.7 million | 523.5 million | 31.2 million |
| Agriculture | 1.2% | 20% | 36.7% | 52% | 1.4% |
| Industrial | 19.2% | 14% | 28.7% | 14% | 18.2% |
| Services | 79.6% | 66% | 34.6% | 34% | 80.4% |
| **Literacy rate** (ability to read and write by age 15) | 99.0% | 88.6% | 92.2% | 61.0% | 99.0% |

|  | UNITED STATES | BRAZIL | CHINA | INDIA | UNITED KINGDOM |
|---|---|---|---|---|---|
| **Exports** Types | $1.497 trillion agricultural products (soybeans, fruit, corn), industrial supplies (organic chemicals), capital goods (transistors, aircraft, motor vehicle parts, computers, telecommunications equipment), consumer goods (automobiles, medicines) | $256 billion transport equipment, iron ore, soybeans, footwear, coffee, autos | $1.904 trillion electrical and other machinery, including data processing equipment, apparel, textiles, iron and steel, optical and medical equipment | $307.2 billion petroleum products, precious stones, machinery, iron and steel, chemicals, vehicles, apparel | $479.2 billion manufactured goods, fuels, chemicals; food, beverages, tobacco |
| **Imports** Types | $2.236 trillion agricultural products, industrial supplies (crude oil), capital goods (computers, telecommunications equipment, motor vehicle parts, office machines, electric power machinery), consumer goods (automobiles, clothing, medicines, furniture, toys) | $226.2 billion machinery, electrical and transport equipment, chemical products, oil, automotive parts, electronics | $1.66 trillion electrical and other machinery, oil and mineral fuels, optical and medical equipment, metal ores, plastics, organic chemicals | $475.3 billion crude oil, precious stones, machinery, fertilizer, iron and steel, chemicals | $639 billion manufactured goods, machinery, fuels; foodstuffs |
| **Top trading partners** (arranged from largest to smallest trade volume) | Exports: Canada, Mexico, China, Japan, UK, Germany<br><br>Imports: China, Canada, Mexico, Japan, Germany | Exports: U.S., Argentina, China, Netherlands, Germany<br><br>Imports: U.S., China, Argentina, Germany, Nigeria | Exports: U.S., Hong Kong, Japan, South Korea, Germany<br><br>Imports: Japan, South Korea, Taiwan, U.S., Germany | Exports: U.S., China, United Arab Emirates, UK<br><br>Imports: China, U.S., Germany, Singapore | Exports: U.S., Germany, France, Ireland, Netherlands, Belgium, Spain, Italy<br><br>Imports: Germany, U.S., China, Netherlands, France, Belgium, Norway, Italy |
| **Foreign investment in other countries** | $2.577 trillion | $171.7 billion | $366 billion | $106.3 billion | $1.705 trillion |
| **Foreign investment within the country** | $2.577 trillion | $539.2 billion | $711.8 billion | $232.7 billion | $1.201 trillion |

*Most recent estimates available.

SOURCE: *CIA World Factbook*, www.cia.gov/library/publications/the-world-factbook.

*If Indian call centers can handle more calls per hour than British call centers, India has an absolute advantage in providing call center services.*

A country has an **absolute advantage** in the production of a good if it can produce more of that good than its trading partner using a given quantity of resources.

A country has a **comparative advantage** in the production of a good if it can produce the good at a lower opportunity cost than its trading partner.

## Absolute Advantage

If one country can produce more of something than another country using a given quantity of resources, the more productive country has an **absolute advantage**. Adam Smith introduced the concept of absolute advantage with examples of two countries producing goods with labor as the resource. Consider the call centers that companies like Microsoft and Delta employ to provide customer assistance and sell things like airline reservations. If workers in Indian call centers can handle 20 calls per hour and workers in British call centers can handle 15 calls per hour, then India has an absolute advantage in providing call center services.

Adam Smith discussed absolute advantage as a basis for trade, suggesting that countries should specialize in those goods in which they have an absolute advantage and trade for the goods they most desire. However, it is possible for one country to have an absolute advantage over its potential trading partners in most or all goods and yet benefit from trade with other countries (as explained in the next section). So having an absolute advantage in producing a particular good does not determine whether that country should import or export that good. An absolute advantage does help a country produce goods at a relatively low financial cost and in relative abundance, for use in trade or for consumption in that country.

## Comparative Advantage

David Ricardo, a classical economist like Adam Smith, developed the concept of *comparative advantage*. When one country can produce a good at a lower opportunity cost than another country, it has a **comparative advantage** in producing that good. Recall that having a lower opportunity cost means that the country gives up less of the next-best alternative good when it produces another unit of the good in question. For example, suppose that the opportunity costs of producing wheat and corn in Britain and the United States are as shown in Table 53.2. For each additional bushel of wheat produced in Britain, 4 fewer bushels of corn can be produced. The opportunity cost of a bushel of wheat is then 4 bushels of corn. The United States can produce a bushel of wheat at an opportunity cost of 2 bushels of corn. In this case the United States has a comparative advantage in wheat production because the United States gives up less corn than Britain to get each bushel of wheat. That is, the United States has a lower opportunity cost.

| Table 53.2 **Opportunity Costs for Britain and the United States** | | |
|---|---|---|
| | **BRITAIN** | **UNITED STATES** |
| Opportunity cost of 1 bushel of wheat | 4 bushels of corn | 2 bushels of corn |
| Opportunity cost of 1 bushel of corn | ¼ bushel of wheat | ½ bushel of wheat |

## Absolute and Comparative Advantages Need Not Go Together

A country can have a comparative advantage in producing a good or service whether or not it has an absolute advantage in producing it. For example, suppose that in one growing season, with the same resources, Britain could produce 4 million bushels of corn if it produced no wheat, and the United States could produce 6 million bushels of corn if it produced no wheat. Alternatively, Britain could produce 1 million bushels of wheat if it produced no corn, and the United States could produce 3 million bushels of wheat if it produced no corn. Because it can produce more wheat or more corn than Britain, the United States has an absolute advantage in producing both goods. However, Britain has a comparative advantage in corn production because it has a lower opportunity cost as shown in Table 53.2: it must forego 1 million bushels of wheat for 4 million bushels of corn, or ¼ bushel of wheat per bushel of corn. The United States must forgo 3 million bushels of wheat for 6 million bushels of corn, or ½ bushel of wheat per bushel of corn.

Because the United States has a comparative advantage in wheat production, Britain has a comparative advantage in corn production. Since Britain gives up 4 bushels of corn per bushel of wheat, each bushel of corn substitutes for only ¼ of a bushel of wheat. The opportunity cost of corn in Britain is thus ¼ of a bushel of wheat. In the United States, where 1 bushel of wheat reduces corn production by 2 bushels of corn, each bushel of corn substitutes for ½ bushel of wheat, so the opportunity cost of a bushel of corn in the United States is ½ bushel of wheat. With the lower opportunity cost of ¼ bushel of wheat, Britain gives up less wheat to get each bushel of corn, so it indeed has a comparative advantage in corn production.

A simple way to find the opportunity cost of, say, corn is to look at what happens when a country switches from making only wheat to making only corn. Suppose Britain can make 1 million bushels of wheat if it produces only wheat, but by foregoing all 1 million bushels of wheat it can make 4 million bushels of corn. Then the opportunity cost of 1 bushel of corn for Britain is

$$\frac{\text{change in quantity of wheat}}{\text{change in quantity of corn}} = \frac{1 \text{ million}}{4 \text{ million}} = \frac{1}{4}$$

In their actual farming practices it is unlikely that a country would go from the extreme of making no corn to the extreme of making no wheat—Britain and the United States produce some of both goods. But looking at the extreme possibilities simplifies opportunity cost calculations.

Ricardo reasoned that whenever a country has a comparative advantage over another country in the production of a good, it is a certainty that *both* countries can benefit from trade. In our example, the United States has a comparative advantage in wheat production and Britain has a comparative advantage in corn production, so the United States should specialize in wheat production and trade it for corn from Britain. Remember that the opportunity cost of 1 bushel of wheat is 4 bushels of corn in Britain and 2 bushels of corn in the United States. If the *terms of trade* are such that 1 bushel of wheat trades for between 2 and 4 bushels of corn, both countries will gain from trade. For example, suppose 1 bushel of wheat from the United States trades for 3 bushels of corn from Britain. Instead of giving up 4 bushels of corn per bushel of wheat as it would without trade, Britain will only give up 3 bushels of corn per bushel of wheat—an improvement for Britain! And rather than giving up ½ bushel of wheat for every bushel of corn as it would without trade, the United States is paying 1 bushel of wheat for 3 bushels of corn, which is only ⅓ bushel

*When a country with a comparative advantage in corn production exports corn to a country with a comparative advantage in something else, both countries can enjoy more of both goods than in the absence of trade.*

of wheat per bushel of corn. So, even the country with an absolute advantage in producing both goods will gain from trade.

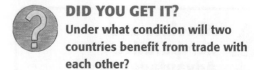

**DID YOU GET IT?**
Under what condition will two countries benefit from trade with each other?

# MODULE 53 REVIEW AND ASSESSMENT

**Summing Up the Key Ideas:** Match the following terms to the correct definitions.

A. Specialize
B. Import

C. Export
D. Commodities

E. Absolute advantage
F. Comparative advantage

_____ 1. To buy a good or service from another country.

_____ 2. When one country can produce a good at a lower opportunity cost than another country.

_____ 3. When a country produces a disproportionate amount of products for consumption and trade.

_____ 4. Standardized raw materials and agricultural products, such as copper and coffee beans.

_____ 5. To sell a good or service to another country.

_____ 6. If one country can produce more of something than another country using a given quantity of resources.

**Analyze:** For each of the following situations, determine, from the standpoint of the United States, whether the good was **imported**, **exported**, or **neither**.

IMPORTED, EXPORTED, OR NEITHER?

1. A shopper in the United States buys a pair of shoes made in China.

_____

2. A customer in the United States buys a car made in the United States.

_____

3. A farmer in India buys a tractor made in the United States.

_____

4. A U.S. oil refinery sells oil to a manufacturer in China.

_____

5. A U.S. firm buys new cars made in Japan.

_____

**Apply:** Determine whether the information provided indicates that Country *A* has an **absolute advantage in producing bananas**, a **comparative advantage in producing bananas**, an **absolute advantage in producing pineapples**, or a **comparative advantage in producing pineapples**.

1. Country *A* gives up 10 bananas for every pineapple it produces and Country *B* gives up 12 bananas for every pineapple it produces.

_____

2. Using the same quantity of resources, Country *A* can produce 3 tons of bananas and Country *B* can produce 2 tons.

_____

3. Country *A* can produce bananas at a lower opportunity cost than Country *B*.

_____

4. Using the same quantity of resources, Country *B* can't produce as many pineapples as Country *A*.

_____

# MODULE 54

# Barriers to Trade

**KEY IDEA:** The benefits of free trade often outweigh the costs.

## OBJECTIVES

- **To identify possible barriers to international trade.**
- **To analyze the reasons why some people seek to limit imports.**
- **To explain how trade agreements promote international trade.**

### Is It Better to Have Fewer Trade Barriers?

Most national governments erect at least some barriers to trade, although trade restrictions have declined in recent decades. Regional trade agreements, organizations set up to promote trade, and *customs zones* with few trade barriers are making trade easier. The exchange of goods and services between trading partners in the absence of government-imposed barriers is called **free trade**. Is free trade good or bad for a country's firms and workers? There are arguments on both sides of the issue. In this module we analyze policies that limit trade.

*"This is great. They're inflatable trade barriers!"*

> Barriers to trade are common but controversial.

## LIMITING TRADE

Since the birth of the United States, Americans have debated the need for trade restrictions to protect young U.S. industries from more-established competitors overseas. Alexander Hamilton, the first secretary of the Treasury, recommended a variety of import taxes, known as import **tariffs** or **duties**, most of which were adopted by Congress.

### Tariffs

The type of tariffs that Hamilton called for are known as **protective tariffs** because they are meant to protect domestic industries from losing consumer dollars to foreign competition. Suppose the cost of a backpack assembled in the United States is $50 and the cost of a backpack imported from Pakistan is $40. If the U.S. government places an import

duty of 25 percent, or $10, on the Pakistani backpack, it will now cost the U.S. consumer $50. The intent of the tariff is to level the playing field by making the imported item at least as expensive as the domestic item, so that domestic consumers have no reason to favor the imported item.

The primary purpose of a **revenue tariff** is to collect money for the federal government. Although any tariff can limit imports or help domestic producers of the same item, a revenue tariff is not designed with these intentions. For example, most European countries do not produce bananas, so they wouldn't want to prohibit banana imports. In fact, more bananas are consumed in Europe than anywhere else in the world. But the European Union does impose a tariff on banana imports from Latin America. The tariff of about $200

**Free trade** is the exchange of goods and services between trading partners in the absence of government-imposed restrictions or charges.

A **tariff** or **duty** is a tax on imports.

A **protective tariff** is a tariff that is meant to protect domestic industries from foreign competition.

A **revenue tariff** is a tariff imposed to generate revenue for the government without necessarily limiting imports or helping domestic producers.

per metric ton is large enough to generate significant revenues without making bananas so expensive that people won't buy them.

At the beginning of the Great Depression, Congress tried to protect U.S. industries by passing the Smoot-Hawley Tariff Act of 1930. The act increased the tariffs on thousands of goods to record levels. Most of the tariffs were specific dollar amounts, such as $1.125 per ton of pig iron. When converted to a percentage of the product's price, the tariffs were, for example, 53.7 percent on glass, 59.8 percent on wool, and 77.2 percent on sugar. In retaliation against these hefty duties, other countries raised their tariffs on imports from the United States. Figure 54.1 shows the dramatic decline of trade that followed. World trade declined by about 66 percent between 1929 and 1934. The Smoot-Hawley tariffs didn't cause the Great Depression, but experts believe they deepened and prolonged it.

In an effort to undo the damage of the Smoot-Hawley Act, Congress passed the Reciprocal Trade Agreements Act of 1934. This law gave the president rather than Congress the power to negotiate trade agreements. The president could reduce tariffs by up to 50 percent if a trading partner agreed to a similar reduction. The use of tariffs has declined ever since.

Early in U.S. history, tariffs provided a majority of the revenue for the U.S. government. In 1825, tariff revenue provided an all-time high of 97.9 percent of government revenues. As the benefits of free trade became apparent and income and payroll taxes were adopted in the early 1900s, the role of tariff revenue diminished. By 1944, tariff revenue amounted to only about 1 percent of federal government revenues, which is still the case today.

## Quotas

Another form of trade barrier, a **quota,** limits the amount of a good that can be imported. This restriction on supply raises the good's price and increases reliance on domestic firms to provide the good. Unlike tariffs, quotas are not a direct source of government revenue.

Consider sugar, which Americans consume at a rate of about 11 million tons per year. To protect domestic sugar-cane and sugar-beet farmers, the U.S. Department of Agriculture (USDA) sets a quota of 1.2 million tons of sugar that can be imported without a substantial tariff. When weather-related problems with domestic supply or increases in domestic demand create a sugar shortage, the USDA limits the resulting spike in prices by raising the quota, as it did twice in 2011.

## Other Trade Barriers

Beyond tariffs and quotas, a variety of other policies limit trade. For example, **voluntary export restraints,** or **VERs,** are self-imposed limits on exports. VERs can help an exporting country avoid more-severe restrictions that would otherwise be imposed by the importing country. For example, to ease pressures within the United States for protective tariffs and quotas on automobile imports

A **quota** limits the amount of a good that can be imported.

A **voluntary export restraint (VER)** is a self-imposed limit on the quantity of exports.

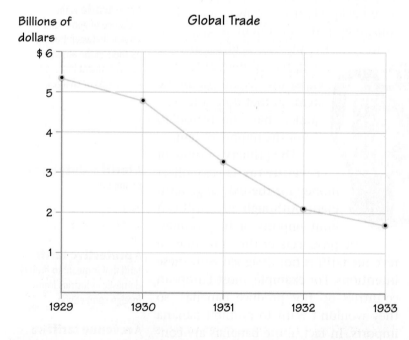

Billions of dollars

Global Trade

**Figure 54.1** The Dramatic Decline of World Trade, 1929–1933
Rising U.S. tariffs and retaliatory tariffs overseas contributed to a downward spiral of trade in the early 1930s.

in the 1980s, Japan agreed to limit itself to exporting 1.68 million cars to the United States each year. In 2005, as the result of an international agreement reached in 1993, worldwide quotas for Chinese textiles were lifted. What followed was a flood of Chinese-made clothing into countries including the United States. In response to U.S. concerns about the impact of these low-priced goods on U.S. manufacturers, China implemented voluntary restraints on textile exports to the United States.

A number of policies limit imports as a side effect rather than a primary purpose. These include product standards, health inspections, harbor and airport permit requirements, customs and border protection procedures, and import-licensing requirements. For example, some pharmaceuticals that are approved for sale in Europe are banned in the United States because they have not passed the rigorous testing standards of the U.S. Food and Drug Administration. Beyond guarding against potential health risks, this policy drives more business to U.S. pharmaceutical companies. Meanwhile, European countries ban milk imports from farmers who follow the common U.S. practice of injecting cows with a controversial growth hormone called rBGH to increase milk production. India is among the countries with a long list of products that must be tested and certified before entering the country. This, too, limits imports.

## Trade Barriers as Strategic Policy

Trade barriers sometimes find their way into political strategies. On the extreme end of strategic trade policies is an **embargo**, which is a government-ordered ban on trade. If you're a history buff you might remember that in 1807, during the Napoleonic Wars, President Thomas Jefferson ordered an embargo against all foreign trade in an effort to protect U.S. neutrality and avoid war. The embargo hurt most sectors of the U.S. economy and was ended in 1809. In 1960, President Dwight Eisenhower ordered an embargo against U.S. trade with, and travel to, Cuba after Fidel Castro established a

Communist government there. Over the next 40 years, efforts to loosen the restrictions met with stiff resistance from exiled Cubans in the United States. However, the twenty-first century brought a new generation of Cuban Americans that was less hard-line. Soon after taking office, President Barack Obama eased travel restrictions for families with relatives in Cuba and listed steps that Cuba must take to have the embargo lifted.

More often, the strategic reason for creating a trade barrier is economic. Just the threat of a quota or tariff can motivate a country to change course and adopt voluntary export restraints. But the economic strategy of trade barriers can also backfire, either by provoking retaliation or by damaging the economies of trading partners who will then buy less overseas. In 2009, Congress proposed a "Buy American" clause in the American Recovery and Reinvestment Act. According to the proposal, recipients of the act's funds for construction projects could only buy U.S.-manufactured iron and steel. The European Union and Canada warned that the policy would start a **trade war**, with each side escalating restrictions to everyone's detriment, as occurred in the 1930s. To defuse the situation, President Barack Obama worked with Congress to exempt the European Union, Canada, Mexico, and several other important trading partners from the policy.

**DID YOU GET IT?**
What are two ways in which the strategy of trade barriers can backfire?

# ARGUMENTS FOR AND AGAINST LIMITS ON TRADE

The practice of limiting foreign trade is called **protectionism.** Among several arguments for protectionism, supporters believe that free trade damages a country's economic independence. There are

An **embargo** is a government-ordered ban on trade.

In a **trade war**, two or more countries retaliate against earlier trade barriers with escalating restrictions on trade.

**Protectionism** is the practice of limiting foreign trade.

also counterarguments and alternative solutions that preserve the benefits of voluntary exchange. In the following sections we will look at the arguments for and against protectionism.

## Protecting "Infant Industries"

According to the "infant industries" argument, new and emerging industries need protection while they develop enough strength and efficiency to face off against foreign competition. India, which is developing its industrial sector, has tariff rates 10 times higher than those of countries like the United States. The intent is to give its industries breathing room as they catch up with those in more-developed countries.

Opponents of the "infant industry" argument point out that the lack of competition provides little incentive for the protected industries to focus on efficiency, quality, or reasonable prices. If new companies are protected against competitors, they may never become competitive. Once protective tariffs or quotas are in place, the industry gains profits by fighting to keep them indefinitely. The trick, then, is to decide when an industry is ready to take off its training wheels and stand up to international competition.

## National Security

There is broad agreement on the need to maintain a strong system of national defense. The steel and oil industries are among those with strategic value for national defense. Without them, we would be unable to build and fuel tanks, airplanes, and other military machines. If foreign competitors undercut domestic prices in critical industries, domestic producers will lose money and may ultimately go bankrupt. This is what

happened to many U.S. steel producers in the second half of the twentieth century. Some people would like to see limits on trade to protect important industries such as these from foreign competition.

There are several concerns about the protectionism solution. One is that it will open a floodgate for industries claiming to be critical to national security. In the event of war, we need food, clothing, electronics, transportation, and so on. It would be difficult to draw the line on protectionism and the problems it presents. Another concern is that protectionism removes incentives for firms to develop efficient production processes. Even the original U.S. steel companies were partly to blame for their lack of competitiveness. They had been slow to adopt new technologies and to look for more innovative ways to run their operations. As a result, they became inefficient and unable to sell steel for the price of foreign-produced steel.

A third concern is that protectionism is more risky and costly than alternative solutions. For those domestic industries that are vital for national security, alternative approaches such as subsidies may be preferable. Policy makers can easily target key industries with subsidies, and they do not raise prices for consumers the way import restrictions do.

## Competing with Foreign Firms That Hire Cheap Labor

Employers in many Asian, Latin American, and Eastern European countries pay their workers wages that are far below typical wages in the United

*India, which is developing its relatively young industrial sector, has tariff rates 10 times higher than those of countries like the United States. The intent is to give its industries breathing room as they catch up with those in more-developed countries.*

States. This practice makes it easier for firms in these countries to charge relatively low prices. The use of trade barriers is seen by some people as a way to help domestic firms compete and thus keep more Americans employed. Labor union leaders are among the most vocal advocates of this position. They believe that unemployment will rise if cheap imported goods are allowed to enter the U.S. market.

If nothing else changes, growth in imports can eliminate jobs. For example, U.S. expenditures on textile imports from China rose from $701 million in January of 2005 to $1.2 billion in January of 2006, immediately after the end of quotas on Chinese textiles. Imports of knit cotton shirts from China, for example, rose from 941,000 units in January of 2005 to a whopping 18.2 million in January of 2006. The U.S. Bureau of Labor Statistics estimates that in the first month after the quotas were lifted, 12,200 U.S. jobs were lost as the result of increased textile imports.

Rather than building artificial barriers to protect industries that have a comparative disadvantage, an alternative approach to this problem is to promote industries that have a comparative advantage. For example, the textile industry in the Philippines experienced a loss of sales in the U.S. market when China increased its exports to the United States. The Filipino solution was not to continue to produce cheap garments like T-shirts but to shift its production to higher-priced garments for higher-end stores. In other words, Filipino manufacturers chose to innovate and specialize in alternative markets in which it held a comparative advantage. This created new jobs to replace those lost in the textile industry.

Japanese automakers followed a similar strategy. Voluntary exports restraints and increasing competition caused Toyota to lose sales of inexpensive small cars in the United States. Toyota then became successful by concentrating on innovative, high-quality cars and trucks of all sizes. Likewise, the United States has pursued its comparative advantages in producing goods such as aircraft, cars, semiconductors (components for electronic circuits), pharmaceuticals, and telecommunications equipment. Even larger are the U.S. service industries, including education, entertainment, tourism, and health care. By transitioning from an economy based on agricultural commodities to an economy that specializes in services and high-tech manufactured goods, the United States has gained more jobs with relatively high salaries.

**DID YOU GET IT?**
In what two ways can a country try to hold on to jobs despite competition from low-priced imports?

## Keeping Jobs at Home

Beyond the potential for job loss due to an increase in imports, jobs can be lost when U.S. firms move their factories overseas. When a firm moves some of its operations to another country, it is called **offshoring**. We have already seen that Facebook did this with its data center. Fruit of the Loom moved some of its production to Honduras, where labor costs are lower. Some firms move to places with more lenient labor regulations, environmental standards, or tax laws. Some manufacturers move their plants closer to sources of raw materials.

Trade barriers could be used to curtail the practice of offshoring. For instance, when production in foreign countries results in the mistreatment of workers or threats to the environment, trade restrictions can limit those problems. Congress has considered bans on imports produced by child labor and *environmental tariffs* for countries whose cost advantages come from less-stringent environmental standards.

However, offshoring can be efficient because of improved access to factors of production. In such cases, economists are reluctant to erect barriers. Protecting domestic industries that are inefficient raises the cost of goods and services, which hurts both consumers and firms

A firm is **offshoring** when it moves some of its operations to another country.

**Dumping** is the practice of exporting goods at a price that is below the price in the exporting country.

A **trade deficit** is the amount by which expenditures on imports exceed receipts from exports.

A **trade surplus** is the amount by which receipts from exports exceed expenditures on imports.

*China was accused of selling solar panels in the United States for less than their price in China. This practice, called dumping, is carried out to drive producers in the importing country out of business.*

that use those imported goods and services. It makes sense to produce goods and services in the country that offers the greatest cost advantages. For example, Toyota makes many of its cars in the United States to benefit from cost advantages and in 2011 employed 29,098 U.S. workers. When U.S. firms move production overseas to reduce costs, the profits are often plowed into innovation, research, and development in the United States. The result is more U.S. jobs in cutting-edge industries, which tend to be relatively high paying.

## Keeping Money at Home

When imports are limited, less money flows out of the country. This promotes domestic spending. If imports decrease by more than exports, this reduces the **trade deficit**—the amount by which expenditures on imports exceed receipts from exports. If receipts from exports exceed expenditures on imports, the country enjoys a **trade surplus**, and by cutting imports the trade surplus is increased.

We have already discussed the risk that trade limits will trigger retaliation from other countries. Note also that a decrease in imports can lead to a decrease in exports. A certain amount of the money that a country's consumers spend on imports comes back to the country in the form of payments for its own exports. For example, when U.S. consumers buy Bolivian products such as coffee, gold, and soybeans, Bolivian firms have more money for the purchase of machinery from the United States and Bolivian workers can buy more food grown by U.S. farmers. In a typical year, Bolivia exports about $696 million worth of goods to the United States, which helps it import about $707 million worth of goods from the United States.

## Dumping

Some trade practices are clearly problematic and are not allowed even under free-trade agreements. As an example, **dumping** is the practice of exporting goods at a price that is below the price in the exporting country. For instance, Brazil has been accused of dumping orange juice on the U.S. market by selling it for less than the price in Brazil. The goal of dumping is to drive competing producers in the importing country out of business. The exporting country can then raise prices on its exports of that good.

Dumping is an unfair and anticompetitive practice outlawed by the World Trade Organization (WTO). The WTO provides a complaint and investigation process to handle accusations of dumping, among other forbidden trade practices. In recent years, Honduras was accused of dumping textiles in the United States, and China was accused of dumping solar panels in the United States, aluminum alloy wheel hubs in the European Union, and shoes in Brazil. The penalty for dumping is the imposition of new, or higher, tariffs on products from the guilty country. For example, in 2009, the United States imposed a tariff on steel pipes from China after dumping incidents.

There is a theme running through the arguments for free trade: competition with foreign producers results in innovation, efficiency, and productivity. With free trade, domestic producers must concentrate on doing what they do best and serving customers with reliable products at reasonable prices. If they do not, it is likely that a competitor will put them out of business. Firms are motivated to develop better technology and production processes that enable them to produce better products at lower prices. With innovation and efficiency, the national economy grows. And with specialization and trade on the basis of comparative advantages, consumers can receive more of all goods and services and enjoy a higher standard of living.

THINKSTOCK

## ECONOMICS IN ACTION

# Is a Foreign Car Always a Foreign Car?

Ford builds the Fiesta in several countries, including Brazil and Mexico, and Nissan makes the Nissan Livina Geniss in China. The Italian carmaker Fiat owns part of U.S. automaker Chrysler, and Opel, a German car company, is owned by General Motors. If you were Brazilian, would the Fiesta be a foreign car? Is the Chrysler Sebring now a foreign car in the United States because the company is partly owned by Fiat?

The source of a car is hard to pin down because automakers, including Ford, Nissan, Fiat, Chrysler, and General Motors, are **multinational corporations** with offices, factories, and dealerships in many countries. It is common to identify a car as "foreign" if the headquarters for the car's manufacturer are located in another country. Toyota is based in Japan, so many people consider the Toyota Camry parked in your neighbors' driveway to be a foreign car even though it was assembled in Georgetown, Kentucky.

However, there is another dimension to the issue. Part of the money that Americans pay for a Toyota Camry goes back to Japan. But part of it goes to the workers in the Georgetown plant where the car was made, the utility company that supplies power to the plant, the transportation companies that ship cars to dealers and car parts to the plant, the car dealership employees, and so on. Even cars built in the United States typically contain parts made all over the world, and some cars made in other countries contain parts made here. Today, most cars are of mixed origin.

If we judge cars according to the number of American manufacturing jobs created by their production, the Toyota Camry is more American than, say, the Ford Escape. The Camry creates 20 American jobs for every 100 cars made, whereas the Escape creates 13.

 **DID YOU GET IT?**
How does the United States benefit from having multinational corporations operating here?

*U.S. car companies make their cars in many different countries.*

# FROM TRADE WARS TO TRADE AGREEMENTS

You've heard it on the schoolyard: "You hit me, so I'll hit you—but harder." Too often this type of exchange escalates into a full-scale fight. A similar game of tit-for-tat can arise between trading partners. In response to a protective or revenue tariff, a country facing new barriers often issues a **retaliatory tariff** intended to avenge the initial tariff. In the case of international trade, the result is a trade war.

In 2009, President Obama imposed a tariff of up to 35 percent on tires imported from China. Days later, China's commerce ministry announced

A **multinational corporation** is a corporation with operations in many countries.

A **retaliatory tariff** is a tariff imposed to punish the trading partner's trade policy.

it would look into whether "certain imported chicken meat products originating from the United States" were being dumped in the Chinese market. If they were, World Trade Organization rules would allow a retaliatory tariff. In 2010, China did indeed impose tariffs of between 50 and 100 percent on chicken imports from the United States. In hopes of avoiding further escalations in the trade war, the United States filed a complaint with the WTO, one of several international organizations and agreements established to control the damage caused by trade wars.

## The General Agreement on Tariffs and Trade

Earlier in this section you read about how the Smoot-Hawley Tariff Act of 1930 and other trade barriers hindered economic growth on an international scale. The General Agreement on Tariffs and Trade (GATT) was established in 1947. Its purpose was to increase world trade after World War II and to end the protectionist strategies of the prewar era. Twenty-three countries signed the original agreement, and by 1994, 128 countries had signed on. The specific goal of GATT was to reduce tariffs and other barriers to trade.

Between 1947 and 1994, the signatories of GATT went through eight rounds of trade negotiations. The Kennedy Round, for example, which took place between 1964 and 1967, resulted in a one-third reduction in tariffs. Also, antidumping measures were enacted for the first time. The final round, the Uruguay Round, took place between 1986 and 1994 with 123 countries participating. In addition to tariff issues related to textiles and agriculture, this round took up the issue of intellectual property rights, genetically modified food, and the environment. This final round ended with the creation of the World Trade Organization to take the place of GATT.

A **free trade zone** is a region within which there are few or no trade restrictions.

## The World Trade Organization

In 1995, the World Trade Organization began operating as a global institution that encourages trade, negotiates trade rules and regulations, and resolves disputes among countries. When a country files a complaint, as the United States did over the Chinese chicken tariffs, a WTO dispute resolution panel investigates the situation and makes a ruling. The 153 member countries of the WTO continue to hammer away on broader trade issues as well. Since 2001, members have been working on the Doha Round of negotiations, meant to provide equitable access to global trade for relatively poor countries.

## Regional Trade Organizations

Many goods are no longer subject to tariffs or quotas on the world market, and trade between countries is freer than it has been since industrialization and trade restrictions began. GATT and the WTO contributed to this progress, but much credit goes to the work of regional trade groups such as the European Union and agreements such as the North American Free Trade Agreement. Figure 54.2 shows the locations of regional organizations that work toward mutual economic development through trade and investment.

## The North American Free Trade Agreement

Some trading partners have established **free trade zones** in which there are few or no trade restrictions. The North American Free Trade Agreement (NAFTA) established the largest free trade zone in the world, linking the United States, Canada, and Mexico. The trade agreement went into effect on January 1, 1994, ending some tariffs and quotas immediately. The rest were phased out over time, and all trade barriers ended on January 1, 2008. By 2007, trade among the three countries had increased to $1.0 trillion, up from $297 billion before NAFTA. U.S. exports to its NAFTA partners totaled $412.4 billion in 2008, up 190 percent from 1993, and U.S. imports from NAFTA partners totaled $555.4 billion, up 268 percent from 1993.

When President Bill Clinton first proposed NAFTA, and throughout congressional hearings on the agreement, labor

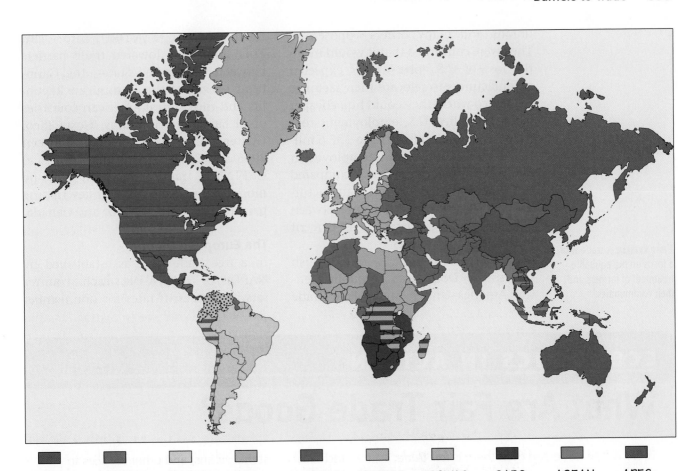

| NAFTA | CAFTA-DR | MERCOSUR | EU | CARICOM | COMESA | ECOWAS | SADC | ASEAN | APEC |
|---|---|---|---|---|---|---|---|---|---|
| North American Free Trade Agreement | Dominican Republic–Central America–United States Free Trade Agreement | Southern Common Market | European Union | Caribbean Community and Common Market | Common Market of Eastern and Southern Africa | Economic Community of West African States | Southern African Development Community | Association of South East Asian Nations | Asia-Pacific Economic Cooperation |

MERCOSUR — **Members**

MERCOSUR — **Associate Members**

| NAFTA | CAFTA-DR | MERCOSUR | EU | CARICOM | COMESA | ECOWAS | SADC | ASEAN | APEC |
|---|---|---|---|---|---|---|---|---|---|
| U.S.A. | Costa Rica | **Members** | Austria | Antigua and Barbuda | Burundi | Benin | Angola | Brunei | Australia |
| Canada | Dominican Republic | Argentina | Belgium | Bahamas | Comoros | Burkina Faso | Botswana | Cambodia | Brunei |
| Mexico | El Salvador | Brazil | Bulgaria | Barbados | Democratic Republic of Congo | Cape Verde | Democratic Republic of Congo | Indonesia | Canada |
| | Guatemala | Paraguay | Cyprus | Belize | Djibouti | Gambia | Lesotho | Laos | Chile |
| | Honduras | Uruguay | Czech Republic | Dominica | Egypt | Ghana | Madagascar | Malaysia | People's Republic of China |
| | Nicaragua | | Denmark | Grenada | Eritrea | Guinea | Malawi | Myanmar | Hong Kong |
| | U.S.A. | **Associate Members** | Estonia | Guyana | Ethiopia | Guinea-Bissau | Mauritius | Philippines | Indonesia |
| | | Bolivia | Finland | Haiti | Kenya | Ivory Coast | Mozambique | Singapore | Japan |
| | | Chile | France | Jamaica | Libya | Liberia | Namibia | Thailand | Republic of Korea |
| | | Colombia | Germany | Montserrat | Madagascar | Mali | South Africa | Vietnam | Malaysia |
| | | Ecuador | Greece | Saint Kitts and Nevis | Malawi | Niger | Swaziland | | Mexico |
| | | Peru | Hungary | Saint Lucia | Mauritius | Nigeria | Tanzania | | New Zealand |
| | | Venezuela | Republic of Ireland | Saint Vincent and the Grenadines | Rwanda | Senegal | Zambia | | Papua New Guinea |
| | | | Italy | Suriname | Seychelles | Sierra Leone | Zimbabwe | | Peru |
| | | | Latvia | Trinidad and Tobago | Sudan | Togo | | | Philippines |
| | | | Lithuania | | Swaziland | | | | Russia |
| | | | Luxembourg | | Uganda | | | | Singapore |
| | | | Malta | | Zambia | | | | Taiwan |
| | | | Netherlands | | Zimbabwe | | | | Thailand |
| | | | Poland | | | | | | U.S.A. |
| | | | Portugal | | | | | | Vietnam |
| | | | Romania | | | | | | |
| | | | Slovakia | | | | | | |
| | | | Slovenia | | | | | | |
| | | | Spain | | | | | | |
| | | | Sweden | | | | | | |
| | | | United Kingdom | | | | | | |

**Figure 54.2** Regional Trade Agreements

Regional trade agreements have flourished throughout the world.

unions and many others opposed it. They were concerned that it would mean the loss of U.S. jobs. Critics expected manufacturers to relocate their factories to Mexico where they could hire cheaper labor. In reality, U.S. employment rose from 110.8 million in 1993 to 137.6 million in 2007. The average unemployment rate was 4.6 percent in 2007, compared to 6.9 percent in 1993. And manufacturing output rose by 58 percent between 1993 and 2006, compared to 42 percent in the previous 13 years.

In 2005, President George W. Bush signed the Dominican Republic–Central America–United States Free Trade Agreement (CAFTA-DR) into law. This agreement lowered trade barriers between the United States, the Caribbean nation of the Dominican Republic, and the Central American countries of El Salvador, Honduras, Costa Rico, Guatemala, and Nicaragua. Between 2005 and 2010, agricultural exports to CAFTA-DR trading partners grew by more than exports to other key trading partners, including Mexico and Canada.

**Fair trade** is trade with a focus on the equitable treatment of farmers and their communities.

### The European Union

In a free trade zone as established by NAFTA or CAFTA-DR, each country sets its own tariff rates for nonmember

---

## ECONOMICS IN ACTION

# What Are Fair Trade Goods?

There is free trade and then there is *fair trade*. You may have seen the term "fair trade" on coffee or another imported item in a store and wondered what it means. Goods with **fair trade** labels have been produced under the standards of a fair trade organization such as Fairtrade International or Equal Exchange. These organizations seek to balance the profit motive with concern for the people who produce the goods and, in some cases, for the environment. The standards require equitable prices and wages, and may include provisions for worker health, safety, and housing, and the right for workers to join labor unions.

Fair trade does not imply free trade—fair trade products may be hit with tariffs and quotas. And free trade does not imply fair trade—the absence of trade barriers does not assure that farmers will be treated fairly.

Fair trade organizations deal directly with the producers when possible, thus cutting out the chain of intermediaries that drive up prices for imported goods. The goal is to direct more money to impoverished farm communities that otherwise receive a tiny fraction of the retail value of their products. Fair trade organizations also provide technical assistance, loans, and other services to help farmers develop their skills and improve their productivity.

Fair trade organizations also educate the buying public about fair trade issues. This includes telling the stories of the producers who provide our food and clothing. The aim of this informational side of fair trade marketing is to help consumers make socially responsible choices.

**DID YOU GET IT?** What is the difference between fair trade and free trade?

*The goals of fair trade organizations include fair wages and safe working environments for farmers and other workers.*

countries. The European Union (EU), however, is a *customs zone*, meaning that the union as a whole sets import duties on goods from non-EU countries. In 1986, all tariffs between member countries were eliminated.

As you can see from Figure 54.2, the EU is made up of 27 countries across all regions of Europe. However, the original organization, which was established in 1957, had just six member countries in Western Europe and was called the Common Market. Its purpose was to integrate economic activities among members. By the mid-1980s, six more countries had joined. In 1993, the Common Market was replaced by the EU, and 15 more countries joined between then and 2004.

The EU is a political as well as an economic organization with a Parliament, Council of Ministers, Court of Justice, and Commission. The Commission is the executive branch of the EU that proposes legislation, implements decisions, and takes care of the day-to-day operations. Citizens of EU nations can move freely across borders and work and live within any EU nation without restrictions. In 2002, 12 EU nations eliminated their own currencies and adopted the **euro** as a common currency; since then 5 more countries have adopted the euro.

The **euro** is the single currency used by 17 of the 27 members of the European Union.

# MODULE 54 REVIEW AND ASSESSMENT

## Summing Up the Key Ideas: Match the following terms to the correct definitions.

A. Free trade
B. Tariff or duty
C. Protective tariff
D. Revenue tariff
E. Quota

F. Voluntary export restraint
G. Embargo
H. Trade war
I. Protectionism
J. Offshoring

K. Trade deficit
L. Trade surplus
M. Dumping
N. Multinational corporation
O. Retaliatory tariff

P. Free trade zone
Q. Euro
R. Fair trade

_____ 1. The common currency adopted by the European Union.

_____ 2. A government-ordered ban on trade.

_____ 3. Tariffs meant to protect domestic industries from the loss of consumers' dollars to foreign competition.

_____ 4. The amount by which expenditures on imports exceed receipts from exports.

_____ 5. A limit on the amount of a good that can be imported.

_____ 6. A type of business with operations in many countries.

_____ 7. A tariff imposed to punish a trading partner's trade policy.

_____ 8. The practice of limiting trade.

_____ 9. The practice of exporting goods at a price that is below the price in the exporting country.

_____ 10. Taxes on imports.

_____ 11. When a firm moves some of its operations to another country.

_____ 12. Self-imposed limits on exports.

_____ 13. Trade with a focus on the equitable treatment of farmers and their communities.

_____ 14. A tax that has as its primary purpose generating money for the federal government without necessarily limiting imports or aiding domestic producers.

_____ 15. The amount by which receipts from exports exceed expenditures on imports.

_____ 16. An area where there are few or no trade restrictions.

_____ 17. An escalation of trade restrictions by trading partners.

_____ 18. The exchange of goods and services between trading partners in the absence of government-imposed restrictions or charges.

## Analyze and Explain

A. Determine whether each of the following events would bring a country closer to a system of **free trade** or closer to **protectionism** and explain your answer.

FREE TRADE OR PROTECTIONISM?

1. A country removes a quota system that has been in place for many years.

_____

2. A country imposes a system of tariffs.

_____

3. A country negotiates an end to a decade-long trade war.

_____

4. A country requires that all prescription drugs that enter the country meet strict standards.

_____

B. Write out the full name of each of the following trade organizations or agreements and briefly explain the mission of each.

| | FULL NAME | MISSION |
| --- | --- | --- |
| 1. GATT | _____ | _____ |
| 2. WTO | _____ | _____ |
| 3. NAFTA | _____ | _____ |
| 4. CAFTA-DR | _____ | _____ |
| 5. EU | _____ | |

**Apply:** Suppose total imports would equal total exports for a country in the absence of the following changes. Determine the effect each change would have on the balance of trade by indicating whether it would create a **trade surplus** or a **trade deficit**.

SURPLUS OR DEFICIT?

1. Exports from a country surge and imports remain constant.

_____

2. Exports from a country plunge and imports rise.

_____

3. Imports into a country expand and exports decline.

_____

4. Imports into a country contract and exports expand.

_____

## MODULE 55

# Foreign Exchange and the Balance of Trade

**KEY IDEA:** The value of a country's currency affects its foreign trade.

**OBJECTIVES**

- To explain the differences between fixed, flexible, and managed exchange rates.
- To identify the effect of weak and strong currencies on a country's trade.
- To explain how countries intervene in foreign exchange markets.
- To analyze the effects of trade deficits.

| USA | USD | 888383 |
| UNITED KINGDOM | GBP | 8Q8888 |
| CANADA | CAD | 888056 |
| CHINA | CNY | 868888 |
| EURO | EUR | 888280 |
| JAPAN | JPY | 888888 |
| SINGAPORE | SGD | 888986 |
| HONG KONG | HKD | 828888 |
| NEW ZEALAND | NZD | 888888 |
| MALAYSIA | MYR | 828888 |
| THAILAND | THB | 888985 |
| INDONESIA | IDR | 888888 |

*Currencies have prices just like goods and services.*

### The Dollar Is Falling

What does it mean to say the dollar is falling? Jeff D. Opdyke and Jane J. Kim mention the impact of the falling dollar on most Americans in their 2007 *Wall Street Journal* article, "Dollar Daze: Investing With a Weak Currency." "Even if you never travel abroad, never buy a foreign car and invest only in American stocks, the falling dollar is potentially a problem for your investments." This refers to the amount of foreign currency a dollar will buy. A falling dollar can be exchanged for less of a foreign currency than previously. If you're planning to buy something on eBay from a seller overseas, you don't want the dollar to fall because if it does, any amount of foreign currency will cost more in terms of dollars. A falling dollar presents broader problems for firms that rely on inputs purchased from other countries. In contrast, people who sell things overseas benefit from a falling dollar because their products become cheaper for foreigners. This module explains the market for foreign currency and the reasons for a rising or falling dollar.

## EXCHANGE RATES

Sometimes it's necessary to buy money with money. For example, American tourists who travel to Spain must buy some euros with their dollars. And when Sears imports Samsung brand televisions made in South Korea, it must first buy the currency accepted in South Korea—the won. The price of one country's currency in terms of another country's currency is called the **foreign exchange rate**. Suppose the foreign exchange rate is $1.45 per euro. That means it will take $1.45 U.S. to buy €1. The rate can also be expressed in terms of euros per dollar as €1/$1.45 = €0.69 per $1.

When the U.S. dollar will buy a relatively small amount of foreign currency, we have a **weak dollar**. We have a **strong dollar** when it will buy a relatively large amount of foreign currency. When the value of one currency rises in relation to another, we say the strengthened currency has *appreciated*.

The United States has a **weak dollar** when it will buy a relatively small amount of foreign currency.

The United States has a **strong dollar** when it will buy a relatively large amount of foreign currency.

A **foreign exchange rate** is the price of one country's currency in terms of another country's currency.

THINKSTOCK

When one currency drops in value relative to another, the weakened currency has *depreciated*.

In Module 54 you read that tariffs increase the price of imported goods. A weak dollar has the same effect: the weaker the dollar, the more dollars it takes to buy enough foreign currency to purchase an imported good. Suppose a U.S. import company wants to buy a shipment of Chinese backpacks that cost 65,000 yuan (the Chinese currency). It will first have to purchase the 65,000 yuan. The number of dollars it takes to buy 65,000 yuan's worth of backpacks may change from day to day, or even minute to minute as the dollar-yuan exchange rate fluctuates. If the exchange rate is 8.125 yuan per dollar, the backpacks will cost 65,000 yuan / (8.125 yuan/$) = $8,000. If the exchange rate is 6.5 yuan per dollar, the same backpacks will cost 65,000 yuan / (6.5 yuan/$) = $10,000.

A weak dollar makes exports less expensive. As a simple example, consider an apple from Washington State that costs $1. If the exchange rate is 8.125 yuan per dollar, the apple will cost the Chinese 8.125 yuan. If the dollar becomes weaker and the exchange rate becomes 6.5 yuan per dollar, the apple will cost 6.5 yuan. Because it lowers the price the Chinese pay for U.S. goods, a weak dollar is good for U.S. exporters. A weak dollar makes imports more expensive, so it is bad for U.S. importers. The opposite is true for a strong dollar—it makes imports less expensive and exports more expensive, so importers like it and exporters don't.

Today, the foreign exchange rates for the U.S. dollar are determined by the supply and demand for dollars in the *foreign exchange markets* for the various currencies. The **foreign exchange markets** are made up of thousands of commercial banks, foreign exchange brokers, central banks, investment firms, and similar financial institutions that buy and

A **foreign exchange market** is a market made up of the many traders of one currency for another.

*A weak dollar increases the price of foreign-made backpacks and other imports.*

sell foreign currencies for their customers or for their own purposes. The foreign exchange market for the dollar in terms of, say, the yuan works just like the market for any good or service, except that the price of dollars is the number of yuan per dollar. When the demand for dollars increases or the supply of dollars decreases, the price of dollars—the number of yuan per dollar—increases. That is, the dollar appreciates. When the demand for dollars decreases or the supply of dollars increases, the price of dollars decreases, so the dollar depreciates. Table 55.1 summarizes these effects.

| Table 55.1 **The Effect of Supply and Demand Shifts on the Exchange Rate** | | |
|---|---|---|
| | **SHIFT** | **FOREIGN CURRENCY PER DOLLAR** |
| Demand for dollars | ⬆ | ⬆ |
| Demand for dollars | ⬇ | ⬇ |
| Supply of dollars | ⬇ | ⬆ |
| Supply of dollars | ⬆ | ⬇ |

©JUANMONINO/ISTOCKPHOTO.COM

# INFLUENCING FOREIGN EXCHANGE RATES

Foreign exchange rates have not always ridden the ups and downs of market supply and demand. In 1944, as World War II seemed to be winding down, the United States and its war allies sought to lay the groundwork for better days ahead. Representatives from 44 nations met in Bretton Woods, New Hampshire, to discuss ways to stabilize the world economy in the postwar era. Out of this meeting came new policies for exchange rate determination and the International Monetary Fund (IMF), an organization with the goal of stabilizing exchange rates, promoting international trade, and strengthening the economies of member countries.

## Fixed Exchange Rates

The Bretton Woods Agreement based the exchange rates for world currencies on the U.S. dollar, which, in turn, was based on the *gold standard*. Under the **gold standard**, a unit of currency can be exchanged for a specified amount of gold. In this case, the United States agreed to exchange dollars for gold at a rate of $35 per ounce. In turn, the other participating countries established ratios of their own currencies to gold, or equivalently, to dollars. For example, suppose the British currency, the *pound*, was equivalent to one tenth of an ounce of gold. Then it would be worth one tenth of the $35-per-ounce dollar value of gold, which is $3.50.

The Bretton Woods Agreement required each country to keep its exchange rate with the dollar stable, thus creating a system of **fixed exchange rates**. If a country's exchange rate varied significantly from the target rate, the central bank of that country would need to intervene in the market by buying or selling currency in order to reestablish the target rate. For example, if the value of the pound became too high, the British central bank could sell pounds in exchange for dollars, thus increasing the supply of pounds and lowering their value. The fixed exchange rates took the uncertainty

out of foreign currency transactions, and the Bretton Woods system worked fairly well for the first two decades.

By the late 1960s, inflation was a growing concern for the United States. Countries that exported goods to the United States began demanding payment in gold for their dollars, fearing that inflation would reduce the value of their dollars. To stop the loss of gold reserves, in 1971, President Richard Nixon suspended the gold standard for the United States. The country would no longer buy back dollars in gold, and the foreign exchange rates for the dollar would be determined by market forces.

### DID YOU GET IT?
Under a fixed exchange rate system, what does a central bank do to keep the exchange rate for its currency close to the target rate?

## Floating Exchange Rates

Like the United States, most countries have now moved to a system of **flexible** or **floating exchange rates**, meaning that the exchange rates for their currency vary according to supply and demand. The floating exchange rates can vary widely. For example, shaken by the uncertainties and policy changes of the recession, the dollar slid from buying 0.81 euros in February of 2009 to buying 0.67 euros in October

Under the **gold standard**, a unit of currency can be exchanged for a specified amount of gold.

Under a **fixed exchange rate** system, the exchange rate between two currencies is kept the same over time.

Under a **flexible** or **floating exchange rate** system, the exchange rate for a currency is determined by supply and demand.

*At the end of World War II, representatives from 44 nations met in Bretton Woods, New Hampshire, to discuss new exchange rate policies and other ways to stabilize the world economy.*

of the same year. Due to the weakened dollar at year-end, Americans paid more for goods manufactured in Europe, and Europeans found bargains on imports from the United States.

### Managed Floating Exchange Rates

Under a **managed floating exchange rate** system, the exchange rate for a currency is determined by supply and demand with occasional central bank intervention.

Under a **managed floating exchange rate** system, rates are not fixed, but the central bank steps in to buy or sell currency when exchange rates fluctuate widely. There are benefits to a relatively stable currency—an economy does not react well when its currency takes a roller coaster ride. Dramatic increases in a currency's value crush export markets because of high prices, and the flood of cheap imports hurts the sales of goods produced domestically. When the value of a currency plummets, the price of

---

## ECONOMICS IN ACTION

# Calculating Foreign Exchange Rates

Suppose you have just landed at Heathrow Airport in London and you want to get British pounds (£) from the ATM. You estimate that you will need £200. To figure out how much this is in U.S. dollars, multiply the number of pounds by the exchange rate in dollars per pound:

pounds × dollars per pound = dollars

£200 × (1.65 $/£) = $330

Now suppose that your parents deposit $50 in your bank account and tell you to treat yourself to some fun on your birthday while in London. To find out how many pounds you can buy with this gift of money, divide the number of dollars by the exchange rate in dollars per pound:

dollars ÷ dollars per pound = pounds

$50 ÷ (1.65 $/£) = £30.30

It's not enough for the £42 afternoon tea at the Ritz Hotel in London, but it's about right for a ticket to the London Eye, a giant Ferris wheel that overlooks the city!

**DID YOU GET IT?**
Use the information in Table 55.2 to convert the following foreign currencies into U.S. dollars: (a) 400 Israeli shekels; (b) 20 Egyptian pounds. Then use the same table to convert $100 into (a) Mexican pesos; (b) Russian rubles.

*The London Eye is a giant Ferris wheel that costs about 20 British pounds to ride. At an exchange rate of $1.65 per pound, that's equivalent to $33.*

critical imports such as oil, machinery, and food can skyrocket. The merits of moderation give a managed floating exchange rate system appeal. Today, most currency markets operate with a mix of floating and managed floating exchange rates. Table 55.2 provides a comparison of exchange rates for the U.S. dollar.

## MONETARY POLICY AND FOREIGN EXCHANGE INTERVENTION

Foreign trade is one determinant of the value of a currency, but it is not the only one. Central banks and speculators buy and sell currency for policy and investment purposes. And when central banks manipulate interest rates, this, too, influences the foreign exchange markets.

### Intervention by the Federal Reserve

Exchange rates have their ups and downs as shown in Figure 55.1. Central banks can help keep fluctuations from getting out of hand. In the United States, the Treasury Department and the Federal Reserve System work together on decisions about intervention in the

| Table 55.2 **The Value of the Dollar Compared to Other Currencies, December 14, 2012** | | |
|---|---|---|
| **COUNTRY** | **U.S. DOLLARS PER UNIT OF FOREIGN CURRENCY** | **UNITS OF FOREIGN CURRENCY PER U.S. DOLLAR** |
| Argentina (peso) | 0.2051 | 4.8738 |
| Brazil (real) | 0.4813 | 2.0781 |
| Mexico (peso) | 0.0783 | 12.7954 |
| Great Britain (pound) | 1.6129 | 0.6200 |
| Europe (euro) | 1.3081 | 0.7645 |
| Russia (ruble) | 0.0326 | 30.6898 |
| China (yuan) | 0.1601 | 6.2473 |
| Japan (yen) | 0.0120 | 83.5430 |
| India (rupee) | 0.0184 | 54.4650 |
| Egypt (pound) | 0.1623 | 6.1726 |
| Iran (rial) | 0.0001 | 12,264.5091 |
| Israel (shekel) | 0.2639 | 3.7895 |
| Kenya (shilling) | 0.0117 | 85.8499 |
| South Africa (rand) | 0.1155 | 8.6597 |

SOURCE: www.xe.com/currency/

foreign exchange markets, but it is the Federal Reserve Bank of New York that actually carries out the plans. The Fed holds stocks of currencies from around the world. To increase the value of the U.S. dollar relative to the British pound,

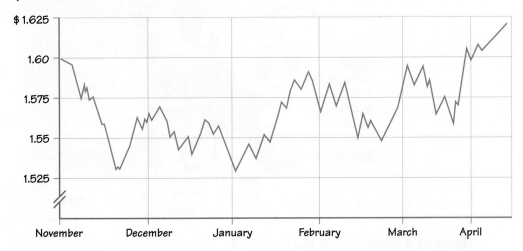

**Figure 55.1** Dollar-Pound Exchange Rate Fluctuations, November 2011–April 2012
*When exchange rates fluctuate too widely, central banks can intervene.*

for example, the Fed could buy dollars with some of its holdings of pounds. This would increase the demand for dollars and increase the supply of pounds. In Table 55.1 we saw that this would raise the value of the dollar and lower the value of the pound. Alternatively, the Fed could sell U.S. dollars in exchange for some other currency, say, the euro. This would increase the supply of dollars and increase the demand for euros, which would lower the value of the dollar and raise the value of the euro.

In addition to buying and selling currency, the Fed can manipulate the value of U.S. currency on the foreign exchange market by changing interest rates. When the Fed raises interest rates, investors from other countries convert more of their currencies into dollars so that they can invest their money in the United States and earn the new, higher interest rates. This increases the demand for dollars and increases the supply of other currencies, thus increasing the

value of the dollar relative to other currencies. The opposite occurs if the Fed lowers interest rates.

## The Eurozone

The euro is the single currency for the *Eurozone*, which is made up of the 17 European Union nations that have joined the European Economic and Monetary Union (EEMU). Figure 55.2 shows the Eurozone. Ten EU nations are not EEMU members, but there are hopes that ultimately all EU nations will eliminate their own currencies and adopt the euro. In joining the Eurozone, participating nations agree to maintain price stability, keep deficits to a specified level, and balance their budgets. They also agree that their central banks will keep interest rates within a certain range.

The adoption of the euro offers EEMU members several advantages. By eliminating the need for exchange rates within the Eurozone, the EEMU members established the type of exchange

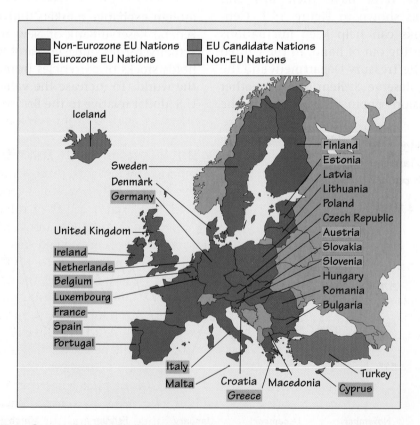

**Figure 55.2** *Countries in the Eurozone*
The Eurozone is made up of the 17 European Union nations that have joined the European Economic and Monetary Union.

rate certainty enjoyed by trading partners under the Bretton Woods system. With all Eurozone goods priced in a single currency, it is easier to compare prices for goods sold in several countries, thus providing more of the benefits of competition. And the single currency eliminates the hassle and expense, also known as the *transaction cost*, of exchanging one currency for another when conducting business in multiple EEMU countries.

There are also enough disadvantages to a common currency to keep countries like Britain, Sweden, and Denmark from wanting to join the Eurozone. Their separate, floating currencies create a cushioning effect for large changes in imports and exports between countries. For example, suppose Britain starts importing far less from Denmark, where the currency is the krone. Because it is buying less from Denmark, Britain will demand fewer krone in exchange for pounds. This shift in krone demand will decrease the value of krone in terms of pounds. With a weaker krone and a stronger pound, Danish goods will be less expensive for British customers to buy. The lower prices for Danish goods in Britain will revive interest and partially offset the effect of the initial decrease in demand. This could not happen with a common currency.

Another disadvantage of a common currency is that the member countries can no longer conduct their own monetary policy, which puts them at the mercy of the European Central Bank. This is problematic, for example, when some countries would benefit from expansionary monetary policy and others might be harmed by it. This was the case during the European debt crisis that started in 2010. While Greece and other countries struggled with tremendous debt, others in the Eurozone worried that the common currency would make it easier for problems to spread across Europe.

**DID YOU GET IT?**
Identify one advantage and one disadvantage of sharing a common currency in the Eurozone.

# THE BALANCE OF TRADE

The **balance of trade** is the difference in value between the total exports and the total imports of a country over a specified period of time. As explained in the previous module, when a country spends more on imports than it receives for exports, it experiences a *trade deficit*. When receipts from exports exceed spending on imports, the country enjoys a *trade surplus*.

The foreign exchange rate for a country's currency affects the country's balance of trade. When the U.S. dollar is weakened, as discussed before, imports from other countries decrease because they cost more, and U.S. exports increase because they cost less. The result is a decrease in the trade deficit or an increase in the trade surplus. In 1975, the dollar was sufficiently weak to bring the United States from a trade deficit of $4.3 billion in the previous year to a trade surplus of $12.4 billion. The United States ran a trade surplus in 13 of the 16 years between 1960 and 1975. Since then, the United States has run a trade deficit in every year, driven in some cases by a strong dollar and increasingly by Americans' appetite for relatively inexpensive goods from overseas.

## The Effects of Trade Deficits

Suppose that in one year, China purchased $100 billion worth of goods from the United States and the United States purchased $100 billion worth of goods from China. This would require the United States to purchase $100 billion worth of yuan using dollars and China to purchase $100 billion using yuan. The two currency transactions would balance each other out, and in the end, neither country would be left holding any of the other country's currency.

In 2011, China purchased $104 billion worth of goods and services from the United States and the United States purchased $399 billion worth of goods and services from China. Our $295 billion trade deficit with China meant that

The **balance of trade** is the difference in value between the total exports and the total imports of a country over a specified period of time.

the United States sent $295 billion dollars to China for the purchase of yuan that were not sent back for the purchase of U.S. exports. To make use of these extra dollars, the Chinese purchased things like U.S. Treasury securities, U.S. real estate, and stakes in the Coca-Cola and Johnson & Johnson corporations. In 2009, Chinese investors purchased a theater in Branson, Missouri, and the Hummer sport utility vehicle brand formerly owned by General Motors.

Concerns over foreign acquisitions of U.S. debt and property lead to support for protectionist policies that limit imports and, if successful, reduce the trade deficit. The opposing view is that foreign investment resulting from a trade deficit can have positive influences. Foreign purchases of securities issued by the Treasury and corporations provide an injection of financial capital that allows governments and firms to finance valuable projects and increase their productive capacity. And foreign purchases of U.S. firms can help struggling firms survive and grow to the benefit of U.S. workers and consumers. Although there are pros and cons, many economists argue that no country should expect to sustain a large and growing trade deficit for the extended future.

# MODULE 55 REVIEW AND ASSESSMENT

## Summing Up the Key Ideas: Match the following terms to the correct definitions.

A. Foreign exchange rate
B. Weak dollar
C. Strong dollar
D. Foreign exchange market
E. Gold standard
F. Fixed exchange rate
G. Flexible exchange rate
H. Managed floating exchange rate
I. Balance of trade
J. Transaction costs

_____ 1. A system under which a unit of currency can be exchanged for a specified amount of gold.

_____ 2. The price of one country's currency in terms of another country's currency.

_____ 3. A market in which supply and demand determine the exchange rate for the U.S. dollar.

_____ 4. A system under which exchange rates for a currency vary according to supply and demand.

_____ 5. When the U.S. dollar will buy a relatively large amount of foreign currency.

_____ 6. The hassle and expense of exchanging one currency for another.

_____ 7. The difference in value between the total exports and the total imports of a country over a specified period of time.

_____ 8. A system under which each country keeps its exchange rate with the dollar stable.

_____ 9. A system under which exchange rates are not fixed, but the central bank steps in to buy or sell currency when exchange rates fluctuate wildly.

_____ 10. When the U.S. dollar will buy a relatively small amount of foreign currency.

## Analyze and Explain

A. Determine whether each of the following is the result of the U.S. dollar becoming **weaker** or **stronger** in the foreign exchange market. Explain your answer.

WEAKER OR STRONGER?

1. Imports become more expensive for U.S. consumers.

_____

2 U.S. exporters have a harder time selling their goods overseas.

_____

B. Suppose each of the following events occurs on a large enough scale to affect the exchange rate for the U.S. dollar. Indicate whether each event causes the U.S. dollar to **appreciate** or **depreciate** and explain your answer.

APPRECIATE OR DEPRECIATE?

1. The Federal Reserve raises interest rates in the United States.

_____

2. The Federal Reserve buys dollars with euros.

_____

3. More Americans visit Europe on vacation.

_____

4. Europeans spend less on goods and services from the United States.

_____

## Apply: Suppose total imports would equal total exports for a country in the absence of the following changes. Determine the effect each change would have on the balance of trade by indicating whether it would create a **trade surplus** or a **trade deficit**.

EFFECT ON BALANCE OF TRADE

1. Imports increase.

_____

2. Exports increase.

_____

3. The value of the country's currency declines.

_____

4. The country's products become less popular in world markets.

_____

5. People living in the country start spending less on foreign goods.

_____

# THE NEW YORK TIMES

# International Trade and World Market

BY BINYAMIN APPELBAUM

In October 2011, Congress passed three long-awaited free trade agreements with South Korea, Colombia and Panama, ending a political standoff that had stretched across two presidencies. The move offered a rare moment of bipartisan accord at a time when Republicans and Democrats were bitterly divided over the role that government ought to play in reviving the sputtering economy.

The passage of the trade deals was important primarily as a political achievement, and for its foreign policy value in solidifying relationships with strategic allies. The economic benefits are projected to be small. A federal agency estimated in 2007 that the impact on employment would be "negligible" and that the deals would increase gross domestic product by about $14.4 billion, or roughly 0.1 percent. Service providers like banks

and law firms are expected to benefit. But many manufacturers, and the textile industry in particular, have argued that they will be disproportionately hurt.

Trade agreements reduce the price of American goods and services in foreign markets—and foreign goods and services here—by eliminating tariffs, or taxes, on those products. Most economists say the overall benefits are substantial, increasing demand and reducing prices. But the outcomes for individuals are much more varied. Consumers may benefit from the availability of cheaper foreign goods even as more expensive American workers are losing their jobs.

The United States has comprehensive free trade agreements with 17 countries, including Mexico and Canada. The agreement with South Korea could increase annual sales of American goods—including dairy products, pork, poultry, chemicals and plastics—by up to $10.9 billion, according to a 2007 estimate by a federal agency, the United States International Trade

Commission. That estimate did not include sales services like banking and legal work, which are also likely to be considerable.

The agreement with Colombia, a much smaller trading partner, would increase annual demand for American goods by about $1.1 billion, the commission estimated. It said the impact of the Panama agreement would be smaller; it did not provide an estimate.

But progress bogged down again over the fate of a modest and obscure benefits program called Trade Adjustment Assistance. The government has long provided benefits to workers who lose jobs to foreign competition, including training programs, money to cover the cost of searching for a job or moving to a new city and tax credits to reduce the cost of health insurance. Congress, under Democratic control, temporarily expanded eligibility for this program in 2009, but Republicans ended the expanded program after taking control of the House.

## DID YOU READ IT?

1) **What are some of the benefits to the United States of the trade agreements made in October 2011?**

2) **What are some of the costs to the United States of the trade agreements made in October 2011?**

## WHAT DO YOU THINK?

1) **Is it a good idea for the United States government to provide special benefits to workers who lose their jobs because of foreign competition? Why or why not?**

2) **How important is international trade to the United States?**

EXCERPTED FROM http://topics.nytimes.com/top/reference/timestopics/subjects/i/international_trade_and_world_market/index.html?scp=1-spot&sq=international%20trade&st=cse

THINKSTOCK

# CHAPTER 18 REVIEW AND SELF-ASSESSMENT

## REVIEW

### Points to Remember

#### MODULE 53: THE BENEFITS OF INTERNATIONAL TRADE

1. The resources held by a particular country position it to **specialize** in certain products by producing a disproportionate amount of those products for consumption and trade.

2. To **import** a good is to purchase it from a seller in another country.

3. To **export** a good is to sell it to a buyer in another country.

4. **Commodities** are standardized raw materials and agricultural products.

5. A country has an **absolute advantage** if it can produce more of something than another country using a given quantity of resources.

6. A country has a **comparative advantage** if can produce a good at a lower opportunity cost than another country.

#### MODULE 54: BARRIERS TO TRADE

7. **Free trade** is the exchange of goods and services between trading partners in the absence of government-imposed restrictions or charges.

8. **Tariffs** or **duties** are taxes on imports.

9. **Protective tariffs** are meant to protect domestic industries from the loss of consumers' dollars to foreign competition.

10. A **revenue tariff** has the primary purpose of generating money for the federal government without necessarily limiting imports or aiding domestic producers.

11. A **quota** limits the amount of a good that can be imported.

12. **Voluntary export restraints (VERs)** are self-imposed limits on exports.

13. An **embargo** is a government-ordered ban on trade.

14. A **trade war** occurs when each trading partner escalates restrictions to trade.

15. **Protectionism** is the practice of limiting foreign trade.

16. **Offshoring** is the practice of a firm moving some of its operations to another country.

17. A **trade deficit** is the amount by which expenditures on imports exceed receipts from exports.

18. A **trade surplus** is the amount by which receipts from exports exceed expenditures on imports.

19. **Dumping** is the practice of exporting goods at a price that is below the price in the exporting country.

20. **Multinational corporations** are businesses with offices, factories, and outlets in many countries.

21. The response to a protective tariff is often a **retaliatory tariff** from the country facing the new barriers, meant to avenge the initial tariff.

22. **Free trade zones** are areas that have few or no trade restrictions.

23. The **euro** is a common currency for the members of the European Union.

24. **Fair trade** is trade with a focus on the equitable treatment of farmers and their communities.

#### MODULE 55: FOREIGN EXCHANGE AND THE BALANCE OF TRADE

25. The price of one country's currency in terms of another country's currency is called the **foreign exchange rate**.

26. When the U.S. dollar will buy a relatively small amount of foreign currency, we have a **weak dollar**.

27. When the U.S. dollar will buy a relatively large amount of foreign currency, we have a **strong dollar**.

28. The foreign exchange rates for the U.S. dollar are determined by the supply and demand for dollars in the **foreign exchange markets** for the various currencies.

29. Under the **gold standard**, a unit of currency can be exchanged for a specified amount of gold.

30. Under a **fixed exchange rate** system, the exchange rate between two currencies is kept the same over time.

31. Under a system of **flexible** or **floating exchange rates**, exchange rates for currency vary according to supply and demand.

32. Under a **managed floating exchange rate** system, rates are not fixed, but the central bank steps in to buy or sell currency when exchange rates fluctuate wildly.

33. The **balance of trade** is the difference in value between the total exports and the total imports of a country over a specified period of time.

## SELF-ASSESSMENT

The following questions are the type your teacher might ask you on a quiz or a test. Practice with these in order to improve your performance on class tests.

### Multiple-Choice Questions

1. Goods and services purchased from abroad are _____, while goods and services sold abroad are _____.

   a. exports; imports
   b. imports; exports
   c. exports; quotas
   d. quotas; factors

2. Suppose that in one month, the United States can produce 10,000 boxes of frozen waffles and no maple syrup or 4,000 gallons of maple syrup and no frozen waffles. In the same period, T.H.E.M. can produce 5,000 boxes of frozen waffles and no maple syrup or 1,000 gallons of maple syrup and no frozen waffles. We then know that

   a. the United States has a comparative advantage in producing frozen waffles.
   b. the United States has a comparative advantage in producing maple syrup.
   c. T.H.E.M. has a comparative advantage in producing maple syrup.
   d. T.H.E.M. has an absolute advantage in producing frozen waffles.

Answer the next two questions based on the following exchange rates.

   Yesterday: 1 peso = $1.25 U.S.
   Today: 1 peso = $1.50 U.S.

3. The peso has

   a. depreciated.
   b. appreciated.
   c. fallen in value relative to the dollar.
   d. not been affected.

4. In countries using the peso as their currency, exports to the United States will

   a. be cheaper.
   b. be more easily afforded by consumers in the United States.
   c. increase in quantity.
   d. be more expensive.

5. If the _____ differ(s) between two countries, this suggests the possibility for mutually advantageous trade.

   a. currency
   b. exchange rate
   c. availability of land, labor, human capital, and physical capital
   d. level of government spending on social programs and national defense

6. Countries that engage in trade will tend to specialize in goods in which they have a(n) _____ and will _____ those goods.

   a. comparative advantage; import
   b. absolute advantage; export
   c. economic profit; import
   d. comparative advantage; export

7. Which of the following is an example of an import quota?

   a. a limit on the number of hockey pucks imported from Canada

   b. regulation by the U.S. government that specifies that each toy from China must meet certain safety guidelines

   c. a tax of $100 on each BMW car produced in the United States

   d. A tax of 10% of the value of each BMW car imported from Germany

8. A tax imposed by a government on imported goods is a(n)

   a. quota.

   b. tariff.

   c. voluntary export restraint (VER).

   d. embargo.

9. Restrictions on free international trade designed to protect domestic industries from foreign competition are

   a. competitive policies.

   b. free-trade policies.

   c. antitrust policies.

   d. protectionist policies.

10. A weak dollar would make

   a. imports and exports more expensive.

   b. just exports more expensive.

   c. just imports more expensive.

   d. imports and exports less expensive.

## Constructed Response Questions

Fill in the blanks to indicate the effects of the following actions.

1. There is an increase in interest rates in the United States but no change in the interest rate in Japan.

   The demand for dollars in the foreign exchange markets _____ (increases/decreases), so the dollar _____ (appreciates/depreciates), while the Japanese yen _____ (appreciates/depreciates).

   This change in exchange rates causes U.S. exports to _____ (increase/decrease) and U.S. imports to _____ (increase/decrease). This change causes the existing trade deficit to _____ (increase/decrease).

2. The European Central Bank buys U.S. dollars with euros.

   The supply of euros in the foreign exchange markets _____ (increases/decreases), so the dollar _____ (appreciates/depreciates), while the euro _____ (appreciates/depreciates).

   This change in exchange rates causes European exports to _____ (increase/decrease) and European imports to _____ (increase/decrease). This change causes an existing trade surplus for Europe to _____ (increase/decrease).

**CHAPTER 19 & YOU** If you care deeply about the poor, you may already cheer for economic development that feeds and clothes the needy. If you ever want to travel the world, you will benefit from economic development that promotes health, sanitation, and transportation systems. But even if you never visit another country, the effects of what other countries do will visit you. Problems with disease, pollution, and war abroad have a way of spreading around the world. On the bright side, history shows that progress in foreign economies can also deliver the delights of new inventions, cures, discoveries, and opportunities for trade to you. So while reducing starvation, solutions to global challenges could improve your health, safety, and financial security.

# Economic Development and Global Challenges

MODULE 56: **Measuring Economic Development**

MODULE 57: **Economic Issues in Developing Countries**

MODULE 58: **Globalization and Its Challenges**

## THE VALUE OF INFORMATION

It's difficult to imagine problems more deserving of attention than those of developing countries. Every four seconds a child dies from problems related to poverty. Across the globe, 1.4 billion people live in extreme poverty. The problems are as complex as they are enormous. As in other areas of economics, incentives influence behavior in developing countries, but which incentives will help the most?

Consider the challenge of increasing school attendance in less-developed countries. In experiments conducted in India, Kenya, Madagascar, and Mexico, researchers studied the effect of various incentives on time spent in school. Their measure of success was the combined additional time spent in school by all affected students. They found that giving financial rewards to parents increased attendance by two to four weeks for every $100 spent. Subsidizing school lunches, uniforms, or tuition increased attendance by one to three years for

*Economic research can help in areas you may not expect—like increasing school attendance in third-world countries.*

every $100 spent. But it was even more effective to provide treatments for intestinal worms. Over 400 million children worldwide suffer infections from intestinal worms, and often they are too sick to attend school. Treating worms increased attendance by 28.6 years per $100 spent.

The attendance experiments show the difference $100 can make and the value of information that compares different ways to allocate money. Uninformed by the economic research, those seeking to promote school attendance might spend their money on rewards for parents rather than deworming students and increase attendance by a few weeks instead of a few decades. But something increased school attendance even more than rewards and deworming: sharing information with parents and students about how much more students earned after completing each level of education. Spreading that information increased attendance by 40 years per $100 spent.

This chapter spreads information on the current state of the world's economies. Module 56 explains the different levels of economic development and the stages of economic growth. Module 57 explores the obstacles people in developing countries face as they pursue a higher standard of living. Module 58 discusses the role of globalization in economic development.

## BOTTOM LINE

Most countries of the world face formidable challenges in developing an economy that can provide satisfactory levels of food, shelter, health care, and education.

*"One day our grandchildren will [have to] go to museums to see what poverty was like."*

*—Muhammad Yunus, founder of Grameen Bank and winner of the Nobel Peace Prize, 2006*

THINKSTOCK

# MODULE 56

# Measuring Economic Development

**KEY IDEA:** Available measures of economic development gauge progress and allow for international comparisons.

**OBJECTIVES**

- **To identify the broad categories of economic development.**
- **To analyze differences in living standards among countries.**
- **To describe the stages of economic development.**

*About 1.75 billion people live in extreme poverty.*

## The Goal of Ending Poverty

We are a long way from realizing Muhammad Yunus's dream of a poverty-free world. And it is not only poor countries that have an interest in making the world poverty-free. Wealthy countries have discovered that it is in their own best interest to help poor countries eradicate hunger, disease, and poverty. At the United Nations Millennium Summit in 2000, 189 of the world's leaders, including those of the 29 richest nations on earth, promised to cut the number of people living in extreme poverty in half by 2015. The *World Bank*—an institution with 187 member countries that provides loans and grants to developing countries—estimates that one out of every four people in developing countries lives in extreme poverty. What is **extreme poverty**? According to the World Bank, it is living on less than $1.25 a day. This module explains measures of progress in the battle against poverty.

# LEVELS OF ECONOMIC DEVELOPMENT

There are several ways to categorize countries on the basis of economic development. The most developed countries are identified as *industrialized* or *developed*. Those whose recent progress has brought them considerable development are labeled *newly industrialized* or *emerging*. And the least developed countries are categorized as *developing* or *less developed*. Here we will use the terms *industrialized*, *newly industrialized*, and *developing* countries.

- A **developing country (DC)** is one with relatively little material wealth, meaning few goods and services are available to the majority of the population. Only a low level of GDP per capita (output per person) is available

to support the standard of living. Compared to industrialized countries, DCs face more poverty, lower levels of literacy, and shorter life expectancies. They also experience higher *infant mortality rates*. The **infant mortality rate** is the number of infants who die in their first year of life out of every 1,000 live births. Gambia, Yemen, and Haiti are among the developing countries. Most people living in extreme poverty live in developing countries in Africa, Asia, and Latin America.

- A **newly industrialized country (NIC)** is one with a rapidly developing capacity for production and an improving standard of living. Typically, large numbers of workers are moving from rural areas to the cities for jobs in the manufacturing sector. More goods

People who live on less than $1.25 per day live in **extreme poverty**.

A **developing country (DC)** is a country with relatively few goods and services available to the majority of the population.

The **infant mortality rate** is the number of infants who die in their first year of life out of every 1,000 live births.

A **newly industrialized country (NIC)** is one with a rapidly developing capacity for production.

THINKSTOCK

and services are becoming available to larger segments of the population, including health care, education, and stoves to replace cooking fires. Such countries include South Africa, Mexico, Malaysia, China, and India.

An **industrialized country (IC)** is one with a relatively high level of material wealth.

• An **industrialized country (IC)** has a relatively high level of economic development and material wealth. Educational and income levels are high, and a high per capita GDP gives industrialized countries a high standard of living. ICs enjoy relatively high literacy rates, long life expectancies, and low infant mortality rates. The United States, France, and Japan are examples of industrialized countries.

**DID YOU GET IT?**
How does a DC differ from an NIC?

# MEASURES FOR COMPARISON

There are several ways to measure economic development. Remember from Chapter 13 that gross domestic product (GDP) is the total value of all final goods and services produced within a country's borders in a given year, and per capita GDP is GDP divided by the population of the country. Per capita GDP is a standard measure of economic development because it is widely available and it provides a good indication of a country's material wealth. The mix of outputs, education, health, and population growth all influence per capita GDP and are influenced by it. In this section we discuss per capita GDP and take a closer look at these related factors.

## Per Capita GDP

Per capita GDP is a common though imperfect measure of progress. This measure doesn't count the value of such things as leisure, clean air, housework, and volunteer work. It rises with expenditures on bad things such as disease and natural disasters as well as on good things like stoves and schools. Nonetheless, per capita GDP is obtainable, objective, and useful as a measure of a country's standard of living—one gauge of economic development.

Table 56.1 shows the population, GDP, per capita GDP, and overall rank of GDP per capita for selected countries. Comparing Egypt and Pakistan,

**Table 56.1** **Per Capita GDP in Selected Countries**

| COUNTRY | POPULATION* | GDP IN U.S. DOLLARS** | PER CAPITA GDP IN U.S. DOLLARS** | RANK IN PER CAPITA GDP AMONG COUNTRIES |
|---|---|---|---|---|
| Brazil | 199,321,413 | $2,476 billion | $12,594 | 102 |
| Burundi | 10,557,259 | 2.3 billion | 271 | 223 |
| Chad | 10,975,648 | 9.4 billion | 823 | 194 |
| China | 1,343,239,923 | 7,318 billion | 5,445 | 122 |
| Egypt | 83,688,164 | 229 billion | 2,781 | 137 |
| Ethiopia | 91,195,675 | 31.7 billion | 374 | 212 |
| France | 65,630,692 | 2,773 billion | 42,377 | 35 |
| Haiti | 9,801,664 | 7.3 billion | 726 | 204 |
| Luxembourg | 509,074 | 59.4 billion | 115,038 | 3 |
| Pakistan | 190,291,129 | 211 billion | 1,194 | 174 |
| Poland | 38,415,284 | 514 billion | 13,463 | 60 |
| United States | 313,847,465 | 15,094 billion | 48,442 | 11 |

* 2012 estimate
** 2011 estimate
SOURCE: *CIA World Factbook*, www.cia.gov/library/publications/the-world-factbook/geos and World Bank.

you can see how the size of a country's population affects the slice of the production "pie" received by the average citizen. These two countries have similar GDPs, but Pakistan's population is more than twice the size of Egypt's. As a result, there is less than half as much GDP per capita in Pakistan as in Egypt, and the average Pakistani receives correspondingly less income and goods. The effect of population size makes it important to focus on per capita GDP rather than simply GDP.

Table 56.1 also exhibits the wide range of per capita GDP figures across countries. In the African country of Burundi, the per capita income is just $271. In the European country of Luxemburg, it is $115,038. Note that the per capita GDP figures do not indicate how wealth is actually distributed within a country. In industrialized countries there are still pockets of people living in poverty, and in developing countries there are typically a small number of extremely wealthy individuals who control large segments of the country's resources. A broader distribution of income is a common goal among citizens and policy makers.

### DID YOU GET IT?

Why doesn't a high per capita GDP for a country indicate that everyone in that country is fairly wealthy?

## The Output Mix

A look at the mix of goods and services produced in a country, what it specializes in for trade, and what it imports from other countries provides a snapshot of its level of industrialization. The economies of most developing countries are based on agriculture. For example, in the African country of Somalia, 60 percent of GDP is made up of agricultural goods, 7 percent is industrial goods, and 33 percent is services. In Somalia, as in many developing countries, a sizable portion of the agricultural production is for **subsistence farming**, meaning that families grow enough for themselves but not enough to sell in the market.

As you would guess, industrialized countries place more emphasis on industrial production and trade. Countries like the United States that have been industrialized for many decades also tend to develop a strong service sector including industries such as health care, education, retail sales, banking, insurance, legal services, and entertainment. In the United States, just 1 percent of GDP comes from the agriculture sector, 19 percent comes from the industrial sector, and 80 percent comes from the services sector. Table 56.2 breaks down GDP by sectors for 12 countries.

**Subsistence farming** produces enough food for the farming families' consumption but not enough to sell in the market.

*The economies of developing countries like Somalia are based on agriculture.*

AP PHOTO

## Literacy

The **literacy rate** is the percentage of people over 15 years old who can read and write. Table 56.2 includes literacy rates and levels of educational attainment for 12 countries.

As suggested by the figures for Burundi, Chad, Ethiopia, Haiti, and Pakistan, literacy and education are areas of weakness for most developing countries. Because of unequal access to education, both literacy rates and educational attainment are generally lower for females than for males in these countries.

Four factors contribute to the low rates of literacy and educational achievement in developing countries:

**1.** The emphasis on agriculture in most developing countries means that children often miss school to work in the fields.

**2.** Families in developing countries tend to have many children. Older girls are kept at home to take care of younger children and older boys are sent out to work, thus ending their educations prematurely.

**3.** As we have seen, many children with diseases such as intestinal worms are not well enough to attend school.

**4.** Most developing countries lack the tax revenues needed to provide tuition-free education through the end of high school, and it is common for high school education to be too expensive for many citizens.

### Table 56.2 Comparing Characteristics of DC, NIC, and IC*

| COUNTRY | PERCENT OF GDP BY SECTOR | LITERACY RATE | EDUCATION LEVEL | INFANT MORTALITY RATE (DEATHS PER 1,000) / RANK** | LIFE EXPECTANCY (YEARS)/ RANK** | POPULATION GROWTH RATE / RANK** |
|---|---|---|---|---|---|---|
| Brazil | Agriculture: 5.5% Industry: 27.5% Services: 67% | 88.6% Male: 88.4% Female: 88.8% | 14 years Male: 14 Female: 14 | 20.5 / 93 | 72.79 / 124 | 0.86% / 131 |
| Burundi | Agriculture: 31% Industry: 21.4% Services: 47.7% | 67.2% Male: 72.9% Female: 61.8% | 11 years Male: 12 Female: 11 | 60.32 / 27 | 59.24 / 191 | 3.104% / 7 |
| Chad | Agriculture: 52.7% Industry: 6.7% Services: 40.6% | 34.5% Male: 45% Female: 24.2% | 7 years Male: 9 Female: 5 | 93.61 / 6 | 48.69 / 222 | 1.98% / 56 |
| China | Agriculture: 10% Industry: 46.6% Services: 43.4% | 92.9% Male: 96% Female: 88.5% | 12 years Male: 11 Female: 12 | 15.62 / 110 | 74.84 / 97 | 0.481% / 152 |
| Egypt | Agriculture: 14.5% Industry: 37.6% Services: 47.6% | 72% Male: 80.3% Female: 63.5% | 11 years Male: 11 Female: 11 | 24.23 / 80 | 72.93 / 122 | 1.922% / 61 |
| Ethiopia | Agriculture: 46.6% Industry: 14.5% Services: 38.9% | 42.7% Male: 50.3% Female: 35.1% | 8 years Male: 9 Female: 8 | 60.9 / 26 | 56.56 / 196 | 2.9% / 12 |
| France | Agriculture: 1.8% Industry: 18.7% Services: 79.5% | 99% Male: 99% Female: 99% | 16 years Male: 16 Female: 16 | 3.4 / 213 | 81.46 / 14 | 0.5% / 150 |

This creates a dilemma. Without an educated workforce, a country does not have the trained technicians and professionals needed to help the country industrialize. But without industrialization, financial and health problems create barriers to the formation of an educated workforce. Newly industrialized countries have solved the problem in part by attracting foreign investment and foreign assistance with both technical expertise and funding.

## Health Care

Most developing countries lack adequate sanitation, hospitals, health-care providers, vaccines, and other medical supplies. Rural areas tend to get their water from wells or larger bodies of water that can be contaminated by human and animal waste. Cities may be growing so fast that

*Life-saving medicine is in short supply in many developing countries.*

**Table 56.2** **Comparing Characteristics of DC, NIC, and IC\* (*continued*)**

| COUNTRY | PERCENT OF GDP BY SECTOR | LITERACY RATE | EDUCATION LEVEL | INFANT MORTALITY RATE (DEATHS PER 1,000) / RANK\*\* | LIFE EXPECTANCY (YEARS)/ RANK\*\* | POPULATION GROWTH RATE / RANK\*\* |
|---|---|---|---|---|---|---|
| Haiti | Agriculture: 25.9%<br>Industry: 18.9%<br>Services: 55.2% | 52.9%<br>Male: 54.8%<br>Female: 51.2% | Not available | 52.44 / 41 | 62.51 / 184 | 0.89% / 126 |
| Luxembourg | Agriculture: 0.4%<br>Industry: 13.6%<br>Services: 86% | 100%<br>Male: 100%<br>Female: 100% | 13 years<br>Male: 13<br>Female: 13 | 4.39/ 192 | 79.75 / 37 | 1.135% / 103 |
| Pakistan | Agriculture: 21.6%<br>Industry: 24.9%<br>Services: 53.4% | 54.9%<br>Male: 68.6%<br>Female: 40.3% | 7 years<br>Male: 8<br>Female: 6 | 61.27/ 25 | 66.35 / 166 | 1.551% / 77 |
| Poland | Agriculture: 3.6%<br>Industry: 33.3%<br>Services: 63% | 99.5%<br>Male: 99.7%<br>Female: 99.4% | 15 years<br>Male: 15<br>Female: 16 | 6.42 / 168 | 76.25 / 78 | −0.075% / 197 |
| United States | Agriculture: 1.2%<br>Industry: 19.2%<br>Services: 79.6% | 99%<br>Male: 99%<br>Female: 99% | 16 years<br>Male: 15<br>Female: 17 | 6 / 173 | 78.49 years/ 51 | 0.9% / 124 |

\*Most recent estimates available
\*\*"Rank" indicates the rank among all countries.
SOURCE: *CIA World Factbook*, www.cia.gov/library/publications/the-world-factbook/geos.

local governments are not able to keep up with needs for clean water and sewer lines. Often, local governments are too poor to supply these services.

Poor nutrition intensifies health problems in developing countries. The limited availability of food makes it difficult to obtain enough calories, vitamins, and minerals. The lack of adequate nutrition and health care contributes to shorter life expectancies and higher rates of infant mortality. The rates of death among older children are also higher than in industrialized countries. HIV/AIDS, malaria, and tuberculosis are among the leading causes of death in developing countries. In industrialized countries, cancer, Alzheimer's disease, and diabetes are relatively common causes of death. Heart disease and stroke are leading killers in rich and poor countries alike. Table 56.2 provides the infant mortality rates and life expectancies in the 12 countries we have been following.

## Population Growth

Figure 56.1 shows the growth in the world population since 1950 and the projected growth over the next several decades. Notice that almost all the growth occurs in developing countries. In the earliest stages of development, countries are characterized by high birth rates and high death rates. As development continues, improvements in food supplies, sanitation, and health care allow a rapid decrease in death rates. Population growth rates are the highest while birth rates remain high and death rates are falling. Decreases in birth rates come later, with improvements in birth control, family planning services, education, and employment opportunities for women.

The period of rapid population growth strains the already limited resources of developing countries, making it all the more difficult for governments to provide enough schools, hospitals, roads, electricity, water, and other essentials. The

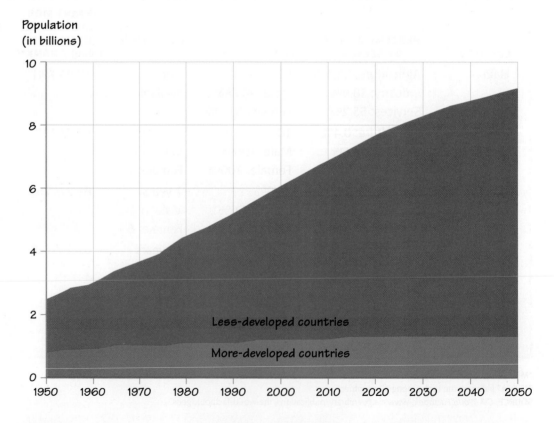

Population
(in billions)

**Figure 56.1** World Population Growth, 1950–2050

Most of the world's population growth occurs in developing countries. This is the result of relatively high birth rates and falling death rates.

SOURCE: United Nations Population Division, *World Population Prospects, The 2008 Revision.*

# ECONOMICS IN ACTION

## Women's Collectives in Developing Countries

Financial independence for women is another deterrent to rapid population growth. Women tend to have fewer children if they are able to support themselves and contribute to the support of their families by starting a business. This is an unintended consequence of the *microfinance* lending programs that help women and other entrepreneurs with start-up money as discussed in Module 57.

Greater economic independence for women also changes the traditional ways of doing things. In many rural areas, women form *collectives* to work together on everything from fishing in India to building storm-resistant roofs in Jamaica. These groups find they can achieve more by pooling their money, which might go to rent land for farming or to buy the materials needed to make fishing nets or crafts. Women's collectives may begin as business enterprises, but they often turn into agents for change in their communities. Some collectives have established funds to help students buy school uniforms; others have interceded to stop child marriages.

While financial independence empowers women and promotes self-confidence, the break with tradition can meet resistance. Push-back comes not only from village leaders whose ideas have been challenged but from family members concerned about the changing roles of women. But with assistance from international organizations and higher-level government officials, women's groups have flourished. The pace of progress can be slow, but women's collectives are bringing financial security to women and change to communities—building schools, opening medical clinics, and casting a broad net to include more women in a growing network of new ideas.

**? DID YOU GET IT?**
**What are two consequences of more women working outside the home in developing countries?**

governments of many developing countries counter population growth with aggressive and controversial family planning campaigns. In China, a policy of fining families with more than one child has prevented over 400 million births since its introduction in 1978. Notice in Table 56.2 that China's population growth rate is now similar to that in the industrialized countries of France and the United States.

There are also cultural reasons for population growth. For example, in traditional societies, children are expected to help support their families and take care of their elders. The high mortality rates for infants and children in developing countries can lead families to have many children in hopes that some will live long enough to assist their aging parents. This reason for large families diminishes as increased health care reduces infant mortality rates. Development also provides sufficient funds for programs such as Social Security to support older citizens, which reduces the need for children to support their parents in old age.

### Per Capita GNI

The World Bank and others use a measure of income that is broader than gross domestic product. **Gross national income (GNI)** is GDP plus net income from interest payments, dividends, and other income from assets in other countries. This net income can be positive or negative. When the Ford Motor Company

**Gross national income** is GDP plus net income from interest payments, dividends, and other income from assets in other countries.

produces and sells cars in Germany, the profit that becomes income for the company's owners in the United States is not part of U.S. GDP because the cars were made in Germany. But the profit is part of U.S. GNI because the income was earned in the United States. And consider the interest that Jamaica pays on its national debt, which exceeds $1.5 trillion. These payments will not affect Jamaica's GDP because they are not part of the value of goods and services, but they will decrease Jamaica's gross national income. The ability to capture transactions such as these makes GNI and *per capita GNI*—GNI divided by the country's population—popular measures of development.

The World Bank uses per capita GNI to classify countries into four income categories. The following values were used in 2011:

- Low: $1,025 or less (35 countries)

- Middle:

  ○ Lower middle: $1,026 to $4,035 (56 countries)

  ○ Upper middle: $4,036 to $12,475 (54 countries)

- High: $12,476 or more (70 countries)

The World Bank classifies the 145 low-income and middle-income countries as developing. Table 56.3 provides a comparison of the per capita GNI of the same 12 countries profiled in Tables 56.1 and 56.2.

**DID YOU GET IT?**
How does GNI differ from GDP?

# STAGES OF ECONOMIC DEVELOPMENT

It is useful to consider simplified stages of economic development as a general guide for what to expect. Although every country develops in its own way, stages resembling these are common. Depending on the circumstances, a country can remain in the same stage for centuries or advance rapidly from one stage to the next.

## Stage 1: Primitive Equilibrium

The stage of **primitive equilibrium** describes a simple economy with no formal markets and often no formal monetary system. Decisions are made on the basis of tradition—things are done as they have always been done. Because there is little investment in capital, the factors of

**Primitive equilibrium** is the initial stage of economic development in which there are no formal markets and decisions are based on tradition.

| COUNTRY | PER CAPITA GNI IN U.S. DOLLARS | WORLD RANK IN GNI PER CAPITA | PER CAPITA GDP IN U.S. DOLLARS | WORLD RANK IN GDP PER CAPITA |
|---|---|---|---|---|
| Brazil | $10,720 | 46 | $11,719 | 72 |
| Burundi | 250 | 163 | 608 | 168 |
| Chad | 690 | 143 | 1,531 | 149 |
| China | 4,940 | 77 | 8,466 | 90 |
| Egypt | 2,600 | 107 | 6,324 | 96 |
| Ethiopia | 400 | 159 | 1,116 | 159 |
| France | 42,420 | 16 | 34,993 | 24 |
| Haiti | 700 | 142 | 1,179 | 156 |
| Luxembourg | 78,130 | 3 | 89,992 | 1 |
| Pakistan | 1,120 | 129 | 2,763 | 127 |
| Poland | 12,480 | 37 | 21,310 | 44 |
| United States | 48,450 | 8 | 48,442 | 9 |

Table 56.3 **Comparing per Capita GNI, 2011**

SOURCE: World Bank.

*The first stage of development is a simple economy in which tradition is the basis for decisions.*

production remain largely unchanged, keeping the economy in this state of equilibrium. Early human societies were in this stage, as are the hunting and gathering tribes of the Amazon rainforest today. Vast rural areas of China, where agriculture is the sole source of income, could be considered in this stage as well.

## Stage 2: Transition

The **transition** stage is not about economic change but about cultural change. People begin to question their traditions and ways of life. They break with old patterns and adopt new customs and traditions. This stage lays the foundation for economic change; it prepares a society for the *takeoff* stage.

In Europe, the Late Middle Ages was a time of transition. Soldiers went off to fight wars called the Crusades and came home with tales of vast wealth, fine silks, and savory spices in foreign lands. Medieval lords looked around their dark, drafty castles and wanted more out of life. Entrepreneurs found ways to spice up the lives of those with money and many became rich merchants in the bargain. Peasant farmers decided there must be a better way to live and escaped to growing cities. These shifts in attitude laid the foundation for the rise of the middle class, the banking system, and business enterprises.

The People's Republic of China is a more recent example of a society in transition. In the late 1970s, weary of three decades of Communist rule, a number of Chinese citizens began to question Communist policies. Some began to demand political rights and economic freedoms. In order to contain potential rebellion, Chinese Communist Party officials eased some economic restrictions. From there, it was not long before private businesses began to spring up. These were the first cracks in the command economy and the beginnings of a system of free enterprise in which firms operate with relatively little government oversight.

Similar stories can be told about other developing and newly industrialized countries that are moving from command economies to mixed economies. These include Vietnam and the former communist countries in Central and Eastern Europe. Even Cuba, the only country with a communist political and economic system in the Western Hemisphere, allows some free enterprise.

## Stage 3: Takeoff

**Takeoff** is a stage of economic growth and abandonment of the primitive equilibrium. Citizens are willing to learn and use new techniques for doing things. New industries develop and expand over time as profits are reinvested in physical capital. Agriculture also expands because new farming methods increase productivity. Households save and invest more of their income. And domestic investment may be supplemented by **foreign aid**—economic or other assistance from another country—and by investments from foreign individuals and multinational corporations. The United States reached the takeoff stage in the mid-1800s. India reached this stage in the mid-1900s.

**Transition** is the stage of economic development in which cultural change lays the foundation for economic change.

**Takeoff** is the stage of economic development in which new industries are formed and profits are reinvested in physical capital to fuel economic growth.

**Foreign aid** is economic or other assistance given by one country to another.

India's growing expenditures on capital, infrastructure, and technology are typical of countries in the semidevelopment stage.

**Semidevelopment** is the stage of economic development in which industries expand and sophisticated technology is widely adopted.

A country at the stage of **high development** produces plenty of goods and services to meet the basic needs of its people.

## Stage 4: Semidevelopment

In the **semidevelopment** stage, industries expand and sophisticated technology becomes widely adopted. Investments in physical and human capital continue to increase, with money from both domestic and foreign sources. Money is spent on infrastructure, education, health care, and similar improvements that affect the quality of life. International trade becomes an increasingly important component of the economy as the country exports goods and services. The result is a greatly expanded economy with less reliance on the agricultural sector and a higher per capita GDP. China, India, Brazil, Malaysia, and South Africa are in this stage of economic development.

## Stage 5: High Development

In the **high development** stage a country produces plenty of goods and services to meet the basic needs of its people. The economy turns to addressing *wants* (travel, toys, electronics) rather than *needs* (food and shelter) with consumer goods and an expanding service sector. Agriculture is less important both for internal consumption and for export. The standard of living is high, and the government focuses on providing public goods such as national defense and the construction and maintenance of the country's infrastructure. The United States, Japan, and the members of the European Union are all examples of countries in the high development stage.

# MODULE 56 REVIEW AND ASSESSMENT

## Summing Up the Key Ideas: Match the following terms to the correct definitions.

A. Extreme poverty
B. Developing country
C. Infant mortality rate
D. Newly industrialized country

E. Industrialized country
F. Subsistence farming
G. Literacy rate
H. Gross national income

I. Primitive equilibrium
J. Transition
K. Takeoff
L. Foreign aid

M. Semidevelopment
N. High development

_____ 1. A country with a rapidly developing capacity for production.

_____ 2. GDP plus net income from interest payments, dividends, and other income from assets in other countries.

_____ 3. The stage of economic development in which a country produces plenty of goods and services to meet the basic needs of its people.

_____ 4. A country with a relatively high level of material wealth.

_____ 5. The percentage of people over 15 years of age who can read and write.

_____ 6. A country with relatively few goods and services available to the majority of the population.

_____ 7. The stage of economic development in which new industries are formed and profits are invested in physical capital to fuel economic growth.

_____ 8. The initial stage of economic development in which there are no formal markets and decisions are based on tradition.

_____ 9. Economic or other assistance given by one country to another.

_____ 10. The number of infants who die in their first year of life out of every 1,000 live births.

_____ 11. The practice of producing just enough food for the farming families' consumption but not enough to sell in the market.

_____ 12. The stage of economic development in which cultural change lays the foundation for economic change.

_____ 13. Refers to people who live on less than $1.25 per day.

_____ 14. The stage of economic development in which industries expand and sophisticated technology is widely adopted.

## Analyze and Explain:

A. Analyze each of the following and determine if the stage of economic development being described is **primitive equilibrium (P)**, **transition (TR)**, **takeoff (TA)**, **semidevelopment (S)** or **high development (H)**.

P, TR, TA, S, OR H?

1. A country finds that its industries are beginning to expand and that the use of advanced technology is becoming more widely accepted.

_____

2. People in the country begin to question traditions and ways of life.

_____

3. A country enjoys the traditional form of economic activity handed down through generations for farming and maintaining their culture and religion.

_____

4. Agriculture expands due to new farming methods.

_____

5. A primitive economy begins the process of developing new industries and reinvesting the profits from those industries to fuel further economic growth.

_____

6. Citizens are willing to learn and use new techniques for doing things.

_____

7. A country enjoys the use of advanced technology, reinvests profits from existing industries, develops new industries, and produces plenty of goods and services to meet the basic needs of the people.

_____

8. This stage lays the foundation for the takeoff stage.

_____

9. The standard of living is high, and the government provides many public goods.

_____

B. List six measures of economic development.

1. _____

2. _____

3. _____

4. _____

5. _____

6. _____

**Apply:** In the following situations, determine if the type of economy described is a **developing country (DC)**, a **newly industrialized country (NIC)**, or an **industrialized country (IC)**.

DC, NIC, OR IC?

1. a country that has vast material wealth, low infant mortality rates, high levels of literacy, and a long life expectancy

_____

2. a country with a very low level of literacy, a very high infant mortality rate, a short life expectancy, and a level of agriculture just above the subsistence level

_____

3. a country with a rapidly developing capacity for production, a low but improving standard of living, an exodus of people from rural areas to urban areas, and more goods and services becoming available to larger segments of the population

_____

# MODULE 57

# Economic Issues in Developing Countries

**KEY IDEA:** Developing and newly industrialized countries face many challenges in expanding their economies and providing public goods to their people.

### OBJECTIVES

- **To explain the theory of income convergence.**
- **To identify the obstacles to economic development in developing and newly industrialized countries.**
- **To discuss the types of foreign aid that developing and newly industrialized countries receive.**

*International aid organizations do their best to assist with the challenges of economic development.*

## Removing Bumps in the Path

You've learned five stages of economic development, but no one said passing through them would be easy. Even the generally slow progress of today's developing countries comes with assistance from committed organizations, governments, and individuals. Organizations such as the Bill and Melinda Gates Foundation spend billions of dollars annually to end poverty and improve health care in developing countries. The 193 member countries of the United Nations sponsor initiatives to fight poverty, such as "Goal 1" of their Millennium Development Goals, which reads, "Assist developing countries, especially in sub-Saharan Africa, to transform subsistence agriculture in order to ensure long-term, sustainable productivity increases and a more diversified economic base." And developmental economists spend their careers addressing challenges related to poverty. In this module we explore the bumps in the path toward development and some efforts to remove them.

## INCOME CONVERGENCE

According to the theory of **income convergence**, the economies of poorer countries will grow faster than those of richer countries. One reason is an expected flow of financial and physical capital from high-income countries to low-income countries. Investors seek to place their capital where it will bring the highest returns, and developing countries ripe for takeoff should provide opportunities that developed countries with ample existing capital do not. The returns, for instance, from building the first rail system in a country are likely to exceed those from building yet another rail system in a country with many.

Manufacturers also invest in developing countries, where labor is abundant and largely untapped markets await the products. For example, when the Finnish cell phone maker Nokia wanted to expand, it chose India as its site, where the population is enormous and the competitors few. Trade and contact with multinational

**Income convergence** is the closing of the per capita income gap between rich and poor countries.

corporations can also help low-income countries get fresh ideas. Interactions among high- and low-income countries often lead to transfers of innovative solutions and technological expertise.

Trade itself is another factor in income convergence. Trade allows high-income (industrialized) countries to specialize in production that is *capital-intensive*, in that a small number of workers accomplish a lot with the help of computers, robots, machines, and heavy equipment. Meanwhile, low-income (developing) countries specialize in relatively simple, *labor-intensive* production such as farming and sewing clothing. As the jobs that do not require intensive training become concentrated in developing countries, rising demand for unskilled labor increases wages in these low-income countries. At the same time, decreasing demand causes wages to fall for unskilled workers in high-income countries.

# OBSTACLES TO ECONOMIC DEVELOPMENT

Unfortunately, incomes are not converging at a desirable rate. Developing countries face a variety of challenges that can be classified as social, financial, governmental, legal, or infrastructure related.

*Persistent violence in the Darfur region of Sudan has devastated lives and held back economic development.*

## Social Issues

Rapid population growth and the associated shortfalls of food, housing, health care, and education present major social issues in developing and newly industrialized countries. Problems with crime, corruption, disease, drought, malnutrition, sanitation, and civil war in some developing countries thwart productivity and ward off the capital investment anticipated by the theory of income convergence.

Low rates of literacy and educational attainment also stand in the way of convergence. The anticipated flow of capital from rich to poor countries is dependent on higher returns from investments in tractors or trains or computers in the countries that lack them than in countries that don't. But if the workforce in a developing country has not received the education required to make good use of capital, the highest returns may still come from investments in the industrialized world.

An industrialized country needs engineers and scientists to design, build, and operate its factories, power plants, and transportation systems. It also needs managers to run businesses; teachers to educate the next generation of workers; and police, lawyers, and judges to maintain the rule of law. But how do you industrialize without making great strides in health and education? And how do you make great strides in health and education without industrialization?

## Financial Issues

Financial problems, worsened by burdens such as foreign debt and farm subsidies in competing countries, add to the workforce issues of developing countries. For instance, this is the case in the African country of Chad. Its farmland and other natural resources are in short supply, as are its financial resources with which to improve or import natural resources. South Africa and Venezuela represent countries rich in natural resources. However, they lack the physical capital needed to take full advantage

MARCO DI LAURO/GETTY IMAGES

of their resources. The cost of building hydroelectric dams for energy production, mines, food processing plants, and fuel refineries may be out of the reach of developing countries. Many resources go untapped. In some cases foreign companies provide the capital needed to develop the resources but then receive most of the profit.

Another problem is the amount of foreign or **external debt** countries accumulate by borrowing from foreign governments, banks, and individuals. Some of this money is borrowed to cover basic needs, and some is for capital investments that will invigorate development. Figure 57.1 illustrates the sizable external debt of countries around the world. The burden of external debt can be crushing even to industrialized countries, as Italy and Greece experienced in recent years. Some countries must keep borrowing money just to pay the interest on their debt, and some countries have little hope of ever repaying their foreign creditors.

To aid countries with debt problems, the International Monetary Fund and the World Bank launched the Heavily Indebted Poor Countries (HIPC) Initiative in 1996. The purpose was "to ensure that no poor country faces a debt that it cannot manage." By 2011, the HIPC had worked out debt reduction packages with 36 countries, amounting to $72 billion in debt-service relief. Of the 36 countries receiving assistance, 30 were on the African continent. In addition, the Multilateral Debt Relief Initiative founded in 2005 provides for the complete elimination of certain debts for countries that complete the HIPC process, particularly in Africa. The Inter-American Development Bank has

**External debt** is debt owed to foreign governments, banks, and individuals.

Legend:
- $0
- 1–1 billion
- 1 billion–20 billion
- 20 billion–100 billion
- 100 billion–200 billion
- 200 billion–500 billion
- 500 billion–1 trillion
- >1 trillion

**Figure 57.1** External Debt by Country (in U.S. Dollars)
The burden of external debt can be crushing even to industrialized countries.

done the same for countries in the Western Hemisphere, such as Haiti, that completed the HIPC process.

Module 27 explained that the governments of many industrialized countries, including the United States, offer farm subsidies to assist the agricultural sector. These payments allow farmers to maintain their own income levels while offering products at artificially low prices. The unsubsidized farmers in developing nations thus have difficulty competing with the prices charged by subsidized farmers in international markets. In calling for additional aid to developing countries in 2003, Prime Minister Tony Blair of Great Britain called on the European Union to end its farm subsidies. Opposition came from France and elsewhere, and both the European Union and the United States continue to subsidize their farmers.

**Capital flight**, the movement of financial capital out of a country, aggravates the challenges of development. Wary of political unrest and economic uncertainty, individuals and firms may move their investments to more stable countries to guard against potentially large losses. In 2011, Russia experienced an estimated $70 billion in capital flight. This loss of capital was part of a global shift of investments from the volatile emerging markets of developing and newly industrialized countries to comparatively safe industrialized countries.

Some forms of capital flight are illegal, as when corrupt leaders take money from the government and hide it in foreign bank accounts. For example, in 2007 Indonesian officials filed suit against former president Suharto for allegedly taking $440 million from a scholarship fund and for reportedly depositing up to $9 billion in an Austrian bank account for personal use. Whether legal or illegal, capital flight represents a leakage of financial capital that could otherwise go toward domestic investment in physical or human capital.

**Capital flight** is the movement of financial capital out of a country, either legally or illegally.

## Government and Legal Issues

Corruption is a global problem, but desperate conditions and inadequate anticorruption programs make developing countries especially vulnerable. Because of the importance of their policy decisions, government officials can be the recipients of bribes from firms seeking to alter policies or gain advantage over competitors. For example, the government of Nigeria recently investigated dealings one of its state governors had with Royal Dutch Shell and Chevron Texaco, multinational oil companies. The companies were suspected of paying bribes to the governor. When successful, bribes and related corruption can derail development efforts by steering policy makers toward what is best for particular individuals and away from what is best for the country.

Developing countries can also struggle with weak laws, or the weak enforcement of laws, meant to protect rights to property, writings, inventions, and ideas. Legal policies for these purposes—property rights, copyrights, patents, and intellectual property rights—are intended to assure those developing land or creations that others cannot take them away. When legal protections are inadequate, people are reluctant to put as much time and effort into projects that contribute to development. Who wants to spend time designing better buildings or writing better books if there are no rewards due to rampant illegal duplication?

Developing countries face the added problem of many families living and farming on land they do not own. The government or a landlord could take possession of the land at any time. This offers little incentive for these families to pay to connect electricity, sewage, or water systems to their homes, or to purchase irrigation systems that would make the land more productive.

Legal restrictions can also hinder development. In some developing countries, women have few civil and legal rights. When a group called the Taliban ruled Afghanistan from 1996 to 2001, for example, women were prohibited from receiving education or working outside the home. In countries with such restrictions, the contributions of women—roughly half their population—are severely limited.

Political instability, including civil wars, is yet another major problem in some areas of the world. For example, the Darfur region of the African country of Sudan has been the center of fighting between the national government and insurgents since the mid-1980s. Other countries that have experienced widespread conflict in the last few decades include Cambodia, El Salvador, Ethiopia, Iraq, Lebanon, Nicaragua, Sierra Leone, and Sri Lanka.

## Infrastructure Issues

Developing countries suffer from a lack of infrastructure and may not have appropriate technology for their needs. A lack of stable electrical grids, water lines, and sewer systems affects the health and productivity of a country's workforce. A primitive transportation infrastructure of mostly dirt roads with few highways, bridges, railroads, and airports impedes the flow of people and goods. There is little value in building a textile factory in the interior of a country if there is no efficient way to get the finished goods to market.

A country without modern machinery, farm equipment, electronics, vehicles, and similar advancements is at a distinct disadvantage when it comes to economic growth. However, as capital is added to the economy, its usefulness depends on how well it fits the country's resources and level of development. Countries with abundant supplies of labor have little need for robots that take the place of workers. Instead, they need things like precision tools and specialized equipment that allow them to make a larger quantity of a wider variety of products. And a textile factory with computerized looms will be of little value if there are frequent power outages or few people who know how to operate and repair the machines.

*Preparations for the 2014 World Cup soccer tournament brought upgraded airports and other new infrastructure to Brazil.*

# FINANCING ECONOMIC DEVELOPMENT

Developing and newly industrialized countries face the puzzle of how to expand their economies when they have few resources to begin with. A possible solution is to accept foreign investments and foreign aid. Industrialized countries and international organizations provide financial assistance to developing countries both because it is good business and because it is morally right.

## Foreign Investment

Foreign investment comes in two flavors: direct and portfolio. **Foreign direct investment** refers to investment from one country to control or significantly influence a business enterprise in another country. For example, Ford built an automobile manufacturing plant in Brazil. Building a factory is one way a company makes a direct investment in another country. Other ways include merging or entering into a joint venture with a foreign company and buying a foreign company. For example, in 2009, Vodafone, a British cell phone company, merged with Vodacom, the South African cell phone company.

**Foreign portfolio investment** is the purchase of foreign corporate bonds or shares of stock in a foreign corporation.

**Foreign direct investment** is investment from one country made to control or significantly influence a business enterprise in another country.

**Foreign portfolio investment** is the purchase of foreign corporate bonds or shares of stock in a foreign corporation.

Investors interested in the emerging markets of newly industrialized countries can buy shares of mutual funds that invest in NIC companies or buy stocks and bonds directly. For example, if you bought shares of stock in Teléfonos de México, a telecommunications firm based in Mexico, you would be engaged in foreign portfolio investment. Many foreign stocks are traded on the U.S. stock exchanges. While the rewards can be great over time, there are also great risks associated with foreign portfolio investment. The social, financial, governmental, and legal challenges in developing and newly industrialized countries can create added uncertainties and erratic stock prices.

## Foreign Aid

Governments and private donors provide billions of dollars' worth of foreign aid to developing countries each year, including economic, technical, medical, and military aid. For example, in 2011 the United States government provided $34.7 billion in foreign aid, which is about 1 percent of the federal budget. Some of the private, nonprofit organizations known as **nongovernmental organizations (NGOs)** specialize in assistance to the people of other countries. Project HOPE, CARE, and Doctors Without Borders are examples of such NGOs.

Economic and technical assistance is targeted to specific programs. For example, the U.S. Agency for International Development (USAID) is the principal U.S. government agency that provides economic aid to other countries. It offers economic assistance through loans and outright grants "to help countries acquire the knowledge and resources that enable development and nurture . . . economic, political, and social institutions," and financing for "economic stabilization programs, supporting peace negotiations, and assisting allies and countries that are in transition to democracy."

Depending on the program, funds may be used for infrastructure construction, such as transportation and communications systems, manufacturing expansion, and education and training to raise the technical competence of workers. Funds may also be used to provide loans to businesses of all sizes. This funding is meant to increase the productive capacity of recipient countries. Since the early 2000s, most U.S. economic assistance has been as grants rather than loans, so that U.S. foreign aid does not add to the debt burden of these countries.

There are also technical assistance programs intended to help the countries increase their per capita GDP. The programs sponsor professionals who train workers in the use of sophisticated machinery, the organization of businesses, and the principles of democratic institutions. These professionals include teachers, engineers, technicians, agricultural experts, and political scientists to advise on the full spectrum of key roles in an industrial economy.

Like the foreign assistance arms of other countries, USAID also provides humanitarian aid. U.S. programs include funding for Child Survival and Health Programs, International Disaster and Famine Assistance, Food Aid, Migration and Refugee Assistance, and the Global HIV/AIDS Initiative.

Military assistance includes both economic and technical aid. For example, the United States gave $5.5 billion in foreign military aid financing in 2012. The financing is typically given with a string attached. It must be used to buy military equipment such as fighter planes and tanks from U.S. manufacturers. This is common for other financial aid as well; it comes back to the giver in the form of sales.

## International Agencies

In addition to national governments and nongovernmental agencies, there are two other important sources of

A **nongovernmental organization (NGO)** is a private, nonprofit organization established for charitable purposes, such as to provide assistance to developing countries.

*Doctors Without Borders is a nongovernmental organization that provides medical care to those whose lives are threatened by violence, neglect, or disaster.*

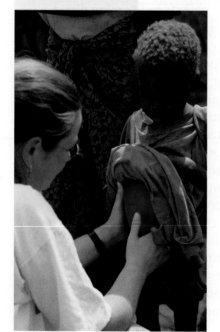

© LOUISE GUBB/CORBIS SABA

foreign assistance—both financial and technical—for developing and newly industrialized countries. One is the World Bank, whose motto is "Working for a World Free of Poverty." The World Bank is made up of the International Bank for Reconstruction and Development (IBRD) and the International Development Association (IDA). The IBRD provides loans and technical assistance to middle-income and creditworthy developing and newly industrialized countries. The poorest countries are helped through the IDA, which provides interest-free loans and grants to these countries.

Together, these agencies support projects across all sectors of a country's economy, including education, health, finance, government, infrastructure, and natural resource management. The IDA emphasizes improvements in agricultural productivity. In Tanzania, IDA support for irrigation and drainage projects has resulted in increases in annual household incomes to about three times preproject levels. After Sierra Leone's 11-year civil war ended in 2002, the IDA provided financing and assistance to help farmers expand the amount of land under cultivation. The IDA also aided the new government in setting up an anticorruption commission and budgeting process, resettling refugees, and retraining former soldiers. IDA-funded projects in Bosnia-Herzegovina helped restore infrastructure and basic services to prewar levels, rebuild 22,000 housing units, and provide loans that created 200,000 jobs.

The second additional source of foreign assistance is the International Monetary Fund (IMF). In collaboration with its 188 member countries, the IMF aids developing and newly industrialized countries. Its goals are "to foster global growth and economic stability," and countries of all types are eligible for assistance. Its primary task is to oversee the international monetary system. This involves monitoring economic developments in all countries around the world and lending money to countries experiencing financial crises. The IMF also provides technical assistance and training in its work with developing and newly industrialized countries to reduce poverty and expand their economies.

## Microfinance

Where people live on a dollar or so per day, money for savings and investment is understandably hard to come by. It is also no surprise that entrepreneurs in developing countries—who typically have limited wealth and few assets to offer as collateral—have difficulty obtaining loans from commercial banks. Innovative lending practices have emerged to address these problems. The most famous is **microfinance** or **microcredit**, which is the provision of small loans to help low-income people start businesses and provide for themselves. In some cases participants, typically groups of women, pool what funds they have to support loans that can be as small as $25 or $50. And sometimes a government or private donors establish the source of funds. A borrower might use the money to buy a few chickens for a new egg production business, to start a catering service that makes lunches for construction workers, or to set up a soda vending machine and a snack booth for villagers.

*Microfinance often involves women pooling their money to make new projects possible.*

**Microfinance (microcredit)** is the provision of small loans to help low-income people start businesses and provide for themselves.

# ECONOMICS IN ACTION

# Muhammad Yunus and Microfinance

*Muhammad Yunus won the Nobel Peace Prize for his work to establish microfinance systems that help poor entrepreneurs.*

What does a handmade stool from Bangladesh and the Nobel Peace Prize have in common? Muhammad Yunus, an economist in Bangladesh. In 2006, Yunus won the Nobel Peace Prize for his work to establish systems of microfinance. These systems lend small amounts of money to entrepreneurs in support of fledgling businesses and self-sufficiency. That is where the handmade stool enters the story.

In 1974, Yunus and some of his students were visiting the small Bangladeshi village of Jobra to study the economy of the rural poor. They came across a woman selling handmade bamboo stools. She told them that she borrowed the money from a moneylender to buy the bamboo. The material for each stool cost her $0.15 plus as much as 10 percent interest on the loan. Her profit on each stool amounted to $0.01. Because her profit was so small, the woman was always in debt and never able to save money to improve her family's situation.

Yunus decided to put economics to work. He lent 42 basket weavers in Jobra what amounted to $27 of his own money at a reasonable interest

rate. The loans enabled the craft workers to expand their small businesses and pull themselves out of poverty. After seeing the success of his first venture, Yunus embarked on a program to spread small loans at reasonable rates to more of Bangladesh's poor. In 1976, Yunus began the Grameen Bank Project with the help of the central bank of Bangladesh and the Bangladeshi government. In 1983, the project became the Grameen Bank. *Grameen* means "rural" or "village."

Five percent of the Grameen Bank is owned by the government, and the other 95 percent is owned by its borrowers. Women make up 96 percent of Grameen's borrowers. Today, 81,379 Bangladeshi villages have access to 2,565 branches of the bank, which has 22,124 employees and 6.61 million borrowers. Every week, Grameen takes in over $35 million in loan payments. With a 96 percent repayment rate, Grameen has the highest repayment rate of any bank in the world. By October 2012, Grameen had lent $12.676 billion to 8.36 million people.

Those initial loans that Yunus made have grown into a worldwide network of microcredit for the poor. Fifty-eight countries now have programs similar to the Grameen Bank. Among them are Canada, France, Norway, the United States, and other industrialized countries. The international Microcredit Summit Campaign estimated in 2007 that 3,200 microcredit lending institutions had reached a total of 100 million borrowers, up from 7.6 million in 1997.

Yunus banked on the reliability, initiative, and hard work of his borrowers, and it paid off for the millions who have pulled themselves and their families out of poverty. For his dedication to this goal, the Nobel Prize committee awarded Yunus and the Grameen Bank the Nobel Peace Prize in 2006.

**DID YOU GET IT?**
**How does microfinancing help poor people to improve their lives?**

# MODULE 57 REVIEW AND ASSESSMENT

**Summing Up the Key Ideas:** Match the following terms to the correct definitions.

A. Income convergence
B. External debt
C. Capital flight

D. Foreign direct investment
E. Foreign portfolio investment

F. Nongovernmental organization
G. Microfinanace (microcredit)

_____ 1. Investment from one country made to control or significantly influence a business enterprise in another country.

_____ 2. A private, nonprofit organization established for charitable purposes, such as to provide assistance to developing countries.

_____ 3. The closing of the per capita income gap between rich and poor countries.

_____ 4. The purchase of foreign corporate bonds or shares of stock in a foreign corporation.

_____ 5. Debt owed to foreign governments, banks, and individuals.

_____ 6. The provision of small loans to help low-income people start businesses and provide for themselves.

_____ 7. The movement of financial capital out of a country, either legally or illegally.

**Analyze and Explain:** Determine if the event described in each of the following situations would lead **toward income convergence** or **away from income convergence** in a developing country.

TOWARD OR AWAY FROM?

1. the flight of capital from areas of political unrest and economic uncertainty

_____

2. the flow of financial and physical capital from high-income countries to low-income countries

_____

3. the expansion of multinational corporations from high-income countries to low-income countries

_____

4. Weak enforcement of laws to protect property, writings, ideas, and inventions results in weak response to development requests.

_____

5. high and increasing external debt in the developing country

_____

6. expanding trade and allowing countries to take advantage of specialization, especially in the areas of capital-intensive and labor-intensive production

_____

7. Farm subsidies worldwide interfere with the market and put unsubsidized farmers at a disadvantage.

_____

8. rapid population growth and associated shortfalls in food, housing, health care, and education in the developing country

_____

9. a move toward political stability and rule of law in the developing country

_____

10. high literacy rates in the developing country

_____

**Apply:** Explain how each of the following can assist with economic development.

1. foreign direct investment

2. foreign portfolio investment

3. nongovernmental organizations

4. USAID

5. the World Bank

6. the International Monetary Fund

7. microfinance

# MODULE 58

# Globalization and Its Challenges

**KEY IDEA:** Globalization is bringing countries closer together in a worldwide network of trade, but it presents a number of challenges, especially for developing and newly industrialized countries.

## OBJECTIVES

- **To identify the characteristics of globalization.**
- **To analyze the challenges that globalization creates for countries.**
- **To explain the role of multinational corporations in globalization.**

## Our Interconnected World

As globalization spreads the flow of goods and resources across national borders, the growing interconnectedness of the world's economies promotes economic expansion. This growth and expansion started long ago. Ancient Middle Easterners created long-distance trade routes long before the first Europeans set sail for Asia. As the known world grew, trade routes lengthened and multiplied. What is different about globalization today is that hundreds of countries now have easy access to each other's markets. Chances are that the shoes you wear, the candy bar you eat, and the TV set you watch were produced in other countries.

Globalization extends the reach of firms, workers, and cultural influence.

Modern telecommunications systems have accelerated the pace of globalization. Today, people in New York can videoconference with business associates in Tokyo or Mexico City without leaving their offices. E-mails flash back and forth around the globe, sending orders for goods and confirming delivery dates. Computers and the Internet have changed how people do business, allowing them to accomplish more tasks more quickly in more places. And with cell phones, no one need ever be out of touch with the workplace. In this module we'll explore the world of globalization.

> *"When foreign companies open a factory or buy a business in a region they also stimulate local commerce and create a demand for more homes, shops, schools, and restaurants. They contribute money to schools, parks and towns, and lure consultants and technicians who provide more jobs."*
>
> —*Micheline Maynard,* The Selling of the American Economy

# CHARACTERISTICS OF GLOBALIZATION

Spurred by the erosion of trade barriers, globalization has brought about growing interdependence among economies. As the markets of distant countries unite, products that were once unique to particular regions—from the mangos of the tropics to the sweaters of Scandinavia—become available in stores around the world. Globalization has both supporters and critics. Let's look at both sides of the debate.

## Global Interdependence

We have seen that when barriers are few, countries tend to specialize and trade. Countries export the goods and services for which they enjoy a comparative advantage and import those made at a lower opportunity cost by other countries. As explained in Module 53, countries participating in trade are able to consume more of all goods than they could produce on their own. These export/import relationships make countries more productive. But they also make countries dependent on one another for the goods and services they do not produce efficiently.

Interdependence can lead to negative consequences. For example, beginning around 2008, the increased use of cereal grains and vegetable oils in biofuels raised the prices of these goods on the world food market. The result was felt in African countries that depend on foreign grain supplies. According to the International Development Agency, the number of people living in poverty in these countries increased dramatically.

## Global Cultural Influence

Some of the criticisms of globalization are cultural. Critics fear that traditional values related to family, religion, and community norms suffer from globalization. Young people may see movies and TV programs and listen to music from industrialized countries and begin to question their own values. The lyrics of rapper Lil Wayne and the storylines of the *Glee* TV series, for example, portray a way of life in sharp contrast with that in Asia, Africa, and most other parts of the world. The threatened loss of cultural identity creates tension among parents and older communities members. Later in this section we'll discuss how multinational corporations have particular influence on cultural change in developing and newly industrialized countries.

> **DID YOU GET IT?**
> How does globalization result in cultural change?

## Global Markets and Standardization

Looking for a flat screen TV? Your local electronics store probably offers models from Panasonic or Sony, both Japanese companies, or Samsung, a South Korean company. Looking for a snack? Your candy bar may have been produced in the United States in a factory owned by Nestlé, a Swiss company. Have an iPod? Did you know that Apple designs its products in the United States but has them manufactured in other countries? The iPod, for example, is assembled in China from parts made in several Asian countries. Apple sells its products around the world and in 2009 introduced the iPhone to the roughly 700,000 cell phones users in China.

Globalization creates many options for the production of goods. A multinational company may manufacture goods in its home country and export them the way Sony and Samsung do or produce goods in the country where they  will be sold, as Nestlé does in the United States. Apple's approach is to **outsource** its production operations to foreign companies and then ship those goods to the countries where they are sold.

Globalization has led to stores all over the world with many of the same products on their shelves. Kellogg's products

To **outsource** production is to contract with foreign firms to produce goods that will be sold by the domestic firm.

are produced in 18 countries and sold in more than 180. Walmart stores operate in 27 countries from Argentina to Zambia. Domino's Pizza is sold in more than 60 countries from Aruba to Wales. And Subway sandwiches are sold in 97 countries from Afghanistan to New Zealand. This standardization of offerings means people across the globe can enjoy the same popular items, such as Kellogg's Corn Flakes. The downside is that multinational brands sometimes squeeze out regional favorites, as when corn flakes replace traditional breakfast foods such as kippers (herring) in the United Kingdom, laverbread (a seaweed dish) in Wales, sopaipillas (fried pastries) in South America, and aloo sabzi (seasoned potato) in India.

*This is a traditional Scottish breakfast complete with haggis (sheep innards) and black pudding (sausage made with congealed animal blood). When globalization puts corn flakes on breakfast tables around the world, there is a loss of regional diversity.*

However, multinational corporations are learning that they can appeal to more customers if they differentiate their products at least to some degree. For instance, Domino's offers pizza topped with squid in Japan, broccoli in Korea, grilled lamb in the Netherlands, and black bean sauce in Guatemala. Nokia phones come with more brightly colored phone cases in India and China, and Nokia uses icons rather than text menus for phones in countries with low literacy

rates. Standardization has the benefit of cutting production costs, but low costs are of no use when products can't be sold because they don't match regional preferences.

# CHALLENGES OF GLOBALIZATION

Globalization can make a number of existing problems worse. Firms can cut costs by exploiting foreign workers. The migration of individuals from country to country causes controversy and resentment. Global competition for the world's limited resources hastens their consumption. And globalization increases the temptation for consumers to neglect the pollution and environmental degradation their choices cause in distant countries. These problems challenge the world's governments, firms, and consumers to act responsibly for the betterment of the global community.

## Worker Exploitation

Many countries have strict laws about the pay, safety, and working conditions of workers. But as firms in those countries offshore or outsource production to cut costs, the result is generally more production in places with lower standards for worker treatment. In some countries, workers earn only a few dollars a day, putting in long hours in poorly ventilated and unsafe factories. Some companies require their workers to live in

*Opponents of globalization worry that it leads to worker exploitation, resource depletion, and pollution.*

company-owned boarding houses with no privacy, little food, and poor sanitation. Critics argue that even though these conditions are endured more or less voluntarily by the workers, prosperous firms have a moral obligation to elevate working conditions to a level that is safe and reasonably comfortable. Over the past few decades companies such as Nike have asked their overseas suppliers to improve the working conditions in their factories. In doing so, they have discovered that the benefits of healthier, happier workers can include higher levels of productivity.

## Migration

Migration is an increasingly controversial issue, especially migration from developing and newly industrialized countries to industrialized countries. The International Organization for Migration (IOM) estimates that currently 214 million people live outside their country of birth. Most people migrate in search of opportunities to work. Many are *forced migrants* who do not want to leave their home countries but have no other choice. For them, migration means not just a better life for their families, but survival; they are leaving behind war, disease, drought, famine, or oppression. Often, migrants are men and women who send home money to help their families and return home when they are able. Others save their money and later bring their families to live with them in the new country.

Some migrants, including those who work in landscaping and agriculture, are seasonal. They travel to another country when there is high demand for their line of work, for example, during the harvest season, and then return home when demand subsides. Others are called *temporary workers* and are allowed into a country on a temporary work permit, which in the United States can be extended for up to six years. These migrants tend to be well-educated men and women seeking further job experience, higher salaries, and better living conditions. For example, it is common for foreign engineers who are needed by the U.S. technology industry to enter the United States as temporary workers.

The International Organization for Migration points out that migration decreases as opportunities increase for decent jobs at home. Where migration is a problem, this motivates aid programs to support economic growth in the countries that are the sources of migrants. The IOM also urges legal safeguards for migrants and respect for the dignity of all people.

Critics fear that migrants will negatively impact a country's culture and society, take jobs away from the native born, strain the resources of the country, and place a burden on taxpayers. Many people on this side of the controversy would like to reduce the levels of legal migration. They also desire larger barriers—sometimes literally in the form of walls between countries—to prevent illegal migration.

Others note that the United States is a nation made up of migrants and the descendants of immigrants. They argue that migrants typically work in jobs that are undesirable to domestic workers, such as harvesting tobacco, or in jobs that go unfilled by domestic workers, helping to fill shortages of physicians, software engineers, medical scientists, and other occupations. Many migrants start businesses, create jobs, and pay income taxes. All pay sales and excise taxes.

 **DID YOU GET IT?**
**Explain one pro and one con of allowing migration.**

## Competition for Resources

In a world of scarce resources, anything that threatens to deplete resources more rapidly deserves scrutiny. Globalization, by extending the reach of producers and consumers around the world, presents such a threat. If countries use resources at home or overseas as if there were no tomorrow, unsustainable practices could lead to deep regrets.

Globalization can occur in sustainable ways. Interdependence can come with international policies that moderate resource use. The spreading of influence can include a spreading of influence to reduce waste, reuse goods, and recycle materials. The trade in global markets can include resource-preserving goods and services such as windmills, hybrid cars, and wood substitutes including bamboo (a type of grass) and lumber alternatives made from recycled plastic. Globalization can also help spread information about reasons and methods for resource conservation.

The resources used to make energy provide an important case study. To industrialize, a country needs far more energy than was required for a more primitive existence. Coal, oil, and natural gas have traditionally contributed most of the energy for economic growth. But global supplies of these *fossil fuels* are limited, and U.S. oil production peaked in the early 1970s. So to make growth sustainable and to avoid the pitfalls of pollution and climate change discussed next, these resources must be managed responsibly.

The available approaches include conservation of known fossil fuels, exploration for new sources of fossil fuels, and adoption of substitutes for fossil fuels. There are ongoing global efforts to develop renewable, nonpolluting sources of energy. Among the options already in use are hydropower from falling water, energy from biomass such as grains and woodchips, solar power from the sun, geothermal power from the earth, and wind power from, well, you guessed it. Each of these alternatives requires capital, such as water turbines, solar panels, and windmills, which is a problem for developing and newly industrialized countries—but so are high oil prices.

The market's pricing mechanism helps moderate resource use. Recall from the supply and demand model that a decrease in supply or an increase in demand will send the price upward. In the case of fossil fuels, rising prices provide added incentives for energy conservation, exploration, and the development of alternative sources. The same is true for other materials tapped more intensely due to industrialization and globalization. The prices of copper, zinc, and bauxite, for example, have risen with more countries competing to buy them.

It takes more than rising prices, however, to constrain resource use to its optimal level. Prices do not reflect the full cost of resource use in terms of environmental damage and losses to future generations. To further moderate resource use, governments adopt policies such as catch limits for fish, logging restrictions in national forests, and taxes on gasoline. The Convention on International Trade in Endangered Species of Wild Fauna and Flora is an example of broader international agreements to protect natural resources.

The Nature Conservancy, the Friends of the Earth, and the Forest Stewardship Council are among the organizations that help countries conserve resources. Conservation International, another example, notes that economic development is "necessary for human well-being" and yet threatens natural resources. The organization provides education and policy assessment to help countries be better stewards of their natural resources as they develop. Likewise, the International Union for Conservation of Nature seeks to inform decision makers in order to improve laws, policies, and institutions that govern natural resources.

## Global Pollution and Climate Change

Pollution is created at every stage of the production process. This includes the extraction of resources from the earth; the transportation of those resources; the processing that creates inputs such as metals, plastics, and textiles; the

*Pollution is a global problem and the United Nations is working on global solutions.*

manufacture of final goods such as refrigerators, toys, and clothing; and the delivery of the finished goods to the stores. Globalization makes it possible for consumers in one country to receive goods manufactured in other countries using resources extracted and processed in other countries. In other words, most of the polluting stages occur far from where the pollution would be evident to the consumers. This makes it easier to ignore the problems of pollution.

Out of sight may mean out of mind, but some types of pollution threaten the entire planet. Carbon dioxide, methane, and nitrous oxide are among the gases that collect in the atmosphere and prevent some of the sun's heat from escaping through the atmosphere and out into space. These *greenhouse gases* are released both from natural sources such as volcanoes and wild animals, and from factories, cars, power plants, and livestock. The results, according to the United Nations–backed Intergovernmental Panel on Climate Change, include global climate change, a slow rising of sea levels, and more intense storms.

The United Nations coordinated the international response to climate change with a series of meetings launched by

**Tradable emission permits** convey the right to emit a certain amount of pollution and can be sold by one firm to another.

the 1992 Earth Summit in Rio de Janeiro, Brazil. In 1997 a meeting in Kyoto, Japan, established an international treaty on the environment known as the Kyoto Protocol. This treaty, which came into effect in 2005 and expired in 2012, required *ratifying countries* (countries that formally consented to the agreement) to reduce their greenhouse gas emissions to meet targets based on each country's level of industrialization. By 2011, 191 countries had ratified the treaty. The United States did not. U.S. policy makers worried that the Kyoto Protocol's limits on pollution would harm the economy by forcing firms to spend money to reduce emissions, thus making U.S. goods less competitive in global markets.

Developing countries did not face the aggressive reduction targets of industrialized nations. If they did, the world's most vulnerable economies would be in a bind. Most of the jobs and economic growth created by investments in less-polluting technology would go to industrialized countries, at the expense of growth efforts and public services in the poorest countries. Proponents of leniency for developing and newly industrialized countries also argued that industrialized countries developed in the absence of pollution limits, so DCs and NICs should be able to as well. However, developing countries account for about 50 percent of greenhouse gas emissions, which creates a dilemma.

One partial solution may be systems of **tradable emission permits**. Under these systems, firms receive permits to emit a certain amount of particular pollutants, such as sulfur dioxide and carbon dioxide. If the targeted amount of sulfur dioxide is 20 billion tons, permits for that quantity are distributed to firms, based on the amount of air pollution created in each region. As set up under the Kyoto Protocol and related systems of tradable permits in the United States and elsewhere, firms that do not use all their permits can sell their extras to firms that want to pollute more than their permits allow.

THINKSTOCK

Relative to inflexible restrictions on the types of pollution-reducing technology each firm must adopt, or limits on the pollution each firm may emit, tradable emission permits have three distinct advantages:

**1.** Firms have incentives to reduce their emissions not just to the mandated level but below it, so that they can sell extra emission permits to other firms.

**2.** Firms have flexibility in how they reduce emissions, so that each firm can innovate and address the problem in the way that best suits their situation.

**3.** The permit market allocates pollution rights to those firms with the most to gain from them—the firms that find it necessary to emit relatively large amounts of pollution in order to produce goods valued by consumers.

Under names that include *carbon trading*, *emissions trading*, and *cap-and-trade*, systems of tradable emissions permits are making their way into global economic policy. The International Emissions Trading Association (IETA) is a partnership of 155 international companies from developing, newly industrialized, and industrialized countries with the mission to "establish a functional international framework for trading in greenhouse gas emission reductions." And the international treaties that replace the Kyoto Protocol are likely to maintain a prominent role for tradable emissions permits.

**DID YOU GET IT?**
What advantages does a system of tradable emissions permits have over a policy requiring each factory to adopt a particular type of technology to reduce pollution?

# MULTINATIONALS AND GLOBALIZATION

Multinational corporations carry the seeds of influence around the globe. As they spread their products and production processes, they plant ideas and values. The McDonald's Corporation, for example, serves more than 64 million customers in 33,000 locations in 119 countries every day. When Toyota builds an auto assembly plant in the United States, it introduces its own management style—emphasizing a flow of new ideas upward from production line workers to management rather than down from management to workers. There is a similar transfer of expectations and methodology when the Ford Motor Company builds an auto plant in Brazil. In these ways, multinational corporations change the way local workers do things.

Table 58.1 lists the 20 largest multinational corporations in the world. As with the other aspects of globalization, the influences of multinational corporations have pros and cons. The trick is to benefit from the trade of new products and ideas while limiting the spread of unwanted cultural change, materialism, unhealthy habits, and environmental damage. There is a gray area surrounding the ideal amount of globalization because change is always accompanied by uncertainty. The controversy comes to a head with protests and pressure on governments to limit the influence of multinational corporations and protect domestic resources and jobs.

Multinational corporations have divided loyalties to stockholders and consumers. Governments are pulled in many directions by firms and individuals. But firms and elected officials share an interest in appealing to consumers and voters, which gives considerable importance to the knowledge and actions of people like you.

| Table 58.1 | **The Top 20 Multinational Corporations in the World, 2012** | |
|---|---|---|
| **COMPANY** | **COUNTRY** | **INDUSTRY** |
| 1. ExxonMobil | United States | Oil and gas |
| 2. JPMorgan Chase | United States | Banking |
| 3. General Electric | United States | Conglomerates |
| 4. Royal Dutch Shell | Netherlands | Oil and gas |
| 5. ICBC | China | Banking |
| 6. HSBC Holdings | United Kingdom | Banking |
| 7. PetroChina | China | Oil and gas |
| 8. Berkshire Hathaway | United States | Diversified financials |
| 9. Wells Fargo | United States | Banking |
| 10. Petrobras-Petroleo Brasil | Brazil | Oil and gas |
| 11. BP | United Kingdom | Oil and gas |
| 12. Chevron | United States | Oil and gas |
| 13. China Construction Bank | China | Banking |
| 14. Citigroup | United States | Banking |
| 15. Gazprom | Russia | Oil and gas |
| 16. Walmart Stores | United States | Retailing |
| 17. Volkswagen Group | Germany | Automobiles |
| 18. Total | France | Oil and gas |
| 19. Agricultural Bank of China | China | Banking |
| 20. BNP Paribas | France | Banking |

SOURCE: *Forbes.com.*

# MODULE 58 REVIEW AND ASSESSMENT

**Summing Up the Key Ideas:** Match the following terms to the correct definitions:

A. Outsource     C. Temporary workers     E. Fossil fuels

B. Forced migration     D. Tradable emission permits     F. Greenhouse gases

_____ 1. Individuals, such as trained engineers for the technology industry, allowed into a country on a temporary work permit.

_____ 2. Carbon dioxide, methane, and nitrous oxide that collect in the atmosphere and prevent some of the sun's heat from escaping out into space.

_____ 3. These are used to convey the right to emit a certain amount of pollution and can be sold by one firm to another.

_____ 4. Those individuals who do not wish to leave their home country but are forced out by war, disease, drought, famine, or oppression.

_____ 5. To contract with foreign firms to produce goods that will be sold by the domestic firm.

_____ 6. Coal, oil, and gas, which are of limited supply and need to be conserved, have traditionally contributed most of the energy for economic growth.

## Analyze and Explain:

A. Determine if each of the following situations would be an example of **outsourcing** for the United States.

OUTSOURCING?

1. An American company produces a product in the United States and exports it to Canada.

_____

2. A British company produces a product in Great Britain and exports it to the United States.

_____

3. An American company contracts to have its product produced overseas and then sells the product around the world.

_____

4. A foreign company contracts to have its product produced in the United States and then sells the product around the world.

_____

B. Provide one example of each of the following characteristics of globalization.

1. global interdependence     _____

2. global cultural influence     _____

3. global standardization     _____

**Apply:** Indicate one pro and one con of each of the following items.

| | PRO | CON |
|---|---|---|
| 1. the migration of workers from one country to another | _____ | _____ |
| 2. the availability of Domino's pizza in 60 countries | _____ | _____ |
| 3. influential multinational corporations | _____ | _____ |

## The Economist

# Drain or gain?

### Poor countries can end up benefiting when their brightest citizens emigrate

MAY 26, 2011

Lots of studies have found that well-educated people from developing countries are particularly likely to emigrate. By some estimates, two-thirds of highly educated Cape Verdeans live outside the country. A big survey of Indian households from 2004 asked about family members who had moved abroad. It found that nearly 40% of emigrants had more than a high school education, compared with around 3.3% of all Indians over the age of 25. This "brain drain" has long bothered policy makers in poor countries. They fear that it hurts their economies, depriving them of much-needed skilled workers who could have taught at their universities, worked in their hospitals, and come up with clever new products for their factories to make.

Many now take issue with this view that migration is costly to a developing economy. Migrants often directly "repay" their homelands through remittances (money sent back home from migrants working abroad). Workers from developing countries remitted a total of $325 billion in 2010, according to the World Bank. In Lebanon, Lesotho, Nepal, Tajikistan, and a few other places, remittances are more than 20% of GDP. A skilled migrant may earn several multiples of what his income would have been had he stayed at home. A study of Romanian migrants to America found that the average emigrant earned almost $12,000 a year more in America than he would have done in his native land, a huge premium for someone from a country where income per person is around $7,500.

It is true that many skilled migrants have been educated and trained partly at the expense of their (often cash-strapped) governments. Some argue that poor countries should therefore rethink how much they spend on higher education. Indians, for example, often debate whether their government should continue to subsidize the Indian Institutes of Technology (IITs), its elite engineering schools, when large numbers of IIT graduates end up in Silicon Valley or on Wall Street. But a new study of remittances sent home by Ghanaian migrants suggests that on average they transfer enough over their working lives to cover the amount spent on educating them several times over.

The possibility of emigration may even have beneficial effects on those who choose to stay, by giving people in poor countries an incentive to invest in education. A study of Cape Verdeans finds that an increase of ten percentage points in young people's perceived probability of emigrating raises the probability of their completing secondary school by around eight points.

Migrants can also affect their home country directly. Migrants may return home, often with skills that would have been hard to pick up had they never gone abroad. The study of Romanian migrants found that returnees earned an average of 12–14 percent more than similar people who had stayed at home. Letting educated people go where they want looks like the brainy option.

---

**DID YOU READ IT?**

1) Why is "brain drain" a concern to developing countries?

2) How might "brain drain" be beneficial to developing countries?

**WHAT DO YOU THINK?**

1) In addition to better economic opportunity, why might a person want to emigrate?

2) Is the life of someone who emigrates difficult? What challenges does someone thinking about emigration face?

EXCERPTED FROM www.economist.com/node/18741763

## AN INTERVIEW WITH Esther Duflo, Author of *Poor Economics: A Radical Rethinking of the Way to Fight Poverty*

**When did you first take an economics class? What was your impression of it?**

It was the equivalent in France of junior year in college. Before that, I was following a very general social science and math track, and I thought I would become a historian. When it was time to really specialize in history, I thought it would be good to try something complementary as well. I hesitated between law and economics, and I eventually took economics. I hated the first class, and in fact my whole first year. We were just doing microeconomics, macroeconomics, and econometrics. I thought micro was pointless because it was so far removed from how people really make decisions, and I suspected macro to have a strong ideological agenda. The only thing I was more interested in was econometrics.

**When did you decide you wanted to become an economist? Why? What attracted you to development economics, in particular?**

After this rather inauspicious start, I was ready to give up economics. I decided to spend my senior year in Russia to write my undergraduate dissertation in history (in France, for the last year in college, in the humanities, you mostly don't need to take classes). I met one of my economics professors in the airport in Moscow when I was waiting for a friend. He suggested I work for him in

Russia, and also for Jeff Sachs, who had a team in Moscow. It was in 1992, and lots of things were happening in Russia. I worked for both of them as a research assistant, and I loved it. So I decided to become an economist. When I came back to France, I had to take one year's worth of exams in about a week, to qualify for a master's program.

**You started the Abdul Latif Jameel Poverty Action Lab at MIT. Can you briefly describe what J-PAL does, and what makes it unique?**

J-PAL is a network of about 60 economics researchers around the world (as I write . . .). We run what is called "randomized controlled trials" to test the effectiveness of policy and programs to help poor people (mainly in developing countries, but not only). This is the equivalent of a drug trial. To test a new drug, you take a group of patients, and you separate it into two parts, randomly. You give a placebo to one half and the new drug to the other, and you collect data. Because the two samples are randomly drawn, you know that the only difference is that one got the drug and the other did not. We do the same thing with policies, ranging from education, to governance, to health, to agriculture. That way we can really say what works and what does not work. For example, imagine you want to know whether it would make a difference to put computers in school to help kids learn math. For a project, we worked in one city in India. We took half the schools there (which we selected randomly) and helped them set up a few computers with software. We then measured progress in math and other disciplines in these schools and in the other half of the schools in the city. After one year we found much more progress in the schools that had received the computers, which shows that it helps them learn.

**In your view, what are the two or three most important findings that have come from J-PAL so far?**

It is hard to point to really isolated projects. It depends a bit what you are interested in. But one of my favorite projects is one where we managed to increase the immunization rates of kids from about 5 percent to almost 40 percent, simply by running monthly immunization camps in the village and providing moms with a kilo of lentils for each vaccine (you can see me talk about it in a talk I gave at Ted: www.ted.com/ talks/esther_duflo_social_experiments_to_fight _poverty.html).

I think the most important overarching lesson, however, is that it is often quite easy to improve a situation dramatically simply by paying closer attention to the detailed way in which programs are designed. Often, good intentions don't translate into good policies, simply because a crucial detail on why people do what they do was forgotten.

**I read that [Irish singer and humanitarian] Bono was very interested in your work. Did he visit the lab? What was your discussion with him like?**

Bono came to J-PAL, but I was not there! I was really bummed. My colleague received him. Bono is very concerned about poverty and thinks the rich world has a real responsibility to help. He first contributed to convince them to forgive debt. Now he wants to get them to do more, with an organization called ONE campaign. But for this it is important to convince people that their dollars can really help, and this is where our approach comes in and he was interested in talking to us.

**What other celebrities or global policy makers have you discussed your research with? Can you point to specific ways in which research**

from J-PAL has influence public policy and the lives of people in developing countries?

Hmm . . . I think we have not done better than Bono. But I do talk to Bill Gates every now and then, and the foundation that he and his wife run (the Bill and Melinda Gates Foundation) has helped our work. Some of the most important people we talk to, however, are people who are likely to be change agents in developing countries. Some of the policies that we have evaluated, and shown to be effective, have been scaled up. For example, many millions of kids are now treated for their intestinal worms after research by J-PAL affiliates showed that this was a very effective way to send them to school. Also, J-PAL research was instrumental in shifting the debate on bed nets and proving that distributing them for free (rather than asking people to pay a little) is the most effective way to proceed. In Rajasthan (India) we have shown that training police officers in investigative methods, and also in "soft skills" (mediation, yoga, etc.) made them more effective and less scary to people: now, money has been given to the State to train *all* their police officers.

**You have been incredibly productive, yet I noticed that you spend a lot of your spare time mountain climbing. Do you think there is any connection between your interest in mountain climbing and your interests in economics?**

Mountain climbing (and also rock climbing, even in a gym) is a wonderful sport. You must be fully absorbed, because your life and that of your partner is on the line. So it helps clear up your mind. Also, I find it somewhat similar to empirical economics: when you are climbing something, you must look ahead and think, will this particular way to go work? Then you must try. Sometimes, it does not work and you have to try again. It is not that different when you are trying to find the explanations for something, or a solution for a real-world problem. It takes patience and creativity and a good dose of humility, because reality easily comes in the way.

# CHAPTER 19 REVIEW AND SELF-ASSESSMENT

## REVIEW

### Points to Remember

**MODULE 56: MEASURING ECONOMIC DEVELOPMENT**

1. People who live on less than $1.25 per day live in **extreme poverty**.

2. A **developing country (DC)** is a country with relatively few goods and services available to the majority of the population.

3. The **infant mortality rate** is the number of infants who die in their first year of life out of every 1,000 live births.

4. A **newly industrialized country (NIC)** is one with a rapidly developing capacity for production.

5. An **industrialized country (IC)** is one with a relatively high level of material wealth.

6. **Subsistence farming** produces enough food for the farming families' consumption but not enough to sell in the market.

7. The **literacy rate** is the percentage of people over 15 years of age who can read and write.

8. **Gross national income** is GDP plus net income from interest payments, dividends, and other income from assets in other countries.

9. **Primitive equilibrium** is the initial stage of economic development in which there are no formal markets and decisions are based on tradition.

10. **Transition** is the stage of economic development in which cultural change lays the foundation for economic change.

11. **Takeoff** is the stage of economic development in which new industries are formed and profits are reinvested in physical capital to fuel economic growth.

12. **Foreign aid** is economic or other assistance given by one country to another.

13. **Semidevelopment** is the stage of economic development in which industries expand and sophisticated technology is widely adopted.

14. A country at the **high development** stage produces plenty of goods and services to meet the basic needs of its people.

**MODULE 57: ECONOMIC ISSUES IN DEVELOPING COUNTRIES**

15. **Income convergence** is the closing of the per capita income gap between rich and poor countries.

16. **External debt** is debt owed to foreign governments, banks, and individuals.

17. **Capital flight** is the movement of financial capital out of a country, either legally or illegally.

18. **Foreign direct investment** is investment from one country made to control or significantly influence a business enterprise in another country.

19. **Foreign portfolio investment** is the purchase of foreign corporate bonds or shares of stock in a foreign corporation.

20. A **nongovernmental organization (NGO)** is a private, nonprofit organization established for charitable purposes, such as to provide assistance to developing nations.

21. **Microfinance (microcredit)** is the provision of small loans to help low-income people start businesses and provide for themselves.

**MODULE 58: GLOBALIZATION AND ITS CHALLENGES**

22. To **outsource** production is to contract with foreign firms to produce goods that will be sold by the domestic firm.

23. **Tradable emission permits** convey the right to emit a certain amount of pollution and can be sold by one firm to another.

## SELF-ASSESSMENT

The following questions are the type your teacher might ask you on a quiz or a test. Practice with these in order to improve your performance on class tests.

### Multiple-Choice Questions

1. The practice of contracting with foreign firms to produce goods that will be sold by the domestic firm is
   a. microfinance.
   b. external debt.
   c. outsourcing.
   d. internal debt.

2. Which of the following indicators would reflect the level of economic development of a country?
   a. life expectancy
   b. literacy level
   c. infant mortality rate
   d. all of the above

Answer the next two questions based on the following description of a country:

Most of the citizens spend their entire waking hours tending the fields by hand just as their ancestors have done, and the people of the country earn the equivalent of $1.15 per day.

3. The stage of economic development this country is experiencing is
   a. primitive equilibrium.
   b. takeoff.
   c. semidevelopment.
   d. high development.

4. The people of this country could be characterized as
   a. living in an industrialized country.
   b. living in extreme poverty.
   c. living in a developed country.
   d. living in a newly industrialized country.

5. Which of the following contributes to economic development?
   a. a low rate of saving and investment
   b. a low literacy rate
   c. a high literacy rate
   d. a high rate of infant mortality

6. According to the theory of income convergence,
   a. differences in real GDP per capita among countries tend to narrow over time.
   b. differences in real GDP per capita among countries tend to increase over time.
   c. differences in real GDP per capita among countries tend to remain constant over time.
   d. differences in real GDP per capita do not have much of an effect on living standards in the long run.

7. Globalization is characterized by which of the following?
   a. an increase in trade barriers
   b. growing interdependence among economies
   c. the protection of cultures from outside influences
   d. a belief that outsourcing will end

8. A high per capita GDP might not indicate that everyone in that country is fairly wealthy because
   a. the country might have a high population.
   b. the country might have a small population.
   c. the country might spend a large amount on national defense.
   d. the wealth might be very unequally distributed.

9. A market-based system to deal with greenhouse gases and other types of pollution associated with economic development is

   a. outsourcing pollution.
   b. tradable emission permits.
   c. capital flight.
   d. external debt.

10. The economic stage of a country that enjoys the use of advanced technology, reinvests profits from existing industries, develops new industries, and produces plenty of goods and services to meet the basic needs of the people would be classed as

    a. primitive equilibrium.
    b. takeoff.
    c. semidevelopment.
    d. high development.

## Constructed Response Question

1. At some point in the future, you might find yourself in charge of creating macroeconomic policies for a developing nation. Answer each of the following as a policy maker.

   a. If your country is just emerging from primitive equilibrium and entering the takeoff stage of development, what would you expect to find happening to income convergence as that process continues?

   b. How would each of the following contribute to economic development?
      i. capital flight
      ii. foreign aid
      iii. direct foreign investment

   c. What are some of the negative effects of rapid economic development?

# Personal Finance Handbook

Personal finance is how you use the principles of finance to manage your money. It covers a range of topics, like earning, budgeting, saving, investing, managing debt, paying taxes, and dealing with financial risks.

We make financial decisions every day. Some of them are small, like which groceries to buy. Some of them are big, like whether to buy a home or how to invest for retirement. Understanding the basics of personal finance will allow you to make wise decisions now and in the future.

You've probably heard the saying "Money doesn't buy happiness." While that's true, how you handle your personal finances can make a huge difference in your quality of life. By managing your money carefully, you'll be more in control and have the freedom to achieve your financial dreams.

# SECTION 1

# Take It to the Bank

**WEB TOOL**
You can use the Electronic Deposit Insurance Estimator (EDIE) at myfdicinsurance.gov to make sure your deposits in various bank accounts are fully covered by the FDIC.

**FINANCIAL FACT**
Since the FDIC was created in 1933 no depositor has lost a cent of insured money as a result of a bank failure. Visit fdic.gov to find out which banks are FDIC insured.

Keeping money in a bank account is a safe and convenient way to make everyday purchases, pay bills, and accumulate savings. Keeping a large amount of cash at home or in your wallet isn't as safe because your money could be lost or stolen.

## OVERVIEW OF BANKS

Banks can be small community institutions that have just one or a few locations. They can also be huge companies with thousands of branch locations all over the country. There are Internet-only banks with no physical location to visit and only a website address. In addition to holding your money, banks also offer a variety of services to improve your financial life.

Banks stay in business by using the money you deposit to make loans. They lend to customers who want to borrow money for big purchases like cars or homes. When you take a loan from a bank you have to pay interest, which is an additional charge on top of the amount you borrow. To stay profitable, a bank must receive more interest from borrowers than it pays out to customers.

### Types of Financial Institutions

When you're ready to open a bank account, there are three main types of institutions to choose from: savings and loan associations, commercial banks, and credit unions.

### Savings and Loan Associations (S&Ls) and Commercial Banks

**Savings and loan associations (S&Ls)** and commercial banks operate under federal and state regulations. They specialize in taking deposits for checking and savings accounts, making home loans (known as mortgages) and other loans, facilitating the flow of money into

and out of accounts, and providing various financial services for individuals and businesses.

Have you ever wondered what would happen to your money if your bank goes out of business or fails? Most banks insure your deposits through the Federal Deposit Insurance Corporation (FDIC) up to the maximum amount allowed by law, which is currently $250,000 per depositor per insured bank.

Having FDIC insurance means if your bank closes for any reason, you can still get your money. You'll know a bank is properly insured if it displays the FDIC logo at a local branch, on advertising materials, or online. To learn more visit fdic.gov.

### Credit Unions

Credit unions are nonprofit organizations owned by their customers, who are called members. Credit union members typically have something in common, like working for the same employer, working in the same profession, or living in the same geographic area. You must qualify to become a member of a credit union and use its financial services.

Credit unions offer many of the same services as commercial banks and S&Ls. Most also offer insurance for your deposits through the National Credit Union Administration (NCUA), which gives the same coverage (up to $250,000 per depositor per insured institution) as the FDIC. Just look for the official NCUA sign at credit union branches and websites. To learn more visit ncua.gov.

### Why Keep Money in a Bank?

While it's possible to keep your money at home and manage your personal finances using a cash-only system, here are five reasons why it's better to use an insured bank or credit union:

1. **Safety**. Money you deposit in a bank account can't be lost, stolen, or destroyed in a natural disaster. Even the best hiding places for money could be found by a thief or be susceptible to a flood or fire.

2. **Insurance**. Deposits covered by FDIC or NCUA insurance are protected by a fund backed by the full faith and credit of the U.S. government. So if your bank closes and can't return your money, the FDIC or NCUA will pay the insured portion of your deposits.

3. **Convenience**. Money in a bank account can be accessed in a variety of ways. You can make deposits by visiting a local branch or setting up electronic direct deposit. Some institutions have remote deposit services where you deposit a paper check by taking a picture of it with a mobile device or scanner and uploading it online.

4. **Low cost**. Different banks offer accounts with a variety of benefits, such as interest paid, debit cards, online banking, account alerts, bill pay, and overdraft protection. Many bank services are free, which makes using a bank to get cash or pay bills less expensive than alternatives, such as a check-cashing service.

5. **Business relationship**. Building a relationship with a bank may give you the opportunity to qualify for premium banking services, loans, and credit cards that can improve your financial future.

# TYPES OF BANK ACCOUNTS

The two main types of bank accounts are deposit accounts and nondeposit accounts.

## Deposit Accounts

Deposit accounts allow you to add or withdraw money at any time. Examples of deposit accounts are checking, savings, and money market accounts.

## Checking Account

A **checking account**, also known as a payment account, is the most common type of bank account. It's a real workhorse that allows you to make purchases or pay bills using paper checks, a debit or check card, online bill pay, automatic transfer, or cash withdrawal from an automatic teller machine (**ATM**). The institution keeps a record of your deposits and withdrawals and sends you a monthly account statement. The best checking accounts offer no fees, no minimum balance requirement, and free checks.

## Savings Account

A **savings account** is a safe place to keep money, and it earns you interest. It doesn't give you as much flexibility or access to your money as a checking account. While there's typically no limit on the number of savings deposits, you can only make up to six withdrawals or transfers per month. Savings accounts typically don't come with paper checks, but they may offer a debit or ATM card that you can use a maximum of three times per month.

If your balance dips below a certain amount, you may be charged a monthly fee. The institution keeps a record of your transactions and sends you a monthly account statement.

Savings accounts are perfect for your short-term savings goals, like a down payment on a car or holiday gift-giving. Interest rates on savings accounts vary, so it's important to shop around locally or online for the highest offers. Interest rates on savings accounts are variable, which means they're subject to change and can decrease after you open an account.

## Money Market Account (MMA)

A money market account has features of both a savings and a checking account. You can make up to six withdrawals or transfers per month, including payments by check, debit card, and online bill pay. You're paid relatively high interest rates, especially if you maintain a high minimum balance, like $5,000 or more.

**FINANCIAL FACT**
Did you know that funds deposited electronically into your bank account are available sooner than those deposited by a paper check?

**FINANCIAL FACT**
Reward checking accounts pay a relatively high rate of interest when you follow certain requirements, such as receiving e-statements, having at least one monthly direct deposit, and using a debit card for a certain number of purchases each month.

Money market accounts are a great choice when you start to accumulate more savings. Interest rates vary and are subject to change, so always do your research to find the best money market account offers.

There are also special types of deposit accounts known as time deposits, where you're restricted from withdrawing your money for a certain period of time.

### Certificate of Deposit (CD)

A certificate of deposit is a time deposit that requires you to give up the use of your money for a fixed term or period of time, such as 3 months, 12 months, or 5 years. In exchange for this restricted access, banks typically pay higher interest rates than for savings or MMAs (where you can withdraw money on demand). In general, the longer the CD term, the higher the interest rate you receive.

For instance, a 6-month CD might pay 1 percent interest and a 5-year CD might pay 3.5 percent. If you take money out of a CD before the end of the term, or maturity date, you generally have to pay a penalty. So before putting money in a CD, be sure you won't need it until after the maturity date and that you understand all the terms.

### Nondeposit Accounts

Many banks offer nondeposit accounts that can be investments, such as stocks, bonds, or mutual funds. It's important to remember that nondeposit products are never insured by the FDIC or NCUA and may lose some or all of their value.

## HOW TO MAINTAIN A CHECKING ACCOUNT

It's important to maintain your checking account on a regular basis so you know exactly how much you have. Never write checks or make debit card purchases that exceed your balance.

### Using ATM and Debit Cards

An **ATM card** allows you to use ATMs to make deposits, check your account balance, transfer funds between accounts, and make cash withdrawals 24 hours a day. You typically have to pay a fee for each ATM cash withdrawal—unless your bank gives you free access to a network of ATMs or reimburses your ATM fees.

A **debit card**, also known as a check card, looks like a credit card because it typically has a MasterCard or VISA logo. A debit card can be used just like an ATM card or to make purchases where accepted by merchants. When you use a debit card, money is transferred immediately from your bank account, reducing your available balance.

### Writing Checks

With the popularity of debit cards and online banking, people don't use paper checks as much anymore. However, if you need to write one it's easy to fill in the blanks. Always write clearly using dark ink and never cross out a mistake—it's better to start over with a fresh check.

1. **Bank name.** This may be preprinted on each check.
2. **Date.** Enter the month, day, and year.
3. **Check number.** If your checks don't have preprinted numbers, label them with consecutive numbers.
4. **Bank ID numbers.** This may be preprinted on each check.

# What Is a Prepaid Card?

A prepaid card may look like a debit or credit card, but it isn't linked to a bank or credit account. Prepaid cards may come loaded with a set value or require you to add money to the card. The card value goes down each time you make a purchase. Prepaid cards have many fees—such as a purchase fee, monthly fees, ATM withdrawal fees, transaction fees, balance inquiry fees, and more—which generally makes them more expensive to use than a bank debit card.

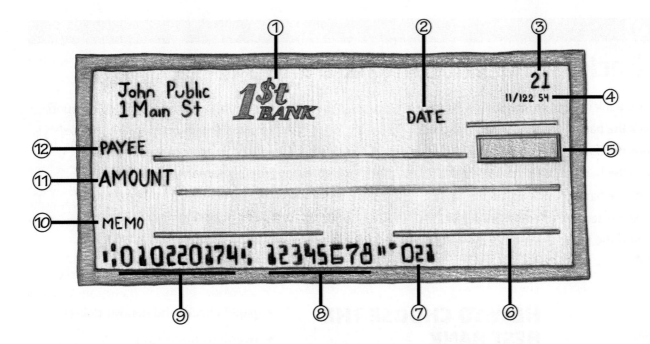

**5. Amount.** Enter the amount to pay in figures.

**6. Signature.** Sign your name exactly as you signed it on documents you completed when you opened the account.

**7. Check number.** This may be pre-printed on each check.

**8. Account number.** This should be preprinted on each check.

**9. Bank routing number.** This should be preprinted on each check to identify your bank.

**10. Memo.** Write a quick note to remind yourself the reason for the check.

**11. Amount of check.** This may be printed on the check for computer processing after the payee takes it to a bank.

**12. Payee.** Enter the person or company to pay.

## Reconciling Your Checking Account

Each month you'll receive a statement that shows activity in your account. The statement should include a reconciliation worksheet that you can follow. Reconciling or balancing your account

## What Is Overdraft Protection?

Having overdraft protection means your debit card purchases and ATM withdrawals will be processed, even if your bank account balance isn't high enough to cover them. You must give written permission for overdraft protection because using it comes with expensive nonsufficient funds (NSF) fees. However, you can opt out of overdraft protection and avoid the potential charges. This means that if you try to use your debit card and your account balance is too low, you will not be permitted to make the purchase.

is the process of making sure the information on the bank statement matches your records. Always keep track of your deposits, checks, debit card purchases, ATM withdrawals, and fees. You can use a paper or digital **check register**. Most financial software programs allow you to automatically download bank and credit card account transactions. Not having to enter each of your transactions manually saves time and makes account reconciliation simple.

# Checklist for Choosing a Bank

Is the bank insured by the FDIC or NCUA?

Does the bank have convenient branches?

Does the bank have convenient ATMs?

Does the bank offer online banking?

Does the bank provide online bill pay?

Does the account offer ATM or debit cards?

What is the fee to use local or out-of-network ATMs?

What is the minimum balance to open an account?

What is the required minimum monthly balance?

What are the monthly account fees?

How many monthly withdrawals are allowed?

Does the account pay interest and how much?

Are account alerts offered for low balances?

Is there overdraft protection and for what fee?

What additional services are available?

## HOW TO CHOOSE THE BEST BANK

Banks provide many financial services and may charge a fee for some of them. Here are common services that banks offer:

- ATM access to checking, savings, and money market accounts
- online banking
- online bill payment
- ATM/debit card
- paper checks and deposit tickets
- overdraft protection
- direct deposit
- safe deposit box
- electronic statements
- account alerts for low balances
- wire transfers
- cashier's checks
- loans

## Common Banking Terms to Know

Banks use jargon, or special words, that you should know. Here are several key banking terms to get familiar with:

**account statement**—a paper or electronic record of account activity, service charges, and fees, issued on a regular basis

**bounced or bad check**—slang for a check that is rejected due to insufficient funds in the account

**check**—a paper form that authorizes a bank to release funds from the payer's account to the payee

**cleared or canceled checks**—paper checks that have been processed and paid by a bank

**deposit slip or ticket**—a printed form you complete that lists cash and checks to be deposited into an account

**direct deposit**—an electronic payment method typically used by an employer or government agency

**electronic payment or transaction**—a deposit or charge to an account that happens without the use of a paper form

**endorsement**—the payee's signature on the back of a paper check that is required to deposit or cash out the funds

**payee**—the person or company to whom a check is made payable

**payer**—the person or company who writes a check or pays another party

**reconciliation**—the process of comparing a bank account statement to your records and resolving any differences

**service charge** (or maintenance charge)—a fee charged by a bank to maintain your account

# SECTION 2

# Get Interested in Money Math

Whether you're shopping at the grocery store, choosing a car loan, or figuring out how much to invest for retirement, managing money comes down to the numbers. Making the best decisions for your personal finances always begins by doing some simple money math.

## PAY ATTENTION TO INTEREST

When you get a credit card or loan for college, the cost you pay to borrow money is called **interest**. Lenders make money by charging interest and borrowers must pay interest on top of the balance they borrow, which is called the **principal**.

When you deposit money in a bank account that pays interest—for example, a savings account or CD—you become the lender and the bank is the borrower. The bank pays you interest for keeping money on deposit.

Interest is typically expressed as an annual percentage rate or APR. To keep more of your money, it's wise to shop around and borrow at the lowest interest rates. Likewise, lend your money for the highest possible interest rates, so you earn more.

## How Simple and Compound Interest Work

But how does your money actually earn interest? There are two basic types of interest: simple interest and compound interest.

## Simple Interest

**Simple interest** is, well, pretty simple! That's because it's calculated on the original principal amount only.

Say you borrow $100 from your friend John at a 5 percent annual rate of simple interest for a term of 3 years. Refer to Table 1 to see how the interest would be calculated for the loan.

Notice that the 5 percent APR is always calculated on the original principal amount of $100. At the end of the third year you have to pay $100 plus $15 in interest. In other words, your $100 loan cost a total of $115.

## Compound Interest

**Compound interest** is more complex because it allows you to earn interest on your original loan amount and on the interest you accumulate over time. You earn interest on a growing principal balance, which allows you to accumulate interest at a much faster rate. Interest can be compounded on any regular schedule, such as annually, semiannually, monthly, or daily.

Say you get the same loan of $100 for 3 years from your friend John, but this time he charges you 5 percent interest that compounds annually. Refer to Table 2 on the next page to see how the interest would be calculated.

Notice that the 5 percent APR is calculated on an increasing principal balance. At the end of the third year you'd owe the original amount of $100 plus interest of $15.76. Your $100 loan cost $115.76 with annual compounding.

**FINANCIAL FACT**

When comparing different bank accounts, always compare APY instead of APR to know which one pays more interest on an annual basis.

| Table 1 **Annual Simple Interest Calculation** | | | | |
|---|---|---|---|---|
| **LOAN YEAR** | **PRINCIPAL AMOUNT (DOLLARS)** | **APR (PERCENT)** | **ANNUAL INTEREST EARNED (DOLLARS)** | **BALANCE DUE (DOLLARS)** |
| 1 | $100 | 5% | $5 | $105 |
| 2 | 100 | 5 | 5 | 110 |
| 3 | 100 | 5 | 5 | 115 |

### Table 2 Annual Compound Interest Calculation

| LOAN YEAR | PRINCIPAL AMOUNT (DOLLARS) | APR (PERCENT) | ANNUAL INTEREST EARNED (DOLLARS) | BALANCE DUE (DOLLARS) |
|---|---|---|---|---|
| 1 | $100 | 5% | $5 | $105 |
| 2 | 105 | 5 | 5.25 | 110.25 |
| 3 | 110.25 | 5 | 5.51 | 115.76 |

**FINANCIAL FACT**

Interest that you earn is considered income, and you may have to pay federal and state tax on it.

**WEB TOOL**

To determine how long it would take to pay off a credit card if you only make the minimum payments, do a web search for "credit card minimum payment calculator" and enter your information.

Let's see how much you'd pay if John charged you 5 percent compounded semi-annually, or every 6 months, shown in Table 3.

At the end of the third year you'd owe the original loan amount of $100 plus $15.97 of interest. With semiannual compounding your $100 loan would cost $115.97. Remember that the more frequent the compounding, the faster the interest grows.

## Annual Percentage Yield (APY)

**Annual percentage yield (APY)** is the amount of interest you'll earn on an annual basis that includes the effect of compounding. APY is expressed as a percentage and will be higher the more often your money compounds.

## What is the Rule of 72?

How long would it take you to double your money through savings and investments? It's easy to figure it out using a handy formula called the **Rule of 72**. If you divide 72 by the interest rate you earn, the answer is the number of years it will take for your initial savings amount to double in value.

For example, if you earn an average annual return of 1 percent on a bank savings account, dividing 1 into 72 tells you

that your money will double in 72 years. But if you earn 6 percent on an investment, your money will take only 12 (72 ÷ 6 = 12) years to double.

You can also estimate the interest rate you'd need to earn to double your money within a set number of years by dividing 72 by the number of years. For instance, if you put $500 in an account that you want to grow to $1,000 in 12 years, you'll need an interest rate of 6 percent (72 ÷ 12 = 6).

# UNDERSTAND CREDIT CARDS

Using credit cards without fully understanding the relevant money math is a recipe for financial disaster. Credit cards start charging interest the day you make a purchase, take a cash advance, or transfer a balance from another account.

You're typically charged a daily rate that's equal to the APR divided by 365 days in a year. Rates may be different for each transaction category and depending on your credit rating. For instance, your APR could be 11.99 percent for new purchases, 23.99 percent for cash advances, and 5 percent for balance transfers. Balances accumulate day after day until you pay them off in full.

### Table 3 Semiannual Compound Interest Calculation

| LOAN YEAR | PRINCIPAL AMOUNT (DOLLARS) | SEMIANNUAL PERCENTAGE RATE (PERCENT) | ANNUAL INTEREST EARNED (DOLLARS) | BALANCE DUE (DOLLARS) |
|---|---|---|---|---|
| 1 (January) | $100 | 2.5% | $2.50 | $102.50 |
| 1 (July) | 102.50 | 2.5 | 2.56 | 105.06 |
| 2 (January) | 105.06 | 2.5 | 2.63 | 107.69 |
| 2 (July) | 107.69 | 2.5 | 2.69 | 110.38 |
| 3 (January) | 110.38 | 2.5 | 2.76 | 113.14 |
| 3 (July) | 113.14 | 2.5 | 2.83 | 115.97 |

You can make a monthly minimum payment and carry over the remaining balance from month to month. But that's not a wise way to manage credit cards because the interest starts racking up. Additionally, if you make a late payment you're charged a fee that gets added to your outstanding balance—and interest is calculated on that amount, too.

The bright spot in using a credit card wisely is that you're given a grace period for new purchases that allows you to avoid all interest charges—if you pay your balance in full by the billing statement due date. Note that there is generally no grace period for cash advances or balance transfers.

Credit cards are a powerful financial tool that can enhance your life if you use them responsibly. But abusing them by making purchases that you can't afford to pay off in full each month can be devastating to your financial future.

## Amortization

Gradually paying off a debt's principal and interest in regular installments over time is called **amortization**. Loans that amortize, such as a car loan or home mortgage, have fixed interest rates and charge equal monthly payments, though each payment is made up of a slightly different amount of principal and interest.

Take a look at Table 4 to see how each payment is split up for the first 6 months on a 30-year $150,000 mortgage with a fixed interest rate of 5 percent.

Notice that each month's beginning loan balance is reduced by the prior month's principal portion paid. The

## Calculate Credit Card Payoff

**Question:** If you buy a TV for $2,000 using a credit card that charges 23.99 percent APR, how long would it take to pay off, if you only make minimum payments of 3 percent of your outstanding balance down to a minimum of $15 per month?

**Answer:** It would take over 16 years! So, if you're 17 years old right now, you'd celebrate your thirty-third birthday before you finally pay off the TV. Due to the credit card interest, the total cost of the TV would actually be $5,328! That's an increase of more than 266 percent on the TV's original purchase price. Only making minimum payments can easily double or triple the price of any item charged to a credit card.

interest portion is slightly lower each month because it's calculated on an ever-decreasing principal balance.

## HOW TO BECOME A MILLIONAIRE

If you think that the only way to become a millionaire is to win the lottery, think again! Due to the power of compounding interest it's easy—if you get an early start. Table 5 on the next page shows you how.

If you start saving and investing just $250 a month as soon as you get your first job, you could amass a million dollars by the time you're in your 60s. But if you wait until you're over 40 years old to get started and invest the same amount, you'd be close to 90 before becoming a millionaire!

### Table 4 **Amortization Schedule**

| PAYMENT MONTH | LOAN BALANCE (DOLLARS) | MONTHLY FIXED PAYMENT (DOLLARS) | INTEREST PORTION OF PAYMENT (DOLLARS) | PRINCIPAL POR- TION OF PAYMENT (DOLLARS) |
|---|---|---|---|---|
| 1 | $150,000 | $805.23 | $625.00 | $180.23 |
| 2 | 149,819.77 | 805.23 | 624.25 | 180.98 |
| 3 | 149,638.78 | 805.23 | 623.49 | 181.74 |
| 4 | 149,457.05 | 805.23 | 622.74 | 182.49 |
| 5 | 149,274.55 | 805.23 | 621.98 | 183.26 |
| 6 | 149,091.30 | 805.23 | 621.21 | 184.02 |

| Table 5 **At What Age Could You Become a Millionaire?** | | | | |
|---|---|---|---|---|
| AGE TO BEGIN SAVING | AMOUNT TO SAVE EACH MONTH (DOLLARS) | AVERAGE APR (PERCENT) | YEARS TO BECOME A MILLIONAIRE | AGE YOU'RE A MILLIONAIRE! |
| 18 | $250 | 7% | 46 | 64 |
| 20 | 250 | 7 | 46 | 66 |
| 25 | 250 | 7 | 45 | 70 |
| 30 | 250 | 7 | 45 | 75 |
| 40 | 250 | 7 | 45 | 86 |

# Millionaire Case Study

Steve and Jessica are both 25 years old and work for the same company. They have the same financial goal: to retire at age 65 with one million dollars to spend. Steve starts contributing to his company's retirement plan right away, but Jessica waits 10 years, until she's 35 years old, to begin investing.

Here's what happens: Steve can reach his million-dollar goal by contributing $400 a month and earning an average 7 percent annual return. But since Jessica gets a late start, she has to contribute much more than Steve. Jessica must contribute $850 a month with the same 7 percent rate of return, to reach her million-dollar goal.

You'll notice that Steve only had to invest $192,000 over a 40-year period to amass over one million dollars. However, Jessica had to invest $306,000, or 60 percent more than Steve, over a 30-year period to accumulate approximately the same amount.

The sooner you start saving and investing, the more you will benefit from the power of compounding interest!

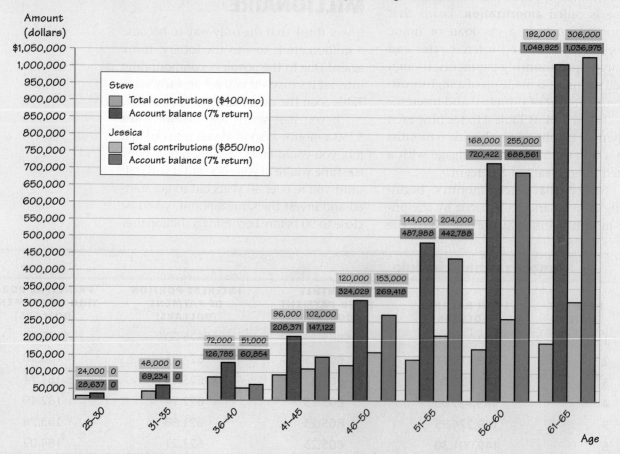

# SECTION 3

# Learn to Earn

How can you earn enough money to cover your expenses and save for the future? It starts by having the education and skills to get a job or start your own business. Every work experience builds your level of knowledge, boosts your resume, helps you know what work you like best, and makes you more attractive to potential employers.

## TYPES OF INCOME

The money you make falls into one of two basic categories: earned income and passive income.

### Earned Income

**Earned income** is the income you receive by working for a company or someone who pays you, or from a business that you own and run. Earned income includes your hourly wages, salaries, tips, commissions, and bonuses. This is the most common way to make money. Of course, if you stop working, you stop earning. However, if you save and invest your earned income wisely, you can turn it into passive income.

### Passive Income

**Passive income** is generated from assets you buy or create, such as financial investments, rental real estate, or something you have created, such as a book or a song. If you buy a house and rent it for more than your mortgage and other expenses, the profit is passive income. If you write and publish a book or a song that pays royalties, that is intellectual property that pays passive income. The benefit of passive income is that you get paid with little or no additional work on your part. That makes it possible to retire and still receive money to pay your everyday living expenses.

## What Is a Resume?

A resume is a summary of your education, skills, and work experience that you submit to a potential employer in person, through the mail, or online. It should be a one-page document that is succinct and well written. At the top of a resume, list your name, address, phone number, and e-mail address. The body should include sections titled "Objective," "Experience," "Skills," and "Education." Tailor each resume to the particular job you apply for so the employer knows you have the skills to be successful.

## GETTING A PAYCHECK

It might surprise you to know that if you get a job earning $600 a week, you don't actually receive $600 a week! Although your gross income or pay will be $600, you'll have payroll taxes deducted from each paycheck before you receive it. You may also have voluntary deductions for workplace benefits such as health insurance, life insurance, and contributions to a retirement account. The remaining amount that you'll have to spend after taxes and deductions is called your **net income** or pay.

When you take a new job, one of the forms you must complete is the W-4. It tells your employer how much tax should be taken out, or withheld, from each of your paychecks. Your **withholding** is based on the number of allowances or exemptions you claim on the W-4 form. The more allowances you claim, the less tax will be taken out.

However, if too little tax is withheld during the year, you'll owe money to the government on tax day. If too much tax is withheld the government will pay a refund, but you will lose the use of your money until the refund payment

**FINANCIAL FACT**

Employers are required to pay 50 percent of FICA on behalf of their employees. If you become your own boss, you must pay self-employment tax, which includes 100 percent of the Social Security and Medicare tax owed.

# Create a Resume

If you applied for a job today, what information could you list on your resume? Create a sample resume using the template below:

YOUR NAME HERE

123 Any Street, City, State, Zip Code

Phone: (000) 000-0000 | Email: yourname@youremail.com

## PROFESSIONAL OBJECTIVE

State the kind of work you want to do and why you are qualified to do it in one or two brief sentences.

Example: To sell technology products and services for a global retailer using my knowledge of electronics and experience in customer service.

Write your objective here:

_____

_____

## EXPERIENCE

List each paid or volunteer experience in order of most recent to oldest. State your title, organization name, dates of service, and a summary of your duties and job responsibilities.

Example: Customer Service, ABC Hardware, 2010–Present

- Assist customers with product selection
- Check out customers on register and accept payment
- Take returns and restock items as needed

Write your job experience here:

_____

_____

_____

_____

_____

_____

_____

_____

_____

_____

_____

_____

_____

_____

## EDUCATION

List each school that you have attended in order of most recent to oldest. State the school name, dates of attendance, and the degree you're studying for or received.

Example: ABC College   2011–Present

　　　　　B.A. Computer Technologies

Write your education here:

_____

_____

_____

_____

_____

_____

_____

_____

_____

_____

_____

## SKILLS & ACHIEVEMENTS

List your skills and any achievements related to your professional objective—they tell an employer why you are best for the job.

Example: Fluent in Spanish, Learn quickly, Pay attention to detail, Strong computer skills, Punctual, Received ABC Hardware's 2010 Most Helpful Employee Award, President of the ABC High School Computer Club

Write your skills & achievements here:

_____

_____

_____

_____

_____

_____

_____

_____

_____

*If you have trouble creating a resume, ask for help from family, friends, or a professional resume writer, who can help you articulate the skills and experiences you have to offer a potential employer.*

# What Is a Job Application?

In addition to your resume, most potential employers require you to complete a job or employment application. The application can be customized by the employer, but it typically asks for personal information, references, and specifics about the job you're applying for. Submitting an impressive resume and application will make you stand out from other applicants.

Here's a tip to save time when you're applying for a job: Complete the sample application below and make a copy to bring with you to each job interview.

# Employment Application Information Sheet

**POSITION APPLYING FOR:**_____

*First Name:* _____ *Middle Initial:*_____ *Last Name:* _____

*Current Address*

*Street and Apt #:* _____*City* _____ *State:* ____ *Zip Code:* _____

*Telephone:*_____ *E-mail:* _____

*Social Security #:* _____ - ____ - _____ *Driver's License #:* _____*State:* ____

*I am an U.S. Citizen or otherwise authorized to work in the United States on an authorized basis:* _____Yes ____No

*Have you ever been convicted of a felony?* _____Yes ____No

**EMPLOYMENT HISTORY**

*Present or Most Recent Employer*

*Employer:*_____ *Address:* _____

*Your Position:* _____ *Salary:* _____

*Duties:* _____

*Dates of Employment:* _____ *to* _____

*Supervisor: Name:* _____*Title:* _____

*May we contact?*_____ Yes _____ No

*Reasons for Leaving:* _____

*Prior Employer*

*Employer:*_____ *Address:* _____

*Your Position:* _____ *Salary:* _____

*Duties:* _____

*Dates of Employment:* _____ *to* _____

*Supervisor: Name:* _____*Title:* _____

*May we contact?*_____ Yes _____ No

*Reasons for Leaving:* _____

## EDUCATION

*High School*

*Name and Address:* _____

*Did you graduate?* _____ *Yes* _____ *No*    *Attended from* _____ *to* _____

*If you did not graduate, did you receive your GED?*                              _____ *Yes* _____ *No*

*Special honors or awards:* _____

*Technical or Vocational School*

*Name and Address:* _____

*Did you graduate?* _____ *Yes* _____ *No*    *Attended from* _____ *to* _____

*If you did not graduate, did you receive your GED?*                              _____ *Yes* _____ *No*

*Special honors or awards:* _____

## REFERENCES

*#I Name:* _____    *Phone:* _____

*Address:* _____

*#2 Name:* _____    *Phone:* _____

*Address:* _____

## POSITION INFORMATION

*Position Applying For:* _____

*How did you hear about this job?* _____

*What hours are you willing to work?* _____    *Would you be able to work weekends?* _____ *Yes* _____ *No*

*When would you would you be able to start?* _____    *Desired salary:* _____ *per* _____

## SKILLS

*Please describe any skills you have in the following area:*

*Computer:* _____

---

arrives. So it is good to have your withholding match the actual amount of tax you'll owe.

Significant events—such as marriage, divorce, the birth or adoption of a child, buying a home, or taking an additional job—will affect how much tax you owe. Any time your personal situation changes, you can file a new W-4 with your employer to make sure the right amount of tax is withheld so you don't have any surprises on tax day. You can learn more by visiting the Internal Revenue Service website at irs.gov and searching for Publication 919, How Do I Adjust My Tax Withholding?

## How Payroll Withholding Works

Employers are required to withhold four different types of tax from your paycheck:

1. **Federal income tax** is paid to the Internal Revenue Service (IRS) for expenses such as salaries of elected

# How Much Income Tax Do You Pay?

The United States has a marginal or progressive tax system, which means that people with more earned income pay tax at a higher rate. A tax bracket is a range of income that's taxed at a certain rate. Currently, there are six federal tax brackets that range from 10 percent up to 35 percent.

Here's a table showing the federal income tax rates for 2011 for a taxpayer who files as a single person:

## Federal Individual Income Tax Rate Single Taxpayers for 2012

| MARGINAL TAX RATE (PERCENT) | TOTAL TAX-ABLE INCOME (DOLLARS) | MARGINAL TAX RATE (DOLLARS) |
|---|---|---|
| 10% | $0 | $8,500 |
| 15 | 8,500 | 34,500 |
| 25 | 34,500 | 83,600 |
| 28 | 83,600 | 174,400 |
| 33 | 174,400 | 379,150 |
| 35 | 379,150 | – |

You'll notice that if you earn $35,000, you're in the 25 percent tax bracket. However, the following shows that your effective or net rate of federal tax rate would be only 14 percent:

| INCOME TAX BRACKET (DOLLARS) | INCOME TAXED (DOLLARS) | TAX RATE (PERCENT) | TAX DUE (DOLLARS) |
|---|---|---|---|
| $0–$8,500 | $8,500 | 10% | $850 |
| 8,500– 34,500 | 26,000 | 15 | 3,900 |
| 34,500–83,600 | 500 | 25 | 125 |
| **Totals** | 35,000 | | 4,875 |

Effective tax rate = $4,875 ÷ $35,000 = 14 percent

There are many variables that affect the amount of tax you must pay, such as tax deductions and tax credits that can significantly reduce your tax liability.

officials, the military, welfare assistance programs, public education, and interest on the national debt.

2. **State income tax** is generally paid to your state's revenue department for expenses such as salaries of state employees and maintenance of state highways and parks. Depending on where you live there may also be payroll deductions for county and city tax.

3. **Social Security tax** provides income for eligible taxpayers who are retired or disabled, or who survive a relative that was receiving benefits. The program's official name is OASDI, which stands for Old-Age, Survivors, and Disability Insurance.

4. **Medicare tax** provides hospital insurance benefits to eligible individuals who are over the age of 65 or have certain medical conditions. Social Security and Medicare taxes are collectively called the Federal Insurance Contributions Act (FICA) tax.

## FILING AN INCOME TAX RETURN

Every year you must complete and submit, or file, a federal tax return by April 15 for income from the prior year. Many states also require a state tax return at the same time. Whether you must file a tax return depends on your income, tax filing status (for example, being single or married), age, and whether you are a dependent. The filing requirements apply even if you don't owe any tax.

If you don't file taxes on time, you'll be charged a late payment penalty, plus interest on any amount owed. Willfully failing to file a return is a serious matter because it's against the law and may result in criminal prosecution.

If you are an unmarried dependent student, you must file a tax return if your earned or unearned income exceeds certain limits. You may also owe tax on certain scholarships and fellowships for education. Tax rules are subject to change each year, so be sure to visit irs.gov and review IRS Publication 501, Exemptions, Standard Deduction and Filing Information, for income limits and up-to-date information.

In January and February, you'll receive official forms from institutions that paid you, such as your employer, bank, or investment brokerage. These forms provide the data you need to complete your taxes. Even if you don't receive income forms, you must still declare all your income on a tax return. So be sure to request any missing information.

Even if your income is below a threshold set by the IRS and you do not have to file, you should file a tax return each year if you can get money back—for instance, if you had income tax withheld from your pay or you qualify for tax credits.

There are four ways to file your federal and state tax returns:

1. **Free File** is tax preparation software provided free of charge at irs.gov for individuals with income below a certain amount. You're guided through a series of questions to calculate your tax liability, and your federal and state returns are filed electronically.

## Not Every State Collects Income Tax

In addition to federal taxes, you may have to pay state tax on your income. Each state has its own tax system. The following nine states don't collect any income tax from income that individuals earn: Alaska, Florida, Nevada, New Hampshire, South Dakota, Tennessee, Texas, Washington, and Wyoming.

2. **Fillable forms** are free online tax forms at irs.gov that you can complete and file electronically without the help of software, regardless of your income. State tax forms are not included.

3. **Tax software** can be purchased to help you prepare your federal and state returns and file them electronically.

4. **Tax preparers** are tax professionals who prepare your federal and state returns and file electronically. Visit irs.gov for a list of authorized e-file providers or ask people you know to recommend a reputable tax accountant.

**WEB TOOL**

Use an online calculator at taxfoundation.org to find out how much federal tax you really pay based on your income and tax filing status.

## SECTION 4

# Save and Invest Money

**FINANCIAL FACT**

If you park money in a savings account, you can't lose your principal—but it could still lose value due to inflation. When prices for goods and services increase, the purchasing power of your money decreases.

Going to college. Buying a car. Starting a business. Retiring from work. Any financial goal or dream that you have can become a reality if you're patient and consistently set aside small amounts of money over time.

Though we tend to use the terms saving and investing interchangeably, they're not the same. The difference has to do with taking financial risk. Investors walk a line between wanting to make money and not wanting to lose money. Saving money in a bank keeps it completely safe but pays a low rate of return. On the other hand, investments that pay higher rates of return come with higher risk—the chance you could lose some or all of your money.

## TYPES OF SAVINGS ACCOUNTS

You will probably earn only a small amount of interest on savings. But the purpose of having them isn't to get rich. Money you need to spend in the short-term for planned purchases and emergencies should be kept in a federally insured savings account so you can't lose it.

There are three basic types of savings accounts you can open at most banks and credit unions: a savings account, a money market account, and a certificate of deposit. Review Section 1 for an explanation of these accounts.

## INVESTING BASICS

Looking at the period from 1928 to 2011, we see that investing money in the stock market has historically rewarded investors with average returns that exceed 10 percent. Even from 2002 to 2011—the decade that includes the most recent economic recession—investors earned approximately 5 percent on average.

So why would you put money in a bank savings account that might earn 0.1 percent to 2 percent instead? Because investing money always involves some amount of risk—the potential to lose money as well as the potential to make money.

Financial analysts make forecasts based on what happened in the past. But they include the disclaimer "Past performance does not guarantee future results." In other words, even the smartest analyst can't predict how much an investment will be worth in the future! Therefore, it's very important to invest with wisdom and caution.

The purpose of investing money is to increase your wealth over a long time so you can afford big, expensive goals like paying for retirement. Whether you should save or invest depends on your time horizon, which is the amount of time between now and when you'll actually need to spend the money. If you have a long time horizon—like 10 years or more—investing makes sense. When you have a short time horizon—like a year or less—stick with an insured savings account.

# What Is the Securities Investor's Protection Corporation (SIPC)?

Investments, or securities, are not guaranteed by any federal agency such as the FDIC. There is no insurance against losing money in an investment. However, the Securities Protection Corporation (SIPC) is a nongovernment entity that gives you limited protection in certain situations. They step in when an investment brokerage fails or fraud is the cause of investor loss. The SIPC replaces missing securities up to $500,000 per customer. You can learn more at sipc.org.

# TYPES OF INVESTMENTS

The earlier you start investing, the more money you'll have to pay for big financial goals. There are four basic types of financial **securities** and products that you can purchase for your investment portfolio. They are stocks, bonds, mutual funds, and exchange-traded funds.

## Stocks

**Stocks** are issued by companies—like Apple, Coca-Cola, and Google—who want to raise money. When you buy shares of a stock, you purchase an ownership interest in a company that can go up or down in value over time. Stocks are bought and sold on exchanges, like the New York Stock Exchange or the NASDAQ, and you can monitor their prices in real time online.

Stocks are one of the riskiest investments because the price per share can be volatile, swinging up or down in a short period of time. People can't be sure about which stocks will increase in value over the short or long term. However, historically, stocks have rewarded investors with higher returns than other major investment classes, like cash or bonds.

## Bonds

**Bonds** are a loan you give to a corporation or government entity, known as the issuer, who wants to raise money for a specific project. Projects paid for by a bond include things such as building a factory or a school. Bonds pay a fixed interest rate over a set period of time. The time can range from weeks to 30 years. In general, interest is higher for longer-term bond terms and for bonds issued by companies with better credit.

Bonds are also called fixed-income investments because the return is guaranteed. In return for that safety, you receive a relatively low rate of return. But these conservative investments still have some risk. For example, an issuer can default on repayment. Agencies such as Standard and Poor's (standardandpoors. com) do research and offer a rating system of bond safety.

## Mutual Funds

**Mutual funds** are products that bundle combinations of investments, such as stocks, bonds, and other securities. They're operated by professional money managers who invest the fund's money according to stated objectives, such as achieving maximum growth or earning fixed income. Mutual fund shares are purchased directly from the fund company and can go up or down in value over time.

In general, mutual funds composed of stock have the greatest potential risk and reward; however, there's a wide range of risk within this category. Mutual funds composed of bonds also have a range of risk but are considered more conservative than stock funds.

## Exchange-Traded Funds (ETFs)

**Exchange-traded funds** are products that bundle combinations of investments—just like mutual funds—but trade like a stock on an exchange throughout the day. There are over a thousand ETFs, and they're growing in popularity due to their flexibility and low cost. The cost to operate an ETF is very low compared to many mutual funds.

Other types of investments include real estate, precious metals (like gold and silver), and businesses, just to name a few. They generally require more expertise and skill to buy and sell than the four types of securities covered here. The drawback to alternative investments is that they aren't as liquid, or sold as easily, as mainstream investments. However, you can still own them when you buy shares of certain mutual funds and ETFs.

## What Is Financial Risk?

To be a successful investor, you need to understand the financial risks of different types of investments and gauge your own tolerance for risk. What seems safe to one person may be deemed very risky by another. Your tolerance for risk is how you react when your investments decline in value. Someone who doesn't like risk is considered risk averse. A risk-averse person is willing to miss out on higher rates

**FINANCIAL FACT**
Bonds issued by the U.S. Treasury are known as treasuries and are backed by the full faith of the federal government, making them one of the safest investments. They have maturities that range from a few days to 30 years. You can learn more at treasurydirect.gov.

**FINANCIAL FACT**
A money market fund is a low-risk, low-return investment—but don't confuse it with a money market deposit account, which is a bank savings account that may be FDIC insured.

of return down the road in exchange for financial safety. A more risk-tolerant person is willing to accept temporary investment losses in exchange for potential higher returns.

# WAYS TO INVEST

You have many choices when it comes to investing your money, but the two most common are brokerage accounts and retirement accounts.

## Brokerage Accounts

**Brokerage accounts** are available at local and online firms that are licensed to place investment orders, such as buying or selling shares of a stock, a mutual fund, or an ETF. You own the assets in a brokerage account and must pay tax each year on the earnings, which are called capital gains.

## Retirement Accounts

**Retirement accounts** are special accounts you can open at a variety of institutions, such as local or online banks and brokerage firms, that allow you to save for retirement and save money on taxes. There are different kinds available for individuals, as part of an employee benefit package at work, and for the self-employed. Investment options include many of the instruments already mentioned, such as such as stocks, bonds, mutual funds, ETFs, or even bank CDs.

When you invest through a retirement account—as opposed to a regular brokerage account—you defer, or avoid paying, tax on your earnings. That means you save money on taxes and have more money for retirement!

The most commonly used retirement accounts include individual retirement arrangements, the 401(k) plan, and the 403(b) plan.

## Individual Retirement Arrangement (IRA)

The IRA is a personal account available to anyone, regardless of age, who has taxable income. You can begin making contributions to an IRA as soon as you get your first job. However, you're in charge of it, not your employer. With a **traditional IRA** you generally don't pay tax on contributions or earnings until after you retire and start taking withdrawals. In other words, taxes on the account are deferred until sometime in the future. With a **Roth IRA**, you pay tax on your contributions up front. However, you never pay tax on them again or on any amount of earnings. You get a huge tax benefit with a Roth because your entire account grows completely tax free!

## 401(k) Plan

The 401(k) plan is a retirement account offered by many companies. You authorize a portion of your wages to be contributed to the plan before income tax is withheld from your paycheck. A 401(k) plan offers participants a set menu of investment choices.

## 403(b) Plan

The 403(b) plan is a retirement account offered by certain organizations such as schools, churches, and hospitals. It's similar to a 401(k) in most aspects.

## Retirement Accounts for Employees

There are two main types of retirement programs found in the workplace: defined benefit plans and defined contribution plans.

- A **defined benefit plan** is funded and managed by an employer and is commonly known as a pension. Employees don't pay into the plan, pick investments, or manage the money in any way. Defined benefit plans give retired workers a specific, defined benefit, such as $800 per month for the rest of their life. The benefit paid depends on various factors, such as age, length of employment, and salary history. These plans have become rare in the workplace because they're expensive to operate. However, some large companies, government agencies, and labor unions offer them.

- A **defined contribution plan** is established by an employer but requires that the employee manage it. They include the 401(k) and 403(b) plans. The retirement benefit that an employee will receive depends on the amount that's invested and the performance of the chosen investments over the years. Defined contribution plans are more common because they're less risky for an employer to administer.

## How Much Will Social Security Pay in Retirement?

As a young person, it's not possible to know exactly how much you'll receive in Social Security retirement benefits. They're calculated based on various factors, such as the current law, your future earnings, the age you elect to start receiving them, and military service.

However, according to the Social Security Administration, the benefit replaces only about 40 percent of your preretirement earnings, if you have average income. At the beginning of 2012, the average monthly benefit for a retired worker was about $1,230. Therefore, it's important not to count on Social Security retirement benefits as your sole source of income during retirement. The program was created as a supplement for personal savings, not as a substitute for having a retirement plan.

## Investing for Education

Just like there are special accounts that allow you to invest for retirement and pay less tax, there are two education savings accounts, or ESAs, to be familiar with: 529 plans and Coverdells.

## What Is Employer Matching?

If you could earn a guaranteed 100 percent return on your money, would you be interested? Many employers match a certain amount of the money you put in a workplace retirement plan. Say your employer matches 100 percent of your contributions to a 401(k) up to 3 percent of your salary. If you earn $30,000 a year and contribute $75 a month or $900 a year, that's a contribution of 3 percent of your salary. With matching, your employer would also contribute $900. So you'd invest $900 and automatically get $900 from your company—an immediate 100 percent return on your money!

- A **529 plan** is a savings or investment vehicle that allows you to contribute money to pay for a student's qualified expenses at a college, university, or vocational school. There are prepaid plans, where you prepay all or a portion of the future cost, and investment plans, where you choose specific investments. Contributions and earnings in a 529 plan grow tax free.

- A **Coverdell** account allows you to contribute money to pay for any level of education, from kindergarten through graduate school. It differs from a 529 plan in that it has more restrictions, such as how much can be contributed each year and the age of the student who will use the funds.

You can learn more about 529s and Coverdells at savingforcollege.com and finaid.org.

**FINANCIAL FACT**
You can reduce risk by diversification, which means owning a variety of investments in your portfolio. When you own multiple types of assets—such as stocks, bonds, and cash—it's unlikely that they would all plummet in value at the same time.

## SECTION 5

# Give Yourself Some Credit

How is it possible to make a major purchase, like a home, if you don't have the cash? The answer is credit. If you're "creditworthy," you can be trusted to borrow money and pay it back over time.

## WHAT IS CREDIT?

Credit is the ability to borrow money that you promise to repay with interest. Credit is an important part of your financial life because it allows you to do the following:

- **Make a large purchase and pay for it over time.** If you don't have enough money saved up to buy a car, having credit allows you to get a loan and repay it over a set period of time.

- **Stay safe in an emergency situation.** If your car breaks down and you don't have enough to pay for the repair, having a credit card or line of credit allows you to get back on the road and repay the balance over time.

- **Avoid having to carry cash or paper checks.** When you're making a large purchase, like a computer or furniture, using a credit card is safer than carrying around a large amount of cash or paper checks that could be stolen.

- **Make online purchases and reservations.** When you need to buy something over the Internet—like books, clothes, or travel reservations—it's convenient to use a credit card.

If you don't have credit, the only way to get a loan or credit card is to have someone with good credit cosign an account. That could be a family member or friend who guarantees to take full responsibility for the debt if you don't repay it. How do you become creditworthy so a potential creditor—such as a bank or credit card company—will allow you to borrow money? While each institution has different guidelines for evaluating a potential borrower, the following five criteria are generally used:

1. **Credit score.** How likely are you to make on-time payments based on your credit history?

2. **Income.** Do you have a steady job and earn enough income to repay a debt?

3. **Debt.** Do you have existing debts? If so, will you have enough money to pay your current debt and make payments on a new debt?

4. **Financial ratios.** How much debt do you have relative to your income?

5. **Collateral.** Will you secure a debt by pledging property (like a car or home) that a lender could sell if you don't make payments?

## Understanding Credit Reports

Your credit history is maintained by three major nationwide credit reporting agencies: Equifax (equifax.com), Experian (experian.com), and TransUnion (transunion.com). These agencies receive information about you and list it on your credit report. They are interested in things such as whether you make payments on time, your outstanding debt balances, and your available **credit limits**. Credit agencies don't make credit decisions; they simply report information provided to them on your credit reports.

Each of your credit reports from the three agencies is slightly different, but they generally contain the following four types of information:

1. **Personal information** includes your name, current and previous addresses, Social Security number, birth date, and employer.

**QUICK TIP**

To stay on top of your credit more than once a year, space out your requests and get a free report from a different credit agency every four months at annualcreditreport.com.

2. **Account information** lists your open accounts and your closed accounts for up to a certain period of time.

3. **Credit inquiries** include a list of companies and employers that have made inquiries about you.

4. **Public information** is data that's available in the public records about you, including bankruptcies, foreclosures, liens for unpaid income taxes, and legal judgments.

The information in your credit report sticks with you for a long time. Credit accounts with negative information, for example, late payments, remain on your credit report for 7 years from the date you originally became past due, even after you close the account or pay it off in full. Credit accounts with positive information remain on your credit report for 10 years after you close the account or pay it off in full.

## Understanding Credit Scores

Just as your schoolwork determines your final grade in various classes, the information in your credit reports is used to calculate your **credit scores**. One of the most confusing things about credit scores is that there isn't just one. Your credit score depends on the particular scoring model that's used to calculate it. Companies can create their own scoring systems or use brand-name scores calculated by other firms, like the **FICO (Fair Isaac Corporation) Score** or the **VantageScore**.

Your credit score is different from the final grade you receive for a class because it isn't figured once and filed away. Your credit score is calculated fresh every time it's requested. Therefore, it's a snapshot of your credit behavior up to that moment in time.

Having a low credit score means you'll be viewed as a risky customer who may not repay a debt. You'll either be turned down for credit or charged an interest rate that's higher than the rate offered to a customer with good credit. Why? In exchange for taking a financial risk on a customer with poor credit, lenders protect themselves financially by charging higher interest rates, which means you have to make higher monthly payments.

The larger a loan, the more poor credit costs you. The table below shows different scenarios for a home mortgage of $150,000 paid for over 30 years.

# How Much Can Poor Credit Cost You?

Susanne has excellent credit and goes to her bank to apply for a $150,000 home mortgage. After a few days the bank's lending representative calls her with good news—she's been approved! She can borrow $150,000 at 3.75 percent APR for a term of 30 years, which makes her monthly payment $694.67. The total amount of interest she'll pay on the loan principal is $100,082.42.

Let's say Susanne didn't have excellent credit and the bank charged her 7.5 percent APR instead of 3.75 percent. At this higher interest rate, her monthly payment would be $1,048.82. She'd pay a total of $227,575.83 in interest—or $127,493.41 more than if her credit was in good shape!

| CREDIT STATUS | APR (PERCENT) | MONTHLY PAYMENT (DOLLARS) | TOTAL INTEREST PAID (DOLLARS) | COST OF HAVING POOR CREDIT (DOLLARS) |
|---|---|---|---|---|
| Excellent | 3.75% | $694.67 | $100,082.42 | $0 |
| Good | 5.00 | 805.23 | 139,883.68 | 39,801.26 |
| Average | 7.50 | 1,048.82 | 227,575.83 | 127,493.41 |

# How to Build Your Credit

It may be difficult to get approved for a credit card before you've established a good credit history. However, everyone over age 18 can get a secured credit card, which can help you build credit for the first time—as long as it reports payment transactions to the credit agencies. With a secured credit card, you must make a refundable upfront deposit (as little as $200) that serves as your credit limit.

**FINANCIAL FACT**

To find out your credit score, you can purchase it from the credit bureau websites, buy your FICO Score at myfico.com, or get several scores for free at creditkarma.com.

Not having excellent credit means you could pay an additional $127,493.41 in interest—on top of the original loan amount of $150,000.

Did you know that having poor credit scores can cost you even if you don't want a loan or credit card? Here are five ways that having poor credit affects your personal finances:

1. **Paying high insurance premiums.** You'll be quoted higher rates from insurance companies because consumers with poor credit are also deemed to be high insurance risks.

2. **Paying high security deposits.** You'll be asked to pay higher deposits for an apartment and for utilities such as power, gas, water, and phone accounts.

3. **Getting declined as a tenant.** You could be turned down for an apartment or house to rent because property managers prefer tenants who demonstrate good payment history.

4. **Getting turned down for government benefits.** You might not qualify for certain types of federal or state benefits that require a good credit history.

5. **Getting denied for a job.** You might be turned down for a job by an employer who requires a credit check. Employers can't get your credit scores or see your entire credit report, but they can find out if you've had credit problems.

## HOW TO ESTABLISH CREDIT

The information in your credit report has a ripple effect throughout your entire financial life. How can you get started building good credit? Knowing how credit scores are calculated can help you improve them.

Each credit scoring model values the information in your credit report differently and uses a unique score range. The popular FICO Score uses a scale from 300 to 850 and values the following five factors:

1. **Payment history** (35%). Making payments for bills and credit accounts on time.

2. **Credit utilization** (30%). Having lower amounts of debt relative to your available credit limits on credit cards and lines of credit.

3. **Length of credit history** (15%). Having credit accounts for a longer period of time.

4. **Type of credit used** (10%). Having a mix of credit types, including loans and credit cards.

5. **Applications for credit** (10%). Having fewer requests for new credit accounts.

To build good credit, focus on actions within your control that have the biggest influence on typical scoring models. These include paying bills on time and not maxing out credit cards. But remember that it takes time to build good credit—it's a marathon, not a sprint!

## HOW TO PROTECT YOUR CREDIT

To protect the integrity of your credit, you should check it on a regular basis. It's up to you to make sure that the information in your credit report is correct. Errors or fraudulent activity can hurt your credit scores without you knowing it.

Checking your credit reports is easy and it never hurts your credit scores. You can purchase your credit report from any of the three credit agencies, but you're entitled to a free report once a year at annualcreditreport.com. You can report inaccuracies or put a stop to fraud by placing a credit alert or **credit freeze** on your credit reports. The Fair Credit Reporting Act (FCRA) is a federal law that regulates how your credit information can be used and your consumer credit rights. You can learn more on the Federal Trade Commission website at ftc.gov.

# SECTION 6

# Borrow without Sorrow

It can be easy to get into financial trouble if you take a loan or make credit card charges that you can't repay. That's why it's important to know how to use debt responsibly and make wise choices that are best for your financial future.

## WHAT TO KNOW ABOUT DEBT

Before you apply for credit or take on any amount of debt, ask yourself some important questions:

• Do I really need this?

• Can I wait until I save enough cash to pay for it?

• What's the total cost of the credit, including interest and fees?

• Can I afford the monthly payments?

There are many different kinds of debt, but they fall into two main categories: installment loans and revolving credit.

## Installment Loan Basics

An **installment loan** is an agreement you make with a creditor to borrow a certain amount of money and repay it in equal monthly payments, or installments, for a set period of time. The length or term of the loan could be very short or in excess of 30 years and may be secured or unsecured.

**Secured loans** are backed by collateral, which is something of value that you pledge to the lender. Collateral protects lenders because they can sell it to repay your debt if you don't make payments as agreed.

**Unsecured loans** are not backed by any collateral. They're often called personal or signature loans because you sign an agreement where you promise to repay the debt.

When you take an installment loan, your monthly payment will depend on three factors:

1. **Principal amount.** The less you borrow, the lower your monthly payment will be.

2. **Interest rate.** The lower the rate, the lower your monthly payment will be.

3. **Loan term.** The longer the term, the lower your monthly payment will be—however, this generally results in paying more total interest.

## Common Types of Installment Loans

Installment loans give consumers money to buy many different products and services, like cars, homes, or a college education.

## Consumer Loans

**Consumer installment loans**, also called personal or signature loans, are commonly used for small purchases, like buying a computer or paying for unexpected expenses. You can apply for an unsecured consumer loan from online lenders, local banks, or credit unions.

## Auto Loans

Loans to buy a new or used vehicle are available from online lenders, local banks, credit unions, and some car dealers. You may be required to make a down payment on the purchase price—especially if you don't have good credit.

For example, if you want to buy a used car that costs $10,000, the lender may require that you pay 20 percent or $2,000 up front in order to borrow the remaining balance of $8,000.

The car you buy becomes collateral for the loan. If you don't make payments as agreed, the lender can repossess, or take, the vehicle to pay off the outstanding loan balance. The lender typically holds the title of the car until the loan is paid in full.

The term or repayment period for a car loan is typically two to seven years. Choosing a longer loan term reduces the monthly payment but can significantly increase the amount of total interest you have to pay.

## Student Loans

There are two main types of unsecured loans you or your parents can get to pay for the cost of tuition, books, and living expenses while you attend college: federal student loans and private student loans.

**Federal student loans** are issued by the federal government and typically don't require a credit check. Most students qualify for some type of federal loan, depending on their income or their parents' financial qualifications. To apply, you must complete the Free Application for Federal Student Aid (FAFSA). You can submit it online at the U.S. Department of Education website at fafsa.ed.gov.

Here are three types of federal student loans:

- **Stafford Loan** is the main federal loan for students, and it can be subsidized by the federal government or unsubsidized. To receive a subsidized Stafford Loan, you must demonstrate financial need. The government pays, or subsidizes, the interest on the loan while you're in school.

  Unsubsidized Stafford Loans require you to pay all the interest; however, you can defer making payments until after graduation. All students, regardless of financial need, can get an unsubsidized Stafford Loan.

- **Perkins Loan** is a subsidized federal loan given to students who have the most financial need. The government pays the loan interest during school and for a nine-month grace period.

- **Parent Loan for Undergraduate Students (PLUS)** is an unsubsidized

federal loan for parents of students. A credit check is made to verify that the parents have no adverse credit history.

**Private student loans** originate from a private lender, such as an online institution, a local bank, or a credit union. Private education loans are generally used to bridge the gap between the cost of college and the amount you can borrow from the government.

Eligibility for a private loan depends on your or your parents' financial qualifications and credit scores. You submit an application directly to a private lender and don't have to complete any federal forms.

## What's Being "Upside Down?"

A new car depreciates, or loses its value, very quickly—especially in the first three years—depending on the make and model. For example, a $20,000 car might be worth only $15,000 after a year. But your outstanding loan balance could be over $16,000 if you made a low or no down payment (depending on the loan terms).

When you owe more for a car than it's worth, you're "upside down" on the loan. If you want to trade or sell the car, you have to pay extra out of pocket to pay off the loan. Making a down payment helps you avoid this common financial problem of being "upside down"—and helps reduce your monthly loan payment. So, even if you have good credit, it's wise to make a down payment on a car loan.

### QUICK TIP

Always shop around for the best auto loan and get preapproved before shopping for a car. That way you'll know how much you can afford and what loan term is best for your situation.

## What's a Car Title?

A car title is a document that shows who purchased a vehicle and lists information including the vehicle identification number (VIN), make, year of manufacture, purchase price, registered owner name and address, and the legal owner if any money is owed. When a car is sold, the title must be transferred to the new owner.

# What's Vehicle Leasing?

Instead of owning a car you can lease one for a set period of time. After the lease term (usually 2, 3, or 4 years) expires, you have to return the vehicle to the leasing company. Monthly lease payments are usually less than loan payments for the same vehicle and term. However, after you pay off a car loan the vehicle belongs to you. You can sell it for cash or continue to drive it for many years without having to make a car payment. That makes purchasing a car more cost effective when you keep it for the long term.

# What Is Foreclosure?

**Foreclosure** is a legal process a home lender uses to recover the balance of a bad debt when a borrower defaults or stops making loan payments as agreed. The lender takes legal title to the property, evicts the borrower(s), and sells the property to pay off the debt.

## QUICK TIP
A good rule of thumb is never to take more total student loan debt than your projected annual starting salary after graduation.

## WEB TOOL
To learn more about completing the FAFSA and paying for college, finaid .org is a leading resource for financial aid—including loans, scholarships, grants, and fellowships.

Private student loans typically have higher interest rates and less repayment flexibility than federal loans. Therefore, always apply for a federal student loan first.

## Home Loans
You can get a home loan or mortgage from online lenders, local banks, or credit unions. They can be used to

- buy real estate, such as a house or condominium,

- buy a parcel of vacant land,

- build a home,

- borrow against a home's value.

There are three main types of home loans:

1. A **purchase loan** is used to buy a home and is secured by the property. You must make a down payment that's typically 5 percent to 20 percent of the purchase price.

The loan term is typically 30 years, but 15- and 20-year mortgages are also common.

2. An **equity loan** is secured by your home and can be used for any purpose. **Equity** is the current market value of your property less the amount of outstanding debt you owe. For instance, if your home is worth $200,000 and your mortgage balance is $140,000, you have $60,000 in equity.

3. A **refinance loan** replaces an existing home loan by paying it off and creating a brand new loan. If you plan to stay in a home for several years, investigate the benefits of refinancing when interest rates decrease. You'll get a lower interest rate with lower monthly payments.

## Revolving Credit Basics
**Revolving credit** is different from an installment loan because it doesn't have a fixed number of payments or a final due date. The account revolves, or stays open indefinitely, as long as you make minimum monthly payments. The lender approves a maximum loan amount, or credit limit, to use at any time. Credit cards, retail store credit cards, and **home equity lines of credit (HELOCs)** are common types of revolving credit.

## Applying for a Credit Card
If you're under age 21, you must show that you have income or an eligible cosigner to qualify for a credit card. The law requires that you receive a Federal Truth in Lending Disclosure Statement from any company that offers you credit. Be sure to read it carefully so you understand the terms and can compare cards based on these features:

- APR for purchases, promotions, cash advances, and balance transfers

- your credit limit

- fees and penalties

- how balances are calculated

- rewards or rebates for purchases
- additional insurance protections

## Managing a Credit Card

A credit card gives you the ability to make purchases now and pay for them later. For example, if you have a credit card with a $1,000 credit limit, you can use it to buy products or services, or take cash advances that total $1,000. That makes credit cards powerful financial tools that can help you in an emergency situation. But credit cards can also devastate your finances if you get over your head in debt that you can't repay.

Because they're so convenient for consumers and come with unsecured risk for lenders, credit cards charge relatively high interest rates that can exceed 30 percent! Every time you make a credit card purchase, you're borrowing money that must be paid back with interest.

### Paying Your Credit Card

Credit cards issue an account statement each month that lists transactions from the previous month. The lowest amount you can pay—your "minimum payment"—varies depending on the card, but may range from 2 percent to 4 percent of your outstanding balance. For instance, if you owe $500, your minimum payment could be 3 percent, or $15. The remaining balance of $485 will continue to accrue interest, in addition to any new transactions you make.

# TIPS TO REDUCE THE COST OF BORROWING

The cost of borrowing money depends on several factors, such as the current interest rates, your credit rating, the APR you're offered, loan fees, and how long it takes you to repay the debt. Here are 10 tips to reduce the cost of borrowing:

1. **Shop around** for the lowest interest rate or APR for a loan or credit card before you accept an offer.

2. **Finance an item based on the total price** (including interest) that you can afford—not just on a monthly payment amount.

3. **Repay loans over a shorter term** so you pay less total interest over the life of a loan.

4. **Pay off credit card purchases in full** each month so you're never charged interest.

5. **Make payments on time** so you're never penalized with expensive late fees or an increased APR on a credit card.

6. **Build a good credit history** so you have high credit scores and will be offered low interest rates by lenders and credit card companies.

7. **Make a bigger down payment** so you'll owe less and receive lower APR offers from auto and home lenders.

8. **Take out federal student loans** before accepting private education loans so you qualify for the most favorable interest rates and repayment terms.

9. **Claim the student loan interest tax deduction** for the allowable amount of interest you pay on education loans each year.

10. **Never take a payday loan** or advance against your next paycheck, because the interest rate can be over 15 percent for just two weeks—which translates into a sky-high APR that can exceed 400 percent!

**QUICK TIP**

If you pay off your entire credit card balance by the due date on your statement each month, you can use a credit card for free because no interest charges accrue during this "grace period."

# SECTION 7

# Manage Your Money

## What Is Social Security?

Social Security is a group of benefits that pays eligible taxpayers who are retired or disabled or survive a relative who was receiving benefits. The funds for Social Security come from taxes withheld from your paycheck. The amount you'll receive in retirement depends on how much you earn during your career, the age you elect to start receiving benefits, and the future financial health of the Social Security system. Visit ssa.gov for more information.

It's easy to build wealth and create financial security if you manage your money wisely. Good money management starts with never spending more than you make. You have to decide what's most important to you and use your financial resources to make your dreams a reality.

Your financial life will always be a balancing act between the short-term gratification of spending versus the long-term benefit of saving. Having the willpower to resist unnecessary spending can really pay off and give you a happy financial future.

## SETTING FINANCIAL GOALS

Financial goals are what you want to do with your money and by when. They can be short-term, like buying a car this year or taking a vacation next summer. Or they can be long-term, like accumulating a large nest egg for retirement so you can stop working when you grow older.

Though you have many years to go, retirement should always be one of your top financial goals because it takes decades to achieve. Financial success doesn't happen overnight—so the earlier you start saving for a huge goal like retirement, the better. Take a few minutes to list your financial goals in order of their priority.

## CREATING A BUDGET

It's easy for everyday purchases like snacks, magazines, and music to get out of control if you're not watching them carefully. Keeping your expenses as low as possible can add up to huge amounts over time. For instance, let's say bringing your lunch to work four days a week saves you $8 a day or $32 a week. If you invested $32 a week for 40 years at a moderate return, you'd have over $330,000!

The best way to take control of your money is to create a budget, or spending plan. A spending plan helps you understand how much money you have and where it goes, so you can prioritize expenses and achieve your short- and long-term financial goals.

Managing money the right way is all about making choices and sacrifices—like whether to spend money on a night out with friends or save it to buy a car. You'll always have many needs and wants competing for your limited financial resources. It's up to you to choose your priorities and decide the best way to spend your money.

### Four Steps to a Preparing a Successful Budget

Knowing exactly how much you have to spend and where you spend it gives you power over your finances. You can keep track of your financial information on paper, using a computer spreadsheet or a mobile app, or by importing transactions from your bank or credit card accounts into a financial program.

Here are four easy steps to creating a successful spending plan:

## STEP #1—Enter your net monthly income.

To stay in control of your money and reach your financial goals, you must know how much money you have coming in each month. Recall that **net income**, or take-home pay, is the amount you have left after taxes and other deductions. Enter this amount at the top of your spending plan because it's what you actually have to spend each month.

## STEP #2—Enter your fixed and variable expenses.

Many people don't achieve financial success because they spend money carelessly. It's critical that you keep a close watch on your spending so it never exceeds your net income. Enter all your expenses below your income.

**Fixed expenses** don't change from month to month and may include your rent, insurance, phone, or a loan payment. **Variable expenses** can change each month or are discretionary, like dining out, transportation, or buying clothes.

Organize your expenses into major categories—such as rent, insurance, groceries, dining out, clothes, and entertainment—and total the amounts.

## STEP #3—Compare your income and expenses.

When you compare your total take-home pay to your total expenses you may be pleased that you have money left over or be disappointed that there's none to spare. Discretionary income is the amount of money you have left over each month after all your essential living expenses are paid.

You must spend less than you make in order to have enough discretionary income to save and invest for your future. Living paycheck to paycheck may satisfy immediate wants and needs, but it won't empower you to achieve financial success.

## STEP #4—Set priorities and make changes.

The final step is to create new spending guidelines. Decide how much you want to allocate toward each of your short- and long-term financial goals and enter them as separate categories in your spending plan. You may need to reduce spending in other categories or find ways to earn extra income to cover all your expenses.

It's up to you to figure out the best way to balance your spending and saving so you enjoy life today but also put away enough money for a safe and secure tomorrow.

## TRACKING YOUR WEALTH

A spending plan is the perfect way to track your income and expenses. But to monitor the big picture of your finances, you need to know your net worth. Your net worth can be summed up in this simple equation:

$$\text{net worth} = \text{assets} - \text{liabilities}$$

**Assets** are items you own that have real value, such as cash in the bank, vehicles, stocks, real estate, personal belongings, and money owed to you. **Liabilities** are your debts and financial obligations to others, such as a car loan, credit card debt, or money you borrowed from a friend.

# What Does "Pay Yourself First" Mean?

"Pay yourself first" is a common saying in personal finance that means saving money should be your top priority. Putting your savings on autopilot is the best way to remove the temptation to spend it! A portion of each paycheck can be automatically deposited in a savings or retirement account before you receive the balance. That way you pay yourself before paying your living expenses or making discretionary purchases.

Take a look at Avery's financial situation and help him create a realistic spending plan that will lead to a better financial future.

# Current Situation

Avery is 24 years old and works in the mail room at a large company. His gross pay is $2,500 per month, which gives him $2,000 in net pay (after taxes and health insurance are taken out). He's been spending more than his take-home pay for a year and has accumulated over $8,000 in credit card debt. Avery can only make the minimum payment on the card and is financing a lifestyle that he can't afford. Additionally, he isn't setting aside any money for emergencies or retirement.

| Avery's Current Monthly Spending* ||
| --- | --- |
| CATEGORY | AMOUNT (DOLLARS) |
| Total after-tax income | $2,000 |
| Fixed expenses | |
| Rent | $700 |
| Utilities | $150 |
| Car loan | $300 |
| Auto insurance | $50 |
| Credit card payment | $200 |
| Variable expenses | |
| Groceries | $500 |
| Dining out | $200 |
| Clothes | $150 |
| Gas | $100 |
| Entertainment | $300 |
| Other | $50 |
| Emergency savings | $0 |
| Retirement savings | $0 |
| Total expenses | $2,700 |

*Avery is adding debt of $700 per month to his credit card by making charges that he can't pay off in full. If he stops making new charges to the credit card, he could make payments of $435 per month to pay it off in two years.

# Financial Goals

Here are Avery's financial goals:

- pay off all credit card debt in two years
- put $100 a month into a bank savings account
- contribute $150 a month to the retirement plan offered at work

*Can you help by creating a realistic spending plan for Avery? You'll need to cut expenses in some categories so he can put money toward his financial goals and never spend more than his take-home pay each month.*

## Avery's New Monthly Spending

| CATEGORY | AMOUNT |
| --- | --- |
| **Total after-tax income** | $2,000 |
| **Fixed expenses** | |
| Rent | $ |
| Utilities | $ |
| Car loan | $ |
| Auto insurance | $ |
| Credit card payment | $ |
| **Variable expenses** | |
| Groceries | $ |
| Dining out | $ |
| Clothes | $ |
| Gas | $ |
| Entertainment | $ |
| Other | $ |
| Emergency savings | $ |
| Retirement savings | $ |
| **Total expenses** | $ |

Create a net worth statement by listing each of your assets and their current value. Then list each of your liabilities and the amount owed. When you subtract your total liabilities from your total assets, you've calculated your net worth!

If you own more assets than you owe in liabilities, your net worth will be a positive number. But if you owe more than you own, your net worth will be a negative number. The goal is to slowly raise your net worth over time by increasing your assets or decreasing your liabilities, so you build wealth.

## PAYING BILLS

Paying bills on time is one of the most important money management tasks. Late payments can result in expensive fees and damage to your credit. Thanks to online banking, it's never been easier to manage bills and pay them on time.

Most local and Internet-only banks offer free bill pay, which allows you to pay any company or individual with the click of a button. If a company you want to pay accepts electronic payments, your funds will transfer electronically. If not, the bill pay service prints and mails a

# CALCULATE NET WORTH

Caroline is 29 years old and runs her own website design business. Take a look at her financial situation and calculate her net worth.

## Caroline's Assets and Liabilities

| CATEGORY | AMOUNT |
| --- | --- |
| Assets | |
| Cash on hand | $100 |
| Cash in checking accounts | $500 |
| Cash in savings accounts | $5,000 |
| Value of retirement accounts (IRAs, workplace retirement plan) | $10,500 |
| Value of investments (stocks, bonds, mutual funds) | $0 |
| Value of vehicles | $10,000 |
| Value of homes | $200,000 |
| Value of household items | $20,000 |
| Value of jewelry | $1,000 |
| Money owed to Caroline | $3,000 |
| **Total assets** | **$** |
| Liabilities | |
| Balance owed on home mortgages | $175,000 |
| Balance owed on vehicle loans | $6,000 |
| Balance owed on student loans | $32,000 |
| Balance owed on other loans | $0 |
| Balance owed on credit cards | $2,000 |
| Outstanding bills | $0 |
| **Total liabilities** | **$** |
| To calculate Caroline's net worth: | |
| **Total assets** | **$** |
| **Less total liabilities** | **$** |
| **= Net worth** | **$** |

paper check on your behalf to any payee in the United States with a mailing address.

E-bills and e-statements can be sent to your e-mail, bill pay center, or both.

You can set up a bill to be paid automatically on a certain date and e-mail you when the transaction is complete. Or you can log on to your bill pay center and manually initiate a payment for up to one year into the future. You can set up reminder alerts for all your recurring bills so no bill due date ever falls through the cracks.

## TIPS TO MANAGE MONEY LIKE A MILLIONAIRE

One of the most surprising facts about wealthy people is that most of them weren't born rich. About 80 percent of the wealthiest people in the United States are first-generation millionaires. They accumulated wealth by working hard, saving, and investing money. That means anyone who is disciplined with his or her money can grow rich. Here are 10 tips to manage your money like a millionaire:

1. **Live below your means.** Saving money—not spending it—is how you grow rich. Wealthy people know that spending less than you make is a choice. The golden ticket to building wealth is to have plenty of discretionary income to save and invest.

2. **Know where your money goes.** If you don't have a spending plan to track your money, you won't know if you're making wise decisions. Getting ahead starts with taking control of your cash flow.

3. **Create an emergency fund.** Having money set aside for unexpected expenses is a safety net that you should never be without. That's how you'll make it through any financial rough patch in your life.

4. **Focus on net worth instead of income.** No matter how much you earn, you can grow rich by slowly increasing your net worth over time.

Even if you have a large income, you can never grow rich if you never set aside money for the future.

5. **Have long-term financial goals.** Wealthy people know what they want to achieve and then work backward so they know exactly what to do each year, month, week, or day to stay on track and meet their goals.

6. **Begin saving for retirement early.** If you think you're too young to start saving for retirement, think again! Creating wealth for your future never happens overnight—unless you have a winning lottery ticket or a big inheritance!

7. **Save and invest at least 15 percent of your income.** Make it a habit to save 15 percent to 20 percent of your income starting with your first job and adjust your lifestyle so you can easily live on the rest.

8. **Automate your savings and investments.** It's easier to save money that you never see. Participate in a workplace retirement account or have your paycheck split between a checking and savings account so your finances are on autopilot.

9. **View money as a tool.** Money is only as useful as what you do with it. So decide what's important to you and use money to achieve your dreams. Push away short-term gratification in favor of important, long-term goals.

10. **Realize when you've made a money mistake.** Everyone makes mistakes with their money from time to time. If you overspend or make unwise decisions, stop and make the choice to get back on track right away.

# SECTION 8

# Protect Yourself from Risk

You get sick and have to go to the emergency room. You get into a car accident and can't work for months. Your apartment gets robbed. While you can't prevent these kinds of catastrophes, you can protect your personal finances by having enough of the right kinds of insurance.

## TYPES OF INSURANCE

Insurance eliminates or reduces the potential financial loss you could experience from an unexpected event. It doesn't help you build wealth—but it protects the income and assets that you work hard for. The types of insurances you should have depend on your age and life circumstances. There are eight major types of insurance: health, disability, life, auto, homeowner's, renter's, long-term care, and umbrella.

### Health Insurance

Without health insurance you could get stuck with a huge bill if you have any kind of medical issue from a broken bone to a chronic illness. Even a quick trip to the emergency room can cost thousands of dollars.

Many employers offer group health insurance, or you can purchase an individual policy on your own. You can stay on your parents' health policy until you're 26 years old.

Visit healthcare.gov to explore your health insurance options.

### Disability Insurance

If you're unable to work due to a disability, accident, or long-term illness, disability insurance replaces a portion of your income while you recuperate. Remember that health insurance only covers your medical bills—not your living expenses.

### Life Insurance

This insurance is more about death than life because it usually kicks in after you're gone. It's important to have life insurance when your death would cause a financial burden for those you leave behind—like a spouse or child.

There are two basic kinds of life insurance—term and permanent:

- **Term life insurance** provides inexpensive coverage for a set period of time, such as 10 or 20 years, and pays the policy's death benefit amount to the beneficiary.

- **Permanent life insurance** provides lifetime coverage that pays a death benefit and accumulates a cash value that you can draw on later in life.

A good rule of thumb is to purchase life insurance with a benefit that's 10 times your income. So if you make $50,000 a year, you might need coverage that would pay your beneficiary $500,000. However, factors such as the number of children you have, your debt, and the lifetime income needs of a surviving partner or spouse are critical considerations.

### Auto Insurance

Most states require you to insure your vehicle. The rates vary depending on your age, driving record, and the vehicle you drive. According to the most recent data, the Toyota Sienna is the least expensive car to insure ($1,111 per year) and the Audi R8 Spyder Quattro Convertible is the most expensive ($3,384 per year). So remember to factor in the cost of insurance when choosing a new ride!

### Homeowner's Insurance

When you have a mortgage, the lender requires you to insure the property. Basic home insurance compensates you for damage to your property or personal belongings caused by natural disasters or theft. Homeowners insurance also includes liability coverage that protects you if someone gets hurt while on your property.

## Renter's Insurance

Your landlord or apartment community may have insurance, but it won't cover your personal belongings. Renters insurance is an inexpensive way to make sure that you're protected against natural disasters, theft, vandalism, and faulty plumbing. A renter's policy can also reimburse your living expenses if you're forced to move out temporarily due to a crisis. And just like with homeowner's insurance, there's a liability portion that keeps you safe if someone is injured on the property.

## Long-Term Care Insurance

If you have a long-term illness or disability that keeps you from taking care of yourself, this insurance pays a certain amount of day-to-day care. Don't confuse it with disability insurance, which only replaces a portion of your lost income.

## Umbrella Insurance

As you build wealth, you may find that you need additional liability insurance protection. An umbrella policy gives you broad coverage from losses above the limits of your existing policies, such as auto or homeowner's insurance.

## EXTENDED PRODUCT WARRANTIES

If you've ever purchased a product like a computer or a TV, the salesperson probably gave you a sales pitch for an **extended product warranty**. These warranties give you additional protection if something breaks after the manufacturer's warranty expires. They can also cover issues that the manufacturer doesn't.

While the added protection of an extended product warranty can come in handy, the cost can be very high.

## What Is an Insurance Deductible?

Many types of insurance—such as health, auto, renter's, and homeowner's—require you to pay a certain amount of expenses before the policy kicks in and covers your remaining costs. This out-of-pocket expense is called your **deductible**. For example, if you have a medical bill for $2,000 and your deductible is $500, then you must pay $500 before the policy will pay the remaining $1,500.

Product warranties are typically very profitable for retailers, who train salespeople to sell them aggressively. If the benefit isn't worth the cost, never let a salesperson talk you into buying something you don't need.

## When to Purchase an Extended Product Warranty

Consider the following to know when you should purchase an extended product warranty:

- **Look at the price of the warranty versus the price of the product.** If you spend $100 for an MP3 player and the extended warranty is $40, that raises the price 40 percent for a relatively inexpensive product. However, spending $150 for a warranty on a $2,000 computer may be worthwhile, since it has many expensive parts that could break.

- **Consider the likelihood you'll need extra coverage.** Will you use the product on a daily basis or in an environment where it could be damaged easily? Does the manufacturer have a reputation for making quality products?

- **Understand the coverage provided.** Does the warranty simply duplicate what's already available from the manufacturer, and how long does it last? What about parts and labor? Are the rules of the warranty clear and do they make sense for your situation? If the coverage is thin or it's too difficult to file a claim, then the warranty would be useless.

- **Remember coverage offered by your credit card.** Many credit cards offer built-in extended warranty coverage as a card benefit. So it might make sense to purchase a product with your credit card to take advantage of the extra protection.

# IDENTITY THEFT

**Identity theft** is a serious and growing crime. It happens when a criminal steals your personal information and uses it to commit fraud. A thief can use data including your name, date of birth, Social Security number, driver's license number, bank account number, or credit card number. Identity theft wreaks havoc on your finances. An identity criminal can open new phone accounts, credit cards, or loans in your name, then go on a spending spree and destroy your credit. Thieves have even filed fictitious tax returns and applied for driver's licenses in their victims' names. Once your identity is jeopardized, getting it corrected can cost time and money.

## Tips to Stay Safe from Identity Theft

Here are 10 tips to help you protect yourself and stay safe from identity theft:

1. **Never carry confidential information you don't need**. Unless you plan to use them, remove your Social Security card, paper checks, and financial cards from your wallet and leave them at home so they can't be lost or stolen.

2. **Don't share your Social Security number**. There are only a few situations where you might need to provide it, such as at a new job, in tax-related matters, or when applying for credit or insurance. Never reveal your confidential information over the phone or Internet to any person or company that you don't trust entirely.

3. **Keep a close watch over your debit and credit cards**. When you hand a financial card to a store clerk or restaurant server, watch to make sure that it isn't copied and get it back as soon as possible. Also, never loan your financial cards to anyone.

4. **Shred all documents with personal information**. Make confetti out of receipts, financial account statements, and unwanted credit card offers before putting them in the garbage. Identity thieves dumpster dive for paperwork and can even use the last few digits of a confidential number against you.

5. **Check your credit reports once a year**. If an identity thief opens an account in your name, it will show up on your credit reports. That's why it's important to review them on a periodic basis at annualcreditreport.com.

6. **Resist clicking on links in e-mails**. Thieves can pose as a legitimate organization—such as the IRS, a bank, or PayPal—and send "phishing" e-mails with links to phony sites that ask for confidential information. Instead of clicking on a hyperlink, enter a website address directly into an Internet browser.

7. **Use a secure Internet connection**. Don't access a website where you enter confidential information using a public computer or an open Wi-Fi connection. Hackers can track what you're doing over an unsecured Internet connection.

8. **Create strong online usernames and passwords**. Each password for your financial accounts should be unique, with no fewer than eight characters made up of uppercase and lowercase letters, numbers, and symbols. They should never include your Social Security number, name, address, or birth date.

9. **Opt for e-bills and e-statements when possible**. Criminals can change your mailing address so they receive your

mail and have access to your personal information. Therefore, reducing the amount of paper documents you send and receive with confidential information is beneficial.

10. **Monitor your bank and credit card accounts**. Review your monthly statements carefully and look out for unauthorized transactions.

It's impossible to completely prevent identity theft; however, when you catch it early you can stop it quickly and with less potential hassle and expense.

# Personal Finance Handbook Glossary

**401(k) plan**: A retirement savings plan established by an employer in which workers can elect to contribute a certain amount of their paychecks on a pretax basis.

**403(b) plan**: A retirement savings plan similar to a 401(k) but established by certain tax-exempt organizations, schools, and churches.

**account number**: Identifies a financial account in various places such as paper checks, deposit slips, credit cards, and account statements.

**account statement**: A paper or electronic record of account activity, service charges, and fees, issued on a regular basis.

**amortization**: Paying off the principal balance and interest of a debt in regular installments over time.

**annual percentage rate (APR)**: The cost of interest charged for a loan or the amount of interest earned on an account each year, expressed as a percentage rate.

**annual percentage yield (APY)**: The amount of interest earned on an account each year, including the effect of compounding, expressed as a percentage rate.

**assets**: Items that have real value, such as cash, vehicles, stocks, real estate, personal belongings, and money owed to you.

**ATM**: Or automated teller machine, is a kiosk or terminal to deposit, withdraw, or transfer money from one account to another 24 hours a day.

**ATM card**: A plastic card with the account owner's name, bank, and account number that can be used at an automatic teller machine to make deposits, check account balances, transfer funds between accounts, and make cash withdrawals 24 hours a day.

**bank**: Financial institution licensed to receive deposits, manage various types of accounts, and make loans.

**bank routing number**: Or routing transit number (RTN), is a nine-digit code used to identify a financial institution for the transfer of funds.

**bill pay**: An online service provided by many financial institutions that allows customers to send payments electronically or by paper check to any company or individual.

**bond**: A loan made to a corporation or government entity that earns interest over a certain period of time.

**bounced or bad check**: Slang for a check that is rejected due to insufficient funds in the account.

**brokerage account**: An account at a licensed brokerage firm that allows an investor to deposit funds and place investment orders.

**cashier's check**: A paper check issued by a bank on a customer account that is recognized as guaranteed funds.

**certificate of deposit (CD)**: A deposit account that earns interest for a set term during which the owner is restricted from withdrawing money without paying a penalty.

**check**: A paper form that authorizes a bank to release funds from the payer's account to the payee.

**checking account**: A financial account that generally allows funds to be used for an unlimited number of purchases using a debit or check card, paper checks, or online bill pay.

**check register**: A paper or digital record of deposits and withdrawals from a financial account.

**cleared or canceled checks**: Paper checks that have been processed and paid by a bank.

**collateral**: An asset put up as security for a loan that typically must be forfeited if the debt is not repaid as agreed.

**compound interest**: Interest paid on a principal amount plus the accumulated interest, which grows at a faster rate than simple interest.

**consumer installment loan**: Money borrowed to pay for personal expenses that must be repaid over a set period of time.

**credit**: The ability to borrow money.

**credit alert**: A message you can add to your credit report that informs potential creditors that you suspect errors due to fraudulent activity.

**credit card**: A plastic card issued by a bank or financial company with the owner's name and account number that gives the cardholder the ability to borrow money up to a set credit limit for purchases that are repaid with interest over time.

**credit freeze**: Prevents new credit and services from being approved in your name without your consent.

**credit limit**: The maximum amount of credit a lender gives a borrower for a revolving credit account, such as a credit card.

**credit score**: A grade used by lenders and merchants to help evaluate a potential customer.

**credit report**: A history of credit information maintained by a national credit reporting agency.

**credit reporting agency**: A business that collects historical information about an individual, from creditors and the public records, and makes it available on a credit report.

**credit union**: A nonprofit financial organization owned by its members who generally work for the same employer.

**credit utilization**: The amount of outstanding debt owed relative to available credit limits on revolving credit accounts.

**creditor**: A person, company, or financial institution that lends money to a borrower who is obligated to repay the debt.

**debit card**: A plastic card with the account owner's name, bank, and account number that allows purchases and ATM cash withdrawals using funds in an account linked to the card.

**deductible**: The amount that must be paid out-of-pocket for expenses before an insurance policy will pay the remaining costs.

**deposit**: Money added to a financial account.

**deposit slip or ticket**: A paper form that lists cash and checks added to an account.

**direct deposit**: An electronic payment method typically used by an employer or government agency.

**diversification**: Spreading financial risk over a variety of savings and investment options.

**earned income**: Is generated by working for a company or person—who pays you hourly wages, salaries, tips, commissions, and bonuses—or from a business that you own and run.

**effective tax rate**: The net rate that a taxpayer pays, calculated as total tax paid divided by taxable income.

**electronic payment or transaction**: A deposit or charge to an account that happens without the use of a paper form.

**emergency fund**: Cash reserves maintained in a safe place that can be used to pay for unexpected expenses.

**employer matching**: Contributions an employer can elect to make to a worker's retirement plan to encourage participation.

**endorsement**: The payee's signature on the back of a paper check that is required to deposit or cash out the funds.

**equity**: The difference between how much a property is worth and how much you owe for it.

**exchange-traded fund (ETF)**: Products that bundle combinations of investments and trade like a stock on an exchange where the price changes throughout the trading day.

**extended product warranty**: A type of insurance consumers can purchase for certain products to pay for covered repairs during a period of time, if not covered by the manufacturer.

**Federal Deposit Insurance Corporation (FDIC)**: Regulations that protect your deposits up to $250,000 per account holder in a failed bank.

**federal income tax**: Is levied by the Internal Revenue Service on the annual earnings of individuals and legal entities.

**FICA (Federal Insurance Contributions Act)**: The law that requires employers and employees to pay tax for the Social Security and Medicare programs.

**FICO (Fair Isaac Corporation) Score**: A credit scoring model that lenders commonly use to assess an applicant's creditworthiness, which is based on information in their credit report.

**fixed expenses**: Amounts you must pay that do not change from month to month.

**foreclosure**: A legal remedy a home lender can use to sell a property to recover losses when a borrower stops making mortgage payments as agreed.

**grace period**: The time a credit card balance can be paid before any interest is charged.

**gross income**: Or gross pay, is total income before tax and voluntary workplace expenses are deducted from a paycheck.

**group health insurance**: A health-care policy that offers benefits to a certain group, such as employees of a company or members of an organization.

**home equity line of credit (HELOC)**: A revolving credit account a homeowner may be approved to open (if there is sufficient equity) that is secured by their home.

**home equity loan**: An installment loan a homeowner may be approved for (if there is sufficient equity) that is secured by their home.

**identity theft**: Fraud committed by a thief who steals personally identifying information.

**income tax return**: The forms used to file income tax with the Internal Revenue Service each year to determine the amount of tax owed or any refund due (if tax was overpaid during the year).

**inflation**: The rate at which prices for goods and services are rising and consumers' purchasing power is falling.

**installment loan**: A loan that is repaid in equal monthly payments or installments over a set period of time.

**insurance**: Products designed to eliminate or limit the risk of potential financial losses.

**interest**: A percentage rate a lender charges you to borrow money or an amount earned from a financial institution on deposits.

**investing**: Committing money to a financial security or a tangible asset with the expectation that it will increase in value, create income, or do both.

**investment portfolio**: A group of investments that an investor owns.

**liabilities**: Financial obligations or debt owed to another party.

**loan**: Money borrowed from a lender with a written promise to repay it, in addition to interest, in the future.

**loan term**: The period of time a borrower is required to make payments to a lender to repay a loan plus interest.

**Medicare**: A federal health program that provides benefits to eligible individuals who are over the age of 65 or have certain medical conditions.

**minimum payment**: The smallest dollar amount that must be paid on a credit account each month.

**money market account (MMA)**: An account that typically requires a minimum balance and pays higher interest than a regular savings account.

**money market fund**: A low-risk, low-return investment fund that should not be confused with a bank money market deposit account.

**mortgage**: A loan to buy, build, or remodel real estate that is secured by the property and repaid over a set term.

**mutual fund**: An investment product that owns a variety of securities (such as stocks and bonds) and is managed by a professional.

**National Credit Union Administration (NCUA)**: A government agency that oversees insurance for deposits at federal credit unions up to $250,000 per depositor.

**net income**: Or net pay, is gross income less taxes and voluntary deductions, also known as take-home pay.

**net worth**: The amount by which assets exceed liabilities for an individual or business entity.

**nondeposit account**: Accounts with products such as stocks, bonds, and mutual funds that are sold by financial institutions but not FDIC insured.

**online banking**: Allows customers to accomplish banking tasks—including making deposits, transferring money between accounts, viewing statements, and paying bills—over the Internet.

**overdraft**: When money is withdrawn from a bank account and the available balance goes below zero.

**overdraft protection**: A service that consumers must authorize in advance that allows overdraft transactions on a debit or ATM card to be processed for a fee. Consumers can opt out of this service, which means that transactions that exceed available funds would be denied at the point of purchase.

**passive income**: Is income generated from assets purchased or created, as opposed to earned income.

**payday loan**: A short-term loan also known as a cash advance loan that's issued at a very high rate of interest.

**payee**: The person or company to whom a check is made payable.

**payer**: The person or company who writes a check or pays another party.

**phishing**: Unsolicited e-mail from criminals (that appear to be from a legitimate source) that attempt to acquire personal information for their illicit financial gain.

**prepaid card**: A plastic payment card issued by a financial institution that can be preloaded with money, but is not linked to a bank or credit account.

**principal**: The amount borrowed or the balance remaining on a loan, not including the interest charges.

**reconciliation**: The process of comparing a bank account statement to your records and resolving any differences.

**refinance**: Paying off an existing loan and replacing it with a new one with more favorable terms.

**retirement account**: A vehicle for saving and investing that typically provides tax advantages when funds are held until the account owner reaches age 59½.

**revolving credit**: A type of debt with no fixed term that allows a borrower to use funds up to a set credit limit for any purpose as long as required minimum payments are made each month.

**Roth IRA (Individual Retirement Arrangement)**: A retirement account for individuals that allows after-tax contributions to grow completely tax free.

**rule of 72**: A formula that gives you a shortcut to estimate how long it will take for savings to double in value given a particular interest rate.

**safe deposit box**: An individually secured container held within a safe or vault at a bank for a renter to store valuable possessions.

**savings**: Money put aside in a safe place for planned purchases and unexpected emergencies.

**savings account**: A financial account that earns interest and allows a limited number of monthly withdrawals.

**savings and loan**: A type of banking institution that specializes in taking deposits, managing checking and savings accounts, and making loans.

**secured credit card**: A type of credit card that requires an up-front deposit as security, which serves as a credit limit and can be used to pay off the debt if a cardholder does not make payments as agreed.

**secured loan**: Debt backed or secured by collateral that a lender can claim and use to pay off the loan if the borrower doesn't repay it as agreed.

**Securities Investor's Protection Corporation (SIPC)**: Insurance that protects investors who lose money due to a brokerage going out of business or failing, for up to $500,000.

**security**: A financial asset that may represent an ownership interest (such as a share of stock), a debt agreement (such as a bond), or a right to ownership (such as a derivative).

**self-employment tax**: The full amount of Social Security and Medicare taxes that individuals who work for themselves must pay to the IRS each year.

**service charge**: Or maintenance charge, is a fee charged by a bank to maintain your account.

**simple interest**: A method of calculating interest that is based on the original principal amount only and ignores the effects of compounding.

**Social Security**: A federal program that provides income for eligible taxpayers who are retired or disabled, or who survive a relative that was receiving benefits.

**spending plan**: A plan for meeting expenses and savings goals in a given period of time.

**stock**: A type of security that represents ownership in a company and is also known as an equity share.

**tax credit**: A type of benefit that allows eligible taxpayers to reduce their tax liability by subtracting an amount from the total tax owed to the government.

**tax deduction**: A type of benefit that allows eligible taxpayers to reduce their tax liability by reducing the amount of income on which tax is calculated.

**traditional IRA (Individual Retirement Arrangement)**: A retirement account for individuals that allows tax on contributions and earnings to be deferred until distribution.

**treasuries**: Loans to the U.S. government for various periods of time that include Treasury bills (T-bills), notes (T-notes), and bonds (T-bonds).

**unsecured loan**: A loan or line of credit that is not backed by collateral.

**VantageScore**: A credit scoring model used to evaluate the creditworthiness of a potential customer, determined by information on a credit report.

**variable expenses**: Amounts you pay each month that are discretionary and not fixed.

**W-4**: A form that must be completed by an employee that tells the employer the correct amount of tax to withhold from each paycheck.

**wire transfer**: An electronic transfer of funds from one person or financial institution to another.

**withdrawal**: Taking money out of a financial account.

**withholding**: Tax taken out of an employee's paycheck before the net amount of funds is received.

# Skills
# Handbook

SECTION 1:   **Critical Thinking Skills**

SECTION 2:   **Data Bank**

SECTION 3:   **Atlas**

SECTION 4:   **Reading Graphs and Other Visual Resources**

SECTION 5:   **Test-Taking Skills**

# SECTION 1

# Critical Thinking Skills

## READING SKILLS

Reading about economics may seem challenging, but following a few steps will help you get the most out of your text. The reading process has three main stages: before reading, during reading, and after reading.

### Before Reading

You can learn a lot about a text even before you begin reading by doing the following:

- **Set a purpose for reading.**
  Think about what you want to learn from your reading. Write this purpose in your notes and use it to guide your reading.

- **Preview the text.**
  Review the title, section headings, photos, and other visual features of the text to find some of the main ideas.

- **Make predictions.**
  Use what you found during your preview to predict the content of the text. Write these predictions with your purpose.

### During Reading

Use your reading purpose and predictions to guide your reading. As you read, add to your notes by completing these steps:

- **Ask questions.**
  Practice active reading by asking yourself questions about the text as you read. Good questions include "What is the author's main point?" and "Why did the author include this information in the text?"

- **Identify main ideas and supporting details.**
  Look for the most important ideas in the text. Then find the details that give facts to support each of these main ideas.

- **Summarize the text.**
  At the end of each section, write a few sentences to summarize what you have read. Be sure to include the main idea sind important supporting details in your notes.

### After Reading

After you finish reading, take a few minutes to check your understanding. Review the purpose for reading and predictions that you wrote before reading. Evaluate whether you met your purpose and if your predictions were correct. Review your section summaries or reread the relevant section to answer any remaining questions.

## READING PRIMARY AND SECONDARY SOURCES

Both primary and secondary sources may provide useful information about economics.

A *primary source* was created by a person who directly witnessed an event. Primary sources may include newspaper articles, journals, and photographs. A *secondary source* was written by someone who was not present at an event. Secondary sources include textbooks, encyclopedias, and historical articles.

### Prepare to Read Primary and Secondary Sources

Identify whether a text is a primary or secondary source by determining who created the source, when it was created, and what it describes or shows.

- **Find the main idea and details.**
  Read closely to determine the primary idea of the text. Find the main idea by listing all the important supporting details and then summarizing them.

- **Look for connections among ideas.**
  Think about how the author organized the text. Look for cause-and-effect and sequence relationships to help you better understand the events and ideas described in the text.

- **Determine credibility and bias.**
  Evaluate whether the author is a reliable source and look for evidence of author bias. Determine whether the author was well informed about the topic of the text. Consider whether the author primarily provides facts or opinions.

## Practice Reading Primary and Secondary Sources

### NEW YORK NEWS

*October 29, 1929*

# STOCK MARKET CRASHES

New York—A massive decline in stock market prices took place yesterday on the New York Stock Exchange. More than 16 million shares changed hands as buyers rushed to sell stocks. The Dow Jones Industrial Average lost 12 percent to close at just 198, down from a high of 381 in September.

Stock prices have been falling for weeks. General Electric closed the day at 210 after peaking at 396 on September 3. RCA hit 505 earlier this year but bottomed out at 26 yesterday. "I'm ruined," investor Andrew Adams told reporters on Wall Street. "I only hope the market recovers soon."

**CHECK YOUR UNDERSTANDING**
Answer the following questions about the practice selection to check your understanding.

**1.** Is the text a primary or secondary source? How can you tell?

**2.** What is the main idea of this text?

**3.** Restate the events of the text using your own words.

## ANALYZING CAUSE AND EFFECT

A *cause* is any event that causes one or more other events to happen. These resulting events are called *effects*. In economics, causes such as shifts in supply may lead to effects such shifts in demand or prices.

### Prepare to Analyze Cause and Effect

Analyzing cause and effect begins with locating pairs or groups of related events. Then, determine the logical relationship between these events.

- **Read closely, looking for keywords.**
  Read the text carefully to find related events. Look for keywords including *because, so, since, therefore, as a result,* and *led to* to help you find related events.

- **Consider the relationship between events.**
  Think about the related events to determine their relationship. Sometimes, events have a cause-and-effect relationship. Other times, they simply occurred in order with no direct cause-and-effect relationship between them.

- **Determine which event caused another to occur.**
  Remember that causes must happen before events. Often, the first event described in a text caused one or more later related events. But you may need to reorder the events described in the text to find the one that came first.

## Practice Analyzing Cause and Effect

Read the following selection. As you read, determine which events were causes and effects and which just occurred in sequence.

Game Co. released its new video game console just before Thanksgiving. Only 115,000 units shipped to stores, but many more consumers wanted the console. As a result, people paid more than the retail price for a console. Two weeks later, XYX released its new console. It produced 500,000 units to sell to consumers.

**CHECK YOUR UNDERSTANDING**
Answer the following questions about the practice selection to check your understanding.

**1.** What are two events that show a cause-and-effect relationship? How can you tell?

**2.** What are two events that just occurred in sequence? How can you tell?

**3.** Predict another possible effect of the cause that you identified.

## USING CONTEXT CLUES

When reading about a complex subject such as economics, you are likely to encounter unfamiliar terms. Using context clues can help you determine the meaning of these words without needing to use a dictionary.

### Prepare to Use Context Clues

Evaluating the text around an unfamiliar term can help you determine its meaning. Keep in mind that your prediction must make sense in the text to be correct.

- **Identify any unfamiliar terms.**
  Note any unfamiliar terms as you read the text. You may wish to write these in your notebook so that you can refer to them later.

- **Read around the unfamiliar terms to determine their context.**
  Read the words and sentences around the unfamiliar terms. Look for words or phrases that can replace the unfamiliar term. Restate the meaning of the sentence or paragraph to help you find the overall idea of the term.

- **Predict a meaning for the term.**
  Substitute the words or phrases you found for the unfamiliar term and reread the sentence. If it makes sense, use this word or phrase to predict a meaning for the term.

## Practice Using Context Clues

Read the following selection. As you read, use context clues to find the meaning of the italicized terms.

> Along with natural resources, machinery, and workers, one important *factor of production* is the creativity of *entrepreneurs*. These individuals provide the ideas and energy needed to transform economic resources and labor into finished goods and services. Entrepreneurs are willing to take economic risks in the hopes of earning profits for their ideas and efforts.

### CHECK YOUR UNDERSTANDING
**Answer the following questions about the practice selection to check your understanding.**

1. Write a definition for the term *factor of production* using your own words.

2. Write a definition for the term *entrepreneur* using your own words.

3. Why are entrepreneurs an important factor of production? Write a sentence or two to answer this question using the italicized terms.

## ANALYZING TEXT STRUCTURE

All texts have a certain text structure, or a pattern on which the text's information is organized. Common text structures include *cause and effect*, *compare and contrast*, *problem and solution*, and *sequence*. Texts may also organize information according to importance, with the most important ideas coming before less important details.

## Prepare to Analyze Text Structure

Analyzing a text to find its structure will help you understand the author's main ideas and identify the most important facts and details in an explanation or analysis.

- **Look for keywords that show text structure.**
  Keywords such as *because*, *likewise*, *however*, *in response*, and *next* all relate to specific types of text structure. Words and phrases including *moreover* and *more importantly* may indicate especially important facts and details.

- **Determine the text structure.**
  Use the keywords you have found to help you make a logical determination about the overall text structure. Keep in mind that text structure can change in each paragraph.

- **Find the most important ideas and facts in the text.**
  Use the text structure to guide you to the most important ideas and facts in the text. Note causes and effects, like and unlike concepts, problems, and so on in your notes.

## Practice Analyzing Text Structure

Read the following selection. As you read, pay close attention to the text structure to help you find the most important ideas.

> Declining demand for goods and services creates a dilemma for producers. Lower demand means lower prices, and lower prices in turn mean lower profits. But producers may attempt to increase demand for older or less desirable offerings. Advertising, for example, is a common way to boost demand.

### CHECK YOUR UNDERSTANDING
**Answer the following questions about the practice selection to check your understanding.**

1. What is the text structure of this paragraph?

2. How does the text structure of the paragraph help you find the most important facts and details?

## ANALYZING MULTIPLE POINTS OF VIEW

Not all economists have the same ideas about the economy. Economists may interpret the same data differently or have varied ideas about how to grow the economy, for example. Learning to analyze multiple points of view will help you better understand these different ideas and form your own ideas.

## Prepare to Analyze Multiple Points of View

To analyze multiple points of view, consider the factors that may influence each speaker's ideas. Think about how those factors shape the speakers' biases or goals.

- **Consider the speakers.**
  Identify the speakers and consider what you already know or can conclude about their ideas. Look for details that identify the speakers' jobs and time period.

- **Identify the speaker's context.**
  Think about the time and place when the speaker was talking or writing. Consider the audience he or she was intending to reach. Identify any possible biases or specific goals that the speaker might have.

- **Compare and contrast viewpoints.**
  Determine the main idea about which speakers are offering ideas. Think about what points the speakers are likely to agree and disagree on.

## Practice Analyzing Multiple Points of View

Read the two quotes below from economists John Maynard Keynes and Ludwig von Mises. As you read, pay close attention to each speaker's ideas.

 **CHECK YOUR UNDERSTANDING**
Answer the following questions about the practice selections to check your understanding.

1. What is the main topic of these quotes?
2. How do Keynes's and von Mises's ideas about this topic differ?

# DETERMINING FACT AND OPINION

A *fact* is any piece of information that can be reliably proven. For example, the statement "member countries of the European Union use the euro" is a fact. In contrast, an *opinion* gives a speaker's unproven ideas about a particular topic. The statement "not all nations should adopt the euro" is an opinion.

## Prepare to Determine Fact and Opinion

Remember that facts can always be proven with data, records, or other evidence. Opinions often vary from person to person because they are based on individuals' beliefs. However, facts may be used to support opinions.

- **Consider whether statements can be proven.**
  As you read, ask yourself, "Can this statement be proven with data or other evidence?" If it can, then the statement must be a fact. If it cannot, it is an opinion.

Capitalism is the astounding belief that the most wickedest of men will do the most wickedest of things for the greatest good of everyone.
—ECONOMIST JOHN MAYNARD KEYNES

The first condition for the establishment of perpetual peace is the general adoption of the principles of laissez-faire capitalism.
—ECONOMIST LUDWIG VON MISES

- **Look for keywords that show opinion.**
  Seek out keywords that indicate opinion. Words such as *should*, *could*, *best*, *worst*, *all*, and *always* may indicate opinion. Loaded adjectives or other judging words also tend to show opinions.

## Practice Determining Fact and Opinion

Read the following selection. As you read, pay close attention to keywords that show fact and opinion.

> Greece became the twelfth country to adopt the euro in 2001. At that time, some European economists warned that the move was risky. Greece should not have been allowed to join the Eurozone. It had high inflation and a great deal of national debt. By the end of the decade, in fact, Greece faced great economic turmoil. The euro was almost certain to fail.
>
> *SOURCE:* http://news.bbc.co.uk/2/hi/business/1095783.stm.

 **CHECK YOUR UNDERSTANDING**
Answer the following questions about the practice selection to check your understanding.

1. What is one fact given in the text above? How can you tell?
2. What is one opinion given in the text above? How can you tell?
3. How does the author use facts to support her ideas?

## DETERMINING BIAS

A bias is the way that a person sees and thinks about a particular topic, similar to his or her point of view. Determining a speaker's bias allows you to better judge his or her ideas fairly for reliability and credibility.

## Prepare to Determine Bias

In order to find bias, you must first identify the speaker. Considering his or her point of view will allow you to gauge whether the arguments are valid.

- **Identify the speaker's context.**
  Look for clues to tell you the place, time, and situation in which the speaker was writing or talking. Consider what values or goals the speaker may have had.

- **Look for facts and opinions.**
  Determine which statements are facts and which are opinions. Remember that facts can be proven but opinions cannot be.

- **Consider how the speaker's bias influences his or her ideas.**
  Pay close attention to the ideas the speaker presents in his or her opinions. Consider how those ideas relate to the speaker's context. Think whether a speaker with a different bias would agree or disagree with the original speaker's ideas.

## Practice Determining Bias

Read the following selection. As you read, pay close attention to information that shows the speaker's bias.

### OP-ED

# SPEND TO SAVE JOBS

Since 2007, unemployment has been a growing problem in the United States. This has been especially true for African Americans, who had an unemployment rate of 15.8 percent at the end of 2011—more than double that of white Americans. Government should spend more money on job-training programs and community education to help this underprivileged group regain its place among U.S. workers.

—Dr. Wallace Smith, professor, African American Studies

*SOURCE:* http://money.cnn.com/2012/01/06/news/economy/black_unemployment_rate/index.htm.

 **CHECK YOUR UNDERSTANDING**
Answer the following questions about the practice selection to check your understanding.

1. What information can you determine about the speaker's context?
2. Summarize the speaker's bias.
3. How does the speaker's bias inform his ideas about government spending?

## EVALUATING ARGUMENTS

Evaluating arguments on the basis of logic, reasoning, and factual evidence helps readers determine the credibility of a text. *Credibility* is the extent to which an author presents a valid, well-informed argument based on reliable facts and details.

## Prepare to Evaluate Arguments

Applying skills in identifying facts and opinion and determining bias will ease the process of evaluating an argument.

- **Identify the speaker's argument.**
  Determine the speaker's main idea. Look for opinions that show the speaker's overall argument and suggest what the speaker wants the reader to believe.

- **Consider the logic and reasoning of the speaker's argument.**
  Study the structure of the argument to find relationships among ideas. Think about how the speaker uses facts and details to support the opinions given in the argument.

- **Determine the validity of evidence.**
  Evaluate whether the speaker mostly backs up the argument with facts or with opinions. Consider the speaker's bias and how it informs his or her ideas. Think about whether the speaker is a reliable source on the topic.

## Practice Evaluating Arguments

Read the following selection. As you read, pay close attention to information that shows the speaker's bias.

---

The global recession that began in the late 2000s has been most devastating for the world's developing countries. World Bank data shows that the developing world received half as much financial aid in 2008 as it had in 2007. This resulted from the lowered global revenues of the developed world. Although developed countries are likely to recover quickly, developing countries face a long, difficult slog forward.

*SOURCE*: www.guardian.co.uk/business/2009/jun/22/world-bank-international-capital-recession.

---

**CHECK YOUR UNDERSTANDING**
**Answer the following questions about the practice selection to check your understanding.**

1. What is the speaker's argument?

2. How logical do you believe the speaker's argument to be? Explain.

3. What is one piece of valid evidence that the speaker uses to support his argument?

## COMPARING TEXTS

Comparing two or more texts on the same topic can help you gain a fuller understanding of that topic. Authors' arguments and the facts they provide can present a more complete picture of a topic than can one text alone. Comparing primary and secondary sources can also provide additional understanding of an event.

## Prepare to Compare Texts

When comparing sources, follow these steps:

- **Identify the sources and authors.**
  Review each source to determine whether it is a primary or secondary source. Consider the purpose of each source. Evaluate each author for credibility and bias.

- **Evaluate the information in each source.**
  Look for facts and opinions in each source. Determine whether the information presented follows a logical argument.

- **Look for relationships between the content of each source.**
  Be sure to consider whether the sources agree with each other or contradict each other on facts and details. If they do not agree, determine which source is more reliable.

## Practice Comparing Texts

Read the following selection. As you read, pay close attention to the relationships between the texts' ideas.

---

I was born in 1978. When I was growing up, I remember buying eggs at the store for just $.79. Today, those same eggs cost almost $2—more than double! Prices have gone up a lot!
—KEISHA JONES, CONSUMER

Inflation rates may vary greatly over the course of several years. During the early 1980s, for example, inflation topped 10 percent annually. But since then, inflation has averaged just 3 percent or 4 percent each year.
—INFLATION JOURNAL

*SOURCE*: CPI Market Basket, Minneapolis Federal Reserve Bank.

---

**CHECK YOUR UNDERSTANDING**
**Answer the following questions about the practice selection to check your understanding.**

1. What type of source is each text? How can you tell?

2. How do these two sources relate? Do they support or contradict each other?

# SECTION 2

# Data Bank

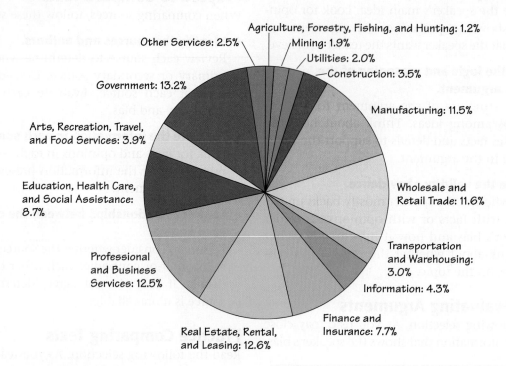

**Figure 1**  U.S. GDP by Industry, 2011

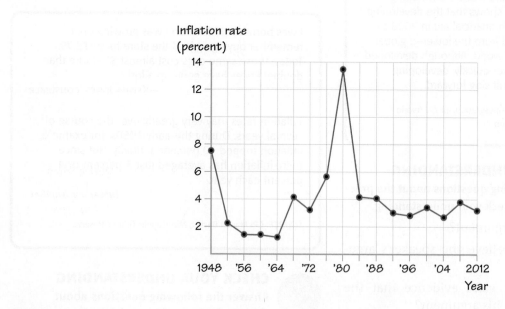

**Figure 2**  U.S. Inflation Rate, 1948–2012

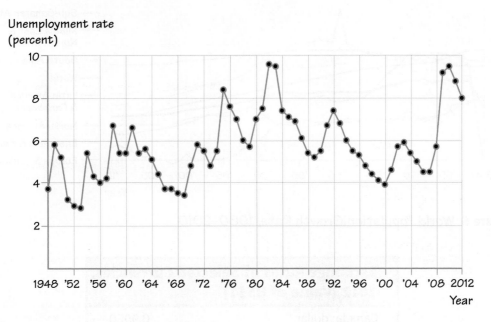

**Figure 3** U.S. Unemployment Rate, 1948–2012

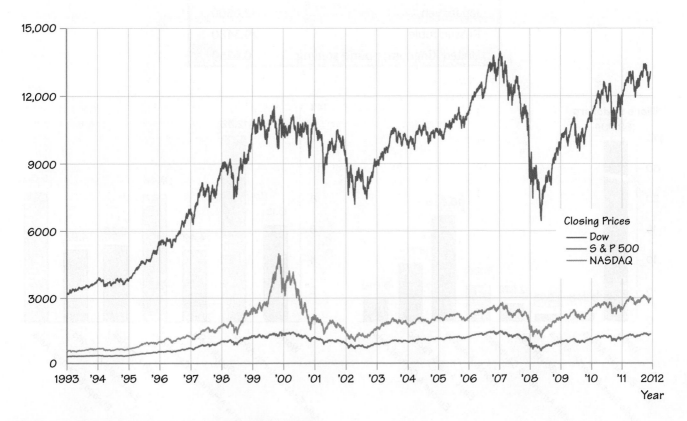

**Figure 4** Stock Market Indicators, 1993–2012

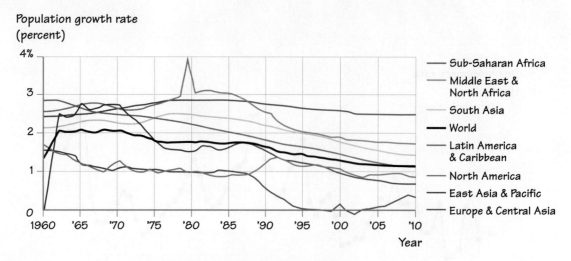

**Figure 5** World Population Growth Rate, 1960–2010

| Exchange Rates of Selected Currencies, 2012 (Value of US$1) | |
|---|---|
| Canada: dollar | 0.9960 |
| China: renminbi | 6.2980 |
| Eurozone: euro | 0.7490 |
| Hong Kong: dollar | 7.7630 |
| India: rupee | 50.8000 |
| Japan: yen | 82.0600 |
| Russia: ruble | 29.3480 |
| United Kingdom: pound sterling | 0.6250 |

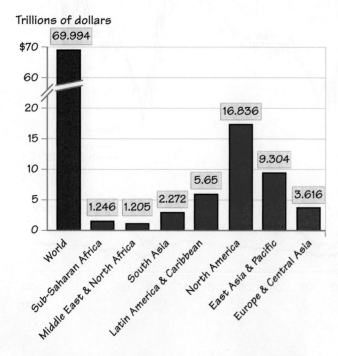

**Figure 6** World Gross Domestic Product, 2010

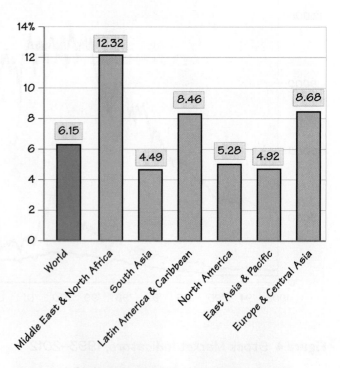

**Figure 7** Global Unemployment Rate, 2005

# SECTION 3

# Atlas

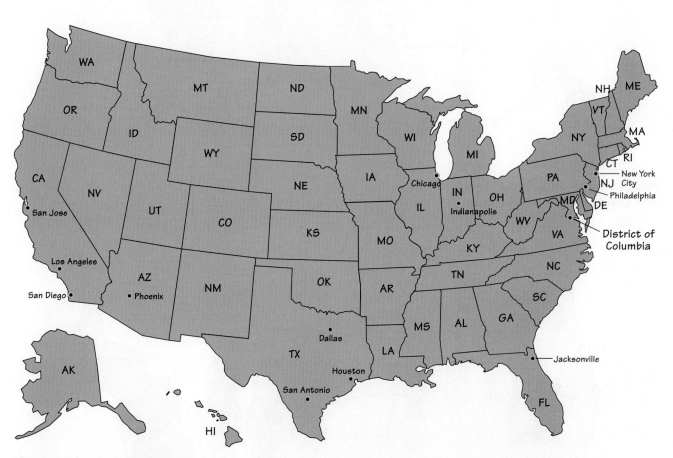

**Figure 8** The United States

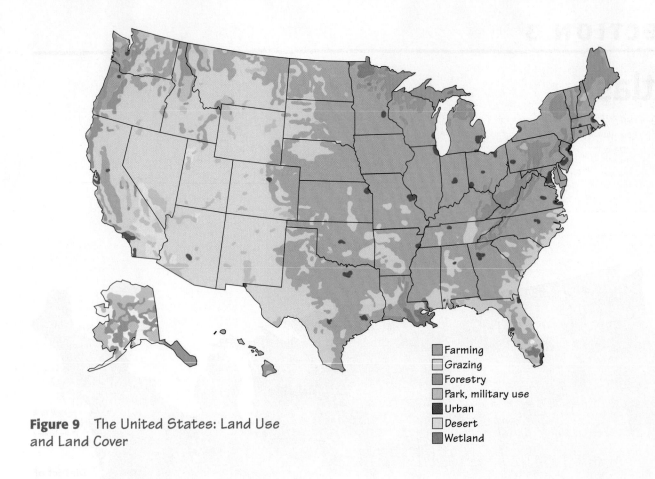

**Figure 9**  The United States: Land Use and Land Cover

☐ Farming
☐ Grazing
☐ Forestry
☐ Park, military use
☐ Urban
☐ Desert
☐ Wetland

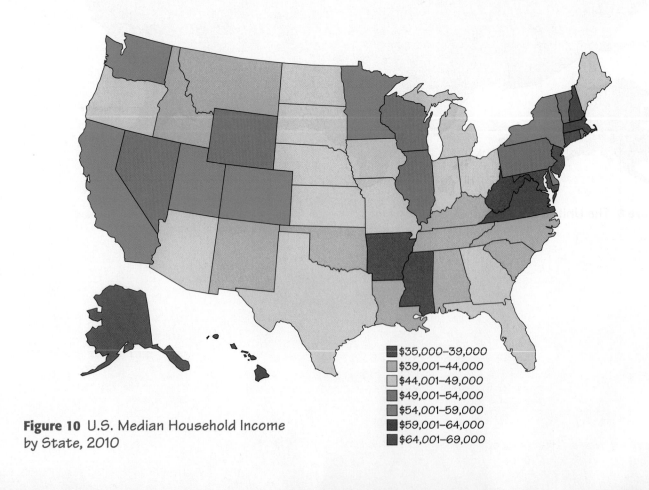

☐ $35,000–39,000
☐ $39,001–44,000
☐ $44,001–49,000
☐ $49,001–54,000
☐ $54,001–59,000
☐ $59,001–64,000
☐ $64,001–69,000

**Figure 10**  U.S. Median Household Income by State, 2010

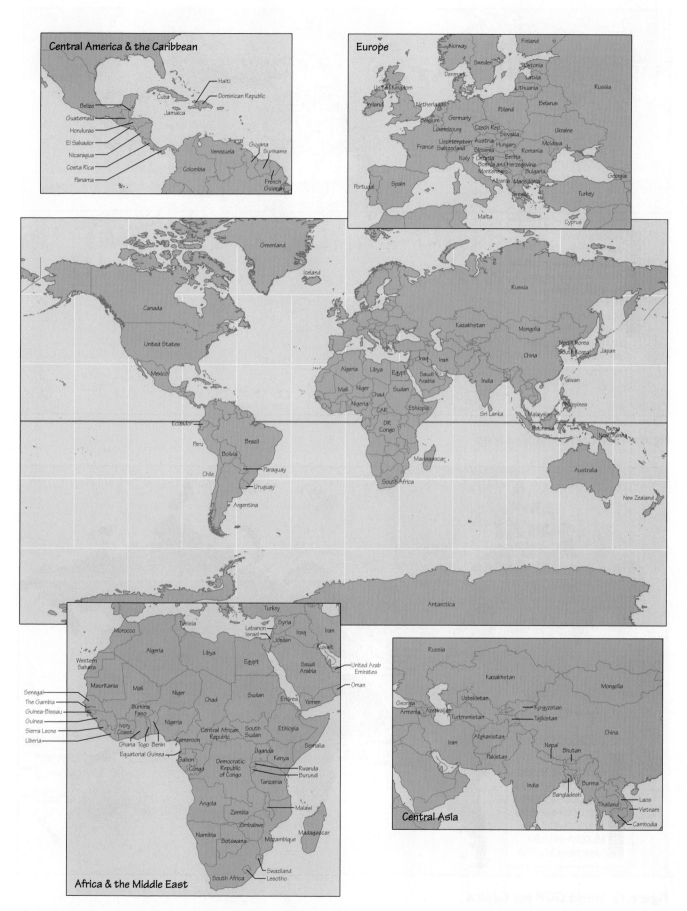

**Figure 11** World Political Map

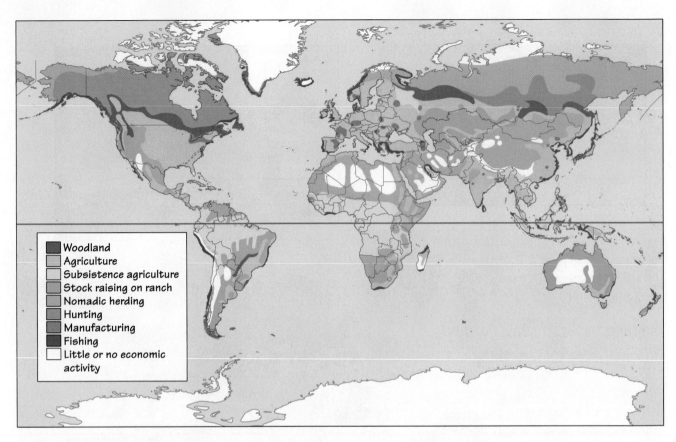

**Figure 12** World Land Use Map

Legend:
- Woodland
- Agriculture
- Subsistence agriculture
- Stock raising on ranch
- Nomadic herding
- Hunting
- Manufacturing
- Fishing
- Little or no economic activity

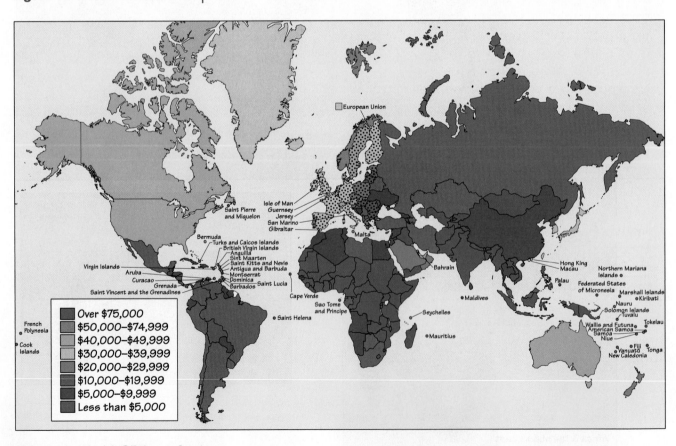

**Figure 13** World GDP per Capita

Legend:
- Over $75,000
- $50,000–$74,999
- $40,000–$49,999
- $30,000–$39,999
- $20,000–$29,999
- $10,000–$19,999
- $5,000–$9,999
- Less than $5,000

# SECTION 4

# Reading Graphs and Other Visual Resources

## READING LINE GRAPHS

Line graphs are visual depictions of numerical values. The line on the graph shows the changing levels of a certain measurement or measurements. Usually, line graphs show change over time. More than one line may appear on a graph to allow the viewer to compare and contrast data.

### Prepare to Read Line Graphs

Learning how to find information on a line graph is important to reading it correctly.

- **Read the title.**
  The title tells the overall purpose of the line graph and explains what the graph shows.

- **Study the horizontal and vertical axes.**
  On a line graph, the vertical axis usually indicates the data that is being compared. This data appears in numerical form. The horizontal axis usually indicates the period of time that the line graph covers. Notice the intervals, or periods, between each entry on the line graph to the right.

- **Determine what the line or lines show.**
  Read the legend or labels on the lines to help you find what each line on the graph represents. Lines that show different information have different colors or patterns to help differentiate them.

- **Analyze the graph data.**
  Look for patterns or significant changes over time in each line. Consider the relationship between each line if more than one appears.

## Practice Reading Line Graphs

Apply the techniques given above as you study this line graph.

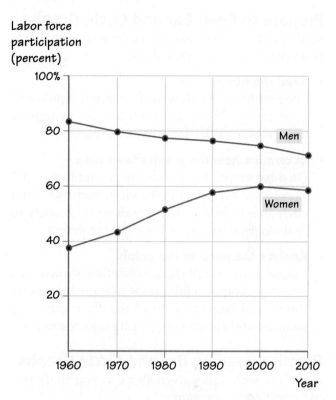

Labor force participation (percent)

**Figure 14** U.S. Labor Force Participation, 1960–2010

 **CHECK YOUR UNDERSTANDING**
Answer the following questions about the line graph to check your understanding.

1. What information does this line graph show?

2. In which year was male labor force participation the highest? In which year was female labor force participation the highest?

3. How has the relationship between male and female labor participation changed over time?

# READING BAR AND CIRCLE GRAPHS

Bar graphs use vertical or horizontal bars to compare numerical data or show change over time. Circle graphs—also called pie graphs—show how parts, or slices, of the complete circle add up to create the whole.

## Prepare to Read Bar and Circle Graphs

Studying the parts of bar and circle graphs will help you understand what they show.

- **Read the title.**
  The graph's title tells what that graph represents. Look for specific details such as time periods or quantities in dollars or millions of people.

- **Determine how the graph shows data.**
  On a bar graph, study the vertical and horizontal axes to see what data is shown in each bar. On a circle graph, look at the key or section labels to find what each piece of the whole represents.

- **Analyze the parts of the graph.**
  Consider the overall change over time shown on a bar graph. Look carefully at the relationship among the various bars or pieces of the circle graphs to compare and contrast the graph's information.

## Practice Reading Bar and Circle Graphs

Apply the techniques given above as you study this bar graph and circle graph.

**CHECK YOUR UNDERSTANDING**
Answer the following questions about the bar and circle graphs to check your understanding.

1. According to the bar graph, how many billions of dollars was the services sector worth in 2010?

2. According to the circle graph, what percentage of the economy was the manufacturing sector in 2010?

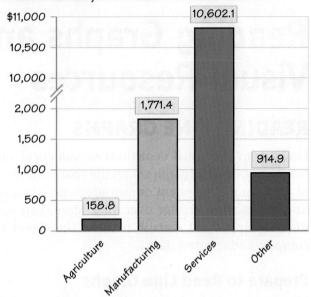

Total value added (billions of dollars)

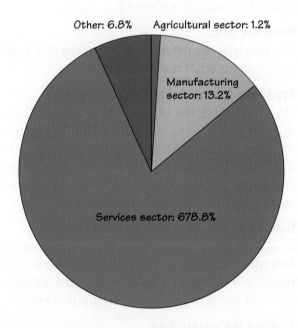

Other: 6.8%  Agricultural sector: 1.2%

Manufacturing sector: 13.2%

Services sector: 678.8%

**Figure 15** U.S. Economy by Sector, 2010

# READING TABLES AND CHARTS

Tables and charts use rows and columns to organize data into categories. Tables usually show data in numbers. Charts usually show data using text.

## Prepare to Read Tables and Charts

Use the table or chart title and headings to guide you to specific information. Then, study the overall table or chart to find broad patterns and trends.

- **Read the title.**

  The title of the table or chart tells what information the visual resource shows. Look for important details such as the years or figures represented on the table or chart.

- **Read the column and row headings.**

  Study the column and row headings to determine the categories into which the table or chart data is organized. Each box contains data that reflects the specific type of information named by the row and column.

- **Analyze the data.**

  Look for patterns or trends among the data shown. Consider the relationships among the information in the table or chart.

## Practice Reading Tables and Charts

Apply the techniques you just learned as you study this chart.

| Typical Education and Training Needed for Selected Jobs | | | |
|---|---|---|---|
| **JOB** | **EDUCATION** | **WORK EXPERIENCE** | **ON-THE-JOB TRAINING** |
| Chief executive | Bachelor's degree | More than 5 years | None |
| Computer support specialist | Some college | None | Midterm on-the-job training |
| Grounds maintenance worker | Less than high school | None | Short-term on-the-job training |
| Human resources manager | Bachelor's degree | 1–5 years | None |
| Pharmacy technician | High school | None | Midterm on-the-job training |

SOURCE: www.bls.gov/emp/ep_table_112.htm.

**CHECK YOUR UNDERSTANDING**

Answer the following questions about the chart to check your understanding.

1. Into what categories is the chart data organized?

2. Which job requires the most education and experience? Which job requires the least?

3. What is one conclusion that can be drawn about the value of education and training based on the chart data?

# READING MAPS

Maps show geographic information and data. In economics, maps are often used to relate economic information at the state, national, or international level. These thematic maps allow viewers to quickly read and analyze spatial data.

## Prepare to Read Maps

Maps show spatial data—information that relates to geographic distribution. Resources, population levels, political borders, and thematic data may all appear in map form.

- **Read the title.**
  The title of the map tells what spatial information the map contains. Look for important details such as the time period or region shown on the map.

- **Study the map key and labels.**
  The map legend, or key, shows the symbols, patterns, or colors used to indicate different data points on the map. Map labels provide more specific information and relate to the location where they appear.

- **Analyze the spatial data.**
  Look for spatial patterns on the map. Consider the relationships among the states, regions, or countries indicated.

## Practice Reading Maps

Apply the techniques you just learned as you study this map.

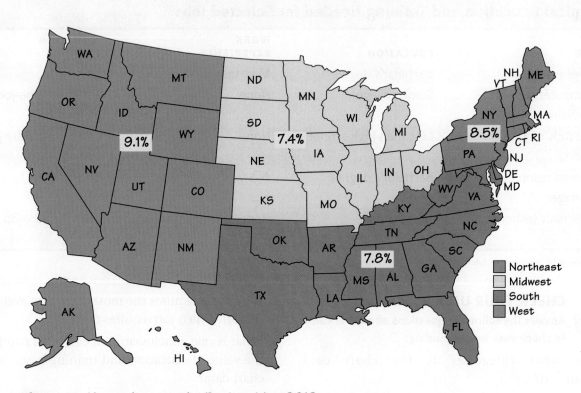

**Figure 16** Unemployment by Region, May 2012

 **CHECK YOUR UNDERSTANDING**
Answer the following questions about the map to check your understanding.

1. What information is shown on this map?

2. What information is given on the map legend?

3. Which region had the highest unemployment rate? Which region had the lowest unemployment rate?

# READING STOCK MARKET REPORTS

Stock markets allow traders to buy and sell shares of a corporation on behalf of individual investors. A stock market report shows the prices and trading details for a series of stocks on any given trading day. The change in the value of an individual share of stock shows the change in the overall value of the corporation it is part of.

## Prepare to Read Stock Market Reports

Stock market reports list many details, such as the stock's name, ticker symbol, annual high and low prices, and daily high and low prices, among other data.

- **Identify the stock.**
  Find the stock's name and ticker symbol. Ticker symbols are shortened versions of the corporation's name.

- **Consider the daily price data.**
  Find the high, low, and closing price. Notice how many shares of the stock were traded on the day of the report. Think about the overall daily change. Positive change represents a rising price, and negative change shows a falling price.

- **Evaluate long-term data.**
  Study the stock's performance over time. Determine the dividends, or amount paid to shareholders per share. Find the stock's yield, or return per share, and price-to-earnings (PE) ratio. Lower ratios usually equate to higher earnings.

## Practice Reading Stock Market Reports

Apply the techniques you just learned as you study this stock report.

| Ticker symbol | C | Company | Citigroup |
|---|---|---|---|
| 52-week high | $43.06 | 52-week low | $21.4 |
| Day high | $27.1 | Day low | $25.6250 |
| Open price | $26.46 | Close price | $26.37 |
| PE ratio | 7.23 | Annual dividend | $0.04 |

SOURCE: www.nasdaq.com/symbol/c/stock-report; www.nasdaq.com/symbol/c/real-time.

 **CHECK YOUR UNDERSTANDING**
Answer the following questions about the stock market report to check your understanding.

1. How does this stock's current price compare to its price over the past year?

2. Is this stock a good investment? Explain your reasoning.

# COMPARING DATA FROM MULTIPLE VISUAL SOURCES

Synthesizing information from multiple visual sources allows the viewer to gain a fuller understanding of the topic those sources address. Learning this skill can help you better analyze economic information.

## Prepare to Compare Data

Looking for relationships among data sources is the key skill needed to master comparing multiple visual sources.

- **Evaluate each source on its own.**
  Apply the techniques needed to evaluate each source. Consider main trends and patterns shown on each source. Look for the core ideas

or concepts each source supports. Determine the strengths and weaknesses of each visual source.

- **Find connections among the sources.**
  Think about how the patterns and information shown on each source connect across sources. Determine what ideas both sources support.

- **Analyze the differences among sources.**
  Sources created at different times or showing related but varying information may show differences. Think about how and why those variations might have occurred.

## Practice Comparing Data

Apply the techniques you just learned as you study these visual resources.

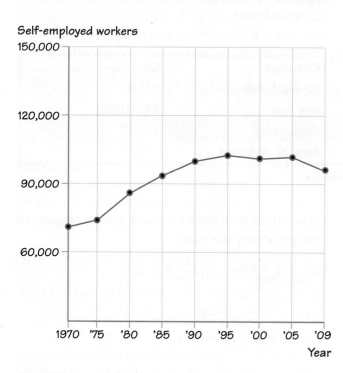

**Figure 17** U.S. Self-Employed Workers, 1970–2009

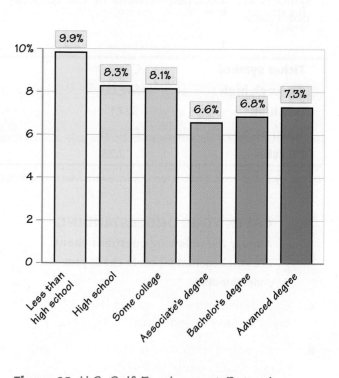

**Figure 18** U.S. Self-Employment Rates by Educational Attainment

**CHECK YOUR UNDERSTANDING**
Answer the following questions about Figures 17 and 18 to check your understanding.

1. What overall topic do both these graphs address?

2. What overall patterns about U.S. self-employment do these graphs suggest?

3. Which graph would better help you trace data about self-employment over time? Why?

# SECTION 5

# Test-Taking Skills

## EFFECTIVELY ANSWERING A MULTIPLE-CHOICE QUESTION

Answering multiple-choice questions may seem challenging, but having a plan to address each question can make the test-taking process less intimidating.

### Parts of a Multiple-Choice Question

All multiple-choice questions are set up in a similar way. Study this question to know what to expect.

> The **question stem** asks the question you must answer.

Which statement best describes the circular flow of income?

> Four or five **answer choices** give just one best response.

a. Money travels back and forth between employers and employees.

b. Businesses, households, and the government exchange money within the economy.

c. Consumers must pay money to producers in order to receive goods and services.

d. The amount of money in the economy changes as a result of supply and demand.

### Steps to Answering a Multiple-Choice Question

Using a consistent method to answer multiple-choice questions will help you do your best on these types of tests.

- **Read the question stem thoroughly.**
  Look for key words such as *most, least, best, not, except, never, usually,* and *always.* Seek out important terms and ideas that underlie the question. Be sure you understand exactly what the question is asking.

- **Read each answer choice carefully.**
  Consider each answer choice one by one. Look for key words in the answer choices. Choices that include words such as *always* or *never* are often wrong.

- **Choose the best answer.**
  Determine which answer choice best fits the question. Make sure that the answer choice addresses the important terms and ideas you identified while reading the question.

### General Practices

Make sure that you mark your answer choice clearly and neatly. If you change an answer, be sure to completely erase your first choice. Use any time at the end of the test to double-check your earlier answers.

## EFFECTIVELY ANSWERING AN ESSAY QUESTION

Essay questions require a well-thought-out response to a deeper, more analytic question than can be answered using a multiple-choice format. Answering an essay question effectively means that you must manage your time well.

### Types of Essay Questions

Essay questions may fall into several categories, including the following:

- **Explanation questions.**
  This question type requires you to thoroughly explain a certain event, idea, or process. Be sure to include all the important facts and details to answer this type of question effectively.

- **Analysis questions.**
  This question type requires you to connect ideas and concepts from different economic areas or time periods. Pay close attention to the relationships among the concepts that appear in the question.

- **Document-based questions.**
  This question type requires analysis of one or more primary and secondary sources. These documents must form the basis for your written response.

## Steps to Answering an Essay Question

Using your time wisely will allow you to plan and write an essay even in a short amount of time. Follow the steps below to make the most of each essay question.

- **Brainstorm and outline.**
  Take a few moments to brainstorm ideas in response to the question. Select your best ideas and use them to create a quick outline. List the main points you plan to make in the outline. This will ensure that you do not forget anything important as you write.

- **Write your response.**
  Use your outline to frame your written response. Do not simply make list of your ideas. Instead, be sure to use complete sentences and to explain your ideas well. Include an introduction and conclusion to reinforce your main points.

- **Revise and clarify.**
  Briefly reread your response. Add any words or decisions needed to make your ideas clear. Correct any major mistakes that make your essay hard to understand.

## General Practices

Always write responses using clear, legible handwriting. Use standard grammar and spelling to make your response easier for the reader to understand. Add missing words or ideas in the margin and connect them to the correct part of the response with an arrow.

# Glossary/Glosario

| English | Español |
| --- | --- |
| **A** | |
| **Absolute advantage**—the ability to produce more of a good than a trading partner using a given quantity of resources. | **Ventaja absoluta**—la capacidad de producir más de un bien que otra persona, usando una cantidad dada de recursos. |
| **ACH (automated clearing house) transfers**—transfers between payers' and payees' accounts carried out without the use of checks on a secure electronic funds-transfer network. | **Transferencias de caja de compensación**—transferencias entre las cuentas de quienes pagan y quienes reciben, efectuadas sin usar cheques, en un red electrónica segura para la transferencia de fondos. |
| **Acquisition**—the purchase by one firm of a controlling interest in another firm. | **Adquisición**—la compra del interés controlador de una empresa por otra. |
| **Active investing**—investing carried out with the goal of outperforming the market. | **Inversiones activas**—inversiones que se realizan con la meta de redituar más que el mercado bursátil. |
| **Adverse selection**—the people with the greatest need for a particular type of insurance are the ones most likely to buy it. | **Selección adversa**—las personas con la mayor necesidad de un tipo específico de seguro son las que más probablemente lo comprarán. |
| **Aggregate demand**—the total amount of domestic output purchased by all sectors of a country's economy, contingent on the price level. | **Demanda agregada**—el monto total de la producción nacional comprada por todos los sectores de la economía de un país, dependiendo del nivel de los precios. |
| **Aggregate supply**—the total output a country's firms are willing and able to produce, contingent on the price level. | **Oferta agregada**—la producción total de todas las empresas del país dispuestas a producir y capaces de hacerlo, dependiendo del nivel de los precios. |
| **Annual percentage rate**—the percentage of the borrowed amount that you would pay in interest if you had the loan for one year. | **Tasa de interés anual**—el porcentaje que se paga en intereses por la cantidad tomada en préstamo, si el préstamo se mantiene durante un año. |
| **Antitrust policy**—a set of laws designed to promote competition in the marketplace. | **Políticas antimonopolio**—conjunto de leyes diseñadas para fomentar la competencia en el mercado. |
| **Asset**—anything of value that is owned or controlled with the expectation that it will provide benefits in the future. | **Activo**—cualquier cosa que sea de valor de lo que se tiene en propiedad o que se controla, con la expectativa de que en un futuro redituará algún beneficio. |
| **Asymmetric information**—an imbalance of information between parties, meaning that one party knows things that the other does not. | **Información asimétrica**—desequilibrio en la información entre partes, o sea, que una parte sabe cosas que la otra ignora. |
| **Automatic stabilizers**—changes in taxation and transfer payments that moderate changes in GDP and do not require authorization from the government. | **Estabilizadores automáticos**—cambios en los pagos de transferencia y de impuestos que moderan los cambios en el PIB y que no requieren la autorización del gobierno. |
| **Average cost**—the total cost of production divided by the quantity of output. | **Costo promedio**—el costo total de la producción, dividida entre la cantidad de la producción. |
| **Average tax rate**—the proportion of a taxpayer's total income that is paid in taxes. | **Gravamen promedio**—la proporción del total de sus ingresos que el contribuyente paga en impuestos. |

## B

**Bailout**—an infusion of money, usually in the form of loans or stock purchases, to keep a firm from failing.

**Rescate financiero**—infusión de dinero, por lo general en la forma de préstamos o la compra de acciones, para impedir que una empresa fracase.

**Balance of trade**—the difference in value between the total exports and the total imports of a country over a specwified period of time.

**Balanza comercial**—la diferencia de valor entre el total de las exportaciones y el total de las importaciones de un país durante un período de tiempo específico.

**Balanced budget**—a budget designed to equate expected revenues with planned expenditures.

**Presupuesto equilibrado**—presupuesto diseñado para que haya equivalencia entre las rentas previstas y los gastos planeados.

**Bank holding companies**—companies that control one or more banks.

**Compañías controladoras de bancos**—empresas que controlan uno o más bancos.

**Barriers to entry**—obstacles that prevent firms from entering particular markets.

**Barreras al ingreso**—obstáculos que les impiden a las empresas incursionar en ciertos mercados definidos.

**Barter**—the exchange of goods or services for other goods or services without the use of money.

**Permutar**—el intercambio de bienes o servicios por otros bienes y servicios, sin que medie un traspaso de dinero.

**Bear market**—a market trend characterized by rapidly declining stock prices.

**Mercado a la baja**—tendencia en el mercado caracterizada por precios de las acciones que están en franca decadencia.

**Behavioral economics**—the branch of economics that uses ideas about decision making from psychology to explain economic behavior.

**Economía conductual**—la rama de la economía que se vale de nociones psicológicas sobre la toma de decisiones para explicar la conducta en asuntos económicos.

**Board of Governors of the Federal Reserve**—the group that manages the operations of the Federal Reserve, made up of members of the Federal Open Market Committee.

**Mesa directiva de la Reserva Federal**—el grupo que administra las operaciones de la Reserva Federal, compuesta de integrantes de la Comisión Federal de Mercados Abiertos.

**Bond**—represents a loan to the bond's issuer in exchange for specified payments to the bond purchaser over time.

**Bono**—representa un préstamo a quien expide el bono con pagos especificados que se le hacen al comprador del bono conforme avanza el tiempo.

**Bubble**—a rapid and unsustainable increase in the price of an asset, such as homes, gold, or stocks.

**Burbuja**—aumento rápido e insostenible en el precio de un activo, tal como viviendas, oro o acciones.

**Budget**—a specific plan for how to spend your money.

**Budget**—plan específico de cómo gastar el dinero.

**Budget deficit**—the difference between the amount of government payments and the amount of government revenues in a particular year when the payments exceed the revenues.

**Déficit presupuestario**—la diferencia entre la cantidad de pagos que hace el gobierno y el monto total de las rentas que percibe el gobierno en un año dado en el que los pagos son mayores que las rentas.

**Budget surplus**—the difference between the amount of government payments and the amount of government revenues in a particular year when the revenues exceed the payments.

**Superávit presupuestario**—la diferencia entre la cantidad de pagos que hace el gobierno y el monto total de las rentas que percibe el gobierno en un año dado en el que las rentas son mayores que los pagos.

**Bull market**—a market trend characterized by steady growth in stock prices.

**Mercado a la alza**—tendencia en el mercado caracterizada por un aumento sostenido en el precio de las acciones.

**Business cycles**—alternating periods of rising and falling real GDP.

**Ciclos económicos**—períodos que se alternan en los que aumenta o cae el PIB real.

**Business ethics**—the examination of standards for "right" and "wrong" behavior by firms.

**Ética empresarial**—el estudio de las normas de lo que se considera conducta "correcta" y conducta "errada" de las empresas.

**Business franchise**—consists of a parent company and numerous associated businesses that sell a standardized good or service.

**Franquicia empresarial**—consiste en una casa matriz y numerosos asociados empresariales que venden un bien o servicio estandarizado.

## C

**Capital**—anything long lasting that is created by humans for use in production.

**Capital**—cualquier cosa de larga duración que es creada por los seres humanos para usar en la producción.

| | |
|---|---|
| **Capital deepening**—an increase in a country's capital per worker. | **Ahondamiento del capital**—aumento en la cantidad de capital por trabajador en un país. |
| **Capital flight**—the movement of financial capital out of a country, either legally or illegally. | **Fuga de capitales**—el desplazamiento de capitales financieros de un país a otro, sea legal o ilegalmente. |
| **Capital market**—a market in which money is lent for one year or more. | **Mercado de capitales**—mercado en el que se presta dinero por un año o más. |
| **Capital stock**—the total amount of physical capital in a country. | **Capital accionario**—la cantidad total de capital físico en un país. |
| **Capitalism**—an economics system in which most resources and businesses are privately owned. | **Capitalismo**—sistema económico en el que la mayoría de los recursos y negocios son de propiedad particular o privada. |
| **Cartel**—a group of firms that agree to work together and act like a monopoly. | **Cartel**—grupo de empresas que conviene en trabajar en conjunto y actuar como monopolio. |
| **Certificate of deposit or CD**—documents a deposit into a financial institution that promises to pay a fixed interest rate for a specified period of time. | **Certificado de depósito**—documenta un depósito que se ha hecho en una institución financiera, la que promete pagar un tasa de interés fija durante un período de tiempo definido. |
| **Change in demand**—a shift of the demand curve (not to be confused with a change in the quantity demanded). | **Cambio en la demanda**—desplazamiento en la curva de la demanda (no se debe confundir con un cambio en la cantidad demandada). |
| **Change in supply**—a shift in the supply curve. | **Cambio en la oferta**—desplazamiento en la curva de la oferta. |
| **Change in the quantity demanded**—a movement along a demand curve caused by a price change (not to be confused with a change in demand). | **Cambio en la cantidad demandada**—desplazamiento a lo largo de la curva de la demanda producido por un cambio en el precio (no se debe confundir con un cambio de la demanda). |
| **Change in the quantity supplied**—a movement along the supply curve. | **Cambio en la cantidad ofertada**—movimiento a lo largo de la curva de la oferta. |
| **Check clearing**—the processes of removing money from the bank account of the person who wrote the check—the payer—and delivering it to the account of the check's recipient—the payee. | **Compensación bancaria**—los procesos mediante los cuales se retira dinero de la cuenta bancaria de la persona que giró el cheque—el pagador—y la persona que recibe el importe del cheque—el beneficiario. |
| **Circular flow diagram**—an illustration of the interactions between key players in the economy. | **Flujograma circular**—ilustración de las interacciones entre los participantes principales de la economía. |
| **Classical economics**—the school of economic thought, dominant from the 1700s to the 1930s, that favors laissez-faire policies with minimal government intervention. | **Economía clásica**—la escuela de pensamientos económicos que dominó desde inicios del siglo XVIII hasta fines de la década de 1930, en la que se favorecen las políticas de *laissez-faire* con mínima intervención del gobierno. |
| **Collateral**—an asset that must be forfeited to the lender if a loan is not paid back. | **Garantía**—activo del que se hace entrega al prestamista si se incumple en el pago del préstamo. |
| **Command economy**—an economic system in which central planners make the important decisions about what, how, and for whom to produce. | **Economía planificada**—sistema económico en el que los planificadores centrales toman las decisiones importantes sobre qué producir, y cómo y para quién producirlo. |
| **Commercial bank**—a bank which accepts deposits from individuals and firms, and provides them with loans in addition to a wide variety of other services. | **Banco comercial**—banco que acepta depósitos de personas y empresas, y que les ofrece préstamos además de toda una serie de otros servicios. |
| **Commodities**—standardized raw materials and agricultural products. | **Insumos**—materia prima estandarizada y productos agrícolas. |
| **Commodity money**—money that has value apart from its use as money. | **Dinero como insumo**—dinero que tiene un valor adicional, aparte de su uso como dinero. |
| **Communism**—a political-economic system under which all resources and businesses are publicly owned and economic decisions are made by central authorities. | **Comunismo**—sistema político y económico según el cual todos los recursos y las empresas son de propiedad pública y las decisiones económicas las toman las autoridades centrales. |

| | |
|---|---|
| **Comparative advantage**—the ability to produce a good at a lower opportunity cost than a trading partner. | **Ventaja comparativa**—la capacidad de producir un bien a un costo de oportunidad más bajo que el de otra persona. |
| **Compensating wage differential**—a premium paid to persuade someone to work in undesirable circumstances. | **Diferencial de sueldos compensatorio**—valor adicional que se paga para convencer a alguien de que trabaje en circunstancias indeseadas. |
| **Complements**—two goods for which an increase in the price of one of the goods leads to a decrease in the demand for the other good. | **Complementos**—dos bienes, en los que el aumento del precio del uno lleva a la disminución de la demanda del otro. |
| **Conglomerate**—a single business enterprise formed by combining firms from unrelated industries. | **Conglomerado**—entidad empresarial conformada al combinar varias empresas en industrias no relacionadas entre sí. |
| **Consumer Price Index (CPI)**—a measure of the overall price level faced by a typical consumer. | **Índice de precios de consumo**—medida del nivel de precios general que enfrenta el consumidor típico. |
| **Contraction**—a phase of the business cycle during which real GDP falls. | **Contracción**—una de las fases del ciclo económico durante la cual el PIB cae. |
| **Contractionary fiscal policy**—any combination of government spending cuts and tax increases meant to slow the economy down. | **Política fiscal de contracción**—cualquier combinación de recortes gubernamentales y aumentos de los impuestos que se implanta con el fin de desacelerar la economía. |
| **Cooperative (co-op)**—a business owned by its members and operated to supply members and others with goods and services. | **Cooperativa**—entidad empresarial de la cual son propietarios sus afiliados y que es manejada de manera que les preste a sus afiliados y a otros de bienes y servicios. |
| **Corporate bond**—a contract between a corporation and the owner of the bond that obligates the corporation to pay the bond's owner a certain amount of money in the future. | **Bono corporativo**—contrato entre una empresa y el propietario del bono, mediante el cual se obliga a la empresa a pagarle a dicho propietario del bono cierta suma de dinero en una fecha en el futuro. |
| **Corporate income tax**—a tax on corporate profit that is paid directly by the corporation. | **Impuesto corporativo sobre los ingresos**—impuesto que pagan directamente las corporaciones sobre sus utilidades corporativas. |
| **Corporate social responsibility (CSR)**—the duties and obligations corporations have to different stakeholders. | **Responsabilidad social corporativa**—los deberes y obligaciones que las corporaciones tienen para con sus diferentes partes interesadas. |
| **Corporation**—a business firm that is itself a legal entity. | **Corporación**—empresa comercial que es una entidad legal individual. |
| **Cover letter**—a short note that tells a potential employer how you heard about the job, why you are interested in it, and why he or she should look at your resume and invite you for an interview. | **Carta de presentación**—breve nota en la que se le comunica al posible empleador que se tiene conocimiento de la vacante y que tiene interés en llenarla. También incluye una explicación de porqué el empleador debe leer su hoja de vida e invitarle a una entrevista. |
| **Credit report**—a record of all the credit card accounts and loans you have, the balances, and whether your bills are paid on time. | **Informe crediticio**—historial de todas las cuentas de tarjetas de crédito y préstamos que usted tiene, los saldos de las mismas y una indicación de si usted paga sus cuentas a tiempo. |
| **Credit union**—a not-for-profit depository institution owned by its members, who are also its customers. | **Cooperativa de crédito**—institución depositaria sin fines de lucro de que es de propiedad de sus afiliados que también son sus clientes. |
| **Crowding-out effect**—the constraint on private sector borrowing that results from higher interest rates due to government borrowing. | **Efecto de exclusión**—la limitación en la obtención de préstamos que resulta del aumento de las tasas de interés atribuible a préstamos que toma el gobierno. |
| **Currency**—paper money and coins. | **Moneda corriente**—dinero en papel y monedas. |
| **Current yield**—the annual coupon payment divided by the price. | **Rendimiento corriente**—el pago anual del cupón dividido entre el precio. |
| **Cyclical unemployment**—joblessness caused by an economic contraction. | **Desempleo cíclico**—la carencia de empleos causada por una contracción económica. |

**D**

| | |
|---|---|
| **Debt financing**—getting money by borrowing. | **Financiamiento de deuda**—obtener dinero a través de préstamos. |

| | |
|---|---|
| **Debt limit**—the highest amount that the national debt can reach, as authorized by Congress. | **Límite de endeudamiento**—el monto máximo que puede alcanzar la deuda nacional, según autorización otorgada por el Congreso. |
| **Deficit spending**—spending in excess of revenues. | **Gastos en déficit**—gastos hechos en exceso de las rentas percibidas. |
| **Deflation**—a decline in the price level. | **Deflación**—disminución en el nivel de precios. |
| **Demand curve**—a graphical representation of the demand schedule for a good, showing the quantity demanded at each price. | **Curva de la demanda**—representación gráfica de la relación de la demanda por un bien, en la que se aprecia la cantidad de la demanda a cada precio. |
| **Demand deposits**—deposits that the depositor is free to withdraw, or "demand," at any time. | **Depósitos exigibles**—depósitos que el depositante puede retirar, con sólo pedirlos o "exigirlos", en cualquier momento. |
| **Demand schedule**—a table that relates the quantity demanded of a particular good to its price. | **Relación de la demanda**—tabla en la que se relaciona la cantidad de la demanda de un bien con su precio. |
| **Demand-side policy**—policy meant to stabilize or stimulate the economy by changing aggregate demand. | **Política que estimula la demanda**—política que tiene por fin estabilizar o estimular la economía mediante el cambio de la demanda agregada. |
| **Depository institution**—a financial institution that obtains money mainly through deposits from clients. | **Institución de depósitos**—institución financiera que obtiene dinero principalmente de los depósitos que hacen sus clientes. |
| **Depreciation**—a fall in value. | **Depreciación**—disminución en el valor. |
| **Depression**—an extremely severe recession. | **Depresión**—recesión extremadamente grave. |
| **Derived demand**—demand for an input that is derived from the demand for the output produced with that input. | **Demanda derivada**—la demanda de un insumo que se deriva de la demanda del producto producido con ese insumo. |
| **Developing country (DC)**—a country with relatively few goods and services available to the majority of the population. | **País en vías de desarrollo**—país con relativamente pocos bienes y servicios al alcance de la mayoría de sus habitantes. |
| **Differentiated products**—goods and services that differ somewhat from other products in the marketplace. | **Productos diferenciados**—bienes y servicios que se distinguen de otros productos en el mercado. |
| **Diminishing marginal productivity**—the decrease in the marginal product of a variable input, such as labor, as more and more of it is combined with a fixed input, such as equipment. | **Productividad marginal en disminución**—la disminución en el producto marginal de un insumo variable, como por ejemplo, la mano de obra, en la medida en que más y más del mismo insumo se combina con un insumo fijo, como por ejemplo, los equipos. |
| **Discount rate**—the interest rate that the Fed charges financial institutions for short-term loans. | **Tasa de descuento**—la tasa de interés que la Reserva Federal cobra a instituciones financieras por préstamos que les hace a corto plazo. |
| **Discouraged workers**—people who would like to work but have given up on their job search. | **Trabajadores desanimados**—personas que quisieran trabajar pero que se han dado por vencidas en su búsqueda de empleo. |
| **Discretionary spending**—government spending that is not required by law; rather, it is authorized annually by Congress and the president. | **Gastos discrecionales**—gastos del gobierno que no son exigidos por ley; son gastos que el Congreso y el presidente autorizan cada año. |
| **Disposable income**—income after taxes have been removed. | **Ingresos disponibles**—ingresos de los que se dispone después de pagados los impuestos. |
| **Dividends**—payments made out of a corporation's profits to owners of its stocks. | **Dividendos**—pagos hechos de las utilidades de una corporación a los propietarios de las acciones de la misma. |
| **Drop-in-the-bucket problem**—no one person's payment for a good is essential, which diminishes each person's incentive to contribute. | **Problema de carencia de valor**—ningún pago individual de una persona por un bien es esencial, lo cual disminuye el incentivo de cada persona a contribuir. |
| **Dumping**—the practice of exporting goods at a price that is below the price in the exporting country. | **Dumping**—la práctica de exportar un bien a un precio que está por debajo del precio de ese bien en el país exportador. |

| E | |
|---|---|
| **Easy money policy**—policy that increases the money supply. | **Política de dinero fácil**—política que aumenta la cantidad de dinero en circulación. |
| **Economic freedom** gives people the ability to make economic decisions for themselves. | **Libertad económica**—le da a las personas la facultad de tomar decisiones económicas por su propia cuenta. |
| **Economic growth**—an increase in the ability to produce goods and services over time. | **Crecimiento económico**—aumento en la capacidad de producir bienes y servicios conforme avanza el tiempo. |
| **Economic infrastructure**—physical capital, such as communications systems and power systems, that provides a basic foundation that users share for many types of economic activity. | **Infraestructura económica**—capital físico, tal como sistemas de comunicaciones y de generación y transmisión de energía eléctrica, que proporciona una base que comparten los usuarios para muchos tipos de actividades económicas. |
| **Economic security**—confidence in the ability to support one's self and one's family. | **Seguridad económica**—confianza en la capacidad propia de darse sustento a uno mismo y a la familia. |
| **Economic system**—an organizational structure for addressing what, how, and for whom to produce. | **Sistema económico**—estructura organizativa para el manejo de lo que se produce, cómo se produce y para quién. |
| **Economics**—the study of choice under conditions of scarcity. | **Economía**—el estudio de las opciones de que se dispone en condiciones de escasez. |
| **Economies of scale**—the cost advantages experienced when, in the long run, an increase in output results in a decrease in average cost. | **Economías de escala**—las ventajas en costo que se experimentan cuando, a la larga, un aumento de la producción resulta en una disminución del costo promedio. |
| **Economy**—a system for coordinating the production and distribution of goods and services. | **Economía**—sistema para coordinar la producción y la distribución de bienes y servicios. |
| **Efficient**—when there is no opportunity to make someone better off without making at least one person worse off. | **Eficiente**—cuando no hay oportunidad de darle una mejor vida a otro sin menguar la calidad de vida de por lo menos una persona. |
| **Efficient market hypothesis**—holds that markets respond to information so efficiently that it is not possible to predict whether the prices of stocks or bonds will rise or fall without inside information. | **Hipótesis del mercado eficiente**—manifiesta que los mercados responden a la información con tal eficiencia que no es posible predecir si los precios de las acciones o de los bonos van a aumentar o disminuir sin contar con información privilegiada. |
| **Elastic demand**—consumers respond to a change in price with a relatively large change in the quantity demanded. | **Demanda elástica**—cuando los consumidores responden a un cambio en el precio con un cambio relativamente grande en la cantidad demandada. |
| **Elasticity of demand**—a measure of how strongly consumers respond to a change in the price of a good, calculated as the percentage change in the quantity demanded divided by the percentage change in price. | **Elasticidad de la demanda**—medida de la fuerza con que responden los consumidores a un cambio en el precio de un bien. Se computa dividiendo el porcentaje de cambio en la cantidad demandada entre el porcentaje de cambio en el precio. |
| **Elasticity of labor demand**—a measure of the responsiveness of the quantity of labor demanded to changes in the wage. | **Elasticidad de la demanda laboral**—medida de la sensibilidad de la cantidad de mano de obra con respecto a cambios que acontecen en los salarios. |
| **Elasticity of supply**—a measure of the responsiveness of the quantity supplied to price changes, calculated by dividing the percentage change in the quantity supplied by the percentage change in price. | **Elasticidad de la oferta**—medida de la sensibilidad de la cantidad ofertada con respecto a cambios en los precios. Se computa dividiendo el porcentaje de cambio en la cantidad ofertada entre el porcentaje de cambio en el precio. |
| **Embargo**—a government-ordered ban on trade. | **Prohibición comercial**—prohibición del comercio impuesta por el gobierno. |
| **Employment discrimination**—the unequal treatment of workers because of characteristics unrelated to job performance. | **Discriminación laboral**—el trato desigual de trabajadores por motivo de características no relacionadas con su desempeño en el empleo. |
| **Entitlement programs**—programs that people are entitled to by law if they meet certain qualifications. | **Programas por derecho ciudadano**—programas a los que el pueblo tiene derecho por ley si cumple con ciertos requisitos. |
| **Entrepreneurship**—the willingness of people to organize, operate, and assume the risks involved with business ventures. | **Espíritu emprendedor**—el deseo y la voluntad de las personas de organizar, manejar y asumir los riesgos que implica una empresa comercial. |

| | |
|---|---|
| **Equilibrium**—in reference to supply and demand, the point at which the quantity supplied equals the quantity demanded. | **Equilibrio**—refiriéndose a la oferta y la demanda, el punto en el que la cantidad de bienes ofertados equivale a la cantidad de bienes demandados. |
| **Equilibrium price**—the price that equates the quantity supplied and the quantity demanded. | **Precio de equilibrio**—el precio que lleva a la equivalencia entre la cantidad ofertada y la cantidad demandado. |
| **Equilibrium quantity**—the quantity that is supplied and demanded at the equilibrium price. | **Cantidad de equilibrio**—la cantidad ofertada y demandada al precio de equilibrio. |
| **Equity**—the quality of being fair and just. | **Igualdad de ánimo**—la calidad de justicia y equidad. |
| **Equity financing**—getting money by selling stock. | **Financiación de capital**—obtención de dinero mediante la venta de acciones. |
| **Euro**—the single currency used by 17 of the 27 members of the European Union. | **Euro**—moneda corriente única utilizada por 17 de los 27 integrantes de la Unión Europea. |
| **Excess demand**—the amount by which the quantity demanded exceeds the quantity supplied. | **Exceso de la demanda**—el monto por el cual la cantidad demandada es mayor que la cantidad ofertada. |
| **Excess supply**—the amount by which the quantity supplied exceeds the quantity demanded. | **Exceso de la oferta**—el monto por el cual la cantidad ofertada es mayor que la cantidad demandada. |
| **Excise tax**—a tax that applies to specific goods, such as cigarettes or gasoline, and is typically assessed as a certain amount of money per unit, rather than a percentage of the price. | **Impuesto de consumo**—impuesto que se aplica a ciertos bienes definidos, tales como cigarrillos o gasolina, y que generalmente se impone como una cierta cantidad de dinero por unidad, en lugar de ser un porcentaje del precio. |
| **Excludable good**—a good that can be consumed by one consumer without making it available to all consumers. | **Bien excluible**—bien que puede ser consumido por un consumidor sin que se tenga que poner a disposición de todos los consumidores. |
| **Expansion**—a phase of the business cycle during which real GDP rises. | **Expansión**—fase del ciclo económico durante el cual el PIB aumenta. |
| **Expansionary fiscal policy**—any combination of government spending and tax cuts meant to spur the economy. | **Política fiscal de expansión**—cualquier combinación de gastos del gobierno y recortes de impuestos que impulsan la economía. |
| **Expenditure approach**—the approach of calculating GDP by adding up expenditures on consumption, investment, government spending, and net exports. | **Enfoque de gastos y erogaciones**—el enfoque para calcular el PIB sumando los gastos en consumo, inversiones, gastos del gobierno y exportaciones netas. |
| **Export**—to sell goods to buyers in another country. | **Exportar**—vender bienes a compradores en otro país. |
| **Exports**—goods, services, and intermediate products bought by people in other countries. | **Exportaciones**—bienes, servicios y productos intermedios comprados por personas en otros países. |
| **External debt**—debt owed to foreign governments, banks, and individuals. | **Deuda externa**—endeudamiento que se le debe a los gobiernos, a los bancos y a las personas de otros países. |
| **Externality**—an effect felt beyond those whose decisions caused the effect. | **Externalidad**—efecto sentido más que por aquellos cuyas decisiones produjeron el efecto. |
| **Extreme poverty**—Conditions in which people live on less than $1.25 per day. | **Pobreza extrema**—Condiciones en las que las personas viven por menos de US$1.25 por día. |

### F

| | |
|---|---|
| **Factor markets**—where resources are exchanged for money. | **Mercados de factores**—en los que los recursos se intercambian por dinero. |
| **Factor payments**—payments for the use of resources. | **Pagos de factores**—pagos efectuados por el uso de recursos. |
| **Fair trade**—trade with a focus on the equitable treatment of farmers and their communities. | **Comercio justo**—comercio que se enfoca en darles un trato justo a los agricultores y sus comunidades. |
| **Federal budget**—a plan for how the federal government will spend money over the coming fiscal year. | **Presupuesto federal**—plan que define cómo el gobierno federal utilizará el dinero durante el siguiente ejercicio fiscal. |
| **Federal funds rate**—the interest rate that commercial banks charge one another for short-term loans. | **Tasa federal de fondos**—la tasa de interés que los bancos comerciales se cobran unos a otros por préstamos a corto plazo. |

| | |
|---|---|
| **Federal Open Market Committee**—the group within the Federal Reserve that creates monetary policy. | **Comisión Federal de Mercados Abiertos**—grupo dentro de la Reserva Federal que crea la política monetaria. |
| **Federal Reserve (the Fed)**—the central bank of the United States. | **Reserva Federal**—banco central de Estados Unidos. |
| **Federal Reserve banks**—banks operated by the Federal Reserve to implement Federal Reserve policies and provide services to member banks and federal government agencies. | **Bancos de la Reserva Federal**—bancos manejados por la Reserva Federal para poner en práctica las políticas de la Reserva Federal y prestar servicios a bancos afiliados y a dependencias del gobierno federal. |
| **Federal Reserve System**—the U.S. central banking system. | **Sistema de Reserva Federal**—el sistema del banco central de Estados Unidos. |
| **Fiat money**—money that has value because the government has ordered that it be accepted in payment of debts. | **Dinero fiduciario**—dinero que tiene valor porque el gobierno ha ordenado que se acepte para el pago de deudas. |
| **Final good or service**—a good or service that is sold to its final user, rather than to a firm that will use it to make something else. | **Bien o servicio final**—bien o servicio que se vende a su usuario final, en lugar de a una empresa que lo convertirá en algo diferente. |
| **Financial intermediary**—an institution that channels money between savers and borrowers. | **Intermediario financiero**—institución que encauza el dinero entre quienes lo ahorran y quienes lo toman prestado. |
| **Firm**—a privately owned organization that produces goods or services and sells them to others. | **Empresa**—entidad de propiedad privada que produce bienes o servicios y se los vende a terceros. |
| **Fiscal agent**—an organization that handles financial duties for another organization, as the Federal Reserve does for the federal government. | **Agente fiscal**—entidad que se encarga de las funciones financieras de otra entidad, tal como la Reserva Federal lo hace para el gobierno federal. |
| **Fiscal policy**—the use of government spending and taxation to pursue economic growth, full employment, and price stability. | **Política fiscal**—el uso de los gastos y los impuestos para lograr el crecimiento económico, el empleo total y la estabilidad de los precios. |
| **Fiscal year**—the period over which the federal budget applies. It begins on October 1 and ends on September 30. | **Año fiscal o ejercicio fiscal**—el período durante el cual se aplica el presupuesto federal. En Estados Unidos comienza el 1 de octubre y termina el 30 de septiembre. |
| **Fixed cost**—the cost of inputs that do not vary with the amount of output produced. | **Costo fijo**—el costo de los insumos que no varía según la cantidad de producción producida. |
| **Fixed exchange rate**—an exchange rate between currencies that is kept the same over time. | **Tipo de cambio fijo**—tipo de cambio entre monedas corrientes que se mantiene igual durante un lapso de tiempo prolongado. |
| **Fixed expenses**—expenses that remain about the same from month to month. | **Gastos fijos**—gastos que permanecen al mismo nivel de mes a mes. |
| **Flat tax**—everyone pays the same share of their income in taxes, regardless of their level of income. | **Impuesto a tasa única**—todos pagan la misma proporción de sus ingresos en impuestos, independientemente de cuál sea su nivel de ingresos. |
| **Flexible or floating exchange rate**—an exchange rate between currencies that is determined by supply and demand. | **Tipo de cambio flexible o flotante**—tipo de cambio entre monedas corrientes que cambia según los principios de oferta y demanda. |
| **Foreign aid**—economic or other assistance given by one country to another. | **Asistencia a países extranjeros**—asistencia económica o de otra índole que un país da a otro. |
| **Foreign direct investment**—investment from one country made to control or significantly influence a business enterprise in another country. | **Inversión directa del extranjero**—inversión proveniente de otro país. Se hace con el fin de controlar o influir de manera significativa una empresa comercial en otro país. |
| **Foreign exchange market**—a market made up of the many traders of one currency for another. | **Mercado de divisas**—mercado compuesto por las muchas personas que se dedican a cambiar la moneda corriente de un país por la de otro. |
| **Foreign exchange rate**—the price of one country's currency in terms of another country's currency. | **Tipo de cambio de divisas**—el precio de la moneda corriente de un país expresado en la moneda corriente de otro país. |

| | |
|---|---|
| **Foreign portfolio investment**—the purchase of foreign corporate bonds or shares of stock in a foreign corporation. | **Inversión en cartera extranjera**—comprar bonos corporativos o acciones bursátiles de una empresa extranjera. |
| **Foreign reserves**—deposits of foreign currencies held by central banks. | **Reservas del extranjero**—depósitos en monedas corrientes extranjeras que se encuentran en la custodia de bancos centrales. |
| **Fractional reserve banking system**—a system under which banks must hold on to a fraction of their deposits and may lend out the rest. | **Sistema de reserva bancaria fraccional**—sistema según el cual todos los bancos tienen que retener una fracción de sus depósitos y pueden prestar el resto. |
| **Free trade**—the exchange of goods and services between trading partners in the absence of government-imposed restrictions or charges. | **Comercio libre**—el intercambio de bienes y servicios sin restricciones ni cargos impuestos por el gobierno. |
| **Free trade zone**—a region within which there are few or no trade restrictions. | **Zona franca**—zona en la que hay pocas o ninguna restricción para el comercio. |
| **Free-enterprise system**—an economic system based on private (individual or business) ownership of resources and voluntary exchange. | **Sistema de empresa libre**—sistema económico basado en la propiedad privada de recursos (sea individual o empresarial) y su intercambio voluntario. |
| **Free-rider problem**—people take advantage of the nonexcludable and nonrival nature of public goods to avoid paying for them. | **Problema de los aprovechados**—las personas no pagan por los bienes públicos porque se aprovechan de su naturaleza no excluible y carente de competencia. |
| **Frictional unemployment**—short-term unemployment that occurs while workers search for the jobs best suited for their skills and interests. | **Desempleo friccional**—desempleo a corto plazo que acontece mientras los trabajadores están en busca de los empleos más adecuados a sus destrezas e intereses. |
| **Full employment**—the level of employment when there is no cyclical unemployment. Due to the existence of other types of unemployment, the achievement of full employment does not mean that every worker is employed. | **Empleo total**—el nivel de empleo cuando no hay desempleo cíclico. Debido a que existen otros tipos de desempleo, el logro de empleo completo no significa que todo el que desea trabajar tiene empleo. |

## G

| | |
|---|---|
| **Globalization**—the broadening access to products, people, businesses, technology, ideas, and money across national borders to create a more integrated and interdependent global economy. | **Globalización**—la ampliación del acceso a productos, personas, negocios, tecnología, ideas y dinero cruzando fronteras nacionales, con el fin de crear una economía global más integrada e interdependiente. |
| **Gold standard**—a monetary system under which a unit of currency, such as a dollar, can be exchanged for a specified amount of gold. | **Patrón oro**—sistema monetario según el cual una unidad de moneda corriente, tal como el dólar estadounidense, se puede intercambiar por un monto preciso de oro. |
| **Goods**—physical items produced in an economy, such as jeans, tennis rackets, popcorn, cars, and homes. | **Bienes**—artículos físicos producidos en una economía, tales como pantalones, raquetas de tenis, maíz, autos y casas. |
| **Government failure**—the inability of government to achieve an efficient outcome. | **Fracaso gubernamental**—la incapacidad del gobierno de lograr un resultado eficiente. |
| **Gross domestic product (GDP)**—the total dollar value of all final goods and services produced within a country's borders in a given year. | **Producto Interno Bruto (PIB)**—el valor total en dólares de todos los bienes y servicios finales producidos dentro de las fronteras de un país durante un ejercicio dado. |
| **Gross income**—the total amount of money you make. | **Ingresos brutos**—el monto total de dinero que un individuo percibe. |
| **Gross national income**—GDP plus net income from interest payments, dividends, and other income from assets in other countries. | **Rentas Internas Brutas**—El PIB más las rentas netas generadas por pagos de interés, dividendos y otras rentas provenientes de activos en otros países. |

## H

| | |
|---|---|
| **Highly developed country**—a country that produces plenty of goods and services to meet the basic needs of its people. | **País altamente desarrollado**—país que produce una abundancia de bienes y servicios para satisfacer las necesidades básicas de su pueblo. |
| **Horizontal equity**—people with the same ability to pay taxes make the same tax payment. | **Equidad horizontal**—las personas con la misma capacidad de pagar impuestos pagan lo mismo en impuestos. |

| | |
|---|---|
| **Horizontal merger**—a combining of two firms that produce the same type of product. | **Fusión horizontal**—combinación de dos empresas que producen el mismo tipo de producto. |
| **Household**—an individual or a group of people who live together and share income, such as you and your family. | **Hogar**—una persona o grupo de personas que conviven y comparten los mismos ingresos, por ejemplo: usted y su familia. |
| **Human capital**—the skills and knowledge of workers. | **Capital humano**—las destrezas y los conocimientos de los trabajadores. |
| **Hyperinflation**—very rapid inflation. | **Hiperinflación**—inflación muy rápida. |

**I**

| | |
|---|---|
| **Identity theft**—any crime involving the wrongful acquisition and use of another person's personal information. | **Robo de la identidad**—delito que implica la adquisición ilícita de los datos personales de otra persona y su uso alevoso. |
| **Imperfect competition**—arises when there is not enough competition among firms to prevent individual firms from raising their price above the equilibrium level determined by supply and demand. | **Competencia imperfecta**—surge cuando no hay suficiente competencia entre empresas para impedir que empresas individuales aumenten su precio por encima del nivel de equilibrio determinado por la oferta y la demanda. |
| **Implementation lag**—the time between the recognition of a problem and the decision about what to do about it. | **Tiempo de implementación**—el lapso de tiempo entre el momento en que se reconoce un problema y el momento en que se decide qué hacer al respecto. |
| **Import**—to purchase goods from sellers in another country. | **Importar**—comprar bienes a vendedores de otro país. |
| **Imports**—goods, services, and intermediate products produced in other countries. | **Importaciones**—bienes, servicios y productos intermedios producidos en otros países. |
| **Incentive**—the prospect of a reward or punishment that influences a decision or motivates greater effort. | **Incentivo**—la perspectiva de recibir un premio o un castigo que influye en una decisión o que motiva a las persones a esforzarse más. |
| **Income approach**—the approach of calculating GDP by adding up all the income earned during the year by people who are involved in the production of goods and services. | **Enfoque de ingresos**—enfoque mediante el cual se computa el PIB sumando todos los ingresos devengados durante el año por personas que participan en la producción de bienes y servicios. |
| **Income convergence**—the closing of the per capita income gap between rich and poor countries. | **Convergencia de ingresos**—el estrechamiento de la brecha en ingresos per capita entre países ricos y países pobres. |
| **Income effect**—the change in consumption that occurs when a price increase causes consumers to feel poorer or when a price decrease causes them to feel richer. | **Efecto de los ingresos**—el cambio en el consumo que ocurre cuando un aumento en el precio motiva a los consumidores a sentirse más pobres o cuando una disminución en el precio los motiva a sentirse más adinerados. |
| **Index fund**—a mutual fund that duplicates the investments in a benchmark index, such as the S&P 500 Index. | **Fondo índice**—fondo mutuo que se ajusta a las inversiones en un índice de referencia, por ejemplo el índice S&P 500. |
| **Industrialized country (IC)**—a country with a relatively high level of material wealth. | **País industrializado**—país con un nivel relativamente alto de riqueza material. |
| **Inelastic demand**—consumers respond to a change in price with a relatively small change in the quantity demanded. | **Demanda inelástica**—los consumidores responden a un cambio en el precio con un cambio relativamente pequeño en la cantidad demandada. |
| **Infant mortality rate**—the number of infants who die in their first year of life out of every 1,000 live births. | **Tasa de mortalidad infantil**—el número de criaturas que fallecen en su primer año de vida entre cada millar de nacimientos vivos. |
| **Inferior good**—a good for which the demand falls when income rises and rises when income falls. | **Bien inferior**—bien para el cual la demanda cae cuando los ingresos aumentan y para el cual la demanda aumenta cuando los ingresos caen. |
| **Inflation**—a rise in the price level. | **Inflación**—aumento en el nivel de precios. |
| **Inflation rate**—the annual percentage increase in the price level. | **Tasa de inflación**—el aumento porcentual anual del nivel de precios. |

| | |
|---|---|
| **Inflation targeting**—the central bank practice of targeting a rate—or range—of inflation for some time in the future and developing monetary policy with that goal in mind. | **Meta de inflación**—práctica del banco central de fijar una tasa meta para la inflación—o una gama de tasas—para algún momento en el futuro y definir una política monetaria teniendo en mente esa meta. |
| **Inputs**—the four types of resources—land, labor, capital, and entrepreneurship—along with anything made with these resources that is then used to make something else, such as cement, steel, lumber, and plastic. | **Insumos**—los cuatro tipos de recursos—tierra, mano de obra, capital y espíritu emprendedor—junto con cualquier cosa que se elabore con estos recursos y que luego se emplea para hacer otra cosa, por ejemplo, cemento, acero, madera o plástico. |
| **Inside lag**—a delay between the onset of a problem and the implementation of a solution. | **Demora interna**—demora entre el inicio de un problema y la implantación de una solución. |
| **Intermediate product**—a product that becomes part of a final good or service, or is used up in the production process. | **Producto intermedio**—producto que se convierte en parte de un bien o servicio final o que se consume totalmente en el proceso de producción. |
| **Intragovernmental debt**—the money the federal government owes to government programs such as Social Security and Medicare. | **Deuda intragubernamental**—dinero que el gobierno federal le debe a programas gubernamentales tales como el Seguro Social y Medicare. |
| **Inventory**—goods that are held in temporary storage. | **Inventario**—bienes que se retienen en almacenaje transitorio. |
| **Investment**—business spending on physical capital, new homes, and inventories. | **Inversión**—gastos empresariales en capital físico, casas nuevas e inventarios. |

### J

| | |
|---|---|
| **Junk bond**—a high-risk, high-interest-rate corporate bond. | **Bono chatarra**—bono corporativo de gran riesgo que reditúa una tasa de interés alta. |

### K

| | |
|---|---|
| **Keynesian economics**—the school of economic thought, named after British economist John Maynard Keynes, that advocates fiscal policy to mend problems with the economy. | **Economía keysiana**—la escuela de pensamiento económica designada con el nombre del economista británico John Maynard Keynes. Propone el uso de políticas fiscales para resolver problemas de la economía. |

### L

| | |
|---|---|
| **Labor**—the time and effort people contribute to the production process. | **Mano de obra**—tiempo y esfuerzo que las personas aportan al proceso de producción. |
| **Labor force**—the combination of the employed workers and the unemployed workers, excluding those in the military or in prison. | **Fuerza laboral**—combinación de los trabajadores empleados y los trabajadores desempleados, con la exclusión de aquéllos que se encuentran en las fuerzas armadas o en la cárcel. |
| **Labor union**—a group of workers who bargain collectively with employers over the terms and conditions of employment. | **Sindicato laboral**—grupo de trabajadores que negocian de manera colectiva con sus empleadores los términos y condiciones de su empleo. |
| **Land**—anything drawn from nature for use in the production of goods or services. | **Tierra**—todo lo que se toma de la naturaleza y se usa para la producción de bienes y servicios. |
| **Law of demand**—the tendency for the price and the quantity demanded to move in opposite directions. | **Ley de demanda**—la tendencia que tienen el precio y la cantidad demandada de desplazarse en sentidos opuestos. |
| **Law of diminishing returns**—there is a general tendency for output to increase at a decreasing rate when additional amounts of an input are used in production, holding the amount of other inputs constant. | **Ley de rendimientos decrecientes**—existe una tendencia general en la que la producción aumenta a un ritmo que se va reduciendo cuando en dicha producción se usan cantidades adicionales de un insumo mientras que la cantidad de los demás insumos permanece constante. |
| **Law of increasing opportunity cost**—states that the opportunity cost of a good rises as more of the good is produced. | **Ley del costo de oportunidad creciente**—declara que el costo de oportunidad de un bien aumenta en la medida en que se produce más de ese bien. |
| **Law of supply**—an increase in the price of a good leads to an increase in the quantity supplied. | **Ley de la oferta**—un aumento en el precio de un bien conlleva un aumento en la cantidad que se oferta. |

| | |
|---|---|
| **Law of unintended consequences**—intervention in a complex system can have surprising and undesirable consequences. | **Ley de las consecuencias imprevistas**—la intervención en un sistema complejo puede causar consecuencias sorpresivas e indeseadas. |
| **Life-cycle approach**—the approach of making riskier investments with higher expected returns early in life and then turning to safer investments with lower returns later in life. | **Enfoque del ciclo de vida**—enfoque según el cual se hacen inversiones más arriesgadas previéndose rendimientos más altos al inicio de la vida y luego se hacen inversiones más seguras con rendimiento más bajos más adelante en la vida de una persona. |
| **Limited liability company (LLC)**—a hybrid business organization that combines features of corporations, partnerships, and sole proprietorships. | **Empresa de responsabilidad limitada**—entidad empresarial híbrida que combina las características de las corporaciones (o sociedades anónimas), las sociedades y las empresas unipersonales. |
| **Literacy rate**—the percentage of people over 15 years of age who can read and write. | **Tasa de alfabetismo**—porcentaje de personas mayores de 15 años de edad que saben leer y escribir. |
| **Logroll**—to work toward the passage of legislation by trading votes with other legislators. | **Reciprocidad de votos**—trabajar hacia la aprobación de proyectos de ley mediante el intercambio de votos con otros legisladores. |
| **Long run**—the period of time in which the quantities of all inputs are variable. | **Largo plazo**—el lapso de tiempo en el que las cantidades de todos los insumos son variables. |

**M**

| | |
|---|---|
| **M1**—a measure of the money supply that includes only the forms of money that are readily available to spend: cash, checking account deposits, and traveler's checks. | **M1**—medida de la oferta de dinero que incluye sólo las formas de dinero que están fácilmente disponibles para utilizar: dinero en efectivo, sumas depositadas en cuentas de cheques y cheques de viajeros. |
| **M2**—a measure of the money supply that includes M1 along with forms of money that are less easily converted to cash. | **M2**—medida de la oferta de dinero que incluye las formas de M1 más las formas de dinero que se convierten fácilmente en dinero en efectivo. |
| **Macroeconomic equilibrium**—when aggregate supply equals aggregate demand. | **Equilibrio macroeconómico**—cuando la oferta agregada es equivalente a la demanda agregada. |
| **Macroeconomics**—the study of the economy as a whole. | **Macroeconomía**—estudio de la economía en su integridad. |
| **Managed floating exchange rate**—a currency exchange rate determined by supply and demand with occasional central bank intervention. | **Tipo de cambio flotante administrado**—tipo de cambio de monedas corrientes que se determina mediante la oferta y la demanda con una intervención ocasional del banco central. |
| **Mandatory spending**—spending that is required by existing law. | **Erogación obligatoria**—gastos que por ley se tienen que hacer. |
| **Marginal benefit**—the additional benefit of doing something one more time. | **Beneficio marginal**—el beneficio adicional que se logra al hacer algo una vez más. |
| **Marginal cost**—the additional cost of doing something one more time. | **Costo marginal**—el costo adicional que se paga al hacer algo una vez más. |
| **Marginal product of labor**—the amount by which total output increases when one more worker is hired. | **Producto marginal de la mano de obra**—la cantidad mediante la cual la producción total aumenta cuando se contrata a un trabajador más. |
| **Marginal revenue**—the additional revenue a firm receives from selling another unit of output. | **Rentas marginales**—las rentas adicionales que percibe una empresa al vender otra unidad de producción. |
| **Marginal tax rate**—the portion of an additional dollar of income that is paid in taxes. | **Gravamen marginal**—la parte de un dólar adicional en ingresos que se paga en impuestos. |
| **Market**—a collection of buyers and sellers, wherever they may be. | **Mercado**—colección de compradores y vendedores, dondequiera que se encuentren. |
| **Market demand curve**—a graphical representation of how the quantity demanded by all consumers in the market varies with the price. | **Curva de la demanda del mercado**—representación gráfica de cómo la cantidad demandada por todos los consumidores en el mercado varía con el precio. |
| **Market demand curve for labor**—shows the total quantity of labor that employers would hire at each wage. | **Curva de la demanda del mercado por mano de obra**—curva en la que se aprecia la cantidad total de mano de obra que los empleadores contratarían a cada nivel salarial. |

| | |
|---|---|
| **Market economy**—an economic system in which most key economic decisions are made by business owners and consumers. | **Economía de mercado**—sistema económico en el que la mayoría de las decisiones económicas importantes las hacen los propietarios de negocios y los consumidores. |
| **Market failure**—the inability of a market to achieve an efficient outcome without government intervention. | **Fracaso del mercado**—la incapacidad del mercado de lograr un resultado eficiente sin contar con la intervención del gobierno. |
| **Market labor supply curve**—shows the total number of hours workers would be willing to supply at each wage. | **Curva de la oferta de mano de obra en el mercado**—curva en la que se aprecia el número total de horas que los trabajadores estarían dispuestos a trabajar a cada nivel salarial. |
| **Market power**—the ability of a firm to change the market price of a good or service. | **Poder del mercado**—la capacidad de una empresa de cambiar el precio que se paga en el mercado por un bien o servicio. |
| **Market structure**—the nature of competition within a market. | **Estructura del mercado**—la naturaleza de la competencia dentro de un mercado. |
| **Market supply curve**—a graphical representation of the quantity supplied by all firms in the market at various prices. | **Curva de oferta en el mercado**—representación gráfica de la cantidad ofertada por todas las empresas en el mercado a precios diversos. |
| **Means-tested programs**—programs for which eligibility depends on the prospective recipients' income. | **Programas que exigen una evaluación financiera**—programas para los cuales el derecho a participar depende de los ingresos de los posibles beneficiarios. |
| **Medium of exchange**—something people acquire for the purpose of payment for goods and services. | **Medio de intercambio**—algo que las personas adquieren con el fin de pagar por bienes y servicios. |
| **Member banks of the Federal Reserve**—banks that are stockholders in their district Federal Reserve bank and help elect the district's board of directors. | **Bancos afiliados a la Reserva Federal**—bancos que son accionistas en su distrito del banco de la Reserva Federal y que ayudan a elegir la junta directiva del distrito. |
| **Menu costs**—the costs of changing prices due to inflation. | **Costos de menú**—los costos de los precios que cambian debido a la inflación. |
| **Merger**—the joining of two firms to form a single, larger firm. | **Fusión**—la unión de dos empresas para formar una sola empresa, de mayor envergadura. |
| **Microeconomics**—the study of how people make decisions and how those decisions affect others in the economy. | **Microeconomía**—estudio de cómo las personas toman decisiones y de cómo tales decisiones afectan a otros en la economía. |
| **Microfinance (microcredit)**—the provision of small loans to help low-income people start businesses and provide for themselves. | **Microfinanzas (microcrédito)**—el otorgamiento de préstamos de menor cuantía que ayudan a personas de bajos ingresos a comenzar un negocio y lograr la independencia económica. |
| **Minimum wage**—a price floor for labor that is set by the government, below which wages are not allowed to fall. | **Salario mínimo**—precio base que se paga por la mano de obra y que es fijado por el gobierno. El salario no puede caer por debajo de dicho nivel. |
| **Mixed economy**—a market economy with significant government involvement and elements of a traditional economy. | **Economía mixta**—economía de mercado con participación significativa del gobierno y con elementos de una economía tradicional. |
| **Model**—a simplified representation of reality. Models help you focus on a few aspects of the real world by stripping away nonessential details. | **Modelo**—representación simplificada de la realidad. Los modelos ayudan a enfocarse en unos pocos aspectos de la vida real al retirar del panorama detalles que no son esenciales. |
| **Monetary policy**—actions taken by the central bank to manage interest rates and the money supply in pursuit of macroeconomic goals. | **Política monetaria**—medidas que toma el banco central a fin de administrar las tasas de interés y la oferta de dinero con miras a lograr metas macroeconómicas. |
| **Monetizing the debt**—the practice of the Federal Reserve creating new money to purchase securities. | **Monetización de la deuda**—la práctica que tiene la Reserva Federal de crear dinero nuevo para comprar títulos valores. |
| **Money**—anything that is widely accepted in exchange for goods and services. | **Dinero**—todo lo que se acepte ampliamente a cambio de bienes y servicios. |

| | |
|---|---|
| **Money factor or lease rate**—a payment similar to an interest rate paid while leasing a car. To approximate the equivalent annual interest rate, multiply the money factor by 2,400. | **Factor dinero o tasa de alquiler**—pago similar al de la tasa de interés que se paga cuando se alquila un vehículo a largo plazo. Para aproximar la tasa de interés anual equivalente, multiplique el factor dinero por 2,400. |
| **Money market**—a market in which money is lent for less than a year. | **Mercado monetario**—mercado en el que el dinero se presta por un plazo de menos de un año. |
| **Money supply**—the amount of money available for the purchase of goods and services. | **Dinero en circulación**—la cantidad de dinero disponible para la compra de bienes y servicios. |
| **Money-market fund**—a mutual fund made up entirely of money-market instruments. | **Fondo del mercado monetario**—fondo mutuo compuesto en su totalidad por instrumentos del mercado monetario. |
| **Monopolist**—the one supplier in a monopoly. | **Monopolista**—el proveedor único en un monopolio. |
| **Monopolistic competition**—a market in which many firms supply similar but not identical goods. | **Competencia monopolística**—mercado en el que muchas empresas abastecen bienes parecidos pero no idénticos. |
| **Monopoly**—a product market served by only one firm. | **Monopolio**—mercado de productos abastecido por una sola empresa. |
| **Multinational corporation**—a company that operates in more than one country. | **Corporación multinacional**—empresa que funciona en más de un país. |
| **Mutual fund**—a collection of investments, such as stocks, bonds, or money-market instruments, selected by a fund manager in accordance with the goals of the particular fund. | **Fondo mutuo**—colección de inversiones, por ejemplo acciones, bonos o instrumentos del mercado monetario, escogidos por un gerente de fondo según los objetivos de ese fondo. |

**N**

| | |
|---|---|
| **National debt**—the amount of money that the federal government has borrowed over time to fund annual budget deficits and has not yet repaid. | **Deuda nacional**—la cantidad de dinero que con el tiempo el gobierno federal ha tomado en préstamo para financiar el déficit presupuestario anual y que todavía no se ha reembolsado. |
| **Natural monopoly**—a market in which high start-up costs make it prohibitively expensive for more than one firm to operate. | **Monopolio natural**—mercado en el que debido a las enormes inversiones iniciales se torna prohibitivamente costoso el funcionamiento de más de una empresa. |
| **Natural rate of unemployment**—the unemployment rate in the absence of cyclical unemployment, around which the actual unemployment rate fluctuates. | **Tasa natural de desempleo**—la tasa de desempleo vista en ausencia del desempleo cíclico, alrededor de la cual fluctúa la tasa de desempleo real. |
| **Needs**—minimal requirements of things such as food, water, and shelter that are necessary for survival. | **Necesidades**—requisitos mínimos de cosas tales como alimentos, agua y vivienda que se necesitan para sobrevivir. |
| **Net benefit**—the benefit of a choice (measured in dollars) minus the cost of the choice. | **Beneficio neto**—el beneficio de una opción (medida en dólares) menos el costo de la opción. |
| **Net income**—the income that you are left with after paying taxes. | **Ingreso neto**—el ingreso que queda disponible después del pago de impuestos. |
| **Newly industrialized country (NIC)**—a country with a rapidly developing capacity for production. | **País recién industrializado**—país con una capacidad de producción en evolución rápida. |
| **Nominal GDP**—values each good at the dollar price it actually sold for in the year in which it was produced. | **PIB Nominal**—valora cada bien al precio en dólares por el cual se vendió en el año en que se produjo. |
| **Nominal interest rate**—the actual rate of interest that a saver will receive and a borrower will pay. | **Tasa de interés nominal**—la tasa de interés real que un ahorrador recibe y que un prestatario paga. |
| **Nongovernmental organization (NGO)**—a private, nonprofit organization established for charitable purposes, such as to provide assistance to developing countries. | **Organización no gubernamental (ONG)**—entidad privada sin fines de lucro, establecida con objetivos de beneficencia, tales como ofrecer asistencia a países en vías de desarrollo. |
| **Nonprofit organization**—a legal entity formed to carry out a "not-for-profit" mission. | **Entidad sin fines de lucro**—entidad jurídica formada para llevar a cabo una misión "que no genere utilidades". |
| **Normal good**—a good for which the demand rises when income rises and falls when income falls. | **Bien normal**—bien para el cual la demanda aumenta cuando los ingresos aumentan y cae cuando los ingresos caen. |

| | |
|---|---|
| **Normative economics**—the study of the way things should be, rather than the way things are. | **Economía normativa**—el estudio de la manera cómo las cosas deben ser en lugar de cómo las cosas son. |

## O

| | |
|---|---|
| **Offshoring**—the relocation of some or all of a firm's operations to another country. | **Extranjerización**—la reubicación de alguna parte o la totalidad de las operaciones de la empresa en otro país. |
| **Oligopolist**—a firm in an oligopoly. | **Oligopolista**—una empresa que existe en un mercado oligopolio. |
| **Oligopoly**—a market with a small number of firms. | **Oligopolio**—mercado con una cantidad pequeña de empresas. |
| **Opportunity cost**—the value of the next-best alternative given up when a choice is made. | **Costo de oportunidad**—el valor de la mejor alternativa que se pasa por alto cuando se escoge una opción. |
| **Outside lag**—the time between a policy action and the resulting effect on the economy. | **Demora externa**—el tiempo entre implantar una medida por política interna y el efecto que resulta en la economía. |
| **Outsource**—to contract with foreign firms to produce goods that will be sold by the domestic firm. | **Tercerizar**—contratar empresas extranjeras para que produzcan bienes que la empresa nacional venderá. |

## P

| | |
|---|---|
| **Partnership**—a for-profit business firm owned by two or more people, called partners, each of whom has a financial interest in the business. | **Sociedad**—empresa comercial con fines de lucro que es propiedad de dos o más personas, denominados socios, cada uno de los cuales tiene un interés económico en las actividades de la empresa. |
| **Passbook savings account**—a savings account that typically has a low or zero minimum balance requirement, pays a relatively low interest rate, and offers easy access to funds. | **Cuenta de ahorros con libreta**—cuenta de ahorros que característicamente tiene un requisito de saldo mínimo muy bajo o de cero, que paga una tasa de interés relativamente baja y que ofrece fácil acceso a los fondos. |
| **Passive investing**—the strategy of duplicating the components of a benchmark index, such as the Dow Jones Industrial Average, and then receiving the same returns as the index (less some minimal expenses). | **Inversiones pasivas**—la estrategia de ajustarse a los componentes de un índice de referencia, tal como el Promedio Industrial Dow Jones, y luego recibir el mismo rendimiento del índice (menos algunos gastos mínimos). |
| **Payroll tax**—a tax collected from employers on the basis of the wages and salaries paid to workers. | **Impuesto sobre la nómina**—impuesto que se les cobra a los empleadores con base en los sueldos y salarios que paga a los trabajadores. |
| **Perfect competition**—the market condition in which there are many firms selling identical goods, firms are free to enter and exit the market, and consumers have full information about the price and availability of goods. | **Competencia perfecta**—condición del mercado en la que hay muchas empresas que venden productos idénticos, en la que las empresas pueden ingresar y salir del mercado libremente, y en la que los consumidores cuentan con toda la información sobre el precio y sobre la disponibilidad de bienes. |
| **Physical capital**—any long-lasting good that is used to make other goods or services. | **Capital físico**—todo bien de larga duración que se utilice para elaborar otros bienes y servicios. |
| **Positive economics**—the study of what the world is like and why it works the way it does. | **Economía positiva**—el estudio de cómo es el mundo y porqué funciona tal como funciona. |
| **Potential output**—the level of real GDP that is produced when there is full employment. | **Producción posible**—el nivel del PIB real que se produce cuando hay empleo total. |
| **Price ceiling**—a government-imposed limit on the highest price firms can charge in a market. | **Precio tope**—límite que ha impuesto el gobierno respecto al precio máximo que las empresas pueden cobrar en el mercado. |
| **Price controls**—policies by which the government sets the prices in an industry. | **Control de precios**—políticas oficiales mediante las cuales el gobierno fija los precios en una industria. |
| **Price discrimination**—the practice of charging different customers different prices for the same good. | **Discriminación por precio**—la práctica de cobrar precios diferentes a clientes diferentes por el mismo bien. |
| **Price floor**—a government-imposed limit below which prices cannot fall. | **Precio base**—límite que ha impuesto el gobierno, por debajo del cual no pueden caer los precios. |

| | |
|---|---|
| **Primary market**—a market in which new assets such as stocks and bonds are sold by their issuers. | **Mercado primario**—mercado en el que los nuevos activos, por ejemplo, las acciones y los bonos, son vendidos por sus emisores. |
| **Primitive equilibrium**—the initial stage of economic development in which there are no formal markets and decisions are based on tradition. | **Equilibrio primitivo**—la etapa inicial del desarrollo económico en la que no hay mercados formales y las decisiones se basan en la tradición. |
| **Principal**—the amount of a deposit or, in the case of a loan, the amount of the loan before any interest is paid. | **Capital**—la cantidad de un depósito o, si se trata de un préstamo, el monto del mismo, antes de que se pague ningún interés. |
| **Principal protection**—assures that every dollar put in will be available to take out. | **Protección del capital**—asegura que todo dólar que se invierta se pueda extraer. |
| **Private good**—a good that can be used by only one person at a time. | **Bien privado**—bien que puede ser aprovechado por una sola persona a la vez. |
| **Product market**—a market for a good that includes all those products that consumers consider to be close substitutes for that good. | **Mercado de productos**—mercado de un bien que incluye todos aquellos productos que los consumidores consideran sustitutos para aquel bien. |
| **Product markets**—where goods and services are exchanged for money. | **Mercados de productos**—mercados en los que los bienes y productos se intercambian por dinero. |
| **Production possibilities frontier (PPF)**—a curve that shows the maximum quantity of one good that can be produced for each possible quantity of another good produced. | **Frontera de posibilidades de producción**—curva en la que se aprecia la cantidad máxima de un bien que puede ser producido en relación con cada cantidad de otro bien producido. |
| **Productivity**—the amount of output the average worker can produce in an hour. | **Productividad**—la cantidad de producción que el trabajador promedio puede producir en una hora. |
| **Profit**—the total revenue a firm receives from selling its product minus the total cost of producing it. | **Utilidades**—el total de rentas que recibe una empresa gracias a la venta de su producto menos el costo total de producirlo. |
| **Profit-maximizing output level**—the amount of output that gives a firm as much profit as possible. | **Nivel de producción que maximiza las utilidades**—la cantidad de producción que le ofrece a la empresa el máximo en utilidades posibles. |
| **Progressive tax**—people with a higher income pay a higher share of their income in taxes. | **Impuesto progresivo**—las personas que tienen mayores ingresos pagan una mayor proporción de sus ingresos en impuestos. |
| **Property right**—a legal claim of ownership. | **Derecho de propiedad**—derecho legítimo a la propiedad. |
| **Property tax**—a required payment made by the owners of property, such as land, buildings, boats, and cars. | **Impuesto catastral**—pago requerido que hacen los dueños de propiedades tales como bienes raíces, edificaciones, barcos y vehículos. |
| **Proportional tax**—everyone pays the same share of their income in taxes, regardless of their level of income. | **Impuesto proporcional**—todos pagan la misma proporción de sus ingresos en impuestos, independientemente de su nivel de ingresos. |
| **Protectionism**—the practice of limiting foreign trade. | **Proteccionismo**—práctica de limitar el comercio con el extranjero. |
| **Protective tariff**—a tariff that is meant to protect domestic industries from foreign competition. | **Arancel protector**—un arancel que tiene por fin proteger las industrias nacionales de la competencia del extranjero. |
| **Public debt**—the money owed to investors by the federal government. | **Deuda pública**—el dinero debido a inversionistas por el gobierno federal. |
| **Public good**—a good or service that can be consumed by many people at once and that other people can't be prevented from using. | **Bien público**—bien o servicio que puede ser aprovechado por muchas personas a la vez y que otras personas no pueden impedir que sea aprovechado. |
| **Public good**—a nonrival and nonexcludable good | **Bien público**—un bien no excluible y sin rivales. |

### Q

| | |
|---|---|
| **Quality of life**—the level of satisfaction gained both from goods and services and from nonmaterial sources of satisfaction, such as leisure time, cultural activities, and personal safety. | **Calidad de vida**—el nivel de satisfacción logrado tanto gracias a los bienes y servicios como gracias a las fuentes de satisfacción no materiales, tales como el tiempo de asueto, las actividades culturales y la seguridad personal. |

| | |
|---|---|
| **Quantity demanded**—the amount of a good that consumers are willing and able to purchase at a particular price within a given period of time. | **Cantidad demandada**—la cantidad de un bien que los consumidores están listos y dispuestos a comprar a un precio dado dentro de un lapso de tiempo definido. |
| **Quantity supplied**—the amount of a good that firms are willing to supply at a particular price over a given period of time. | **Cantidad ofertada**—la cantidad de un bien que las empresas están dispuestas a ofertar a un precio dado dentro de un lapso de tiempo definido. |
| **Quota**—a limit on the amount of a good that can be imported. | **Límite**—límite de la cantidad de un bien que se puede importar. |

**R**

| | |
|---|---|
| **Ration**—to provide each person with a fixed quantity. | **Racionar**—suministrarle a cada persona una cantidad fija. |
| **Rational decision**—a decision that benefits the decision maker as much as possible. | **Decisión racional**—decisión que beneficia al máximo posible a quien toma la decisión. |
| **Rationing**—the placement of limits on the amount of goods each person can purchase. | **Racionamiento**—la colocación de límites en la cantidad de bienes que cada persona puede comprar. |
| **Real GDP**—measures total production in dollars after removing the distorting effect of price changes. | **PIB real**—mide la producción total en dólares luego de retirar el efecto distorsionador de los cambios de precio. |
| **Real GDP per capita**—output per person, calculated as real GDP divided by the total population. | **PIB real per capita**—producción por persona, calculada al dividir el PIB real entre la cantidad total de habitantes. |
| **Real interest rate**—the nominal interest rate minus the expected rate of inflation. | **Tasa de interés real**—la tasa de interés nominal menos la tasa de inflación prevista. |
| **Recession**—a contraction severe enough to last several months or longer and have widespread effects on production, real income, employment, and sales across the economy. | **Recesión**—contracción de suficiente gravedad que dura varios meses o más y que tiene efectos generalizados en la producción, en los ingresos reales, en el nivel de empleo y en las ventas, impactando toda la economía. |
| **Recognition lag**—the time it takes economists and government officials to realize that the economy is experiencing a problem. | **Demora en el reconocimiento**—el tiempo que les toma a los economistas y funcionarios del gobierno reconocer que la economía está experimentando un problema. |
| **Regressive tax**—people with a higher income pay a lower share of their income in taxes. | **Impuesto regresivo**—las personas que perciben ingresos más altos pagan una menor proporción de sus ingresos en impuestos. |
| **Regulatory capture**—the control of a regulatory agency by the industry it is supposed to regulate. | **Captura reglamentaria**—la industria que una dependencia oficial debe reglamentar controla la dependencia. |
| **Rent seeking**—the pursuit of profit by shifting existing gains rather than by creating new gains for society. | **Manipulación de rentas**—lograr utilidades mediante la manipulación de la riqueza existente en lugar de crear ganancias nuevas para la sociedad. |
| **Representative money**—money that has no value of its own but can be exchanged for something of value. | **Dinero representativo**—dinero que no tiene un valor intrínseco pero que se puede intercambiar por algo de valor. |
| **Research and development**—activities firms conduct to discover or improve products or procedures. | **Investigación y desarrollo**—actividades que realizan las empresas con miras a descubrir mejoras o a mejorar sus productos o procedimientos. |
| **Reservation price**—the highest price a consumer is willing to pay to own one more unit of a product. | **Precio de reserva**—el precio más alto que el consumidor está dispuesto a pagar para ser propietario una unidad de producto más. |
| **Reservation wage**—the lowest wage for which a worker would accept a job. | **Salario de reserva**—el salario más bajo por el cual un trabajador aceptaría un empleo. |
| **Reserve requirement**—the percentage of deposits that banks must hold as reserves. | **Requisito de reserva**—el porcentaje de los depósitos que los bancos tienen que retener como reservas. |
| **Residual value**—the value assigned to a car at the end of its lease period. | **Valor residual**—el valor que se le ha asignado a un vehículo al concluir su período de alquiler a largo plazo. |
| **Resources**—the basic elements from which all goods and services are produced. | **Recursos**—los elementos básicos a partir de los cuales se producen todos los bienes y servicios. |

**Resume**—a brief document that summarizes your education, work experience, and skills. | **Hoja de vida**—documento en el que se resumen la experiencia laboral y las destrezas de la persona.

**Retaliatory tariff**—a tariff imposed to punish the trading partner's trade policy. | **Arancel de represalia**—arancel impuesto para castigar la política comercial de alguien con quien se comercia.

**Revenue tariff**—a tariff imposed to generate revenue for the government without necessarily limiting imports or helping U.S. producers. | **Arancel de rentas**—arancel que se impone para generarle rentas al gobierno sin pensar en limitar las importaciones ni en ayudar a los productores estadounidenses.

**Risk tolerance**—the ability to accept and absorb losses. | **Tolerancia a los riesgos**—la capacidad de aceptar y absorber pérdidas.

**Rival**—one person's consumption of the good makes it impossible for others to consume it. | **Rival**—debido a que una persona consume el bien, se les imposibilita a otros consumirlo.

**Rule of law**—the principle that no person is above the law. | **Imperio de la ley**—el principio que manifiesta que ninguna persona está exenta del cumplimiento de la ley.

## S

**Sales tax**—a payment collected from consumers by firms when a taxed good or service is purchased and then passed on to the government. | **Impuesto sobre las ventas**—pago que las empresas les cobran a los consumidores cuando compran un bien o servicio gravable. Dicha suma se le transfiere al gobierno.

**Savings and loan associations (S&Ls)**—depository institutions, similar to savings banks, that specialize in loans for the purchase of homes. | **Cajas de ahorro y crédito**—instituciones depositarias parecidas a los bancos de ahorro, que se especializan en préstamos para la compra de hogares.

**Savings bank**—a depository institution that specializes in loans for the purchase of homes and other real estate. | **Caja de ahorros**—institución depositaria que se especializa en préstamos para la compra de hogares y otros bienes inmuebles.

**Scarcity**—the lack of a sufficient supply to meet all desires. | **Escasez**—la carencia de suficiente abastecimiento para satisfacer todos los deseos.

**Seasonal unemployment**—a loss of jobs due to a change of seasons. | **Desempleo por temporada**—la pérdida de empleos debido al cambio de temporada o estación del año.

**Secondary market**—a market in which investors buy and sell financial assets that have already been purchased at least once. | **Mercado secundario**—mercado en el que los inversionistas compran y venden activos financieros que ya han sido comprados por lo menos en una ocasión anterior.

**Self-interested**—a term used to describe an individual who makes decisions for his or her own benefit. | **Interés propio**—vocablos que se usan para describir a una persona que toma decisiones para su beneficio propio.

**Semidevelopment**—the stage of economic development in which industries expand and sophisticated technology is widely adopted. | **Semidesarrollo**—etapa en el desarrollo económico en la que las industrias se amplían y adoptan de manera generalizada tecnologías avanzadas.

**Services**—activities produced in an economy, such as education, entertainment, and health care. | **Servicios**—actividades producidas en una economía, tales como la educación, las diversiones y la atención de la salud.

**Servicing the debt**—payment of interest on the national debt. | **Servicio de la deuda**—pago de los intereses debidos por la deuda nacional.

**Shift of the demand curve**—a change in the amount people are willing and able to buy at every price. | **Desplazamiento de la curva de la demanda**—cambio en la cantidad que las personas están dispuestas y listas a comprar a diferentes precios.

**Shift of the supply curve**—the result of a change in the quantity supplied at every price, not to be confused with a movement along the supply curve, which is the result of a change in the price. | **Desplazamiento de la curva de la oferta**—el resultado de un cambio en la cantidad ofertada a cada precio, que no se debe confundir con un desplazamiento a lo largo de la curva de la oferta, el cual es el resultado de un cambio en el precio.

**Shoe leather costs**—the costs of time and effort involved in frequent trips to the bank or ATM to avoid holding much cash during periods of high inflation. | **Costos de transacciones**—los costos del tiempo y el esfuerzo que implican viajes frecuentes al banco o al cajero automático a fin de evitar retener mucho efectivo durante períodos de inflación alta.

| | |
|---|---|
| **Short run**—the period of time during which the quantity of at least one input is fixed. | **Corto plazo**—el lapso de tiempo durante el cual la cantidad de por lo menos un insumo es una cantidad fija. |
| **Shortage**—when an excess demand for a product persists for a significant period of time. | **Insuficiencia**—cuando un exceso de la demanda por un producto persiste por un período de tiempo significativo. |
| **Short-termism**—a tendency to place too much weight on immediate benefits and not enough weight on longer-term benefits and costs. | **Cortoplazismo**—tendencia a sopesar demasiado los beneficios inmediatos y no darle mayor importancia a los beneficios y los costos que se obtienen en el largo plazo. |
| **Sin taxes**—taxes imposed to discourage undesired behavior, such as the use of tobacco products. | **Impuestos por vicios**—Los impuestos por vicios desaniman las conductas indeseadas, como por ejemplo la práctica del tabaquismo. |
| **Social safety net**—any form of government assistance for those with financial needs. | **Red de seguridad social**—cualquier forma de asistencia gubernamental para aquellos que sufren necesidades económicas. |
| **Socialism**—an economic system under which most resources and businesses are publicly owned and economic decisions are made by groups of workers and consumers. | **Socialismo**—sistema económico según el cual la mayoría de los recursos y negocios son de dominio público y las decisiones económicas las toman grupos de trabajadores y consumidores. |
| **Society**—a collection of people who share a common bond, such as those living in a city, a country, or even the entire world. | **Sociedad**—colección de personas que comparten un vínculo común, como por ejemplo los que residen en una ciudad, un país o hasta en el mundo entero. |
| **Sole proprietorship**—a business firm owned by one person, the proprietor. | **Empresa unipersonal**—empresa comercial que es propiedad de una persona, el dueño. |
| **Specialization**—the production of a disproportionate amount of a particular good for consumption and trade. | **Especialización**—la producción de una cantidad desproporcionada de un bien concreto para consumirlo o comerciarlo. |
| **Stagflation**—a combination of unemployment and sluggish economic growth, high inflation, and high unemployment. | **Estanflación**—combinación de un crecimiento económico lento, con inflación alta, y desempleo alto. |
| **Standard of living**—the level of material wealth as measured by the availability of goods and services. | **Estándar de vida**—nivel de riqueza material medida según la disponibilidad de bienes y servicios. |
| **Status quo bias**—the tendency to keep things the way they are. | **Sesgo del estatu quo**—tendencia de mantener las cosas tal como están. |
| **Sticky prices**—prices that move to their equilibrium values very slowly. | **Precios resistentes al cambio**—precios que se desplazan hacia sus valores de equilibrio muy lentamente. |
| **Stock**—represents partial ownership of a company. | **Acciones**—representan propiedad parcial de una empresa. |
| **Store of value**—something that can be saved and will hold its value relatively well over time. | **Valor en almacenaje**—algo que se puede guardar y que retendrá su valor relativamente bien en el tiempo. |
| **Strong dollar**—This describes the U.S. dollar when it will purchase a relatively large amount of foreign currency due to the current exchange rate. | **Dólar fuerte**—descripción del dólar estadounidense cuando puede comprar una cantidad relativamente grande de divisas debido al tipo de cambio vigente. |
| **Structural unemployment**—a mismatch between job seekers and the types of jobs available. | **Desempleo estructural**—desajuste entre las personas que buscan empleo y los tipos de empleo que hay disponibles. |
| **Subsistence farming**—farming that produces enough food for the farming families' consumption but not enough to sell in the market. | **Agricultura de subsistencia**—actividad agrícola que produce suficiente alimento para satisfacer el consumo de las familias de los agricultores pero no suficiente para vender en el mercado. |
| **Substitutes**—two goods for which an increase in the price of one of the goods leads to an increase in the demand for the other. | **Sustitutos**—dos bienes para los cuales un aumento en el precio de uno de los bienes conlleva un aumento en la demanda por el otro. |
| **Substitution effect**—the change in consumption that arises when an increase in the price of a good causes a consumer to switch away from that good and toward other goods that do not experience a price increase. Likewise, a decrease in the price of a good causes consumers to switch toward that good. | **Efecto de sustitución**—cambio en el consumo que surge cuando un aumento en el precio de un bien obliga al consumidor a alejarse de ese bien y acercarse a otros bienes que no experimentan un aumento del precio. Igualmente, una disminución en el precio de un bien obliga a los consumidores a pasarse a ese bien. |

| | |
|---|---|
| **Sunk costs**—costs that have been paid and cannot be recovered. | **Costos hundidos**—costos que se han pagado y que no se pueden recuperar. |
| **Supply curve**—a graphical representation of the supply schedule, showing the quantity a firm will supply at each price. | **Curva de la oferta**—representación gráfica de la relación de la oferta, en la que se aprecia la cantidad que una empresa puede abastecer a cada nivel de precio. |
| **Supply schedule**—a table listing the quantity of a good that will be supplied at specified prices. | **Relación de la oferta**—tabla en la que se relaciona la cantidad de un bien que se ofrecerá a precios especificados. |
| **Supply-side policy**—policy meant to stimulate the economy by increasing aggregate supply. | **Política que estimula la oferta**—política que tiene por objeto estimular la economía mediante el aumento de la oferta agregada. |
| **Surplus**—when an excess supply of a product persists for a significant period of time. | **Superávit**—cuando un exceso de la oferta de un producto persiste por un lapso de tiempo significativo. |
| **Sustainability**—the ability to continue actions indefinitely. | **Sostenibilidad**—la capacidad de continuar las acciones indefinidamente. |

## T

| | |
|---|---|
| **Takeoff**—the stage of economic development in which new industries are formed and profits are reinvested in physical capital to fuel economic growth. | **Despegue**—la etapa del desarrollo económico en la que se forman industrias nuevas y las utilidades se reinvierten en capital físico a fin de estimular el crecimiento económico. |
| **tariff (or duty)**—a tax on imports. | **arancel**—impuesto sobre las importaciones. |
| **Tax base**—the value of taxed assets, or of economic activity subject to a particular type of tax. | **Base imponible**—el valor de los activos gravados o el valor de la actividad económica sujeta a un impuesto específico. |
| **Tax rate**—a specific percentage of the tax base that is paid in taxes. | **Gravamen**—porcentaje específico de la base imponible que se paga en impuestos. |
| **Tax return**—a form you will complete and submit to the government when you pay your income taxes. It contains the information used to determine the amount of taxes you owe. | **Declaración de renta**—formulario que se completa y se le entrega al gobierno cuando se pagan los impuestos sobre la renta (o ingresos). Contiene la información que se usa para determinar la cantidad de impuestos que debe pagar cada cual. |
| **Taxes**—required payments to the government. | **Impuestos**—pagos al gobierno que se le exigen al contribuyente. |
| **Thrift**—a depository institution established to encourage saving and can be a savings and loan association, a credit union, or a savings bank. | **Institución de ahorros**—institución depositaria establecida para fomentar los ahorros. Puede ser una caja de ahorros y préstamos, una cooperativa de crédito o un banco de ahorros. |
| **Tight money policy**—policy that decreases the money supply. | **Política monetaria apretada**—política mediante la cual se disminuye el dinero en circulación. |
| **Total cost**—fixed cost plus variable cost. | **Costo total**—los costos fijos más los costos variables. |
| **Total employment**—the total number of employed workers in an economy, whether they work part time or full time. | **Empleo total**—el número total de trabajadores empleados en una economía, sean empleos de dedicación total o dedicación parcial. |
| **Total revenue**—all the money consumers spend on a good, and firms receive for a good, during a particular period of time: it is the price of the good multiplied by the quantity of the good sold. | **Rentas totales**—todo el dinero que los consumidores usan en un bien y que las empresas reciben por un bien, durante un período definido de tiempo: el precio del bien multiplicado por la cantidad del bien que se vendió. |
| **Total unemployment**—the number of workers in an economy who are actively seeking jobs but not actually working. | **Desempleo total**—el número de trabajadores en una economía que activamente están buscando empleo pero que no están trabajando. |
| **Tradable emission permits**—permits that convey the right to emit a certain amount of pollution. The permits can be sold by one firm to another. | **Permisos de emisión comerciables**—permisos que otorgan el derecho de emitir cierta cantidad de contaminación. Los permisos pueden ser vendidos por una empresa a otra. |
| **Trade deficit**—the amount by which expenditures on imports exceed receipts from exports. | **Déficit comercial**—la cantidad por la cual lo que se paga por las importaciones es mayor que lo que se recibe por las exportaciones. |

| | |
|---|---|
| **Trade surplus**—the amount by which receipts from exports exceed expenditures on imports. | **Superávit comercial**—la cantidad por la cual lo que se recibe por las exportaciones es mayor que lo que se paga por las importaciones. |
| **Trade war**—a conflict between two or more countries involving escalating restrictions on trade as retaliation against earlier trade barriers. | **Guerra comercial**—conflicto entre dos o más países en el que se van aumentando las restricciones para el comercio como represalia contra barreras comerciales impuestas anteriormente. |
| **Tradeoff**—when you give up one thing to get something else. | **Compensación**—cuando se deja de obtener una cosa para obtener otra. |
| **Traditional economy**—an economic system in which decisions about resources are made by habit, custom, superstition, or religious tradition. | **Economía tradicional**—sistema económico en el que las decisiones sobre los recursos se toman por costumbre, hábito, superstición o tradición religiosa. |
| **Tragedy of the commons**—nonexcludable but rival goods become overused. | **Tragedia de los comunes**—bienes no excluibles pero rivales que se usan en exceso. |
| **Transfer payments**—payments for which the government receives no goods or services in return. | **Pagos por transferencia**—pagos a cambio de los cuales el gobierno no recibe ni bienes ni servicios. |
| **Transition**—the stage of economic development in which cultural change lays the foundation for economic change. | **Transición**—la etapa del desarrollo económico en la cual el cambio cultural forma los cimientos para el cambio económico. |
| **Treasury bill (T-bill)**—a security issued by the U.S. Treasury that matures in 4, 13, 26, or 52 weeks. | **Título del Tesoro**—título valor emitido por el Tesoro estadounidense y cuyo vencimiento es a los 4, 13, 26 o 52 semanas. |
| **Treasury bond (T-bond)**—a U.S. Treasury security that pays interest in the form of coupon payments and matures in 30 years. | **Bono del Tesoro**—título valor emitido por el Tesoro estadounidense que paga intereses en la forma de pagos por cupón y cuyo vencimiento es a los 30 años. |
| **Treasury Inflation-Protected Securities (TIPS)**—U.S. Treasury securities that protect investors against inflation because the amount to be repaid rises with inflation. | **Títulos del Tesoro protegidos contra la inflación**—títulos del Tesoro estadounidense que protegen a los inversionistas contra la inflación debido a que la cantidad que se reembolsará aumenta con la inflación. |
| **Treasury note (T-note)**—a U.S. Treasury security that pays interest in the form of coupon payments and matures in 2, 3, 5, or 10 years. | **Pagaré del Tesoro**—título del Tesoro estadounidense que paga intereses en la forma de pagos por cupón y cuyo vencimiento es a los 2, 3, 5 o 10 años. |

## U

| | |
|---|---|
| **Underemployed**—workers who would like to work more hours or prefer a job that better matches their skills. | **Subempleados**—trabajadores que quisieran trabajar más horas o que preferirían un empleo que concuerde más con sus destrezas. |
| **Underground economy**—business activity conducted without the knowledge of the government. | **Economía subterránea**—actividad comercial que se lleva a cabo sin conocimiento del gobierno. |
| **Unemployment rate**—the percentage of the labor force without a paid job. | **Tasa de desempleo**—el porcentaje de la fuerza laboral que está sin empleo pagado. |
| **Unit of account**—a standard measure used to set prices and make economic calculations. | **Unidad de cuenta**—medida normalizada que se usa para fijar precios y para realizar cómputos económicos. |
| **Unit-elastic demand**—consumers respond to a change in price by decreasing the quantity demanded by the same percentage. | **Demanda elástica por unidad**—los consumidores responden a un cambio en el precio disminuyendo la cantidad de su demanda por el mismo porcentaje. |

## V

| | |
|---|---|
| **Value of the marginal product**—the marginal product multiplied by the price of the output being produced. | **Valor del producto marginal**—el producto marginal multiplicado por el precio de la producción que se está produciendo. |
| **Variable cost**—the cost of inputs that do vary with the amount of output produced. | **Costo variable**—el costo de los insumos que varía según la cantidad de producción. |
| **Variable expenses**—expenses that can change frequently at your discretion. | **Gastos variables**—gastos que se pueden cambiar con frecuencia según la discreción de cada cual. |
| **Vertical equity**—people who have a greater ability to pay taxes make a larger tax payment. | **Equidad vertical**—las personas con una mayor capacidad para pagar impuestos pagan una mayor cantidad de impuestos. |

| | |
|---|---|
| **Vertical merger**—a combining of firms that operate at different stages in the production of a good. | **Fusión vertical**—combinación de empresas que funcionan en diferentes niveles de la producción de un bien. |
| **Voluntary export restraint (VER)**—a self-imposed limit on the quantity of exports. | **Límite de exportación voluntario**—límite autoimpuesto en la cantidad de las exportaciones. |

## W

| | |
|---|---|
| **Wants**—things that are desired but are not essential to life. | **Deseos**—cosas que se desean pero que no son esenciales para la vida. |
| **Weak dollar**—This describes the U.S. dollar when it will purchase a relatively small amount of foreign currency due to the current exchange rate. | **Dólar débil**—descripción del dólar estadounidense cuando puede comprar una cantidad relativamente pequeña de divisas debido al tipo de cambio vigente. |
| **Wealth**—the sum of everything a person owns minus what the person owes to others. | **Riqueza**—la suma de todo lo que es de propiedad de una persona menos lo que dicha persona debe a otros. |

# Reviewers

Jan Abel, Independence High School, CA
Christopher Adams, Carroll High School, IN
Laura Adams, Kirbyville High School, TX
Joy Alford, Early County High School, GA
Laura Ambrose, Clarke Central High School, GA
Linda Ames, Granite City High School, Il
Danny Ams, Obion County Central High
	School, TN
Ike Anders, Lindale High School, TX
Anita Anderson, Alcovy High School, GA
Christine Anderson, Pearland High School, TX
Mischell Anderson, A. J. Dimond
	High School, AK
Jackie Angel, Milton High School, GA
Stephen Arel, Fargo South High School, ND
Jody Arnold, Harker Heights High School, TX
Tom Avvakumovits, Cupertino High School, CA
Andrea Badger, Lynbrook High School, CA
Rick Baguley, Homewood High School, AL
Debra Ballweg, Verona Area High School, WI
Ricky D. Balthrop, L. D. Bell High School, TX
Craig Bancroft, West High School, IA
Christopher Bangs, Canby High School, OR
Wade Barnett, Lawrence County
	High School, TN
John Barthold, New Albany Senior
	High School, IN
Jay Bauer, West Aurora High School, Il
Andy Baxa, McCallum High School, TX
Bradley Beilfuss, Thornridge High School, Il
William Belew, Northwest High School, NE
Tim Belshe, Waynesville High School, MO
Christopher Benestad, Saint John's
	High School, MA
Joanne Benjamin, Los Gatos High School, CA
Lisa Bergman, Princeton High School, NJ
Scott Bersin, John L. Miller Great Neck North
	High School, NY
Ralph Bild, Borah High School, ID
Ronald Bishop, Brandywine Community
	Schools, MI
Sherry Blackmon, Arab High School, AL
Eric Bloom, Palo Alto Senior High School, CA
Joe Bogar, Chesaning Union High School, MI
Susan Bolly, Nicolet High School, WI
Ave Maria Bortz, Southwestern Academy, CA
Matthew Bosworth, Mooresville High School, IN
Deborah Bourgeois, West Mesquite
	High School, TX
Alan Bradshaw, Mirabeau B. Lamar Senior High
	School, TX
J. B. Brafford, American Institute for
	Learning, TX
George Branch, Michigan City High School, IN
Patricia Brazill, Irondequoit High School, NY

David Bremer, Las Lomas High School, CA
Kathleen Brennan, Mount Saint Mary
	Academy, NJ
Staci Brick, Alexis I. DuPont High School, DE
Catherine Bridges, Queen City High School, TX
Tony Brock, Cumberland County
	High School, TN
Darcy Brodison, Coronado High School, AZ
Megan Brooks, Franklin High School, MD
Richard Brooks, Clarence High School, NY
Diane Bryant, Sandusky High School, OH
Kim Burney, Russellville City Schools, AL
Susan Burton, Gordon Central High School, GA
Brian Busen, Cedar Springs High School, MI
Amy Bushey, Dow High School, MI
Jeffrey Butch, Octorara High School, PA
Shannon Butler, Huntsville High School, AL
Gary Byrne, Olathe East High School, KS
Diana Cabana, Oviedo High School, FL
Rosco Campbell, Pendleton High School, SC
Dale Candelaria, Atwater High School, CA
Adrian Cantu, Weslaco High School, TX
Janet Cartwright, Antioch High School, TN
Greg Casper, Canton South High School, OH
Mark Catlett, Ballard High School, KY
Ginny Chambliss, Lake Highlands
	High School, TX
Marion Cherne, Glynn Academy, GA
Aster Chin, Lowell High School, CA
Deborah Chont, Albuquerque High School, NM
Mary Chowenhill, Robert E. Lee High School, FL
Janis Christopher, Sequoia Continuation High
	School, CA
Daria Clark, Valley View High School, CA
Fred Cole, Marquette Area Public
	School District, MI
Matthew Cole, Livonia High School, NY
Candee Collins, Pine Tree High School, TX
Josh Collins, Rocky Mountain High School, WY
Waunda Comeaux, Westport Senior High
	School, MO
Sidney Conrad, Norris High School, NE
Patrick Conroy, Clarkstown South
	High School, NY
Sarah Cook, Rockwall High School, TX
Robert Cooms, Startford Senior High School, TX
Denise Corbin, Madison Consolidated High
	School, IN
Joseph Cortese, Homer High School, NY
Jack Couch, Brooklyn Technical High School, NY
Scott Craig, Seaholm High School, MI
Andrew Crane, Southwest High School, WI
Frank Crivello, Clinton Community School
	District, WI
Kimberly Cross, Frankston High School, TX

Donna Crow, Pampa High School, TX
Denny Crum, Oak Hill High School, IN
John Czepiel, Avon Board of Education, CT
Chris Dabney, Escambia County
	High School, AL
James Dacus, Colleyville Heritage
	High School, TX
Bruce Damasio, Liberty High School, MD
Patrick Davis, Thompson High School, AL
Tyler Dean, Forney High School, TX
Monte DeArmoun, Northwood-Kensett High
	School, IA
Vanessa DeCoteau, Century High School, ND
Mark Decourcy, Sandy Creek High School, GA
Katherine DeForge, Marcellus Central School
	District, NY
Gary De Leon, Canutillo High School, TX
Kim Denson, Tara High School, LA
Judith Depew, Dakota High School, MI
Robert Diamant, Federal Reserve Bank of New
	York, NY
Patrick Diemer, Pennfield High School, MI
Thomas Dillabough, Caro High School, MI
Robert Dittmer, Abraham Lincoln
	High School, IA
Kyleen Dobbs, Pflugerville High School, TX
Kevin Donahue, Eisenhower High School, MI
Shawn Donovan, Thornton Fractional South
	High School, Il
Denise Douglas, Tulare Western High School, CA
John Downey, Royal High School, CA
Steve Dubreuil, J. R. Arnold High School, FL
Dana Duenzen, Woodbridge High School, CA
Richard Duncan, Kelso Redirection Academy, LA
Julie Dvorak, Warren Township High School, Il
Bertrand Eckelhoefer, La Sierra High School, CA
Maria Edlin, Middle Tennessee State University, TN
Jessica Erhardt, Rigby High School, ID
Anthony Ethridge, Thornton Township High
	School, Il
Elizabeth Ewing, Mayde Creek High School, TX
David Faerber, Glen Oaks High School, LA
Sharon Fangman, Vega Junior High/High
	School, TX
John Feckanin, Livingston School Districts 4
	and 1, MT
Arthur Feeley, Edward Little Senior
	High School, ME
Elayne Feldman, Fridley Independent School
	District 14, MN
Jason Feller, Kaufman High School, TX
Tawni Ferrarini, Northern Michigan
	University, MI
Jaime Festa-Daigle, Lake Havasu High School, AZ
Carol Fisher, Hastings High School, TX

Steve Flinn, La Sierra High School, CA

Philip Foisy, Potsdam High School, NY

Donald Fortner, Munster High School, IN

Kelli Fournier, Louisa-Muscatine Junior/Senior High School, IA

Michelle Foutz, Carmel High School, IN

Raymond Frisbie, Anderson High School, CA

John Gambs, Red Oak Senior High School, IA

Susan Gattis, Hamshire-Fannett High School, TX

David Gavron, Wayland High School, MA

Craig Ghessi, Fleetwood Area High School, PA

John Gibson, Indiana University Northwest, IN

Thomas W. Glaser, Hialeah-Miami Lakes Senior High School, FL

Ron Goyette, Bell High School, TX

Carl Graham, Westfield High School, TX

Mary Gray, Bastrop High School, TX

Nathan Green, West Anchorage High School, AK

John Gregg, Westside High School, GA

Rebecca Griffith, Avery County High School, NC

Lesa Grooms, Maynard Junior/Senior High School, AR

Luke Groser, Shorewood High School, WI

David Grote, Dorman High School, SC

Gloria Guzman, Monsignor Pace High School, FL

Paul Hadfield, Paducah Tilghman High School, KY

Franklin Hagler, Ore City High School, TX

Susan Haglin, Carl Hayden Community High School, AZ

Levi Hahn, A. J. Dimond High School, AK

Judy Haley, Pine Tree High School, TX

Dan Halladay, Fountain Central Junior/Senior High School, IN

John W. Hamann, McAllen High School, TX

Lawrence Hanover, Pinecrest High School, NC

Brett Hardin, Campbell High School, GA

Leslie Harmon, Newberry High School, SC

Brian Hart, Sanger High School, TX

Bill Hasty, Fairview High School, OK

Timothy Hatcher, Murray County High School, GA

Jimmy Haynes, Van Alstyne High School, TX

Marc Hefke, Marquette Senior High School, MI

Karen Hense, Pflugerville High School, TX

Tevi Henson, West Hall High School, GA

Rico Hernandez, Notre Dame High School, CA

Staci Herrin, Benjamin Bosse High School, IN

Tim Hetrich, Wyomissing Junior/Senior High School, PA

Jim Hill, Lamphere School District, MI

Susan Hirsch, East Wake High School, NC

Matthew Hirvela, Southfield-Lathrup High School, MI

John Hoch, Thomas More School, WI

Sheila Hocutt-Remington, Brookwood High School, AL

Christine Hodges, Ozona High School, TX

Andrew Hofer, Decatur Central High School, IN

Mary Beth Hollas, Lamar Consolidated High School, TX

Thomas Hornish, Westfield High School, NJ

Lisa Howard, Del Norte High School, CA

Jeffrey Howell, Reavis Township High School District 220, Il

Carla Hubbard, Harris County High School, GA

Linda Hubbs, Dalton High School, GA

Tom Hubner, Addison Trail High School, Il

Brenda Hudnall, Plano West Senior High School, TX

Donald Huey, Ganesha High School, CA

Woodrow W. Hughes Jr., Converse College, SC

Derek Huntley, Western High School, MI

Vicki Hyneman, Pahokee Middle Senior High School, FL

Scott Immerfall, Marion Independent School District, IA

Martin Inde, Willis High School, TX

Cheryl Irwin, West Vigo High School, IN

Maleah Ivie, Butte County High School, ID

Todd Jacobson, Creston High School, IA

James Jiles, Lucy Ragsdale High School, NC

Andrew Johnson, Avon High School, IN

Dan Johnson, Lincoln High School, IA

Mike Johnson, Southeast Polk High School, IA

Shawn Johnson, Knox High School, IN

Phillip Jones, Central High School, TN

Jackie Joseph, Taylor High School, TX

Joy Joyce, University of Illinois at Chicago, Il

Chris Kahler, Harborfields High School, NY

Martha Kavanaugh, Hamburg Central School District, NY

Martha Kelly, Woodruff High School, Il

Gina Kerbel, George S. Parker High School, WI

Leslie Kieschnick, Rockwall High School, TX

Michael Kieselbach, Moorhead High School, MN

Leah Kifoyle, Mountain Brook High School, AL

Jabe Kile, Marcellus Senior High School, NY

Jack Klein, Idaho Falls High School, ID

Jeff Klinger, Montesano Junior/Senior High School, WA

Bill Klugh, Seneca High School, SC

John Knaff, Memphis University School, TN

Julia Knoff, Scripps Ranch High School, CA

Mary Kohelis, Brooke High School, OH

Gail Kohn, Grapvine High School, TX

Calvin Korab, Frenship High School, TX

Stan Kramer, Blanchet Catholic High School, OR

Richard Kuhn, Marlington High School, OH

Jenny Kuhns, Fullerton Union High School, CA

Kali Kurdy, Borah High School, ID

John Labno, Orestimba High School, CA

K. Langston, Brookland High School, AR

K. Lantow, Peshtigo School District, WI

Patrick Lapid, Convent of Sacred Heart High School, CA

Carol Larson, Bartlett High School, AK

Nancy La Spina, Bastrop High School, TX

Riza Laudin, Herricks High School, NY

William Moses Ledford, Bertie High School, NC

Conor Lefere, Parchment High School, MI

Erik Lewis, Templeton High School, CA

Rhonda Bernyce Lewis, South Garland High School, TX

Vernell Lewis, Murrah High School, MS

Richard Liebman, Lake Worth High School, FL

Chris Ljunggren, Billing Senior High School, MT

Leonard Lockwood, Oak Ridge High School, TX

Dean Longwell, Hampton High School, PA

Jane S. Lopus, California State University, East Bay, CA

Tim Loreman, Smiths High School, AL

Daryl Lowery, Jemison High School, AL

Raymond Lucas, Ygnacio Valley High School, CA

Kurt Luedke, Slinger High School, WI

Kay Majors, Pittsburg High School, TX

David Maloney, Manchester High School, CT

Rick Martin, Sequoyah High School, GA

Ross Martin, South Vigo High School, IN

Miguel Martinez Jr., Archbishop Riordan High School, CA

Melissa Marvin, James E. Taylor High School, TX

John Masiello, Matawan Regional High School, NJ

Mark Maxwell, Lufkin High School, TX

James McCalip, Jack E. Singley Academy, TX

James McCall, Firebaugh High School, CA

Jan McPherson, Hoopa Valley High School, CA

Eleanor McSwiggin, Mother of Mercy High School, OH

Sally Meek, Plano West Senior High School, TX

Cliff Meixner, Fossil Ridge High School, TX

Jeff Melton, Kings Mountain High School, NC

Kenneth Mengani, World Journalism Preparatory School, NY

James Meskill, Reavis High School, Il

Sue Messino, John Glenn High School, OH

Susan Miller, Eleanor Roosevelt High School, NY

Chris Miller, Patrick Henry High School, CA

Bettie Millikan, Paris High School, TX

Michael Milush, Stow High School, OH

Dudley Mitchell, McLean County High School, KY

John Mitchell, Community High School, TX

Judy Mitchell, Thomas Moore Prep-Marian High School, KS

R. Mitchell, Cocke County High School, TN

Rose Molina, Huntington Beach High School, CA

Joseph Moll, Jac-Cen-Del Community School District, IN

James Morley, Huntsville High School, TX

JuLee Morse, East High School, AK

Kenneth Moryl, La Porte High School, IN

Clarence Moses, Lyons High School, KS

Daniel Mumbrue, Lake Shore High School, MI

Joan Mundy-Klement, Half Hollow Hills High School West, NY

Tige Munoz, King City High School, CA

Christopher Murphy, Wiregrass Ranch High School, FL

Alan Musante, Oviedo High School, FL

Barbara Mussman, Grant Park High School, Il

David Nach, Mountain Pointe High School, AZ

Halehma Naseer, Alief Elsik High School, TX

Bradford Ness, Marathon High School, WI

Ed Newman, South Ripley Junior/Senior High School, IN

Faith Newton, Ronald Reagan High School, TX

Michael Nickerson, Pulaski High School, WI

Gary Nielsen, Antonian College Preparatory High School, TX

Marty Nienstedt, Haven High School, KS

James Norris, Osseo Senior High School, MN

Elizabeth Nowak, High School of Economics and Finance, NY

Libby Nowak, High School of Economics and Finance, NY

David E. O'Connor, Edwin O. Smith High School, CN

Joyce O'Dell, Orrick High School, MO

Timothy G. O'Driscoll, University of Wisconsin-Milwaukee, WI

Marisol Ortega, Calexico High School, CA

Michele Otte, Kiel High School, WI

Heidi Painter, Folsom High School, Prairie City Campus, CA

Michael Palfy, Poinciana High School, FL

Kurt Parker, Campbellsport High School, WI

Michael Pasqua, Arcadia High School, CA

Jefferey Payne, Flint Central High School, MI

Matt Pedlow, Chelsea High School, MI

James Perry, Lincoln High School, NE

Wayne Pfeifer, Kellogg High School, ID

Michael Phiel, Salem High School, GA

Sean Phillips, Blissfield High School, MI

James Plouffe, Rockdale County High School, GA

Randy Plummer, Gering High School, NE

Keith Poulsen, Atlantic High School, FL

Cara Prentiss, New Horizon Continuation High School, CA

Patrick Preudhomme, Eastern Alamance High School, NC

Michael Prewitt, Eastern Hills High School, TX

Leslie Priebe, Hagerman Junior/Senior High School, ID

Steve Prusack, Altmar Parish Williamstown High School, NY

Daniel Quinn, Grosse Pointe North High School, MI

Michael Quinn, Lake Travis High School, TX

Kyle Race, Greene High School, NY

Daniel Radzicki, Oceanside High School, NY

Randolph Ramlall, Education Place, MN

Brett Ramsey, Wink High School, TX

Eric Rayle, Portage Central High School, MI

M. J. Regennitter, Copley-Fairlawn City School District, OH

Michael Reneau, Macon County High School, GA

Gary Revale, Sharon City School District, PA

Tiffany Rhodes, Richlands High School, NC

Rebecca Richardson, Allen High School, TX

Brian Richter, Sterling High School, KS

Ken Ripp, Memorial Eau Claire High School, WI

Ron Rishagen, Saint Bernard High School, CA

Charles D. Robbins, Brooks High School, AL

Kenneth Roberson, Oelwein Community School District, IA

Claire Roberts, Bandera High School, TX

David Robinson, Diboll High School, TX

Jen Roesch, Windsor High School, MO

Alicia Ross, Blue Ridge High School, PA

Molly Rothert, Verona Junior/Senior High School, MO

Karen Russell, Columbus North High School, IN

Kenneth Sadjak, eAchieve Academy, WI

Ruben Salazar, La Pryor High School, TX

Richard Sanders, Oran High School, MO

David Santos, Gettysburg College, PA

Michael Satcher, Horn Lake High School, MS

Ken Savaglia, Burlington High School, WI

Ann Scharfenberg, New Richmond High School, WI

Eliot Scher, White Plains High School, NY

Michael Scherck, Baraboo High School, WI

Scott Schifeling, Manual High School, Il

William Schlink, Cinco Ranch High School, TX

Pamela M. Schmitt, United States Naval Academy, MD

Bill Schreier, Wheaton-Warrenville South High School, Il

Mark Scott, Harrison High School, IN

Nell Scrivener, Ozark High School, MO

L. Rodney Scudder, Granby Memorial High School, CT

Francis Seery, Cordova High School, TN

Ann Semler, North Shore Senior High School, TX

Ron Settle, Blue Springs High School, MO

Marvin Shagam, Thacher School, CA

Brian Shank, Ponderosa High School, CA

Bonnie Shanks, Jefferson Davis High School, AL

Kathy Simmons, Canyon High School, TX

Stephen Simmons, Traverse City Area Public Schools, MI

Dan Simonson, Kettle Moraine High School, WI

Sean Keary Sims, Bell High School, TX

Peter Singer, Duncanville High School, TX

Mike Skytland, Bismarck High School, ND

Gail Sloan, Whitehouse High School, TX

Linda Smith, Rockwall High School, TX

Mike Smith, Ralston High School, NE

Monica Soileau, Notre Dame High School, LA

James Spellicy, Lowell High School, CA

David Stark, Brainerd Senior High School, MN

Ann Stefanov, Forest City Regional Junior/Senior High School, PA

Dennis Stephen, Centerville Abington Senior High School, IN

Julie Stodghill, Troup County High School, GA

Steve Styers, Huntley High School, Il

Barbara Sullivan, Williamsville High School, Il

Mark Swancoat, Downey High School, CA

Jonathan Sweemer, NJ

Judy Swirczynski, Wylie High School, TX

Susan Syme, Athens High School, MI

Janet Tavares, Apponequet Regional High School, MA

Kyle Taylor, Russellville City Schools, AL

Alice Temnick, Cactus Shadows High School, AZ

Kathy Terrell, Shenandoah High School, IN

Jay Thatcher, East High School, AK

Betty Thomas, El Campo High School, TX

David Thompson, Southwest High School, CA

Hugh Thompson, Hawken High School, OH

Ron Toomey, Newbury Park High School, CA

Jim Tostrud, Monroe High School, WI

Rick Toward, Bemidji High School, MN

Mary Beth Townsend, Henry Sibley High School, MN

Shawn Trapuzzano, Trinity High School, PA

Jerry Treat, Rose Hill High School, KS

Pete Trevino, San Diego High School, TX

Paul Trevizo, Townview Magnet High School, TX

Dan Tricarico, East Davidson High School, NC

Terri Tubbs, Carbon County School District, UT

Joan Uhrick, Byron Area High School, MI

Anna Vanlandingham, Lake Mary High School, FL

Pam Vaughn, Houston Independent School District, TX

Keith Venturoni, Richardson Independent School District, TX

Belinda Wade, Brentwood High School, TN

Douglas Wadley, Bradley-Bourbonnais Community High School District 307, Il

Jacob Wadsworth, Hillcrest High School, MO

Dianne Waggoner, Monahans High School, TX

David Wallace, Lebanon High School, NH

Gary Waller, Franklin High School, TN

Karen Warren, Canyon High School, TX

Danny Wasson, Demopolis High School, AL

Alyssa Watson, Lincoln Southwest High School, NE

Brian Weaver, Big Rapids High School, MI

Robbie Sue Weaver, Palomar College, CA

Craig Weems, Cedar Park High School, TX

Elizabeth Weidman, Clear Creek High School, TX

Peter Weinburgh, Keller Central High School, TX

Don Weir, Lawrence Central High School, IN

Rick Weller, Marble Hill School for International Studies, NY

John Wells, West Hill High School, NY

Jeff Westendorf, Roosevelt High School, IA

Betty Jo Western, Delta Technical Center, UT

Paul White, Markesan High School, WI

Gordon Whiting, Elgin High School, Il

Barb Wicks, Campbell County High School, WY

John Wietlispach, Joliet Central High School, Il

Jeff Williams, Coffee High School, GA

Keith Williams, Newark Valley High School, NY

Morris Williams, Holly Pond High School, AL

Stephen Williams, Plymouth Canton High School, MI

Amy Willis, Liberty Fund Inc., IN

Keturah Wineinger, Brownsboro High School, TX

Russ Winton, Livingston High School, CA

Leslie Wolfson, Pingry School, NJ

John Worrell, Dondero High School, MI

Phyllis Worsham, Clements High School, TX

Gillian Wright, Ticonderoga High School, NY

Dan Wucherer, Waupun High School, WI

Douglas Young, Croton-Harmon High School, NY

Donald Yuhouse, Greensburg Central Catholic High School, PA

Linda Zeigler, Don Antonio Lugo High School, CA

Betty B. Zielinski, Saint Mary's Preparatory High School, MI

# Index

Note: Headings and page numbers in bold indicate definitions.